D0590016

Collins
German
Dictionary

HarperCollins Publishers
Westerhill Road
Bishopbriggs
Glasgow
G64 2QT
Great Britain

Second Edition 2007

Previously published as Collins Pocket
German Dictionary

Reprint 10 9 8 7 6 5 4 3 2 1 0

© William Collins Sons & Co. Ltd 1990
© HarperCollins Publishers 1996,
1998, 1999, 2001, 2007

ISBN-13 978-0-00-725343-2
ISBN-10 0-00-725343-5

www.collins.co.uk

A catalogue record for this book is
available from the British Library

HarperCollins Publishers, 10 East
53rd Street, New York, NY 10022

COLLINS POCKET GERMAN DICTIONARY.
Fourth US Edition 2007

ISBN-13 978-0-06-114186-7
ISBN-10 0-06-114186-0

Library of Congress Cataloging-in-
Publication Data has been applied for

www.harpercollins.com

Dictionary text typeset by
RefineCatch Ltd, Bungay, Suffolk

Supplement text typeset by
Davidson's Prepress, Glasgow

Printed in Italy by
Rotolito Lombarda S.p.A.

Acknowledgements
We would like to thank those autho[r]
and publishers who kindly gave
permission for copyright material t[o]
be used in the Collins Word Web. W[e]
would also like to thank Times
Newspapers Ltd for providing
valuable data.

GENERAL EDITOR
Maree Airlie

CONTRIBUTORS
Daphne Day
Horst Kopleck
Joyce Littlejohn

EDITORIAL COORDINATION
Susie Beattie

SERIES EDITOR
Lorna Knight

This book is set in Collins Fedra, a
typeface specially created for Collins
Dictionaries by Peter Bil'ak

INHALT		CONTENTS	

WARENZEICHEN

Warenzeichen, die unseres Wissens eingetragene Warenzeichen darstellen, sind als solche gekennzeichnet. Es ist jedoch zu beachten, dass weder das Vorhandensein noch das Fehlen derartiger Kennzeichnungen die Rechtslage hinsichtlich eingetragener Warenzeichen berührt.

NOTE ON TRADEMARKS

Words which we have reason to believe constitute trademarks have been designated as such. However, neither the presence nor the absence of such designation should be regarded as affecting the legal status of any trademark.

William Collins' dream of knowledge for all began with the publication of his first book in 1819. A self-educated mill worker, he not only enriched millions of lives, but also founded a flourishing publishing house. Today, staying true to this spirit, Collins books are packed with inspiration, innovation, and practical expertise. They place you at the centre of a world of possibility and give you exactly what you need to explore it.

Language is the key to this exploration, and at the heart of Collins Dictionaries is language as it is really used. New words, phrases, and meanings spring up every day, and all of them are captured and analysed by the Collins Word Web. Constantly updated, and with over 2.5 billion entries, this living language resource is unique to our dictionaries.

Words are tools for life. And a Collins Dictionary makes them work for you.

Collins. Do more.

EINFÜHRUNG

Wir freuen uns sehr, dass Sie sich zum Kauf eines Collins Wörterbuchs Deutsch entschlossen haben. Wir wünschen Ihnen viel Spaß beim Gebrauch in der Schule, zu Hause, im Urlaub und im Beruf.

Diese Einführung wird Ihnen einige nützliche Hinweise dazu geben, wie Sie am besten von Ihrem neuen Wörterbuch profitieren. Schließlich bietet Ihnen das Wörterbuch nicht nur Stichwörter und Übersetzungen, sondern auch zahlreiche Zusatzinformationen in jedem einzelnen Eintrag. Mit Hilfe all dieser Informationen können Sie zum einen modernes Deutsch lesen und verstehen, zum anderen auch aktiv auf Deutsch kommunizieren.

Das Collins Wörterbuch Deutsch gibt Ihnen vor dem eigentlichen Wörterbuchtextteil selbst eine Liste aller verwendeten Abkürzungen sowie eine Übersicht zu Aussprache und Gebrauch phonetischer Umschrift. Darüber hinaus finden Sie noch eine Auflistung zu den regelmäßigen deutschen Substantivendungen sowie zu unregelmäßigen englischen und deutschen Verben. Auf den letzten Seiten Ihres Wörterbuchs finden Sie in einem „kleinen Reise-ABC" zahlreiche nützliche Phrasen für verschiedenste Situationen am Urlaubsort.

WIE FINDE ICH WAS?

Die verschiedenen Schriftarten, Schriftgrößen, Symbole, Abkürzungen und Klammern helfen Ihnen dabei, sich innerhalb der Informationen, die das Wörterbuch bietet, zurechtzufinden. Die Konventionen, die diesem Wörterbuch zugrunde liegen, sowie auch der Gebrauch verschiedener Symbole werden im Folgenden näher erläutert.

STICHWÖRTER

Die Wörter, die Sie in Ihrem Wörterbuch nachschlagen, die Stichwörter, sind in alphabetischer Reihenfolge angeordnet. Sie sind **fett** gedruckt und in blauer Farbe, sodass Sie sie schnell finden. Die Stichwörter, die rechts und links oben auf jeder Seite erscheinen, sind das jeweils erste Stichwort einer Seite, wenn es sich dabei um eine linke Seite handelt, bzw. das letzte Stichwort einer Seite, wenn es sich um eine rechte Seite handelt. Informationen zu Form und Gebrauch des jeweiligen Stichworts

werden im Anschluss an die Lautschrift in Klammern angegeben. Normalerweise sind diese Angaben in abgekürzter Form
und *kursiver Schrift* (z.B. *(fam)* für umgangssprachlich oder *(Comm)*
als Sachgebietsangabe für Wirtschaft).

Wo es sich anbietet, werden zusammengehörige Wörter und
Wortgruppen in einem Eintrag zusammengefasst (z.B. **gather**,
gathering; **höflich**, **Höflichkeit**). Hierbei sind die Stichwörter
innerhalb des Nests von der Schriftgröße etwas kleiner als das erste
Stichwort. Geläufige Ausdrücke, in denen das Stichwort vor-
kommt, erscheinen ebenfalls **fett**, aber in einer anderen
Schriftgröße. Die Tilde (~) steht hierbei für das Hauptstichwort
am Anfang eines Eintrags. So steht beispielsweise im Eintrag
‚Mitte' der Ausdruck ‚**~ Juni**' für ‚**Mitte Juni**'.

PHONETISCHE UMSCHRIFT

Die Aussprache jedes Stichworts findet sich in phonetischer
Umschrift in eckigen Klammern jeweils direkt hinter dem
Stichwort selbst (z.B. **mountain** ['mauntɪn]). Eine Liste der Laut-
schriftzeichen mit Erklärungen finden Sie auf S. xi.

BEDEUTUNGEN

Die Übersetzung der Stichwörter ist in Normalschrift angegeben.
Gibt es mehrere Bedeutungen oder Gebrauchsmöglichkeiten, so
sind diese durch einen Strichpunkt voneinander zu unterscheiden. Sie finden oft weitere Angaben in Klammern vor den
jeweiligen Übersetzungen. Diese zeigen Ihnen typische Kontexte
auf, in denen das Stichwort verwendet werden kann (z.B.
breakup *(of meeting, organisation)*), oder sie liefern Synonyme (z.B.
fit *(suitable)*).

GRAMMATISCHE HINWEISE

Die Wortartangabe finden Sie als Abkürzung und in *kursiver Schrift*
direkt hinter der Ausspracheinformation zum jeweiligen
Stichwort (z.B. *vt*, *adj*, *n*).

Die Genusangaben zu deutschen Substantiven werden wie folgt
angegeben: *m* für Maskulinum, *f* für Femininum und *nt* für
Neutrum. Darüber hinaus finden Sie neben dem Stichwort in
Klammern Genitiv- und Pluralform (**Abenteuer** *(-s, -)*).

Die Genusangabe zur deutschen Übersetzung findet sich ebenfalls in *kursiver Schrift* direkt hinter dem Hauptbestandteil der
Übersetzung.

INTRODUCTION

We are delighted you have decided to buy the Collins German Dictionary and hope you will enjoy and benefit from using it at school, at home, on holiday or at work.

This introduction gives you a few tips on how to get the most out of your dictionary - not simply from its comprehensive wordlist but also from the information provided in each entry. This will help you to read and understand modern German, as well as to communicate and express yourself in the language.

The Collins German Dictionary begins by listing the abbreviations used in the text and illustrating the sounds shown by the phonetic symbols. Next you will find regular German noun endings and English irregular verbs followed by a section on German irregular verbs. Finally, the new Phrasefinder supplement gives you hundreds of useful phrases which are intended to give you practical help in everyday situations when travelling.

USING YOUR COLLINS DICTIONARY

A wealth of information is presented in the dictionary, using various typefaces, sizes of type, symbols, abbreviations and brackets. The conventions and symbols used are explained in the following sections.

HEADWORDS

The words you look up in the dictionary – 'headwords' – are listed alphabetically. They are printed in **colour** for rapid identification. The headwords appearing at the top of each page indicate the first (if it appears on a left-hand page) and last word (if it appears on a right-hand page) dealt with on the page in question.

Information about the usage or form of certain headwords is given in brackets after the phonetic spelling. This usually appears in abbreviated form and in italics (e.g. (*fam*), (*Comm*)).

Where appropriate, words related to headwords are grouped in the same entry (**gather**, **gathering**; **höflich**, **Höflichkeit**) in a slightly smaller bold type than the headword. Common expressions in which the headword appears are shown in a different size of bold roman type. The swung dash, ~, represents the main headword at the start of each entry. For example, in the entry for 'Mitte', the phrase '~ Juni' should be read **Mitte Juni**.

PHONETIC SPELLINGS

The phonetic spelling of each headword (indicating its pronunciation) is given in square brackets immediately after the headword (e.g. mountain ['maʊntɪn]). A list of these spellings is given on page xi.

MEANINGS

Headword translations are given in ordinary type and, where more than one meaning or usage exists, they are separated by a semicolon. You will often find other words in italics in brackets before the translations. These offer suggested contexts in which the headword might appear (e.g. **breakup** (*of meeting, organisation*)) or provide synonyms (e.g. **fit** (*suitable*)).

GRAMMATICAL INFORMATION

Parts of speech are given in abbreviated form in italics after the phonetic spellings of headwords (e.g. *vt*, *adj*, *n*).

Genders of German nouns are indicated as follows: *m* for a masculine, *f* for a feminine, and *nt* for a neuter noun. Genitive and plural forms of nouns are also shown next to the headword (**Abenteuer** (-*s*, -)).

The gender of the German translation appears in *italics* immediately following the key element of the translation.

auch	*a.*	also
Abkürzung	*abk, abbr*	abbreviation
Akronym	*acr*	acronym
Adjektiv	*adj*	adjective
Adverb	*adv*	adverb
Landwirtschaft	*Agr*	agriculture
Akkusativ	*akk*	accusative
Akronym	*akr*	acronym
Anatomie	*Anat*	anatomy
Artikel	*art*	article
Bildende Künste	*Art*	fine arts
Astronomie, Astrologie	*Astr*	astronomy, astrology
Auto, Verkehr	*Auto*	automobiles, traffic
Luftfahrt	*Aviat*	aviation
Biologie	*Bio*	biology
Botanik	*Bot*	botany
britisch	*BRIT*	British
schweizerisch	*CH*	Swiss
Chemie	*Chem*	chemistry
Film	*Cine*	cinema
Wirtschaft	*Comm*	commerce
Konjunktion	*conj*	conjunction
Dativ	*dat*	dative
Eisenbahn	*Eisenb*	railways
Elektrizität	*Elek, Elec*	electricity
besonders	*esp*	especially
und so weiter	*etc*	et cetera
etwas	*etw*	
Femininum	*f*	feminine
umgangssprachlich	*fam*	familiar, informal
übertragen	*fig*	figurative
Finanzen, Börse	*Fin*	finance
Fotografie	*Foto*	photography
Gastronomie	*Gastr*	cooking, gastronomy
Genitiv	*gen*	genitive
Geographie, Geologie	*Geo*	geography, geology
Geschichte	*Hist*	history
Imperativ	*imper*	imperative
Imperfekt	*imperf*	past tense
Informatik und Computer	*Inform*	computing
Interjektion, Ausruf	*interj*	interjection
unveränderlich	*inv*	invariable
unregelmäßig	*irr*	irregular
jemand, jemandem	*jd, jdm*	
jemanden, jemandes	*jdn, jds*	
Rechtsprechung	*Jur*	law

Konjunktion	*konj*	conjunction
Bildende Künste	*Kunst*	fine arts
Sprachwissenschaft, Grammatik	*Ling*	linguistics, grammar
Maskulinum	*m*	masculine
Mathematik	*Math*	mathematics
Medizin	*Med*	medicine
Meteorologie	*Meteo*	meteorology
Maskulinum und Femininum	*mf*	masculine and feminine
Militär	*Mil*	military
Musik	*Mus*	music
Substantiv	*n*	noun
Seefahrt	*Naut*	nautical, naval
Neutrum	*nt*	neuter
Zahlwort	*num*	numeral
oder	*o*	or
pejorativ, abwertend	*pej*	pejorative
Physik	*Phys*	physics
Plural	*pl*	plural
Politik	*Pol*	politics
Partizip Perfekt	*pp*	past participle
Präfix	*pref*	prefix
Präposition	*prep*	preposition
Pronomen	*pron*	pronoun
1. Vergangenheit	*pt*	past tense
Eisenbahn	*Rail*	railways
Religion	*Rel*	religion
siehe	*s.*	see
	sb	someone, somebody
schottisch	*Scot*	Scottish
Singular	*sing*	singular
Skisport	*Ski*	skiing
	sth	something
Technik	*Tech*	technology
Nachrichtentechnik	*Tel*	telecommunications
Theater	*Theat*	theatre
Fernsehen	*TV*	television
Typographie, Buchdruck	*Typo*	printing
unpersönlich	*unpers*	impersonal
(nord)amerikanisch	*US*	(North) American
Verb	*vb*	verb
Hilfsverb	*vb aux*	auxiliary verb
intransitives Verb	*vi*	intransitive verb
reflexives Verb	*vr*	reflexive verb
transitives Verb	*vt*	transitive verb
vulgär	*vulg*	vulgar
Zoologie	*Zool*	zoology
ungefähre Entsprechung	≈	cultural equivalent
abtrennbares Präfix	|	separable prefix

Lautschrift   Phonetic symbols

[:] Längezeichen, length mark
['] Betonung, stress mark
[*] Bindungs-R, 'r' pronounced before a vowel

alle Vokallaute sind nur ungefähre Entsprechungen
all vowel sounds are approximate only

Vokale und Diphthonge

plant, arm, father	[ɑ:]	Bahn
fiancé	[ɑ̃:]	Ensemble
life	[aɪ]	weit
house	[au]	Haut
man, sad	[æ]	
but, son	[ʌ]	Butler
get, bed	[e]	Metall
name, lame	[eɪ]	
ago, better	[ə]	bitte
bird, her	[ɜ:]	
there, care	[ɛə]	mehr
it, wish	[ɪ]	Bischof
bee, me, beat, belief	[i:]	viel
here	[ɪə]	Bier
no, low	[əʊ]	
not, long	[ɒ]	Post
law, all	[ɔ:]	Mond
boy, oil	[ɔɪ]	Heu
push, look	[ʊ]	Pult
you, do	[u:]	Hut
poor, sure	[ʊə]	

Konsonanten

been, blind	[b]	Ball
do, had	[d]	dann
jam, object	[dʒ]	
father, wolf	[f]	Fass
go, beg	[g]	Gast
house	[h]	Herr
youth, Indian	[j]	ja
keep, milk	[k]	kalt
lamp, oil, ill	[l]	Last
man, am	[m]	Mast
no, manner	[n]	Nuss
long, sing	[ŋ]	lang

El Niño	[ɲ]	El Niño
paper, happy	[p]	Pakt
red, dry	[r]	rot
stand, sand, yes	[s]	Rasse
ship, station	[ʃ]	Schal
tell, fat	[t]	Tal
thank, death	[θ]	
this, father	[ð]	
church, catch	[tʃ]	Rutsch
voice, live	[v]	was
water, we, which	[w]	
loch	[x]	Bach
zeal, these, gaze	[z]	Hase
pleasure	[ʒ]	Genie

REGULAR GERMAN NOUN ENDINGS

nominative		genitive	plural		nominative		genitive	plural
-ade	f	-ade	-aden		-ist	m	-isten	-isten
-ant	m	-anten	-anten		-ium	nt	-iums	-ien
-anz	f	-anz	-anzen		-ius	m	-ius	-iusse
-ar	m	-ars	-are		-ive	f	-ive	-iven
-är	m	-ärs	-äre		-keit	f	-keit	-keiten
-at	nt	-at(e)s	-ate		-lein	nt	-leins	-lein
-atte	f	-atte	-atten		-ling	m	-lings	-linge
-chen	nt	-chens	-chen		-ment	nt	-ments	-mente
-ei	f	-ei	-eien		-mus	m	-mus	-men
-elle	f	-elle	-ellen		-nis	f	-nis	-nisse
-ent	m	-enten	-enten		-nis	nt	-nisses	-nisse
-enz	f	-enz	-enzen		-nom	m	-nomen	-nomen
-ette	f	-ette	-etten		-rich	m	-richs	-riche
-eur	m	-eurs	-eure		-schaft	f	-schaft	-schaften
-euse	f	-euse	-eusen		-sel	nt	-sels	-sel
-heit	f	-heit	-heiten		-tät	f	-tät	-täten
-ie	f	-ie	-ien		-tiv	nt, m	-tivs	-tive
-ik	f	-ik	-iken		-tor	m	-tors	-toren
-in	f	-in	-innen		-tum	m, nt	-tums	-tümer
-ine	f	-ine	-inen		-ung	f	-ung	-ungen
-ion	f	-ion	-ionen		-ur	f	-ur	-uren

Substantive, die mit einem geklammerten 'r' oder 's' enden (z.B. **Ange-stellte(r)** *mf*, **Beamte(r)** *m*, **Gute(s)** *nt*) werden wie Adjektive dekliniert:

Nouns listed with an 'r' or an 's' in brackets (eg **Angestellte(r)** *mf*, **Beamte(r)** *m*, **Gute(s)** *nt*) take the same endings as adjectives:

der Angestellte *m*	**die Angestellte** *f*	**die Angestellten** *pl*
ein Angestellter *m*	**eine Angestellte** *f*	**Angestellte** *pl*
der Beamte *m*		**die Beamten** *pl*
ein Beamter *m*		**Beamte** *pl*
das Gute *nt*		
ein Gutes *nt*		

UNREGELMÄßIGE ENGLISCHE VERBEN

present	past tense	past participle	present	past tense	past participle
arise	arose	arisen	drink	drank	drunk
(arising)			drive	drove	driven
awake	awoke	awaked	(driving)		
(awaking)			eat	ate	eaten
be (am, is,	was, were	been	fall	fell	fallen
are; being)			feed	fed	fed
bear	bore	born(e)	feel	felt	felt
beat	beat	beaten	fight	fought	fought
become	became	become	find	found	found
(becoming)			flee	fled	fled
begin	began	begun	fling	flung	flung
(beginning)			fly (flies)	flew	flown
bend	bent	bent	forbid	forbade	forbidden
bet (betting)	bet	bet	(forbidding)		
bid (bidding)	bid	bid	foresee	foresaw	foreseen
bind	bound	bound	forget	forgot	forgotten
bite (biting)	bit	bitten	(forgetting)		
bleed	bled	bled	forgive	forgave	forgiven
blow	blew	blown	(forgiving)		
break	broke	broken	freeze	froze	frozen
breed	bred	bred	(freezing)		
bring	brought	brought	get	got	got,
build	built	built	(getting)		(US) gotten
burn	burnt	burnt	give	gave	given
	(o burned)	(o burned)	(giving)		
burst	burst	burst	go (goes)	went	gone
buy	bought	bought	grind	ground	ground
can	could	(been able)	grow	grew	grown
cast	cast	cast	hang	hung (o	hung (o
catch	caught	caught		hanged)	hanged)
choose	chose	chosen	have (has;	had	had
(choosing)			having)		
cling	clung	clung	hear	heard	heard
come	came	come	hide	hid	hidden
(coming)			(hiding)		
cost	cost	cost	hit (hitting)	hit	hit
creep	crept	crept	hold	held	held
cut (cutting)	cut	cut	hurt	hurt	hurt
deal	dealt	dealt	keep	kept	kept
dig (digging)	dug	dug	kneel	knelt (o	knelt (o
do (does)	did	done		kneeled)	kneeled)
draw	drew	drawn	know	knew	known
dream	dreamed	dreamed	lay	laid	laid
	(o dreamt)	(o dreamt)	lead	led	led

present	past tense	past participle	present	past tense	past participle
lean	leant (o leaned)	leant (o leaned)	shoot	shot	shot
			show	showed	shown
leap	leapt (o leaped)	leapt (o leaped)	shrink	shrank	shrunk
			shut (shutting)	shut	shut
learn	learnt (o learned)	learnt (o learned)	sing	sang	sung
leave (leaving)	left	left	sink	sank	sunk
			sit (sitting)	sat	sat
lend	lent	lent	sleep	slept	slept
let (letting)	let	let	slide (sliding)	slid	slid
lie (lying)	lay	lain			
light	lit (o lighted)	lit (o lighted)	sling	slung	slung
			slit (slitting)	slit	slit
lose (losing)	lost	lost	smell	smelt (o smelled)	smelt (o smelled)
make (making)	made	made			
may	might	–	sow	sowed	sown (o sowed)
mean	meant	meant	speak	spoke	spoken
meet	met	met	speed	sped (o speeded)	sped (o speeded)
mow	mowed	mown (o mowed)			
			spell	spelt (o spelled)	spelt (o spelled)
must	(had to)	(had to)	spend	spent	spent
pay	paid	paid	spin (spinning)	spun	spun
put (putting)	put	put			
quit (quitting)	quit (o quitted)	quit (o quitted)	spit (spitting)	spat	spat
read	read	read	split (splitting)	split	split
rid (ridding)	rid	rid			
ride (riding)	rode	ridden	spoil	spoiled (o spoilt)	spoiled (o spoilt)
ring	rang	rung			
rise (rising)	rose	risen	spread	spread	spread
run (running)	ran	run	spring	sprang	sprung
			stand	stood	stood
saw	sawed	sawn	steal	stole	stolen
say	said	said	stick	stuck	stuck
see	saw	seen	sting	stung	stung
seek	sought	sought	stink	stank	stunk
sell	sold	sold	strike (striking)	struck	struck
send	sent	sent			
set (setting)	set	set	strive (striving)	strove	striven
shake (shaking)	shook	shaken			
			swear	swore	sworn
shall	should	–	sweep	swept	swept
shine (shining)	shone	shone	swell	swelled	swollen (o swelled)

present	past tense	past participle	present	past tense	past participle
swim (swimming)	swam	swum	wake (waking)	woke (o waked)	woken (o waked)
swing	swung	swung	wear	wore	worn
take (taking)	took	taken	weave (weaving)	wove (o weaved)	woven (o weaved)
teach	taught	taught	weep	wept	wept
tear	tore	torn	win (winning)	won	won
tell	told	told			
think	thought	thought	wind	wound	wound
throw	threw	thrown	write (writing)	wrote	written
thrust	thrust	thrust			
tread	trod	trodden			

IRREGULAR GERMAN VERBS

Infinitiv	Präsens 2., 3. Singular	Imperfekt	Partizip Perfekt
backen	bäckst, bäckt	backte o buk	gebacken
befehlen	befiehlst, befiehlt	befahl	befohlen
beginnen	beginnst, beginnt	begann	begonnen
beißen	beißt, beißt	biss	gebissen
bergen	birgst, birgt	barg	geborgen
betrügen	betrügst, betrügt	betrog	betrogen
biegen	biegst, biegt	bog	gebogen
bieten	bietest, bietet	bot	geboten
binden	bindest, bindet	band	gebunden
bitten	bittest, bittet	bat	gebeten
blasen	bläst, bläst	blies	geblasen
bleiben	bleibst, bleibt	blieb	geblieben
braten	brätst, brät	briet	gebraten
brechen	brichst, bricht	brach	gebrochen
brennen	brennst, brennt	brannte	gebrannt
bringen	bringst, bringt	brachte	gebracht
denken	denkst, denkt	dachte	gedacht
dringen	dringst, dringt	drang	gedrungen
dürfen	darfst, darf	durfte	gedurft
erschrecken	erschrickst, erschrickt	erschrak	erschrocken
essen	isst, isst	aß	gegessen
fahren	fährst, fährt	fuhr	gefahren
fallen	fällst, fällt	fiel	gefallen
fangen	fängst, fängt	fing	gefangen
finden	findest, findet	fand	gefunden
fliegen	fliegst, fliegt	flog	geflogen
fließen	fließt, fließt	floss	geflossen
fressen	frisst, frisst	fraß	gefressen
frieren	frierst, friert	fror	gefroren
geben	gibst, gibt	gab	gegeben
gehen	gehst, geht	ging	gegangen
gelingen	–, gelingt	gelang	gelungen
gelten	giltst, gilt	galt	gegolten
genießen	genießt, genießt	genoss	genossen
geschehen	–, geschieht	geschah	geschehen
gewinnen	gewinnst, gewinnt	gewann	gewonnen
gießen	gießt, gießt	goss	gegossen
gleichen	gleichst, gleicht	glich	geglichen
gleiten	gleitest, gleitet	glitt	geglitten
graben	gräbst, gräbt	grub	gegraben
greifen	greifst, greift	griff	gegriffen
haben	hast, hat	hatte	gehabt
halten	hältst, hält	hielt	gehalten
hängen	hängst, hängt	hing	gehangen

Infinitiv	Präsens 2., 3. Singular	Imperfekt	Partizip Perfekt
heben	hebst, hebt	hob	gehoben
heißen	heißt, heißt	hieß	geheißen
helfen	hilfst, hilft	half	geholfen
kennen	kennst, kennt	kannte	gekannt
klingen	klingst, klingt	klang	geklungen
kommen	kommst, kommt	kam	gekommen
können	kannst, kann	konnte	gekonnt
kriechen	kriechst, kriecht	kroch	gekrochen
laden	lädst, lädt	lud	geladen
lassen	lässt, lässt	ließ	gelassen
laufen	läufst, läuft	lief	gelaufen
leiden	leidest, leidet	litt	gelitten
leihen	leihst, leiht	lieh	geliehen
lesen	liest, liest	las	gelesen
liegen	liegst, liegt	lag	gelegen
lügen	lügst, lügt	log	gelogen
mahlen	mahlst, mahlt	mahlte	gemahlen
meiden	meidest, meidet	mied	gemieden
messen	misst, misst	maß	gemessen
mögen	magst, mag	mochte	gemocht
müssen	musst, muss	musste	gemusst
nehmen	nimmst, nimmt	nahm	genommen
nennen	nennst, nennt	nannte	genannt
pfeifen	pfeifst, pfeift	pfiff	gepfiffen
raten	rätst, rät	riet	geraten
reiben	reibst, reibt	rieb	gerieben
reißen	reißt, reißt	riss	gerissen
reiten	reitest, reitet	ritt	geritten
rennen	rennst, rennt	rannte	gerannt
riechen	riechst, riecht	roch	gerochen
rufen	rufst, ruft	rief	gerufen
saufen	säufst, säuft	soff	gesoffen
saugen	saugst, saugt	sog o saugte	gesogen o gesaugt
schaffen	schaffst, schafft	schuf	geschaffen
scheiden	scheidest, scheidet	schied	geschieden
scheinen	scheinst, scheint	schien	geschienen
schieben	schiebst, schiebt	schob	geschoben
schießen	schießt, schießt	schoss	geschossen
schlafen	schläfst, schläft	schlief	geschlafen
schlagen	schlägst, schlägt	schlug	geschlagen
schleichen	schleichst, schleicht	schlich	geschlichen
schließen	schließt, schließt	schloss	geschlossen
schmeißen	schmeißt, schmeißt	schmiss	geschmissen
schmelzen	schmilzt, schmilzt	schmolz	geschmolzen
schneiden	schneidest, schneidet	schnitt	geschnitten

Infinitiv	Präsens 2., 3. Singular	Imperfekt	Partizip Perfekt
schreiben	schreibst, schreibt	schrieb	geschrieben
schreien	schreist, schreit	schrie	geschrie(e)n
schweigen	schweigst, schweigt	schwieg	geschwiegen
schwellen	schwillst, schwillt	schwoll	geschwollen
schwimmen	schwimmst, schwimmt	schwamm	geschwommen
schwören	schwörst, schwört	schwor	geschworen
sehen	siehst, sieht	sah	gesehen
sein	bist, ist	war	gewesen
senden	sendest, sendet	sandte	gesandt
singen	singst, singt	sang	gesungen
sinken	sinkst, sinkt	sank	gesunken
sitzen	sitzt, sitzt	saß	gesessen
sollen	sollst, soll	sollte	gesollt
sprechen	sprichst, spricht	sprach	gesprochen
springen	springst, springt	sprang	gesprungen
stechen	stichst, sticht	stach	gestochen
stehen	stehst, steht	stand	gestanden
stehlen	stiehlst, stiehlt	stahl	gestohlen
steigen	steigst, steigt	stieg	gestiegen
sterben	stirbst, stirbt	starb	gestorben
stinken	stinkst, stinkt	stank	gestunken
stoßen	stößt, stößt	stieß	gestoßen
streichen	streichst, streicht	strich	gestrichen
streiten	streitest, streitet	stritt	gestritten
tragen	trägst, trägt	trug	getragen
treffen	triffst, trifft	traf	getroffen
treiben	treibst, treibt	trieb	getrieben
treten	trittst, tritt	trat	getreten
trinken	trinkst, trinkt	trank	getrunken
tun	tust, tut	tat	getan
verderben	verdirbst, verdirbt	verdarb	verdorben
vergessen	vergisst, vergisst	vergaß	vergessen
verlieren	verlierst, verliert	verlor	verloren
verschwinden	verschwindest, verschwindet	verschwand	verschwunden
verzeihen	verzeihst, verzeiht	verzieh	verziehen
wachsen	wächst, wächst	wuchs	gewachsen
wenden	wendest, wendet	wandte	gewandt
werben	wirbst, wirbt	warb	geworben
werden	wirst, wird	wurde	geworden
werfen	wirfst, wirft	warf	geworfen
wiegen	wiegst, wiegt	wog	gewogen
wissen	weißt, weiß	wusste	gewusst
wollen	willst, will	wollte	gewollt
ziehen	ziehst, zieht	zog	gezogen
zwingen	zwingst, zwingt	zwang	gezwungen

à *prep +akk* at ... each; **4 Tickets ~ 8 Euro** 4 tickets at 8 euros each

A *abk* = **Autobahn** ≈ M (*Brit*), ≈ I (*US*)

Aal (-(e)s, -e) *m* eel

SCHLÜSSELWORT

ab *prep +dat* from; **Kinder ab 12 Jahren** children from the age of 12; **ab morgen** from tomorrow; **ab sofort** as of now

▷ *adv* **1** off; **links ab** to the left; **der Knopf ist ab** the button has come off; **ab nach Hause!** off you go home

2 (*zeitlich*) **von da ab** from then on; **von heute ab** from today, as of today

3 (*auf Fahrplänen*) **München ab 12.20** leaving Munich 12.20

4 ab und zu *o* **an** now and then *o* again

ab|bauen *vt* (*Zelt*) to take down; (*verringern*) to reduce

ab|beißen *irr vt* to bite off

ab|bestellen *vt* to cancel

ab|biegen *irr vi* to turn off; (*Straße*) to bend; **nach links/rechts ~** to turn left/right

Abbildung *f* illustration

ab|blasen *irr vt* (*fig*) to call off

ab|blenden *vt, vi* (*Auto*) (**die Scheinwerfer**) **~** to dip (*Brit*) (*o* to dim (*US*)) one's headlights; **Abblendlicht** *nt* dipped (*Brit*) (*o* dimmed (*US*)) headlights *pl*

ab|brechen *irr vt* to break off; (*Gebäude*) to pull down; (*aufhören*) to stop; (*Computerprogramm*) to abort

ab|bremsen *vi* to brake, to slow down

ab|bringen *irr vt*: **jdn von einer Idee ~** to talk sb out of an idea; **jdn vom Thema ~** to get sb away from the subject; **davon lasse ich mich nicht ~** nothing will make me change my mind about it

ab|buchen *vt* to debit (*von* to)

ab|danken *vi* to resign

ab|drehen *vt* (*Gas, Wasser*) to turn off; (*Licht*) to switch off ▷ *vi* (*Schiff, Flugzeug*) to change course

Abend (-s, -e) *m* evening; **am ~** in the evening; **zu ~ essen** to have dinner; **heute/morgen/gestern ~** this/tomorrow/yesterday evening; **guten ~!** good evening; **Abendbrot** *nt* supper; **Abendessen** *nt* dinner; **Abendgarderobe** *f* evening dress (*o* gown); **Abendkasse** *f* box office; **Abendkleid** *nt* evening dress (*o* gown); **Abendmahl** *nt*: **das ~** (Holy) Communion; **abends** *adv* in the evening; **montags ~** on Monday evenings

Abenteuer (-s, -) *nt* adventure; **Abenteuerurlaub** *m* adventure holiday

aber _conj_ but; _(jedoch)_ however; **oder ~** alternatively; **~ ja!** (but) of course; **das ist ~ nett von Ihnen** that's really nice of you

abergläubisch _adj_ superstitious

ab|fahren _irr vi_ to leave _(o to depart)_ _(nach for)_; _(Ski)_ to ski down; **Abfahrt** _f_ departure; _(von Autobahn)_ exit; _(Ski)_ descent; _(Piste)_ run; **Abfahrtslauf** _m_ _(Ski)_ downhill; **Abfahrtszeit** _f_ departure time

Abfall _m_ waste; _(Müll)_ rubbish _(Brit)_, garbage _(US)_; **Abfalleimer** _m_ rubbish bin _(Brit)_, garbage can _(US)_

abfällig _adj_ disparaging; **~ von jdm sprechen** to make disparaging remarks about sb

ab|färben _vi_ _(Wäsche)_ to run; _(fig)_ to rub off

ab|fertigen _vt_ _(Pakete)_ to prepare for dispatch; _(an der Grenze)_ to clear; **Abfertigungsschalter** _m_ _(am Flughafen)_ check-in desk

ab|finden _irr vt_ to pay off ▷ _vr_: **sich mit etw ~** to come to terms with sth; **Abfindung** _f_ _(Entschädigung)_ compensation; _(von Angestellten)_ redundancy payment

ab|fliegen _irr vi_ _(Flugzeug)_ to take off; _(Passagier a.)_ to fly off; **Abflug** _m_ departure; _(Start)_ takeoff; **Abflughalle** _f_ departure lounge; **Abflugzeit** _f_ departure time

Abfluss _m_ drain; _(am Waschbecken)_ plughole _(Brit)_; **Abflussrohr** _nt_ waste pipe; _(außen)_ drainpipe

ab|fragen _vt_ to test; _(Inform)_ to call up

ab|führen _vi_ _(Med)_ to have a laxative effect ▷ _vt_ _(Steuern, Gebühren)_ to pay; **jdn ~ lassen** to take sb into custody; **Abführmittel** _nt_ laxative

Abgabe _f_ handing in; _(von Ball)_ pass; _(Steuer)_ tax; _(einer Erklärung)_ making; **abgabenfrei** _adj_ tax-free; **abgabenpflichtig** _adj_ liable to tax

Abgase _pl_ _(Auto)_ exhaust fumes _pl_; **Abgas(sonder)untersuchung** _f_ exhaust emission test

ab|geben _irr vt_ _(Gepäck, Schlüssel)_ to leave _(bei with)_; _(Schularbeit etc)_ to hand in; _(Wärme)_ to give off; _(Erklärung, Urteil)_ to make ▷ _vr_: **sich mit jdm ~** to associate with sb; **sich mit etw ~** to bother with sth

abgebildet _adj_: **wie oben ~** as shown above

ab|gehen _irr vi_ _(Post)_ to go; _(Knopf etc)_ to come off; _(abgezogen werden)_ to be taken off; _(Straße)_ to branch off; **von der Schule ~** to leave school; **sie geht mir ab** I really miss her; **was geht denn hier ab?** _(fam)_ what's going on here?

abgehetzt _adj_ exhausted, shattered

abgelaufen _adj_ _(Pass)_ expired; _(Zeit, Frist)_ up; **die Milch ist ~** the milk is past its sell-by date

abgelegen _adj_ remote

abgemacht _interj_ OK, it's a deal, that's settled, then

abgeneigt _adj_ **einer Sache** _(dat)_ **~ sein** to be averse to sth; **ich wäre nicht ~, das zu tun** I wouldn't mind doing that

Abgeordnete(r) _mf_ Member of Parliament

abgepackt _adj_ prepacked

abgerissen _adj_: **der Knopf ist ~** the button has come off

abgesehen _adj_: **es auf jdn/etw ~ haben** to be after sb/sth; **~ von** apart from

abgespannt _adj_ _(Person)_ exhausted, worn out

abgestanden adj stale; (Bier) flat
abgestorben adj (Pflanze) dead; (Finger) numb
abgestumpft adj (Person) insensitive
abgetragen adj (Kleidung) worn
ab|gewöhnen vt: **jdm etw ~** to cure sb of sth; **sich etw ~** to give sth up
ab|haken vt to tick off; **das (Thema) ist schon abgehakt** that's been dealt with
ab|halten irr vt (Versammlung) to hold; **jdn von etw ~** (fernhalten) to keep sb away from sth; (hindern) to keep sb from sth
abhanden adj: **~ kommen** to get lost
Abhang m slope
ab|hängen vt (Bild) to take down; (Anhänger) to uncouple; (Verfolger) to shake off ▷ irr vi: **von jdm/etw ~** to depend on sb/sth; **das hängt davon ab, ob ...** it depends (on) whether ...; **abhängig** adj dependent (von on)
ab|hauen irr vt (abschlagen) to cut off ▷ vi (fam: verschwinden) to clear off; **hau ab!** get lost!, beat it!
ab|heben irr vt (Geld) to withdraw; (Telefonhörer, Spielkarte) to pick up ▷ vi (Flugzeug) to take off; (Rakete) to lift off; (Karten) to cut
ab|holen vt to collect; (am Bahnhof etc) to meet; (mit dem Auto) to pick up; **Abholmarkt** m cash and carry
ab|horchen vt (Med) to listen to
ab|hören vt (Vokabeln) to test; (Telefongespräch) to tap; (Tonband etc) to listen to
Abitur (-s, -e) nt German school-leaving examination, ≈ A-levels (Brit), ≈ High School Diploma (US)

▪ **ABITUR**
▪
▪ The **Abitur** is the German
▪ school-leaving examination
▪ which is taken at the age of 18
▪ or 19 by pupils at a **Gymnasium**.
▪ It is taken in four subjects and is
▪ necessary for entry to
▪ university.

ab|kaufen vt: **jdm etw ~** to buy sth from sb; **das kauf ich dir nicht ab!** (fam: glauben) I don't believe you
ab|klingen irr vi (Schmerz) to ease; (Wirkung) to wear off
ab|kommen irr vi to get away; **von der Straße ~** to leave the road; **von einem Plan ~** to give up a plan; **vom Thema ~** to stray from the point
Abkommen (-s, -) nt agreement
ab|koppeln vt (Anhänger) to unhitch
ab|kratzen vt to scrape off ▷ vi (fam: sterben) to kick the bucket, to croak
ab|kühlen vi, vt to cool down ▷ vr: **sich ~** to cool down
ab|kürzen vt (Wort) to abbreviate; **den Weg ~** to take a short cut; **Abkürzung** f (Wort) abbreviation; (Weg) short cut
ab|laden irr vt to unload
Ablage f (für Akten) tray; (Aktenordnung) filing system
Ablauf m (Abfluss) drain; (von Ereignissen) course; (einer Frist, Zeit) expiry; **ab|laufen** irr vi (abfließen) to drain away; (Ereignisse) to happen; (Frist, Zeit, Pass) to expire
ab|legen vt to put down; (Kleider) to take off; (Gewohnheit) to get out of; (Prüfung) to take, to sit; (Akten) to file away ▷ vi (Schiff) to cast off
ab|lehnen vt to reject; (Einladung) to decline; (missbilligen)

to disapprove of; (*Bewerber*) to turn down ▷ *vi* to decline

ab|lenken *vt* to distract; **jdn von der Arbeit ~** to distract sb from their work; **vom Thema ~** to change the subject; **Ablenkung** *f* distraction

ab|lesen *vt* (*Text, Rede*) to read; **das Gas/den Strom ~** to read the gas/electricity meter

ab|liefern *vt* to deliver

ab|machen *vt* (*entfernen*) to take off; (*vereinbaren*) to agree; **Abmachung** *f* agreement

ab|melden *vt* (*Zeitung*) to cancel; (*Auto*) to take off the road ▷ *vr*: **sich ~** to give notice of one's departure; (*im Hotel*) to check out; (*vom Verein*) to cancel one's membership

ab|messen *irr vt* to measure

ab|nehmen *irr vt* to take off, to remove; (*Hörer*) to pick up; (*Führerschein*) to take away; (*Geld*) to get (*jdm* out of sb); (*kaufen, umg: glauben*) to buy (*jdm* from sb) ▷ *vi* to decrease; (*schlanker werden*) to lose weight; (*Tel*) to pick up the phone; **fünf Kilo ~** to lose five kilos

Abneigung *f* dislike (*gegen* of); (*stärker*) aversion (*gegen* to)

ab|nutzen *vt* to wear out ▷ *vr*: **sich ~** to wear out

Abonnement (*-s, -s*) *nt* subscription; **Abonnent(in)** *m(f)* subscriber; **abonnieren** *vt* to subscribe to

ab|raten *irr vi*: **jdn von etw ~** to advise sb against sth

ab|räumen *vt*: **den Tisch ~** to clear the table; **das Geschirr ~** to clear away the dishes; (*Preis etc*) to walk off with

Abrechnung *f* settlement; (*Rechnung*) bill

ab|regen *vr*: **sich ~** (*fam*) to calm

(*o to cool*) down; **reg dich ab!** take it easy

Abreise *f* departure; **ab|reisen** *vi* to leave (*nach* for); **Abreisetag** *m* day of departure

ab|reißen *irr vt* (*Haus*) to pull down; (*Blatt*) to tear off; **den Kontakt nicht ~ lassen** to stay in touch ▷ *vi* (*Knopf etc*) to come off

ab|runden *vt*: **eine Zahl nach oben/unten ~** to round a number up/down

abrupt *adj* abrupt

ABS *nt abk* = **Antiblockiersystem** (*Auto*) ABS

Abs. *abk* = **Absender** from

ab|sagen *vt* to cancel, to call off; (*Einladung*) to turn down ▷ *vi* (*ablehnen*) to decline; **ich muss leider ~** I'm afraid I can't come

Absatz *m* (*Comm*) sales *pl*; (*neuer Abschnitt*) paragraph; (*Schuh*) heel

ab|schaffen *vt* to abolish, to do away with

ab|schalten *vt, vi* (*a. fig*) to switch off

ab|schätzen *vt* to estimate; (*Lage*) to assess

abscheulich *adj* disgusting

ab|schicken *vt* to send off

ab|schieben *irr vt* (*ausweisen*) to deport

Abschied (*-(e)s, -e*) *m* parting; **~ nehmen** to say good-bye (*von jdm* to sb); **Abschiedsfeier** *f* farewell party

Abschlagszahlung *f* interim payment

Abschleppdienst *m* (*Auto*) breakdown service; **ab|schleppen** *vt* to tow; **Abschleppseil** *nt* towrope; **Abschleppwagen** *m* breakdown truck (*Brit*), tow truck (*US*)

ab|schließen *irr vt* (*Tür*) to lock; (*beenden*) to conclude, to finish; (*Vertrag, Handel*) to conclude;

Abschluss m (Beendigung) close, conclusion; (von Vertrag, Handel) conclusion

ab|schmecken vt (kosten) to taste; (würzen) to season

ab|schminken vr: **sich ~** to take one's make-up off ▷ vt (fam) **sich** (dat) **etw ~** to get sth out of one's mind

ab|schnallen vr: **sich ~** to undo one's seatbelt

ab|schneiden irr vt to cut off ▷ vi: **gut/schlecht ~** to do well/badly

Abschnitt m (von Buch, Text) section; (Kontrollabschnitt) stub

ab|schrauben vt to unscrew

ab|schrecken vt to deter, to put off

ab|schreiben irr vt to copy (bei, von from, off); (verloren geben) to write off; (Comm: absetzen) to deduct

abschüssig adj steep

ab|schwächen vt to lessen; (Behauptung, Kritik) to tone down

ab|schwellen irr vi (Entzündung) to go down; (Lärm) to die down

absehbar adj foreseeable; **in ~er Zeit** in the foreseeable future; **ab|sehen** irr vt (Ende, Folgen) to foresee ▷ vi: **von etw ~** to refrain from sth

abseits adv out of the way; (Sport) offside ▷ prep +gen away from; **Abseits** nt (Sport) offside; **Abseitsfalle** f (Sport) offside trap

ab|senden irr vt to send off; (Post) to post; **Absender(in)** (-s, -) m(f) sender

ab|setzen vt (Glas, Brille etc) to put down; (aussteigen lassen) to drop (off); (Comm) to sell; (Fin) to deduct; (streichen) to drop ▷ vr: **sich ~** (sich entfernen) to clear off; (sich ablagern) to be deposited

Absicht f intention; **mit ~** on purpose; **absichtlich** adj intentional, deliberate

absolut adj absolute

ab|specken vi (fam) to lose weight

ab|speichern vt (Inform) to save

ab|sperren vt to block (o to close) off; (Tür) to lock; **Absperrung** f (Vorgang) blocking (o closing) off; (Sperre) barricade

ab|spielen vt (CD etc) to play ▷ vr: **sich ~** to happen

ab|springen irr vi to jump down/off; (von etw Geplantem) to drop out (von of)

ab|spülen vt to rinse; (Geschirr) to wash (up)

Abstand m distance; (zeitlich) interval; **~ halten** to keep one's distance

ab|stauben vt, vi to dust; (fam: stehlen) to pinch

Abstecher (-s, -) m detour

ab|steigen irr vi (vom Rad etc) to get off, to dismount; (in Gasthof) to stay (in +dat at)

ab|stellen vt (niederstellen) to put down; (Auto) to park; (ausschalten) to turn (o to switch) off; (Missstand, Unsitte) to stop; **Abstellraum** m store room

Abstieg (-(e)s, -e) m (vom Berg) descent; (Sport) relegation

ab|stimmen vi to vote ▷ vt (Termine, Ziele) to fit in (auf +akk with); **Dinge aufeinander ~** to coordinate things ▷ vr: **sich ~** to come to an agreement (o arrangement)

abstoßend adj repulsive

abstrakt adj abstract

ab|streiten irr vt to deny

Abstrich m (Med) smear; **~e machen** to cut back (an +dat on); (weniger erwarten) to lower one's sights

Absturz m fall; (Aviat, Inform)

crash; **ab|stürzen** vi to fall;
(Aviat, Inform) to crash
absurd adj absurd
Abszess (-es, -e) m abscess
ab|tauen vt, vi to thaw;
(Kühlschrank) to defrost
Abtei (-, -en) f abbey
Abteil (-(e)s, -e) nt compartment
Abteilung f (in Firma, Kaufhaus)
department; (in Krankenhaus)
section
ab|treiben irr vt (Kind) to abort
▷ vi to be driven off course; (Med:
Abtreibung vornehmen) to carry out
an abortion; (Abtreibung vornehmen
lassen) to have an abortion;
Abtreibung f abortion
ab|trocknen vt to dry
ab|warten vt to wait for; **das
bleibt abzuwarten** that remains
to be seen ▷ vi to wait
abwärts adv down
Abwasch (-(e)s) m washing-up;
ab|waschen irr vt (Schmutz) to
wash off; (Geschirr) to wash (up)
Abwasser (-s, Abwässer) nt
sewage
ab|wechseln vr: **sich ~** to
alternate; **sich mit jdm ~** to take
turns with sb; **abwechselnd** adv
alternately; **Abwechslung** f
change; **zur ~** for a change
ab|weisen irr vt to turn away;
(Antrag) to turn down; **abweisend**
adj unfriendly
abwesend adj absent;
Abwesenheit f absence
ab|wiegen irr vt to weigh (out)
ab|wimmeln vt (fam) **jdn ~** to
get rid of sb, to give sb the elbow
ab|wischen vt (Gesicht, Tisch etc)
to wipe; (Schmutz) to wipe off
ab|zählen vt to count; (Geld) to
count out
Abzeichen nt badge
ab|zeichnen vt to draw, to copy;
(Dokument) to initial ▷ vr: **sich**

~ to stand out; (fig: bevorstehen) to
loom
ab|ziehen irr vt to take off; (Bett)
to strip; (Schlüssel) to take out;
(subtrahieren) to take away, to
subtract ▷ vi to go away
Abzug m (Foto) print; (Öffnung)
vent; (Truppen) withdrawal;
(Betrag) deduction; **nach ~ der
Kosten** charges deducted;
abzüglich prep +gen minus;
~ 20% Rabatt less 20% discount
ab|zweigen vi to branch off ▷ vt
to set aside; **Abzweigung** f
junction
Accessoires pl accessories pl
ach interj oh; **~ so!** oh, I see;
~ was! (Überraschung) really?;
(Ärger) don't talk nonsense
Achse (-, -n) f axis; (Auto) axle
Achsel (-, -n) f shoulder;
(Achselhöhle) armpit
Achsenbruch m (Auto) broken
axle
acht num eight; **heute in ~ Tagen**
in a week('s time), a week from
today
Acht (-) f: **sich in ~ nehmen** to be
careful (vor +dat of), to watch out
(vor +dat for); **etw außer ~ lassen**
to disregard sth
achte(r, s) adj eighth; siehe auch
dritte; **Achtel** (-s, -) nt (Bruchteil)
eighth; (Wein etc) eighth of a litre;
(Glas Wein) ≈ small glass
achten vt to respect ▷ vi to pay
attention (auf +akk to)
Achterbahn f big dipper, roller
coaster
acht|geben irr vi to take care
(auf +akk of)
achthundert num eight
hundred; **achtmal** adv eight
times
Achtung f attention; (Ehrfurcht)
respect ▷ interj look out
achtzehn num eighteen;

achtzehnte(r, s) *adj*
eighteenth; *siehe auch* **dritte**;
achtzig *num* eighty; **in den ~er
Jahren** in the eighties;
achtzigste(r, s) *adj* eightieth
Acker (*-s, Äcker*) *m* field
Action (*-, -s*) *f* (*fam*) action;
Actionfilm *m* action film
Adapter (*-s, -*) *m* adapter
addieren *vt* to add (up)
Adel (*-s*) *m* nobility; **adelig** *adj*
noble
Ader (*-, -n*) *f* vein
Adjektiv *nt* adjective
Adler (*-s, -*) *m* eagle
adoptieren *vt* to adopt;
Adoption *f* adoption;
Adoptiveltern *pl* adoptive
parents *pl*; **Adoptivkind** *nt*
adopted child
Adrenalin (*-s*) *nt* adrenalin
Adressbuch *nt* directory;
(*persönliches*) address book;
Adresse (*-, -n*) *f* address;
adressieren *vt* to address (*an
+akk* to)
Advent (*-s, -*) *m* Advent;
Adventskranz *m* Advent wreath
Adverb *nt* adverb
Aerobic (*-s*) *nt* aerobics *sing*
Affäre (*-, -n*) *f* affair
Affe (*-n, -n*) *m* monkey
Afghanistan (*-s*) *nt*
Afghanistan
Afrika (*-s*) *nt* Africa;
Afrikaner(in) (*-s, -*) *m(f)* African;
afrikanisch *adj* African
After (*-s, -*) *m* anus
Aftershave (*-(s), -s*) *nt*
aftershave
AG (*-, -s*) *f abk* =
Aktiengesellschaft plc (*Brit*),
corp. (*US*)
Agent(in) *m(f)* agent; **Agentur**
f agency
aggressiv *adj* aggressive
Ägypten (*-s*) *nt* Egypt

ah *interj* ah, ooh
äh *interj* (*Sprechpause*) er, um;
(*angeekelt*) ugh
aha *interj* I see, aha
ähneln *vi +dat* to be like, to
resemble ▷ *vr:* **sich ~** to be alike (*o
similar*)
ahnen *vt* to suspect; **du ahnst es
nicht!** would you believe it?
ähnlich *adj* similar (*dat* to); **jdm
~ sehen** to look like sb;
Ähnlichkeit *f* similarity
Ahnung *f* idea; (*Vermutung*)
suspicion; **keine ~!** no idea;
ahnungslos *adj* unsuspecting
Ahorn (*-s, -e*) *m* maple
Aids (*-*) *nt* Aids; **aidskrank** *adj*
suffering from Aids; **Aidstest** *m*
Aids test
Airbag (*-s, -s*) *m* (*Auto*) airbag;
Airbus *m* airbus
Akademie (*-, -n*) *f* academy;
Akademiker(in) (*-s, -*) *m(f)*
(university) graduate
akklimatisieren *vr:* **sich ~** to
acclimatize oneself
Akkordeon (*-s, -s*) *nt* accordion
Akku (*-s, -s*) *m* (storage) battery
Akkusativ *m* accusative (case)
Akne (*-, -*) *f* acne
Akrobat(in) (*-s, -en*) *m(f)* acrobat
Akt (*-(e)s, -e*) *m* act; (*Kunst*) nude
Akte (*-, -n*) *f* file; **etw zu den ~n
legen** (*a. fig*) to file sth away;
Aktenkoffer *m* briefcase
Aktie (*-, -n*) *f* share;
Aktiengesellschaft *f* public
limited company (*Brit*),
corporation (*US*)
Aktion *f* (*Kampagne*) campaign;
(*Einsatz*) operation
Aktionär(in) (*-s, -e*) *m(f)*
shareholder
aktiv *adj* active; **aktivieren** *vt*
to activate
aktualisieren *vt* to update;
aktuell *adj* (*Thema*) topical;

(*modern*) up-to-date; (*Problem*) current; **nicht mehr ~** no longer relevant

Akupunktur f acupuncture

akustisch *adj* acoustic; **Akustik** f acoustics *sing*

akut *adj* acute

AKW (-*s*, -*s*) *nt* abk = **Atomkraftwerk** nuclear power station

Akzent (-(*e*)*s*, -*e*) *m* accent; (*Betonung*) stress; **mit starkem schottischen ~** with a strong Scottish accent

akzeptieren *vt* to accept

Alarm (-(*e*)*s*, -*e*) *m* alarm; **Alarmanlage** f alarm system; **alarmieren** *vt* to alarm; **die Polizei ~** to call the police

Albanien (-*s*) *nt* Albania

Albatros (-*ses*, -*se*) *m* albatross

albern *adj* silly

Albtraum *m* nightmare

Album (-*s*, *Alben*) *nt* album

Algen *pl* algae *pl*; (*Meeresalgen*) seaweed *sing*

Algerien (-*s*) *nt* Algeria

Alibi (-*s*, -*s*) *nt* alibi

Alimente *pl* maintenance *sing*

Alkohol (-*s*, -*e*) *m* alcohol; **alkoholfrei** *adj* non-alcoholic; **~es Getränk** soft drink; **Alkoholiker(in)** (-*s*, -) *m(f)* alcoholic; **alkoholisch** *adj* alcoholic; **Alkoholtest** *m* breathalyser® test (*Brit*), alcohol test

All (-*s*) *nt* universe

 SCHLÜSSELWORT

alle(r, s) *adj* 1 (*sämtliche*) all; **wir alle** all of us; **alle Kinder waren da** all the children were there; **alle Kinder mögen ...** all children like ...; **alle beide** both of us/them; **sie kamen alle** they all came; **alles Gute** all the best; **alles**

in allem all in all

2 (*mit Zeit- oder Maßangaben*) every; **alle vier Jahre** every four years; **alle fünf Meter** every five metres

▷ *pron* everything; **alles, was er sagt** everything he says, all that he says

▷ *adv* (*zu Ende, aufgebraucht*) finished; **die Milch ist alle** the milk's all gone, there's no milk left; **etw alle machen** to finish sth up

Allee (-, -*n*) f avenue

allein *adj*, *adv* alone; (*ohne Hilfe*) on one's own, by oneself; **nicht ~** (*nicht nur*) not only; **alleinerziehend** *adj*: **~e Mutter** single mother; **Alleinerziehende(r)** *mf* single mother/father/parent; **alleinstehend** *adj* single, unmarried

allerbeste(r, s) *adj* very best

allerdings *adv* (*zwar*) admittedly; (*gewiss*) certainly, sure (*US*)

allererste(r, s) *adj* very first; **zu allererst** first of all

Allergie f allergy; **Allergiker(in)** (-*s*, -) *m(f)* allergy sufferer; **allergisch** *adj* allergic (*gegen* to)

allerhand *adj inv* (*fam*) all sorts of; **das ist doch ~!** (*Vorwurf*) that's the limit

Allerheiligen (-) *nt* All Saints' Day

allerhöchste(r, s) *adj* very highest; **allerhöchstens** *adv* at the very most; **allerlei** *adj inv* all sorts of; **allerletzte(r, s)** *adj* very last; **allerwenigste(r, s)** *adj* very least

alles *pron* everything; **~ in allem** all in all; *siehe auch* **alle**

Alleskleber (-*s*, -) *m* all-purpose glue

allgemein *adj* general; **im Allgemeinen** in general; **Allgemeinarzt** *m*,

Allgemeinärztin *f* GP (*Brit*), family practitioner (*US*)
Alligator (*-s, -en*) *m* alligator
alljährlich *adj* annual
allmählich *adj* gradual ▷ *adv* gradually
Allradantrieb *m* all-wheel drive
Alltag *m* everyday life; **alltäglich** *adj* everyday; (*gewöhnlich*) ordinary; (*tagtäglich*) daily
allzu *adv* all too
Allzweckreiniger (*-s, -*) *m* multi-purpose cleaner
Alpen *pl*: **die ~** the Alps *pl*
Alphabet (*-(e)s, -e*) *nt* alphabet; **alphabetisch** *adj* alphabetical
Alptraum *m siehe* **Albtraum**

⬤ **SCHLÜSSELWORT**

als *konj* 1 (*zeitlich*) when; (*gleichzeitig*) as; **damals, als ...** (in the days) when ...; **gerade, als ...** just as ...
2 (*in der Eigenschaft*) than; **als Antwort** as an answer; **als Kind** as a child
3 (*bei Vergleichen*) than; **ich kam später als er** I came later than he (did) *o* later than him; **lieber ... als ...** rather ... than ...; **nichts als Ärger** nothing but trouble
4 **als ob/wenn** as if

also *konj* (*folglich*) so, therefore ▷ *adv, interj* so; **~ gut** (*o* **schön**)! okay then
alt *adj* old; **wie ~ sind Sie?** how old are you?; **28 Jahre ~** 28 years old; **vier Jahre älter** four years older
Altar (*-(e)s, Altäre*) *m* altar
Alter (*-s, -*) *nt* age; (*hohes*) old age; **im ~ von** at the age of; **er ist in meinem ~** he's my age
alternativ *adj* alternative; (*umweltbewusst*) ecologically minded; (*Landwirtschaft*) organic; **Alternative** *f* alternative
Altersheim *nt* old people's home
Altglas *nt* used glass; **Altglascontainer** *m* bottle bank; **altmodisch** *adj* old-fashioned; **Altpapier** *nt* waste paper; **Altstadt** *f* old town
Alt-Taste *f* Alt key
Alufolie *f* tin (*o* kitchen) foil
Aluminium (*-s*) *nt* aluminium (*Brit*), aluminum (*US*)
Alzheimerkrankheit *f* Alzheimer's (disease)
am *kontr von* **an dem**; **~ 2. Januar** on January 2(nd); **~ Morgen** in the morning; **~ Strand** on the beach; **~ Bahnhof** at the station; **was gefällt Ihnen ~ besten?** what do you like best?; **~ besten bleiben wir hier** it would be best if we stayed here
Amateur(in) *m(f)* amateur
ambulant *adj* outpatient; **kann ich ~ behandelt werden?** can I have it done as an outpatient?; **Ambulanz** *f* (*Krankenwagen*) ambulance; (*in der Klinik*) outpatients' department
Ameise (*-, -n*) *f* ant
amen *interj* amen
Amerika (*-s*) *nt* America; **Amerikaner(in)** (*-s, -*) *m(f)* American; **amerikanisch** *adj* American
Ampel (*-, -n*) *f* traffic lights *pl*
Amphitheater *nt* amphitheatre
Amsel (*-, -n*) *f* blackbird
Amt (*-(e)s, Ämter*) *nt* (*Dienststelle*) office, department; (*Posten*) post; **amtlich** *adj* official; **Amtszeichen** *nt* (*Tel*) dialling tone (*Brit*), dial tone (*US*)
amüsant *adj* amusing; **amüsieren** *vt* to amuse ▷ *vr*: **sich ~** to enjoy oneself, to have a good time

○ SCHLÜSSELWORT

an prep +dat **1** (räumlich) (wo?) at; (auf, bei) on; (nahe bei) near; **an diesem Ort** at this place; **an der Wand** on the wall; **zu nahe an etw** too near to sth; **unten am Fluss** down by the river; **Köln liegt am Rhein** Cologne is on the Rhine

2 (zeitlich: wann?) on; **an diesem Tag** on this day; **an Ostern** at Easter

3 **arm an Fett** low in fat; **an etw sterben** to die of sth; **an (und für) sich** actually

▷ prep +akk **1** (räumlich: wohin?) to; **er ging ans Fenster** he went (over) to the window; **etw an die Wand hängen/schreiben** to hang/write sth on the wall

2 (woran?) **an etw denken** to think of sth

3 (gerichtet an) to; **ein Gruß/eine Frage an dich** greetings/a question to you

▷ adv **1** (ungefähr) about; **an die hundert** about a hundred

2 (auf Fahrplänen) **Frankfurt an 18.30** arriving Frankfurt 18.30

3 (ab) **von dort/heute an** from there/today onwards

4 (angeschaltet, angezogen) on; **das Licht ist an** the light is on; **ohne etwas an** with nothing on; siehe auch **am**

anal adj anal
analog adj analogous; (Inform) analog
Analyse (-, -n) f analysis; **analysieren** vt to analyse
Ananas (-, - o -se) f pineapple
an|baggern vt (fam) to chat up (Brit), to come on to (US)
Anbau m (Agr) cultivation; (Gebäude) extension; **an|bauen** vt (Agr) to cultivate; (Gebäudeteil) to build on
an|behalten irr vt to keep on
anbei adv enclosed; **~ sende ich ...** please find enclosed ...
an|beten vt to worship
an|bieten irr vt to offer ▷ vr: **sich ~** to volunteer
an|binden irr vt to tie up
Anblick m sight
an|braten irr vt to brown
an|brechen irr vt to start; (Vorräte, Ersparnisse) to break into; (Flasche, Packung) to open ▷ vi to start; (Tag) to break; (Nacht) to fall
an|brennen irr vt, vi to burn; **das Fleisch schmeckt angebrannt** the meat tastes burnt
an|bringen irr vt (herbeibringen) to bring; (befestigen) to fix, to attach
Andacht (-, -en) f devotion; (Gottesdienst) prayers pl
an|dauern vi to continue, to go on; **andauernd** adj continual
Andenken (-s, -) nt memory; (Gegenstand) souvenir
andere(r, s) adj (weitere) other; (verschieden) different; (folgend) next; **am ~n Tag** the next day; **von etw/jmd ~m sprechen** to talk about sth/sb else; **unter ~m** among other things; **andererseits** adv on the other hand
ändern vt to alter, to change ▷ vr: **sich ~** to change
andernfalls adv otherwise
anders adv differently (als from); **jemand/irgendwo ~** someone/somewhere else; **sie ist ~ als ihre Schwester** she's not like her sister; **es geht nicht ~** there's no other way; **anders(he)rum** adv the other way round; **anderswo** adv somewhere else
anderthalb num one and a half

Änderung f change, alteration
an|deuten vt to indicate; (Wink geben) to hint at
Andorra (-s) nt Andorra
Andrang m: **es herrschte großer ~** there was a huge crowd
an|drohen vt: **jdm etw ~** to threaten sb with sth
aneinander adv at/on/to one another (o each other); **~ denken** think of each other; **sich ~ gewöhnen** to get used to each other; **aneinander|geraten** irr vi to clash; **aneinander|legen** vt to put together
an|erkennen irr vt (Staat, Zeugnis etc) to recognize; (würdigen) to appreciate; **Anerkennung** f recognition; (Würdigung) appreciation
an|fahren irr vt (fahren gegen) to run into; (Ort, Hafen) to stop (o call) at; (liefern) to deliver; **jdn ~** (fig: schimpfen) to jump on sb ▷ vi to start; (losfahren) to drive off
Anfall m (Med) attack; **anfällig** adj delicate; (Maschine) temperamental; **~ für** prone to
Anfang (-(e)s, Anfänge) m beginning, start; **zu/am ~** to start with; **~ Mai** at the beginning of May; **sie ist ~ 20** she's in her early twenties; **an|fangen** irr vt, vi to begin, to start; **damit kann ich nichts ~** that's no use to me; **Anfänger(in)** (-s, -) m(f) beginner; **anfangs** adv at first; **Anfangsbuchstabe** m first (o initial) letter
an|fassen vt (berühren) to touch ▷ vi: **kannst du mal mit ~?** can you give me a hand?
Anflug m (Aviat) approach; (Hauch) trace
an|fordern vt to demand; **Anforderung** f request (von for); (Anspruch) demand

Anfrage f inquiry
an|freunden vr: **sich mit jdm ~** to make (o to become) friends with sb
an|fühlen vr: **sich ~** to feel; **es fühlt sich gut an** it feels good
Anführungszeichen pl quotation marks pl
Angabe f (Tech) specification; (fam: Prahlerei) showing off; (Tennis) serve; **~n** pl (Auskunft) particulars pl; **die ~n waren falsch** (Info) the information was wrong; **an|geben** irr vt (Name, Grund) to give; (zeigen) to indicate; (bestimmen) to set ▷ vi (fam: prahlen) to boast; (Sport) to serve; **Angeber(in)** (-s, -) m(f) (fam) show-off; **angeblich** adj alleged
angeboren adj inborn
Angebot nt offer; (Comm) supply (an +dat of); **~ und Nachfrage** supply and demand
angebracht adj appropriate
angebunden adj: **kurz ~** curt
angeheitert adj tipsy
an|gehen irr vt to concern; **das geht dich nichts an** that's none of your business; **ein Problem ~** to tackle a problem; **was ihn angeht** as far as he's concerned, as for him ▷ vi (Feuer) to catch; (fam: beginnen) to begin; **angehend** adj prospective
Angehörige(r) mf relative
Angeklagte(r) mf accused, defendant
Angel (-, -n) f fishing rod; (an der Tür) hinge
Angelegenheit f affair, matter
Angelhaken m fish hook; **angeln** vt to catch ▷ vi to fish; **Angeln** (-s) nt angling, fishing; **Angelrute** (-, -n) f fishing rod
angemessen adj appropriate, suitable

angenehm adj pleasant; **~!** (bei Vorstellung) pleased to meet you

angenommen adj assumed ▷ conj: **~, es regnet, was machen wir dann?** suppose it rains, what do we do then?

angesehen adj respected

angesichts prep +gen in view of, considering

Angestellte(r) mf employee

angetan adj: **von jdm/etw ~ sein** to be impressed by (o taken with) sb/sth

angewiesen adj: **auf jdn/etw ~ sein** to be dependent on sb/sth

an|gewöhnen vt: **sich etw ~** to get used to doing sth; **Angewohnheit** f habit

Angina (-, Anginen) f tonsillitis; **Angina Pectoris** (-) f angina

Angler(in) (-s, -) m(f) angler

Angora (-s) nt angora

an|greifen irr vt to attack; (anfassen) to touch; (beschädigen) to damage; **Angriff** m attack; **etw in ~ nehmen** to get started on sth

Angst (-, Ängste) f fear; **~ haben** to be afraid (o scared) (vor +dat of); **jdm ~ machen** to scare sb; **ängstigen** vt to frighten ▷ vr: **sich ~** to worry (um, wegen +dat about); **ängstlich** adj nervous; (besorgt) worried

an|haben irr vt (Kleidung) to have on, to wear; (Licht) to have on

an|halten irr vi to stop; (andauern) to continue; **anhaltend** adj continuous; **Anhalter(in)** (-s, -) m(f) hitch-hiker; **per ~ fahren** to hitch-hike

anhand prep +gen with; **~ von** by means of

an|hängen vt to hang up; (Eisenb: Wagen) to couple; (Zusatz) to add (on); **jdm etw ~** (fam: unterschieben) to pin sth on sb;

Anhänger (-s, -) m (Auto) trailer; (am Koffer) tag; (Schmuck) pendant; **Anhänger(in)** (-s, -) m(f) supporter; **Anhängerkupplung** f towbar; **anhänglich** adj affectionate (pej) clinging

Anhieb m: **auf ~** straight away; **das kann ich nicht auf ~ sagen** I can't say offhand

an|himmeln vt to worship, to idolize

an|hören vt to listen to ▷ vr: **sich ~** to sound; **das hört sich gut an** that sounds good

Animateur(in) m(f) host/hostess

Anis (-es, -e) m aniseed

Anker (-s, -) m anchor; **ankern** vt, vi to anchor; **Ankerplatz** m anchorage

an|klicken vt (Inform) to click on

an|klopfen vi to knock (an +akk on)

an|kommen irr vi to arrive; **bei jdm gut ~** to go down well with sb; **es kommt darauf an** it depends (ob on whether); **darauf kommt es nicht an** that doesn't matter

an|kotzen vt (vulg) **es kotzt mich an** it makes me sick

an|kreuzen vt to mark with a cross

an|kündigen vt to announce

Ankunft (-, Ankünfte) f arrival; **Ankunftszeit** f arrival time

Anlage f (Veranlagung) disposition; (Begabung) talent; (Park) gardens pl, grounds pl; (zu Brief etc) enclosure; (Stereoanlage) stereo (system); (Tech) plant; (Fin) investment

Anlass (-es, Anlässe) m cause (zu for); (Ereignis) occasion; **aus diesem ~** for this reason; **an|lassen** irr vt (Motor) to start; (Licht, Kleidung) to leave on;

Anlasser (-s, -) m (Auto) starter; **anlässlich** prep +gen on the occasion of

Anlauf m run-up; **an|laufen** irr vi to begin; (Film) to open; (Fenster) to mist up; (Metall) to tarnish

an|legen vt to put (an +akk against/on); (Schmuck) to put on; (Garten) to lay out; (Geld) to invest; (Gewehr) to aim (auf +akk at); **es auf etw** (akk) **~** to be out for sth ▷ vi (Schiff) to berth, to dock ▷ vr: **sich mit jdm ~** (fam) to pick a quarrel with sb; **Anlegestelle** f moorings pl

an|lehnen vt to lean (an +akk against); (Tür) to leave ajar ▷ vr: **sich ~** to lean (an +akk against)

an|leiern vt: **etw ~** (fam) to get sth going

Anleitung f instructions pl

Anliegen (-s, -) nt matter; (Wunsch) request

Anlieger(in) (-s, -) m(f) resident; **~ frei** residents only

an|lügen irr vt to lie to

an|machen vt (befestigen) to attach; (einschalten) to switch on; (Salat) to dress; (fam: aufreizen) to turn on; (fam: ansprechen) to chat up (Brit), to come on to (US); (fam: beschimpfen) to have a go at

Anmeldeformular nt application form; (bei Amt) registration form; **an|melden** vt (Besuch etc) to announce ▷ vr: **sich ~** (beim Arzt etc) to make an appointment; (bei Amt, für Kurs etc) to register; **Anmeldeschluss** m deadline for applications, registration deadline; **Anmeldung** f registration; (Antrag) application

an|nähen vt: **einen Knopf (an den Mantel) ~** to sew a button on (one's coat)

annähernd adv roughly; **nicht ~** nowhere near

Annahme (-, -n) f acceptance; (Vermutung) assumption, **annehmbar** adj acceptable; **an|nehmen** irr vt to accept; (Namen) to take; (Kind) to adopt; (vermuten) to suppose, to assume

Annonce (-, -n) f advertisement

an|öden vt (fam) to bore stiff (o silly)

annullieren vt to cancel

anonym adj anonymous

Anorak (-s, -s) m anorak

an|packen vt (Problem, Aufgabe) to tackle; **mit ~** to lend a hand

an|passen vt (fig) to adapt (dat to) ▷ vr: **sich ~** to adapt (an +akk to)

an|pfeifen irr vt (Fußballspiel) **das Spiel ~** to start the game; **Anpfiff** m (Sport) (starting) whistle; (Beginn) kick-off; (fam: Tadel) roasting

an|probieren vt to try on

Anrede f form of address; **an|reden** vt to address

an|regen vt to stimulate; **Anregung** f stimulation; (Vorschlag) suggestion

Anreise f journey; **an|reisen** vi to arrive; **Anreisetag** m day of arrival

Anreiz m incentive

an|richten vt (Speisen) to prepare; (Schaden) to cause

Anruf m call; **Anrufbeantworter** (-s, -) m answering machine, answerphone; **an|rufen** irr vt (Tel) to call, to phone, to ring (Brit)

ans kontr von **an das**

Ansage f announcement; (auf Anrufbeantworter) recorded message; **an|sagen** vt to announce; **angesagt sein** to be recommended; (modisch sein) to be the in thing

an|schaffen vt to buy
an|schauen vt to look at
Anschein m appearance; **dem** (o **allem**) **~ nach ...** it looks as if ...; **den ~ erwecken, hart zu arbeiten** to give the impression of working hard; **anscheinend** adj apparent ▷ adv apparently
an|schieben irr vt: **könnten Sie mich mal ~?** (Auto) could you give me a push?
Anschlag m notice; (Attentat) attack; **an|schlagen** irr vt (Plakat) to put up; (beschädigen) to chip ▷ vi (wirken) to take effect; **mit etw an etw** (akk) **~** to bang sth against sth
an|schließen irr vt (Elek, Tech) to connect (an +akk to); (mit Stecker) to plug in ▷ vi, vr (sich) **an etw** (akk) **~** (Gebäude etc) to adjoin sth; (zeitlich) to follow sth ▷ vr: **sich ~** to join (jdm/einer Gruppe sb/a group); **anschließend** adj adjacent; (zeitlich) subsequent ▷ adv afterwards; **~ an** (+akk) following; **Anschluss** m (Elek, Eisenb) connection; (von Wasser, Gas etc) supply; **im ~ an** (+akk) following; **kein ~ unter dieser Nummer** (Tel) the number you have dialled has not been recognized; **Anschlussflug** m connecting flight
an|schnallen vt (Skier) to put on ▷ vr: **sich ~** to fasten one's seat belt
Anschrift f address
an|schwellen irr vi to swell (up)
an|sehen irr vt to look at; (bei etw zuschauen) to watch; **jdn/etw als etw ~** to look on sb/sth as sth; **das sieht man ihm an** he looks it
an sein irr vi siehe **an**
an|setzen vt (Termin) to fix; (zubereiten) to prepare ▷ vi (anfangen) to start, to begin; **zu**

etw ~ to prepare to do sth
Ansicht f (Meinung) view, opinion; (Anblick) sight; **meiner ~ nach** in my opinion; **zur ~** on approval; **Ansichtskarte** f postcard
ansonsten adv otherwise
an|spielen vi **auf etw** (akk) **~** to allude to sth; **Anspielung** f allusion (auf +akk to)
an|sprechen irr vt to speak to; (gefallen) to appeal to ▷ vi **auf etw** (akk) **~** (Patient) to respond to sth; **ansprechend** adj attractive; **Ansprechpartner(in)** m(f) contact
an|springen irr vi (Auto) to start
Anspruch m claim; (Recht) right (auf +akk to); **etw in ~ nehmen** to take advantage of sth; **~ auf etw haben** to be entitled to sth; **anspruchslos** adj undemanding; (bescheiden) modest; **anspruchsvoll** adj demanding
Anstalt (-, -en) f institution
Anstand m decency; **anständig** adj decent; (fig, fam) proper; (groß) considerable
an|starren vt to stare at
anstatt prep +gen instead of
an|stecken vt to pin on; (Med) to infect; **jdn mit einer Erkältung ~** to pass one's cold on to sb ▷ vr: **ich habe mich bei ihm angesteckt** I caught it from him ▷ vi (fig) to be infectious; **ansteckend** adj infectious; **Ansteckungsgefahr** f danger of infection
an|stehen irr vi (in Warteschlange) to queue (Brit), to stand in line (US); (erledigt werden müssen) to be on the agenda
anstelle prep +gen instead of
an|stellen vt (einschalten) to turn on; (Arbeit geben) to employ; (machen) to do; **was hast du**

wieder angestellt? what have you been up to now? ▷ *vr:* **sich ~** to queue (*Brit*), to stand in line (*US*); (*fam*) **stell dich nicht so an!** stop making such a fuss

Anstoß *m* impetus; (*Sport*) kick-off; **an|stoßen** *irr vt* to push; (*mit Fuß*) to kick ▷ *vi* to knock, to bump; (*mit Gläsern*) to drink (a toast) (*auf +akk* to); **anstößig** *adj* offensive; (*Kleidung etc*) indecent

an|strengen *vt* to strain ▷ *vr:* **sich ~** to make an effort; **anstrengend** *adj* tiring

Antarktis *f* Antarctic

Anteil *m* share (*an +dat* in); **~ nehmen an** (*+dat*) (*mitleidig*) to sympathize with; (*sich interessieren*) to take an interest in

Antenne (*-, -n*) *f* aerial

Antibabypille *f:* **die ~** the pill; **Antibiotikum** (*-s, Antibiotika*) *nt* (*Med*) antibiotic

antik *adj* antique

Antilope (*-, -n*) *f* antelope

Antiquariat *nt* (*für Bücher*) second-hand bookshop

Antiquitäten *pl* antiques *pl*; **Antiquitätenhändler(in)** *m(f)* antique dealer

an|törnen *vt* (*fam*) to turn on

Antrag (*-(e)s, Anträge*) *m* proposal; (*Pol*) motion; (*Formular*) application form; **einen ~ stellen auf** (*+akk*) to make an application for

an|treffen *irr vt* to find

an|treiben *irr vt* (*Tech*) to drive; (*anschwemmen*) to wash up; **jdn zur Arbeit ~** to make sb work

an|treten *irr vt:* **eine Reise ~** to set off on a journey

Antrieb *m* (*Tech*) drive; (*Motivation*) impetus

an|tun *irr vt:* **jdm etwas ~** to do sth to sb; **sich** (*dat*) **etwas ~** (*Selbstmord begehen*) to kill

oneself

Antwort (*-, -en*) *f* answer, reply; **um ~ wird gebeten** RSVP (*répondez s'il vous plaît*); **antworten** *vi* to answer, to reply; **jdm ~** to answer sb; **auf etw** (*akk*) **~** to answer sth

an|vertrauen *vt:* **jdm etw ~** to entrust sb with sth

Anwalt (*-s, Anwälte*) *m*, **Anwältin** *f* lawyer

an|weisen *irr vt* (*anleiten*) to instruct; (*zuteilen*) to allocate (*jdm etw* sth to sb); **Anweisung** *f* instruction; (*von Geld*) money order

an|wenden *irr vt* to use; (*Gesetz, Regel*) to apply; **Anwender(in)** (*-s, -*) *m(f)* user; **Anwendung** *f* use; (*Inform*) application

anwesend *adj* present; **Anwesenheit** *f* presence

an|widern *vt* to disgust

Anwohner(in) (*-s, -*) *m(f)* resident

Anzahl *f* number (*an +dat* of); **an|zahlen** *vt* to pay a deposit on; **100 Euro ~** to pay 100 euros as a deposit; **Anzahlung** *f* deposit

Anzeichen *nt* sign; (*Med*) symptom

Anzeige (*-, -n*) *f* (*Werbung*) advertisement; (*elektronisch*) display; (*bei Polizei*) report; **an|zeigen** *vt* (*Temperatur, Zeit*) to indicate, to show; (*elektronisch*) to display; (*bekannt geben*) to announce; **jdn/einen Autodiebstahl bei der Polizei ~** to report sb/a stolen car to the police

an|ziehen *irr vt* to attract; (*Kleidung*) to put on; (*Schraube, Seil*) to tighten ▷ *vr:* **sich ~** to get dressed; **anziehend** *adj* attractive

Anzug *m* suit

anzüglich *adj* suggestive

an|zünden *vt* to light; (*Haus etc*)

to set fire to

an|zweifeln vt to doubt

Aperitif (-s, -s (o -e)) m aperitif

Apfel (-s, Äpfel) m apple;
Apfelbaum m apple tree;
Apfelkuchen m apple cake;
Apfelmus nt apple purée;
Apfelsaft m apple juice;
Apfelsine f orange; **Apfelwein** m cider

Apostroph (-s, -e) m apostrophe

Apotheke (-, -n) f chemist's (shop) (Brit), pharmacy (US);
apothekenpflichtig adj only available at the chemist's (o pharmacy); **Apotheker(in)** (-s, -) m(f) chemist (Brit), pharmacist (US)

Apparat (-(e)s, -e) m (piece of) apparatus; (Tel) telephone; (Radio, TV) set; **am ~!** (Tel) speaking; **am ~ bleiben** (Tel) to hold the line

Appartement (-s, -s) nt studio flat (Brit) (o apartment (US))

Appetit (-(e)s, -e) m appetite; **guten ~!** bon appétit; **appetitlich** adj appetizing

Applaus (-es, -e) m applause

Aprikose (-, -n) f apricot

April (-(s), -e) m April; siehe auch Juni; **~, ~!** April fool!; **Aprilscherz** (-es, -e) m April fool's joke

apropos adv by the way; **~ Urlaub ...** while we're on the subject of holidays ...

Aquajogging nt aqua jogging; **Aquaplaning** (-(s)) nt aquaplaning

Aquarell (-s, -e) nt watercolour

Aquarium (-s, Aquarien) nt aquarium

Äquator (-s, -) m equator

Araber(in) (-s, -) m(f) Arab; **arabisch** adj Arab; (Ziffer, Sprache) Arabic; (Meer, Wüste) Arabian

Arbeit (-, -en) f work; (Stelle) job; (Erzeugnis) piece of work; **arbeiten** vi to work; **Arbeiter(in)** (-s, -) m(f) worker; (ungelernt) labourer;

Arbeitgeber(in) (-s, -) m(f) employer; **Arbeitnehmer(in)** (-s, -) m(f) employee; **Arbeitsagentur** f job agency (Brit), unemployment agency (US); **Arbeitsamt** nt job centre (Brit), employment office (US); **Arbeitserlaubnis** f work permit; **arbeitslos** adj unemployed; **Arbeitslose(r)** mf unemployed person; **die ~n** pl the unemployed pl; **Arbeitslosengeld** nt (income-related) unemployment benefit, job-seeker's allowance (Brit); **Arbeitslosenhilfe** f (non-income related) unemployment benefit; **Arbeitslosigkeit** f unemployment; **Arbeitsplatz** m job; (Ort) workplace; **Arbeitsspeicher** m (Inform) main memory; **Arbeitszeit** f working hours pl; **Arbeitszimmer** nt study

Archäologe (-n, -n) m, **Archäologin** f archaeologist

Architekt(in) (-en, -en) m(f) architect; **Architektur** f architecture

Archiv (-s, -e) nt archives pl

arg adj bad; (schrecklich) awful ▷ adv (sehr) terribly

Argentinien (-s) nt Argentina

Ärger (-s) m annoyance; (stärker) anger; (Unannehmlichkeiten) trouble; **ärgerlich** adj (zornig) angry; (lästig) annoying; **ärgern** vt to annoy ▷ vr: **sich ~** to get annoyed

Argument (-s, -e) nt argument

Arktis (-) f Arctic

arm adj poor

Arm (-(e)s, -e) m arm; (Fluss) branch

Armaturenbrett nt instrument panel; (Auto) dashboard

Armband nt bracelet;

Armbanduhr f (wrist)watch
Armee (-, -n) f army
Ärmel (-s, -) m sleeve;
Ärmelkanal m (English) Channel
Armut (-) f poverty
Aroma (-s, Aromen) nt aroma
arrogant adj arrogant
Arsch (-es, Ärsche) m (vulg) arse
(Brit), ass (US); **Arschloch** nt
(vulg: Person) arsehole (Brit),
asshole (US)
Art (-, -en) f (Weise) way; (Sorte)
kind, sort; (bei Tieren) species;
nach ~ des Hauses à la maison;
auf diese ~ (und Weise) in this
way; **das ist nicht seine ~** that's
not like him
Arterie (-, -n) f artery
artig adj good, well-behaved
Artikel (-s, -) m (Ware) article,
item; (Zeitung) article
Artischocke (-, -n) f artichoke
Artist(in) (-en, -en) m(f) (circus)
performer
Arznei f medicine; **Arzt** (-es,
Ärzte) m doctor; **Arzthelfer(in)**
m(f) doctor's assistant; **Ärztin** f
(female) doctor; **ärztlich** adj
medical; **sich ~ behandeln lassen**
to undergo medical treatment
Asche (-, -n) f ashes pl; (von
Zigarette) ash; **Aschenbecher** m
ashtray; **Aschermittwoch** m
Ash Wednesday
Asiat(in) (-en, -en) m(f) Asian;
asiatisch adj Asian; **Asien** (-s) nt
Asia
Aspekt (-(e)s, -e) m aspect
Asphalt (-(e)s, -e) m asphalt
Aspirin® (-s, -e) nt aspirin
aß imperf von **essen**
Ass (-es, -e) nt (Karten, Tennis) ace
Assistent(in) m(f) assistant
Ast (-(e)s, Äste) m branch
Asthma (-s) nt asthma
Astrologie f astrology;
Astronaut(in) (-en, -en) m(f)

astronaut; **Astronomie** f
astronomy
ASU (-, -s) f abk =
Abgassonderuntersuchung
exhaust emission test
Asyl (-s, -e) nt asylum; (Heim)
home; (für Obdachlose) shelter;
Asylant(in) m(f), **Asylbe-
werber(in)** m(f) asylum seeker
Atelier (-s, -s) nt studio
Atem (-s) m breath;
atemberaubend adj breathtaking; **Atembeschwerden** pl
breathing difficulties pl; **atemlos**
adj breathless; **Atempause** f
breather
Athen nt Athens
Äthiopien (-s) nt Ethiopia
Athlet(in) (-en, -en) m(f) athlete
Atlantik (-s) m Atlantic (Ocean)
Atlas (- o Atlasses, Atlanten) m
atlas
atmen vt, vi to breathe; **Atmung**
f breathing
Atom (-s, -e) nt atom;
Atombombe f atom bomb;
Atomkraftwerk nt nuclear
power station; **Atommüll** m
nuclear waste; **Atomwaffen** pl
nuclear weapons pl
Attentat (-(e)s, -e) nt
assassination (auf +akk of);
(Versuch) assassination attempt
Attest (-(e)s, -e) nt certificate
attraktiv adj attractive
Attrappe (-, -n) f dummy
ätzend adj (fam) revolting;
(schlecht) lousy
au interj ouch; **~ ja!** yeah
Aubergine (-, -n) f aubergine,
eggplant (US)

⭕ SCHLÜSSELWORT

auch adv **1** (ebenfalls) also, too, as
well; **das ist auch schön** that's
nice too o as well; **er kommt — ich**

auch he's coming — so am I, me too; **auch nicht** not ... either; **ich auch nicht** nor I, me neither; **oder auch** or; **auch das noch!** not that as well!
2 (*selbst, sogar*) even; **auch wenn das Wetter schlecht ist** even if the weather is bad; **ohne auch nur zu fragen** without even asking
3 (*wirklich*) really; **du siehst müde aus—bin ich auch** you look tired— (so) I am; **so sieht es auch aus** it looks like it too
4 (*auch immer*) **wer auch** whoever; **was auch** whatever; **wie dem auch sei** be that as it may; **wie sehr er sich auch bemühte** however much he tried

audiovisuell *adj* audiovisual

O SCHLÜSSELWORT

auf *prep* +*dat* (*wo?*) on; **auf dem Tisch** on the table; **auf der Reise** on the way; **auf der Post/dem Fest** at the post office/party; **auf der Straße** on the road; **auf dem Land/der ganzen Welt** in the country/the whole world
▷ *prep* +*akk* **1** (*wohin?*) on(to); **auf den Tisch** on(to) the table; **auf die Post gehen** to go to the post office; **auf das Land** into the country; **etw auf einen Zettel schreiben** to write sth on a piece of paper
2 auf Deutsch in German; **auf Lebenszeit** for my/his lifetime; **bis auf ihn** except for him; **auf einmal** at once; **auf seinen Vorschlag (hin)** at his suggestion
▷ *adv* **1** (*offen*) open; **auf sein** (*fam*) (*Tür, Geschäft*) to be open; **das Fenster ist auf** the window is open

2 (*hinauf*) up; **auf und ab** up and down; **auf und davon** up and away; **auf!** (*los!*) come on!
3 (*aufgestanden*) up; **auf sein** to be up; **ist er schon auf?** is he up yet?
▷ *konj*: **auf dass** (so) that

auf|atmen *vi* to breathe a sigh of relief
auf|bauen *vt* (*errichten*) to put up; (*schaffen*) to build up; (*gestalten*) to construct; (*gründen*) to found, to base (*auf* +*akk* on); **sich eine Existenz ~** to make a life for oneself
auf|bewahren *vt* to keep, to store
auf|bleiben *irr vi* (*Tür, Laden etc*) to stay open; (*Mensch*) to stay up
auf|blenden *vi, vt*: (**die Scheinwerfer**) **~** to put one's headlights on full beam
auf|brechen *irr vt* to break open
▷ *vi* to burst open; (*gehen*) to leave; (*abreisen*) to set off
auf|drängen *vt*: **jdm etw ~** to force sth on sb ▷ *vr*: **sich ~** to intrude (*jdm* on sb); **aufdringlich** *adj* pushy
aufeinander *adv* (*übereinander*) on top of each other; **~ achten** to look after each other; **~ vertrauen** to trust each other; **aufeinander|folgen** *vi* to follow one another; **aufeinander|prallen** *vi* to crash into one another
Aufenthalt *m* stay; (*Zug*) stop; **Aufenthaltsgenehmigung** *f* residence permit; **Aufenthaltsraum** *m* lounge
auf|essen *irr vt* to eat up
auf|fahren *irr vi* (*Auto*) to run (*o* to crash) (*auf* +*akk* into); (*herankommen*) to drive up; **Auffahrt** *f* (*am Haus*) drive; (*Autobahn*) slip road (*Brit*), ramp (*US*); **Auffahrunfall** *m* rear-end

collision; (*mehrere Fahrzeuge*) pile-up

auf|fallen *irr vi* to stand out; **jdm ~** to strike sb; **das fällt gar nicht auf** nobody will notice; **auffallend** *adj* striking; **auffällig** *adj* conspicuous; (*Kleidung, Farbe*) striking

auf|fangen *irr vt* (*Ball*) to catch; (*Stoß*) to cushion

auf|fassen *vt* to understand; **Auffassung** *f* view; (*Meinung*) opinion; (*Auslegung*) concept; (*Auffassungsgabe*) grasp

auf|fordern *vt* (*befehlen*) to call upon; (*bitten*) to ask

auf|frischen *vt* (*Kenntnisse*) to brush up

auf|führen *vt* (*Theat*) to perform; (*in einem Verzeichnis*) to list; (*Beispiel*) to give ▷ *vr*: **sich ~** (*sich benehmen*) to behave; **Aufführung** *f* (*Theat*) performance

Aufgabe *f* job, task; (*Schule*) exercise; (*Hausaufgabe*) homework

Aufgang *m* (*Treppe*) staircase

auf|geben *irr vt* (*verzichten auf*) to give up; (*Paket*) to post; (*Gepäck*) to check in; (*Bestellung*) to place; (*Inserat*) to insert; (*Rätsel, Problem*) to set ▷ *vi* to give up

auf|gehen *irr vi* (*Sonne, Teig*) to rise; (*sich öffnen*) to open; (*klar werden*) to dawn (*jdm* on sb)

aufgelegt *adj*: **gut/schlecht ~** in a good/bad mood

aufgeregt *adj* excited

aufgeschlossen *adj* open(minded)

aufgeschmissen *adj* (*fam*) in a fix

aufgrund, auf Grund *prep* +*gen* on the basis of; (*wegen*) because of

auf|haben *irr vt* (*Hut etc*) to have on; **viel ~** (*Schule*) to have a lot of homework to do ▷ *vi* (*Geschäft*) to be open

auf|halten *irr vt* (*jdn*) to detain; (*Entwicklung*) to stop; (*Tür, Hand*) to hold open; (*Augen*) to keep open ▷ *vr*: **sich ~** (*wohnen*) to live; (*vorübergehend*) to stay

auf|hängen *irr vt* to hang up

auf|heben *irr vt* (*vom Boden etc*) to pick up; (*aufbewahren*) to keep

auf|holen *vt* (*Zeit*) to make up ▷ *vi* to catch up

auf|hören *vi* to stop; **~, etw zu tun** to stop doing sth

auf|klären *vt* (*Geheimnis etc*) to clear up; **jdn ~** to enlighten sb; (*sexuell*) to tell sb the facts of life

Aufkleber (*-s, -*) *m* sticker

auf|kommen *irr vi* (*Wind*) to come up; (*Zweifel, Gefühl*) to arise; (*Mode etc*) to appear on the scene; **für den Schaden ~** to pay for the damage

auf|laden *irr vt* to load; (*Handy etc*) to charge; (*Handykarte etc*) to top up; **Aufladegerät** *nt* charger

Auflage *f* edition; (*von Zeitung*) circulation; (*Bedingung*) condition

auf|lassen *vt* (*Hut, Brille*) to keep on; (*Tür*) to leave open

Auflauf *m* (*Menschen*) crowd; (*Speise*) bake

auf|legen *vt* (*CD, Schminke etc*) to put on; (*Hörer*) to put down ▷ *vi* (*Tel*) to hang up

auf|leuchten *vi* to light up

auf|lösen *vt* (*in Flüssigkeit*) to dissolve ▷ *vr*: **sich ~** (*in Flüssigkeit*) to dissolve; **der Stau hat sich aufgelöst** traffic is back to normal; **Auflösung** *f* (*von Rätsel*) solution; (*von Bildschirm*) resolution

auf|machen *vt* to open; (*Kleidung*) to undo ▷ *vr*: **sich ~** to set out (*nach* for)

aufmerksam *adj* attentive; **jdn auf etw** (*akk*) **~ machen** to draw sb's attention to sth;

Aufmerksamkeit f attention; (Konzentration) attentiveness; (Geschenk) small token

auf|muntern vt (ermutigen) to encourage; (aufheitern) to cheer up

Aufnahme (-, -n) f (Foto) photo(graph); (einzelne) shot; (in Verein, Krankenhaus etc) admission; (Beginn) beginning; (auf Tonband etc) recording; **Aufnahmeprüfung** f entrance exam; **auf|nehmen** irr vt (in Krankenhaus, Verein etc) to admit; (Musik) to record; (beginnen) to take up; (in Liste) to include; (begreifen) to take in; **mit jdm Kontakt ~** to get in touch with sb

auf|passen vi (aufmerksam sein) to pay attention; (vorsichtig sein) to take care; **auf jdn/etw ~** to keep an eye on sb/sth

Aufprall (-s, -e) m impact; **auf|prallen** vi **auf etw** (akk) **~** to hit sth, to crash into sth

Aufpreis m extra charge

auf|pumpen vt to pump up

Aufputschmittel nt stimulant

auf|räumen vt, vi (Dinge) to clear away; (Zimmer) to tidy up

aufrecht adj upright

auf|regen vt to excite; (ärgern) to annoy ▷ vr: **sich ~** to get worked up; **aufregend** adj exciting; **Aufregung** f excitement

auf|reißen irr vt (Tüte) to tear open; (Tür) to fling open; (fam: Person) to pick up

Aufruf m (Aviat, Inform) call; (öffentlicher) appeal; **auf|rufen** irr vt (auffordern) to call upon (zu for); (Namen) to call out; (Aviat) to call; (Inform) to call up

auf|runden vt (Summe) to round up

aufs kontr von **auf das**

Aufsatz m essay

auf|schieben irr vt (verschieben) to postpone; (verzögern) to put off; (Tür) to slide open

Aufschlag m (auf Preis) extra charge; (Tennis) service; **auf|schlagen** irr vt (öffnen) to open; (verletzen) to cut open; (Zelt) to pitch, to put up; (Lager) to set up ▷ vi (Tennis) to serve; **auf etw** (+akk) **~** (aufprallen) to hit sth

auf|schließen irr vt to unlock, to open up ▷ vi (aufrücken) to close up

auf|schneiden irr vt to cut open; (in Scheiben) to slice ▷ vi (angeben) to boast, to show off

Aufschnitt m (slices pl of) cold meat; (bei Käse) (assorted) sliced cheeses pl

auf|schreiben irr vt to write down

Aufschrift f inscription; (Etikett) label

Aufschub m (Verzögerung) delay; (Vertagung) postponement

Aufsehen (-s) nt stir; **großes ~ erregen** to cause a sensation; **Aufseher(in)** (-s, -) m(f) guard; (im Betrieb) supervisor; (im Museum) attendant; (im Park) keeper

auf sein irr vi siehe **auf**

auf|setzen vt to put on; (Dokument) to draw up ▷ vi (Flugzeug) to touch down

Aufsicht f supervision; (bei Prüfung) invigilation; **die ~ haben** to be in charge

auf|spannen vt (Schirm) to put up

auf|sperren vt (Mund) to open wide; (aufschließen) to unlock

auf|springen irr vi to jump (auf +akk onto); (hochspringen) to jump up; (sich öffnen) to spring open

auf|stehen irr vi to get up; (Tür) to be open

auf|stellen vt (aufrecht stellen) to

put up; (*aufreihen*) to line up; (*nominieren*) to put up; (*Liste, Programm*) to draw up; (*Rekord*) to set up

Aufstieg (-(e)s, -e) m (*auf Berg*) ascent; (*Fortschritt*) rise; (*beruflich, im Sport*) promotion

Aufstrich m spread

auf|tanken vt, vi (*Auto*) to tank up; (*Flugzeug*) to refuel

auf|tauchen vi to turn up; (*aus Wasser etc*) to surface; (*Frage, Problem*) to come up

auf|tauen vt (*Speisen*) to defrost ▷ vi to thaw; (*fig: Person*) to unbend

Auftrag (-(e)s, Aufträge) m (*Comm*) order; (*Arbeit*) job; (*Anweisung*) instructions pl; (*Aufgabe*) task; **im ~ von** on behalf of; **auf|tragen** irr vt (*Salbe etc*) to apply; (*Essen*) to serve

auf|treten irr vi to appear; (*Problem*) to come up; (*sich verhalten*) to behave; **Auftritt** m (*des Schauspielers*) entrance; (*fig: Szene*) scene

auf|wachen vi to wake up

auf|wachsen irr vi to grow up

Aufwand (-(e)s) m expenditure; (*Kosten a.*) expense; (*Anstrengung*) effort; **aufwändig** adj costly; **das ist zu ~** that's too much trouble

auf|wärmen vt to warm up ▷ vr: **sich ~** to warm up

aufwärts adv upwards; **mit etw geht es ~** things are looking up for sth

auf|wecken vt to wake up

aufwendig adj siehe **aufwändig**

auf|wischen vt to wipe up; (*Fußboden*) to wipe

auf|zählen vt to list

auf|zeichnen vt to sketch; (*schriftlich*) to jot down; (*auf Band etc*) to record; **Aufzeichnung** f

(*schriftlich*) note; (*Tonband etc*) recording; (*Film*) record

auf|ziehen irr vt (*öffnen*) to pull open; (*Uhr*) to wind (up); (*fam: necken*) to tease; (*Kinder*) to bring up; (*Tiere*) to rear ▷ vi (*Gewitter*) to come up

Aufzug m (*Fahrstuhl*) lift (*Brit*), elevator (*US*); (*Kleidung*) get-up; (*Theat*) act

Auge (-s, -n) nt eye; **jdm etw aufs ~ drücken** (*fam*) to force sth on sb; **ins ~ gehen** (*fam*) to go wrong; **unter vier ~n** in private; **etw im ~ behalten** to keep sth in mind; **Augenarzt** m, **Augenärztin** f eye specialist, eye doctor (*US*); **Augenblick** m moment; **im ~** at the moment; **Augenbraue** (-, -n) f eyebrow; **Augenbrauenstift** m eyebrow pencil; **Augenfarbe** f eye colour; **seine ~** the colour of his eyes; **Augenlid** nt eyelid; **Augen- optiker(in)** (-s, -) m(f) optician; **Augentropfen** pl eyedrops pl; **Augenzeuge** m, **Augenzeugin** f eyewitness

August (-(e)s o -, -e) m August; **siehe auch Juni**

Auktion f auction

 SCHLÜSSELWORT

aus prep +dat **1** (*räumlich*) out of; (*von ... her*) from; **er ist aus Berlin** he's from Berlin; **aus dem Fenster** out of the window
2 (*gemacht/hergestellt aus*) made of; **ein Herz aus Stein** a heart of stone
3 (*auf Ursache deutend*) out of; **aus Mitleid** out of sympathy; **aus Erfahrung** from experience; **aus Spaß** for fun
4 aus ihr wird nie etwas she'll never get anywhere

▷ *adv* **1** (*zu Ende*) finished, over; **aus sein** to be over; **aus und vorbei** over and done with
2 (*ausgeschaltet, ausgezogen*) out; (*Aufschrift an Geräten*) off; **aus sein** (*nicht brennen*) to be out; (*abgeschaltet sein: Radio, Herd*) to be off; **Licht aus!** lights out!
3 (*nicht zu Hause*) **aus sein** to be out
4 (*in Verbindung mit von*) **von Rom aus** from Rome; **vom Fenster aus** out of the window; **von sich aus** (*selbstständig*) of one's own accord; **von ihm aus** as far as he's concerned

Aus (-) *nt* (*Sport*) touch; (*fig*) end
aus|atmen *vi* to breathe out
aus|bauen *vt* (*Haus, Straße*) to extend; (*Motor etc*) to remove
aus|bessern *vt* to repair; (*Kleidung*) to mend
aus|bilden *vt* to educate; (*Lehrling etc*) to train; (*Fähigkeiten*) to develop; **Ausbildung** *f* education; (*von Lehrling etc*) training; (*von Fähigkeiten*) development
Ausblick *m* view; (*fig*) outlook
aus|brechen *irr vi* to break out; **in Tränen ~** to burst into tears; **in Gelächter ~** to burst out laughing
aus|breiten *vt* to spread (out); (*Arme*) to stretch out ▷ *vr*: **sich ~** to spread
Ausbruch *m* (*Krieg, Seuche etc*) outbreak; (*Vulkan*) eruption; (*Gefühle*) outburst; (*von Gefangenen*) escape
aus|buhen *vt* to boo
Ausdauer *f* perseverance; (*Sport*) stamina
aus|dehnen *vt* to stretch; (*fig: Macht*) to extend
aus|denken *irr vt* **sich** (*dat*) **etw ~** to come up with sth

Ausdruck *m* (*Ausdrücke*) expression ▷ *m* (*Ausdrucke, Computerausdruck*) print-out; **aus|drucken** *vt* (*Inform*) to print (out)
aus|drücken *vt* (*formulieren*) to express; (*Zigarette*) to put out; (*Zitrone etc*) to squeeze ▷ *vr*: **sich ~** to express oneself; **ausdrücklich** *adj* express ▷ *adv* expressly
auseinander *adv* (*getrennt*) apart; **~ schreiben** to write as separate words; **auseinander|gehen** *irr vi* (*Menschen*) to separate; (*Meinungen*) to differ; (*Gegenstand*) to fall apart; **auseinander|halten** *irr vt* to tell apart; **auseinander|setzen** *vt* (*erklären*) to explain; **auseinander|setzen** *vr*: **sich ~** (*sich beschäftigen*) to look (mit at); (*sich streiten*) to argue (mit with); **Auseinandersetzung** *f* (*Streit*) argument; (*Diskussion*) debate
Ausfahrt *f* (*des Zuges etc*) departure; (*Autobahn, Garage etc*) exit
aus|fallen *irr vi* (*Haare*) to fall out; (*nicht stattfinden*) to be cancelled; (*nicht funktionieren*) to break down; (*Strom*) to be cut off; (*Resultat haben*) to turn out; **groß/klein ~** (*Kleidung, Schuhe*) to be too big/too small
ausfindig machen *vt* to discover
aus|flippen *vi* (*fam*) to freak out
Ausflug *m* excursion, outing; **Ausflugsziel** *nt* destination
Ausfluss *m* (*Med*) discharge
aus|fragen *vt* to question
Ausfuhr (-, -en) *f* export
aus|führen *vt* (*verwirklichen*) to carry out; (*Person*) to take out; (*Comm*) to export; (*darlegen*) to explain

ausführlich adj detailed ▷ adv in detail

aus|füllen vt to fill up; (Fragebogen etc) to fill in (o out)

Ausgabe f (Geld) expenditure; (Inform) output; (Buch) edition; (Nummer) issue

Ausgang m way out, exit; (Flugsteig) gate; (Ende) end; (Ergebnis) result; „**kein ~"** "no exit"

aus|geben irr vt (Geld) to spend; (austeilen) to distribute; **jdm etw ~** (spendieren) to buy sb sth ▷ vr: **sich für etw/jdn ~** to pass oneself off as sth/sb

ausgebucht adj fully booked

ausgefallen adj (ungewöhnlich) unusual

aus|gehen irr vi (abends etc) to go out; (Benzin, Kaffee etc) to run out; (Haare) to fall out; (Feuer, Licht etc) to go out; (Resultat haben) to turn out; **davon ~, dass** to assume that; **ihm ging das Geld aus** he ran out of money

ausgelassen adj exuberant

ausgeleiert adj worn out

ausgenommen conj, prep +gen o dat except

ausgerechnet adv: **~ du** you of all people; **~ heute** today of all days

ausgeschildert adj signposted

ausgeschlafen adj: **bist du ~?** have you had enough sleep?

ausgeschlossen adj (unmöglich) impossible, out of the question

ausgesprochen adj (absolut) out-and-out; (unverkennbar) marked ▷ adv extremely; **~ gut** really good

ausgezeichnet adj excellent

ausgiebig adj (Gebrauch) thorough; (Essen) substantial

aus|gießen irr vt (Getränk) to pour out; (Gefäß) to empty

aus|gleichen irr vt to even out ▷ vi (Sport) to equalize

Ausguss m (Spüle) sink; (Abfluss) outlet

aus|halten irr vt to bear, to stand; **nicht auszuhalten sein** to be unbearable ▷ vi to hold out

aus|händigen vt: **jdm etw ~** to hand sth over to sb

Aushang m notice

Aushilfe f temporary help; (im Büro) temp

aus|kennen irr vr: **sich ~** to know a lot (bei, mit about); (an einem Ort) to know one's way around

aus|kommen irr vi: **gut/schlecht mit jdm ~** to get on well/badly with sb; **mit etw ~** to get by with sth

Auskunft (-, Auskünfte) f information; (nähere) details pl; (Schalter) information desk; (Tel) (directory) enquiries sing (kein Artikel, Brit), information (US)

aus|lachen vt to laugh at

aus|laden irr vt (Gepäck etc) to unload; **jdn ~** (Gast) to tell sb not to come

Auslage f window display; **~n** pl (Kosten) expenses

Ausland nt foreign countries pl; **im/ins ~** abroad; **Ausländer(in)** (-s, -) m(f) foreigner; **ausländerfeindlich** adj hostile to foreigners, xenophobic; **ausländisch** adj foreign; **Auslandsgespräch** nt international call; **Auslandskrankenschein** m health insurance certificate for foreign countries, ≈ E111 (Brit); **Auslandsschutzbrief** m international (motor) insurance cover (documents pl)

aus|lassen irr vt to leave out; (Wort etc a.) to omit; (überspringen) to skip; (*Wut, Ärger*) to vent (*an +dat* on) ▷ vr **sich über etw** (*akk*) **~** to speak one's mind about sth

aus|laufen *irr vi* (*Flüssigkeit*) to run out; (*Tank etc*) to leak; (*Schiff*) to leave port; (*Vertrag*) to expire

aus|legen *vt* (*Waren*) to display; (*Geld*) to lend; (*Text etc*) to interpret; (*technisch ausstatten*) to design (*für, auf +akk* for)

aus|leihen *irr vt* (*verleihen*) to lend; **sich** (*dat*) **etw ~** to borrow sth

aus|loggen *vi* (*Inform*) to log out (*o off*)

aus|lösen *vt* (*Explosion, Alarm*) to set off; (*hervorrufen*) to cause; **Auslöser** (*-s, -*) *m* (*Foto*) shutter release

aus|machen *vt* (*Licht, Radio*) to turn off; (*Feuer*) to put out; (*Termin, Preis*) to fix; (*vereinbaren*) to agree; (*Anteil darstellen, betragen*) to represent; (*bedeuten*) to matter; **macht es Ihnen etwas aus, wenn ...?** would you mind if ...?; **das macht mir nichts aus** I don't mind

Ausmaß *nt* extent

Ausnahme (*-, -n*) *f* exception; **ausnahmsweise** *adv* as an exception, just this once

aus|nutzen *vt* (*Zeit, Gelegenheit, Einfluss*) to use; (*jdn, Gutmütigkeit*) to take advantage of

aus|packen *vt* to unpack

aus|probieren *vt* to try (out)

Auspuff (*-(e)s, -e*) *m* (*Tech*) exhaust; **Auspuffrohr** *nt* exhaust (pipe); **Auspufftopf** *m* (*Auto*) silencer (*Brit*), muffler (*US*)

aus|rauben *vt* to rob

aus|räumen *vt* (*Dinge*) to clear away; (*Schrank, Zimmer*) to empty; (*Bedenken*) to put aside

aus|rechnen *vt* to calculate, to work out

Ausrede *f* excuse

aus|reden *vi* to finish speaking ▷ *vt*: **jdm etw ~** to talk sb out of sth

ausreichend *adj* sufficient, satisfactory; (*Schulnote*) ≈ D

Ausreise *f* departure; **bei der ~** on leaving the country; **Ausreiseerlaubnis** *f* exit visa; **aus|reisen** *vi* to leave the country

aus|reißen *irr vt* to tear out ▷ *vi* to come off; (*fam: davonlaufen*) to run away

aus|renken *vt* **sich** (*dat*) **den Arm ~** to dislocate one's arm

aus|richten *vt* (*Botschaft*) to deliver; (*Gruß*) to pass on; (*erreichen*) **ich konnte bei ihr nichts ~** I couldn't get anywhere with her; **jdm etw ~** to tell sb sth

aus|rufen *irr vt* (*über Lautsprecher*) to announce; **jdn ~ lassen** to page sb; **Ausrufezeichen** *nt* exclamation mark

aus|ruhen *vi* to rest ▷ *vr*: **sich ~** to rest

Ausrüstung *f* equipment

aus|rutschen *vi* to slip

aus|schalten *vt* to switch off; (*fig*) to eliminate

Ausschau *f*: **~ halten** to look out (*nach* for)

aus|scheiden *irr vt* (*Med*) to give off, to secrete ▷ *vi* to leave (*aus etw* sth); (*Sport*) to be eliminated

aus|schlafen *irr vi* to have a lie-in ▷ *vr*: **sich ~** to have a lie-in ▷ *vt* to sleep off

Ausschlag *m* (*Med*) rash; **den ~ geben** (*fig*) to tip the balance; **aus|schlagen** *vt* (*Zahn*) to knock out; (*Einladung*) to turn down ▷ *vi* (*Pferd*) to kick out; **ausschlaggebend** *adj* decisive

aus|schließen *irr vt* to lock out; (*fig*) to exclude; **ausschließlich**

adv exclusively ▷ *prep* +*gen* excluding

Ausschnitt *m* (*Teil*) section; (*von Kleid*) neckline; (*aus Zeitung*) cutting

Ausschreitungen *pl* riots *pl*

aus|schütten *vt* (*Flüssigkeit*) to pour out; (*Gefäß*) to empty

aus|sehen *irr vi* to look; **krank ~** to look ill; **gut ~** (*Person*) to be good-looking; (*Sache*) to be looking good; **es sieht nach Regen aus** it looks like rain; **es sieht schlecht aus** things look bad

aus sein *irr vi siehe* **aus**

außen *adv* outside; **nach ~** outwards; **von ~** from (the) outside; **Außenbordmotor** *m* outboard motor; **Außenminister(in)** *m(f)* foreign minister, Foreign Secretary (*Brit*); **Außenseite** *f* outside; **Außenseiter(in)** *m(f)* outsider; **Außenspiegel** *m* wing mirror (*Brit*), side mirror (*US*)

außer *prep* +*dat* (*abgesehen von*) except (for); **nichts ~** nothing but; **~ Betrieb** out of order; **~ sich sein** to be beside oneself (*vor* with); **~ Atem** out of breath ▷ *conj* (*ausgenommen*) except; **~ wenn** unless; **~ dass** except; **außerdem** *conj* besides

äußere(r, s) *adj* outer, external

außergewöhnlich *adj* unusual ▷ *adv* exceptionally; **~ kalt** exceptionally cold; **außerhalb** *prep* +*gen* outside

äußerlich *adj* external

äußern *vt* to express; (*zeigen*) to show ▷ *vr*: **sich ~** to give one's opinion; (*sich zeigen*) to show itself

außerordentlich *adj* extraordinary; **außerplanmäßig** *adj* unscheduled

äußerst *adv* extremely;

äußerste(r, s) *adj* utmost; (*räumlich*) farthest; (*Termin*) last possible

Äußerung *f* remark

aus|setzen *vt* (*Kind, Tier*) to abandon; (*Belohnung*) to offer; **ich habe nichts daran auszusetzen** I have no objection to it ▷ *vi* (*aufhören*) to stop; (*Pause machen*) to drop out; (*beim Spiel*) to miss a turn

Aussicht *f* (*Blick*) view; (*Chance*) prospect; **aussichtslos** *adj* hopeless; **Aussichtsplattform** *f* observation platform; **Aussichtsturm** *m* observation tower

Aussiedler(in) (-s, -) *m(f)* émigré (*person of German descent from Eastern Europe*)

aus|spannen *vi* (*erholen*) to relax ▷ *vt*: **er hat ihm die Freundin ausgespannt** (*fam*) he's nicked his girlfriend

aus|sperren *vt* to lock out ▷ *vr*: **sich ~** to lock oneself out

Aussprache *f* (*von Wörtern*) pronunciation; (*Gespräch*) (*frank*) discussion; **aus|sprechen** *irr vt* to pronounce; (*äußern*) to express ▷ *vr*: **sich ~** to talk (*über*+*akk* about) ▷ *vi* (*zu Ende sprechen*) to finish speaking

aus|spülen *vt* to rinse (out)

Ausstattung *f* (*Ausrüstung*) equipment; (*Einrichtung*) furnishings *pl*; (*von Auto*) fittings *pl*

aus|stehen *irr vt* to endure; **ich kann ihn nicht ~** I can't stand him ▷ *vi* (*noch nicht da sein*) to be outstanding

aus|steigen *irr vi* to get out (*aus* of); **aus dem Bus/Zug ~** to get off the bus/train; **Aussteiger(in)** *m(f)* dropout

aus|stellen *vt* to display; (*auf Messe, in Museum etc*) to exhibit;

(fam: ausschalten) to switch off; *(Scheck etc)* to make out; *(Pass etc)* to issue; **Ausstellung** *f* exhibition

aus|sterben *irr vi* to die out

aus|strahlen *vt* to radiate; *(Programm)* to broadcast; **Ausstrahlung** *f (Radio, TV)* broadcast; *(fig: von Person)* charisma

aus|strecken *vr:* **sich ~** to stretch out ▷ *vt (Hand)* to reach out *(nach for)*

aus|suchen *vt* to choose

Austausch *m* exchange; **aus|tauschen** *vt* to exchange *(gegen for)*

aus|teilen *vt* to distribute; *(aushändigen)* to hand out

Auster *(-, -n)* *f* oyster; **Austernpilz** *m* oyster mushroom

aus|tragen *irr vt (Post)* to deliver; *(Wettkampf)* to hold

Australien *(-s)* *nt* Australia; **Australier(in)** *(-s, -)* *m(f)* Australian; **australisch** *adj* Australian

aus|trinken *irr vt (Glas)* to drain; *(Getränk)* to drink up ▷ *vi* to finish one's drink

aus|trocknen *vi* to dry out; *(Fluss)* to dry up

aus|üben *vt (Beruf, Sport)* to practise; *(Einfluss)* to exert

Ausverkauf *m* sale; **ausverkauft** *adj (Karten, Artikel)* sold out

Auswahl *f* selection, choice *(an +dat of)*; **aus|wählen** *vt* to select, to choose

aus|wandern *vi* to emigrate

auswärtig *adj (nicht am/vom Ort)* not local; *(ausländisch)* foreign; **auswärts** *adv (außerhalb der Stadt)* out of town; *(Sport)* **~ spielen** to play away; **Auswärtsspiel** *nt* away match

aus|wechseln *vt* to replace; *(Sport)* to substitute

Ausweg *m* way out

aus|weichen *irr vi* to get out of the way; **jdm/einer Sache ~** to move aside for sb/sth; *(fig)* to avoid sb/sth

Ausweis *(-es, -e)* *m (Personalausweis)* identity card, ID; *(für Bibliothek etc)* card; **aus|weisen** *irr vt* to expel ▷ *vr:* **sich ~** to prove one's identity; **Ausweiskontrolle** *f* ID check; **Ausweispapiere** *pl* identification documents *pl*

auswendig *adv* by heart

aus|wuchten *vt (Auto: Räder)* to balance

aus|zahlen *vt (Summe)* to pay (out); *(Person)* to pay off ▷ *vr:* **sich ~** to be worth it

aus|zeichnen *vt (ehren)* to honour; *(Comm)* to price ▷ *vr:* **sich ~** to distinguish oneself

aus|ziehen *irr vt (Kleidung)* to take off ▷ *vr:* **sich ~** to undress ▷ *vi (aus Wohnung)* to move out

Auszubildende(r) *mf* trainee

authentisch *adj* authentic, genuine

Auto *(-s, -s)* *nt* car; **~ fahren** to drive; **Autoatlas** *m* road atlas; **Autobahn** *f* motorway *(Brit)*, freeway *(US)*; **Autobahnauffahrt** *f* motorway access road *(Brit)*, on-ramp *(US)*; **Autobahnausfahrt** *f* motorway exit *(Brit)*, off-ramp *(US)*; **Autobahngebühr** *f* toll; **Autobahnkreuz** *nt* motorway interchange; **Autobahnring** *m* motorway ring *(Brit)*, beltway *(US)*; **Autobombe** *f* car bomb; **Autofähre** *f* car ferry; **Autofahrer(in)** *m(f)* driver, motorist; **Autofahrt** *f* drive

Autogramm *(-s, -e)* *nt* autograph

Automarke f make of car
Automat (-en, -en) m vending machine
Automatik (-, -en) f (Auto) automatic transmission; **Automatikschaltung** f automatic gear change (Brit) (o shift (US)); **Automatikwagen** m automatic
automatisch adj automatic ▷ adv automatically
Automechaniker(in) m(f) car mechanic; **Autonummer** f registration (Brit) (o license (US)) number; **Autoradio** nt car radio; **Autoreifen** m car tyre; **Autoreisezug** m Motorail train® (Brit), auto train (US); **Autorennen** nt motor racing; (einzelnes Rennen) motor race; **Autoschlüssel** m car key; **Autotelefon** nt car phone; **Autounfall** m car accident; **Autoverleih** m, **Autovermietung** f car hire (Brit) (o rental (US)); (Firma) car hire (Brit) (o rental (US)) company; **Autowaschanlage** f car wash; **Autowerkstatt** f car repair shop, garage; **Autozubehör** nt car accessories pl
Avocado (-, -s) f avocado
Axt (-, Äxte) f axe
Azubi (-s, -s) m (-, -s) f akr = **Auszubildende** trainee

b

B abk = **Bundesstraße**
Baby (-s, -s) nt baby; **Babybett** nt cot (Brit), crib (US); **Babyfläschchen** nt baby's bottle; **Babynahrung** f baby food; **Babysitter(in)** m(f) babysitter; **Babysitz** m child seat; **Babywickelraum** m baby-changing room
Bach (-(e)s, Bäche) m stream
Backblech nt baking tray (Brit), cookie sheet (US)
Backbord nt port (side)
Backe (-, -n) f cheek
backen (backte, gebacken) vt, vi to bake
Backenzahn m molar
Bäcker(in) (-s, -) m(f) baker; **Bäckerei** f bakery; (Laden) baker's (shop)
Backofen m oven; **Backpulver** nt baking powder
Backspace-Taste f (Inform)

backspace key
Backstein *m* brick
Backwaren *pl* bread, cakes and pastries *pl*
Bad (-(e)s, Bäder) *nt* bath; (Schwimmen) swim; (Ort) spa; **ein ~ nehmen** to have (o take) a bath; **Badeanzug** *m* swimsuit, swimming costume (Brit); **Badehose** *f* swimming trunks *pl*; **Badekappe** *f* swimming cap; **Bademantel** *m* bathrobe; **Bademeister(in)** *m(f)* pool attendant; **Bademütze** *f* swimming cap
baden *vi* to have a bath; (schwimmen) to swim, to bathe (Brit) ▷ *vt* to bath (Brit), to bathe (US)
Baden-Württemberg (-s) *nt* Baden-Württemberg
Badeort *m* spa; **Badesachen** *pl* swimming things *pl*; **Badeschaum** *m* bubble bath, bath foam; **Badetuch** *nt* bath towel; **Badewanne** *f* bath (tub); **Badezeug** *nt* swimming gear; **Badezimmer** *nt* bathroom
Badminton *nt* badminton
baff *adj*: **~ sein** (fam) to be flabbergasted (o gobsmacked)
Bagger (-s, -) *m* excavator; **Baggersee** *m* artificial lake in quarry etc, used for bathing
Bahamas *pl*: **die ~** the Bahamas *pl*
Bahn (-, -en) *f* (Eisenbahn) railway (Brit), railroad (US); (Rennbahn) track; (für Läufer) lane; (Astr) orbit; **Deutsche ~** Germany's main railway operator; **bahnbrechend** *adj* groundbreaking; **BahnCard®** (-, -s) *f* rail card (allowing 50% or 25% reduction on tickets); **Bahnfahrt** *f* railway (Brit) (o railroad (US)) journey; **Bahnhof** *m* station; **am** (o **auf dem**) **~** at the station;

Bahnlinie *f* railway (Brit) (o railroad (US)) line; **Bahnpolizei** *f* railway (Brit) (o railroad (US)) police; **Bahnsteig** (-(e)s, -e) *m* platform; **Bahnstrecke** *f* railway (Brit) (o railroad (US)) line; **Bahnübergang** *m* level crossing (Brit), grade crossing (US)
Bakterien *pl* bacteria *pl*, germs *pl*
bald *adv* (zeitlich) soon; (beinahe) almost; **bis ~!** see you soon (o later); **baldig** *adj* quick, speedy
Balkan (-s) *m*: **der ~** the Balkans *pl*
Balken (-s, -) *m* beam
Balkon (-s, -s o -e) *m* balcony
Ball (-(e)s, Bälle) *m* ball; (Tanz) dance, ball
Ballett (-s) *nt* ballet
Ballon (-s, -s) *m* balloon
Ballspiel *nt* ball game
Ballungsgebiet *nt* conurbation
Baltikum (-s) *nt*: **das ~** the Baltic States *pl*
Bambus (-ses, -se) *m* bamboo; **Bambussprossen** *pl* bamboo shoots *pl*
banal *adj* banal; (Frage, Bemerkung) trite
Banane (-, -n) *f* banana
band *imperf von* **binden**
Band (-(e)s, Bände) *m* (Buch) volume ▷ (-(e)s, Bänder) *nt* (aus Stoff) ribbon, tape; (Fließband) production line; (Tonband) tape; (Anat) ligament; **etw auf ~ aufnehmen** to tape sth ▷ (-, -s) *f* (Musikgruppe) band
Bandage (-, -n) *f* bandage; **bandagieren** *vt* to bandage
Bande (-, -n) *f* (Gruppe) gang
Bänderriss *m* (Med) torn ligament
Bandscheibe *f* (Anat) disc; **Bandwurm** *m* tapeworm
Bank (-, Bänke) *f* (Sitzbank) bench ▷ (-, -en) *f* (Fin) bank

Bankautomat *m* cash dispenser; **Bankkarte** *f* bank card; **Bankkonto** *nt* bank account; **Bankleitzahl** *f* bank sort code; **Banknote** *f* banknote; **Bankverbindung** *f* (*Kontonummer etc*) banking (*o* account) details *pl*

bar *adj*: **~es Geld** cash; **etw** (**in**) **~ bezahlen** to pay sth (in) cash

Bar (-, -s) *f* bar

Bär (-en, -en) *m* bear

barfuß *adj* barefoot

barg *imperf von* **bergen**

Bargeld *nt* cash; **bargeldlos** *adj* non-cash

Barkeeper (-s, -) *m*, **Barmann** *m* barman, bartender (*US*)

barock *adj* baroque

Barometer (-s, -) *m* barometer

barsch *adj* brusque

Barsch (-(e)s, -e) *m* perch

Barscheck *m* open (*o* uncrossed) cheque

Bart (-(e)s, Bärte) *m* beard; **bärtig** *adj* bearded

Barzahlung *f* cash payment

Basar (-s, -e) *m* bazaar

Baseballmütze *f* baseball cap

Basel (-s) *nt* Basle

Basilikum (-s) *nt* basil

Basis (-, Basen) *f* basis

Baskenland *nt* Basque region

Basketball *m* basketball

Bass (-es, Bässe) *m* bass

basta *interj*: **und damit ~!** and that's that

basteln *vt* to make ▷ *vi* to make things, to do handicrafts

bat *imperf von* **bitten**

Batterie *f* battery; **batteriebetrieben** *adj* battery-powered

Bau (-(e)s) *m* (*Bauen*) building, construction; (*Aufbau*) structure; (*Baustelle*) building site ▷ *m* (*Baue*) (*Tier*) burrow ▷ *m* (*Bauten*) (*Gebäude*) building; **Bauarbeiten** *pl* construction work *sing*; (*Straßenbau*) roadworks *pl* (*Brit*), roadwork (*US*); **Bauarbeiter(in)** *m(f)* construction worker

Bauch (-(e)s, Bäuche) *m* stomach; **Bauchnabel** *m* navel; **Bauchredner(in)** *m(f)* ventriloquist; **Bauchschmerzen** *pl* stomach-ache *sing*; **Bauchspeicheldrüse** *f* pancreas; **Bauchtanz** *m* belly dance; (*das Tanzen*) belly dancing; **Bauchweh** (-s) *nt* stomach-ache

bauen *vt, vi* to build; (*Tech*) to construct

Bauer (-n *o* -s, -n) *m* farmer; (*Schach*) pawn; **Bäuerin** *f* farmer; (*Frau des Bauern*) farmer's wife; **Bauernhof** *m* farm

baufällig *adj* dilapidated; **Baujahr** *adj* year of construction; **der Wagen ist ~ 2002** the car is a 2002 model, the car was made in 2002

Baum (-(e)s, Bäume) *m* tree

Baumarkt *m* DIY centre

Baumwolle *f* cotton

Bauplatz *m* building site; **Baustein** *m* (*für Haus*) stone; (*Spielzeug*) brick; (*fig*) element; **elektronischer ~** chip; **Baustelle** *f* building site; (*bei Straßenbau*) roadworks *pl* (*Brit*), roadwork (*US*); **Bauteil** *nt* prefabricated part; **Bauunternehmer(in)** *m(f)* building contractor; **Bauwerk** *nt* building

Bayern (-s) *nt* Bavaria

beabsichtigen *vt* to intend

beachten *vt* (*Aufmerksamkeit schenken*) to pay attention to; (*Vorschrift etc*) to observe; **nicht ~** to ignore; **beachtlich** *adj* considerable

Beachvolleyball *nt* beach volleyball

Beamte(r) (-n, -n) m, **Beamtin** f
official; (*Staatsbeamter*) civil
servant
beanspruchen vt to claim; (*Zeit,
Platz*) to take up; **jdn ~** to keep sb
busy
beanstanden vt to complain
about; **Beanstandung** f
complaint
beantragen vt to apply for
beantworten vt to answer
bearbeiten vt to work; (*Material,
Daten*) to process; (*Chem*) to treat;
(*Fall etc*) to deal with; (*Buch etc*) to
revise; (*fam: beeinflussen wollen*) to
work on; **Bearbeitungsgebühr** f
handling (*o service*) charge
beatmen vt: **jdn ~** to give sb
artificial respiration
beaufsichtigen vt to supervise;
(*bei Prüfung*) to invigilate
beauftragen vt to instruct; **jdn
mit etw ~** to give sb the job of
doing sth
Becher (-s, -) m mug; (*ohne
Henkel*) tumbler; (*für Jogurt*) pot;
(*aus Pappe*) tub
Becken (-s, -) nt basin; (*Spüle*)
sink; (*zum Schwimmen*) pool; (*Mus*)
cymbal; (*Anat*) pelvis
bedanken vr: **sich ~** to say thank
you; **sich bei jdm für etw ~** to
thank sb for sth
Bedarf (-(e)s) m need (*an +dat
for*); (*Comm*) demand (*an +dat for*);
je nach ~ according to demand;
bei ~ if necessary;
Bedarfshaltestelle f request
stop, flag stop (*US*)
bedauerlich adj regrettable;
bedauern vt to regret;
(*bemitleiden*) to feel sorry for;
bedauernswert adj (*Zustände*)
regrettable; (*Mensch*) unfortunate
bedeckt adj covered; (*Himmel*)
overcast
bedenken irr vt to consider;

Bedenken (-s, -) nt (*Überlegen*)
consideration; (*Zweifel*) doubt;
(*Skrupel*) scruples pl; **bedenklich**
adj dubious; (*Zustand*) serious
bedeuten vt to mean; **jdm
nichts/viel ~** to mean nothing/a
lot to sb; **bedeutend** adj
important; (*beträchtlich*)
considerable; **Bedeutung** f
meaning; (*Wichtigkeit*) importance
bedienen vt to serve; (*Maschine*)
to operate ▷ vr: **sich ~** (*beim Essen*)
to help oneself; **Bedienung** f
service; (*Kellner/Kellnerin*)
waiter/waitress; (*Verkäufer(in)*)
shop assistant; (*Zuschlag*) service
(charge); **Bedienungsanleitung**
f operating instructions pl;
Bedienungshandbuch nt
instruction manual; **Bedingung** f
condition; **unter der ~, dass** on
condition that; **unter diesen ~en**
under these circumstances
bedrohen vt to threaten
Bedürfnis nt need
beeilen vr: **sich ~** to hurry
beeindrucken vt to impress
beeinflussen vt to influence
beeinträchtigen vt to affect
beenden vt to end; (*fertigstellen*)
to finish
beerdigen vt to bury;
Beerdigung f burial; (*Feier*)
funeral
Beere (-, -n) f berry;
(*Traubenbeere*) grape
Beet (-(e)s, -e) nt bed
befahl imperf von **befehlen**
befahrbar adj passable; (*Naut*)
navigable; **befahren** irr vt
(*Straße*) to use; (*Pass*) to drive over;
(*Fluss etc*) to navigate ▷ adj:
stark/wenig ~ busy/quiet
Befehl (-(e)s, -e) m order; (*Inform*)
command; **befehlen** (*befahl,
befohlen*) vt to order; **jdm ~, etw
zu tun** to order sb to do sth ▷ vi

to give orders

befestigen vt to fix; (mit Schnur, Seil) to attach; (mit Klebestoff) to stick

befeuchten vt to moisten

befinden irr vr: **sich ~** to be

befohlen pp von **befehlen**

befolgen vt (Rat etc) to follow

befördern vt (transportieren) to transport; (beruflich) to promote; **Beförderung** f transport; (beruflich) promotion; **Beförderungsbedingungen** pl conditions pl of carriage

Befragung f questioning; (Umfrage) opinion poll

befreundet adj friendly; **~ sein** to be friends (mit jdm with sb)

befriedigen vt to satisfy; **befriedigend** adj satisfactory; (Schulnote) ≈ C; **Befriedigung** f satisfaction

befristet adj limited (auf +akk to)

befruchten vt to fertilize; (fig) to stimulate

Befund (-(e)s, -e) m findings pl; (Med) diagnosis

befürchten vt to fear

befürworten vt to support

begabt adj gifted, talented; **Begabung** f talent, gift

begann imperf von **beginnen**

begegnen vi to meet (jdm sb), to meet with (einer Sache dat sth)

begehen irr vt (Straftat) to commit; (Jubiläum etc) to celebrate

begehrt adj sought-after; (Junggeselle) eligible

begeistern vt to fill with enthusiasm; (inspirieren) to inspire ▷ vr: **sich für etw ~** to be/get enthusiastic about sth; **begeistert** adj enthusiastic

Beginn (-(e)s) m beginning; **zu ~** at the beginning; **beginnen** (begann, begonnen) vt, vi to start, to begin

beglaubigen vt to certify; **Beglaubigung** f certification

begleiten vt to accompany; **Begleiter(in)** m(f) companion; **Begleitung** f company; (Mus) accompaniment

beglückwünschen vt to congratulate (zu on)

begonnen pp von **beginnen**

begraben irr vt to bury; **Begräbnis** nt burial; (Feier) funeral

begreifen irr vt to understand

Begrenzung f boundary; (fig) restriction

Begriff (-(e)s, -e) m concept; (Vorstellung) idea; **im ~ sein, etw zu tun** to be on the point of doing sth; **schwer von ~ sein** to be slow on the uptake

begründen vt (rechtfertigen) to justify; **Begründung** f explanation; (Rechtfertigung) justification

begrüßen vt to greet; (willkommen heißen) to welcome; **Begrüßung** f greeting; (Empfang) welcome

behaart adj hairy

behalten irr vt to keep; (im Gedächtnis) to remember; **etw für sich ~** to keep sth to oneself

Behälter (-s, -) m container

behandeln vt to treat; **Behandlung** f treatment

behaupten vt to claim, to maintain ▷ vr: **sich ~** to assert oneself; **Behauptung** f claim

beheizen vt to heat

behelfen irr vr: **sich mit/ohne etw ~** to make do with/without sth

beherbergen vt to accommodate

beherrschen vt (Situation, Gefühle) to control; (Instrument) to master ▷ vr: **sich ~** to control

oneself; **Beherrschung** f control
(*über +akk* of); **die ~ verlieren** to
lose one's self-control
behilflich adj helpful; **jdm ~ sein**
to help sb (*bei* with)
behindern vt to hinder; (*Verkehr,
Sicht*) to obstruct; **Behinderte(r)**
mf disabled person;
behindertengerecht adj suitable
for disabled people
Behörde (-, -n) f authority; **die
~n** pl the authorities pl

O SCHLÜSSELWORT

bei prep +dat **1** (*nahe bei*) near; (*zum
Aufenthalt*) at, with; (*unter,
zwischen*) among; **bei München**
near Munich; **bei uns** at our place;
beim Friseur at the hairdresser's;
bei seinen Eltern wohnen to live
with one's parents; **bei einer
Firma arbeiten** to work for a
firm; **etw bei sich haben** to have
sth on one; **jdn bei sich haben** to
have sb with one; **bei Goethe** in
Goethe; **beim Militär** in the army
2 (*zeitlich*) at, on; (*während*) during;
(*Zustand, Umstand*) in; **bei Nacht** at
night; **bei Nebel** in fog; **bei Regen**
if it rains; **bei solcher Hitze** in
such heat; **bei meiner Ankunft** on
my arrival; **bei der Arbeit** when
I'm *etc* working; **beim Fahren**
while driving

bei|behalten irr vt to keep
Beiboot nt dinghy
bei|bringen irr vt: **jdm etw
~** (*mitteilen*) to break sth to sb;
(*lehren*) to teach sb sth
beide(s) pron both; **meine ~n
Brüder** my two brothers, both my
brothers; **wir ~** both (*o* the two) of
us; **keiner von ~** neither of them;
alle ~ both (of them); **~s ist sehr
schön** both are very nice; **30**

~ (*beim Tennis*) 30 all
beieinander adv together
Beifahrer(in) m(f) passenger;
Beifahrerairbag m passenger
airbag; **Beifahrersitz** m
passenger seat
Beifall (-(e)s) m applause
beige adj inv beige
Beigeschmack m aftertaste
Beil (-(e)s, -e) nt axe
Beilage f (*Gastr*) side dish;
(*Gemüse*) vegetables pl; (*zu Buch etc*)
supplement
beiläufig adj casual ▷ adv
casually
Beileid nt condolences pl; (**mein**)
herzliches ~ please accept my
sincere condolences
beiliegend adj enclosed
beim kontr von **bei dem**
Bein (-(e)s, -e) nt leg
beinah(e) adv almost, nearly
beinhalten vt to contain
Beipackzettel m instruction
leaflet
beisammen adv together;
Beisammensein (-s) nt
get-together
beiseite adv aside;
beiseite|legen vt: **etw ~** (*sparen*)
to put sth by
Beispiel (-(e)s, -e) nt example;
sich (*dat*) **an jdm/etw ein
~ nehmen** to take sb/sth as an
example; **zum ~** for example
beißen (*biss, gebissen*) vt to bite
▷ vi to bite; (*stechen: Rauch, Säure*)
to sting ▷ vr: **sich ~** (*Farben*) to
clash
Beitrag (-(e)s, Beiträge) m
contribution; (*für Mitgliedschaft*)
subscription; (*Versicherung*)
premium; **bei|tragen** irr vt, vi to
contribute (*zu* to)
bekannt adj well-known; (*nicht
fremd*) familiar; **mit jdm ~ sein** to
know sb; **~ geben** to announce;

jdn mit jdm ~ machen to introduce sb to sb; **Bekannte(r)** *mf* friend; *(entfernter)* acquaintance; **bekanntlich** *adv* as everyone knows; **Bekanntschaft** *f* acquaintance

bekiffen *vr:* **sich ~** *(fam)* to get stoned

beklagen *vr:* **sich ~** to complain

Bekleidung *f* clothing

bekommen *irr vt* to get; *(erhalten)* to receive; *(Kind)* to have; *(Zug, Grippe)* to catch, to get; **wie viel ~ Sie dafür?** how much is that? ▷ *vi:* **jdm ~** *(Essen)* to agree with sb; **wir ~ schon** *(bedient werden)* we're being served

beladen *irr vt* to load

Belag *(-(e)s, Beläge) m* coating; *(auf Zähnen)* plaque; *(auf Zunge)* fur

belasten *vt* to load; *(Körper)* to strain; *(Umwelt)* to pollute; *(fig: mit Sorgen etc)* to burden; *(Comm: Konto)* to debit; *(Jur)* to incriminate

belästigen *vt* to bother; *(stärker)* to pester; *(sexuell)* to harass; **Belästigung** *f* annoyance; **sexuelle ~** sexual harassment

belebt *adj* *(Straße etc)* busy

Beleg *(-(e)s, -e) m* *(Comm)* receipt; *(Beweis)* proof; **belegen** *vt* *(Brot)* to spread; *(Platz)* to reserve; *(Kurs, Vorlesung)* to register for; *(beweisen)* to prove

belegt *adj* *(Tel)* engaged *(Brit)*, busy *(US)*; *(Hotel)* full; *(Zunge)* coated; **~es Brötchen** sandwich; **der Platz ist ~** this seat is taken; **Belegzeichen** *nt* *(Tel)* engaged tone *(Brit)*, busy tone *(US)*

beleidigen *vt* to insult; *(kränken)* to offend; **Beleidigung** *f* insult; *(Jur)* slander; *(schriftliche)* libel

beleuchten *vt* to light; *(bestrahlen)* to illuminate; *(fig)* to examine; **Beleuchtung** *f* lighting; *(Bestrahlung)* illumination

Belgien *(-s) nt* Belgium; **Belgier(in)** *(-s, -) m(f)* Belgian; **belgisch** *adj* Belgian

belichten *vt* to expose; **Belichtung** *f* exposure; **Belichtungsmesser** *(-s, -) m* light meter

Belieben *nt:* **(ganz) nach ~** (just) as you wish

beliebig *adj:* **jedes ~e Muster** any pattern; **jeder ~e** anyone ▷ *adv:* **~ lange** as long as you like; **~ viel** as many (*o* much) as you like

beliebt *adj* popular; **sich bei jdm ~ machen** to make oneself popular with sb

beliefern *vt* to supply

bellen *vi* to bark

Belohnung *f* reward

Belüftung *f* ventilation

belügen *irr vt* to lie to

bemerkbar *adj* noticeable; **sich ~ machen** *(Mensch)* to attract attention; *(Zustand)* to become noticeable; **bemerken** *vt* *(wahrnehmen)* to notice; *(sagen)* to remark; **bemerkenswert** *adj* remarkable; **Bemerkung** *f* remark

bemitleiden *vt* to pity

bemühen *vr:* **sich ~** to try (hard), to make an effort; **Bemühung** *f* effort

bemuttern *vt* to mother

benachbart *adj* neighbouring

benachrichtigen *vt* to inform; **Benachrichtigung** *f* notification

benachteiligen *vt* to (put at a) disadvantage; *(wegen Rasse etc)* to discriminate against

benehmen *irr vr:* **sich ~** to behave; **Benehmen** *(-s) nt* behaviour

beneiden *vt* to envy; **jdn um etw ~** to envy sb sth

Beneluxländer *pl* Benelux countries *pl*

benommen *adj* dazed
benötigen *vt* to need
benutzen *vt* to use;
  Benutzer(in) *(-s, -)* *m(f)* user;
  benutzerfreundlich *adj* user-friendly; **Benutzerhandbuch** *nt*
  user's guide; **Benutzerkennung** *f*
  user ID; **Benutzeroberfläche** *f*
  (Inform) user/system interface;
  Benutzung *f* use;
  Benutzungsgebühr *f* (hire)
  charge
Benzin *(-s, -e)* *nt* *(Auto)* petrol
  (Brit), gas *(US)*; **Benzingutschein**
  m petrol *(Brit)* *(o* gas *(US))* coupon;
  Benzinkanister *m* petrol *(Brit)* *(o*
  gas *(US))* can; **Benzinpumpe** *f*
  petrol *(Brit)* *(o* gas *(US))* pump;
  Benzintank *m* petrol *(Brit)* *(o* gas
  (US)) tank; **Benzinuhr** *f* fuel
  gauge
beobachten *vt* to observe;
  Beobachtung *f* observation
bequem *adj* comfortable;
  (Ausrede) convenient; *(faul)* lazy;
  machen Sie es sich ~ make
  yourself at home; **Bequemlichkeit**
  f comfort; *(Faulheit)* laziness
beraten *irr vt* to advise;
  (besprechen) to discuss ▷ *vr:* **sich**
  ~ to consult; **Beratung** *f* advice;
  (bei Arzt etc) consultation
berauben *vt* to rob
berechnen *vt* to calculate;
  (Comm) to charge; **berechnend**
  adj *(Mensch)* calculating
berechtigen *vt* to entitle *(zu* to);
  (fig) to justify; **berechtigt** *adj*
  justified; **zu etw ~ sein** to be
  entitled to sth
bereden *vt* *(besprechen)* to discuss
Bereich *(-(e)s, -e)* *m* area;
  (Ressort, Gebiet) field
bereisen *vt* to travel through
bereit *adj* ready; **zu etw ~ sein** to
  be ready for sth; **sich ~ erklären,**
  etw zu tun to agree to do sth

bereiten *vt* to prepare; *(Kummer)*
  to cause; *(Freude)* to give
bereit|legen *vt* to lay out
bereit|machen *vr:* **sich ~** to get
  ready
bereits *adv* already
Bereitschaft *f* readiness;
  ~ haben *(Arzt)* to be on call
bereit|stehen *vi* to be ready
bereuen *vt* to regret
Berg *(-(e)s, -e)* *m* mountain;
  (kleiner) hill; **in die ~e fahren** to go
  to the mountains; **bergab** *adv*
  downhill; **bergauf** *adv* uphill;
  Bergbahn *f* mountain railway
  (Brit) *(o* railroad *(US))*
bergen *(barg, geborgen)* *vt* *(retten)*
  to rescue; *(enthalten)* to contain
Bergführer(in) *m(f)* mountain
  guide; **Berghütte** *f* mountain hut;
  bergig *adj* mountainous;
  Bergschuh *m* climbing boot;
  Bergsteigen *(-s)* *nt*
  mountaineering; **Bergsteiger(in)**
  (-s, -) *m(f)* mountaineer;
  Bergtour *f* mountain hike
Bergung *f* *(Rettung)* rescue; *(von*
  Toten, Fahrzeugen) recovery
Bergwacht *(-, -en)* *f* mountain
  rescue service; **Bergwerk** *nt*
  mine
Bericht *(-(e)s, -e)* *m* report;
  berichten *vt, vi* to report
berichtigen *vt* to correct
Bermudadreieck *nt* Bermuda
  triangle; **Bermudainseln** *pl*
  Bermuda *sing;* **Bermudashorts**
  pl Bermuda shorts *pl*
Bernstein *m* amber
berüchtigt *adj* notorious,
  infamous
berücksichtigen *vt* to take into
  account; *(Antrag, Bewerber)* to
  consider
Beruf *(-(e)s, -e)* *m* occupation;
  (akademischer) profession;
  (Gewerbe) trade; **was sind Sie von**

~? what do you do (for a living)?;
beruflich adj professional
Berufsausbildung f vocational
training; **Berufsschule** f
vocational college; **berufstätig**
adj employed; **Berufsverkehr** m
commuter traffic
beruhigen vt to calm ▷ vr: **sich
~** (Mensch, Situation) to calm down;
beruhigend adj reassuring;
Beruhigungsmittel nt sedative
berühmt adj famous
berühren vt to touch;
(gefühlsmäßig bewegen) to move;
(betreffen) to affect; (flüchtig
erwähnen) to mention, to touch on
▷ vr: **sich ~** to touch
besaufen irr vr: **sich ~** (fam) to
get plastered
beschädigen vt to damage
beschäftigen vt to occupy;
(beruflich) to employ ▷ vr: **sich mit
etw ~** to occupy oneself with sth;
(sich befassen) to deal with sth;
beschäftigt adj busy, occupied;
Beschäftigung f (Beruf)
employment; (Tätigkeit)
occupation; (geistige)
preoccupation (mit with)
Bescheid (-(e)s, -e) m
information; **~ wissen** to be
informed (o know) (über +akk
about); **ich weiß ~** I know; **jdm
~ geben** (o sagen) to let sb know
bescheiden adj modest
bescheinigen vt to certify;
(bestätigen) to acknowledge;
Bescheinigung f certificate;
(Quittung) receipt
bescheißen irr vt (vulg) to cheat
(um out of)
bescheuert adj (fam, pej) crazy
beschimpfen vt (mit
Kraftausdrücken) to swear at
Beschiss (-es) m: **das ist ~** (vulg)
that's a rip-off; **beschissen** adj
(vulg) shitty

beschlagnahmen vt to
confiscate
Beschleunigung f acceleration;
Beschleunigungsspur f
acceleration lane
beschließen irr vt to decide on;
(beenden) to end; **Beschluss** m
decision
beschränken vt to limit, to
restrict (auf +akk to) ▷ vr: **sich ~** to
restrict oneself (auf +akk to);
Beschränkung f limitation,
restriction
beschreiben irr vt to describe;
(Papier) to write on; **Beschreibung**
f description
beschuldigen vt to accuse (gen
of); **Beschuldigung** f
accusation
beschummeln vt, vi (fam) to
cheat (um out of)
beschützen vt to protect (vor
+dat from)
Beschwerde (-, -n) f complaint;
~n pl (Leiden) trouble sing;
beschweren vt to weight down;
(fig) to burden ▷ vr: **sich ~** to
complain
beschwipst adj tipsy
beseitigen vt to remove;
(Problem) to get rid of; (Müll) to
dispose of; **Beseitigung** f
removal; (von Müll) disposal
Besen (-s, -) m broom
besetzen vt (Haus, Land) to
occupy; (Platz) to take; (Posten) to
fill; (Rolle) to cast; **besetzt** adj
full; (Tel) engaged (Brit), busy (US);
(Platz) taken; (WC) engaged;
Besetztzeichen nt engaged tone
(Brit), busy tone (US)
besichtigen vt (Museum) to visit;
(Sehenswürdigkeit) to have a look at;
(Stadt) to tour
besiegen vt to defeat
Besitz (-es) m possession;
(Eigentum) property; **besitzen** irr

vt to own; (*Eigenschaft*) to have;
Besitzer(in) (*-s, -*) *m(f)* owner
besoffen *adj* (*fam*) plastered
besondere(r, s) *adj* special;
(*bestimmt*) particular;
(*eigentümlich*) peculiar; **nichts ~s**
nothing special; **Besonderheit** *f*
special feature; (*besondere*
Eigenschaft) peculiarity; **besonders**
adv especially, particularly;
(*getrennt*) separately
besorgen *vt* (*beschaffen*) to get
(*jdm* for sb); (*kaufen a.*) to purchase;
(*erledigen: Geschäfte*) to deal with
besprechen *irr vt* to discuss;
Besprechung *f* discussion;
(*Konferenz*) meeting; **Besprech-**
ungsraum *m* consultation
room
besser *adj* better; **es geht ihm**
~ he feels better; **~ gesagt** or
rather; **~ werden** to improve;
bessern *vt* to improve ▷ *vr*: **sich**
~ to improve; (*Mensch*) to mend
one's ways; **Besserung** *f*
improvement; **gute ~!** get well
soon
beständig *adj* constant; (*Wetter*)
settled
Bestandteil *m* component
bestätigen *vt* to confirm;
(*Empfang, Brief*) to acknowledge;
Bestätigung *f* confirmation; (*von*
Brief) acknowledgement
beste(r, s) *adj* best; **das ~ wäre,**
wir ... it would be best if we ...
▷ *adv*: **sie singt am ~n** she sings
best; **so ist es am ~n** it's best that
way; **am ~n gehst du gleich** you'd
better go at once
bestechen *irr vt* to bribe;
Bestechung *f* bribery
Besteck (*-(e)s, -e*) *nt* cutlery
bestehen *irr vi* to be, to exist;
(*andauern*) to last; **~ auf** (*+dat*) to
insist on; **~ aus** to consist of ▷ *vt*
(*Probe, Prüfung*) to pass; (*Kampf*) to

win
bestehlen *irr vt* to rob
bestellen *vt* to order; (*reservieren*)
to book; (*Grüße, Auftrag*) to pass on
(*jdm* to sb); (*kommen lassen*) to send
for; **Bestellnummer** *f* order
number; **Bestellung** *f* (*Comm*)
order; (*das Bestellen*) ordering
bestens *adv* very well
bestimmen *vt* to determine;
(*Regeln*) to lay down; (*Tag, Ort*) to
fix; (*ernennen*) to appoint;
(*vorsehen*) to mean (*für* for);
bestimmt *adj* definite; (*gewiss*)
certain; (*entschlossen*) firm ▷ *adv*
definitely; (*wissen*) for sure;
Bestimmung *f* (*Verordnung*)
regulation; (*Zweck*) purpose
Best.-Nr. *abk* = **Bestellnummer**
order number
bestrafen *vt* to punish
bestrahlen *vt* to illuminate;
(*Med*) to treat with radiotherapy
bestreiten *irr vt* (*leugnen*) to
deny
Bestseller (*-s, -*) *m* bestseller
bestürzt *adj* dismayed
Besuch (*-(e)s, -e*) *m* visit; (*Mensch*)
visitor; **~ haben** to have visitors/a
visitor; **besuchen** *vt* to visit;
(*Schule, Kino etc*) to go to;
Besucher(in) (*-s, -*) *m(f)* visitor;
Besuchszeit *f* visiting hours *pl*
betäuben *vt* (*Med*) to
anaesthetize; **Betäubung** *f*
anaesthetic; **örtliche ~** local
anaesthetic; **Betäubungsmittel**
nt anaesthetic
Bete (*-, -n*) *f*: **Rote ~** beetroot
beteiligen *vr* **sich an etw** (*dat*)
~ to take part in sth, to participate
in sth ▷ *vt* **jdn an etw** (*dat*) **~** to
involve sb in sth; **Beteiligung** *f*
participation; (*Anteil*) share;
(*Besucherzahl*) attendance
beten *vi* to pray
Beton (*-s, -s*) *m* concrete

betonen *vt* to stress;
(*hervorheben*) to emphasize;
Betonung *f* stress; (*fig*)
emphasis

Betr. *abk* = **Betreff** re

Betracht *m*: **in ~ ziehen** to take
into consideration; **in ~ kommen**
to be a possibility; **nicht in
~ kommen** to be out of the
question; **betrachten** *vt* to look
at; **~ als** to regard as; **beträchtlich**
adj considerable

Betrag (*-(e)s, Beträge*) *m* amount,
sum; **betragen** *irr vt* to amount
(*o* come) to ⊳ *vr*: **sich ~** to behave

betreffen *irr vt* to concern;
(*Regelung etc*) to affect; **was mich
betrifft** as for me; **betreffend** *adj*
relevant, in question

betreten *irr vt* to enter; (*Bühne
etc*) to step onto; „**Betreten
verboten**" "keep off/out"

betreuen *vt* to look after;
(*Reisegruppe, Abteilung*) to be in
charge of; **Betreuer(in)** (*-s, -*) *m(f)*
(*Pfleger*) carer; (*von Kind*) child
minder; (*von Reisegruppe*)
groupleader

Betrieb (*-(e)s, -e*) *m* (*Firma*) firm;
(*Anlage*) plant; (*Tätigkeit*)
operation; (*Treiben*) bustle; **außer
~ sein** to be out of order; **in ~ sein**
to be in operation; **betriebsbereit**
adj operational; **Betriebsrat** *m*
(*Gremium*) works council;
Betriebssystem *nt* (*Inform*)
operating system

betrinken *irr vr*: **sich ~** to get
drunk

betroffen *adj* (*bestürzt*) shaken;
von etw ~ werden/sein to be
affected by sth

betrog *imperf von* **betrügen**;
betrogen *pp von* **betrügen**

Betrug (*-(e)s*) *m* deception; (*Jur*)
fraud; **betrügen** (*betrog, betrogen*)
vt to deceive; (*Jur*) to defraud;

(*Partner*) to cheat on; **Betrüger(in)**
(*-s, -*) *m(f)* cheat

betrunken *adj* drunk

Bett (*-(e)s, -en*) *nt* bed; **ins** (*o* **zu**)
~ gehen to go to bed; **das
~ machen** to make the bed;
Bettbezug *m* duvet cover;
Bettdecke *f* blanket

betteln *vi* to beg

Bettlaken *nt* sheet

Bettler(in) (*-s, -*) *m(f)* beggar

Bettsofa *nt* sofa bed; **Betttuch**
nt sheet; **Bettwäsche** *f* bed
linen; **Bettzeug** *nt* bedding

beugen *vt* to bend ⊳ *vr*: **sich ~** to
bend; (*sich fügen*) to submit (*dat* to)

Beule (*-, -n*) *f* (*Schwellung*) bump;
(*Delle*) dent

beunruhigen *vt* to worry ⊳ *vr*:
sich ~ to worry

beurteilen *vt* to judge

Beute (*-*) *f* (*von Dieb*) booty, loot;
(*von Tier*) prey

Beutel (*-s, -*) *m* bag

Bevölkerung *f* population

bevollmächtigt *adj* authorized
(*zu etw* to do sth)

bevor *conj* before; **bevor|stehen**
irr vi (*Schwierigkeiten*) to lie ahead;
(*Gefahr*) to be imminent; **jdm
~** (*Überraschung etc*) to be in store
for sb; **bevorstehend** *adj*
forthcoming; **bevorzugen** *vt* to
prefer

bewachen *vt* to guard; **bewacht**
adj: **~er Parkplatz** supervised car
park (*Brit*), guarded parking lot
(*US*)

bewegen *vt* to move; **jdn dazu ~,
etw zu tun** to get sb to do sth
⊳ *vr*: **sich ~** to move; **es bewegt
sich etwas** (*fig*) things are
beginning to happen; **Bewegung**
f movement; (*Phys*) motion;
(*innere*) emotion; (*körperlich*)
exercise; **Bewegungsmelder**
(*-s, -*) *m* sensor (*which reacts to*

movement)

Beweis *(-es, -e)* m proof; *(Zeugnis)* evidence; **beweisen** *irr vt* to prove; *(zeigen)* to show

bewerben *irr vr:* **sich ~** to apply *(um* for); **Bewerbung** f application; **Bewerbungsunterlagen** *pl* application documents *pl*

bewilligen *vt* to allow; *(Geld)* to grant

bewirken *vt* to cause, to bring about

bewohnen *vt* to live in; **Bewohner(in)** *(-s, -)* m(f) inhabitant; *(von Haus)* resident

bewölkt *adj* cloudy, overcast; **Bewölkung** f clouds *pl*

bewundern *vt* to admire; **bewundernswert** *adj* admirable

bewusst *adj* conscious; *(absichtlich)* deliberate; **sich** *(dat)* **einer Sache** *(gen)* **~ sein** to be aware of sth ▷ *adv* consciously; *(absichtlich)* deliberately; **bewusstlos** *adj* unconscious; **Bewusstlosigkeit** f unconsciousness; **Bewusstsein** *(-s)* nt consciousness; **bei ~** conscious

bezahlen *vt* to pay; *(Ware, Leistung)* to pay for; **kann ich bar/mit Kreditkarte ~?** can I pay cash/by credit card?; **sich bezahlt machen** to be worth it; **Bezahlung** f payment

bezeichnen *vt (kennzeichnen)* to mark; *(nennen)* to call; *(beschreiben)* to describe; **Bezeichnung** f *(Name)* name; *(Begriff)* term

beziehen *irr vt (Bett)* to change; *(Haus, Position)* to move into; *(erhalten)* to receive; *(Zeitung)* to take; **einen Standpunkt ~** *(fig)* to take up a position ▷ *vr:* **sich ~** to refer *(auf +akk* to); **Beziehung** f *(Verbindung)* connection; *(Verhältnis)* relationship; **~en**

haben *(vorteilhaft)* to have connections (*o* contacts); **in dieser ~** in this respect; **beziehungsweise** *adv* or; *(genauer gesagt)* or rather

Bezirk *(-(e)s, -e)* m district

Bezug *(-(e)s, Bezüge)* m *(Überzug)* cover; *(von Kopfkissen)* pillowcase; **in ~ auf** *(+akk)* with regard to; **bezüglich** *prep +gen* concerning

bezweifeln *vt* to doubt

BH *(-s, -s)* m bra

Bhf. *abk* = **Bahnhof** station

Biathlon *(-s, -s)* m biathlon

Bibel *(-, -n)* f Bible

Biber *(-s, -)* m beaver

Bibliothek *(-, -en)* f library

biegen *(bog, gebogen)* vt to bend ▷ *vr:* **sich ~** to bend ▷ *vi* to turn *(in +akk* into); **Biegung** f bend

Biene *(-, -n)* f bee

Bier *(-(e)s, -e)* nt beer; **helles ~** ≈ lager *(Brit)*, beer *(US)*; **dunkles ~** ≈ brown ale *(Brit)*, dark beer *(US)*; **zwei ~, bitte!** two beers, please; **Biergarten** m beer garden; **Bierzelt** nt beer tent

bieten *(bot, geboten)* vt to offer; *(bei Versteigerung)* bid; **sich** *(dat)* **etw ~ lassen** to put up with sth ▷ *vr:* **sich ~** *(Gelegenheit)* to present itself *(dat* to)

Bikini *(-s, -s)* m bikini

Bild *(-(e)s, -er)* nt picture; *(gedankliches)* image; *(Foto)* photo

bilden *vt* to form; *(geistig)* to educate; *(ausmachen)* to constitute ▷ *vr:* **sich ~** *(entstehen)* to form; *(lernen)* to educate oneself

Bilderbuch nt picture book

Bildhauer(in) *(-s, -)* m(f) sculptor

Bildschirm m screen; **Bildschirmschoner** *(-s, -)* m screensaver; **Bildschirmtext** m viewdata, videotext

Bildung f formation; *(Wissen,*

Benehmen) education;
Bildungsurlaub *m* educational holiday; (*von Firma*) study leave
Billard *nt* billiards *sing*
billig *adj* cheap; (*gerecht*) fair
Billigflieger *m* budget airline
Billigflug *m* cheap flight
Binde (-, -n) *f* bandage; (*Armbinde*) band; (*Damenbinde*) sanitary towel (*Brit*), sanitary napkin (*US*)
Bindehautentzündung *f* conjunctivitis
binden (*band, gebunden*) *vt* to tie; (*Buch*) to bind; (*Soße*) to thicken
Bindestrich *m* hyphen
Bindfaden *m* string
Bindung *f* bond, tie; (*Skibindung*) binding
Bio- *in zW* bio-; **Biokost** *f* health food

○ **BIOLADEN**
○
○ A **Bioladen** is a shop which
○ specializes in selling
○ environmentally friendly
○ products such as
○ phosphate-free washing
○ powders, recycled paper and
○ organically grown vegetables.

Biologie *f* biology; **biologisch** *adj* biological; (*Anbau*) organic
Birke (-, -n) *f* birch
Birne (-, -n) *f* (*Obst*) pear; (*Elek*) (light) bulb

 SCHLÜSSELWORT

bis *prep +akk, adv* **1** (*zeitlich*) till, until; (*bis spätestens*) by; **Sie haben bis Dienstag Zeit** you have until *o* till Tuesday; **bis Dienstag muss es fertig sein** it must be ready by Tuesday; **bis auf Weiteres** until further notice; **bis in die Nacht**

into the night; **bis bald/gleich** see you later/soon
2 (*räumlich*) (up) to; **ich fahre bis Köln** I'm going to *o* I'm going as far as Cologne; **bis an unser Grundstück** (right *o* up) to our plot; **bis hierher** this far
3 (*bei Zahlen*) up to; **bis zu** up to
4 bis auf etw *akk* (*außer*) except sth; (*einschließlich*) including sth
▷ *konj* **1** (*mit Zahlen*) to; **10 bis 20** 10 to 20
2 (*zeitlich*) till, until; **bis es dunkel wird** till *o* until it gets dark; **von … bis …** from … to …

Bischof (-s, *Bischöfe*) *m* bishop
bisher *adv* up to now, so far
Biskuit (-(e)s, -s *o* -e) *nt* sponge
biss *imperf von* **beißen**
Biss (-es, -e) *m* bite
bisschen *adj:* **ein ~** a bit of; **ein ~ Salz/Liebe** a bit of salt/love; **ich habe kein ~ Hunger** I'm not a bit hungry ▷ *adv:* **ein ~** a bit; **kein ~** not at all
bissig *adj* (*Hund*) vicious; (*Bemerkung*) cutting
Bit (-s, -s) *nt* (*Inform*) bit
bitte *interj* please; (*wie*) **~?** (I beg your) pardon?; **~ (schön)!** (*als Antwort auf Dank*) you're welcome, that's alright; **hier, ~** here you are; **Bitte** (-, -n) *f* request; **bitten** (*bat, gebeten*) *vt, vi* to ask (*um* for)
bitter *adj* bitter
Blähungen *pl* (*Med*) wind *sing*
blamieren *vr:* **sich ~** to make a fool of oneself ▷ *vt:* **jdn ~** to make sb look a fool
Blankoscheck *m* blank cheque
Blase (-, -n) *f* bubble; (*Med*) blister; (*Anat*) bladder
blasen (*blies, geblasen*) *vi* to blow; **jdm einen ~** (*vulg*) to give sb a blow job
Blasenentzündung *f* cystitis

blass adj pale

Blatt (-(e)s, Blätter) nt leaf; (von Papier) sheet; **blättern** vi (Inform) to scroll; **in etw** (dat) **~ to** leaf through sth; **Blätterteig** m puff pastry; **Blattsalat** m green salad; **Blattspinat** m spinach

blau adj blue; (fam: betrunken) plastered; (Gastr) boiled; **~es Auge** black eye; **~er Fleck** bruise; **Blaubeere** f bilberry, blueberry; **Blaulicht** nt flashing blue light; **blau|machen** vi to skip work; (in Schule) to skip school; **Blauschimmelkäse** m blue cheese

Blazer (-s, -) m blazer

Blech (-(e)s, -e) nt sheet metal; (Backblech) baking tray (Brit), cookie sheet (US); **Blechschaden** m (Auto) damage to the bodywork

Blei (-(e)s, -e) nt lead

bleiben (blieb, geblieben) vi to stay; **lass das ~!** stop it; **das bleibt unter uns** that's (just) between ourselves; **mir bleibt keine andere Wahl** I have no other choice

bleich adj pale; **bleichen** vt to bleach

bleifrei adj (Benzin) unleaded; **bleihaltig** adj (Benzin) leaded

Bleistift m pencil

Blende (-, -n) f (Foto) aperture

Blick (-(e)s, -e) m look; (kurz) glance; (Aussicht) view; **auf den ersten ~** at first sight; **einen ~ auf etw** (akk) **werfen** to have a look at sth; **blicken** vi to look; **sich ~ lassen** to show up

blieb imperf von **bleiben**

blies imperf von **blasen**

blind adj blind; (Glas etc) dull; **Blinddarm** m appendix; **Blinddarmentzündung** f appendicitis; **Blinde(r)** mf blind person/man/woman; **die ~n** pl

the blind pl; **Blindenhund** m guide dog; **Blindenschrift** f braille

blinken vi (Stern, Lichter) to twinkle; (aufleuchten) to flash; (Auto) to indicate; **Blinker** (-s, -) m (Auto) indicator (Brit), turn signal (US)

blinzeln vi (mit beiden Augen) to blink; (mit einem Auge) to wink

Blitz (-es, -e) m (flash of) lightning; (Foto) flash; **blitzen** vi (Foto) to use a/the flash; **es blitzte und donnerte** there was thunder and lightning; **Blitzlicht** nt flash

Block (-(e)s, Blöcke) m (a. fig) block; (von Papier) pad; **Blockflöte** f recorder; **Blockhaus** nt log cabin; **blockieren** vt to block ▷ vi to jam; (Räder) to lock; **Blockschrift** f block letters pl

blöd adj stupid; **blödeln** vi (fam) to fool around

Blog (-s, -s) nt (Inform) blog

blond adj blond; (Frau) blonde

 SCHLÜSSELWORT

bloß adj 1 (unbedeckt) bare; (nackt) naked; **mit der bloßen Hand** with one's bare hand; **mit bloßem Auge** with the naked eye
2 (alleinig, nur) mere; **der bloße Gedanke** the very thought; **bloßer Neid** sheer envy
▷ adv only, merely; **lass das bloß!** just don't do that!; **wie ist das bloß passiert?** how on earth did that happen?

blühen vi to bloom; (fig) to flourish

Blume (-, -n) f flower; (von Wein) bouquet; **Blumengeschäft** nt florist's (shop); **Blumenkohl** m cauliflower; **Blumenladen** m flower shop; **Blumenstrauß** m bunch of flowers; **Blumentopf** *m* flowerpot; **Blumenvase** *f* vase

Bluse (-, -*n*) *f* blouse

Blut (-(*e*)*s*) *nt* blood; **Blutbild** *nt* blood count; **Blutdruck** *m* blood pressure; **Blutorange** *f* blood orange

Blüte (-, -*n*) *f* (*Pflanzenteil*) flower, bloom; (*Baumblüte*) blossom; (*fig*) prime

bluten *vi* to bleed

Blütenstaub *m* pollen

Bluter (-*s*, -) *m* (*Med*) haemophiliac; **Bluterguss** *m* haematoma; (*blauer Fleck*) bruise; **Blutgruppe** *f* blood group; **blutig** *adj* bloody; **Blutkonserve** *f* unit of stored blood; **Blutprobe** *f* blood sample; **Blutspende** *f* blood donation; **Bluttransfusion** *f* blood transfusion; **Blutung** *f* bleeding; **Blutvergiftung** *f* blood poisoning; **Blutwurst** *f* black pudding (*Brit*), blood sausage (*US*)

BLZ *abk* = **Bankleitzahl**

Bob (-*s*, -*s*) *m* bob(sleigh)

Bock (-(*e*)*s*, Böcke) *m* (*Reh*) buck; (*Schaf*) ram; (*Gestell*) trestle; (*Sport*) vaulting horse; **ich hab keinen ~ (drauf)** (*fam*) I don't feel like it

Boden (-*s*, Böden) *m* ground; (*Fußboden*) floor; (*von Meer, Fass*) bottom; (*Speicher*) attic; **Bodennebel** *m* ground mist; **Bodenpersonal** *nt* ground staff; **Bodenschätze** *pl* mineral resources *pl*

Bodensee *m*: **der ~** Lake Constance

Body (-*s*, -*s*) *m* body; **Bodybuilding** (-*s*) *nt* bodybuilding

bog *imperf von* **biegen**

Bogen (-*s*, -) *m* (*Biegung*) curve; (*in der Architektur*) arch; (*Waffe, Instrument*) bow; (*Papier*) sheet

Bohne (-, -*n*) *f* bean; **grüne ~n** *pl* green (*o* French (*Brit*)) beans *pl*; **weiße ~n** *pl* haricot beans *pl*; **Bohnenkaffee** *m* real coffee; **Bohnensprosse** *f* bean sprout

bohren *vt* to drill; **Bohrer** (-*s*, -) *m* drill

Boiler (-*s*, -) *m* water heater

Boje (-, -*n*) *f* buoy

Bolivien (-*s*) *nt* Bolivia

Bombe (-, -*n*) *f* bomb

Bon (-*s*, -*s*) *m* (*Kassenzettel*) receipt; (*Gutschein*) voucher, coupon

Bonbon (-*s*, -*s*) *nt* sweet (*Brit*), candy (*US*)

Bonus (- *o* -*ses*, -*se o* Boni) *m* bonus; (*Punktvorteil*) bonus points *pl*; (*Schadenfreiheitsrabatt*) no-claims bonus

Boot (-(*e*)*s*, -*e*) *nt* boat; **Bootsverleih** *m* boat hire (*Brit*) (*o* rental (*US*))

Bord (-(*e*)*s*, -*e*) *m*: **an ~ (eines Schiffes)** on board (a ship); **an ~ gehen** (*Schiff*) to go on board; (*Flugzeug*) to board; **von ~ gehen** to disembark; **Bordcomputer** *m* dashboard computer

Bordell (-*s*, -*e*) *nt* brothel

Bordkarte *f* boarding card

Bordstein *m* kerb (*Brit*), curb (*US*)

borgen *vt* to borrow; **jdm etw ~** to lend sb sth; **sich** (*dat*) **etw ~** to borrow sth

Börse (-, -*n*) *f* stock exchange; (*Geldbörse*) purse

bös *adj siehe* **böse**; **bösartig** *adj* malicious; (*Med*) malignant

Böschung *f* slope; (*Uferböschung*) embankment

böse *adj* bad; (*stärker*) evil; (*Wunde*) nasty; (*zornig*) angry; **bist du mir ~?** are you angry with me?

boshaft *adj* malicious

Bosnien (-*s*) *nt* Bosnia; **Bosnien-Herzegowina** (-*s*) *nt*

Bosnia-Herzegovina
böswillig *adj* malicious
bot *imperf von* **bieten**
botanisch *adj*: **~er Garten** botanical gardens *pl*
Botschaft *f* message; (*Pol*) embassy; **Botschafter(in)** *m(f)* ambassador
Botsuana (-s) *nt* Botswana
Bouillon (-, -s) *f* stock
Boutique (-, -n) *f* boutique
Bowle (-, -n) *f* punch
Box (-, -en) *f* (*Behälter, Pferdebox*) box; (*Lautsprecher*) speaker; (*bei Autorennen*) pit
boxen *vi* to box; **Boxer** (-s, -) *m* (*Hund, Sportler*) boxer; **Boxershorts** *pl* boxer shorts *pl*; **Boxkampf** *m* boxing match
Boykott (-s, -e) *m* boycott
brach *imperf von* **brechen**
brachte *imperf von* **bringen**
Brainstorming (-s) *nt* brainstorming
Branchenverzeichnis *nt* yellow pages® *pl*
Brand (-(e)s, Brände) *m* fire; **einen ~ haben** (*fam*) to be parched
Brandenburg (-s) *nt* Brandenburg
Brandsalbe *f* ointment for burns
Brandung *f* surf
Brandwunde *f* burn
brannte *imperf von* **brennen**
Brasilien (-s) *nt* Brazil
braten (briet, gebraten) *vt* to roast; (*auf dem Rost*) to grill; (*in der Pfanne*) to fry; **Braten** (-s, -) *m* roast; (*roher*) joint; **Bratensoße** *f* gravy; **Brathähnchen** *nt* roast chicken; **Bratkartoffeln** *pl* fried potatoes *pl*; **Bratpfanne** *f* frying pan; **Bratspieß** *m* spit; **Bratwurst** *f* fried sausage; (*gegrillte*) grilled sausage
Brauch (-s, Bräuche) *m* custom
brauchen *vt* (*nötig haben*) to need

(*für, zu* for); (*erfordern*) to require; (*Zeit*) to take; (*gebrauchen*) to use; **wie lange wird er ~?** how long will it take him?; **du brauchst es nur zu sagen** you only need to say; **das braucht (seine) Zeit** it takes time; **ihr braucht es nicht zu tun** you don't have (*o* need) to do it; **sie hätte nicht zu kommen ~** she needn't have come
brauen *vt* to brew; **Brauerei** *f* brewery
braun *adj* brown; (*von Sonne*) tanned; **Bräune** (-, -n) *f* brownness; (*von Sonne*) tan; **Bräunungsstudio** *nt* tanning studio
Brause (-, -n) *f* (*Dusche*) shower; (*Getränk*) fizzy drink (*Brit*), soda (*US*)
Braut (-, Bräute) *f* bride; **Bräutigam** (-s, -e) *m* bridegroom
brav *adj* (*artig*) good, well-behaved
bravo *interj* well done
BRD (-) *f abk* = **Bundesrepublik Deutschland** FRG

- BRD
-
- The **BRD** is the official name for
- the Federal Republic of
- Germany. It comprises 16
- **Länder** (see **Land**). It was the
- name given to the former West
- Germany as opposed to East
- Germany (the **DDR**). The two
- Germanies were reunited on 3rd
- October 1990.

brechen (brach, gebrochen) *vt* to break; (*erbrechen*) to bring up; **sich** (*dat*) **den Arm ~** to break one's arm ▷ *vi* to break; (*erbrechen*) to vomit, to be sick; **Brechreiz** *m* nausea
Brei (-(e)s, -e) *m* (*Breimasse*) mush, pulp; (*Haferbrei*) porridge; (*für

Kinder) pap
breit *adj* wide; (*Schultern*) broad;
zwei Meter ~ two metres wide;
Breite (-, -n) *f* breadth; (*bei Maßangaben*) width; (*Geo*) latitude;
der ~ nach widthways;
Breitengrad *m* (degree of) latitude
Bremen (-s) *nt* Bremen
Bremsbelag *m* brake lining;
Bremse (-, -n) *f* brake; (*Zool*) horsefly; **bremsen** *vi* to brake
▷ *vt* (*Auto*) to brake; (*fig*) to slow down; **Bremsflüssigkeit** *f* brake fluid; **Bremslicht** *nt* brake light; **Bremspedal** *nt* brake pedal;
Bremsspur *f* tyre marks *pl*;
Bremsweg *m* braking distance
brennen (*brannte*, *gebrannt*) *vi* to burn; (*in Flammen stehen*) to be on fire; **es brennt!** fire!; **mir ~ die Augen** my eyes are smarting; **das Licht ~ lassen** to leave the light on; **Brennholz** *nt* firewood;
Brennnessel *f* stinging nettle;
Brennspiritus *m* methylated spirits *pl*; **Brennstab** *m* fuel rod; **Brennstoff** *m* fuel
Brett (-(e)s, -er) *nt* board; (*länger*) plank; (*Regal*) shelf; (*Spielbrett*) board; **Schwarzes ~** notice board, bulletin board (*US*); **~er** *pl* (*ski*) skis *pl*; **Brettspiel** *nt* board game
Brezel (-, -n) *f* pretzel
Brief (-(e)s, -e) *m* letter;
Briefbombe *f* letter bomb;
Brieffreund(in) *m(f)* penfriend, pen pal; **Briefkasten** *m* letterbox (*Brit*), mailbox (*US*);
elektronischer ~ electronic mailbox; **Briefmarke** *f* stamp;
Briefpapier *nt* writing paper;
Brieftasche *f* wallet;
Briefträger(in) *m(f)* postman/-woman; **Briefumschlag** *m* envelope; **Briefwaage** *f* letter scales *pl*

briet *imperf von* **braten**
Brille (-, -n) *f* glasses *pl*;
(*Schutzbrille*) goggles *pl*; **Brillenetui** *nt* glasses case
bringen (*brachte*, *gebracht*) *vt* (*herbringen*) to bring; (*mitnehmen, vom Sprecher weg*) to take; (*holen, herbringen*) to get, to fetch; (*Theat, Cine*) to show; (*Radio, TV*) to broadcast; **~ Sie mir bitte noch ein Bier** could you bring me another beer, please?; **jdn nach Hause ~** to take sb home; **jdn dazu ~, etw zu tun** to make sb do sth; **jdn auf eine Idee ~** to give sb an idea
Brise (-, -n) *f* breeze
Brite (-n, -n) *m*, **Britin** *f* British person, Briton; **er ist ~** he is British; **die ~n** the British; **britisch** *adj* British
Brocken (-s, -) *m* bit; (*größer*) lump, chunk
Brokkoli *m* broccoli
Brombeere *f* blackberry
Bronchitis (-) *f* bronchitis
Bronze (-, -n) *f* bronze
Brosche (-, -n) *f* brooch
Brot (-(e)s, -e) *nt* bread; (*Laib*) loaf;
Brotaufstrich *m* spread;
Brötchen *nt* roll; **Brotzeit** *f* (*Pause*) break; (*Essen*) snack;
~ machen to have a snack
Browser (-s, -) *m* (*Inform*) browser
Bruch (-(e)s, Brüche) *m* (*Brechen*) breaking; (*Bruchstelle; mit Partei, Tradition etc*) break; (*Med: Eingeweidebruch*) rupture, hernia; (*Knochenbruch*) fracture; (*Math*) fraction; **brüchig** *adj* brittle
Brücke (-, -n) *f* bridge
Bruder (-s, Brüder) *m* brother
Brühe (-, -n) *f* (*Suppe*) (clear) soup; (*Grundlage*) stock; (*pej: Getränk*) muck; **Brühwürfel** *m* stock cube

brüllen vi to roar; (Stier) to bellow; (vor Schmerzen) to scream (with pain)

brummen vi (Bär, Mensch) to growl; (brummeln) to mutter; (Insekt) to buzz; (Motor, Radio) to drone ▷ vt to growl

brünett adj brunette

Brunnen (-s, -) m fountain; (tief) well; (natürlich) spring

Brust (-, Brüste) f breast; (beim Mann) chest; **Brustschwimmen** (-s) nt breaststroke; **Brustwarze** f nipple

brutal adj brutal

brutto adv gross

BSE (-) nt abk = **bovine spongiforme Enzephalopathie** BSE

Bube (-n, -n) m boy, lad; (Karten) jack

Buch (-(e)s, Bücher) nt book

Buche (-, -n) f beech (tree)

buchen vt to book; (Betrag) to enter

Bücherei f library

Buchfink m chaffinch

Buchhalter(in) m(f) accountant

Buchhandlung f bookshop

Büchse (-, -n) f tin (Brit), can

Buchstabe (-ns, -n) m letter; **buchstabieren** vt to spell

Bucht (-, -en) f bay

Buchung f booking; (Comm) entry

Buckel (-s, -) m hump

bücken vr: **sich ~** to bend down

Buddhismus (-) m Buddhism

Bude (-, -n) f (auf Markt) stall; (fam: Wohnung) pad, place

Büfett (-s, -s) nt sideboard; **kaltes ~** cold buffet

Büffel (-s, -) m buffalo

Bügel (-s, -) m (Kleidung) hanger; (Steigbügel) stirrup; (Brille) sidepiece; (von Skilift) T-bar; **Bügelbrett** nt ironing board;

Bügeleisen nt iron; **Bügelfalte** f crease; **bügelfrei** adj non-iron; **bügeln** vt, vi to iron

buh interj boo

Bühne (-, -n) f stage; **Bühnenbild** nt set

Bulgare (-n, -n) m, **Bulgarin** f Bulgarian; **Bulgarien** (-s) nt Bulgaria; **bulgarisch** adj Bulgarian; **Bulgarisch** nt Bulgarian

Bulimie f bulimia

Bulle (-n, -n) m bull; (fam: Polizist) cop

Bummel (-s, -) m stroll; **bummeln** vi to stroll; (trödeln) to dawdle; (faulenzen) to loaf around; **Bummelzug** m slow train

bums interj bang

bumsen vi (vulg) to screw

Bund (-(e)s, Bünde) m (von Hose, Rock) waistband; (Freundschaftsbund) bond; (Organisation) association; (Pol) confederation; **der ~** (fam: Bundeswehr) the army ▷ (-(e)s, -e) nt bunch; (von Stroh etc) bundle

Bundes- in zW Federal; (auf Deutschland bezogen a.) German; **Bundeskanzler(in)** m(f) Chancellor; **Bundesland** nt state, Land; **Bundesliga** f: **erste/zweite ~** First/Second Division; **Bundespräsident(in)** m(f) President; **Bundesrat** m (in Deutschland) Upper House (of the German Parliament); (in der Schweiz) Council of Ministers; **Bundesregierung** f Federal Government; **Bundesrepublik** f Federal Republic; **~ Deutschland** Federal Republic of Germany; **Bundesstraße** f ≈ A road (Brit), ≈ state highway (US); **Bundestag** m Lower House (of the German Parliament); **Bundeswehr** f (German) armed forces pl

Bündnis *nt* alliance
Bungalow (-s, -s) *m* bungalow
Bungeejumping (-s) *nt* bungee jumping
bunt *adj* colourful; (*von Programm etc*) varied; **~e Farben** bright colours ▷ *adv* (*anstreichen*) in bright colours; **Buntstift** *m* crayon, coloured pencil
Burg (-, -en) *f* castle
Bürger(in) (-s, -) *m(f)* citizen; **bürgerlich** *adj* (*Rechte, Ehe etc*) civil; (*vom Mittelstand*) middle-class; (*pej*) bourgeois; **Bürgermeister(in)** *m(f)* mayor; **Bürgersteig** (-(e)s, -e) *m* pavement (*Brit*), sidewalk (*US*)
Büro (-s, -s) *nt* office; **Büroklammer** *f* paper clip
Bürokratie *f* bureaucracy
Bursche (-n, -n) *m* lad; (*Typ*) guy
Bürste (-, -n) *f* brush; **bürsten** *vt* to brush
Bus (-ses, -se) *m* bus; (*Reisebus*) coach (*Brit*), bus; **Busbahnhof** *m* bus station
Busch (-(e)s, Büsche) *m* bush; (*Strauch*) shrub
Busen (-s, -) *m* breasts *pl*, bosom
Busfahrer(in) *m(f)* bus driver; **Bushaltestelle** *f* bus stop

Businessclass (-) *f* business class
Busreise *f* coach tour (*Brit*), bus tour
Bußgeld *nt* fine
Büstenhalter (-s, -) *m* bra
Busverbindung *f* bus connection
Butter (-) *f* butter; **Butterbrot** *nt* slice of bread and butter; **Butterkäse** *m type of mild, full-fat cheese*; **Buttermilch** *f* buttermilk; **Butterschmalz** *nt* clarified butter
Button (-s, -s) *m* badge (*Brit*), button (*US*)
b. w. *abk* = **bitte wenden** pto
Byte (-s, -s) *nt* byte
bzw. *adv abk* = **beziehungsweise**

C

ca. adv abk = **circa** approx
Cabrio (-s, -s) nt convertible
Café (-s, -s) nt café
Cafeteria (-, -s) f cafeteria
Call-Center (-s, -) nt call centre
campen vi to camp; **Camping** (-s) nt camping; **Campingbus** m camper; **Campingplatz** m campsite, camping ground (US)
Cappuccino (-s, -) m cappuccino
Carving (-s) nt (Ski) carving; **Carvingski** m carving ski
CD (-, -s) f abk = **Compact Disc** CD; **CD-Brenner** (-s, -) m CD burner, CD writer; **CD-Player** (-s, -) m CD player; **CD-ROM** (-, -s) f abk = **Compact Disc Read Only Memory** CD-ROM; **CD-ROM-Laufwerk** nt CD-ROM drive, **CD-Spieler** m CD player
Cello (-s, -s o Celli) nt cello
Celsius nt celsius; **20 Grad ~** 20 degrees Celsius, 68 degrees Fahrenheit
Cent (-, -s) m (von Dollar und Euro) cent
Chamäleon (-s, -s) nt chameleon
Champagner (-s, -) m champagne
Champignon (-s, -s) m mushroom
Champions League (-, -s) f Champions League
Chance (-, -n) f chance; **die ~n stehen gut** the prospects are good
Chaos (-) nt chaos; **Chaot(in)** (-en, -en) m(f) (fam) disorganized person, scatterbrain; **chaotisch** adj chaotic
Charakter (-s, -e) m character; **charakteristisch** adj characteristic (für of)
Charisma (-s, Charismen o Charismata) nt charisma
charmant adj charming
Charterflug m charter flight; **chartern** vt to charter
Chat (-s, -s) m (Inform) chat; **chatten** vi (Inform) to chat
checken vt (überprüfen) to check; (fam: verstehen) to get
Check-in (-s, -s) m check-in; **Check-in-Schalter** m check-in desk
Chef(in) (-s, -s) m(f) boss; **Chefarzt** m, **Chefärztin** f senior consultant (Brit), medical director (US)
Chemie (-) f chemistry; **chemisch** adj chemical; **~e Reinigung** dry cleaning
Chemotherapie f chemotherapy
Chicoree (-s) m chicory
Chiffre (-, -n) f (Geheimzeichen) cipher; (in Zeitung) box number
Chile (-s) nt Chile
Chili (-s, -s) m chilli

China (-s) nt China; **Chinakohl** m Chinese leaves pl (Brit), bok choy (US); **Chinarestaurant** nt Chinese restaurant; **Chinese** (-n, -n) m Chinese; **Chinesin** (-, -nen) f Chinese (woman); **sie ist ~** she's Chinese; **chinesisch** adj Chinese; **Chinesisch** nt Chinese

Chip (-s, -s) m (Inform) chip; **Chipkarte** f smart card

Chips pl (Kartoffelchips) crisps pl (Brit), chips pl (US)

Chirurg(in) (-en, -en) m(f) surgeon

Chlor (-s) nt chlorine

Choke (-s, -s) m choke

Cholera (-) f cholera

Cholesterin (-s) nt cholesterol

Chor (-(e), Chöre) m choir; (Theat) chorus

Choreografie f choreography

Christ(in) (-en, -en) m(f) Christian; **Christbaum** m Christmas tree; **Christi Himmelfahrt** f the Ascension (of Christ); **Christkind** nt baby Jesus; (das Geschenke bringt) ≈ Father Christmas, Santa Claus; **christlich** adj Christian

Chrom (-s) nt chrome; (Chem) chromium

chronisch adj chronic

chronologisch adj chrono-logical ▷ adv in chronological order

Chrysantheme (-, -n) f chrysanthemum

circa adv about, approximately

City (-) f city centre, downtown (US)

Clementine (-, -n) f clementine

clever adj clever, smart

Clique (-, -n) f group; (pej) clique; **David und seine ~** David and his lot o crowd

Clown (-s, -s) m clown

Club (-s, -s) m club; **Cluburlaub** m club holiday (Brit), club vacation (US)

Cocktail (-s, -s) m cocktail; **Cocktailtomate** f cherry tomato

Cognac (-s) m cognac

Cola (-, -s) f Coke®, cola

Comic (-s, -s) m comic strip; (Heft) comic

Compact Disc (-, -s) f compact disc

Computer (-s, -) m computer; **Computerfreak** m computer nerd; **computergesteuert** adj computer-controlled; **Computer-grafik** f computer graphics pl; **computerlesbar** adj machine-readable; **Computerspiel** nt computer game; **Computer-tomografie** f computer tomography, scan; **Computer-virus** m computer virus

Container (-s, -) m (zum Transport) container; (für Bauschutt etc) skip

Control-Taste f control key

Cookie (-s, -s) nt (Inform) cookie

cool adj (fam) cool

Cornflakes pl cornflakes pl

Couch (-, -en) f couch; **Couchtisch** m coffee table

Coupé (-s, -s) nt coupé

Coupon (-s, -s) m coupon

Cousin (-s, -s) m cousin; **Cousine** f cousin

Crack (-s) nt (Droge) crack

Creme (-, -s) f cream; (Gastr) mousse

Creutzfeld-Jakob-Krankheit f Creutzfeld-Jakob disease, CJD

Croissant (-s, -s) nt croissant

Curry (-s) m curry powder ▷ (-s) nt (indisches Gericht) curry; **Currywurst** f fried sausage with ketchup and curry powder

Cursor (-s, -) m (Inform) cursor

Cybercafé nt cybercafé; **Cyberspace** (-) m cyberspace

d

da adv 1 (örtlich) there; (hier) here; **da draußen** out there; **da sein** to be there; **da bin ich** here I am; **da, wo** where; **ist noch Milch da?** is there any milk left?
2 (zeitlich) then; (folglich) so
3 **da haben wir Glück gehabt** we were lucky there; **da kann man nichts machen** nothing can be done about it
▷ konj (weil) as, since

dabei adv (räumlich) close to it; (zeitlich) at the same time; (obwohl, doch) though; **sie hörte Radio und rauchte** ~ she was listening to the radio and smoking (at the same time); ~ **fällt mir ein ...** that reminds me ...; ~ **kam es zu einem Unfall** this led to an accident; **... und** ~ **hat er gar keine Ahnung** ...

even though he has no idea; **ich finde nichts** ~ I don't see anything wrong with it; **es bleibt** ~ that's settled; ~ **sein** (anwesend) to be present; (beteiligt) to be involved; **ich bin** ~! count me in; **er war gerade** ~ **zu gehen** he was just (o on the point of) leaving

dabei|bleiben irr vi to stick with it; **ich bleibe dabei** I'm not changing my mind

dabei|haben irr vt: **er hat seine Schwester dabei** he's brought his sister; **ich habe kein Geld dabei** I haven't got any money on me

Dach (-(e)s, Dächer) nt roof; **Dachboden** m attic, loft; **Dachgepäckträger** m roofrack; **Dachrinne** f gutter

Dachs (-es, -e) m badger

dachte imperf von **denken**

Dackel (-s, -) m dachshund

dadurch adv (räumlich) through it; (durch diesen Umstand) in that way; (deshalb) because of that, for that reason ▷ conj: ~, **dass** because; ~, **dass er hart arbeitete** (indem) by working hard

dafür adv for it; (anstatt) instead; ~ **habe ich 50 Euro bezahlt** I paid 50 euros for it; **ich bin** ~ **zu bleiben** I'm for (o in favour of) staying; ~ **ist er ja da** that's what he's there for; **er kann nichts** ~ he can't help it

dagegen adv against it; (im Vergleich damit) in comparison; (bei Tausch) for it; **ich habe nichts** ~ I don't mind

daheim adv at home

daher adv (räumlich) from there; (Ursache) that's why ▷ conj (deshalb) that's why

dahin adv (räumlich) there; (zeitlich) then; (vergangen) gone; **bis** ~ (zeitlich) till then; (örtlich) up to there; **bis** ~ **muss die Arbeit fertig**

sein the work must be finished by
then
dahinter *adv* behind it;
~ kommen to find out
dahinterkommen *vi* to find
out
Dahlie *f* dahlia
Dalmatiner (-s, -) *m* dalmatian
damals *adv* at that time, then
Dame (-, -n) *f* lady; (*Karten*)
queen; (*Spiel*) draughts *sing* (*Brit*),
checkers *sing* (*US*); **Damenbinde**
f sanitary towel (*Brit*), sanitary
napkin (*US*); **Damenkleidung** *f*
ladies' wear; **Damentoilette** *f*
ladies' toilet (*o* restroom (*US*))
damit *adv* with it; (*begründend*) by
that; **was meint er ~?** what does
he mean by that?; **genug ~!** that's
enough ▷ *conj* so that
Damm (-(e)s, Dämme) *m* dyke;
(*Staudamm*) dam; (*am Hafen*) mole;
(*Bahn-, Straßendamm*)
embankment
Dämmerung *f* twilight; (*am
Morgen*) dawn; (*am Abend*) dusk
Dampf (-(e)s, Dämpfe) *m* steam;
(*Dunst*) vapour; **Dampfbad** *nt*
Turkish bath; **Dampfbügeleisen**
nt steam iron; **dampfen** *vi* to
steam
dämpfen *vt* (*Gastr*) to steam;
(*Geräusch*) to deaden; (*Begeisterung*)
to dampen
Dampfer (-s, -) *m* steamer
Dampfkochtopf *m* pressure
cooker
danach *adv* after that; (*zeitlich a.*)
afterwards; (*demgemäß*)
accordingly; **mir ist nicht ~** I don't
feel like it; **~ sieht es aus** that's
what it looks like
Däne (-n, -n) *m* Dane
daneben *adv* beside it; (*im
Vergleich*) in comparison
Dänemark (-s) *nt* Denmark;
Dänin *f* Dane, Danish

woman/girl; **dänisch** *adj*
Danish; **Dänisch** *nt* Danish
dank *prep* +*dat o gen* thanks to;
Dank (-(e)s) *m* thanks *pl*; **vielen
~!** thank you very much; **jdm
~ sagen** to thank sb; **dankbar**
adj grateful; (*Aufgabe*) rewarding;
danke *interj* thank you, thanks;
nein ~! no, thank you; **~, gerne!**
yes, please; **~, gleichfalls!** thanks,
and the same to you; **danken** *vi*:
jdm für etw ~ to thank sb for sth;
nichts zu ~! you're welcome
dann *adv* then; **bis ~!** see you
(later); **~ eben nicht** okay, forget
it, suit yourself
daran *adv* (*räumlich*) on it;
(*befestigen*) to it; (*stoßen*) against
it; **es liegt ~, dass ...** it's
because ...
darauf *adv* (*räumlich*) on it;
(*zielgerichtet*) towards it; (*danach*)
afterwards; **es kommt ganz ~ an,
ob ...** it all depends whether ...;
ich freue mich ~ I'm looking
forward to it; **am Tag ~** the next
day; **~ folgend** (*Tag, Jahr*) next,
following
darauffolgend *adj* (*Tag, Jahr*)
next, following
daraus *adv* from it; **was ist
~ geworden?** what became of it?
darin *adv* in it; **das Problem liegt
~, dass ...** the basic problem is
that ...
Darlehen (-s, -) *nt* loan
Darm (-(e)s, Därme) *m* intestine;
(*Wurstdarm*) skin; **Darmgrippe** *f*
gastroenteritis
dar|stellen *vt* to represent;
(*Theat*) to play; (*beschreiben*) to
describe; **Darsteller(in)** *m(f)*
actor/actress; **Darstellung** *f*
representation; (*Beschreibung*)
description
darüber *adv* (*räumlich*) above it,
over it; (*fahren*) over it; (*mehr*)

more; (*währenddessen*) meanwhile; (*sprechen, streiten, sich freuen*) about it

darum *adv* (*deshalb*) that's why; **es geht ~, dass ...** the point (*o* thing) is that ...

darunter *adv* (*räumlich*) under it; (*dazwischen*) among them; (*weniger*) less; **was verstehen Sie ~?** what do you understand by that?; **~ fallen** to be included

darunterfallen *vi* to be included

das *art* the; **~ Auto da** that car; **er hat sich ~ Bein gebrochen** he's broken his leg; **vier Euro ~ Kilo** four euros a kilo ▷ *pron* that (one), this (one); (*relativ, Sache*) that, which; (*relativ, Person*) who, that; (*demonstrativ*) this/that one; **~ Auto da** that car; **ich nehme ~ da** I'll take that one; **~ Auto, ~ er kaufte** the car (that (*o* which)) he bought; **~ Mädchen, ~ nebenan wohnt** the girl who (*o* that) lives next door; **~ heißt** that is; **~ sind Amerikaner** they're American

da sein *irr vi siehe* **da**

dass *conj* that; **so ~** so that; **es sei denn, ~** unless; **ohne ~ er grüßte** without saying hello

dasselbe *pron* the same

Datei *f* (*Inform*) file; **Dateimanager** *m* file manager

Daten *pl* data *pl*; **Datenbank** *f* database; **Datenmissbrauch** *m* misuse of data; **Datenschutz** *m* data protection; **Datenträger** *m* data carrier; **Datenverarbeitung** *f* data processing

datieren *vt* to date

Dativ *m* dative (case)

Dattel (-, -n) *f* date

Datum (-s, *Daten*) *nt* date

Dauer (-, -n) *f* duration; (*Länge*) length; **auf die ~** in the long run; **für die ~ von zwei Jahren** for (a

period of) two years;

Dauerauftrag *m* (*Fin*) standing order; **dauerhaft** *adj* lasting; (*Material*) durable; **Dauerkarte** *f* season ticket; **dauern** *vi* to last; (*Zeit benötigen*) to take; **es hat sehr lange gedauert, bis er ...** it took him a long time to ...; **wie lange dauert es denn noch?** how much longer will it be?; **das dauert mir zu lange** I can't wait that long; **dauernd** *adj* lasting; (*ständig*) constant ▷ *adv* always, constantly; **er lachte ~** he kept laughing; **unterbrich mich nicht ~** stop interrupting me; **Dauerwelle** *f* perm (*Brit*), permanent (*US*)

Daumen (-s, -) *m* thumb

Daunendecke *f* eiderdown

davon *adv* of it; (*räumlich*) away; (*weg von*) from it; (*Grund*) because of it; **ich hätte gerne ein Kilo ~** I'd like one kilo of that; **~ habe ich gehört** I've heard of it; (*Geschehen*) I've heard about it; **das kommt ~, wenn ...** that's what happens when ...; **was habe ich ~?** what's the point?; **auf und ~** up and away; **davon|laufen** *irr vi* to run away

davor *adv* (*räumlich*) in front of it; (*zeitlich*) before; **ich habe Angst ~** I'm afraid of it

dazu *adv* (*zusätzlich*) on top of that, as well; (*zu diesem Zweck*) for it, for that purpose; **ich möchte Reis ~** I'd like rice with it; **und ~ noch** and in addition; **~ fähig sein, etw zu tun** to be capable of doing sth; **wie kam es ~?** how did it happen?; **dazu|gehören** *vi* to belong to it; **dazu|kommen** *irr vi* (*zu jdm ~*) to join sb; **kommt noch etwas dazu?** anything else?

dazwischen *adv* in between; (*Unterschied etc*) between them; (*in einer Gruppe*) among them

dazwischen|kommen *irr vi*:
wenn nichts dazwischenkommt
if all goes well; **mir ist etwas
dazwischengekommen**
something has cropped up

DDR (-) *f abk* = **Deutsche
Demokratische Republik** (*Hist*)
GDR

dealen *vi* (*fam: mit Drogen*) to deal
in drugs; **Dealer(in)** (-s, -) *m(f)*
(*fam*) dealer, pusher

Deck (-(e)s, -s o -e) *nt* deck

Decke (-, -n) *f* cover; (*für Bett*)
blanket; (*für Tisch*) tablecloth; (*von
Zimmer*) ceiling

Deckel (-s, -) *m* lid

decken *vt* to cover; (*Tisch*) to lay,
to set ▷ *vr*: **sich ~** (*Interessen*) to
coincide; (*Aussagen*) to correspond
▷ *vi* (*den Tisch decken*) to lay (o set)
the table

Decoder (-s, -) *m* decoder

defekt *adj* faulty; **Defekt** (-(e)s,
-e) *m* fault, defect

definieren *vt* to define;
Definition (-, -en) *f* definition

deftig *adj* (*Preise*) steep; **ein ~es
Essen** a good solid meal

dehnbar *adj* flexible, elastic;
dehnen *vt* to stretch ▷ *vr*: **sich
~** to stretch

Deich (-(e)s, -e) *m* dyke

dein *pron* (*adjektivisch*) your;
deine(r, s) *pron* (*substantivisch*)
yours, of you; **deiner** *pron gen
von* **du**; of you; **deinetwegen** *adv*
(*wegen dir*) because of you; (*dir
zuliebe*) for your sake; (*um dich*)
about you

deinstallieren *vt* (*Programm*) to
uninstall

Dekolleté (-s, -s) *nt* low neckline

Dekoration *f* decoration; (*in
Laden*) window dressing;
dekorativ *adj* decorative;
dekorieren *vt* to decorate;
(*Schaufenster*) to dress

Delfin (-s, -e) *m* dolphin

delikat *adj* (*lecker*) delicious;
(*heikel*) delicate

Delikatesse (-, -n) *f* delicacy

Delle (-, -en) *f* (*fam*) dent

Delphin (-s, -e) *m* dolphin

dem *dat sing von* **der/das**; **wie
~ auch sein mag** be that as it may

demnächst *adv* shortly, soon

Demo (-, -s) *f* (*fam*) demo

Demokratie (-, -n) *f* democracy;
demokratisch *adj* democratic

demolieren *vt* to demolish

Demonstration *f* demonstration; **demonstrieren** *vt, vi* to
demonstrate

den *art akk sing, dat pl von* **der**; **sie
hat sich ~ Arm gebrochen** she's
broken her arm ▷ *pron* him;
(*Sache*) that one; (*relativ: Person*)
who, that, whom; (*relativ: Sache*)
which, that; **~ hab ich schon ewig
nicht mehr gesehen** I haven't
seen him in ages ▷ *pron* (*Person*)
who, that, whom; (*Sache*) which,
that; **der Typ, auf ~ sie steht** the
guy (who) she fancies; **der Berg,
auf ~ wir geklettert sind** the
mountain (that) we climbed

denkbar *adj*: **das ist ~** that's
possible ▷ *adv*: **~ einfach**
extremely simple; **denken** (*dachte,
gedacht*) *vt, vi* to think (*über +akk*
about); **an jdn/etw ~** to think of
sb/sth; (*sich erinnern,
berücksichtigen*) to remember
sb/sth; **woran denkst Du?** what
are you thinking about?; **denk an
den Kaffee!** don't forget the coffee
▷ *vr*: **sich ~** (*sich vorstellen*) to
imagine; **das kann ich mir ~** I can
(well) imagine

Denkmal (-s, *Denkmäler*) *nt*
monument; **Denkmalschutz** *m*
monument preservation; **unter
~ stehen** to be listed

denn *conj* for, because ▷ *adv*

then; (*nach Komparativ*) than; **was ist ~?** what's wrong?; **ist das ~ so schwierig?** is it really that difficult?

dennoch *conj* still, nevertheless

Deo (*-s, -s*) *nt*, **Deodorant** (*-s, -s*) *nt* deodorant; **Deoroller** *m* roll-on deodorant; **Deospray** *m o nt* deodorant spray

Deponie (*-, -n*) *f* waste disposal site, tip

Depressionen *pl*: **an ~ leiden** to suffer from depression *sing*; **deprimieren** *vt* to depress

○ SCHLÜSSELWORT

der (*f* **die**, *nt* **das**, *gen* **des, der, des,** *dat* **dem, der, dem,** *akk* **den, die, das,** *pl* **die**) *def art* the; **der Rhein** the Rhine; **der Klaus** (*fam*) Klaus; **die Frau** (*im Allgemeinen*) women; **der Tod/das Leben** death/life; **der Fuß des Berges** the foot of the hill; **gib es der Frau** give it to the woman; **er hat sich die Hand verletzt** he has hurt his hand
▷ *relativ pron* (*bei Menschen*) who, that; (*bei Tieren, Sachen*) which, that; **der Mann, den ich gesehen habe** the man who *o* whom *o* that I saw
▷ *demonstrativ pron* he/she/it (*jener, dieser*) that; (*pl*) those; **der/die war es** it was him/her; **der mit der Brille** the one with glasses; **ich will den (da)** I want that one

derart *adv* so; (*solcher Art*) such; **derartig** *adj*: **ein ~er Fehler** such a mistake, a mistake like that

deren *gen von* **die** ▷ *pron* (*Person*) her; (*Sache*) its; (*Plural*) their ▷ *pron* (*Person*) whose; (*Sache*) of which; **meine Freundin und ~ Mutter** my

friend and her mother; **das sind ~ Sachen** that's their stuff; **die Frau, ~ Tochter ...** the woman whose daughter ...; **ich bin mir ~ bewusst** I'm aware of that

dergleichen *pron*: **und ~ mehr** and the like, and so on; **nichts ~** no such thing

derjenige *pron* the one; **~, der** (*relativ*) the one who (*o* that)

dermaßen *adv* so much; (*mit Adj*) so

derselbe *pron* the same (person/thing)

deshalb *adv* therefore; **~ frage ich ja** that's why I'm asking

Design (*-s, -s*) *nt* design; **Designer(in)** (*-s, -*) *m(f)* designer

Desinfektionsmittel *nt* disinfectant; **desinfizieren** *vt* to disinfect

dessen *gen von* **der, das** ▷ *pron* (*Person*) his; (*Sache*) its; **ich bin mir ~ bewusst** I'm aware of that
▷ *pron* (*Person*) whose; (*Sache*) of which; **mein Freund und ~ Mutter** my friend and his mother; **der Mann, ~ Tochter ...** the man whose daughter ...; **ich bin mir ~ bewusst** I'm aware of that

Dessert (*-s, -s*) *nt* dessert; **zum** (*o* **als**) **~** for dessert

destilliert *adj* distilled

desto *adv*: **je eher, ~ besser** the sooner, the better

deswegen *conj* therefore

Detail (*-s, -s*) *nt* detail; **ins ~ gehen** to go into detail

Detektiv(in) (*-s, -e*) *m(f)* detective

deutlich *adj* clear; (*Unterschied*) distinct

deutsch *adj* German; **Deutsch** *nt* German; **auf ~** in German; **ins ~e übersetzen** to translate into German; **Deutsche(r)** *mf*

German; **Deutschland** *nt*
Germany
Devise (-, -n) *f* motto; **~n** *pl* (*Fin*)
foreign currency *sing*;
Devisenkurs *m* exchange rate
Dezember (-(s), -) *m* December;
siehe auch **Juni**
dezent *adj* discreet
d.h. *abk von* **das heißt** i.e.
(*gesprochen: i.e. oder that is*)
Dia (-s, -s) *nt* slide
Diabetes (-, -) *m* (*Med*) diabetes;
Diabetiker(in) (-s, -) *m(f)*
diabetic
Diagnose (-, -n) *f* diagnosis
diagonal *adj* diagonal
Dialekt (-(e)s, -e) *m* dialect
Dialog (-(e)s, -e) *m* dialogue;
(*Inform*) dialog
Dialyse (-, -n) *f* (*Med*) dialysis
Diamant *m* diamond
Diaprojektor *m* slide projector
Diät (-, -en) *f* diet; **eine ~ machen**
to be on a diet; (*anfangen*) to go on
a diet
dich *pron akk von* **du** you;
~ (selbst) (*reflexiv*) yourself; **pass
auf ~ auf** look after yourself; **reg
~ nicht auf** don't get upset
dicht *adj* dense; (*Nebel*) thick;
(*Gewebe*) close; (*wasserdicht*)
watertight; (*Verkehr*) heavy ▷ *adv*:
~ an/bei close to; **~ bevölkert**
densely populated
Dichter(in) (-s, -) *m(f)* poet;
(*Autor*) writer
Dichtung *f* (*Auto*) gasket;
(*Dichtungsring*) washer; (*Gedichte*)
poetry
Dichtungsring *m* (*Tech*) washer
dick *adj* thick; (*Person*) fat; **jdn
~ haben** to be sick of sb;
Dickdarm *m* colon; **Dickkopf** *m*
stubborn (*o* pig-headed) person;
Dickmilch *f* sour milk
die *art* the; **~ arme Sarah** poor
Sarah ▷ *pron* (*sing, Person, als*

Subjekt) she; (*Person, als Subjekt,
Plural*) they; (*Person, als Objekt*) her;
(*Person, als Objekt, Plural*) them;
(*Sache*) that (one), this (one);
(*Plural*) those (ones); (*Sache, Plural*)
those (ones); (*relativ, auf Person*)
who, that; (*relativ, auf Sache*)
which, that; **~ mit den langen
Haaren** the one (*o* her) with the
long hair; **sie war ~ erste, ~ es
erfuhr** she was the first to know;
ich nehme ~ da I'll take that
one/those ▷ *pl von* **der, die, das**
Dieb(in) (-(e)s, -e) *m(f)* thief;
Diebstahl (-(e)s, Diebstähle) *m*
theft; **Diebstahlsicherung** *f*
burglar alarm
diejenige *pron* the one; **~, die**
(*relativ*) the one who (*o* that); **~n** *pl*
those *pl*, the ones
Diele (-, -n) *f* hall
Dienst (-(e)s, -e) *m* service; **außer
~** retired; **~ haben** to be on duty
Dienstag *m* Tuesday; *siehe auch*
Mittwoch; **dienstags** *adv* on
Tuesdays; *siehe auch* **mittwochs**
Dienstbereitschaft *f*: **~ haben**
(*Arzt*) to be on call; **diensthabend**
adj: **der ~e Arzt** the doctor on
duty; **Dienstleistung** *f* service;
dienstlich *adj* official; **er ist
~ unterwegs** he's away on
business; **Dienstreise** *f* business
trip; **Dienststelle** *f* department;
Dienstwagen *m* company car;
Dienstzeit *f* office hours *pl*; (*Mil*)
period of service
diesbezüglich *adj* (*formell*) on
this matter
diese(r, s) *pron* this (one); *pl*
these; **~ Frau** this woman; **~r
Mann** this man; **~s Mädchen** this
girl; **~ Leute** these people; **ich
nehme ~/~n/~s** (*hier*) I'll take this
one; (*dort*) I'll take that one; **ich
nehme ~** *pl* (*hier*) I'll take these
(ones); (*dort*) I'll take those (ones)

Diesel (-s, -) m (Auto) diesel
dieselbe pron the same; **es sind immer ~n** it's always the same people
Dieselmotor m diesel engine; **Dieselöl** nt diesel (oil)
diesig adj hazy, misty
diesmal adv this time
Dietrich (-s, -e) m skeleton key
Differenz (-, -en) f difference
digital adj digital; **Digital-** in zW (Anzeige etc) digital; **Digitalfernsehen** nt digital television, digital TV; **Digitalkamera** f digital camera
Diktat (-(e)s, -e) nt dictation
Diktatur f dictatorship
Dill (-s) m dill
DIN abk = **Deutsche Industrienorm** DIN; **~ A4** A4
Ding (-(e)s, -e) nt thing; **vor allen ~en** above all; **der Stand der ~e** the state of affairs; **das ist nicht mein ~** (fam) it's not my sort of thing (o cup of tea); **Dingsbums** (-) nt (fam) thingy, thingummybob
Dinkel (-s, -) m (Bot) spelt
Dinosaurier (-s, -) m dinosaur
Diphtherie (-, -n) f diphtheria
Diplom (-(e)s, -e) nt diploma
Diplomat(in) (-en, -en) m(f) diplomat
dir pron dat von **du** (to) you; **hat er ~ geholfen?** did he help you?; **ich werde es ~ erklären** I'll explain it to you; (reflexiv) **wasch ~ die Hände** go and wash your hands; **ein Freund von ~** a friend of yours
direkt adj direct; (Frage) straight; **~e Verbindung** through service ▷ adv directly; (sofort) immediately; **~ am Bahnhof** right next to the station; **Direktflug** m direct flight
Direktor(in) m(f) director; (Schule) headmaster/-mistress

(Brit), principal (US)
Direktübertragung f live broadcast
Dirigent(in) m(f) conductor; **dirigieren** vt to direct; (Mus) to conduct
Discman® (-s, -s) m Discman®
Diskette f disk, diskette; **Diskettenlaufwerk** nt disk drive
Diskjockey (-s, -s) m disc jockey; **Disko** (-, -s) f (fam) disco, club; **Diskothek** (-, -en) f discotheque, club
diskret adj discreet
diskriminieren vt to discriminate against
Diskussion f discussion; **diskutieren** vt, vi to discuss
Display (-s, -s) nt display
disqualifizieren vt to disqualify
Distanz f distance
Distel (-, -n) f thistle
Disziplin (-, -en) f discipline
divers adj various
dividieren vt to divide (durch by); **8 dividiert durch 2 ist 4** 8 divided by 2 is 4
DJ (-s, -s) m abk = **Diskjockey** DJ

 SCHLÜSSELWORT

doch adv **1** (dennoch) after all; (sowieso) anyway; **er kam doch noch** he came after all; **du weißt es ja doch besser** you know better than I do anyway; **und doch ...** and yet ...
2 (als bejahende Antwort) yes I do/it does etc; **das ist nicht wahr — doch!** that's not true — yes it is!
3 (auffordernd) **komm doch** do come; **lass ihn doch** just leave him; **nicht doch!** oh no!
4 **sie ist doch noch so jung** but she's still so young; **Sie wissen doch, wie das ist** you know how

it is(, don't you?); **wenn doch** if
only
▷ *konj (aber)* but; *(trotzdem)* all the
same; **und doch hat er es getan**
but still he did it

Doktor(in) *m(f)* doctor
Dokument *nt* document;
Dokumentarfilm *m* docu-
mentary (film); **dokumentieren**
vt to document;
Dokumentvorlage *f (Inform)*
document template
Dolch *(-(e)s, -e) m* dagger
Dollar *(-(s), -) m* dollar
dolmetschen *vt, vi* to interpret;
Dolmetscher(in) *(-s, -) m(f)*
interpreter
Dolomiten *pl* Dolomites *pl*
Dom *(-(e)s, -e) m* cathedral
Domäne *(-, -n) f* domain,
province; *(Inform: Med)* domain
Dominikanische Republik *f*
Dominican Republic
Domino *(-s, -s) nt* dominoes *sing*
Donau *(-) f* Danube
Döner *(-s, -) m*, **Döner Kebab**
(-(s), -s) m doner kebab
Donner *(-s, -) m* thunder;
donnern *vi*: **es donnert** it's
thundering
Donnerstag *m* Thursday; *siehe
auch* **Mittwoch**; **donnerstags**
adv on Thursdays; *siehe auch*
mittwochs
doof *adj (fam)* stupid
dopen *vt* to dope; **Doping** *(-s) nt*
doping; **Dopingkontrolle** *f*
drugs test
Doppel *(-s, -) nt* duplicate; *(Sport)*
doubles *sing*; **Doppelbett** *nt*
double bed; **Doppeldecker** *m*
double-decker; **Doppelhaushälfte** *f* semi-detached house
(Brit), duplex *(US)*; **doppelklicken**
vi to double-click; **Doppelname**
m double-barrelled name;

Doppelpunkt *m* colon;
Doppelstecker *m* two-way
adaptor; **doppelt** *adj* double; **in
~er Ausführung** in duplicate;
Doppelzimmer *nt* double room
Dorf *(-(e)s, Dörfer) nt* village
Dorn *(-(e)s, -en) m (Bot)* thorn
Dörrobst *nt* dried fruit
Dorsch *(-(e)s, -e) m* cod
dort *adv* there; **~ drüben** over
there; **dorther** *adv* from there
Dose *(-, -n) f* box; *(Blechdose)* tin
(Brit), can; *(Bierdose)* can
dösen *vi* to doze
Dosenbier *nt* canned beer;
Dosenmilch *f* canned milk,
tinned milk *(Brit)*; **Dosenöffner**
m tin opener *(Brit)*, can opener
Dotter *(-s, -) m (egg)* yolk
downloaden *vt* to download
Downsyndrom *(-(e)s, -e) nt*
(Med) Down's syndrome
Dozent(in) *m(f)* lecturer
Dr. *abk* = **Doktor**
Drache *(-n, -n) m* dragon;
Drachen *(-s, -) m (Spielzeug)* kite;
(Sport) hang-glider;
Drachenfliegen *(-s) nt*
hang-gliding; **Drachenflieger(in)**
(-s, -) m(f) hang-glider
Draht *(-(e)s, Drähte) m* wire;
Drahtseilbahn *f* cable railway
Drama *(-s, Dramen) nt* drama;
dramatisch *adj* dramatic
dran *adv (fam) kontr von* **daran**;
gut ~ sein *(reich)* to be well-off;
(glücklich) to be fortunate;
(gesundheitlich) to be well;
schlecht ~ sein to be in a bad way;
wer ist ~? whose turn is it?; **ich
bin ~** it's my turn; **bleib ~!** *(Tel)*
hang on
drang *imperf von* **dringen**
Drang *(-(e)s, Dränge) m (Trieb)*
urge *(nach* for); *(Druck)* pressure
drängeln *vt, vi* to push
drängen *vt (schieben)* to push;

(*antreiben*) to urge ▷ *vi* (*eilig sein*)
to be urgent; (*Zeit*) to press; **auf
etw** (*akk*) **~** to press for sth
dran|kommen *irr vi*: **wer
kommt dran?** who's turn is it?,
who's next?
drauf (*fam*) *kontr von* **darauf**;
gut/schlecht ~ sein to be in a
good/bad mood
Draufgänger(in) (*-s, -*) *m(f)*
daredevil
drauf|kommen *irr vi* to
remember; **ich komme nicht
drauf** I can't think of it
drauf|machen *vi* (*fam*) **einen
~** to go on a binge
draußen *adv* outside
Dreck (*-(e)s*) *m* dirt, filth; **dreckig**
adj dirty, filthy
drehen *vt, vi* to turn; (*Zigaretten*)
to roll; (*Film*) to shoot ▷ *vr*: **sich
~** to turn; (*um Achse*) to rotate; **sich
~ um** (*handeln von*) to be about
Drehstrom *m* three-phase
current; **Drehtür** *f* revolving
door; **Drehzahlmesser** *m* rev
counter
drei *num* three; **~ viertel voll**
three-quarters full; **es ist ~ viertel
neun** it's a quarter to nine; **Drei**
(*-, -en*) *f* three; (*Schulnote*) ≈ C;
Dreieck *nt* triangle; **dreieckig**
adj triangular; **dreifach** *adj*
triple ▷ *adv* three times;
dreihundert *num* three hundred;
Dreikönigstag *m* Epiphany;
dreimal *adv* three times; **Dreirad**
nt tricycle; **dreispurig** *adj*
three-lane
dreißig *num* thirty; **dreißigste(r,
s)** *adj* thirtieth; *siehe auch* **dritte**
Dreiviertelstunde *f*: **eine
~** three quarters of an hour
dreizehn *num* thirteen;
dreizehnte(r, s) *adj* thirteenth;
siehe auch **dritte**
dressieren *vt* to train

Dressing (*-s, -s*) *nt* (*salad*)
dressing
Dressman (*-s, Dressmen*) *m* (*male*)
model
Dressur (*-, -en*) *f* training
drin (*fam*) *kontr von* **darin** in it;
mehr war nicht ~ that was the
best I could do
dringen (*drang, gedrungen*) *vi*
(*Wasser, Licht, Kälte*) to penetrate
(*durch* through, *in +akk* into); **auf
etw** (*akk*) **~** to insist on sth;
dringend, **dringlich** *adj* urgent
drinnen *adv* inside
dritt *adv*: **wir sind zu ~** there are
three of us; **dritte(r, s)** *adj* third;
die Dritte Welt the Third World; **7.
Juni** 7(th) June (*gesprochen: the
seventh of June*); **am 7. Juni** on 7(th)
June, on June 7(th) (*gesprochen: on
the seventh of June*); **München, den
7. Juni** Munich, June 7(th); **Drittel**
(*-s, -*) *nt* (*Bruchteil*) third; **drittens**
adv thirdly
Droge (*-, -n*) *f* drug;
drogenabhängig, **drogensüchtig**
adj addicted to drugs
Drogerie *f* chemist's (*Brit*),
drugstore (*US*); **Drogeriemarkt**
m discount chemist's (*Brit*) (*o*
drugstore (*US*))

● **DROGERIE**
●
● The **Drogerie** as opposed to the
● **Apotheke** sells medicines not
● requiring a prescription. It
● tends to be cheaper and also
● sells cosmetics, perfume and
● toiletries.

drohen *vi* to threaten (*jdm* sb);
mit etw ~ to threaten to do sth
dröhnen *vi* (*Motor*) to roar;
(*Stimme, Musik*) to boom; (*Raum*) to
resound
Drohung *f* threat

Drossel *(-, -n)* f thrush
drüben *adv* over there; *(auf der anderen Seite)* on the other side
drüber *(fam)* kontr von **darüber**
Druck *(-(e)s, Drücke)* m *(Phys)* pressure; *(fig: Belastung)* stress; **jdn unter ~ setzen** to put sb under pressure ▷ *(-(e)s, -e)* m *(Typo: Vorgang)* printing; *(Produkt, Schriftart)* print; **Druckbuchstabe** m block letter; **in ~n schreiben** to print; **drucken** *vt, vi* to print
drücken *vt, vi (Knopf, Hand)* to press; *(zu eng sein)* to pinch; *(fig: Preise)* to keep down; **jdm etw in die Hand ~** to press sth into sb's hand ▷ *vr* **sich vor etw** *(dat)* **~** to get out of sth; **drückend** *adj* oppressive
Drucker *(-s, -)* m *(Inform)* printer; **Druckertreiber** m printer driver
Druckknopf m press stud *(Brit)*, snap fastener *(US)*; **Drucksache** f printed matter; **Druckschrift** f block letters *pl*
drunten *adv* down there
drunter *(fam)* kontr von **darunter**
Drüse *(-, -n)* f gland
Dschungel *(-s, -)* m jungle
du *pron* you; **bist ~ es?** is it you?; **wir sind per ~** we're on first-name terms
Dübel *(-s, -)* m Rawlplug®
ducken *vt* to duck ▷ *vr:* **sich ~** to duck
Dudelsack m bagpipes *pl*
Duett *(-s, -e)* nt duet
Duft *(-(e)s, Düfte)* m scent; **duften** *vi* to smell nice; **es duftet nach ...** it smells of ...
dulden *vt* to tolerate
dumm *adj* stupid; **Dummheit** f stupidity; *(Tat)* stupid thing; **Dummkopf** m idiot
dumpf *adj (Ton)* muffled; *(Erinnerung)* vague; *(Schmerz)* dull
Düne *(-, -n)* f dune

Dünger *(-s, -)* m fertilizer
dunkel *adj* dark; *(Stimme)* deep; *(Ahnung)* vague; *(rätselhaft)* obscure; *(verdächtig)* dubious; **im Dunkeln tappen** *(fig)* to be in the dark; **dunkelblau** *adj* dark blue; **dunkelblond** *adj* light brown; **dunkelhaarig** *adj* dark-haired; **Dunkelheit** f darkness
dünn *adj* thin; *(Kaffee)* weak
Dunst *(-es, Dünste)* m haze; *(leichter Nebel)* mist; *(Chem)* vapour
dünsten *vt (Gastr)* to steam
Duo *(-s, -s)* nt duo
Dur *(-)* nt *(Mus)* major (key); **in G-~** in G major

 SCHLÜSSELWORT

durch *prep +akk* **1** *(hindurch)* through; **durch den Urwald** through the jungle; **durch die ganze Welt reisen** to travel all over the world
2 *(mittels)* through, by (means of); *(aufgrund)* due to, owing to; **Tod durch Herzschlag/den Strang** death from a heart attack/by hanging; **durch die Post** by post; **durch seine Bemühungen** through his efforts
▷ *adv* **1** *(hindurch)* through; **die ganze Nacht durch** all through the night; **den Sommer durch** during the summer; **8 Uhr durch** past 8 o'clock; **durch und durch** completely
2 *(durchgebraten etc)* **(gut) durch** well-done

durchaus *adv* absolutely; **~ nicht** not at all
Durchblick m view; **den ~ haben** *(fig)* to know what's going on; **durch|blicken** *vi* to look through; *(fam: verstehen)* to understand *(bei etw* sth); **etw**

~ lassen (*fig*) to hint at sth
Durchblutung *f* circulation
durch|brennen *irr vi* (*Sicherung*) to blow; (*Draht*) to burn through; (*fam: davonlaufen*) to run away
durchdacht *adv*: **gut ~** well thought-out
durch|drehen *vt* (*Fleisch*) to mince ▷ *vi* (*Räder*) to spin; (*fam: nervlich*) to crack up
durcheinander *adv* in a mess; (*fam: verwirrt*) confused; **Durcheinander** (*-s*) *nt* (*Verwirrung*) confusion; (*Unordnung*) mess; **durcheinander|bringen** *irr vt* to mess up; (*verwirren*) to confuse; **durcheinander|reden** *vi* to talk all at the same time; **durcheinander|trinken** *irr vi* to mix one's drinks
Durchfahrt *f* way through; **„~ verboten!"** "no thoroughfare"
Durchfall *m* (*Med*) diarrhoea
durch|fallen *irr vi* to fall through; (*in Prüfung*) to fail
durch|fragen *vr*: **sich ~** to ask one's way
durch|führen *vt* to carry out
Durchgang *m* passage; (*Sport*) round; (*bei Wahl*) ballot; **Durchgangsverkehr** *m* through traffic
durchgebraten *adj* well done
durchgefroren *adj* frozen to the bone
durch|gehen *irr vi* to go through (*durch etw* sth); (*ausreißen: Pferd*) to break loose; (*Mensch*) to run away; **durchgehend** *adj* (*Zug*) through; **~ geöffnet** open all day
durch|halten *irr vi* to hold out ▷ *vt* (*Tempo*) to keep up; **etw ~** (*bis zum Schluss*) to see sth through
durch|kommen *irr vi* to get through; (*Patient*) to pull through

durch|lassen *irr vt* (*jdn*) to let through; (*Wasser*) to let in
durch|lesen *irr vt* to read through
durchleuchten *vt* to X-ray
durch|machen *vt* to go through; (*Entwicklung*) to undergo; **die Nacht ~** to make a night of it, to have an all-nighter
Durchmesser (*-s, -*) *m* diameter
Durchreise *f* journey through; **auf der ~** passing through; (*Güter*) in transit; **Durchreisevisum** *nt* transit visa
durch|reißen *irr vt, vi* to tear (in two)
durchs *kontr von* **durch das**
Durchsage (*-, -n*) *f* announcement
durchschauen *vt* (*jdn, Lüge*) to see through
durch|schlagen *irr vr*: **sich ~** to struggle through
durch|schneiden *irr vt* to cut (in two)
Durchschnitt *m* (*Mittelwert*) average; **im ~** on average; **durchschnittlich** *adj* average ▷ *adv* (*im Durchschnitt*) on average; **Durchschnittsgeschwindigkeit** *f* average speed
durch|setzen *vt* to get through ▷ *vr*: **sich ~** (*Erfolg haben*) to succeed; (*sich behaupten*) to get one's way
durchsichtig *adj* transparent, see-through
durch|stellen *vt* (*Tel*) to put through
durch|streichen *irr vt* to cross out
durchsuchen *vt* to search (*nach* for); **Durchsuchung** *f* search
durchwachsen *adj* (*Speck*) streaky; (*fig: mittelmäßig*) so-so
Durchwahl *f* direct dialling; (*Nummer*) extension

durch|ziehen *irr vt (Plan)* to
carry through
Durchzug *m* draught

 SCHLÜSSELWORT

dürfen *unreg vi* **1** *(Erlaubnis haben)*
to be allowed to; **ich darf das** I'm
allowed to (do that); **darf ich?** may
I?; **darf ich ins Kino?** can *o* may I
go to the cinema?; **es darf
geraucht werden** you may smoke
2 *(in Verneinungen)* **er darf das
nicht** he's not allowed to (do that);
das darf nicht geschehen that
must not happen; **da darf sie sich
nicht wundern** that shouldn't
surprise her
3 *(in Höflichkeitsformeln)* **darf ich
Sie bitten, das zu tun?** may *o*
could I ask you to do that?; **was
darf es sein?** what can I do for
you?
4 *(können)* **das dürfen Sie mir
glauben** you can believe me
5 *(Möglichkeit)* **das dürfte genug
sein** that should be enough; **es
dürfte Ihnen bekannt sein,
dass ...** as you will probably
know ...

dürftig *adj (ärmlich)* poor;
(unzulänglich) inadequate
dürr *adj* dried-up; *(Land)* arid;
(mager) skinny
Durst *(-(e)s) m* thirst; **~ haben** to
be thirsty; **durstig** *adj* thirsty
Dusche *(-, -n) f* shower; **duschen**
vi to have a shower ▷ *vr*: **sich ~** to
have a shower; **Duschgel** *nt*
shower gel; **Duschvorhang** *m*
shower curtain
Düse *(-, -n) f* nozzle; *(Tech)* jet;
Düsenflugzeug *nt* jet (aircraft)
Dussel *(-s, -) m (fam)* dope;
duss(e)lig *adj (fam)* stupid

düster *adj* dark; *(Gedanken,
Zukunft)* gloomy
Dutyfreeshop *(-s, -s) m* duty-
-free shop
Dutzend *(-s, -e) nt* dozen
duzen *vt to address as "du"* ▷ *vr*:
sich ~ (mit jdm) *to address each
other as "du"*, to be on first-name
terms
DVD *(-, -s) f abk =* **Digital
Versatile Disk** DVD; **DVD-Player**
(-s, -) m DVD player;
DVD-Rekorder *(-s, -) m* DVD
recorder
dynamisch *adj* dynamic
Dynamo *(-s, -s) m* dynamo
D-Zug *m* fast train

e

precious stone

EDV (-) f abk = **elektronische Datenverarbeitung** EDP

Efeu (-s) m ivy

Effekt (-s, -e) m effect

egal adj: **das ist ~** it doesn't matter; **das ist mir ~** I don't care, it's all the same to me; **~ wie teuer** no matter how expensive

egoistisch adj selfish

ehe conj before

Ehe (-, -n) f marriage; **Ehefrau** f wife; (verheiratete Frau) married woman; **Eheleute** pl married couple sing

ehemalig adj former; **ehemals** adv formerly

Ehemann m husband; (verheirateter Mann) married man; **Ehepaar** nt married couple

eher adv (früher) sooner; (lieber) rather, sooner; (mehr) more; **je ~, desto besser** the sooner the better

Ehering m wedding ring

eheste(r, s) adj (früheste) first ▷ adv: **am ~n** (am wahrscheinlichsten) most likely

Ehre (-, -n) f honour; **ehren** vt to honour; **ehrenamtlich** adj voluntary; **Ehrengast** m guest of honour; **Ehrenwort** nt word of honour; **~!** I promise; **ich gebe dir mein ~** I give you my word

ehrgeizig adj ambitious

ehrlich adj honest

Ei (-(e)s, -er) nt egg; **hart gekochtes/weiches ~** hard-boiled/soft-boiled egg

Eiche (-, -n) f oak (tree); **Eichel** (-, -n) f acorn

Eichhörnchen nt squirrel

Eid (-(e)s, -e) m oath

Eidechse (-, -n) f lizard

Eierbecher m eggcup; **Eierstock** m ovary; **Eieruhr** f egg timer

Eifersucht f jealousy;

Ebbe (-, -n) f low tide

eben adj level; (glatt) smooth ▷ adv just; (bestätigend) exactly

Ebene (-, -n) f plain; (fig) level

ebenfalls adv also, as well; (Antwort: gleichfalls!) you too; **ebenso** adv just as; **~ gut** just as well; **~ viel** just as much

Eber (-s, -) m boar

EC (-, -s) m abk = **Eurocityzug**

Echo (-s, -s) nt echo

echt adj (Leder, Gold) real, genuine; **ein ~er Verlust** a real loss

EC-Karte f ≈ debit card

Ecke (-, -n) f corner; (Math) angle; **an der ~** at the corner; **gleich um die ~** just round the corner; **eckig** adj rectangular; **Eckzahn** m canine

Economyclass (-) f coach (class), economy class

Ecstasy (-) f (Droge) ecstasy

edel adj noble; **Edelstein** m

eifersüchtig *adj* jealous (*auf +akk* of)

Eigelb (-(*e*)*s*, -) *nt* egg yolk

eigen *adj* own; (*typisch*) characteristic (*jdm* of sb); (*eigenartig*) peculiar; **eigenartig** *adj* peculiar; **Eigenschaft** *f* quality; (*Chem, Phys*) property; (*Merkmal*) characteristic

eigentlich *adj* actual, real ▷ *adv* actually, really; **was denken Sie sich ~ dabei?** what on earth do you think you're doing?

Eigentum *nt* property; **Eigentümer(in)** *m(f)* owner; **Eigentumswohnung** *f* owner-occupied flat (*Brit*), condominium (*US*)

eignen *vr*: **sich ~ für** to be suited for; **er würde sich als Lehrer ~** he'd make a good teacher

Eilbrief *m* express letter, special-delivery letter; **Eile** (-) *f* hurry; **eilen** *vi* (*dringend sein*) to be urgent; **es eilt nicht** there's no hurry; **eilig** *adj* hurried; (*dringlich*) urgent; **es ~ haben** to be in a hurry

Eimer (-*s*, -) *m* bucket

ein *adv*: **nicht ~ noch aus wissen** not to know what to do; **~ - aus** (*Schalter*) on - off

ein(e) *art* a; (*vor gesprochenem Vokal*) an; **~ Mann** a man; **~ Apfel** an apple; **~e Stunde** an hour; **~ Haus** a house; **~ (gewisser) Herr Miller** a (certain) Mr Miller; **~es Tages** one day

einander *pron* one another, each other

ein|arbeiten *vt* to train ▷ *vr*: **sich ~** to get used to the work

ein|atmen *vt, vi* to breathe in

Einbahnstraße *f* one-way street

ein|bauen *vt* to build in; (*Motor etc*) to install, to fit; **Einbauküche**

f fitted kitchen

ein|biegen *irr vi* to turn (*in +akk* into)

ein|bilden *vt*: **sich** (*dat*) **etw ~** to imagine sth

ein|brechen *irr vi* (*in Haus*) to break in; (*Dach etc*) to fall in, to collapse; **Einbrecher(in)** (-*s*, -) *m(f)* burglar

ein|bringen *irr vt* (*Ernte*) to bring in; (*Gewinn*) to yield; **jdm etw ~** to bring (*o earn*) sb sth ▷ *vr* **sich in** (*akk*) **etw ~** to make a contribution to sth

Einbruch *m* (*Haus*) break-in, burglary; **bei ~ der Nacht** at nightfall

Einbürgerung *f* naturalization

ein|checken *vt* to check in

ein|cremen *vt* to put some cream on ▷ *vr*: **sich ~** to put some cream on

eindeutig *adj* clear, obvious ▷ *adv* clearly; **~ falsch** clearly wrong

ein|dringen *irr vi* (*gewaltsam*) to force one's way in (*in +akk -to*); (*in Haus*) to break in (*in +akk -to*); (*Gas, Wasser*) to get in (*in +akk -to*)

Eindruck *m* impression; **großen ~ auf jdn machen** to make a big impression on sb

eine(r, s) *pron* one; (*jemand*) someone; **~r meiner Freunde** one of my friends; **~r nach dem andern** one after the other

eineiig *adj* (*Zwillinge*) identical

eineinhalb *num* one and a half

einerseits *adv* on the one hand

einfach *adj* (*nicht kompliziert*) simple; (*Mensch*) ordinary; (*Essen*) plain; (*nicht mehrfach*) single; **~e Fahrkarte** single ticket (*Brit*), one-way ticket (*US*) ▷ *adv* simply; (*nicht mehrfach*) once

Einfahrt *f* (*Vorgang*) driving in; (*eines Zuges*) arrival; (*Ort*) entrance

Einfall m (*Idee*) idea; **ein|fallen** *irr vi* (*Licht etc*) to fall in; (*einstürzen*) to collapse; **ihm fiel ein, dass ...** it occurred to him that ...; **ich werde mir etwas ~ lassen** I'll think of something; **was fällt Ihnen ein!** what do you think you're doing?

Einfamilienhaus *nt* detached house

einfarbig *adj* all one colour; (*Stoff etc*) self-coloured

Einfluss m influence

ein|frieren *irr vt, vi* to freeze

ein|fügen *vt* to fit in; (*zusätzlich*) to add; (*Inform*) to insert; **Einfügetaste** f (*Inform*) insert key

Einfuhr (-, -en) f import; **Einfuhrbestimmungen** *pl* import regulations *pl*

ein|führen *vt* to introduce; (*Ware*) to import; **Einführung** f introduction

Eingabe f (*Dateneingabe*) input; **Eingabetaste** f (*Inform*) return (*o* enter) key

Eingang m entrance; **Eingangshalle** f entrance hall, lobby (*US*)

ein|geben *irr vt* (*Daten etc*) to enter, to key in

eingebildet *adj* imaginary; (*eitel*) arrogant

Eingeborene(r) *mf* native

ein|gehen *irr vi* (*Sendung, Geld*) to come in, to arrive; (*Tier, Pflanze*) to die; (*Stoff*) to shrink; **auf etw** (*akk*) **~ to agree to sth; **auf jdn ~ to respond to sb *⊳ vt* (*Vertrag*) to enter into; (*Wette*) to make; (*Risiko*) to take

eingelegt *adj* (*in Essig*) pickled

eingeschaltet *adj* (switched) on

eingeschlossen *adj* locked in; (*inklusive*) included

ein|gewöhnen *vr*: **sich ~ to settle in

ein|gießen *irr vt* to pour

ein|greifen *irr vi* to intervene; **Eingriff** m intervention; (*Operation*) operation

ein|halten *irr vt* (*Versprechen etc*) to keep

einheimisch *adj* (*Produkt, Mannschaft*) local; **Einheimische(r)** *mf* local

Einheit f (*Geschlossenheit*) unity; (*Maß*) unit; **einheitlich** *adj* uniform

ein|holen *vt* (*Vorsprung aufholen*) to catch up with; (*Verspätung*) to make up for; (*Rat, Erlaubnis*) to ask for

Einhorn *nt* unicorn

einhundert *num* one (*o* a) hundred

einig *adj* (*vereint*) united; **sich** (*dat*) **~ sein** to agree

einige *pron pl* some; (*mehrere*) several *⊳ adj* some; **nach ~er Zeit** after some time; **~e hundert Euro** some hundred euros

einigen *vr*: **sich ~ to agree (*auf +akk* on)

einigermaßen *adv* fairly, quite; (*leidlich*) reasonably

einiges *pron* something; (*ziemlich viel*) quite a bit; (*mehreres*) a few things; **es gibt noch ~ zu tun** there's still a fair bit to do

Einkauf m purchase; **Einkäufe** (**machen**) (to do one's) shopping; **ein|kaufen** *vt* to buy *⊳ vi* to go shopping; **Einkaufsbummel** m shopping trip; **Einkaufstasche** f, **Einkaufstüte** f shopping bag; **Einkaufswagen** m shopping trolley (*Brit*) (*o* cart (*US*)); **Einkaufszentrum** *nt* shopping centre (*Brit*) (*o* mall (*US*))

ein|klemmen *vt* to jam; **er hat sich** (*dat*) **den Finger eingeklemmt** he got his finger caught

Einkommen (-s, -) *nt* income

ein|laden *irr vt* (*jdn*) to invite; (*Gegenstände*) to load; **jdn zum Essen ~** to take sb out for a meal; **ich lade dich ein** (*bezahle*) it's my treat; **Einladung** *f* invitation

Einlass (*-es, Einlässe*) *m* admittance; **~ ab 18 Uhr** doors open at 6 pm; **ein|lassen** *irr vr* **sich mit jdm/auf etw** (*akk*) **~** to get involved with sb/sth

ein|leben *vr*: **sich ~** to settle down

ein|legen *vt* (*Film etc*) to put in; (*marinieren*) to marinate; **eine Pause ~** to take a break

ein|leiten *vt* to start; (*Maßnahmen*) to introduce; (*Geburt*) to induce; **Einleitung** *f* introduction; (*von Geburt*) induction

ein|leuchten *vi*: **jdm ~** to be (*o* become) clear to sb; **einleuchtend** *adj* clear

ein|loggen *vi* (*Inform*) to log on (*o* in)

ein|lösen *vt* (*Scheck*) to cash; (*Gutschein*) to redeem; (*Versprechen*) to keep

einmal *adv* once; (*früher*) before; (*in Zukunft*) some day; (*erstens*) first; **~ im Jahr** once a year; **noch ~** once more, again; **ich war schon ~ hier** I've been here before; **warst du schon ~ in London?** have you ever been to London?; **nicht ~** not even; **auf ~** suddenly; (*gleichzeitig*) at once; **einmalig** *adj* unique; (*einmal geschehend*) single; (*prima*) fantastic

ein|mischen *vr*: **sich ~** to interfere (*in +akk* with)

Einnahme (*-, -n*) *f* (*Geld*) takings *pl*; (*von Medizin*) taking; **ein|nehmen** *irr vt* (*Medizin*) to take; (*Geld*) to take in; (*Standpunkt, Raum*) to take up; **jdn für sich ~** to win sb over

ein|ordnen *vt* to put in order; (*klassifizieren*) to classify; (*Akten*) to file ⊳ *vr*: **sich ~** (*Auto*) to get in lane; **sich rechts/links ~** to get into the right/left lane

ein|packen *vt* to pack (up)

ein|parken *vt, vi* to park

ein|planen *vt* to allow for

ein|prägen *vt*: **sich** (*dat*) **etw ~** to remember (*o* memorize) sth

ein|räumen *vt* (*Bücher, Geschirr*) to put away; (*Schrank*) to put things in

ein|reden *vt*: **jdm/sich etw ~** to talk sb/oneself into (believing) sth

ein|reiben *irr vt*: **sich mit etw ~** to rub sth into one's skin

ein|reichen *vt* to hand in; (*Antrag*) to submit

Einreise *f* entry; **Einreisebestimmungen** *pl* entry regulations *pl*; **Einreiseerlaubnis** *f*, **Einreisegenehmigung** *f* entry permit; **ein|reisen** *vi* to enter (*in ein Land* a country); **Einreisevisum** *nt* entry visa

ein|renken *vt* (*Arm, Bein*) to set

ein|richten *vt* (*Wohnung*) to furnish; (*gründen*) to establish, to set up; (*arrangieren*) to arrange ⊳ *vr*: **sich ~** (*in Haus*) to furnish one's home; (*sich vorbereiten*) to prepare oneself (*auf +akk* for); (*sich anpassen*) to adapt (*auf +akk* to); **Einrichtung** *f* (*Wohnung*) furnishings *pl*; (*öffentliche Anstalt*) institution; (*Schwimmbad etc*) facility

eins *num* one; **Eins** (*-, -en*) *f* one; (*Schulnote*) ≈ A

einsam *adj* lonely

ein|sammeln *vt* to collect

Einsatz *m* (*Teil*) insert; (*Verwendung*) use; (*Spieleinsatz*) stake; (*Risiko*) risk; (*Mus*) entry

ein|schalten *vt* (*Elek*) to switch on

ein|schätzen vt to estimate, to assess
ein|schenken vt to pour
ein|schiffen vr: **sich ~** to embark (*nach* for)
ein|schlafen irr vi to fall asleep, to drop off; **mir ist der Arm eingeschlafen** my arm's gone to sleep
ein|schlagen irr vt (*Fenster*) to smash; (*Zähne, Schädel*) to smash in; (*Weg, Richtung*) to take ▷ vi to hit (*in etw akk* sth, *auf jdn* sb); (*Blitz*) to strike; (*Anklang finden*) to be a success
ein|schließen irr vt (*jdn*) to lock in; (*Gegenstand*) to lock away; (*umgeben*) to surround; (*fig: beinhalten*) to include; **einschließlich** adv inclusive ▷ prep +gen including; **von Montag bis ~ Freitag** from Monday up to and including Friday, Monday through Friday (US)
ein|schränken vt to limit, to restrict; (*verringern*) to cut down on ▷ vr: **sich ~** to cut down (on expenditure)
ein|schreiben irr vr: **sich ~** to register; (*Schule*) to enrol; **Einschreiben** (*-s, -*) nt registered letter; **etw per ~ schicken** to send sth by special delivery
ein|schüchtern vt to intimidate
ein|sehen irr vt (*verstehen*) to see; (*Fehler*) to recognize; (*Akten*) to have a look at
einseitig adj one-sided
ein|senden irr vt to send in
ein|setzen vt to put in; (*in Amt*) to appoint; (*Geld*) to stake; (*verwenden*) to use ▷ vi (*beginnen*) to set in; (*Mus*) to enter, to come in ▷ vr: **sich ~** to work hard; **sich für jdn/etw ~** to support sb/sth
Einsicht f insight; **zu der**

~ kommen, dass ... to come to realize that ...
ein|sperren vt to lock up
ein|spielen vt (*Geld*) to bring in
ein|springen irr vi (*aushelfen*) to step in (*für* for)
Einspruch m objection (*gegen* to)
einspurig adj single-lane
Einstand m (*Tennis*) deuce
ein|stecken vt to pocket; (*Elek: Stecker*) to plug in; (*Brief*) to post, to mail (US); (*mitnehmen*) to take; (*hinnehmen*) to swallow
ein|steigen irr vi (*in Auto*) to get in; (*in Bus, Zug, Flugzeug*) to get on; (*sich beteiligen*) to get involved
ein|stellen vt (*beenden*) to stop; (*Geräte*) to adjust; (*Kamera*) to focus; (*Sender, Radio*) to tune in; (*unterstellen*) to put; (*in Firma*) to employ, to take on ▷ vr: **sich auf jdn/etw ~** to adapt to sb/prepare oneself for sth; **Einstellung** f (*von Gerät*) adjustment; (*von Kamera*) focusing; (*von Arbeiter*) taking on; (*Meinung*) attitude
ein|stürzen vi to collapse
eintägig adj one-day
ein|tauschen vt to exchange (*gegen* for)
eintausend num one (*o a*) thousand
ein|teilen vt (*in Teile*) to divide (up) (*in +akk* into); (*Zeit*) to organize
eintönig adj monotonous
Eintopf m stew
ein|tragen irr vt (*in eine Liste*) to put down, to enter ▷ vr: **sich ~** to put one's name down, to register
ein|treffen irr vi to happen; (*ankommen*) to arrive
ein|treten irr vi (*hineingehen*) to enter (*in etw akk* sth); (*in Klub, Partei*) to join (*in etw akk* sth); (*sich ereignen*) to occur; **~ für** to support; **Eintritt** m admission; „**~ frei**"

"admission free"; **Eintrittskarte** f (entrance) ticket; **Eintrittspreis** m admission charge

einverstanden interj okay, all right ▷ adj: **mit etwas ~ sein** to agree to sth, to accept sth

Einwanderer m, **Einwanderin** f immigrant; **ein|wandern** vi to immigrate

einwandfrei adj perfect, flawless

Einwegflasche f non-returnable bottle

ein|weichen vt to soak

ein|weihen vt (Gebäude) to inaugurate, to open; **jdn in etw** (akk) **~** to let sb in on sth; **Einweihungsparty** f house-warming party

ein|werfen irr vt (Ball, Bemerkung etc) to throw in; (Brief) to post, to mail (US); (Geld) to put in, to insert; (Fenster) to smash

ein|wickeln vt to wrap up; (fig) **jdn ~** to take sb in

Einwohner(in) (-s, -) m(f) inhabitant; **Einwohnermeldeamt** nt registration office for residents

Einwurf m (Öffnung) slot; (Sport) throw-in

Einzahl f singular

ein|zahlen vt to pay in (auf ein Konto -to an account)

Einzel (-s, -) nt (Tennis) singles sing; **Einzelbett** nt single bed; **Einzelfahrschein** m single ticket (Brit), one-way ticket (US); **Einzelgänger(in)** m(f) loner; **Einzelhandel** m retail trade; **Einzelkind** nt only child

einzeln adj individual; (getrennt) separate; (einzig) single; **~e ...** several ..., some ...; **der/die Einzelne** the individual; **im Einzelnen** in detail ▷ adv separately; (verpacken, aufführen) individually; **~ angeben** to specify; **~ eintreten** to enter one

by one

Einzelzimmer nt single room; **Einzelzimmerzuschlag** m single-room supplement

ein|ziehen irr vt: **den Kopf ~** to duck ▷ vi (in ein Haus) to move in

einzig adj only; (einzeln) single; (einzigartig) unique; **kein ~er Fehler** not a single mistake; **das Einzige** the only thing; **der/die Einzige** the only person ▷ adv only; **die ~ richtige Lösung** the only correct solution; **einzigartig** adj unique

Eis (-es, -) nt ice; (Speiseeis) ice-cream; **Eisbahn** f ice(skating) rink; **Eisbär** m polar bear; **Eisbecher** m (ice-cream) sundae; **Eisberg** m iceberg; **Eisbergsalat** m iceberg lettuce; **Eiscafé** nt, **Eisdiele** f ice-cream parlour

Eisen (-s, -) nt iron; **Eisenbahn** f railway (Brit), railroad (US); **eisern** adj iron

eisgekühlt adj chilled; **Eishockey** nt ice hockey; **Eiskaffee** m iced coffee; **eiskalt** adj ice-cold; (Temperatur) freezing; **Eiskunstlauf** m figure skating; **eis|laufen** irr vi to skate; **Eisschokolade** f iced chocolate; **Eisschrank** m fridge, ice-box (US); **Eistee** m iced tea; **Eiswürfel** m ice cube; **Eiszapfen** m icicle

eitel adj vain

Eiter (-s) m pus

Eiweiß (-es, -e) nt egg white; (Chem, Bio) protein

ekelhaft, **ek(e)lig** adj disgusting, revolting; **ekeln** vr: **sich ~** to be disgusted (vor +dat at)

EKG (-s, -s) nt abk = **Elektrokardiogramm** ECG

Ekzem (-s, -e) nt (Med) eczema

elastisch adj elastic

Elch (-(e)s, -e) m elk;
(nordamerikanischer) moose
Elefant m elephant
elegant adj elegant
Elektriker(in) (-s, -) m(f) electrician; **elektrisch** adj electric;
Elektrizität f electricity;
Elektroauto nt electric car;
Elektrogerät nt electrical
appliance; **Elektrogeschäft** nt
electrical shop; **Elektroherd** m
electric cooker; **Elektromotor** m
electric motor; **Elektronik** f
electronics sing; **elektronisch** adj
electronic; **Elektrorasierer** (-s, -)
m electric razor
Element (-s, -e) nt element
elend adj miserable; **Elend** (-(e)s)
nt misery
elf num eleven; **Elf** (-, -en) f
(Sport) eleven
Elfenbein nt ivory
Elfmeter m (Sport) penalty (kick)
elfte(r, s) adj eleventh; siehe auch
dritte
Ell(en)bogen m elbow
Elster (-, -n) f magpie
Eltern pl parents pl
EM f abk = **Europameisterschaft**
European Championship(s)
E-Mail (-, -s) f (Inform) e-mail;
jdm eine ~ schicken to e-mail sb,
to send sb an e-mail; **jdm etwas
per ~ schicken** to e-mail sth to sb;
E-Mail-Adresse f e-mail address;
e-mailen vt to e-mail
Emoticon (-s, -s) nt emoticon
emotional adj emotional
empfahl imperf von **empfehlen**
empfand imperf von **empfinden**
Empfang (-(e)s, Empfänge) m
(Rezeption; Veranstaltung)
reception; (Erhalten) receipt; **in
~ nehmen** to receive; **empfangen**
(empfing, empfangen) vt to receive;
Empfänger(in) (-s, -) m(f)
recipient; (Adressat) addressee ▷ m

(Tech) receiver; **Empfäng-
nisverhütung** f contraception;
Empfangshalle f reception area
empfehlen (empfahl, empfohlen)
vt to recommend; **Empfehlung** f
recommendation
empfinden (empfand, empfunden)
vt to feel; **empfindlich** adj
(Mensch) sensitive; (Stelle) sore;
(reizbar) touchy; (Material) delicate
empfing imperf von **empfangen**
empfohlen pp von **empfehlen**
empfunden pp von **empfinden**
empört adj indignant (über +akk
at)
Ende (-s, -n) nt end; (Film, Roman)
ending; **am ~** at the end;
(schließlich) in the end; **~ Mai** at
the end of May; **~ der**
Achtzigerjahre in the late
eighties; **sie ist ~ zwanzig** she's in
her late twenties; **zu ~** over,
finished; **enden** vi to end; **der
Zug endet hier** this service (o
train) terminates here; **endgültig**
adj final; (Beweis) conclusive
Endivie f endive
endlich adv at last, finally; (am
Ende) eventually; **Endspiel** nt
final; (Endrunde) finals pl;
Endstation f terminus; **Endung**
f ending
Energie f energy; **~ sparend**
energy-saving; **Energiebedarf** m
energy requirement;
Energieverbrauch m energy
consumption
energisch adj (entschlossen)
forceful
eng adj narrow; (Kleidung) tight;
(fig: Freundschaft, Verhältnis) close;
das wird ~ (fam: zeitlich) we're
running out of time, it's getting
tight ▷ adv: **~ befreundet sein** to
be close friends
engagieren vt to engage ▷ vr:
sich ~ to commit oneself, to be

committed (*für* to)

Engel (*-s, -*) *m* angel

England *nt* England;
Engländer(in) (*-s, -*) *m(f)*
Englishman/-woman; **die ~** *pl* the
English *pl*; **englisch** *adj* English;
(*Gastr*) rare; **Englisch** *nt* English;
ins ~e übersetzen to translate
into English

Enkel (*-s, -*) *m* grandson; **Enkelin**
f granddaughter

enorm *adj* enormous; (*fig*)
tremendous

Entbindung *f* (*Med*) delivery

entdecken *vt* to discover;
Entdeckung *f* discovery

Ente (*-, -n*) *f* duck

Enter-Taste *f* (*Inform*) enter (*o*
return) key

entfernen *vt* to remove; (*Inform*)
to delete ▷ *vr*: **sich ~** to go away;
entfernt *adj* distant; **15 km von X
~** 15 km away from X; **20 km
voneinander ~** 20 km apart;
Entfernung *f* distance; **aus der
~** from a distance

entführen *vt* to kidnap;
Entführer(in) *m(f)* kidnapper;
Entführung *f* kidnapping

entgegen *prep* +*dat* contrary to
▷ *adv* towards; **dem Wind
~** against the wind;
entgegengesetzt *adj* (*Richtung*)
opposite; (*Meinung*) opposing;
entgegen|kommen *irr vi*: **jdm
~** to come to meet sb; (*fig*) to
accommodate sb;
entgegenkommend *adj* (*Verkehr*)
oncoming; (*fig*) obliging

entgegnen *vt* to reply (*auf* +*akk*
to)

entgehen *irr vi*: **jdm ~** to escape
sb's notice; **sich** (*dat*) **etw ~ lassen**
to miss sth

entgleisen *vi* (*Eisenb*) to be
derailed; (*fig: Mensch*) to
misbehave

Enthaarungscreme *f* hair
remover

enthalten *irr vt* (*Behälter*) to
contain; (*Preis*) to include ▷ *vr*:
sich ~ to abstain (*gen* from)

entkoffeiniert *adj*
decaffeinated

entkommen *irr vi* to escape

entkorken *vt* to uncork

entlang *prep* +*akk o dat* **~ dem
Fluss, den Fluss ~** along the river;
entlang|gehen *irr vi* to walk
along

entlassen *irr vt* (*Patient*) to
discharge; (*Arbeiter*) to dismiss

entlasten *vt*: **jdn ~** (*Arbeit
abnehmen*) to relieve sb of some of
his/her work

entmutigen *vt* to discourage

entnehmen *vt* to take (*dat* from)

entrahmt *adj* (*Milch*) skimmed

entschädigen *vt* to
compensate; **Entschädigung** *f*
compensation

entscheiden *irr vt, vi* to decide
▷ *vr*: **sich ~** to decide; **sich
für/gegen etw ~** to decide
on/against sth; **wir haben uns
entschieden, nicht zu gehen** we
decided not to go; **das
entscheidet sich morgen** that'll
be decided tomorrow;
entscheidend *adj* decisive;
(*Stimme*) casting; (*Frage, Problem*)
crucial; **Entscheidung** *f*
decision

entschließen *irr vr*: **sich ~** to
decide (*zu, für* on), to make up
one's mind; **Entschluss** *m*
decision

entschuldigen *vt* to excuse
▷ *vr*: **sich ~** to apologize; **sich bei
jdm für etw ~** to apologize to sb
for sth ▷ *vi*: **entschuldige!, ~ Sie!**
(*vor einer Frage*) excuse me;
(*Verzeihung!*) (I'm) sorry, excuse me
(*US*); **Entschuldigung** *f* apology;

(*Grund*) excuse; **jdn um ~ bitten** to apologize to sb; **~!** (*bei Zusammenstoß*) (I'm) sorry, excuse me (*US*); (*vor einer Frage*) excuse me; (*wenn man etw nicht verstanden hat*) (I beg your) pardon?

entsetzlich *adj* dreadful, appalling

entsorgen *vt* to dispose of

entspannen *vt* (*Körper*) to relax; (*Pol: Lage*) to ease ▷ *vr:* **sich ~** to relax; (*fam*) to chill out; **Entspannung** *f* relaxation

entsprechen *irr vi* +*dat* to correspond to; (*Anforderungen, Wünschen etc*) to comply with; **entsprechend** *adj* appropriate ▷ *adv* accordingly ▷ *prep* +*dat* according to, in accordance with

entstehen *vi* (*Schwierigkeiten*) to arise; (*gebaut werden*) to be built; (*hergestellt werden*) to be created

enttäuschen *vt* to disappoint; **Enttäuschung** *f* disappointment

entweder *conj*: **~ ... oder ...** either ... or ...; **~ oder!** take it or leave it

entwerfen *irr vt* (*Möbel, Kleider*) to design; (*Plan, Vertrag*) to draft

entwerten *vt* to devalue; (*Fahrschein*) to cancel; **Entwerter** (*-s, -*) *m* ticket-cancelling machine

entwickeln *vt* (*a. Foto*) to develop; (*Mut, Energie*) to show, to display ▷ *vr:* **sich ~** to develop; **Entwicklung** *f* development; (*Foto*) developing; **Entwicklungshelfer(in)** (*-s, -*) *m(f)* development worker; **Entwicklungsland** *nt* developing country

Entwurf *m* outline; (*Design*) design; (*Vertragsentwurf, Konzept*) draft

entzückend *adj* delightful, charming

Entzug *m* withdrawal;

(*Behandlung*) detox; **Entzugserscheinung** *f* withdrawal symptom

entzünden *vr:* **sich ~** to catch fire; (*Med*) to become inflamed; **Entzündung** *f* (*Med*) inflammation

Epidemie (*-, -n*) *f* epidemic

Epilepsie (*-, -n*) *f* epilepsy

epilieren *vt* to remove body hair, to depilate; **Epiliergerät** *nt* Ladyshave®

er *pron* (*Person*) he; (*Sache*) it; **er ist's** it's him; **wo ist mein Mantel? — ~ ist ...** where's my coat? — it's ...

Erbe (*-n, -n*) *m* heir ▷ (*-s*) *nt* inheritance; (*fig*) heritage; **erben** *vt* to inherit; **Erbin** *f* heiress; **erblich** *adj* hereditary

erbrechen *irr vt* to vomit ▷ *vr:* **sich ~** to vomit; **Erbrechen** *nt* vomiting

Erbschaft *f* inheritance

Erbse (*-, -n*) *f* pea

Erdapfel *m* potato; **Erdbeben** *nt* earthquake; **Erdbeere** *f* strawberry; **Erde** (*-, -n*) *f* (*Planet*) earth; (*Boden*) ground; **Erdgas** *nt* natural gas; **Erdgeschoss** *nt* ground floor (*Brit*), first floor (*US*); **Erdkunde** *f* geography; **Erdnuss** *f* peanut; **Erdöl** *nt* (mineral) oil; **Erdrutsch** *m* landslide; **Erdteil** *m* continent

ereignen *vr:* **sich ~** to happen, to take place; **Ereignis** *nt* event

erfahren *irr vt* to learn, to find out; (*erleben*) to experience ▷ *adj* experienced; **Erfahrung** *f* experience

erfinden *irr vt* to invent; **erfinderisch** *adj* inventive, creative; **Erfindung** *f* invention

Erfolg (*-(e)s, -e*) *m* success; (*Folge*) result; **~ versprechend** promising; **viel ~!** good luck;

erfolglos *adj* unsuccessful;
erfolgreich *adj* successful
erforderlich *adj* necessary
erforschen *vt* to explore;
(*untersuchen*) investigate
erfreulich *adj* pleasing, pleasant;
(*Nachricht*) good;
erfreulicherweise *adv*
fortunately
erfrieren *irr vi* to freeze to death;
(*Pflanzen*) to be killed by frost
Erfrischung *f* refreshment
erfüllen *vt* (*Raum*) to fill; (*Bitte,
Wunsch etc*) to fulfil ▷ *vr*: **sich ~** to
come true
ergänzen *vt* (*hinzufügen*) to add;
(*vervollständigen*) to complete ▷ *vr*:
sich ~ to complement one
another; **Ergänzung** *f*
completion; (*Zusatz*) supplement
ergeben *irr vt* (*Betrag*) to come
to; (*zum Ergebnis haben*) to result in
▷ *irr vr*: **sich ~** to surrender;
(*folgen*) to result (*aus* from) ▷ *adj*
devoted; (*demütig*) humble
Ergebnis *nt* result
ergreifen *irr vt* to seize; (*Beruf*) to
take up; (*Maßnahme, Gelegenheit*) to
take; (*rühren*) to move
erhalten *irr vt* (*bekommen*) to
receive; (*bewahren*) to preserve;
gut ~ sein to be in good
condition; **erhältlich** *adj*
available
erheblich *adj* considerable
erhitzen *vt* to heat (up)
erhöhen *vt* to raise; (*verstärken*)
to increase ▷ *vr*: **sich ~** to
increase
erholen *vr*: **sich ~** to recover; (*sich
ausruhen*) to have a rest; **erholsam**
adj restful; **Erholung** *f* recovery;
(*Entspannung*) relaxation, rest
erinnern *vt* to remind (*an +akk*
of) ▷ *vr*: **sich ~** to remember (*an
etw akk* sth); **Erinnerung** *f*
memory; (*Andenken*) souvenir;

(*Mahnung*) reminder
erkälten *vr*: **sich ~** to catch a
cold; **erkältet** *adj*: (**stark**) **~ sein**
to have a (bad) cold; **Erkältung** *f*
cold
erkennen *irr vt* to recognize;
(*sehen, verstehen*) to see; **~, dass ...**
to realize that ...; **erkenntlich**
adj: **sich ~ zeigen** to show one's
appreciation
Erker (*-s, -*) *m* bay
erklären *vt* to explain; (*kundtun*)
to declare; **Erklärung** *f*
explanation; (*Aussage*) declaration
erkundigen *vr*: **sich ~** to enquire
(*nach* about)
erlauben *vt* to allow, to permit;
jdm ~, etw zu tun to allow (*o*
permit*) sb to do sth; **sich** (*dat*) **etw
~** to permit oneself sth; **~ Sie(,
dass ich rauche)?** do you mind (if I
smoke)?; **was ~ Sie sich?** what do
you think you're doing?; **Erlaubnis**
f permission
Erläuterung *f* explanation; (*zu
Text*) comment
erleben *vt* to experience; (*schöne
Tage etc*) to have; (*Schlimmes*) to go
through; (*miterleben*) to witness;
(*noch miterleben*) to live to see;
Erlebnis *nt* experience
erledigen *vt* (*Angelegenheit,
Aufgabe*) to deal with; (*fam:
ruinieren*) to finish; **erledigt** *adj*
(*beendet*) finished; (*gelöst*) dealt
with; (*fam: erschöpft*) whacked,
knackered (*Brit*)
erleichtert *adj* relieved
Erlös (*-es, -e*) *m* proceeds *pl*
ermahnen *vt* (*warnend*) to warn
ermäßigt *adj* reduced;
Ermäßigung *f* reduction
ermitteln *vt* to find out; (*Täter*)
to trace ▷ *vi* (*Jur*) to investigate
ermöglichen *vt* to make
possible (*dat* for)
ermorden *vt* to murder

ermüdend adj tiring
ermutigen vt to encourage
ernähren vt to feed; (Familie)
to support ▷ vr: **sich ~** to
support oneself; **sich ~ von** to
live on; **Ernährung** f (Essen)
food; **Ernährungsberater(in)**
m(f) nutritional (o dietary)
adviser
erneuern vt to renew;
(restaurieren) to restore; (renovieren)
to renovate; (auswechseln) to
replace
ernst adj serious ▷ adv: **jdn/etw**
~ nehmen take sb/sth seriously;
Ernst (-es) m seriousness; **das ist**
mein ~ I'm quite serious; **im ~?**
seriously?; **ernsthaft** adj serious
▷ adv seriously
Ernte (-, -n) f harvest;
Erntedankfest nt harvest festival
(Brit), Thanksgiving (Day) (US: 4.
Donnerstag im November); **ernten**
vt to harvest; (Lob etc) to earn
erobern vt to conquer
eröffnen vt to open; **Eröffnung**
f opening
erogen adj erogenous
erotisch adj erotic
erpressen vt (jdn) to blackmail;
(Geld etc) to extort; **Erpressung** f
blackmail; (von Geld) extortion
erraten irr vt to guess
erregen vt to excite; (sexuell) to
arouse; (ärgern) to annoy;
(hervorrufen) to arouse ▷ vr: **sich**
~ to get worked up; **Erreger** (-s, -)
m (Med) germ; (Virus) virus
erreichbar adj: **~ sein** to be
within reach; (Person) to be
available; **das Stadtzentrum ist**
zu Fuß/mit dem Wagen leicht
~ the city centre is within easy
walking/driving distance;
erreichen vt to reach; (Zug etc) to
catch
Ersatz (-es) m replacement; (auf

Zeit) substitute; (Ausgleich)
compensation; **Ersatzreifen** m
(Auto) spare tyre; **Ersatzteil** nt
spare (part)
erscheinen irr vi to appear;
(wirken) to seem
erschöpft adj exhausted;
Erschöpfung f exhaustion
erschrecken vt to frighten
▷ (erschrak, erschrocken) vi to get a
fright; **erschreckend** adj
alarming; **erschrocken** adj
frightened
erschwinglich adj affordable
ersetzen vt to replace; (Auslagen)
to reimburse

O SCHLÜSSELWORT

erst adv **1** first; **mach erst mal die**
Arbeit fertig finish your work
first; **wenn du das erst mal**
hinter dir hast once you've got
that behind you
2 (nicht früher als, nur) only; (nicht
bis) not till; **erst gestern** only
yesterday; **erst morgen** not until
tomorrow; **erst als** only when, not
until; **wir fahren erst später**
we're not going until later; **er ist**
(gerade) erst angekommen he's
only just arrived
3 wäre er doch erst zurück! if
only he were back!

erstatten vt (Kosten) to refund;
Bericht ~ to report (über +akk on);
Anzeige gegen jdn ~ to report sb
to the police
erstaunlich adj astonishing;
erstaunt adj surprised
erstbeste(r, s) adj: **das ~ Hotel**
any old hotel; **der Erstbeste** just
anyone
erste(r, s) adj first; siehe auch
dritte; zum ~n Mal for the first
time; **er wurde Erster** he came

first; **auf den ~n Blick** at first sight
erstens adv first(ly), in the first place
ersticken vi (Mensch) to suffocate; **in Arbeit ~** to be snowed under with work
erstklassig adj first-class; **erstmals** adv for the first time
erstrecken vr: **sich ~** to extend, to stretch (auf +akk to; über +akk over)
ertappen vt to catch
erteilen vt (Rat, Erlaubnis) to give
Ertrag (-(e)s, Erträge) m yield; (Gewinn) proceeds pl; **ertragen** irr vt (Schmerzen) to bear, to stand; (dulden) to put up with; **erträglich** adj (nicht zu schlecht) tolerable
ertrinken irr vi to drown
erwachsen adj grown-up; **~ werden** to grow up; **Erwachsene(r)** mf adult, grown-up
erwähnen vt to mention
erwarten vt to expect; (warten auf) to wait for; **ich kann den Sommer kaum ~** I can hardly wait for the summer
erwerbstätig adj employed
erwidern vt to reply; (Gruß, Besuch) to return
erwischen vt (fam) to catch (bei etw doing sth)
erwünscht adj desired; (willkommen) welcome
Erz (-es, -e) nt ore
erzählen vt to tell (jdm etw sb sth); **Erzählung** f story, tale
erzeugen vt to produce; (Strom) to generate; **Erzeugnis** nt product
erziehen irr vt to bring up; (geistig) to educate; (Tier) to train; **Erzieher(in)** (-s, -) m(f) educator; (Kindergarten) (nursery school)

teacher; **Erziehung** f upbringing; (Bildung) education
es pron (Sache, im Nom und Akk) it; (Baby, Tier) he/she; **ich bin ~** it's me; **~ ist kalt** it's cold; **~ gibt ...** there is .../there are ...; **ich hoffe ~** I hope so; **ich kann ~** I can do it
Escape-Taste f (Inform) escape key
Esel (-s, -) m donkey
Espresso (-s, -) m espresso
essbar adj edible; **essen** (aß, gegessen) vt, vi to eat; **zu Mittag/Abend ~** to have lunch/dinner; **was gibt's zu ~?** what's for lunch/dinner?; **~ gehen** to eat out; **gegessen sein** (fig, fam) to be history; **Essen** (-s, -) nt (Mahlzeit) meal; (Nahrung) food
Essig (-s, -e) m vinegar
Esslöffel m dessert spoon; **Esszimmer** nt dining room
Estland nt Estonia
Etage (-, -n) f floor, storey; **in** (o **auf**) **der ersten ~** on the first (Brit) (o second (US)) floor; **Etagenbett** nt bunk bed
Etappe (-, -n) f stage
ethnisch adj ethnic
Etikett (-(e)s, -e) nt label
etliche pron pl several, quite a few; **etliches** pron quite a lot
etwa adv (ungefähr) about; (vielleicht) perhaps; (beispielsweise) for instance
etwas pron something; (verneinend, fragend) anything; (ein wenig) a little; **~ Neues** something/anything new; **~ zu essen** something to eat; **~ Salz** some salt; **wenn ich noch ~ tun kann ...** if I can do anything else ... ▷ adv a bit, a little; **~ mehr** a little more
EU (-) f abk = **Europäische Union** EU
euch pron akk, dat von **ihr**; you, (to)

you; **~ (selbst)** (*reflexiv*) yourselves; **wo kann ich ~ treffen?** where can I meet you?; **sie schickt es ~** she'll send it to you; **ein Freund von ~** a friend of yours; **setzt ~ bitte** please sit down; **habt ihr ~ amüsiert?** did you enjoy yourselves?

euer *pron* (*adjektivisch*) your; **~ David** (*am Briefende*) Yours, David ▷ *pron gen von* **ihr**; of you; **euere(r, s)** *pron siehe* **eure**

Eule (-, -n) *f* owl

eure(r, s) *pron* (*substantivisch*) yours; **das ist ~** that's yours; **euretwegen** *adv* (*wegen euch*) because of you; (*euch zuliebe*) for your sake; (*um euch*) about you

Euro (-, -) *m* (*Währung*) euro; **Eurocent** *m* eurocent; **Eurocity** (-(s), -s) *m*, **Eurocityzug** *m* European Intercity train; **Europa** (-s) *nt* Europe; **Europäer(in)** (-s, -) *m(f)* European; **europäisch** *adj* European; **Europäische Union** European Union; **Europameister(in)** *m(f)* European champion; (*Mannschaft*) European champions *pl*; **Europaparlament** *nt* European Parliament

Euter (-s, -) *nt* udder

evangelisch *adj* Protestant

eventuell *adj* possible ▷ *adv* possibly, perhaps

ewig *adj* eternal; **er hat ~ gebraucht** it took him ages; **Ewigkeit** *f* eternity

Ex *mf* ex

Ex- *in zW* ex-, former; **~frau** ex-wife; **~freund** *m* ex-boyfriend; **~minister** former minister

exakt *adj* precise

Examen (-s, -) *nt* exam

Exemplar (-s, -e) *nt* specimen; (*Buch*) copy

Exil (-s, -e) *nt* exile

Existenz *f* existence; (*Unterhalt*) livelihood, living; **existieren** *vi* to exist

exklusiv *adj* exclusive; **exklusive** *adv*, *prep* +*gen* excluding

exotisch *adj* exotic

Experte (-n, -n) *m*, **Expertin** *f* expert

explodieren *vi* to explode; **Explosion** *f* explosion

Export (-(e)s, -e) *m* export; **exportieren** *vt* to export

Express (-es) *m*, **Expresszug** *m* express (train)

extra *adj inv* (*fam: gesondert*) separate; (*zusätzlich*) extra ▷ *adv* (*gesondert*) separately; (*speziell*) specially; (*absichtlich*) on purpose; **Extra** (-s, -s) *nt* extra

extrem *adj* extreme ▷ *adv* extremely; **~ kalt** extremely cold

exzellent *adj* excellent

Eyeliner (-s, -) *m* eyeliner

f

fabelhaft adj fabulous, marvellous

Fabrik f factory

Fach (-(e)s, Fächer) nt compartment; (Schulfach, Sachgebiet) subject; **Facharzt** m, **Fachärztin** f specialist; **Fachausdruck** (-s, Fachausdrücke) m technical term

Fächer (-s, -) m fan

Fachfrau f specialist, expert; **Fachmann** (-leute) m specialist, expert; **Fachwerkhaus** nt half-timbered house

Fackel (-, -n) f torch

fad(e) adj (Essen) bland; (langweilig) dull

Faden (-s, Fäden) m thread

fähig adj capable (zu, gen of); **Fähigkeit** f ability

Fahndung f search

Fahne (-, -n) f flag

Fahrausweis m ticket

Fahrbahn f road; (Spur) lane

Fähre (-, -n) f ferry

fahren (fuhr, gefahren) vt to drive; (Rad) to ride; (befördern) to drive, to take; **50 km/h ~** to drive at (o do) 50 kph ▷ vi (sich bewegen) to go; (Autofahrer) to drive; (Schiff) to sail; (abfahren) to leave; **mit dem Auto/Zug ~** to go by car/train; **rechts ~!** keep to the right; **Fahrer(in)** (-s, -) m(f) driver; **Fahrerairbag** m driver airbag; **Fahrerflucht** f: **~ begehen** to fail to stop after an accident; **Fahrersitz** m driver's seat

Fahrgast m passenger; **Fahrgeld** nt fare; **Fahrgemeinschaft** f car pool; **Fahrkarte** f ticket; **Fahrkartenautomat** m ticket machine; **Fahrkartenschalter** m ticket office

fahrlässig adj negligent

Fahrlehrer(in) m(f) driving instructor; **Fahrplan** m timetable; **Fahrplanauszug** m individual timetable; **fahrplanmäßig** adj (Eisenb) scheduled; **Fahrpreis** m fare; **Fahrpreisermäßigung** f fare reduction; **Fahrrad** nt bicycle; **Fahrradschlauch** m bicycle tube; **Fahrradschloss** nt bicycle lock; **Fahrradverleih** m cycle hire (Brit) (o rental (US)); **Fahrradweg** m cycle path; **Fahrschein** m ticket; **Fahrscheinautomat** m ticket machine; **Fahrscheinentwerter** m ticket-cancelling machine; **Fahrschule** f driving school; **Fahrschüler(in)** m(f) learner (driver) (Brit), student driver (US); **Fahrspur** f lane; **Fahrstreifen** m lane; **Fahrstuhl** m lift (Brit), elevator (US)

Fahrt (-, -en) f journey; (kurz) trip; (Auto) drive; **auf der ~ nach London** on the way to London; **nach drei Stunden ~** after travelling for three hours; **gute ~!** have a good trip; **Fahrtkosten** *pl* travelling expenses *pl*; **Fahrtrichtung** *f* direction of travel

fahrtüchtig *f* (*Person*) fit to drive; (*Fahrzeug*) roadworthy

Fahrtunterbrechung *f* break in the journey, stop

Fahrverbot *nt*: **~ erhalten/ haben** to be banned from driving; **Fahrzeug** *nt* vehicle; **Fahrzeugbrief** *m* (vehicle) registration document; **Fahrzeughalter(in)** *m(f)* registered owner; **Fahrzeugpapiere** *pl* vehicle documents *pl*

fair *adj* fair

Fakultät *f* faculty

Falke (-n, -n) *m* falcon

Fall (-(e)s, *Fälle*) *m* (*Sturz*) fall; (*Sachverhalt, juristisch*) case; **auf jeden ~, auf alle Fälle** in any case; (*bestimmt*) definitely; **auf keinen ~** on no account; **für den ~, dass ...** in case ...

Falle (-, -n) *f* trap

fallen (*fiel, gefallen*) *vi* to fall; **etw ~ lassen** to drop sth

fällig *adj* due

falls *adv* if; (*für den Fall, dass*) in case

Fallschirm *m* parachute; **Fallschirmspringen** *nt* parachuting, parachute jumping; **Fallschirmspringer(in)** *m(f)* parachutist

falsch *adj* (*unrichtig*) wrong; (*unehrlich, unecht*) false; (*Schmuck*) fake; **~ verbunden** sorry, wrong number; **fälschen** *vt* to forge; **Falschfahrer(in)** *m(f)* person driving the wrong way on the motorway; **Falschgeld** *nt* counterfeit money; **Fälschung** *f* forgery, fake

Faltblatt *nt* leaflet

Falte (-, -n) *f* (*Knick*) fold; (*Haut*) wrinkle; (*Rock*) pleat; (*Bügel*) crease; **falten** *vt* to fold; **faltig** *adj* (*zerknittert*) creased; (*Haut, Gesicht*) wrinkled

Familie *f* family; **Familienangehörige(r)** *mf* family member; **Familienname** *m* surname; **Familienstand** *m* marital status

Fan (-s, -s) *m* fan

fand *imperf von* **finden**

fangen (*fing, gefangen*) *vt* to catch ▷ *vr*: **sich ~** (*nicht fallen*) to steady oneself; (*fig*) to compose oneself

Fantasie *f* imagination

fantastisch *adj* fantastic

Farbdrucker *m* colour printer; **Farbe** (-, -n) *f* colour; (*zum Malen etc*) paint; (*für Stoff*) dye; **färben** *vt* to colour; (*Stoff, Haar*) to dye; **Farbfernsehen** *nt* colour television; **Farbfilm** *m* colour film; **farbig** *adj* coloured; **Farbkopierer** *m* colour copier; **farblos** *adj* colourless; **Farbstoff** *m* dye; (*für Lebensmittel*) colouring

Farn (-(e)s, -e) *m* fern

Fasan (-(e)s, -e(n)) *m* pheasant

Fasching (-s, -e) *m* carnival, Mardi Gras (US); **Faschingsdienstag** (-s, -e) *m* Shrove Tuesday, Mardi Gras (US)

Faschismus *m* fascism

Faser (-, -n) *f* fibre

Fass (-es, *Fässer*) *nt* barrel; (*Öl*) drum

fassen *vt* (*ergreifen*) to grasp; (*enthalten*) to hold; (*Entschluss*) to take; (*verstehen*) to understand; **nicht zu ~!** unbelievable ▷ *vr*: **sich ~** to compose oneself; **Fassung** *f* (*Umrahmung*) mount; (*Brille*) frame; (*Lampe*) socket; (*Wortlaut*) version; (*Beherrschung*) composure; **jdn aus der ~ bringen**

to throw sb; **die ~ verlieren** to lose one's cool

fast *adv* almost, nearly

fasten *vi* to fast; **Fastenzeit** *f*: **die ~** (*christlich*) Lent; (*muslimisch*) Ramadan

Fast Food (-s) *nt* fast food

Fastnacht *f* (*Fasching*) carnival

fatal *adj* (*verhängnisvoll*) disastrous; (*peinlich*) embarrassing

faul *adj* (*Obst, Gemüse*) rotten; (*Mensch*) lazy; (*Ausreden*) lame; **faulen** *vi* to rot

faulenzen *vi* to do nothing, to hang around; **Faulheit** *f* laziness

faulig *adj* rotten; (*Geruch, Geschmack*) foul

Faust (-, *Fäuste*) *f* fist; **Fausthandschuh** *m* mitten

Fax (-, -(e)) *nt* fax; **faxen** *vi, vt* to fax; **Faxgerät** *nt* fax machine; **Faxnummer** *f* fax number

FCKW (-, -s) *nt abk =* **Fluorchlorkohlenwasserstoff** CFC

Februar (-(s), -e) *m* February; *siehe auch* **Juni**

Fechten *nt* fencing

Feder (-, -n) *f* feather; (*Schreibfeder*) (pen-)nib; (*Tech*) spring; **Federball** *m* (*Ball*) shuttlecock; (*Spiel*) badminton; **Federung** *f* suspension

Fee (-, -n) *f* fairy

fegen *vi, vt* to sweep

fehl *adj*: **~ am Platz** (*o* **Ort**) out of place

fehlen *vi* (*abwesend sein*) to be absent; **etw fehlt jdm** sb lacks sth; **was fehlt ihm?** what's wrong with him?; **du fehlst mir** I miss you; **es fehlt an ...** there's no...

Fehler (-s, -) *m* mistake, error; (*Mangel, Schwäche*) fault; **Fehlermeldung** *f* (*Inform*) error message

Fehlzündung *f* (*Auto*) misfire

Feier (-, -n) *f* celebration; (*Party*) party; **Feierabend** *m* end of the working day; **~ haben** to finish work; **nach ~** after work; **feierlich** *adj* solemn; **feiern** *vt, vi* to celebrate, to have a party; **Feiertag** *m* holiday; **gesetzlicher ~** public (*o* bank (*Brit*) *o* legal (*US*)) holiday

feig(e) *adj* cowardly

Feige (-, -n) *f* fig

Feigling *m* coward

Feile (-, -n) *f* file

fein *adj* fine; (*vornehm*) refined; **~!** great!; **das schmeckt ~** that tastes delicious

Feind(in) (-(e)s, -e) *m(f)* enemy; **feindlich** *adj* hostile

Feinkost (-) *f* delicacies *pl*; **Feinkostladen** *m* delicatessen; **Feinschmecker(in)** (-s, -) *m(f)* gourmet; **Feinstaub** *m* particulate matter; **Feinwaschmittel** *nt* washing powder for delicate fabrics

Feld (-(e)s, -er) *nt* field; (*Schach*) square; (*Sport*) pitch; **Feldsalat** *m* lamb's lettuce; **Feldweg** *m* path across the fields

Felge (-, -n) *f* (wheel) rim

Fell (-(e)s, -e) *nt* fur; (*von Schaf*) fleece

Fels (-en, -en) *m*, **Felsen** (-s, -) *m* rock; (*Klippe*) cliff; **felsig** *adj* rocky

feminin *adj* feminine; **Femininum** (-s, *Feminina*) *nt* (*Ling*) feminine noun

feministisch *adj* feminist

Fenchel (-s, -) *m* fennel

Fenster (-s, -) *nt* window; **Fensterbrett** *nt* windowsill; **Fensterladen** *m* shutter; **Fensterplatz** *m* windowseat; **Fensterscheibe** *f* windowpane

Ferien *pl* holidays *pl* (*Brit*), vacation *sing* (*US*); **~ haben/ machen** to be/go on holiday (*Brit*)

flambiert adj flambé(ed)
Flamme (-, -n) f flame
Flanell (-s) m flannel
Flasche (-, -n) f bottle; **eine ~ sein** (fam) to be useless; **Flaschenbier** nt bottled beer; **Flaschenöffner** m bottle opener; **Flaschenpfand** nt deposit; **Flaschentomate** f plum tomato
flatterhaft adj fickle; **flattern** vi to flutter
flauschig adj fluffy
Flausen pl (fam) daft ideas pl
Flaute (-, -n) f calm; (Comm) recession
Flechte (-, -n) f plait; (Med) scab; (Bot) lichen; **flechten** (flocht, geflochten) vt to plait; (Kranz) to bind
Fleck (-(e)s, -e) m, **Flecken** (-s, -) m spot; (Schmutz) stain; (Stoff~) patch; (Makel) blemish; **Fleckentferner** (-s, -) m stain remover; **fleckig** adj spotted; (mit Schmutzflecken) stained
Fledermaus f bat
Fleisch (-(e)s) nt flesh; (Essen) meat; **Fleischbrühe** f meat stock; **Fleischer(in)** (-s, -) m(f) butcher; **Fleischerei** f butcher's (shop); **Fleischtomate** f beef tomato
fleißig adj diligent, hard-working
flennen vi (fam) to cry, to howl
flexibel adj flexible
flicken vt to mend; **Flickzeug** nt repair kit
Flieder (-s, -) m lilac
Fliege (-, -n) f fly; (Krawatte) bow tie
fliegen (flog, geflogen) vt, vi to fly
Fliese (-, -n) f tile
Fließband nt conveyor belt; (als Einrichtung) production (o assembly) line; **fließen** (floss, geflossen) vi to flow; **fließend** adj (Rede, Deutsch) fluent; (Übergänge) smooth; **~(es) Wasser** running water
Flipper (-s, -) m pinball machine; **flippern** vi to play pinball
flippig adj (fam) eccentric
flirten vi to flirt
Flitterwochen pl honeymoon sing
flocht imperf von **flechten**
Flocke (-, -n) f flake
flog imperf von **fliegen**
Floh (-(e)s, Flöhe) m flea; **Flohmarkt** m flea market
Flop (-s, -s) m flop
Floskel (-, -n) f empty phrase
floss imperf von **fließen**
Floß (-es, Flöße) nt raft
Flosse (-, -n) f fin; (Schwimmflosse) flipper
Flöte (-, -n) f flute; (Blockflöte) recorder
flott adj lively; (elegant) smart; (Naut) afloat
Fluch (-(e)s, Flüche) m curse; **fluchen** vi to swear, to curse
Flucht (-, -en) f flight; **flüchten** vi to flee (vor +dat from); **flüchtig** adj: **ich kenne ihn nur ~** I don't know him very well at all; **Flüchtling** m refugee
Flug (-(e)s, Flüge) m flight; **Flugbegleiter(in)** (-s, -) m(f) flight attendant; **Flugblatt** nt leaflet
Flügel (-s, -) m wing; (Mus) grand piano
Fluggast m passenger (on a plane); **Fluggesellschaft** f airline; **Flughafen** m airport; **Fluglotse** m air-traffic controller; **Flugnummer** f flight number; **Flugplan** m flight schedule; **Flugplatz** m airport; (klein) airfield; **Flugschein** m plane ticket; **Flugschreiber** m flight recorder, black box; **Flugsteig** (-s, -e) m gate; **Flugstrecke** f air route; **Flugticket** nt plane ticket; **Flugverbindung** f flight

connection; **Flugverkehr** *m* air traffic; **Flugzeit** *f* flying time; **Flugzeug** *nt* plane; **Flugzeugentführung** *f* hijacking

Flunder (-, -*n*) *f* flounder

Fluor (-*s*) *nt* fluorine

Flur (-(*e*)*s*, -*e*) *m* hall

Fluss (-*es*, *Flüsse*) *m* river; (*Fließen*) flow

flüssig *adj* liquid; **Flüssigkeit** (-, -*en*) *f* liquid; **Flüssigseife** *f* liquid soap

flüstern *vt*, *vi* to whisper

Flut (-, -*en*) *f* (*a. fig*) flood; (*Gezeiten*) high tide; **Flutlicht** *nt* floodlight

Fohlen (-*s*, -) *nt* foal

Föhn (-(*e*)*s*, -*e*) *m* hairdryer; (*Wind*) foehn; **föhnen** *vt* to dry; (*beim Friseur*) to blow-dry

Folge (-, -*n*) *f* (*Reihe, Serie*) series *sing*; (*Aufeinanderfolge*) sequence; (*Fortsetzung eines Romans*) instalment; (*Fortsetzung einer Fernsehserie*) episode; (*Auswirkung*) result; **etw zur ~ haben** to result in sth; **~n haben** to have consequences; **folgen** *vi* to follow (*jdm* sb); (*gehorchen*) to obey (*jdm* sb); **jdm ~ können** (*fig*) to be able to follow sb; **folgend** *adj* following; **folgendermaßen** *adv* as follows; **folglich** *adv* consequently

Folie *f* foil; (*für Projektor*) transparency

Fön® *m siehe* **Föhn**

Fondue (-*s*, -*s*) *nt* fondue

fönen *vt siehe* **föhnen**

fordern *vt* to demand

fördern *vt* to promote; (*unterstützen*) to help

Forderung *f* demand

Forelle *f* trout

Form (-, -*en*) *f* form; (*Gestalt*) shape; (*Gussform*) mould; (*Backform*) baking tin (*Brit*) (*o pan* (*US*)); **in ~ sein** to be in good form; **Formalität** *f* formality; **Format** *nt* format; **von internationalem ~** of international standing; **formatieren** *vt* (*Diskette*) to format; (*Text*) to edit

Formblatt *nt* form; **formen** *vt* to form, to shape; **förmlich** *adj* formal; (*buchstäblich*) real; **formlos** *adj* informal; **Formular** (-*s*, -*e*) *nt* form; **formulieren** *vt* to formulate

forschen *vi* to search (*nach* for); (*wissenschaftlich*) to (do) research; **Forscher(in)** *m(f)* researcher; **Forschung** *f* research

Förster(in) (-*s*, -) *m(f)* forester; (*für Wild*) gamekeeper

fort *adv* away; (*verschwunden*) gone; **fort|bewegen** *vt* to move away ▷ *vr*: **sich ~** to move; **Fortbildung** *f* further education; (*im Beruf*) further training; **fort|fahren** *irr vi* to go away; (*weitermachen*) to continue; **fort|gehen** *irr vi* to go away; **fortgeschritten** *adj* advanced; **Fortpflanzung** *f* reproduction

Fortschritt *m* progress; **~e machen** to make progress; **fortschrittlich** *adj* progressive

fort|setzen *vt* to continue; **Fortsetzung** *f* continuation; (*folgender Teil*) instalment; **~ folgt** to be continued

Foto (-*s*, -*s*) *nt* photo ▷ (-*s*, -*s*) *m* (*Fotoapparat*) camera; **Fotograf(in)** (-*en*, -*en*) *m(f)* photographer; **Fotografie** *f* photography; (*Bild*) photograph; **fotografieren** *vt* to photograph ▷ *vi* to take photographs; **Fotohandy** *nt* camera phone; **Fotokopie** *f* photocopy; **fotokopieren** *vt* to photocopy

Foul (-*s*, -*s*) *nt* foul

Foyer (-*s*, -*s*) *nt* foyer

Fr. f abk = **Frau** Mrs; (unverheiratet, neutral) Ms

Fracht (-, -en) f freight; (Naut) cargo; (Preis) carriage; **Frachter** (-s, -) m freighter

Frack (-(e)s, Fräcke) m tails pl

Frage (-, -n) f question; **das ist eine ~ der Zeit** that's a matter (o question) of time; **das kommt nicht in ~** that's out of the question; **Fragebogen** m questionnaire; **fragen** vt, vi to ask; **Fragezeichen** nt question mark; **fragwürdig** adj dubious

Franken (-s, -) m (Schweizer Währung) Swiss franc ▷ (-s) nt (Land) Franconia

frankieren vt to stamp; (maschinell) to frank

Frankreich (-s) nt France; **Franzose** (-n, -n) m, **Französin** f Frenchman/-woman; **die ~n** pl the French pl; **französisch** adj French; **Französisch** nt French

fraß imperf von **fressen**

Frau (-, -en) f woman; (Ehefrau) wife; (Anrede) Mrs; (unverheiratet, neutral) Ms; **Frauenarzt** m, **Frauenärztin** f gynaecologist; **Frauenbewegung** f women's movement; **frauenfeindlich** adj misogynous; **Frauenhaus** nt refuge (for battered women)

Fräulein nt (junge Dame) young lady; (veraltet als Anrede) Miss

Freak (-s, -s) m (fam) freak

frech adj cheeky; **Frechheit** f cheek; **so eine ~!** what a cheek

Freeclimbing (-s) nt free climbing

frei adj free; (Straße) clear; (Mitarbeiter) freelance; **ein ~er Tag** a day off; **~e Arbeitsstelle** vacancy; **Zimmer ~** room(s) to let (Brit), room(s) for rent (US); **im Freien** in the open air; **Freibad** nt open-air (swimming) pool;

freiberuflich adj freelance; **freig(i)ebig** adj generous; **Freiheit** f freedom; **Freikarte** f free ticket; **frei|lassen** irr vt to (set) free

freilich adv of course

Freilichtbühne f open-air theatre; **frei|machen** vr: **sich ~** to undress; **frei|nehmen** irr vt **sich** (dat) **einen Tag ~** to take a day off; **Freisprechanlage** f hands-free phone; **Freistoß** m free kick

Freitag m Friday; siehe auch **Mittwoch**; **freitags** adv on Fridays; siehe auch **mittwochs**

freiwillig adj voluntary

Freizeichen nt (Tel) ringing tone

Freizeit f spare (o free) time; **Freizeithemd** nt sports shirt; **Freizeitkleidung** f leisure wear; **Freizeitpark** m leisure park

fremd adj (nicht vertraut) strange; (ausländisch) foreign; (nicht eigen) someone else's; **Fremde(r)** mf (Unbekannter) stranger; (Ausländer) foreigner; **fremdenfeindlich** adj anti-foreigner, xenophobic; **Fremdenführer(in)** m(f) (tourist) guide; **Fremdenverkehr** m tourism; **Fremdenverkehrsamt** nt tourist information office; **Fremdenzimmer** nt (guest) room; **Fremdsprache** f foreign language; **Fremdsprachen-kenntnisse** pl knowledge sing of foreign languages; **Fremdwort** nt foreign word

Frequenz f (Radio) frequency

fressen (fraß, gefressen) vt, vi (Tier) to eat; (Mensch) to guzzle

Freude (-, -n) f joy, delight; **freuen** vt to please; **es freut mich, dass ...** I'm pleased that ... ▷ vr: **sich ~** to be pleased (über +akk about); **sich auf etw** (akk) **~** to look forward to sth

Freund (-(e)s, -e) m friend; (in Beziehung) boyfriend; **Freundin** f friend; (in Beziehung) girlfriend; **freundlich** adj friendly; (liebenswürdig) kind; **freundlicherweise** adv kindly; **Freundlichkeit** f friendliness; (Liebenswürdigkeit) kindness; **Freundschaft** f friendship

Frieden (-s, -) m peace; **Friedhof** m cemetery; **friedlich** adj peaceful

frieren (fror, gefroren) vt, vi to freeze; **ich friere, es friert mich** I'm freezing

Frikadelle f rissole

Frisbee® nt, **Frisbeescheibe®** f frisbee®

frisch adj fresh; (lebhaft) lively; **„~ gestrichen"** "wet paint"; **sich ~ machen** to freshen up; **Frischhaltefolie** f clingfilm® (Brit), plastic wrap (US); **Frischkäse** m cream cheese

Friseur(in) (-s, -e) m(f) hairdresser; **frisieren** vt: **jdn ~** to do sb's hair ▷ vr: **sich ~** to do one's hair

Frist (-, -en) f period; (Zeitpunkt) deadline; **innerhalb einer ~ von zehn Tagen** within a ten-day period; **eine ~ einhalten** to meet a deadline; **die ~ ist abgelaufen** the deadline has expired; **fristgerecht** adj, adv within the specified time; **fristlos** adj: **~e Entlassung** dismissal without notice

Frisur f hairdo, hairstyle

frittieren vt to deep-fry

Frl. f abk = **Fräulein** Miss

froh adj happy; **~e Weihnachten!** Merry Christmas

fröhlich adj happy, cheerful

Fronleichnam (-(e)s) m Corpus Christi

frontal adj frontal

fror imperf von **frieren**

Frosch (-(e)s, Frösche) m frog

Frost (-(e)s, Fröste) m frost; **bei ~** in frosty weather; **Frostschutzmittel** nt anti-freeze

Frottee nt terry(cloth); **Frottier(hand)tuch** nt towel

Frucht (-, Früchte) f (a. fig) fruit; (Getreide) corn; **Fruchteis** nt fruit-flavoured ice-cream; **Früchtetee** m fruit tea; **fruchtig** adj fruity; **Fruchtpresse** f juicer; **Fruchtsaft** m fruit juice; **Fruchtsalat** m fruit salad

früh adj, adv early; **heute ~** this morning; **um fünf Uhr ~** at five (o'clock) in the morning; **~ genug** soon enough; **früher** adj earlier; (ehemalig) former ▷ adv formerly, in the past; **frühestens** adv at the earliest

Frühjahr nt, **Frühling** m spring; **Frühlingsrolle** f spring roll; **Frühlingszwiebel** f spring onion (Brit), scallion (US)

frühmorgens adv early in the morning

Frühstück nt breakfast; **frühstücken** vi to have breakfast; **Frühstücksbüfett** nt breakfast buffet; **Frühstücksfernsehen** nt breakfast television; **Frühstücksspeck** m bacon

frühzeitig adj early

Frust (-s) m (fam) frustration; **frustrieren** vt to frustrate

Fuchs (-es, Füchse) m fox

fühlen vt, vi to feel ▷ vr: **sich ~** to feel

fuhr imperf von **fahren**

führen vt to lead; (Geschäft) to run; (Name) to bear; (Buch) to keep ▷ vi to lead, to be in the lead ▷ vr: **sich ~** to behave; **Führerschein** m driving licence (Brit), driver's license (US); **Führung** f leadership; (eines Unternehmens)

management; (*Mil*) command; (*in Museum, Stadt*) guided tour; **in ~ liegen** to be in the lead
füllen *vt* to fill; (*Gastr*) to stuff ▷ *vr*: **sich ~** to fill
Füller (*-s, -*) *m*, **Füllfederhalter** (*-s, -*) *m* fountain pen
Füllung *f* filling
Fund (*-(e)s, -e*) *m* find; **Fundbüro** *nt* lost property office (*Brit*), lost and found (*US*); **Fundsachen** *pl* lost property *sing*
fünf *num* five; **Fünf** (*-, -en*) *f* five; (*Schulnote*) ≈ E; **fünfhundert** *num* five hundred; **fünfmal** *adv* five times; **fünfte(r, s)** *adj* fifth; *siehe auch* **dritte**; **Fünftel** (*-s, -*) *nt* (*Bruchteil*) fifth; **fünfzehn** *num* fifteen; **fünfzehnte(r, s)** *adj* fifteenth; *siehe auch* **dritte**; **fünfzig** *num* fifty; **fünfzigste(r, s)** *adj* fiftieth
Funk (*-s*) *m* radio; **über ~** by radio
Funke (*-ns, -n*) *m* spark; **funkeln** *vi* to sparkle
Funkgerät *nt* radio set; **Funktaxi** *nt* radio taxi, radio cab
Funktion *f* function; **funktionieren** *vi* to work, to function; **Funktionstaste** *f* (*Inform*) function key
für *prep* +*akk* for; **was ~ (ein) ...?** what kind (*o* sort) of ...?; **Tag ~ Tag** day after day
Furcht (*-*) *f* fear; **furchtbar** *adj* terrible; **fürchten** *vt* to be afraid of, to fear ▷ *vr*: **sich ~** to be afraid (*vor* +*dat* of); **fürchterlich** *adj* awful
füreinander *adv* for each other
fürs *kontr von* **für das**
Fürst(in) (*-en, -en*) *m(f)* prince/princess; **Fürstentum** *nt* principality; **fürstlich** *adj* (*fig*) splendid
Furunkel (*-s, -*) *nt* boil

Furz (*-es, -e*) *m* (*vulg*) fart; **furzen** *vi* (*vulg*) to fart
Fuß (*-es, Füße*) *m* foot; (*von Glas, Säule etc*) base; (*von Möbel*) leg; **zu ~** on foot; **zu ~ gehen** to walk; **Fußball** *m* football (*Brit*), soccer; **Fußballmannschaft** *f* football (*Brit*) (*o* soccer) team; **Fußballplatz** *m* football pitch (*Brit*), soccer field (*US*); **Fußballspiel** *nt* football (*Brit*) (*o* soccer) match; **Fußballspieler(in)** *m(f)* footballer (*Brit*), soccer player; **Fußboden** *m* floor; **Fußgänger(in)** (*-s, -*) *m(f)* pedestrian; **Fußgängerüberweg** *m* pedestrian crossing (*Brit*), crosswalk (*US*); **Fußgängerzone** *f* pedestrian precinct (*Brit*) (*o* zone (*US*)); **Fußgelenk** *nt* ankle; **Fußpilz** *m* athlete's foot; **Fußtritt** *m* kick; **jdm einen ~ geben** to give sb a kick, to kick sb; **Fußweg** *m* footpath
Futon (*-s, -s*) *m* futon
Futter (*-s, -*) *nt* feed; (*Heu etc*) fodder; (*Stoff*) lining; **füttern** *vt* to feed; (*Kleidung*) to line
Futur (*-s, -e*) *nt* (*Ling*) future (tense)
Fuzzi (*-s, -s*) *m* (*fam*) guy

g

(*Durchgang*) passage; (*Auto*) gear; **den zweiten ~ einlegen** to change into second (gear); **etw in ~ bringen** to get sth going; **Gangschaltung** f gears pl; **Gangway** (-, -s) f (*Aviat*) steps pl; (*Naut*) gangway

Gans (-, *Gänse*) f goose; **Gänseblümchen** nt daisy; **Gänsehaut** f goose pimples pl (*Brit*), goose bumps pl (*US*)

ganz adj whole; (*vollständig*) complete; **~ Europa** all of Europe; **sein ~es Geld** all his money; **den ~en Tag** all day; **die ~e Zeit** all the time ▷ adv quite; (*völlig*) completely; **es hat mir ~ gut gefallen** I quite liked it; **~ schön viel** quite a lot; **~ und gar nicht** not at all; **das ist etwas ~ anderes** that's a completely different matter; **ganztägig** adj all-day; (*Arbeit, Stelle*) full-time

gar adj done, cooked ▷ adv at all; **~ nicht/nichts/keiner** not/nothing/nobody at all; **~ nicht schlecht** not bad at all

Garage (-, -n) f garage

Garantie f guarantee; **garantieren** vt to guarantee

Garderobe (-, -n) f (*Kleidung*) wardrobe; (*Abgabe*) cloakroom

Gardine f curtain

Garn (-(e)s, -e) nt thread

Garnele (-, -n) f shrimp

garnieren vt to decorate; (*Speisen*) to garnish

Garten (-s, *Gärten*) m garden; **Gärtner(in)** (-s, -) m(f) gardener; **Gärtnerei** f nursery; (*Gemüsegärtnerei*) market garden (*Brit*), truck farm (*US*)

Garzeit f cooking time

Gas (-es, -e) nt gas; **~ geben** (*Auto*) to accelerate; (*fig*) to get a move on; **Gasanzünder** m gas lighter; **Gasbrenner** m gas burner;

gab imperf von **geben**

Gabe (-, -n) f gift

Gabel (-, -n) f fork; **Gabelung** f fork

gaffen vi to gape

Gage (-, -n) f fee

gähnen vi to yawn

Galerie f gallery

Galle (-, -n) f gall; (*Organ*) gall bladder; **Gallenstein** m gallstone

Galopp (-s) m gallop; **galoppieren** vi to gallop

galt imperf von **gelten**

Gameboy® (-s, -s) m Gameboy®

gammeln vi to loaf (o hang) around; **Gammler(in)** (-s, -) m(f) layabout

gang adj: **~ und gäbe sein** to be quite normal

Gang (-(e)s, *Gänge*) m walk; (*im Flugzeug*) aisle; (*Essen, Ablauf*) course; (*Flur etc*) corridor;

Gasflasche f gas bottle;
Gasheizung f gas heating;
Gasherd m gas stove, gas cooker
(*Brit*); **Gaskocher** (*-s, -*) m
camping stove; **Gaspedal** nt
accelerator, gas pedal (*US*)
Gasse (*-, -n*) f alley
Gast (*-es, Gäste*) m guest; **Gäste
haben** to have guests;
Gastarbeiter(in) m(f) foreign
worker; **Gästebett** nt spare bed;
Gästebuch nt visitors' book;
Gästehaus nt guest house;
Gästezimmer nt guest room;
gastfreundlich adj hospitable;
Gastgeber(in) (*-s, -*) m(f) host/
hostess; **Gasthaus** nt, **Gasthof** m
inn; **Gastland** nt host country
Gastritis (*-*) f gastritis
Gastronomie f (*Gewerbe*)
catering trade
Gastspiel nt (*Sport*) away game;
Gaststätte f restaurant;
(*Trinklokal*) pub (*Brit*), bar;
Gastwirt(in) m(f) landlord/-lady
GAU (*-s, -s*) m akr = **größter
anzunehmender Unfall** MCA
Gaumen (*-s, -*) m palate
Gaze (*-, -n*) f gauze
geb. adj abk = **geboren** b. ▷ adj
abk = **geborene** née; siehe **geboren**
Gebäck (*-(e)s, -e*) nt pastries pl;
(*Kekse*) biscuits pl (*Brit*), cookies pl
(*US*)
gebacken pp von **backen**
Gebärdensprache f sign
language
Gebärmutter f womb
Gebäude (*-s, -*) nt building
geben (*gab, gegeben*) vt, vi to give
(*jdm etw* sb sth, sth to sb); (*Karten*)
to deal; **lass dir eine Quittung
~** ask for a receipt ▷ vt impers: **es
gibt** there is/are; (*in Zukunft*) there
will be; **das gibt's nicht** I don't
believe it ▷ vr: **sich ~** (*sich
verhalten*) to behave, to act; **das**

gibt sich wieder it'll sort itself out
Gebet (*-(e)s, -e*) nt prayer
gebeten pp von **bitten**
Gebiet (*-(e)s, -e*) nt area;
(*Hoheitsgebiet*) territory; (*fig*) field
gebildet adj educated; (*belesen*)
well-read
Gebirge (*-s, -*) nt mountains pl;
gebirgig adj mountainous
Gebiss (*-es, -e*) nt teeth pl;
(*künstlich*) dentures pl; **gebissen**
pp von **beißen**; **Gebissreiniger** m
denture tablets pl
Gebläse (*-s, -*) nt fan, blower
geblasen pp von **blasen**
geblieben pp von **bleiben**
gebogen pp von **biegen**
geboren pp von **gebären** ▷ adj
born; **Andrea Jordan, geborene
Christian** Andrea Jordan, née
Christian
geborgen pp von **bergen** ▷ adj
secure, safe
geboten pp von **bieten**
gebracht pp von **bringen**
gebrannt pp von **brennen**
gebraten pp von **braten**
gebrauchen vt to use;
Gebrauchsanweisung f direc-
tions pl for use; **gebrauchsfertig**
adj ready to use; **gebraucht** adj
used; **etw ~ kaufen** to buy sth
secondhand; **Gebrauchtwagen**
m secondhand (o used) car
gebräunt adj tanned
gebrochen pp von **brechen**
Gebühr (*-, -en*) f charge; (*Maut*)
toll; (*Honorar*) fee; **Gebühren-
einheit** f (*Tel*) unit;
gebührenfrei adj free of charge;
(*Telefonnummer*) freefone® (*Brit*),
toll-free (*US*); **gebührenpflichtig**
adj subject to charges; **~e Straße**
toll road
gebunden pp von **binden**
Geburt (*-, -en*) f birth; **gebürtig**
adj: **er ist ~er Schweizer** he is

Swiss by birth; **Geburtsdatum**
nt date of birth; **Geburtsjahr** *nt*
year of birth; **Geburtsname** *m*
birth name; (*einer Frau*) maiden
name; **Geburtsort** *m* birthplace;
Geburtstag *m* birthday;
herzlichen Glückwunsch zum ~!
Happy Birthday; **Geburtsurkunde**
f birth certificate
Gebüsch (-(e)s, -e) *nt* bushes *pl*
gedacht *pp von* **denken**
Gedächtnis *nt* memory; **im**
~ behalten to remember
Gedanke (-ns, -n) *m* thought;
sich (*dat*) **über etw** (*akk*) **~n**
machen to think about sth;
(*besorgt*) to be worried about sth;
Gedankenstrich *m* dash
Gedeck (-(e)s, -e) *nt* place
setting; (*Speisenfolge*) set meal
Gedenkstätte *f* memorial;
Gedenktafel *f* commemorative
plaque
Gedicht (-(e)s, -e) *nt* poem
Gedränge (-s) *nt* crush, crowd
gedrungen *pp von* **dringen**
Geduld (-) *f* patience; **geduldig**
adj patient
gedurft *pp von* **dürfen**
geehrt *adj*: **Sehr ~er Herr Young**
Dear Mr Young
geeignet *adj* suitable
Gefahr (-, -en) *f* danger; **auf**
eigene ~ at one's own risk; **außer**
~ out of danger; **gefährden** *vt* to
endanger
gefahren *pp von* **fahren**
gefährlich *adj* dangerous
Gefälle (-s, -) *nt* gradient, slope
gefallen *pp von* **fallen** ▷ *irr vi*:
jdm ~ to please sb; **er/es gefällt**
mir I like him/it; **sich** (*dat*) **etw**
~ lassen to put up with sth
Gefallen (-s, -) *m* favour; **jdm**
einen ~ tun to do sb a favour
gefälligst *adv* ..., will you!; **sei**
~ still! be quiet, will you!

gefangen *pp von* **fangen**
Gefängnis *nt* prison
Gefäß (-es, -e) *nt* (*Behälter*)
container, receptacle; (*Anat, Bot*)
vessel
gefasst *adj* composed, calm; **auf**
etw (*akk*) **~ sein** to be prepared (*o*
ready) for sth
geflochten *pp von* **flechten**
geflogen *pp von* **fliegen**
geflossen *pp von* **fließen**
Geflügel (-s) *nt* poultry
gefragt *adj* in demand
gefressen *pp von* **fressen**
Gefrierbeutel *m* freezer bag;
gefrieren *irr vi* to freeze;
Gefrierfach *nt* freezer
compartment; **Gefrierschrank**
m (upright) freezer; **Gefriertruhe**
f (chest) freezer
gefroren *pp von* **frieren**
Gefühl (-(e)s, -e) *nt* feeling
gefunden *pp von* **finden**
gegangen *pp von* **gehen**
gegeben *pp von* **geben**;
gegebenenfalls *adv* if need
be

 SCHLÜSSELWORT

gegen *prep +akk* **1** against; **nichts**
gegen jdn haben to have nothing
against sb; **X gegen Y** (*Sport, Jur*) X
versus Y; **ein Mittel gegen**
Schnupfen something for colds
2 (*in Richtung auf*) towards; **gegen**
Osten to(wards) the east; **gegen**
Abend towards evening; **gegen**
einen Baum fahren to drive into a
tree
3 (*ungefähr*) round about; **gegen 3**
Uhr around 3 o'clock
4 (*gegenüber*) towards; (*ungefähr*)
around; **gerecht gegen alle** fair to
all
5 (*im Austausch für*) for; **gegen bar**
for cash; **gegen Quittung** against

a receipt
6 (*verglichen mit*) compared with

Gegend (-, -en) f area; **hier in der ~** around here
gegeneinander adv against one another
Gegenfahrbahn f opposite lane; **Gegenmittel** nt remedy (*gegen* for); **Gegenrichtung** f opposite direction; **Gegensatz** m contrast; **im ~ zu** in contrast to; **gegensätzlich** adj conflicting; **gegenseitig** adj mutual; **sich ~ helfen** to help each other
Gegenstand m object; (*Thema*) subject
Gegenteil nt opposite; **im ~** on the contrary; **gegenteilig** adj opposite, contrary
gegenüber prep +dat opposite; (*zu jdm*) to(wards); (*angesichts*) in the face of ▷ adv opposite; **gegenüber|stehen** vt to face; (*Problemen*) to be faced with; **gegenüber|stellen** vt to confront (*dat* with); (*fig*) compare (*dat* with)
Gegenverkehr m oncoming traffic; **Gegenwart** (-) f present (tense)
Gegenwind m headwind
gegessen pp von **essen**
geglichen pp von **gleichen**
geglitten pp von **gleiten**
Gegner(in) (-s, -) m(f) opponent
gegolten pp von **gelten**
gegossen pp von **gießen**
gegraben pp von **graben**
gegriffen pp von **greifen**
gehabt pp von **haben**
Gehackte(s) nt mince(d meat) (*Brit*), ground meat (*US*)
Gehalt (-(e)s, -e) m content ▷ (-(e)s, Gehälter) nt salary
gehalten pp von **halten**
gehangen pp von **hängen**
gehässig adj spiteful, nasty

gehauen pp von **hauen**
gehbehindert adj: **sie ist ~** she can't walk properly
geheim adj secret; **etw ~ halten** to keep sth secret; **Geheimnis** nt secret; (*rätselhaft*) mystery; **geheimnisvoll** adj mysterious; **Geheimnummer** f, **Geheimzahl** f (*von Kreditkarte*) PIN number
geheißen pp von **heißen**
gehen (*ging, gegangen*) vt, vi to go; (*zu Fuß*) to walk; (*funktionieren*) to work; **über die Straße ~** to cross the street; **~ nach** (*Fenster*) to face ▷ vi impers: **wie geht es (dir)?** how are you (o things)?; **mir/ihm geht es gut** I'm/he's (doing) fine; **geht das?** is that possible?; **geht's noch?** can you still manage?; **es geht** not too bad, OK; **das geht nicht** that's not on; **es geht um ...** it's about ...
Gehirn (-(e)s, -e) nt brain; **Gehirnerschütterung** f concussion
gehoben pp von **heben**
geholfen pp von **helfen**
Gehör (-(e)s) nt hearing
gehorchen vi to obey (*jdm* sb)
gehören vi to belong (*jdm* to sb); **wem gehört das Buch?** whose book is this?; **gehört es dir?** is it yours? ▷ vr impers: **das gehört sich nicht** it's not done
gehörlos adj deaf
gehorsam adj obedient
Gehsteig m
Gehweg (-s, -e) m pavement (*Brit*), sidewalk (*US*)
Geier (-s, -) m vulture
Geige (-, -n) f violin
geil adj randy (*Brit*), horny (*US*); (*fam: toll*) fantastic
Geisel (-, -n) f hostage
Geist (-(e)s, -er) m spirit; (*Gespenst*) ghost; (*Verstand*) mind; **Geisterbahn** f ghost train, tunnel

of horror (US); **Geisterfahrer(in)**
m(f) person driving the wrong way on
the motorway
geizig adj stingy
gekannt pp von **kennen**
geklungen pp von **klingen**
geknickt adj (fig) dejected
gekniffen pp von **kneifen**
gekommen pp von **kommen**
gekonnt pp von **können** ▷ adj
skilful
gekrochen pp von **kriechen**
Gel (-s, -s) nt gel
Gelächter (-s, -) nt laughter
geladen pp von **laden** ▷ adj
loaded; (Elek) live; (fig) furious
gelähmt adj paralysed
Gelände (-s, -) nt land, terrain;
(Fabrik, Sportgelände) grounds pl;
(Baugelände) site
Geländer (-s, -) nt railing;
(Treppengeländer) banister
Geländewagen m off-road
vehicle
gelang imperf von **gelingen**
gelassen pp von **lassen** ▷ adj
calm, composed
Gelatine f gelatine
gelaufen pp von **laufen**
gelaunt adj: **gut/schlecht ~** in a
good/bad mood
gelb adj yellow; (Ampel) amber,
yellow (US); **gelblich** adj
yellowish; **Gelbsucht** f jaundice
Geld (-(e)s, -er) nt money;
Geldautomat m cash machine (o
dispenser (Brit), ATM (US));
Geldbeutel m, **Geldbörse** f
purse; **Geldbuße** f fine;
Geldschein m (bank)note (Brit),
bill (US); **Geldstrafe** f fine;
Geldstück nt coin; **Geldwechsel**
m exchange of money; (Ort)
bureau de change;
Geldwechselautomat m,
Geldwechsler (-s, -) m change
machine

Gelee (-s, -s) nt jelly
gelegen pp von **liegen** ▷ adj
situated; (passend) convenient;
etw kommt jdm ~ sth is
convenient for sb
Gelegenheit f opportunity;
(Anlass) occasion
gelegentlich adj occasional
▷ adv occasionally; (bei
Gelegenheit) some time (or other)
Gelenk (-(e)s, -e) nt joint
gelernt adj skilled
gelesen pp von **lesen**
geliehen pp von **leihen**
gelingen (gelang, gelungen) vi to
succeed; **es ist mir gelungen, ihn
zu erreichen** I managed to get
hold of him
gelitten pp von **leiden**
gelockt adj curly
gelogen pp von **lügen**
gelten (galt, gegolten) vt (wert
sein) to be worth; **jdm viel/wenig
~** to mean a lot/not to mean much
to sb ▷ vi (gültig sein) to be valid;
(erlaubt sein) to be allowed; **jdm
~** (gemünzt sein auf) to be meant for
(o aimed at) sb; **etw ~ lassen** to
accept sth; **als etw ~** to be
considered to be sth;
Geltungsdauer f: **eine ~ von
fünf Tagen haben** to be valid for
five days
gelungen pp von **gelingen**
gemahlen pp von **mahlen**
Gemälde (-s, -) nt painting,
picture
gemäß prep +dat in accordance
with ▷ adj appropriate (dat to)
gemein adj (niederträchtig) mean,
nasty; (gewöhnlich) common
Gemeinde (-, -n) f district,
community; (Pfarrgemeinde)
parish; (Kirchengemeinde)
congregation
gemeinsam adj joint, common
▷ adv together, jointly; **das Haus**

gehört uns beiden ~ the house belongs to both of us

Gemeinschaft *f* community; **~ Unabhängiger Staaten** Commonwealth of Independent States

gemeint *pp von* **meinen**; **das war nicht so ~** I didn't mean it like that

gemessen *pp von* **messen**

gemieden *pp von* **meiden**

gemischt *adj* mixed

gemocht *pp von* **mögen**

Gemüse (*-s, -*) *nt* vegetables *pl*; **Gemüsehändler(in)** *m(f)* greengrocer

gemusst *pp von* **müssen**

gemustert *adj* patterned

gemütlich *adj* comfortable, cosy; (*Mensch*) good-natured, easy-going; **mach es dir ~** make yourself at home

genannt *pp von* **nennen**

genau *adj* exact, precise ▷ *adv* exactly, precisely; **~ in der Mitte** right in the middle; **es mit etw ~ nehmen** to be particular about sth; **~ genommen** strictly speaking; **ich weiß es ~** I know for certain (*o* for sure); **genauso** *adv* exactly the same (way); **~ gut/viel/viele Leute** just as well/much/many people (*wie* as)

genehmigen *vt* to approve; **sich** (*dat*) **etw ~** to indulge in sth; **Genehmigung** *f* approval

Generalkonsulat *nt* consulate general

Generation *f* generation

Genf (*-s*) *nt* Geneva; **~er See** Lake Geneva

Genforschung *f* genetic research

genial *adj* brilliant

Genick (*-(e)s, -e*) *nt* (back of the) neck

Genie (*-s, -s*) *nt* genius

genieren *vr*: **sich ~** to feel awkward; **ich geniere mich vor ihm** he makes me feel embarrassed

genießen (*genoss, genossen*) *vt* to enjoy

Genitiv *m* genitive (case)

genmanipuliert *adj* genetically modified, GM

genommen *pp von* **nehmen**

genoss *imperf von* **genießen**

genossen *pp von* **genießen**

Gentechnik *f* genetic technology; **gentechnisch** *adv*: **~ verändert** genetically modified, GM

genug *adv* enough

genügen *vi* to be enough (*jdm* for sb); **danke, das genügt** thanks, that's enough (*o* that will do)

Genuss (*-es, Genüsse*) *m* pleasure; (*Zusichnehmen*) consumption

geöffnet *adj* (*Geschäft etc*) open

Geografie *f* geography

Geologie *f* geology

Georgien (*-s*) *nt* Georgia

Gepäck (*-(e)s*) *nt* luggage (*Brit*), baggage; **Gepäckabfertigung** *f* luggage (*Brit*) (*o* baggage) check-in; **Gepäckablage** *f* luggage (*Brit*) (*o* baggage) rack; **Gepäckannahme** *f* (*zur Beförderung*) luggage (*Brit*) (*o* baggage) office; (*zur Aufbewahrung*) left-luggage office (*Brit*), baggage checkroom (*US*); **Gepäckaufbewahrung** *f* left-luggage office (*Brit*), baggage checkroom (*US*); **Gepäckausgabe** *f* luggage (*Brit*) (*o* baggage) office; (*am Flughafen*) baggage reclaim; **Gepäckband** *nt* luggage (*Brit*) (*o* baggage) conveyor; **Gepäckkontrolle** *f* luggage (*Brit*) (*o* baggage) check; **Gepäckstück** *nt* item of luggage (*Brit*) (*o* baggage (*US*)); **Gepäckträger** *m* porter; (*an Fahrrad*) carrier;

Gepäckversicherung f luggage (*Brit*) (o baggage) insurance; **Gepäckwagen** m luggage van (*Brit*), baggage car (*US*)
gepfiffen pp von **pfeifen**
gepflegt adj well-groomed; (*Park*) well looked after
gequollen pp von **quellen**

 SCHLÜSSELWORT

gerade adj straight; (*aufrecht*) upright; **eine gerade Zahl** an even number
▷ adv **1** (*genau*) just, exactly; (*speziell*) especially; **gerade deshalb** that's just o exactly why; **das ist es ja gerade!** that's just it!; **gerade du** you especially; **warum gerade ich?** why me (of all people)?; **jetzt gerade nicht!** not now!; **gerade neben** right next to
2 (*eben, soeben*) just; **er wollte gerade aufstehen** he was just about to get up; **gerade erst** only just; **gerade noch** (only) just

geradeaus adv straight ahead
gerannt pp von **rennen**
geraspelt adj grated
Gerät (-(e)s, -e) nt device, gadget; (*Werkzeug*) tool; (*Radio, Fernseher*) set; (*Zubehör*) equipment
geraten pp von **raten** ▷ irr vi to turn out; **gut/schlecht ~** to turn out well/badly; **an jdn ~** to come across sb; **in etw** (*akk*) **~** to get into sth
geräuchert adj smoked
geräumig adj roomy
Geräusch (-(e)s, -e) nt sound; (*unangenehm*) noise
gerecht adj fair; (*Strafe, Belohnung*) just; **jdm/einer Sache ~ werden** to do justice to sb/sth
gereizt adj irritable

Gericht (-(e)s, -e) nt (*Jur*) court; (*Essen*) dish
gerieben pp von **reiben**
gering adj small; (*unbedeutend*) slight; (*niedrig*) low; (*Zeit*) short; **geringfügig** adj slight, minor ▷ adv slightly
gerissen pp von **reißen**
geritten pp von **reiten**
gern(e) adv willingly, gladly; **etw ~ tun** to like doing sth; **~ geschehen** you're welcome; **gern|haben, gern mögen** irr vt to like
gerochen pp von **riechen**
Gerste (-, -n) f barley; **Gerstenkorn** nt (*im Auge*) stye
Geruch (-(e)s, Gerüche) m smell
Gerücht (-(e)s, -e) nt rumour
gerufen pp von **rufen**
Gerümpel (-s) nt junk
gerungen pp von **ringen**
Gerüst (-(e)s, -e) nt (*auf Bau*) scaffolding; (*Gestell*) trestle; (*fig*) framework (*zu* of)
gesalzen pp von **salzen**
gesamt adj whole, entire; (*Kosten*) total; (*Werke*) complete; **Gesamtschule** f ≈ comprehensive school
gesandt pp von **senden**
Gesäß (-es, -e) nt bottom
geschaffen pp von **schaffen**
Geschäft (-(e)s, -e) nt business; (*Laden*) shop; (*Geschäftsabschluss*) deal; **geschäftlich** adj commercial ▷ adv on business; **Geschäftsfrau** f businesswoman; **Geschäftsführer(in)** m(f) managing director; (*von Laden*) manager; **Geschäftsleitung** f executive board; **Geschäftsmann** m businessman; **Geschäftsreise** f business trip; **Geschäftsstraße** f shopping street; **Geschäftszeiten** pl business (o opening) hours pl

geschehen (*geschah, geschehen*) *vi* to happen

Geschenk (*-(e)s, -e*) *nt* present, gift; **Geschenkgutschein** *m* gift voucher; **Geschenkpapier** *nt* gift-wrapping paper, giftwrap

Geschichte (*-, -n*) *f* story; (*Sache*) affair; (*Hist*) history

geschickt *adj* skilful

geschieden *pp von* **scheiden** ▷ *adj* divorced

geschienen *pp von* **scheinen**

Geschirr (*-(e)s, -e*) *nt* crockery; (*zum Kochen*) pots and pans *pl*; (*von Pferd*) harness; **~ spülen** to do (*o* wash) the dishes, to do the washing-up (*Brit*);
Geschirrspülmaschine *f* dishwasher; **Geschirrspülmittel** *nt* washing-up liquid (*Brit*), dishwashing liquid (*US*);
Geschirrtuch *nt* tea towel (*Brit*), dish towel (*US*)

geschissen *pp von* **scheißen**

geschlafen *pp von* **schlafen**

geschlagen *pp von* **schlagen**

Geschlecht (*-(e)s, -er*) *nt* sex; (*Ling*) gender; **Geschlechtskrankheit** *f* sexually transmitted disease, STD; **Geschlechtsorgan** *nt* sexual organ;
Geschlechtsverkehr *m* sexual intercourse

geschlichen *pp von* **schleichen**

geschliffen *pp von* **schleifen**

geschlossen *adj* closed

Geschmack (*-(e)s, Geschmäcke*) *m* taste; **geschmacklos** *adj* tasteless; **Geschmack(s)sache** *f*: **das ist ~** that's a matter of taste; **geschmackvoll** *adj* tasteful

geschmissen *pp von* **schmeißen**

geschmolzen *pp von* **schmelzen**

geschnitten *pp von* **schneiden**

geschoben *pp von* **schieben**

Geschoss (*-es, -e*) *nt* (*Stockwerk*) floor

geschossen *pp von* **schießen**

Geschrei (*-s*) *nt* cries *pl*; (*fig*) fuss

geschrieben *pp von* **schreiben**

geschrie(e)n *pp von* **schreien**

geschützt *adj* protected

Geschwätz (*-es*) *nt* chatter; (*Klatsch*) gossip; **geschwätzig** *adj* talkative, gossipy

geschweige *adv*: **~ (denn)** let alone

geschwiegen *pp von* **schweigen**

Geschwindigkeit *f* speed; (*Phys*) velocity; **Geschwindigkeitsbegrenzung** *f* speed limit

Geschwister *pl* brothers and sisters *pl*

geschwollen *adj* (*angeschwollen*) swollen; (*Rede*) pompous

geschwommen *pp von* **schwimmen**

geschworen *pp von* **schwören**

Geschwulst (*-, Geschwülste*) *f* growth

Geschwür (*-(e)s, -e*) *nt* ulcer

gesehen *pp von* **sehen**

gesellig *adj* sociable; **Gesellschaft** *f* society; (*Begleitung*) company; (*Abend~*) party; **~ mit beschränkter Haftung** limited company (*Brit*), limited corporation (*US*)

gesessen *pp von* **sitzen**

Gesetz (*-es, -e*) *nt* law; **gesetzlich** *adj* legal; **~er Feiertag** public (*o* bank (*Brit*) *o* legal (*US*)) holiday; **gesetzwidrig** *adj* illegal

Gesicht (*-(e)s, -er*) *nt* face; (*Miene*) expression; **mach doch nicht so ein ~!** stop pulling such a face!; **Gesichtscreme** *f* face cream; **Gesichtswasser** *nt* toner

gesoffen *pp von* **saufen**

gesogen *pp von* **saugen**

gespannt *adj* tense; (*begierig*) eager; **ich bin ~, ob ...** I wonder if ...; **auf etw/jdn ~ sein** to look forward to sth/to seeing sb

Gespenst (-(e)s, -er) nt ghost

gesperrt adj closed

gesponnen pp von **spinnen**

Gespräch (-(e)s, -e) nt talk, conversation; (Diskussion) discussion; (Anruf) call

gesprochen pp von **sprechen**

gesprungen pp von **springen**

Gestalt (-, -en) f form, shape; (Mensch) figure

gestanden pp von **stehen, gestehen**

Gestank (-(e)s) m stench

gestatten vt to permit, to allow; **~ Sie?** may I?

Geste (-, -n) f gesture

gestehen irr vt to confess

gestern adv yesterday; **~ Abend/Morgen** yesterday evening/morning

gestiegen pp von **steigen**

gestochen pp von **stechen**

gestohlen pp von **stehlen**

gestorben pp von **sterben**

gestört adj disturbed; (Empfang) poor

gestoßen pp von **stoßen**

gestreift adj striped

gestrichen pp von **streichen**

gestritten pp von **streiten**

gestunken pp von **stinken**

gesund adj healthy; **wieder ~ werden** to get better; **Gesundheit** f health; **~!** bless you!; **gesundheitsschädlich** adj unhealthy

gesungen pp von **singen**

gesunken pp von **sinken**

getan pp von **tun**

getragen pp von **tragen**

Getränk (-(e)s, -e) nt drink; **Getränkeautomat** m drinks machine; **Getränkekarte** f list of drinks

Getreide (-s, -) nt cereals pl, grain

getrennt adj separate; **~ leben** to live apart; **~ zahlen** to pay separately

getreten pp von **treten**

Getriebe (-s, -) nt (Auto) gearbox

getrieben pp von **treiben**

Getriebeschaden m gearbox damage

getroffen pp von **treffen**

getrunken pp von **trinken**

Getue nt fuss

geübt adj experienced

gewachsen pp von **wachsen** ▷ adj: **jdm/einer Sache ~ sein** to be a match for sb/up to sth

Gewähr (-) f guarantee; **keine ~ übernehmen für** to accept no responsibility for

Gewalt (-, -en) f (Macht) power; (Kontrolle) control; (große Kraft) force; (~taten) violence; **mit aller ~** with all one's might; **gewaltig** adj tremendous; (Irrtum) huge

gewandt pp von **wenden** ▷ adj (flink) nimble; (geschickt) skilful

gewann imperf von **gewinnen**

gewaschen pp von **waschen**

Gewebe (-s, -) nt (Stoff) fabric; (Bio) tissue

Gewehr (-(e)s, -e) nt rifle, gun

Geweih (-(e)s, -e) nt antlers pl

gewellt adj (Haare) wavy

gewendet pp von **wenden**

Gewerbe (-s, -) nt trade; **Gewerbegebiet** nt industrial estate (Brit) (o park (US)); **gewerblich** adj commercial

Gewerkschaft f trade union

gewesen pp von **sein**

Gewicht (-(e)s, -e) nt weight; (fig) importance

gewiesen pp von **weisen**

Gewinn (-(e)s, -e) m profit; (bei Spiel) winnings pl; **gewinnen** (gewann, gewonnen) vt to win; (erwerben) to gain; (Kohle, Öl) to extract ▷ vi to win; (profitieren) to gain; **Gewinner(in)** (-s, -) m(f) winner

gewiss adj certain ▷ adv certainly

Gewissen (-s, -) nt conscience; **ein gutes/schlechtes ~ haben** to have a clear/bad conscience

Gewitter (-s, -) nt thunderstorm; **gewittern** vi impers: **es gewittert** it's thundering

gewogen pp von **wiegen**

gewöhnen vt **jdn an etw** (akk) ~ to accustom sb to sth ▷ vr: **sich an jdn/etw ~** to get used (o accustomed) to sb/sth; **Gewohnheit** f habit; (Brauch) custom; **gewöhnlich** adj usual; (durchschnittlich) ordinary; (pej) common; **wie ~** as usual; **gewohnt** adj usual; **etw ~ sein** to be used to sth

Gewölbe (-s, -) nt (Deckengewölbe) vault

gewonnen pp von **gewinnen**

geworben pp von **werben**

geworden pp von **werden**

geworfen pp von **werfen**

Gewürz (-es, -e) nt spice; **Gewürznelke** f clove; **gewürzt** adj seasoned

gewusst pp von **wissen**

Gezeiten pl tides pl

gezogen pp von **ziehen**

gezwungen pp von **zwingen**

Gibraltar (-s) nt Gibraltar

Gicht (-) f gout

Giebel (-s, -) m gable

gierig adj greedy

gießen (goss, gegossen) vt to pour; (Blumen) to water; (Metall) to cast; **Gießkanne** f watering can

Gift (-(e)s, -e) nt poison; **giftig** adj poisonous

Gigabyte nt gigabyte

Gin (-s, -s) m gin

ging imperf von **gehen**

Gin Tonic (-(s), -s) m gin and tonic

Gipfel (-s, -) m summit, peak; (Pol) summit; (fig: Höhepunkt) height

Gips (-es, -e) m (a. Med) plaster; **Gipsbein** nt: **sie hat ein ~** she's got her leg in plaster; **Gipsverband** m plaster cast

Giraffe (-, -n) f giraffe

Girokonto nt current account (Brit), checking account (US)

Gitarre (-, -n) f guitar

Gitter (-s, -) nt bars pl

glänzen vi (a. fig) to shine; **glänzend** adj shining; (fig) brilliant

Glas (-es, Gläser) nt glass; (Marmelade) jar; **zwei ~ Wein** two glasses of wine; **Glascontainer** m bottle bank; **Glaser(in)** m(f) glazier; **Glasscheibe** f pane (of glass); **Glassplitter** m splinter of glass

Glasur f glaze; (Gastr) icing

glatt adj smooth; (rutschig) slippery; (Lüge) downright; **Glatteis** nt (black) ice

Glatze (-, -n) f bald head; (fam: Skinhead) skinhead

glauben vt, vi to believe (an +akk in); (meinen) to think; **jdm ~** to believe sb

gleich adj equal; (identisch) same, identical; **alle Menschen sind ~** all people are the same; **es ist mir ~** it's all the same to me ▷ adv equally; (sofort) straight away; (bald) in a minute; **~ groß/alt** the same size/age; **~ nach/an** right after/at; **Gleichberechtigung** f equal rights pl; **gleichen** (glich, geglichen) vi: **jdm/einer Sache ~** to be like sb/sth ▷ vr: **sich ~** to be alike; **gleichfalls** adv likewise; **danke ~!** thanks, and the same to you; **gleichgültig** adj indifferent; **gleichmäßig** adj regular; (Verteilung) even, equal;

gleichzeitig *adj* simultaneous ▷ *adv* at the same time

Gleis (-es, -e) *nt* track, rails *pl*; (*Bahnsteig*) platform

gleiten (*glitt, geglitten*) *vi* to glide; (*rutschen*) to slide; **Gleitschirmfliegen** (-s) *nt* paragliding

Gletscher (-s, -) *m* glacier; **Gletscherskifahren** *nt* glacier skiing; **Gletscherspalte** *f* crevasse

glich *imperf von* **gleichen**

Glied (-(e)s, -er) *nt* (*Arm, Bein*) limb; (*von Kette*) link; (*Penis*) penis; **Gliedmaßen** *pl* limbs *pl*

glitschig *adj* slippery

glitt *imperf von* **gleiten**

glitzern *vi* to glitter; (*Sterne*) to twinkle

Glocke (-, -n) *f* bell; **Glockenspiel** *nt* chimes *pl*

Glotze (-, -n) *f* (*fam: TV*) box; **glotzen** *vi* (*fam*) to stare

Glück (-(e)s) *nt* luck; (*Freude*) happiness; **~ haben** to be lucky; **viel ~!** good luck; **zum ~** fortunately; **glücklich** *adj* lucky; (*froh*) happy; **glücklicherweise** *adj* fortunately; **Glückwunsch** *m* congratulations *pl*; **herzlichen ~ zur bestandenen Prüfung** congratulations on passing your exam; **herzlichen ~ zum Geburtstag!** Happy Birthday

Glühbirne *f* light bulb; **glühen** *vi* to glow; **Glühwein** *m* mulled wine

GmbH (-, -s) *f abk* = **Gesellschaft mit beschränkter Haftung** ≈ Ltd (*Brit*), ≈ Inc (*US*)

Gokart (-(s), -s) *m* go-kart

Gold (-(e)s) *nt* gold; **golden** *adj* gold; (*fig*) golden; **Goldfisch** *m* goldfish; **Goldmedaille** *f* gold medal; **Goldschmied(in)** *m(f)*

goldsmith

Golf (-(e)s, -e) *m* gulf; **der ~ von Biskaya** the Bay of Biscay ▷ (-s) *nt* golf; **Golfplatz** *m* golf course; **Golfschläger** *m* golf club

Gondel (-, -n) *f* gondola; (*Seilbahn*) cable-car

gönnen *vt*: **ich gönne es ihm** I'm really pleased for him; **sich** (*dat*) **etw ~** to allow oneself sth

goss *imperf von* **gießen**

gotisch *adj* Gothic

Gott (-es, Götter) *m* God; (*Gottheit*) god; **Gottesdienst** *m* service; **Göttin** *f* goddess

Grab (-(e)s, Gräber) *nt* grave

graben (*grub, gegraben*) *vt* to dig; **Graben** (-s, Gräben) *m* ditch

Grabstein *m* gravestone

Grad (-(e)s, -e) *m* degree; **wir haben 30 ~ Celsius** it's 30 degrees Celsius, it's 86 degrees Fahrenheit; **bis zu einem gewissen ~** up to a certain extent

Graf (-en, -en) *m* count; (*in Großbritannien*) earl

Graffiti *pl* graffiti *sing*

Grafik (-, -en) *f* graph; (*Kunstwerk*) graphic; (*Illustration*) diagram; **Grafikkarte** *f* (*Inform*) graphics card; **Grafikprogramm** *nt* (*Inform*) graphics software

Gräfin (-, -nen) *f* countess

Gramm (-s) *nt* gram(me)

Grammatik *f* grammar

Grapefruit (-, -s) *f* grapefruit

Graphik *f siehe* **Grafik**

Gras (-es, Gräser) *nt* grass

grässlich *adj* horrible

Gräte (-, -n) *f* (fish)bone

gratis *adj, adv* free (of charge)

gratulieren *vi*: **jdm** (**zu etw**) **~** to congratulate sb (on sth); (**ich**) **gratuliere!** congratulations!

grau *adj* grey, gray (*US*); **grauhaarig** *adj* grey-haired

grausam *adj* cruel

gravierend adj (Fehler) serious
greifen (griff, gegriffen) vt to seize; **zu etw ~** (fig) to resort to sth ▷ vi (Regel etc) to have an effect (bei on)
grell adj harsh
Grenze (-, -n) f boundary; (Staat) border; (Schranke) limit; **grenzen** vi to border (an +akk on); **Grenzkontrolle** f border control; **Grenzübergang** m border crossing point; **Grenzverkehr** m border traffic
Grieche (-n, -n) m Greek; **Griechenland** nt Greece; **Griechin** f Greek; **griechisch** adj Greek; **Griechisch** nt Greek
griesgrämig adj grumpy
Grieß (-es, -e) m (Gastr) semolina
griff imperf von **greifen**
Griff (-(e)s, -e) m grip; (Tür etc) handle; **griffbereit** adj handy
Grill (-s, -s) m grill; (im Freien) barbecue
Grille (-, -n) f cricket
grillen vt to grill ▷ vi to have a barbecue; **Grillfest** nt, **Grillfete** f barbecue; **Grillkohle** f charcoal
grinsen vi to grin; (höhnisch) to sneer
Grippe (-, -n) f flu; **Grippeschutzimpfung** f flu vaccination
grob adj coarse; (Fehler, Verstoß) gross; (Einschätzung) rough
Grönland (-s) nt Greenland
groß adj big, large; (hoch) tall; (fig) great; (Buchstabe) capital; (erwachsen) grown-up; **im Großen und Ganzen** on the whole ▷ adv greatly; **großartig** adj wonderful
Großbritannien (-s) nt (Great) Britain
Großbuchstabe m capital letter
Größe (-, -n) f size; (Länge) height; (fig) greatness; **welche**
~ haben Sie? what size do you take?
Großeltern pl grandparents pl; **Großhandel** m wholesale trade; **Großmarkt** m hypermarket; **Großmutter** f grandmother; **Großraum** m: **der ~ Manchester** Greater Manchester; **groß|schreiben** irr vt to write with a capital letter; **Großstadt** f city; **Großvater** m grandfather; **großzügig** adj generous; (Planung) on a large scale
Grotte (-, -n) f grotto
grub imperf von **graben**
Grübchen nt dimple
Grube (-, -n) f pit
grüezi interj (schweizerisch) hello
Gruft (-, -en) f vault
grün adj green; **~er Salat** lettuce; **~e Bohnen** French beans; **der ~e Punkt** symbol for recyclable packaging; **im ~en Bereich** hunky-dory

• **GRÜNER PUNKT**
•
• The **grüner Punkt** is the green
• spot symbol which appears on
• packaging, indicating that the
• packaging should not be
• thrown into the normal
• household refuse but kept
• separate to be recycled through
• the **DSD** (Duales System
• Deutschland) system. The
• recycling is financed by licences
• bought by the manufacturer
• from the 'DSD' and the cost of
• this is often passed on to the
• consumer.

Grünanlage f park
Grund (-(e)s, Gründe) m (Ursache) reason; (Erdboden) ground; (See, Gefäß) bottom; (Grundbesitz) land, property; **aus gesundheitlichen**

Gründen for health reasons; **im ~e** basically; **aus diesem ~** for this reason

gründen vt to found; **Gründer(in)** m(f) founder

Grundgebühr f basic charge; **Grundgesetz** nt (German) Constitution

gründlich adj thorough

Gründonnerstag m Maundy Thursday

grundsätzlich adj fundamental, basic; **sie kommt ~ zu spät** she's always late; **Grundschule** f primary school; **Grundstück** nt plot; (Anwesen) estate; (Baugrundstück) site; **Grundwasser** nt ground water

Grüne(r) mf (Pol) Green; **die ~n** the Green Party

Gruppe (-, -n) f group; **Gruppenermäßigung** f group discount; **Gruppenreise** f group tour

Gruß (-es, Grüße) m greeting; **viele Grüße** best wishes; **Grüße an** (+akk) regards to; **mit freundlichen Grüßen** Yours sincerely (Brit), Sincerely yours (US); **sag ihm einen schönen ~ von mir** give him my regards; **grüßen** vt to greet; **grüß deine Mutter von mir** give your mother my regards; **Julia lässt (euch) ~** Julia sends (you) her regards

gucken vi to look

Gulasch (-(e)s, -e) nt goulash

gültig adj valid

Gummi (-s, -s) m o nt rubber; **Gummiband** nt rubber (o elastic (Brit)) band; **Gummibärchen** pl gums pl (in the shape of a bear) (Brit), gumdrops pl (in the shape of a bear) (US); **Gummihandschuhe** pl rubber gloves pl; **Gummistiefel** m wellington (boot) (Brit), rubber boot (US)

günstig adj favourable; (Preis) good

gurgeln vi to gurgle; (im Mund) to gargle

Gurke (-, -n) f cucumber; **saure ~** gherkin

Gurt (-(e)s, -e) m belt

Gürtel (-s, -) m belt; (Geo) zone; **Gürtelrose** f shingles sing

GUS (-) f akr = **Gemeinschaft Unabhängiger Staaten** CIS

◯ SCHLÜSSELWORT

gut adj good; **alles Gute** all the best; **also gut** all right then
▷ adv well; **gut gehen** to work, to come off; **es geht jdm gut** sb's doing fine; **gut gemeint** well meant; **gut schmecken** to taste good; **jdm guttun** to do sb good; **gut, aber ...** OK, but ...; **(na) gut, ich komme** all right, I'll come; **gut drei Stunden** a good three hours; **das kann gut sein** that may well be; **lass es gut sein** that'll do

Gutachten (-s, -) nt report; **Gutachter(in)** (-s, -) m(f) expert

gutartig adj (Med) benign

Güter pl goods pl; **Güterbahnhof** m goods station; **Güterzug** m goods train

gutgläubig adj trusting; **Guthaben** (-s) nt (credit) balance

gutmütig adj good-natured

Gutschein m voucher; **Gutschrift** f credit

Gymnasium nt ≈ grammar school (Brit), ≈ high school (US)

Gymnastik f exercises pl, keep-fit

Gynäkologe m, **Gynäkologin** f gynaecologist

Gyros (-, -) nt doner kebab

h

you mind if ...?; **was hast du denn?** what's the matter (with you)?

Haben nt (Comm) credit

Habicht (-(e)s, -e) m hawk

Hacke (-, -n) f (im Garten) hoe; (Ferse) heel; **hacken** vt to chop; (Loch) to hack; (Erde) to hoe; **Hacker(in)** (-s, -) m(f) (Inform) hacker; **Hackfleisch** nt mince(d meat) (Brit), ground meat (US)

Hafen (-s, Häfen) m harbour; (großer) port; **Hafenstadt** f port

Hafer (-s, -) m oats pl; **Haferflocken** pl rolled oats pl

Haft (-) f custody; **haftbar** adj liable, responsible; **haften** vi to stick; ~ **für** to be liable (o responsible) for; **Haftnotiz** f Post-it®; **Haftpflichtver-sicherung** f third party insurance; **Haftung** f liability

Hagebutte (-, -n) f rose hip

Hagel (-s) m hail; **hageln** vi impers to hail

Hahn (-(e)s, Hähne) m cock; (Wasserhahn) tap (Brit), faucet (US); **Hähnchen** nt cockerel; (Gastr) chicken

Hai(fisch) (-(e)s, -e) m shark

häkeln vi, vt to crochet; **Häkelnadel** f crochet hook

Haken (-s, -) m hook; (Zeichen) tick

halb adj half; ~ **eins** half past twelve; (fam) half twelve; **eine ~e Stunde** half an hour; ~ **offen** half-open; **Halbfinale** nt semifinal; **halbieren** vt to halve; **Halbinsel** f peninsula; **Halbjahr** nt half-year; **halbjährlich** adj half-yearly; **Halbmond** m (Astr) half-moon; (Symbol) crescent; **Halbpension** f half board; **halbseitig** adj: ~ **gelähmt** paralyzed on one side; **halbtags**

Haar (-(e)s, -e) nt hair; **um ein** ~ nearly; **sich** (dat) **die ~e schneiden lassen** to have one's hair cut; **Haarbürste** f hairbrush; **Haarfestiger** m setting lotion; **Haargel** nt hair gel; **haarig** adj hairy; (fig) nasty; **Haarschnitt** m haircut; **Haarspange** f hair slide (Brit), barrette (US); **Haarspliss** m split ends pl; **Haarspray** nt hair spray; **Haartrockner** (-s, -) m hairdryer; **Haarwaschmittel** nt shampoo; **Haarwasser** nt hair tonic

haben (hatte, gehabt) vt, vaux to have; **Hunger/Angst** ~ to be hungry/afraid; **Ferien** ~ to be on holiday (Brit) (o vacation (US)); **welches Datum** ~ **wir heute?** what's the date today?; **ich hätte gerne ...** I'd like ...; **hätten Sie etwas dagegen, wenn ...?** would *adv* (*arbeiten*) part-time; **halbwegs** *adv* (*leidlich*) reasonably; **Halbzeit** *f* half; (*Pause*) half-time

half *imperf von* **helfen**; **Hälfte** (-, -n) *f* half

Halle (-, -n) *f* hall; **Hallenbad** *nt* indoor (swimming) pool

hallo *interj* hello, hi

Halogenlampe *f* halogen lamp; **Halogenscheinwerfer** *m* halogen headlight

Hals (-es, Hälse) *m* neck; (*Kehle*) throat; **Halsband** *nt* (*für Tiere*) collar; **Halsentzündung** *f* sore throat; **Halskette** *f* necklace; **Hals-Nasen-Ohren-Arzt** *m*, **Hals-Nasen-Ohren-Ärztin** *f* ear, nose and throat specialist; **Halsschmerzen** *pl* sore throat *sing*; **Halstuch** *nt* scarf

halt *interj* stop ▷ *adv*: **das ist ~ so** that's just the way it is; **Halt** (-(e)s, -e) *m* stop; (*fester*) hold; (*innerer*) stability

haltbar *adj* durable; (*Lebensmittel*) non-perishable; **Haltbarkeitsdatum** *nt* best-before date

halten (*hielt, gehalten*) *vt* to keep; (*festhalten*) to hold; **~ für** to regard as; **~ von** to think of; **den Elfmeter ~** to save the penalty; **eine Rede ~** to give (*o* make) a speech ▷ *vi* to hold; (*frisch bleiben*) to keep; (*stoppen*) to stop; **zu jdm ~** to stand by sb ▷ *vr*: **sich ~** (*frisch bleiben*) to keep; (*sich behaupten*) to hold out

Haltestelle *f* stop; **Halteverbot** *nt*: **hier ist ~** you can't stop here

Haltung *f* (*Körper*) posture; (*fig*) attitude; (*Selbstbeherrschung*) composure; **~ bewahren** to keep one's composure

Hamburg (-s) *nt* Hamburg; **Hamburger** (-s, -) *m* (*Gastr*) hamburger

Hammelfleisch *nt* mutton

Hammer (-s, Hämmer) *m* hammer; (*fig, fam: Fehler*) howler; **das ist der ~** (*unerhört*) that's a bit much

Hämorr(ho)iden *pl* haemorrhoids *pl*, piles *pl*

Hamster (-s, -) *m* hamster

Hand (-, Hände) *f* hand; **jdm die ~ geben** to shake hands with sb; **jdn bei der ~ nehmen** to take sb by the hand; **eine ~ voll Reis/Leute** a handful of rice/people; **zu Händen von** attention; **Handarbeit** *f* (*Schulfach*) handicraft; **~ sein** to be handmade; **Handball** *m* handball; **Handbremse** *f* handbrake; **Handbuch** *nt* handbook, manual; **Handcreme** *f* hand cream; **Händedruck** *m* handshake

Handel (-s) *m* trade; (*Geschäft*) transaction; **handeln** *vi* to act; (*Comm*) to trade; **~ von** to be about ▷ *vr impers*: **sich ~ um** to be about; **es handelt sich um ...** it's about ...; **Handelskammer** *f* chamber of commerce; **Handelsschule** *f* business school

Handfeger (-s, -) *m* brush; **Handfläche** *f* palm; **Handgelenk** *nt* wrist; **handgemacht** *adj* handmade; **Handgepäck** *nt* hand luggage (*Brit*) (*o* baggage)

Händler(in) (-s, -) *m(f)* dealer

handlich *adj* handy

Handlung *f* act, action; (*von Roman, Film*) plot

Handschellen *pl* handcuffs *pl*; **Handschrift** *f* handwriting; **Handschuh** *m* glove; **Handschuhfach** *nt* glove compartment; **Handtasche** *f* handbag, purse (*US*); **Handtuch** *nt* towel; **Handwerk** *nt* trade; (*Kunst~*) craft; **Handwerker** (-s, -)

m workman

Handy (-s, -s) *nt* mobile (phone) (*Brit*), cell phone (*US*); **Handynummer** *f* mobile number (*Brit*), cell phone number (*US*)

Hanf (-(e)s) *m* hemp

Hang (-(e)s, Hänge) *m* (*Abhang*) slope; (*fig*) tendency

Hängebrücke *f* suspension bridge; **Hängematte** *f* hammock

hängen (hing, gehangen) *vi* to hang; **an der Wand/an der Decke ~** to hang on the wall/from the ceiling; **an jdm ~** (*fig*) to be attached to sb; **~ bleiben** to get caught (*an +dat* on); (*fig*) to get stuck ▷ *vt* to hang (*an +akk* on)

Hantel (-, -n) *f* dumbbell

Hardware (-, -s) *f* (*Inform*) hardware

Harfe (-, -n) *f* harp

harmlos *adj* harmless

harmonisch *adj* harmonious

Harn (-(e)s, -e) *m* urine; **Harnblase** *f* bladder

Harpune (-, -n) *f* harpoon

hart *adj* hard; (*fig*) harsh; **zu jdm ~ sein** to be hard on sb; **~ gekocht** (*Ei*) hard-boiled; **hartnäckig** *adj* stubborn

Haschee (-s, -s) *nt* hash

Haschisch (-) *nt* hashish

Hase (-n, -n) *m* hare

Haselnuss *f* hazelnut

Hasenscharte *f* (*Med*) harelip

Hass (-es) *m* hatred (*auf, gegen +akk* of), hate; **einen ~ kriegen** (*fam*) to see red; **hassen** *vt* to hate

hässlich *adj* ugly; (*gemein*) nasty

Hast (-) *f* haste, hurry; **hastig** *adj* hasty

hatte *imperf von* **haben**

Haube (-, -n) *f* hood; (*Mütze*) cap; (*Auto*) bonnet (*Brit*), hood (*US*)

Hauch (-(e)s, -e) *m* breath; (*Luft~*)

breeze; (*fig*) trace; **hauchdünn** *adj* (*Schicht, Scheibe*) wafer-thin

hauen (*haute, gehauen*) *vt* to hit

Haufen (-s, -) *m* pile; **ein ~ Geld** (*viel Geld*) a lot of money

häufig *adj* frequent ▷ *adv* frequently, often

Haupt- *in zW* main; **Hauptbahnhof** *m* central (*o* main) station; **Hauptdarsteller(in)** *m(f)* leading actor/lady; **Haupteingang** *m* main entrance; **Hauptgericht** *nt* main course; **Hauptgeschäftszeiten** *pl* peak shopping hours *pl*; **Hauptgewinn** *m* first prize

Häuptling *m* chief

Hauptquartier *nt* headquarters *pl*; **Hauptreisezeit** *f* peak tourist season; **Hauptrolle** *f* leading role; **Hauptsache** *f* main thing; **hauptsächlich** *adv* mainly, chiefly; **Hauptsaison** *f* high (*o* peak) season; **Hauptsatz** *m* main clause; **Hauptschule** *f* ≈ secondary school (*Brit*), ≈ junior high school (*US*); **Hauptspeicher** *m* (*Inform*) main storage (*o* memory); **Hauptstadt** *f* capital; **Hauptstraße** *f* main road; (*im Stadtzentrum*) main street; **Hauptverkehrszeit** *f* rush hour

Haus (-es, Häuser) *nt* house; **nach ~e** home; **zu ~e** at home; **jdn nach ~e bringen** to take sb home; **bei uns zu ~e** (*Heimat*) where we come from; (*Familie*) in my family; (*Haus*) at our place; **Hausarbeit** *f* housework; **Hausaufgabe** *f* (*Schule*) homework; **~n** *pl* homework *sing*; **Hausbesitzer(in)** (-s, -) *m(f)* house owner; (*Vermieter*) landlord/-lady; **Hausbesuch** *m* home visit; **Hausbewohner(in)** (-s, -) *m(f)* occupar **Hausflur** *m* hall; **Hausfrau** *f* housewife; **hausgemacht** adj homemade; **Haushalt** m household; (Pol) budget; **Hausherr(in)** m(f) host/hostess; (Vermieter) landlord/-lady

häuslich adj domestic

Hausmann m house-husband; **Hausmannskost** f good plain cooking; **Hausmeister(in)** m(f) caretaker (Brit), janitor (US); **Hausnummer** f house number; **Hausordnung** f (house) rules pl; **Hausschlüssel** m front-door key; **Hausschuh** m slipper; **Haustier** nt pet; **Haustür** f front door

Haut (-, Häute) f skin; (Tier) hide; **Hautarzt** m, **Hautärztin** f dermatologist; **Hautausschlag** m skin rash; **Hautcreme** f skin cream; **Hautfarbe** f skin colour; **Hautkrankheit** f skin disease

Hawaii (-s) nt Hawaii

Hbf. abk = **Hauptbahnhof** central station

Hebamme (-, -n) f midwife

Hebel (-s, -) m lever

heben (hob, gehoben) vt to raise, to lift

Hebräisch (-) nt Hebrew

Hecht (-(e)s, -e) m pike

Heck (-(e)s, -e) nt (von Boot) stern; (von Auto) rear; **Heckantrieb** m rear-wheel drive

Hecke (-, -n) f hedge

Heckklappe f tailgate; **Hecklicht** nt tail-light; **Heckscheibe** f rear window

Hefe (-, -n) f yeast

Heft (-(e)s, -e) nt notebook, exercise book; (Ausgabe) issue

heftig adj violent; (Kritik, Streit) fierce

Heftklammer f paper clip; **Heftpflaster** nt plaster (Brit), Band-Aid® (US)

Heide (-, -n) f heath, moor; **Heidekraut** nt heather

Heidelbeere f bilberry, blueberry

heidnisch adj (Brauch) pagan

heikel adj (Angelegenheit) awkward; (wählerisch) fussy

heil adj (Sache) in one piece, intact; (Person) unhurt; **heilbar** adj curable

Heilbutt (-(e)s, -e) m halibut

heilen vt to cure ▷ vi to heal

heilig adj holy; **Heiligabend** m Christmas Eve; **Heilige(r)** mf saint

Heilmittel n remedy, cure (gegen for); **Heilpraktiker(in)** (-s, -) m(f) non-medical practitioner

heim adv home; **Heim** (-(e), -e) nt home

Heimat (-, -en) f home (town/country); **Heimatland** nt home country

heim|fahren irr vi to drive home; **Heimfahrt** f journey home; **heimisch** adj (Bevölkerung, Brauchtum) local; (Tiere, Pflanzen) native; **heim|kommen** irr vi to come (o return) home

heimlich adj secret

Heimreise f journey home; **Heimspiel** nt (Sport) home game; **Heimvorteil** m (Sport) home advantage; **Heimweg** m way home; **Heimweh** (-s) nt homesickness; **~ haben** to be homesick; **Heimwerker(in)** m(f) DIY enthusiast

Heirat (-, -en) f marriage; **heiraten** vi to get married ▷ vt to marry; **Heiratsantrag** m proposal; **er hat ihr einen ~ gemacht** he proposed to her

heiser adj hoarse

heiß adj hot; (Diskussion) heated; **mir ist ~** I'm hot

heißen (hieß, geheißen) vi to be called; (bedeuten) to mean; **ich heiße Tom** my name is Tom; **wie**

~ Sie? what's your name?; **wie heißt sie mit Nachnamen?** what's her surname?; **wie heißt das auf Englisch?** what's that in English? ▷ *vi impers:* **es heißt** (*man sagt*) it is said; **es heißt in dem Brief ...** it says in the letter ...; **das heißt** that is

Heißluftherd *m* fan-assisted oven

heiter *adj* cheerful; (*Wetter*) bright

heizen *vt* to heat; **Heizkissen** *m* (*Med*) heated pad; **Heizkörper** *m* radiator; **Heizöl** *nt* fuel oil; **Heizung** *f* heating

Hektar (*-s, -*) *nt* hectare

Hektik (*-, -en*) *f:* **nur keine ~!** take it easy; **hektisch** *adj* hectic

Held (*-en, -en*) *m* hero; **Heldin** *f* heroine

helfen (*half, geholfen*) *vi* to help; (*jdm bei etw* sb with sth); (*nützen*) to be of use; **sie weiß sich** (*dat*) **zu ~** she can manage ▷ *vi impers:* **es hilft nichts, du musst ...** it's no use, you have to ...; **Helfer(in)** *m(f)* helper; (*Mitarbeiter*) assistant

Helikopter-Skiing (*-s*) *nt* heliskiing, helicopter skiing

hell *adj* bright; (*Farbe*) light; (*Hautfarbe*) fair; **hellblau** *adj* light blue; **hellblond** *adj* ash-blond; **hellgelb** *adj* pale yellow; **hellgrün** *adj* light green; **Hellseher(in)** *m(f)* clairvoyant

Helm (*-(e)s, -e*) *m* helmet; **Helmpflicht** *f* compulsory wearing of helmets

Hemd (*-(e)s, -en*) *nt* shirt; (*Unter~*) vest

hemmen *vt* to check; (*behindern*) to hamper; **gehemmt sein** to be inhibited; **Hemmung** *f* (*psychisch*) inhibition; **sie hatte keine ~, ihn zu betrügen** she had no scruples about deceiving him; (*moralisch*) scruple

Henkel (*-s, -*) *m* handle

Henna (*-s*) *nt* henna

Henne (*-, -n*) *f* hen

Hepatitis (*-, Hepatitiden*) *f* hepatitis

 SCHLÜSSELWORT

her *adv* **1** (*Richtung*) **komm her zu mir** come here (to me); **von England her** from England; **von weit her** from a long way away; **her damit!** hand it over!; **wo hat er das her?** where did he get that from?; **wo bist du her?** where do you come from?
2 (*Blickpunkt*) **von der Form her** as far as the form is concerned
3 (*zeitlich*) **das ist 5 Jahre her** that was 5 years ago; **ich kenne ihn von früher her** I know him from before

herab *adv* down; **herablassend** *adj* (*Bemerkung*) condescending; **herab|sehen** *irr vt:* **auf jdn ~** to look down on sb; **herab|setzen** *vt* to reduce; (*fig*) to disparage

heran *adv:* **näher ~!** come closer; **heran|kommen** *irr vi:* to approach; **~ an** (*+akk*) to be able to get at; (*fig*) to be able to get hold of; **heran|wachsen** *irr vi* to grow up

herauf *adv* up; **herauf|beschwören** *irr vt* to evoke; (*verursachen*) to cause; **herauf|ziehen** *irr vt* to pull up ▷ *vi* to approach; (*Sturm*) to gather

heraus *adv* out; **heraus|bekommen** *irr vt* (*Geheimnis*) to find out; (*Rätsel*) to solve; **ich bekomme noch zwei Euro heraus** I've got two euros change to come; **heraus|bringen** *irr vt* to bring out; **heraus|finden**

irr vt to find out; **heraus|fordern**
vt to challenge; **Herausforderung**
f challenge; **heraus|geben** irr vt
(Buch) to edit; (veröffentlichen) to
publish; **jdm zwei Euro ~** to give
sb two euros change; **geben Sie
mir bitte auf 20 Euro heraus**
could you give me change for 20
euros, please?; **heraus|holen** vt
to get out (aus of); **heraus|-
kommen** irr vi to come
out; **dabei kommt nichts heraus**
nothing will come of it;
heraus|stellen vr: **sich ~** to turn
out (als to be); **heraus|ziehen** irr
vt to pull out
Herbst (-(e)s, -e) m autumn, fall
(US)
Herd (-(e)s, -e) m cooker, stove
Herde (-, -n) f herd; (Schafe) flock
herein adv in; **~!** come in;
herein|fallen irr vi: **wir sind auf
einen Betrüger hereingefallen**
we were taken in by a swindler;
herein|legen vt: **jdn ~** (fig) to
take sb for a ride
Herfahrt f journey here; **auf der
~** on the way here
Hergang m course (of events);
schildern Sie mir den ~ tell me
what happened
Hering (-s, -e) m herring
her|kommen irr vi to come; **wo
kommt sie her?** where does she
come from?
Heroin (-s) nt heroin
Herpes (-) m (Med) herpes
Herr (-(e)n, -en) m (vor Namen) Mr;
(Mann) gentleman; (Adliger, Gott)
Lord; **mein ~!** sir; **meine ~en!**
gentlemen; **Sehr geehrte Damen
und ~en** Dear Sir or Madam;
herrenlos adj (Gepäckstück)
abandoned; (Tier) stray;
Herrentoilette f men's toilet,
gents
her|richten vt to prepare

herrlich adj marvellous, splendid
Herrschaft f rule; (Macht) power;
meine ~en! ladies and gentlemen!
herrschen vi to rule; (bestehen) to
be
her|stellen vt to make;
(industriell) to manufacture;
Hersteller(in) m(f) manufacturer; **Herstellung** f
production
herüber adv over
herum adv around; (im Kreis)
round; **um etw ~** around sth; **du
hast den Pulli falsch ~ an** you're
wearing your sweater inside out;
anders ~ the other way round;
herum|fahren irr vi to drive
around; **herum|führen** vt: **jdn in
der Stadt ~** to show sb around the
town ▷ vi: **die Straße führt um
das Zentrum herum** the road
goes around the city centre;
herum|kommen irr vi: **sie ist
viel in der Welt herum-
gekommen** she's been
around the world; **um etw
~** (vermeiden) to get out of sth;
herum|kriegen vt to talk round;
herum|treiben irr vr: **sich ~** to
hang around
herunter adv down;
heruntergekommen adj (Gebäude,
Gegend) run-down; (Person)
down-at-heel; **herunter|handeln**
vt to get down; **herunter|holen**
vt to bring down;
herunter|kommen irr vi to come
down; **herunter|laden** irr vt
(Inform) to download
hervor adv out; **hervor|bringen**
irr vt to produce; (Wort) to utter;
hervor|heben irr vt to
emphasize, to stress;
hervorragend adj excellent;
hervor|rufen irr vt to cause, to
give rise to
Herz (-ens, -en) nt heart; (Karten)

hearts pl; **von ganzem ~en** wholeheartedly; **sich** (dat) **etw zu ~en nehmen** to take sth to heart; **Herzanfall** m heart attack; **Herzbeschwerden** pl heart trouble sing; **Herzfehler** m heart defect; **herzhaft** adj (Essen) substantial; **~ lachen** to have a good laugh; **Herzinfarkt** m heart attack; **Herzklopfen** (-s) nt (Med) palpitations pl; **ich hatte ~** (**vor Aufregung**) my heart was pounding (with excitement); **herzkrank** adj: **sie ist ~** she's got a heart condition; **herzlich** adj (Empfang, Mensch) warm; **~en Glückwunsch** congratulations

Herzog(in) (-s, Herzöge) m(f) duke/duchess

Herzschlag m heartbeat; (Herzversagen) heart failure; **Herzschrittmacher** m pacemaker; **Herzstillstand** m cardiac arrest

Hessen (-s) nt Hessen

heterosexuell adj heterosexual; **Heterosexuelle(r)** mf heterosexual

Hetze (-, -n) f (Eile) rush; **hetzen** vt to rush ▷ vr: **sich ~** to rush

Heu (-(e)s) nt hay

heuer adv this year

heulen vi to howl; (weinen) to cry

Heuschnupfen m hay fever; **Heuschrecke** (-, -n) f grasshopper; (größer) locust

heute adv today; **~ Abend/früh** this evening/morning; **~ Nacht** tonight; (letzte Nacht) last night; **~ in acht Tagen** a week (from) today; **sie hat bis ~ nicht bezahlt** she hasn't paid to this day; **heutig** adj: **die ~e Zeitung/Generation** today's paper/generation; **heutzutage** adv nowadays

Hexe (-, -n) f witch; **Hexenschuss** m lumbago

hielt imperf von **halten**

hier adv here; **~ entlang** this way; **ich bin auch nicht von ~** I'm a stranger here myself; **hier|bleiben** irr vi to stay here; **hier|lassen** irr vt to leave here; **hierher** adv here; **das gehört nicht ~** that doesn't belong here; **hiermit** adv with this; **hierzulande** adv in this country

hiesig adj local

hieß imperf von **heißen**

Hi-Fi-Anlage f hi-fi (system)

high adj (fam) high; **Highlife** (-s) nt high life; **~ machen** to live it up; **Hightech** (-s) nt high tech

Hilfe (-, -n) f help; (für Notleidende, finanziell) aid; **~!** help!; **Erste ~ leisten** to give first aid; **um ~ bitten** to ask for help; **hilflos** adj helpless; **hilfsbereit** adj helpful; **Hilfsmittel** nt aid

Himbeere f raspberry

Himmel (-s, -) m sky; (Rel) heaven; **Himmelfahrt** f Ascension; **Himmelsrichtung** f direction; **himmlisch** adj heavenly

◯ **SCHLÜSSELWORT**

hin adv **1** (Richtung) **hin und zurück** there and back; **hin und her** to and fro; **bis zur Mauer hin** up to the wall; **wo ist er hin?** where has he gone?; **Geld hin, Geld her** money or no money
2 (auf ... hin) **auf meine Bitte hin** at my request; **auf seinen Rat hin** on the basis of his advice
3 mein Glück ist hin my happiness has gone

hinab adv down; **hinab|gehen** irr vi to go down

hinauf adv up; **hinauf|gehen** irr

vi, vt to go up; **hinauf|steigen** *irr vi* to climb (up)

hinaus *adv* out; **hinaus|gehen** *irr vi* to go out; **das Zimmer geht auf den See hinaus** the room looks out onto the lake; **~ über** (+*akk*) to exceed; **hinaus|laufen** *irr vi* to run out; **~ auf** (+*akk*) to come to, to amount to; **hinaus|schieben** *irr vi* to put off, to postpone; **hinaus|werfen** *irr vt* to throw out; (*aus Firma*) to fire, to sack (*Brit*); **hinaus|zögern** *vr:* **sich ~** to take longer than expected

Hinblick *m* **in** (*o* **im**) **~ auf** (+*akk*) with regard to; (*wegen*) in view of

hin|bringen *irr vt:* **ich bringe Sie hin** I'll take you there

hindern *vt* to prevent; **jdn daran ~, etw zu tun** to stop (*o* prevent) sb from doing sth; **Hindernis** *nt* obstacle

Hinduismus *m* Hinduism

hindurch *adv* through; **das ganze Jahr ~** throughout the year, all year round; **die ganze Nacht ~** all night (long)

hinein *adv* in; **hinein|gehen** *irr vi* to go in; **~ in** (+*akk*) to go into, to enter; **hinein|passen** *vi* to fit in; **~ in** (+*akk*) to fit into

hin|fahren *irr vi* to go there ▷ *vt* to take there; **Hinfahrt** *f* outward journey

hin|fallen *irr vi* to fall (down)

Hinflug *m* outward flight

hing *imperf von* **hängen**

hin|gehen *irr vi* to go there; (*Zeit*) to pass; **hin|halten** *irr vt* to hold out; (*warten lassen*) to put off

hinken *vi* to limp; **der Vergleich hinkt** the comparison doesn't work

hin|knien *vr:* **sich ~** to kneel down; **hin|legen** *vt* to put down ▷ *vr:* **sich ~** to lie down; **hin|nehmen** *irr vt* (*fig*) to put up

with, to take; **Hinreise** *f* outward journey; **hin|setzen** *vr:* **sich ~** to sit down; **hinsichtlich** *prep* +*gen* with regard to; **hin|stellen** *vt* to put (down) ▷ *vr:* **sich ~** to stand

hinten *adv* at the back; (*im Auto*) in the back; (*dahinter*) behind

hinter *prep* +*dat o akk* behind; (*nach*) after; **~ jdm her sein** to be after sb; **etw ~ sich** (*akk*) **bringen** to get sth over (and done) with; **Hinterachse** *f* rear axle; **Hinterausgang** *m* rear exit; **Hinterbein** *nt* hind leg; **Hinterbliebene(r)** *mf* dependant; **hintere(r, s)** *adj* rear, back; **hintereinander** *adv* (*in einer Reihe*) one behind the other; (*hintereinander her*) one after the other; **drei Tage ~** three days running (*o* in a row); **Hintereingang** *m* rear entrance; **Hintergedanke** *m* ulterior motive; **hintergehen** *irr vt* to deceive; **Hintergrund** *m* background; **hinterher** *adv* (*zeitlich*) afterwards; **los, ~!** come on, after him/her/them; **Hinterkopf** *m* back of the head; **hinterlassen** *vt* to leave; **jdm eine Nachricht ~** to leave a message for sb; **hinterlegen** *vt* to leave (*bei* with)

Hintern (-, -) *m* (*fam*) backside, bum

Hinterradantrieb *m* (*Auto*) rear-wheel drive; **Hinterteil** *nt* back (part); (*Hintern*) behind; **Hintertür** *f* back door

hinüber *adv* over; **~ sein** (*fam: kaputt*) to be ruined; (*verdorben*) to have gone bad; **hinüber|gehen** *irr vi* to go over

hinunter *adv* down; **hinunter|gehen** *irr vi, vt* to go down; **hinunter|schlucken** *vt* (*a. fig*) to swallow

Hinweg *m* outward journey

hinweg|setzen *vr* **sich über etw** (*akk*) **~** to ignore sth

Hinweis (*-es, -e*) *m* (*Andeutung*) hint; (*Anweisung*) instruction; (*Verweis*) reference; **hin|weisen** *irr vi* **jdn auf etw** (*acc*) **~** to point sth out to sb; **jdn nochmal auf etw ~** to remind sb of sth

hinzu *adv* in addition; **hinzu|fügen** *vt* to add; **hinzu|kommen** *irr vi*: **zu jdm ~** to join sb; **es war kalt, hinzu kam, dass es auch noch regnete** it was cold, and on top of that it was raining

Hirn (*-(e)s, -e*) *nt* brain; (*Verstand*) brains *pl*; **Hirnhautentzündung** *f* meningitis; **hirnverbrannt** *adj* crazy

Hirsch (*-(e)s, -e*) *m* deer; (*als Speise*) venison

Hirse (*-, -n*) *f* millet

Hirte (*-n, -n*) *m* shepherd

historisch *adj* historical

Hit (*-s, -s*) *m* (*fig, Mus, Inform*) hit; **Hitliste** *f*, **Hitparade** *f* charts *pl*

Hitze (*-*) *f* heat; **hitzebeständig** *adj* heat-resistant; **Hitzewelle** *f* heatwave; **hitzig** *adj* hot-tempered; (*Debatte*) heated; **Hitzschlag** *m* heatstroke

HIV (*-(s), -(s)*) *nt abk* = **Human Immunodeficiency Virus** HIV; **HIV-negativ** *adj* HIV-negative; **HIV-positiv** *adj* HIV-positive

H-Milch *f* long-life milk

hob *imperf von* **heben**

Hobby (*-s, -s*) *nt* hobby

Hobel (*-s, -*) *m* plane

hoch *adj* high; (*Baum, Haus*) tall; (*Schnee*) deep; **der Zaun ist drei Meter ~** the fence is three metres high; **~ auflösend** high-resolution; **~ begabt** extremely gifted; **das ist mir zu ~** that's above my head;

~ soll sie leben!, sie lebe ~! three cheers for her; **4 ~ 2 ist 16** 4 squared is 16; **4 ~ 5** 4 to the power of 5

Hoch (*-s, -s*) *nt* (*Ruf*) cheer; (*Meteo*) high; **hochachtungsvoll** *adv* (*in Briefen*) Yours faithfully; **Hochbetrieb** *m*: **es herrscht ~** they/we are extremely busy; **Hochdeutsch** *nt* High German; **Hochgebirge** *nt* high mountains *pl*; **Hochgeschwindigkeitszug** *m* high-speed train; **Hochhaus** *nt* high rise; **hoch|heben** *irr vt* to lift (up); **hochprozentig** *adj* (*Alkohol*) high-proof; **Hochsaison** *f* high season; **Hochschule** *f* college; (*Universität*) university; **hochschwanger** *adj* heavily pregnant; **Hochsommer** *m* midsummer; **Hochspannung** *f* great tension; (*Elek*) high voltage; **Hochsprung** *m* high jump

höchst *adv* highly, extremely; **höchste(r, s)** *adj* highest; (*äußerste*) extreme; **höchstens** *adv* at the most; **Höchstgeschwindigkeit** *f* maximum speed; **Höchstparkdauer** *f* maximum stay

Hochstuhl *m* high chair

höchstwahrscheinlich *adv* very probably

Hochwasser *nt* high water; (*Überschwemmung*) floods *pl*; **hochwertig** *adj* high-quality

Hochzeit (*-, -en*) *f* wedding; **Hochzeitsnacht** *f* wedding night; **Hochzeitsreise** *f* honeymoon; **Hochzeitstag** *m* wedding day; (*Jahrestag*) wedding anniversary

hocken *vi* to squat, to crouch

Hocker (*-s, -*) *m* stool

Hockey (*-s*) *nt* hockey

Hoden (*-s, -*) *m* testicle

Hof (*-(e)s, Höfe*) *m* (*Hinterhof*) yard;

(*Innenhof*) courtyard; (*Bauernhof*) farm; (*Königshof*) court

hoffen *vi* to hope (*auf +akk* for); **ich hoffe es** I hope so; **hoffentlich** *adv* hopefully; **~ nicht** I hope not; **Hoffnung** *f* hope; **hoffnungslos** *adj* hopeless

höflich *adj* polite; **Höflichkeit** *f* politeness

hohe(r, s) *adj siehe* **hoch**

Höhe (-, -n) *f* height; (*Anhöhe*) hill; (*einer Summe*) amount; **in einer ~ von 5000 Metern** at an altitude of 5,000 metres; (*Flughöhe*) altitude; **Höhenangst** *f* vertigo

Höhepunkt *m* (*einer Reise*) high point; (*einer Veranstaltung*) highlight; (*eines Films; sexuell*) climax

höher *adj, adv* higher

hohl *adj* hollow

Höhle (-, -n) *f* cave

holen *vt* to get, to fetch; (*abholen*) to pick up; (*Atem*) to catch; **die Polizei ~** to call the police; **jdn/etw ~ lassen** to send for sb/sth

Holland *nt* Holland; **Holländer(in)** (-s, -) *m(f)* Dutchman/ -woman; **holländisch** *adj* Dutch

Hölle (-, -n) *f* hell

Hologramm *nt* hologram

holperig *adj* bumpy

Holunder (-s, -) *m* elder

Holz (-es, *Hölzer*) *nt* wood; **Holzboden** *m* wooden floor; **hölzern** *adj* wooden; **holzig** *adj* (*Stängel*) woody; **Holzkohle** *f* charcoal

Homebanking (-s) *nt* home banking, online banking; **Homepage** (-, -s) *f* home page; **Hometrainer** *m* exercise machine

Homoehe *f* (*fam*) gay marriage

homöopathisch *adj* homeopathic

homosexuell *adj* homosexual; **Homosexuelle(r)** *mf* homosexual

Honig (-s, -e) *m* honey; **Honigmelone** *f* honeydew melon

Honorar (-s, -e) *nt* fee

Hopfen (-s, -) *m* (*Bot*) hop; (*beim Brauen*) hops *pl*

hoppla *interj* whoops, oops

horchen *vi* to listen (*auf +akk* to); (*an der Tür*) to eavesdrop

hören *vt, vi* (*passiv, mitbekommen*) to hear; (*zufällig*) to overhear; (*aufmerksam zuhören; Radio, Musik*) to listen to; **ich habe schon viel von Ihnen gehört** I've heard a lot about you; **Hörer** *m* (*Tel*) receiver; **Hörer(in)** *m(f)* listener; **Hörgerät** *nt* hearing aid

Horizont (-(e)s, -e) *m* horizon; **das geht über meinen ~** that's beyond me

Hormon (-s, -e) *nt* hormone

Hornhaut *f* hard skin; (*des Auges*) cornea

Hornisse (-, -n) *f* hornet

Horoskop (-s, -e) *nt* horoscope

Hörsaal *m* lecture hall; **Hörsturz** *m* acute hearing loss; **Hörweite** *f*: **in/außer ~** within/out of earshot

Höschenwindel (-, -n) *f* nappy (*Brit*), diaper (*US*)

Hose (-, -n) *f* trousers *pl* (*Brit*), pants *pl* (*US*); (*Unterhose*) (under)pants *pl*; **eine ~** a pair of trousers/pants; **kurze ~** (pair of) shorts *pl*; **Hosenanzug** *m* trouser suit (*Brit*), pantsuit (*US*); **Hosenschlitz** *m* fly, flies (*Brit*); **Hosentasche** *f* trouser pocket (*Brit*), pant pocket (*US*); **Hosenträger** *m* braces *pl* (*Brit*), suspenders *pl* (*US*)

Hospital (-s, *Hospitäler*) *nt* hospital

Hotdog (-s, -s) *nt o m* hot dog

Hotel (-s, -s) nt hotel; **in welchem ~ seid ihr?** which hotel are you staying at?; **Hoteldirektor(in)** m(f) hotel manager; **Hotelkette** f hotel chain; **Hotelzimmer** nt hotel room

Hotline (-, -s) f hot line

Hubraum m cubic capacity

hübsch adj (Mädchen, Kind, Kleid) pretty; (gutaussehend; Mann, Frau) good-looking, cute

Hubschrauber (-s, -) m helicopter

Huf (-(e)s, -e) m hoof; **Hufeisen** nt horseshoe

Hüfte (-, -n) f hip

Hügel (-s, -) m hill; **hügelig** adj hilly

Huhn (-(e)s, Hühner) nt hen; (Gastr) chicken; **Hühnchen** nt chicken; **Hühnerauge** nt corn; **Hühnerbrühe** f chicken broth

Hülle (-, -n) f cover; (für Ausweis) case; (Zellophan) wrapping

Hummel (-, -n) f bumblebee

Hummer (-s, -) m lobster; **Hummerkrabbe** f king prawn

Humor (-s) m humour; **~ haben** to have a sense of humour; **humorvoll** adj humorous

humpeln vi hobble

Hund (-(e)s, -e) m dog; **Hundeleine** f dog lead (Brit), dog leash (US)

hundert num hundred; **Hundertjahrfeier** f centenary; **hundertprozentig** adj, adv one hundred per cent; **hundertste(r, s)** adj hundredth

Hündin f bitch

Hunger (-s) m hunger; **~ haben/bekommen** to be/get hungry; **hungern** vi to go hungry; (ernsthaft, dauernd) to starve

Hupe (-, -n) f horn; **hupen** vi to sound one's horn

Hüpfburg f bouncy castle®; **hüpfen** vi to hop; (springen) to jump

Hürde (-, -n) f hurdle

Hure (-, -n) f whore

hurra interj hooray

husten vi to cough; **Husten** (-s) m cough; **Hustenbonbon** nt cough sweet; **Hustensaft** m cough mixture

Hut (-(e)s, Hüte) m hat

hüten vt to look after ▷ vr: **sich ~** to watch out; **sich ~, etw zu tun** to take care not to do sth; **sich ~ vor** (+dat) to beware of

Hütte (-, -n) f hut, cottage; **Hüttenkäse** m cottage cheese

Hyäne (-, -n) f hyena

Hydrant m hydrant

hygienisch adj hygienic

Hyperlink (-s, -s) m hyperlink

Hypnose (-, -n) f hypnosis; **Hypnotiseur(in)** m(f) hypnotist; **hypnotisieren** vt to hypnotize

Hypothek (-, -en) f mortgage

hysterisch adj hysterical

i

i. A. *abk* = **im Auftrag** pp
IC (-, -s) *m abk* = **Intercityzug**
Intercity (train)
ICE (-, -s) *m abk* = **Intercityexpresszug** *German high-speed train*
ich *pron* I; **~ bin's** it's me; **~ nicht** not me; **du und ~** you and me; **hier bin ~!** here I am; **~ Idiot!** stupid me
Icon (-s, -s) *nt* (*Inform*) icon
IC-Zuschlag *m* Intercity supplement
ideal *adj* ideal; **Ideal** (-s, -e) *nt* ideal
Idee (-, -n) *f* idea
identifizieren *vt* to identify
▷ *vr:* **sich mit jdm/etw ~** to identify with sb/sth
identisch *adj* identical
Idiot(in) (-en, -en) *m(f)* idiot; **idiotisch** *adj* idiotic
Idol (-s, -e) *nt* idol
Idylle *f* idyll; **idyllisch** *adj* idyllic

Igel (-s, -) *m* hedgehog
ignorieren *vt* to ignore
ihm *pron dat sing von* **er/es**; (to) him, (to) it; **wie geht es ~?** how is he?; **ein Freund von ~** a friend of his ▷ *pron dat von* **es**; (to) it
ihn *pron akk sing von* **er**; (*Person*) him; (*Sache*) it
ihnen *pron dat pl von* **sie**; (to) them; **wie geht es ~?** how are they?; **ein Freund von ~** a friend of theirs
Ihnen *pron dat sing u pl von* **Sie**; (to) you; **wie geht es ~?** how are you?; **ein Freund von ~** a friend of yours

SCHLÜSSELWORT

ihr *pron* **1** (*nom pl*) you; **ihr seid es** it's you
2 (*dat von sie*) to her; **gib es ihr** give it to her; **er steht neben ihr** he is standing beside her
▷ *possessiv pron* **1** (*sg*) her; (*bei Tieren, Dingen*) its; **ihr Mann** her husband
2 (*pl*) their; **die Bäume und ihre Blätter** the trees and their leaves

Ihr *pron von* **Sie**; (*adjektivisch*) your; **~(e) XY** (*am Briefende*) Yours, XY
ihre(r, s) *pron* (*substantivisch, sing*) hers; (*pl*) theirs; **das ist ~/~r/ihr(e)s** that's hers; (*pl*) that's theirs
Ihre(r, s) *pron* (*substantivisch*) yours; **das ist ~/~r/Ihr(e)s** that's yours
ihretwegen *adv* (*wegen ihr*) because of her; (*ihr zuliebe*) for her sake; (*um sie*) about her; (*von ihr aus*) as far as she is concerned
▷ *adv* (*wegen ihnen*) because of them; (*ihnen zuliebe*) for their sake; (*um sie*) about them; (*von ihnen aus*)

as far as they are concerned;
Ihretwegen adv (wegen Ihnen)
because of you; (Ihnen zuliebe) for
your sake; (um Sie) about you; (von
Ihnen aus) as far as you are
concerned
Ikone (-, -n) f icon
illegal adj illegal
Illusion f illusion; **sich** (dat) **~en
machen** to delude oneself;
illusorisch adj illusory
Illustration f illustration
Illustrierte (-n, -n) f (glossy)
magazine
im kontr von **in dem**; **~ Bett** in bed;
~ Fernsehen on TV; **~ Radio** on
the radio; **~ Bus/Zug** on the
bus/train; **~ Januar** in January;
~ Stehen (while) standing up
Imbiss (-es, -e) m snack;
Imbissbude f, **Imbissstube** f
snack bar
Imbusschlüssel m hex key
immer adv always; **~ mehr** more
and more; **~ wieder** again and
again; **~ noch** still; **~ noch nicht**
still not; **für ~** forever; **~ wenn
ich …** every time I …; **~ schöner/
trauriger** more and
more beautiful/sadder and
sadder; **was/wer/wo/wann**
(**auch**) **~** whatever/whoever/
wherever/whenever; **immerhin**
adv after all; **immerzu** adv all the
time
Immigrant(in) m(f) immigrant
Immobilien pl property sing, real
estate sing; **Immobilien-
makler(in)** m(f) estate
agent (Brit), realtor (US)
immun adj immune (gegen to);
Immunschwäche f immunodeficiency; **Immun-
schwächekrankheit** f immune
deficiency syndrome;
Immunsystem nt immune
system

impfen vt to vaccinate; **ich muss
mich gegen Pocken ~ lassen** I've
got to get myself vaccinated
against smallpox; **Impfpass** m
vaccination card; **Impfstoff** m
vaccine; **Impfung** f vaccination
imponieren vi to impress (jdm
sb)
Import (-(e)s, -e) m import;
importieren vt to import
impotent adj impotent
imstande adj: **~ sein** to be
in a position; (fähig) to be
able

O SCHLÜSSELWORT

in prep +akk **1** (räumlich: wohin?) in,
into; **in die Stadt** into town; **in die
Schule gehen** to go to school
2 (zeitlich) **bis ins 20. Jahrhundert**
into o up to the 20th century
▷ prep +dat **1** (räumlich: wo?) in; **in
der Stadt** in town; **in der Schule
sein** to be at school
2 (zeitlich: wann?) **in diesem Jahr**
this year; (in jenem Jahr) in that
year; **heute in zwei Wochen** two
weeks today

inbegriffen adj included
indem conj: **sie gewann, ~ sie
mogelte** she won by cheating
Inder(in) (-s, -) m(f) Indian
Indianer(in) (-s, -) m(f)
American Indian, Native
American; **indianisch** adj
American Indian, Native American
Indien (-s) nt India
indirekt adj indirect
indisch adj Indian
indiskret adj indiscreet
individuell adj individual
Indonesien (-s) nt Indonesia
Industrie f industry; **Industrie-
in** zW industrial; **Industriegebiet**
nt industrial area; **industriell** adj

industrial

ineinander *adv* in(to) one another (*o* each other)

Infarkt (-(e)s, -e) *m* (*Herzinfarkt*) heart attack

Infektion *f* infection; **Infektionskrankheit** *f* infectious disease; **infizieren** *vt* to infect ▷ *vr*: **sich ~** to be infected

Info (-, -s) *f* (*fam*) info

infolge *prep* +*gen* as a result of, owing to; **infolgedessen** *adv* consequently

Infomaterial *nt* (*fam*) bumf, info

Informatik *f* computer science; **Informatiker(in)** (-s, -) *m(f)* computer scientist

Information *f* information; **Informationsschalter** *m* information desk; **informieren** *vt* to inform; **falsch ~** to misinform ▷ *vr*: **sich ~** to find out (*über* +*akk* about)

infrage *adv*: **das kommt nicht ~** that's out of the question; **etw ~ stellen** to question sth

Infrastruktur *f* infrastructure

Infusion *f* infusion

Ingenieur(in) *m(f)* engineer

Ingwer (-s) *m* ginger

Inhaber(in) (-s, -) *m(f)* owner; (*Haus~*) occupier; (*von Lizenz*) holder; (*Fin*) bearer

Inhalt (-(e)s, -e) *m* contents *pl*; (*eines Buchs etc*) content; (*Math*) volume; (*Flächeninhalt*) area; **Inhaltsangabe** *f* summary; **Inhaltsverzeichnis** *nt* table of contents

Initiative *f* initiative; **die ~ ergreifen** to take the initiative

Injektion *f* injection

inklusive *adv, prep* inclusive (*gen* of)

inkonsequent *adj* inconsistent

Inland *nt* (*Pol, Comm*) home; **im ~** at home; (*Geo*) inland;

inländisch *adj* domestic; **Inlandsflug** *m* domestic flight; **Inlandsgespräch** *nt* national call

Inliner *pl*, **Inlineskates** *pl* (*Sport*) Rollerblades® *pl*, in-line skates *pl*

innen *adv* inside; **Innenarchitekt(in)** *m(f)* interior designer; **Innenhof** *m* (inner) courtyard; **Innenminister(in)** *m(f)* minister of the interior, Home Secretary (*Brit*); **Innenseite** *f* inside; **Innenspiegel** *m* rearview mirror; **Innenstadt** *f* town centre; (*von Großstadt*) city centre

innere(r, s) *adj* inner; (*im Körper, inländisch*) internal; **Innere(s)** *nt* inside; (*Mitte*) centre; (*fig*) heart

Innereien *pl* innards *pl*

innerhalb *adv, prep* +*gen* within; (*räumlich*) inside

innerlich *adj* internal; (*geistig*) inner

innerste(r, s) *adj* innermost

Innovation *f* innovation; **innovativ** *adj* innovative

inoffiziell *adj* unofficial; (*zwanglos*) informal

ins *kontr von* **in das**

Insasse (-n, -n) *m*, **Insassin** *f* (*Auto*) passenger; (*Anstalt*) inmate

insbesondere *adv* particularly, in particular

Inschrift *f* inscription

Insekt (-(e)s, -en) *nt* insect, bug (*US*); **Insektenschutzmittel** *nt* insect repellent; **Insektenstich** *m* insect bite

Insel (-, -n) *f* island

Inserat *nt* advertisement

insgesamt *adv* altogether, all in all

Insider(in) (-s, -) *m(f)* insider

insofern *adv* in that respect; (*deshalb*) (and) so ▷ *conj* if; **~ als** in so far as

Installateur(in) *m(f)* *(Klempner)*
plumber; *(Elektroinstallateur)*
electrician; **installieren** *vt*
(Inform) to install
Instinkt *(-(e)s, -e) m* instinct
Institut *(-(e)s, -e) nt* institute
Institution *f* institution
Instrument *nt* instrument
Insulin *(-s) nt* insulin
Inszenierung *f* production
intakt *adj* intact
intellektuell *adj* intellectual
intelligent *adj* intelligent;
Intelligenz *f* intelligence
intensiv *adj* *(gründlich)* intensive;
(Gefühl, Schmerz) intense;
Intensivkurs *m* crash course;
Intensivstation *f* intensive care
unit
interaktiv *adj* interactive
Intercityexpress(zug) *m* German
high-speed train; **Intercityzug** *m*
Intercity (train);
Intercityzuschlag *m* Intercity
supplement
interessant *adj* interesting;
Interesse *(-s, -n) nt* interest;
~ haben an (+dat) to be interested
in; **interessieren** *vt* to interest
▷ *vr:* **sich ~** to be interested *(für* in)
Interface *(-, -s) nt* *(Inform)*
interface
Internat *nt* boarding school
international *adj* international
Internet *(-s) nt* internet, net; **im
~ on the internet; **im ~ surfen** to
surf the net; **Internetanschluss**
m internet connection;
Internetauktion *f* internet
auction; **Internetcafé** *nt*
internet café, cybercafé;
Internetfirma *f* dotcom
company; **Internethandel** *m*
e-commerce; **Internetseite** *f*
web page; **Internetzugang** *m*
internet access
interpretieren *vt* to interpret

(als as)
Interpunktion *f* punctuation
Interview *(-s, -s) nt* interview;
interviewen *vt* to interview
intim *adj* intimate
intolerant *adj* intolerant
investieren *vt* to invest
inwiefern *adv* in what way; *(in
welchem Ausmaß)* to what extent;
inwieweit *adv* to what extent
inzwischen *adv* meanwhile
Irak *(-(s)) m:* **(der) ~** Iraq
Iran *(-(s)) m:* **(der) ~** Iran
Ire *(-n, -n) m* Irishman
irgend *adv:* **~ so ein Idiot** some
idiot; **wenn ~ möglich** if at all
possible; **irgendein** *pron,*
irgendeine(r, s) *adj* some;
(fragend, im Bedingungssatz; beliebig)
any; **irgendetwas** *pron*
something; *(fragend, im
Bedingungssatz)* anything;
irgendjemand *pron* somebody;
(fragend, im Bedingungssatz)
anybody; **irgendwann** *adv*
sometime; *(zu beliebiger Zeit)* any
time; **irgendwie** *adv* somehow;
irgendwo *adv* somewhere;
(fragend, im Bedingungssatz)
anywhere
Irin *f* Irishwoman; **irisch** *adj*
Irish; **Irland** *nt* Ireland
ironisch *adj* ironic
irre *adj* crazy, mad; *(toll)* terrific;
Irre(r) *mf* lunatic; **irreführen** *irr*
vt to mislead; **irremachen** *vt* to
confuse; **irren** *vi* to be mistaken;
(umherirren) to wander ▷ *vr:* **sich
~** to be mistaken; **wenn ich mich
nicht irre** if I'm not mistaken; **sich
in der Nummer ~** *(Telefon)* to get
the wrong number; **irrsinnig** *adj*
mad, crazy; **Irrtum** *(-s, -tümer) m*
mistake, error; **irrtümlich** *adj*
mistaken ▷ *adv* by mistake
ISBN *(-) nt abk = **industrial
standard business network** ISBN

▷ (-) *f abk* = **Internationale Standard Buchnummer** ISBN
Ischias (-) *m* sciatica
ISDN (-) *nt abk* = **integrated services digital network** ISDN
Islam (-s) *m* Islam; **islamisch** *adj* Islamic
Island *nt* Iceland; **Isländer(in)** (-s, -) *m(f)* Icelander; **isländisch** *adj* Icelandic; **Isländisch** *nt* Icelandic
Isolierband *nt* insulating tape; **isolieren** *vt* to isolate; (*Elek*) to insulate
Isomatte *f* thermomat, karrymat®
Israel (-s) *nt* Israel; **Israeli** (-(s), -(s)) *m* (-, -(s)) *f* Israeli; **israelisch** *adj* Israeli
IT (-) *f abk* = **Informationstechnologie** IT
Italien (-s) *nt* Italy; **Italiener(in)** (-s, -) *m(f)* Italian; **italienisch** *adj* Italian; **Italienisch** *nt* Italian

j

○ SCHLÜSSELWORT

ja *adv* **1** yes; **haben Sie das gesehen? — ja** did you see it? — yes(, I did); **ich glaube ja** (yes,) I think so
2 (*fragend*) really?; **ich habe gekündigt — ja?** I've quit — have you?; **du kommst, ja?** you're coming, aren't you?
3 sei ja vorsichtig do be careful; **Sie wissen ja, dass ...** as you know, ...; **tu das ja nicht!** don't do that!; **ich habe es ja gewusst** I just knew it; **ja, also ...** well you see ...
Jacht (-, -en) *f* yacht; **Jachthafen** *m* marina
Jacke (-, -n) *f* jacket; (*Wolljacke*) cardigan
Jackett (-s, -s *o* -e) *nt* jacket
Jagd (-, -en) *f* hunt; (*Jagen*) hunting; **jagen** *vi* to hunt ▷ *vt* to

hunt; (*verfolgen*) to chase; **Jäger(in)**
m(f) hunter
Jaguar (*-s, -e*) *m* jaguar
Jahr (*-(e)s, -e*) *nt* year; **ein halbes
~** six months *pl*; **Anfang der
neunziger ~e** in the early nineties;
mit sechzehn ~en at (the age of)
sixteen; **Jahrestag** *m*
anniversary; **Jahreszahl** *f* date,
year; **Jahreszeit** *f* season;
Jahrgang *m* (*Wein*) year, vintage;
der ~ 1989 (*Personen*) those born in
1989; **Jahrhundert** (*-s, -e*) *nt*
century; **jährlich** *adj* yearly,
annual; **Jahrmarkt** *m* fair;
Jahrtausend *nt* millennium;
Jahrzehnt *nt* decade
jähzornig *adj* hot-tempered
Jakobsmuschel *f* scallop
Jalousie *f* (venetian) blind
Jamaika (*-s*) *nt* Jamaica
jämmerlich *adj* pathetic
jammern *vi* to moan
Januar (*-(s), -e*) *m* January; *siehe
auch* **Juni**
Japan (*-s*) *nt* Japan; **Japaner(in)**
(*-s, -*) *m(f)* Japanese; **japanisch**
adj Japanese; **Japanisch** *nt*
Japanese
jaulen *vi* to howl
jawohl *adv* yes (of course)
Jazz (*-*) *m* jazz

 SCHLÜSSELWORT

je *adv* 1 (*jemals*) ever; **hast du so
was je gesehen?** did you ever see
anything like it?
2 (*jeweils*) every, each; **sie zahlten
je 3 Euro** they paid 3 euros each
▷ *konj* 1 **je nach** depending on; **je
nachdem** it depends; **je nachdem,
ob ...** depending on whether ...
2 **je eher, desto** *o* **umso besser**
the sooner the better

Jeans (*-, -*) *f* jeans *pl*

jede(r, s) *unbest Zahlwort*
(*insgesamt gesehen*) every; (*einzeln
gesehen*) each; (*jede(r, s) beliebige*)
any; **~s Mal** every time, each time;
~n zweiten Tag every other day;
sie hat an ~m Finger einen Ring
she's got a ring on each finger; **~r
Computer reicht aus** any
computer will do; **bei ~m Wetter**
in any weather ▷ *pron* everybody;
(*jeder Einzelne*) each; **~r von
euch/uns** each of you/us;
jedenfalls *adv* in any case;
jederzeit *adv* at any time;
jedesmal *adv* every time
jedoch *adv* however
jemals *adv* ever
jemand *pron* somebody; (*in Frage
und Verneinung*) anybody
Jemen (*-(s)*) *m* Yemen
jene(r, s) *adj* that, those *pl*
▷ *pron* that (one), those *pl*
jenseits *adv* on the other side
▷ *prep* +*gen* on the other side of;
(*fig*) beyond
Jetlag (*-s*) *m* jet lag
jetzig *adj* present
jetzt *adv* now; **erst ~** only now;
~ gleich right now; **bis ~** so far, up
to now; **von ~ an** from now on
jeweils *adv*: **~ zwei zusammen**
two at a time; **zu ~ 5 Euro** at 5
euros each
Job (*-s, -s*) *m* job; **jobben** *vi*
(*fam*) to work, to have a job
Jod (*-(e)s*) *nt* iodine
joggen *vi* to jog; **Jogging** (*-s*) *nt*
jogging; **Jogginganzug** *m*
jogging suit, tracksuit;
Jogginghose *f* jogging pants *pl*
Jog(h)urt (*-s, -s*) *m o nt* yoghurt
Johannisbeere *f*: **Schwarze
~** blackcurrant; **Rote ~** redcurrant
Joint (*-s, -s*) *m* (*fam*) joint
jonglieren *vi* to juggle
Jordanien (*-s*) *nt* Jordan
Journalist(in) *m(f)* journalist

Joystick (-s, -s) m (Inform)
joystick
jubeln vi to cheer
Jubiläum (-s, Jubiläen) nt jubilee;
(Jahrestag) anniversary
jucken vi to itch ▷ vt: **es juckt
mich am Arm** my arm is itching;
das juckt mich nicht (fam) I
couldn't care less; **Juckreiz** m
itch
Jude (-n, -n) m, **Jüdin** f Jew; **sie
ist Jüdin** she's Jewish; **jüdisch** adj
Jewish
Judo (-(s)) nt judo
Jugend (-) f youth; **jugendfrei**
adj: **ein ~er Film** a U-rated film
(Brit), a G-rated film (US); **ein
nicht ~er Film** an X-rated film;
Jugendgruppe f youth group;
Jugendherberge (-, -n) f youth
hostel; **Jugendherbergsausweis**
m youth hostel card; **jugendlich**
adj youthful; **Jugendliche(r)** mf
young person; **Jugendstil** m art
nouveau; **Jugendzentrum** nt
youth centre
Jugoslawien (-s) nt (Hist)
Yugoslavia; **das ehemalige ~** the
former Yugoslavia
Juli (-(s), -s) m July; siehe auch **Juni**
jung adj young
Junge (-n, -n) m boy
Junge(s) (-n, -n) nt young animal;
die ~n pl the young pl
Jungfrau f virgin; (Astr) Virgo
Junggeselle (-n, -n) m bachelor;
Junggesellin f single woman
Juni (-(s), -s) m June; **im ~** in June;
am 4. ~ on 4(th) June, on June
4(th) (gesprochen: on the fourth of
June); **Anfang/Mitte/Ende ~** at
the beginning/in the middle/at
the end of June;
letzten/nächsten ~ last/next
June
Jupiter (-s) m Jupiter
Jura ohne Artikel (Studienfach) law;

~ studieren to study law;
Jurist(in) m(f) lawyer; **juristisch**
adj legal
Justiz (-) f justice;
Justizminister(in) m(f) minister
of justice
Juwel (-s, -en) nt jewel;
Juwelier(in) (-s, -e) m(f) jeweller

k

Kabel (-s, -) nt (Elek) wire; (stark) cable; **Kabelfernsehen** nt cable television

Kabeljau (-s, -e o -s) m cod

Kabine f cabin; (im Schwimmbad) cubicle

Kabrio (-s, -s) nt convertible

Kachel (-, -n) f tile; **Kachelofen** m tiled stove

Käfer (-s, -) m beetle, bug (US)

Kaff (-s, -s) nt dump, hole

Kaffee (-s, -s) m coffee; **~ kochen** to make some coffee; **Kaffeefilter** m coffee filter; **Kaffeekanne** f coffeepot; **Kaffeeklatsch** (-(e)s, -e) m chat over coffee and cakes, coffee klatch (US); **Kaffeelöffel** m coffee spoon; **Kaffeemaschine** f coffee maker (o machine); **Kaffeetasse** f coffee cup

Käfig (-s, -e) m cage

kahl adj (Mensch, Kopf) bald; (Baum, Wand) bare

Kahn (-(e)s, Kähne) m boat; (Lastkahn) barge

Kai (-s, -e o -s) m quay

Kaiser (-s, -) m emperor; **Kaiserin** f empress; **Kaiserschnitt** m (Med) caesarean (section)

Kajak (-s, -s) nt kayak; **Kajakfahren** nt kayaking

Kajal (-s) m kohl

Kajüte (-, -n) f cabin

Kakao (-s, -s) m cocoa; (Getränk) (hot) chocolate

Kakerlake (-, -n) f cockroach

Kaki (-, -s) f kaki

Kaktee (-, -n) f, **Kaktus** (-, -se) m cactus

Kalb (-(e)s, Kälber) nt calf; **Kalbfleisch** nt veal; **Kalbsbraten** m roast veal; **Kalbsschnitzel** nt veal cutlet; (paniert) escalope of veal

Kalender (-s, -) m calendar; (Taschenkalender) diary

Kalk (-(e)s, -e) m lime; (in Knochen) calcium

Kalorie f calorie; **kalorienarm** adj low-calorie

kalt adj cold; **mir ist (es) ~** I'm cold; **kaltblütig** adj cold-blooded; **Kälte** (-) f cold; (fig) coldness

kam imperf von **kommen**

Kambodscha (-s) nt Cambodia

Kamel (-(e)s, -e) nt camel

Kamera (-, -s) f camera

Kamerad(in) (-en, -en) m(f) friend; (als Begleiter) companion

Kamerafrau f, **Kameramann** m camerawoman/-man

Kamille (-, -n) f camomile; **Kamillentee** m camomile tea

Kamin (-s, -e) m (außen) chimney; (innen) fireplace

Kamm (-(e)s, Kämme) m comb; (Berg) ridge; (Hahn) crest; **kämmen** vr **sich ~, sich** (dat) **die Haare ~** to comb one's hair; **Kammermusik** f chamber music

Kampf (-(e)s, Kämpfe) m fight; (Schlacht) battle; (Wettbewerb) contest; (fig: Anstrengung) struggle; **kämpfen** vi to fight (für, um for); **Kampfsport** m martial art

Kanada (-s) nt Canada; **Kanadier(in)** (-s, -) m(f) Canadian; **kanadisch** adj Canadian

Kanal (-s, Kanäle) m (Fluss) canal; (Rinne, TV) channel; (für Abfluss) drain; **der ~** (Ärmelkanal) the (English) Channel; **Kanalinseln** pl Channel Islands pl; **Kanalisation** f sewerage system; **Kanaltunnel** m Channel Tunnel

Kanarienvogel m canary

Kandidat(in) (-en, -en) m(f) candidate

Kandis(zucker) (-) m rock candy

Känguru (-s, -s) nt kangaroo

Kaninchen nt rabbit

Kanister (-s, -) m can

Kännchen nt pot; **ein ~ Kaffee/Tee** a pot of coffee/tea; **Kanne** (-, -n) f (Krug) jug; (Kaffeekanne) pot; (Milchkanne) churn; (Gießkanne) can

kannte imperf von **kennen**

Kante (-, -n) f edge

Kantine f canteen

Kanton (-s, -e) m canton

Kanu (-s, -s) nt canoe

Kanzler(in) (-s, -) m(f) chancellor

Kap (-s, -s) nt cape

Kapazität f capacity; (Fachmann) authority

Kapelle f (Gebäude) chapel; (Mus) band

Kaper (-, -n) f caper

kapieren vt, vi (fam) to understand; **kapiert?** got it?

Kapital (-s, -e o -ien) nt capital

Kapitän (-s, -e) m captain

Kapitel (-s, -) nt chapter

Kappe (-, -n) f cap

Kapsel (-, -n) f capsule

kaputt adj (fam) broken; (Mensch) exhausted; **kaputt|gehen** irr vi to break; (Schuhe) to fall apart; (Firma) to go bust; (Stoff) to wear out; **kaputt|machen** vt to break; (jdn) to wear out

Kapuze (-, -n) f hood

Kap Verde (-s) nt Cape Verde

Karaffe (-, -n) f carafe; (mit Stöpsel) decanter

Karamell (-s) m caramel, toffee

Karaoke (-(s)) nt karaoke

Karat (-s, -e) nt carat

Karate (-s) nt karate

Kardinal (-s, Kardinäle) m cardinal

Karfreitag m Good Friday

kariert adj checked; (Papier) squared

Karies (-) f (tooth) decay

Karikatur f caricature

Karneval (-s, -e o -s) m carnival

Kärnten (-s) nt Carinthia

Karo (-s, -s) nt square; (Karten) diamonds pl

Karosserie f (Auto) body(work)

Karotte (-, -n) f carrot
Karpfen (-s, -) m carp
Karriere (-, -n) f career
Karte (-, -n) f card; (*Landkarte*) map; (*Speisekarte*) menu; (*Eintrittskarte, Fahrkarte*) ticket; **mit ~ bezahlen** to pay by credit card; **~n spielen** to play cards; **die ~n mischen/geben** to shuffle/deal the cards
Kartei f card index; **Karteikarte** f index card
Kartenspiel nt card game; **Kartentelefon** nt cardphone; **Kartenvorverkauf** m advance booking
Kartoffel (-, -n) f potato; **Kartoffelbrei** m mashed potatoes pl; **Kartoffelchips** pl crisps pl (*Brit*), chips pl (*US*); **Kartoffelpuffer** m potato cake (*made from grated potatoes*); **Kartoffelpüree** nt mashed potatoes pl; **Kartoffelsalat** m potato salad
Karton (-s, -s) m cardboard; (*Schachtel*) (cardboard) box
Kartusche (-, -n) f cartridge
Karussell (-s, -s) nt roundabout (*Brit*), merry-go-round
Kaschmir (-s, e) m (*Stoff*) cashmere
Käse (-s, -) m cheese; **Käsekuchen** m cheesecake; **Käseplatte** f cheeseboard
Kasino (-s, -s) nt (*Spielkasino*) casino
Kaskoversicherung f comprehensive insurance
Kasper(l) (-s, -) m Punch; (*fig*) clown; **Kasperl(e)theater** nt (*Vorstellung*) Punch and Judy show; (*Gebäude*) Punch and Judy theatre
Kasse (-, -n) f (*in Geschäft*) till, cash register; (*im Supermarkt*) checkout; (*Geldkasten*) cashbox; (*Theater*) box office; (*Kino*) ticket office; (*Krankenkasse*) health insurance; (*Spar~*) savings bank; **Kassenbon** (-s, -s) m, **Kassenzettel** m receipt
Kassette f (small) box; (*Tonband*) cassette; **Kassettenrekorder** m cassette recorder
kassieren vt to take ▷ vi: **darf ich ~?** would you like to pay now?; **Kassierer(in)** m(f) cashier
Kastanie f chestnut
Kasten (-s, Kästen) m (*Behälter*) box; (*Getränkekasten*) crate
Kat m abk = **Katalysator**
Katalog (-(e)s, -e) m catalogue
Katalysator m (*Auto*) catalytic converter; (*Phys*) catalyst
Katar (-s) nt Qatar
Katarr(h) (-s, -e) m catarrh
Katastrophe (-, -n) f catastrophe, disaster
Kategorie (-, -n) f category
Kater (-s, -) m tomcat; (*fam: nach zu viel Alkohol*) hangover
Kathedrale (-, -n) f cathedral
Katholik(in) m(f) Catholic; **katholisch** adj Catholic
Katze (-, -n) f cat
Kauderwelsch (-(s)) nt (*unverständlich*) gibberish; (*Fachjargon*) jargon
kauen vt, vi to chew
Kauf (-(e)s, Käufe) m purchase; (*Kaufen*) buying; **ein guter ~** a bargain; **etw in ~ nehmen** to put up with sth; **kaufen** vt to buy; **Käufer(in)** m(f) buyer; **Kauffrau** f businesswoman; **Kaufhaus** nt department store; **Kaufmann** m businessman; (*im Einzelhandel*) shopkeeper (*Brit*), storekeeper (*US*); **Kaufpreis** m purchase price; **Kaufvertrag** m purchase agreement
Kaugummi m chewing gum
Kaulquappe (-, -n) f tadpole

kaum *adv* hardly, scarcely
Kaution *f* deposit; (*Jur*) bail
Kaviar *m* caviar
KB (-, -) *nt*, **Kbyte** (-, -) *nt abk* =
  Kilobyte KB
Kebab (-(s), -s) *m* kebab
Kegel (-s, -) *m* skittle; (*beim
  Bowling*) pin; (*Math*) cone;
  Kegelbahn *f* bowling alley;
  kegeln *vi* to play skittles; (*bowlen*)
  to bowl
Kehle (-, -n) *f* throat; **Kehlkopf**
  m larynx
Kehre (-, -n) *f* sharp bend
kehren *vt* (*fegen*) to sweep
Keilriemen *m* (*Auto*) fan belt
kein *pron* no, not ... any; **ich habe
  ~ Geld** I have no money, I don't
  have money; **~ Mensch** no one; **du
  bist ~ Kind mehr** you're not a
  child any more; **keine(r, s)** *pron*
  (*Person*) no one, nobody; (*Sache*)
  not ... any, none; **~r von ihnen**
  none of them; (*bei zwei
  Personen/Sachen*) neither of them;
  ich will keins von beiden I don't
  want either (of them); **keinesfalls**
  adv on no account, under no
  circumstances
Keks (-es, -e) *m* biscuit (*Brit*),
  cookie (*US*); **jdm auf den ~ gehen**
  (*fam*) to get on sb's nerves
Keller (-s, -) *m* cellar; (*Geschoss*)
  basement
Kellner (-s, -) *m* waiter;
  Kellnerin *f* waitress
Kenia (-s) *nt* Kenya
kennen (*kannte, gekannt*) *vt* to
  know; **wir ~ uns seit 1990** we've
  known each other since 1990; **wir
  ~ uns schon** we've already met;
  kennst du mich noch? do you
  remember me?; **kennen|lernen**
  vt to get to know; **sich ~** to get to
  know each other; (*zum ersten Mal*)
  to meet
Kenntnis *f* knowledge; **seine ~se**

his knowledge
Kennwort *nt* (*a. Inform*)
  password; **Kennzeichen** *nt*
  mark, sign; (*Auto*) number plate
  (*Brit*), license plate (*US*);
  besondere ~ distinguishing
  marks
Kerl (-s, -e) *m* guy, bloke (*Brit*)
Kern (-(e)s, -e) *m* (*Obst*) pip;
  (*Pfirsich, Kirsche etc*) stone; (*Nuss*)
  kernel; (*Atomkern*) nucleus; (*fig*)
  heart, core
Kernenergie *f* nuclear energy;
  Kernkraft *f* nuclear power;
  Kernkraftwerk *nt* nuclear power
  station
Kerze (-, -n) *f* candle; (*Zündkerze*)
  plug
Ket(s)chup (-(s), -s) *m o nt*
  ketchup
Kette (-, -n) *f* chain; (*Halskette*)
  necklace
keuchen *vi* to pant;
  Keuchhusten *m* whooping
  cough
Keule (-, -n) *f* club; (*Gastr*) leg;
  (*von Hähnchen a.*) drumstick
Keyboard (-s, -s) *nt* (*Mus*)
  keyboard
Kfz *nt abk* = **Kraftfahrzeug**
Kfz-Brief *m* ≈ logbook
Kfz-Steuer *f* ≈ road tax (*Brit*),
  vehicle tax (*US*)
KG (-, -s) *f abk* =
  Kommanditgesellschaft limited
  partnership
Kichererbse *f* chick pea
kichern *vi* to giggle
Kickboard® (-s, -s) *nt* micro
  scooter
Kicker (-s, -) *m* (*Spiel*) table
  football (*Brit*), foosball (*US*)
kidnappen *vt* to kidnap
Kidney-Bohne *f* kidney bean
Kiefer (-s, -) *m* jaw ▷ (-, -n) *f*
  pine; **Kieferchirurg(in)** *m(f)* oral
  surgeon

Kieme (-, -n) f gill
Kies (-es, -e) m gravel; **Kiesel**
(-s, -) m, **Kieselstein** m pebble
kiffen vi (fam) to smoke pot
Kilo (-s, -(s)) nt kilo; **Kilobyte** nt
kilobyte; **Kilogramm** nt
kilogram; **Kilometer** m
kilometre; **Kilometerstand** m
≈ mileage; **Kilometerzähler** m
≈ mileometer; **Kilowatt** nt
kilowatt
Kind (-(e)s, -er) nt child; **sie
bekommt ein ~** she's having a
baby; **Kinderarzt** m,
Kinderärztin f paediatrician;
Kinderbetreuung f childcare;
Kinderbett nt cot (Brit), crib (US);
Kinderfahrkarte f child's ticket;
Kindergarten m nursery school,
kindergarten; **Kindergärtner(in)**
m(f) nursery-school teacher;
Kindergeld nt child benefit;
Kinderkrankheit f children's
illness; **Kinderkrippe** f crèche
(Brit), daycare center (US);
Kinderlähmung f polio;
Kindermädchen nt nanny (Brit),
nurse(maid); **kindersicher** adj
childproof; **Kindersicherung** f
childproof safety catch; (an Flasche)
childproof cap; **Kindersitz** m
child seat; **Kindertagesstätte** nt
day nursery; **Kinderteller** m (im
Restaurant) children's portion;
Kinderwagen m pram (Brit),
baby carriage (US); **Kinderzimmer**
nt children's (bed)room; **Kindheit**
f childhood; **kindisch** adj
childish; **kindlich** adj childlike
Kinn (-(e)s, -e) nt chin
Kino (-s, -s) nt cinema (Brit),
movie theater (US); **ins ~ gehen** to
go to the cinema (Brit) (o to the
movies (US))
Kiosk (-(e)s, -e) m kiosk
Kippe f (fam: Zigarettenstummel)
cigarette end, fag end (Brit)

kippen vi to tip over ▷ vt to tilt;
(Regierung, Minister) to topple
Kirche (-, -n) f church;
Kirchturm m church tower; (mit
Spitze) steeple
Kirmes (-, -sen) f fair
Kirsche (-, -n) f cherry;
Kirschtomate f cherry tomato
Kissen (-s, -) nt cushion;
(Kopfkissen) pillow; **Kissenbezug**
m cushion cover; (für Kopfkissen)
pillowcase
Kiste (-, -n) f box; (Truhe) chest
KITA (-, -s) f abk =
Kindertagesstätte day-care
centre (Brit), day-care center (US)
kitschig adj kitschy, cheesy
kitzelig adj (a. fig) ticklish;
kitzeln vt, vi to tickle
Kiwi (-, -s) f (Frucht) kiwi (fruit)
Klage (-, -n) f complaint; (Jur)
lawsuit; **klagen** vi to complain
(über +akk about, bei to); **kläglich**
adj wretched
Klammer (-, -n) f (in Text)
bracket; (Büroklammer) clip;
(Wäscheklammer) peg (Brit),
clothespin (US); (Zahnklammer)
brace; **Klammeraffe** m (fam)
at-sign, @; **klammern** vr: **sich
~** to cling (an +akk to)
klang imperf von **klingen**
Klang (-(e)s, Klänge) m sound
Klappbett nt folding bed
klappen vi impers (gelingen) to
work; **es hat gut geklappt** it went
well
klappern vi to rattle; (Geschirr) to
clatter; **Klapperschlange** f
rattlesnake
Klappfahrad nt folding bicycle;
Klappstuhl m folding chair
klar adj clear; **sich** (dat) **im Klaren
sein** to be clear (über +akk about);
alles ~? everything okay?
klären vt (Flüssigkeit) to purify;
(Probleme, Frage) to clarify ▷ vr:

sich ~ to clear itself up
Klarinette (-, -n) f clarinet
klar|kommen irr vi: **mit etw ~** to cope with something; **kommst du klar?** are you managing all right?; **mit jdm ~** to get along with sb; **klar|machen** vt: **jdm etw ~** to make sth clear to sb; **klar|stellen** vt to clarify
Klärung f (von Frage, Problem) clarification
klasse adj inv (fam) great, brilliant
Klasse (-, -n) f class; (Schuljahr) form (Brit), grade (US); **erster ~ reisen** to travel first class; **in welche ~ gehst du?** which form (Brit) (o grade (US)) are you in?; **Klassenarbeit** f test; **Klassenlehrer(in)** m(f) class teacher; **Klassenzimmer** nt classroom
Klassik f (Zeit) classical period; (Musik) classical music
Klatsch (-(e)s, -e) m (Gerede) gossip; **klatschen** vi (schlagen) to smack; (Beifall) to applaud, to clap; (reden) to gossip; **Klatschmohn** m (corn) poppy; **klatschnass** adj soaking (wet)
Klaue (-, -n) f claw; (fam: Schrift) scrawl; **klauen** vt (fam) to pinch
Klavier (-s, -e) nt piano
Klebeband nt adhesive tape; **kleben** vt to stick (an +akk to) ▷ vi (klebrig sein) to be sticky; **klebrig** adj sticky; **Klebstoff** m glue; **Klebstreifen** m adhesive tape
Klecks (-es, -e) m blob; (Tinte) blot
Klee (-s) m clover
Kleid (-(e)s, -er) nt (Frauen~) dress; **~er** pl (Kleidung) clothes pl; **Kleiderbügel** m coat hanger; **Kleiderschrank** m wardrobe (Brit), closet (US); **Kleidung** f clothing
klein adj small, little; (Finger) little; **mein ~er Bruder** my little (o

younger) brother; **als ich noch ~ war** when I was a little boy/girl; **etw ~ schneiden** to chop sth up; **Kleinanzeige** f classified ad; **Kleinbuchstabe** m small letter; **Kleinbus** m minibus; **Kleingeld** nt change; **Kleinigkeit** f trifle; (Zwischenmahlzeit) snack; **Kleinkind** nt toddler; **klein|schreiben** vt (mit kleinem Anfangsbuchstaben) to write with a small letter; **Kleinstadt** f small town
Kleister (-s, -) m paste
Klempner(in) m(f) plumber
klettern vi to climb
Klettverschluss m Velcro® fastening
klicken vi (a. Inform) to click
Klient(in) (-en, -en) m(f) client
Klima (-s, -s) nt climate; **Klimaanlage** f air conditioning; **klimatisiert** adj air-conditioned
Klinge (-, -n) f blade
Klingel (-, -n) f bell; **klingeln** vi to ring
klingen (klang, geklungen) vi to sound
Klinik f clinic; (Krankenhaus) hospital
Klinke (-, -n) f handle
Klippe (-, -n) f cliff; (im Meer) reef; (fig) hurdle
Klischee (-s, -s) nt (fig) cliché
Klo (-s, -s) nt (fam) loo (Brit), john (US); **Klobrille** f toilet seat; **Klopapier** nt toilet paper
klopfen vt, vi to knock; (Herz) to thump
Kloß (-es, Klöße) m (im Hals) lump; (Gastr) dumpling
Kloster (-s, Klöster) nt (für Männer) monastery; (für Frauen) convent
Klub (-s, -s) m club
klug adj clever
knabbern vt, vi to nibble

Knäckebrot nt crispbread
knacken vt, vi to crack
Knall (-(e)s, -e) m bang; **knallen** vi to bang
knapp adj (kaum ausreichend) scarce; (Sieg) narrow; **~ bei Kasse sein** to be short of money; **~ zwei Stunden** just under two hours
Knauf (-s, Knäufe) m knob
kneifen (kniff, gekniffen) vt, vi to pinch; (sich drücken) to back out (vor +dat of); **Kneifzange** f pincers pl
Kneipe (-, -n) f (fam) pub (Brit), bar
Knete (-) f (fam: Geld) dough; **kneten** vt to knead; (formen) to mould
knicken vt, vi (brechen) to break; (Papier) to fold; **geknickt sein** (fig) to be downcast
Knie (-s, -) nt knee; **in die ~ gehen** to bend one's knees; **Kniebeuge** f knee bend; **Kniegelenk** nt knee joint; **Kniekehle** f back of the knee; **knien** vi to kneel; **Kniescheibe** f kneecap; **Knieschoner** (-s, -) m, **Knieschützer** (-s, -) m knee pad; **Kniestrumpf** m knee-length sock
kniff imperf von **kneifen**
knipsen vt to punch; (Foto) to snap ▷ vi (Foto) to take snaps
knirschen vt to crunch; **mit den Zähnen ~** to grind one's teeth
knitterfrei adj non-crease; **knittern** vi to crease
Knoblauch m garlic; **Knoblauchbrot** nt garlic bread; **Knoblauchzehe** f clove of garlic
Knöchel (-s, -) m (Finger) knuckle; (Fuß) ankle
Knochen (-s, -) m bone; **Knochenbruch** m fracture; **Knochenmark** nt marrow
Knödel (-s, -) m dumpling
Knollensellerie m celeriac

Knopf (-(e)s, Knöpfe) m button; **Knopfdruck** m: **auf ~** at the touch of a botton; **Knopfloch** nt buttonhole
Knospe (-, -n) f bud
knoten vt to knot; **Knoten** (-s, -) m knot; (Med) lump
Know-how (-(s)) nt know-how, expertise
knurren vi (Hund) to growl; (Magen) to rumble; (Mensch) to grumble
knusprig adj crisp; (Keks) crunchy
knutschen vi (fam) to smooch
k. o. adj inv (Sport) knocked out; (fig) knackered
Koalition f coalition
Koch (-(e)s, Köche) m cook; **Kochbuch** nt cookery book, cookbook; **kochen** vt, vi to cook; (Wasser) to boil; (Kaffee, Tee) to make; **Köchin** f cook; **Kochlöffel** m wooden spoon; **Kochnische** f kitchenette; **Kochplatte** f hotplate; **Kochrezept** nt recipe; **Kochtopf** m saucepan
Kode (-s, -s) m code
Köder (-s, -) m bait
Koffein (-s) nt caffeine; **koffeinfrei** adj decaffeinated
Koffer (-s, -) m (suit)case; **Kofferraum** m (Auto) boot (Brit), trunk (US)
Kognak (-s, -s) m brandy
Kohl (-(e)s, -e) m cabbage
Kohle (-, -n) f coal; (Holzkohle) charcoal; (Chem) carbon; (fam: Geld) cash, dough; **Kohlehydrat** nt carbohydrate; **Kohlendioxid** nt carbon dioxide; **Kohlensäure** f (in Getränken) fizz; **ohne ~** still, non-carbonated (US); **mit ~** sparkling, carbonated (US); **Kohletablette** f charcoal tablet
Kohlrabi (-(s), -(s)) m kohlrabi
Koje (-, -n) f cabin; (Bett) bunk

Kokain (-s) nt cocaine
Kokosnuss f coconut
Kolben (-s, -) m (Tech) piston; (Mais~) cob
Kolik (-, -en) f colic
Kollaps (-es, -e) m collapse
Kollege (-n, -n) m, **Kollegin** f colleague
Köln (-s) nt Cologne
Kolonne (-, -n) f convoy; **in ~ fahren** to drive in convoy
Kölsch (-, -) nt (Bier) (strong) lager (from the Cologne region)
Kolumbien (-s) nt Columbia
Koma (-s, -s) nt coma
Kombi (-(s), -s) m estate (car) (Brit), station wagon (US); **Kombination** f combination; (Folgerung) deduction; (Hemdhose) combinations pl; (Aviat) flying suit; **kombinieren** vt to combine ▷ vi to reason; (vermuten) to guess; **Kombizange** f (pair of) pliers pl
Komfort (-s) m conveniences pl; (Bequemlichkeit) comfort
Komiker(in) m(f) comedian, comic; **komisch** adj funny
Komma (-s, -s) nt comma
Kommanditgesellschaft f limited partnership
kommen (kam, gekommen) vi to come; (näher kommen) to approach; (passieren) to happen; (gelangen, geraten) to get; (erscheinen) to appear; (in die Schule, das Gefängnis etc) to go; **~ lassen** to send for; **zu sich ~** to come round (o to); **zu etw ~** (bekommen) to acquire sth; (Zeit dazu finden) to get round to sth; **wer kommt zuerst?** who's first?; **kommend** adj coming; **~e Woche** next week; **in den ~en Jahren** in the years to come
Kommentar m commentary; **kein ~** no comment
Kommilitone (-n, -n) m, **Kommilitonin** f fellow student

Kommissar(in) m(f) inspector
Kommode (-, -n) f chest of drawers
Kommunikation f communication
Kommunion f (Rel) communion
Kommunismus m communism
Komödie f comedy
kompakt adj compact
Kompass (-es, -e) m compass
kompatibel adj compatible
kompetent adj competent
komplett adj complete
Kompliment nt compliment; **jdm ein ~ machen** to pay sb a compliment; **~!** congratulations
Komplize (-n, -n) m accomplice
kompliziert adj complicated
Komponist(in) m(f) composer
Kompost (-(e)s, -e) m compost; **Komposthaufen** m compost heap; **kompostierbar** adj biodegradable
Kompott (-(e)s, -e) nt stewed fruit
Kompresse (-, -n) f compress
Kompromiss (-es, -e) m compromise
Kondensmilch f condensed milk, evaporated milk
Kondition f (Leistungsfähigkeit) condition; **sie hat eine gute ~** she's in good shape
Konditorei f cake shop; (mit Café) café
Kondom (-s, -e) nt condom
Konfektionsgröße f size
Konferenz f conference
Konfession f religion; (christlich) denomination
Konfetti (-(s)) nt confetti
Konfirmation f (Rel) confirmation
Konfitüre (-, -n) f jam
Konflikt (-(e)s, -e) m conflict
konfrontieren vt to confront
Kongo (-s) m Congo

Kongress (-es, -e) m conference;
der ~ (Parlament der USA)
Congress
König (-(e)s, -e) m king; **Königin**
f queen; **königlich** adj royal;
Königreich nt kingdom
Konkurrenz f competition

⊙ SCHLÜSSELWORT

können (pt **konnte**, pp **gekonnt** o
(als Hilfsverb) **können**) vt, vi **1** to be
able to; **ich kann es machen** I can
do it, I am able to do it; **ich kann
es nicht machen** I can't do it, I'm
not able to do it; **ich kann nicht ...**
I can't ..., I cannot ...; **ich kann
nicht mehr** I can't go on
2 (wissen, beherrschen) to know;
können Sie Deutsch? can you
speak German?; **er kann gut
Englisch** he speaks English well;
sie kann keine Mathematik she
can't do mathematics
3 (dürfen) to be allowed to; **kann
ich gehen?** can I go?; **könnte ich
...?** could I ...?; **kann ich mit?** (fam)
can I come with you?
4 (möglich sein) **Sie könnten recht
haben** you may be right; **das kann
sein** that's possible; **kann sein**
maybe

konsequent adj consistent;
Konsequenz f consequence
konservativ adj conservative
Konserven pl tinned food sing
(Brit), canned food sing;
Konservendose f tin (Brit), can
konservieren vt to preserve;
Konservierungsmittel nt
preservative
Konsonant m consonant
Konsul(in) (-s, -n) m(f) consul;
Konsulat nt consulate
Kontakt (-(e)s, -e) m contact;
kontaktarm adj: **er ist ~** he lacks

contact with other people;
kontaktfreudig adj sociable;
Kontaktlinsen pl contact lenses
pl
Kontinent m continent
Konto (-s, Konten) nt account;
Kontoauszug m (bank)
statement;
Kontoauszugsdrucker m
bank-statement machine;
Kontoinhaber(in) m(f) account
holder; **Kontonummer** f
account number; **Kontostand** m
balance
Kontrabass m double bass
Kontrast (-(e)s, -e) m contrast
Kontrolle (-, -n) f control;
(Aufsicht) supervision;
(Passkontrolle) passport control;
kontrollieren vt to control;
(nachprüfen) to check
Konzentration f concentra-
tion; **Konzentrationslager** nt
(Hist) concentration camp;
konzentrieren vt to concentrate
▷ vr: **sich ~** to concentrate
Konzept (-(e)s, -e) nt rough draft;
jdn aus dem ~ bringen to put sb
off
Konzern (-(e)s, -e) m firm
Konzert (-(e)s, -e) nt concert;
(Stück) concerto; **Konzertsaal** m
concert hall
koordinieren vt to coordinate
Kopf (-(e)s, Köpfe) m head; **pro
~** per person; **sich den
~ zerbrechen** to rack one's brains;
Kopfhörer m headphones pl;
Kopfkissen nt pillow; **Kopfsalat**
m lettuce; **Kopfschmerzen** pl
headache sing; **Kopfstütze** f
headrest; **Kopftuch** nt
headscarf; **kopfüber** adv
headfirst
Kopie f copy; **kopieren** vt (a.
Inform) to copy; **Kopierer** (-s, -) m,
Kopiergerät nt copier

Kopilot(in) *m(f)* co-pilot
Koralle (-, -n) *f* coral
Koran (-s) *m* (*Rel*) Koran
Korb (-(e)s, Körbe) *m* basket; **jdm einen ~ geben** (*fig*) to turn sb down
Kord (-(e)s, -e) *m* corduroy
Kordel (-, -n) *f* cord
Kork (-(e)s, -e) *m* cork; **Korken** (-s, -) *m* cork; **Korkenzieher** (-s, -) *m* corkscrew
Korn (-(e)s, Körner) *nt* grain; **Kornblume** *f* cornflower
Körper (-s, -) *m* body; **Körperbau** *m* build; **Körpergeruch** *m* body odour; **Körpergröße** *f* height; **körperlich** *adj* physical; **Körperteil** *m* part of the body; **Körperverletzung** *f* physical injury
korrekt *adj* correct
Korrespondent(in) *m(f)* correspondent; **Korrespondenz** *f* correspondence
korrigieren *vt* to correct
Kosmetik *f* cosmetics *pl*; **Kosmetikkoffer** *m* vanity case; **Kosmetiksalon** *m* beauty parlour; **Kosmetiktuch** *nt* paper tissue
Kost (-) *f* (*Nahrung*) food; (*Verpflegung*) board
kostbar *adj* precious; (*teuer*) costly, expensive
kosten *vt* to cost ▷ *vt*, *vi* (*versuchen*) to taste; **Kosten** *pl* costs *pl*, cost; (*Ausgaben*) expenses *pl*; **auf ~ von** at the expense of; **kostenlos** *adj* free (of charge); **Kostenvoranschlag** *m* estimate
köstlich *adj* (*Essen*) delicious; (*Einfall*) delightful; **sich ~ amüsieren** to have a marvellous time
Kostprobe *f* taster; (*fig*) sample; **kostspielig** *adj* expensive
Kostüm (-s, -e) *nt* costume;

(*Damenkostüm*) suit
Kot (-(e)s) *m* excrement
Kotelett (-(e)s, -e o -s) *nt* chop, cutlet
Koteletten *pl* sideboards *pl* (*Brit*), sideburns *pl* (*US*)
Kotflügel *m* (*Auto*) wing
kotzen *vi* (*vulg*) to puke, to throw up
Krabbe (-, -n) *f* shrimp; (*größer*) prawn; (*Krebs*) crab
krabbeln *vi* to crawl
Krach (-(e)s, -s o -e) *m* crash; (*andauernd*) noise; (*fam*: *Streit*) row
Kraft (-, Kräfte) *f* strength; (*Pol*, *Phys*) force; (*Fähigkeit*) power; (*Arbeits~*) worker; **in ~ treten** to come into effect; **Kraftausdruck** *m* swearword; **Kraftfahrzeug** *nt* motor vehicle; **Kraftfahrzeugbrief** *m* ≈ logbook; **Kraftfahrzeugschein** *m* vehicle registration document; **Kraftfahrzeugsteuer** *f* ≈ road tax (*Brit*), vehicle tax (*US*); **Kraftfahrzeugversicherung** *f* car insurance; **kräftig** *adj* strong; (*gesund*) healthy; (*Farben*) intense, strong; **Kraftstoff** *m* fuel; **Kraftwerk** *nt* power station
Kragen (-s, -) *m* collar
Krähe (-, -n) *f* crow
Kralle (-, -n) *f* claw; (*Parkkralle*) wheel clamp
Kram (-(e)s) *m* stuff
Krampf (-(e)s, Krämpfe) *m* cramp; (*zuckend*) spasm; **Krampfader** *f* varicose vein
Kran (-(e)s, Kräne) *m* crane
Kranich (-s, -e) *m* (*Zool*) crane
krank *adj* ill, sick
kränken *vt* to hurt
Krankengymnastik *f* physiotherapy; **Krankenhaus** *nt* hospital; **Krankenkasse** *f* health insurance; **Krankenpfleger** (-s, -) *m* (male) nurse;

Krankenschein m health insurance certificate; **Krankenschwester** f nurse; **Krankenversicherung** f health insurance; **Krankenwagen** m ambulance; **Krankheit** f illness; (durch Infektion hervorgerufen) disease

Kränkung f insult

Kranz (-es, Kränze) m wreath

krass adj crass; (fam: toll) wicked

kratzen vt, vi to scratch; **Kratzer** (-s, -) m scratch

kraulen vi (schwimmen) to do the crawl ▷ vt (streicheln) to pet

Kraut (-(e)s, Kräuter) nt plant; (Gewürz) herb; (Gemüse) cabbage; **Kräuter** pl herbs pl; **Kräuterbutter** f herb butter; **Kräutertee** m herbal tea; **Krautsalat** m coleslaw

Krawatte f tie

kreativ adj creative

Krebs (-es, -e) m (Zool) crab; (Med) cancer; (Astr) Cancer

Kredit (-(e)s, -e) m credit; **auf ~** on credit; **einen ~ aufnehmen** to take out a loan; **Kreditkarte** f credit card

Kreide (-, -n) f chalk

Kreis (-es, -e) m circle; (Bezirk) district

kreischen vi to shriek; (Bremsen, Säge) to screech

Kreisel (-s, -) m (Spielzeug) top; (Verkehrskreisel) roundabout (Brit), traffic circle (US)

Kreislauf m (Med) circulation; (fig: der Natur etc) cycle; **Kreislaufstörungen** pl (Med) **ich habe ~** I've got problems with my circulation; **Kreisverkehr** m roundabout (Brit), traffic circle (US)

Kren (-s) m horseradish

Kresse (-, -n) f cress

Kreuz (-es, -e) nt cross; (Anat) small of the back; (Karten) clubs pl;

mir tut das ~ weh I've got backache; **Kreuzband** nt cruciate ligament; **kreuzen** vt to cross ▷ vr: **sich ~** to cross ▷ vi (Naut) to cruise; **Kreuzfahrt** f cruise; **Kreuzgang** m cloisters pl; **Kreuzotter** (-, -n) f adder; **Kreuzschlitzschraubenzieher** m Phillips® screwdriver; **Kreuzschlüssel** m (Auto) wheel brace; **Kreuzschmerzen** pl backache sing; **Kreuzung** f (Verkehrskreuzung) crossroads sing, intersection; (Züchtung) cross; **Kreuzworträtsel** nt crossword (puzzle)

kriechen (kroch, gekrochen) vi to crawl; (unauffällig) to creep; (fig, pej) (**vor jdm**) **~** to crawl (to sb); **Kriechspur** f crawler lane

Krieg (-(e)s, -e) m war

kriegen vt (fam) to get; (erwischen) to catch; **sie kriegt ein Kind** she's having a baby; **ich kriege noch Geld von dir** you still owe me some money

Krimi (-s, -s) m (fam) thriller; **Kriminalität** f criminality; **Kriminalpolizei** f detective force, ≈ CID (Brit), ≈ FBI (US); **Kriminalroman** m detective novel; **kriminell** adj criminal

Krippe (-, -n) f (Futterkrippe) manger; (Weihnachtskrippe) crib (Brit), crèche (US); (Kinderkrippe) crèche (Brit), daycare center (US)

Krise (-, -n) f crisis

Kristall (-s, -e) m crystal ▷ (-s) nt (Glas) crystal

Kritik f criticism; (Rezension) review; **Kritiker(in)** m(f) critic; **kritisch** adj critical

kritzeln vt, vi to scribble, to scrawl

Kroate (-n, -n) m Croat; **Kroatien** (-s) nt Croatia; **Kroatin** f Croat; **kroatisch** adj Croatian;

Kroatisch nt Croatian

kroch imperf von **kriechen**

Krokodil (-s, -e) nt crocodile

Krokus (-, - o -se) m crocus

Krone (-, -n) f crown;
Kronleuchter m chandelier

Kropf (-(e)s, Kröpfe) m (Med)
goitre; (von Vogel) crop

Kröte (-, -n) f toad

Krücke (-, -n) f crutch

Krug (-(e)s, Krüge) m jug;
(Bierkrug) mug

Krümel (-s, -) m crumb

krumm adj crooked

Krüppel (-s, -) m cripple

Kruste (-, -n) f crust

Kruzifix (-es, -e) nt crucifix

Kuba (-s) nt Cuba

Kübel (-s, -) m tub; (Eimer) bucket

Kubikmeter m cubic metre

Küche (-, -n) f kitchen; (Kochen)
cooking

Kuchen (-s, -) m cake; (mit
Teigdeckel) pie; **Kuchengabel** f
cake fork

Küchenmaschine f food
processor; **Küchenpapier** nt
kitchen roll; **Küchenschrank** m
(kitchen) cupboard

Kuckuck (-s, -e) m cuckoo

Kugel (-, -n) f ball; (Math) sphere;
(Mil) bullet; (Weihnachtskugel)
bauble; **Kugellager** nt ball
bearing; **Kugelschreiber** m
(ball-point) pen, biro® (Brit);
Kugelstoßen (-s) nt shot put

Kuh (-, Kühe) f cow

kühl adj cool; **Kühlakku** (-s, -s) m
ice pack; **Kühlbox** f cool box;
kühlen vt to cool; **Kühler** (-s, -)
m (Auto) radiator; **Kühlerhaube**
f (Auto) bonnet (Brit), hood (US);
Kühlschrank m fridge,
refrigerator; **Kühltasche** f cool
bag; **Kühltruhe** f freezer;
Kühlwasser nt (Auto) radiator
water

Kuhstall m cowshed

Küken (-s, -) nt chick

Kuli (-s, -s) m (fam: Kugelschreiber)
pen, biro® (Brit)

Kulisse (-, -n) f scenery

Kult (-s, -e) m cult; **Kultfigur** f
cult figure

Kultur f culture; (Lebensform)
civilization; **Kulturbeutel** m
toilet bag (Brit), washbag;
kulturell adj cultural

Kümmel (-s, -) m caraway
seeds pl

Kummer (-s) m grief, sorrow

kümmern vr: **sich um jdn ~** to
look after sb; **sich um etw ~** to see
to sth ▷ vt to concern; **das
kümmert mich nicht** that doesn't
worry me

Kumpel (-s, -) m (fam) mate, pal

Kunde (-n, -n) m customer;
Kundendienst m after-sales (o
customer) service;
Kunden(kredit)karte f storecard, chargecard; **Kunden-
nummer** f customer number

kündigen vi to hand in one's
notice; (Mieter) to give notice that
one is moving out; **jdm ~** to give
sb his/her notice; (Vermieter) to
give sb notice to quit ▷ vt to
cancel; (Vertrag) to terminate; **jdm
die Stellung ~** to give sb his/her
notice; **jdm die Wohnung ~** to
give sb notice to quit; **Kündigung**
f (Arbeitsverhältnis) dismissal;
(Vertrag) termination;
(Abonnement) cancellation; (Frist)
notice; **Kündigungsfrist** f
period of notice

Kundin f customer; **Kundschaft**
f customers pl

künftig adj future

Kunst (-, Künste) f art; (Können)
skill; **Kunstausstellung** f art
exhibition; **Kunstgewerbe** nt arts
and crafts pl; **Künstler(in)** (-s, -)

m(f) artist; **künstlerisch** *adj* artistic

künstlich *adj* artificial

Kunststoff *m* synthetic material; **Kunststück** *nt* trick; **Kunstwerk** *nt* work of art

Kupfer *(-s, -)* *nt* copper

Kuppel *(-, -n)* *f* dome

kuppeln *vi (Auto)* to operate the clutch; **Kupplung** *f* coupling; *(Auto)* clutch

Kur *(-, -en)* *f* course of treatment; *(am Kurort)* cure

Kür *(-, -en)* *f (Sport)* free programme

Kurbel *(-, -n)* *f* crank; *(von Rollo, Fenster)* winder

Kürbis *(-ses, -se)* *m* pumpkin

Kurierdienst *m* courier service

kurieren *vt* to cure

Kurort *m* health resort

Kurs *(-es, -e)* *m* course; *(Fin)* rate; *(Wechselkurs)* exchange rate

kursiv *adj* italic ▷ *adv* in italics

Kursleiter(in) *m(f)* course tutor; **Kursteilnehmer(in)** *m(f)* (course) participant; **Kurswagen** *m* *(Eisenb)* through carriage

Kurve *(-, -n)* *f* curve; *(Straßenkurve)* bend; **kurvenreich** *adj (Straße)* winding

kurz *adj* short; *(zeitlich a.)* brief; **~ vorher/darauf** shortly before/after; **kannst du ~ kommen?** could you come here for a minute?; **~ gesagt** in short; **kurzärmelig** *adj* short-sleeved; **kürzen** *vt* to cut short; *(in der Länge)* to shorten; *(Gehalt)* to reduce; **kurzerhand** *adv* on the spot; **kurzfristig** *adj* short-term; **das Konzert wurde ~ abgesagt** the concert was called off at short notice; **Kurzgeschichte** *f* short story; **kurzhaarig** *adj* short-haired; **kürzlich** *adv* recently; **Kurzparkzone** *f* short-stay *(Brit)* *(o* short-term *(US))* parking zone; **Kurzschluss** *m* *(Elek)* short circuit; **kurzsichtig** *adj* short-sighted; **Kurztrip** *m* trip, break; **Kurzurlaub** *m* short holiday *(Brit)*, short vacation *(US)*; **Kurzwelle** *f* short wave

Kusine *f* cousin

Kuss *(-es, Küsse)* *m* kiss; **küssen** *vt* to kiss ▷ *vr*: **sich ~** to kiss

Küste *(-, -n)* *f* coast; *(Ufer)* shore; **Küstenwache** *f* coastguard

Kutsche *(-, -n)* *f* carriage; *(geschlossene)* coach

Kuvert *(-s, -s)* *nt* envelope

Kuvertüre *(-, -n)* *f* coating

Kuwait *(-s)* *nt* Kuwait

KZ *(-s, -s)* *nt* *abk* = **Konzentrationslager** *(Hist)* concentration camp

Labor (-s, -e o -s) nt lab

Labyrinth (-s, -e) nt maze

Lache (-, -n) f (Pfütze) puddle; (Blut~, Öl~) pool

lächeln vi to smile; **Lächeln** (-s) nt smile; **lachen** vi to laugh; **lächerlich** adj ridiculous

Lachs (-es, -e) m salmon

Lack (-(e)s, -e) m varnish; (Farblack) lacquer; (an Auto) paint; **lackieren** vt to varnish; (Auto) to spray; **Lackschaden** m scratch (on the paintwork)

Ladegerät nt (battery) charger; **laden** (lud, geladen) vt (a. Inform) to load; (einladen) to invite; (Handy etc) to charge

Laden (-s, Läden) m shop; (Fensterladen) shutter; **Ladendieb(in)** m(f) shoplifter; **Ladendiebstahl** m shoplifting; **Ladenschluss** m closing time

Ladung f load; (Naut, Aviat) cargo; (Jur) summons sing

lag imperf von **liegen**

Lage (-, -n) f position, situation; (Schicht) layer; **in der ~ sein zu** to be in a position to

Lager (-s, -) nt camp; (Comm) warehouse; (Tech) bearing; **Lagerfeuer** nt campfire; **lagern** vi (Dinge) to be stored; (Menschen) to camp ▷ vt to store

Lagune f lagoon

lahm adj lame; (langweilig) dull; **lähmen** vt to paralyse; **Lähmung** f paralysis

Laib (-s, -e) m loaf

Laie (-n, -n) m layman

Laken (-s, -) nt sheet

Lakritze (-, -n) f liquorice

Lamm (-(e)s, Lämmer) nt lamb

Lampe (-, -n) f lamp; (Glühbirne) bulb; **Lampenfieber** nt stage fright; **Lampenschirm** m lampshade

Lampion (-s, -s) m Chinese lantern

Land (-(e)s, Länder) nt (Gelände) land; (Nation) country; (Bundesland) state, Land; **auf dem ~(e)** in the country

● **LAND**
●
● A **Land** (plural **Länder**) is a
● member state of the **BRD**. There
● are 16 **Länder**, namely
● Baden-Württemberg, Bayern,
● Berlin, Brandenburg, Bremen,
● Hamburg, Hessen,
● Mecklenburg-Vorpommern,
● Niedersachsen,
● Nordrhein-Westfalen,
● Rheinland-Pfalz, Saarland,
● Sachsen, Sachsen-Anhalt,
● Schleswig-Holstein and
● Thüringen. Each "Land" has its
● own parliament and
● constitution.

Landebahn f runway; **landen** vt, vi to land; (Schiff) to dock

Länderspiel nt international (match)

Landesgrenze f national border, frontier; **Landesinnere** nt interior; **landesüblich** adj customary; **Landeswährung** f national currency; **landesweit** adj nationwide

Landhaus nt country house; **Landkarte** f map; **Landkreis** m administrative region, ≈ district

ländlich adj rural

Landschaft f countryside; (schöne) scenery; (Kunst) landscape; **Landstraße** f country road, B road (Brit)

Landung f landing; **Landungsbrücke** f, **Landungssteg** m gangway

Landwirt(in) m(f) farmer; **Landwirtschaft** f agriculture, farming; **landwirtschaftlich** adj agricultural

lang adj long; (Mensch) tall; **ein zwei Meter ~er Tisch** a table two metres long; **den ganzen Tag ~** all day long; **die Straße ~** along the street; **langärmelig** adj long-sleeved; **lange** adv (for) a long time; **ich musste ~ warten** I had to wait (for) a long time; **ich bleibe nicht ~** I won't stay long; **es ist ~ her, dass wir uns gesehen haben** it's a long time since we saw each other; **Länge** (-, -n) f length; (Geo) longitude

langen vi (fam: ausreichen) to be enough; (fam: fassen) to reach (nach for); **mir langt's** I've had enough

Langeweile f boredom

langfristig adj long-term ▷ adv in the long term

Langlauf m cross-country skiing

längs prep +gen **die Bäume ~ der Straße** the trees along(side) the road ▷ adv: **die Streifen laufen ~ über das Hemd** the stripes run lengthways down the shirt

langsam adj slow ▷ adv slowly

Langschläfer(in) (-s, -) m(f) late riser

längst adv: **das ist ~ fertig** that was finished a long time ago; **sie sollte ~ da sein** she should have been here long ago; **als sie kam, waren wir ~ weg** when she arrived we had long since left

Langstreckenflug m long-haul flight

Languste (-, -n) f crayfish, crawfish (US)

langweilen vt to bore; **ich langweile mich** I'm bored; **langweilig** adj boring; **Langwelle** f long wave

Laos (-) nt Laos

Lappen (-s, -) m cloth, rag; (Staublappen) duster

läppisch adj silly; (Summe) ridiculous

Laptop (-s, -s) m laptop

Lärche (-, -n) f larch

Lärm (-(e)s) m noise

las imperf von **lesen**

Lasche (-, -n) f flap

Laser (-s, -) m laser; **Laserdrucker** m laser printer

⊙ SCHLÜSSELWORT

lassen (pt **ließ**, pp **gelassen** o (als Hilfsverb) **lassen**) vt **1** (unterlassen) to stop; (momentan) to leave; **lass das (sein)!** don't (do it)!; (hör auf!) stop it!; **lass mich!** leave me alone; **lassen wir das!** let's leave it; **er kann das Trinken nicht lassen** he can't stop drinking

2 (zurücklassen) to leave; **etw lassen, wie es ist** to leave sth (just) as it is

3 (*überlassen*) **jdn ins Haus lassen** to let sb into the house
▷ *vi* ; **lass mal, ich mache das schon** leave it, I'll do it
▷ *Hilfsverb* **1** (*veranlassen*) **etw machen lassen** to have *o* get sth done; **sich** *dat* **etw schicken lassen** to have sth sent (to one)
2 (*zulassen*) **jdn etw wissen lassen** to let sb know sth; **das Licht brennen lassen** to leave the light on; **jdn warten lassen** to keep sb waiting; **das lässt sich machen** that can be done
3 lass uns gehen let's go

lässig *adj* casual
Last (-, *-en*) *f* load; (*Bürde*) burden; (*Naut, Aviat*) cargo
Laster (-*s, -*) *nt* vice; (*fam*) truck, lorry (*Brit*)
lästern *vi*: **über jdn/etw ~** to make nasty remarks about sb/sth
lästig *adj* annoying; (*Person*) tiresome
Last-Minute-Angebot *nt* last-minute offer; **Last-Minute-Flug** *m* last-minute flight; **Last-Minute-Ticket** *nt* last-minute ticket
Lastwagen *m* truck, lorry (*Brit*)
Latein (-*s*) *nt* Latin
Laterne (-, *-n*) *f* lantern; (*Straßenlaterne*) streetlight
Latte (-, *-n*) *f* slat; (*Sport*) bar
Latz (-*es, Lätze*) *m* bib; **Lätzchen** *nt* bib; **Latzhose** *f* dungarees *pl*
lau *adj* (*Wind, Luft*) mild
Laub (-*(e)s*) *nt* foliage; **Laubfrosch** *m* tree frog; **Laubsäge** *f* fretsaw
Lauch (-*(e)s, -e*) *m* leeks *pl*; **eine Stange ~** a leek; **Lauchzwiebel** *f* spring onions *pl* (*Brit*), scallions *pl* (*US*)
Lauf (-*(e)s, Läufe*) *m* run; (*Wettlauf*) race; (*Entwicklung*) course; (*von

Gewehr) barrel; **Laufbahn** *f* career;
laufen (*lief, gelaufen*) *vi, vt* to run; (*gehen*) to walk; (*funktionieren*) to work; **mir läuft die Nase** my nose is running; **was läuft im Kino?** what's on at the cinema?; **wie läuft's so?** how are things?;
laufend *adj* running; (*Monat, Ausgaben*) current; **auf dem Laufenden sein/halten** to be/to keep up-to-date; **Läufer** (-*s, -*) *m* (*Teppich*) rug; (*Schach*) bishop; **Läufer(in)** *m(f)* (*Sport*) runner; **Laufmasche** *f* ladder (*Brit*), run (*US*); **Laufwerk** *nt* (*Inform*) drive
Laune (-, *-n*) *f* mood; **gute/schlechte ~ haben** to be in a good/bad mood; **launisch** *adj* moody
Laus (-, *Läuse*) *f* louse
lauschen *vi* to listen; (*heimlich*) to eavesdrop
laut *adj* loud ▷ *adv* loudly; (*lesen*) aloud ▷ *prep* +*gen o dat* according to
läuten *vt, vi* to ring
lauter *adv* (*fam: nichts als*) nothing but
Lautsprecher *m* loudspeaker; **Lautstärke** *f* loudness; (*Radio, TV*) volume
lauwarm *adj* lukewarm
Lava (-, *Laven*) *f* lava
Lavendel (-*s, -*) *m* lavender
Lawine *f* avalanche
LCD-Anzeige *f* LCD-display
leasen *vt* to lease; **Leasing** (-*s*) *nt* leasing
leben *vt, vi* to live; (*am Leben sein*) to be alive; **wie lange ~ Sie schon hier?** how long have you been living here?; **von ... ~** (*Nahrungsmittel etc*) to live on ...; (*Beruf, Beschäftigung*) to make one's living from ...; **Leben** (-*s, -*) *nt* life; **lebend** *adj* living; **lebendig** *adj* alive; (*lebhaft*) lively;

Leukoplast® (-(e)s, -e) nt
Elastoplast® (Brit), Band-Aid®
(US)
Leute pl people pl
Lexikon (-s, Lexika) nt encyclo-
paedia (Brit), encyclopedia (US);
(Wörterbuch) dictionary
Libanon (-s) m: **der ~** Lebanon
Libelle f dragonfly
liberal adj liberal
Libyen (-s) nt Libya
Licht (-(e)s, -er) nt light;
Lichtblick m ray of hope;
lichtempfindlich adj sensitive to
light; **Lichempfindlichkeit** f
(Foto) speed; **Lichthupe** f: **die
~ betätigen** to flash one's lights;
Lichtjahr nt light year;
Lichtmaschine f dynamo;
Lichtschalter m light switch;
Lichtschranke f light barrier;
Lichtschutzfaktor m sun
protection factor, SPF
Lichtung f clearing
Lid (-(e)s, -er) nt eyelid;
Lidschatten m eyeshadow
lieb adj (nett) nice; (teuer, geliebt)
dear; (liebenswert) sweet; **das ist
~ von dir** that's nice of you; **Lieber
Herr X** Dear Mr X; **Liebe** (-, -n) f
love; **lieben** vt to love; (sexuell) to
make love to; **liebenswürdig** adj
kind; **lieber** adv rather; **ich
möchte ~ nicht** I'd rather not;
welches ist dir ~? which one do
you prefer?; siehe auch **gern, lieb**;
Liebesbrief m love letter;
Liebeskummer m: **~ haben** to be
lovesick; **Liebespaar** nt lovers pl;
liebevoll adj loving;
Liebhaber(in) (-s, -) m(f) lover;
lieblich adj lovely; (Wein) sweet;
Liebling m darling; (Günstling)
favourite; **Lieblings-** in zW
favourite; **liebste(r, s)** adj
favourite; **liebsten** adv: **am
~ esse ich ...** my favourite food

is ...; **am ~ würde ich bleiben** I'd
really like to stay
Liechtenstein (-s) nt
Liechtenstein
Lied (-(e)s, -er) nt song; (Rel) hymn
lief imperf von **laufen**
Lieferant(in) m(f) supplier
lieferbar adj available
liefern vt to deliver; (beschaffen)
to supply
Lieferschein m delivery note;
Lieferung f delivery;
Lieferwagen m delivery van
Liege (-, -n) f (beim Arzt) couch;
(Notbett) campbed; (Gartenliege)
lounger; **liegen** (lag, gelegen) vi to
lie; (sich befinden) to be; **mir liegt
nichts/viel daran** it doesn't
matter to me/it matters a lot to
me; **woran liegt es nur, dass ...?**
why is it that ...?; **~ bleiben**
(Mensch) to stay lying down; (im
Bett) to stay in bed; (Ding) to be left
(behind); **~ lassen** (vergessen) to
leave behind; **Liegestuhl** m deck
chair; **Liegestütz** m press-up
(Brit), push-up (US); **Liegewagen**
m (Eisenb) couchette car
lieh imperf von **leihen**
ließ imperf von **lassen**
Lift (-(e)s, -e o -s) m lift, elevator
(US)
Liga (-, Ligen) f league, division
light adj (Cola) diet; (fettarm)
low-fat; (kalorienarm) low-calorie;
(Zigaretten) mild
Likör (-s, -e) m liqueur
lila adj inv purple
Lilie f lily
Limette (-, -n) f lime
Limo (-, -s) f (fam) fizzy drink
(Brit), soda (US); **Limonade** f
fizzy drink (Brit), soda (US); (mit
Zitronengeschmack) lemonade
Limone (-, -n) f lime
Limousine (-, -n) f saloon (car)
(Brit), sedan (US); (fam) limo

Linde (-, -n) f lime tree
lindern vt to relieve, to soothe
Lineal (-s, -e) nt ruler
Linie f line; **Linienflug** m
scheduled flight; **liniert** adj
ruled, lined
Link (-s, -s) m (Inform) link
Linke (-n, -n) f left-hand side;
(Hand) left hand; (Pol) left (wing);
linke(r, s) adj left; **auf der ~n
Seite** on the left, on the left-hand
side; **links** adv on the left;
~ abbiegen to turn left; **~ von** to
the left of; **~ oben** at the top left;
Linkshänder(in) (-s, -) m(f) left-
hander; **linksherum** adv to the
left, anticlockwise; **Linksverkehr**
m driving on the left
Linse (-, -n) f lentil; (optisch) lens
Lippe (-, -n) f lip; **Lipgloss** nt lip
gloss; **Lippenstift** m lipstick
lispeln vi to lisp
List (-, -en) f cunning; (Trick)
trick
Liste (-, -n) f list
Litauen (-s) nt Lithuania
Liter (-s, -) m o nt litre
literarisch adj literary; **Literatur**
f literature
Litschi (-, -s) f lychee, litchi
litt imperf von **leiden**
live adv (Radio, TV) live
Lizenz f licence
Lkw (-(s), -(s)) m abk =
Lastkraftwagen truck, lorry (Brit);
Lkw-Maut f heavy goods vehicle
toll
Lob (-(e)s) nt praise; **loben** vt to
praise
Loch (-(e)s, Löcher) nt hole;
lochen vt to punch; **Locher** (-s, -)
m (hole) punch
Locke (-, -n) f curl; **locken** vt
(anlocken) to lure; (Haare) to curl;
Lockenstab m curling tongs pl
(Brit), curling irons pl (US);
Lockenwickler (-s, -) m curler

locker adj (Schraube, Zahn) loose;
(Haltung) relaxed; (Person)
easy-going; **das schaffe ich
~** (fam) I'll manage it, no problem;
lockern vt to loosen ▷ vr: **sich
~** to loosen
lockig adj curly
Löffel (-s, -) m spoon; **einen
~ Mehl zugeben** add a spoonful of
flour; **Löffelbiskuit** (-s, -s) m
sponge finger
log imperf von **lügen**
Loge (-, -n) f (Theat) box
logisch adj logical
Logo (-s, -s) nt logo
Lohn (-(e)s, Löhne) m reward;
(Arbeitslohn) pay, wages pl
lohnen vr: **sich ~** to be worth it;
es lohnt sich nicht zu warten it's
no use waiting
Lohnerhöhung f pay rise (Brit),
pay raise (US); **Lohnsteuer** f
income tax
Lokal (-(e)s, -e) nt (Gaststätte)
restaurant; (Kneipe) pub (Brit), bar
Lokomotive f locomotive
London (-s) nt London
Lorbeer (-s, -en) m laurel;
Lorbeerblatt nt (Gastr) bay leaf
los adj loose; **~!** go on!; **jdn/etw
~ sein** to be rid of sb/sth; **was ist
~?** what's the matter?, what's up?;
dort ist nichts/viel ~ there's
nothing/a lot going on there
Los (-es, -e) nt (Schicksal) lot, fate;
(Lotterie etc) ticket
los|binden irr vt to untie
löschen vt (Feuer, Licht) to put
out, to extinguish; (Durst) to
quench; (Tonband) to erase; (Daten,
Zeile) to delete; **Löschtaste** f
delete key
lose adj loose
Lösegeld nt ransom
losen vi to draw lots
lösen vt (lockern) to loosen;
(Rätsel) to solve; (Chem) to

mahlen *(mahlte, gemahlen)* vt to grind

Mahlzeit f meal; *(für Baby)* feed ▷ *interj (guten Appetit)* enjoy your meal

Mähne *(-, -n)* f mane

mahnen vt to urge; **jdn schriftlich ~** to send sb a reminder; **Mahngebühr** f fine; **Mahnung** f warning; *(schriftlich)* reminder

Mai *(-(s), -e)* m May; *siehe auch* **Juni**; **Maifeiertag** m May Day; **Maiglöckchen** nt lily of the valley; **Maikäfer** m cockchafer

Mail *(-, -s)* f e-mail; **jdm eine~ schicken** to mail sb, to e-mail sb; **Mailbox** f *(Inform)* mailbox; **mailen** vi, vt to e-mail

Mais *(-es, -e)* m maize, corn *(US)*; **Maiskolben** m corn cob; *(Gastr)* corn on the cob

Majestät *(-, -en)* f Majesty

Majonäse *(-, -n)* f mayonnaise

Majoran *(-s, -e)* m marjoram

makaber adj macabre

Make-up *(-s, -s)* nt make-up

Makler(in) *(-s, -)* m(f) broker; *(Immobilienmakler)* estate agent *(Brit)*, Realtor® *(US)*

Makrele *(-, -n)* f mackerel

Makro *(-s, -s)* nt *(Inform)* macro

Makrone *(-, -n)* f macaroon

mal adv *(beim Rechnen)* times, multiplied by; *(beim Messen)* by; *(fam: einmal = früher)* once; *(einmal = zukünftig)* some day; **4 ~ 3 ist 12** 4 times 3 is (o equals) twelve; **da habe ich ~ gewohnt** I used to live there; **irgendwann ~ werde ich dort hinfahren** I'll go there one day; **das ist nun ~ so** well, that's just the way it is (o goes); **Mal** *(-(e)s, -e)* nt *(Zeitpunkt)* time; *(Markierung)* mark; **jedes ~** every time; **ein paar ~** a few times; **ein einziges ~** just once

Malaria *(-)* f malaria

Malaysia *(-s)* nt Malaysia

Malbuch nt colouring book

Malediven pl Maldives pl

malen vt, vi to paint; **Maler(in)** *(-s, -)* m(f) painter; **Malerei** f painting; **malerisch** adj picturesque

Mallorca *(-s)* nt Majorca, Mallorca

mal|nehmen irr vt to multiply *(mit* by)

Malta *(-s)* nt Malta

Malventee m mallow tea

Malz *(-es)* nt malt; **Malzbier** nt malt beer

Mama *(-, -s)* f mum(my) *(Brit)*, mom(my) *(US)*

man pron you; *(förmlich)* one; *(jemand)* someone, somebody; *(die Leute)* they, people pl; **wie schreibt ~ das?** how do you spell that?; **~ hat ihr das Fahrrad gestohlen** someone stole her bike; **~ sagt, dass ...** they (o people) say that ...

managen vt *(fam)* to manage; **Manager(in)** *(-s, -)* m(f) manager

manche(r, s) adj many a; *(mit pl)* a number of, some ▷ pron *(einige)* some; *(viele)* many; **~ Politiker** many politicians pl, many a politician; **manchmal** adv sometimes

Mandant(in) m(f) client

Mandarine f mandarin, tangerine

Mandel *(-, -n)* f almond; **~n** *(Anat)* tonsils pl; **Mandelentzündung** f tonsillitis

Manege *(-, -n)* f ring

Mangel *(-s, Mängel)* m *(Fehlen)* lack; *(Knappheit)* shortage *(an +dat* of); *(Fehler)* defect, fault; **mangelhaft** adj *(Ware)* faulty; *(Schulnote)* ≈ E

Mango *(-, -s)* f mango

Mangold *(-s)* m mangel(wurzel)

Manieren *pl* manners *pl*

Maniküre (-, -n) *f* manicure

manipulieren *vt* to manipulate

Manko (-s, -s) *nt* deficiency

Mann (-(e)s, Männer) *m* man; (*Ehemann*) husband; **Männchen** *nt*: **es ist ein ~** (*Tier*) it's a he; **männlich** *adj* masculine; (*Bio*) male

Mannschaft *f* (*Sport, fig*) team; (*Naut, Aviat*) crew

Mansarde (-, -n) *f* attic

Manschettenknopf *m* cufflink

Mantel (-s, Mäntel) *m* coat; (*Tech*) casing, jacket

Mappe (-, -n) *f* briefcase; (*Aktenmappe*) folder

Maracuja (-, -s) *f* passion fruit

Marathon (-s, -s) *m* marathon

Märchen *nt* fairy tale

Marder (-s, -) *m* marten

Margarine *f* margarine

Marienkäfer *m* ladybird (*Brit*), ladybug (*US*)

Marihuana (-s) *nt* marijuana

Marille (-, -n) *f* apricot

Marinade *f* marinade

Marine *f* navy

marinieren *vt* to marinate

Marionette *f* puppet

Mark (-(e)s) *nt* (*Knochenmark*) marrow; (*Fruchtmark*) pulp

Marke (-, -n) *f* (*Warensorte*) brand; (*Fabrikat*) make; (*Briefmarke*) stamp; (*Essenmarke*) voucher, ticket; (*aus Metall etc*) disc; (*Messpunkt*) mark; **Markenartikel** *m* branded item, brand name product; **Markenzeichen** *nt* trademark

markieren *vt* to mark; **Markierung** *f* marking; (*Zeichen*) mark

Markise (-, -n) *f* awning

Markt (-(e)s, Märkte) *m* market; **auf den ~ bringen** to launch; **Markthalle** *f* covered market;

Marktlücke *f* gap in the market; **Marktplatz** *m* market piace; **Marktwirtschaft** *f* market economy

Marmelade *f* jam; (*Orangenmarmelade*) marmalade

Marmor (-s, -e) *m* marble; **Marmorkuchen** *m* marble cake

Marokko (-s) *nt* Morocco

Marone (-, -n) *f* chestnut

Mars (-) *m* Mars

Marsch (-(e)s, Märsche) *m* march

Märtyrer(in) (-s, -) *m(f)* martyr

März (-(es), -e) *m* March; *siehe auch* **Juni**

Marzipan (-s, -e) *nt* marzipan

Maschine *f* machine; (*Motor*) engine; **maschinell** *adj* mechanical, machine-; **Maschinenbau** *m* mechanical engineering

Masern *pl* (*Med*) measles *sing*

Maske (-, -n) *f* mask; **Maskenball** *m* fancy-dress ball; **maskieren** *vr*: **sich ~** (*Maske aufsetzen*) to put on a mask; (*verkleiden*) to dress up

Maskottchen *nt* mascot

maß *imperf von* **messen**

Maß (-es, -e) *nt* measure; (*Mäßigung*) moderation; (*Grad*) degree, extent; **~e** (*Person*) measurements; (*Raum*) dimensions; **in gewissem/hohem ~e** to a certain/high degree; **in zunehmendem ~e** increasingly

Mass (-, -(en)) *f* (*Bier*) litre of beer

Massage (-, -n) *f* massage

Masse (-, -n) *f* mass; (*von Menschen*) crowd; (*Großteil*) majority; **massenhaft** *adv* masses (*o* loads) of; **am See sind ~ Mücken** there are masses of mosquitoes at the lake; **Massenkarambolage** *f* pile-up; **Massenmedien** *pl* mass media *pl*; **Massenproduktion** *f* mass

production; **Massentourismus**
m mass tourism
Masseur(in) *m(f)*
masseur/masseuse
maßgeschneidert *adj* (*Kleidung*) made-to-measure
massieren *vt* to massage
mäßig *adj* moderate
massiv *adj* solid; (*fig*) massive
maßlos *adj* extreme
Maßnahme (-, -n) *f* measure,
step
Maßstab *m* rule, measure; (*fig*)
standard; **im ~ von 1:5** on a scale
of 1:5
Mast (-(e)s, -e(n)) *m* mast; (*Elek*)
pylon
Material (-s, -ien) *nt* material;
(*Arbeitsmaterial*) materials *pl*;
materialistisch *adj* materialistic
Materie *f* matter; **materiell** *adj*
material
Mathematik *f* mathematics
sing; **Mathematiker(in)** *m(f)*
mathematician
Matinee (-, -ien) *f* ≈ matinee
Matratze (-, -n) *f* mattress
Matrose (-n, -n) *m* sailor
Matsch (-(e)s) *m* mud; (*Schnee*)
slush; **matschig** *adj* (*Boden*)
muddy; (*Schnee*) slushy; (*Obst*)
mushy
matt *adj* weak; (*glanzlos*) dull;
(*Foto*) matt; (*Schach*) mate
Matte (-, -n) *f* mat
Matura (-) *f* Austrian
school-leaving examination; ≈
A-levels (*Brit*), ≈ High School
Diploma (*US*)
Mauer (-, -n) *f* wall
Maul (-(e)s, Mäuler) *nt* mouth;
(*fam*) gob; **halt's ~!** shut your face
(*o* gob); **Maulbeere** *f* mulberry;
Maulesel *m* mule; **Maulkorb** *m*
muzzle; **Maul- und Klauenseuche**
f foot-and-mouth disease;
Maulwurf *m* mole

Maurer(in) (-s, -) *m(f)* bricklayer
Mauritius (-) *nt* Mauritius
Maus (-, Mäuse) *f* mouse;
Mausefalle *f* mousetrap;
Mausklick (-s, -s) *m* mouse click;
Mauspad (-s, -s) *nt* mouse mat (*o*
pad); **Maustaste** *f* mouse key (*o*
button)
Maut (-, -en) *f* toll; **Mautgebühr**
f toll; **mautpflichtig** *adj*: **~e
Straße** toll road, turnpike (*US*);
Mautstelle *f* tollbooth, tollgate;
Mautstraße *f* toll road, turnpike
(*US*)
maximal *adv*: **ihr habt ~ zwei
Stunden Zeit** you've got two
hours at (the) most; **~ vier Leute** a
maximum of four people
Mayonnaise *f siehe* **Majonäse**
Mazedonien (-s) *nt* Macedonia
MB (-, -) *nt*, **Mbyte** (-, -) *nt abk* =
Megabyte MB
Mechanik *f* mechanics *sing*;
(*Getriebe*) mechanics *pl*;
Mechaniker(in) (-s, -) *m(f)* mechanic;
mechanisch *adj* mechanical;
Mechanismus *m* mechanism
meckern *vi* (*Ziege*) to bleat; (*fam:
schimpfen*) to moan
Mecklenburg-Vorpommern
(-s) *nt* Mecklenburg-Western
Pomerania
Medaille (-, -n) *f* medal
Medien *pl* media *pl*
Medikament *nt* medicine
Meditation *f* meditation;
meditieren *vi* to meditate
medium *adj* (*Steak*) medium
Medizin (-, -en) *f* medicine (*gegen*
for); **medizinisch** *adj* medical
Meer (-(e)s, -e) *nt* sea; **am ~** by
the sea; **Meerenge** *f* straits *pl*;
Meeresfrüchte *pl* seafood *sing*;
Meeresspiegel *m* sea level;
Meerrettich *m* horseradish;
Meerschweinchen *nt* guinea
pig; **Meerwasser** *nt* seawater

Megabyte *nt* megabyte;
Megahertz *nt* megahertz
Mehl *(-(e)s, -e) nt* flour;
Mehlspeise *f* sweet dish made from flour, eggs and milk
mehr *pron, adv* more; **~ will ich nicht ausgeben** I don't want to spend any more, that's as much as I want to spend; **was willst du ~?** what more do you want? ▷ *adv:* **immer ~** (**Leute**) more and more (people); **~ als fünf Minuten** more than five minutes; **je ~ ..., desto besser** the more ..., the better; **ich kann nicht ~ stehen** I can't stand any more (o longer); **es ist kein Brot ~ da** there's no bread left; **nie ~** never again; **mehrdeutig** *adj* ambiguous; **mehrere** *pron* several; **mehreres** *pron* several things; **mehrfach** *adj* multiple; (*wiederholt*) repeated;
Mehrfachstecker *m* multiple plug; **Mehrheit** *f* majority; **mehrmals** *adv* repeatedly; **mehrsprachig** *adj* multilingual; **Mehrwegflasche** *f* returnable bottle, deposit bottle; **Mehrwertsteuer** *f* value added tax, VAT; **Mehrzahl** *f* majority; (*Plural*) plural
meiden (*mied, gemieden*) *vt* to avoid
Meile *(-, -n) f* mile
mein *pron* (*adjektivisch*) my; **meine(r, s)** *pron* (*substantivisch*) mine
meinen *vt, vi* (*glauben, der Ansicht sein*) to think; (*sagen*) to say; (*sagen wollen, beabsichtigen*) to mean; **das war nicht so gemeint** I didn't mean it like that
meinetwegen *adv* (*wegen mir*) because of me; (*mir zuliebe*) for my sake; (*von mir aus*) as far as I'm concerned
Meinung *f* opinion; **meiner**

~ nach in my opinion;
Meinungsumfrage *f* opinion poll; **Meinungsverschiedenheit** *f* disagreement (*über +akk* about)
Meise *(-, -n) f* tit; **eine ~ haben** (*fam*) to be crazy
Meißel *(-s, -) m* chisel
meist *adv* mostly; **meiste(r, s)** *pron* (*adjektivisch*) most; **die ~n** (**Leute**) most people; **die ~ Zeit** most of the time; **das ~** (**davon**) most of it; **die ~n von ihnen** most of them; (*substantivisch*) most of them; **am ~n** (the) most; **meistens** *adv* mostly; (*zum größten Teil*) for the most part
Meister(in) *(-s, -) m(f)* master; (*Sport*) champion; **Meisterschaft** *f* championship; **Meisterwerk** *nt* masterpiece
melden *vt* to report ▷ *vr:* **sich ~** to report (*bei* to); (*Schule*) to put one's hand up; (*freiwillig*) to volunteer; (*auf etw, am Telefon*) to answer; **Meldung** *f* announcement; (*Bericht*) report; (*Inform*) message
Melodie *f* tune, melody
Melone *(-, -n) f* melon
Memoiren *pl* memoirs *pl*
Menge *(-, -n) f* quantity; (*Menschen*) crowd; **eine ~** (*große Anzahl*) a lot (*gen* of); **Mengenrabatt** *m* bulk discount
Meniskus *(-, Menisken) m* meniscus
Mensa *(-, Mensen) f* canteen, cafeteria (US)
Mensch *(-en, -en) m* human being, man; (*Person*) person; **kein ~** nobody; **~!** (*bewundernd*) wow!; (*verärgert*) bloody hell!; **Menschenmenge** *f* crowd; **Menschenrechte** *pl* human rights *pl*; **Menschenverstand** *m:* **gesunder ~** common sense; **Menschheit** *f* humanity,

mankind; **menschlich** adj human; (human) humane

Menstruation f menstruation

Mentalität f mentality, mindset

Menthol (-s) nt menthol

Menü (-s, -s) nt set meal; (Inform) menu; **Menüleiste** f (Inform) menu bar

Merkblatt nt leaflet; **merken** vt (bemerken) to notice; **sich** (dat) **etw ~** to remember sth; **Merkmal** nt feature

Merkur (-s) m Mercury

merkwürdig adj odd

Messbecher m measuring jug

Messe (-, -n) f fair; (Rel) mass; **Messebesucher(in)** m(f) visitor to a/the fair; **Messegelände** nt exhibition site

messen (maß, gemessen) vt to measure; (Temperatur, Puls) to take ▷ vr: **sich ~** to compete; **sie kann sich mit ihm nicht ~** she's no match for him

Messer (-s, -) nt knife

Messgerät nt measuring device, gauge

Messing (-s) nt brass

Metall (-s, -e) nt metal

Meteorologe m, **Meteorologin** f meteorologist

Meter (-s, -) m o nt metre; **Metermaß** nt tape measure

Methode (-, -n) f method

Metzger(in) (-s, -) m(f) butcher; **Metzgerei** f butcher's (shop)

Mexiko (-s) nt Mexico

MEZ f abk = **mitteleuropäische Zeit** CET

miau interj miaow

mich pron akk von **ich** me; **~ (selbst)** (reflexiv) myself; **stell dich hinter ~** stand behind me; **ich fühle ~ wohl** I feel fine

mied imperf von **meiden**

Miene (-, -n) f look, expression

mies adj (fam) lousy

Miesmuschel f mussel

Mietauto nt siehe **Mietwagen**; **Miete** (-, -n) f rent; **mieten** vt to rent; (Auto) to hire (Brit), to rent (US); **Mieter(in)** (-s, -) m(f) tenant; **Mietshaus** nt block of flats (Brit), apartment house (US); **Mietvertrag** m rental agreement; **Mietwagen** m hire car (Brit), rental car (US); **sich** (dat) **einen ~ nehmen** to hire (Brit) (o rent (US)) a car

Migräne (-, -n) f migraine

Migrant(in) (-en, -en) m(f) migrant (worker)

Mikrofon (-s, -e) nt microphone

Mikrowelle (-, -n) f, **Mikrowellenherd** m microwave (oven)

Milch (-) f milk; **Milcheis** nt ice-cream (made with milk); **Milchglas** nt (dickes, trübes Glas) frosted glass; **Milchkaffee** m milky coffee; **Milchprodukte** pl dairy products pl; **Milchpulver** nt powdered milk; **Milchreis** m rice pudding; **Milchshake** m milk shake; **Milchstraße** f Milky Way

mild adj mild; (Richter) lenient; (freundlich) kind

Militär (-s) nt military, army

Milliarde (-, -n) f billion; **Milligramm** nt milligram; **Milliliter** m millilitre; **Millimeter** m millimetre; **Million** f million; **Millionär(in)** m(f) millionaire

Milz (-, -en) f spleen

Mimik f facial expression(s)

Minderheit f minority

minderjährig adj underage

minderwertig adj inferior; **Minderwertigkeitskomplex** m inferiority complex

Mindest- in zW minimum; **mindeste(r, s)** adj least; **mindestens** adv at least; **Mindesthaltbarkeitsdatum** nt best-before date, sell-by date (*Brit*)

Mine (-, -n) *f* mine; (*Bleistift*) lead; (*Kugelschreiber*) refill

Mineralwasser *nt* mineral water

Minibar *f* minibar; **Minigolf** *nt* miniature golf, crazy golf (*Brit*)

minimal *adj* minimal

Minimum (-s, *Minima*) *nt* minimum

Minirock *m* miniskirt

Minister(in) (-s, -) *m(f)* minister; **Ministerium** *nt* ministry; **Ministerpräsident(in)** *m(f)* (*von Bundesland*) Minister President (*Prime Minister of a Bundesland*)

minus *adv* minus; **Minus** (-, -) *nt* deficit; **im ~ sein** to be in the red; (*Konto*) to be overdrawn

Minute (-, -n) *f* minute

Minze (-, -n) *f* mint

Mio. *nt abk von* **Million(en)** m

mir *pron dat von* **ich** (to) me; **kannst du ~ helfen?** can you help me?; **kannst du es ~ erklären?** can you explain it to me?; **ich habe ~ einen neuen Rechner gekauft** I bought (myself) a new computer; **ein Freund von ~** a friend of mine

Mirabelle (-, -n) *f* mirabelle (*small yellow plum*)

mischen *vt* to mix; (*Karten*) to shuffle; **Mischmasch** *m* (*fam*) hotchpotch; **Mischung** *f* mixture (*aus* of)

missachten *vt* to ignore; **Missbrauch** *m* abuse; (*falscher Gebrauch*) misuse; **missbrauchen** *vt* to misuse (*zu* for); (*sexuell*) to abuse; **Misserfolg** *m* failure; **Missgeschick** *nt* (*Panne*) mishap; **misshandeln** *vt* to ill-treat

Mission *f* mission

misslingen (*misslang, misslungen*) *vi* to fail; **der Versuch ist mir misslungen** my attempt failed;

misstrauen *vt +dat* to distrust; **Misstrauen** (-s) *nt* mistrust, suspicion (*gegenüber* of); **misstrauisch** *adj* distrustful; (*argwöhnisch*) suspicious; **Missverständnis** *nt* misunder-standing; **missverstehen** *irr vt* to misunderstand

Mist (-(e)s) *m* (*fam*) rubbish; (*von Kühen*) dung; (*als Dünger*) manure

Mistel (-, -n) *f* mistletoe

mit *prep +dat* with; (*mittels*) by; **~ der Bahn** by train; **~ der Kreditkarte bezahlen** to pay by credit card; **~ 10 Jahren** at the age of 10; **wie wärs ~ ...?** how about ...? ▷ *adv* along, too; **wollen Sie ~?** do you want to come along?

Mitarbeiter(in) *m(f)* (*Angestell-ter*) employee; (*an Projekt*) collaborator; (*freier*) freelancer

mit|bekommen *irr vt* (*fam: aufschnappen*) to catch; (*hören*) to hear; (*verstehen*) to get

mit|benutzen *vt* to share

Mitbewohner(in) *m(f)* (*in Wohnung*) flatmate (*Brit*), roommate (*US*)

mit|bringen *irr vt* to bring along; **Mitbringsel** (-s, -) *nt* small present

miteinander *adv* with one another; (*gemeinsam*) together

mit|erleben *vt* to see (with one's own eyes)

Mitesser (-s, -) *m* blackhead

Mitfahrgelegenheit *f* ≈ lift, ride (*US*); **Mitfahrzentrale** *f* *agency for arranging lifts*

mit|geben *irr vt:* **jdm etw ~** to give sb sth (to take along)

Mitgefühl *nt* sympathy

mit|gehen *irr vi* to go/come along

mitgenommen *adj* worn out, exhausted

Mitglied *nt* member

Mörder(in) (-s, -) *m(f)* murderer/murderess

morgen *adv* tomorrow; **~ früh** tomorrow morning

Morgen (-s, -) *m* morning; **am ~** in the morning; **Morgenmantel** *m*, **Morgenrock** *m* dressing gown; **Morgenmuffel** *m*: **er ist ein ~** he's not a morning person; **morgens** *adv* in the morning; **um 3 Uhr ~** at 3 (o'clock) in the morning, at 3 am

Morphium (-s) *nt* morphine

morsch *adj* rotten

Mosaik (-s, -e(n)) *nt* mosaic

Mosambik (-s) *nt* Mozambique

Moschee (-, -n) *f* mosque

Moskau (-s) *nt* Moscow

Moskito (-s, -s) *m* mosquito; **Moskitonetz** *nt* mosquito net

Moslem (-s, -s) *m*, **Moslime** (-, -n) *f* Muslim

Most (-(e)s, -e) *m* (unfermented) fruit juice; (*Apfelwein*) cider

Motel (-s, -s) *nt* motel

motivieren *vt* to motivate

Motor *m* engine; (*Elek*) motor; **Motorboot** *nt* motorboat; **Motorenöl** *nt* engine oil; **Motorhaube** *f* bonnet (*Brit*), hood (*US*); **Motorrad** *nt* motorbike, motorcycle; **Motorradfahrer(in)** *m(f)* motorcyclist; **Motorroller** *m* (motor) scooter; **Motorschaden** *m* engine trouble

Motte (-, -n) *f* moth

Motto (-s, -s) *nt* motto

Mountainbike (-s, -s) *nt* mountain bike

Möwe (-, -n) *f* (sea)gull

MP3-Player (-s, -) *m* MP3 player

Mrd. *f abk* = **Milliarde(n)**

MS (-) *f abk* = **multiple Sklerose** MS

Mücke (-, -n) *f* midge; (*tropische*) mosquito; **Mückenstich** *m* mosquito bite

müde *adj* tired

muffig *adj* (*Geruch*) musty; (*Gesicht, Mensch*) grumpy

Mühe (-, -n) *f* trouble, pains *pl*; **sich** (*dat*) **große ~ geben** to go to a lot of trouble

muhen *vi* to moo

Mühle (-, -n) *f* mill; (*Kaffeemühle*) grinder

Müll (-(e)s) *m* rubbish (*Brit*), garbage (*US*); **Müllabfuhr** *f* rubbish (*Brit*) (*o* garbage (*US*)) disposal

Mullbinde *f* gauze bandage

Müllcontainer *m* waste container; **Mülldeponie** *f* rubbish (*Brit*) (*o* garbage (*US*)) dump; **Mülleimer** *m* rubbish bin (*Brit*), garbage can (*US*); **Mülltonne** *f* dustbin (*Brit*), garbage can (*US*); **Mülltrennung** *f* sorting and collecting household waste according to type of material; **Müllverbrennungsanlage** *f* incineration plant; **Müllwagen** *m* dustcart (*Brit*), garbage truck (*US*)

multikulturell *adj* multicultural

Multimedia- *in zW* multimedia

Multiple-Choice-Verfahren *nt* multiple choice

multiple Sklerose (-n, -n) *f* multiple sclerosis

Multiplexkino *nt* multiplex (cinema)

multiplizieren *vt* to multiply (*mit* by)

Mumie *f* mummy

Mumps (-) *m* mumps *sing*

München (-s) *nt* Munich

Mund (-(e)s, *Münder*) *m* mouth; **halt den ~!** shut up; **Mundart** *f* dialect; **Munddusche** *f* dental water jet

münden *vi* to flow (*in +akk* into)

Mundgeruch *m* bad breath; **Mundharmonika** (-, -s) *f* mouth organ

mündlich *adj* oral
Mundschutz *m* mask;
   Mundwasser *nt* mouthwash
Munition *f* ammunition
Münster (-s, -) *nt* minster,
   cathedral
munter *adj* lively
Münzautomat *m* vending
   machine; **Münze** (-, -n) *f* coin;
   Münzeinwurf *m* slot;
   Münzrückgabe *f* coin return;
   Münztelefon *nt* pay phone;
   Münzwechsler *m* change
   machine
murmeln *vt, vi* to murmur, to
   mutter
Murmeltier *nt* marmot
mürrisch *adj* sullen, grumpy
Mus (-es, -e) *nt* puree
Muschel (-, -n) *f* mussel; (~*schale*)
   shell
Museum (-s, *Museen*) *nt*
   museum
Musical (-s, -s) *nt* musical
Musik *f* music; **musikalisch** *adj*
   musical; **Musiker(in)** (-s, -) *m(f)*
   musician; **Musikinstrument** *nt*
   musical instrument; **musizieren**
   vi to play music
Muskat (-(e)s) *m* nutmeg
Muskel (-s, -n) *m* muscle;
   Muskelkater *m*: **~ haben** to be
   stiff; **Muskelriss** *m* torn muscle;
   Muskelzerrung *f* pulled muscle;
   muskulös *adj* muscular
Müsli (-s, -) *nt* muesli
Muslim(in) (-s, -s) *m(f)* Muslim
Muss (-) *nt* must

SCHLÜSSELWORT

müssen (*pt* **musste**, *pp* **gemusst**
o (*als Hilfsverb*) **müssen**) *vi*
1 (*Zwang*) must; (*nur im Präsens*) to
have to; **ich muss es tun** I must do
it, I have to do it; **ich musste es
tun** I had to do it; **er muss es**

nicht tun he doesn't have to do it;
muss ich? must I?, do I have to?;
wann müsst ihr zur Schule?
when do you have to go to
school?; **er hat gehen müssen** he
(has) had to go; **muss das sein?** is
that really necessary?; **ich muss
mal** (*fam*) I need the toilet
2 (*sollen*) **das musst du nicht tun!**
you oughtn't to *o* shouldn't do
that; **Sie hätten ihn fragen
müssen** you should have asked
him
3 es muss geregnet haben it
must have rained; **es muss nicht
wahr sein** it needn't be true

Muster (-s, -) *nt* (*Dessin*) pattern,
design; (*Probe*) sample; (*Vorbild*)
model; **mustern** *vt* to have a
close look at; **jdn ~** to look sb up
and down
Mut (-(e)s) *m* courage; **jdm
~ machen** to encourage sb; **mutig**
adj brave, courageous
Mutter (-, *Mütter*) *f* mother
▷ (-, -n) *f* (*Schraubenmutter*) nut;
Muttersprache *f* mother
tongue; **Muttertag** *m* Mother's
Day; **Mutti** *f* mum(my) (*Brit*),
mom(my) (*US*)
mutwillig *adj* deliberate
Mütze (-, -n) *f* cap
MwSt. *abk* = **Mehrwertsteuer**
VAT
Myanmar (-s) *nt* Myanmar

n

na *interj*: **~ also!**, **~ bitte!** see?, what did I tell you?; **~ ja** well; **~ und?** so what?

Nabel (-s, -) *m* navel

SCHLÜSSELWORT

nach *prep* +*dat* **1** (*örtlich*) to; **nach Berlin** to Berlin; **nach links/rechts** (to the) left/right; **nach oben/hinten** up/back

2 (*zeitlich*) after; **einer nach dem anderen** one after the other; **nach Ihnen!** after you!; **zehn (Minuten) nach drei** ten (minutes) past three

3 (*gemäß*) according to; **nach dem Gesetz** according to the law; **dem Namen nach** judging by his/her name; **nach allem, was ich weiß** as far as I know

▷ *adv*: **ihm nach!** after him!; **nach**

und nach gradually, little by little; **nach wie vor** still

nach|ahmen *vt* to imitate

Nachbar(in) (-n, -n) *m(f)* neighbour; **Nachbarschaft** *f* neighbourhood

nach|bestellen *vt* to order some more

nachdem *conj* after; (*weil*) since; **je ~ (ob/wie)** depending on (whether/how)

nach|denken *irr vi* to think (*über* +*akk* about); **nachdenklich** *adj* thoughtful

nacheinander *adv* one after another (*o* the other)

Nachfolger(in) (-s, -) *m(f)* successor

nach|forschen *vt* to investigate

Nachfrage *f* inquiry; (*Comm*) demand; **nach|fragen** *vi* to inquire

nach|geben *irr vi* to give in (*jdm* to sb)

Nachgebühr *f* surcharge; (*für Briefe etc*) excess postage

nach|gehen *irr vi* to follow (*jdm* sb); (*erforschen*) to inquire (*einer Sache dat* into sth); **die Uhr geht (zehn Minuten) nach** this watch is (ten minutes) slow

nachher *adv* afterwards; **bis ~!** see you later

Nachhilfe *f* extra tuition

nach|holen *vt* to catch up with; (*Versäumtes*) to make up for

nach|kommen *irr vi* to follow; **einer Verpflichtung** (*dat*) **~** to fulfil an obligation

nach|lassen *irr vt* (*Summe*) to take off ▷ *vi* to decrease, to ease off; (*schlechter werden*) to deteriorate; **nachlässig** *adj* negligent, careless

nach|laufen *irr vi* to run after, to chase (*jdm* sb)

nach|lösen vt: **eine Fahrkarte ~** to buy a ticket on the bus/train

nach|machen vt to imitate, to copy (jdm etw sth from sb); (fälschen) to counterfeit

Nachmittag m afternoon; **heute ~** this afternoon; **am ~** in the afternoon; **nachmittags** adv in the afternoon; **um 3 Uhr ~** at 3 (o'clock) in the afternoon, at 3 pm

Nachnahme (-, -n) f cash on delivery; **per ~** COD

Nachname m surname

nach|prüfen vt to check

nach|rechnen vt to check

Nachricht (-, -en) f (piece of) news sing; (Mitteilung) message; **Nachrichten** pl news sing

Nachsaison f off-season

nach|schauen vi: **jdm ~** to gaze after sb ▷ vt (prüfen) to check

nach|schicken vt to forward

nach|schlagen irr vt to look up

nach|sehen irr vt (prüfen) to check

Nachspeise f dessert

nächstbeste(r, s) adj: **der ~ Zug/Job** the first train/job that comes along; **nächste(r, s)** adj next; (nächstgelegen) nearest

Nacht (-, Nächte) f night; **in der ~** during the night; (bei Nacht) at night; **Nachtclub** m nightclub; **Nachtdienst** m night duty; **~ haben** (Apotheke) to be open all night

Nachteil m disadvantage

Nachtflug m night flight; **Nachtfrost** m overnight frost; **Nachthemd** nt (für Damen) nightdress; (für Herren) nightshirt

Nachtigall (-, -en) f nightingale

Nachtisch m dessert, sweet (Brit), pudding (Brit); **Nachtleben** nt nightlife

nach|tragen irr vt: **jdm etw ~** (übel nehmen) to hold sth against sb

nachträglich adv: **~ alles Gute zum Geburtstag!** Happy belated birthday

nachts adv at night; **um 11 Uhr ~** at 11 (o'clock) at night, at 11 pm; **um 2 Uhr ~** at 2 (o'clock) in the morning, at 2 am; **Nachtschicht** f night shift; **Nachttarif** m off-peak rate; **Nachttisch** m bedside table; **Nachtzug** m night train

Nachweis (-es, -e) m proof

Nachwirkung f after-effect

nach|zahlen vi to pay extra ▷ vt: **20 Euro ~** to pay 20 euros extra

nach|zählen vt to check

Nacken (-s, -) m (nape of the) neck

nackt adj naked; (Tatsachen) plain, bare; **Nacktbadestrand** m nudist beach

Nadel (-, -n) f needle; (Stecknadel) pin; **Nadelstreifen** pl pinstripes pl

Nagel (-s, Nägel) m nail; **Nagelbürste** f nail brush; **Nagelfeile** f nail-file; **Nagellack** m nail varnish (o polish); **Nagellackentferner** (-s, -) m nail-varnish (o nail-polish) remover; **Nagelschere** f nail scissors pl

nah(e) adj, adv (räumlich) near(by); (zeitlich) near; (Verwandte, Freunde) close; **Nähe** (-) f (Umgebung) vicinity; **in der ~** nearby; **in der ~ von** near to; **nahe|gehen** irr vi: **jdm ~** to upset sb; **nahe|legen** vt: **jdm etw ~** to suggest sth to sb; **nahe|liegen** irr vi to be obvious ▷ prep +dat near (to), close to

nähen vt, vi to sew

nähere(r, s) adj (Erklärung, Erkundigung) more detailed; **die ~ Umgebung** the immediate area;

Nähere(s) nt details pl; **nähern** vr: **sich ~** to approach
nahezu adv virtually, almost
nahm imperf von **nehmen**
Nähmaschine f sewing machine
nahrhaft adj nourishing, nutritious; **Nahrung** f food; **Nahrungsmittel** nt food
Naht (-, Nähte) f seam; (Med) stitches pl, suture; (Tech) join
Nahverkehr m local traffic; **Nahverkehrszug** m local train
Nähzeug nt sewing kit
naiv adj naive
Name (-ns, -n) m name
nämlich adv that is to say, namely; (denn) since
nannte imperf von **nennen**
Napf (-(e)s, Näpfe) m bowl, dish
Narbe (-, -n) f scar
Narkose (-, -n) f anaesthetic
Narzisse (-, -n) f narcissus
naschen vt, vi to nibble; **Naschkatze** f (fam) nibbler; **eine ~ sein** to have a sweet tooth
Nase (-, -n) f nose; **Nasenbluten** (-s) nt nosebleed; **~ haben** to have a nosebleed; **Nasenloch** nt nostril; **Nasentropfen** pl nose drops pl
Nashorn nt rhinoceros
nass adj wet; **Nässe** (-) f wetness; **nässen** vi (Wunde) to weep
Nation (-, -en) f nation; **national** adj national; **Nationalfeiertag** m national holiday; **Nationalhymne** (-, -n) f national anthem; **Nationalität** f nationality; **Nationalmannschaft** f national team; **Nationalpark** m National Park; **Nationalspieler(in)** m(f) international (player)
NATO (-) f abk = **North Atlantic Treaty Organization** NATO, Nato
Natur f nature; **Naturkost** f health food; **natürlich** adj natural ▷ adv naturally; (selbstverständlich) of course; **Naturpark** m nature reserve; **naturrein** adj natural, pure; **Naturschutz** m conservation; **Naturschutzgebiet** nt nature reserve; **Naturwissenschaft** f (natural) science; **Naturwissenschaftler(in)** m(f) scientist
Navigationssystem nt (Auto) navigation system
n. Chr. abk = **nach Christus** AD
Nebel (-s, -) m fog, mist; **nebelig** adj foggy, misty; **Nebelscheinwerfer** m foglamp; **Nebelschlussleuchte** f (Auto) rear foglight
neben prep +akk o dat next to; (außer) apart from, besides; **nebenan** adv next door; **Nebenausgang** m side exit; **nebenbei** adv at the same time; (außerdem) additionally; (beiläufig) incidentally; **nebeneinander** adv side by side; **Nebeneingang** m side entrance; **Nebenfach** nt subsidiary subject
nebenher adv (zusätzlich) besides; (gleichzeitig) at the same time; (daneben) alongside
Nebenkosten pl extra charges pl, extras pl; **Nebensache** f minor matter; **nebensächlich** adj minor; **Nebensaison** f low season; **Nebenstraße** f side street; **Nebenwirkung** f side effect
neblig adj foggy, misty
necken vt to tease
Neffe (-n, -n) m nephew
negativ adj negative; **Negativ** nt (Foto) negative
nehmen (nahm, genommen) vt to take; **wie man's nimmt** it depends on how you look at it; **den Bus/Zug ~** to take the bus/train; **jdn/etw ernst ~** to

take sb/sth seriously; **etw zu sich ~** to eat sth; **jdn zu sich ~** to have sb come and live with one; **jdn an die Hand ~** to take sb by the hand

neidisch _adj_ envious

neigen _vi:_ **zu etw ~** to tend towards sth; **Neigung** _f (des Geländes)_ slope; _(Tendenz)_ inclination; _(Vorliebe)_ liking

nein _adv_ no

Nektarine _f_ nectarine

Nelke (-, -n) _f_ carnation; _(Gewürz)_ clove

nennen _(nannte, genannt) vt_ to name; _(mit Namen)_ to call

Neonazi (-s, -s) _m_ neo-Nazi

Nepal (-s) _nt_ Nepal

Neptun (-s) _m_ Neptune

Nerv (-s, -en) _m_ nerve; **jdm auf die ~en gehen** to get on sb's nerves; **nerven** _vt:_ **jdn ~** _(fam)_ to get on sb's nerves; **Nervenzusammenbruch** _m_ nervous breakdown; **nervös** _adj_ nervous

Nest (-(e)s, -er) _nt_ nest; _(pej: Ort)_ dump

nett _adj_ nice; _(freundlich)_ kind; **sei so ~ und ...** do me a favour and ...

netto _adv_ net

Netz (-es, -e) _nt_ net; _(für Einkauf)_ string bag; _(System)_ network; _(Stromnetz)_ mains, power _(US)_; **Netzanschluss** _m_ mains connection; **Netzbetreiber(in)** _m(f)_ network operator; _(Inform)_ Internet (_o_ Net) operator; **Netzgerät** _nt_ power pack; **Netzkarte** _f_ season ticket; **Netzwerk** _nt (Inform)_ network; **Netzwerkkarte** _f_ network card

neu _adj_ new; _(Sprache, Geschichte)_ modern; **die ~esten Nachrichten** the latest news; **Neubau** _m_ new building; **neuerdings** _adv_ recently; **Neueröffnung** _f (Geschäft)_ new business;

Neuerung _f_ innovation; _(Reform)_ reform

Neugier _f_ curiosity; **neugierig** _adj_ curious _(auf +akk_ about); **ich bin ~, ob ...** I wonder whether _(o_ if) ...; **ich bin ~ , was du dazu sagst** I'll be interested to hear what you have to say about it

Neuheit _f_ novelty; **Neuigkeit** _f_ news _sing;_ **eine ~** a piece of news; **Neujahr** _nt_ New Year; **prosit ~!** Happy New Year; **neulich** _adv_ recently, the other day; **Neumond** _m_ new moon

neun _num_ nine; **neunhundert** _num_ nine hundred; **neunmal** _adv_ nine times; **neunte(r, s)** _adj_ ninth; _siehe auch_ **dritte**; **Neuntel** (-s, -) _nt_ ninth; **neunzehn** _num_ nineteen; **neunzehnte(r, s)** _adj_ nineteenth; _siehe auch_ **dritte**; **neunzig** _num_ ninety; **in den ~er Jahren** in the nineties; **Neunzigerjahre** _pl_ nineties _pl;_ **neunzigste(r, s)** _adj_ ninetieth

neureich _adj_ nouveau riche

Neurologe _m_, **Neurologin** _f_ neurologist; **Neurose** (-, -n) _f_ neurosis; **neurotisch** _adj_ neurotic

Neuseeland _nt_ New Zealand

Neustart _m (Inform)_ restart, reboot

neutral _adj_ neutral

neuwertig _adj_ nearly new

Nicaragua (-s) _nt_ Nicaragua

 SCHLÜSSELWORT

nicht _adv_ **1** _(Verneinung)_ not; **er ist es nicht** it's not him, it isn't him; **er raucht nicht** _(gerade)_ he isn't smoking; _(gewöhnlich)_ he doesn't smoke; **ich kann das nicht — ich auch nicht** I can't do it — neither _o_ nor can I; **es regnet nicht mehr** it's not raining any more; **nicht rostend** stainless

2 (*Bitte, Verbot*) **nicht!** don't!, no!;
nicht berühren! do not touch!;
nicht doch! don't!
3 (*rhetorisch*) **du bist müde, nicht
(wahr)?** you're tired, aren't you?;
das ist schön, nicht (wahr)? it's
nice, isn't it?
4 was du nicht sagst! the things
you say!

Nichte (-, -n) *f* niece
Nichtraucher(in) *m(f)* non-
smoker; **Nichtraucherabteil** *nt*
non-smoking compartment;
Nichtraucherzone *f* non-
smoking area
nichts *pron* nothing; **für ~ und
wieder ~** for nothing at all; **ich
habe ~ gesagt** I didn't say
anything; **macht ~** never mind
Nichtschwimmer(in) *m(f)*
non-swimmer
nichtssagend *adj* meaningless
nicken *vi* to nod
Nickerchen *nt* nap
nie *adv* never; **~ wieder** (*o* **mehr**)
never again; **fast ~** hardly ever
nieder *adj* (*niedrig*) low; (*gering*)
inferior ▷ *adv* down;
niedergeschlagen *adj* depressed;
Niederlage *f* defeat
Niederlande *pl* Netherlands *pl*;
Niederländer(in) *m(f)* Dutch-
man/Dutchwoman;
niederländisch *adj* Dutch;
Niederländisch *nt* Dutch
Niederlassung *f* branch
Niederösterreich *nt* Lower
Austria; **Niedersachsen** *nt*
Lower Saxony
Niederschlag *m* (*Meteo*)
precipitation; (*Regen*) rainfall
niedlich *adj* sweet, cute
niedrig *adj* low; (*Qualität*)
inferior
niemals *adv* never
niemand *pron* nobody, no one;

ich habe ~en gesehen I haven't
seen anyone; **~ von ihnen** none of
them
Niere (-, -n) *f* kidney;
Nierenentzündung *f* kidney
infection; **Nierensteine** *pl*
kidney stones *pl*
nieseln *vi impers* to drizzle;
Nieselregen *m* drizzle
niesen *vi* to sneeze
Niete (-, -n) *f* (*Los*) blank; (*Reinfall*)
flop; (*pej: Mensch*) failure; (*Tech*) rivet
Nigeria (-s) *nt* Nigeria
Nikotin (-s) *nt* nicotine
Nilpferd *nt* hippopotamus
nippen *vi* to sip; **an etw** (*dat*) **~** to
sip sth
nirgends *adv* nowhere
Nische (-, -n) *f* niche
Niveau (-s, -s) *nt* level; **sie hat
~** she's got class
nobel *adj* (*großzügig*) generous;
(*fam: luxuriös*) classy, posh;
Nobelpreis *m* Nobel Prize

SCHLÜSSELWORT

noch *adv* **1** (*weiterhin*) still; **noch
nicht** not yet; **noch nie** never
(yet); **noch immer** *o* **immer noch**
still; **bleiben Sie doch noch** stay a
bit longer
2 (*in Zukunft*) still, yet; **das kann
noch passieren** that might still
happen; **er wird noch kommen**
he'll come (yet)
3 (*nicht später als*) **noch vor einer
Woche** only a week ago; **noch am
selben Tag** the very same day;
noch im 19. Jahrhundert as late
as the 19th century; **noch heute**
today
4 (*zusätzlich*) **wer war noch da?**
who else was there?; **noch einmal**
once more, again; **noch dreimal**
three more times; **noch einer**
another one

5 (*bei Vergleichen*) **noch größer** even bigger; **das ist noch besser** that's better still; **und wenn es noch so schwer ist** however hard it is

6 Geld noch und noch heaps (and heaps) of money; **sie hat noch und noch versucht, ...** she tried again and again to ...
▷ *konj*: **weder A noch B** neither A nor B

nochmal(s) *adv* again, once more
Nominativ *m* nominative (case)
Nonne (-, -n) *f* nun
Nonstop-Flug *m* nonstop flight
Nord north; **Nordamerika** *nt* North America; **Norddeutschland** *nt* Northern Germany; **Norden** (-s) *m* north; **im ~ Deutschlands** in the north of Germany; **Nordeuropa** *nt* Northern Europe
Nordic Walking *nt* (*Sport*) Nordic Walking
Nordirland *nt* Northern Ireland; **nordisch** *adj* (*Völker, Sprache*) Nordic; **Nordkorea** (-s) *nt* North Korea; **nördlich** *adj* northern; (*Kurs, Richtung*) northerly; **Nordost(en)** *m* northeast; **Nordpol** *m* North Pole; **Nordrhein-Westfalen** (-s) *nt* North Rhine-Westphalia; **Nordsee** *f* North Sea; **nordwärts** *adv* north, northwards; **Nordwest(en)** *m* northwest; **Nordwind** *m* north wind
nörgeln *vi* to grumble
Norm (-, -en) *f* norm; (*Größenvorschrift*) standard
normal *adj* normal; **Normalbenzin** *nt* regular (petrol (*Brit*) o gas (*US*)); **normalerweise** *adv* normally
normen *vt* to standardize
Norwegen (-s) *nt* Norway;

Norweger(in) *m(f)* Norwegian; **norwegisch** *adj* Norwegian; **Norwegisch** *nt* Norwegian
Not (-, *Nöte*) *f* need; (*Armut*) poverty; (*Elend*) hardship; (*Bedrängnis*) trouble; (*Mangel*) want; (*Mühe*) trouble; (*Zwang*) necessity; **zur ~** if necessary; (*gerade noch*) just about
Notar(in) *m(f)* public notary; **notariell** *adj*: **~ beglaubigt** attested by a notary
Notarzt *m*, **Notärztin** *f* emergency doctor; **Notarztwagen** *m* emergency ambulance; **Notaufnahme** *f* A&E, casualty (*Brit*), emergency room (*US*); **Notausgang** *m* emergency exit; **Notbremse** *f* emergency brake; **Notdienst** *m* emergency service, after-hours service; **notdürftig** *adj* scanty; (*behelfsmäßig*) makeshift
Note (-, -n) *f* note; (*in Schule*) mark, grade (*US*); (*Mus*) note
Notebook (-(s), -s) *nt* (*Inform*) notebook
Notfall *m* emergency; **notfalls** *adv* if necessary
notieren *vt* to note down
nötig *adj* necessary; **etw ~ haben** to need sth
Notiz (-, -en) *f* note; (*Zeitungs~*) item; **Notizblock** *m* notepad; **Notizbuch** *nt* notebook
Notlage *f* crisis; (*Elend*) plight; **notlanden** *vi* to make a forced (o emergency) landing; **Notlandung** *f* emergency landing; **Notruf** *m* emergency call; **Notrufnummer** *f* emergency number; **Notrufsäule** *f* emergency telephone
notwendig *adj* necessary
Nougat (-s, -s) *m* od *nt* nougat
November (-(s), -) *m* November; *siehe auch* **Juni**

Nr. *abk* = **Nummer** No., no.
Nu *m*: **im ~** in no time
nüchtern *adj* sober; (*Magen*)
empty
Nudel (-, -n) *f* noodle; **~n** *pl*
(*italienische*) pasta *sing*
null *num* zero; (*Tel*) O (*Brit*), zero
(*US*); **~ Fehler** no mistakes; **~ Uhr**
midnight; **Null** (-, *-en*) *f* nought,
zero; (*pej: Mensch*) dead loss;
Nulltarif *m*: **zum ~** free of charge
Numerus clausus (-) *m*
restriction on the number of students
allowed to study a particular subject
Nummer (-, -n) *f* number;
nummerieren *vt* to number;
Nummernschild *nt* (*Auto*)
number plate (*Brit*), license plate
(*US*)
nun *adv* now; **von ~ an** from now
on ▷ *interj* well; **~ gut!** all right,
then; **es ist ~ mal so** that's the
way it is
nur *adv* only; **nicht ~ ..., sondern**
auch ... not only ..., but also ...;
~ Anna nicht except Anna
Nürnberg (*-s*) *nt* Nuremberg
Nuss (-, *Nüsse*) *f* nut;
Nussknacker (*-s*, -) *m* nutcracker; **Nuss-Nougat-Creme** *f*
chocolate nut cream
Nutte (-, -n) *f* (*fam*) tart
nutz, **nütze** *adj*: **zu nichts ~ sein**
to be useless; **nutzen**, **nützen** *vt*
to use (*zu etw for sth*); **was nützt**
es? what use is it? ▷ *vi* to be of
use; **das nützt nicht viel** that
doesn't help much; **es nützt**
nichts(, es zu tun) it's no use
(doing it); **Nutzen** (*-s*, -) *m*
usefulness; (*Gewinn*) profit;
nützlich *adj* useful
Nylon (*-s*) *nt* nylon

O

o *interj* oh
O *abk* = **Ost** E
Oase (-, -n) *f* oasis
ob *conj* if, whether; **so als ~** as if;
er tut so, als ~ er krank wäre he's
pretending to be sick; **und ~!** you
bet
obdachlos *adj* homeless
oben *adv* (*am oberen Ende*) at the
top; (*obenauf*) on (the) top; (*im*
Haus) upstairs; (*in einem Text*)
above; **~ erwähnt** (*o genannt*)
above-mentioned; **mit dem**
Gesicht nach ~ face up; **da ~** up
there; **von ~ bis unten** from top to
bottom; **siehe ~** see above
Ober (*-s*, -) *m* waiter
obere(r, s) *adj* upper, top
Oberfläche *f* surface;
oberflächlich *adj* superficial;
Obergeschoss *nt* upper floor
oberhalb *adv*, *prep* +*gen* above
Oberhemd *nt* shirt; **Oberkörper**

m upper body; **Oberlippe** *f* upper lip; **Oberösterreich** *nt* Upper Austria; **Oberschenkel** *m* thigh

oberste(r, s) *adj* very top, topmost

Oberteil *nt* top; **Oberweite** *f* bust/chest measurement

obig *adj* above(-mentioned)

Objekt (*-(e)s, -e*) *nt* object

objektiv *adj* objective; **Objektiv** *nt* lens

obligatorisch *adj* compulsory, obligatory

Oboe (*-, -n*) *f* oboe

Observatorium *nt* observatory

Obst (*-(e)s*) *nt* fruit; **Obstkuchen** *m* fruit tart; **Obstsalat** *m* fruit salad

obszön *adj* obscene

obwohl *conj* although

Ochse (*-n, -n*) *m* ox; **Ochsenschwanzsuppe** *f* oxtail soup

ocker *adj* ochre

öd(e) *adj* waste; (*unbebaut*) barren; (*fig*) dull

oder *conj* or; **~ aber** or else; **er kommt doch, ~?** he's coming, isn't he?

Ofen (*-s, Öfen*) *m* oven; (*Heizofen*) heater; (*Kohleofen*) stove; (*Herd*) cooker, stove; **Ofenkartoffel** *f* baked (*o* jacket) potato

offen *adj* open; (*aufrichtig*) frank; (*Stelle*) vacant ▷ *adv* frankly; **~ gesagt** to be honest

offenbar *adj* obvious; **offensichtlich** *adj* evident, obvious

öffentlich *adj* public; **Öffentlichkeit** *f* (*Leute*) public; (*einer Versammlung etc*) public nature

offiziell *adj* official

offline *adv* (*Inform*) offline

öffnen *vt* to open ▷ *vr*: **sich ~** to open; **Öffner** (*-s, -*) *m* opener;

Öffnung *f* opening; **Öffnungszeiten** *pl* opening times *pl*

oft *adv* often; **schon ~** many times; **öfter** *adv* more often (*o* frequently); **öfters** *adv* often, frequently

ohne *conj, prep +akk* without; **~ weiteres** without a second thought; (*sofort*) immediately; **~ ein Wort zu sagen** without saying a word; **~ mich** count me out

Ohnmacht (*-machten*) *f* unconsciousness; (*Hilflosigkeit*) helplessness; **in ~ fallen** to faint; **ohnmächtig** *adj* unconscious; **sie ist ~** she has fainted

Ohr (*-(e)s, -en*) *nt* ear; (*Gehör*) hearing

Öhr (*-(e)s, -e*) *nt* eye

Ohrenarzt *m*, **Ohrenärztin** *f* ear specialist; **Ohrenschmerzen** *pl* earache; **Ohrentropfen** *pl* ear drops *pl*; **Ohrfeige** *f* slap (in the face); **Ohrläppchen** *nt* earlobe; **Ohrringe** *pl* earrings *pl*

oje *interj* oh dear

okay *interj* OK, okay

Ökoladen *m* health food store; **ökologisch** *adj* ecological; **~e Landwirtschaft** organic farming

ökonomisch *adj* economic; (*sparsam*) economical

Ökosystem *nt* ecosystem

Oktanzahl *f* (*bei Benzin*) octane rating

Oktober (*-(s), -*) *m* October; *siehe auch* **Juni**

⬤ **OKTOBERFEST**
⬤
⬤ The annual October beer
⬤ festival, the **Oktoberfest**,
⬤ takes place in Munich on a
⬤ huge field where beer tents,
⬤ roller coasters and many other

amusements are set up. People
sit at long wooden tables, drink
beer from enormous litre beer
mugs, eat pretzels and listen
to brass bands. It is a great
attraction for tourists and locals
alike.

Öl (-(e)s, -e) nt oil; **Ölbaum** m
olive tree; **ölen** vt to oil; (Tech) to
lubricate; **Ölfarbe** f oil paint;
Ölfilter m oil filter; **Ölgemälde**
nt oil painting; **Ölheizung** f
oil-fired central heating; **ölig** adj
oily

oliv adj inv olive-green; **Olive**
(-, -n) f olive; **Olivenöl** nt olive
oil

Ölmessstab m dipstick; **Ölofen**
m oil stove; **Ölpest** f oil
pollution; **Ölsardine** f sardine in
oil; **Ölstandanzeiger** m (Auto)
oil gauge; **Ölteppich** m oil slick;
Ölwechsel m oil change

Olympiade f Olympic Games pl;
olympisch adj Olympic

Oma f, **Omi** (-s, -s) f grandma,
gran(ny)

Omelett (-(e)s, -s) nt, **Omelette**
f omelette

Omnibus m bus

onanieren vi to masturbate

Onkel (-s, -) m uncle

online adv (Inform) online;
Onlinedienst m (Inform) online
service

OP (-s, -s) m abk =
Operationssaal operating
theatre (Brit) (o room (US))

Opa m, **Opi** (-s, -s) m grandpa,
grandad

Open-Air-Konzert nt open-air
concert

Oper (-, -n) f opera; (Gebäude)
opera house

Operation f operation

Operette f operetta

operieren vi to operate ▷ vt to
operate on

Opernhaus nt opera house,
opera; **Opernsänger(in)** m(f)
opera singer

Opfer (-s, -) nt sacrifice; (Mensch)
victim; **ein ~ bringen** to make a
sacrifice

Opium (-s) nt opium

Opposition f opposition

Optiker(in) (-s, -) m(f) optician

optimal adj optimal, optimum

optimistisch adj optimistic

oral adj oral; **Oralverkehr** m
oral sex

orange adj inv orange; **Orange**
(-, -n) f orange; **Orangenmarmelade** f marmalade;
Orangensaft m orange juice

Orchester (-s, -) nt orchestra

Orchidee (-, -n) f orchid

Orden (-s, -) m (Rel) order; (Mil)
decoration

ordentlich adj (anständig)
respectable; (geordnet) tidy, neat;
(fam: annehmbar) not bad; (fam:
tüchtig) proper ▷ adv properly

ordinär adj common, vulgar;
(Witz) dirty

ordnen vt to sort out; **Ordner**
(-s, -) m (bei Veranstaltung)
steward; (Aktenordner) file;
Ordnung f order; (Geordnetsein)
tidiness; (**geht**) **in ~!** (that's) all
right; **mit dem Drucker ist etwas
nicht in ~** there's something
wrong with the printer

Oregano (-s) m oregano

Organ (-s, -e) nt organ; (Stimme)
voice

Organisation f organization;
organisieren vt to organize;
(fam: beschaffen) to get hold of
▷ vr: **sich ~** to organize

Organismus m organism

Orgasmus m orgasm

Orgel (-, -n) f organ

Orgie f orgy
orientalisch adj oriental
orientieren vr: **sich ~** to get
one's bearings; **Orientierung** f
orientation; **Orientierungssinn**
m sense of direction
original adj original; (echt)
genuine; **Original** (-s, -e) nt
original
originell adj original; (komisch)
witty
Orkan (-(e)s, -e) m hurricane
Ort (-(e)s, -e) m place; (Dorf)
village; **an ~ und Stelle, vor ~** on
the spot
Orthopäde (-n, -n) m,
Orthopädin f orthopaedist
örtlich adj local; **Ortschaft** f
village, small town; **Ortsgespräch**
nt local call; **Ortstarif** m local
rate; **Ortszeit** f local time

- **OSSI**
-
- **Ossi** is a colloquial and rather
- derogatory word used to
- describe a German from the
- former **DDR**.

Ost east; **Ostdeutschland** nt
(als Landesteil) Eastern Germany;
(Hist) East Germany; **Osten** (-s) m
east
Osterei nt Easter egg;
Osterglocke f daffodil;
Osterhase m Easter bunny;
Ostermontag m Easter Monday;
Ostern (-, -) nt Easter; **an** (o **zu**)
~ at Easter; **frohe ~** Happy Easter
Österreich (-s) nt Austria;
Österreicher(in) (-s, -) m(f) Austrian;
österreichisch adj Austrian
Ostersonntag m Easter Sunday
Osteuropa nt Eastern Europe;
Ostküste f east coast; **östlich**
adj eastern; (Kurs, Richtung)
easterly; **Ostsee** f: **die ~** the

Baltic (Sea); **Ostwind** m
east(erly) wind
OSZE (-) f abk = **Organisation für
Sicherheit und Zusammenarbeit
in Europa** OSCE
Otter (-s, -) m otter
out adj (fam) out; **outen** vt to
out
oval adj oval
Overheadprojektor m overhead projector
Ozean (-s, -e) m ocean; **der Stille
~** the Pacific (Ocean)
Ozon (-s) nt ozone;
Ozonbelastung f ozone level;
Ozonloch nt hole in the ozone
layer; **Ozonschicht** f ozone
layer; **Ozonwerte** pl ozone
levels pl

p

paar adj inv **ein ~** a few; **ein ~ Mal** a few times; **ein ~ Äpfel** some apples

Paar (-(e)s, -e) nt pair; (Ehepaar) couple; **ein ~ Socken** a pair of socks

pachten vt to lease

Päckchen nt package; (Zigaretten) packet; (zum Verschicken) small parcel; **packen** vt to pack; (fassen) to grasp, to seize; (fam: schaffen) to manage; (fig: fesseln) to grip; **Packpapier** nt brown paper; **Packung** f packet, pack (US); **Packungsbeilage** f package insert, patient information leaflet

Pädagoge (-n, -n) m, **Pädagogin** f teacher; **pädagogisch** adj educational; **~e Hochschule** college of education

Paddel (-s, -) nt paddle; **Paddelboot** nt canoe; **paddeln**

vi to paddle

Paket (-(e)s, -e) nt packet; (Postpaket) parcel; (Inform) package; **Paketbombe** f parcel bomb; **Paketkarte** f dispatch form (to be filled in with details of the sender and the addressee when handing in a parcel at the post office)

Pakistan (-s) nt Pakistan

Palast (-es, Paläste) m palace

Palästina (-s) nt Palestine; **Palästinenser(in)** (-s, -) m(f) Palestinian

Palatschinken pl filled pancakes pl

Palette f (von Maler) palette; (Ladepalette) pallet; (Vielfalt) range

Palme (-, -n) f palm (tree); **Palmsonntag** m Palm Sunday

Pampelmuse (-, -n) f grapefruit

pampig adj (fam: frech) cheeky; (breiig) gooey

Panda(bär) (-s, -s) m panda

Pandemie (-, -n) f pandemic

panieren vt (Gastr) to coat with breadcrumbs; **paniert** adj breaded

Panik f panic

Panne (-, -n) f (Auto) breakdown; (Missgeschick) slip; **Pannendienst** m, **Pannenhilfe** f breakdown (o rescue) service

Pant(h)er (-s, -) m panther

Pantomime (-, -n) f mime

Panzer (-s, -) m (Panzerung) armour (plating); (Mil) tank

Papa (-s, -s) m dad(dy), pa (US)

Papagei (-s, -en) m parrot

Papaya (-, -s) f papaya

Papier (-s, -e) nt paper; **~e** pl (Ausweispapiere) papers pl; (Dokumente, Urkunden) papers pl, documents pl; **Papiercontainer** m paper bank; **Papierformat** nt paper size; **Papiergeld** nt paper money; **Papierkorb** m wastepaper basket; (Inform)

recycle bin; **Papiertaschentuch** nt (paper) tissue; **Papiertonne** f paper bank

Pappbecher m paper cup; **Pappe** (-, -n) f cardboard; **Pappkarton** m cardboard box; **Pappteller** m paper plate

Paprika (-s, -s) m (Gewürz) paprika; (Schote) pepper

Papst (-(e)s, Päpste) m pope

Paradeiser (-s, -) m tomato

Paradies (-es, -e) nt paradise

Paragliding (-s) nt paragliding

Paragraph (-en, -en) m paragraph; (Jur) section

parallel adj parallel

Paranuss f Brazil nut

Parasit (-en, -en) m parasite

parat adj ready; **etw ~ haben** to have sth ready

Pärchen nt couple

Parfüm (-s, -s o -e) nt perfume; **Parfümerie** f perfumery; **parfümieren** vt to scent, to perfume

Pariser (-s, -) m (fam: Kondom) rubber

Park (-s, -s) m park

Park-and-ride-System nt park-and-ride system; **Parkbank** f park bench; **Parkdeck** nt parking level; **parken** vt, vi to park

Parkett (-s, -e) nt parquet flooring; (Theat) stalls pl (Brit), parquet (US)

Parkhaus nt multi-storey car park (Brit), parking garage (US)

parkinsonsche Krankheit f Parkinson's disease

Parkkralle f (Auto) wheel clamp; **Parklicht** nt parking light; **Parklücke** f parking space; **Parkplatz** m (für ein Auto) parking space; (für mehrere Autos) car park (Brit), parking lot (US); **Parkscheibe** f parking disc; **Parkscheinautomat** m pay point; (Parkscheinausgabegerät) ticket machine; **Parkuhr** f parking meter; **Parkverbot** nt (Stelle) no-parking zone; **hier ist ~** you can't park here

Parlament nt parliament

Parmesan (-s) m Parmesan (cheese)

Partei f party

Parterre (-s, -s) nt ground floor (Brit), first floor (US)

Partie f part; (Spiel) game; (Mann, Frau) catch; **mit von der ~ sein** to be in on it

Partitur f (Mus) score

Partizip (-s, -ien) nt participle

Partner(in) (-s, -) m(f) partner; **Partnerschaft** f partnership; **eingetragene ~** civil partnership; **Partnerstadt** f twin town

Party (-, -s) f party; **Partymuffel** (-s, -) m party pooper; **Partyservice** m catering service

Pass (-es, Pässe) m pass; (Ausweis) passport

passabel adj reasonable

Passagier (-s, -e) m passenger

Passamt nt passport office

Passant(in) m(f) passer-by; **Passbild** nt passport photo

passen vi (Größe) to fit; (Farbe, Stil) to go (zu with); (auf Frage) to pass; **passt (es) dir morgen?** does tomorrow suit you?; **das passt mir gut** that suits me fine; **passend** adj suitable; (zusammenpassend) matching; (angebracht) fitting; (Zeit) convenient; **haben Sie es nicht ~?** (Kleingeld) have you got the right change?

passieren vi to happen

passiv adj passive

Passkontrolle f passport control

Passwort nt password

Paste (-, -n) f paste

Pastellfarbe f pastel colour
Pastete (-, -n) f (warmes Gericht) pie; (Pastetchen) vol-au-vent; (ohne Teig) pâté
Pastor, in (-s, -en) m(f) minister, vicar
Pate (-n, -n) m godfather; **Patenkind** nt godchild
Patient(in) m(f) patient
Patin f godmother
Patrone (-, -n) f cartridge
patsch interj splat; **patschnass** adj soaking wet
pauschal adj (Kosten) inclusive; (Urteil) sweeping; **Pauschale** (-, -n) f, **Pauschalgebühr** f flat rate (charge); **Pauschalpreis** m flat rate; (für Hotel, Reise) all-inclusive price; **Pauschalreise** f package tour
Pause (-, -n) f break; (Theat) interval; (Kino etc) intermission; (Innehalten) pause
Pavian (-s, -e) m baboon
Pavillon (-s, -s) m pavilion
Pay-TV (-s) nt pay-per-view television, pay TV
Pazifik (-s) m Pacific (Ocean)
PC (-s, -s) m abk = **Personal Computer** PC
Pech (-s, -e) nt (fig) bad luck; ~ **haben** to be unlucky; ~ **gehabt!** tough (luck)
Pedal (-s, -e) nt pedal
Pediküre (-, -en) f pedicure
Peeling (-s, -s) nt (facial/body) scrub
peinlich adj (unangenehm) embarrassing, awkward; (genau) painstaking; **es war mir sehr ~** I was totally embarrassed
Peitsche (-, -n) f whip
Pelikan (-s, -e) m pelican
Pellkartoffeln pl potatoes pl boiled in their skins
Pelz (-es, -e) m fur; **pelzig** adj (Zunge) furred

pendeln vi (Zug, Bus) to shuttle; (Mensch) to commute; **Pendelverkehr** m shuttle traffic; (für Pendler) commuter traffic; **Pendler(in)** (-s, -) m(f) commuter
penetrant adj sharp; (Mensch) pushy
Penis (-, -se) m penis
Pension f (Geld) pension; (Ruhestand) retirement; (für Gäste) guesthouse, B&B; **pensioniert** adj retired; **Pensionsgast** m guest (in a guesthouse)
Peperoni (-, -) f chilli
per prep +akk by, per; (pro) per; (bis) by
perfekt adj perfect
Pergamentpapier nt grease-proof paper
Periode (-, -n) f period
Perle (-, -n) f (a. fig) pearl
perplex adj dumbfounded
Person (-, -en) f person; **ein Tisch für drei ~en** a table for three; **Personal** (-s) nt staff, personnel; (Bedienung) servants pl; **Personalausweis** m identity card; **Personalien** pl particulars pl; **Personenschaden** m injury to persons; **Personenwaage** f (bathroom) scales pl; **Personenzug** m passenger train; **persönlich** adj personal; (auf Briefen) private ▷ adv personally; (selbst) in person; **Persönlichkeit** f personality
Peru (-s) nt Peru
Perücke (-, -n) f wig
pervers adj perverted
pessimistisch adj pessimistic
Pest (-) f plague
Petersilie f parsley
Petroleum (-s) nt paraffin (Brit), kerosene (US)
Pfad (-(e)s, -e) m path; **Pfadfinder** (-s, -) m boy scout;

Pfadfinderin f girl guide
Pfahl (-(e)s, Pfähle) m post, stake
Pfand (-(e)s, Pfänder) nt security; (Flaschenpfand) deposit; (im Spiel) forfeit; **Pfandflasche** f returnable bottle
Pfanne (-, -n) f (frying) pan
Pfannkuchen m pancake
Pfarrei f parish; **Pfarrer(in)** (-s, -) m(f) priest
Pfau (-(e)s, -en) m peacock
Pfeffer (-s, -) m pepper; **Pfefferkuchen** m gingerbread; **Pfefferminze** (-e) f peppermint; **Pfefferminztee** m peppermint tea; **Pfeffermühle** f pepper mill; **pfeffern** vt to put pepper on/in; **Pfefferstreuer** (-s, -) m pepper pot
Pfeife (-, -n) f whistle; (für Tabak, von Orgel) pipe; **pfeifen** (pfiff, gepfiffen) vt, vi to whistle
Pfeil (-(e)s, -e) m arrow
Pfeiltaste f (Inform) arrow key
Pferd (-(e)s, -e) nt horse; **Pferdeschwanz** m (Frisur) ponytail; **Pferdestall** m stable; **Pferdestärke** f horsepower
pfiff imperf von **pfeifen**
Pfifferling m chanterelle
Pfingsten (-, -) nt Whitsun, Pentecost (US); **Pfingstmontag** m Whit Monday; **Pfingstsonntag** m Whit Sunday, Pentecost (US)
Pfirsich (-s, -e) m peach
Pflanze (-, -n) f plant; **pflanzen** vt to plant; **Pflanzenfett** nt vegetable fat
Pflaster (-s, -) nt (für Wunde) plaster, Band Aid® (US); (Straßenpflaster) road surface, pavement (US)
Pflaume (-, -n) f plum
Pflege (-, -n) f care; (Krankenpflege) nursing; (von Autos, Maschinen) maintenance; **pflegebedürftig** adj in need of

care; **pflegeleicht** adj easy-care; (fig) easy to handle; **pflegen** vt to look after; (Kranke) to nurse; (Beziehungen) to foster; (Fingernägel, Gesicht) to take care of; (Daten) to maintain; **Pflegepersonal** nt nursing staff; **Pflegeversicherung** f long-term care insurance
Pflicht (-, -en) f duty; (Sport) compulsory section; **pflichtbewusst** adj conscientious; **Pflichtfach** nt (Schule) compulsory subject; **Pflichtversicherung** f compulsory insurance
pflücken vt to pick
Pforte (-, -n) f gate; **Pförtner(in)** (-s, -) m(f) porter
Pfosten (-s, -) m post
Pfote (-, -n) f paw
pfui interj ugh
Pfund (-(e)s, -e) nt pound
pfuschen vi (fam) to be sloppy
Pfütze (-, -n) f puddle
Phantasie f siehe **Fantasie**; **phantastisch** adj siehe **fantastisch**
Phase (-, -n) f phase
Philippinen pl Philippines pl
Philosophie f philosophy
Photo nt siehe **Foto**
pH-neutral adj pH-balanced; **pH-Wert** m pH-value
Physalis (-, Physalen) f physalis
Physik f physics sing
physisch adj physical
Pianist(in) (-en, -en) m(f) pianist
Pickel (-s, -) m pimple; (Werkzeug) pickaxe; (Berg~) ice-axe
Picknick (-s, -e o -s) nt picnic; **ein ~ machen** to have a picnic
piepsen vi to chirp
piercen vt: **sich die Nase ~ lassen** to have one's nose pierced; **Piercing** (-s) nt (body) piercing
pieseln vi (fam) to pee

Pik (-, -) nt (Karten) spades pl
pikant adj spicy
Pilates nt (Sport) Pilates
Pilger(in) m(f) pilgrim;
  Pilgerfahrt f pilgrimage
Pille (-, -n) f pill; **sie nimmt die
  ~** she's on the pill
Pilot(in) (-en, -en) m(f) pilot
Pilz (-es, -e) m (essbar) mushroom;
  (giftig) toadstool; (Med) fungus
PIN (-, -s) f PIN (number)
pingelig adj (fam) fussy
Pinguin (-s, -e) m penguin
Pinie f pine; **Pinienkern** m pine
  nut
pink adj shocking pink
pinkeln vi (fam) to pee
Pinsel (-s, -) m (paint)brush
Pinzette f tweezers pl
Pistazie f pistachio
Piste (-, -n) f (Ski) piste; (Aviat)
  runway
Pistole (-, -n) f pistol
Pixel (-s) nt (Inform) pixel
Pizza (-, -s) f pizza; **Pizzaservice**
  m pizza delivery service; **Pizzeria**
  (-, Pizzerien) f pizzeria
Pkw (-(s), -(s)) m abk =
  Personenkraftwagen car
Plakat nt poster
Plakette f (Schildchen) badge;
  (Aufkleber) sticker
Plan (-(e)s, Pläne) m plan; (Karte)
  map; **planen** vt to plan
Planet (-en, -en) m planet;
  Planetarium nt planetarium
planmäßig adj scheduled
Plan(t)schbecken nt paddling
  pool; **plan(t)schen** vi to splash
  around
Planung f planning
Plastik f sculpture ▷ (-s) nt
  (Kunststoff) plastic; **Plastikfolie** f
  plastic film; **Plastiktüte** f
  plastic bag
Platin (-s) nt platinum
platsch interj splash

platt adj flat; (fam: überrascht)
  flabbergasted; (fig: geistlos) flat,
  boring
Platte (-, -n) f (Foto, Tech, Gastr)
  plate; (Steinplatte) flag;
  (Schallplatte) record;
  Plattenspieler m record player
Plattform f platform; **Plattfuß**
  m flat foot; (Reifen) flat (tyre)
Platz (-es, Plätze) m place;
  (Sitzplatz) seat; (freier Raum) space,
  room; (in Stadt) square; (Sportplatz)
  playing field; **nehmen Sie ~** please
  sit down, take a seat; **ist dieser
  ~ frei?** is this seat taken?;
  Platzanweiser(in) m(f)
  usher/usherette
Plätzchen nt spot; (Gebäck)
  biscuit
platzen vi to burst; (Bombe) to
  explode
Platzkarte f seat reservation;
  Platzreservierung f seat
  reservation; **Platzverweis** m: **er
  erhielt einen ~** he was sent off;
  Platzwunde f laceration, cut
plaudern vi to chat, to talk
pleite adj (fam) broke; **Pleite**
  (-, -n) f (Bankrott) bankruptcy;
  (fam: Reinfall) flop
Plombe (-, -n) f lead seal;
  (Zahnplombe) filling; **plombieren**
  vt (Zahn) to fill
plötzlich adj sudden ▷ adv suddenly,
  all at once
plump adj clumsy; (Hände)
  ungainly; (Körper) shapeless
plumps interj thud; (in Flüssigkeit)
  plop
Plural (-s, -e) m plural
plus adv plus; **fünf ~ sieben ist
  zwölf** five plus seven is (o are)
  twelve; **zehn Grad ~** ten degrees
  above zero; **Plus** (-, -) nt plus;
  (Fin) profit; (Vorteil) advantage
Plüsch (-(e)s, -e) m plush
Pluto (-) m Pluto

PLZ *abk* = **Postleitzahl** postcode (*Brit*), zip code (*US*)

Po (*-s, -s*) *m* (*fam*) bottom, bum

Pocken *pl* smallpox *sing*

poetisch *adj* poetic

Pointe (*-, -n*) *f* punch line

Pokal (*-s, -e*) *m* goblet; (*Sport*) cup

pökeln *vt* to pickle

Pol (*-s, -e*) *m* pole

Pole (*-n, -n*) *m* Pole; **Polen** (*-s*) *nt* Poland

Police (*-, -n*) *f* (insurance) policy

polieren *vt* to polish

Polin *f* Pole, Polish woman

Politik *f* politics *sing*; (*eine bestimmte*) policy; **Politiker(in)** *m(f)* politician; **politisch** *adj* political

Politur *f* polish

Polizei *f* police *pl*; **Polizeibeamte(r)** *m*, **Polizeibeamtin** *f* police officer; **polizeilich** *adj* police; **sie wird ~ gesucht** the police are looking for her; **Polizeirevier** *nt*, **Polizeiwache** *f* police station; **Polizeistunde** *f* closing time; **Polizeiwache** *f* police station; **Polizist(in)** *m(f)* policeman/ -woman

Pollen (*-s, -*) *m* pollen; **Pollenflug** (*-s*) *m* pollen count

polnisch *adj* Polish; **Polnisch** *nt* Polish

Polo (*-s*) *nt* polo; **Polohemd** *nt* polo shirt

Polster (*-s, -*) *nt* cushion; (*Polsterung*) upholstery; (*in Kleidung*) padding; (*fig: Geld*) reserves *pl*; **Polstergarnitur** *f* living-room suite; **Polstermöbel** *pl* upholstered furniture *sing*; **polstern** *vt* to upholster; (*Kleidung*) to pad

Polterabend *m* party prior to a wedding, at which old crockery is smashed to bring good luck

poltern *vi* (*Krach machen*) to crash; (*schimpfen*) to rant

Polyester (*-s, -*) *m* polyester

Polypen *pl* (*Med*) adenoids *pl*

Pommes frites *pl* chips *pl* (*Brit*), French fries *pl* (*US*)

Pony (*-s, -s*) *m* (*Frisur*) fringe (*Brit*), bangs *pl* (*US*) ▷ (*-s, -s*) *nt* (*Pferd*) pony

Popcorn (*-s*) *nt* popcorn

Popmusik *f* pop (music)

populär *adj* popular

Pore (*-, -n*) *f* pore

Pornografie *f* pornography

Porree (*-s, -s*) *m* leeks *pl*; **eine Stange ~** a leek

Portemonnaie, **Portmonee** (*-s, -s*) *nt* purse

Portier (*-s, -s*) *m* porter; *siehe auch* **Pförtner**

Portion *f* portion, helping

Porto (*-s, -s*) *nt* postage

Portrait, **Porträt** (*-s, -s*) *nt* portrait

Portugal (*-s*) *nt* Portugal; **Portugiese** (*-n, -n*) *m* Portuguese; **Portugiesin** (*-, -nen*) *f* Portuguese; **portugiesisch** *adj* Portuguese; **Portugiesisch** *nt* Portuguese

Portwein (*-s, -e*) *m* port

Porzellan (*-s, -e*) *nt* china

Posaune (*-, -n*) *f* trombone

Position *f* position

positiv *adj* positive

Post® (*-, -en*) *f* post office; (*Briefe*) post (*Brit*), mail; **Postamt** *nt* post office; **Postanweisung** *f* postal order (*Brit*), money order (*US*); **Postbank** *f* German post office bank; **Postbote** *m*, **-botin** *f* postman/-woman

Posten (*-s, -*) *m* post, position; (*Comm*) item; (*auf Liste*) entry

Poster (*-s, -*) *nt* poster

Postfach *nt* post-office box, PO box; **Postkarte** *f* postcard;

postlagernd adv poste restante; **Postleitzahl** f postcode (Brit), zip code (US)

postmodern adj postmodern

Postsparkasse f post office savings bank; **Poststempel** m postmark; **Postweg** m: **auf dem ~** by mail

Potenz f (Math) power; (eines Mannes) potency

PR (-, -s) f abk = **Public Relations** PR

prächtig adj splendid

prahlen vi to boast, to brag

Praktikant(in) m(f) trainee; **Praktikum** (-s, Praktika) nt practical training; **praktisch** adj practical; **~er Arzt** general practitioner

Praline f chocolate

Prämie f (bei Versicherung) premium; (Belohnung) reward; (von Arbeitgeber) bonus

Präparat nt (Med) medicine; (Bio) preparation

Präservativ nt condom

Präsident(in) m(f) president

Praxis (-, Praxen) f practice; (Behandlungsraum) surgery; (von Anwalt) office; **Praxisgebühr** f surgery surcharge

präzise adj precise, exact

predigen vt, vi to preach; **Predigt** (-, -en) f sermon

Preis (-es, -e) m (zu zahlen) price; (bei Sieg) prize; **den ersten ~ gewinnen** to win first prize; **Preisausschreiben** nt competition

Preiselbeere f cranberry

preisgünstig adj inexpensive; **Preislage** f price range; **Preisliste** f price list; **Preisschild** nt price tag; **Preisträger(in)** m(f) prizewinner; **preiswert** adj inexpensive

Prellung f bruise

Premiere (-, -n) f premiere, first night

Premierminister(in) m(f) prime minister, premier

Prepaidhandy nt prepaid mobile (Brit), prepaid cell phone (US); **Prepaidkarte** f prepaid card

Presse (-, -n) f press

pressen vt to press

prickeln vi to tingle

Priester(in) (-s, -) m(f) priest/(woma~ priest

Primel (-, -n) f primrose

primitiv adj primitive

Prinz (-en, -en) m prince; **Prinzessin** f princess

Prinzip (-s, -ien) nt principle; **im ~** basically; **aus ~** on principle

Priorität f priority

privat adj private; **Privatfernsehen** nt commercial television; **Privatgrundstück** nt private property; **privatisieren** vt to privatize

pro prep +akk per; **5 Euro ~ Stück/Person** 5 euros each/per person; **Pro** (-s) nt pro

Probe (-, -n) f test; (Teststück) sample; (Theat) rehearsal; **Probefahrt** f test drive; **eine ~ machen** to go for a test drive; **Probezeit** f trial period; **probieren** vt, vi to try; (Wein, Speise) to taste, to sample

Problem (-s, -e) nt problem

Produkt (-(e)s, -e) nt product; **Produktion** f production; (produzierte Menge) output; **produzieren** vt to produce

Professor(in) (-s, -en) m(f) professor

Profi (-s, -s) m pro

Profil (-s, -e) nt profile; (von Reifen, Schuhsohle) tread

Profit (-(e)s, -e) m profit; **profitieren** vi to profit (von from)

Prognose (-, -n) f prediction; (*Wetter*) forecast

Programm (-s, -e) nt programme; (*Inform*) program; (*TV*) channel; **Programmheft** nt programme; **programmieren** vt to program; **Programmierer(in)** (-s, -) m(f) programmer; **Programmkino** nt arts (o repertory (*US*)) cinema

Projekt (-(e)s, -e) nt project

Projektor m projector

Promenade (-, -n) f promenade

Promille (-(s), -) nt (blood) alcohol level; **0,8 ~** 0,08 per cent; **Promillegrenze** f legal alcohol limit

prominent adj prominent; **Prominenz** f VIPs pl, prominent figures pl; (*fam: Stars*) the glitterati pl

Propeller (-s, -) m propeller

prosit interj cheers

Prospekt (-(e)s, -e) m leaflet, brochure

prost interj cheers

Prostituierte(r) mf prostitute

Protest (-(e)s, -e) m protest

Protestant(in) m(f) Protestant; **protestantisch** adj Protestant

protestieren vi to protest (*gegen* against)

Prothese (-, -n) f artificial arm/leg; (*Gebiss*) dentures pl

Protokoll (-s, -e) nt (*bei Sitzung*) minutes pl; (*diplomatisch, Inform*) protocol; (*bei Polizei*) statement

protzen vi to show off; **protzig** adj flashy

Proviant (-s, -e) m provisions pl

Provider (-s, -) m (*Inform*) (service) provider

Provinz (-, -en) f province

Provision f (*Comm*) commission

provisorisch adj provisional; **Provisorium** (-s, Provisorien) nt stopgap; (*Zahn*) temporary filling

provozieren vt to provoke

Prozent (-(e)s, -e) nt per cent

Prozess (-es, -e) m (*Vorgang*) process; (*Jur*) trial; (*Rechtsfall*) (court) case; **prozessieren** vi to go to law (*mit* against)

Prozession f procession

Prozessor (-s, -en) m (*Inform*) processor

prüde adj prudish

prüfen vt to test; (*nachprüfen*) to check; **Prüfung** f (*Schule*) exam; (*Überprüfung*) check; **eine ~ machen** (*Schule*) to take an exam

Prügelei f fight; **prügeln** vt to beat ▷ vr: **sich ~** to fight

PS abk = **Pferdestärke** hp; = **Postskript(um)** PS

pseudo- präf pseudo; **Pseudokrupp** (-s) m (*Med*) pseudocroup; **Pseudonym** (-s, -e) nt pseudonym

pst interj ssh

Psychiater(in) (-s, -) m(f) psychiatrist; **psychisch** adj psychological; (*Krankheit*) mental; **Psychoanalyse** f psychoanalysis; **Psychologe** (-n, -n) m, **Psychologin** f psychologist; **Psychologie** f psychology

Psychopharmaka pl mind-affecting drugs pl, psychotropic drugs pl; **psychosomatisch** adj psychosomatic; **Psychoterror** m psychological intimidation; **Psychotherapie** f psychotherapy

Pubertät f puberty

Publikum (-s) nt audience; (*Sport*) crowd

Pudding (-s, -e o -s) m blancmange

Pudel (-s, -) m poodle

Puder (-s, -) m powder; **Puderzucker** m icing sugar

Puerto Rico (-s) nt Puerto Rico

Pulli (-s, -s) m, **Pullover** (-s, -) m sweater, pullover, jumper (*Brit*)

rechnen vt, vi to calculate; **~ mit** to expect; (*bauen auf*) to count on ▷ vr: **sich ~** to pay off, to turn out to be profitable; **Rechner** (*-s, -*) m calculator; (*Computer*) computer; **Rechnung** f calculation(s); (*Comm*) bill (*Brit*), check (*US*); **die ~, bitte!** can I have the bill, please?; **das geht auf meine ~** this is on me

recht adj (*richtig, passend*) right; **~ haben** to be right; **jdm ~ geben** to agree with sb; **mir soll's ~ sein** it's alright by me; **mir ist es ~** I don't mind ▷ adv really, quite; (*richtig*) right(ly); **ich weiß nicht ~** I don't really know; **es geschieht ihm ~** it serves him right

Recht (*-(e)s, -e*) nt right; (*Jur*) law

Rechte (*-n, -n*) f right-hand side; (*Hand*) right hand; (*Pol*) right (wing); **rechte(r, s)** adj right; **auf der ~n Seite** on the right, on the right-hand side; **Rechte(s)** nt right thing; **etwas/nichts ~s** something/nothing proper

Rechteck (*-s, -e*) nt rectangle; **rechteckig** adj rectangular

rechtfertigen vt to justify ▷ vr: **sich ~** to justify oneself

rechtlich adj legal; **rechtmäßig** adj legal, lawful

rechts adv on the right; **~ abbiegen** to turn right; **~ von** to the right of; **~ oben** at the top right

Rechtsanwalt m, **-anwältin** f lawyer

Rechtschreibung f spelling

Rechtshänder(in) (*-s, -*) m(f) right-hander; **rechtsherum** adv to the right, clockwise; **rechtsradikal** adj (*Pol*) extreme right-wing

Rechtsschutzversicherung f legal costs insurance

Rechtsverkehr m driving on the right

rechtswidrig adj illegal

rechtwinklig adj right-angled; **rechtzeitig** adj timely ▷ adv in time

recycelbar adj recyclable; **recyceln** vt to recycle; **Recycling** (*-s*) nt recycling; **Recyclingpapier** nt recycled paper

Redakteur(in) m(f) editor; **Redaktion** f editing; (*Leute*) editorial staff; (*Büro*) editorial office(s)

Rede (*-, -n*) f speech; (*Gespräch*) talk; **eine ~ halten** to make a speech; **reden** vi to talk, to speak ▷ vt to say; (*Unsinn etc*) to talk; **Redewendung** f idiom; **Redner(in)** m(f) speaker

reduzieren vt to reduce

Referat (*-s, -e*) nt paper; **ein ~ halten** to give a paper (*über +akk* on)

reflektieren vt to reflect

Reform (*-, -en*) f reform; **Reformhaus** nt health food shop; **reformieren** vt to reform

Regal (*-s, -e*) nt shelf; (*Möbelstück*) shelves pl

Regel (*-, -n*) f rule; (*Med*) period; **regelmäßig** adj regular; **regeln** vt to regulate, to control; (*Angelegenheit*) to settle ▷ vr: **sich von selbst ~** to sort itself out; **Regelung** f regulation

Regen (*-s, -*) m rain; **Regenbogen** m rainbow; **Regenmantel** m raincoat; **Regenrinne** f gutter; **Regenschauer** m shower; **Regenschirm** m umbrella; **Regenwald** m rainforest; **Regenwurm** m earthworm

Regie f direction

regieren vt, vi to govern, to rule;

Regierung f government; (von Monarch) reign
Region f region; **regional** adj regional
Regisseur(in) m(f) director
registrieren vt to register; (bemerken) to notice
regnen vi impers to rain; **regnerisch** adj rainy
regulär adj regular; **regulieren** vt to regulate, to adjust
Reh (-(e)s, -e) nt deer; (Fleisch) venison
Rehabilitationszentrum nt (Med) rehabilitation centre
Reibe (-, -n) f, **Reibeisen** nt grater; **reiben** (rieb, gerieben) vt to rub; (Gastr) to grate; **reibungslos** adj smooth
reich adj rich
Reich (-(e)s, -e) nt empire; (eines Königs) kingdom
reichen vi to reach; (genügen) to be enough, to be sufficient (jdm for sb) ▷ vt to hold out; (geben) to pass, to hand; (anbieten) to offer
reichhaltig adj ample, rich; **reichlich** adj (Trinkgeld) generous; (Essen) ample; ~ **Zeit** plenty of time; **Reichtum** (-s, -tümer) m wealth
reif adj ripe; (Mensch, Urteil) mature
Reif (-(e)s) m (Raureif) hoarfrost ▷ (-(e)s, -e) m (Ring) ring, hoop
reifen vi to mature; (Obst) to ripen
Reifen (-s, -) m ring, hoop; (von Auto) tyre; **Reifendruck** m tyre pressure; **Reifenpanne** m puncture; **Reifenwechsel** m tyre change
Reihe (-, -n) f row; (von Tagen etc, fam: Anzahl) series sing; **der ~ nach** one after the other; **er ist an der ~** it's his turn; **Reihenfolge** f

order, sequence; **Reihenhaus** nt terraced house (Brit), row house (US)
Reiher (-s, -) m heron
rein (fam) kontr von **herein, hinein** ▷ adj pure; (sauber) clean
Reinfall m (fam) letdown; **rein|fallen** irr vi (fam) **auf etw** (akk) ~ to fall for sth
reinigen vt to clean; **Reinigung** f cleaning; (Geschäft) (dry) cleaner's; **Reinigungsmittel** nt cleaning agent, cleaner
rein|legen vt: **jdn ~** to take sb for a ride
Reis (-es, -e) m rice
Reise (-, -n) f journey; (auf Schiff) voyage; **Reiseapotheke** f first-aid kit; **Reisebüro** nt travel agent's; **Reisebus** m coach; **Reiseführer(in)** m(f) (Mensch) courier; (Buch) guide(book); **Reisegepäck** nt luggage (Brit), baggage; **Reisegesellschaft** f (Veranstalter) tour operator; **Reisegruppe** f tourist party; (mit Reisebus) coach party; **Reiseleiter(in)** m(f) courier; **reisen** vi to travel; ~ **nach** to go to; **Reisende(r)** mf traveller; **Reisepass** m passport; **Reiseroute** f route, itinerary; **Reiserücktrittversicherung** f holiday cancellation insurance; **Reisescheck** m traveller's cheque; **Reisetasche** f holdall (Brit), carryall (US); **Reiseveranstalter** m tour operator; **Reiseverkehr** m holiday traffic; **Reiseversicherung** f travel insurance; **Reiseziel** nt destination
Reiskocher (-s, -) m rice steamer
reißen (riss, gerissen) vt, vi to tear; (ziehen) to pull, to drag; (Witz) to crack

Reißnagel m drawing pin (Brit), thumbtack (US); **Reißverschluss** m zip (Brit), zipper (US); **Reißzwecke** f drawing pin (Brit), thumbtack (US)

reiten (ritt, geritten) vt, vi to ride; **Reiter(in)** m(f) rider; **Reithose** f riding breeches pl; **Reitsport** m riding; **Reitstiefel** m riding boot

Reiz (-es, -e) m stimulus; (angenehm) charm; (Verlockung) attraction; **reizen** vt to stimulate; (unangenehm) to annoy; (verlocken) to appeal to, to attract; **reizend** adj charming; **Reizgas** nt irritant gas; **Reizung** f irritation

Reklamation f complaint

Reklame (-, -n) f advertising; (Einzelwerbung) advertisement; (im Fernsehen) commercial

reklamieren vi to complain (wegen about)

Rekord (-(e)s, -e) m record

relativ adj relative ▷ adv relatively

relaxen vi to relax, to chill out

Religion f religion; **religiös** adj religious

Remoulade (-, -n) f tartar sauce

Renaissance f renaissance, revival; (Hist) Renaissance

Rennbahn f racecourse; (Auto) racetrack; **rennen** (rannte, gerannt) vt, vi to run; **Rennen** (-s, -) nt running; (Wettbewerb) race; **Rennfahrer(in)** m(f) racing driver; **Rennrad** nt racing bike; **Rennwagen** m racing car

renommiert adj famous, noted (wegen, für for)

renovieren vt to renovate; **Renovierung** f renovation

rentabel adj profitable

Rente (-, -n) f pension; **Rentenversicherung** f pension scheme

Rentier nt reindeer

rentieren vr: **sich ~** to pay, to be profitable

Rentner(in) (-s, -) m(f) pensioner, senior citizen

Reparatur f repair; **Reparaturwerkstatt** f repair shop; (Auto) garage; **reparieren** vt to repair

Reportage f report; **Reporter(in)** (-s, -) m(f) reporter

Reptil (-s, -ien) nt reptile

Republik f republic

Reservat (-s, -e) nt nature reserve; (für Ureinwohner) reservation; **Reserve** (-, -n) f reserve; **Reservekanister** m spare can; **Reserverad** nt (Auto) spare wheel; **reservieren** vt to reserve; **Reservierung** f reservation

resignieren vi to give up; **resigniert** adj resigned

Respekt (-(e)s) m respect; **respektieren** vt to respect

Rest (-(e)s, -e) m rest, remainder; (Überreste) remains pl; **der ~ ist für Sie** (zur Bedienung) keep the change

Restaurant (-s, -s) nt restaurant

restaurieren vt to restore

Restbetrag m balance; **restlich** adj remaining; **restlos** adj complete

Resultat nt result

retten vt to save, to rescue

Rettich (-s, -e) m radish (large white or red variety)

Rettung f rescue; (Hilfe) help; (Rettungsdienst) ambulance service; **Rettungsboot** nt lifeboat; **Rettungshubschrauber** m rescue helicopter; **Rettungsring** m lifebelt, life preserver (US); **Rettungswagen** m ambulance

Reue (-) f remorse; (Bedauern)

regret; **reuen** vt: **es reut ihn** he regrets it

revanchieren vr: **sich ~** (sich rächen) to get one's own back, to get one's revenge; (für Hilfe etc) to return the favour

Revolution f revolution

Rezept (-(e)s, -e) nt (Gastr) recipe; (Med) prescription; **rezeptfrei** adj over-the-counter, non-prescription

Rezeption f (im Hotel) reception

rezeptpflichtig adj available only on prescription

R-Gespräch nt reverse-charge (Brit) (o collect (US)) call

Rhabarber (-s) m rhubarb

Rhein (-s) m Rhine; **Rheinland-Pfalz** (-) nt Rhineland-Palatinate

Rheuma (-s) nt rheumatism

Rhythmus m rhythm

richten vt (lenken) to direct (auf +akk to); (Waffe, Kamera) to point (auf +akk at); (Brief, Anfrage) to address (an +akk to); (einstellen) to adjust; (instand setzen) to repair; (zurechtmachen) to prepare ▷ vr: **sich ~ nach** (Regel etc) to keep to; (Mode, Beispiel) to follow; (abhängen von) to depend on

Richter(in) (-s, -) m(f) judge

Richtgeschwindigkeit f recommended speed

richtig adj right, correct; (echt) proper ▷ adv (fam: sehr) really; **richtig|stellen** vt: **etw ~** (berichtigen) to correct sth

Richtlinie f guideline

Richtung f direction; (Tendenz) tendency

rieb imperf von **reiben**

riechen (roch, gerochen) vt, vi to smell; **nach etw ~** to smell of sth; **an etw** (dat) **~** to smell sth

rief imperf von **rufen**

Riegel (-s, -) m bolt; (Gastr) bar

Riemen (-s, -) m strap; (Gürtel) belt

Riese (-n, -n) m giant; **Riesengarnele** f king prawn; **riesengroß** adj gigantic, huge; **Riesenrad** nt big wheel; **riesig** adj enormous, huge

riet imperf von **raten**

Riff (-(e)s, -e) nt reef

Rind (-(e)s, -er) nt cow; (Bulle) bull; (Gastr) beef; **~er** pl cattle pl

Rinde (-, -n) f (Baum) bark; (Käse) rind; (Brot) crust

Rinderbraten m roast beef; **Rinderwahn(sinn)** m mad cow disease; **Rindfleisch** nt beef

Ring (-(e)s, -e) m ring; (Straße) ring road; **Ringbuch** nt ring binder

ringen (rang, gerungen) vi to wrestle; **Ringer(in)** m(f) wrestler; **Ringfinger** m ring finger; **Ringkampf** m wrestling match; **ringsherum** adv round about

Rippe (-, -n) f rib; **Rippenfellentzündung** f pleurisy

Risiko (-s, -s o Risiken) nt risk; **auf eigenes ~** at one's own risk; **riskant** adj risky; **riskieren** vt to risk

riss imperf von **reißen**

Riss (-es, -e) m tear; (in Mauer, Tasse etc) crack; **rissig** adj cracked; (Haut) chapped

ritt imperf von **reiten**

Ritter (-s, -) m knight

Rivale (-n, -n) m, **Rivalin** f rival

Rizinusöl nt castor oil

Robbe (-, -n) f seal

Roboter (-s, -) m robot

robust adj robust

roch imperf von **riechen**

Rock (-(e)s, Röcke) m skirt

Rockband f (Musikgruppe) rock band; **Rockmusik** f rock (music)

Rodelbahn f toboggan run;
  rodeln vi to toboggan
Roggen (-s, -) m rye;
  Roggenbrot nt rye bread
roh adj raw; (Mensch) coarse,
  crude; **Rohkost** f raw vegetables
  and fruit pl
Rohr (-(e)s, -e) nt pipe; (Bot) cane;
  (Schilf) reed; **Röhre** (-, -n) f tube;
  (Leitung) pipe; (Elek) valve;
  (Backröhre) oven; **Rohrzucker** m
  cane sugar
Rohstoff m raw material
Rokoko (-s) nt rococo
Rolle (-, -n) f (etw
  Zusammengerolltes) roll; (Theat) role
rollen vt, vi to roll
Roller (-s, -) m scooter
Rollerblades® pl Rollerblades®
  pl; **Rollerskates** pl roller skates
  pl
Rollkragenpullover m polo-
  neck (Brit) (o turtleneck (US))
  sweater; **Rollladen** m, **Rollo**
  (-s, -s) m (roller) shutters pl;
  Rollschuh m roller skate;
  Rollstuhl m wheelchair;
  rollstuhlgerecht adj suitable
  for wheelchairs; **Rolltreppe** f
  escalator
Roman (-s, -e) m novel
Romantik f romance;
  romantisch adj romantic
römisch-katholisch adj Roman
  Catholic
röntgen vt to X-ray;
  Röntgenaufnahme f,
  Röntgenbild nt X-ray;
  Röntgenstrahlen pl X-rays pl
rosa adj inv pink
Rose (-, -n) f rose
Rosenkohl m (Brussels) sprouts
  pl
Rosé(wein) m rosé (wine)
rosig adj rosy
Rosine f raisin
Rosmarin (-s) m rosemary

Rosskastanie f horse chestnut
Rost (-(e)s, -e) m rust; (zum Braten)
  grill, gridiron; **Rostbratwurst** f
  grilled sausage; **rosten** vi to
  rust; **rösten** vt to roast, to grill;
  (Brot) to toast; **rostfrei** adj
  rustproof; (Stahl) stainless; **rostig**
  adj rusty; **Rostschutz** m
  rustproofing
rot adj red; **~ werden** to blush;
  Rote Karte red card; **Rote Bete**
  beetroot; **bei Rot über die Ampel
  fahren** to jump the lights; **das
  Rote Kreuz** the Red Cross
Röteln pl German measles sing
röten vt to redden ▷ vr: **sich ~** to
  redden
rothaarig adj red-haired
rotieren vi to rotate; **am
  Rotieren sein** (fam) to be rushing
  around like a mad thing
Rotkehlchen nt robin; **Rotkohl**
  m, **Rotkraut** nt red cabbage;
  Rotlichtviertel nt red-light
  district; **Rotwein** m red wine
Rouge (-s, -s) nt rouge
Route (-, -n) f route
Routine f experience; (Trott)
  routine
Rubbellos nt scratchcard;
  rubbeln vt to rub
Rübe (-, -n) f turnip; **Gelbe
  ~** carrot; **Rote ~** beetroot
rüber (fam) kontr von **herüber,
  hinüber**
rückbestätigen vt (Flug etc) to
  reconfirm
rücken vt, vi to move; **könntest
  du ein bisschen ~?** could you
  move over a bit?
Rücken (-s, -) m back;
  Rückenlehne f back(rest);
  Rückenmark nt spinal cord;
  Rückenschmerzen pl backache
  sing; **Rückenschwimmen** (-s) nt
  backstroke; **Rückenwind** m
  tailwind

Rückerstattung f refund;
Rückfahrkarte f return ticket
(Brit), round-trip ticket (US);
Rückfahrt f return journey;
Rückfall m relapse; **Rückflug** m
return flight; **Rückgabe** f return;
rückgängig adj: **etw ~ machen**
to cancel sth; **Rückgrat** (-(e)s, -e)
nt spine, backbone; **Rückkehr**
(-, -en) f return; **Rücklicht** nt
rear light; **Rückreise** f return
journey; **auf der ~** on the way
back

Rucksack m rucksack, backpack;
Rucksacktourist(in) m(f)
backpacker

Rückschritt m step back;
Rückseite f back; (hinterer Teil)
rear; **siehe ~** see overleaf;
Rücksicht f consideration;
~ nehmen auf (+akk) to show
consideration for; **rücksichtslos**
adj inconsiderate; (Fahren)
reckless; (unbarmherzig) ruthless;
rücksichtsvoll adj considerate;
Rücksitz m back seat;
Rückspiegel m (Auto) rear-view
mirror; **Rückstand** m: **sie sind
zwei Tore im ~** they're two goals
down; **im ~ sein mit** (Arbeit, Miete)
to be behind with; **Rücktaste** f
backspace key; **Rückvergütung**
f refund; **rückwärts** adv
backwards, back; **Rückwärtsgang** m (Auto) reverse (gear);
Rückweg m return journey, way
back; **Rückzahlung** f repayment

Ruder (-s, -) nt oar; (Steuer)
rudder; **Ruderboot** nt rowing
boat (Brit), rowboat (US); **rudern**
vt, vi to row

Ruf (-(e)s, -e) m call, cry; (Ansehen)
reputation; **rufen** (rief, gerufen) vt,
vi to call; (schreien) to cry;
Rufnummer f telephone number

Ruhe (-) f rest; (Ungestörtheit)
peace, quiet; (Gelassenheit, Stille)
calm; (Schweigen) silence; **lass
mich in ~!** leave me alone; **ruhen**
vi to rest; **Ruhestand** m
retirement; **im ~ sein** to be retired;
Ruhestörung f disturbance of
the peace; **Ruhetag** m closing
day; **montags ~ haben** to be
closed on Mondays

ruhig adj quiet; (bewegungslos)
still; (Hand) steady; (gelassen) calm

Ruhm (-(e)s) m fame, glory

Rührei nt scrambled egg(s);
rühren vt to move; (umrühren) to
stir ▷ vr: **sich ~** to move; (sich
bemerkbar machen) to say
something; **rührend** adj
touching, moving; **Rührung** f
emotion

Ruine (-, -n) f ruin; **ruinieren** vt
to ruin

rülpsen vi to burp, to belch

rum (fam) kontr von **herum**

Rum (-s, -s) m rum

Rumänien (-s) nt Romania

Rummel (-s) m (Trubel) hustle
and bustle; (Jahrmarkt) fair;
(Medienrummel) hype;
Rummelplatz m fairground

rumoren vi: **es rumort in
meinem Bauch/Kopf** my
stomach is rumbling/my head is
spinning

Rumpf (-(e)s, Rümpfe) m (Anat)
trunk; (Aviat) fuselage; (Naut)
hull

rümpfen vt: **die Nase ~** to turn
one's nose up (über at)

Rumpsteak nt rump steak

rund adj round ▷ adv (etwa)
around; **~ um etw** (a)round sth;
Runde (-, -n) f round; (in Rennen)
lap; **Rundfahrt** f tour (durch of);
Rundfunk m broadcasting;
(Rundfunkanstalt) broadcasting
service; **im ~** on the radio;
Rundgang m tour (durch of); (von
Wächter) round

rundlich *adj* plump; **Rundreise** *f* tour (*durch* of)
runter (*fam*) *kontr von* **herunter, hinunter**; **runterscrollen** *vt* (*Inform*) to scroll down
runzeln *vt*: **die Stirn ~** to frown; **runzelig** *adj* wrinkled
ruppig *adj* gruff
Rüsche (-, -n) *f* frill
Ruß (-es) *m* soot
Russe (-n, -n) *m* Russian
Rüssel (-s, -) *m* (*Elefant*) trunk; (*Schwein*) snout
Russin *f* Russian; **russisch** *adj* Russian; **Russisch** *nt* Russian; **Russland** *nt* Russia
Rüstung *f* (*mit Waffen*) arming; (*Ritterrüstung*) armour; (*Waffen*) armaments *pl*
Rutsch (-(e)s, -e) *m*: **guten ~ (ins neue Jahr)!** Happy New Year; **Rutschbahn** *f*, **Rutsche** *f* slide; **rutschen** *vi* to slide; (*ausrutschen*) to slip; **rutschig** *adj* slippery
rütteln *vt, vi* to shake

S

S *abk* = **Süd** S
s. *abk* = **siehe** see; = **Seite** p.
Saal (-(e)s, Säle) *m* hall; (*für Sitzungen*) room
Saarland *nt* Saarland
sabotieren *vt* to sabotage
Sache (-, -n) *f* thing; (*Angelegenheit*) affair, business; (*Frage*) matter; **bei der ~ bleiben** to keep to the point; **sachkundig** *adj* competent; **Sachlage** *f* situation; **sachlich** *adj* (*objektiv*) objective; (*nüchtern*) matter-of-fact; (*inhaltlich*) factual; **sächlich** *adj* (*Ling*) neuter; **Sachschaden** *m* material damage
Sachsen (-s) *nt* Saxony; **Sachsen-Anhalt** (-s) *nt* Saxony-Anhalt
sacht(e) *adv* softly, gently
Sachverständige(r) *mf* expert
Sack (-(e)s, Säcke) *m* sack; (*pej:*

Mensch) bastard, bugger;
Sackgasse *f* dead end, cul-de-sac
Safe (*-s, -s*) *m* safe
Safer Sex *m* safe sex
Safran (*-s, -e*) *m* saffron
Saft (*-(e)s, Säfte*) *m* juice; **saftig**
adj juicy
Sage (*-, -n*) *f* legend
Säge (*-, -n*) *f* saw; **Sägemehl** *nt*
sawdust
sagen *vt, vi* to say (*jdm* to sb),
to tell (*jdm* sb); **wie sagt man ...
auf Englisch?** what's ... in
English?
sägen *vt, vi* to saw
sagenhaft *adj* legendary; (*fam:
großartig*) fantastic
sah *imperf von* **sehen**
Sahne (*-*) *f* cream
Saison (*-, -s*) *f* season;
außerhalb der ~ out of season
Saite (*-, -n*) *f* string
Sakko (*-s, -s*) *nt* jacket
Salami (*-, -s*) *f* salami
Salat (*-(e)s, -e*) *m* salad;
(*Kopfsalat*) lettuce; **Salatbar** *f*
salad bar; **Salatschüssel** *f* salad
bowl; **Salatsoße** *f* salad
dressing
Salbe (*-, -n*) *f* ointment
Salbei (*-s*) *m* sage
Salmonellenvergiftung *f*
salmonella (poisoning)
salopp *adj* (*Kleidung*) casual;
(*Sprache*) slangy
Salsamusik *f* salsa (music)
Salto (*-s, -s*) *m* somersault
Salz (*-es, -e*) *nt* salt; **salzarm** *adj*
low-salt; **salzen** (*salzte, gesalzen*)
vt to salt; **Salzgurke** *f* pickled
gherkin; **Salzhering** *m* pickled
herring; **salzig** *adj* salty;
Salzkartoffeln *pl* boiled potatoes
pl; **Salzstange** *f* pretzel stick;
Salzstreuer *m* salt cellar (*Brit*) (*o*
shaker (*US*)); **Salzwasser** *nt* salt
water

Samba (*-, -s*) *f* samba
Samen (*-s, -*) *m* seed; (*Sperma*)
sperm
sammeln *vt* to collect;
Sammler(in) *m(f)* collector;
Sammlung *f* collection;
(*Ansammlung, Konzentration*)
concentration
Samstag *m* Saturday; *siehe auch*
Mittwoch; **samstags** *adv* on
Saturdays; *siehe auch* **mittwochs**
samt *prep +dat* (along) with,
together with
Samt (*-(e)s, -e*) *m* velvet
sämtliche(r, s) *adj* all (the)
Sanatorium (*-s, Sanatorien*) *nt*
sanatorium (*Brit*), sanitarium (*US*)
Sand (*-(e)s, -e*) *m* sand
Sandale (*-, -n*) *f* sandal
sandig *adj* sandy; **Sandkasten**
m sandpit (*Brit*), sandbox (*US*);
Sandpapier *nt* sandpaper;
Sandstrand *m* sandy beach
sandte *imperf von* **senden**
sanft *adj* soft, gentle
sang *imperf von* **singen**;
Sänger(in) (*-s, -*) *m(f)* singer
Sangria (*-, -s*) *f* sangria
sanieren *vt* to redevelop;
(*Gebäude*) to renovate; (*Betrieb*) to
restore to profitability
sanitär *adj* sanitary; **~e Anlagen**
pl sanitation
Sanitäter(in) (*-s, -*) *m(f)* ambu-
lance man/woman, paramedic
sank *imperf von* **sinken**
Sankt Gallen (*-s*) *nt* St Gallen
Saphir (*-s, -e*) *m* sapphire
Sardelle *f* anchovy
Sardine *f* sardine
Sarg (*-(e)s, Särge*) *m* coffin
saß *imperf von* **sitzen**
Satellit (*-en, -en*) *m* satellite;
Satellitenfernsehen *nt* satellite
TV; **Satellitenschüssel** *f* (*fam*)
satellite dish
Satire (*-, -n*) *f* satire (*auf +akk* on)

foam (rubber); **Schaumwein** *m* sparkling wine

Schauplatz *m* scene; **Schauspiel** *nt* spectacle; (*Theat*) play; **Schauspieler(in)** *m(f)* actor/actress

Scheck (*-s, -s*) *m* cheque; **Scheckheft** *nt* chequebook; **Scheckkarte** *f* cheque card

Scheibe (*-, -n*) *f* disc; (*von Brot, Käse etc*) slice; (*Glasscheibe*) pane; **Scheibenbremse** *f* (*Auto*) disc brake; **Scheibenwaschanlage** *f* (*Auto*) windscreen (*Brit*) (*o* windshield (*US*)) washer unit; **Scheibenwischer** (*-s, -*) *m* (*Auto*) windscreen (*Brit*) (*o* windshield (*US*)) wiper

Scheich (*-s, -s*) *m* sheik(h)

Scheide (*-, -n*) *f* (*Anat*) vagina

scheiden (*schied, geschieden*) *vt* (*trennen*) to separate; (*Ehe*) to dissolve; **sich ~ lassen** to get a divorce; **sie hat sich von ihm ~ lassen** she divorced him; **Scheidung** *f* divorce

Schein (*-(e)s, -e*) *m* light; (*Anschein*) appearance; (*Geld*) (bank)note; **scheinbar** *adj* apparent; **scheinen** (*schien, geschienen*) *vi* (*Sonne*) to shine; (*den Anschein haben*) to seem; **Scheinwerfer** (*-s, -*) *m* flood-light; (*Theat*) spotlight; (*Auto*) headlight

Scheiß- *in zW* (*vulg*) damned, bloody (*Brit*); **Scheiße** (*-*) *f* (*vulg*) shit, crap; **scheißegal** *adj* (*vulg*) **das ist mir ~** I don't give a damn (*o* toss); **scheißen** (*schiss, geschissen*) *vi* (*vulg*) to shit

Scheitel (*-s, -*) *m* parting (*Brit*), part (*US*)

scheitern *vi* to fail (*an +dat* because of)

Schellfisch *m* haddock

Schema (*-s, -s o Schemata*) *nt* scheme, plan; (*Darstellung*) diagram

Schenkel (*-s, -*) *m* thigh

schenken *vt* to give; **er hat es mir geschenkt** he gave it to me (as a present); **sich** (*dat*) **etw ~** (*fam: weglassen*) to skip sth

Scherbe (*-, -n*) *f* broken piece, fragment

Schere (*-, -n*) *f* scissors *pl*; (*groß*) shears *pl*; **eine ~** a pair of scissors/shears

Scherz (*-es, -e*) *m* joke

scheu *adj* shy

scheuen *vr* **sich ~ vor** (*+dat*) to be afraid of, to shrink from ▷ *vt* to shun ▷ *vi* (*Pferd*) to shy

scheuern *vt* to scrub; **jdm eine ~** (*fam*) to slap sb in the face

Scheune (*-, -n*) *f* barn

scheußlich *adj* dreadful

Schi (*-s, -er*) *m* siehe **Ski**

Schicht (*-, -en*) *f* layer; (*in Gesellschaft*) class; (*in Fabrik etc*) shift

schick *adj* stylish, chic

schicken *vt* to send ▷ *vr*: **sich ~** (*sich beeilen*) to hurry up

Schickimicki (*-(s), -s*) *m* (*fam*) trendy

Schicksal (*-s, -e*) *nt* fate

Schiebedach *nt* (*Auto*) sunroof; **schieben** (*schob, geschoben*) *vt, vi* to push; **die Schuld auf jdn ~** to put the blame on sb; **Schiebetür** *f* sliding door

schied *imperf von* **scheiden**

Schiedsrichter(in) *m(f)* referee; (*Tennis*) umpire; (*Schlichter*) arbitrator

schief *adj* crooked; (*Blick*) funny ▷ *adv* crooked(ly); **schief|gehen** *irr vi* (*fam: misslingen*) to go wrong

schielen *vi* to squint

schien *imperf von* **scheinen**

Schienbein *nt* shin

Schiene (*-, -n*) *f* rail; (*Med*) splint

schier *adj* pure; *(fig)* sheer ▷ *adv* nearly, almost

schießen *(schoss, geschossen)* vt to shoot; *(Ball)* to kick; *(Tor)* to score; *(Foto)* to take ▷ *vi* to shoot *(auf +akk* at)

Schiff *(-(e)s, -e)* nt ship; *(in Kirche)* nave; **Schifffahrt** *f* shipping; **Schiffsreise** *f* voyage

schikanieren *vt* to harass; *(Schule)* to bully

Schild *(-(e)s, -e)* m *(Schutz)* shield ▷ *(-(e)s, -er)* nt sign; **was steht auf dem ~?** what does the sign say?

Schilddrüse *f* thyroid gland

schildern *vt* to describe

Schildkröte *f* tortoise; *(Wasserschildkröte)* turtle

Schimmel *(-s, -)* m mould; *(Pferd)* white horse; **schimmeln** *vi* to go mouldy

schimpfen *vt* to tell off ▷ *vi (sich beklagen)* to complain; **mit jdm ~** to tell sb off; **Schimpfwort** *nt* swearword

Schinken *(-s, -)* m ham

Schirm *(-(e)s, -e)* m *(Regenschirm)* umbrella; *(Sonnenschirm)* parasol, sunshade

schiss *imperf von* **scheißen**

Schlacht *(-, -en)* f battle; **schlachten** *vt* to slaughter; **Schlachter(in)** *(-s, -)* m(f) butcher

Schlaf *(-(e)s)* m sleep; **Schlafanzug** *m* pyjamas pl; **Schlafcouch** *f* bed settee

Schläfe *(-, -n)* f temple

schlafen *(schlief, geschlafen)* vi to sleep; **schlaf gut!** sleep well; **hast du gut geschlafen?** did you sleep all right?; **er schläft noch** he's still asleep; **~ gehen** to go to bed

schlaff *adj* slack; *(kraftlos)* limp; *(erschöpft)* exhausted

Schlafgelegenheit *f* place to sleep; **Schlaflosigkeit** *f*

sleeplessness; **Schlafmittel** *nt* sleeping pill; **schläfrig** *adj* sleepy

Schlafsaal *m* dormitory; **Schlafsack** *m* sleeping bag; **Schlaftablette** *f* sleeping pill; **er ist eine richtige ~** *(fam: langweilig)* he's such a bore; **Schlafwagen** *m* sleeping car, sleeper; **Schlafzimmer** *nt* bedroom

Schlag *(-(e)s, Schläge)* m blow; *(Puls)* beat; *(Elek)* shock; *(fam: Portion)* helping; *(Art)* kind, type; **Schlagader** *f* artery; **Schlaganfall** *m (Med)* stroke; **schlagartig** *adj* sudden

schlagen *(schlug, geschlagen)* vt to hit; *(besiegen)* to beat; *(Sahne)* to whip; **jdn zu Boden ~** to knock sb down ▷ *vi (Herz)* to beat; *(Uhr)* to strike; **mit dem Kopf gegen etw ~** to bang one's head against sth ▷ *vr:* **sich ~** to fight

Schläger *(-s, -)* m *(Sport)* bat; *(Tennis)* racket; *(Golf)* (golf) club; *(Hockey)* hockey stick; *(Mensch)* brawler; **Schlägerei** *f* fight, brawl

schlagfertig *adj* quick-witted; **Schlagloch** *nt* pothole; **Schlagsahne** *f* whipping cream; *(geschlagen)* whipped cream; **Schlagzeile** *f* headline; **Schlagzeug** *nt* drums pl; *(in Orchester)* percussion

Schlamm *(-(e)s, -e)* m mud

schlampig *adj (fam)* sloppy

schlang *imperf von* **schlingen**

Schlange *(-, -n)* f snake; *(von Menschen)* queue *(Brit)*, line *(US)*; **~ stehen** to queue *(Brit)*, to stand in line *(US)*; **Schlangenlinie** *f* wavy line; **in ~n fahren** to swerve about

schlank *adj* slim

schlapp *adj* limp; *(locker)* slack

Schlappe *(-, -n)* f *(fam)* setback

schlau adj clever, smart; (raffiniert) crafty, cunning
Schlauch (-(e)s, Schläuche) m hose; (in Reifen) inner tube; **Schlauchboot** nt rubber dinghy
schlecht adj bad; **mir ist ~** I feel sick; **die Milch ist ~** the milk has gone off ▷ adv badly; **es geht ihm ~** he's having a hard time; (gesundheitlich) he's not feeling well; (finanziell) he's pretty hard up; **schlecht|machen** vt: **jdn ~** (herabsetzen) to run sb down
schleichen (schlich, geschlichen) vi to creep
Schleier (-s, -) m veil
Schleife (-, -n) f (Inform, Aviat, Elek) loop; (Band) bow
schleifen vt (ziehen, schleppen) to drag ▷ (schliff, geschliffen) vt (schärfen) to grind; (Edelstein) to cut
Schleim (-(e)s, -e) m slime; (Med) mucus; **Schleimer** (-s, -) m (fam) creep; **Schleimhaut** f mucous membrane
schlendern vi to stroll
schleppen vt to drag; (Auto, Schiff) to tow; (tragen) to lug; **Schlepplift** m ski tow
Schleswig-Holstein (-s) nt Schleswig-Holstein
Schleuder (-, -n) f catapult; (für Wäsche) spin-dryer; **schleudern** vt to hurl; (Wäsche) to spin-dry ▷ vi (Auto) to skid; **Schleudersitz** m ejector seat
schlich imperf von **schleichen**
schlicht adj simple, plain
schlichten vt (Streit) to settle
schlief imperf von **schlafen**
schließen (schloss, geschlossen) vt, vi to close, to shut; (beenden) to close; (Freundschaft, Ehe) to enter into; (folgern) to infer (aus from) ▷ vr: **sich ~** to close, to shut; **Schließfach** nt locker

schließlich adv finally; (schließlich doch) after all
schliff imperf von **schleifen**
schlimm adj bad; **schlimmer** adj worse; **schlimmste(r, s)** adj worst; **schlimmstenfalls** adv at (the) worst
Schlinge (-, -n) f loop; (Med) sling
Schlips (-es, -e) m tie
Schlitten (-s, -) m sledge, toboggan; (mit Pferden) sleigh; **Schlittenfahren** (-s) nt tobogganing
Schlittschuh m ice skate; **~ laufen** to ice-skate
Schlitz (-es, -e) m slit; (für Münze) slot; (an Hose) flies pl
schloss imperf von **schließen**
Schloss (-es, Schlösser) nt lock; (Burg) castle
Schlosser(in) m(f) mechanic
Schlucht (-, -en) f gorge, ravine
schluchzen vi to sob
Schluck (-(e)s, -e) m swallow; **Schluckauf** (-s) m hiccups pl; **schlucken** vt, vi to swallow
schludern vi (fam) to do sloppy work
schlug imperf von **schlagen**
Schlüpfer (-s, -) m panties pl
schlürfen vt, vi to slurp
Schluss (-es, Schlüsse) m end; (Schlussfolgerung) conclusion; **am ~** at the end; **mit jdm ~ machen** to finish (o split up) with sb
Schlüssel (-s, -) m (a. fig) key; **Schlüsselbein** nt collarbone; **Schlüsselbund** m bunch of keys; **Schlüsseldienst** m key-cutting service; **Schlüsselloch** nt keyhole
Schlussfolgerung f conclusion; **Schlusslicht** nt tail-light; (fig) tail-ender; **Schlussverkauf** m clearance sale
schmächtig adj frail
schmal adj narrow; (Mensch, Buch etc) slim; (karg) meagre

Schmalz (-es, -e) nt dripping, lard; (fig: Sentimentalitäten) schmaltz

schmatzen vi to eat noisily

schmecken vt, vi to taste (nach of); **es schmeckt ihm** he likes it; **lass es dir ~!** bon appétit

Schmeichelei f flattery; **schmeichelhaft** adj flattering; **schmeicheln** vi: **jdm ~** to flatter sb

schmeißen (schmiss, geschmissen) vt (fam) to chuck, to throw

schmelzen (schmolz, geschmolzen) vt, vi to melt; (Metall, Erz) to smelt; **Schmelzkäse** m cheese spread

Schmerz (-es, -en) m pain; (Trauer) grief; **~en haben** to be in pain; **~en im Rücken haben** to have a pain in one's back; **schmerzen** vt, vi to hurt; **Schmerzensgeld** nt compensation; **schmerzhaft**, **schmerzlich** adj painful; **schmerzlos** adj painless; **Schmerzmittel** nt painkiller; **schmerzstillend** adj painkilling; **Schmerztablette** f painkiller

Schmetterling m butterfly

Schmied(in) (-(e)s, -e) m(f) blacksmith; **schmieden** vt to forge; (Pläne) to make

schmieren vt to smear; (ölen) to lubricate, to grease; (bestechen) to bribe ▷ vt, vi (unsauber schreiben) to scrawl; **Schmiergeld** nt (fam) bribe; **schmierig** adj greasy; **Schmierseife** f soft soap

Schminke (-, -n) f make-up; **schminken** vr: **sich ~** to put one's make-up on

schmiss imperf von **schmeißen**

schmollen vi to sulk; **schmollend** adj sulky

schmolz imperf von **schmelzen**

Schmuck (-(e)s, -e) m jewellery (Brit), jewelry (US); (Verzierung) decoration; **schmücken** vt to decorate

schmuggeln vt, vi to smuggle

schmunzeln vi to smile

schmusen vi to (kiss and) cuddle

Schmutz (-es) m dirt, filth; **schmutzig** adj dirty

Schnabel (-s, Schnäbel) m beak, bill; (Ausguss) spout

Schnake (-, -n) f mosquito

Schnalle (-, -n) f buckle

Schnäppchen nt (fam) bargain; **schnappen** vt (fangen) to catch ▷ vi: **nach Luft ~** to gasp for breath; **Schnappschuss** m (Foto) snap(shot)

Schnaps (-es, Schnäpse) m schnapps

schnarchen vi to snore

schnaufen vi to puff, to pant

Schnauzbart m moustache; **Schnauze** (-, -n) f snout, muzzle; (Ausguss) spout; (fam: Mund) trap; **die ~ voll haben** to have had enough

schnäuzen vr: **sich ~** to blow one's nose

Schnecke (-, -n) f snail; **Schneckenhaus** nt snail's shell

Schnee (-s) m snow; **Schneeball** m snowball; **Schneebob** m snowmobile; **Schneebrille** f snow goggles pl; **Schneeflocke** f snowflake; **Schneegestöber** (-s, -) nt snow flurry; **Schneeglöckchen** nt snowdrop; **Schneegrenze** f snowline; **Schneekanone** f snow thrower; **Schneekette** f (Auto) snow chain; **Schneemann** m snowman; **Schneepflug** m snowplough; **Schneeregen** m sleet; **Schneeschmelze** f thaw; **Schneesturm** m snowstorm, blizzard; **Schneetreiben** nt light blizzards pl; **Schneewehe** f snowdrift

Schneide (-, -n) f edge; (Klinge) blade; **schneiden** (schnitt, geschnitten) vt to cut; **sich** (dat) **die Haare ~ lassen** to have one's hair cut ▷ vr: **sich ~** to cut oneself; **Schneider(in)** (-s, -) m(f) tailor; (für Damenmode) dressmaker; **Schneiderin** f dressmaker; **Schneidezahn** m incisor

schneien vi impers to snow

schnell adj quick, fast ▷ adv quickly, fast; **mach ~!** hurry up; **Schnelldienst** m express service; **Schnellhefter** m loose-leaf binder; **Schnellimbiss** m snack bar; **Schnellkochtopf** m pressure cooker; **Schnellreinigung** f express dry cleaning; (Geschäft) express (dry) cleaner's; **Schnellstraße** f expressway; **Schnellzug** m fast train

schneuzen vr siehe **schnäuzen**

schnitt imperf von **schneiden**

Schnitt (-(e)s, -e) m cut; (Schnittpunkt) intersection; (Querschnitt) (cross) section; (Durchschnitt) average; (eines Kleides) style; **Schnitte** (-, -n) f slice; (belegt) sandwich; **Schnittkäse** m cheese slices pl; **Schnittlauch** m chives pl; **Schnittmuster** nt pattern; **Schnittstelle** f (Inform, fig) interface; **Schnittwunde** f cut, gash

Schnitzel (-s, -) nt (Papier) scrap; (Gastr) escalope

schnitzen vt to carve

Schnorchel (-s, -) m snorkel; **schnorcheln** vi to go snorkelling, to snorkel

schnüffeln vi to sniff

Schnuller (-s, -) m dummy (Brit), pacifier (US)

Schnulze (-, -n) f (Film, Roman) weepie

Schnupfen (-s, -) m cold

schnuppern vi to sniff

Schnur (-, Schnüre) f string, cord; (Elek) lead; **schnurlos** adj (Telefon) cordless

Schnurrbart m moustache

schnurren vi to purr

Schnürsenkel (-s, -) m shoelace

schob imperf von **schieben**

Schock (-(e)s, -e) m shock; **unter ~ stehen** to be in a state of shock; **schockieren** vt to shock

Schokolade f chocolate; **Schokoriegel** m chocolate bar

Scholle (-, -n) f (Fisch) plaice; (Eis) ice floe

SCHLÜSSELWORT

schon adv 1 (bereits) already; **er ist schon da** he's there already, he's already there; **ist er schon da?** is he there yet?; **warst du schon einmal da?** have you ever been there?; **ich war schon einmal da** I've been there before; **das war schon immer so** that has always been the case; **schon oft** often; **hast du schon gehört?** have you heard?

2 (bestimmt) all right; **du wirst schon sehen** you'll see (all right); **das wird schon noch gut** that'll be OK

3 (bloß) just; **allein schon das Gefühl ...** just the very feeling ...; **schon der Gedanke** the very thought; **wenn ich das schon höre** I only have to hear that

4 (einschränkend) **ja schon, aber ...** yes (well), but ...

5 **schon möglich** possible; **schon gut!** OK!; **du weißt schon** you know; **komm schon!** come on!

schön adj beautiful; (nett) nice; (Frau) beautiful, pretty; (Mann) beautiful, handsome; (*Wetter*) fine; **~e Grüße** best wishes; **~es Wochenende** have a nice weekend

schonen *vt* (*pfleglich behandeln*) to look after ▷ *vr*: **sich ~** to take it easy

Schönheit *f* beauty

Schonkost *f* light diet

schöpfen *vt* to scoop; (*mit Kelle*) to ladle; **Schöpfkelle** *f*, **Schöpflöffel** *m* ladle

Schöpfung *f* creation

Schoppen (-s, -) *m* glass (of wine)

Schorf (-(e)s, -e) *m* scab

Schorle (-, -n) *f* spritzer

Schornstein *m* chimney; **Schornsteinfeger(in)** (-s, -) *m(f)* chimney sweep

schoss *imperf von* **schießen**

Schoß (-es, Schöße) *m* lap

Schotte (-n, -n) *m* Scot, Scotsman; **Schottin** *f* Scot, Scotswoman; **schottisch** *adj* Scottish, Scots; **Schottland** *nt* Scotland

schräg *adj* slanting; (*Dach*) sloping; (*Linie*) diagonal; (*fam: unkonventionell*) wacky

Schrank (-(e)s, Schränke) *m* cupboard; (*Kleiderschrank*) wardrobe (*Brit*), closet (*US*)

Schranke (-, -n) *f* barrier

Schrankwand *f* wall unit

Schraube (-, -n) *f* screw; **schrauben** *vt* to screw; **Schraubendreher** (-s, -) *m* screwdriver; **Schraubenschlüssel** *m* spanner; **Schraubenzieher** (-s, -) *m* screwdriver; **Schraubverschluss** *m* screw top, screw cap

Schreck (-(e)s, -e) *m*, **Schrecken** (-s, -) *m* terror; (*Angst*) fright; **jdm einen ~ einjagen** to give sb a fright; **schreckhaft** *adj* jumpy; **schrecklich** *adj* terrible, dreadful

Schrei (-(e)s, -e) *m* scream; (*Ruf*) shout

Schreibblock *m* writing pad; **schreiben** (*schrieb, geschrieben*) *vt*, *vi* to write; (*buchstabieren*) to spell; **wie schreibt man ...?** how do you spell ...?; **Schreiben** (-s, -) *nt* writing; (*Brief*) letter; **Schreibfehler** *m* spelling mistake; **schreibgeschützt** *adj* (*Diskette*) write-protected; **Schreibtisch** *m* desk; **Schreibwaren** *pl* stationery *sing*; **Schreibwarenladen** *m* stationer's

schreien (*schrie, geschrie(e)n*) *vt*, *vi* to scream; (*rufen*) to shout

Schreiner(in) *m(f)* joiner; **Schreinerei** *f* joiner's workshop

schrie *imperf von* **schreien**

schrieb *imperf von* **schreiben**

Schrift (-, -en) *f* writing; (*Handschrift*) handwriting; (*Schriftart*) typeface; (*Schrifttyp*) font; **schriftlich** *adj* written ▷ *adv* in writing; **würden Sie uns das bitte ~ geben?** could we have that in writing, please?; **Schriftsteller(in)** (-s, -) *m(f)* writer

Schritt (-(e)s, -e) *m* step; **~ für ~** step by step; **~e gegen etw unternehmen** to take steps against sth; **Schrittgeschwindigkeit** *f* walking speed; **Schrittmacher** *m* (*Med*) pacemaker

Schrott (-(e)s, -e) *m* scrap metal; (*fig*) rubbish

schrubben *vi*, *vt* to scrub; **Schrubber** (-s, -) *m* scrubbing brush

schrumpfen *vi* to shrink

Schubkarren (-s, -) *m* wheelbarrow; **Schublade** *f* drawer

schubsen *vt* to shove, to push

schüchtern *adj* shy

schuf *imperf von* **schaffen**

Schuh (-(e)s, -e) *m* shoe;
 Schuhcreme *f* shoe polish;
 Schuhgeschäft *nt* shoe shop;
 Schuhgröße *f* shoe size;
 Schuhlöffel *m* shoehorn
Schulabschluss *m* school-
 leaving qualification
schuld *adj*: **wer ist ~ daran?**
 whose fault is it?; **er ist ~** it's his
 fault, he's to blame; **Schuld** (-) *f*
 guilt; (*Verschulden*) fault; **~ haben**
 to be to blame (*an +dat* for); **er hat
 ~** it's his fault; **sie gibt mir die
 ~ an dem Unfall** she blames me
 for the accident; **schulden** *vt* to
 owe (*jdm etw* sb sth); **Schulden** *pl*
 debts *pl*; **~ haben** to be in debt;
 ~ machen to run up debts; **seine
 ~ bezahlen** to pay off one's debts;
 schuldig *adj* guilty (*an +dat* of);
 (*gebührend*) due; **jdm etw ~ sein** to
 owe sb sth
Schule (-, -n) *f* school; **in der ~** at
 school; **in die ~ gehen** to go to
 school; **Schüler(in)** (-s, -) *m(f)*
 (*jüngerer*) pupil; (*älterer*) student;
 Schüleraustausch *m* school
 exchange; **Schulfach** *nt* subject;
 Schulferien *pl* school holidays *pl*
 (*Brit*) (*o* vacation (*US*)); **schulfrei**
 adj: **morgen ist ~** there's no school
 tomorrow; **Schulfreund(in)** *m(f)*
 schoolmate; **Schuljahr** *nt* school
 year; **Schulkenntnisse** *pl*: **~ in
 Französisch** school(-level) French;
 Schulklasse *f* class; **Schul-
 leiter(in)** *m(f)* headmaster/
 headmistress (*Brit*), principal (*US*)
Schulter (-, -n) *f* shoulder;
 Schulterblatt *nt* shoulder blade
Schulung *f* training;
 (*Veranstaltung*) training course
schummeln *vi* (*fam*) to cheat
Schuppe (-, -n) *f* (*von Fisch*) scale;
 schuppen *vt* to scale ▷ *vr*: **sich
 ~** to peel; **Schuppen** *pl* (*im Haar*)
 dandruff *sing*

Schürfwunde *f* graze
Schürze (-, -n) *f* apron
Schuss (-es, *Schüsse*) *m* shot; **mit
 einem ~ Wodka** with a dash of
 vodka
Schüssel (-, -n) *f* bowl
Schuster(in) (-s, -) *m(f)*
 shoemaker
Schutt (-(e)s) *m* rubble
Schüttelfrost *m* shivering fit;
 schütteln *vt* to shake ▷ *vr*: **sich
 ~** to shake
schütten *vt* to pour; (*Zucker, Kies
 etc*) to tip ▷ *vi impers* to pour
 (down)
Schutz (-es) *m* protection (*gegen,
 vor* against, from); (*Unterschlupf*)
 shelter; **jdn in ~ nehmen** to stand
 up for sb; **Schutzblech** *nt*
 mudguard; **Schutzbrief** *m* travel
 insurance document for drivers;
 Schutzbrille *f* (safety) goggles *pl*
Schütze (-n, -n) *m* (*beim Fußball*)
 scorer; (*Astr*) Sagittarius
schützen *vt*: **jdn gegen/vor etw
 ~** to protect sb against/from sth;
 Schutzimpfung *f* inoculation,
 vaccination
schwach *adj* weak; **~e Augen**
 poor eyesight *sing*; **Schwäche**
 (-, -n) *f* weakness; **Schwachstelle**
 f weak point; **Schwachstrom** *m*
 low-voltage current
Schwager (-s, *Schwäger*) *m*
 brother-in-law; **Schwägerin** *f*
 sister-in-law
Schwalbe (-, -n) *f* swallow; (*beim
 Fußball*) dive
schwamm *imperf von*
 schwimmen
Schwamm (-(e)s, *Schwämme*) *m*
 sponge; **~ drüber!** (*fam*) let's forget
 it!
Schwan (-(e)s,
 Schwäne) *m* swan
schwanger *adj* pregnant; **im
 vierten Monat ~ sein** to be four

months pregnant; **Schwanger-schaft** f pregnancy; **Schwanger-schaftsabbruch** m abortion; **Schwangerschaftstest** m pregnancy test

schwanken vi to sway; (*Preise, Zahlen*) to fluctuate; (*zögern*) to hesitate; (*taumeln*) to stagger; **ich schwanke zwischen A und B** I can't decide between A and B

Schwanz (*-es, Schwänze*) m tail; (*vulg: Penis*) cock

Schwarm (*-(e)s, Schwärme*) m swarm; (*fam: angehimmelte Person*) heartthrob; **schwärmen** vi to swarm; **~ für** to be mad about

schwarz adj black; **mir wurde ~ vor Augen** everything went black; **Schwarzarbeit** f illicit work; **Schwarzbrot** nt black bread; **schwarz|fahren** irr vi to travel without a ticket; (*ohne Führerschein*) to drive without a licence; **Schwarzfahrer(in)** m(f) fare-dodger; **Schwarzmarkt** m black market; **schwarz|sehen** irr vi (*fam: pessimistisch sein*) to be pessimistic (*für* about); **Schwarzwald** m Black Forest; **schwarzweiß** adj black and white; **Schwarzwurzel** f black salsify

schwatzen vi to chatter; **Schwätzer(in)** (*-s, -*) m(f) chatterbox; (*Schwafler*) gasbag; (*Klatschmaul*) gossip

Schwebebahn f suspension railway; **schweben** vi to float; (*hoch*) to soar

Schwede (*-n, -n*) m Swede; **Schweden** (*-s*) nt Sweden; **Schwedin** f Swede; **schwedisch** adj Swedish; **Schwedisch** nt Swedish

Schwefel (*-s*) m sulphur

schweigen (*schwieg, geschwiegen*) vi to be silent; (*nicht mehr reden*) to

stop talking; **Schweigen** (*-s*) nt silence; **Schweigepflicht** f duty of confidentiality; **die ärztliche ~** medical confidentiality

Schwein (*-(e)s, -e*) nt pig; (*fam: Glück*) luck; (*fam: gemeiner Mensch*) swine; **Schweinebraten** m roast pork; **Schweinefleisch** nt pork; **Schweinerei** f mess; (*Gemeinheit*) dirty trick

Schweiß (*-es*) m sweat

schweißen vt, vi to weld

Schweiz (*-*) f: **die ~** Switzerland; **Schweizer(in)** (*-s, -*) m(f) Swiss; **Schweizerdeutsch** nt Swiss German; **schweizerisch** adj Swiss

Schwelle (*-, -n*) f doorstep; (*a. fig*) threshold

schwellen vi to swell (up); **Schwellung** f swelling

schwer adj heavy; (*schwierig*) difficult, hard; (*schlimm*) serious, bad; **er ist ~ zu verstehen** it's difficult to understand what he's saying ▷ adv (*sehr*) really; (*verletzt etc*) seriously, badly; **etw ~ nehmen** to take sth hard; **Schwerbehinderte(r)** mf severely disabled person; **schwer|fallen** irr vi (*Schwierigkeiten bereiten*) **jdm ~** to be difficult for sb; **schwerhörig** adj hard of hearing

Schwert (*-(e)s, -er*) nt sword; **Schwertlilie** f iris

Schwester (*-, -n*) f sister; (*Med*) nurse

schwieg imperf von **schweigen**

Schwiegereltern pl parents-in-law pl; **Schwiegermutter** f mother-in-law; **Schwiegersohn** m son-in-law; **Schwiegertochter** f daughter-in-law; **Schwiegervater** m father-in-law

schwierig adj difficult, hard; **Schwierigkeit** f difficulty; **in ~en kommen** to get into trouble; **jdm**

~en machen to make things difficult for sb
Schwimmbad *nt* swimming pool; **Schwimmbecken** *nt* swimming pool; **schwimmen** (*schwamm, geschwommen*) *vi* to swim; (*treiben*) to float; (*fig: unsicher sein*) to be all at sea; **Schwimmer(in)** *m(f)* swimmer; **Schwimmflosse** *f* flipper; **Schwimmflügel** *m* water wing; **Schwimmreifen** *m* rubber ring; **Schwimmweste** *f* life jacket
Schwindel (*-s*) *m* dizziness; (*Anfall*) dizzy spell; (*Betrug*) swindle; **schwindelfrei** *adj*: **nicht ~ sein** to suffer from vertigo; **~ sein** to have a head for heights; **schwindlig** *adj* dizzy; **mir ist ~** I feel dizzy
Schwips *m*: **einen ~ haben** to be tipsy
schwitzen *vi* to sweat
schwoll *imperf von* **schwellen**
schwor *imperf von* **schwören**
schwören (*schwor, geschworen*) *vt, vi* to swear; **einen Eid ~** to take an oath
schwul *adj* gay
schwül *adj* close
Schwung (*-(e)s, Schwünge*) *m* swing; (*Triebkraft*) momentum; (*fig: Energie*) energy; (*fam: Menge*) batch; **in ~ kommen** to get going
Schwur (*-s, Schwüre*) *m* oath
scrollen *vi* (*Inform*) to scroll
sechs *num* six; **Sechs** (*-, -en*) *f* six; (*Schulnote*) ≈ F; **Sechserpack** *m* sixpack; **sechshundert** *num* six hundred; **sechsmal** *adv* six times; **sechste(r, s)** *adj* sixth; *siehe auch* **dritte**; **Sechstel** (*-s, -*) *nt* sixth; **sechzehn** *num* sixteen; **sechzehnte(r, s)** *adj* sixteenth; *siehe auch* **dritte**; **sechzig** *num* sixty; **in den ~er Jahren** in the

sixties; **sechzigste(r, s)** *adj* sixtieth
Secondhandladen *m* second-hand shop
See (*-, -n*) *f* sea; **an der ~** by the sea ▷ (*-s, -n*) *m* lake; **Seegang** *m* waves; **hoher/schwerer/leichter ~** rough/heavy/calm seas *pl*; **Seehund** *m* seal; **Seeigel** *m* sea urchin; **seekrank** *adj* seasick
Seele (*-, -n*) *f* soul
Seeleute *pl* seamen *pl*, sailors *pl*
seelisch *adj* mental, psychological
Seelöwe *m* sea lion; **Seemann** *m* sailor, seaman; **Seemeile** *f* nautical mile; **Seemöwe** *f* seagull; **Seenot** *f* distress (at sea); **Seepferdchen** *nt* sea horse; **Seerose** *f* water lily; **Seestern** *m* starfish; **Seezunge** *f* sole
Segel (*-s, -*) *nt* sail; **Segelboot** *nt* yacht; **Segelfliegen** (*-s*) *nt* gliding; **Segelflugzeug** *nt* glider; **segeln** *vt, vi* to sail; **Segelschiff** *nt* sailing ship
sehbehindert *adj* partially sighted
sehen (*sah, gesehen*) *vt, vi* to see; (*in bestimmte Richtung*) to look; **gut/schlecht ~** to have good/bad eyesight; **auf die Uhr ~** to look at one's watch; **kann ich das mal ~?** can I have a look at it?; **wir ~ uns morgen!** see you tomorrow; **ich kenne sie nur vom Sehen** I only know her by sight; **Sehenswürdigkeiten** *pl* sights *pl*
Sehne (*-, -n*) *f* tendon; (*an Bogen*) string
sehnen *vr*: **sich ~** to long (*nach* for)
Sehnenscheidenentzündung *f* (*Med*) tendovaginitis;

Sehnenzerrung f (Med) pulled tendon

Sehnsucht f longing; **sehnsüchtig** adj longing

sehr adv (vor Adjektiv, Adverb) very; (mit Verben) a lot, very much; **zu ~** too much

seicht adj shallow

Seide (-, -n) f silk

Seife (-, -n) f soap; **Seifenoper** f soap (opera); **Seifenschale** f soap dish

Seil (-(e)s, -e) nt rope; (Kabel) cable; **Seilbahn** f cable railway

⊙ SCHLÜSSELWORT

sein¹ (pt **war**, pp **gewesen**) vi 1 to be; **ich bin** I am; **du bist** you are; **er/sie/es ist** he/she/it is; **wir sind/ihr seid/sie sind** we/you/they are; **wir waren** we were; **wir sind gewesen** we have been

2 **seien Sie nicht böse** don't be angry; **sei so gut und ...** be so kind as to ...; **das wäre gut** that would o that'd be a good thing; **wenn ich Sie wäre** if I were o was you; **das wär's** that's all, that's it; **morgen bin ich in Rom** tomorrow I'll o I will o I shall be in Rome; **waren Sie mal in Rom?** have you ever been to Rome?

3 **wie ist das zu verstehen?** how is that to be understood?; **er ist nicht zu ersetzen** he cannot be replaced; **mit ihr ist nicht zu reden** you can't talk to her

4 **mir ist kalt** I'm cold; **was ist?** what's the matter?, what is it?; **ist was?** is something the matter?; **es sei denn, dass ...** unless ...; **wie dem auch sei** be that as it may; **wie wäre es mit ...?** how o what about ...?; **lass das sein!** stop that!

sein² pron possessiv von **er**; (adjektivisch) his ▷ pron possessiv von **es**; (adjektivisch) its; (adjektivisch, männlich) his; (weiblich) her; (sächlich) its; **das ist ~e Tasche** that's his bag; **jeder hat ~e Sorgen** everyone has their problems; **seine(r, s)** pron possessiv von **er**; (substantivisch) his ▷ pron possessiv von **es**; (substantivisch) its; (substantivisch, männlich) his; (weiblich) hers; **das ist ~r/~s/~s** that's his/hers; **seiner** pron gen von **er**; of him ▷ pron gen von **es**; of it; **seinetwegen** adv (wegen ihm) because of him; (ihm zuliebe) for his sake; (um ihn) about him; (von ihm aus) as far as he is concerned

seit conj (bei Zeitpunkt) since; (bei Zeitraum) for; **er ist ~ Montag hier** he's been here since Monday; **er ist ~ einer Woche hier** he's been here for a week; **~ langem** for a long time; **seitdem** adv, conj since

Seite (-, -n) f side; (in Buch) page; **zur ~ gehen** to step aside; **Seitenairbag** m side-impact airbag; **Seitenaufprallschutz** m (Auto) side-impact protection; **Seitensprung** m affair; **Seitenstechen** (-s) nt: **~ haben/bekommen** to have/get a stitch; **Seitenstraße** f side street; **Seitenstreifen** m hard shoulder (Brit), shoulder (US); **Seitenwind** m crosswind

seither adv since (then)

seitlich adj side

Sekretär(in) m(f) secretary; **Sekretariat** (-s, -e) nt secretary's office

Sekt (-(e)s, -e) m sparkling wine (similar to champagne)

Sekte (-, -n) f sect

Sekunde (-, -n) f second;
Sekundenkleber (-s, -) m superglue; **Sekundenschnelle** f: **es
geschah alles in ~** it was all over
in a matter of seconds

O SCHLÜSSELWORT

selbst pron 1 **ich/er/wir selbst** I
myself/he himself/we ourselves;
sie ist die Tugend selbst she's
virtue itself; **er braut sein Bier
selbst** he brews his own beer; **wie
geht's? — gut, und selbst?** how
are things? — fine, and yourself?
2 (ohne Hilfe) alone, on
my/his/one's etc own; **von selbst**
by itself; **er kam von selbst** he
came of his own accord; **selbst
gemacht** home-made
▷ adv even; **selbst wenn** even if;
selbst Gott even God (himself)

selbständig adj siehe
selbstständig
Selbstauslöser (-s, -) m (Foto)
self-timer; **Selbstbedienung** f
self-service; **Selbstbefriedigung** f
masturbation;
Selbstbeherrschung f
self-control; **Selbstbeteiligung** f
(einer Versicherung) excess;
selbstbewusst adj
(self-)confident; **Selbstbräuner**
(-s, -) m self-tanning lotion;
selbstgemacht adj self-made;
selbstklebend adj self-adhesive;
Selbstlaut m vowel; **Selbstmord**
m suicide; **Selbstmordattentat**
nt suicide bombing; **Selbstmord-
attentäter(in)** m(f) suicide
bomber; **selbstsicher** adj
self-assured; **selbstständig** adj
independent; (arbeitend)
self-employed; **Selbstverpflegung**
f self-catering;
selbstverständlich adj obvious;

ich halte das für ~ I take that for
granted ▷ adv naturally;
Selbstvertrauen nt
self-confidence
Sellerie (-s, -(s)) m (-, -n) f (Knollensellerie) celeriac; (Stangensellerie)
celery
selten adj rare ▷ adv seldom,
rarely
seltsam adj strange;
~ schmecken/riechen to
taste/smell strange
Semester (-s, -) nt semester;
Semesterferien pl vacation sing
Semikolon (-s, Semikola) nt
semicolon
Seminar (-s, -e) nt seminar
Semmel (-, -n) f roll;
Semmelbrösel pl breadcrumbs
Senat (-(e)s, -e) m senate
senden (sandte, gesandt) vt to
send ▷ vt, vi (Radio, TV) to
broadcast; **Sender** (-s, -) m (TV)
channel; (Radio) station; (Anlage)
transmitter; **Sendung** f (Radio,
TV) broadcasting; (Programm)
programme
Senf (-(e)s, -e) m mustard
Senior(in) m(f) senior citizen;
Seniorenpass m senior citizen's
travel pass
senken vt to lower ▷ vr: **sich
~ senken** to sink
senkrecht adj vertical
Sensation (-, -en) f sensation
sensibel adj sensitive
sentimental adj sentimental
separat adj separate
September (-(s), -) m
September; siehe auch **Juni**
Serbien (-s) nt Serbia
Serie f series sing
seriös adj (ernsthaft) serious;
(anständig) respectable
Serpentine f hairpin (bend)
Serum (-s, Seren) nt serum
Server (-s, -) m (Inform) server

Service (-(s), -) nt (Geschirr)
service ▷ (-, -s) m service
servieren vt, vi to serve
Serviette f napkin, serviette
Servolenkung f (Auto) power
steering
Sesam (-s, -s) m sesame seeds pl
Sessel (-s, -) m armchair;
Sessellift m chairlift
Set (-s, -s) m o nt set; (Tischset)
tablemat
setzen vt to put; (Baum etc) to
plant; (Segel) to set ▷ vr: **sich ~** to
settle; (hinsetzen) to sit down; **~ Sie
sich doch** please sit down
Seuche (-, -n) f epidemic
seufzen vt, vi to sigh
Sex (-(es)) m sex; **Sexismus** m
sexism; **sexistisch** adj sexist;
Sextourismus m sex tourism;
Sexualität f sexuality; **sexuell**
adj sexual
Seychellen pl Seychelles pl
sfr abk = **Schweizer Franken** Swiss
franc(s)
Shampoo (-s, -s) nt shampoo
Shareware (-, -s) f (Inform)
shareware
Shorts pl shorts pl
Shuttlebus m shuttle bus

 SCHLÜSSELWORT

sich pron **1** (akk) **er/sie/es ... sich**
he/she/it ... himself/herself/itself;
sie pl/**man ... sich** they/one ...
themselves/oneself; **Sie ... sich**
you ... yourself/yourselves pl; **sich
wiederholen** to repeat
oneself/itself
2 (dat) **er/sie/es ... sich** he/she/it
... to himself/herself/itself; **sie**
pl/**man ... sich** they/one ... to
themselves/oneself; **Sie ... sich**
you ... to yourself/yourselves pl;
**sie hat sich einen Pullover
gekauft** she bought herself a

jumper; **sich die Haare waschen**
to wash one's hair
3 (mit Präposition) **haben Sie Ihren
Ausweis bei sich?** do you have
your pass on you?; **er hat nichts
bei sich** he's got nothing on him;
sie bleiben gern unter sich they
keep themselves to themselves
4 (einander) each other, one
another; **sie bekämpfen sich** they
fight each other o one another
5 dieses Auto fährt sich gut this
car drives well; **hier sitzt es sich
gut** it's good to sit here

sicher adj safe (vor +dat from);
(gewiss) certain (gen of);
(zuverlässig) reliable; (selbstsicher)
confident; **aber ~!** of course, sure;
Sicherheit f safety; (Aufgabe von
Sicherheitsbeamten) (Fin) security;
(Gewissheit) certainty;
(Selbstsicherheit) confidence; **mit
~** definitely; **Sicherheitsabstand**
m safe distance; **Sicherheitsgurt**
m seat belt; **sicherheitshalber**
adv just to be on the safe side;
Sicherheitsnadel f safety pin;
Sicherheitsvorkehrung f safety
precaution; **sicherlich** adv
certainly; (wahrscheinlich) probably
sichern vt to secure (gegen
against); (schützen) to protect;
(Daten) to back up; **Sicherung** f
(Sichern) securing; (Vorrichtung)
safety device; (an Waffen) safety
catch; (Elek) fuse; (Inform) backup;
die ~ ist durchgebrannt the fuse
has blown
Sicht (-) f sight; (Aussicht) view;
sichtbar adj visible; **sichtlich**
adj evident, obvious;
Sichtverhältnisse pl visibility
sing; **Sichtweite** f: **in/außer
~** within/out of sight
sie pron (3. Person sing) she; (3.
Person pl) they; (akk von sing) her;

(akk von pl) them; (für eine Sache) it; **da ist ~ ja** there she is; **da sind ~ ja** there they are; **ich kenne ~** (Frau) I know her; (mehrere Personen) I know them; **~ lag gerade noch hier** (meine Jacke, Uhr) it was here just a minute ago; **ich hab ~ gefunden** (meine Jacke, Uhr) I've found it; **hast du meine Brille/Hose gesehen? — ich kann ~ nirgends finden** have you seen my glasses/trousers? — I can't find them anywhere

Sie pron (Höflichkeitsform, Nom und Akk) you

Sieb (-(e)s, -e) nt sieve; (Teesieb) strainer

sieben num seven; **siebenhundert** num seven hundred; **siebenmal** adv seven times; **siebte(r, s)** adj seventh; siehe auch **dritte**; **Siebtel** (-s, -) nt seventh; **siebzehn** num seventeen; **siebzehnte(r, s)** adj seventeenth; siehe auch **dritte**; **siebzig** num seventy; **in den ~er Jahren** in the seventies; **siebzigste(r, s)** adj seventieth

Siedlung (-, -en) f (Wohngebiet) housing estate (Brit) (o development (US))

Sieg (-(e)s, -e) m victory; **siegen** vi to win; **Sieger(in)** (-s, -) m(f) winner; **Siegerehrung** f presentation ceremony

siehe imper see

siezen vt to address as "Sie"

Signal (-s, -e) nt signal

Silbe (-, -n) f syllable

Silber (-s) nt silver; **Silberhochzeit** f silver wedding; **Silbermedaille** f silver medal

Silikon (-s, -e) nt silicone

Silvester (-s, -) nt, **Silvesterabend** m New Year's Eve, Hogmanay (Scot)

○ **SILVESTER**
○
○ **Silvester** is the German name
○ for New Year's Eve. Although
○ not an official holiday, most
○ businesses close early and
○ shops shut at midday. Most
○ Germans celebrate in the
○ evening and at midnight they
○ let off fireworks and rockets;
○ the revelry usually lasts until the
○ early hours of the morning.

Simbabwe (-s) nt Zimbabwe

simpel adj simple

simultan adj simultaneous

simsen vt, vi (fam) to text

Sinfonie (-, -n) f symphony; **Sinfonieorchester** nt symphony orchestra

Singapur (-s) nt Singapore

singen (sang, gesungen) vt, vi to sing; **richtig/falsch ~** to sing in tune/out of tune

Single (-, -s) f (CD) single ▷ (-s, -s) m (Mensch) single

Singular m singular

sinken (sank, gesunken) vi to sink; (Preise etc) to fall, to go down

Sinn (-(e)s, -e) m (Denken) mind; (Wahrnehmung) sense; (Bedeutung) sense, meaning; **~ machen** to make sense; **das hat keinen ~** it's no use; **sinnlich** adj sensuous; (erotisch) sensual; (Wahrnehmung) sensory; **sinnlos** adj (unsinnig) stupid; (Verhalten) senseless; (zwecklos) pointless; (bedeutungslos) meaningless; **sinnvoll** adj meaningful; (vernünftig) sensible

Sirup (-s, -e) m syrup

Sitte (-, -n) f custom

Situation f situation

Sitz (-es, -e) m seat; **sitzen** (saß, gesessen) vi to sit; (Bemerkung, Schlag) to strike home; (Gelerntes) to have sunk in; **der Rock sitzt**

gut the skirt is a good fit;
Sitzgelegenheit f place to sit
down; **Sitzplatz** m seat; **Sitzung**
f meeting
Sizilien (-s) nt Sicily
Skandal (-s, -e) m scandal
Skandinavien (-s) nt
Scandinavia
Skateboard (-s, -s) nt
skateboard
Skelett (-s, -e) nt skeleton
skeptisch adj sceptical
Ski (-s, -er) m ski; **~ laufen** (o
fahren) to ski; **Skianzug** m ski
suit; **Skibrille** f ski goggles pl;
Skifahren (-s) nt skiing; **Skigebiet**
(-s, -e) nt skiing area; **Skihose** f
skiing trousers pl; **Skikurs** m
skiing course; **Skilanglauf** m
cross-country skiing; **Skiläufer(in)**
m(f) skier; **Skilehrer(in)** m(f) ski
instructor; **Skilift** m ski-lift
Skinhead (-s, -s) m skinhead
Skipiste f ski run; **Skischanze**
(-, -n) f ski jump; **Skischuh** m
ski boot; **Skischule** f ski school;
Skispringen (-s, -n) nt ski
jumping; **Skistiefel** (-s, -) m ski
boot; **Skistock** m ski pole;
Skiträger m ski rack; **Skiurlaub**
m skiing holiday (Brit) (o vacation
(US))
Skizze (-, -n) f sketch
Skonto (-s, -s) m o nt discount
Skorpion (-s, -e) m (Zool)
scorpion; (Astr) Scorpio
Skulptur (-, -en) f sculpture
S-Kurve f double bend
Slalom (-s, -s) m slalom
Slip (-s, -s) m (pair of) briefs pl;
Slipeinlage f panty liner
Slowakei (-) f Slovakia;
slowakisch adj Slovakian;
Slowakische Republik Slovak
Republic; **Slowakisch** nt
Slovakian
Slowenien (-s) nt Slovenia;

slowenisch adj Slovenian;
Slowenisch nt Slovenian
Smiley (-s, -s) m smiley
Smog (-s) m smog; **Smogalarm**
m smog alert
Smoking (-s, -s) m dinner jacket
(Brit), tuxedo (US)
SMS nt abk = **Short Message
Service** ▷ f (Nachricht) text
message; **ich schicke dir eine ~** I'll
text you, I'll send you a text
(message)
Snowboard (-s, -s) nt snow-
board; **Snowboardfahren** (-s) nt
snowboarding;
Snowboardfahrer(in) m(f)
snowboarder

SCHLÜSSELWORT

SO adv **1** (so sehr) so; **so groß/schön**
etc so big/nice etc; **so groß/schön
wie ...** as big/nice as ...; **so viel
(wie)** as much as; **rede nicht so
viel** don't talk so much; **so weit
sein** to be ready; **so weit wie** o **als
möglich** as far as possible; **ich bin
so weit zufrieden** by and large I'm
quite satisfied; **so wenig (wie)** as
little (as); **das hat ihn so
geärgert, dass ...** that annoyed
him so much that ...; **so einer wie
ich** somebody like me; **na so was!**
well, well!
2 (auf diese Weise) like this; **mach
es nicht so** don't do it like that; **so
oder so** in one way or the other;
und so weiter and so on; **... oder
so was** ... or something like that;
das ist gut so that's fine
3 (fam) (umsonst) **ich habe es so
bekommen** I got it for nothing
▷ konj: **sodass** so that; **so wie es
jetzt ist** as things are at the
moment
▷ excl: **so?** really?; **so, das wär's**
so, that's it then

s. o. *abk* = **siehe oben** see above

sobald *conj* as soon as

Socke (-, -n) *f* sock

Sodbrennen (-s) *nt* heartburn

Sofa (-s, -s) *nt* sofa

sofern *conj* if, provided (that)

soff *imperf von* **saufen**

sofort *adv* immediately, at once; **Sofortbildkamera** *f* instant camera

Softeis *nt* soft ice-cream

Software (-, -s) *f* software

sog *imperf von* **saugen**

sogar *adv* even; **kalt, ~ sehr kalt** cold, in fact very cold

sogenannt *adj* so-called

Sohle (-, -n) *f* sole

Sohn (-(e)s, Söhne) *m* son

Soja (-, Sojen) *f* soya; **Sojasprossen** *pl* bean sprouts *pl*

solang(e) *conj* as long as

Solarium *nt* solarium

Solarzelle *f* solar cell

solche(r, s) *pron* such; **eine ~ Frau, solch eine Frau** such a woman, a woman like that; **~ Sachen** things like that, such things; **ich habe ~ Kopfschmerzen** I've got such a headache; **ich habe ~n Hunger** I'm so hungry

Soldat(in) (-en, -en) *m(f)* soldier

solidarisch *adj* showing solidarity; **sich ~ erklären mit** to declare one's solidarity with

solid(e) *adj* solid; (*Leben, Mensch*) respectable

Soll (-(s), (-s)) *nt* (*Fin*) debit; (*Arbeitsmenge*) quota, target

SCHLÜSSELWORT

sollen (*pt* **sollte**, *pp* **gesollt** *o* (*als Hilfsverb*) **sollen**) *Hilfsverb* **1** (*Pflicht, Befehl*) to be supposed to; **du hättest nicht gehen sollen** you shouldn't have gone, you oughtn't to have gone; **soll ich?** shall I?; **soll ich dir helfen?** shall I help you?; **sag ihm, er soll warten** tell him he's to wait; **was soll ich machen?** what should I do?

2 (*Vermutung*) **sie soll verheiratet sein** she's said to be married; **was soll das heißen?** what's that supposed to mean?; **man sollte glauben, dass ...** you would think that ...; **sollte das passieren, ...** if that should happen ...

▷ *vt, vi*: **was soll das?** what's all this?; **das sollst du nicht** you shouldn't do that; **was soll's?** what the hell!

Solo (-s, -) *nt* solo

Sommer (-s, -) *m* summer; **Sommerfahrplan** *m* summer timetable; **Sommerferien** *pl* summer holidays *pl* (Brit) (*o* vacation *sing* (US)); **sommerlich** *adj* summery; (Sommer-) summer; **Sommerreifen** *m* normal tyre; **Sommersprossen** *pl* freckles *pl*; **Sommerzeit** *f* summertime; (*Uhrzeit*) daylight saving time

Sonderangebot *nt* special offer; **sonderbar** *adj* strange, odd; **Sondermarke** *f* special stamp; **Sondermaschine** *f* special plane; **Sondermüll** *m* hazardous waste

sondern *conj* but; **nicht nur ..., ~ auch** not only ..., but also

Sonderpreis *m* special price; **Sonderschule** *f* special school; **Sonderzeichen** *nt* (*Inform*) special character; **Sonderzug** *m* special train

Song (-s, -s) *m* song

Sonnabend *m* Saturday; *siehe auch* **Mittwoch**; **sonnabends** *adv* on Saturdays; **~ morgens** on Saturday mornings; *siehe auch* **mittwochs**

Sonne (-, -n) f sun; **sonnen** vr:
sich ~ to sunbathe;
Sonnenallergie f sun allergy;
Sonnenaufgang m sunrise;
Sonnenblume f sunflower;
Sonnenblumenkern m sunflower seed; **Sonnenbrand** m
sunburn; **Sonnenbrille** f
sunglasses pl, shades pl;
Sonnencreme f sun cream;
Sonnendach nt (an Haus)
awning; (Auto) sunroof; **Sonnen-
deck** nt sun deck; **Sonnenmilch** f
suntan lotion; **Sonnenöl** nt
suntan oil; **Sonnenschein** m
sunshine; **Sonnenschirm** m
parasol, sunshade; **Sonnenschutz-
creme** f sunscreen; **Sonnenstich**
m sunstroke; **Sonnenstudio** nt
solarium; **Sonnenuhr** f sundial;
Sonnenuntergang m sunset;
sonnig adj sunny

Sonntag m Sunday; siehe auch
Mittwoch; **sonntags** adv on
Sundays; siehe auch **mittwochs**

sonst adv, conj (außerdem) else;
(andernfalls) otherwise, (or) else;
(mit Pron, in Fragen) else;
(normalerweise) normally, usually;
~ noch etwas? anything else?;
~ nichts nothing else

sooft conj whenever

Sopran (-s, -e) m soprano

Sorge (-, -n) f worry; (Fürsorge)
care; **sich** (dat) **um jdn ~n machen**
to be worried about sb; **sorgen**
vi: **für jdn ~** to look after sb; **für
etw ~** to take care of sth, to see to
sth ▷ vr: **sich ~** to worry (um
about); **sorgfältig** adj careful

sortieren vt to sort (out)

Sortiment nt assortment

sosehr conj however much

Soße (-, -n) f sauce; (zu Braten)
gravy

Soundkarte f (Inform) sound
card

Souvenir (-s, -s) nt souvenir

soviel conj as far as

soweit conj as far as

sowie conj (wie auch) as well as;
(sobald) as soon as

sowohl conj: **~ ... als** (o **wie**) **auch**
both ... and

sozial adj social; **Sozialhilfe** f
income support (Brit), welfare
(aid) (US); **Sozialismus** m
socialism; **Sozialversicherung** f
social security; **Sozialwohnung**
f council flat (Brit),
state-subsidized apartment (US)

Soziologie f sociology

sozusagen adv so to speak

Spachtel (-s, -) m spatula

Spag(h)etti pl spaghetti sing

Spalte (-, -n) f crack; (Gletscher)
crevasse; (in Text) column

spalten vt to split ▷ vr: **sich ~** to
split

Spange (-, -n) f clasp;
(Haarspange) hair slide (Brit),
barrette (US)

Spanien (-s) nt Spain;
Spanier(in) (-s, -) m(f) Spaniard;
spanisch adj Spanish; **Spanisch**
nt Spanish

spann imperf von **spinnen**

spannen vt (straffen) to tighten;
(befestigen) to brace ▷ vi to be
tight

spannend adj exciting, gripping;
Spannung f tension; (Elek)
voltage; (fig) suspense

Sparbuch nt savings book;
(Konto) savings account; **sparen**
vt, vi to save

Spargel (-s, -) m asparagus;
Spargelsuppe f asparagus soup

Sparkasse f savings bank;
Sparkonto nt savings account

spärlich adj meagre; (Bekleidung)
scanty

sparsam adj economical;
Sparschwein nt piggy bank

Spaß (-es, Späße) m joke; (Freude) fun; **es macht mir ~** I enjoy it, it's (great) fun; **viel ~!** have fun

spät adj, adv late; **zu ~ kommen** to be late

Spaten (-s, -) m spade

später adj, adv later; **spätestens** adv at the latest; **Spätlese** f late vintage (wine); **Spätvorstellung** f late-night performance

Spatz (-en, -en) m sparrow

spazieren vi to stroll, to walk; **~ gehen** to go for a walk; **Spaziergang** m walk

Specht (-(e)s, -e) m woodpecker

Speck (-(e)s, -e) m bacon fat; (durchwachsen) bacon

Spedition f (für Umzug) removal firm

Speiche (-, -n) f spoke

Speichel (-s) m saliva

Speicher (-s, -) m storehouse; (Dachboden) attic; (Inform) memory; **speichern** vt (Inform) to store; (sichern) to save

Speise (-, -n) f food; (Gericht) dish; **Speisekarte** f menu; **Speiseröhre** f gullet, oesophagus; **Speisesaal** m dining hall; **Speisewagen** m dining car

Spende (-, -n) f donation; **spenden** vt to donate, to give

spendieren vt: **jdm etw ~** to treat sb to sth

Sperre (-, -n) f barrier; (Verbot) ban; **sperren** vt to block; (Sport) to suspend; (verbieten) to ban

Sperrgepäck nt bulky luggage; **Sperrmüll** m bulky refuse; **Sperrstunde** f closing time; **Sperrung** f closing

Spesen pl expenses pl

spezialisieren vr: **sich ~** to specialize (auf +akk in); **Spezialist(in)** m(f) specialist; **Spezialität** f speciality (Brit),

specialty (US); **speziell** adj special ▷ adv especially

Spiegel (-s, -) m mirror; **Spiegelei** nt fried egg (sunny-side up (US)); **spiegelglatt** adj very slippery; **Spiegelreflexkamera** f reflex camera

Spiel (-(e)s, -e) nt game; (Tätigkeit) play(ing); (Karten) pack, deck; (Tech) (free) play; **Spielautomat** m (ohne Geldgewinn) gaming machine; (mit Geldgewinn) slot machine; **spielen** vt, vi to play; (um Geld) to gamble; (Theat) to perform, to act; **Klavier ~** to play the piano; **spielend** adv easily; **Spieler(in)** (-s, -) m(f) player; (um Geld) gambler; **Spielfeld** nt (für Fußball, Hockey) field; (für Basketball) court; **Spielfilm** m feature film; **Spielkasino** nt casino; **Spielplatz** m playground; **Spielraum** m room to manoeuvre; **Spielregel** f rule; **sich an die ~n halten** to stick to the rules; **Spielsachen** pl toys pl; **Spielzeug** nt toys pl; (einzelnes) toy

Spieß (-es, -e) m spear; (Bratspieß) spit; **Spießer(in)** (-s, -) m(f) square, stuffy type; **spießig** adj square, uncool

Spikes pl (Sport) spikes pl; (Auto) studs pl

Spinat (-(e)s, -e) m spinach

Spinne (-, -n) f spider; **spinnen** (spann, gesponnen) vt, vi to spin; (fam: Unsinn reden) to talk rubbish; (verrückt sein) to be crazy; **du spinnst!** you must be mad; **Spinnwebe** (-, -n) f cobweb

Spion(in) (-s, -e) m(f) spy; **spionieren** vi to spy; (fig) to snoop around

Spirale (-, -n) f spiral; (Med) coil

Spirituosen pl spirits pl, liquor sing (US)

Spiritus (-, -se) m spirit
spitz adj (Nase, Kinn) pointed; (Bleistift, Messer) sharp; (Winkel) acute; **Spitze** (-, -n) f point; (von Finger, Nase) tip; (Bemerkung) taunt, dig; (erster Platz) lead; (Gewebe) lace; **Spitzer** (-s, -) m pencil sharpener; **Spitzname** m nickname
Spliss (-) m split ends pl
sponsern vt to sponsor; **Sponsor(in)** (-s, -en) m(f) sponsor
spontan adj spontaneous
Sport (-(e)s, -e) m sport; ~ **treiben** to do sport; **Sportanlage** f sports grounds pl; **Sportart** f sport; **Sportbekleidung** f sportswear; **Sportgeschäft** nt sports shop; **Sporthalle** f gymnasium, gym; **Sportlehrer(in)** (-s, -) m(f) sports instructor; (Schule) PE teacher; **Sportler(in)** (-s, -) m(f) sports-man/-woman; **sportlich** adj sporting; (Mensch) sporty; **Sportplatz** m playing field; **Sporttauchen** nt (skin-)diving; (mit Gerät) scuba-diving; **Sportverein** m sports club; **Sportwagen** m sports car
sprach imperf von **sprechen**
Sprache (-, -n) f language; (Sprechen) speech; **Sprachenschule** f language school; **Sprachführer** m phrasebook; **Sprachkenntnisse** pl knowledge sing of languages; **gute englische ~ haben** to have a good knowledge of English; **Sprachkurs** m language course; **Sprachunterricht** m language teaching
sprang imperf von **springen**
Spray (-s, -s) m o nt spray
Sprechanlage f intercom; **sprechen** (sprach, gesprochen) vt, vi

to speak (jdn, mit jdm to sb); (sich unterhalten) to talk (mit to, über, von about); ~ **Sie Deutsch?** do you speak German?; **kann ich bitte mit David ~?** (am Telefon) can I speak to David, please?; **Sprecher(in)** m(f) speaker; (Ansager) announcer; **Sprechstunde** f consultation; (Arzt) surgery hours pl; (Anwalt etc) office hours pl; **Sprechzimmer** nt consulting room
Sprengstoff m explosive
Sprichwort nt proverb
Springbrunnen m fountain
springen (sprang, gesprungen) vi to jump; (Glas) to crack; (mit Kopfsprung) to dive
Sprit (-(e)s, -e) m (fam: Benzin) petrol (Brit), gas (US)
Spritze (-, -n) f (Gegenstand) syringe; (Injektion) injection; (an Schlauch) nozzle; **spritzen** vt to spray; (Med) to inject ▷ vi to splash; (Med) to give injections
Spruch (-(e)s, Sprüche) m saying
Sprudel (-s, -) m sparkling mineral water; (süßer) fizzy drink (Brit), soda (US); **sprudeln** vi to bubble
Sprühdose f aerosol (can); **sprühen** vt, vi to spray; (fig) to sparkle; **Sprühregen** m drizzle
Sprung (-(e)s, Sprünge) m jump; (Riss) crack; **Sprungbrett** nt springboard; **Sprungschanze** f ski jump; **Sprungturm** m diving platforms pl
Spucke (-) f spit; **spucken** vt, vi to spit; (fam: sich erbrechen) to vomit; **Spucktüte** f sick bag
spuken vi (Geist) to walk; **hier spukt es** this place is haunted
Spülbecken nt sink
Spule (-, -n) f spool; (Elek) coil
Spüle (-, -n) f sink; **spülen** vt, vi to rinse; (Geschirr) to wash up;

(*Toilette*) to flush; **Spülmaschine**
f dishwasher; **Spülmittel** *nt*
washing-up liquid (*Brit*),
dishwashing liquid (*US*); **Spültuch**
nt dishcloth; **Spülung** *f* (*von WC*)
flush

Spur (-, -en) *f* trace; (*Fußspur,
Radspur*) track; (*Fährte*) trail;
(*Fahrspur*) lane; **die ~ wechseln** to
change lanes *pl*

spüren *vt* to feel; (*merken*) to
notice; **Spürhund** *m* sniffer dog

Squash (-) *nt* squash;
Squashschläger *m* squash racket

Sri Lanka (-s) *nt* Sri Lanka

Staat (-(*e*)*s*, -en) *m* state;
staatlich *adj* state(-); (*vom Staat
betrieben*) state-run;
Staatsangehörigkeit *f*
nationality; **Staatsanwalt** *m*,
-anwältin *f* prosecuting counsel
(*Brit*), district attorney (*US*);
Staatsbürger(in) *m(f)* citizen;
Staatsbürgerschaft *f* nationality; **doppelte ~** dual nationality;
Staatsexamen *nt* final exam
*taken by trainee teachers, medical and
law students*

Stab (-(*e*)*s*, Stäbe) *m* rod; (*Gitter*)
bar; **Stäbchen** *nt* (*Essstäbchen*)
chopstick; **Stabhochsprung** *m*
pole vault

stabil *adj* stable; (*Möbel*) sturdy

stach *imperf von* **stechen**

Stachel (-s, -n) *m* spike; (*von Tier*)
spine; (*von Insekten*) sting;
Stachelbeere *f* gooseberry;
Stacheldraht *m* barbed wire;
stachelig *adj* prickly

Stadion (-s, Stadien) *nt* stadium

Stadt (-, Städte) *f* town; (*groß*)
city; **in der ~** in town;
Stadtautobahn *f* urban
motorway (*Brit*) (*o* expressway
(*US*)); **Stadtbummel** (-s, -) *m*:
einen ~ machen to go round
town; **Stadtführer** *m* (*Heft*) city

guide; **Stadtführung** *f* city
sightseeing tour; **Stadthalle** *f*
municipal hall; **städtisch** *adj*
municipal; **Stadtmauer** *f* city
wall(s); **Stadtmitte** *f* town/city
centre, downtown (*US*);
Stadtplan *m* (street) map;
Stadtrand *m* outskirts *pl*;
Stadtrundfahrt *f* city tour;
Stadtteil *m*, **Stadtviertel** *nt*
district, part of town;
Stadtzentrum *nt* town/city
centre, downtown (*US*)

stahl *imperf von* **stehlen**

Stahl (-(*e*)*s*, Stähle) *m* steel

Stall (-(*e*)*s*, Ställe) *m* stable;
(*Kaninchen*) hutch; (*Schweine*)
pigsty; (*Hühner*) henhouse

Stamm (-(*e*)*s*, Stämme) *m* (*Baum*)
trunk; (*von Menschen*) tribe;
stammen *vi*: **~ aus** to come from;
Stammgast *m* regular (guest);
Stammkunde *m*, **Stammkundin**
f regular (customer); **Stammtisch**
m *table reserved for regulars*

stampfen *vt, vi* to stamp; (*mit
Werkzeug*) to pound; (*stapfen*) to
tramp

stand *imperf von* **stehen**

Stand (-(*e*)*s*, Stände) *m* (*Wasser,
Benzin*) level; (*Stehen*) standing
position; (*Zustand*) state;
(*Spielstand*) score; (*auf Messe etc*)
stand; (*Klasse*) class; **im ~e sein** to
be in a position; (*fähig*) to be able

Stand-by-Betrieb *m* stand-by;
Stand-by-Ticket *nt* stand-by
ticket

Ständer (-s, -) *m* (*Gestell*) stand;
(*fam: Erektion*) hard-on

Standesamt *nt* registry office

ständig *adj* permanent;
(*ununterbrochen*) constant,
continual

Standlicht *nt* sidelights *pl* (*Brit*),
parking lights *pl* (*US*); **Standort**
m position; **Standpunkt** *m*

standpoint; **Standspur** f (Auto) hard shoulder (Brit), shoulder (US)

Stange (-, -n) f stick; (Stab) pole; (Metall) bar; (Zigaretten) carton; **Stangenbohne** f runner (Brit) (o string (US)) bean; **Stangenbrot** nt French stick; **Stangensellerie** m celery

stank imperf von **stinken**

Stapel (-s, -) m pile

Star (-(e)s, -e) m (Vogel) starling; (Med) cataract ▷ (-s, -s) m (in Film etc) star

starb imperf von **sterben**

stark adj strong; (heftig, groß) heavy; (Maßangabe) thick; **Stärke** (-, -n) f strength; (Dicke) thickness; (Wäschestärke, Speisestärke) starch; **stärken** vt to strengthen; (Wäsche) to starch; **Starkstrom** m high-voltage current; **Stärkung** f strengthening; (Essen) refreshment

starr adj stiff; (unnachgiebig) rigid; (Blick) staring

starren vi to stare

Start (-(e)s, -e) m start; (Aviat) takeoff; **Startautomatik** f automatic choke; **Startbahn** f runway; **starten** vt, vi to start; (Aviat) to take off; **Starthilfekabel** nt jump leads pl (Brit), jumper cables pl (US); **Startmenü** nt (Inform) start menu

Station f (Haltestelle) stop; (Bahnhof) station; (im Krankenhaus) ward; **stationär** adj stationary; **~e Behandlung** in-patient treatment; **jdn ~ behandeln** to treat sb as an in-patient

Statistik f statistics pl

Stativ nt tripod

statt conj, prep +gen o dat instead of; **~ zu arbeiten** instead of working

statt|finden irr vi to take place

Statue (-, -n) f statue

Statusleiste f, **Statuszeile** f (Inform) status bar

Stau (-(e)s, -e) m (im Verkehr) (traffic) jam; **im ~ stehen** to be stuck in a traffic jam

Staub (-(e)s) m dust; **~ wischen** to dust; **staubig** adj dusty; **staubsaugen** vt, vi to vacuum, to hoover (Brit); **Staubsauger** m vacuum cleaner, Hoover® (Brit); **Staubtuch** nt duster

Staudamm m dam

staunen vi to be astonished (über +akk at)

Stausee m reservoir; **Stauung** f (von Wasser) damming-up; (von Blut, Verkehr) congestion; **Stauwarnung** f traffic report

Std. abk = **Stunde** h

Steak (-s, -s) nt steak

stechen (stach, gestochen) vt, vi (mit Nadel etc) to prick; (mit Messer) to stab; (mit Finger) to poke; (Biene) to sting; (Mücke) to bite; (Sonne) to burn; (Kartenspiel) to trump; **Stechen** (-s, -) nt sharp pain, stabbing pain; **Stechmücke** f mosquito

Steckdose f socket; **stecken** vt to put; (Nadel) to stick; (beim Nähen) to pin ▷ vi (festsitzen) to be stuck; (Nadeln) to be (sticking); **der Schlüssel steckt** the key is in the door; **Stecker** (-s, -) m plug; **Steckrübe** f swede (Brit), rutabaga (US)

Steg (-s, -e) m bridge

stehen (stand, gestanden) vi to stand (zu by); (sich befinden) to be; (stillstehen) to have stopped; **was steht im Brief?** what does it say in the letter?; **jdm (gut) ~** to suit sb; **~ bleiben** (Uhr) to stop; **~ lassen** to leave ▷ vi impers: **wie steht's?** (Sport) what's the score?

stehlen (*stahl, gestohlen*) *vt* to steal

Stehplatz *m* (*im Konzert etc*) standing ticket

Steiermark (-) *f* Styria

steif *adj* stiff

steigen (*stieg, gestiegen*) *vi* (*Preise, Temperatur*) to rise; (*klettern*) to climb; **~ in/auf** (+*akk*) to get in/on

steigern *vt* to increase ▷ *vr*: **sich ~** to increase

Steigung *f* incline, gradient

steil *adj* steep; **Steilhang** *m* steep slope; **Steilküste** *f* steep coast

Stein (-(e)s, -e) *m* stone; **Steinbock** *m* (*Zool*) ibex; (*Astr*) Capricorn; **steinig** *adj* stony; **Steinschlag** *m* falling rocks *pl*

Stelle (-, -n) *f* place, spot; (*Arbeit*) post, job; (*Amt*) office; **ich an deiner ~** if I were you; **auf der ~** straightaway; **stellen** *vt* to put; (*Uhr etc*) to set (*auf* +*akk* to); (*zur Verfügung stellen*) to provide ▷ *vr*: **sich ~** (*bei Polizei*) to give oneself up; **sich schlafend ~** to pretend to be asleep; **Stellenangebot** *nt* job offer, vacancy; **stellenweise** *adv* in places; **Stellenwert** *m* (*fig*) status; **einen hohen ~ haben** to play an important role; **Stellplatz** *m* parking space; **Stellung** *f* position; **zu etw ~ nehmen** to comment on sth; **Stellvertreter(in)** *m(f)* representative; (*amtlich*) deputy; (*von Arzt*) locum (*Brit*), locum tenens (*US*)

Stempel (-s, -) *m* stamp; **stempeln** *vt* to stamp; (*Briefmarke*) to cancel

sterben (*starb, gestorben*) *vi* to die

Stereoanlage *f* stereo (system)

steril *adj* sterile; **sterilisieren** *vt* to sterilize

Stern (-(e)s, -e) *m* star; **ein Hotel mit vier ~en** a four-star hotel; **Sternbild** *nt* constellation; (*Sternzeichen*) star sign, sign of the zodiac; **Sternfrucht** *f* star fruit; **Sternschnuppe** (-, -n) *f* shooting star; **Sternwarte** (-e, -n) *f* observatory; **Sternzeichen** *nt* star sign, sign of the zodiac; **welches ~ bist du?** what's your star sign?

stets *adv* always

Steuer (-s, -) *nt* (*Auto*) steering wheel ▷ (-, -n) *f* tax; **Steuerberater(in)** *m(f)* tax adviser; **Steuerbord** *nt* starboard; **Steuererklärung** *f* tax declaration; **steuerfrei** *adj* tax-free; (*Waren*) duty-free; **Steuerknüppel** *m* control column; (*Aviat, Inform*) joystick; **steuern** *vt, vi* to steer; (*Flugzeug*) to pilot; (*Entwicklung, Tonstärke*) (*Inform*) to control; **steuerpflichtig** *adj* taxable; **Steuerung** *f* (*Auto*) steering; (*Vorrichtung*) controls *pl*; (*Aviat*) piloting; (*fig*) control; **Steuerungstaste** *f* (*Inform*) control key

Stich (-(e)s, -e) *m* (*von Insekt*) sting; (*von Mücke*) bite; (*durch Messer*) stab; (*beim Nähen*) stitch; (*Färbung*) tinge; (*Kartenspiel*) trick; (*Kunst*) engraving

sticken *vt, vi* to embroider

Sticker (-s, -) *m* sticker

Stickerei *f* embroidery

stickig *adj* stuffy, close

Stiefbruder *m* stepbrother

Stiefel (-s, -) *m* boot

Stiefmutter *f* stepmother

Stiefmütterchen *nt* pansy

Stiefschwester *f* stepsister; **Stiefsohn** *m* stepson; **Stieftochter** *f* stepdaughter; **Stiefvater** *m* stepfather

stieg *imperf von* **steigen**

Stiege (-, -n) f steps pl
Stiel (-(e)s, -e) m handle; (Bot)
stalk; **ein Eis am ~** an ice lolly
(Brit), a Popsicle® (US)
Stier (-(e)s, -e) m (Zool) bull; (Astr)
Taurus; **Stierkampf** m bullfight
stieß imperf von **stoßen**
Stift (-(e)s, -e) m (aus Holz) peg;
(Nagel) tack; (zum Schreiben) pen;
(Farbstift) crayon; (Bleistift) pencil
Stil (-s, -e) m style
still adj quiet; (unbewegt) still
stillen vt (Säugling) to breast-feed
still|halten irr vi to keep still;
still|stehen irr vi to stand still
Stimme (-, -n) f voice; (bei Wahl)
vote
stimmen vi to be right; **stimmt!**
that's right; **hier stimmt was
nicht** there's something wrong
here; **stimmt so!** (beim Bezahlen)
keep the change
Stimmung f mood; (Atmosphäre)
atmosphere
Stinkefinger m (fam) **jdm den
~ zeigen** to give sb the finger (o
bird (US))
stinken (stank, gestunken) vi to
stink (nach of)
Stipendium nt scholarship; (als
Unterstützung) grant
Stirn (-, -en) f forehead;
Stirnhöhle f sinus
Stock (-(e)s, Stöcke) m stick; (Bot)
stock ▷ m (Stockwerke) floor,
storey; **Stockbett** nt bunk bed;
Stöckelschuhe pl high-heels;
Stockwerk nt floor; **im ersten
~** on the first floor (Brit), on the
second floor (US)
Stoff (-(e)s, -e) m (Gewebe)
material; (Materie) matter; (von
Buch etc) subject (matter); (fam:
Rauschgift) stuff
stöhnen vi to groan (vor with)
stolpern vi to stumble, to trip
stolz adj proud

stopp interj hold it; (Moment mal!)
hang on a minute; **stoppen** vt, vi
to stop; (mit Uhr) to time;
Stoppschild nt stop sign;
Stoppuhr f stopwatch
Stöpsel (-s, -) m plug; (für
Flaschen) stopper
Storch (-(e)s, Störche) m stork
stören vt to disturb; (behindern)
to interfere with; **darf ich dich
kurz ~?** can I trouble you for a
minute?; **stört es dich, wenn ...?**
do you mind if ...?
stornieren vt to cancel;
Stornogebühr f cancellation fee
Störung f disturbance; (in der
Leitung) fault
Stoß (-es, Stöße) m (Schub) push;
(Schlag) blow; (mit Fuß) kick;
(Haufen) pile; **Stoßdämpfer** (-s, -)
m shock absorber
stoßen (stieß, gestoßen) vt (mit
Druck) to shove, to push; (mit
Schlag) to knock; (mit Fuß) to kick;
(anstoßen) to bump; (zerkleinern) to
pulverize ▷ vr: **sich ~** to bang
oneself; **sich ~ an** (+dat) (fig) to
take exception to
Stoßstange f (Auto) bumper
stottern vt, vi to stutter
Str. abk von **Straße** St, Rd
Strafe (-, -n) f punishment;
(Sport) penalty; (Gefängnisstrafe)
sentence; (Geldstrafe) fine; **strafen**
vt to punish; **Straftat** f
(criminal) offence; **Strafzettel** m
ticket
Strahl (-s, -en) m ray, beam;
(Wasser) jet; **strahlen** vi to
radiate; (fig) to beam
Strähne (-, -n) f strand; (weiß,
gefärbt) streak
Strand (-(e)s, Strände) m beach;
am ~ on the beach; **Strandcafé**
nt beach café; **Strandkorb** m
wicker beach chair with a hood;
Strandpromenade f promenade

strapazieren vt (Material) to be hard on; (Mensch, Kräfte) to be a strain on

Straße (-, -n) f road; (in der Stadt) street; **Straßenarbeiten** pl roadworks pl (Brit), road repairs pl (US); **Straßenbahn** f tram (Brit), streetcar (US); **Straßencafé** nt pavement café (Brit), sidewalk café (US); **Straßenfest** nt street party; **Straßenglätte** f slippery roads pl; **Straßenkarte** f road map; **Straßenrand** m: **am ~** at the roadside; **Straßenschild** nt street sign; **Straßensperre** f roadblock; **Straßenverhältnisse** pl road conditions pl

Strategie (-, -n) f strategy

Strauch (-(e)s, Sträucher) m bush, shrub; **Strauchtomate** f vine-ripened tomato

Strauß (-es, Sträuße) m bunch; (als Geschenk) bouquet ▷ m (Strauße) (Vogel) ostrich

Strecke (-, -n) f route; (Entfernung) distance; (Eisenb) line

strecken vt to stretch ▷ vr: **sich ~** to stretch

streckenweise adv (teilweise) in parts; (zeitweise) at times

Streich (-(e)s, -e) m trick, prank

streicheln vt to stroke

streichen (strich, gestrichen) vt (anmalen) to paint; (berühren) to stroke; (auftragen) to spread; (durchstreichen) to delete; (nicht genehmigen) to cancel

Streichholz nt match; **Streichholzschachtel** f matchbox; **Streichkäse** m cheese spread

Streifen (-s, -) m (Linie) stripe; (Stück) strip; (Film) film

Streifenwagen m patrol car

Streik (-(e)s, -s) m strike; **streiken** vi to be on strike

Streit (-(e)s, -e) m argument (um, wegen about, over); **streiten** (stritt, gestritten) vi to argue (um, wegen about, over) ▷ vr: **sich ~** to argue (um, wegen about, over)

streng adj (Blick) severe; (Lehrer) strict; (Geruch) sharp

Stress (-es) m stress; **stressen** vt to stress (out); **stressig** adj (fam) stressful

Stretching (-(e)s) nt (Sport) stretching exercises pl

streuen vt to scatter; **die Straßen ~** to grit the roads; (mit Salz) to put salt down on the roads; **Streufahrzeug** nt gritter lorry (Brit), salt truck (US)

strich imperf von **streichen**

Strich (-(e)s, -e) m (Linie) line; **Stricher** (-s) m (fam: Strichjunge) rent boy (Brit), boy prostitute; **Strichkode** (-s, -s) m bar code; **Stricherin** f (fam: Strichmädchen) hooker; **Strichpunkt** m semicolon

Strick (-(e)s, -e) m rope

stricken vt, vi to knit; **Strickjacke** f cardigan; **Stricknadel** f knitting needle

String (-s, -s) m, **Stringtanga** m G-string

Stripper(in) m(f) stripper; **Striptease** (-) m striptease

stritt imperf von **streiten**

Stroh (-(e)s) nt straw; **Strohdach** nt thatched roof; **Strohhalm** m (drinking) straw

Strom (-(e)s, Ströme) m river; (fig) stream; (Elek) current; **Stromanschluss** m connection; **Stromausfall** m power failure

strömen vi to stream, to pour; **Strömung** f current

Stromverbrauch m power consumption; **Stromzähler** m electricity meter

Strophe (-, -n) f verse

Strudel (-s, -) *m* (*in Fluss*) whirlpool; (*Gebäck*) strudel

Struktur *f* structure; (*von Material*) texture

Strumpf (-(e)s, Strümpfe) *m* (*Damenstrumpf*) stocking; (*Socke*) sock; **Strumpfhose** *f* (pair of) tights *pl* (Brit), pantyhose (US)

Stück (-(e)s, -e) *nt* piece; (*von Zucker*) lump; (*etwas*) bit; (*Zucker*) lump; (*Theat*) play; **ein ~ Käse** a piece of cheese

Student(in) *m(f)* student; **Studentenausweis** *m* student card; **Studentenwohnheim** *nt* hall of residence (Brit), dormitory (US); **Studienabschluss** *m* qualification (*at the end of a course of higher education*); **Studienfahrt** *f* study trip; **Studienplatz** *m* university/college place; **studieren** *vt*, *vi* to study; **Studium** *nt* studies *pl*; **während seines ~s** while he is/was studying

Stufe (-, -n) *f* step; (*Entwicklungsstufe*) stage

Stuhl (-(e)s, Stühle) *m* chair

stumm *adj* silent; (*Med*) dumb

stumpf *adj* blunt; (*teilnahmslos, glanzlos*) dull; **stumpfsinnig** *adj* dull

Stunde (-, -n) *f* hour; (*Unterricht*) lesson; **eine halbe ~** half an hour; **Stundenkilometer** *m*: **80 ~** 80 kilometres an hour; **stundenlang** *adv* for hours; **Stundenlohn** *m* hourly wage; **Stundenplan** *m* timetable; **stündlich** *adj* hourly

Stuntman (-s, Stuntmen) *m* stuntman; **Stuntwoman** (-, Stuntwomen) *f* stuntwoman

stur *adj* stubborn; (*stärker*) pigheaded

Sturm (-(e)s, Stürme) *m* storm; **stürmen** *vi* (*Wind*) to blow hard; (*rennen*) to storm; **Stürmer(in)** *m(f)* striker, forward; **Sturmflut** *f* storm tide; **stürmisch** *adj* stormy; (*fig*) tempestuous; (*Zeit*) turbulent; (*Liebhaber*) passionate; (*Beifall, Begrüßung*) tumultuous; **Sturmwarnung** *f* gale warning

Sturz (-es, Stürze) *m* fall; (*Pol*) overthrow; **stürzen** *vt* (*werfen*) to hurl; (*Pol*) to overthrow; (*umkehren*) to overturn ▷ *vi* to fall; (*rennen*) to dash; **Sturzhelm** *m* crash helmet

Stute (-, -n) *f* mare

Stütze (-, -n) *f* support; (*Hilfe*) help; (*fam: Arbeitslosenunter-stützung*) dole (Brit), welfare (US)

stützen *vt* to support; (*Ellbogen*) to prop

stutzig *adj* perplexed, puzzled; (*misstrauisch*) suspicious

Styropor® (-s) *nt* polystyrene (Brit), styrofoam (US)

subjektiv *adj* subjective

Substanz (-, -en) *f* substance

subtrahieren *vt* to subtract

Subvention *f* subsidy; **subventionieren** *vt* to subsidize

Suche *f* search (*nach* for); **auf der ~ nach etw sein** to be looking for sth; **suchen** *vt* to look for; (*Inform*) to search ▷ *vi* to look, to search (*nach* for); **Suchmaschine** *f* (*Inform*) search engine

Sucht (-, Süchte) *f* mania; (*Med*) addiction; **süchtig** *adj* addicted; **Süchtige(r)** *mf* addict

Süd south; **Südafrika** *nt* South Africa; **Südamerika** *nt* South America; **Süddeutschland** *nt* Southern Germany; **Süden** (-s) *m* south; **im ~ Deutschlands** in the south of Germany; **Südeuropa** *nt* Southern Europe; **Südkorea** (-s) *nt* South Korea; **südlich** *adj* southern; (*Kurs, Richtung*) southerly; **Verkehr in ~er**

Richtung southbound traffic; **Südost(en)** m southeast; **Südpol** m South Pole; **Südstaaten** pl (der USA) the Southern States pl, the South sing; **südwärts** adv south, southwards; **Südwest(en)** m southwest; **Südwind** m south wind

Sülze (-, -n) f jellied meat

Summe (-, -n) f sum; (Gesamtsumme) total

summen vi, vt to hum; (Insekt) to buzz

Sumpf (-(e)s, Sümpfe) m marsh; (subtropischer) swamp; **sumpfig** adj marshy

Sünde (-, -n) f sin

super adj (fam) super, great; **Super** (-s) nt (Benzin) four star (petrol) (Brit), premium (US); **Supermarkt** m supermarket

Suppe (-, -n) f soup; **Suppengrün** nt bunch of herbs and vegetables for flavouring soup; **Suppenlöffel** m soup spoon; **Suppenschüssel** f soup tureen; **Suppentasse** f soup cup; **Suppenteller** m soup plate; **Suppenwürfel** m stock cube

Surfbrett nt surfboard; **surfen** vi to surf; **im Internet ~** to surf the Internet; **Surfer(in)** (-s, -) m(f) surfer

Surrealismus m surrealism

Sushi (-s, -s) nt sushi

süß adj sweet; **süßen** vt to sweeten; **Süßigkeit** f (Bonbon etc) sweet (Brit), candy (US); **Süßkartoffel** f sweet potato (Brit), yam (US); **süßsauer** adj sweet-and-sour; **Süßspeise** f dessert; **Süßstoff** m sweetener; **Süßwasser** nt fresh water

Sweatshirt (-s, -s) nt sweatshirt

Swimmingpool (-s, -s) m (swimming) pool

Sylvester nt siehe **Silvester**

Symbol (-s, -e) nt symbol; **Symbolleiste** f (Inform) toolbar

Symmetrie (-, -n) f symmetry; **symmetrisch** adj symmetrical

sympathisch adj nice; **jdn ~ finden** to like sb

Symphonie (-, -n) f symphony

Symptom (-s, -e) nt symptom (für of)

Synagoge (-, -n) f synagogue

synchronisiert adj (Film) dubbed; **Synchronstimme** f dubbing voice

Synthetik (-, -en) f synthetic (fibre); **synthetisch** adj synthetic

Syrien (-s) nt Syria

System (-s, -e) nt system; **systematisch** adj systematic; **Systemsteuerung** f (Inform) control panel

Szene (-, -n) f scene

t

Tabak (-s, -e) m tobacco;
Tabakladen m tobacconist's
Tabelle f table
Tablett (-s, -s) nt tray
Tablette f tablet, pill
Tabulator m tabulator, tab
Tacho(meter) (-s, -) m (Auto)
speedometer
Tafel (-, -n) f (a. Math) table;
(Anschlagtafel) board; (Wandtafel)
blackboard; (Schiefer~) slate;
(Gedenktafel) plaque; **eine
~ Schokolade** a bar of chocolate;
Tafelwasser nt table water;
Tafelwein m table wine
Tag (-(e)s, -e) m day; (Tageslicht)
daylight; **guten ~!** good
morning/afternoon; **am ~** during
the day; **sie hat ihre ~e** she's got
her period; **eines ~es** one day;
~ der Arbeit Labour Day;
Tagebuch nt diary; **tagelang**
adj for days (on end);

Tagesanbruch m daybreak;
Tagesausflug m day trip;
Tagescreme f day cream;
Tagesdecke f bedspread;
Tagesgericht nt dish of the day;
Tageskarte f (Fahrkarte) day
ticket; **die ~** (Speisekarte) today's
menu; **Tageslicht** nt daylight;
Tagesmutter f child minder;
Tagesordnung f agenda;
Tagestour f day trip;
Tageszeitung f daily newspaper;
täglich adj, adv daily; **tags(über)**
adv during the day; **Tagung** f
conference
Tai Chi (-) nt tai chi
Taille (-, -n) f waist
Taiwan (-s) nt Taiwan
Takt (-(e)s, -e) m (Taktgefühl) tact;
(Mus) time
Taktik (-, -en) f tactics pl
taktlos adj tactless; **taktvoll** adj
tactful
Tal (-(e)s, Täler) nt valley
Talent (-(e)s, -e) nt talent;
talentiert adj talented
Talkmaster(in) (-s, -) m(f) talk-show
host; **Talkshow** (-, -s) f talkshow
Tampon (-s, -s) m tampon
Tandem (-s, -s) nt tandem
Tang (-s, -e) m seaweed
Tanga (-s, -s) m thong
Tank (-s, -s) m tank;
Tankanzeige f fuel gauge;
Tankdeckel m fuel cap; **tanken** vi
to get some petrol (Brit) (o gas
(US)); (Aviat) to refuel; **Tanker**
(-s, -) m (oil) tanker; **Tankstelle** f
petrol station (Brit), gas station
(US); **Tankwart(in)** (-s, -e) m(f)
petrol pump attendant (Brit), gas
station attendant (US)
Tanne (-, -n) f fir; **Tannenzapfen**
m fir cone
Tansania (-s) nt Tanzania
Tante (-, -n) f aunt;
Tante-Emma-Laden m corner

shop (Brit), grocery store (US)

Tanz (-es, Tänze) m dance; **tanzen** vi, vi to dance; **Tänzer(in)** m(f) dancer; **Tanzfläche** f dance floor; **Tanzkurs** m dancing course; **Tanzlehrer(in)** m(f) dancing instructor; **Tanzstunde** f dancing lesson

Tapete (-, -n) f wallpaper; **tapezieren** vt, vi to wallpaper

Tarantel (-, -n) f tarantula

Tarif (-s, -e) m tariff, (scale of) fares/charges pl

Tasche (-, -n) f bag; (Hosentasche) pocket; (Handtasche) bag (Brit), purse (US)

Taschen- in zW pocket; **Taschenbuch** nt paperback; **Taschendieb(in)** m(f) pickpocket; **Taschengeld** nt pocket money; **Taschenlampe** f torch (Brit), flashlight (US); **Taschenmesser** nt penknife; **Taschenrechner** m pocket calculator; **Taschentuch** nt handkerchief

Tasse (-, -n) f cup; **eine ~ Kaffee** a cup of coffee

Tastatur f keyboard; **Taste** (-, -n) f button; (von Klavier, Computer) key; **Tastenkombination** f (Inform) shortcut

tat imperf von **tun**

Tat (-, -en) f action

Tatar (-s, -s) nt raw minced beef

Täter(in) (-s, -) m(f) culprit

tätig adj active; **in einer Firma ~ sein** to work for a firm; **Tätigkeit** f activity; (Beruf) occupation

tätowieren vt to tattoo; **Tätowierung** f tattoo (an +dat on)

Tatsache f fact; **tatsächlich** adj actual ▷ adv really

Tau (-(e)s, -e) nt (Seil) rope ▷ (-(e)s) m dew

taub adj deaf; (Füße etc) numb (vor Kälte with cold)

Taube (-, -n) f pigeon; (Turtel~, fig: Friedenssymbol) dove

taubstumm adj deaf-and-dumb; **Taubstumme(r)** mf deaf-mute

tauchen vt to dip ▷ vi to dive; (Naut) to submerge; **Tauchen** (-s) nt diving; **Taucher(in)** (-s, -) m(f) diver; **Taucheranzug** m diving (o wet) suit; **Taucherbrille** f diving goggles pl; **Tauchermaske** f diving mask; **Tauchkurs** m diving course; **Tauchsieder** (-s, -) m portable immersion coil for heating water

tauen vi impers to thaw

Taufe (-, -n) f baptism; **taufen** vt to baptize; (nennen) to christen

taugen vi to be suitable (für for); **nichts ~** to be no good

Tausch (-(e)s, -e) m exchange; **tauschen** vt to exchange, to swap

täuschen vt to deceive ▷ vi to be deceptive ▷ vr: **sich ~** to be wrong; **täuschend** adj deceptive; **Täuschung** f deception; (optisch) illusion

tausend num a thousand; **vier~** four thousand; **~ Dank!** thanks a lot; **tausendmal** adv a thousand times; **tausendste(r, s)** adj thousandth; **Tausendstel** (-s, -) nt (Bruchteil) thousandth

Taxi nt taxi; **Taxifahrer(in)** m(f) taxi driver; **Taxistand** m taxi rank (Brit), taxi stand (US)

Team (-s, -s) nt team; **Teamarbeit** f team work; **teamfähig** adj able to work in a team

Technik f technology; (angewandte) engineering; (Methode) technique; **Techniker(in)** (-s, -) m(f) engineer; (Sport, Mus) technician;

technisch *adj* technical
Techno (-s) *m* (*Mus*) techno
Teddybär *m* teddy bear
Tee (-s, -s) *m* tea; **Teebeutel** *m* teabag; **Teekanne** *f* teapot; **Teelöffel** *m* teaspoon
Teer (-(e)s, -e) *m* tar
Teesieb *nt* tea strainer; **Teetasse** *f* teacup
Teich (-(e)s, -e) *m* pond
Teig (-(e)s, -e) *m* dough; **Teigwaren** *pl* pasta *sing*
Teil (-(e)s, -e) *m* part; (*Anteil*) share; **zum** ~ partly ▷ (-(e)s, -e) *nt* part; (*Bestandteil*) component; **teilen** *vt* to divide; (*mit jdm*) to share (*mit* with); **20 durch 4** ~ to divide 20 by 4 ▷ *vr*: **sich** ~ to divide
Teilkaskoversicherung *f* third party, fire and theft insurance
teilmöbliert *adj* partly furnished
Teilnahme (-, -n) *f* participation (*an +dat* in); **teil|nehmen** *irr vi* to take part (*an +dat* in); **Teilnehmer(in)** (-s, -) *m(f)* participant
teils *adv* partly; **teilweise** *adv* partially, in part; **Teilzeit** *f*: ~ **arbeiten** to work part-time
Teint (-s, -s) *m* complexion
Tel. *abk von* **Telefon** tel.
Telefon (-s, -e) *nt* telephone; **Telefonanruf** *m*, **Telefonat** *nt* (tele)phone call; **Telefonanschluss** *m* telephone connection; **Telefonauskunft** *f* directory enquiries *pl* (*Brit*), directory assistance (*US*); **Telefonbuch** *nt* telephone directory; **Telefongebühren** *pl* telephone charges *pl*; **Telefongespräch** *nt* telephone conversation; **telefonieren** *vi*: **ich telefoniere gerade (mit ...)** I'm on the phone (to ...); **telefonisch** *adj* telephone; (*Benachrichtigung*) by telephone;

Telefonkarte *f* phonecard; **Telefonnummer** *f* (tele)phone number; **Telefonrechnung** *f* phone bill; **Telefonverbindung** *f* telephone connection; **Telefonzelle** *f* phone box (*Brit*), phone booth; **Telefonzentrale** *f* switchboard; **über die** ~ through the switchboard
Telegramm *nt* telegram; **Teleobjektiv** *nt* telephoto lens; **Teleshopping** (-s) *nt* teleshopping; **Teleskop** (-s, -e) *nt* telescope
Teller (-s, -) *m* plate
Tempel (-s, -) *m* temple
Temperament *nt* temperament; (*Schwung*) liveliness; **temperamentvoll** *adj* lively
Temperatur *f* temperature; **bei ~en von 30 Grad** at temperatures of 30 degrees; ~ **haben** to have a temperature; ~ **bei jdm messen** to take sb's temperature
Tempo (-s, -s) *nt* (*Geschwindigkeit*) speed; **Tempolimit** (-s, -s) *nt* speed limit
Tempotaschentuch® *nt* (*Papiertaschentuch*) (paper) tissue, ≈ Kleenex®
Tendenz *f* tendency; (*Absicht*) intention
Tennis (-) *nt* tennis; **Tennisball** *m* tennis ball; **Tennisplatz** *m* tennis court; **Tennisschläger** *m* tennis racket; **Tennisspieler(in)** *m(f)* tennis player
Tenor (-s, Tenöre) *m* tenor
Teppich (-s, -e) *m* carpet; **Teppichboden** *m* (wall-to-wall) carpet
Termin (-s, -e) *m* (*Zeitpunkt*) date; (*Frist*) deadline; (*Arzttermin etc*) appointment
Terminal (-s, -s) *nt* (*Inform, Aviat*) terminal
Terminkalender *m* diary;

Terminplaner m (in Buchform) personal organizer, Filofax®; (Taschencomputer) personal digital assistant, PDA

Terpentin (-s, -e) nt turpentine, turps sing

Terrasse (-, -n) f terrace; (hinter einem Haus) patio

Terror (-s) m terror; **Terroranschlag** m terrorist attack; **terrorisieren** vt to terrorize; **Terrorismus** m terrorism; **Terrorist(in)** m(f) terrorist

Tesafilm® m ≈ sellotape® (Brit), ≈ Scotch tape® (US)

Test (-s, -s) m test

Testament nt will; **das Alte/Neue ~** the Old/New Testament

testen vt to test; **Testergebnis** nt test results pl

Tetanus (-) m tetanus; **Tetanusimpfung** f (anti-)tetanus injection

teuer adj expensive, dear (Brit)

Teufel (-s, -) m devil; **was/wo zum ~** what/where the devil; **Teufelskreis** m vicious circle

Text (-(e)s, -e) m text; (Liedertext) words pl, lyrics pl; **Textmarker** (-s, -) m highlighter; **Textverarbeitung** f word processing; **Textverarbeitungsprogramm** nt word processing program

Thailand nt Thailand

Theater (-s, -) nt theatre; (fam) fuss; **ins ~ gehen** to go to the theatre; **Theaterkasse** f box office; **Theaterstück** nt (stage) play; **Theatervorstellung** f (stage) performance

Theke (-, -n) f (Schanktisch) bar; (Ladentisch) counter

Thema (-s, Themen) nt subject, topic; **kein ~!** no problem

Themse (-) f Thames

Theologie f theology

theoretisch adj theoretical; **~ stimmt das** that's right in theory; **Theorie** f theory

Therapeut(in) m(f) therapist; **Therapie** f therapy; **eine ~ machen** to undergo therapy

Thermalbad nt thermal bath; (Ort) thermal spa; **Thermometer** (-s, -) nt thermometer

Thermosflasche® f, **Thermoskanne®** f Thermos® (flask); **Thermostat** (-(e)s, -e) m thermostat

These (-, -n) f theory

Thron (-(e)s, -e) m throne

Thunfisch m tuna

Thüringen (-s) nt Thuringia

Thymian (-s, -e) m thyme

Tick (-(e)s, -s) m tic; (Eigenart) quirk; (Fimmel) craze; **ticken** vi to tick; **er tickt nicht ganz richtig** he's off his rocker

Ticket (-s, -s) nt (plane) ticket

tief adj deep (Ausschnitt, Ton, Sonne) low; **2 Meter ~** 2 metres deep; **Tief** (-s, -s) nt (Meteo) low; (seelisch) depression; **Tiefdruck** m (Meteo) low pressure; **Tiefe** (-, -n) f depth; **Tiefgarage** f underground car park (Brit) (o garage (US)); **tiefgekühlt** adj frozen; **Tiefkühlfach** nt freezer compartment; **Tiefkühlkost** f frozen food; **Tiefkühltruhe** f freezer; **Tiefpunkt** m low

Tier (-(e)s, -e) nt animal; **Tierarzt** m, **Tierärztin** f vet; **Tiergarten** m zoo; **Tierhandlung** f pet shop; **Tierheim** nt animal shelter; **tierisch** adj animal ▷ adv (fam) really; **~ ernst** deadly serious; **ich hatte ~ Angst** I was dead scared; **Tierkreiszeichen** nt sign of the zodiac; **Tierpark** m zoo; **Tierquälerei** f cruelty to animals;

Tierschützer(in) (-s, -) m(f) animal rights campaigner; **Tierversuch** m animal experiment

Tiger (-s, -) m tiger

timen vt to time; **Timing** (-s) nt timing

Tinte (-, -n) f ink; **Tintenfisch** m cuttlefish; (klein) squid; (achtarmig) octopus; **Tintenfischringe** pl calamari pl; **Tintenstrahldrucker** m ink-jet printer

Tipp (-s, -s) m tip; **tippen** vt, vi to tap; (fam: schreiben) to type; (fam: raten) to guess

Tirol (-s) nt Tyrol

Tisch (-(e)s, -e) m table; **Tischdecke** f tablecloth; **Tischlerei** f joiner's workshop; (Arbeit) joinery; **Tischtennis** nt table tennis; **Tischtennisschläger** m table-tennis bat

Titel (-s, -) m title; **Titelbild** nt cover picture

Toast (-(e)s, -s) m toast; **toasten** vt to toast; **Toaster** (-s, -) m toaster

Tochter (-, Töchter) f daughter

Tod (-(e)s, -e) m death; **Todesopfer** nt casualty; **Todesstrafe** f death penalty; **todkrank** adj terminally ill; (sehr krank) seriously ill; **tödlich** adj deadly, fatal; **er ist ~ verunglückt** he was killed in an accident; **todmüde** adj (fam) dead tired; **todsicher** adj (fam) dead certain

Tofu (-(s)) m tofu, bean curd

Toilette f toilet, restroom (US); **Toilettenpapier** nt toilet paper

toi, toi, toi interj good luck

tolerant adj tolerant (gegen of)

toll adj mad; (Treiben) wild; (fam: großartig) great; **Tollkirsche** f deadly nightshade; **Tollwut** f rabies sing

Tomate (-, -n) f tomato; **Tomatenmark** nt tomato purée (Brit) (o paste (US)); **Tomatensaft** m tomato juice

Tombola (-, -s) f raffle, tombola (Brit)

Ton (-(e)s, -e) m (Erde) clay ▷ m (Töne; Laut) sound; (Mus) note; (Redeweise) tone; (Farbton, Nuance) shade; **Tonband** nt tape; **Tonbandgerät** nt tape recorder

tönen vi to sound ▷ vt to shade; (Haare) to tint

Toner (-s, -) m toner; **Tonerkassette** f toner cartridge

Tonne (-, -n) f (Fass) barrel; (Gewicht) tonne, metric ton

Tontechniker(in) m(f) sound engineer

Tönung f hue; (für Haar) rinse

Top (-s, -s) nt top

Topf (-(e)s, Töpfe) m pot

Töpfer(in) (-s, -) m(f) potter; **Töpferei** f pottery; (Gegenstand) piece of pottery

Tor (-(e)s, -e) nt gate; (Sport) goal; **ein ~ schießen** to score a goal; **Torhüter(in)** m(f) goalkeeper

torkeln vi to stagger

Tornado (-s, -s) m tornado

Torschütze m, **Torschützin** f (goal)scorer

Torte (-, -n) f cake; (Obsttorte) flan; (Sahnetorte) gateau

Torwart(in) (-s, -e) m(f) goalkeeper

tot adj dead; **~er Winkel** blind spot

total adj total, complete; **Totalschaden** m complete write-off

Tote(r) mf dead man/woman; (Leiche) corpse; **töten** vt, vi to kill; **Totenkopf** m skull

tot|lachen vr: **sich ~** to kill oneself laughing

Toto (-s, -s) m o nt pools pl

tot|schlagen *irr vt* to beat to death; **die Zeit ~** to kill time
Touchscreen (-s, -s) *m* touch screen
Tour (-, -en) *f* trip; (*Rundfahrt*) tour; **eine ~ nach York machen** to go on a trip to York; **Tourenski** *m* touring ski
Tourismus *m* tourism; **Tourist(in)** *m(f)* tourist; **Touristenklasse** *f* tourist class; **touristisch** *adj* tourist; (*pej*) touristy
traben *vi* to trot
Tournee (-, -n) *f* tour
Tracht (-, -en) *f* (*Kleidung*) traditional costume
Trackball (-s, -s) *m* (*Inform*) trackball
Tradition *f* tradition; **traditionell** *adj* traditional
traf *imperf von* **treffen**
Trafik (-, -en) *f* tobacconist's
Tragbahre (-, -n) *f* stretcher
tragbar *adj* portable
träge *adj* sluggish, slow
tragen (trug, getragen) *vt* to carry; (*Kleidung, Brille, Haare*) to wear; (*Namen, Früchte*) to bear; **Träger** (-s, -) *m* (*an Kleidung*) strap; (*Hosen~*) braces *pl* (*Brit*), suspenders *pl* (*US*); (*in der Architektur*) beam; (*Stahl~, Eisen~*) girder
Tragfläche *f* wing; **Tragflügelboot** *nt* hydrofoil
tragisch *adj* tragic; **Tragödie** *f* tragedy
Trainer(in) (-s, -) *m(f)* trainer, coach; **trainieren** *vt, vi* to train; (*jdn a.*) to coach; (*Übung*) to practise; **Training** (-s, -s) *nt* training; **Trainingsanzug** *m* tracksuit
Traktor *m* tractor
Trambahn *f* tram (*Brit*), streetcar (*US*)

trampen *vi* to hitchhike; **Tramper(in)** *m(f)* hitchhiker
Träne (-, -n) *f* tear; **tränen** *vi* to water; **Tränengas** *nt* teargas
trank *imperf von* **trinken**
Transfusion *f* transfusion
Transitverkehr *m* transit traffic; **Transitvisum** *nt* transit visa
Transplantation *f* transplant; (*Hauttransplantation*) graft
Transport (-(e)s, -e) *m* transport; **transportieren** *vt* to transport; **Transportmittel** *nt* means *sing of* transport; **Transportunternehmen** *nt* haulage firm
Transvestit (-en, -en) *m* transvestite
trat *imperf von* **treten**
Traube (-, -n) *f* (*einzelne Beere*) grape; (*ganze Frucht*) bunch of grapes; **Traubensaft** *m* grape juice; **Traubenzucker** *m* glucose
trauen *vi*: **jdm/einer Sache ~** to trust sb/sth; **ich traute meinen Ohren nicht** I couldn't believe my ears ▷ *vr*: **sich ~** to dare ▷ *vt* to marry; **sich ~ lassen** to get married
Trauer (-) *f* sorrow; (*für Verstorbenen*) mourning
Traum (-(e)s, Träume) *m* dream; **träumen** *vt, vi* to dream (*von* of, about); **traumhaft** *adj* dreamlike; (*fig*) wonderful
traurig *adj* sad (*über +akk* about)
Trauschein *m* marriage certificate; **Trauung** *f* wedding ceremony; **Trauzeuge** *m*, **Trauzeugin** *f* witness (*at wedding ceremony*), ≈ best man/maid of honour
Travellerscheck *m* traveller's cheque
treffen (traf, getroffen) *vr*: **sich ~** to meet ▷ *vt, vi* to hit; (*Bemerkung*) to hurt; (*begegnen*) to

meet; (*Entscheidung*) to make; (*Maßnahmen*) to take; **Treffen** (-s, -) *nt* meeting; **Treffer** (-s, -) *m* (*Tor*) goal; **Treffpunkt** *m* meeting place

treiben (*trieb, getrieben*) *vt* to drive; (*Sport*) to do ▷ *vi* (*im Wasser*) to drift; (*Pflanzen*) to sprout; (*Tee, Kaffee*) to be diuretic; **Treiber** (-s, -) *m* (*Inform*) driver

Treibgas *nt* propellant; **Treibhaus** *nt* greenhouse; **Treibstoff** *m* fuel

trennen *vt* to separate; (*teilen*) to divide ▷ *vr*: **sich ~** to separate; **sich von jdm ~** to leave sb; **sich von etw ~** to part with sth; **Trennung** *f* separation

Treppe (-, -n) *f* stairs *pl*; (*im Freien*) steps *pl*; **Treppengeländer** *nt* banister; **Treppenhaus** *nt* staircase

Tresen (-s, -) *m* (*in Kneipe*) bar; (*in Laden*) counter

Tresor (-s, -e) *m* safe

Tretboot *nt* pedal boat; **treten** (*trat, getreten*) *vi* to step; **mit jdm in Verbindung ~** to get in contact with sb ▷ *vt* to kick; (*nieder~*) to tread

treu *adj* (*gegenüber Partner*) faithful; (*Kunde, Fan*) loyal; **Treue** (-) *f* (*eheliche*) faithfulness; (*von Kunde, Fan*) loyalty

Triathlon (-s, -s) *m* triathlon

Tribüne (-, -n) *f* stand; (*Rednertribüne*) platform

Trick (-s, -e *o* -s) *m* trick; **Trickfilm** *m* cartoon

trieb *imperf von* **treiben**

Trieb (-(e)s, -e) *m* urge; (*Instinkt*) drive; (*Neigung*) inclination; (*an Baum etc*) shoot; **Triebwerk** *nt* engine

Trikot (-s, -s) *nt* shirt, jersey

Trimm-Dich-Pfad *m* fitness trail

trinkbar *adj* drinkable; **trinken** (*trank, getrunken*) *vt, vi* to drink; **einen ~ gehen** to go out for a drink; **Trinkgeld** *nt* tip; **Trinkhalm** *m* (drinking) straw; **Trinkwasser** *nt* drinking water

Trio (-s, -s) *nt* trio

Tripper (-s, -) *m* gonorrhoea

Tritt (-(e)s, -e) *m* (*Schritt*) step; (*Fußtritt*) kick; **Trittbrett** *nt* running board

Triumph (-(e)s, -e) *m* triumph; **triumphieren** *vi* to triumph (*über* +*akk* over)

trivial *adj* trivial

trocken *adj* dry; **Trockenhaube** *f* hair-dryer; **Trockenheit** *f* dryness; **trocken|legen** *vt* (*Baby*) to change; **trocknen** *vt, vi* to dry; **Trockner** (-s, -) *m* dryer

Trödel (-s) *m* (*fam*) junk; **Trödelmarkt** *m* flea market

trödeln *vi* (*fam*) to dawdle

Trommel (-, -n) *f* drum; **Trommelfell** *nt* eardrum; **trommeln** *vt, vi* to drum

Trompete (-, -n) *f* trumpet

Tropen *pl* tropics *pl*

Tropf (-(e)s, -e) *m* (*Med*) drip; **am ~ hängen** to be on a drip; **tröpfeln** *vi* to drip; **es tröpfelt** it's drizzling; **tropfen** *vt, vi* to drip; **Tropfen** (-s, -) *m* drop; **tropfenweise** *adv* drop by drop; **tropfnass** *adj* dripping wet; **Tropfsteinhöhle** *f* stalactite cave

tropisch *adj* tropical

Trost (-es) *m* consolation, comfort; **trösten** *vt* to console, to comfort; **trostlos** *adj* bleak; (*Verhältnisse*) wretched; **Trostpreis** *m* consolation prize

Trottoir (-s, -s) *nt* pavement (*Brit*), sidewalk (*US*)

trotz *prep* +*gen o dat* in spite of; **Trotz** (-es) *m* defiance; **trotzdem** *adv* nevertheless ▷ *conj* although;

trotzig adj defiant

trüb adj dull; (Flüssigkeit, Glas) cloudy; (fig) gloomy

Trüffel (-, -n) f truffle

trug imperf von **tragen**

trügerisch adj deceptive

Truhe (-, -n) f chest

Trümmer pl wreckage sing; (Bau~) ruins pl

Trumpf (-(e)s, Trümpfe) m trump

Trunkenheit f intoxication; **~ am Steuer** drink driving (Brit), drunk driving (US)

Truthahn m turkey

Tscheche (-n, -n) m, **Tschechin** f Czech; **Tschechien** (-s) nt Czech Republic; **tschechisch** adj Czech; **Tschechische Republik** Czech Republic; **Tschechisch** nt Czech

Tschetschenien (-s) nt Chechnya

tschüs(s) interj bye

T-Shirt (-s, -s) nt T-shirt

Tube (-, -n) f tube

Tuberkulose (-, -n) f tuberculosis, TB

Tuch (-(e)s, Tücher) nt cloth; (Halstuch) scarf; (Kopftuch) headscarf

tüchtig adj competent; (fleißig) efficient; (fam: kräftig) good

Tugend (-, -en) f virtue; **tugendhaft** adj virtuous

Tulpe (-, -n) f tulip

Tumor (-s, -en) m tumour

tun (tat, getan) vt (machen) to do; (legen) to put; **was tust du da?** what are you doing?; **das tut man nicht** you shouldn't do that; **jdm etw ~** (antun) to do sth to sb; **das tut es auch** that'll do ▷ vi to act; **so ~, als ob** to act as if ▷ vr impers: **es tut sich etwas/viel** something/a lot is happening

Tuner (-s, -) m tuner

Tunesien (-s) nt Tunisia

Tunfisch m siehe **Thunfisch** tuna

Tunnel (-s, -s o -) m tunnel

Tunte (-, -n) f (pej, fam) fairy

tupfen vt, vi to dab; (mit Farbe) to dot; **Tupfen** (-s, -) m dot

Tür (-, -en) f door; **vor/an der ~** at the door; **an die ~ gehen** to answer the door

Türke (-n, -n) m Turk; **Türkei** (-) f: **die ~** Turkey; **Türkin** f Turk

Türkis (-es, -e) m turquoise

türkisch adj Turkish; **Türkisch** nt Turkish

Turm (-(e)s, Türme) m tower; (spitzer Kirchturm) steeple; (Sprung~) diving platform; (Schach) rook, castle

turnen vi to do gymnastics; **Turnen** (-s) nt gymnastics sing; (Schule) physical education, PE; **Turner(in)** m(f) gymnast; **Turnhalle** f gym(nasium); **Turnhose** f gym shorts pl

Turnier (-s, -e) nt tournament

Turnschuh m gym shoe, sneaker (US)

Türschild nt doorplate; **Türschloss** nt lock

tuscheln vt, vi to whisper

Tussi (-, -s) f (pej, fam) chick

Tüte (-, -n) f bag

TÜV (-s, -s) m akr = **Technischer Überwachungsverein** ≈ MOT (Brit), vehicle inspection (US)

- **TÜV**
- The **TÜV** is the organization
- responsible for checking the
- safety of machinery, particularly
- vehicles. Cars over three years
- old have to be examined every
- two years for their safety and
- for their exhaust emissions.
- **TÜV** is also the name given to
- the test itself.

TÜV-Plakette *f* badge attached to a vehicle's numberplate, indicating that it has passed the "TÜV"

Tweed (*-s*, *-s*) *m* tweed

Typ (*-s*, *-en*) *m* type; (*Auto*) model; (*Mann*) guy, bloke

Typhus (*-*) *m* typhoid

typisch *adj* typical (*für* of); **ein ~er Fehler** a common mistake; **~ Marcus!** that's just like Marcus; **~ amerikanisch!** that's so American

u. *abk* = **und**

u. a. *abk* = **und andere(s)** and others; = **unter anderem, unter anderen** among other things

u. A. w. g. *abk* = **um Antwort wird gebeten** RSVP

U-Bahn *f* underground (*Brit*), subway (*US*)

übel *adj* bad; (*moralisch*) wicked; **mir ist ~** I feel sick; **diese Bemerkung hat er mir ~ genommen** he took offence at my remark; **Übelkeit** *f* nausea

üben *vt, vi* to practise

 SCHLÜSSELWORT

über *prep* +*dat* **1** (*räumlich*) over, above; **zwei Grad über null** two degrees above zero
2 (*zeitlich*) over; **über der Arbeit einschlafen** to fall asleep over one's work

▷ prep +akk **1** (räumlich) over; (hoch über auch) above; (quer über auch) across

2 (zeitlich) over; **über Weihnachten** over Christmas; **über kurz oder lang** sooner or later

3 (mit Zahlen) **Kinder über 12 Jahren** children over o above 12 years of age; **ein Scheck über 200 Euro** a cheque for 200 euros

4 (auf dem Wege) via; **nach Köln über Aachen** to Cologne via Aachen; **ich habe es über die Auskunft erfahren** I found out from information

5 (betreffend) about; **ein Buch über ...** a book about o on ...; **über jdn/etw lachen** to laugh about o at sb/sth

6 Macht über jdn haben to have power over sb; **sie liebt ihn über alles** she loves him more than everything

▷ adv over; **über und über** over and over; **den ganzen Tag über** all day long; **jdm in etw** dat **über sein** to be superior to sb in sth

überall adv everywhere
überanstrengen vr: **sich ~** to overexert oneself
überbacken adj: (mit Käse) **~** au gratin; **überbelichten** vt (Foto) to overexpose; **überbieten** irr vt to outbid; (übertreffen) to surpass; (Rekord) to break
Überbleibsel (-s, -) nt remnant
Überblick m overview; (fig: in Darstellung) survey; (Fähigkeit zu verstehen) grasp (über +akk of)
überbuchen vt to overbook; **Überbuchung** f overbooking
überdurchschnittlich adj above average
übereinander adv on top of each other; (sprechen etc) about

each other
überein|stimmen vi to agree (mit with)
überempfindlich adj hypersensitive
überfahren irr vt (Auto) to run over; **Überfahrt** f crossing
Überfall m (Banküberfall) robbery; (Mil) raid; (auf jdn) assault; **überfallen** irr vt to attack; (Bank) to raid
überfällig adj overdue
überfliegen irr vt to fly over; (Buch) to skim through
Überfluss m overabundance, excess (an +dat of); **überflüssig** adj superfluous
überfordern vt to demand too much of; (Kräfte) to overtax; **da bin ich überfordert** (bei Antwort) you've got me there
Überführung f (Brücke) flyover (Brit), overpass (US)
überfüllt adj overcrowded
Übergabe f handover
Übergang m crossing; (Wandel, Überleitung) transition; **Übergangslösung** f temporary solution, stopgap
übergeben irr vt to hand over
▷ vr: **sich ~** to be sick, to vomit
Übergepäck nt excess baggage
Übergewicht nt excess weight; **(10 Kilo) ~ haben** to be (10 kilos) overweight
überglücklich adj overjoyed; (fam) over the moon
Übergröße f outsize
überhaupt adv at all; (im Allgemeinen) in general; (besonders) especially; **was willst du ~?** what is it you want?
überheblich adj arrogant
überholen vt to overtake; (Tech) to overhaul; **Überholspur** f overtaking (Brit) (o passing (US)) lane; **überholt** adj outdated

Überholverbot *nt*: **hier herrscht ~** you can't overtake here
überhören *vt* to miss, not to catch; (*absichtlich*) to ignore; **überladen** *irr vt* to overload ▷ *adj* (*fig*) cluttered; **überlassen** *irr vt*: **jdm etw ~** to leave sth to sb; **über|laufen** *irr vi* (*Flüssigkeit*) to overflow
überleben *vt, vi* to survive; **Überlebende(r)** *mf* survivor
überlegen *vt* to consider; **sich** (*dat*) **etw ~** to think about sth; **er hat es** (*dat*) **anders überlegt** he's changed his mind ▷ *adj* superior (*dat* to); **Überlegung** *f* consideration
überm *kontr von* **über dem**
übermäßig *adj* excessive
übermorgen *adv* the day after tomorrow
übernächste(r, s) *adj*: **~ Woche** the week after next
übernachten *vi* to spend the night (*bei jdm* at sb's place); **übernächtigt** *adj* bleary-eyed, very tired; **Übernachtung** *f* overnight stay; **~ mit Frühstück** bed and breakfast
übernehmen *irr vt* to take on; (*Amt, Geschäft*) to take over ▷ *vr*: **sich ~** to take on too much
überprüfen *vt* to check; **Überprüfung** *f* check; (*Überprüfen*) checking
überqueren *vt* to cross
überraschen *vt* to surprise; **Überraschung** *f* surprise
überreden *vt* to persuade; **er hat mich überredet** he talked me into it
überreichen *vt* to hand over
übers *kontr von* **über das**
überschätzen *vt* to overestimate; **überschlagen** *irr vt* (*berechnen*) to estimate; (*auslassen: Seite*) to skip ▷ *vr*: **sich**

~ to somersault; (*Auto*) to overturn; (*Stimme*) to crack; **überschneiden** *irr vr*: **sich ~** (*Linien etc*) to intersect; (*Termine*) to clash
Überschrift *f* heading
Überschwemmung *f* flood
Übersee *f*: **nach/in ~** overseas
übersehen *irr vt* (*Gelände*) to look (out) over; (*nicht beachten*) to overlook
übersetzen *vt* to translate (*aus* from, *in* +*akk* into); **Übersetzer(in)** (*-s, -*) *m(f)* translator; **Übersetzung** *f* translation
Übersicht *f* overall view; (*Darstellung*) survey; **übersichtlich** *adj* clear
überstehen *irr vt* (*durchstehen*) to get over; (*Winter etc*) to get through
Überstunden *pl* overtime *sing*
überstürzt *adj* hasty
überteuert *adj* overpriced
übertragbar *adj* transferable; (*Med*) infectious; **übertragen** *irr vt* to transfer (*auf* +*akk* to); (*Radio*) to broadcast; (*Krankheit*) to transmit ▷ *vr* to spread (*auf* +*akk* to) ▷ *adj* figurative; **Übertragung** *f* (*Radio*) broadcast; (*von Daten*) transmission
übertreffen *irr vt* to surpass
übertreiben *irr vt, vi* to exaggerate, to overdo; **Übertreibung** *f* exaggeration; **übertrieben** *adj* exaggerated, overdone
überwachen *vt* to supervise; (*Verdächtigen*) to keep under surveillance
überwand *imperf von* **überwinden**
überweisen *irr vt* to transfer; (*Patienten*) to refer (*an* +*akk* to); **Überweisung** *f* transfer; (*von Patienten*) referral

überwiegend adv mainly
überwinden (*überwand, überwunden*) vt to overcome ▷ vr: **sich ~** to make an effort, to force oneself; **überwunden** pp von **überwinden**
Überzelt nt flysheet
überzeugen vt to convince; **Überzeugung** f conviction
überziehen irr vt (*bedecken*) to cover; (*Jacke etc*) to put on; (*Konto*) to overdraw; **die Betten frisch ~** to change the sheets
üblich adj usual
übrig adj remaining; **ist noch Saft ~?** is there any juice left?; **die Übrigen** pl the rest pl; **im Übrigen** besides; **~ bleiben** to be left (over); **mir blieb nichts anderes ~(, als zu gehen)** I had no other choice (but to go); **übrigens** adv besides; (*nebenbei bemerkt*) by the way; **übrig|haben** irr vt: **für jdn etwas ~** (*fam: jdn mögen*) to have a soft spot for sb
Übung f practice; (*im Sport, Aufgabe etc*) exercise
Ufer (-s, -) nt (*Fluss*) bank; (*Meer, See*) shore; **am ~** on the bank/shore
Ufo (-(s), -s) nt akr = **unbekanntes Flugobjekt** UFO
Uhr (-, -en) f clock; (*am Arm*) watch; **wie viel ~ ist es?** what time is it?; **1 ~** 1 o'clock; **20 ~** 8 o'clock, 8 pm; **Uhrzeigersinn** m: **im ~** clockwise; **gegen den ~** anticlockwise (*Brit*), counterclockwise (*US*); **Uhrzeit** f time (of day)
Ukraine (-) f: **die ~** the Ukraine
UKW abk = **Ultrakurzwelle** VHF
Ulme (-, -n) f elm
Ultrakurzwelle f very high frequency; **Ultraschallaufnahme** f (*Med*) scan

○ SCHLÜSSELWORT

um prep +akk **1** (*um herum*) (a)round; **um Weihnachten** around Christmas; **er schlug um sich** he hit about him
2 (*mit Zeitangabe*) at; **um acht (Uhr)** at eight (o'clock)
3 (*mit Größenangabe*) by; **etw um 4 cm kürzen** to shorten sth by 4 cm; **um 10% teurer** 10% more expensive; **um vieles besser** better by far; **um so besser** so much the better
4 der Kampf um den Titel the battle for the title; **um Geld spielen** to play for money; **Stunde um Stunde** hour after hour; **Auge um Auge** an eye for an eye
▷ prep +gen: **um ... willen** for the sake of ...; **um Gottes willen** for goodness' o (*stärker*) God's sake
▷ konj: **um ... zu** (in order) to ...; **zu klug, um zu ...** too clever to ...; **siehe umso**
▷ adv **1** (*ungefähr*) about; **um (die) 30 Leute** about o around 30 people
2 (*vorbei*) **die 2 Stunden sind um** the two hours are up

umarmen vt to embrace
Umbau m rebuilding; (*zu etwas*) conversion (*zu into*); **um|bauen** vt to rebuild; (*zu etwas*) to convert (*zu into*)
um|blättern vt, vi to turn over
um|bringen irr vt to kill
um|buchen vi to change one's reservation/flight
um|drehen vt to turn (round); (*obere Seite nach unten*) to turn over ▷ vr: **sich ~** to turn (round); **Umdrehung** f turn; (*Phys, Auto*) revolution
um|fahren irr vt to knock down

um|fallen *irr vi* to fall over
Umfang *m (Ausmaß)* extent; *(von Buch)* size; *(Reichweite)* range; *(Math)* circumference;
umfangreich *adj* extensive
Umfeld *nt* environment
Umfrage *f* survey
Umgang *m* company; *(mit jdm)* dealings *pl*; **umgänglich** *adj* sociable; **Umgangssprache** *f* colloquial language, slang
Umgebung *f* surroundings *pl*; *(Milieu)* environment; *(Personen)* people around one
umgehen *irr vi (Gerücht)* to go round; **~ (können) mit** (know how to) handle ▷ *irr vt* to avoid; *(Schwierigkeit, Verbot)* to get round
um|gehen *irr vi*: **mit etw ~** to handle sth; **Umgehungsstraße** *f* bypass
umgekehrt *adj* reverse; *(gegenteilig)* opposite ▷ *adv* the other way round; **und ~** and vice versa
um|hören *vr*: **sich ~** to ask around; **um|kehren** *vi* to turn back ▷ *vt* to reverse; *(Kleidungsstück)* to turn inside out; **um|kippen** *vt* to tip over ▷ *vi* to overturn; *(fig)* to change one's mind; *(fam: ohnmächtig werden)* to pass out
Umkleidekabine *f* changing cubicle *(Brit)*, dressing room *(US)*; **Umkleideraum** *m* changing room
Umkreis *m* neighbourhood; **im ~ von** within a radius of
um|leiten *vt* to divert; **Umleitung** *f* diversion
um|rechnen *vt* to convert *(in +akk* into); **Umrechnung** *f* conversion; **Umrechnungskurs** *m* rate of exchange
Umriss *m* outline
um|rühren *vi, vt* to stir

ums *kontr von* **um das**
Umsatz *m* turnover
um|schalten *vi* to turn over
Umschlag *m* cover; *(Buch)* jacket; *(Med)* compress; *(Brief)* envelope
Umschulung *f* retraining
um|sehen *irr vr*: **sich ~** to look around; *(suchen)* to look out *(nach* for)
umso *adv* all the; **~ mehr** all the more; **~ besser** so much the better
umsonst *adv (vergeblich)* in vain; *(gratis)* for nothing
Umstand *m* circumstance; **Umstände** *(pl) (fig)* fuss; **in anderen Umständen sein** to be pregnant; **jdm Umstände machen** to cause sb a lot of trouble; **machen Sie bitte keine Umstände** please, don't put yourself out; **unter diesen/ keinen Umständen** under these/no circumstances; **unter Umständen** possibly; **umständlich** *adj (Methode)* complicated; *(Ausdrucksweise)* long-winded; *(Mensch)* ponderous; **Umstandsmode** *f* maternity wear
um|steigen *irr vi* to change (trains/buses)
um|stellen *vt (an anderen Ort)* to change round; *(Tech)* to convert ▷ *vr*: **sich ~** to adapt *(auf +akk* to); **Umstellung** *f* change; *(Umgewöhnung)* adjustment; *(Tech)* conversion
Umtausch *m* exchange; **um|tauschen** *vt* to exchange; *(Währung)* to change
Umweg *m* detour
Umwelt *f* environment; **Umweltbelastung** *f* ecological damage; **umweltbewusst** *adj* environmentally aware;

umweltfreundlich adj environment-friendly; **Umweltpapier** nt recycled paper; **umweltschädlich** adj harmful to the environment; **Umweltschutz** m environmental protection; **Umweltschützer(in)** (-s, -) m(f) environmentalist; **Umweltverschmutzung** f pollution; **umweltverträglich** adj environment-friendly

um|werfen irr vt to knock over; (fig: ändern) to upset; (fig, fam: jdn) to flabbergast

um|ziehen irr vt to change ▷ vr: **sich ~** to change ▷ vi to move (house); **Umzug** m (Straßenumzug) procession; (Wohnungsumzug) move

unabhängig adj independent; **Unabhängigkeitstag** m Independence Day, Fourth of July (US)

unabsichtlich adv unintentionally

unangenehm adj unpleasant; **Unannehmlichkeit** f inconvenience; **~en** pl trouble sing

unanständig adj indecent; **unappetitlich** adj (Essen) unappetizing; (abstoßend) off-putting; **unbeabsichtigt** adj unintentional; **unbedeutend** adj insignificant, unimportant; (Fehler) slight

unbedingt adj unconditional ▷ adv absolutely

unbefriedigend adj unsatisfactory; **unbegrenzt** adj unlimited; **unbekannt** adj unknown; **unbeliebt** adj unpopular; **unbemerkt** adj unnoticed; **unbequem** adj (Stuhl, Mensch) uncomfortable; (Regelung) inconvenient; **unbeständig** adj (Wetter) unsettled; (Lage) unstable;

(Mensch) unreliable; **unbestimmt** adj indefinite; **unbeteiligt** adj (nicht dazugehörig) uninvolved; (innerlich nicht berührt) indifferent, unconcerned; **unbewacht** adj unguarded; **unbewusst** adj unconscious; **unbezahlt** adj unpaid; **unbrauchbar** adj useless

und conj and; **~ so weiter** and so on; **na ~?** so what?

undankbar adj (Person) ungrateful; (Aufgabe) thankless; **undenkbar** adj inconceivable; **undeutlich** adj indistinct; **undicht** adj leaky; **uneben** adj uneven; **unecht** adj (Schmuck etc) fake; **unehelich** adj (Kind) illegitimate; **unendlich** adj endless; (Math) infinite; **unentbehrlich** adj indispensable; **unentgeltlich** adj free (of charge)

unentschieden adj undecided; **~ enden** (Sport) to end in a draw

unerfreulich adj unpleasant

unerhört adj unheard-of; (Bitte) outrageous; **unerlässlich** adj indispensable; **unerträglich** adj unbearable; **unerwartet** adj unexpected

unerwünscht adj unwelcome; (Eigenschaften) undesirable; **unfähig** adj incompetent; **~ sein, etw zu tun** to be incapable of doing sth; **unfair** adj unfair

Unfall m accident; **Unfallbericht** m accident report; **Unfallflucht** f failure to stop after an accident; **Unfallhergang** m: **den ~ schildern** to give details of the accident; **Unfallstation** f casualty ward; **Unfallstelle** f scene of the accident; **Unfallversicherung** f accident insurance

unfreundlich adj unfriendly

Ungarn (-s) nt Hungary

Ungeduld f impatience;
ungeduldig adj impatient
ungeeignet adj unsuitable
ungefähr adj approximate ▷ adv
approximately; **~ 10 Kilometres**
about 10 kilometres; **wann ~?**
about what time?; **wo ~?**
whereabouts?
ungefährlich adj harmless;
(sicher) safe
ungeheuer adj huge ▷ adv (fam)
enormously; **Ungeheuer** (-s, -) nt
monster
ungehorsam adj disobedient
(gegenüber to)
ungelegen adj inconvenient;
ungemütlich adj unpleasant;
(Mensch) disagreeable;
ungenießbar adj inedible;
(Getränk) undrinkable;
ungenügend adj unsatisfactory;
(Schulnote) ≈ F; **ungepflegt** adj
(Garten) untended; (Aussehen)
unkempt; (Hände) neglected;
ungerade adj odd
ungerecht adj unjust;
ungerechtfertigt adj unjusti-
fied; **Ungerechtigkeit** f
injustice, unfairness
ungern adv reluctantly;
ungeschickt adj clumsy;
ungeschminkt adj without
make-up; **ungesund** adj
unhealthy; **ungewiss** adj
uncertain; **ungewöhnlich** adj
unusual
Ungeziefer (-s) nt vermin pl
ungezogen adj ill-mannered
ungezwungen adj relaxed
ungiftig adj non-toxic
unglaublich adj incredible
Unglück (-(e)s, -e) nt (Unheil)
misfortune; (Pech) bad luck;
(Unglücksfall) disaster; (Verkehrs~)
accident; **das bringt ~** that's
unlucky; **unglücklich** adj
unhappy; (erfolglos) unlucky;

(unerfreulich) unfortunate;
unglücklicherweise adv
unfortunately
ungültig adj invalid
ungünstig adj inconvenient
unheilbar adj incurable; **~ krank
sein** to be terminally ill
unheimlich adj eerie ▷ adv (fam)
incredibly
unhöflich adj impolite
uni adj plain
Uni (-, -s) f uni
Uniform (-, -en) f uniform
Universität f university
Unkenntnis f ignorance
unklar adj unclear
Unkosten pl expenses pl;
Unkostenbeitrag m contribution (towards expenses)
Unkraut nt weeds pl, ~art, weed
unlogisch adj illogical
unmissverständlich adj
unambiguous
unmittelbar adj immediate;
~ darauf immediately afterwards
unmöbliert adj unfurnished
unmöglich adj impossible
unnahbar adj unapproachable
unnötig adj unnecessary
UNO (-) f akr = **United Nations
Organization** UN
unordentlich adj untidy;
Unordnung f disorder
unpassend adj inappropriate;
(Zeit) inconvenient; **unpersönlich**
adj impersonal; **unpraktisch** adj
impractical
Unrecht nt wrong; **zu ~** wrongly;
im ~ sein to be wrong; **unrecht**
adj wrong; **~ haben** to be
wrong
unregelmäßig adj irregular;
unreif adj unripe; **unruhig** adj
restless; **~ schlafen** to have a bad
night
uns pron akk, dat von **wir**; us, (to)
us; **~ (selbst)** (reflexiv) ourselves;

sehen Sie ~? can you see us?; **er schickte es ~** he sent it to us; **lasst ~ in Ruhe** leave us alone; **ein Freund von ~** a friend of ours; **wir haben ~ hingesetzt** we sat down; **wir haben ~ amüsiert** we enjoyed ourselves; **wir mögen ~** we like each other

unscharf adj (*Foto*) blurred, out of focus

unscheinbar adj insignificant; (*Aussehen*) unprepossessing

unschlüssig adj undecided

unschuldig adj innocent

unser pron (*adjektivisch*) our ▷ pron gen von **wir**; of us; **unsere(r, s)** pron (*substantivisch*) ours; **unseretwegen** adv (*wegen uns*) because of us; (*uns zuliebe*) for our sake; (*um uns*) about us; (*von uns aus*) as far as we are concerned

unseriös adj dubious; **unsicher** adj (*ungewiss*) uncertain; (*Person, Job*) insecure

Unsinn m nonsense

unsterblich adj immortal; **~ verliebt** madly in love

unsympathisch adj unpleasant; **er ist mir ~** I don't like him

unten adv below; (*im Haus*) downstairs; (*an der Treppe etc*) at the bottom; **nach ~** down

SCHLÜSSELWORT

unter prep +dat **1** (*räumlich, mit Zahlen*) under; (*drunter*) underneath, below; **unter 18 Jahren** under 18 years
2 (*zwischen*) among(st); **sie waren unter sich** they were by themselves; **einer unter ihnen** one of them; **unter anderem** among other things
▷ prep +akk under, below

Unterarm m forearm

unterbelichtet adj (*Foto*) underexposed

Unterbewusstsein nt subconscious

unterbrechen irr vt to interrupt; **Unterbrechung** f interruption; **ohne ~** nonstop

unterdrücken vt to suppress; (*Leute*) to oppress

unterdurchschnittlich adj below average

untere(r, s) adj lower

untereinander adv (*räumlich*) one below the other; (*gegenseitig*) each other; (*miteinander*) among themselves/yourselves/ourselves

Unterführung f underpass

untergehen irr vi to go down; (*Sonne*) to set; (*Volk*) to perish; (*Welt*) to come to an end; (*im Lärm*) to be drowned out

Untergeschoss nt basement; **Untergewicht** nt: (**3 Kilo) ~ haben** to be (3 kilos) underweight; **Untergrund** m foundation; (*Pol*) underground; **Untergrundbahn** f underground (*Brit*), subway (*US*)

unterhalb adv, prep +gen below; **~ von**

Unterhalt m maintenance; **unterhalten** irr vt to maintain; (*belustigen*) to entertain ▷ vr: **sich ~** to talk; (*sich belustigen*) to enjoy oneself; **Unterhaltung** f (*Belustigung*) entertainment; (*Gespräch*) talk, conversation

Unterhemd nt vest (*Brit*), undershirt (*US*); **Unterhose** f underpants pl; (*für Damen*) briefs pl

unterirdisch adj underground

Unterkiefer m lower jaw

Unterkunft (-, -künfte) f accommodation

Unterlage f (*Beleg*) document; (*Schreibunterlage*) pad

unterlassen *irr vt*: **es ~, etw zu tun** (*versäumen*) to fail to do sth; (*bleiben lassen*) to refrain from doing sth

unterlegen *adj* inferior (*dat* to); (*besiegt*) defeated

Unterleib *m* abdomen

Unterlippe *f* lower lip

Untermiete *f*: **zur ~ wohnen** to be a subtenant; **Untermieter(in)** *m(f)* subtenant

unternehmen *irr vt* (*Reise*) to go on; (*Versuch*) to make; **etwas ~ to** do something (*gegen* about); **Unternehmen** (*-s, -*) *nt* undertaking; (*Comm*) company; **Unternehmensberater(in)** (*-s, -*) *m(f)* management consultant; **Unternehmer(in)** (*-s, -*) *m(f)* entrepreneur

Unterricht (*-(e)s, -e*) *m* lessons *pl*; **unterrichten** *vt* to teach

unterschätzen *vt* to underestimate

unterscheiden *irr vt* to distinguish (*von* from, *zwischen* +*dat* between) ⊳ *vr*: **sich ~** to differ (*von* from)

Unterschenkel *m* lower leg

Unterschied (*-(e)s, -e*) *m* difference; **im ~ zu dir** unlike you; **unterschiedlich** *adj* different

unterschreiben *irr vt* to sign; **Unterschrift** *f* signature

Untersetzer (*-s, -*) *m* tablemat; (*für Gläser*) coaster

unterste(r, s) *adj* lowest, bottom

unter|stellen *vr*: **sich ~** to take shelter

unterstellen *vt* (*rangmäßig*) to subordinate (*dat* to); (*fig*) to impute (*jdm etw* sth to sb)

unterstreichen *irr vt* (*a. fig*) to underline

Unterstrich *m* (*Inform*) underscore

unterstützen *vt* to support; **Unterstützung** *f* support

untersuchen *vt* (*Med*) to examine; (*Polizei*) to investigate; **Untersuchung** *f* examination; (*polizeiliche*) investigation

untertags *adv* during the day

Untertasse *f* saucer

Unterteil *nt* lower part, bottom

Untertitel *m* subtitle

untervermieten *vt* to sublet

Unterwäsche *f* underwear

unterwegs *adv* on the way

unterzeichnen *vt* to sign

untreu *adj* unfaithful

untröstlich *adj* inconsolable; **unüberlegt** *adj* ill-considered ⊳ *adv* without thinking; **unüblich** *adj* unusual; **unverantwortlich** *adj* irresponsible; (*unentschuldbar*) inexcusable

unverbindlich *adj* not binding; (*Antwort*) noncommittal ⊳ *adv* (*Comm*) without obligation

unverbleit *adj* unleaded; **unverheiratet** *adj* unmarried, single; **unvermeidlich** *adj* unavoidable; **unvernünftig** *adj* silly; **unverschämt** *adj* impudent; **unverständlich** *adj* incomprehensible; **unverträglich** *adj* (*Person*) quarrelsome; (*Essen*) indigestible

unverwüstlich *adj* indestructible; (*Mensch*) irrepressible

unverzeihlich *adj* unpardonable; **unverzüglich** *adj* immediate; **unvollständig** *adj* incomplete; **unvorsichtig** *adj* careless

unwahrscheinlich *adj* improbable, unlikely ⊳ *adv* (*fam*) incredibly

Unwetter *nt* thunderstorm

unwichtig *adj* unimportant

unwiderstehlich *adj* irresistible

Verband m (Med) bandage; (Bund) association; **Verband(s)kasten** m first-aid box; **Verband(s)zeug** nt dressing material

verbergen irr vt to hide (vor +dat from) ▷ vr: **sich ~** to hide (vor +dat from)

verbessern vt to improve; (berichtigen) to correct ▷ vr: **sich ~** to improve; (berichtigen) to correct oneself; **Verbesserung** f improvement; (Berichtigung) correction

verbiegen irr vi to bend ▷ vr: **sich ~** to bend

verbieten irr vt to forbid; **jdm ~, etw zu tun** to forbid sb to do sth

verbinden irr vt to connect; (kombinieren) to combine; (Med) to bandage; **können Sie mich mit ... ~?** (Tel) can you put me through to ...?; **ich verbinde** (Tel) I'm putting you through ▷ vr (Chem) **sich ~** to combine

verbindlich adj binding; (freundlich) friendly; **Verbindung** f connection

verbleit adj leaded

verblüffen vt to amaze

verblühen vi to fade

verborgen adj hidden

Verbot (-(e)s, -e) nt ban (für, von on); **verboten** adj forbidden; **es ist ~** it's not allowed; **es ist ~, hier zu parken** you're not allowed to park here; **Rauchen ~** no smoking

verbrannt adj burnt

Verbrauch (-(e)s) m consumption; **verbrauchen** vt to use up; **Verbraucher(in)** (-s, -) m(f) consumer

Verbrechen (-s, -) nt crime; **Verbrecher(in)** (-s, -) m(f) criminal

verbreiten vt to spread ▷ vr: **sich ~** to spread

verbrennen irr vt to burn; **Verbrennung** f burning; (in Motor) combustion

verbringen irr vt to spend

verbunden adj: **falsch ~** sorry, wrong number

Verdacht (-(e)s) m suspicion; **verdächtig** adj suspicious; **verdächtigen** vt to suspect

verdammt interj (fam) damn

verdanken vt: **jdm etw ~** to owe sth to sb

verdarb imperf von **verderben**

verdauen vt (a. fig) to digest; **verdaulich** adj digestible; **das ist schwer ~** that is hard to digest; **Verdauung** f digestion

Verdeck (-(e)s, -e) nt top

verderben (verdarb, verdorben) vt to spoil; (schädigen) to ruin; (moralisch) to corrupt; **es sich** (dat) **mit jdm ~** to get into sb's bad books; **ich habe mir den Magen verdorben** I've got an upset stomach ▷ vi (Lebensmittel) to go off

verdienen vt to earn; (moralisch) to deserve; **Verdienst** (-(e)s, -e) m earnings pl ▷ (-(e)s, -e) nt merit; (Leistung) service (um to sb)

verdoppeln vt to double

verdorben pp von **verderben** ▷ adj spoilt; (geschädigt) ruined; (moralisch) corrupt

verdrehen vt to twist; (Augen) to roll; **jdm den Kopf ~** (fig) to turn sb's head

verdünnen vt to dilute

verdunsten vi to evaporate

verdursten vi to die of thirst

verehren vt to admire; (Rel) to worship; **Verehrer(in)** (-s, -) m(f) admirer

Verein (-(e)s, -e) m association; (Klub) club

vereinbar adj compatible

vereinbaren *vt* to arrange; **Vereinbarung** *f* agreement, arrangement
vereinigen *vt* to unite ▷ *vr*: **sich ~** to unite; **Vereinigtes Königreich** *nt* United Kingdom; **Vereinigte Staaten (von Amerika)** *pl* United States *sing* (of America); **Vereinigung** *f* union; (*Verein*) association; **Vereinte Nationen** *pl* United Nations *pl*
vereisen *vi* (*Straße*) to freeze over; (*Fenster*) to ice up ▷ *vt* (*Med*) to freeze
vererben *vt*: **jdm etw ~** to leave sth to sb; (*Bio*) to pass sth on to sb ▷ *vr*: **sich ~** to be hereditary; **vererblich** *adj* hereditary
verfahren *irr vi* to proceed ▷ *vr*: **sich ~** to get lost; **Verfahren** (*-s, -*) *nt* procedure; (*Tech*) method; (*Jur*) proceedings *pl*
verfallen *irr vi* to decline; (*Haus*) to be falling apart; (*Fin*) to lapse; (*Fahrkarte etc*) to expire; **~ in** (*+akk*) to lapse into; **Verfallsdatum** *nt* expiry (*Brit*) (*o* expiration (*US*)) date; (*von Lebensmitteln*) best-before date
verfärben *vr*: **sich ~** to change colour; (*Wäsche*) to discolour
Verfasser(in) (*-s, -*) *m(f)* author, writer; **Verfassung** *f* (*gesundheitlich*) condition; (*Pol*) constitution
verfaulen *vi* to rot
verfehlen *vt* to miss
verfeinern *vt* to refine
Verfilmung *f* film (*o* screen) version
verfluchen *vt* to curse
verfolgen *vt* to pursue; (*Pol*) to persecute
verfügbar *adj* available; **verfügen** *vi* **über etw** (*akk*) **~** to have sth at one's disposal;

Verfügung *f* order; **jdm zur ~ stehen** to be at sb's disposal; **jdm etw zur ~ stellen** to put sth at sb's disposal
verführen *vt* to tempt; (*sexuell*) to seduce; **verführerisch** *adj* seductive
vergangen *adj* past; **~e Woche** last week; **Vergangenheit** *f* past
Vergaser (*-s, -*) *m* (*Auto*) carburettor
vergaß *imperf von* **vergessen**
vergeben *irr vt* to forgive (*jdm etw* sb for sth); (*weggeben*) to award, to allocate; **vergebens** *adv* in vain; **vergeblich** *adv* in vain ▷ *adj* vain, futile
vergehen *irr vi* to pass ▷ *vr*: **sich an jdm ~** to indecently assault sb; **Vergehen** (*-s, -*) *nt* offence
Vergeltung *f* retaliation
vergessen (*vergaß, vergessen*) *vt* to forget; **vergesslich** *adj* forgetful
vergeuden *vt* to squander, to waste
vergewaltigen *vt* to rape; **Vergewaltigung** *f* rape
vergewissern *vr*: **sich ~** to make sure
vergiften *vt* to poison; **Vergiftung** *f* poisoning
Vergissmeinnicht (*-(e)s, -e*) *nt* forget-me-not
Vergleich (*-(e)s, -e*) *m* comparison; (*Jur*) settlement; **im ~ zu** compared to (*o* with); **vergleichen** *irr vt* to compare (*mit* with)
Vergnügen (*-s, -*) *nt* pleasure; **viel ~!** enjoy yourself; **vergnügt** *adj* cheerful; **Vergnügungspark** *m* amusement park
vergoldet *adj* gold-plated
vergriffen *adj* (*Buch*) out of print; (*Ware*) out of stock

vergrößern *vt* to enlarge; (*Menge*) to increase; (*mit Lupe*) to magnify; **Vergrößerung** *f* enlargement; (*Menge*) increase; (*mit Lupe*) magnification; **Vergrößerungsglas** *nt* magnifying glass

verh. *adj abk* = **verheiratet** married

verhaften *vt* to arrest

verhalten *irr vr*: **sich ~** (*sich benehmen*) to behave; (*Sache*) to be; **Verhalten** (*-s*) *nt* behaviour

Verhältnis *nt* relationship (*zu* with); (*Math*) ratio; **~se** *pl* circumstances *pl*, conditions *pl*; **im ~ von 1 zu 2** in a ratio of 1 to 2; **verhältnismäßig** *adj* relative ▷ *adv* relatively

verhandeln *vi* to negotiate (*über etw akk* sth); **Verhandlung** *f* negotiation

verheimlichen *vt* to keep secret (*jdm* from sb)

verheiratet *adj* married

verhindern *vt* to prevent; **sie ist verhindert** she can't make it

Verhör (*-(e)s, -e*) *nt* interrogation; (*gerichtlich*) examination; **verhören** *vt* to interrogate; (*bei Gericht*) to examine ▷ *vr*: **sich ~** to mishear

verhungern *vi* to starve to death

verhüten *vt* to prevent; **Verhütung** *f* prevention; (*mit Pille, Kondom etc*) contraception; **Verhütungsmittel** *nt* contraceptive

verirren *vr*: **sich ~** to get lost

Verkauf *m* sale; **verkaufen** *vt* to sell; **zu ~** for sale; **Verkäufer(in)** *m(f)* seller; (*beruflich*) salesperson; (*in Laden*) shop assistant (*Brit*), salesperson (*US*); **verkäuflich** *adj* for sale

Verkehr (*-s, -e*) *m* traffic; (*Sex*) intercourse; (*Umlauf*) circulation; **verkehren** *vi* (*Bus etc*) to run; **~ in** to frequent; **~ mit** to associate (*o* mix) with; **Verkehrsampel** *f* traffic lights *pl*; **Verkehrsamt** *nt* tourist information office; **verkehrsfrei** *adj* traffic-free; **Verkehrsfunk** *m* travel news *sing*; **Verkehrsinsel** *f* traffic island; **Verkehrsmeldung** *f* traffic report; **Verkehrsmittel** *nt* means *sing* of transport; **öffentliche ~** *pl* public transport *sing*; **Verkehrsschild** *nt* traffic sign; **Verkehrstote(r)** *mf* road casualty; **die Zahl der ~n** the number of deaths on the road; **Verkehrsunfall** *m* road accident; **Verkehrszeichen** *nt* traffic sign

verkehrt *adj* wrong; (*verkehrt herum*) the wrong way round; (*Pullover etc*) inside out; **du machst es ~** you're doing it wrong

verklagen *vt* to take to court

verkleiden *vt* to dress up (*als* as) ▷ *vr*: **sich ~** to dress up (*als* as); (*um unerkannt zu bleiben*) to disguise oneself; **Verkleidung** *f* (*Karneval*) fancy dress; (*um nicht erkannt zu werden*) disguise

verkleinern *vt* to reduce; (*Zimmer, Gebiet etc*) to make smaller

verkneifen *irr vt*: **sich** (*dat*) **etw ~** (*Lachen*) to stifle sth; (*Schmerz*) to hide sth; (*sich versagen*) to do without sth; **verkommen** *irr vi* to deteriorate; (*Mensch*) to go downhill ▷ *adj* (*Haus*) dilapidated; (*moralisch*) depraved; **verkraften** *vt* to cope with

verkratzt *adj* scratched

verkühlen *vr*: **sich ~** to get a chill

verkürzen *vt* to shorten

Verlag (*-(e)s, -e*) *m* publishing company

verlangen *vt* (*fordern*) to

demand; (*wollen*) to want; (*Preis*) to ask; (*Qualifikation*) to require; (*erwarten*) to ask (*von of*); (*fragen nach*) to ask for; (*Pass etc*) to ask to see; **~ Sie Herrn X** ask for Mr X ▷ *vi*: **~ nach** to ask for

verlängern *vt* to extend; (*Pass, Erlaubnis*) renew; **Verlängerung** *f* extension; (*Sport*) extra time; (*von Pass, Erlaubnis*) renewal; **Verlängerungsschnur** *f* extension cable; **Verlängerungswoche** *f* extra week

verlassen *irr vt* to leave ▷ *irr vr*: **sich ~** to rely (*auf +akk on*) ▷ *adj* desolate; (*Mensch*) abandoned; **verlässlich** *adj* reliable

Verlauf *m* course; **verlaufen** *irr vi* (*Weg, Grenze*) to run (*entlang along*); (*zeitlich*) to pass; (*Farben*) to run ▷ *vr*: **sich ~** to get lost; (*Menschenmenge*) to disperse

verlegen *vt* to move; (*verlieren*) to mislay; (*Buch*) to publish ▷ *adj* embarrassed; **Verlegenheit** *f* embarrassment; (*Situation*) difficulty

Verleih (*-(e)s, -e*) *m* (*Firma*) hire company (*Brit*), rental company (*US*); **verleihen** *irr vt* to lend; (*vermieten*) to hire (out) (*Brit*), to rent (out) (*US*); (*Preis, Medaille*) to award

verleiten *vt*: **jdn dazu ~, etw zu tun** to induce sb to do sth

verlernen *vt* to forget

verletzen *vt* to injure; (*fig*) to hurt; **Verletzte(r)** *mf* injured person; **Verletzung** *f* injury; (*Verstoß*) violation

verlieben *vr*: **sich ~** to fall in love (*in jdn with sb*); **verliebt** *adj* in love

verlieren (*verlor, verloren*) *vt, vi* to lose

verloben *vr*: **sich ~** to get engaged (*mit to*); **Verlobte(r)** *mf* fiancé/fiancée; **Verlobung** *f* engagement

verlor *imperf von* **verlieren**

verloren *pp von* **verlieren** ▷ *adj* lost; (*Eier*) poached; **~ gehen** to go missing

verlosen *vt* to raffle; **Verlosung** *f* raffle

Verlust (*-(e)s, -e*) *m* loss

vermehren *vt* to multiply; (*Menge*) to increase ▷ *vr*: **sich ~** to multiply; (*Menge*) to increase

vermeiden *irr vt* to avoid

vermeintlich *adj* supposed

vermieten *vt* to rent (out), to let (out) (*Brit*); (*Auto*) to hire (out) (*Brit*), to rent (out) (*US*); **Vermieter(in)** *m(f)* landlord/-lady

vermischen *vt* to mix ▷ *vr*: **sich ~** to mix

vermissen *vt* to miss; **vermisst** *adj* missing; **jdn als ~ melden** to report sb missing

Vermittlung *f* (*bei Streit*) mediation; (*Herbeiführung*) arranging; (*Stelle*) agency

Vermögen (*-s, -*) *nt* fortune

vermuten *vt* to suppose; (*argwöhnen*) to suspect; **vermutlich** *adj* probable ▷ *adv* probably; **Vermutung** *f* supposition; (*Verdacht*) suspicion

vernachlässigen *vt* to neglect

vernichten *vt* to destroy; **vernichtend** *adj* (*fig*) crushing; (*Blick*) withering; (*Kritik*) scathing

Vernunft (*-*) *f* reason; **ich kann ihn nicht zur ~ bringen** I can't make him see reason; **vernünftig** *adj* sensible; (*Preis*) reasonable

veröffentlichen *vt* to publish

verordnen *vt* (*Med*) to prescribe; **Verordnung** *f* order; (*Med*) prescription

verpachten *vt* to lease (out) (*an +akk to*)

verpacken vt to pack; (*einwickeln*) to wrap up

Verpackung f packaging; **Verpackungskosten** pl packing charges pl

verpassen vt to miss

verpflegen vt to feed; **Verpflegung** f feeding; (*Kost*) food; (*in Hotel*) board

verpflichten vt to oblige; (*anstellen*) to engage ▷ vr: **sich ~** to commit oneself (*etw zu tun* to doing sth)

verprügeln vt to beat up

verraten irr vt to betray; (*Geheimnis*) to divulge; **aber nicht ~!** but don't tell anyone ▷ vr: **sich ~** to give oneself away

verrechnen vt: **~ mit** to set off against ▷ vr: **sich ~** to miscalculate; **Verrechnungsscheck** m crossed cheque (*Brit*), check for deposit only (*US*)

verregnet adj rainy

verreisen vi to go away (*nach* to); **sie ist (geschäftlich) verreist** she's away (on business); **verrenken** vt to contort; (*Med*) to dislocate; **sich** (*dat*) **den Knöchel ~** to sprain (*o* twist) one's ankle; **verringern** vt to reduce

verrostet adj rusty

verrückt adj mad, crazy; **es macht mich ~** it's driving me mad

versagen vi to fail; **Versagen** (*-s*) nt failure; **Versager(in)** (*-s, -*) m(f) failure

versalzen irr vt to put too much salt in/on

versammeln vt to assemble, to gather ▷ vr: **sich ~** to assemble, to gather; **Versammlung** f meeting

Versand (*-(e)s*) m dispatch; (*Abteilung*) dispatch department; **Versandhaus** nt mail-order company

versäumen vt to miss; (*unterlassen*) to neglect; **~, etw zu tun** to fail to do sth

verschätzen vr: **sich ~** to miscalculate

verschenken vt to give away; (*Chance*) to waste

verschicken vt to send off

verschieben vt irr (*auf später*) to postpone, to put off; (*an anderen Ort*) to move

verschieden adj (*unterschiedlich*) different; (*mehrere*) various; **sie sind ~ groß** they are of different sizes; **Verschiedene** pl various people/things pl; **Verschiedenes** various things pl

verschimmelt adj mouldy

verschlafen irr vt to sleep through; (*fig*) to miss ▷ vi to oversleep

verschlechtern vr: **sich ~** to deteriorate, to get worse; **Verschlechterung** f deterioration

Verschleiß (*-es*) m wear and tear

verschließbar adj lockable; **verschließen** irr vt to close; (*mit Schlüssel*) to lock

verschlimmern vt to make worse ▷ vr: **sich ~** to get worse

verschlossen adj locked; (*fig*) reserved

verschlucken vt to swallow ▷ vr: **sich ~** to choke (*an +dat* on)

Verschluss m lock; (*von Kleid*) fastener; (*Foto*) shutter; (*Stöpsel*) stopper

verschmutzen vt to get dirty; (*Umwelt*) to pollute

verschnaufen vi: **ich muss mal ~** I need to get my breath back

verschneit adj snow-covered

verschnupft adj: **~ sein** to have a cold; (*fam: beleidigt*) to be peeved

verschonen vt to spare (*jdn mit etw* sb sth)

verschreiben *irr vt* (*Med*) to prescribe;
verschreibungspflichtig *adj* available only on prescription
verschwand *imperf von* **verschwinden**
verschweigen *irr vt* to keep secret; **jdm etw ~** to keep sth from sb
verschwenden *vt* to waste; **Verschwendung** *f* waste
verschwiegen *adj* discreet; (*Ort*) secluded
verschwinden (*verschwand, verschwunden*) *vi* to disappear, to vanish; **verschwinde!** get lost!;
verschwunden *pp von* **verschwinden**
Versehen (-s, -) *nt*: **aus ~** by mistake; **versehentlich** *adv* by mistake
versenden *irr vt* to send off
versessen *adj* **~ auf** (+*akk*) mad about
versetzen *vt* to transfer; (*verpfänden*) to pawn; (*fam: bei Verabredung*) to stand up ▷ *vr*: **sich in jdn** (*o* **jds Lage**) **~** to put oneself in sb's place
verseuchen *vt* to contaminate
versichern *vt* to insure; (*bestätigen*) to assure; **versichert sein** to be insured;
Versichertenkarte *f* health-insurance card; **Versicherung** *f* insurance; **Versicherungskarte** *f*: **grüne ~** green card (*Brit*), insurance document for driving abroad; **Versicherungspolice** *f* insurance policy
versilbert *adj* silver-plated
versinken *irr vi* to sink
Version *f* version
versöhnen *vt* to reconcile ▷ *vr*: **sich ~** to become reconciled
versorgen *vt* to provide, to supply (*mit* with); (*Familie*) to look after ▷ *vr*: **sich ~** to look after oneself; **Versorgung** *f* provision; (*Unterhalt*) maintenance; (*für Alter etc*) benefit
verspäten *vr*: **sich ~** to be late; **verspätet** *adj* late; **Verspätung** *f* delay; (**eine Stunde**) **~ haben** to be (an hour) late
versprechen *irr vt* to promise ▷ *vr*: **ich habe mich versprochen** I didn't mean to say that
Verstand *m* mind; (*Vernunft*) (common) sense; **den ~ verlieren** to lose one's mind; **verständigen** *vt* to inform ▷ *vr*: **sich ~** to communicate; (*sich einigen*) to come to an understanding; **Verständigung** *f* communication; **verständlich** *adj* understandable; **Verständnis** *nt* understanding (*für* of); (*Mitgefühl*) sympathy; **verständnisvoll** *adj* understanding
verstauchen *vt* to sprain; **verstaucht** *pp von* **verstauchen** sprained
Versteck (-(e)s, -e) *nt* hiding place; **~ spielen** to play hide-and-seek; **verstecken** *vt* to hide (*vor* +*dat* from) ▷ *vr*: **sich ~** to hide (*vor* +*dat* from)
verstehen *irr vt* to understand; **falsch ~** to misunderstand ▷ *vr*: **sich ~** to get on (*mit* with)
Versteigerung *f* auction
verstellbar *adj* adjustable; **verstellen** *vt* to move; (*Uhr*) to adjust; (*versperren*) to block; (*Stimme, Handschrift*) to disguise ▷ *vr*: **sich ~** to pretend, to put on an act
verstopfen *vt* to block up; (*Med*) to constipate; **Verstopfung** *f* obstruction; (*Med*) constipation
Verstoß *m* infringement, violation (*gegen* of)

Versuch (-(e)s, -e) m attempt; (wissenschaftlich) experiment; **versuchen** vt to try
vertauschen vt to exchange; (versehentlich) to mix up
verteidigen vt to defend; **Verteidiger(in)** (-s, -) m(f) (Sport) defender; (Jur) defence counsel; **Verteidigung** f defence
verteilen vt to distribute
Vertrag (-(e)s, Verträge) m contract; (Pol) treaty
vertragen irr vt to stand, to bear ▷ vr: **sich ~** to get along (with each other); (sich aussöhnen) to make it up
verträglich adj (Mensch) good-natured; (Speisen) digestible
vertrauen vi: **jdm/einer Sache ~** to trust sb/sth; **Vertrauen** (-s) nt trust (in +akk in, zu in); **ich habe kein ~ zu ihm** I don't trust him; **ich hab's ihm im ~ gesagt** I told him in confidence; **vertraulich** adj (geheim) confidential; **vertraut** adj: **sich mit etw ~ machen** to familiarize oneself with sth
vertreten irr vt to represent; (Ansicht) to hold; **Vertreter(in)** (-s, -) m(f) representative
Vertrieb (-(e)s, -e) m (Abteilung) sales department
vertrocknen vi to dry up
vertun irr vr: **sich ~** to make a mistake
vertuschen vt to cover up
verunglücken vi to have an accident; **tödlich ~** to be killed in an accident
verunsichern vt to make uneasy
verursachen vt to cause
verurteilen vt to condemn
vervielfältigen vt to make copies of
verwählen vr: **sich ~** to dial the wrong number

verwalten vt to manage; (behördlich) to administer; **Verwalter(in)** (-s, -) m(f) manager; (Vermögens~) trustee; **Verwaltung** f management; (amtlich) administration
verwandt adj related (mit to); **Verwandte(r)** mf relative, relation; **Verwandtschaft** f relationship; (Menschen) relations pl
verwarnen vt to warn; (Sport) to caution
verwechseln vt to confuse (mit with); (halten für) to mistake (mit for)
verweigern vt to refuse
verwenden vt to use; (Zeit) to spend; **Mühe auf etw** (akk) **~ to** take trouble over sth; **Verwendung** f use
verwirklichen vt to realize; **sich selbst ~** to fulfil oneself
verwirren vt to confuse; **Verwirrung** f confusion
verwitwet adj widowed
verwöhnen vt to spoil
verwunderlich adj surprising; **Verwunderung** f astonishment
verwüsten vt to devastate
verzählen vr: **sich ~** to miscount
verzehren vt to consume
Verzeichnis nt (Liste) list; (Katalog) catalogue; (in Buch) index; (Inform) directory
verzeihen (verzieh, verziehen) vt, vi to forgive (jdm etw sb for sth); **~ Sie bitte, ...** (vor Frage etc) excuse me, ...; **~ Sie die Störung** sorry to disturb you; **Verzeihung** f: **~!** sorry; **~, ...** (vor Frage etc) excuse me, ...; **(jdn) um ~ bitten** to apologize (to sb)
verzichten vi **auf etw** (akk) **~ to** do without sth; (aufgeben) to give sth up

verzieh *imperf von* **verzeihen**
verziehen *pp von* **verzeihen**
verziehen *irr vt* (*Kind*) to spoil;
das Gesicht ~ to pull a face ▷ *vr:*
sich ~ to go out of shape; (*Gesicht*)
to contort; (*verschwinden*) to
disappear
verzieren *vt* to decorate
verzögern *vt* to delay ▷ *vr:* **sich**
~ to be delayed; **Verzögerung** *f*
delay
verzweifeln *vi* to despair (*an*
+dat of); **verzweifelt** *adj*
desperate; **Verzweiflung** *f*
despair
Veterinär(in) (*-s, -e*) *m(f)* veter-
inary surgeon (*Brit*), veterinarian
(*US*)
Vetter (*-s, -n*) *m* cousin
vgl. *abk =* **vergleiche** cf
Viagra® (*-s*) *nt* Viagra®
Vibrator (*-s, -en*) *m* vibrator;
vibrieren *vi* to vibrate
Video (*-s, -s*) *nt* video; **auf**
~ aufnehmen to video; **Videoclip**
(*-s, -s*) *m* video clip; **Videofilm**
m video; **Videogerät** *nt* video
(recorder); **Videokamera** *f* video
camera; **Videokassette** *f* video
(cassette); **Videorekorder** *m*
video recorder; **Videospiel** *nt*
video game; **Videothek** (*-, -en*) *f*
video library
Vieh (*-(e)s*) *nt* cattle
viel *pron* a lot (of), lots of; **~ Arbeit**
a lot of work, lots of work; **~e**
Leute a lot of people, lots of
people, many people; **zu ~** too
much; **zu ~e** too many; **sehr ~** a
great deal of; **sehr ~e** a great
many; **ziemlich ~/~e** quite a lot
of; **nicht ~** not much, not a lot of;
nicht ~e not many, not a lot of
▷ *pron* a lot; **sie sagt nicht ~** she
doesn't say a lot; **nicht ~** not
much, not a lot of; **nicht ~e** not
many, not a lot of; **gibt es ~?** is

there much?, is there a lot?; **gibt**
es ~e? are there many?, are there a
lot? ▷ *adv* a lot; **er geht ~ ins Kino**
he goes a lot to the cinema; **sehr**
~ a great deal; **ziemlich ~** quite a
lot; **~ besser** much better;
~ teurer much more expensive;
~ zu ~ far too much
vielleicht *adv* perhaps; **~ ist sie**
krank perhaps she's ill, she might
be ill; **weißt du ~, wo er ist?** do
you know where he is (by any
chance)?
vielmal(s) *adv* many times;
danke ~s many thanks; **vielmehr**
adv rather; **vielseitig** *adj* very
varied; (*Mensch, Gerät*) versatile
vier *num* four; **auf allen ~en** on all
fours; **unter ~ Augen** in private,
privately; **Vier** (*-, -en*) *f* four;
(*Schulnote*) ≈ D; **Vierbettzimmer**
nt four-bed room; **Viereck** (*-(e)s,*
-e) *nt* four-sided figure; (*Quadrat*)
square; **viereckig** *adj* four-sided;
(*quadratisch*) square; **vierfach**
adj: **die ~e Menge** four times the
amount; **vierhundert** *num* four
hundred; **viermal** *adv* four
times; **vierspurig** *adj* four-lane
viert *adv:* **wir sind zu ~** there are
four of us; **vierte(r, s)** *adj* fourth;
siehe auch **dritte**
Viertel (*-s, -*) *nt* (*Stadtviertel*)
quarter, district; (*Bruchteil*)
quarter; (*Viertelliter*) quarter-litre;
(*Uhrzeit*) quarter; **~ vor/nach drei**
a quarter to/past three; **viertel**
drei a quarter past two; **drei**
viertel drei a quarter to three;
Viertelfinale *nt* quarter-final;
vierteljährlich *adj* quarterly;
Viertelstunde *f* quarter of an
hour
vierzehn *num* fourteen; **in**
~ Tagen in two weeks, in a
fortnight (*Brit*); **vierzehntägig** *adj*
two-week, fortnightly (*Brit*);

vierzehnte(r, s) adj fourteenth;
siehe auch **dritte**; **vierzig** num
forty; **vierzigste(r, s)** adj
fortieth
Vietnam (-s) nt Vietnam
Vignette f (Autobahn~)
motorway (Brit) (o freeway (US))
permit
Villa (-, Villen) f villa
violett adj purple
Violine f violin
Virus (-, Viren) m o nt virus
Visitenkarte f card
Visum (-s, Visa o Visen) nt visa
Vitamin (-s, -e) nt vitamin
Vitrine (-, -n) f (glass) cabinet;
(Schaukasten) display case
Vogel (-s, Vögel) m bird;
Vogelgrippe f bird flu, avian flu;
vögeln vi, vt (vulg) to screw
Voicemail (-, -s) f voice mail
Vokal (-s, -e) m vowel
Volk (-(e)s, Völker) nt people pl;
(Nation) nation; **Volksfest** nt
festival; (Jahrmarkt) funfair;
Volkshochschule f adult
education centre; **Volkslied** nt
folksong; **Volksmusik** f folk
music; **volkstümlich** adj (einfach
und beliebt) popular; (herkömmlich)
traditional; (Kunst) folk
voll adj full (von of); **voll**|**machen**
vt to fill (up); **voll**|**tanken** vi to
fill up
Vollbart m beard; **Vollbremsung**
f: **eine ~ machen** to slam on
the brakes; **vollends** adv
completely
Volleyball m volleyball
Vollgas nt: **mit ~** at full throttle;
~ geben to step on it
völlig adj complete ▷ adv
completely
volljährig adj of age;
Vollkaskoversicherung f fully
comprehensive insurance;
vollklimatisiert adj fully

air-conditioned; **vollkommen**
adj perfect; **~er Unsinn** complete
rubbish ▷ adv completely
Vollkornbrot nt wholemeal
(Brit) (o whole wheat (US)) bread
Vollmacht (-, -en) f authority;
(Urkunde) power of attorney
Vollmilch f full-fat milk (Brit),
whole milk (US);
Vollmilchschokolade f milk
chocolate; **Vollmond** m full
moon; **Vollnarkose** f general
anaesthetic; **Vollpension** f full
board
vollständig adj complete
Volltreffer m direct hit;
Vollwertkost f wholefood;
vollzählig adj complete
Volt (-, -) nt volt
Volumen (-s, -) nt volume
vom kontr von **von dem** (räumlich,
zeitlich, Ursache) from; **ich kenne
sie nur ~ Sehen** I only know her by
sight

von prep +dat **1** (Ausgangspunkt)
from; **von ... bis** from ... to; **von
morgens bis abends** from
morning till night; **von ... nach**
from ... to ...; **von ... an** from ...;
von ... aus from ...; **von dort aus**
from there; **etw von sich aus tun**
to do sth of one's own accord; **von
mir aus** (fam) if you like, I don't
mind; **von wo/wann ...?**
where/when ... from?
2 (Ursache, im Passiv) by; **ein
Gedicht von Schiller** a poem by
Schiller; **von etw müde** tired from
sth
3 (als Genitiv) of; **ein Freund von
mir** a friend of mine; **nett von dir**
nice of you; **jeweils zwei von zehn**
two out of every ten
4 (über) about; **er erzählte vom**

Urlaub he talked about his holiday **5 von wegen!** (*fam*) no way!

voneinander *adv* from each other

 SCHLÜSSELWORT

vor *prep* +*dat* **1** (*räumlich*) in front of; **vor der Kirche links abbiegen** turn left before the church **2** (*zeitlich*) before; **ich war vor ihm da** I was there before him; **vor 2 Tagen** 2 days ago; **5 (Minuten) vor 4** 5 (minutes) to 4; **vor Kurzem** a little while ago **3** (*Ursache*) with; **vor Wut/Liebe** with rage/love; **vor Hunger sterben** to die of hunger; **vor lauter Arbeit** because of work **4 vor allem, vor allen Dingen** most of all
▷ *prep* +*akk* (*räumlich*) in front of
▷ *adv*: **vor und zurück** backwards and forwards

voran|gehen *irr vi* to go ahead; **einer Sache** (*dat*) **~** to precede sth; **voran|kommen** *irr vi* to make progress
Vorarlberg (*-s*) *nt* Vorarlberg
voraus *adv* ahead ; **im Voraus** in advance; **voraus|fahren** *irr vi* to drive on ahead; **vorausgesetzt** *conj* provided (that); **Voraussage** *f* prediction; (*Wetter*) forecast; **voraus|sagen** *vt* to predict; **voraus|sehen** *irr vt* to foresee; **voraus|sein** *irr vi*: **jdm ~** to be ahead of sb; **voraus|setzen** *vt* to assume; **Voraussetzung** *f* requirement, prerequisite; **voraussichtlich** *adj* expected
▷ *adv* probably; **voraus|zahlen** *vt* to pay in advance
Vorbehalt (*-(e)s, -e*) *m* reservation; **vor|behalten** *irr vt*:

sich/jdm etw ~ to reserve sth (for oneself)/for sb
vorbei *adv* past, over, finished; **vorbei|bringen** *irr vt* to drop by (*o in*); **vorbei|fahren** *irr vi* to drive past; **vorbei|gehen** *irr vi* to pass by, to go past; (*verstreichen, aufhören*) to pass; **vorbei|kommen** *irr vi* to drop by; **vorbei|lassen** *irr vt*: **kannst du die Leute ~?** would you let these people past?; **lässt du mich bitte mal vorbei?** can I get past, please?; **vorbei|reden** *vi*: **aneinander ~** to talk at cross-purposes
vor|bereiten *vt* to prepare ▷ *vr*: **sich ~** to get ready (*auf* +*akk, für* for); **Vorbereitung** *f* preparation
vor|bestellen *vt* to book in advance; (*Essen*) to order in advance; **Vorbestellung** *f* booking, reservation
vor|beugen *vi* to prevent (*dat* sth); **vorbeugend** *adj* preventive; **Vorbeugung** *f* prevention
Vorbild *nt* (*role*) model; **vorbildlich** *adj* model, ideal
Vorderachse *f* front axle; **vordere(r, s)** *adj* front; **Vordergrund** *m* foreground; **Vorderradantrieb** *m* (*Auto*) front-wheel drive; **Vorderseite** *f* front; **Vordersitz** *m* front seat; **Vorderteil** *m o nt* front (part)
Vordruck *m* form
voreilig *adj* hasty, rash; **~e Schlüsse ziehen** to jump to conclusions; **voreingenommen** *adj* biased
vor|enthalten *irr vt*: **jdm etw ~** to withhold sth from sb
vorerst *adv* for the moment
vor|fahren *irr vi* (*vorausfahren*) to drive on ahead; **vor das Haus ~** to drive up to the house; **fahren Sie bis zur Ampel vor** drive as far as the traffic lights

Vorfahrt f (*Auto*) right of way;
~ **achten** give way (*Brit*), yield
(*US*); **Vorfahrtsschild** nt give
way (*Brit*) (o yield (*US*)) sign;
Vorfahrtsstraße f major road

Vorfall m incident

vor|führen vt to demonstrate;
(*Film*) to show; (*Theaterstück, Trick*)
to perform

Vorgänger(in) m(f) predecessor

vor|gehen irr vi (*vorausgehen*) to
go on ahead; (*nach vorn*) to go
forward; (*handeln*) to act, to
proceed; (*Uhr*) to be fast; (*Vorrang
haben*) to take precedence;
(*passieren*) to go on; **Vorgehen** (-s)
nt procedure

Vorgesetzte(r) mf superior

vorgestern adv the day before
yesterday

vor|haben irr vt to plan; **hast du
schon was vor?** have you got
anything on?; **ich habe vor, nach
Rom zu fahren** I'm planning to go
to Rome

vor|halten irr vt: **jdm etw ~** to
accuse sb of sth

Vorhand f forehand

vorhanden adj existing;
(*erhältlich*) available

Vorhang m curtain

Vorhaut f foreskin

vorher adv before; **zwei Tage
~** two days before; **~ essen wir**
we'll eat first; **Vorhersage** f
forecast; **vorher|sehen** irr vt to
foresee

vorhin adv just now, a moment
ago

Vorkenntnisse pl previous
knowledge *sing*

vor|kommen irr vi (*nach vorne
kommen*) to come forward;
(*geschehen*) to happen; (*sich finden*)
to occur; (*scheinen*) to seem (to
be); **sich** (*dat*) **dumm ~** to feel
stupid

Vorlage f model

vor|lassen irr vt: **jdn ~** to let sb
go first

vorläufig adj temporary

vor|lesen irr vt to read out

Vorlesung f lecture

vorletzte(r, s) adj last but one;
am ~n Samstag (on) the Saturday
before last

Vorliebe f preference

vor|machen vt: **kannst du es
mir ~?** can you show me how to do
it?; **jdm etwas ~** (*fig: täuschen*) to
fool sb

vor|merken vt to note down;
(*Plätze*) to book

Vormittag m morning; **am ~** in
the morning; **heute ~** this
morning; **vormittags** adv in the
morning; **um 9 Uhr ~** at 9 (o'clock)
in the morning, at 9 am

vorn(e) adv in front; **von
~ anfangen** to start at the
beginning; **nach ~** to the front;
weiter ~ further up; **von ~ bis
hinten** from beginning to end

Vorname m first name; **wie
heißt du mit ~?** what's your first
name?

vornehm adj (*von Rang*)
distinguished; (*Benehmen*) refined;
(*fein, elegant*) elegant

vor|nehmen irr vt **sich** (*dat*) **etw
~** to start on sth; **sich** (*dat*) **~, etw
zu tun** (*beschließen*) to decide to do
sth

vornherein adv: **von ~** from the
start

Vorort m suburb

vorrangig adj priority

Vorrat m stock, supply; **vorrätig**
adj in stock

Vorrecht nt privilege

Vorruhestand m early
retirement

Vorsaison f early season

Vorsatz m intention; (*Jur*) intent;

vorsätzlich *adj* intentional; *(Jur)* premeditated

Vorschau *f* preview; *(Film)* trailer

Vorschlag *m* suggestion, proposal; **vorschlagen** *irr vt* to suggest, to propose; **ich schlage vor, dass wir gehen** I suggest we go

vor|schreiben *irr vt (befehlen)* to stipulate; **jdm etw ~** to dictate sth to sb

Vorschrift *f* regulation, rule; *(Anweisung)* instruction; **vorschriftsmäßig** *adj* correct

Vorschule *f* nursery school, pre-school *(US)*

Vorsicht *f* care; **~!** look out; *(Schild)* caution; **~ Stufe!** mind the step; **vorsichtig** *adj* careful; **vorsichtshalber** *adv* just in case

Vorsorge *f* precaution; *(Vorbeugung)* prevention; **Vorsorgeuntersuchung** *f* checkup; **vorsorglich** *adv* as a precaution

Vorspann (*-(e)s, -e*) *m* credits *pl*

Vorspeise *f* starter

Vorsprung *m* projection; *(Abstand)* lead

vor|stellen *vt (bekannt machen)* to introduce; *(Uhr)* to put forward; *(vor etw)* to put in front; **sich** *(dat)* **etw ~** to imagine sth; **Vorstellung** *f (Bekanntmachen)* introduction; *(Theat)* performance; *(Gedanke)* idea; **Vorstellungsgespräch** *nt* interview

vor|täuschen *vt* to feign

Vorteil *m* advantage *(gegenüber* over); **die Vor- und Nachteile** the pros and cons; **vorteilhaft** *adj* advantageous

Vortrag (*-(e)s, Vorträge*) *m* talk *(über +akk* on); *(akademisch)* lecture; **einen ~ halten** to give a talk

vorüber *adv* over; **vorüber|gehen** *irr vi* to pass; **vorübergehend** *adj* temporary

▷ *adv* temporarily, for the time being

Vorurteil *nt* prejudice

Vorverkauf *m* advance booking

vor|verlegen *vt* to bring forward

Vorwahl *f (Tel)* dialling code *(Brit)*, area code *(US)*

Vorwand (*-(e)s, Vorwände*) *m* pretext, excuse; **unter dem ~, dass** with the excuse that

vorwärts *adv* forward; **vorwärts|gehen** *irr vi (fig)* to progress

vorweg *adv* in advance; **vorweg|nehmen** *irr vt* to anticipate

Vorweihnachtszeit *f* pre-Christmas period, run-up to Christmas *(Brit)*

vor|werfen *irr vt*: **jdm etw ~** to accuse sb of sth

vorwiegend *adv* mainly

Vorwort *nt* preface

Vorwurf *m* reproach; **sich** *(dat)* **Vorwürfe machen** to reproach oneself; **jdm Vorwürfe machen** to accuse sb; **vorwurfsvoll** *adj* reproachful

vor|zeigen *vt* to show

vorzeitig *adj* premature, early

vor|ziehen *irr vt (lieber haben)* to prefer

Vorzug *m* preference; *(gute Eigenschaft)* merit; *(Vorteil)* advantage

vorzüglich *adj* excellent

vulgär *adj* vulgar

Vulkan (*-s, -e*) *m* volcano; **Vulkanausbruch** *m* volcanic eruption

W

W *abk* = **West** W

Waage (-, -n) *f* scales *pl*; (*Astr*) Libra; **waagerecht** *adj* horizontal

wach *adj* awake; **~ werden** to wake up; **Wache** (-, -n) *f* guard

Wachs (-es, -e) *nt* wax

wachsen (*wuchs, gewachsen*) *vi* to grow

wachsen *vt* (*Skier*) to wax

Wachstum *nt* growth

Wachtel (-, -n) *f* quail

Wächter(in) (-s, -) *m(f)* guard; (*auf Parkplatz*) attendant

wackelig *adj* wobbly; (*fig*) shaky; **Wackelkontakt** *m* loose connection; **wackeln** *vi* (*Stuhl*) to be wobbly; (*Zahn, Schraube*) to be loose; **mit dem Kopf ~** to waggle one's head

Wade (-, -n) *f* (*Anat*) calf

Waffe (-, -n) *f* weapon

Waffel (-, -n) *f* waffle; (*Keks, Eiswaffel*) wafer

wagen *vt* to risk; **es ~, etw zu tun** to dare to do sth

Wagen (-s, -) *m* (*Auto*) car; (*Eisenb*) carriage; **Wagenheber** (-s, -) *m* jack; **Wagentyp** *m* model, make

Wahl (-, -en) *f* choice; (*Pol*) election

wählen *vt* to choose; (*Tel*) to dial; (*Pol*) to vote for; (*durch Wahl ermitteln*) to elect ▷ *vi* to choose; (*Tel*) to dial; (*Pol*) to vote; **Wähler(in)** (-s, -) *m(f)* voter; **wählerisch** *adj* choosy

Wahlkampf *m* election campaign; **wahllos** *adv* at random; **Wahlwiederholung** *f* redial

Wahnsinn *m* madness; **~!** amazing!; **wahnsinnig** *adj* insane, mad ▷ *adv* (*fam*) incredibly

wahr *adj* true; **das darf doch nicht ~ sein!** I don't believe it; **nicht ~?** that's right, isn't it?

während *prep* +*gen* during ▷ *conj* while; **währenddessen** *adv* meanwhile, in the meantime

Wahrheit *f* truth

wahrnehmbar *adj* noticeable, perceptible; **wahr|nehmen** *irr vt* to perceive

Wahrsager(in) (-s, -) *m(f)* fortune-teller

wahrscheinlich *adj* probable, likely ▷ *adv* probably; **ich komme ~ zu spät** I'll probably be late; **Wahrscheinlichkeit** *f* probability

Währung *f* currency

Wahrzeichen *nt* symbol

Waise (-, -n) *f* orphan

Wal (-(e)s, -e) *m* whale

Wald (-(e)s, Wälder) *m* wood; (*groß*) forest; **Waldbrand** *m* forest fire; **Waldsterben** (-s) *nt* forest dieback

Wales (-) nt Wales; **Waliser(in)** m(f) Welshman/Welshwoman; **walisisch** adj Welsh; **Walisisch** nt Welsh

Walkie-Talkie (-(s), -s) nt walkie-talkie

Walkman® (-s, -s) m walkman®, personal stereo

Wall (-(e)s, Wälle) m embankment

Wallfahrt f pilgrimage; **Wallfahrtsort** m place of pilgrimage

Walnuss f walnut

Walross (-es, -e) nt walrus

wälzen vt to roll; (Bücher) to pore over; (Probleme) to deliberate on ▷ vr: **sich ~** to wallow; (vor Schmerzen) to roll about; (im Bett) to toss and turn

Walzer (-s, -) m waltz

Wand (-, Wände) f wall; (Trenn~) partition; (Berg~) (rock) face

Wandel (-s) m change; **wandeln** vt to change ▷ vr: **sich ~** to change

Wanderer (-s, -) m, **Wanderin** f hiker; **Wanderkarte** f hiking map; **wandern** vi to hike; (Blick) to wander; (Gedanken) to stray; **Wanderschuh** m walking shoe; **Wanderstiefel** m hiking boot; **Wanderung** f hike; **eine ~ machen** to go on a hike; **Wanderweg** m walking (o hiking) trail

Wandleuchte f wall lamp; **Wandmalerei** f mural; **Wandschrank** m built-in cupboard (Brit), closet (US)

wandte imperf von **wenden**

Wange (-, -n) f cheek

wann adv when; **seit ~ ist sie da?** how long has she been here?; **bis ~ bleibt ihr?** how long are you staying?

Wanne (-, -n) f (bath) tub

Wappen (-s, -) nt coat of arms

war imperf von **sein**

warb imperf von **werben**

Ware (-, -n) f product; **~n** goods pl; **Warenhaus** nt department store; **Warenprobe** f sample; **Warenzeichen** nt trademark

warf imperf von **werfen**

warm adj warm; (Essen) hot; **~ laufen** to warm up; **mir ist es zu ~** I'm too warm; **Wärme** (-, -n) f warmth; **wärmen** vt to warm; (Essen) to warm (o to heat) up ▷ vi (Kleidung, Sonne) to be warm ▷ vr: **sich ~** to warm up; (gegenseitig) to keep each other warm; **Wärmflasche** f hot-water bottle; **Warmstart** m (Inform) warm start

Warnblinkanlage f (Auto) warning flasher; **Warndreieck** nt (Auto) warning triangle; **warnen** vt to warn (vor +dat about, of); **Warnung** f warning

Warteliste f waiting list; **warten** vi to wait (auf +akk for); **warte mal!** wait (o hang on) a minute ▷ vt (Tech) to service

Wärter(in) m(f) attendant

Wartesaal m, **Wartezimmer** nt waiting room

Wartung f service; (das Warten) servicing

warum adv why

Warze (-, -n) f wart

was pron what; (fam: etwas) something; **~ kostet das?** what does it cost? how much is it?; **~ für ein Auto ist das?** what kind of car is that?; **~ für eine Farbe/Größe?** what colour/size?; **~?** (fam: wie bitte?) what?; **~ ist/gibt's?** what is it? what's up? **du weißt, ~ ich meine** you know what I mean; **~ (auch) immer** whatever; **soll ich dir ~ mitbringen?** do you want me to bring you anything?; **alles, ~ er hat** everything he's got

Waschanlage f (Auto) car wash; **waschbar** adj washable; **Waschbär** m raccoon; **Waschbecken** nt washbasin

Wäsche (-, -n) f washing; (schmutzig) laundry; (Bettwäsche) linen; (Unterwäsche) underwear; **in der ~** in the wash; **Wäscheklammer** f clothes peg (Brit) (o pins (US)); **Wäscheleine** f clothesline

waschen (wusch, gewaschen) vt, vi to wash; **Waschen und Legen** shampoo and set ▷ vr: **sich ~** to (have a) wash; **sich** (dat) **die Haare ~** to wash one's hair

Wäscherei f laundry; **Wäscheständer** m clothes horse; **Wäschetrockner** m tumble-drier

Waschgelegenheit f washing facilities pl; **Waschlappen** m flannel (Brit), washcloth (US); (fam: Mensch) wet blanket; **Waschmaschine** f washing machine; **Waschmittel** nt, **Waschpulver** nt washing powder; **Waschraum** m washroom; **Waschsalon** (-s, -s) m launderette (Brit), laundromat (US); **Waschstraße** f car wash

Wasser (-s, -) nt water; **fließendes ~** running water; **Wasserball** m (Sport) water polo; **Wasserbob** m jet ski; **wasserdicht** adj watertight; (Uhr etc) waterproof; **Wasserfall** m waterfall; **Wasserfarbe** f watercolour; **wasserfest** adj watertight, waterproof; **Wasserhahn** m tap (Brit), faucet (US); **wässerig** adj watery; **Wasserkessel** (-s, -) m kettle; **Wasserkocher** (-s, -) m electric kettle; **Wasserleitung** f water pipe; **wasserlöslich** adj water-soluble; **Wassermann** m (Astr) Aquarius; **Wassermelone** f

water melon; **Wasserrutschbahn** f water chute; **Wasserschaden** m water damage; **wasserscheu** adj scared of water; **Wasserski** nt water-skiing; **Wasserspiegel** m surface of the water; (Wasserstand) water level; **Wassersport** m water sports pl; **wasserundurchlässig** adj watertight, waterproof; **Wasserverbrauch** m water consumption; **Wasserversorgung** f water supply; **Wasserwaage** f spirit level; **Wasserwerk** nt waterworks pl

waten vi to wade

Watt (-(e)s, -en) nt (Geo) mud flats pl ▷ (-s, -) nt (Elek) watt

Watte (-, -n) f cotton wool; **Wattepad** (-s, -s) m cotton pad; **Wattestäbchen** nt cotton bud, Q-tip® (US)

WC (-s, -s) nt toilet, restroom (US); **WC-Reiniger** m toilet cleaner

Web (-s) nt (Inform) Web; **Webseite** f (Inform) web page

Wechsel (-s, -) m change; (Spieler~: Sport) substitution; **Wechselgeld** nt change; **wechselhaft** adj (Wetter) changeable; **Wechseljahre** pl menopause sing; **Wechselkurs** m exchange rate; **wechseln** vt to change; (Blicke) to exchange; **Geld ~** to change some money; (in Kleingeld) to get some change; **Euro in Pfund ~** to change euros into pounds ▷ vi to change; **kannst du ~?** can you change this?; **Wechselstrom** m alternating current, AC; **Wechselstube** f bureau de change

Weckdienst m wake-up call service; **wecken** vt to wake (up);

Wecker (-s, -) m alarm clock; **Weckruf** m wake-up call

wedeln vi (Ski) to wedel; **mit etw ~ to** wave sth; **mit dem Schwanz ~ to** wag its tail; **der Hund wedelte mit dem Schwanz** the dog wagged its tail

weder conj: **~ ... noch ...** neither ... nor ...

weg adv (entfernt, verreist) away; (los, ab) off; **er war schon ~** he had already left (o gone); **Hände ~!** hands off; **weit ~** a long way away (o off)

Weg (-(e)s, -e) m way; (Pfad) path; (Route) route; **jdn nach dem ~ fragen** to ask sb the way; **auf dem ~ sein** to be on the way

weg|bleiben irr vi to stay away; **weg|bringen** irr vt to take away

wegen prep +gen o dat because of

weg|fahren irr vi to drive away; (abfahren) to leave; (in Urlaub) to go away; **Wegfahrsperre** f (Auto) (engine) immobilizer; **weg|gehen** irr vi to go away; **weg|kommen** irr vi to get away; (fig) **gut/schlecht ~** to come off well/badly; **weg|lassen** irr vt to leave out; **weg|laufen** irr vi to run away; **weg|legen** vt to put aside; **weg|machen** vt (fam) to get rid of; **weg|müssen** irr vi: **ich muss weg** I've got to go; **weg|nehmen** irr vt to take away; **weg|räumen** vt to clear away; **weg|rennen** irr vi to run away; **weg|schicken** vt to send away; **weg|schmeißen** irr vt to throw away; **weg|sehen** irr vi to look away; **weg|tun** irr vt to put away

Wegweiser (-s, -) m signpost

weg|werfen irr vt to throw away; **weg|wischen** vt to wipe off; **weg|ziehen** irr vi to move (away)

weh adj sore; siehe auch **wehtun**

wehen vt, vi to blow; (Fahne) to flutter

Wehen pl labour pains pl

Wehrdienst m military service

wehren vr: **sich ~** to defend oneself

weh|tun irr vi to hurt; **jdm/sich ~** to hurt sb/oneself

Weibchen nt: **es ist ein ~** (Tier) it's a she; **weiblich** adj feminine; (Bio) female

weich adj soft; **~ gekocht** (Ei) soft-boiled

Weichkäse m soft cheese; (Streichkäse) cheese spread; **weichlich** adj soft; (körperlich) weak; **Weichspüler** (-s, -) m (für Wäsche) (fabric) softener

Weide (-, -n) f (Baum) willow; (Grasfläche) meadow

weigern vr: **sich ~** to refuse; **Weigerung** f refusal

Weiher (-s, -) m pond

Weihnachten (-, -) nt Christmas; **Weihnachtsabend** m Christmas Eve; **Weihnachtsbaum** m Christmas tree; **Weihnachtsfeier** f Christmas party; **Weihnachtsferien** pl Christmas holidays pl (Brit), Christmas vacation sing (US); **Weihnachtsgeld** nt Christmas bonus; **Weihnachtsgeschenk** nt Christmas present; **Weihnachtskarte** f Christmas card; **Weihnachtslied** nt Christmas carol; **Weihnachtsmann** m Father Christmas, Santa (Claus)

● **WEIHNACHTSMARKT**
●
● The **Weihnachtsmarkt** is a
● market held in most large
● towns in Germany in the weeks
● prior to Christmas. People visit
● it to buy presents, toys and

- Christmas decorations, and to
- enjoy the festive atmosphere.
- Food and drink associated with
- the Christmas festivities can
- also be eaten and drunk there,
- for example, gingerbread and
- mulled wine.

Weihnachtsstern m (*Bot*)
poinsettia; **Weihnachtstag** m:
erster ~ Christmas Day; **zweiter
~** Boxing Day; **Weihnachtszeit** f
Christmas season
weil *conj* because
Weile (-) f while, short time; **es
kann noch eine ~ dauern** it could
take some time
Wein (-(e)s, -e) m wine; (*Pflanze*)
vine; **Weinbeere** f grape;
Weinberg m vineyard;
Weinbergschnecke f snail;
Weinbrand m brandy
weinen *vt, vi* to cry
Weinglas *nt* wine glass;
Weinkarte f wine list;
Weinkeller m wine cellar;
Weinlese (-, -n) f vintage;
Weinprobe f wine tasting;
Weintraube f grape
weise *adj* wise
Weise (-, -n) f manner, way; **auf
diese (Art und) ~** this way
weisen (*wies, gewiesen*) *vt* to
show
Weisheit f wisdom;
Weisheitszahn m wisdom
tooth
weiß *adj* white; **Weißbier** *nt* ≈
wheat beer; **Weißbrot** *nt* white
bread; **weißhaarig** *adj*
white-haired; **Weißkohl** m,
Weißkraut *nt* (white) cabbage;
Weißwein m white wine
weit *adj* wide; (*Begriff*) broad;
(*Reise, Wurf*) long; (*Kleid*) loose; **wie
~ ist es ...?** how far is it ...?; **so
~ sein** to be ready ▷ *adv* far;

~ verbreitet widespread;
~ gereist widely travelled; **~ offen**
wide open; **das geht zu ~** that's
going too far, that's pushing it
weiter *adj* wider; (~ *weg*) farther
(away); (*zusätzlich*) further; **~e
Informationen** further
information *sing* ▷ *adv* further; **~!**
go on; (*weitergehen!*) keep moving;
~ nichts/niemand
nothing/nobody else; **und so
~** and so on; **weiter|arbeiten** *vi*
to carry on working;
Weiterbildung f further training
(*o education*); **weiter|empfehlen**
irr vt to recommend;
weiter|erzählen *vt*: **nicht ~!**
don't tell anyone; **weiter|fahren**
irr vi to go on (*nach* to, *bis* as far
as); **weiter|geben** *irr vt* to pass
on; **weiter|gehen** *irr vi* to go on;
weiter|helfen *irr vi*: **jdm ~** to
help sb; **weiterhin** *adv*: **etw
~ tun** to go on doing sth;
weiter|machen *vt, vi* to
continue; **weiter|reisen** *vi* to
continue one's journey
weitgehend *adj* considerable
▷ *adv* largely; **weitsichtig** *adj*
long-sighted; (*fig*) far-sighted;
Weitsprung m long jump;
Weitwinkelobjektiv *nt* (*Foto*)
wide-angle lens
Weizen (-s, -) m wheat;
Weizenbier *nt* ≈ wheat beer

 SCHLÜSSELWORT

welche(r, s) *interrogativ pron*
which; **welcher von beiden?**
which (one) of the two?; **welchen
hast du genommen?** which (one)
did you take?; **welche eine ...!**
what a ...!; **welche Freude!** what
joy! ▷ *indef pron* some; (*in Fragen*)
any; **ich habe welche** I have some;
haben Sie welche? do you have

any? ▷ *relativ pron* (*bei Menschen*) who; (*bei Sachen*) which, that; **welche(r, s) auch immer** whoever/whichever/whatever

welk *adj* withered; **welken** *vi* to wither

Welle (-, -n) *f* wave; **Wellengang** *m* waves *pl*; **starker ~** heavy seas *pl*; **Wellenlänge** *f* (*a. fig*) wavelength; **Wellenreiten** *nt* surfing; **Wellensittich** (-s, -e) *m* budgerigar, budgie; **wellig** *adj* wavy

Wellness *f* health and beauty (*Brit*), wellness (*US*)

Welpe (-n, -n) *m* puppy

Welt (-, -en) *f* world; **auf der ~** in the world; **auf die ~ kommen** to be born; **Weltall** *nt* universe; **weltbekannt, weltberühmt** *adj* world-famous; **Weltkrieg** *m* world war; **Weltmacht** *f* world power; **Weltmeister(in)** *m(f)* world champion; **Weltmeisterschaft** *f* world championship; (*im Fußball*) World Cup; **Weltraum** *m* space; **Weltreise** *f* trip round the world; **Weltrekord** *m* world record; **Weltstadt** *f* metropolis; **weltweit** *adj* worldwide, global

wem *pron dat von* **wer** who ... to, (to) whom; **~ hast du's gegeben?** who did you give it to?; **~ gehört es?** who does it belong to?, whose is it?; **~ auch immer es gehört** whoever it belongs to

wen *pron akk von* **wer** who, whom; **~ hast du besucht?** who did you visit?; **~ möchten Sie sprechen?** who would you like to speak to?

Wende (-, -n) *f* turning point; (*Veränderung*) change; **die ~** (*Hist*) the fall of the Berlin Wall; **Wendekreis** *m* (*Auto*) turning circle

Wendeltreppe *f* spiral staircase

wenden (*wendete o wandte, gewendet o gewandt*) *vt, vi* to turn (round); (*um 180°*) to make a U-turn; **sich an jdn ~** to turn to sb; **bitte ~!** please turn over, PTO ▷ *vr*: **sich ~** to turn; **sich an jdn ~** to turn to sb

wenig *pron, adv* little; **~(e)** *pl* few; (**nur**) **ein** (**klein**) **~** (just) a little (bit); **ein ~ Zucker** a little bit of sugar, a little sugar; **wir haben ~ Zeit** we haven't got much time; **zu ~** too little; *pl* too few; **nur ~ wissen** only a few know ▷ *adv*: **er spricht ~** he doesn't talk much; **~ bekannt** little known; **wenige** *pron pl* few *pl*; **wenigste(r, s)** *adj* least; **wenigstens** *adv* at least

○ SCHLÜSSELWORT

wenn *konj* **1** (*falls, bei Wünschen*) if; **wenn auch ..., selbst wenn ...** even if ...; **wenn ich doch ...** if only I ...
2 (*zeitlich*) when; **immer wenn** whenever

wennschon *adv*: **na ~?** so what?

wer *pron* who; **~ war das?** who was that?; **~ von euch** which (one) of you? ▷ *pron* anybody who, anyone who; **~ das glaubt, ist dumm** anyone who believes that is stupid; **~ auch immer** whoever ▷ *pron* somebody, someone; (*in Fragen*) anybody, anyone; **ist da ~?** is (there) anybody there?

Werbefernsehen *nt* TV commercials *pl*; **Werbegeschenk** *nt* promotional gift; **werben** (*warb, geworben*) *vt* to win; (*Mitglied*) to recruit ▷ *vi* to advertise; **Werbespot** (-s, -s) *m* commercial; **Werbung** *f* advertising

○ SCHLÜSSELWORT

werden (pt **wurde**, pp **geworden** o (bei Passiv) **worden**) vi to become; **was ist aus ihm/aus der Sache geworden?** what became of him/it?; **es ist nichts/gut geworden** it came to nothing/turned out well; **es wird Nacht/Tag** it's getting dark/light; **mir wird kalt** I'm getting cold; **mir wird schlecht** I feel ill; **Erster werden** to come o be first; **das muss anders werden** that'll have to change; **rot/zu Eis werden** to turn red/to ice; **was willst du (mal) werden?** what do you want to be?; **die Fotos sind gut geworden** the photos have come out nicely

▷ als Hilfsverb **1** (bei Futur) **er wird es tun** he will o he'll do it; **er wird das nicht tun** he will not o he won't do it; **es wird gleich regnen** it's going to rain

2 (bei Konjunktiv) **ich würde ...** I would ...; **er würde gern ...** he would o he'd like to ...; **ich würde lieber ...** I would o I'd rather ...

3 (bei Vermutung) **sie wird in der Küche sein** she will be in the kitchen

4 (bei Passiv) **gebraucht werden** to be used; **er ist erschossen worden** he has o he's been shot; **mir wurde gesagt, dass ...** I was told that ...

werfen (**warf**, **geworfen**) vt to throw

Werft (-, -en) f shipyard, dockyard

Werk (-(e)s, -e) nt (Kunstwerk, Buch etc) work; (Fabrik) factory; (Mechanismus) works pl; **Werkstatt** (-, -stätten) f workshop; (Auto)

garage; **Werktag** m working day; **werktags** adv on weekdays, during the week; **Werkzeug** nt tool; **Werkzeugkasten** m toolbox

wert adj worth; **es ist etwa 50 Euro ~** it's worth about 50 euros; **das ist nichts ~** it's worthless; **Wert** (-(e)s, -e) m worth; (Zahlen~) (Fin) value; **~ legen auf** (+akk) to attach importance to; **es hat doch keinen ~** (Sinn) it's pointless; **Wertangabe** f declaration of value; **Wertbrief** m insured letter; **Wertgegenstand** m valuable object; **wertlos** adj worthless; **Wertmarke** f token; **Wertpapiere** pl securities pl; **Wertsachen** pl valuables pl; **Wertstoff** m recyclable waste; **wertvoll** adj valuable

Wesen (-s, -) nt being; (Natur, Charakter) nature

wesentlich adj significant; (beträchtlich) considerable ▷ adv considerably

weshalb adv why

Wespe (-, -n) f wasp; **Wespenstich** m wasp sting

wessen pron gen von **wer**; whose

○ WESSI
○
○ A **Wessi** is a colloquial and often
○ derogatory word used to
○ describe a German from the
○ former West Germany. The
○ expression 'Besserwessi' is used
○ by East Germans to describe a
○ West German who is considered
○ to be a know-all.

West west; **Westdeutschland** nt (als Landesteil) Western Germany; (Hist) West Germany

Weste (-, -n) f waistcoat (Brit), vest (US); (Wollweste) cardigan

Westen (-s) m west; **im ~ Englands** in the west of England; **der Wilde ~** the Wild West; **Westeuropa** nt Western Europe; **Westküste** f west coast; **westlich** adj western; (Kurs, Richtung) westerly; **Westwind** m west(erly) wind

weswegen adv why

Wettbewerb m competition; **Wettbüro** nt betting office; **Wette** (-, -n) f bet; **eine ~ abschließen** to make a bet; **die ~ gilt!** you're on; **wetten** vt, vi to bet (auf +akk on); **ich habe mit ihm gewettet, dass ...** I bet him that ...; **ich wette mit dir um 50 Euro** I'll bet you 50 euros; **~, dass?** wanna bet?

Wetter (-s, -) nt weather; **Wetterbericht** m, **Wettervorhersage** f weather forecast; **Wetterkarte** f weather map; **Wetterlage** f weather situation; **Wettervorhersage** f weather forecast

Wettkampf m contest; **Wettlauf** m race; **Wettrennen** nt race

WG (-, -s) f abk = **Wohngemeinschaft**

Whirlpool® (-s, -s) m jacuzzi®

Whisky (-s, -s) m (schottisch) whisky; (irisch, amerikanisch) whiskey

wichtig adj important

wickeln vt (Schnur) to wind (um round); (Schal, Decke) to wrap (um round); **ein Baby ~** to change a baby's nappy (Brit) (o diaper (US)); **Wickelraum** m baby-changing room; **Wickeltisch** m baby-changing table

Widder (-s, -) m (Zool) ram; (Astr) Aries sing

wider prep +akk against

widerlich adj disgusting

widerrufen irr vt to withdraw; (Auftrag, Befehl etc) to cancel

widersprechen irr vi to contradict (jdm sb); **Widerspruch** m contradiction

Widerstand m resistance; **widerstandsfähig** adj resistant (gegen to)

widerwärtig adj disgusting

widerwillig adj unwilling, reluctant

widmen vt to dedicate ▷ vr: **sich jdm/etw ~** to devote oneself to sb/sth; **Widmung** f dedication

⭕ SCHLÜSSELWORT

wie adv how; **wie groß/schnell?** how big/fast?; **wie wär's?** how about it?; **wie ist er?** what's he like?; **wie gut du das kannst!** you're very good at it; **wie bitte?** pardon?; (entrüstet) I beg your pardon!; **und wie!** and how!; **wie viel** how much; **wie viele Menschen** how many people; **wie weit** to what extent

▷ konj **1** (bei Vergleichen) **so schön wie ...** as beautiful as ...; **wie schon sagte** as I said; **wie du** like you; **singen wie ein ...** to sing like a ...; **wie (zum Beispiel)** such as (for example)

2 (zeitlich) **wie er das hörte, ging er** when he heard that he left; **er hörte, wie der Regen fiel** he heard the rain falling

wieder adv again; **~ ein(e) ...** another ...; **~ erkennen** to recognize; **etw ~ gutmachen** to make up for sth; **~ verwerten** to recycle

wieder|bekommen irr vt to get back

wiederholen vt to repeat;
Wiederholung f repetition
Wiederhören nt (Tel) **auf**
~ goodbye
wieder|kommen irr vi to come
back
wieder|sehen irr vt to see
again; (wieder treffen) to meet
again; **Wiedersehen** (-s) nt
reunion; **auf ~!** goodbye
Wiedervereinigung f
reunification
Wiege (-, -n) f cradle; **wiegen**
(wog, gewogen) vt, vi (Gewicht) to
weigh
Wien (-s) nt Vienna
wies imperf von **weisen**
Wiese (-, -n) f meadow
Wiesel (-s, -) nt weasel
wieso adv why
wievielmal adv how often;
wievielte(r, s) adj: **zum ~n Mal?**
how many times?; **den
Wievielten haben wir heute?**
what's the date today?; **am
Wievielten hast du Geburtstag?**
which day is your birthday?
wieweit conj to what extent
wild adj wild
Wild (-(e)s) nt game
wildfremd adj (fam) **ein ~er
Mensch** a complete (o total)
stranger; **Wildleder** nt suede;
Wildpark m game park;
Wildschwein nt (wild) boar;
Wildwasserfahren (-s) nt
whitewater canoeing (o
rafting)
Wille (-ns, -n) m will
willen prep +gen **um ... ~** for the
sake of ...; **um Himmels ~!**
(vorwurfsvoll) for heaven's sake;
(betroffen) goodness me
willkommen adj welcome
Wimper (-, -n) f eyelash;
Wimperntusche f mascara
Wind (-(e)s, -e) m wind

Windel (-, -n) f nappy (Brit),
diaper (US)
windgeschützt adj sheltered
from the wind; **windig** adj windy;
(fig) dubious; **Windjacke** f
windcheater; **Windmühle** f
windmill; **Windpocken** pl
chickenpox sing;
Windschutzscheibe f (Auto)
windscreen (Brit), windshield (US);
Windstärke f wind force;
Windsurfen (-s) nt windsurfing;
Windsurfer(in) m(f) windsurfer
Winkel (-s, -) m (Math) angle;
(Gerät) set square; (in Raum)
corner; **im rechten ~ zu** at right
angles to
winken vt, vi to wave
Winter (-s, -) m winter;
Winterausrüstung f (Auto)
winter equipment;
Winterfahrplan m winter
timetable; **winterlich** adj
wintry; **Wintermantel** m winter
coat; **Winterreifen** m winter
tyre; **Winterschlussverkauf** m
winter sales pl; **Wintersport** m
winter sports pl
Winterzeit f (Uhrzeit) winter
time (Brit), standard time (US)
winzig adj tiny
wir pron we; **~ selbst** we
ourselves; **~ alle** all of us; **~ drei**
the three of us; **~ sind's** it's us;
~ nicht not us
Wirbel (-s, -) m whirl; (Trubel)
hurly-burly; (Aufsehen) fuss; (Anat)
vertebra; **Wirbelsäule** f spine
wirken vi to be effective;
(erfolgreich sein) to work; (scheinen)
to seem
wirklich adj real; **Wirklichkeit** f
reality
wirksam adj effective; **Wirkung**
f effect
wirr adj confused; **Wirrwarr** (-s)
m confusion

Wirsing (-s) m savoy cabbage
Wirt (-(e)s, -e) m landlord; **Wirtin** f landlady
Wirtschaft f (Comm) economy; (Gaststätte) pub; **wirtschaftlich** adj (Pol, Comm) economic; (sparsam) economical
Wirtshaus nt pub
wischen vt, vi to wipe; **Wischer** (-s, -) m wiper
wissen (wusste, gewusst) vt to know; **weißt du schon, …?** did you know …?; **woher weißt du das?** how do you know?; **das musst du selbst ~** that's up to you; **Wissen** (-s) nt knowledge
Wissenschaft f science; **Wissenschaftler(in)** (-s, -) m(f) scientist; (Geisteswissenschaftler) academic; **wissenschaftlich** adj scientific; (geisteswissenschaftlich) academic
Witwe (-, -n) f widow; **Witwer** (-s, -) m widower
Witz (-(e)s, -e) m joke; **mach keine ~e!** you're kidding!; **das soll wohl ein ~ sein** you've got to be joking; **witzig** adj funny
wo adv where; **zu einer Zeit, ~ …** at a time when …; **überall, ~ ich hingehe** wherever I go ▷ conj: **jetzt, ~ du da bist** now that you're here; **~ ich dich gerade spreche** while I'm talking to you; **woanders** adv somewhere else
wobei adv: **~ mir einfällt …** which reminds me …
Woche (-, -n) f week; **während** (o **unter**) **der ~** during the week; **einmal die ~** once a week; **Wochenende** nt weekend; **am ~** at (Brit) (o **on** (US)) the weekend; **wir fahren übers ~ weg** we're going away for the weekend; **Wochenendhaus** nt weekend cottage; **Wochenendtrip** m weekend trip; **Wochenendurlaub**

m weekend break; **Wochenkarte** f weekly (season) ticket; **wochenlang** adv for weeks (on end); **Wochenmarkt** m weekly market; **Wochentag** m weekday; **wöchentlich** adj, adv weekly
Wodka (-s, -s) m vodka
wodurch adv: **~ unterscheiden sie sich?** what's the difference between them?; **~ hast du es gemerkt?** how did you notice?; **wofür** adv (relativ) for which; (Frage) what … for; **~ brauchst du das?** what do you need that for?
wog imperf von **wiegen**
woher adv where … from; **wohin** adv where … to

SCHLÜSSELWORT

wohl adv **1 wohl oder übel** whether one likes it or not **2** (wahrscheinlich) probably; (gewiss) certainly; (vielleicht) perhaps; **sie ist wohl zu Hause** she's probably at home; **das ist doch wohl nicht dein Ernst!** surely you're not serious; **das mag wohl sein** that may well be; **ob das wohl stimmt?** I wonder if that's true; **er weiß das sehr wohl** he knows that perfectly well

Wohl (-(e)s) nt: **zum ~!** cheers; **wohlbehalten** adv safe and sound; **wohl|fühlen** vr: **sich ~** (zufrieden) to feel happy; (gesundheitlich) to feel well; **Wohlstand** m prosperity, affluence; **wohl|tun** irr vi: **jdm ~** to do sb good; **Wohlwollen** nt goodwill
Wohnblock m block of flats (Brit), apartment house (US); **wohnen** vi to live; **Wohngemeinschaft** f shared flat

(Brit) (o apartment (US)); **ich wohne in einer ~** I share a flat (o apartment); **wohnhaft** adj resident; **Wohnküche** f kitchen-cum-living-room; **Wohnmobil** (-s, -e) nt camper, RV (US); **Wohnort** m place of residence; **Wohnsitz** m place of residence; **Wohnung** f flat (Brit), apartment (US); **Wohnungstür** f front door; **Wohnwagen** m caravan; **Wohnzimmer** nt living room

Wolf (-(e)s, Wölfe) m wolf
Wolke (-, -n) f cloud; **Wolkenkratzer** m skyscraper; **wolkenlos** adj cloudless; **wolkig** adj cloudy
Wolldecke f (woollen) blanket; **Wolle** (-, -n) f wool

SCHLÜSSELWORT

wollen (pt **wollte**, pp **gewollt** o (als Hilfsverb) **wollen**) vt, vi to want; **ich will nach Hause** I want to go home; **er will nicht** he doesn't want to; **er wollte das nicht** he didn't want it; **wenn du willst** if you like; **ich will, dass du mir zuhörst** I want you to listen to me
▷ Hilfsverb: **er will ein Haus kaufen** he wants to buy a house; **ich wollte, ich wäre ...** I wish I were ...; **etw gerade tun wollen** to be going to do sth

Wolljacke f cardigan
womit adv what ... with; **~ habe ich das verdient?** what have I done to deserve that?
womöglich adv possibly
woran adv: **~ denkst du?** what are you thinking of?; **~ ist er gestorben?** what did he die of?; **~ sieht man das?** how can you tell?

worauf adv: **~ wartest du?** what are you waiting for?
woraus adv: **~ ist das gemacht?** what is it made of?
Workshop (-s, -s) m workshop
World Wide Web nt World Wide Web
Wort (-(e)s, Wörter) nt (Vokabel) word ▷ (-(e)s, -e) nt (Äußerung) word; **mit anderen ~en** in other words; **jdn beim ~ nehmen** to take sb at his/her word; **Wörterbuch** nt dictionary; **wörtlich** adj literal
worüber adv: **~ redet sie?** what is she talking about?
worum adv: **~ gehts?** what is it about?
worunter adv: **~ leidet er?** what is he suffering from?
wovon adv (relativ) from which; **~ redest du?** what are you talking about?; **wozu** adv (relativ) to/for which; (interrogativ) what ... for/to; (warum) why; **~?** what for?; **~ brauchst du das?** what do you need it for?; **~ soll das gut sein?** what's it for?; **~ hast du Lust?** what do you feel like doing?
Wrack (-(e)s, -s) nt wreck
Wucher (-s) m profiteering; **das ist ~!** that's daylight robbery!
wuchs imperf von **wachsen**
wühlen vi to rummage; (Tier) to root; (Maulwurf) to burrow
Wühltisch m bargain counter
wund adj sore; **Wunde** (-, -n) f wound
Wunder (-s, -) nt miracle; **es ist kein ~** it's no wonder; **wunderbar** adj wonderful, marvellous; **Wunderkerze** f sparkler; **Wundermittel** nt wonder cure; **wundern** vr: **sich ~** to be surprised (über +akk at) ▷ vt to surprise; **wunderschön** adj

beautiful; **wundervoll** *adj* wonderful

Wundsalbe *f* antiseptic ointment; **Wundstarrkrampf** *m* tetanus

Wunsch (-*(e)s, Wünsche*) *m* wish (*nach* for); **wünschen** *vt* to wish; **sich** (*dat*) **etw ~** to want sth; **ich wünsche dir alles Gute** I wish you all the best; **wünschenswert** *adj* desirable

wurde *imperf von* **werden**

Wurf (-*s, Würfe*) *m* throw; (*Zool*) litter

Würfel (-*s, -*) *m* dice; (*Math*) cube; **würfeln** *vi* to throw (the dice); (*Würfel spielen*) to play dice ▷ *vt* (*Zahl*) to throw; (*Gastr*) to dice; **Würfelzucker** *m* lump sugar

Wurm (-*(e)s, Würmer*) *m* worm

Wurst (-*, Würste*) *f* sausage; **das ist mir ~** (*fam*) I couldn't care less

Würstchen *nt* frankfurter

Würze (-*, -n*) *f* seasoning, spice

Wurzel (-*, -n*) *f* root; **Wurzelbehandlung** *f* root canal treatment

würzen *vt* to season, to spice; **würzig** *adj* spicy

wusch *imperf von* **waschen**

wusste *imperf von* **wissen**

wüst *adj* (*unordentlich*) chaotic; (*ausschweifend*) wild; (*öde*) desolate; (*fam: heftig*) terrible

Wüste (-*, -n*) *f* desert

Wut (-*) *f* rage, fury; **ich habe eine ~ auf ihn** I'm really mad at him; **wütend** *adj* furious

WWW (-*) *nt abk* = **World Wide Web** WWW

X-Beine *pl* knock-knees *pl*; **x-beinig** *adj* knock-kneed

x-beliebig *adj*: **ein ~es Buch** any book (you like)

x-mal *adv* umpteen times

Xylophon (-*s, -e*) *nt* xylophone

Y Z

Yoga (-(s)) *m o nt* yoga
Yuppie (-s, -s) *m* (-, -s) *f* yuppie

zackig *adj* (*Linie etc*) jagged; (*fam: Tempo*) brisk
zaghaft *adj* timid
zäh *adj* tough; (*Flüssigkeit*) thick
Zahl (-, -en) *f* number; **zahlbar** *adj* payable; **zahlen** *vt, vi* to pay; **~ bitte!** could I have the bill (*Brit*) (*o* check (*US*)) please?; **bar ~** to pay cash; **zählen** *vt, vi* to count (*auf +akk* on); **~ zu** to be one of; **Zahlenschloss** *nt* combination lock; **Zähler** (-s, -) *m* (*Gerät*) counter; (*für Strom, Wasser*) meter; **zahlreich** *adj* numerous; **Zahlung** *f* payment; **Zahlungsanweisung** *f* money order; **Zahlungsbedingungen** *pl* terms *pl* of payment
zahm *adj* tame; **zähmen** *vt* to tame
Zahn (-(e)s, Zähne) *m* tooth; **Zahnarzt** *m*, **Zahnärztin** *f* dentist; **Zahnbürste** *f*

toothbrush; **Zahncreme** f
toothpaste; **Zahnersatz** m
dentures pl; **Zahnfleisch** nt gums
pl; **Zahnfleischbluten** nt bleeding
gums pl; **Zahnfüllung** f filling;
Zahnklammer f brace;
Zahnpasta f, **Zahnpaste** f
toothpaste; **Zahnradbahn** f rack
railway (Brit) (o railroad (US));
Zahnschmerzen pl toothache
sing; **Zahnseide** f dental floss;
Zahnspange f brace;
Zahnstocher (-s, -) m toothpick
Zange (-, -n) f pliers pl;
(Zuckerzange) tongs pl; (Beißzange,
Zool) pincers pl; (Med) forceps pl
zanken vi to quarrel ▷ vr: **sich
~** to quarrel
Zäpfchen nt (Anat) uvula; (Med)
suppository
zapfen vt (Bier) to pull; **Zapfsäule**
f petrol (Brit) (o gas (US)) pump
zappeln vi to wriggle; (unruhig
sein) to fidget
zappen vi to zap, to channel-hop
zart adj (weich, leise) soft; (Braten
etc) tender; (fein, schwächlich)
delicate; **zartbitter** adj
(Schokolade) plain, dark
zärtlich adj tender, affectionate;
Zärtlichkeit f tenderness; **~en** pl
hugs and kisses pl
Zauber (-s, -) m magic; (Bann)
spell; **Zauberei** f magic; **Zauberer**
(-s, -) m magician; (Künstler)
conjuror; **Zauberformel** f (magic)
spell; **zauberhaft** adj enchanting;
Zauberin f sorceress;
Zauberkünstler(in) m(f)
magician, conjuror; **Zaubermittel**
nt magic cure; **zaubern** vi to do
magic; (Künstler) to do conjuring
tricks; **Zauberspruch** m (magic)
spell
Zaun (-(e)s, Zäune) m fence
z. B. abk = **zum Beispiel** e.g., eg
Zebra (-s, -s) nt zebra;

Zebrastreifen m zebra crossing
(Brit), crosswalk (US)
Zecke (-, -n) f tick
Zehe (-, -n) f toe; (Knoblauch)
clove; **Zehennagel** m toenail;
Zehenspitze f tip of the toes
zehn num ten; **Zehnerkarte** f
ticket valid for ten trips; **Zehnkampf**
m decathlon; **Zehnkämpfer(in)**
m(f) decathlete; **zehnmal** adv ten
times; **zehntausend** num ten
thousand; **zehnte(r, s)** adj
tenth; siehe auch **dritte**; **Zehntel**
(-s, -) nt (Bruchteil) tenth;
Zehntelsekunde f tenth of a
second
Zeichen (-s, -) nt sign;
(Schriftzeichen) character;
Zeichenblock m sketch pad;
Zeichenerklärung f key;
Zeichensetzung f punctuation;
Zeichensprache f sign language;
Zeichentrickfilm m cartoon
zeichnen vt, vi to draw;
Zeichnung f drawing
Zeigefinger m index finger;
zeigen vt to show; **sie zeigte uns
die Stadt** she showed us around
the town; **zeig mal!** let me see
▷ vi to point (auf +akk to, at) ▷ vr:
sich ~ to show oneself; **es wird
sich ~** time will tell; **Zeiger** (-s, -)
m pointer; (Uhr) hand
Zeile (-, -n) f line
Zeit (-, -en) f time; **ich habe keine
~** I haven't got time; **lass dir ~** take
your time; **das hat ~** there's no
rush; **von ~ zu ~** from time to
time; **Zeitansage** f (Tel)
speaking clock (Brit), correct time
(US); **Zeitarbeit** f temporary
work; **zeitgenössisch** adj
contemporary, modern; **zeitgleich**
adj simultaneous ▷ adv at exactly
the same time; **zeitig** adj early;
Zeitkarte f season ticket;
zeitlich adj (Reihenfolge)

chronological; **es passt ~ nicht** it isn't a convenient time; **ich schaff es ~ nicht** I'm not going to make it; **Zeitlupe** f slow motion; **Zeitplan** m schedule; **Zeitpunkt** m point in time; **Zeitraum** m period (of time); **Zeitschrift** f magazine; (*wissenschaftliche*) periodical

Zeitung f newspaper; **es steht in der ~** it's in the paper(s); **Zeitungsanzeige** f newspaper advertisement; **Zeitungsartikel** m newspaper article; **Zeitungskiosk** m, **Zeitungsstand** m newsstand

Zeitunterschied m time difference; **Zeitverschiebung** f time lag; **Zeitvertreib** (-(e)s, -e) m: **zum ~** to pass the time; **zeitweise** adv occasionally; **Zeitzone** f time zone

Zelle (-, -n) f cell

Zellophan® (-s) nt cellophane®

Zelt (-(e)s, -e) nt tent; **zelten** vi to camp, to go camping; **Zeltplatz** m campsite, camping site

Zement (-(e)s, -e) m cement

Zentimeter m o nt centimetre

Zentner (-s, -) m (metric) hundredweight; (*in Deutschland*) fifty kilos; (*in Österreich und der Schweiz*) one hundred kilos

zentral adj central; **Zentrale** (-, -n) f central office; (*Tel*) exchange; **Zentralheizung** f central heating; **Zentralverriegelung** f (*Auto*) central locking; **Zentrum** (-s, *Zentren*) nt centre

zerbrechen irr vt, vi to break; **zerbrechlich** adj fragile

Zeremonie (-, -n) f ceremony

zergehen irr vi to dissolve; (*schmelzen*) to melt

zerkleinern vt to cut up; (*zerhacken*) to chop (up);

zerkratzen vt to scratch; **zerlegen** vt to take to pieces; (*Fleisch*) to carve; (*Gerät, Maschine*) to dismantle; **zerquetschen** vt to squash; **zerreißen** irr vt to tear to pieces ▷ vi to tear

zerren vt to drag; **sich** (*dat*) **einen Muskel ~** to pull a muscle ▷ vi to tug (*an +dat* at); **Zerrung** f (*Med*) pulled muscle

zerschlagen irr vt to smash ▷ vr: **sich ~** to come to nothing

zerschneiden irr vt to cut up

zerstören vt to destroy; **Zerstörung** f destruction

zerstreuen vt to scatter; (*Menge*) to disperse; (*Zweifel etc*) to dispel ▷ vr: **sich ~** (*Menge*) to disperse; **zerstreut** adj scattered; (*Mensch*) absent-minded; (*kurzfristig*) distracted

zerteilen vt to split up

Zertifikat (-(e)s, -e) nt certificate

Zettel (-s, -) m piece of paper; (*Notizzettel*) note

Zeug (-(e)s, -e) nt (*fam*) stuff; (*Ausrüstung*) gear; **dummes ~** nonsense

Zeuge (-n, -n) m, **Zeugin** f witness

Zeugnis nt certificate; (*Schule*) report; (*Referenz*) reference

z. H(d). abk = **zu Händen von** attn

zickig adj (*fam*) touchy, bitchy

Zickzack (-(e)s, -e) m: **im ~ fahren** to zigzag (across the road)

Ziege (-, -n) f goat

Ziegel (-s, -) m brick; (*Dach*) tile

Ziegenkäse m goat's cheese; **Ziegenpeter** m mumps

ziehen (*zog, gezogen*) vt to draw; (*zerren*) to pull; (*Spielfigur*) to move; (*züchten*) to rear ▷ vi (*zerren*) to pull; (*sich bewegen*) to move; (*Rauch, Wolke etc*) to drift; **den Tee**

~ lassen to let the tea stand ▷ *vi impers*: **es zieht** there's a draught ▷ *vr*: **sich ~** (*Treffen, Rede*) to drag on

Ziel (-(e)s, -e) *nt* (*Reise*) destination; (*Sport*) finish; (*Absicht*) goal, aim; **zielen** *vi* to aim (*auf +akk* at); **Zielgruppe** *f* target group; **ziellos** *adj* aimless; **Zielscheibe** *f* target

ziemlich *adj* considerable; **ein ~es Durcheinander** quite a mess; **mit ~er Sicherheit** with some certainty ▷ *adv* rather, quite; **~ viel** quite a lot

zierlich *adj* dainty; (*Frau*) petite

Ziffer (-, -n) *f* figure; **arabische/römische ~n** *pl* Arabic/Roman numerals *pl*; **Zifferblatt** *nt* dial, face

zig *adj* (*fam*) umpteen

Zigarette *f* cigarette; **Zigarettenautomat** *m* cigarette machine; **Zigarettenpapier** *nt* cigarette paper; **Zigarettenschachtel** *f* cigarette packet; **Zigarettenstummel** *m* cigarette end; **Zigarillo** (-s, -s) *m* cigarillo; **Zigarre** (-, -n) *f* cigar

Zigeuner(in) (-s, -) *m(f)* gipsy

Zimmer (-s, -) *nt* room; **haben Sie ein ~ für zwei Personen?** do you have a room for two?; **Zimmerlautstärke** *f* reasonable volume; **Zimmermädchen** *nt* chambermaid; **Zimmermann** *m* carpenter; **Zimmerpflanze** *f* house plant; **Zimmerschlüssel** *m* room key; **Zimmerservice** *m* room service; **Zimmervermittlung** *f* accommodation agency

Zimt (-(e)s, -e) *m* cinnamon; **Zimtstange** *f* cinnamon stick

Zink (-(e)s) *nt* zinc

Zinn (-(e)s) *nt* (*Element*) tin; (*legiertes*) pewter

Zinsen *pl* interest *sing*

Zipfel (-s, -) *m* corner; (*spitz*) tip; (*Hemd*) tail; (*Wurst*) end; **Zipfelmütze** *f* pointed hat

zirka *adv* about, approximately

Zirkel (-s, -) *m* (*Math*) (pair of) compasses *pl*

Zirkus (-, -se) *m* circus

zischen *vi* to hiss

Zitat (-(e)s, -e) *nt* quotation (*aus* from); **zitieren** *vt* to quote

Zitronat *nt* candied lemon peel; **Zitrone** (-, -n) *f* lemon; **Zitronenlimonade** *f* lemonade; **Zitronensaft** *m* lemon juice

zittern *vi* to tremble (*vor +dat* with)

zivil *adj* civilian; (*Preis*) reasonable; **Zivil** (-s) *nt* plain clothes *pl*; (*Mil*) civilian clothes *pl*; **Zivildienst** *m* community service (*for conscientious objectors*)

zocken *vi* (*fam*) to gamble

Zoff (-s) *m* (*fam*) trouble

zog *imperf von* **ziehen**

zögerlich *adj* hesitant; **zögern** *vi* to hesitate

Zoll (-(e)s, Zölle) *m* customs *pl*; (*Abgabe*) duty; **Zollabfertigung** *f* customs clearance; **Zollamt** *nt* customs office; **Zollbeamte(r)** *m*, **-beamtin** *f* customs official; **Zollerklärung** *f* customs declaration; **zollfrei** *adj* duty-free; **Zollgebühren** *pl* customs duties *pl*; **Zollkontrolle** *f* customs check; **Zöllner(in)** *m(f)* customs officer; **zollpflichtig** *adj* liable to duty

Zone (-, -n) *f* zone

Zoo (-s, -s) *m* zoo

Zoom (-s, -s) *nt* zoom (shot); (*Objektiv*) zoom (lens)

Zopf (-(e)s, Zöpfe) *m* plait (*Brit*), braid (*US*)

Zorn (-(e)s) *m* anger; **zornig** *adj* angry (*über etw akk* about sth, *auf jdn* with sb)

zu prep +dat **1** (örtlich) to; **zum Bahnhof/Arzt gehen** to go to the station/doctor; **zur Schule/Kirche gehen** to go to school/church; **sollen wir zu euch gehen?** shall we go to your place?; **sie sah zu ihm hin** she looked towards him; **zum Fenster herein** through the window; **zu meiner Linken** to o on my left

2 (zeitlich) at; **zu Ostern** at Easter; **bis zum 1. Mai** until May 1st; (nicht später als) by May 1st; **zu meiner Zeit** in my time

3 (Zusatz) with; **Wein zum Essen trinken** to drink wine with one's meal; **sich zu jdm setzen** to sit down beside sb; **setz dich doch zu uns** (come and) sit with us; **Anmerkungen zu etw** notes on sth

4 (Zweck) for; **Wasser zum Waschen** water for washing; **Papier zum Schreiben** paper to write on; **etw zum Geburtstag bekommen** to get sth for one's birthday

5 (Veränderung) into; **zu etw werden** to turn into sth; **jdn zu etw machen** to make sb (into) sth; **zu Asche verbrennen** to burn to ashes

6 (mit Zahlen) **3 zu 2** (Sport) 3-2; **das Stück zu 5 Euro** at 5 euros each; **zum ersten Mal** for the first time

7 zu meiner Freude etc to my joy etc; **zum Glück** luckily; **zu Fuß** on foot; **es ist zum Weinen** it's enough to make you cry

▷ konj to; **etw zu essen** sth to eat; **um besser sehen zu können** in order to see better; **ohne es zu wissen** without knowing it; **noch zu bezahlende Rechnungen** bills that are still to be paid

▷ adv **1** (allzu) too; **zu sehr** too much; **zu viel** too much; **zu wenig** too little

2 (örtlich) toward(s); **er kam auf mich zu** he came up to me

3 (geschlossen) shut, closed; **die Geschäfte haben zu** the shops are closed; **„auf/zu"** (Wasserhahn etc) "on/off"

4 (fam) (los) **nur zu!** just keep on!; **mach zu!** hurry up!

zuallererst adv first of all; **zuallerletzt** adv last of all
Zubehör (-(e)s, -e) nt accessories pl
zu|bereiten vt to prepare; **Zubereitung** f preparation
zu|binden irr vt to do (o tie) up
Zucchini pl courgettes pl (Brit), zucchini pl (US)
züchten vt (Tiere) to breed; (Pflanzen) to grow
zucken vi to jerk; (krampfhaft) to twitch; (Strahl etc) to flicker; **mit den Schultern ~** to shrug (one's shoulders)
Zucker (-s, -) m sugar; (Med) diabetes sing; **Zuckerdose** f sugar bowl; **zuckerkrank** adj diabetic; **Zuckerrohr** nt sugar cane; **Zuckerrübe** f sugar beet; **Zuckerwatte** f candy-floss (Brit), cotton candy (US)
zu|decken vt to cover up
zu|drehen vt to turn off
zueinander adv to one other; (mit Verb) together; **zueinander|halten** irr vi to stick together
zuerst adv first; (zu Anfang) at first; **~ einmal** first of all
Zufahrt f access; (Einfahrt) drive(way); **Zufahrtsstraße** f access road; (Autobahn) slip road (Brit), ramp (US)

Zufall m chance; (Ereignis) coincidence; **durch ~** by accident; **so ein ~!** what a coincidence; **zufällig** adj chance ▷ adv by chance; **weißt du ~, ob ...?** do you happen to know whether ...?

zufrieden adj content(ed); (befriedigt) satisfied; **lass sie ~** leave her alone (o in peace); **zufrieden|geben** irr vr: **sich mit etw ~** to settle for sth; **Zufriedenheit** f contentment; (Befriedigtsein) satisfaction; **zufrieden|stellen** vt: **sie ist schwer zufriedenzustellen** she is hard to please

zu|fügen vt to add (dat to); **jdm Schaden/Schmerzen ~** to cause sb harm/pain

Zug (-(e)s, Züge) m (Eisenb) train; (Luft) draught; (Ziehen) pull; (Gesichtszug) feature; (Schach) move; (Charakterzug) trait; (an Zigarette) puff, drag; (Schluck) gulp

Zugabe f extra; (in Konzert etc) encore

Zugabteil nt train compartment

Zugang m access; **„kein ~!"** "no entry!"

Zugauskunft f (Stelle) train information office/desk; **Zugbegleiter(in)** m(f) guard (Brit), conductor (US)

zu|geben irr vt (zugestehen) admit; **zugegeben** adv admittedly

zu|gehen irr vi (schließen) to shut; **auf jdn/etw ~** to walk towards sb/sth; **dem Ende ~** to be coming to a close ▷ vi impers (sich ereignen) to happen; **es ging lustig zu** we/they had a lot of fun; **dort geht es streng zu** it's strict there

Zügel (-s, -) m rein

Zugführer(in) m(f) guard (Brit), conductor (US)

zugig adj draughty

zügig adj speedy

Zugluft f draught

Zugpersonal nt train staff

zu|greifen irr vi (fig) to seize the opportunity; (beim Essen) to help oneself; **~ auf** (+akk) (Inform) to access

Zugrestauraunt nt dining car, diner (US)

Zugriffsberechtigung f (Inform) access right

zugrunde adv: **~ gehen** to perish; **~ gehen an** (+dat) (sterben) to die of

Zugschaffner(in) m(f) ticket inspector; **Zugunglück** nt train crash

zugunsten prep +gen o dat in favour of

Zugverbindung f train connection

zu|haben irr vi to be closed

zu|halten irr vt **sich** (dat) **die Nase ~** to hold one's nose; **sich** (dat) **die Ohren ~** to hold one's hands over one's ears; **die Tür ~** to hold the door shut

Zuhause (-s) nt home

zu|hören vi to listen (dat to); **Zuhörer(in)** m(f) listener

zu|kleben vt to seal

zu|kommen irr vi to come up (auf +akk to); **jdm etw ~ lassen** to give/send sb sth; **etw auf sich** (akk) **~ lassen** to take sth as it comes

zu|kriegen vt: **ich krieg den Koffer nicht zu** I can't shut the case

Zukunft (-, Zukünfte) f future; **zukünftig** adj future ▷ adv in future

zu|lassen irr vt (hereinlassen) to admit; (erlauben) to permit; (Auto) to license; (fam: nicht öffnen) to keep shut; **zulässig** adj permissible, permitted

zuletzt *adv* finally, at last
zuliebe *adv*: **jdm ~** for sb's sake
zum *kontr von* **zu dem**; **~ dritten Mal** for the third time; **~ Scherz** as a joke; **~ Trinken** for drinking
zu|machen *vt* to shut; (*Kleidung*) to do up ▷ *vi* to shut
zumindest *adv* at least
zu|muten *vt*: **jdm etw ~** to expect sth of sb ▷ *vr* **sich** (*dat*) **zu viel ~** to overdo things
zunächst *adv* first of all; **~ einmal** to start with
Zunahme (-, -n) *f* increase
Zuname *m* surname, last name
zünden *vt, vi* (*Auto*) to ignite, to fire; **Zündkabel** *f* (*Auto*) ignition cable; **Zündkerze** *f* (*Auto*) spark plug; **Zündschloss** *nt* ignition lock; **Zündschlüssel** *m* ignition key; **Zündung** *f* ignition
zu|nehmen *irr vi* to increase; (*Mensch*) to put on weight ▷ *vt*: **5 Kilo ~** to put on 5 kilos
Zunge (-, -n) *f* tongue
Zungenkuss *m* French kiss
zunichte|machen *vt* (*zerstören*) to ruin
zunutze *adv* **sich** (*dat*) **etw ~ machen** to make use of sth
zu|parken *vt* to block
zur *kontr von* **zu der**
zurecht|finden *irr vr*: **sich ~** to find one's way around;
zurecht|kommen *irr vi* to cope (*mit etw* with sth);
zurecht|machen *vt* to prepare ▷ *vr*: **sich ~** to get ready
Zürich (-s) *nt* Zurich
zurück *adv* back
zurück|bekommen *irr vt* to get back; **zurück|blicken** *vi* to look back (*auf +akk* at); **zurück|bringen** *irr vt* (*hierhin*) to bring back; (*woandershin*) to take back; **zurück|erstatten** *vt* to refund; **zurück|fahren** *irr vi* to go back;

zurück|geben *irr vt* to give back; (*antworten*) to answer;
zurück|gehen *irr vi* to go back; (*zeitlich*) to date back (*auf +akk* to)
zurück|halten *irr vt* to hold back; (*hindern*) to prevent ▷ *vr*: **sich ~** to hold back;
zurückhaltend *adj* reserved
zurück|holen *vt* to fetch back; **zurück|kommen** *irr vi* to come back; **auf etw** (*akk*) **~** to return (*o* get back) to sth; **zurück|lassen** *irr vt* to leave behind; **zurück|legen** *vt* to put back; (*Geld*) to put by; (*reservieren*) to keep back; (*Strecke*) to cover; **zurück|nehmen** *irr vt* to take back; **zurück|rufen** *irr vt* to call back; **zurück|schicken** *vt* to send back; **zurück|stellen** *vt* to put back; **zurück|treten** *irr vi* to step back; (*von Amt*) to retire; **zurück|verlangen** *vt*: **etw ~** to ask for sth back; **zurück|zahlen** *vt* to pay back
zurzeit *adv* at present
Zusage *f* promise; (*Annahme*) acceptance; **zu|sagen** *vt* to promise ▷ *vi* to accept; **jdm ~** (*gefallen*) to appeal to sb
zusammen *adv* together
Zusammenarbeit *f* collaboration; **zusammen|arbeiten** *vi* to work together
zusammen|brechen *irr vi* to collapse; (*psychisch*) to break down; **Zusammenbruch** *m* collapse; (*psychischer*) breakdown
zusammen|fassen *vt* to summarize; (*vereinigen*) to unite; **zusammenfassend** *adj* summarizing ▷ *adv* to summarize; **Zusammenfassung** *f* summary
zusammen|gehören *vi* to belong together; **zusammen|halten** *irr vi* to stick together

Zusammenhang m connection; **im/aus dem ~** in/out of context; **zusammen|hängen** irr vi to be connected; **zusammenhängend** adj coherent; **zusammenhang(s)los** adj incoherent

zusammen|klappen vi, vt to fold up

zusammen|knüllen vt to screw up

zusammen|kommen irr vi to meet; (sich ereignen) to happen together; **zusammen|legen** vt to fold up ▷ vi (Geld sammeln) to club together; **zusammen|nehmen** irr vt to summon up; **alles zusammengenommen** all in all ▷ vr: **sich ~** to pull oneself together; (fam) to get a grip, to get one's act together; **zusammen|passen** vi to go together; (Personen) to be suited; **zusammen|rechnen** vt to add up

Zusammensein (-s) nt get-together

zusammen|setzen vt to put together ▷ vr: **sich ~ aus** to be composed of; **Zusammensetzung** f composition

Zusammenstoß m crash, collision; **zusammen|stoßen** irr vi to crash (mit into)

zusammen|zählen vt to add up

zusammen|ziehen irr vi (in Wohnung etc) to move in together

Zusatz m addition; **zusätzlich** adj additional ▷ adv in addition

zu|schauen vi to watch; **Zuschauer(in)** (-s, -) m(f) spectator; **die ~** (pl) (Theat) the audience sing; **Zuschauertribüne** f stand

zu|schicken vt to send

Zuschlag m extra charge; (Fahrkarte) supplement

zuschlagpflichtig adj subject to an extra charge; (Eisenb) subject to a supplement

zu|schließen irr vt to lock up

zu|sehen irr vi to watch (jdm sb); **~, dass** (dafür sorgen) to make sure that

zu|sichern vt: **jdm etw ~** to assure sb of sth

Zustand m state, condition; **sie bekommt Zustände, wenn sie das sieht** (fam) she'll have a fit if she sees that

zustande adv: **~ bringen** to bring about; **~ kommen** to come about

zuständig adj (Behörde) relevant; **~ für** responsible for

Zustellung f delivery

zu|stimmen vi to agree (einer Sache dat to sth, jdm with sb); **Zustimmung** f approval

zu|stoßen irr vi (fig) to happen (jdm to sb)

Zutaten pl ingredients pl

zu|trauen vt: **jdm etw ~** to think sb is capable of sth; **das hätte ich ihm nie zugetraut** I'd never have thought he was capable of it; **ich würde es ihr ~** (etw Negatives) I wouldn't put it past her; **Zutrauen** (-s) nt confidence (zu in); **zutraulich** adj trusting; (Tier) friendly

zu|treffen irr vi to be correct; **~ auf** (+akk) to apply to; **Zutreffendes bitte streichen** please delete as applicable

Zutritt m entry; (Zugang) access; **~ verboten!** no entry

zuverlässig adj reliable; **Zuverlässigkeit** f reliability

Zuversicht f confidence; **zuversichtlich** adj confident

zuvor adv before; (zunächst) first; **zuvor|kommen** irr vi: **jdm ~** to

beat sb to it; **zuvorkommend**
adj obliging
Zuwachs (*-es, Zuwächse*) *m*
increase, growth; (*fam: Baby*)
addition to the family
zuwider *adv*: **es ist mir ~** I hate (*o*
detest) it
zuzüglich *prep +gen* plus
zwang *imperf von* **zwingen**
Zwang (*-(e)s, Zwänge*) *m* (*innerer*)
compulsion; (*Gewalt*) force
zwängen *vt* to squeeze (*in +akk*
into) ▷ *vr*: **sich ~** to squeeze (*in*
+akk into)
zwanglos *adj* informal
zwanzig *num* twenty;
zwanzigste(r, s) *adj* twentieth;
siehe auch **dritte**
zwar *adv*: **und ~ ...** (*genauer*) ...,
to be precise; **das ist ~ schön,**
aber ... it is nice, but ...; **ich kenne**
ihn ~, aber ... I know him all right,
but ...
Zweck (*-(e)s, -e*) *m* purpose;
zwecklos *adj* pointless
zwei *num* two; **Zwei** (*-, -en*) *f*
two; (*Schulnote*) ≈ B;
Zweibettzimmer *nt* twin room;
zweideutig *adj* ambiguous;
(*unanständig*) suggestive;
zweifach *adj, adv* double
Zweifel (*-s, -*) *m* doubt;
zweifellos *adv* undoubtedly;
zweifeln *vi* to doubt (*an etw dat*
sth); **Zweifelsfall** *m*: **im ~** in case
of doubt
Zweig (*-(e)s, -e*) *m* branch
Zweigstelle *f* branch
zweihundert *num* two hundred;
zweimal *adv* twice; **zweisprachig**
adj bilingual; **zweispurig** *adj*
(*Auto*) two-lane; **zweit** *adv*: **wir**
sind zu ~ there are two of us;
zweite(r, s) *adj* second; *siehe*
auch **dritte eine ~ Portion** a
second helping; **zweitens** *adv*
secondly; (*bei Aufzählungen*)

second; **zweitgrößte(r, s)** *adj*
second largest; **Zweitschlüssel**
m spare key
Zwerchfell *nt* diaphragm
Zwerg(in) (*-(e)s, -e*) *m(f)* dwarf
Zwetschge (*-, -n*) *f* plum
zwicken *vt* to pinch
Zwieback (*-(e)s, -e*) *m* rusk
Zwiebel (*-, -n*) *f* onion; (*von*
Blume) bulb; **Zwiebelsuppe** *f*
onion soup
Zwilling (*-s, -e*) *m* twin; **~e** (*pl*)
(*Astr*) Gemini *sing*
zwingen (*zwang, gezwungen*) *vt*
to force
zwinkern *vi* to blink; (*absichtlich*)
to wink
zwischen *prep +akk o dat*
between
Zwischenablage *f* (*Inform*)
clipboard
zwischendurch *adv* in between
Zwischenfall *m* incident
Zwischenlandung *f* stopover
zwischenmenschlich *adj*
interpersonal
Zwischenraum *m* space
Zwischenstopp (*-s, -s*) *m*
stopover
Zwischensumme *f* subtotal
Zwischenzeit *f*: **in der ~** in the
meantime
zwitschern *vt, vi* to twitter, to
chirp
zwölf *num* twelve; **zwölfte(r, s)**
adj twelfth; *siehe auch* **dritte**
Zylinder (*-s, -*) *m* cylinder; (*Hut*)
top hat
zynisch *adj* cynical
Zypern (*-s*) *nt* Cyprus
Zyste (*-, -n*) *f* cyst

German in focus

Introduction

German in focus gives you an introduction to various aspects of Germany, Austria and other German-speaking areas. The following pages help you get to know the countries where the language is spoken and the people who speak it.

Practical language tips and helpful notes on common translation difficulties will enable you to become a more confident German speaker. A useful correspondence section gives you all the information you need to be able to communicate effectively.

We've also included a number of links to useful websites, which will give you the opportunity to read more about German-speaking Europe and the German language.

We hope you will enjoy using your *German in focus* supplement. We are sure it will help you find out more about German and German speakers and become more confident in writing and speaking German.

Los gehts!

Germany and its regions

Germany and its regions

The ten biggest German cities

City	Name of inhabitants	Population
Berlin	die Berliner	3,275,000
Hamburg	die Hamburger	1,686,000
München	die Münchner	1,185,400
Köln	die Kölner	965,300
Frankfurt	die Frankfurter	648,400
Essen	die Essener	588,800
Dortmund	die Dortmunder	587,600
Stuttgart	die Stuttgarter	581,100
Düsseldorf	die Düsseldorfer	568,900
Bremen	die Bremer	527,900

Berlin was the capital of Germany between 1871 and 1945. After the second world war, until 1990, Germany was divided into West Germany and East Germany. This division was mirrored in Berlin, which was divided by a wall into western and eastern sectors. Germany (including Berlin) was reunified in 1990, and in 1999 Berlin again became the capital of the whole country.

Germany is a republic made up of 16 federal states (*Länder*). Many of these states have long histories. Three cities have Land status: Berlin and the Free Hanseatic Cities of Bremen and Hamburg. The other 13 Länder are regions: Baden-Württemberg, Bavaria, Brandenburg, Hesse, Mecklenburg-Pomerania, North Rhine-Westphalia, Rhineland-Palatinate, Saarland, Saxony, Saxony Anhalt, Lower Saxony, Schleswig-Holstein, Thuringia.

The head of the German state is the President (*der Bundespräsident*) and the head of government is the Chancellor (*der Bundeskanzler*). The feminine form of this word (*die Bundeskanzlerin*) was used for the first time in 2005, when Germany got a woman chancellor.

A useful link is:
www.tatsachen-ueber-deutschland.de
Federal Foreign Office – Facts about Germany

A snapshot of Germany

- In area, Germany (357,045 km²) is a third bigger than the UK (244,110 km²).

- The population of Germany is about 82.5 million, a third more than that of the UK. The birth rate is low (1.4 children per woman).

- The German economy is the biggest in the EU and one of the biggest in the world.

- The Rhine, which rises in Switzerland and flows into the North Sea in Holland is 1,320 km long. Most of this great river is in Germany (865 km).

- There are almost equal numbers of Roman Catholics and Protestants in Germany.

- Germany's highest mountain is the Zugspitze (2962 m).

- Germany has borders with nine other countries: Denmark, Holland, Belgium, Luxembourg, France, Switzerland, Austria, the Czech Republic and Poland.

- German beer is famous for its purity and high quality. There are hundreds of small independent breweries which produce distinctive beers. The Oktoberfest in Munich is a two-week beer festival attended by 6 million people.

Some useful links are:
www.destatis.de
Federal statistical office
www.muenchen.de
Munich tourist office

Austria and its regions

Switzerland and its regions

Swiss Cantons
1. APPENZELL AUSSERRHODEN
2. APPENZELL INNERRHODEN
3. FRIBOURG
4. VAUD

FRANKREICH

DEUTSCHLAND

ÖSTERREICH

ITALIEN

Basel
BERN
BASELLANDSCHAFT
JURA • Delemont
SOLOTHURN
SCHAFFHAUSEN
Frauenfeld • THURGAU
AARGAU
Aarau
ZÜRICH
• Zürich
SANKT
• St Gallen
1 2
GALLEN
NEUCHÂTEL
LUZERN
ZUG
Luzern •
NIDWALDEN
OBWALDEN
SCHWYZ
GLARUS
URI
LIECHTENSTEIN
3 4
3
• Bern
BERN
• Fribourg
FRIBOURG
VAUD
• Lausanne
Vorderrhein
• Chur
GRAUBÜNDEN
Inn
GENÈVE
• Genève
Rhône
Sion • VALAIS
TICINO
Bellinzona •

Aare
Rhein
Rhein

©Collins Bartholomew Ltd 2006

7

A snapshot of Austria and Switzerland

- German is the main language in Austria, and is spoken by 65% of the population in Switzerland.

- Austria has an area of 83,870 km². A quarter of the 8 million inhabitants live in or around the capital, Vienna (Wien).

- Austria is a member of the EU, and uses the euro, while Switzerland remains outside the EU and retains the Swiss franc as its currency.

- Austria is a federal republic consisting of nine states. Switzerland too is a federal state, made up of 26 cantons. Its official name is the Swiss Confederation. The letters CH on the back of Swiss cars stand for the Latin version: Confoederatio Helvetica.

- Austria's highest mountain is the Großglockner (3 797m).

- Switzerland's highest mountain is the Dufourspitze (4 643m): it's just within Switzerland's boundary with Italy.

- Switzerland has an area of only 41,290 km², about half that of Austria, but its population is only slightly less than that of Austria – about 7.5m.

- There are three official languages in Switzerland – German, French and Italian. 21% of the population speak French, and 7% Italian. There is a fourth national language, Romansch, which is spoken by less than 1% of the Swiss population. The population also includes a large number of foreign workers.

- Switzerland's biggest city is Zürich, (about 1.3 million), but the capital is Bern (just under a million).

- Banking is one of Switzerland's most important industries. The secrecy of Swiss banks is legendary.

Some useful links are:
www.bfs.admin.ch
Swiss Federal Statistical Office
www.austria.org
Austrian Press and Information Service

Varieties of German

The type of German we are taught is Standard German or *Hochdeutsch*.
There are many regional dialects, though, no more so than in Austria and
Switzerland where you may encounter a variety of words and expressions
which do not correspond to Standard German. Here are a few examples:

Austrian German (Österreichisch)	English	Standard German
die Aschanti	peanut	*die Erdnuss*
das Beisel	(small) pub	*das Wirtshaus*
das Best	prize	*der Preis*
die Bim	tram	*die Straßenbahn*
der Karfiol	cauliflower	*der Blumenkohl*
die Marille	apricot	*die Aprikose*
das Obers	cream	*die Sahne*
der Paradeiser	tomato	*die Tomate*
die Ribisel	(red)currant	*die Johannisbeere*

Some of the words listed below are used both by people speaking
Standard German in Switzerland and by people speaking *Schweizerdeutsch*.
This is a spoken dialect, while Standard German is the written language of
German-speaking Switzerland.

Swiss German (Schweizerdeutsch)	English	Standard German
der Abwart	caretaker	*der Hausmeister*
das Bébé	baby	*das Baby*
das Billett	ticket	*die (Fahr)karte*
der Goalie	goalkeeper	*der Torwart*
grüezi!	hello!	*guten Tag!*
das Morgenessen	breakfast	*das Frühstück*
parkieren	to park	*parken*
die Serviertochter	waitress	*die Kellnerin*
salü!	hi!	*hallo!*
das Velo	bicycle	*das Fahrrad*

German words used in English

English was originally a Germanic language, and many of the oldest words in English are the same as, or very similar to, German words, for example, hand (*Hand*), man (*Mann*), house (*Haus*), garden (*Garten*), father (*Vater*), mother (*Mutter*), to have (*haben*), to sing (*singen*), to bring (*bringen*), to run (*rennen*).

In more recent times English has borrowed words from German such as delicatessen, kindergarten, blitz, angst, schadenfreude, lager, hamburger, rucksack.

It is often possible to work out how these words came about. For example, in German lager means 'storeroom', and Lagerbier was so called because it was kept for a while. Rucksacks are carried on your back, the German for back being *der Rücken*. Schadenfreude combines the words for misfortune (*der Schaden*) and pleasure (*die Freude*), and is a neat way of describing enjoyment of someone else's misfortune.

As in other languages some very familiar words used in English are the names of German inventors and scientists, for example Rudolf Diesel who invented the diesel engine, Daniel Fahrenheit who invented the alcohol thermometer and Hans Geiger, a nuclear physicist.

English words used in German

With the spread of English as a global means of communication, English terms have become very common in the German language.

Many of these terms mean the same in both languages:

das Baby	*die Software*
der Computer	*der Stress*
die Hardware	*das T-Shirt*
die Hitparade	*das WC*
das Internet	*der Western*
das Interview	*der Yuppie*

But be careful – others often have either totally different meanings in German and English, or they sound English but aren't proper English at all:

der Beamer	digital projector
die Box	(stereo) speaker
das Handy	mobile phone
der Oldtimer	vintage car
der Pullunder	tank top
der Slip	briefs, panties
der Smoking	dinner jacket
der Talkmaster	talk-show host
der Twen	twentysomething

Some informal German

We all use different language styles depending on the situation we find ourselves in.

When you visit a German-speaking country, you're sure to hear some informal expressions in everyday situations.

Here are some examples of informal German words:

bescheuert	crazy
flennen	to cry
geil	fantastic
die Glotze	television
das Klo	toilet
der Knast	prison
die Kneipe	pub
die Kohle	money
quatschen	to talk
schummeln	to cheat
tschüs(s)	bye bye
der Typ	guy
der Zoff	trouble

Informal language is marked very clearly in the dictionary to help you choose the appropriate word or phrase.

> *Be careful!*
> Be careful when using items marked 'informal' (*fam*) in your dictionary, and avoid ones marked 'offensive' (*vulg*) altogether.

Improving your pronunciation

There are a number of different methods you can use to improve your pronunciation and increase your confidence in speaking German:

- listen to German radio
- watch German-language films
- chat with German speakers

Some useful links are:
www.ard.de/radio/
A choice of German radio stations, plus information about cultural events.
www.dw-world.de/
Deutsche Welle, the equivalent of the BBC World Service.

Some points to help you with your pronunciation

Letters which are peculiar to German:

- **ä** is pronounced like English 'a' in '**ba**re'.

- **ö** is pronounced similar to English 'ea' in '**ea**rn'.

- **ü** is pronounced like French 'u' – round your lips and say 'ee'.

- **ß** is pronounced like English 's' in '**s**ing'.

Also note the following:

- **j** is usually pronounced like English 'y' in '**y**et'

- **v** is usually pronounced like 'f'.

- **w** is pronounced like 'v'.

Improving your fluency

Conversational words and phrases

In English we insert lots of words and phrases, such as *so, then, by the way*, into our conversation, to give our thoughts a structure and often to show our attitude. The German words below do the same thing. If you use them they will make you sound more fluent and natural.

- **also**
  Kommst du **also** mit (ja oder nein)?
  (=so, then)
  Also, wie ich schon sagte, ... (=well)

- **übrigens**
  Übrigens, du schuldest mir Geld.
  (=by the way)
  Ich habe sie **übrigens** gestern getroffen.
  (=by the way)

- **schließlich**
  Er hat es mir **schließlich** doch gesagt.
  (=eventually)
  Sie ist **schließlich** erst drei Jahre alt.
  (=after all)

- **stimmt!, stimmts?**
  Er ist doch in Australien. – **Stimmt!**
  (=correct!, that's right!)
  Du hast mich belogen, **stimmts?**
  (=right?)

- **wirklich**
  Bist du mir böse? – Nicht **wirklich**.
  (=really)
  Das hat mich **wirklich** geärgert.
  (=really)

- **jedenfalls**
  Es ist **jedenfalls** schon zu spät.
  (=anyhow)
  Er hat nichts gesagt, **jedenfalls** nichts Neues. (=anyway)

- **eigentlich**
  Wer hat das Spiel **eigentlich** gewonnen? (=actually)
  Bist du müde? – **Eigentlich** nicht.
  (=really)

- **nämlich**
  Wir bleiben zu Hause, es ist **nämlich** sehr regnerisch. (=since)
  Er ist **nämlich** mein bester Freund.
  (=you see)

- **überhaupt**
  Hörst du mir **überhaupt** zu? (=at all)
  Ich habe **überhaupt** keinen Grund dazu. (=whatsoever)

Improving your fluency

Varying the words you use to get your message across will make you sound more fluent in German. For example, you already know *Ich mag diesen Film*, but for a change you could say *Dieser Film gefällt mir* to mean the same thing. Here are some other suggestions:

Saying what you like or dislike

Die CD *hat mir sehr gut gefallen*.	I loved ...
Der Englandurlaub *hat uns Spaß gemacht*.	We enjoyed ...
Ich mag ihn.	I like ...
Ich mag keinen Fisch.	I don't like ...
Ich hasse Fußball.	I hate ...
Ich kann ihn nicht ausstehen.	I can't stand ...

Expressing your opinion

Ich denke, dass wir gehen sollten.	I think ...
Ich glaube, er hat richtig gehandelt.	I think ...
Ich meine, wir sollten es versuchen.	I think ...
Ich bin sicher, dass er gelogen hat.	I'm sure ...
Meiner Meinung nach hat er einen Fehler gemacht.	In my opinion ...

Agreeing or disagreeing

Du hast recht.	You're right.
Ich stimme Ihnen zu.	I agree with you.
Ich bin ganz Ihrer Meinung.	I totally agree with you.
Er hat unrecht.	He's wrong.
Ich bin anderer Meinung.	I disagree.

Correspondence

The following section on correspondence has been designed to help you communicate confidently in written as well as spoken German. Sample letters, e-mails and sections on text messaging and making telephone calls will ensure that you have all the vocabulary you need to correspond successfully in German.

Text messaging

Abbreviation	German	English
8ung	*Achtung*	look out
akla	*alles klar*	okay
bb	*bis bald*	see you soon
DaD	*denk an dich*	thinking of you
div	*danke im Voraus*	thanks in advance
GA	*Gruß an*	love/greetings to
GiE	*Ganz im Ernst*	seriously
GLG	*Ganz liebe Grüße*	love
gn8	*gute Nacht*	good night
GuK, G&K	*Gruß und Kuss*	love and kisses
ild	*Ich liebe dich*	I love you
mediwi	*melde dich wieder*	get in touch
mfg	*mit freundlichen Grüßen*	yours
rumian	*ruf mich an*	call me
sfh	*Schluss für heute*	enough for today
siw	*soweit ich weiß*	as far as I know
sTn	*schönen Tag noch*	have a nice day
sz	*schreib zurück*	write back
vlg	*viele Grüße*	love/greetings
vv	*viel Vergnügen*	have fun

Writing an e-mail

Hallo Markus,

hattest du vergessen, dass wir uns gestern treffen wollten? Anke und ich waren da und haben über eine Stunde lang auf dich gewartet. Bitte melde dich so bald wie möglich bei mir, sodass wir einen neuen Termin vereinbaren können.
Viele Grüße
Thomas

Datei (f)	file		*Allen antworten*	reply to all
Bearbeiten	to edit		*Weiterleiten*	to forward
Ansicht (f)	to view		*Anlage (f)*	attachment
Extras (ntpl)	tools		*An*	to
Verfassen	to compose		*Cc*	cc (carbon copy)
Hilfe (f)	help		*Bcc*	bcc (blind carbon copy)
Senden	to send		*Betreff (m)*	subject
Neue Nachricht (f)	new message		*Von*	from
Antworten	reply to sender		*Datum (nt)*	date

17

Here is some additional useful Internet vocabulary:

abmelden	to sign off	klicken	to click
anmelden	to sign in	Links (mpl)	links
ausloggen	to log off	Menü (nt)	menu
ausschneiden	to cut	Monitor (m)	monitor
Breitband (nt)	broadband	Ordner (m)	folder
Browser (m)	browser	Papierkorb (m)	recycle bin
chatten	to chat	Pfeiltasten (fpl)	arrow keys
Datenbank (f)	database	speichern	to save
doppelklicken	to double-click	suchen	to search
drucken	to print	Suchmaschine (f)	search engine
einfügen	to paste	(im Internet) surfen	to surf (the Net)
einloggen	to log on	Tabellenkalkulation (f)	spreadsheet
ersetzen	to replace	Tastatur (f)	keyboard
FAQ (nt)	FAQ	Verzeichnis (nt)	directory
Favoriten (mpl)	favourites	Webseite (f)	web page
Fenster (nt)	window	Website (f)	website
herunterladen	to download	weiter	forward
Homepage (f)	home page	(World Wide) Web (nt)	the (World-Wide) Web
Icon (nt)	icon	zurück	back
Internet (nt)	Internet		
Internetprovider (m)	Internet Service Provider		

Writing a personal letter

Town/city you are writing from, and the date; your full address is not given → Köln, 24. September 2006

Liebe Tante Erika,   No capital for start of letter

ich möchte mich ganz herzlich für dein tolles Geburtstagsgeschenk bedanken. Diese DVD habe ich mir schon seit langem gewünscht. Colin Farrell war schon immer mein Lieblingsschauspieler, und ich habe mir den Film bereits zweimal angesehen.

Den Sommerurlaub habe ich mit meiner Freundin in Frankreich verbracht. Aber in den nächsten Monaten muss ich mich intensiv auf mein Abitur vorbereiten. Ich hoffe, dass ich danach in München Medizin studieren kann. Vielleicht gehe ich aber zuvor noch für ein Jahr ins Ausland.

Ich habe gehört, dass Onkel Heinz vor kurzem krank war. Ich hoffe, es geht ihm inzwischen besser, und meine Eltern und ich freuen uns auf unseren Besuch bei euch im Oktober.

Viele Grüße

Jens

Writing a personal letter

Other ways of starting a personal letter	Other ways of ending a personal letter
Liebe Freunde	*Herzliche Grüße*
Liebe Anita, lieber Andreas	*Alles Gute*
Liebe Eltern	*Viele Grüße auch von ...*

Some useful phrases

Vielen Dank für deinen Brief.	Thank you for your letter.
Es war schön, von dir zu hören.	It was great to hear from you.
Tut mir Leid, dass ich erst jetzt antworte.	I'm sorry I didn't reply sooner.
Bitte grüße Silvia von mir.	Give my love to Silvia.
Mutti sendet viele Grüße.	Mum sends her best wishes.
Bitte schreib mir bald.	Please write soon.

Writing a formal letter

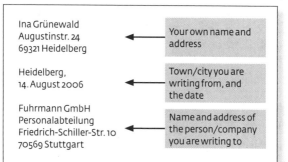

Ina Grünewald
Augustinstr. 24
69321 Heidelberg

→ Your own name and address

Heidelberg,
14. August 2006

→ Town/city you are writing from, and the date

Fuhrmann GmbH
Personalabteilung
Friedrich-Schiller-Str. 10
70569 Stuttgart

→ Name and address of the person/company you are writing to

Sehr geehrte Damen und Herren,

ich beziehe mich auf Ihr Stellenangebot in der Stuttgarter Zeitung vom 12. August und möchte mich als Fremdsprachenkorrespondentin in Ihrer Firma bewerben.

Ich verfüge über ausgezeichnete Englisch- und Französischkenntnisse sowie Grundkenntnisse in den Sprachen Spanisch und Portugiesisch. Darüber hinaus habe ich gute Erfahrung bei der Texterfassung am PC (ca. 220 Anschläge pro Minute).

Weitere Einzelheiten entnehmen Sie bitte dem beigefügten Lebenslauf.

Mit freundlichen Grüßen

Ina Grünewald

Writing a formal letter

Other ways of starting a formal letter	Other ways of ending a formal letter
Sehr geehrter Herr Franzen,	*... und verbleibe mit freundlichen*
Sehr geehrte Frau Meinhardt,	*Grüßen*
Sehr geehrter Herr Dr. Bleibtreu,	*Mit freundlichem Gruß*
Sehr geehrter Herr Professor,	*Hochachtungsvoll*

Some useful phrases

Vielen Dank für Ihr Schreiben vom ...	Thank you for your letter of ...
Mit Bezug auf ...	With reference to ...
Anbei schicke ich Ihnen ...	Please find enclosed ...
Ich würde mich freuen, von Ihnen zu hören.	I look forward to hearing from you ...
Ich danke Ihnen im Voraus für ...	Thank you in advance for ...

This is the dative form of "Herr" – the word "an" (=to) is assumed. If writing to a woman, use "Frau".

Herrn

Prof. Günter Seiffarth

Salamanderstr. 57

04989 Leipzig

DEUTSCHLAND

The house number comes after the street name, and the postcode comes before the name of the town.

Making a call

Asking for information

Was ist die Vorwahl für Freiburg?	What's the code for Freiburg?
Wie bekomme ich eine Amtsleitung?	How do I get an outside line?
Können Sie mir die Durchwahl für Herrn Faltermeier geben?	Could you give me the extension number for Mr Faltermeier?

When your number answers

Hallo! Ist Barbara da?	Hello! Is Barbara there?
Kann ich bitte mit Peter Martin sprechen?	Could I speak to Peter Martin, please?
Spreche ich mit Frau Schuster?	Is that Ms/Mrs Schuster?
Könnten Sie sie bitten, mich zurückzurufen?	Could you ask her to call me back?
Ich rufe in einer halben Stunde wieder an.	I'll call back in half an hour.
Kann ich bitte eine Nachricht hinterlassen?	Could I leave a message, please?

When you answer the telephone

Wer spricht bitte?	Who's speaking?
Hier ist Marion.	It's Marion speaking.
Am Apparat.	Speaking.

What you may hear

Wer ist am Apparat?	Who shall I say is calling?
Ich stelle durch.	I'm putting you through now.
Bitte bleiben Sie am Apparat.	Please hold.
Es meldet sich niemand.	There's no reply.
Es ist besetzt.	The line is engaged (Brit)/busy (US).
Möchten Sie eine Nachricht hinterlassen?	Would you like to leave a message?

If you have a problem

Tut mir Leid, ich habe mich verwählt.	Sorry, I dialled the wrong number.
Die Verbindung ist sehr schlecht.	This is a very bad line.
Ich kann Sie nur schlecht verstehen.	You're breaking up.
Mein Akku ist fast leer.	My battery's low.
Ich kann Sie nicht verstehen.	I can't hear you.

Saying your phone number

To tell someone your phone number in German, you usually divide the number up into pairs instead of saying each digit separately. For example:

0180 45 23 12

null-eins / achtzig / fünfundvierzig / dreiundzwanzig / zwölf

If there's an extra number, you say that first. For example:

238 47 32 94

zwei / achtunddreißig / siebenundvierzig / zweiunddreißig / vierundneunzig

German phrases and sayings

In German, as in many languages, people use vivid expressions based on images from their experience of real life. We've grouped the common expressions below according to the type of image they use. For fun, we have given you the word-for-word translation as well as the true English equivalent.

Fruit and vegetables

für einen Apfel und ein Ei
    word for word:
→ dirt cheap, as a bargain
for an apple and an egg

mit ihm ist nicht gut Kirschen essen
    word for word:
→ it's best not to tangle with him
you can't eat cherries with him

das macht den Kohl nicht fett
    word for word:
→ that won't be much help
it won't fatten the cabbage

sich die Radieschen von unten ansehen
    word for word:
→ to be pushing up the daisies
to look at the radishes from below

Animals and birds

da liegt der Hund begraben
    word for word:
→ that's the real problem
that's where the dog is buried

die Spatzen pfeifen es von den Dächern
    word for word:
→ it's common knowledge
the sparrows are whistling it from the rooftops

wo sich Hase und Fuchs gute Nacht sagen
    word for word:
→ in the middle of nowhere
where hare and fox bid each other good night

German phrases and sayings

die Katze im Sack kaufen → to buy a pig in a poke
    word for word: *to buy the cat in the bag*
die Sau rauslassen → to let one's hair down
    word for word: *to let the sow go*

The weather

das ist Schnee von gestern → it's old hat
    word for word: *it's yesterday's snow*
ein Gesicht wie drei Tage
Regenwetter → a miserable face
    word for word: *a face like three days' rain*
ein Sturm im Wasserglas → a storm in a teacup
    word for word: *a storm in a glass of water*
etwas in den Wind schreiben → to give something up for lost
    word for word: *to write something in the wind*
es regnet Bindfäden → it's bucketing down
    word for word: *it's raining pieces of string*

Parts of the body

sich den Kopf zerbrechen → to rack one's brains
    word for word: *to break one's head*
Hals über Kopf → head over heels
    word for word: *neck over head*
sich kein Bein ausreißen → not to overstrain oneself
    word for word: *not to tear one's leg off*
es brennt mir auf der Zunge → I'm dying to say it
    word for word: *it burns on my tongue*
auf großem Fuß leben → to live the high life
    word for word: *to live on a big foot*

German phrases and sayings

Clothes

mir platzt der Kragen → this is the last straw for me
    word for word: *my collar is bursting*

das ist Jacke wie Hose → it doesn't make the slightest difference

    word for word: *it's like jacket like trousers*

jemandem auf den Schlips treten → to tread on somebody's toes
    word for word: *to step on somebody's tie*

das sind zwei Paar Stiefel → they are two completely different things

    word for word: *they are two pairs of boots*

eine weiße Weste haben → to have a clean record
    word for word: *to have a white waistcoat*

Colours

das Blaue vom Himmel versprechen → to promise the moon
    word for word: *to promise the blue off the sky*

sie sind sich nicht grün → there's no love lost between them

    word for word: *they are not green to each other*

du kannst warten, bis du schwarz wirst → you can wait till the cows come home
    word for word: *you can wait till you go black*

eine Fahrt ins Blaue → a mystery tour
    word for word: *a journey into the blue*

sich eine goldene Nase verdienen → to make a mint
    word for word: *to earn a golden nose*

Some common translation difficulties

On the following pages we have shown some of the translation difficulties that you are most likely to come across. We hope that the tips we have given will help you to avoid these common pitfalls when writing and speaking German.

Du or Sie?

In German the word for 'you' depends on who you are talking to:

• To a person you know well, or to a child, use *du*:

  Will **you** lend me this CD? → *Kannst du mir diese CD leihen?*

• To more than one person you know well, or a group of children, use *ihr*:

  Do **you** understand, children? → *Versteht ihr das, Kinder?*

• To a person or people you do not know so well, use *Sie*:

  Have **you** met my wife? → *Kennen Sie meine Frau?*

> **Getting friendly**
> When you get to know someone, they may ask you:
> *Wollen wir uns duzen?* → Shall we use '*du*' to each other?

Singular versus plural

A word that is singular in English may be plural in German, and vice versa. Check in the dictionary if you are not sure:

Singular:	*Plural:*
headache	→ *die* Kopfschmerz**en**
Plural:	*Singular:*
my trouser**s**	→ *meine* Hose

27

Some common translation difficulties

'There is' and 'there are'

In German, when meaning 'to exist', these are both translated by *es gibt*:

There is no God. → *Es gibt keinen Gott.*
There are two reasons for this. → *Es gibt zwei Gründe dafür.*

In other contexts the most appropriate German verb is used – note that this is not necessarily *sein* (to be):

There is someone at the door. → *Jemand ist an der Tür.*
There are five books on the table. → *Fünf Bücher liegen auf dem Tisch.*

Word order

Word order in German sentences is much more variable than in English. If, for example, a German sentence begins with something other than the subject, the position of subject and verb will change:

Today **we** don't **have** any lessons. → *Heute haben wir keinen Unterricht.*
At 3 o'clock **my uncle** will **come** → *Um 3 Uhr kommt mein Onkel zu*
for a visit. *Besuch.*

This applies in particular to questions:

Why **are**n't **you** at school? → *Warum bist du nicht in der Schule?*
Where **did he** go? → *Wohin ist er gegangen?*

It is also worth noting the word order in clauses beginning with words like *that*, *if*, *because* and so on, where in German the verb always comes last:

I know that **she is** a teacher. → *Ich weiß, dass sie Lehrerin ist.*
I like him because **he** always **buys** me → *Ich mag ihn, weil er mir immer*
presents. *Geschenke kauft.*

Some common translation difficulties

Translating 'to'

The translation of 'to' varies a lot in German:

- When indicating a direction, 'to' is translated by *nach*:

the train **to** London	→ *der Zug **nach** London*
to the left	→ ***nach** links*

- But when you are talking about the time, *nach* would in fact mean 'past' – for 'to' you must use *vor*:

five **to** ten	→ *fünf **vor** zehn*

- When talking about going to a particular place or visiting a particular person, use *zu*:

We drove **to** the station.	→ *Wir fuhren **zum** Bahnhof.*
I'm going **to** Anne's house.	→ *Ich gehe **zu** Anne.*

- When you mean 'in order to', use *um...zu*:

He's going into town **(in order) to** buy a present.	→ *Er geht in die Stadt, **um** ein Geschenk **zu** kaufen.*

- In front of verbs, it is shown by the verb ending (*-en* or *-n*):

to eat	→ *ess**en***
to fish	→ *angel**n***

Translating 'to be'

'To be' usually corresponds to *sein*, but remember:

- In phrases describing how you feel, you sometimes use *haben*:

to be hungry/thirsty	→ *Hunger/Durst **haben***
to be afraid	→ *Angst **haben***

- To talk about your health, use *gehen*:

I**'m** very well, thank you	→ *Es **geht** mir sehr gut, danke.*

Some common translation difficulties

Translating 'to have'

'To have' usually corresponds to **haben**, but remember that while in English 'to have' is always used to form the perfect tense, in German many verbs take **sein** instead:

They **have** arrived	→ *Sie **sind** angekommen.*
She **has** gone to Berlin.	→ *Sie **ist** nach Berlin gegangen.*

Translating 'to go'

'To go' is normally translated by **gehen**, but if you are talking about various modes of transport, this may change:

• When talking about going by car, train or boat, use **fahren**:

We're **going** to Calais tomorrow.	→ *Morgen **fahren** wir nach Calais.*
My car won't **go**.	→ *Mein Auto **fährt** nicht.*

• When talking about going by plane, use **fliegen**:

This plane **goes** to Toronto.	→ *Dieses Flugzeug **fliegt** nach Toronto.*

Translating 'to know'

In German, there are two ways of translating 'to know'. It is important not to get them confused:

• When talking about knowing facts, use **wissen**:

Do you **know** how this works?	→ ***Weißt** du, wie das funktioniert?*
I don't **know**.	→ *Ich **weiß** nicht.*

• When talking about knowing people and places, use **kennen**:

I **know** Berlin well.	→ *Ich **kenne** Berlin gut.*
Do you **know** her?	→ ***Kennst** du sie?*

Some common translation difficulties

Translating 'to put'

German tends to be a lot more specific than English when talking about putting things in certain places:

- When putting something down flat, use *legen*:

    Put the book in the drawer. → *Leg das Buch in die Schublade.*
    Where shall I **put** my things? → *Wohin soll ich meine Sachen legen?*

- When putting something upright, use *stellen*:

    Put the book on the shelf. → *Stell das Buch ins Regal.*
    She **put** the vase on the table. → *Sie stellte die Vase auf den Tisch.*

- When 'to put' means 'to sit' or 'to place', use *setzen*:

    She **put** the child on the chair. → *Sie setzte das Kind auf den Stuhl.*
    Put the red ball behind the black one. → *Setz die rote Kugel hinter die schwarze.*

Translating '-ing'

Unlike English, German does not distinguish between the simple and continuous form of verbs. The simple form is used for both:

    He smok**es** cigarettes. → *Er raucht Zigaretten.*
    He is smok**ing** a cigarette. → *Er raucht eine Zigarette.*

If you want to emphasize that somebody is doing something at this very moment, you have to add the word *gerade*.

    He is smok**ing** a cigarette. → *Er raucht gerade eine Zigarette.*

a

abandon [əˈbændən] vt
(desert) verlassen; (give up)
aufgeben

abbey [ˈæbɪ] n Abtei f

abbreviate [əˈbriːvɪeɪt] vt
abkürzen; **abbreviation**
[əbriːvɪˈeɪʃən] n Abkürzung f

ABC [ˈeɪbiːˈsiː] n (a. fig) Abc nt

abdicate [ˈæbdɪkeɪt] vi (king)
abdanken; **abdication**
[æbdɪˈkeɪʃən] n Abdankung f

abdomen [ˈæbdəmən] n Unterleib m

ability [əˈbɪlɪtɪ] n Fähigkeit f;
able [ˈeɪbl] adj fähig; **to be ~ to
do sth** etw tun können

abnormal [æbˈnɔːml] adj
anormal

aboard [əˈbɔːd] adv, prep an Bord
+gen

abolish [əˈbɒlɪʃ] vt abschaffen

aborigine [æbəˈrɪdʒɪniː] n Ur-
einwohner(in) m(f) (Australiens)

abort [əˈbɔːt] vt (Med: foetus)
abtreiben; (Space: mission)
abbrechen; **abortion** [əˈbɔːʃən] n
Abtreibung f

KEYWORD

a [eɪ, ə; æn, ən] (before vowel or
silent h: **an**) indef art **1** ein,
eine; **a woman** eine Frau; **a
book** ein Buch; **an eagle** ein
Adler; **she's a doctor** sie ist
Ärztin

2 (instead of the number "one") ein,
eine; **a year ago** vor einem Jahr; **a
hundred/thousand** etc **pounds**
(ein) hundert/(ein) tausend etc
Pfund

3 (in expressing ratios, prices etc) pro;
3 a day/week 3 pro Tag/Woche, 3
am Tag/in der Woche; **10 km an
hour** 10 km pro Stunde/in der
Stunde

AA abbr = **Automobile
Association** britischer
Automobilklub, ≈ ADAC m

aback adv: **taken ~** erstaunt

KEYWORD

about [əˈbaʊt] adv **1**
(approximately) etwa, ungefähr;
about a hundred/thousand etc
etwa hundert/tausend etc; **at
about 2 o'clock** etwa um 2 Uhr;
I've just about finished ich bin
gerade fertig

2 (referring to place) herum, umher;
to leave things lying about
Sachen herumliegen lassen; **to
run/walk** etc **about**
herumrennen/gehen etc

3 to be about to do sth im Begriff
sein, etw zu tun; **he was about to
go to bed** er wollte gerade ins Bett
gehen

▷ prep **1** (relating to) über +akk; **a book about London** ein Buch über London; **what is it about?** worum geht es?; (book etc) wovon handelt es?; **we talked about it** wir haben darüber geredet; **what** o **how about doing this?** wollen wir das machen?
2 (referring to place) um (... herum); **to walk about the town** in der Stadt herumgehen; **her clothes were scattered about the room** ihre Kleider waren über das ganze Zimmer verstreut

above [əˈbʌv] adv oben; **children aged 8 and ~** Kinder ab 8 Jahren; **on the floor ~** ein Stockwerk höher ▷ prep über; **~ 40 degrees** über 40 Grad; **~ all** vor allem ▷ adj obig

abroad [əˈbrɔːd] adv im Ausland; **to go ~** ins Ausland gehen

abrupt [əˈbrʌpt] adj (sudden) plötzlich, abrupt

abscess [ˈæbsɪs] n Geschwür nt

absence [ˈæbsəns] n Abwesenheit f; **absent** [ˈæbsənt] adj abwesend; **to be ~** fehlen; **absent-minded** adj zerstreut

absolute [ˈæbsəluːt] adj absolut; (power) unumschränkt; (rubbish) vollkommen, total; **absolutely** adv absolut; (true, stupid) vollkommen; **~!** genau!; **you're ~ right** du hast/Sie haben völlig recht

absorb [əbˈzɔːb] vt absorbieren; (fig: information) in sich aufnehmen; **absorbed** adj: **~ in sth** in etw vertieft; **absorbent** adj absorbierend; **~ cotton** (US) Watte f; **absorbing** adj (fig) faszinierend, fesselnd

abstain [əbˈsteɪn] vi: **to ~ (from voting)** sich (der Stimme) enthalten

abstract [ˈæbstrækt] adj abstrakt

absurd [əbˈsɜːd] adj absurd

abundance [əˈbʌndəns] n Reichtum m (of an +dat)

abuse [əˈbjuːs] n (rude language) Beschimpfungen pl; (mistreatment) Missbrauch m ▷ [əˈbjuːz] vt (misuse) missbrauchen; **abusive** [əˈbjuːsɪv] adj beleidigend

AC abbr = **alternating current** Wechselstrom m ▷ abbr = **air conditioning** Klimaanlage

a/c abbr = **account** Kto.

academic [ækəˈdemɪk] n Wissenschaftler(in) m(f) ▷ adj akademisch, wissenschaftlich

accelerate [ækˈseləreɪt] vi (car etc) beschleunigen; (driver) Gas geben; **acceleration** [əkseləˈreɪʃən] n Beschleunigung f; **accelerator** [əkˈseləreɪtə*] n Gas(pedal) nt

accent [ˈæksent] n Akzent m

accept [əkˈsept] vt annehmen; (agree to) akzeptieren; (responsibility) übernehmen; **acceptable** [əkˈseptəbl] adj annehmbar

access [ˈækses] n Zugang m; (Inform) Zugriff m; **accessible** [əkˈsesəbl] adj (leicht) zugänglich/erreichbar; (place) (leicht) erreichbar

accessory [əkˈsesərɪ] n Zubehörteil nt

access road n Zufahrtsstraße f

accident [ˈæksɪdənt] n Unfall m; **by ~** zufällig; **accidental** [æksɪˈdentl] adj unbeabsichtigt; (meeting) zufällig; (death) durch Unfall; **~ damage** Unfallschaden m; **accident-prone** adj vom Pech verfolgt

acclimatize [əˈklaɪmətaɪz] vt: **to ~ oneself** sich gewöhnen (to an +akk)

accommodate [əˈkɒmədeɪt] vt unterbringen; **accommodation(s)** [əkɒməˈdeɪʃən(z)] n Unterkunft f

accompany [əˈkʌmpənɪ] vt begleiten

accomplish [əˈkʌmplɪʃ] vt erreichen

accord [əˈkɔːd] n: **of one's own ~** freiwillig; **according to** prep nach, laut +dat

account [əˈkaʊnt] n (in bank etc) Konto nt; (narrative) Bericht m; **on ~ of** wegen; **on no ~** auf keinen Fall; **to take into ~** berücksichtigen, in Betracht ziehen; **accountant** [əˈkaʊntənt] n Buchhalter(in) m(f); **account for** vt (explain) erklären; (expenditure) Rechenschaft ablegen für; **account number** n Kontonummer f

accumulate [əˈkjuːmjʊleɪt] vt ansammeln ▷ vi sich ansammeln

accuracy [ˈækjʊrəsɪ] n Genauigkeit f; **accurate** [ˈækjʊrɪt] adj genau

accusation [ækjʊˈzeɪʃən] n Anklage f, Beschuldigung f

accusative [əˈkjuːzətɪv] n Akkusativ m

accuse [əˈkjuːz] vt beschuldigen; (Jur) anklagen (of wegen +gen); **~ sb of doing sth** jdn beschuldigen, etw getan zu haben; **accused** n (Jur) Angeklagte(r) mf

accustom [əˈkʌstəm] vt gewöhnen (to an +akk); **accustomed** adj gewohnt; **to get ~ to sth** sich an etw akk gewöhnen

ace [eɪs] n Ass nt ▷ adj Star-

ache [eɪk] n Schmerz m ▷ vi wehtun

achieve [əˈtʃiːv] vt erreichen; **achievement** n Leistung f

acid [ˈæsɪd] n Säure f ▷ adj sauer; **~ rain** saurer Regen

acknowledge [əkˈnɒlɪdʒ] vt (recognize) anerkennen; (admit) zugeben; (receipt of letter etc) bestätigen; **acknowledgement** n Anerkennung f; (of letter) Empfangsbestätigung f

acne [ˈæknɪ] n Akne f

acorn [ˈeɪkɔːn] n Eichel f

acoustic [əˈkuːstɪk] adj akustisch; **acoustics** [əˈkuːstɪks] npl Akustik f

acquaintance [əˈkweɪntəns] n (person) Bekannte(r) mf

acquire [əˈkwaɪə*] vt erwerben, sich aneignen; **acquisition** [ækwɪˈzɪʃn] n (of skills etc) Erwerb m; (object) Anschaffung f

acrobat [ˈækrəbæt] n Akrobat(in) m(f)

across [əˈkrɒs] prep über +akk; **he lives ~ the street** er wohnt auf der anderen Seite der Straße ▷ adv hinüber, herüber; **100m ~** 100m breit

act [ækt] n (deed) Tat f; (Jur: law) Gesetz nt; (Theat) Akt m; (fig: pretence) Schau f; **it's all an ~** es ist alles nur Theater; **to be in the ~ of doing sth** gerade dabei sein, etw zu tun ▷ vi (take action) handeln; (behave) sich verhalten; (Theat) spielen; **to ~ as** (person) fungieren als; (thing) dienen als ▷ vt (a part) spielen

action [ˈækʃən] n (of play, novel etc) Handlung f; (in film etc) Action f; (Mil) Kampf m; **to take ~** etwas unternehmen; **out of ~** (machine) außer Betrieb; **to put a plan into ~** einen Plan in die Tat umsetzen; **action replay** n (Sport, TV) Wiederholung f

activate [ˈæktɪveɪt] vt aktivieren; **active** [ˈæktɪv] adj aktiv; (child) lebhaft; **activity** [ækˈtɪvɪtɪ] n Aktivität f; (occupation) Beschäftigung f; (organized event) Veranstaltung f

actor ['æktə°] n Schauspieler(in) m(f); **actress** ['æktrɪs] n Schauspielerin f

actual ['æktjʊəl] adj wirklich; **actually** adv eigentlich; (said in surprise) tatsächlich

acupuncture ['ækjʊpʌŋktʃə°] n Akupunktur f

acute [ə'kju:t] adj (pain) akut; (sense of smell) fein; (Math: angle) spitz

ad [æd] abbr = **advertisement**

AD abbr = **Anno Domini** nach Christi, n. Chr.

adapt [ə'dæpt] vi sich anpassen (to +dat) ▷ vt anpassen (to +dat); (rewrite) bearbeiten (for für); **adaptable** adj anpassungsfähig; **adaptation** n (of book etc) Bearbeitung f; **adapter** n (Elec) Zwischenstecker m, Adapter m

add [æd] vt (ingredient) hinzufügen; (numbers) addieren; **add up** vi (make sense) stimmen ▷ vt (numbers) addieren

addict ['ædɪkt] n Süchtige(r) mf; **addicted** [ə'dɪktɪd] adj: ~ to alcohol/drugs alkohol-/ drogensüchtig

addition [ə'dɪʃən] n Zusatz m; (to bill) Aufschlag m; (Math) Addition f; **in** ~ außerdem, zusätzlich (to zu); **additional** adj zusätzlich, weiter; **additive** ['ædɪtɪv] n Zusatz m; **add-on** ['ædɒn] n Zusatzgerät nt

address [ə'dres] n Adresse f ▷ vt (letter) adressieren; (person) anreden

adequate ['ædɪkwɪt] adj (appropriate) angemessen; (sufficient) ausreichend; (time) genügend

adhesive [əd'hi:sɪv] n Klebstoff m; **adhesive tape** n Klebstreifen m

adjacent [ə'dʒeɪsənt] adj benachbart

adjective ['ædʒəktɪv] n Adjektiv nt

adjoining [ə'dʒɔɪnɪŋ] adj benachbart, Neben-

adjust [ə'dʒʌst] vt einstellen; (put right also) richtig stellen; (speed, flow) regulieren; (in position) verstellen ▷ vi sich anpassen (to +dat); **adjustable** adj verstellbar

admin [əd'mɪn] n (fam) Verwaltung f; **administration** [ədmɪnɪs'treɪʃən] n Verwaltung f; (Pol) Regierung f

admirable ['ædmərəbl] adj bewundernswert; **admiration** [ædmɪ'reɪʃən] n Bewunderung f; **admire** [əd'maɪə°] vt bewundern

admission [əd'mɪʃən] n (entrance) Zutritt m; (to university etc) Zulassung f; (fee) Eintritt m; (confession) Eingeständnis nt; **admission charge, admission fee** n Eintrittspreis m; **admit** [əd'mɪt] vt (let in) hereinlassen (to in +akk); (to university etc) zulassen; (confess) zugeben, gestehen; **to be ~ted to hospital** ins Krankenhaus eingeliefert werden

adolescent [ædə'lesnt] n Jugendliche(r) mf

adopt [ə'dɒpt] vt (child) adoptieren; (idea) übernehmen; **adoption** [ə'dɒptʃn] n (of child) Adoption f; (of idea) Übernahme f

adorable [ə'dɔ:rəbl] adj entzückend; **adore** [ə'dɔ:°] vt anbeten; (person) über alles lieben, vergöttern

adult ['ædʌlt] adj (person) erwachsen; (film etc) für Erwachsene ▷ n Erwachsene(r) mf

adultery [ə'dʌltəri] n Ehebruch m

advance [əd'vɑ:ns] n (money) Vorschuss m; (progress) Fortschritt

m; **in ~** im Voraus; **to book in ~**
vorbestellen ▷ *vi* (*move forward*)
vorrücken ▷ *vt* (*money*)
vorschießen; **advance booking** *n*
Reservierung *f*; (*Theat*) Vorverkauf
m; **advanced** *adj* (*modern*)
fortschrittlich; (*course, study*) für
Fortgeschrittene; **advance**
payment *n* Vorauszahlung *f*

advantage [əd'vɑ:ntɪdʒ] *n*
Vorteil *m*; **to take ~ of** (*exploit*)
ausnutzen; (*profit from*) Nutzen
ziehen aus; **it's to your ~** es ist in
deinem/Ihrem Interesse

adventure [əd'ventʃə*] *n*
Abenteuer *nt*; **adventure holiday**
n Abenteuerurlaub *m*; **adventure**
playground *n* Abenteuerspiel-
platz *m*; **adventurous**
[əd'ventʃərəs] *adj* (*person*)
abenteuerlustig

adverb ['ædvɜ:b] *n* Adverb *nt*

adverse ['ædvɜ:s] *adj* (*conditions*
etc) ungünstig; (*effect, comment etc*)
negativ

advert ['ædvɜ:t] *n* Anzeige *f*;
advertise ['ædvətaɪz] *vt* werben
für; (*in newspaper*) inserieren; (*job*)
ausschreiben ▷ *vi* Reklame
machen; (*in newspaper*)
annoncieren; (*for* für);
advertisement [əd'vɜ:tɪsmənt]
n Werbung *f*; (*announcement*)
Anzeige *f*; **advertising** *n*
Werbung *f*

advice [əd'vaɪs] *n* Rat(schlag) *m*;
word *o* **piece of ~** Ratschlag *m*;
take my ~ hör auf mich;
advisable [əd'vaɪzəbl] *adj* rat-
sam; **advise** [əd'vaɪz] *vt* raten
(*sb* jdm); **to ~ sb to do sth/not to**
do sth jdm zuraten/abraten, etw
zu tun

Aegean [iː'dʒiːən] *n*: **the ~** (**Sea**)
die Ägäis

aerial ['ɛərɪəl] *n* Antenne *f* ▷ *adj*
Luft-

aerobatics [ɛərəʊ'bætɪks] *npl*
Kunstfliegen *nt*

aerobics [ɛə'rəʊbɪks] *nsing*
Aerobic *nt*

aeroplane ['ɛərəpleɪn] *n*
Flugzeug *nt*

afaik *abbr* = **as far as I know**;
(*SMS*) ≈ soweit ich weiß

affair [ə'fɛə*] *n* (*matter, business*)
Sache *f*, Angelegenheit *f*; (*scandal*)
Affäre *f*; (*love affair*) Verhältnis *nt*

affect [ə'fekt] *vt* (*influence*)
(ein)wirken auf +*akk*; (*health,*
organ) angreifen; (*move deeply*)
berühren; (*concern*) betreffen;
affection [ə'fekʃən] *n* Zuneigung
f; **affectionate** [ə'fekʃnɪt] *adj*
liebevoll

affluent ['æfluənt] *adj*
wohlhabend

afford [ə'fɔːd] *vt* sich leisten; **I**
can't ~ it ich kann es mir nicht
leisten; **affordable** [ə'fɔːdəbl]
adj erschwinglich

Afghanistan [æf'gænɪstæn] *n*
Afghanistan *nt*

aforementioned
[əfɔː'menʃənd] *adj* oben genannt

afraid [ə'freɪd] *adj*: **to be ~** Angst
haben (*of vor* +*dat*); **to be ~ that ...**
fürchten, dass ...; **I'm ~ I don't**
know das weiß ich leider nicht

Africa ['æfrɪkə] *n* Afrika *nt*;
African *adj* afrikanisch ▷ *n*
Afrikaner(in) *m(f)*; **African**
American, **Afro-American** *n*
Afroamerikaner(in) *m(f)*

after ['ɑːftə*] *prep* nach; **ten**
~ five (*US*) zehn nach fünf; **to be**
~ sb/sth (*following, seeking*) hinter
jdm/etw her sein; **~ all**
schließlich; (*in spite of everything*)
(schließlich) doch ▷ *conj*
nachdem ▷ *adv*: **soon ~** bald
danach; **aftercare** *n*
Nachbehandlung *f*; **after-effect** *n*
Nachwirkung *f*

afternoon n Nachmittag m; **~, good ~** guten Tag!; **in the ~** nachmittags

afters npl Nachtisch m; **after-sales service** n Kundendienst m; **after-shave (lotion)** n Rasierwasser nt; **afterwards** adv nachher; (after that) danach

again [ə'gen] adv wieder; (one more time) noch einmal; **not ~!** (nicht) schon wieder; **~ and ~** immer wieder; **the same ~ please** das Gleiche noch mal bitte

against [ə'genst] prep gegen; **~ my will** wider Willen; **~ the law** unrechtmäßig, illegal

age [eidʒ] n Alter nt; (period of history) Zeitalter nt; **at the ~ of four** im Alter von vier (Jahren); **what ~ is she?, what is her ~?** wie alt ist sie?; **to come of ~** volljährig werden; **under ~** minderjährig ▷ vi altern, alt werden; **aged** adj: **~ thirty** dreißig Jahre alt; **a son ~ twenty** ein zwanzigjähriger Sohn ▷ adj ['eidʒid] (elderly) betagt; **age group** n Altersgruppe f; **ageism** n Diskriminierung f aufgrund des Alters; **age limit** n Altersgrenze f

agency ['eidʒənsɪ] n Agentur f

agenda [ə'dʒendə] n Tagesordnung f

agent ['eidʒənt] n (Comm) Vertreter(in) m(f); (for writer, actor etc) Agent(in) m(f)

aggression [ə'greʃn] n Aggression f; **aggressive** [ə'gresɪv] adj aggressiv

agitated adj aufgeregt; **to get ~** sich aufregen

AGM abbr = **Annual General Meeting** JHV f

ago [ə'gəʊ] adv: **two days ~** heute vor zwei Tagen; **not long ~** (erst) vor Kurzem

agonize ['ægənaɪz] vi sich den Kopf zerbrechen (over über dat); **agonizing** adj qualvoll; **agony** ['ægənɪ] n Qual f

agree [ə'griː] vt (date, price etc) vereinbaren; **to ~ to do sth** sich bereit erklären, etw zu tun; **to ~ that ...** sich dat einig sein, dass ...; (decide) beschließen, dass ...; (admit) zugeben, dass ... ▷ vi (have same opinion, correspond) übereinstimmen (with mit); (consent) zustimmen; (come to an agreement) sich einigen (about, on auf +akk); (food) **not to ~ with sb** jdm nicht bekommen; **agreement** n (agreeing) Übereinstimmung f; (contract) Abkommen nt, Vereinbarung f

agricultural [ægrɪ'kʌltʃərəl] adj landwirtschaftlich, Landwirtschafts-; **agriculture** ['ægrɪkʌltʃə*] n Landwirtschaft f

ahead [ə'hed] adv: **to be ~** führen, vorne liegen; **~ of** vor +dat; **to be ~ of sb** (person) jdm voraus sein; (thing) vor jdm liegen; **to be 3 metres ~** 3 Meter Vorsprung haben

aid [eid] n Hilfe f; **in ~ of** zugunsten +gen; **with the ~ of** mithilfe +gen ▷ vt helfen +dat; (support) unterstützen

Aids [eidz] n acr = **acquired immune deficiency syndrome** Aids nt

aim [eim] vt (gun, camera) richten (at auf +akk) ▷ vi: **to ~ at** (with gun etc) zielen auf +akk; (fig) abzielen auf +akk; **to ~ to do sth** beabsichtigen, etw zu tun ▷ n Ziel nt

air [ɛə*] n Luft f; **in the open ~** im Freien; (Radio, TV) **to be on the ~** (programme) auf Sendung sein;

(station) senden ▷ vt lüften;
airbag n (Auto) Airbag m;
air-conditioned adj mit
Klimaanlage; **air-conditioning** n
Klimaanlage f; **aircraft** n
Flugzeug nt; **airfield** n Flugplatz
m; **air force** n Luftwaffe f;
airgun n Luftgewehr nt;
airline n Fluggesellschaft f;
airmail n Luftpost f; **by ~** mit
Luftpost; **airplane** n (US)
Flugzeug nt; **air pollution** n
Luftverschmutzung f; **airport** n
Flughafen m; **airsick** adj
luftkrank; **airtight** adj luftdicht;
air-traffic controller n Fluglotse
m, Fluglotsin f; **airy** adj luftig;
(manner) lässig
aisle [aɪl] n Gang m; (in church)
Seitenschiff nt; **~ seat** Sitz m am
Gang
ajar [ə'dʒɑːʳ] adj (door) angelehnt
alarm [ə'lɑːm] n (warning) Alarm
m; (bell etc) Alarmanlage f ▷ vt
beunruhigen; **alarm clock** n
Wecker m; **alarmed** adj (protected)
alarmgesichert; **alarming** adj
beunruhigend
Albania [æl'beɪnɪə] n Albanien
nt; **Albanian** adj albanisch ▷ n
(person) Albaner(in) m(f); (language)
Albanisch nt
album ['ælbəm] n Album nt
alcohol ['ælkəhɒl] n Alkohol m;
alcohol-free adj alkoholfrei;
alcoholic [ælkə'hɒlɪk] adj (drink)
alkoholisch ▷ n Alkoholiker(in)
m(f); **alcoholism** n Alkoholismus
m
ale [eɪl] n Ale nt (helles englisches
Bier)
alert [ə'lɜːt] adj wachsam ▷ n
Alarm m ▷ vt warnen (to vor +dat)
algebra ['ældʒɪbrə] n Algebra f
Algeria [æl'dʒɪərɪə] n Algerien nt
alibi ['ælɪbaɪ] n Alibi nt
alien ['eɪlɪən] n (foreigner)

Ausländer(in) m(f); (from space)
Außerirdische(r) mf
align [ə'laɪn] vt ausrichten (with
auf +akk)
alike [ə'laɪk] adj, adv gleich;
(similar) ähnlich
alive [ə'laɪv] adj lebendig; **to
keep sth ~** etw am Leben
erhalten; **he's still ~** er lebt noch

KEYWORD

all [ɔːl] adj alle(r, s); **all day/night**
den ganzen Tag/die ganze Nacht;
all men are equal alle Menschen
sind gleich; **all five came** alle fünf
kamen; **all the books/food** die
ganzen Bücher/das ganze Essen;
all the time die ganze Zeit (über);
all his life sein ganzes Leben
(lang)
▷ pron **1** alles; **I ate it all, I ate all of
it** ich habe alles gegessen; **all of
us/the boys went** wir gingen
alle/alle Jungen gingen; **we all sat
down** wir setzten uns alle
2 (in phrases) **above all** vor allem;
after all schließlich; **at all: not at
all** (in answer to question)
überhaupt nicht; (in answer to
thanks) gern geschehen; **I'm not at
all tired** ich bin überhaupt nicht
müde; **anything at all will do** es
ist egal, welche(r, s); **all in all** alles
in allem
▷ adv ganz; **all alone** ganz allein;
it's not as hard as all that so
schwer ist es nun auch wieder
nicht; **all the more/the better**
umso mehr/besser; **all but** fast;
the score is 2 all es steht 2 zu 2

allegation [ælɪ'geɪʃən] n
Behauptung f; **alleged** adj
angeblich
allergic [ə'lɜːdʒɪk] adj allergisch

(*to* gegen); **allergy** ['ælədʒɪ] *n*
Allergie *f*
alleviate [ə'liːvɪeɪt] *vt* (*pain*)
lindern
alley ['ælɪ] *n* (enge) Gasse;
(*passage*) Durchgang *m*; (*bowling*)
Bahn *f*
alliance [ə'laɪəns] *n* Bündnis *nt*
alligator ['ælɪgeɪtə*] *n* Alligator
m
all-night *adj* (*café, cinema*) die
ganze Nacht geöffnet
allocate ['æləkeɪt] *vt* zuweisen,
zuteilen (*to dat*)
allotment *n* (*plot*)
Schrebergarten *m*
allow [ə'laʊ] *vt* (*permit*) erlauben
(*sb* jdm); (*grant*) bewilligen; (*time*)
einplanen; **allow for** *vt*
berücksichtigen; (*cost etc*)
einkalkulieren; **allowance** *n* (*from
state*) Beihilfe *f*; (*from parent*)
Unterhaltsgeld *nt*
all right ['ɔːl'raɪt] *adj* okay, in
Ordnung; **I'm ~** mir geht's gut
▷ *adv* (*satisfactorily*) ganz gut
▷ *interj* okay
all-time *adj* (*record, high*) aller
Zeiten
allusion [ə'luːʒn] *n* Anspielung *f*
(*to* auf +*akk*)
ally ['ælaɪ] *n* Verbündete(r) *mf*;
(*Hist*) Alliierte(r) *mf*
almond ['ɑːmənd] *n* Mandel *f*
almost ['ɔːlməʊst] *adv* fast
alone [ə'ləʊn] *adj, adv* allein
along [ə'lɒŋ] *prep* entlang
+*akk*; **~ the river** den Fluss
entlang; (*position*) am Fluss
entlang ▷ *adv* (*onward*) weiter;
~ with zusammen mit; **all ~** die
ganze Zeit, von Anfang an;
alongside *prep* neben +*dat* ▷ *adv*
(*walk*) nebenher
aloud [ə'laʊd] *adv* laut
alphabet ['ælfəbet] *n* Alphabet
nt

alpine ['ælpaɪn] *adj* alpin; **Alps**
[ælps] *npl* die **~** die Alpen
already [ɔːl'redɪ] *adv* schon,
bereits
Alsace ['ælsæs] *n* Elsass *nt*;
Alsatian [æl'seɪʃən] *adj*
elsässisch ▷ *n* Elsässer(in) *m(f)*;
(*Brit: dog*) Schäferhund *m*
also ['ɔːlsəʊ] *adv* auch
altar ['ɔːltə*] *n* Altar *m*
alter ['ɔːltə*] *vt* ändern;
alteration [ɔːltə'reɪʃən] *n*
Änderung *f*; **~s** (*to building*) Umbau
m
alternate [ɔːl'tɜːnət] *adj*
abwechselnd ▷ ['ɔːltəneɪt] *vi*
abwechseln (*with* mit);
alternating current *n*
Wechselstrom *m*
alternative [ɔːl'tɜːnətɪv] *adj*
Alternativ- ▷ *n* Alternative *f*
although [ɔːl'ðəʊ] *conj* obwohl
altitude ['æltɪtjuːd] *n* Höhe *f*
altogether [ɔːltə'geðə*] *adv* (*in
total*) insgesamt; (*entirely*) ganz
und gar
aluminium, aluminum (*US*)
[æljʊ'mɪnɪəm, ə'luːmɪnəm] *n*
Aluminium *nt*
always ['ɔːlweɪz] *adv* immer
am [æm] *present of* **be**; bin
am, a.m. *abbr* = **ante meridiem**
vormittags, vorm.
amateur ['æmətə*] *n* Ama-
teur(in) *m(f)* ▷ *adj* Amateur-;
(*theatre, choir*) Laien-
amaze [ə'meɪz] *vt* erstaunen;
amazed *adj* erstaunt (*at* über
+*akk*); **amazing** *adj* erstaunlich
Amazon ['æməzən] *n*: **~ (river)**
Amazonas *m*
ambassador [æm'bæsədə*] *n*
Botschafter *m*
amber ['æmbə*] *n* Bernstein *m*
ambiguity [æmbɪ'gjuːtɪ] *n*
Zweideutigkeit *f*; **ambiguous**
[æm'bɪgjʊəs] *adj* zweideutig

ambition [æm'bɪʃən] n Ambition f; (ambitious nature) Ehrgeiz m; **ambitious** [æm'bɪʃəs] adj ehrgeizig

ambulance ['æmbjʊləns] n Krankenwagen m

amend [ə'mend] vt (law etc) ändern

America [ə'merɪkə] n Amerika nt; **American** adj amerikanisch ▷ n Amerikaner(in) m(f); **native ~** Indianer(in) m(f)

amiable ['eɪmɪəbl] adj liebenswürdig

amicable ['æmɪkəbl] adj freundlich; (relations) freundschaftlich; (Jur: settlement) gütlich

amnesia [æm'niːzɪə] n Gedächtnisverlust m

among(st) [ə'mʌŋ(st)] prep unter +dat

amount [ə'maʊnt] n (quantity) Menge f; (of money) Betrag m; **a large/small ~ of ...** ziemlich viel/wenig ... ▷ vi: **to ~ to** (total) sich belaufen auf +akk

amp, ampere [æmp, 'æmpɛə˚] n Ampere nt

amplifier ['æmplɪfaɪə˚] n Verstärker m

amputate ['æmpjʊteɪt] vt amputieren

Amtrak® ['æmtræk] n amerikanische Eisenbahngesellschaft

amuse [ə'mjuːz] vt amüsieren; (entertain) unterhalten; **amused** adj: **I'm not ~** das finde ich gar nicht lustig; **amusement** n (enjoyment) Vergnügen nt; (recreation) Unterhaltung f; **amusement arcade** n Spielhalle f; **amusement park** n Vergnügungspark m; **amusing** adj amüsant

an [æn, ən] art ein(e)

anaemic [ə'niːmɪk] adj blutarm

anaesthetic [ænɪs'θetɪk] n Narkose f; (substance) Narkosemittel nt

analyse, analyze ['ænəlaɪz] vt analysieren; **analysis** [ə'nælɪsɪs] n Analyse f

anatomy [ə'nætəmɪ] n Anatomie f; (structure) Körperbau m

ancestor ['ænsestə˚] n Vorfahr m

anchor ['æŋkə˚] n Anker m ▷ vt verankern; **anchorage** n Ankerplatz m

anchovy ['æntʃəvɪ] n Sardelle f

ancient ['eɪnʃənt] adj alt; (fam: person, clothes etc) uralt

and [ænd, ənd] conj und

Andorra [æn'dɔːrə] n Andorra nt

anemic adj (US) see **anaemic**

anesthetic n (US) see **anaesthetic**

angel ['eɪndʒəl] n Engel m

anger ['æŋgə˚] n Zorn m ▷ vt ärgern

angina, angina pectoris [æn'dʒaɪnə('pektərɪs)] n Angina Pectoris f

angle ['æŋgl] n Winkel m; (fig) Standpunkt m

angler ['æŋglə˚] n Angler(in) m(f); **angling** ['æŋglɪŋ] n Angeln nt

angry ['æŋgrɪ] adj verärgert; (stronger) zornig; **to be ~ with sb** auf jdn böse sein

angular ['æŋgjʊlə˚] adj eckig; (face) kantig

animal ['ænɪməl] n Tier nt; **animal rights** npl Tierrechte pl

animated ['ænɪmeɪtɪd] adj lebhaft; **~ film** Zeichentrickfilm m

aniseed ['ænɪsiːd] n Anis m

ankle ['æŋkl] n (Fuß)knöchel m

annex ['æneks] n Anbau m

anniversary [ænɪ'vɜːsərɪ] n Jahrestag m

announce [ə'naʊns] vt bekannt geben; (officially) bekannt machen; (on radio, TV etc) (Radio,

TV) ansagen; **announcement** n
Bekanntgabe f; (official)
Bekanntmachung f; (Radio, TV)
Ansage f; **announcer** n (Radio, TV)
Ansager(in) m(f)
annoy [ə'nɔɪ] vt ärgern;
annoyance n Ärger m; **annoyed**
adj ärgerlich; **to be ~ with sb**
(**about sth**) sich über jdn (über
etw) ärgern; **annoying** adj
ärgerlich; (person) lästig, nervig
annual ['ænjʊəl] adj jährlich
▷ n Jahrbuch nt
anonymous [ə'nɒnɪməs] adj
anonym
anorak ['ænəræk] n Anorak m;
(Brit fam: pej) Freak m
anorexia [ænə'reksɪə] n Mager-
sucht f; **anorexic** adj
magersüchtig
another [ə'nʌðə*] adj, pron
(different) ein(e) andere(r, s);
(additional) noch eine(r, s); **let me
put it ~ way** lass es mich anders
sagen
answer ['ɑːnsə*] n Antwort f (to
auf +akk); (solution) Lösung f (gen
▷ vi antworten; (on phone) sich
melden ▷ vt (person) antworten
+dat; (letter, question) beantworten;
(telephone) gehen an +akk,
abnehmen; (door) öffnen; **answer
back** vi widersprechen;
answering machine,
answerphone n Anrufbeant-
worter m
ant [ænt] n Ameise f
Antarctic [ænt'ɑːktɪk] n
Antarktis f; **Antarctic Circle** n
südlicher Polarkreis
antelope ['æntɪləʊp] n Antilope f
antenna [æn'tenə] (pl **antennae**)
n (Zool) Fühler m; (Radio) Antenne f
anti- ['æntɪ] pref Anti-, anti-;
antibiotic ['æntɪbaɪ'ɒtɪk] n
Antibiotikum nt
anticipate [æn'tɪsɪpeɪt] vt (expect:

trouble, question) erwarten,
rechnen mit; **anticipation**
[æntɪsɪ'peɪʃən] n Erwartung f
anticlimax [æntɪ'klaɪmæks] n
Enttäuschung f; **anticlockwise**
[æntɪ'klɒkwaɪz] adv entgegen
dem Uhrzeigersinn
antidote ['æntɪdəʊt] n Gegenmittel nt; **antifreeze** n
Frostschutzmittel nt
Antipodes [æn'tɪpədiːz] npl
Australien und Neuseeland
antiquarian [æntɪ'kwɛərɪən]
adj: **~ bookshop** Antiquariat nt
antique [æn'tiːk] n Antiquität f
▷ adj antik; **antique shop** n
Antiquitätengeschäft nt
anti-Semitism [æntɪ'semɪtɪzm]
n Antisemitismus m; **antiseptic**
[æntɪ'septɪk] n Antiseptikum nt
▷ adj antiseptisch; **antisocial** adj
(person) ungesellig; (behaviour)
unsozial, asozial
antlers ['æntləz] npl Geweih nt
anxiety [æŋ'zaɪətɪ] n Sorge f
(about um); **anxious** ['æŋkʃəs] adj
besorgt (about um); (apprehensive)
ängstlich

KEYWORD

any ['enɪ] adj **1** (in questions etc)
have you any butter? haben Sie
(etwas) Butter?; **have you any
children?** haben Sie Kinder?; **if
there are any tickets left** falls
noch Karten da sind
2 (with negative) **I haven't any
money/books** ich habe kein
Geld/keine Bücher
3 (no matter which) jede(r, s)
(beliebige); **any colour (at all)**
jede beliebige Farbe; **choose any
book you like** nehmen Sie ein
beliebiges Buch
4 (in phrases) **in any case** in jedem

Fall; **any day now** jeden Tag; **at any moment** jeden Moment; **at any rate** auf jeden Fall
▷ *pron* **1** (*in questions etc*) **have you got any?** haben Sie welche?; **can any of you sing?** kann (irgend)einer von euch singen?
2 (*with negative*) **I haven't any (of them)** ich habe keinen/keines (davon)
3 (*no matter which one(s)*): **take any of those books (you like)** nehmen Sie irgendeines dieser Bücher
▷ *adv* **1** (*in questions etc*) **do you want any more soup/ sandwiches?** möchten Sie noch Suppe/Brote?; **are you feeling any better?** fühlen Sie sich etwas besser?
2 (*with negative*) **I can't hear him any more** ich kann ihn nicht mehr hören

anybody *pron* (*whoever one likes*) irgendjemand; (*everyone*) jeder; (*in question*) jemand; **anyhow** *adv*: **I don't want to talk about it, not now ~** ich möchte nicht darüber sprechen, jedenfalls nicht jetzt; **they asked me not to go, but I went ~** sie baten mich, nicht hinzugehen, aber ich bin trotzdem hingegangen; **anyone** *pron* (*whoever one likes*) irgendjemand; (*everyone*) jeder; (*in question*) jemand; **isn't there ~ you can ask?** gibt es denn niemanden, den du fragen kannst/den Sie fragen können?; **anyplace** *adv* (*US*) irgendwo; (*direction*) irgendwohin; (*everywhere*) überall

KEYWORD

anything ['enɪθɪŋ] *pron* **1** (*in questions etc*) (irgend)etwas; **can you see anything?** können Sie etwas sehen?
2 (*with negative*) **I can't see anything** ich kann nichts sehen
3 (*no matter what*) **you can say anything you like** Sie können sagen, was Sie wollen; **anything will do** irgendetwas (wird genügen), irgendeine(r, s) (wird genügen); **he'll eat anything** er isst alles

anytime *adv* jederzeit; **anyway** *adv*: **I didn't want to go there ~** ich wollte da sowieso nicht hingehen; **thanks ~** trotzdem danke; **~, as I was saying, ...** jedenfalls, wie ich schon sagte, ...; **anywhere** *adv* irgendwo; (*direction*) irgendwohin; (*everywhere*) überall
apart [ə'pɑːt] *adv* auseinander; **~ from** außer; **live ~** getrennt leben
apartment [ə'pɑːtmənt] *n* (*esp US*) Wohnung *f*; **apartment block** *n* (*esp US*) Wohnblock *m*
ape [eɪp] *n* (Menschen)affe *m*
aperitif [ə'perɪtɪf] *n* Aperitif *m*
aperture ['æpətjʊə°] *n* Öffnung *f*; (*Foto*) Blende *f*
apologize [ə'pɒlədʒaɪz] *vi* sich entschuldigen; **apology** *n* Entschuldigung *f*
apostrophe [ə'pɒstrəfɪ] *n* Apostroph *m*
appalled [ə'pɔːld] *adj* entsetzt (*at* über +*akk*); **appalling** *adj* entsetzlich
apparatus [æpə'reɪtəs] *n* Apparat *m*; (*piece of apparatus*) Gerät *nt*
apparent [ə'pærənt] *adj* (*obvious*) offensichtlich (*to* für); (*seeming*) scheinbar; **apparently** *adv* anscheinend
appeal [ə'piːl] *vi* (dringend)

bitten (for um, to +akk); (Jur)
Berufung einlegen; **to ~ to sb** (be
attractive) jdm zusagen ▷ n Aufruf
m (to an +akk); (Jur) Berufung f;
(attraction) Reiz m; **appealing** adj
ansprechend, attraktiv

appear [ə'pɪə°] vi erscheinen;
(Theat) auftreten; (seem) scheinen;
appearance n Erscheinen nt;
(Theat) Auftritt m; (look) Aussehen
nt

appendicitis [əpendɪ'saɪtɪs] n
Blinddarmentzündung f;
appendix [ə'pendɪks] n Blinddarm m; (to book) Anhang m

appetite ['æpɪtaɪt] n Appetit m;
(fig: desire) Verlangen nt; (sexual)
Lust f; **appetizing** ['æpɪtaɪzɪŋ]
adj appetitlich, appetitanregend

applause [ə'plɔ:z] n Beifall m,
Applaus m

apple ['æpl] n Apfel m; **apple
crumble** n mit Streuseln bestreutes
Apfeldessert; **apple juice** n
Apfelsaft m; **apple pie** n
gedeckter Apfelkuchen m; **apple
puree, apple sauce** n Apfelmus
nt; **apple tart** n Apfelkuchen m;
apple tree n Apfelbaum m

appliance [ə'plaɪəns] n Gerät nt;
applicable [ə'plɪkəbl] adj
anwendbar; (on forms) zutreffend;
applicant ['æplɪkənt] n Bewer-
ber(in) m(f); **application**
[æplɪ'keɪʃən] n (request) Antrag m
(for auf +akk); (for job) Bewerbung f
(for um); **application form** n
Anmeldeformular nt; **apply**
[ə'plaɪ] vi (be relevant) zutreffen (to
auf +akk); (for job etc) sich
bewerben (for um) ▷ vt (cream,
paint etc) auftragen; (put into
practice) anwenden; (brakes)
betätigen

appoint [ə'pɔɪnt] vt (to post)
ernennen; **appointment** n
Verabredung f; (at doctor, hairdresser

etc, in business) Termin m; **by
~** nach Vereinbarung

appreciate [ə'pri:ʃɪeɪt] vt (value)
zu schätzen wissen; (understand)
einsehen; **to be much ~d** richtig
gewürdigt werden ▷ vi (increase in
value) im Wert steigen;
appreciation [əpri:ʃɪ'eɪʃən] n
(esteem) Anerkennung f,
Würdigung f; (of person also)
Wertschätzung f

apprehensive [æprɪ'hensɪv] adj
ängstlich

apprentice [ə'prentɪs] n Lehr-
ling m

approach [ə'prəʊtʃ] vi sich
nähern ▷ vt (place) sich nähern
+dat; (person) herantreten an +akk;
(problem) angehen

appropriate [ə'prəʊprɪət] adj
passend; (to occasion) angemessen;
(remark) treffend; **appropriately**
adv passend; (expressed) treffend

approval [ə'pru:vəl] n (show of
satisfaction) Anerkennung f;
(permission) Zustimmung f (of zu);
approve [ə'pru:v] vt billigen
▷ vi: **to ~ of sth/sb** etw
billigen/von jdm etwas halten; **I
don't ~** ich missbillige das

approx [ə'prɒks] abbr =
approximately ca.; **approximate**
[ə'prɒksɪmɪt] adj ungefähr;
approximately adv ungefähr,
circa

apricot ['eɪprɪkɒt] n Aprikose f

April ['eɪprəl] n April m; see also
September

apron ['eɪprən] n Schürze f

aptitude [æptɪtjuːd] n Begabung
f

aquaplaning ['ækwəpleɪnɪŋ] n
(Auto) Aquaplaning nt

aquarium [ə'kwɛərɪəm] n
Aquarium nt

Aquarius [ə'kwɛərɪəs] n (Astr)
Wassermann m

Arab ['ærəb] n Araber(in) m(f); (horse) Araber m; **Arabian** [ə'reɪbɪən] adj arabisch; **Arabic** ['ærəbɪk] n (language) Arabisch nt ⊳ adj arabisch

arbitrary ['ɑːbɪtrərɪ] adj willkürlich

arcade [ɑː'keɪd] n Arkade f; (shopping arcade) Einkaufspassage f

arch [ɑːtʃ] n Bogen m

archaeologist, archeologist (US) [ɑːkɪ'ɒlədʒɪst] n Archäologe m, Archäologin f; **archaeology, archeology** (US) [ɑːkɪ'ɒlədʒɪ] n Archäologie f

archaic [ɑː'keɪɪk] adj veraltet

archbishop [ɑːtʃ'bɪʃəp] n Erzbischof m

archery ['ɑːtʃərɪ] n Bogenschießen nt

architect ['ɑːkɪtekt] n Architekt(in) m(f); **architecture** [ɑːkɪ'tektʃə] n Architektur f

archive(s) ['ɑːkaɪv(z)] n(pl) Archiv nt

archway ['ɑːtʃweɪ] n Torbogen m

Arctic ['ɑːktɪk] n Arktis f; **Arctic Circle** n nördlicher Polarkreis

are [ə, unstressed ɑː*] present of **be**

area ['ɛərɪə] n (region, district) Gebiet nt, Gegend f; (amount of space) Fläche f; (part of building etc) Bereich m, Zone f; (fig: field) Bereich m; **the London ~** der Londoner Raum; **area code** n (US) Vorwahl f

aren't [ɑːnt] contr of **are not**

Argentina [ɑːdʒən'tiːnə] n Argentinien nt

argue ['ɑːgjuː] vi streiten (about, over über +akk); **to ~ that ...** behaupten, dass ...; **to ~ for/against ...** sprechen für/gegen ...; **argument** n (reasons) Argument nt; (quarrel)

Streit m; **to have an ~** sich streiten

Aries ['ɛəriːz] nsing (Astr) Widder m

arise [ə'raɪz] (**arose, arisen**) vi sich ergeben, entstehen; (problem, question, wind) aufkommen

aristocracy [ærɪs'tɒkrəsɪ] n (class) Adel m; **aristocrat** ['ærɪstəkræt] n Adlige(r) mf; **aristocratic** [ærɪstə'krætɪk] adj aristokratisch, adlig

arm [ɑːm] n Arm m; (sleeve) Ärmel m; (of armchair) Armlehne f ⊳ vt bewaffnen; **armchair** ['ɑːmtʃɛə*] n Lehnstuhl m

armed [ɑːmd] adj bewaffnet

armpit ['ɑːmpɪt] n Achselhöhle f

arms [ɑːmz] npl Waffen pl

army ['ɑːmɪ] n Armee f, Heer nt

A road ['eɪrəʊd] n (Brit) ≈ Bundesstraße f

aroma [ə'rəʊmə] n Duft m, Aroma nt; **aromatherapy** [ərəʊmə'θerəpɪ] n Aromatherapie f

arose [ə'rəʊz] pt of **arise**

around [ə'raʊnd] adv herum, umher; (present) hier (irgendwo); (approximately) ungefähr; (with time) gegen; **he's ~ somewhere** er ist hier irgendwo in der Nähe ⊳ prep (surrounding) um ... (herum); (about in) in ... herum

arr. abbr = **arrival**, **arrives** Ank.

arrange [ə'reɪndʒ] vt (put in order) (an)ordnen; (alphabetically) ordnen; (artistically) arrangieren; (agree to: meeting etc) vereinbaren, festsetzen; (holidays) festlegen; (organize) planen; **to ~ that ...** es so einrichten, dass ...; **we ~d to meet at eight o'clock** wir haben uns für acht Uhr verabredet; **it's all ~d** es ist alles arrangiert; **arrangement** n (layout) Anordnung f; (agreement)

Vereinbarung f, Plan m; **make ~s** Vorbereitungen treffen

arrest [ə'rest] vt (person) verhaften ▷ n Verhaftung f; **under ~** verhaftet

arrival [ə'raɪvəl] n Ankunft f; **new ~** (person) Neuankömmling m; **arrivals** n (airport) Ankunftshalle f; **arrive** [ə'raɪv] vi ankommen (at bei, in +dat); **to ~ at a solution** eine Lösung finden

arrogant ['ærəgənt] adj arrogant

arrow ['ærəʊ] n Pfeil m

arse [ɑːs] n (vulg) Arsch m

art [ɑːt] n Kunst f, **the ~s** (pl) Geisteswissenschaften pl

artery ['ɑːtəri] n Schlagader f, Arterie f

art gallery n Kunstgalerie f, Kunstmuseum nt

arthritis [ɑː'θraɪtɪs] n Arthritis f

artichoke ['ɑːtɪtʃəʊk] n Artischocke f

article ['ɑːtɪkl] n Artikel m; (object) Gegenstand m

artificial [ɑːtɪ'fɪʃəl] adj künstlich, Kunst-; (smile etc) gekünstelt

artist ['ɑːtɪst] n Künstler(in) m(f); **artistic** [ɑː'tɪstɪk] adj künstlerisch

KEYWORD

as [æz, əz] conj **1** (referring to time) als; **as the years went by** mit den Jahren; **he came in as I was leaving** als er hereinkam, ging ich gerade; **as from tomorrow** ab morgen

2 (in comparisons) **as big as** so groß wie; **twice as big as** zweimal so groß wie; **as much/many as** so viel/so viele wie; **as soon as** sobald

3 (since, because) da; **he left early as he had to be home by 10** er

ging früher, da er um 10 zu Hause sein musste

4 (referring to manner, way) wie; **do as you wish** mach was du willst; **as she said** wie sie sagte

5 (concerning) **as for** o **to that** was das betrifft o angeht

6 as if o **though** als ob ▷ prep als; see also **long**; **he works as a driver** er arbeitet als Fahrer; see also **such**; **he gave it to me as a present** er hat es mir als Geschenk gegeben; see also **well**

asap [eɪeseɪ'piː, 'eɪsæp] acr = **as soon as possible** möglichst bald

ascertain [æsə'teɪn] vt feststellen

ash [æʃ] n (dust) Asche f; (tree) Esche f

ashamed [ə'ʃeɪmd] adj beschämt; **to be ~ (of sb/sth)** sich (für jdn/etw) schämen

ashore [ə'ʃɔː*] adv an Land

ashtray ['æʃtreɪ] n Aschenbecher m

Asia ['eɪʃə] n Asien nt; **Asian** adj asiatisch ▷ n Asiat(in) m(f)

aside [ə'saɪd] adv beiseite, zur Seite; **~ from** (esp US) außer

ask [ɑːsk] vt, vi fragen; (question) stellen; (request) bitten um; (invite) einladen; **to ~ sb the way** jdn nach dem Weg fragen; **to ~ sb to do sth** jdn darum bitten, etw zu tun; **ask for** vt bitten um

asleep [ə'sliːp] adj, adv: **to be ~** schlafen; **to fall ~** einschlafen

asparagus [əs'pærəgəs] n Spargel m

aspect ['æspekt] n Aspekt m

aspirin ['æsprɪn] n Aspirin® nt

ass [æs] n (a. fig) Esel m; (US vulg) Arsch m

assassinate [ə'sæsɪneɪt] vt ermorden; **assassination**

[əˈsæsɪneɪʃn] n Ermordung f;
~ attempt Attentat nt
assault [əˈsɔːlt] n Angriff m; (Jur)
Körperverletzung f ▷ vt
überfallen, herfallen über +akk
assemble [əˈsembl] vt (parts)
zusammensetzen; (people)
zusammenrufen ▷ vi sich
versammeln; **assembly**
[əˈsemblɪ] n (of people)
Versammlung f; (putting together)
Zusammensetzen nt; **assembly
hall** n Aula f
assert [əˈsɜːt] vt behaupten;
assertion [əˈsɜːʃən] n Behauptung f
assess [əˈses] vt einschätzen;
assessment n Einschätzung f
asset [ˈæset] n Vermögenswert
m; (fig) Vorteil m; **~s** pl Vermögen
nt
assign [əˈsaɪn] vt zuweisen;
assignment n Aufgabe f;
(mission) Auftrag m
assist [əˈsɪst] vt helfen +dat;
assistance n Hilfe f; **assistant** n
Assistent(in) m(f), Mitarbeiter(in)
m(f); (in shop) Verkäufer(in) m(f);
assistant referee n (Sport)
Schiedsrichterassistent(in) m(f)
associate [əˈsəʊʃɪeɪt] vt
verbinden (with mit); **association**
[əsəʊsɪˈeɪʃən] n (organization)
Verband m, Vereinigung f; **in
~ with ...** in Zusammenarbeit
mit ...
assorted [əˈsɔːtɪd] adj gemischt;
assortment n Auswahl f (of an
+dat); (of sweets) Mischung f
assume [əˈsjuːm] vt annehmen
(that ... dass ...); (role, responsibility)
übernehmen; **assumption**
[əˈsʌmpʃən] n Annahme f
assurance [əˈʃʊərəns] n Versicherung f; (confidence) Zuversicht
f; **assure** [əˈʃʊəʳ] vt (say
confidently) versichern +dat; **to**

~ sb of sth jdm etw zusichern; **to
be ~d of sth** einer Sache sicher
sein
asterisk [ˈæstərɪsk] n Sternchen
nt
asthma [ˈæsmə] n Asthma nt
astonish [əˈstɒnɪʃ] vt erstaunen;
astonished adj erstaunt (at
über); **astonishing** adj
erstaunlich; **astonishment** n
Erstaunen nt
astound [əˈstaʊnd] vt sehr
erstaunen; **astounding** adj
erstaunlich
astray [əˈstreɪ] adv: **to go ~**
(letter etc) verloren gehen;
(person) vom Weg abkommen; **to
lead ~** irreführen, verführen
astrology [əsˈtrɒlədʒɪ] n
Astrologie f
astronaut [ˈæstrənɔːt] n Astro-
naut(in) m(f)
astronomy [əsˈtrɒnəmɪ] n
Astronomie f
asylum [əˈsaɪləm] n (home)
Anstalt f; (political asylum) Asyl nt;
asylum seeker n
Asylbewerber(in) m(f)

KEYWORD

at [æt] prep **1** (referring to position,
direction) an +dat; bei +dat; (with
place) in +dat; **at the top** an der
Spitze; **at home/school** zu Hause,
zuhause (österreichisch,
schweizerisch)/in der Schule; **at the
baker's** beim Bäcker; **to look at
sth** auf etw akk blicken; **to throw
sth at sb** etw nach jdm werfen
2 (referring to time) **at 4 o'clock** um
4 Uhr; **at night** bei Nacht; **at
Christmas** zu Weihnachten; **at
times** manchmal
3 (referring to rates, speed etc) **at £1 a
kilo** zu £1 pro Kilo; **two at a time**

zwei auf einmal; **at 50 km/h** mit 50 km/h
4 (*referring to manner*) **at a stroke** mit einem Schlag; **at peace** in Frieden
5 (*referring to activity*) **to be at work** bei der Arbeit sein; **to play at cowboys** Cowboy spielen; **to be good at sth** gut in etw *dat* sein
6 (*referring to cause*)
shocked/surprised/annoyed at sth schockiert/überrascht/verärgert über etw *akk*; **I went at his suggestion** ich ging auf seinen Vorschlag hin

ate [et, eɪt] *pt of* **eat**
athlete ['æθli:t] *n* Athlet(in) *m(f)*; (*track and field*) Leichtathlet(in) *m(f)*; (*sportsman*) Sportler(in) *m(f)*; **~'s foot** Fußpilz *m*; **athletic** [æθ'letɪk] *adj* sportlich; (*build*) athletisch; **athletics** *npl* Leichtathletik *f*
Atlantic [ət'læntɪk] *n*: **the ~** (**Ocean**) der Atlantik
atlas ['ætləs] *n* Atlas *m*
ATM *abbr* = **automated teller machine** Geldautomat *m*
atmosphere ['ætməsfɪə*] *n* Atmosphäre *f*; (*fig*) Stimmung *f*
atom ['ætəm] *n* Atom *nt*; **atom(ic) bomb** *n* Atombombe *f*; **atomic** [ə'tɒmɪk] *adj* Atom-; **~ energy** Atomenergie *f*; **~ power** Atomkraft *f*
A to Z® ['eɪtə'zed] *n* Stadtplan *m* (*in Buchform*)
atrocious [ə'trəʊʃəs] *adj* grauenhaft; **atrocity** [ə'trɒsɪtɪ] *n* Grausamkeit *f*; (*deed*) Gräueltat *f*
attach [ə'tætʃ] *vt* befestigen, anheften (*to an* +*dat*); **to ~ importance to sth** Wert auf etw *akk* legen; **to be ~ed to sb/sth** an jdm/etw hängen; **attachment** [ə'tætʃmənt] *n* (*affection*)

Zuneigung *f*; (*Inform*) Attachment *nt*, Anhang *m*, Anlage *f*
attack [ə'tæk] *vt*, *vi* angreifen ▷ *n* Angriff +*akk* (*on auf m*); (*Med*) Anfall *m*
attempt [ə'tempt] *n* Versuch *m*; **to make an ~ to do sth** versuchen, etw zu tun ▷ *vt* versuchen
attend [ə'tend] *vt* (*go to*) teilnehmen an +*dat*; (*lectures, school*) besuchen ▷ *vi* (*be present*) anwesend sein; **attend to** *vt* sich kümmern um; (*customer*) bedienen; **attendance** *n* (*presence*) Anwesenheit *f*; (*people present*) Teilnehmerzahl *f*; **attendant** *n* (*in car park etc*) Wächter(in) *m(f)*; (*in museum*) Aufseher(in) *m(f)*
attention [ə'tenʃən] *n* Aufmerksamkeit *f*; (**your**) **~ please** Achtung!; **to pay ~ to sth** etw beachten; **to pay ~ to sb** jdm aufmerksam zuhören; (*listen*) jdm/etw aufmerksam zuhören; **for the ~ of ...** zu Händen von ...; **attentive** [ə'tentɪv] *adj* aufmerksam
attic ['ætɪk] *n* Dachboden *m*; (*lived in*) Mansarde *f*
attitude ['ætɪtju:d] *n* (*mental*) Einstellung *f* (*to, towards* zu); (*more general, physical*) Haltung *f*
attorney [ə'tɜ:nɪ] *n* (*US: lawyer*) Rechtsanwalt *m*, Rechtsanwältin *f*
attract [ə'trækt] *vt* anziehen; (*attention*) erregen; **to be ~ed to o by sb** sich zu jdm hingezogen fühlen; **attraction** [ə'trækʃən] *n* Anziehungskraft *f*; (*thing*) Attraktion *f*; **attractive** *adj* attraktiv; (*thing, idea*) reizvoll
aubergine ['əʊbəʒi:n] *n* Aubergine *f*
auction ['ɔ:kʃən] *n* Versteigerung *f*, Auktion *f* ▷ *vt* versteigern

audible ['ɔːdɪbl] adj hörbar
audience ['ɔːdɪəns] n Publikum nt; (Radio) Zuhörer pl; (TV) Zuschauer pl
audio ['ɔːdɪəʊ] adj Ton-
audition [ɔːˈdɪʃən] n Probe f ▷ vi (Theat) vorspielen, vorsingen
auditorium [ɔːdɪˈtɔːrɪəm] n Zuschauerraum m
Aug abbr = **August**
August ['ɔːgəst] n August m; see also **September**
aunt [ɑːnt] n Tante f
au pair [əʊˈpeə*] n Aupairmädchen nt, Aupairjunge m
Australia [ɒˈstreɪlɪə] n Australien nt; **Australian** adj australisch ▷ n Australier(in) m(f)
Austria ['ɒstrɪə] n Österreich nt; **Austrian** adj österreichisch ▷ n Österreicher(in) m(f)
authentic [ɔːˈθentɪk] adj echt; (signature) authentisch; **authenticity** [ɔːθenˈtɪsɪtɪ] n Echtheit f
author ['ɔːθə*] n Autor(in) m(f); (of report etc) Verfasser(in) m(f)
authority [ɔːˈθɒrɪtɪ] n (power, expert) Autorität f; **an ~ on sth** eine Autorität auf dem Gebiet einer Sache; **the authorities** (pl) die Behörden pl; **authorize** ['ɔːθəraɪz] vt (permit) genehmigen; **to be ~d to do sth** offiziell berechtigt sein, etw zu tun
auto ['ɔːtəʊ] (pl -s) n (US) Auto nt
autobiography [ɔːtəʊbaɪˈɒgrəfɪ] n Autobiographie f; **autograph** ['ɔːtəgrɑːf] n Autogramm nt
automatic [ɔːtəˈmætɪk] adj automatisch; **~ gear change** (Brit), **~ gear shift** (US) Automatikschaltung f ▷ n (car) Automatikwagen m
automobile ['ɔːtəməbiːl] n (US) Auto(mobil) nt; **autotrain**

['ɔːtəʊtreɪn] n (US) Autoreisezug m
autumn ['ɔːtəm] n (Brit) Herbst m
auxiliary [ɔːgˈzɪlɪərɪ] adj Hilfs-; **~ verb** Hilfsverb nt ▷ n Hilfskraft f
availability [əveɪləˈbɪlɪtɪ] n (of product) Lieferbarkeit f; (of resources) Verfügbarkeit f; **available** adj erhältlich; (existing) vorhanden; (product) lieferbar; (person) erreichbar; **to be/make ~ to sb** jdm zur Verfügung stehen/stellen; **they're only ~ in black** es gibt sie nur in Schwarz, sie sind nur in Schwarz erhältlich
avalanche ['ævəlɑːnʃ] n Lawine f
Ave abbr = **avenue**
avenue ['ævənjuː] n Allee f
average ['ævrɪdʒ] n Durchschnitt m; **on ~** im Durchschnitt ▷ adj durchschnittlich; **~ speed** Durchschnittsgeschwindigkeit f; **of ~ height** von mittlerer Größe
avian flu ['eɪvɪənˈfluː] n Vogelgrippe f
aviation [eɪvɪˈeɪʃən] n Luftfahrt f
avocado [ævəˈkɑːdəʊ] (pl -s) n Avocado f
avoid [əˈvɔɪd] vt vermeiden; **to ~ sb** jdm aus dem Weg gehen; **avoidable** adj vermeidbar
awake [əˈweɪk] (**awoke, awoken**) vi aufwachen ▷ adj wach
award [əˈwɔːd] n (prize) Preis m; (for bravery etc) Auszeichnung f ▷ vt zuerkennen (to sb jdm); (present) verleihen (to sb jdm)
aware [əˈweə*] adj bewusst; **to be ~ of sth** sich dat einer Sache gen bewusst sein; **I was not ~ that …** es war mir nicht klar, dass …
away [əˈweɪ] adv weg; **to look ~** wegsehen; **he's ~** er ist nicht da; (on a trip) er ist verreist; (from school, work) er fehlt; (Sport) **they**

are (**playing**) ~ sie spielen auswärts; (*with distance*) **three miles** ~ drei Meilen (von hier) entfernt; **to work** ~ drauflos arbeiten

awful ['ɔːfʊl] *adj* schrecklich, furchtbar; **awfully** *adv* furchtbar

awkward ['ɔːkwəd] *adj* (*clumsy*) ungeschickt; (*embarrassing*) peinlich; (*difficult*) schwierig

awning ['ɔːnɪŋ] *n* Markise *f*

awoke [ə'wəʊk] *pt of* **awake**; **awoken** [ə'wəʊkən] *pp of* **awake**

ax (*US*), **axe** [æks] *n* Axt *f*

axle ['æksl] *n* (*Tech*) Achse *f*

BA *abbr* = **Bachelor of Arts**

BSc *abbr* = **Bachelor of Science**

babe [beɪb] *n* (*fam*) Baby *nt*; (*fam: affectionate*) Schatz *m*, Kleine(r) *mf*

baby ['beɪbɪ] *n* Baby *nt*; (*of animal*) Junge(s) *nt*; (*fam: affectionate*) Schatz *m*, Kleine(r) *mf*; **to have a** ~ ein Kind bekommen; **it's your** ~ (*fam: responsibility*) das ist dein Bier; **baby carriage** *n* (*US*) Kinderwagen *m*; **baby food** *n* Babynahrung *f*; **babyish** *adj* kindisch; **baby shower** *n* (*US*) *Party für die werdende Mutter*; **baby-sit** *irr vi* babysitten; **baby-sitter** *n* Babysitter(in) *m(f)*

bachelor ['bætʃələ°] *n* Junggeselle *m*; **Bachelor of Arts/Science** *erster akademischer Grad,* ≈ Magister/Diplom; **bachelorette** *n* Junggesellin *f*; **bachelorette party** *n* (*US*)

Junggesellinnenabschied; **bachelor party** n (US) Junggesellenabschied
back [bæk] n (of person, animal) Rücken m; (of house, coin etc) Rückseite f; (of chair) Rückenlehne f; (of car) Rücksitz m; (of train) Ende nt; (Sport: defender) Verteidiger(in) m(f); **at the ~ of ...**, (US) **in ~ of** (inside) hinten in ...; (outside) hinter ...; **~ to front** verkehrt herum ▷ vt (support) unterstützen; (car) rückwärtsfahren ▷ vi (go backwards) rückwärtsgehen o rückwärtsfahren ▷ adj Hinter-; **~ wheel** Hinterrad nt ▷ adv zurück; **they're ~** sie sind wieder da; **back away** vi sich zurückziehen; **back down** vi nachgeben; **back up** vi (car etc) zurücksetzen ▷ vt (support) unterstützen; (Inform) sichern; (car) zurückfahren
backache n Rückenschmerzen pl; **backbone** n Rückgrat nt; **backdate** vt zurückdatieren; **backdoor** n Hintertür f; **backfire** vi (plan) fehlschlagen; (Auto) fehlzünden; **background** n Hintergrund m; **backhand** n (Sport) Rückhand f; **backlog** n (of work) Rückstand m; **backpack** n (US) Rucksack m; **backpacker** n Rucksacktourist(in) m(f); **backpacking** n Rucksacktourismus m; **back seat** n Rücksitz m; **backside** n (fam) Po m; **back street** n Seitensträßchen nt; **backstroke** n Rückenschwimmen nt; **back-up** n (support) Unterstützung f; **~ (copy)** (Inform) Sicherungskopie f; **backward** adj (child) zurückgeblieben; (region) rückständig; **~ movement** Rückwärtsbewegung f; **backwards** adv rückwärts; **backyard** n Hinterhof m

bacon ['beɪkən] n Frühstücksspeck m
bacteria [bæk'tɪərɪə] npl Bakterien pl
bad [bæd] (**worse, worst**) adj schlecht, schlimm; (smell) übel; **I have a ~ back** mir tut der Rücken weh; **I'm ~ at maths/sport** ich bin schlecht in Mathe/Sport; **to go ~** schlecht werden, verderben
badge [bædʒ] n Abzeichen nt
badger ['bædʒə*] n Dachs m
badly ['bædlɪ] adv schlecht; **~ wounded** schwer verwundet; **to need sth ~** etw dringend brauchen; **bad-tempered** ['bæd'tempəd] adj schlecht gelaunt
bag [bæg] n (small) Tüte f; (larger) Beutel m; (handbag) Tasche f; **my ~s** (luggage) mein Gepäck
baggage ['bægɪdʒ] n Gepäck nt; **baggage allowance** n Freigepäck nt; **baggage (re)claim** n Gepäckrückgabe f
baggy ['bægɪ] adj (zu) weit; (trousers, suit) ausgebeult
bag lady ['bægleɪdɪ] n Stadtstreicherin f
bagpipes ['bægpaɪps] npl Dudelsack m
Bahamas [bə'hɑːməz] npl: **the ~** die Bahamas pl
bail [beɪl] n (money) Kaution f
bait [beɪt] n Köder m
bake [beɪk] vt, vi backen; **baked beans** npl weiße Bohnen in Tomatensoße; **baked potato** (pl **-es**) n in der Schale gebackene Kartoffel, Ofenkartoffel f; **baker** n Bäcker(in) m(f); **bakery** ['beɪkərɪ] n Bäckerei f; **baking powder** n Backpulver nt
balance ['bæləns] n (equilibrium) Gleichgewicht nt ▷ vt (make up for) ausgleichen; **balanced** adj

ausgeglichen; **balance sheet** n
Bilanz f
balcony ['bælkənɪ] n Balkon m
bald [bɔːld] adj kahl; **to be ~** eine
Glatze haben
Balkans ['bɔːlkənz] npl: **the ~**
der Balkan, die Balkanländer pl
ball [bɔːl] n Ball m; **to have a ~**
(fam) sich prima amüsieren
ballet ['bæleɪ] n Ballett nt; **ballet
dancer** n Balletttänzer(in) m(f)
balloon [bə'luːn] n (Luft)ballon
m
ballot ['bælət] n (geheime)
Abstimmung; **ballot box** n
Wahlurne f; **ballot paper** n
Stimmzettel m
ballpoint (pen) ['bɔːlpɔɪnt] n
Kugelschreiber m
ballroom ['bɔːlruːm] n Tanzsaal
m
Baltic ['bɔːltɪk] adj: **~ Sea** Ostsee
f; **the ~ States** die baltischen
Staaten
Baltics ['bɔːltɪks] n: **the ~** das
Baltikum nt
bamboo [bæm'buː] n Bambus m;
bamboo shoots npl
Bambussprossen pl
ban [bæn] n Verbot nt ▷ vt
verbieten
banana [bə'nɑːnə] n Banane f;
he's ~s er ist völlig durchgeknallt;
banana split n Bananensplit nt
band [bænd] n (group) Gruppe f;
(of criminals) Bande f; (Mus) Kapelle
f; (pop, rock etc) Band f; (strip) Band
nt
bandage ['bændɪdʒ] n Verband
m; (elastic) Bandage f ▷ vt
verbinden
B & B abbr = **bed and breakfast**
bang [bæŋ] n (noise) Knall m;
(blow) Schlag m ▷ vt, vi knallen;
(door) zuschlagen, zuknallen;
banger ['bæŋə*] n (Brit fam:
firework) Knallkörper m; (sausage)

Würstchen nt; (fam: old car)
Klapperkiste f
bangs [bæŋz] npl (US: of hair)
Pony m
banish ['bænɪʃ] vt verbannen
banister(s) ['bænɪstə*] n (Treppen)geländer nt
bank [bæŋk] n (Fin) Bank f; (of
river etc) Ufer nt; **bank account** n
Bankkonto nt; **bank balance** n
Kontostand m; **bank card** n
Bankkarte f; **bank code** n
Bankleitzahl f; **bank holiday** n
gesetzlicher Feiertag

● **BANK HOLIDAY**
●
● Als **bank holiday** wird in
● Großbritannien ein gesetzlicher
● Feiertag bezeichnet, an dem die
● Banken geschlossen sind. Die
● meisten dieser Feiertage,
● abgesehen von Weihnachten
● und Ostern, fallen auf Montage
● im Mai und August. An diesen
● langen Wochenenden (bank
● holiday weekends) fahren viele
● Briten in Urlaub, sodass dann
● auf den Straßen, Flughäfen und
● bei der Bahn sehr viel Betrieb
● ist.

bank manager n Filialleiter(in)
m(f); **banknote** n Banknote f
bankrupt vt ruinieren; **to go
~** Pleite gehen
bank statement n
Kontoauszug m
baptism ['bæptɪzəm] n Taufe f;
baptize ['bæptaɪz] vt taufen
bar [bɑː*] n (for drinks) Bar f; (less
smart) Lokal nt; (rod) Stange f; (of
chocolate etc) Riegel m, Tafel f; (of
soap) Stück nt; (counter) Theke f
▷ prep außer; **~ none** ohne
Ausnahme
barbecue ['bɑːbɪkjuː] n (device)

Grill m; (*party*) Barbecue nt, Grillfete f; **to have a ~** grillen

barbed wire ['bɑːbd'waɪə°] n Stacheldraht m

barber ['bɑːbə°] n (Herren)friseur m

bar code ['bɑːkəud] n Strichkode m

bare [beə°] adj nackt; **~ patch** kahle Stelle; **barefoot** adj, adv barfuß; **bareheaded** adj, adv ohne Kopfbedeckung; **barely** adv kaum; (*with age*) knapp

bargain ['bɑːgɪn] n (*cheap offer*) günstiges Angebot, Schnäppchen nt; (*transaction*) Geschäft nt; **what a ~** das ist aber günstig! ▷ vi (ver)handeln

barge [bɑːdʒ] n (*for freight*) Lastkahn m; (*unpowered*) Schleppkahn m

bark [bɑːk] n (*of tree*) Rinde f; (*of dog*) Bellen nt ▷ vi (*dog*) bellen

barley ['bɑːlɪ] n Gerste f

barmaid ['bɑːmeɪd] n Barkeeperin f; **barman** ['bɑːmən] (pl **-men**) n Barkeeper m

barn [bɑːn] n Scheune f

barometer [bə'rɒmɪtə°] n Barometer nt

baroque [bə'rɒk] adj barock, Barock-

barracks ['bærəks] npl Kaserne f

barrel ['bærəl] n Fass nt; **barrel organ** n Drehorgel f

barricade [bærɪ'keɪd] n Barrikade f

barrier ['bærɪə°] n (*obstruction*) Absperrung f, Barriere f; (*across road etc*) Schranke f

barrow ['bærəu] n (*cart*) Schubkarren m

bartender ['bɑːtendə°] n (US) Barkeeper(in) m(f)

base [beɪs] n Basis f; (*of lamp, pillar etc*) Fuß m; (*Mil*) Stützpunkt m ▷ vt gründen (*on* auf +*akk*); **to be ~d on sth** auf etw *dat* basieren; **baseball** n Baseball m; **baseball cap** n Baseballmütze f; **basement** n Kellergeschoss nt

bash [bæʃ] (*fam*) n Schlag m; (*fam*) Party f ▷ vt hauen

basic ['beɪsɪk] adj einfach; (*fundamental*) Grund-; (*importance, difference*) grundlegend; (*in principle*) grundsätzlich; **the accomodation is very ~** die Unterkunft ist sehr bescheiden; **basically** adv im Grunde; **basics** npl: **the ~** das Wesentliche

basil ['bæzl] n Basilikum nt

basin ['beɪsn] n (*for washing, valley*) (Wasch)becken nt

basis ['beɪsɪs] n Basis f; **on the ~ of** aufgrund +*gen*; **on a monthly ~** monatlich

basket ['bɑːskɪt] n Korb m; **basketball** n Basketball m

Basque [bæsk] n (*person*) Baske m, Baskin f; (*language*) Baskisch nt ▷ adj baskisch

bass [beɪs] n (Mus) Bass m; (Zool) Barsch m ▷ adj (Mus) Bass-

bastard ['bɑːstəd] n (vulg: *awful person*) Arschloch nt

bat [bæt] n (Zool) Fledermaus f; (Sport: *cricket, baseball*) Schlagholz nt; (*table tennis*) Schläger m

batch [bætʃ] n Schwung m; (fam: *of letters, books etc*) Stoß m

bath [bɑːθ] n Bad nt; (*tub*) Badewanne f; **to have a ~** baden ▷ vt (*child etc*) baden

bathe [beɪð] vt, vi (*wound etc*) baden; **bath foam** ['bɑːθfəum] n Badeschaum m; **bathing cap** n Badekappe f; **bathing costume, bathing suit** (US) n Badeanzug m

bathmat ['bɑːθmæt] n Badevorleger m; **bathrobe** n Bademantel m; **bathroom** n Bad(ezimmer) nt; **baths** [bɑːðz] npl (Schwimm)bad

nt; **bath towel** *n* Badetuch *nt*;
bathtub *n* Badewanne *f*

baton ['bætən] *n* (*Mus*) Taktstock
m; (*police*) Schlagstock *m*

batter ['bætə°] *n* Teig *m* ▷ *vt*
heftig schlagen; **battered** *adj*
übel zugerichtet; (*hat, car*)
verbeult; (*wife, baby*) misshandelt

battery ['bætərɪ] *n* (*Elec*) Batterie
f; **battery charger** *n* Ladegerät *nt*

battle ['bætl] *n* Schlacht *f*; (*fig*)
Kampf *m* (*for* um +*akk*); **battlefield**
n Schlachtfeld *nt*; **battlements**
npl Zinnen *pl*

Bavaria [bə'vɛərɪə] *n* Bayern *nt*;
Bavarian *adj* bay(e)risch ▷ *n*
Bayer(in) *m(f)*

bay [beɪ] *n* (*of sea*) Bucht *f*; (*on
house*) Erker *m*; (*tree*) Lorbeerbaum
m; **bay leaf** *n* Lorbeerblatt *nt*; **bay
window** *n* Erkerfenster *nt*

BBC *abbr* = **British Broadcasting
Corporation** BBC *f*

BC *abbr* = **before Christ** vor Christi
Geburt, v. Chr.

O **KEYWORD**

be [biː] (*pt* **was**, **were**, *pp* **been**) *vb
aux* **1** (*with present participle: forming
continuous tenses*): **what are you
doing?** was machst du (gerade)?;
it is raining es regnet; **I've been
waiting for you for hours** ich
warte schon seit Stunden auf dich
2 (*with pp: forming passives*): **to be
killed** getötet werden; **the thief
was nowhere to be seen** der Dieb
war nirgendwo zu sehen
3 (*in tag questions*) **it was fun,
wasn't it?** es hat Spaß gemacht,
nicht wahr?
4 (+*to* +*infin*) **the house is to be
sold** das Haus soll verkauft
werden; **he's not to open it** er darf
es nicht öffnen
▷ *vb* +*complement* **1** (*usu*) sein; **I'm

tired ich bin müde; **I'm hot/cold**
mir ist heiß/kalt; **he's a doctor** er
ist Arzt; **2 and 2 are 4** 2 und 2 ist 0
sind 4; **she's tall/pretty** sie ist
groß/hübsch; **be careful/quiet**
sei vorsichtig/ruhig
2 (*of health*) **how are you?** wie geht
es dir?; **he's very ill** er ist sehr
krank; **I'm fine now** jetzt geht es
mir gut
3 (*of age*) **how old are you?** wie alt
bist du?; **I'm sixteen (years old)**
ich bin sechzehn (Jahre alt)
4 (*cost*) **how much was the meal?**
was 0 wie viel hat das Essen
gekostet?; **that'll be £5.75, please**
das macht £5.75, bitte
▷ *vi* **1** (*exist, occur etc*) sein; **is there
a God?** gibt es einen Gott?; **be
that as it may** wie dem auch sei;
so be it also gut
2 (*referring to place*) sein; **I won't be
here tomorrow** ich werde morgen
nicht hier sein
3 (*referring to movement*) **where
have you been?** wo bist du
gewesen?; **I've been in the
garden** ich war im Garten
▷ *impers vb* **1** (*referring to time,
distance, weather*) sein; **it's 5
o'clock** es ist 5 Uhr; **it's 10 km to
the village** es sind 10 km bis zum
Dorf; **it's too hot/cold** es ist zu
heiß/kalt
2 (*emphatic*) **it's me** ich bin's; **it's
the postman** es ist der Briefträger

beach [biːtʃ] *n* Strand *m*;
beachwear *n* Strandkleidung *f*

bead [biːd] *n* (*of glass, wood etc*)
Perle *f*; (*drop*) Tropfen *m*

beak [biːk] *n* Schnabel *m*

beam [biːm] *n* (*of wood etc*) Balken
m; (*of light*) Strahl *m* ▷ *vi* (*smile etc*)
strahlen

bean [biːn] *n* Bohne *f*; **bean curd**
n Tofu *m*

bear [bɛə*] (**bore, borne**) vt
(carry) tragen; (tolerate) ertragen
▷ n Bär m; **bearable** adj
erträglich

beard [bɪəd] n Bart m

beast [biːst] n Tier nt; (brutal
person) Bestie f; (disliked person)
Biest nt

beat [biːt] (**beat, beaten**) vt
schlagen; (as punishment) prügeln;
to ~ sb at tennis jdn im Tennis
schlagen ▷ n (of heart, drum etc)
Schlag m; (Mus) Takt m; (type of
music) Beat m; **beat up** vt
zusammenschlagen

beaten [ˈbiːtn] pp of **beat**; **off the
~ track** abgelegen

beautiful [ˈbjuːtɪfʊl] adj schön;
(splendid) herrlich; **beauty** [ˈbjuːtɪ]
n Schönheit f; **beauty spot** n
(place) lohnendes Ausflugsziel

beaver [ˈbiːvə*] n Biber m

became [bɪˈkeɪm] pt of **become**

because [bɪˈkɒz] adv, conj weil
▷ prep: **~ of** wegen +gen o dat

become [bɪˈkʌm] (**became,
become**) vi werden; **what's ~ of
him?** was ist aus ihm geworden?

bed [bed] n Bett nt; (in garden)
Beet nt; **bed and breakfast** n
Übernachtung f mit Frühstück;
bedclothes npl Bettwäsche f;
bedding n Bettzeug nt; **bed linen**
n Bettwäsche f; **bedroom** n
Schlafzimmer nt; **bed-sit(ter)** n
(fam) möblierte
Einzimmerwohnung; **bedspread**
n Tagesdecke f; **bedtime** n
Schlafenszeit f

bee [biː] n Biene f

beech [biːtʃ] n Buche f

beef [biːf] n Rindfleisch nt;
beefburger n Hamburger m; **beef
tomato** (pl **-es**) n Fleischtomate
f

beehive [ˈbiːhaɪv] n Bienenstock
m

been [biːn] pp of **be**

beer [bɪə*] n Bier nt; **beer garden**
n Biergarten m

beetle [ˈbiːtl] n Käfer m

beetroot [ˈbiːtruːt] n Rote Bete

before [bɪˈfɔː*] prep vor; **the year
~ last** vorletztes Jahr; **the day
~ yesterday** vorgestern ▷ conj
bevor ▷ adv (of time) vorher; **have
you been there ~?** waren
Sie/warst du schon einmal dort?;
beforehand adv vorher

beg [beg] vt: **to ~ sb to do sth** jdn
inständig bitten, etw zu tun ▷ vi
(beggar) betteln (for um +akk)

began [bɪˈgæn] pt of **begin**

beggar [ˈbegə*] n Bettler(in) m(f)

begin [bɪˈgɪn] (**began, begun**) vt,
vi anfangen, beginnen; **to ~ to do
sth** anfangen, etw zu tun;
beginner n Anfänger(in) m(f);
beginning n Anfang m

begun [bɪˈgʌn] pp of **begin**

behalf [bɪˈhɑːf] n: **on ~ of, in ~ of**
(US) im Namen/Auftrag von; **on
my ~** für mich

behave [bɪˈheɪv] vi sich
benehmen; **~ yourself!** benimm
dich!; **behavior** (US), **behaviour**
[bɪˈheɪvjə*] n Benehmen nt

behind [bɪˈhaɪnd] prep hinter;
to be ~ time Verspätung haben
▷ adv hinten; **to be ~ with one's
work** mit seiner Arbeit im
Rückstand sein ▷ n (fam)
Hinterteil nt

beige [beɪʒ] adj beige

being [ˈbiːɪŋ] n (existence) Dasein
nt; (person) Wesen nt

Belarus [beləˈrʊs] n Weißruss-
land nt

belch [beltʃ] n Rülpser m ▷ vi
rülpsen

belfry [ˈbelfrɪ] n Glockenturm m

Belgian [ˈbeldʒən] adj belgisch
▷ n Belgier(in) m(f); **Belgium**
[ˈbeldʒəm] n Belgien nt

belief [bɪ'liːf] n Glaube m (in an +akk); (conviction) Überzeugung f; **it's my ~ that ...** ich bin der Überzeugung, dass ...; **believe** [bɪ'liːv] vt glauben; **believe in** vi glauben an +akk; **believer** n (Rel) Gläubige(r) mf

bell [bel] n (church) Glocke f; (bicycle, door) Klingel f; **bellboy** ['belbɔɪ] n (esp US) Page m

bellows ['beləʊz] npl (for fire) Blasebalg m

belly ['belɪ] n Bauch m; **bellyache** n Bauchweh nt ▷ vi (fam) meckern; **belly button** n (fam) Bauchnabel m; **bellyflop** n (fam) Bauchklatscher m

belong [bɪ'lɒŋ] vi gehören (to sb jdm); (to club) angehören +dat; **belongings** npl Habe f

below [bɪ'ləʊ] prep unter ▷ adv unten

belt [belt] n (round waist) Gürtel m; (safety belt) Gurt m; **below the ~** unter der Gürtellinie ▷ vi (fam: go fast) rasen, düsen; **beltway** n (US) Umgehungsstraße f

bench [bentʃ] n Bank f

bend [bend] n Biegung f; (in road) Kurve f ▷ vt (bent, bent) (curve) biegen; (head, arm) beugen ▷ vi sich biegen; (person) sich beugen; **bend down** vi sich bücken

beneath [bɪ'niːθ] prep unter ▷ adv darunter

beneficial [benɪ'fɪʃl] adj gut, nützlich (to für); **benefit** ['benɪfɪt] n (advantage) Vorteil m; (profit) Nutzen m; **for your/his ~** deinetwegen/seinetwegen; **unemployment ~** Arbeitslosengeld nt ▷ vt guttun +dat ▷ vi Nutzen ziehen (from aus)

benign [bɪ'naɪn] adj (person) gütig; (climate) mild; (Med) gutartig

bent [bent] pt, pp of **bend** ▷ adj krumm; (fam) korrupt

beret ['bereɪ] n Baskenmütze f

Bermuda [bə'mjuːdə] n **the ~s** pl die Bermudas pl ▷ adj **~ shorts** pl Bermudashorts pl; **the ~ triangle** das Bermudadreieck

berry ['berɪ] n Beere f

berth [bɜːθ] n (for ship) Ankerplatz m; (in ship) Koje f; (in train) Bett nt ▷ vt am Kai festmachen ▷ vi anlegen

beside [bɪ'saɪd] prep neben; **~ the sea/lake** am Meer/See; **besides** [bɪ'saɪdz] prep außer ▷ adv außerdem

besiege [bɪ'siːdʒ] vt belagern

best [best] adj beste(r, s); **my ~ friend** mein bester o engster Freund; **the ~ thing (to do) would be to ...** das Beste wäre zu ...; (on food packaging) **~ before ...** ▷ n mindestens haltbar bis ... ▷ n der/die/das Beste; **all the ~** alles Gute; **to make the ~ of it** das Beste daraus machen ▷ adv am besten; **I like this ~** das mag ich am liebsten; **best-before date** n Mindesthaltbarkeitsdatum nt; **best man** ['best'mæn] (pl **men**) n Trauzeuge m; **bestseller** ['bestselə°] n Bestseller m

bet [bet] n (**bet, bet**) vt, vi wetten (on auf +akk); **I ~ him £5 that ...** ich habe mit ihm um 5 Pfund gewettet, dass ...; **you ~** (fam) und ob!; **I ~ he'll be late** er kommt mit Sicherheit zu spät ▷ n Wette f

betray [bɪ'treɪ] vt verraten; **betrayal** n Verrat m

better ['betə°] adj, adv besser; **to get ~** (healthwise) sich erholen, wieder gesund werden; (improve) sich verbessern; **I'm much ~ today** es geht mir heute viel besser; **you'd ~ go** du solltest/Sie sollten lieber gehen; **a change for the ~** eine Wendung zum Guten

betting ['betɪŋ] n Wetten nt; **betting shop** n Wettbüro nt

between [bɪ'twiːn] prep zwischen; (among) unter; **~ you and me, ...** unter uns gesagt, ... ▷ adv: (in) ~ dazwischen

beverage ['bevərɪdʒ] n (formal) Getränk nt

beware [bɪ'weə*] vt: **to ~ of sth** sich vor etw +dat hüten; **"~ of the dog"** „Vorsicht, bissiger Hund!"

bewildered [bɪ'wɪldəd] adj verwirrt

beyond [bɪ'jɒnd] prep (place) jenseits +gen; (time) über ... hinaus; (out of reach) außerhalb +gen; **it's ~ me** da habe ich keine Ahnung, da bin ich überfragt ▷ adv darüber hinaus

bias ['baɪəs] n (prejudice) Vorurteil nt, Voreingenommenheit f

bias(s)ed adj voreingenommen

bib [bɪb] n Latz m

Bible ['baɪbl] n Bibel f

bicycle ['baɪsɪkl] n Fahrrad nt

bid [bɪd] (bid, bid) vt (offer) bieten ▷ n (attempt) Versuch m; (offer) Gebot nt

big [bɪg] adj groß; **it's no ~ deal** (fam) es ist nichts Besonderes; **big dipper** n (Brit) Achterbahn f; **big-headed** [bɪg'hedɪd] adj eingebildet

bike [baɪk] n (fam) Rad nt

bikini [bɪ'kiːnɪ] n Bikini m

bilberry ['bɪlbərɪ] n Heidelbeere f

bilingual [baɪ'lɪŋgwəl] adj zweisprachig

bill [bɪl] n (account) Rechnung f; (US: banknote) Banknote f; (Pol) Gesetzentwurf m; (Zool) Schnabel m; **billfold** ['bɪlfəʊld] n (US) Brieftasche f

billiards ['bɪliədz] nsing Billard nt; **billiard table** Billardtisch m

billion ['bɪliən] n Milliarde f

bin [bɪn] n Behälter m; (rubbish bin) (Müll)eimer m; (for paper) Papierkorb m

bind [baɪnd] (**bound, bound**) vt binden; (bind together) zusammenbinden; (wound) verbinden; **binding** n (ski) Bindung f; (book) Einband m

binge [bɪndʒ] n (fam: drinking) Sauferei f; **to go on a ~** auf Sauftour gehen

bingo ['bɪŋgəʊ] n Bingo nt

binoculars [bɪ'nɒkjʊləz] npl Fernglas nt

biodegradable ['baɪəʊdɪ'greɪdəbl] adj biologisch abbaubar

biography [baɪ'ɒgrəfɪ] n Biografie f

biological [baɪə'lɒdʒɪkəl] adj biologisch; **biology** [baɪ'ɒlədʒɪ] n Biologie f

birch [bɜːtʃ] n Birke f

bird [bɜːd] n Vogel m; (Brit fam: girl, girlfriend) Tussi f; **bird flu** n Vogelgrippe f; **bird watcher** n Vogelbeobachter(in) m(f)

birth [bɜːθ] n Geburt f; **birth certificate** n Geburtsurkunde f; **birth control** n Geburtenkontrolle f; **birthday** n Geburtstag m; **happy ~** herzlichen Glückwunsch zum Geburtstag; **birthday card** n Geburtstagskarte f; **birthday party** n Geburtstagsfeier f; **birthplace** n Geburtsort m

biscuit ['bɪskɪt] n (Brit) Keks m

bisexual [baɪ'seksjʊəl] adj bisexuell

bishop ['bɪʃəp] n Bischof m; (in chess) Läufer m

bit [bɪt] pt of **bite** ▷ n (piece) Stück(chen) nt; (Inform) Bit nt; **a ~ (of ...)** (small amount) ein bisschen ...; **a ~ tired** etwas müde;

~ by ~ allmählich; (*time*) **for a ~** ein Weilchen; **quite a ~** (*a lot*) ganz schön viel

bitch [bɪtʃ] *n* (*dog*) Hündin *f*; (*pej: woman*) Miststück *nt*, Schlampe *f*; **son of a ~** (*US: vulg*) Hurensohn *m*, Scheißkerl *m*; **bitchy** *adj* gemein, zickig

bite [baɪt] (**bit, bitten**) *vt, vi* beißen ▷ *n* Biss *m*; (*mouthful*) Bissen *m*; (*insect*) Stich *m*; **to have a ~** eine Kleinigkeit essen; **bitten** *pp of* **bite**

bitter ['bɪtə*] *adj* bitter; (*memory etc*) schmerzlich ▷ *n* (*Brit: beer*) halbdunkles Bier; **bitter lemon** *n* Bitter Lemon *nt*

bizarre [bɪ'zɑː*] *adj* bizarr

black [blæk] *adj* schwarz; **blackberry** *n* Brombeere *f*; **blackbird** *n* Amsel *f*; **blackboard** *n* (Wand)tafel *f*; **black box** *n* (*Aviat*) Flugschreiber *m*; **blackcurrant** *n* Schwarze Johannisbeere; **black eye** *n* blaues Auge; **Black Forest** *n* Schwarzwald *m*; **Black Forest gateau** *n* Schwarzwälder Kirschtorte *f*; **blackmail** *n* Erpressung *f* ▷ *vt* erpressen; **black market** *n* Schwarzmarkt *m*; **blackout** *n* (*Med*) Ohnmacht *f*; **to have a ~** ohnmächtig werden; **black pudding** *n* ≈ Blutwurst *f*; **Black Sea** *n*: **the ~** das Schwarze Meer; **blacksmith** *n* Schmied(in) *m(f)*; **black tie** *n* Abendanzug *m*, Smoking *m*; **is it ~?** ist/besteht da Smokingzwang?

bladder ['blædə*] *n* Blase *f*

blade [bleɪd] *n* (*of knife*) Klinge *f*; (*of propeller*) Blatt *nt*; (*of grass*) Halm *m*

blame [bleɪm] *n* Schuld *f* ▷ *vt*: **to ~ sth on sb** jdm die Schuld an etw *dat* geben; **he is to ~** er ist daran schuld

bland [blænd] *adj* (*taste*) fade; (*comment*) nichtssagend

blank [blæŋk] *adj* (*page, space*) leer, unbeschrieben; (*look*) ausdruckslos; **~ cheque** Blankoscheck *m*

blanket ['blæŋkɪt] *n* (Woll)decke *f*

blast [blɑːst] *n* (*of wind*) Windstoß *m*; (*of explosion*) Druckwelle *f* ▷ *vt* (*blow up*) sprengen; **~!** (*fam*) Mist!, verdammt!

blatant ['bleɪtənt] *adj* (*undisguised*) offen; (*obvious*) offensichtlich

blaze [bleɪz] *vi* lodern; (*sun*) brennen ▷ *n* (*building*) Brand *m*; (*other fire*) Feuer *nt*; **a ~ of colour** eine Farbenpracht

blazer ['bleɪzə*] *n* Blazer *m*

bleach [bliːtʃ] *n* Bleichmittel *nt* ▷ *vt* bleichen

bleak [bliːk] *adj* öde, düster; (*future*) trostlos

bleary ['blɪərɪ] *adj* (*eyes*) trübe, verschlafen

bleed [bliːd] (**bled, bled**) *vi* bluten

blend [blend] *n* Mischung *f* ▷ *vt* mischen ▷ *vi* sich mischen; **blender** *n* Mixer *m*

bless [bles] *vt* segnen; **~ you!** Gesundheit!; **blessing** *n* Segen *m*

blew [bluː] *pt of* **blow**

blind [blaɪnd] *adj* blind; (*corner*) unübersichtlich; **to turn a ~ eye to sth** bei etw ein Auge zudrücken ▷ *n* (*for window*) Rollo *nt* ▷ *vt* blenden; **blind alley** *n* Sackgasse *f*; **blind spot** *n* (*Auto*) toter Winkel; (*fig*) schwacher Punkt

blink [blɪŋk] *vi* blinzeln; (*light*) blinken

bliss [blɪs] *n* (Glück)seligkeit *f*

blister ['blɪstə*] *n* Blase *f*

blizzard [ˈblɪzəd] *n* Schneesturm *m*

bloated [ˈbləʊtɪd] *adj* aufgedunsen

block [blɒk] *n* (*of wood, stone, ice*) Block *m*, Klotz *m*; (*of buildings*) Häuserblock *m*; **~ of flats** (*Brit*) Wohnblock *m* ▷ *vt* (*road etc*) blockieren; (*pipe, nose*) verstopfen; **blockage** [ˈblɒkɪdʒ] *n* Verstopfung *f*; **blockbuster** [ˈblɒkbʌstə°] *n* Knüller *m*; **block letters** *npl* Blockschrift *f*

blog [blɒg] *n* (*Inform*) Blog *nt*

bloke [bləʊk] *n* (*Brit fam*) Kerl *m*, Typ *m*

blond(e) [blɒnd] *adj* blond ▷ *n* (*person*) Blondine *f*, blonder Typ

blood [blʌd] *n* Blut *nt*; **blood count** *n* Blutbild *nt*; **blood donor** *n* Blutspender(in) *m(f)*; **blood group** *n* Blutgruppe *f*; **blood orange** *n* Blutorange *f*; **blood poisoning** *n* Blutvergiftung *f*; **blood pressure** *n* Blutdruck *m*; **blood sample** *n* Blutprobe *f*; **bloodsports** *npl* Sportarten, bei denen Tiere getötet werden; **bloodthirsty** *adj* blutrünstig; **bloody** *adj* (*Brit fam*) verdammt, Scheiß-; (*literal sense*) blutig

bloom [bluːm] *n* Blüte *f* ▷ *vi* blühen

blossom [ˈblɒsəm] *n* Blüte *f* ▷ *vi* blühen

blot [blɒt] *n* (*of ink*) Klecks *m*; (*fig*) Fleck *m*

blouse [blaʊz] *n* Bluse *f*; **big girl's ~** (*fam*) Schwächling *m*, femininer Typ

blow [bləʊ] *n* Schlag *m* ▷ *vi, vt* (**blew, blown**) (*wind*) wehen, blasen; (*person: trumpet etc*) blasen; **to ~ one's nose** sich *dat* die Nase putzen; **blow out** *vt* (*candle etc*) ausblasen; **blow up** *vi* explodieren ▷ *vt* sprengen; (*balloon, tyre*) aufblasen; (*Foto: enlarge*) vergrößern; **blow-dry** *vt* föhnen; **blowjob** *n* (*fam*) **to give sb a ~** jdm einen blasen; **blown** [bləʊn] *pp of* **blow**; **blow-out** *n* (*Auto*) geplatzter Reifen

BLT *n abbr* = **bacon, lettuce and tomato sandwich** mit Frühstücksspeck, Kopfsalat und Tomaten belegtes Sandwich

blue [bluː] *adj* blau; (*fam: unhappy*) trübsinnig, niedergeschlagen; (*film*) pornografisch; (*joke*) anzüglich; (*language*) derb; **bluebell** *n* Glockenblume *f*; **blueberry** *n* Blaubeere *f*; **blue cheese** *n* Blauschimmelkäse *m*; **blues** *npl*: **the ~** (*Mus*) der Blues; **to have the ~** (*fam*) niedergeschlagen sein

blunder [ˈblʌndə°] *n* Schnitzer *m*

blunt [blʌnt] *adj* (*knife*) stumpf; (*fig*) unverblümt; **bluntly** *adv* geradeheraus

blurred [blɜːd] *adj* verschwommen, unklar

blush [blʌʃ] *vi* erröten

board [bɔːd] *n* (*of wood*) Brett *nt*; (*committee*) Ausschuss *m*; (*of firm*) Vorstand *m*; **~ and lodging** Unterkunft und Verpflegung; **on ~** an Bord ▷ *vt* (*train, bus*) einsteigen in +*akk*; (*ship*) an Bord gehen; **boarder** *n* Pensionsgast *m*; (*school*) Internatsschüler(in) *m(f)*; **board game** *n* Brettspiel *nt*; **boarding card, boarding pass** *n* Bordkarte *f*, Einsteigekarte *f*; **boarding school** *n* Internat *nt*; **board meeting** *n* Vorstandssitzung *f*; **boardroom** *n* Sitzungssaal *m* (des Vorstands)

boast [bəʊst] *vi* prahlen (*about* mit) ▷ *n* Prahlerei *f*

boat [bəʊt] *n* Boot *nt*; (*ship*) Schiff *nt*; **boatman** *n* (*hirer*)

Bootsverleiher m; **boat race** n
Regatta f; **boat train** n Zug m mit
Schiffsanschluss
bob(sleigh) ['bɒbsleɪ] n Bob m
bodily ['bɒdɪlɪ] adj körperlich
▷ adv (forcibly) gewaltsam; **body**
['bɒdɪ] n Körper m; (dead) Leiche f;
(of car) Karosserie f; **bodybuilding**
n Bodybuilding nt; **bodyguard** n
Leibwächter m; (group) Leibwache
f; **body jewellery** n
Intimschmuck m; **body odour** n
Körpergeruch m; **body piercing** n
Piercing nt; **bodywork** n
Karosserie f
boil [bɔɪl] vt, vi kochen ▷ n (Med)
Geschwür nt; **boiler** n Boiler m;
boiling adj (water etc) kochend
(heiß); **I was ~** (hot) mir war
fürchterlich heiß; (with rage) ich
kochte vor Wut; **boiling point** n
Siedepunkt m
bold [bəʊld] adj kühn, mutig;
(colours) kräftig; (type) fett
Bolivia [bə'lɪvɪə] n Bolivien nt
bolt [bəʊlt] n (lock) Riegel m;
(screw) Bolzen m ▷ vt verriegeln
bomb [bɒm] n Bombe f ▷ vt
bombardieren
bond [bɒnd] n (link) Bindung f;
(Fin) Obligation f
bone [bəʊn] n Knochen m; (of
fish) Gräte f; **boner** n (US fam)
Schnitzer m; (vulg: erection) Ständer
m
bonfire ['bɒnfaɪə°] n Feuer nt
(im Freien)
bonnet ['bɒnɪt] n (Brit Auto)
Haube f; (for baby) Häubchen nt
bonny ['bɒnɪ] adj (esp Scottish)
hübsch
bonus ['bəʊnəs] n Bonus m,
Prämie f
boo [bu:] vt auspfeifen,
ausbuhen ▷ vi buhen ▷ n Buhruf
m
book [bʊk] n Buch nt; (of tickets,

stamps) Heft nt ▷ vt (ticket etc)
bestellen; (hotel, flight etc) buchen;
(Sport) verwarnen; **fully ~ed** (**up**)
ausgebucht; (performance)
ausverkauft; **book in** vt
eintragen; **to be ~ed in at a hotel**
ein Zimmer in einem Hotel
bestellt haben; **bookcase** n
Bücherregal nt; **booking** n
Buchung f; **booking office** n
(Rail) Fahrkartenschalter m; (Theat)
Vorverkaufsstelle f; **book-keeping**
n Buchhaltung f; **booklet** n
Broschüre f; **bookmark** n (a.
Inform) Lesezeichen nt; **bookshelf**
n Bücherbord nt; **bookshelves**
Bücherregal nt; **bookshop**,
bookstore n (esp US)
Buchhandlung f
boom [bu:m] n (of business)
Boom m; (noise) Dröhnen nt ▷ vi
(business) boomen; (fam) florieren;
(voice etc) dröhnen
boomerang ['bu:məræŋ] n
Bumerang m
boost [bu:st] n Auftrieb m ▷ vt
(production, sales) ankurbeln;
(power, profits etc) steigern;
booster (injection) n
Wiederholungsimpfung f
boot [bu:t] n Stiefel m; (Brit Auto)
Kofferraum m ▷ vt (Inform) laden,
booten
booth [bu:ð] n (at fair etc) Bude f;
(at trade fair etc) Stand m
booze [bu:z] n (fam) Alkohol m
▷ vi (fam) saufen
border ['bɔːdə°] n Grenze f; (edge)
Rand m; **north/south of the**
Border in Schottland/England;
borderline n Grenze f
bore [bɔː°] pt of **bear** ▷ vt (hole
etc) bohren; (person) langweilen
▷ n (person) Langweiler(in) m(f),
langweiliger Mensch; (thing)
langweilige Sache; **bored** adj: **to**
be ~ sich langweilen; **boredom** n

Langeweile f; **boring** adj
langweilig

born [bɔːn] adj: **he was ~ in London** er ist in London geboren

borne [bɔːn] pp of **bear**

borough ['bʌrə] n Stadtbezirk m

borrow ['bɒrəʊ] vt borgen

Bosnia-Herzegovina
['bɒznɪəhɜːtsəgəʊ'viːnə] n
Bosnien-Herzegowina nt; **Bosnian**
['bɒznɪən] adj bosnisch ▷ n
Bosnier(in) m(f)

boss [bɒs] n Chef(in) m(f), Boss
m; **boss around** vt
herumkommandieren; **bossy** adj
herrisch

botanical [bə'tænɪkəl] adj botanisch; **~ garden(s)** botanischer
Garten

both [bəʊθ] adj beide; **~ the
books** beide Bücher ▷ pron
(people) beide; (things) beides;
~ (of) the boys die beiden Jungs; **I
like ~ of them** ich mag sie (alle)
beide ▷ adv: **~ X and Y** sowohl X
als auch Y

bother ['bɒðəʳ] vt ärgern,
belästigen; **it doesn't ~ me** das
stört mich nicht; **he can't be ~ed
with details** mit Details gibt er
sich nicht ab; **I'm not ~ed** das ist
mir egal ▷ vi sich kümmern
(about um); **don't ~** (das ist) nicht
nötig, lass es! ▷ n (trouble) Mühe f;
(annoyance) Ärger m

bottle ['bɒtl] n Flasche f ▷ vt (in
Flaschen) abfüllen; **bottle out** vi
(fam) den Mut verlieren, aufgeben;
bottle bank n Altglascontainer
m; **bottled** adj in Flaschen; **~ beer**
Flaschenbier nt; **bottleneck** n
(fig) Engpass m; **bottle opener** n
Flaschenöffner m

bottom ['bɒtəm] n (of container)
Boden m; (underside) Unterseite f;
(fam: of person) Po m; **at the ~ of
the sea/table/page** auf dem

Meeresgrund/am Tabellen-
ende/unten auf der Seite ▷ adj
unterste(r, s); **to be ~ of the
class/league** Klassen-
letzte(r)/Tabellenletzte(r) sein;
~ gear (Auto) erster Gang

bought [bɔːt] pt, pp of **buy**

bounce [baʊns] vi (ball)
springen, aufprallen; (cheque)
platzen; **~ up and down** (person)
herumhüpfen; **bouncy** adj (ball)
gut springend; (person) munter;
bouncy castle® n Hüpfburg f

bound [baʊnd] pt, pp of **bind**
▷ adj (tied up) gebunden; (obliged)
verpflichtet; **to be ~ to do sth** (sure
to) etw bestimmt tun (werden);
(have to) etw tun müssen; **it's ~ to
happen** es muss so kommen; **to
be ~ for ...** auf dem Weg nach ...
sein; **boundary** ['baʊndərɪ] n
Grenze f

bouquet [bʊ'keɪ] n (flowers)
Strauß m; (of wine) Blume f

boutique [buːˈtiːk] n Boutique f

bow [bəʊ] n (ribbon) Schleife f;
(instrument, weapon) Bogen m
▷ [baʊ] vi sich verbeugen ▷ [baʊ]
n (with head) Verbeugung f; (of
ship) Bug m

bowels ['baʊəlz] npl Darm m

bowl [bəʊl] n (basin) Schüssel f;
(shallow) Schale f; (for animal) Napf
m ▷ vt, vi (in cricket) werfen

bowler ['bəʊləʳ] n (in cricket)
Werfer(in) m(f); (hat) Melone f

bowling ['bəʊlɪŋ] n Kegeln nt;
bowling alley n Kegelbahn f;
bowling green n Rasen m zum
Bowling-Spiel; **bowls** [bəʊlz]
nsing (game) Bowling-Spiel nt

bow tie [bəʊ'taɪ] n Fliege f

box [bɒks] n Schachtel f;
(cardboard) Karton m; (bigger)
Kasten m; (space on form) Kästchen
nt; (Theat) Loge f; **boxer** n
Boxer(in) m(f); **boxers, boxer**

shorts npl Boxershorts pl; **boxing** n (Sport) Boxen nt; **Boxing Day** n zweiter Weihnachtsfeiertag

- **BOXING DAY**
-
- **Boxing Day** ist ein Feiertag in
- Großbritannien. Fällt
- Weihnachten auf ein
- Wochenende, wird der Feiertag
- am nächsten Wochentag
- nachgeholt. Der Name geht auf
- einen alten Brauch zurück:
- früher erhielten Händler und
- Lieferanten an diesem Tag ein
- Geschenk, die sogenannte
- Christmas Box.

boxing gloves npl Boxhandschuhe pl; **boxing ring** n Boxring m
box number n Chiffre f
box office n (cinema, theatre) Kasse f
boy [bɔɪ] n Junge m
boycott ['bɔɪkɒt] n Boykott m ▷ vt boykottieren
boyfriend ['bɔɪfrend] n (fester) Freund m; **boy scout** n Pfadfinder m
bra [brɑː] n BH m
brace [breɪs] n (on teeth) Spange f
bracelet ['breɪslɪt] n Armband nt
braces ['breɪsɪz] npl (Brit) Hosenträger pl
bracket ['brækɪt] n (in text) Klammer f; (Tech) Träger m ▷ vt einklammern
brag [bræg] vi angeben
Braille [breɪl] n Blindenschrift f
brain [breɪn] n (Anat) Gehirn nt; (mind) Verstand m; **~s** (pl) (intelligence) Grips m; **brainwave** n Geistesblitz m; **brainy** adj schlau, clever
braise [breɪz] vt schmoren
brake [breɪk] n Bremse f ▷ vi

bremsen; **brake fluid** n Bremsflüssigkeit f; **brake light** n Bremslicht nt; **brake pedal** n Bremspedal nt
branch [brɑːntʃ] n (of tree) Ast m; (of family, subject) Zweig m; (of firm) Filiale f, Zweigstelle f; **branch off** vi (road) abzweigen
brand [brænd] n (Comm) Marke f
brand-new ['brænd'njuː] adj (funkel)nagelneu
brandy ['brændɪ] n Weinbrand m
brass [brɑːs] n Messing nt; (Brit fam: money) Knete f; **brass band** n Blaskapelle f
brat [bræt] n (pej, fam) Gör nt
brave [breɪv] adj tapfer, mutig; **bravery** ['breɪvərɪ] n Mut m
brawl [brɔːl] n Schlägerei f
brawn [brɔːn] n (strength) Muskelkraft f; (Gastr) Sülze f; **brawny** adj muskulös
Brazil [brə'zɪl] n Brasilien nt; **Brazilian** adj brasilianisch ▷ n Brasilianer(in) m(f); **brazil nut** n Paranuss f
bread [bred] n Brot nt; **breadbin** (Brit), **breadbox** (US) n Brotkasten m; **breadcrumbs** npl Brotkrumen pl; (Gastr) Paniermehl nt; **breaded** adj paniert; **breadknife** n Brotmesser nt
breadth [bredθ] n Breite f
break [breɪk] n (fracture) Bruch m; (rest) Pause f; (short holiday) Kurzurlaub m; **give me a ~** gib mir eine Chance, hör auf damit! ▷ vt (**broke, broken**) (fracture) brechen; (in pieces) zerbrechen; (toy, device) kaputt machen; (promise) nicht halten; (silence) brechen; (law) verletzen; (journey) unterbrechen; (news) mitteilen (to sb jdm); **I broke my leg** ich habe mir das Bein gebrochen; **he broke it to her gently** er hat es ihr schonend beigebracht ▷ vi (come apart)

(auseinander)brechen; (*in pieces*) zerbrechen; (*toy, device*) kaputtgehen; (*person*) zusammenbrechen; (*day, dawn*) anbrechen; (*news*) bekannt werden; **break down** *vi* (*car*) eine Panne haben; (*machine*) versagen; (*person*) zusammenbrechen; **break in** *vi* (*burglar*) einbrechen; **break into** *vt* einbrechen in +*akk*; **break off** *vi*, *vt* abbrechen; **break out** *vi* ausbrechen; **to ~ in a rash** einen Ausschlag bekommen; **break up** *vi* aufbrechen; (*meeting, organisation*) sich auflösen; (*marriage*) in die Brüche gehen; (*couple*) sich trennen; **school breaks up on Friday** am Freitag beginnen die Ferien ▷ *vt* aufbrechen; (*marriage*) zerstören; (*meeting*) auflösen; **breakable** *adj* zerbrechlich; **breakage** *n* Bruch *m*; **breakdown** *n* (*of car*) Panne *f*; (*of machine*) Störung *f*; (*of person, relations, system*) Zusammenbruch *m*; **breakdown service** *n* Pannendienst *m*; **breakdown truck** *n* Abschleppwagen *m*

breakfast ['brekfəst] *n* Frühstück *nt*; **to have ~** frühstücken; **breakfast cereal** *n* Cornflakes, Muesli etc; **breakfast television** *n* Frühstücksfernsehen *nt*

break-in ['breɪkɪn] *n* Einbruch *m*; **breakup** ['breɪkʌp] *n* (*of meeting, organization*) Auflösung *f*; (*of marriage*) Zerrüttung *f*

breast [brest] *n* Brust *f*; **breastfeed** *vt* stillen; **breaststroke** *n* Brustschwimmen *nt*

breath [breθ] *n* Atem *m*; **out of ~** außer Atem; **breathalyse**, **breathalyze** ['breθəlaɪz] *vt* (ins Röhrchen) blasen lassen; **breathalyser**, **breathalyzer** *n* Promillemesser *m*; **breathe** [briːð]

vt, *vi* atmen; **breathe in** *vt*, *vi* einatmen; **breathe out** *vt*, *vi* ausatmen; **breathless** ['breθlɪs] *adj* atemlos; **breathtaking** ['breθteɪkɪŋ] *adj* atemberaubend

bred [bred] *pt*, *pp of* **breed**

breed [briːd] *n* (*race*) Rasse *f* ▷ *vi* (**bred, bred**) sich vermehren ▷ *vt* züchten; **breeder** *n* Züchter(in) *m(f)*; (*fam*) Hetero *m*; **breeding** *n* (*of animals*) Züchtung *f*; (*of person*) (gute) Erziehung *f*

breeze [briːz] *n* Brise *f*

brevity ['brevɪtɪ] *n* Kürze *f*

brew [bruː] *vt* (*beer*) brauen; (*tea*) kochen; **brewery** *n* Brauerei *f*

bribe ['braɪb] *n* Bestechungsgeld *nt* ▷ *vt* bestechen; **bribery** ['braɪbərɪ] *n* Bestechung *f*

brick [brɪk] *n* Backstein *m*; **bricklayer** *n* Maurer(in) *m(f)*

bride [braɪd] *n* Braut *f*; **bridegroom** *n* Bräutigam *m*; **bridesmaid** *n* Brautjungfer *f*

bridge [brɪdʒ] *n* Brücke *f*; (*cards*) Bridge *nt*

brief [briːf] *adj* kurz ▷ *vt* instruieren (*on* über +*akk*); **briefcase** *n* Aktentasche *f*; **briefs** *npl* Slip *m*

bright [braɪt] *adj* hell; (*colour*) leuchtend; (*cheerful*) heiter; (*intelligent*) intelligent; (*idea*) glänzend; **brighten up** *vt* aufhellen; (*person*) aufheitern ▷ *vi* sich aufheitern; (*person*) fröhlicher werden

brilliant ['brɪljənt] *adj* (*sunshine, colour*) strahlend; (*person*) brillant; (*idea*) glänzend; (*Brit fam*) **it was ~** es war fantastisch

brim [brɪm] *n* Rand *m*

bring [brɪŋ] (**brought, brought**) *vt* bringen; (*with one*) mitbringen; **bring about** *vt* herbeiführen, bewirken; **bring back** *vt* zurückbringen; (*memories*) wecken; **bring down** *vt* (*reduce*)

senken; (*government etc*) zu Fall
bringen; **bring in** vt
hereinbringen; (*introduce*)
einführen; **bring out** vt
herausbringen; **bring round**,
bring to vt wieder zu sich
bringen; **bring up** vt (*child*)
aufziehen; (*question*) zur Sprache
bringen
brisk [brɪsk] *adj* (*trade*) lebhaft;
(*wind*) frisch
bristle ['brɪsl] *n* Borste *f*
Brit [brɪt] *n* (*fam*) Brite *m*, Britin *f*;
Britain ['brɪtn] *n* Großbritannien
nt; **British** ['brɪtɪʃ] *adj* britisch;
the ~ Isles (*pl*) die Britischen
Inseln *pl* ▷ *n* **the ~** (*pl*) die Briten *pl*
brittle ['brɪtl] *adj* spröde
broad [brɔːd] *adj* breit; (*accent*)
stark; **in ~ daylight** am helllichten
Tag ▷ (*US fam*) Frau *f*
B road ['biːrəʊd] *n* (*Brit*) ≈
Landstraße *f*
broadcast ['brɔːdkɑːst] *n*
Sendung *f* ▷ *irr vt, vi* senden;
(*event*) übertragen
broaden ['brɔːdn] *vt*: **to ~ the
mind** den Horizont erweitern;
broad-minded *adj* tolerant
broccoli ['brɒkəlɪ] *n* Brokkoli *pl*
brochure ['brəʊʃjʊəʳ] *n* Prospekt
m, Broschüre *f*
broke [brəʊk] *pt of* **break** ▷ *adj*
(*Brit fam*) pleite; **broken**
['brəʊkən] *pp of* **break**;
broken-hearted *adj* untröstlich
broker ['brəʊkəʳ] *n* Makler(in)
m(f)
brolly ['brɒlɪ] *n* (*Brit*) Schirm *m*
bronchitis [brɒŋ'kaɪtɪs] *n*
Bronchitis *f*
bronze [brɒnz] *n* Bronze *f*
brooch [brəʊtʃ] *n* Brosche *f*
broom [bruːm] *n* Besen *m*
Bros [brɒs] *abbr* = **brothers** Gebr.
broth [brɒθ] *n* Fleischbrühe *f*
brothel ['brɒθl] *n* Bordell *nt*

brother ['brʌðəʳ] *n* Bruder *m*; **~s**
(*pl*) (*Comm*) Gebrüder *pl*; **brother-
in-law** (*pl* **brothers-in-law**) *n*
Schwager *m*
brought [brɔːt] *pt, pp of* **bring**
brow [braʊ] *n* (*eyebrow*)
(Augen)braue *f*; (*forehead*) Stirn *f*
brown [braʊn] *adj* braun; **brown
bread** *n* Mischbrot *nt*; (*wholemeal*)
Vollkornbrot *nt*; **brownie**
['braʊnɪ] *n* (*Gastr*) Brownie *m*;
(*Brit*) *junge Pfadfinderin*; **brown
paper** *n* Packpapier *nt*; **brown
rice** *n* Naturreis *m*; **brown sugar**
n brauner Zucker
browse [braʊz] *vi* (*in book*)
blättern; (*in shop*) schmökern,
herumschauen; **browser** *n*
(*Inform*) Browser *m*
bruise [bruːz] *n* blauer Fleck
▷ *vt*: **to ~ one's arm** sich *dat* einen
blauen Fleck (am Arm) holen
brunette [bruːˈnet] *n* Brünette
f
brush [brʌʃ] *n* Bürste *f*; (*for
sweeping*) Handbesen *m*; (*for
painting*) Pinsel *m* ▷ *vt* bürsten;
(*sweep*) fegen; **to ~ one's teeth**
sich *dat* die Zähne putzen; **brush
up** *vt* (*French etc*) auffrischen
Brussels sprouts
[brʌslˈspraʊts] *npl* Rosenkohl *m*,
Kohlsprossen *pl*
brutal ['bruːtl] *adj* brutal;
brutality [bruːˈtælɪtɪ] *n* Bru-
talität *f*
BSE *abbr* = **bovine spongiform
encephalopathy** BSE *f*
bubble ['bʌbl] *n* Blase *f*; **bubble
bath** *n* Schaumbad *nt*,
Badeschaum *m*; **bubbly** ['bʌblɪ]
adj sprudelnd; (*person*)
temperamentvoll ▷ *n* (*fam*)
Schampus *m*
buck [bʌk] *n* (*animal*) Bock *m*; (*US
fam*) Dollar *m*
bucket ['bʌkɪt] *n* Eimer *m*

● **BUCKINGHAM PALACE**

Der **Buckingham Palace** ist die offizielle Londoner Residenz der britischen Monarchen und liegt am St James's Park. Der Palast wurde 1703 für den Herzog von Buckingham erbaut, 1762 von George III gekauft, zwischen 1821 und 1836 von John Nash umgebaut und Anfang des 20. Jahrhunderts teilweise neu gestaltet. Teile des Buckingham Palace sind heute der Öffentlichkeit zugänglich.

buckle ['bʌkl] n Schnalle f ▷ vi (Tech) sich verbiegen ▷ vt zuschnallen

bud [bʌd] n Knospe f

Buddhism ['bʊdɪzəm] n Buddhismus m; **Buddhist** adj buddhistisch ▷ n Buddhist(in) m(f)

buddy ['bʌdɪ] n (fam) Kumpel m

budget ['bʌdʒɪt] n Budget nt ▷ adj preisgünstig; **budget airline** n Billigflieger m

budgie ['bʌdʒɪ] n Wellensittich m

buff [bʌf] adj (US) muskulös; **in the ~** nackt ▷ n (enthusiast) Fan m

buffalo ['bʌfələʊ] (pl -es) n Büffel m

buffer ['bʌfə*] n (a. Inform) Puffer m

buffet ['bʊfeɪ] n (food) (kaltes) Büfett nt

bug [bʌg] n (Inform) Bug m, Programmfehler m; (listening device) Wanze f; (US: insect) Insekt nt; (fam: illness) Infektion f ▷ vt (fam) nerven

bugger ['bʌgə*] n (vulg) Scheißkerl m ▷ interj (vulg) Scheiße f; **bugger off** vi (vulg) abhauen, Leine ziehen

buggy® ['bʌgɪ] n (for baby) Buggy® m

build [bɪld] (**built, built**) vt bauen; **build up** vt aufbauen; **builder** n Bauunternehmer(in) m(f); **building** n Gebäude nt; **building site** n Baustelle f; **building society** n Bausparkasse f

built pt, pp of **build**; **built-in** adj (cupboard) Einbau-, eingebaut

bulb [bʌlb] n (Bot) (Blumen)zwiebel f; (Elec) Glühbirne f

Bulgaria [bʌl'gɛərɪə] n Bulgarien nt; **Bulgarian** adj bulgarisch ▷ n (person) Bulgare m, Bulgarin f; (language) Bulgarisch nt

bulimia [bə'lɪmɪə] n Bulimie f

bulk [bʌlk] n (size) Größe f; (greater part) Großteil m (of +gen); **in ~** en gros; **bulky** adj (goods) sperrig; (person) stämmig

bull [bʊl] n Stier m; **bulldog** n Bulldogge f; **bulldoze** ['bʊldəʊz] vt planieren; **bulldozer** n Planierraupe f

bullet ['bʊlɪt] n Kugel f

bulletin ['bʊlɪtɪn] n Bulletin nt; (announcement) Bekanntmachung f; (Med) Krankenbericht m; **bulletin board** n (US: Inform) schwarzes Brett

bullfight ['bʊlfaɪt] n Stierkampf m; **bullshit** n (fam) Scheiß m

bully ['bʊlɪ] n Tyrann m

bum [bʌm] n (Brit fam: backside) Po m; (US: vagrant) Penner m; (worthless person) Rumtreiber m; **bum around** vi herumgammeln

bumblebee ['bʌmblbiː] n Hummel f

bumf [bʌmf] n (fam) Infomaterial nt, Papierkram m

bump [bʌmp] n (fam: swelling) Beule f; (road) Unebenheit f; (blow) Stoß m ▷ vt stoßen; **to ~ one's head** sich dat den Kopf anschlagen (on an +dat); **bump into** vt stoßen gegen; (fam: meet)

(zufällig) begegnen +dat; **bumper**
n (Auto) Stoßstange f ▷ adj
(edition etc) Riesen-; (crop etc)
Rekord-; **bumpy** ['bʌmpɪ] adj
holp(e)rig

bun [bʌn] n süßes Brötchen

bunch [bʌntʃ] n (of flowers)
Strauß m; (fam: of people) Haufen m;
~ **of keys** Schlüsselbund m; ~ **of
grapes** Weintraube f

bundle ['bʌndl] n Bündel nt

bungalow ['bʌŋgələʊ] n Bungalow m

bungee jumping ['bʌndʒɪ-
dʒʌmpɪŋ] n Bungeejumping nt

bunk [bʌŋk] n Koje f; **bunk
bed(s)** n(pl) Etagenbett nt

bunker ['bʌŋkə*] n (Mil) Bunker
m

bunny ['bʌnɪ] n Häschen nt

buoy [bɔɪ] n Boje f; **buoyant**
['bɔɪənt] adj (floating)
schwimmend

BUPA ['buːpə] abbr (Brit) private
Krankenkasse

burden ['bɜːdn] n Last f

bureau ['bjuːrəʊ] n Büro nt;
(government department) Amt nt;
bureaucracy [bjʊˈrɒkrəsɪ] n
Bürokratie f; **bureaucratic**
[bjuːrəˈkrætɪk] adj bürokratisch;
bureau de change ['bjuːrəʊ də
ʃãːnʒ] n Wechselstube f

burger ['bɜːgə*] n Hamburger m

burglar ['bɜːglə*] n Einbre-
cher(in) m(f); **burglar alarm** n
Alarmanlage f; **burglarize** vt (US)
einbrechen in +akk; **burglary** n
Einbruch m; **burgle** ['bɜːgl] vt
einbrechen in +akk

burial ['berɪəl] n Beerdigung f

burn [bɜːn] (burnt o burned,
burnt o burned) vt verbrennen;
(food, slightly) anbrennen; **to
~ one's hand** sich dat die Hand
verbrennen ▷ vi brennen ▷ n
(injury) Brandwunde f; (on material)

verbrannte Stelle; **burn down** vt,
vi abbrennen

burp [bɜːp] vi rülpsen ▷ vt (baby)
aufstoßen lassen

bursary ['bɜːsərɪ] n Stipendium nt

burst [bɜːst] (burst, burst) vt
platzen lassen ▷ vi platzen;
to ~ into tears in Tränen
ausbrechen

bury ['berɪ] vt begraben; (in grave)
beerdigen; (hide) vergraben

bus [bʌs] n Bus m; **bus driver** n
Busfahrer(in) m(f)

bush [bʊʃ] n Busch m

business ['bɪznɪs] n Geschäft nt;
(enterprise) Unternehmen nt;
(concern, affair) Sache f; **I'm here on
~** ich bin geschäftlich hier; **it's
none of your ~** das geht dich
nichts an; **business card** n
Visitenkarte f; **business class** n
(Aviat) Businessclass f;
businessman (pl -men) n
Geschäftsmann m; **business
studies** npl Betriebswirtschaft-
slehre f; **businesswoman** (pl
-women) n Geschäftsfrau f

bus service n Busverbindung f;
bus shelter n Wartehäuschen nt;
bus station n Busbahnhof m; **bus
stop** n Bushaltestelle f

bust [bʌst] n Büste f ▷ adj
(broken) kaputt; **to go ~** Pleite
gehen; **bust-up** n (fam) Krach m

busy ['bɪzɪ] adj beschäftigt;
(street, place) belebt; (esp US:
telephone) besetzt; **~ signal** (US)
Besetztzeichen nt

O KEYWORD

but [bʌt, bət] conj 1 (yet) aber; **not
X but Y** nicht X sondern Y
2 (however) **I'd love to come, but
I'm busy** ich würde gern kommen,
bin aber beschäftigt
3 (showing disagreement, surprise etc)

but that's fantastic! (aber) das ist ja fantastisch!
▷ prep (apart from, except): **nothing but trouble** nichts als Ärger; **no-one but him can do it** niemand außer ihm kann es machen; **but for you/your help** ohne dich/deine Hilfe; **anything but that** alles, nur das nicht
▷ adv (just, only) **she's but a child** sie ist noch ein Kind; **had I but known** wenn ich es nur gewusst hätte; **I can but try** ich kann es immerhin versuchen; **all but finished** so gut wie fertig

butcher ['bʊtʃə*] n Fleischer(in) m(f), Metzger(in) m(f)
butler ['bʌtlə*] n Butler m
butt [bʌt] (US fam) n Hintern m
butter ['bʌtə*] n Butter f ▷ vt buttern; **buttercup** n Butterblume f; **butterfly** n Schmetterling m
buttocks ['bʌtəks] npl Gesäß nt
button ['bʌtn] n Knopf m; (badge) Button m ▷ vt zuknöpfen; **buttonhole** n Knopfloch nt
buy [baɪ] n Kauf m ▷ vt (**bought, bought**) kaufen (from von); **he bought me a ring** er hat mir einen Ring gekauft; **buyer** n Käufer(in) m(f)
buzz [bʌz] n Summen nt; **to give sb a ~** (fam) jdn anrufen ▷ vi summen; **buzzer** ['bʌzə*] n Summer m; **buzz word** n (fam) Modewort nt

○ **KEYWORD**

by [baɪ] prep **1** (referring to cause, agent) von, durch; **killed by lightning** vom Blitz getötet; **a painting by Picasso** ein Gemälde von Picasso
2 (referring to method, manner) **by**
bus/car/train mit dem Bus/Auto/Zug; **to pay by cheque** per Scheck bezahlen; **by moonlight** bei Mondschein; **by saving hard, he ...** indem er eisern sparte, ... er ...
3 (via, through) über +akk; **he came in by the back door** er kam durch die Hintertür herein
4 (close to, past) bei, an +dat; **a holiday by the sea** ein Urlaub am Meer; **she rushed by me** sie eilte an mir vorbei
5 (not later than) **by 4 o'clock** bis 4 Uhr; **by this time tomorrow** morgen um diese Zeit; **by the time I got here it was too late** als ich hier ankam, war es zu spät
6 (during) **by day** bei Tag
7 (amount) **by the kilo/metre** kiloweise/meterweise; **paid by the hour** stundenweise bezahlt
8 (math, measure) **to divide by 3** durch 3 teilen; **to multiply by 3** mit 3 malnehmen; **a room 3 metres by 4** ein Zimmer 3 mal 4 Meter; **it's broader by a metre** es ist (um) einem Meter breiter
9 (according to) nach; **it's all right by me** von mir aus gern
10 (all) **by oneself** etc ganz allein
11 by the way übrigens
▷ adv **1** see **go**; **pass** etc
2 by and by irgendwann; (with past tenses) nach einiger Zeit; **by and large** (on the whole) im Großen und Ganzen

bye-bye ['baɪ'baɪ] interj (fam) Wiedersehen, tschüss
by-election n Nachwahl f; **bypass** n Umgehungsstraße f; (Med) Bypass m; **byproduct** n Nebenprodukt nt; **byroad** n Nebenstraße f; **bystander** n Zuschauer(in) m(f)
byte [baɪt] n Byte nt

C

C [siː] *abbr* = **Celsius** C

c *abbr* = **circa** ca

cab [kæb] *n* Taxi *nt*

cabbage ['kæbɪdʒ] *n* Kohl *m*

cabin ['kæbɪn] *n* (*Naut*) Kajüte *f*; (*Aviat*) Passagierraum *m*; (*wooden house*) Hütte *f*; **cabin crew** *n* Flugbegleitpersonal *nt*; **cabin cruiser** *n* Kajütboot *nt*

cabinet ['kæbɪnɪt] *n* Schrank *m*; (*for display*) Vitrine *f*; (*Pol*) Kabinett *nt*

cable ['keɪbl] *n* (*Elec*) Kabel *nt*; **cable-car** *n* Seilbahn *f*; **cable railway** *n* Drahtseilbahn *f*; **cable television**, **cablevision** (*US*) *n* Kabelfernsehen *nt*

cactus ['kæktəs] *n* Kaktus *m*

CAD *abbr* = **computer-aided design** CAD *nt*

Caesarean [siːˈzɛərɪən] *adj*: **~** (**section**) Kaiserschnitt *m*

café ['kæfeɪ] *n* Café *nt*; **cafeteria** [kæfɪˈtɪərɪə] *n* Cafeteria *f*; **cafetiere** [kæfəˈtjɛə°] *n* Kaffeebereiter *m*

cage [keɪdʒ] *n* Käfig *m*

Cairo ['kaɪərəʊ] *n* Kairo *nt*

cake [keɪk] *n* Kuchen *m*; **cake shop** *n* Konditorei *f*

calamity [kəˈlæmɪtɪ] *n* Katastrophe *f*

calculate ['kælkjʊleɪt] *vt* berechnen; (*estimate*) kalkulieren; **calculating** *adj* berechnend; **calculation** [kælkjʊˈleɪʃən] *n* Berechnung *f*; (*estimate*) Kalkulation *f*; **calculator** ['kælkjʊleɪtə°] *n* Taschenrechner *m*

calendar ['kælɪndə°] *n* Kalender *m*

calf [kɑːf] (*pl* **calves**) *n* Kalb *nt*; (*Anat*) Wade *f*

California [kælɪˈfɔːnɪə] *n* Kalifornien *nt*

call [kɔːl] *vt* rufen; (*name, describe as*) nennen; (*Tel*) anrufen; (*Inform, Aviat*) aufrufen; **what's this ~ed?** wie heißt das?; **that's what I ~ service** das nenne ich guten Service ▷ *vi* (*shout*) rufen (*for help* um Hilfe); (*visit*) vorbeikommen; **to ~ at the doctor's** beim Arzt vorbeigehen; (*of train*) **to ~ at ...** in ... halten ▷ *n* (*shout*) Ruf *m*; (*Tel*) Anruf *m*; (*Inform, Aviat*) Aufruf *m*; **to make a ~ telefonieren; to give sb a ~** jdn anrufen; **to be on ~** Bereitschaftsdienst haben; **call back** *vt, vi* zurückrufen; **call for** *vt* (*come to pick up*) abholen; (*demand, require*) verlangen; **call off** *vt* absagen

call centre *n* Callcenter *nt*; **caller** *n* Besucher(in) *m(f)*; (*Tel*) Anrufer(in) *m(f)*

calm [kɑːm] *n* Stille *f*; (*also of person*) Ruhe *f*; (*of sea*) Flaute *f* ▷ *vt*

beruhigen ▷ adj ruhig; **calm down** vi sich beruhigen
calorie ['kælərɪ] n Kalorie f
calves [kɑːvz] pl of **calf**
Cambodia [kæm'bəʊdɪə] n Kambodscha nt
camcorder ['kæmkɔːdə°] n Camcorder m
came [keɪm] pt of **come**
camel ['kæməl] n Kamel nt
camera ['kæmərə] n Fotoapparat m, Kamera f; **camera phone** ['kæmərəfəʊn] n Fotohandy nt
camomile ['kæməmaɪl] n Kamille f
camouflage ['kæməflɑːʒ] n Tarnung f
camp [kæmp] n Lager nt; (camping place) Zeltplatz m ▷ vi zelten, campen ▷ adj (fam) theatralisch, tuntig
campaign [kæm'peɪn] n Kampagne f; (Pol) Wahlkampf m ▷ vi sich einsetzen (for/against für/gegen)
campbed ['kæmpbed] n Campingliege f; **camper** ['kæmpə°] n (person) Camper(in) m(f); (van) Wohnmobil nt; **camping** ['kæmpɪŋ] n Zelten nt, Camping nt; **campsite** ['kæmpsaɪt] n Zeltplatz m, Campingplatz m
campus ['kæmpəs] n (of university) Universitätsgelände nt, Campus m

○ **KEYWORD**

can [kæn] (negative **cannot**, **can't**, conditional **could**) vb aux **1** (be able to, know how to) können; **I can see you tomorrow, if you like** ich könnte Sie morgen sehen, wenn Sie wollen; **I can swim** ich kann schwimmen; **can you speak German?** sprechen Sie Deutsch?

2 (may) können, dürfen; **could I have a word with you?** könnte ich Sie kurz sprechen?

Canada ['kænədə] n Kanada nt; **Canadian** [kə'neɪdjən] adj kanadisch ▷ n Kanadier(in) m(f)
canal [kə'næl] n Kanal m
canary [kə'nɛərɪ] n Kanarienvogel m
cancel ['kænsəl] vt (plans) aufgeben; (meeting, event) absagen; (Comm: order etc) stornieren; (contract) kündigen; (Inform) löschen; (Aviat: flight) streichen; **to be ~led** (event, train, bus) ausfallen; **cancellation** [kænsə'leɪʃən] n Absage f; (Comm) Stornierung f; (Aviat) gestrichener Flug
cancer ['kænsə°] n (Med) Krebs m; **Cancer** n (Astr) Krebs m
candid ['kændɪd] adj (person, conversation) offen
candidate ['kændɪdət] n (for post) Bewerber(in) m(f); (Pol) Kandidat(in) m(f)
candle ['kændl] n Kerze f; **candlelight** n Kerzenlicht nt; **candlestick** n Kerzenhalter m
candy ['kændɪ] n (US) Bonbon nt; (quantity) Süßigkeiten pl; **candy-floss** n (Brit) Zuckerwatte f
cane [keɪn] n Rohr nt; (stick) Stock m
cannabis ['kænəbɪs] n Cannabis m
canned [kænd] adj Dosen-
cannot ['kænɒt] contr of **can not**
canny ['kænɪ] adj (shrewd) schlau
canoe [kə'nuː] n Kanu nt; **canoeing** n Kanufahren nt
can opener ['kænəʊpnə°] n Dosenöffner m
canopy ['kænəpɪ] n Baldachin m; (awning) Markise f; (over entrance) Vordach nt

can't [kɑːnt] *contr of* **can not**

canteen [kæn'tiːn] *n* (*in factory*) Kantine *f*; (*in university*) Mensa *f*

canvas ['kænvəs] *n* (*for sails, shoes*) Segeltuch *nt*; (*for tent*) Zeltstoff *m*; (*for painting*) Leinwand *f*

canvass ['kænvəs] *vi* um Stimmen werben (*for* für)

canyon ['kænjən] *n* Felsenschlucht *f*; **canyoning** ['kænjənɪŋ] *n* Canyoning *nt*

cap [kæp] *n* Mütze *f*; (*lid*) Verschluss *m*, Deckel *m*

capability [keɪpə'bɪlɪtɪ] *n* Fähigkeit *f*; **capable** ['keɪpəbl] *adj* fähig; **to be ~ of sth** zu etw fähig (*o* imstande) sein; **to be ~ of doing sth** etw tun können

capacity [kə'pæsɪtɪ] *n* (*of building, container*) Fassungsvermögen *nt*; (*ability*) Fähigkeit *f*; (*function*) **in his ~ as ...** in seiner Eigenschaft als ...

cape [keɪp] *n* (*garment*) Cape *nt*, Umhang *m*; (*Geo*) Kap *nt*

caper ['keɪpə*] *n* (*for cooking*) Kaper *f*

capital ['kæpɪtl] *n* (*Fin*) Kapital *nt*; (*letter*) Großbuchstabe *m*; **~ (city)** Hauptstadt *f*; **capitalism** *n* Kapitalismus *m*; **capital punishment** *n* die Todesstrafe

Capricorn ['kæprɪkɔːn] *n* (*Astr*) Steinbock *m*

capsize [kæp'saɪz] *vi* kentern

capsule ['kæpsjuːl] *n* Kapsel *f*

captain ['kæptɪn] *n* Kapitän *m*; (*army*) Hauptmann *m*

caption ['kæpʃən] *n* Bildunterschrift *f*

captive ['kæptɪv] *n* Gefangene(r) *mf*; **capture** ['kæptʃə*] *vt* (*person*) fassen, gefangen nehmen; (*town etc*) einnehmen; (*Inform: data*) erfassen ▷ *n* Gefangennahme *f*; (*Inform*) Erfassung *f*

car [kɑː*] *n* Auto *nt*; (*US Rail*) Wagen *m*

carafe [kə'ræf] *n* Karaffe *f*

caramel ['kærəmel] *n* Karamelle *f*

caravan ['kærəvæn] *n* Wohnwagen *m*; **caravan site** *n* Campingplatz *m* für Wohnwagen

caraway (seed) ['kærəweɪ] *n* Kümmel *m*

carbohydrate [kɑːbəʊ'haɪdreɪt] *n* Kohle(n)hydrat *nt*

car bomb *n* Autobombe *f*

carbon ['kɑːbən] *n* Kohlenstoff *m*

car boot sale *n auf einem* Parkplatz stattfindender Flohmarkt

carburettor, carburetor (*US*) ['kɑːbjʊretə*] *n* Vergaser *m*

card [kɑːd] *n* Karte *f*; (*material*) Pappe *f*; **cardboard** *n* Pappe *f*; **~ (box)** Karton *m*; (*smaller*) Pappschachtel *f*; **card game** *n* Kartenspiel *nt*

cardigan ['kɑːdɪgən] *n* Strickjacke *f*

card index *n* Kartei *f*; **cardphone** ['kɑːdfəʊn] *n* Kartentelefon *nt*

care [kɛə*] *n* (*worry*) Sorge *f*; (*carefulness*) Sorgfalt *f*; (*looking after things, people*) Pflege *f*; **with ~** sorgfältig; (*cautiously*) vorsichtig; **to take ~** (*watch out*) vorsichtig sein; (*in address*) **~ of** bei; **to take ~ of** sorgen für, sich kümmern um ▷ *vi*: **I don't ~** es ist mir egal; **to ~ about sth** Wert auf etw *akk* legen; **he ~s about her** sie liegt ihm am Herzen; **care for** *vt* (*look after*) sorgen für, sich kümmern um; (*like*) mögen

career [kə'rɪə*] *n* Karriere *f*, Laufbahn *f*; **career woman** (*pl* **women**) *n* Karrierefrau *f*; **careers adviser** *n* Berufsberater(in) *m(f)*

carefree ['kɛəfriː] *adj* sorgenfrei; **careful, carefully** *adj, adv* sorgfältig; (*cautious, cautiously*)

vorsichtig; **careless, carelessly**
adj, adv nachlässig; (*driving etc*)
leichtsinnig; (*remark*)
unvorsichtig; **carer** ['kɛərə*] *n*
Betreuer(in) *m(f)*, Pfleger(in) *m(f)*;
caretaker ['kɛəteɪkə*] *n* Haus-
meister(in) *m(f)*; **careworker** *n*
Pfleger(in) *m(f)*
car-ferry ['kɑːfɛrɪ] *n* Autofähre *f*
cargo ['kɑːgəʊ] (*pl* **-(e)s**) *n*
Ladung *f*
car hire, car hire company *n*
Autovermietung *f*
Caribbean [kærɪ'biːən] *n* Karibik
f ▷ *adj* karibisch
caring ['kɛərɪŋ] *adj* mitfühlend;
(*parent, partner*) liebevoll; (*looking
after sb*) fürsorglich
car insurance *n*
Kraftfahrzeugversicherung *f*
carnation [kɑː'neɪʃən] *n* Nelke *f*
carnival ['kɑːnɪvəl] *n* Volksfest
nt; (*before Lent*) Karneval *m*
carol ['kærəl] *n* Weihnachtslied *nt*
carp [kɑːp] *n* (*fish*) Karpfen *m*
car park *n* (*Brit*) Parkplatz *m*;
(*multi-storey car park*) Parkhaus *nt*
carpenter ['kɑːpəntə*] *n* Zimmermann *m*
carpet ['kɑːpɪt] *n* Teppich *m*
car phone *n* Autotelefon *nt*;
carpool *n* Fahrgemeinschaft *f*;
(*vehicles*) Fuhrpark *m* ▷ *vi* eine
Fahrgemeinschaft bilden; **car
rental** *n* Autovermietung *f*
carriage ['kærɪdʒ] *n* (*Brit Rail:
coach*) Wagen *m*; (*compartment*)
Abteil *nt*; (*horse-drawn*) Kutsche *f*;
(*transport*) Beförderung *f*;
carriageway *n* (*Brit: on road*)
Fahrbahn *f*
carrier ['kærɪə*] *n* (*Comm*)
Spediteur(in) *m(f)*; **carrier bag** *n*
Tragetasche *f*
carrot ['kærət] *n* Karotte *f*
carry ['kærɪ] *vt* tragen; (*in vehicle*)
befördern; (*have on one*) bei sich

haben; **carry on** *vi* (*continue*)
weitermachen; (*fam: make a scene*)
ein Theater machen ▷ *vt*
(*continue*) fortführen; **to ~ on
working** weiter arbeiten; **carry
out** *vt* (*orders, plan*) ausführen,
durchführen
carrycot *n* Babytragetasche *f*
carsick ['kɑːsɪk] *adj:* **he gets
~** ihm wird beim Autofahren übel
cart [kɑːt] *n* Wagen *m*, Karren *m*;
(*US: shopping trolley*)
Einkaufswagen *m*
carton ['kɑːtən] *n* (*Papp*)karton
m; (*of cigarettes*) Stange *f*
cartoon [kɑː'tuːn] *n* Cartoon *m* o
nt; (*one drawing*) Karikatur *f*; (*film*)
(Zeichen)trickfilm *m*
cartridge ['kɑːtrɪdʒ] *n* (*for film*)
Kassette *f*; (*for gun, pen, printer*)
Patrone *f*; (*for copier*) Kartusche *f*
carve [kɑːv] *vt, vi* (*wood*)
schnitzen; (*stone*) meißeln; (*meat*)
schneiden, tranchieren; **carving** *n*
(*in wood*) Schnitzerei *f*; (*in stone*)
Skulptur *f*; (*Ski*) Carving *nt*
car wash *n* Autowaschanlage *f*
case [keɪs] *n* (*crate*) Kiste *f*; (*box*)
Schachtel *f*; (*for jewels*) Schatulle *f*;
(*for spectacles*) Etui *nt*; (*Jur, matter*)
Fall *m*; **in ~ falls**; **in that ~** in dem
Fall; **in ~ of fire** bei Brand; **it's a
~ of ...** es handelt sich hier um ...
cash [kæʃ] *n* Bargeld *nt*; **in ~** bar;
~ on delivery per Nachnahme
▷ *vt* (*cheque*) einlösen; **cash desk**
n Kasse *f*; **cash dispenser** *n*
Geldautomat *m*; **cashier** [kæ'ʃɪə*]
n Kassierer(in) *m(f)*; **cash
machine** *n* (*Brit*) Geldautomat *m*
cashmere ['kæʃmɪə*] *n* Kasch-
mirwolle *f*
cash payment *n* Barzahlung *f*;
cashpoint *n* (*Brit*) Geldautomat *m*
casing ['keɪsɪŋ] *n* Gehäuse *nt*
casino [kə'siːnəʊ] (*pl* **-s**) *n*
Kasino *nt*

cask [kɑːsk] n Fass nt
casserole ['kæsərəʊl] n Kasserole f; (food) Schmortopf m
cassette [kæ'set] n Kassette f; **cassette recorder** n Kassettenrekorder m
cast [kɑːst] (**cast, cast**) vt (throw) werfen; (Theat, Cine) besetzen; (roles) verteilen ▷ n (Theat, Cine) Besetzung f; (Med) Gipsverband m; **cast off** vi (Naut) losmachen
caster ['kɑːstə*] n: **~ sugar** Streuzucker m
castle ['kɑːsl] n Burg f
castrate [kæs'treɪt] vt kastrieren
casual ['kæʒjʊəl] adj (arrangement, remark) beiläufig; (attitude, manner) (nach)lässig, zwanglos; (dress) leger; (work, earnings) Gelegenheits-; (look, glance) flüchtig; **~ wear** Freizeitkleidung f; **~ sex** Gelegenheitssex m; **casually** adv (remark, say) beiläufig; (meet) zwanglos; (dressed) leger
casualty ['kæʒjʊəltɪ] n Verletzte(r) mf; (dead) Tote(r) mf; (department in hospital) Notaufnahme f
cat [kæt] n Katze f; (male) Kater m
catalog (US), **catalogue** ['kætəlɒg] n Katalog m ▷ vt katalogisieren
cataract ['kætərækt] n Wasserfall m; (Med) grauer Star
catarrh [kə'tɑː*] n Katarr(h) m
catastrophe [kə'tæstrəfɪ] n Katastrophe f
catch [kætʃ] n (fish etc) Fang m ▷ vt (**caught, caught**) fangen; (thief) fassen; (train, bus etc) nehmen; (not miss) erreichen; **to ~ a cold** sich erkälten; **to ~ fire** Feuer fangen; **I didn't ~ that** das habe ich nicht verstanden; **catch on** vi (become popular) Anklang finden; **catch up** vt, vi: **to ~ with**

sb jdn einholen; **to ~ on sth** etw nachholen; **catching** adj ansteckend
category ['kætɪgərɪ] n Kategorie f
cater ['keɪtə*] vi die Speisen und Getränke liefern (for für); **cater for** vt (have facilities for) eingestellt sein auf +akk; **catering** n Versorgung f mit Speisen und Getränken, Gastronomie f; **catering service** n Partyservice m
caterpillar ['kætəpɪlə*] n Raupe f
cathedral [kə'θiːdrəl] n Kathedrale f, Dom m
Catholic ['kæθəlɪk] adj katholisch ▷ Katholik(in) m(f)
cat nap n (Brit) kurzer Schlaf; **cat's eyes** ['kætsaɪz] npl (in road) Katzenaugen pl, Reflektoren pl
catsup ['kætsəp] n (US) Ketschup nt o m
cattle ['kætl] npl Vieh nt
caught [kɔːt] pt, pp of **catch**
cauliflower ['kɒlɪflaʊə*] n Blumenkohl m; **cauliflower cheese** n Blumenkohl m in Käsesoße
cause [kɔːz] n (origin) Ursache f (of für); (reason) Grund m (for zu); (purpose) Sache f; **for a good ~** für wohltätige Zwecke; **no ~ for alarm/complaint** kein Grund zur Aufregung/Klage ▷ vt verursachen
causeway ['kɔːzweɪ] n Damm m
caution ['kɔːʃən] n Vorsicht f; (Jur, Sport) Verwarnung f ▷ vt (ver)warnen; **cautious** ['kɔːʃəs] adj vorsichtig
cave [keɪv] n Höhle f; **cave in** vi einstürzen
cavity ['kævɪtɪ] n Hohlraum m; (in tooth) Loch nt
cayenne (pepper) [keɪ'en] n Cayennepfeffer m

CCTV *abbr* = **closed circuit television** Video-überwachungsanlage *f*

CD *abbr* = **Compact Disc** CD *f*; **CD player** *n* CD-Spieler *m*; **CD-ROM** *abbr* = **Compact Disc Read Only Memory** CD-ROM *f*; **CD-RW** *abbr* = **Compact Disc Rewritable** CD-RW *f*

cease [siːs] *vi* aufhören ▷ *vt* beenden; **to ~ doing sth** aufhören, etw zu tun; **cease fire** *n* Waffenstillstand *m*

ceiling ['siːlɪŋ] *n* Decke *f*

celebrate ['selɪbreɪt] *vt, vi* feiern; **celebrated** *adj* gefeiert; **celebration** [selɪ'breɪʃən] *n* Feier *f*; **celebrity** [sɪ'lebrɪtɪ] *n* Berühmtheit *f*, Star *m*

celeriac [sə'lerɪæk] *n* (Knollen)sellerie *m* o *f*; **celery** ['selərɪ] *n* (Stangen)sellerie *m* o *f*

cell [sel] *n* Zelle *f*; (US) see **cellphone**

cellar ['selə*] *n* Keller *m*

cello ['tʃeləʊ] (*pl* **-s**) *n* Cello *nt*

cellphone ['selfəʊn], **cellular phone** ['seljʊlə* 'fəʊn] *n* Mobiltelefon *nt*, Handy *nt*

Celt [kelt] *n* Kelte *m*, Keltin *f*; **Celtic** ['keltɪk] *adj* keltisch ▷ *n* (*language*) Keltisch *nt*

cement [sɪ'ment] *n* Zement *m*

cemetery ['semɪtrɪ] *n* Friedhof *m*

censorship ['sensəʃɪp] *n* Zensur *f*

cent [sent] *n* (*of dollar, euro etc*) Cent *m*

center *n* (US) see **centre**

centiliter (US), **centilitre** ['sentɪliːtə*] *n* Zentiliter *m*; **centimeter** (US), **centimetre** ['sentɪmiːtə*] *n* Zentimeter *m*

central ['sentrəl] *adj* zentral; **Central America** *n* Mittelamerika *nt*; **Central Europe** *n* Mitteleuropa *nt*; **central heating** *n* Zentralheizung *f*; **centralize** *vt* zentralisieren; **central locking** *n* (*Auto*) Zentralverriegelung *f*; **central reservation** *n* (*Brit*) Mittelstreifen *m*; **central station** *n* Hauptbahnhof *m*

centre ['sentə*] *n* Mitte *f*; (*building, of city*) Zentrum *nt* ▷ *vt* zentrieren; **centre forward** *n* (*Sport*) Mittelstürmer *m*

century ['sentjʊrɪ] *n* Jahrhundert *nt*

ceramic [sɪ'ræmɪk] *adj* keramisch

cereal ['sɪərɪəl] *n* (*any grain*) Getreide *nt*; (*breakfast cereal*) Frühstücksflocken *pl*

ceremony ['serɪmənɪ] *n* Feier *f*, Zeremonie *f*

certain ['sɜːtən] *adj* sicher (*of +gen*); (*particular*) bestimmt; **for ~** mit Sicherheit; **certainly** *adv* sicher; (*without doubt*) bestimmt; **~!** aber sicher!; **~ not** ganz bestimmt nicht!

certificate [sə'tɪfɪkɪt] *n* Bescheinigung *f*; (*in school, of qualification*) Zeugnis *nt*; **certify** ['sɜːtɪfaɪ] *vt, vi* bescheinigen

cervical smear ['sɜːvɪkəl smɪə*] *n* Abstrich *m*

CFC *abbr* = **chlorofluorocarbon** FCKW *nt*

chain [tʃeɪn] *n* Kette *f* ▷ *vt*: **to ~ (up)** anketten; **chain reaction** *n* Kettenreaktion *f*; **chain store** *n* Kettenladen *m*

chair [tʃeə*] *n* Stuhl *m*; (*university*) Lehrstuhl *m*; (*armchair*) Sessel *m*; (*chairperson*) Vorsitzende(r) *mf*; **chairlift** *n* Sessellift *m*; **chairman** (*pl* **-men**) *n* Vorsitzende(r) *m*; (*of firm*) Präsident *m*; **chairperson** *n* Vorsitzende(r) *mf*; (*of firm*) Präsident(in) *m(f)*; **chairwoman**

(*pl* **-women**) *n* Vorsitzende *f*; (*of firm*) Präsidentin *f*

chalet ['ʃæleɪ] *n* (*in mountains*) Berghütte *f*; (*holiday dwelling*) Ferienhäuschen *nt*

chalk [tʃɔːk] *n* Kreide *f*

challenge ['tʃælɪndʒ] *n* Herausforderung *f* ▷ *vt* (*person*) herausfordern; (*statement*) bestreiten

chambermaid ['tʃeɪmbə*meɪd] *n* Zimmermädchen *nt*

chamois leather ['ʃæmwɑː'leðə*] *n* (*for windows*) Fensterleder *nt*

champagne [ʃæm'peɪn] *n* Champagner *m*

champion ['tʃæmpɪən] *n* (*Sport*) Meister(in) *m(f)*; **championship** *n* Meisterschaft *f*

chance [tʃɑːns] *n* (*fate*) Zufall *m*; (*possibility*) Möglichkeit *f*; (*opportunity*) Gelegenheit *f*; (*risk*) Risiko *nt*; **by ~** zufällig; **he doesn't stand a ~** (**of winning**) er hat keinerlei Chance(, zu gewinnen)

chancellor ['tʃɑːnsələ*] *n* Kanzler(in) *m(f)*

chandelier [ʃændɪ'lɪə*] *n* Kronleuchter *m*

change [tʃeɪndʒ] *vt* verändern; (*alter*) ändern; (*money, wheel, nappy*) wechseln; (*exchange*) (um)tauschen; **to ~ one's clothes** sich umziehen; **to ~ trains** umsteigen; **to ~ gear** (*Auto*) schalten ▷ *vi* sich ändern; (*esp outwardly*) sich verändern; (*get changed*) sich umziehen ▷ *n* Veränderung *f*; (*alteration*) Änderung *f*; (*money*) Wechselgeld *nt*; (*coins*) Kleingeld *nt*; **for a ~** zur Abwechslung; **can you give me ~ for £10?** können Sie mir auf 10 Pfund herausgeben?; **change down** *vi* (*Brit Auto*) herunterschalten; **change over** *vi*

sich umstellen (*to* auf +*akk*); **change up** *vi* (*Brit Auto*) hochschalten

changeable *adj* (*weather*) veränderlich, wechselhaft; **change machine** *n* Geldwechsler *m*; **changing room** *n* Umkleideraum *m*

channel ['tʃænl] *n* Kanal *m*; (*Radio, TV*) Kanal *m*, Sender *m*; **the** (**English**) **Channel** der Ärmelkanal; **the Channel Islands** die Kanalinseln; **the Channel Tunnel** der Kanaltunnel; **channel-hopping** *n* Zappen *nt*

chaos ['keɪɒs] *n* Chaos *nt*; **chaotic** [keɪ'ɒtɪk] *adj* chaotisch

chap [tʃæp] *n* (*Brit fam*) Bursche *m*, Kerl *m*

chapel ['tʃæpəl] *n* Kapelle *f*

chapped ['tʃæpt] *adj* (*lips*) aufgesprungen

chapter ['tʃæptə*] *n* Kapitel *nt*

character ['kærəktə*] *n* Charakter *m*, Wesen *nt*; (*in a play, novel etc*) Figur *f*; (*Typo*) Zeichen *nt*; **he's a real ~** er ist ein echtes Original; **characteristic** [kærəktə'rɪstɪk] *n* typisches Merkmal

charcoal ['tʃɑːkəʊl] *n* Holzkohle *f*

charge [tʃɑːdʒ] *n* (*cost*) Gebühr *f*; (*Jur*) Anklage *f*; **free of ~** gratis, kostenlos; **to be in ~ of** verantwortlich sein für ▷ *vt* (*money*) verlangen; (*Jur*) anklagen; (*battery*) laden; **charge card** *n* Kundenkreditkarte *f*

charity ['tʃærɪtɪ] *n* (*institution*) wohltätige Organisation *f*; **a collection for ~** eine Sammlung für wohltätige Zwecke; **charity shop** *n* Geschäft einer 'charity', in dem freiwillige Helfer gebrauchte Kleidung, Bücher etc verkaufen

charm [tʃɑːm] *n* Charme *m* ▷ *vt* bezaubern; **charming** *adj* reizend, charmant

chart [tʃɑːt] *n* Diagramm *nt*; (*map*) Karte *f*; **the ~s** *pl* die Charts, die Hitliste

charter ['tʃɑːtə*] *n* Urkunde *f* ▷ *vt* (*Naut, Aviat*) chartern; **charter flight** *n* Charterflug *m*

chase [tʃeɪs] *vt* jagen, verfolgen ▷ *n* Verfolgungsjagd *f*; (*hunt*) Jagd *f*

chassis ['ʃæsɪ] *n* (*Auto*) Fahrgestell *nt*

chat [tʃæt] *vi* plaudern; (*Inform*) chatten ▷ *n* Plauderei *f*; **chat up** *vt* anmachen, anbaggern; **chatroom** *n* (*Inform*) Chatroom *m*; **chat show** *n* Talkshow *f*; **chatty** *adj* geschwätzig

chauffeur ['ʃəʊfə*] *n* Chauffeur(in) *m(f)*, Fahrer(in) *m(f)*

cheap [tʃiːp] *adj* billig; (*of poor quality*) minderwertig

cheat [tʃiːt] *vt, vi* betrügen; (*in school, game*) mogeln

Chechen ['tʃetʃen] *adj* tschetschenisch ▷ *n* Tschetschene *m*, Tschetschenin *f*; **Chechnya** ['tʃetʃnɪə] *n* Tschetschenien *nt*

check [tʃek] *vt* (*examine*) überprüfen (*for* auf +*akk*); (*Tech: adjustment etc*) kontrollieren; (*US: tick*) abhaken; (*Aviat: luggage*) einchecken; (*US: coat*) abgeben ▷ *n* (*examination, restraint*) Kontrolle *f*; (*US: restaurant bill*) Rechnung *f*; (*pattern*) Karo(muster) *nt*; (*US*) *see* **cheque**; **check in** *vt, vi* (*Aviat*) einchecken; (*into hotel*) sich anmelden; **check out** *vi* sich abmelden, auschecken; **check up** *vi* nachprüfen; **to ~ on sb** Nachforschungen über jdn anstellen

checkers ['tʃekəz] *nsing* (*US*) Damespiel *nt*

check-in ['tʃekɪn] *n* (*airport*) Check-in *m*; (*hotel*) Anmeldung *f*; **check-in desk** *n*

Abfertigungsschalter *m*; **checking account** *n* (*US*) Scheckkonto *nt*; **check list** *n* Kontrollliste *f*; **checkout** *n* (*supermarket*) Kasse *f*; **checkout time** *n* (*hotel*) Abreise(zeit) *f*; **checkpoint** *n* Kontrollpunkt *m*; **checkroom** *n* (*US*) Gepäckaufbewahrung *f*; **checkup** *n* (*Med*) (ärztliche) Untersuchung

cheddar ['tʃedə*] *n* Cheddarkäse *m*

cheek [tʃiːk] *n* Backe *f*, Wange *f*; (*insolence*) Frechheit *f*; **what a ~** so eine Frechheit!; **cheekbone** *n* Backenknochen *m*; **cheeky** *adj* frech

cheer [tʃɪə*] *n* Beifallsruf *m*; **~s** (*when drinking*) prost!; (*Brit fam: thanks*) danke; (*Brit: goodbye*) tschüs ▷ *vt* zujubeln +*dat* ▷ *vi* jubeln; **cheer up** *vt* aufmuntern ▷ *vi* fröhlicher werden; **~!** Kopf hoch!; **cheerful** ['tʃɪəfʊl] *adj* fröhlich

cheese [tʃiːz] *n* Käse *m*; **cheeseboard** *n* Käsebrett *nt*; (*as course*) (gemischte) Käseplatte; **cheesecake** *n* Käsekuchen *m*

chef [ʃef] *n* Koch *m*; (*in charge of kitchen*) Küchenchef(in) *m(f)*

chemical ['kemɪkəl] *adj* chemisch ▷ Chemikalie *f*; **chemist** ['kemɪst] *n* (*pharmacist*) Apotheker(in) *m(f)*; (*industrial chemist*) Chemiker(in) *m(f)*; **~'s** (**shop**) Apotheke *f*; **chemistry** *n* Chemie *f*

cheque [tʃek] *n* (*Brit*) Scheck *m*; **cheque account** *n* (*Brit*) Girokonto *nt*; **cheque book** *n* (*Brit*) Scheckheft *nt*; **cheque card** *n* (*Brit*) Scheckkarte *f*

chequered ['tʃekəd] *adj* kariert

cherish ['tʃerɪʃ] *vt* (*look after*) liebevoll sorgen für; (*hope*) hegen; (*memory*) bewahren

cherry ['tʃerɪ] n Kirsche f; **cherry tomato** (pl **-es**) n Kirschtomate f

chess [tʃes] n Schach nt; **chessboard** n Schachbrett nt

chest [tʃest] n Brust f; (box) Kiste f; **~ of drawers** Kommode f

chestnut ['tʃesnʌt] n Kastanie f

chew [tʃuː] vt, vi kauen; **chewing gum** n Kaugummi m

chick [tʃɪk] n Küken nt; **chicken** n Huhn nt; (food: roast) Hähnchen nt; (coward) Feigling m; **chicken breast** n Hühnerbrust f; **chicken Kiev** n paniertes Hähnchen, mit Knoblauchbutter gefüllt; **chickenpox** n Windpocken pl; **chickpea** n Kichererbse f

chicory ['tʃɪkərɪ] n Chicorée f

chief [tʃiːf] n (of department etc) Leiter(in) m(f); (boss) Chef(in) m(f); (of tribe) Häuptling m ▷ adj Haupt-; **chiefly** adv hauptsächlich

child [tʃaɪld] (pl **children**) n Kind nt; **child abuse** n Kindesmisshandlung f; **child allowance**, **child benefit** (Brit) n Kindergeld nt; **childbirth** n Geburt f, Entbindung f; **childhood** n Kindheit f; **childish** adj kindisch; **child lock** n Kindersicherung f; **childproof** adj kindersicher; **children** ['tʃɪldrən] pl of **child**; **child seat** n Kindersitz m

Chile ['tʃɪlɪ] n Chile nt

chill [tʃɪl] n Kühle f; (Med) Erkältung f ▷ vt (wine) kühlen; **chill out** vi (fam) chillen, relaxen; **chilled** adj gekühlt

chilli ['tʃɪlɪ] n Pepperoni pl; (spice) Chili m; **chilli con carne** ['tʃɪlɪkɔn'kɑːnɪ] n Chili con carne nt

chilly ['tʃɪlɪ] adj kühl, frostig

chimney ['tʃɪmnɪ] n Schornstein m; **chimneysweep** n Schornsteinfeger(in) m(f)

chimpanzee [tʃɪmpæn'ziː] n Schimpanse m

chin [tʃɪn] n Kinn nt

china ['tʃaɪnə] n Porzellan nt

China ['tʃaɪnə] n China nt; **Chinese** [tʃaɪ'niːz] adj chinesisch ▷ n (person) Chinese m, Chinesin f; (language) Chinesisch nt; **Chinese leaves** npl Chinakohl m

chip [tʃɪp] n (of wood etc) Splitter m; (damage) angeschlagene Stelle; (Inform) Chip m; **~s** (Brit: potatoes) Pommes (frites) pl; (US: crisps) Kartoffelchips pl ▷ vt anschlagen, beschädigen; (fam), **chip shop** n Frittenbude f

chiropodist [kɪ'rɔpədɪst] n Fußpfleger(in) m(f)

chirp [tʃɜːp] vi zwitschern

chisel ['tʃɪzl] n Meißel m

chitchat ['tʃɪttʃæt] n Gerede nt

chives [tʃaɪvz] npl Schnittlauch m

chlorine ['klɔːriːn] n Chlor nt

chocaholic, **chocoholic** [tʃɒkə'hɒlɪk] n Schokoladenfreak m; **choc-ice** ['tʃɒkaɪs] n Eis nt mit Schokoladenüberzug; **chocolate** ['tʃɒklɪt] n Schokolade f; (chocolate-coated sweet) Praline f; **a bar of ~** eine Tafel Schokolade; **a box of ~s** eine Schachtel Pralinen; **chocolate cake** n Schokoladenkuchen m; **chocolate sauce** n Schokoladensoße f

choice [tʃɔɪs] n Wahl f; (selection) Auswahl f ▷ adj auserlesen; (product) Qualitäts-

choir ['kwaɪə*] n Chor m

choke [tʃəʊk] vi sich verschlucken; (Sport) die Nerven verlieren ▷ vt erdrosseln ▷ n (Auto) Choke m

cholera ['kɒlərə] n Cholera f
cholesterol [kə'lestərəl] n Cholesterin nt
choose [tʃuːz] (**chose, chosen**) vt wählen; (pick out) sich aussuchen; **there are three to ~ from** es stehen drei zur Auswahl
chop [tʃɒp] vt (zer)hacken; (meat etc) klein schneiden ▷ n (meat) Kotelett nt; **to get the ~** gefeuert werden; **chopper** n Hackbeil nt; (fam: helicopter) Hubschrauber m; **chopsticks** npl Essstäbchen pl
chorus ['kɔːrəs] n Chor m; (in song) Refrain m
chose, chosen [tʃəʊz, 'tʃəʊzn] pt, pp of **choose**
chowder ['tʃaʊdə*] n (US) dicke Suppe mit Meeresfrüchten
christen ['krɪsn] vt taufen; **christening** n Taufe f; **Christian** ['krɪstɪən] adj christlich ▷ n Christ(in) m(f); **Christian name** n (Brit) Vorname m
Christmas ['krɪsməs] n Weihnachten pl; **Christmas bonus** n Weihnachtsgeld nt; **Christmas card** n Weihnachtskarte f; **Christmas carol** n Weihnachtslied nt; **Christmas Day** n der erste Weihnachtstag; **Christmas Eve** n Heiligabend m; **Christmas pudding** n Plumpudding m; **Christmas tree** n Weihnachtsbaum m
chronic ['krɒnɪk] adj (Med, fig) chronisch; (fam: very bad) miserabel
chrysanthemum [krɪ'sænθɪməm] n Chrysantheme f
chubby ['tʃʌbɪ] adj (child) pummelig; (adult) rundlich
chuck [tʃʌk] vt (fam) schmeißen; **chuck in** vt (fam: job) hinschmeißen; **chuck out** vt (fam) rausschmeißen; **chuck up** vi (fam) kotzen
chunk [tʃʌŋk] n Klumpen m; (of bread) Brocken m; (of meat) Batzen m; **chunky** adj (person) stämmig
Chunnel ['tʃʌnəl] n (fam) Kanaltunnel m
church [tʃɜːtʃ] n Kirche f; **churchyard** n Kirchhof m
chute [ʃuːt] n Rutsche f
chutney ['tʃʌtnɪ] n Chutney m
CIA abbr = **Central Intelligence Agency** (US) CIA f
CID abbr = **Criminal Investigation Department** (Brit) ≈ Kripo f
cider ['saɪdə*] n ≈ Apfelmost m
cigar [sɪ'gɑː*] n Zigarre f; **cigarette** [sɪgə'ret] n Zigarette f
cinema ['sɪnəmə] n Kino nt
cinnamon ['sɪnəmən] n Zimt m
circle ['sɜːkl] n Kreis m ▷ vi kreisen; **circuit** ['sɜːkɪt] n Rundfahrt f; (on foot) Rundgang m; (for racing) Rennstrecke f; (Elec) Stromkreis m; **circular** ['sɜːkjʊlə*] adj (kreis)rund, kreisförmig ▷ n Rundschreiben nt; **circulation** [sɜːkjʊ'leɪʃən] n (of blood) Kreislauf m; (of newspaper) Auflage f
circumstances ['sɜːkəmstənsəz] npl (facts) Umstände pl; (financial condition) Verhältnisse pl; **in/under the ~** unter den Umständen; **under no ~** auf keinen Fall
circus ['sɜːkəs] n Zirkus m
cissy ['sɪsɪ] n (fam) Weichling m
cistern ['sɪstən] n Zisterne f; (of WC) Spülkasten m
citizen ['sɪtɪzn] n Bürger(in) m(f); (of nation) Staatsangehörige(r) mf; **citizenship** n Staatsangehörigkeit f
city ['sɪtɪ] n Stadt f; (large) Großstadt f; **the ~** (London's financial centre) die (Londoner)

City; **city centre** n Innenstadt f,
Zentrum nt
civil ['sɪvl] adj (of town) Bürger-;
(of state) staatsbürgerlich; (not
military) zivil; **civil ceremony** n
standesamtliche Hochzeit; **civil
engineering** n Hoch- und Tiefbau
m, Bauingenieurwesen nt; **civilian**
[sɪ'vɪljən] n Zivilist(in) m(f);
civilization [sɪvɪlaɪ'zeɪʃən] n
Zivilisation f, Kultur f; **civilized**
['sɪvɪlaɪzd] adj zivilisiert,
kultiviert; **civil partnership** n
eingetragene Partnerschaft; **civil
rights** npl Bürgerrechte pl; **civil
servant** n (Staats)beamte(r) m,
(Staats)beamtin f; **civil service** n
Staatsdienst m; **civil war** n
Bürgerkrieg m
CJD abbr = **Creutzfeld-Jakob
disease** Creutzfeld-
Jakob-Krankheit f
cl abbr = **centilitre(s)** cl
claim [kleɪm] vt beanspruchen;
(apply for) beantragen; (demand)
fordern; (assert) behaupten (that
dass) ▷ n (demand) Forderung f
(for für); (right) Anspruch m (to auf
+akk); **~ for damages**
Schadenersatzforderung f; **to
make** o **put in a ~** (insurance)
Ansprüche geltend machen;
claimant n Antragsteller(in) m(f)
clam [klæm] n Venusmuschel f;
clam chowder n (US) dicke
Muschelsuppe (mit Sellerie, Zwiebeln
etc)
clap [klæp] vi (Beifall) klatschen
claret ['klærɪt] n roter
Bordeaux(wein)
clarify ['klærɪfaɪ] vt klären
clarinet [klærɪ'net] n Klarinette f
clarity ['klærɪtɪ] n Klarheit f
clash [klæʃ] vi (physically)
zusammenstoßen (with mit);
(argue) sich auseinandersetzen
(with mit); (fig: colours) sich beißen

▷ n Zusammenstoß m; (argument)
Auseinandersetzung f
clasp [klɑːsp] n (on belt) Schnalle f
class [klɑːs] n Klasse f ▷ vt
einordnen, einstufen
classic ['klæsɪk] adj (mistake,
example etc) klassisch ▷ n
Klassiker m; **classical** ['klæsɪkəl]
adj (music, ballet etc) klassisch
classification [klæsɪfɪ'keɪʃn] n
Klassifizierung f; **classify**
['klæsɪfaɪ] vt klassifizieren;
classified advertisement
Kleinanzeige f
classroom ['klɑːsrʊm] n Klassenzimmer nt
classy ['klɑːsɪ] adj (fam) nobel,
exklusiv
clatter ['klætə°] vi klappern
clause [klɔːz] n (Ling) Satz m; (Jur)
Klausel f
claw [klɔː] n Kralle f
clay [kleɪ] n Lehm m; (for pottery)
Ton m
clean [kliːn] adj sauber;
~ driving licence Führerschein
ohne Strafpunkte ▷ vt sauber
machen; (carpet etc) reinigen;
(window, shoes, vegetables) putzen;
(wound) säubern; **clean up** vt
sauber machen ▷ vi aufräumen;
cleaner n (person) Putzmann m,
Putzfrau f; (substance) Putzmittel
nt; **~'s** (firm) Reinigung f
cleanse [klenz] vt reinigen;
(wound) säubern; **cleanser** n
Reinigungsmittel nt
clear ['klɪə°] adj klar; (distinct)
deutlich; (conscience) rein; (free,
road etc) frei; **to be ~ about sth**
sich über etw im Klaren sein
▷ adv: **to stand ~** zurücktreten
▷ vt (road, room etc) räumen; (table)
abräumen; (Jur: find innocent)
freisprechen (of von) ▷ vi (fog,
mist) sich verziehen; (weather)
aufklaren; **clear away** vt

wegräumen; (*dishes*) abräumen;
clear off *vi* (*fam*) abhauen; **clear
up** *vi* (*tidy up*) aufräumen;
(*weather*) sich aufklären ▷ *vt*
(*room*) aufräumen; (*litter*)
wegräumen; (*matter*) klären

clearance sale *n*
Räumungsverkauf *m*; **clearing** *n*
Lichtung *f*; **clearly** *adv* klar;
(*speak, remember*) deutlich;
(*obviously*) eindeutig; **clearout**
n Entrümpelungsaktion *f*;
clearway *n* (*Brit*) Straße *f* mit
Halteverbot nt

clench [klentʃ] *vt* (*fist*) ballen;
(*teeth*) zusammenbeißen

clergyman ['klɜːdʒɪmən] (*pl
-men*) *n* Geistliche(r) *m*;
clergywoman ['klɜːdʒɪwʊmən] (*pl
-women*) *n* Geistliche *f*

clerk [klɑːk], (*US*) [klɜːk] *n* (*in
office*) Büroangestellte(r) *mf*; (*US:
salesperson*) Verkäufer(in) *m(f)*

clever ['klevə*] *adj* schlau, klug;
(*idea*) clever

cliché ['kliːʃeɪ] *n* Klischee nt

click [klɪk] *n* Klicken nt; (*Inform*)
Mausklick *m* ▷ *vi* klicken; **to ~ on
sth** (*Inform*) etw anklicken; **it ~ed**
(*fam*) ich hab's/er hat's etc
geschnallt, es hat gefunkt, es hat
Klick gemacht; **they ~ed** sie haben
sich gleich verstanden; **click on** *vt*
(*Inform*) anklicken

client ['klaɪənt] *n* Kunde *m*,
Kundin *f*; (*Jur*) Mandant(in) *m(f)*

cliff [klɪf] *n* Klippe *f*

climate ['klaɪmɪt] *n* Klima nt

climax ['klaɪmæks] *n* Höhepunkt
m

climb [klaɪm] *vi* (*person*) klettern;
(*aircraft, sun*) steigen; (*road*)
ansteigen ▷ *vt* (*mountain*)
besteigen; (*tree etc*) klettern auf
+*akk* ▷ *n* Aufstieg *m*; **climber** *n*
(*mountaineer*) Bergsteiger(in) *m(f)*;
climbing *n* Klettern nt,

Bergsteigen nt; **climbing frame** *n*
Klettergerüst nt

cling [klɪŋ] (**clung, clung**) *vi*
sich klammern (*to an* +*akk*); **cling
film®** *n* Frischhaltefolie *f*

clinic ['klɪnɪk] *n* Klinik *f*; **clinical**
adj klinisch

clip [klɪp] *n* Klammer *f* ▷ *vt* (*fix*)
anklemmen (*to an* +*akk*;
(*fingernails*) schneiden; **clipboard**
n Klemmbrett nt; **clippers** npl
Schere *f*; (*for nails*) Zwicker *m*

cloak [kləʊk] *n* Umhang *m*;
cloakroom *n* (*for coats*)
Garderobe *f*

clock [klɒk] *n* Uhr *f*; (*Auto: fam*)
Tacho *m*; **round the ~** rund um die
Uhr; **clockwise** *adv* im
Uhrzeigersinn

clog [klɒg] *n* Holzschuh *m* ▷ *vt*
verstopfen

cloister ['klɔɪstə*] *n* Kreuzgang
m

clone [kləʊn] *n* Klon *m* ▷ *vt*
klonen

close [kləʊs] *adj* nahe (*to* +*dat*);
(*friend, contact*) eng; (*resemblance*)
groß; **~ to the beach** in der Nähe
des Strandes; **~ win** knapper Sieg;
on ~r examination bei näherer o
genauerer Untersuchung ▷ *adv*
[kləʊs] dicht; **he lives ~ by** er
wohnt ganz in der Nähe ▷ *vt*
[kləʊz] schließen; (*road*) sperren;
(*discussion, matter*) abschließen-
▷ *vi* [kləʊz] schließen
rtri; *n* [kləʊz] Ende nt; **close
down** *vi* schließen; (*factory*)
stillgelegt werden ▷ *vt* (*shop*)
schließen; (*factory*) stilllegen;
closed *adj* (*road*) gesperrt;
(*shop etc*) geschlossen; **closed
circuit television** *n*
Videoüberwachungsanlage *f*;
closely *adv* (*related*) eng, nah;
(*packed, follow*) dicht; (*attentively*)
genau

closet ['klɒzɪt] n (esp US) Schrank m

close-up ['kləʊsʌp] n Nahaufnahme f

closing ['kləʊzɪŋ] adj: ~ **date** letzter Termin; (for competition) Einsendeschluss m; ~ **time** (of shop) Ladenschluss m; (Brit: of pub) Polizeistunde f

closure ['kləʊʒə*] n Schließung f; Abschluss m; **to look for** ~ mit etw abschließen wollen

clot [klɒt] (**blood**) ~ Blutgerinnsel nt; (fam: idiot) Trottel m ▷ vi (blood) gerinnen

cloth [klɒθ] n (material) Tuch nt; (for cleaning) Lappen m

clothe [kləʊð] vt kleiden; **clothes** [kləʊðz] npl Kleider pl, Kleidung f; **clothes line** n Wäscheleine f; **clothes peg**, **clothespin** (US) n Wäscheklammer f; **clothing** ['kləʊðɪŋ] n Kleidung f

clotted ['klɒtɪd] adj: ~ **cream** dicke Sahne (aus erhitzter Milch)

cloud [klaʊd] n Wolke f; **cloudy** adj (sky) bewölkt; (liquid) trüb

clove [kləʊv] n Gewürznelke f; ~ **of garlic** Knoblauchzehe f

clover ['kləʊvə*] n Klee m; **cloverleaf** (pl -**leaves**) n Kleeblatt nt

clown [klaʊn] n Clown m

club [klʌb] n (weapon) Knüppel m; (society) Klub m, Verein m; (nightclub) Disko f; (golf club) Golfschläger m; ~**s** (Cards) Kreuz nt; **clubbing** n: **to go** ~ in die Disko gehen; **club class** n (Aviat) Businessclass f

clue [klu:] n Anhaltspunkt m, Hinweis m; **he hasn't a** ~ er hat keine Ahnung

clumsy ['klʌmzɪ] adj unbeholfen, ungeschickt

clung [klʌŋ] pt, pp of **cling**

clutch [klʌtʃ] n (Auto) Kupplung f ▷ vt umklammern; (book etc) an sich akk klammern

cm abbr = **centimetre(s)** cm

c/o abbr = **care of** bei

Co abbr = **company** Co

coach [kəʊtʃ] n (Brit: bus) Reisebus m; (Rail) (Personen)wagen m; (Sport: trainer) Trainer(in) m(f) ▷ vt Nachhilfeunterricht geben +dat; (Sport) trainieren; **coach (class)** n (Aviat) Economyclass f; **coach driver** n Busfahrer(in) m(f); **coach party** n Reisegruppe f (Bus) ; **coach station** n Busbahnhof m; **coach trip** n Busfahrt f; (tour) Busreise f

coal [kəʊl] n Kohle f

coalition [kəʊə'lɪʃən] n (Pol) Koalition f

coalmine ['kəʊlmaɪn] n Kohlenbergwerk nt; **coalminer** n Bergarbeiter m

coast [kəʊst] n Küste f; **coastguard** n Küstenwache f; **coastline** n Küste f

coat [kəʊt] n Mantel m; (jacket) Jacke f; (on animals) Fell nt, Pelz m; (of paint) Schicht f; ~ **of arms** Wappen nt; **coathanger** n Kleiderbügel m; **coating** n Überzug m; (layer) Schicht f

cobble(stone)s ['kɒbl(stəʊn)z] npl Kopfsteine pl; (surface) Kopfsteinpflaster nt

cobweb ['kɒbweb] n Spinnennetz nt

cocaine [kə'keɪn] n Kokain nt

cock [kɒk] n Hahn m; (vulg: penis) Schwanz m; **cock up** vt (Brit fam) vermasseln, versauen; **cockerel** ['kɒkərəl] n junger Hahn

cockle ['kɒkl] n Herzmuschel f

cockpit ['kɒkpɪt] n (in plane, racing car) Cockpit nt; **cockroach** ['kɒkrəʊtʃ] n Kakerlake f; **cocktail**

['kɒkteɪl] n Cocktail m; **cock-up**
n (Brit fam) **to make a ~ of sth** bei
etw Mist bauen; **cocky** ['kɒkɪ]
adj großspurig, von sich selbst
überzeugt
cocoa ['kəʊkəʊ] n Kakao m
coconut ['kəʊkənʌt] n Kokosnuss f
cod [kɒd] n Kabeljau m
COD abbr = **cash on delivery** per
Nachnahme
code [kəʊd] n Kode m
coeducational
[kəʊedjʊ'keɪʃənl] adj (school)
gemischt
coffee ['kɒfɪ] n Kaffee m; **coffee
bar** n Café nt; **coffee break** n
Kaffeepause f; **coffee maker** n
Kaffeemaschine f; **coffee pot** n
Kaffeekanne f; **coffee shop** n Café
nt; **coffee table** n Couchtisch m
coffin ['kɒfɪn] n Sarg m
coil [kɔɪl] n Rolle f; (Elec) Spule f;
(Med) Spirale f
coin [kɔɪn] n Münze f
coincide [kəʊɪn'saɪd] vi (happen
together) zusammenfallen (with
mit); **coincidence** [kəʊ'ɪnsɪdəns]
n Zufall m
coke [kəʊk] n Koks m; **Coke®**
Cola f
cola ['kəʊlə] n Cola f
cold [kəʊld] adj kalt; **I'm ~** mir ist
kalt, ich friere ▷ n Kälte f; (illness)
Erkältung f, Schnupfen m; **to
catch a ~** sich erkälten; **cold box**
n Kühlbox f; **cold sore** n Herpes
m; **cold turkey** n (fam)
Totalentzug m; (symptoms)
Entzugserscheinungen pl
coleslaw ['kəʊlslɔː] n Krautsalat
m
collaborate [kə'læbəreɪt] vi
zusammenarbeiten (with mit);
collaboration [kəlæbə'reɪʃən] n
Zusammenarbeit f; (of one party)
Mitarbeit f

collapse [kə'læps] vi zusammenbrechen; (building etc)
einstürzen ▷ n Zusammenbruch
m; (of building) Einsturz m;
collapsible [kə'læpsəbl] adj
zusammenklappbar, Klapp-
collar ['kɒlə*] n Kragen m; (for
dog, cat) Halsband nt; **collarbone**
n Schlüsselbein nt
colleague ['kɒliːg] n Kollege m,
Kollegin f
collect [kə'lekt] vt sammeln;
(fetch) abholen ▷ vi sich sammeln;
collect call n (US) R-Gespräch nt;
collected adj (works) gesammelt;
(person) gefasst; **collector** n
Sammler(in) m(f); **collection**
[kə'lekʃən] n Sammlung f; (Rel)
Kollekte f; (from postbox) Leerung f
college ['kɒlɪdʒ] n (residential)
College nt; (specialist)
Fachhochschule f; (vocational)
Berufsschule f; (US: university)
Universität f; **to go to ~** (US)
studieren
collide [kə'laɪd] vi zusammenstoßen; **collision** [kə'lɪʒən]
n Zusammenstoß m
colloquial [kə'ləʊkwɪəl] adj
umgangssprachlich
Cologne [kə'ləʊn] n Köln nt
colon ['kəʊlən] n (punctuation
mark) Doppelpunkt m
colonial [kə'ləʊnɪəl] adj Kolo-
nial-; **colonize** ['kɒlənaɪz] vt
kolonisieren; **colony** ['kɒlənɪ] n
Kolonie f
color n (US), **colour** ['kʌlə*] n
Farbe f; (of skin) Hautfarbe f ▷ vt
anmalen; (bias) färben;
colour-blind adj farbenblind;
coloured adj farbig; (biased)
gefärbt; **colour film** n Farbfilm
m; **colourful** adj (lit, fig) bunt;
(life, past) bewegt; **colouring** n (in
food etc) Farbstoff m; (complexion)
Gesichtsfarbe f; **colourless** adj

(*lit, fig*) farblos; **colour photo(graph)** *n* Farbfoto *nt*; **colour television** *n* Farbfernsehen *nt*

column ['kɒləm] *n* Säule *f*; (*of print*) Spalte *f*

comb [kəʊm] *n* Kamm *m* ▷ *vt* kämmen; **to ~ one's hair** sich kämmen

combination [kɒmbɪ'neɪʃən] *n* Kombination *f*; (*mixture*) Mischung *f* (*of* aus); **combine** [kəm'baɪn] *vt* verbinden (*with* mit); (*two things*) kombinieren

come [kʌm] (**came, come**) *vi* kommen; (*arrive*) ankommen; (*on list, in order*) stehen; (*with adjective: become*) werden; **~ and see us** besuchen Sie uns mal; **coming** ich komm ja schon!; **to ~ first/second** erster/zweiter werden; **to ~ true** wahr werden; **to ~ loose** sich lockern; **the years to ~** die kommenden Jahre; **there's one more to ~** es kommt noch eins/noch einer; **how ~ ...?** (*fam*) wie kommt es, dass ...?; **~ to think of it** (*fam*) wo es mir gerade einfällt; **come across** *vt* (*find*) stoßen auf +*akk*; **come back** *vi* zurückkommen; **I'll ~ to that** ich komme darauf zurück; **come down** *vi* herunterkommen; (*rain, snow, price*) fallen; **come from** *vi* (*result*) kommen von; **where do you ~?** wo kommen Sie her?; **I ~ London** ich komme aus London; **come in** *vi* hereinkommen; (*arrive*) ankommen; (*in race*) **to ~ fourth** Vierter werden; **come off** *vi* (*button, handle etc*) abgehen; (*succeed*) gelingen; **to ~ well/badly** gut/schlecht wegkommen; **come on** *vi* (*progress*) vorankommen; **~!** komm!; (*hurry*) beeil dich!; (*encouraging*) los!; **come out** *vi*

herauskommen; (*photo*) was werden; (*homosexual*) sich outen; **come round** *vi* (*visit*) vorbeikommen; (*regain consciousness*) wieder zu sich kommen; **come to** *vi* (*regain consciousness*) wieder zu sich kommen ▷ *vt* (*sum*) sich belaufen auf +*akk*; **when it comes to ...** wenn es um ... geht; **come up** *vi* hochkommen; (*sun, moon*) aufgehen; **to ~ (for discussion)** zur Sprache kommen; **come up to** *vt* (*approach*) zukommen auf +*akk*; (*water*) reichen bis zu; (*expectations*) entsprechen +*dat*; **come up with** *vt* (*idea*) haben; (*solution, answer*) kommen auf +*akk*; **to ~ a suggestion** einen Vorschlag machen

comedian [kə'miːdɪən] *n* Komiker(in) *m(f)*

comedown ['kʌmdaʊn] *n* Abstieg *m*

comedy ['kɒmədɪ] *n* Komödie *f*, Comedy *f*

comfort ['kʌmfət] *n* Komfort *m*; (*consolation*) Trost *m* ▷ *vt* trösten; **comfortable** *adj* bequem; (*income*) ausreichend; (*temperature, life*) angenehm; **comforting** *adj* tröstlich

comic ['kɒmɪk] *n* (*magazine*) Comic(heft) *nt*; (*comedian*) Komiker(in) *m(f)* ▷ *adj* komisch

coming ['kʌmɪŋ] *adj* kommend; (*event*) bevorstehend

comma ['kɒmə] *n* Komma *nt*

command [kə'mɑːnd] *n* Befehl *m*; (*control*) Führung *f*; (*Mil*) Kommando *nt* ▷ *vt* befehlen +*dat*

commemorate [kə'meməreɪt] *vt* gedenken +*gen*; **commemoration** [kəmemə'reɪʃən] *n*: **in ~ of** in Gedenken an +*akk*

comment ['kɒment] *n* (*remark*)

Bemerkung f; (note) Anmerkung f;
(official) Kommentar m (on zu); **no
~ kein Kommentar ▷ vi** sich
äußern (on zu); **commentary**
['kɒməntrɪ] n Kommentar m (on
zu); (TV, Sport) Livereportage f;
commentator ['kɒmənteɪtə°] n
Kommentator(in) m(f); (TV, Sport)
Reporter(in) m(f)

commerce ['kɒmɜːs] n Handel
m; **commercial** [kə'mɜːʃəl] adj
kommerziell; (training)
kaufmännisch; **~ break**
Werbepause f; **~ vehicle**
Lieferwagen m ▷ n (TV)
Werbespot m

commission [kə'mɪʃən] n
Auftrag m; (fee) Provision f;
(reporting body) Kommission f ▷ vt
beauftragen

commit [kə'mɪt] vt (crime)
begehen ▷ vr: **to ~ oneself**
(undertake) sich verpflichten (to
zu); **commitment** n
Verpflichtung f; (Pol) Engagement
nt

committee [kə'mɪtɪ] n Ausschuss m, Komitee nt

commodity [kə'mɒdɪtɪ] n Ware
f

common ['kɒmən] adj (experience) allgemein, alltäglich;
(shared) gemeinsam; (widespread,
frequent) häufig; (pej)
gewöhnlich, ordinär; **to have
sth in ~** etw gemein haben ▷ n
(Brit: land) Gemeindewiese f;
commonly adv häufig,
allgemein; **commonplace** adj
alltäglich; (pej) banal;
commonroom n Gemeinschafts-
raum m; **Commons** n (Brit Pol)
the (House of) ~ das Unterhaus;
common sense n gesunder
Menschenverstand;
Commonwealth n Commonwealth nt; **~ of Independent
States** Gemeinschaft f
Unabhängiger Staaten

communal ['kɒmjʊnl] adj
gemeinsam; (of a community)
Gemeinschafts-, Gemeinde-

communicate [kə'mjuːnɪkeɪt]
vi kommunizieren (with mit);
communication
[kəmjuːnɪ'keɪʃən] n Kom-
munikation f, Verständigung f;
communications satellite n
Nachrichtensatellit m;
communications technology n
Nachrichtentechnik f;
communicative adj gesprächig

communion [kə'mjuːnɪən] n:
(Holy) Communion Heiliges
Abendmahl; (Catholic)
Kommunion f

communism ['kɒmjʊnɪzəm] n
Kommunismus m; **communist**
['kɒmjʊnɪst] adj kommunistisch
▷ n Kommunist(in) m(f)

community [kə'mjuːnɪtɪ] n
Gemeinschaft f; **community
centre** n Gemeindezentrum nt;
community service n (Jur)
Sozialdienst m

commutation ticket
[kɒmjʊ'teɪʃəntɪkɪt] n (US)
Zeitkarte f; **commute** [kə'mjuːt]
vi pendeln; **commuter** n
Pendler(in) m(f)

compact [kəm'pækt] adj kompakt ▷ ['kɒmpækt] n (for
make-up) Puderdose f; (US: car) ≈
Mittelklassewagen m; **compact
camera** n Kompaktkamera f;
compact disc n Compact Disc f,
CD f

companion [kəm'pænɪən] n
Begleiter(in) m(f)

company ['kʌmpənɪ] n
Gesellschaft f; (Comm) Firma f;
to keep sb ~ jdm Gesellschaft
leisten; **company car** n
Firmenauto nt

comparable ['kɒmpərəbl] *adj* vergleichbar (*with, to* mit)

comparative [kəm'pærətɪv] *adj* relativ ▷ *n* (*Ling*) Komparativ *m*; **comparatively** *adv* verhältnismäßig

compare [kəm'pεə°] *vt* vergleichen (*with, to* mit); **~d with** o **to** im Vergleich zu; **beyond ~** unvergleichlich; **comparison** [kəm'pærɪsn] *n* Vergleich *m*; **in ~ with** im Vergleich mit (*o* zu)

compartment [kəm'pɑːtmənt] *n* (*Rail*) Abteil *nt*; (*in desk etc*) Fach *nt*

compass ['kʌmpəs] *n* Kompass *m*; **~es** *pl* Zirkel *m*

compassion [kəm'pæʃən] *n* Mitgefühl *nt*

compatible [kəm'pætɪbl] *adj* vereinbar (*with* mit); (*Inform*) kompatibel; **we're not ~** wir passen nicht zueinander

compensate ['kɒmpenseɪt] *vt* (*person*) entschädigen (*for* für) ▷ *vi*: **to ~ for sth** Ersatz für etw leisten; (*make up for*) etw ausgleichen; **compensation** [kɒmpen'seɪʃən] *n* Entschädigung *f*; (*money*) Schadenersatz *m*; (*Jur*) Abfindung *f*

compete [kəm'piːt] *vi* konkurrieren (*for* um); (*Sport*) kämpfen (*for* um); (*take part*) teilnehmen (*in* an +*dat*)

competence ['kɒmpɪtəns] *n* Fähigkeit *f*; (*Jur*) Zuständigkeit *f*; **competent** *adj* fähig; (*Jur*) zuständig

competition [kɒmpɪ'tɪʃən] *n* (*contest*) Wettbewerb *m*; (*Comm*) Konkurrenz *f* (*for* um); **competitive** [kəm'petɪtɪv] *adj* (*firm, price, product*) konkurrenzfähig; **competitor** [kəm'petɪtə°] *n* (*Comm*) Konkurrent(in) *m(f)*; (*Sport*) Teilnehmer(in) *m(f)*

complain [kəm'pleɪn] *vi* klagen; (*formally*) sich beschweren (*about* über +*akk*); **complaint** *n* Klage *f*; Beanstandung *f*; (*formal*) Beschwerde *f*; (*Med*) Leiden *nt*

complement *vt* ergänzen

complete [kəm'pliːt] *adj* vollständig; (*finished*) fertig; (*failure, disaster*) total; (*happiness*) vollkommen; **are we ~?** sind wir vollzählig? ▷ *vt* vervollständigen; (*finish*) beenden; (*form*) ausfüllen; **completely** *adv* völlig; **not ~ ...** nicht ganz ...

complex ['kɒmpleks] *adj* komplex; (*task, theory etc*) kompliziert ▷ *n* Komplex *m*

complexion [kəm'plekʃən] *n* Gesichtsfarbe *f*, Teint *m*

complicated ['kɒmplɪkeɪtɪd] *adj* kompliziert; **complication** ['kɒmplɪkeɪʃən] *n* Komplikation *f*

compliment ['kɒmplɪmənt] *n* Kompliment *nt*; **complimentary** [kɒmplɪ'mentərɪ] *adj* lobend; (*free of charge*) Gratis-; **~ ticket** Freikarte *f*

comply [kəm'plaɪ] *vi*: **to ~ with the regulations** den Vorschriften entsprechen

component [kəm'pəunənt] *n* Bestandteil *m*

compose [kəm'pəuz] *vt* (*music*) komponieren; **to ~ oneself** sich zusammennehmen; **composed** *adj* gefasst; **to be ~ of** bestehen aus; **composer** *n* Komponist(in) *m(f)*; **composition** [kɒmpə'zɪʃən] *n* (*of a group*) Zusammensetzung *f*; (*Mus*) Komposition *f*

comprehend [kɒmprɪ'hend] *vt* verstehen; **comprehension** [kɒmprɪ'henʃən] *n* Verständnis *nt*

comprehensive [kɒmprɪ'hensɪv] *adj* umfassend; **~ school** Gesamtschule *f*

compress [kəm'pres] *vt*
komprimieren

comprise [kəm'praɪz] *vt*
umfassen, bestehen aus

compromise ['kɒmprəmaɪz] *n*
Kompromiss *m* ▷ *vi* einen
Kompromiss schließen

compulsory [kəm'pʌlsərɪ] *adj*
obligatorisch; **~ subject**
Pflichtfach *nt*

computer [kəm'pju:tə°] *n*
Computer *m*; **computer-aided** *adj*
computergestützt;
computer-controlled *adj* rech-
nergesteuert; **computer game** *n*
Computerspiel *nt*;
computer-literate *adj*: **to be**
~ mit dem Computer umgehen
können; **computer scientist** *n*
Informatiker(in) *m(f)*; **computing**
n (*subject*) Informatik *f*

con [kɒn] (*fam*) *n* Schwindel *m*
▷ *vt* betrügen (*out of* um)

conceal [kən'si:l] *vt* verbergen
(*from* vor +*dat*)

conceivable [kən'si:vəbl] *adj*
denkbar, vorstellbar; **conceive**
[kən'si:v] *vt* (*imagine*) sich
vorstellen; (*child*) empfangen

concentrate ['kɒnsəntreɪt] *vi*
sich konzentrieren (*on* auf +*akk*);
concentration [kɒnsən'treɪʃən]
n Konzentration *f*

concept ['kɒnsept] *n* Begriff *m*

concern [kən'sɜ:n] *n* (*affair*)
Angelegenheit *f*; (*worry*) Sorge *f*;
(*Comm: firm*) Unternehmen *nt*; **it's**
not my ~ das geht mich nichts an;
there's no cause for ~ kein Grund
zur Beunruhigung ▷ *vt* (*affect*)
angehen; (*have connection with*)
betreffen; (*be about*) handeln von;
those ~ed die Betroffenen; **as far**
as I'm ~ed was mich betrifft;
concerned *adj* (*anxious*) besorgt;
concerning *prep* bezüglich,
hinsichtlich +*gen*

concert ['kɒnsət] *n* Konzert *nt*;
~ hall Konzertsaal *m*

concession [kən'seʃən] *n* Zu-
geständnis *nt*; (*reduction*)
Ermäßigung *f*

concise [kən'saɪs] *adj* knapp
gefasst, prägnant

conclude [kən'klu:d] *vt* (*end*)
beenden, (ab)schließen; (*infer*)
folgern (*from* aus); **to ~ that ...** zu
dem Schluss kommen, dass ...;
conclusion [kən'klu:ʒən] *n*
Schluss *m*, Schlussfolgerung *f*

concrete ['kɒŋkri:t] *n* Beton *m*
▷ *adj* konkret

concussion [kɒn'kʌʃən] *n*
Gehirnerschütterung *f*

condemn [kən'dem] *vt*
verdammen; (*esp Jur*)
verurteilen

condensed milk *n*
Kondensmilch *f*, Dosenmilch *f*

condition [kən'dɪʃən] *n* (*state*)
Zustand *m*; (*requirement*)
Bedingung *f*; **on ~ that ...** unter
der Bedingung, dass ...; **~s** *pl*
(*circumstances, weather*)
Verhältnisse *pl*; **conditional** *adj*
bedingt; (*Ling*) Konditional-;
conditioner *n* Weichspüler *m*; (*for*
hair) Pflegespülung *f*

condo ['kɒndəʊ] (*pl* **-s**) *n* see
condominium

condolences [kən'dəʊlənsɪz]
npl Beileid *nt*

condom ['kɒndəm] *n* Kondom *nt*

condominium [kɒndə'mɪnɪəm]
n (*US: apartment*)
Eigentumswohnung *f*

conduct ['kɒndʌkt] *n* (*behaviour*)
Verhalten *nt* ▷ [kən'dʌkt] *vt*
führen, leiten; (*orchestra*)
dirigieren; **conductor**
[kən'dʌktə°] *n* (*of orchestra*)
Dirigent(in) *m(f)*; (*Brit: in bus*)
Schaffner(in) *m(f)*; (*US: on train*)
Zugführer(in) *m(f)*

cone [kəʊn] n Kegel m; (for ice cream) Waffeltüte f; (fir cone) (Tannen)zapfen m

conference ['kɒnfərəns] n Konferenz f

confess [kən'fes] vt, vi: **to ~ that ...** gestehen, dass ...; **confession** [kən'feʃən] n Geständnis nt; (Rel) Beichte f

confetti [kən'fetɪ] n Konfetti nt

confidence ['kɒnfɪdəns] n Vertrauen nt (in zu); (assurance) Selbstvertrauen nt; **confident** adj (sure) zuversichtlich (that ... dass ...), überzeugt (of von); (self-assured) selbstsicher; **confidential** [kɒnfɪ'denʃəl] adj vertraulich

confine [kən'faɪn] vt beschränken (to auf +akk)

confirm [kən'fɜːm] vt bestätigen; **confirmation** [kɒnfə'meɪʃən] n Bestätigung f; (Rel) Konfirmation f; **confirmed** adj überzeugt; (bachelor) eingefleischt

confiscate ['kɒnfɪskeɪt] vt beschlagnahmen, konfiszieren

conflict ['kɒnflɪkt] n Konflikt m

confuse [kən'fjuːz] vt verwirren; (sth with sth) verwechseln (with mit); (several things) durcheinanderbringen; **confused** adj (person) konfus, verwirrt; (account) verworren; **confusing** adj verwirrend; **confusion** [kən'fjuːʒən] n Verwirrung f; (of two things) Verwechslung f; (muddle) Chaos nt

congested [kən'dʒestɪd] adj verstopft; (overcrowded) überfüllt; **congestion** [kən'dʒestʃən] n Stau m

congratulate [kən'grætjʊleɪt] vt gratulieren (on zu); **congratulations** [kəngrætjʊ'leɪʃənz] npl Glückwünsche pl; **~!** gratuliere!, herzlichen Glückwunsch!

congregation [kɒngrɪ'geɪʃən] n (Rel) Gemeinde f

congress ['kɒngres] n Kongress m; (US) **Congress** der Kongress; **congressman** (pl **-men**), **congresswoman** (pl **-women**) n (US) Mitglied nt des Repräsentantenhauses

conifer ['kɒnɪfə°] n Nadelbaum m

conjunction [kən'dʒʌŋkʃən] n (Ling) Konjunktion f; **in ~ with** in Verbindung mit

conk out [kɒŋk 'aʊt] vi (fam: appliance, car) den Geist aufgeben, streiken; (person: die) ins Gras beißen

connect [kə'nekt] vt verbinden (with, to mit); (Elec, Tech: appliance etc) anschließen (to an +akk) ▷ vi (train, plane) Anschluss haben (with an +akk); **~ing flight** Anschlussflug m; **~ing train** Anschlusszug m; **connection** [kə'nekʃən] n Verbindung f; (link) Zusammenhang m; (for train, plane, electrical appliance) Anschluss m (with, to an +akk); (business etc) Beziehung f; **in ~ with** in Zusammenhang mit; **bad ~** (Tel) schlechte Verbindung; (Elec) Wackelkontakt m; **connector** n (Inform: computer) Stecker m

conscience ['kɒnʃəns] n Gewissen nt; **conscientious** [kɒnʃɪ'enʃəs] adj gewissenhaft

conscious ['kɒnʃəs] adj (act) bewusst; (Med) bei Bewusstsein; **to be ~** bei Bewusstsein sein; **consciousness** n Bewusstsein nt

consecutive [kən'sekjʊtɪv] adj aufeinanderfolgend

consent [kən'sent] n Zustimmung f ▷ vi zustimmen (to dat)

consequence ['kɒnsɪkwəns] n
Folge f, Konsequenz f;
consequently ['kɒnsɪkwəntlɪ]
adv folglich, deshalb

conservation [kɒnsə'veɪʃən] n
Erhaltung f; (nature conservation)
Naturschutz m; **conservation
area** n Naturschutzgebiet nt

conservative, (Pol) **Conservative**
[kən'sɜːvətɪv] adj konservativ

conservatory [kən'sɜːvətrɪ] n
(greenhouse) Gewächshaus nt;
(room) Wintergarten m

consider [kən'sɪdə*] vt (reflect
on) nachdenken über, sich
überlegen; (take into account) in
Betracht ziehen; (regard) halten
für; **he is ~ed (to be) ...** er gilt als
...; **considerable** [kən'sɪdərəbl]
adj beträchtlich; **considerate**
[kən'sɪdərɪt] adj aufmerksam,
rücksichtsvoll; **consideration**
[kənsɪdə'reɪʃən] n (thoughtfulness)
Rücksicht f; (thought) Überlegung
f; **to take sth into ~** etw in
Betracht ziehen; **considering**
[kən'sɪdərɪŋ] prep in Anbetracht
+gen ▷ conj da

consist [kən'sɪst] vi: **to ~ of ...**
bestehen aus ...

consistent [kən'sɪstənt] adj
(behaviour, process etc)
konsequent; (statements)
übereinstimmend; (argument)
folgerichtig; (performance, results)
beständig

consolation [kɒnsə'leɪʃən] n
Trost m; **console** [kən'səʊl] vt
trösten

consolidate [kən'sɒlɪdeɪt] vt
festigen

consonant ['kɒnsənənt] n
Konsonant m

conspicuous [kən'spɪkjʊəs] adj
auffällig, auffallend

conspiracy [kən'spɪrəsɪ] n
Komplott nt; **conspire**
[kən'spaɪə*] vi sich verschwören
(against gegen)

constable ['kʌnstəbl] n (Brit)
Polizist(in) m(f)

Constance ['kɒnstəns] n Konstanz nt; **Lake ~** der Bodensee

constant ['kɒnstənt] adj (continual) ständig, dauernd;
(unchanging: temperature etc)
gleichbleibend; **constantly** adv
dauernd

consternation [kɒnstə'neɪʃən]
n (dismay) Bestürzung f

constituency [kən'stɪtjʊənsɪ]
n Wahlkreis m

constitution [kɒnstɪ'tjuːʃən] n
Verfassung f; (of person)
Konstitution f

construct [kən'strʌkt] vt bauen;
construction [kən'strʌkʃən] n
(process, result) Bau m; (method)
Bauweise f; **under ~** im Bau
befindlich; **construction site** n
Baustelle f; **construction worker**
n Bauarbeiter(in) m(f)

consulate ['kɒnsjʊlət] n Konsulat nt

consult [kən'sʌlt] vt um Rat
fragen; (doctor) konsultieren;
(book) nachschlagen in +dat;
consultant n (Med) Facharzt m,
Fachärztin f; **consultation**
[kɒnsəl'teɪʃən] n Beratung f;
(Med) Konsultation f; **~ room**
Besprechungsraum;
Sprechzimmer

consume [kən'sjuːm] vt verbrauchen; (food) konsumieren;
consumer n Verbraucher(in)
m(f); **consumer-friendly** adj
verbraucherfreundlich

contact ['kɒntækt] n (touch)
Berührung f; (communication)
Kontakt m; (person) Kontaktperson
f; **to be/keep in ~ (with sb)** (mit
jdm) in Kontakt sein/bleiben ▷ vt
sich in Verbindung setzen mit;

contact lenses npl Kontaktlinsen pl

contagious [kən'teɪdʒəs] adj ansteckend

contain [kən'teɪn] vt enthalten; **container** n Behälter m; (for transport) Container m

contaminate [kən'tæmɪneɪt] vt verunreinigen; (chemically) verseuchen; **~d by radiation** strahlenverseucht, verstrahlt; **contamination** [kəntæmɪ'neɪʃən] n Verunreinigung f; (by radiation) Verseuchung f

contemporary [kən'tempərərɪ] adj zeitgenössisch

contempt [kən'tempt] n Verachtung f; **contemptuous** adj verächtlich; **to be ~** voller Verachtung sein (of für)

content [kən'tent] adj zufrieden

content(s) ['kɒntent(s)] n pl Inhalt m

contest ['kɒntest] n (Wett)kampf m (for um); (competition) Wettbewerb m ▷ [kən'test] vt kämpfen um +akk; (dispute) bestreiten; **contestant** [kən'testənt] n Teilnehmer(in) m(f)

context ['kɒntekst] n Zusammenhang m; **out of ~** aus dem Zusammenhang gerissen

continent ['kɒntɪnənt] n Kontinent m, Festland nt; **the Continent** (Brit) das europäische Festland, der Kontinent; **continental** [kɒntɪ'nentl] adj kontinental; **~ breakfast** kleines Frühstück mit Brötchen und Marmelade, Kaffee oder Tee

continual [kən'tɪnjʊəl] adj (endless) ununterbrochen; (constant) dauernd, ständig; **continually** adv dauernd; (again and again) immer wieder; **continuation** [kəntɪnjʊ'eɪʃən] n

Fortsetzung f; **continue** [kən'tɪnjuː] vi weitermachen (with mit); (esp talking) fortfahren (with mit); (travelling) weiterfahren; (state, conditions) fortdauern, anhalten ▷ vt fortsetzen; **to be ~d** Fortsetzung folgt; **continuous** [kən'tɪnjʊəs] adj (endless) ununterbrochen; (constant) ständig

contraceptive [kɒntrə'septɪv] n Verhütungsmittel nt

contract ['kɒntrækt] n Vertrag m

contradict [kɒntrə'dɪkt] vt widersprechen +dat; **contradiction** [kɒntrə'dɪkʃən] n Widerspruch m

contrary ['kɒntrərɪ] n Gegenteil nt; **on the ~** im Gegenteil ▷ adj: **~ to** entgegen +dat

contrast ['kɒntrɑːst] n Kontrast m, Gegensatz m; **in ~ to** im Gegensatz zu ▷ [kən'trɑːst] vt entgegensetzen

contribute [kən'trɪbjuːt] vt, vi beitragen (to zu); (money) spenden (to für); **contribution** [kɒntrɪ'bjuːʃən] n Beitrag m

control [kən'trəʊl] vt (master) beherrschen; (temper etc) im Griff haben; (esp Tech) steuern; **to ~ oneself** sich beherrschen ▷ n Kontrolle f; (mastery) Beherrschung f; (esp Tech) Steuerung f; **~s** pl (knobs, switches etc) Bedienungselemente pl; (collectively) Steuerung f; **to be out of ~** außer Kontrolle sein; **control knob** n Bedienungsknopf m; **control panel** n Schalttafel f

controversial [kɒntrə'vɜːʃəl] adj umstritten

convalesce [kɒnvə'les] vi gesund werden; **convalescence** n Genesung f

convenience [kən'viːnɪəns] n (quality, thing) Annehmlichkeit f; **at**

your ~ wann es Ihnen passt; **with all modern ~s** mit allem Komfort; **convenience food** n Fertiggericht nt; **convenient** adj günstig, passend

convent ['kɒnvənt] n Kloster nt

convention [kən'venʃən] n (custom) Konvention f; (meeting) Konferenz f; **the Geneva Convention** die Genfer Konvention; **conventional** adj herkömmlich, konventionell

conversation [kɒnvə'seɪʃən] n Gespräch nt, Unterhaltung f

conversion [kən'vɜːʃən] n Umwandlung f (into in +akk); (of building) Umbau m (into zu); (calculation) Umrechnung f; **conversion table** n Umrechnungstabelle f; **convert** [kən'vɜːt] vt umwandeln; (person) bekehren; (Inform) konvertieren; **to ~ into euros** in Euro umrechnen; **convertible** n (Auto) Kabrio nt ▷ adj umwandelbar

convey [kən'veɪ] vt (carry) befördern; (feelings) vermitteln; **conveyor belt** n Förderband nt, Fließband nt

convict [kən'vɪkt] vt verurteilen (of wegen) ▷ ['kɒnvɪkt] n Strafgefangene(r) mf; **conviction** n (Jur) Verurteilung f; (strong belief) Überzeugung f

convince [kən'vɪns] vt überzeugen (of von); **convincing** adj überzeugend

cook [kʊk] vt, vi kochen ▷ n Koch m, Köchin f; **cookbook** n Kochbuch nt; **cooker** n Herd m; **cookery** n Kochkunst f; **~ book** Kochbuch nt; **cookie** n (US) Keks m; **cooking** n Kochen nt; (style of cooking) Küche f

cool [kuːl] adj kühl, gelassen; (fam: brilliant) cool, stark ▷ vt, vi (ab)kühlen; **~ it** reg dich ab! ▷ n:

to keep/lose one's ~ (fam) ruhig bleiben/durchdrehen; **cool down** vi abkühlen; (calm down) sich beruhigen

cooperate [kəʊ'ɒpəreɪt] vi zusammenarbeiten, kooperieren; **cooperation** [kəʊɒpə'reɪʃən] n Zusammenarbeit f, Kooperation f; **cooperative** [kəʊ'ɒpərətɪv] adj hilfsbereit ▷ n Genossenschaft f

coordinate [kəʊ'ɔːdɪneɪt] vt koordinieren

cop [kɒp] n (fam: policeman) Bulle m

cope [kəʊp] vi zurechtkommen, fertig werden (with mit)

Copenhagen [kəʊpən'heɪgən] n Kopenhagen nt

copier ['kɒpɪə°] n Kopierer m

copper ['kɒpə°] n Kupfer nt; (Brit fam: policeman) Bulle m; (fam: coin) Kupfermünze f; **~s** Kleingeld nt

copy ['kɒpɪ] n Kopie f; (of book) Exemplar nt ▷ vt kopieren; (imitate) nachahmen; **copyright** n Urheberrecht nt

coral ['kɒrəl] n Koralle f

cord [kɔːd] n Schnur f; (material) Kordsamt m; **cordless** ['kɔːdlɪs] adj (phone) schnurlos

core [kɔː°] n (a. fig) Kern m; (of apple, pear) Kerngehäuse nt; **core business** n Kerngeschäft nt

cork [kɔːk] n (material) Kork m; (stopper) Korken m; **corkscrew** ['kɔːkskruː] n Korkenzieher m

corn [kɔːn] n Getreide nt, Korn nt; (US: maize) Mais m; (on foot) Hühnerauge nt; **~ on the cob** (gekochter) Maiskolben; **corned beef** n Cornedbeef nt

corner ['kɔːnə°] n Ecke f; (on road) Kurve f; (Sport) Eckstoß m ▷ vt in die Enge treiben; **corner shop** n Laden m an der Ecke

cornflakes ['kɔːfleɪks] npl Cornflakes pl

Cornish ['kɔ:nɪʃ] adj kornisch; **~ pasty** mit Fleisch und Kartoffeln gefüllte Pastete; **Cornwall** ['kɔ:nwəl] n Cornwall nt

coronation [kɒrə'neɪʃən] n Krönung f

corporation [kɔ:pə'reɪʃən] n (US Comm) Aktiengesellschaft f

corpse [kɔ:ps] n Leiche f

correct [kə'rekt] adj (accurate) richtig; (proper) korrekt ▷ vt korrigieren, verbessern; **correction** (esp written) Korrektur f

correspond [kɒrɪ'spɒnd] vi entsprechen (to dat); (two things) übereinstimmen; (exchange letters) korrespondieren; **corresponding** adj entsprechend

corridor ['kɒrɪdɔ:*] n (in building) Flur m; (in train) Gang m

corrupt [kə'rʌpt] adj korrupt

cosmetic [kɒz'metɪk] adj kosmetisch; **cosmetics** npl Kosmetika pl; **cosmetic surgeon** n Schönheitschirurg(in) m(f); **cosmetic surgery** n Schönheitschirurgie f

cosmopolitan [kɒzmə'pɒlɪtən] adj international; (attitude) weltoffen

cost [kɒst] (cost, cost) vt kosten ▷ n Kosten pl; **at all ~s, at any ~** um jeden Preis; **~ of living** Lebenshaltungskosten pl; **costly** adj kostspielig

costume ['kɒstju:m] n (Theat) Kostüm nt

cosy ['kəʊzɪ] adj gemütlich

cot [kɒt] n (Brit) Kinderbett nt; (US) Campingliege f

cottage ['kɒtɪdʒ] n kleines Haus; (country cottage) Landhäuschen nt; **cottage cheese** n Hüttenkäse m; **cottage pie** n Hackfleisch mit Kartoffelbrei überbacken

cotton ['kɒtn] n Baumwolle f;

cotton candy n (US) Zuckerwatte f; **cotton wool** n (Brit) Watte f

couch [kaʊtʃ] n Couch f; (sofa) Sofa nt; **couchette** [ku:'ʃet] n Liegewagen(platz) m

cough [kɒf] vi husten ▷ n Husten m; **cough mixture** n Hustensaft m; **cough sweet** n Hustenbonbon nt

could [kʊd] pt of can konnte; conditional könnte; **~ you come earlier?** könntest du/könnten Sie früher kommen?

couldn't contr of could not

council ['kaʊnsl] n (Pol) Rat m; (local ~) Gemeinderat m; (town ~) Stadtrat m; **council estate** n Siedlung f des sozialen Wohnungsbaus; **council house** n Sozialwohnung f; **councillor** ['kaʊnsɪlə*] n Gemeinderat m, Gemeinderätin f; **council tax** n Gemeindesteuer f

count [kaʊnt] vt, vi zählen; (include) mitrechnen ▷ n Zählung f; (noble) Graf m; **count on** vt (rely on) sich verlassen auf +akk; (expect) rechnen mit

counter ['kaʊntə*] n (in shop) Ladentisch m; (in café) Theke f; (in bank, post office) Schalter m; **counter attack** n Gegenangriff m ▷ vi zurückschlagen; **counter-clockwise** adv (US) entgegen dem Uhrzeigersinn

counterpart ['kaʊntəpɔ:t] n Gegenstück nt (of zu)

countess n Gräfin f

countless ['kaʊntlɪs] adj zahllos, unzählig

country ['kʌntrɪ] n Land nt; **in the ~** auf dem Land(e); **in this ~** hierzulande; **country cousin** n (fam) Landei nt; **country dancing** n Volkstanz m; **country house** n Landhaus nt; **countryman** n (compatriot) Landsmann m;

country music n Countrymusic f;
country road n Landstraße f;
countryside n Landschaft f; (rural area) Land nt
county ['kaʊntɪ] n (Brit) Grafschaft f; (US) Verwaltungsbezirk m; **county town** n (Brit) ≈ Kreisstadt f
couple ['kʌpl] n Paar nt; **a ~ of** ein paar
coupon ['ku:pɒn] n (voucher) Gutschein m
courage ['kʌrɪdʒ] n Mut m; **courageous** [kə'reɪdʒəs] adj mutig
courgette [kʊə'ʒet] n (Brit) Zucchini f
courier ['kʊrɪə*] n (for tourists) Reiseleiter(in) m(f); (messenger) Kurier m
course [kɔ:s] n (of study) Kurs m; (for race) Strecke f; (Naut, Aviat) Kurs m; (at university) Studiengang m; (in meal) Gang m; **of ~** natürlich; **in the ~ of** während
court [kɔ:t] n (Sport) Platz m; (Jur) Gericht nt
courteous ['kɜ:tɪəs] adj höflich; **courtesy** ['kɜ:təsɪ] n Höflichkeit f; **~ bus/coach** (gebührenfreier) Zubringerbus
courthouse ['kɔ:thaʊs] n (US) Gerichtsgebäude nt; **court order** n Gerichtsbeschluss m; **courtroom** n Gerichtssaal m
courtyard ['kɔ:tjɑ:d] n Hof m
cousin ['kʌzn] n (male) Cousin m; (female) Cousine f
cover ['kʌvə*] vt bedecken (in, with mit); (distance) zurücklegen; (loan, costs) decken ▷ n (for bed etc) Decke f; (of cushion) Bezug m; (lid) Deckel m; (of book) Umschlag m; (**insurance**) ~ Versicherungsschutz m; **cover up** vt zudecken; (error etc) vertuschen; **coverage** n Berichterstattung f (of über +akk);

cover charge n Kosten pl für ein Gedeck; **covering** n Decke f; **covering letter** n Begleitbrief m; **cover story** n (newspaper) Titelgeschichte f
cow [kaʊ] n Kuh f
coward ['kaʊəd] n Feigling m; **cowardly** adj feig(e)
cowboy ['kaʊbɔɪ] n Cowboy m
coy [kɔɪ] adj gespielt schüchtern, kokett
cozy ['kəʊzɪ] adj (US) gemütlich
CPU abbr = **central processing unit** Zentraleinheit f
crab [kræb] n Krabbe f
crabby ['kræbɪ] adj mürrisch, reizbar
crack [kræk] n Riss m; (in pottery, glass) Sprung m; (drug) Crack nt; **to have a ~ at sth** etw ausprobieren ▷ vi (pottery, glass) einen Sprung bekommen; (wood, ice etc) einen Riss bekommen; **to get ~ing** (fam) loslegen ▷ vt (bone) anbrechen; (nut, code) knacken
cracker ['krækə*] n (biscuit) Kräcker m; (Christmas ~) Knallbonbon nt; **crackers** adj (fam) verrückt, bekloppt; **he's ~** er hat nicht alle Tassen im Schrank
crackle ['krækl] vi knistern; (telephone, radio) knacken; **crackling** n (Gastr) Kruste f (des Schweinebratens)
cradle ['kreɪdl] n Wiege f
craft [krɑ:ft] n Handwerk nt; (art) Kunsthandwerk nt; (Naut) Boot nt; **craftsman** (pl **-men**) n Handwerker m; **craftsmanship** n Handwerkskunst f; (ability) handwerkliches Können
crafty ['krɑ:ftɪ] adj schlau
cram [kræm] vt stopfen (into in +akk); **to be ~med with ...** mit ... vollgestopft sein ▷ vi (revise for exam) pauken (for für)
cramp [kræmp] n Krampf m

cranberry ['krænbərı] n Preiselbeere f
crane [kreɪn] n (machine) Kran m;
(bird) Kranich m
crap [kræp] n (vulg) Scheiße f;
(rubbish) Mist m ▷ adj beschissen,
Scheiß-
crash [kræʃ] vi einen Unfall
haben; (two vehicles)
zusammenstoßen; (plane,
computer) abstürzen; (economy)
zusammenbrechen; **to ~ into sth**
gegen etw knallen ▷ vt einen
Unfall haben mit ▷ n (car) Unfall
m; (train) Unglück nt; (collision)
Zusammenstoß m; (Aviat, Inform)
Absturz m; (noise) Krachen nt;
crash barrier n Leitplanke f;
crash course n Intensivkurs m;
crash helmet n Sturzhelm m;
crash landing n Bruchlandung f
crate [kreɪt] n Kiste f; (of beer)
Kasten m
crater ['kreɪtə°] n Krater m
craving [kreɪvɪŋ] n starkes
Verlangen, Bedürfnis nt
crawl [krɔːl] vi kriechen; (baby)
krabbeln ▷ n (swimming) Kraul nt;
crawler lane n Kriechspur f
crayfish ['kreɪfɪʃ] n Languste f
crayon ['kreɪən] n Buntstift m
crazy ['kreɪzɪ] adj verrückt (about
nach)
cream [kriːm] n (from milk)
Sahne f, Rahm m; (polish, cosmetic)
Creme f ▷ adj cremefarben;
cream cake n (small)
Sahnetörtchen nt; (big) Sahnetorte
f; **cream cheese** n Frischkäse m;
creamer n Kaffeeweißer m;
cream tea n (Brit) Nachmittagstee
mit Törtchen, Marmelade und
Schlagsahne; **creamy** adj sahnig
crease [kriːs] n Falte f ▷ vt
falten; (untidy) zerknittern
create [krɪ'eɪt] vt schaffen;
(cause) verursachen; **creative**

[kriː'eɪtɪv] adj schöpferisch;
(person) kreativ; **creature**
['kriːtʃə°] n Geschöpf nt
crèche [kreʃ] n Kinderkrippe f
credible ['kredɪbl] adj (person)
glaubwürdig; **credibility** n
Glaubwürdigkeit f
credit ['kredɪt] n (Fin: amount
allowed) Kredit m; (amount
possessed) Guthaben nt;
(recognition) Anerkennung f; **~s** (of
film) Abspann m; **credit card** n
Kreditkarte f
creep [kriːp] (**crept, crept**) vi
kriechen; **creeps** n: **he gives me
the ~** er ist mir nicht ganz
geheuer; **creepy** ['kriːpɪ] adj
(frightening) gruselig, unheimlich
crept [krept] pt, pp of **creep**
cress [kres] n Kresse f
crest [krest] n Kamm m; (coat of
arms) Wappen nt
crew [kruː] n Besatzung f,
Mannschaft f
crib [krɪb] n (US) Kinderbett nt
cricket ['krɪkɪt] n (insect) Grille f;
(game) Kricket nt
crime [kraɪm] n Verbrechen nt;
criminal ['krɪmɪnl] n Verbre-
cher(in) m(f) ▷ adj kriminell,
strafbar
cripple ['krɪpl] n Krüppel m ▷ vt
verkrüppeln, lähmen
crisis ['kraɪsɪs] n (pl **crises**) n Krise
f
crisp [krɪsp] adj knusprig; **crisps**
npl (Brit) Chips pl; **crispbread** n
Knäckebrot nt
criterion [kraɪ'tɪərɪən] n Krite-
rium nt; **critic** ['krɪtɪk] n
Kritiker(in) m(f); **critical** adj
kritisch; **critically** adv kritisch;
~ ill/injured schwer
krank/verletzt; **criticism**
['krɪtɪsɪzəm] n Kritik f; **criticize**
['krɪtɪsaɪz] vt kritisieren
Croat ['krəʊæt] n Kroate m,

Kroatin f; **Croatia** [krəʊˈeɪʃə] n
Kroatien nt; **Croatian** [krəʊˈeɪʃən]
adj kroatisch
crockery [ˈkrɒkərɪ] n Geschirr nt
crocodile [ˈkrɒkədaɪl] n Krokodil
nt
crocus [ˈkrəʊkəs] n Krokus m
crop [krɒp] n (harvest) Ernte f;
crops npl Getreide nt; **crop up** vi
auftauchen
croquette [krəˈket] n Krokette f
cross [krɒs] n Kreuz nt; **to mark
sth with a ~** etw ankreuzen ▷ vt
(road, river etc) überqueren; (legs)
übereinanderschlagen; **it ~ed my
mind** es fiel mir ein; **to ~ one's
fingers** die Daumen drücken
▷ adj ärgerlich, böse; **cross out** vt
durchstreichen
crossbar n (of bicycle) Stange f;
(Sport) Querlatte f; **cross-country**
adj: **~ running** Geländelauf m;
~ skiing Langlauf m;
cross-examination n Kreuz-
verhör nt; **cross-eyed** adj: **to be
~** schielen; **crossing** n (crossroads)
(Straßen)kreuzung f; (for
pedestrians) Fußgängerüberweg m;
(on ship) Überfahrt f; **crossroads**
nsing o pl Straßenkreuzung f; **cross
section** n Querschnitt m;
crosswalk n (US)
Fußgängerüberweg m; **crossword
(puzzle)** n Kreuzworträtsel nt
crouch [kraʊtʃ] vi hocken
crouton [ˈkruːtɒn] n Croûton m
crow [krəʊ] n Krähe f
crowbar [ˈkrəʊbɑː°] n Brecheisen
nt
crowd [kraʊd] n Menge f ▷ vi
sich drängen (into in +akk; round
um); **crowded** adj überfüllt
crown [kraʊn] n Krone f ▷ vt
krönen; (fam) **and to ~ it all ...** und
als Krönung ...
crucial [ˈkruːʃəl] adj
entscheidend

crude [kruːd] adj primitiv;
(humour, behaviour) derb, ordinär
▷ n: **~ (oil)** Rohöl nt
cruel [ˈkrʊəl] adj grausam (to zu,
gegen); (unfeeling) gefühllos;
cruelty n Grausamkeit f; **~ to
animals** Tierquälerei f
cruise [kruːz] n Kreuzfahrt f ▷ vi
(ship) kreuzen; (car) mit
Reisegeschwindigkeit fahren;
cruise liner n Kreuzfahrtschiff nt;
cruise missile n
Marschflugkörper m; **cruising
speed** n Reisegeschwindigkeit f
crumb [krʌm] n Krume f
crumble [ˈkrʌmbl] vt, vi
zerbröckeln ▷ n mit Streuseln
überbackenes Kompott
crumpet [ˈkrʌmpɪt] n weiches
Hefegebäck zum Toasten; (fam:
attractive woman) Schnecke f
crumple [ˈkrʌmpl] vt
zerknittern
crunchy [ˈkrʌntʃɪ] adj (Brit)
knusprig
crusade [kruːˈseɪd] n Kreuzzug
m
crush [krʌʃ] vt zerdrücken;
(finger etc) quetschen; (spices,
stone) zerstoßen ▷ n: **to have a
~ on sb** in jdn verknallt sein;
crushing adj (defeat, remark)
vernichtend
crust [krʌst] n Kruste f; **crusty**
adj knusprig
crutch [krʌtʃ] n Krücke f
cry [kraɪ] vi (call) rufen; (scream)
schreien; (weep) weinen ▷ n (call)
Ruf m; (louder) Schrei m
crypt [krɪpt] n Krypta f
crystal [ˈkrɪstl] n Kristall m
cu abbr = **see you** (SMS, e-mail) bis
bald
Cuba [ˈkjuːbə] n Kuba nt
cube [kjuːb] n Würfel m
cubic [ˈkjuːbɪk] adj Kubik-
cubicle [ˈkjuːbɪkl] n Kabine f

cuckoo ['kʊkuː] n Kuckuck m
cucumber ['kjuːkʌmbə°] n
Salatgurke f
cuddle ['kʌdl] vt in den Arm
nehmen; (amorously) schmusen
mit ▷ n Liebkosung f, Umarmung
f; **to have a ~** schmusen; **cuddly**
adj verschmust; **cuddly toy** n
Plüschtier nt
cuff [kʌf] n Manschette f; (US:
trouser ~) Aufschlag m; **off the**
~ aus dem Stegreif; **cufflink** n
Manschettenknopf m
cuisine [kwɪˈziːn] n Kochkunst f,
Küche f
cul-de-sac ['kʌldəsæk] n (Brit)
Sackgasse f
culprit ['kʌlprɪt] n Schuldige(r)
mf; (fig) Übeltäter(in) m(f)
cult [kʌlt] n Kult m
cultivate ['kʌltɪveɪt] vt (Agr:
land) bebauen; (crop) anbauen;
cultivated adj (person) kultiviert,
gebildet
cultural ['kʌltʃərəl] adj kulturell,
Kultur-; **culture** ['kʌltʃə°] n
Kultur f; **cultured** adj gebildet,
kultiviert; **culture vulture** (Brit
fam) n Kulturfanatiker(in) m(f)
cumbersome ['kʌmbəsəm] adj
(object) unhandlich
cumin ['kʌmɪn] n Kreuzkümmel
m
cunning ['kʌnɪŋ] adj schlau;
(person a.) gerissen
cup [kʌp] n Tasse f; (prize) Pokal
m; **it's not his ~ of tea** das ist
nicht sein Fall; **cupboard** ['kʌbəd]
n Schrank m; **cup final** n
Pokalendspiel nt; **cup tie** n
Pokalspiel nt
cupola ['kjuːpələ] n Kuppel f
curable ['kjʊərəbəl] adj heilbar
curb [kɜːb] n (US) see **kerb**
curd [kɜːd] n: **~ cheese, ~s** ≈
Quark m
cure [kjʊə°] n Heilmittel nt (for

gegen); (process) Heilung f ▷ vt
heilen; (Gastr) pökeln; (smoke)
räuchern
curious ['kjʊərɪəs] adj neugierig;
(strange) seltsam
curl [kɜːl] n Locke f ▷ vi sich
kräuseln; **curly** adj lockig
currant ['kʌrənt] n (dried)
Korinthe f; (red, black)
Johannisbeere f
currency ['kʌrənsɪ] n Währung
f; **foreign ~** Devisen pl
current ['kʌrənt] n (in water)
Strömung f; (electric ~) Strom m
▷ adj (issue, affairs) aktuell,
gegenwärtig; (expression) gängig;
current account n Girokonto nt;
currently adv zur Zeit
curriculum [kəˈrɪkjʊləm] n
Lehrplan m; **curriculum vitae**
[kəˈrɪkjʊləmˈviːtaɪ] n (Brit)
Lebenslauf m
curry ['kʌrɪ] n Currygericht nt;
curry powder n Curry(pulver) nt
curse [kɜːs] vi (swear) fluchen (at
auf +akk) ▷ n Fluch m
cursor ['kɜːsə°] n (Inform) Cursor
m
curt [kɜːt] adj schroff, kurz
angebunden
curtain ['kɜːtn] n Vorhang m; **it**
was ~s for Benny für Benny war
alles vorbei
curve [kɜːv] n Kurve f ▷ vi einen
Bogen machen; **curved** adj
gebogen
cushion ['kʊʃən] n Kissen nt
custard ['kʌstəd] n dicke
Vanillesoße, die warm oder kalt zu
vielen englischen Nachspeisen
gegessen wird
custom ['kʌstəm] n Brauch m;
(habit) Gewohnheit f; **customary**
['kʌstəmrɪ] adj üblich;
custom-built adj nach
Kundenangaben gefertigt;
customer ['kʌstəmə°] n Kunde

m, Kundin f; **customer loyalty card** n Kundenkarte f; **customer service** n Kundendienst m

customs ['kʌstəmz] npl (organization, location) Zoll m; **to pass through ~** durch den Zoll gehen; **customs officer** n Zollbeamte(r) m, Zollbeamtin f

cut [kʌt] (**cut, cut**) vt schneiden; (cake) anschneiden; (wages, benefits) kürzen; (prices) heruntersetzen; **I ~ my finger** ich habe mir in den Finger geschnitten ▷ n Schnitt m; (wound) Schnittwunde f; (reduction) Kürzung f (in gen); **price/tax ~** Preissenkung/Steuersenkung f; **to be a ~ above the rest** eine Klasse besser als die anderen sein; **cut back** vt (workforce etc) reduzieren; **cut down** vt (tree) fällen; **to ~ on sth** etwas einschränken; **cut in** vi (Auto) scharf einscheren; **to ~ on sb** jdn schneiden; **cut off** vt abschneiden; (gas, electricity) abdrehen, abstellen; (Tel) **I was ~** ich wurde unterbrochen

cutback n Kürzung f

cute [kjuːt] adj putzig, niedlich; (US: shrewd) clever

cutlery ['kʌtlərɪ] n Besteck nt

cutlet ['kʌtlɪt] n (pork) Kotelett nt; (veal) Schnitzel nt

cut-price adj verbilligt

cutting ['kʌtɪŋ] n (from paper) Ausschnitt m; (of plant) Ableger m ▷ adj (comment) verletzend

CV abbr = **curriculum vitae**

cwt abbr = **hundredweight** ≈ Zentner, Ztr.

cybercafé [saɪbə'kæfeɪ] n Internetcafé nt; **cyberspace** n Cyberspace m

cycle ['saɪkl] n Fahrrad nt ▷ vi Rad fahren; **cycle lane**, **cycle path** n Radweg m; **cycling** n

Radfahren nt; **cyclist** ['saɪklɪst] n Radfahrer(in) m(f)

cylinder ['sɪlɪndə*] n Zylinder m

cynical ['sɪnɪkəl] adj zynisch

cypress ['saɪprɪs] n Zypresse f

Cypriot ['sɪprɪət] adj zypriotisch ▷ n Zypriote m, Zypriotin f; **Cyprus** ['saɪprəs] n Zypern nt

czar [zɑː*] n Zar m; **czarina** [zaˈriːnə] n Zarin f

Czech [tʃek] adj tschechisch ▷ n (person) Tscheche m, Tschechin f; (language) Tschechisch nt; **Czech Republic** n Tschechische Republik, Tschechien nt

d

dab [dæb] vt (wound, nose etc) betupfen (with mit)

dachshund ['dækshund] n Dackel m

dad(dy) ['dæd(ı)] n Papa m, Vati m; **daddy-longlegs** nsing (Brit) Schnake; (US) Weberknecht m

daffodil ['dæfədıl] n Osterglocke f

daft [dɑ:ft] adj (fam) blöd, doof

dahlia ['deılıə] n Dahlie f

daily ['deılı] adj, adv täglich ▷ n (paper) Tageszeitung f

dairy ['dɛərı] n (on farm) Molkerei f; **dairy products** npl Milchprodukte pl

daisy ['deızı] n Gänseblümchen nt

dam [dæm] n Staudamm m ▷ vt stauen

damage ['dæmıdʒ] n Schaden m; **~s** pl (Jur) Schadenersatz m ▷ vt beschädigen; (reputation, health) schädigen, schaden +dat

damn [dæm] adj (fam) verdammt ▷ vt (condemn) verurteilen; **~ (it)!** verflucht! ▷ n: **he doesn't give a ~** es ist ihm völlig egal

damp [dæmp] adj feucht ▷ n Feuchtigkeit f; **dampen** ['dæmpən] vt befeuchten

dance [dɑ:ns] n Tanz m; (event) Tanzveranstaltung f ▷ vi tanzen; **dance floor** n Tanzfläche f; **dancer** n Tänzer(in) m(f); **dancing** n Tanzen nt

dandelion ['dændılaıən] n Löwenzahn m

dandruff ['dændrəf] n Schuppen pl

Dane [deın] n Däne m, Dänin f

danger ['deındʒə°] n Gefahr f; **~ (sign)** Achtung!; **to be in ~** in Gefahr sein; **dangerous** adj gefährlich

Danish ['deınıʃ] adj dänisch ▷ n (language) Dänisch nt; **the ~** pl die Dänen; **Danish pastry** n Plundergebäck nt

Danube ['dænju:b] n Donau f

dare [dɛə°] vi: **to ~ (to) do sth** es wagen, etw zu tun; **I didn't ~ ask** ich traute mich nicht, zu fragen; **how ~ you** was fällt dir ein!; **daring** adj (person) mutig; (film, clothes etc) gewagt

dark [dɑ:k] adj dunkel; (gloomy) düster, trübe; (sinister) finster; **~ chocolate** Bitterschokolade f; **~ green/blue** dunkelgrün/dunkelblau ▷ n Dunkelheit f; **in the ~** im Dunkeln; **dark glasses** npl Sonnenbrille f; **darkness** n Dunkelheit nt

darling ['dɑ:lıŋ] n Schatz m; (also favourite) Liebling m

darts [dɑ:ts] nsing (game) Darts nt

dash [dæʃ] vi stürzen, rennen

▷ vt: **to ~ hopes** Hoffnungen zerstören ▷ n (in text) Gedankenstrich m; (of liquid) Schuss m; **dashboard** n Armaturenbrett nt

data ['deɪtə] npl Daten pl; **data bank, data base** n Datenbank f; **data capture** n Datenerfassung f; **data processing** n Datenverarbeitung f; **data protection** n Datenschutz m

date [deɪt] n Datum nt; (for meeting, delivery etc) Termin m; (with person) Verabredung f; (with girlfriend/boyfriend etc) Date nt; (fruit) Dattel f; **what's the ~ (today)?** der Wievielte ist heute?; **out of ~** veraltet; **up to ~** adj (news) aktuell; (fashion) zeitgemäß ▷ vt (letter etc) datieren; (person) gehen mit; **dated** adj altmodisch; **date of birth** n Geburtsdatum nt; **dating agency** n Partnervermittlung f

dative ['deɪtɪv] n Dativ m

daughter ['dɔːtə°] n Tochter f; **daughter-in-law** (pl **daughters-in-law**) n Schwiegertochter f

dawn [dɔːn] n Morgendämmerung f ▷ vi dämmern; **it ~ed on me** mir ging ein Licht auf

day [deɪ] n Tag m; **one ~** eines Tages; **by ~** bei Tage; **~ after ~, ~ by ~** Tag für Tag; **the ~ after/ before** am Tag danach/zuvor; **the ~ before yesterday** vorgestern; **the ~ after tomorrow** übermorgen; **these ~s** heutzutage; **in those ~s** damals; **let's call it a ~** Schluss für heute!; **daybreak** n Tagesanbruch m; **day-care center** (US), **day-care centre** n (Brit) Kita f (Kindertagesstätte); **daydream** n Tagtraum m ▷ vi (mit offenen Augen) träumen; **daylight** n

Tageslicht nt; **in ~** bei Tage; **day nursery** n Kita f (Kindertagesstätte); **day return** n (Brit Rail) Tagesrückfahrkarte f; **daytime** n: **in the ~** bei Tage, tagsüber; **daytrip** n Tagesausflug m

dazed [deɪzd] adj benommen

dazzle ['dæzl] vt blenden; **dazzling** adj blendend, glänzend

dead [dɛd] adj tot; (limb) abgestorben ▷ adv genau; (fam) total, völlig; **~ tired** adj todmüde; **~ slow** (sign) Schritt fahren; **dead end** n Sackgasse f; **deadline** n Termin m; (period) Frist f; **~ for applications** Anmeldeschluss m; **deadly** adj tödlich ▷ adv: **~ dull** todlangweilig

deaf [dɛf] adj taub; **deafen** vt taub machen; **deafening** adj ohrenbetäubend

deal [diːl] n (**dealt, dealt**) vt, vi (cards) geben, austeilen ▷ n (business ~) Geschäft nt; (agreement) Abmachung f; **it's a ~** abgemacht!; **a good/great ~ of** ziemlich/sehr viel; **deal in** vt handeln mit; **deal with** vt (matter) sich beschäftigen mit; (book, film) behandeln; (successfully: person, problem) fertig werden mit; (matter) erledigen; **dealer** n (Comm) Händler(in) m(f); (drugs) Dealer(in) m(f); **dealings** npl (Comm) Geschäfte pl

dealt [dɛlt] pt, pp of **deal**

dear [dɪə°] adj lieb, teuer; **Dear Sir or Madam** Sehr geehrte Damen und Herren; **Dear David** Lieber David ▷ n Schatz m; (as address) mein Schatz, Liebling; **dearly** adv (love) (heiß und) innig; (pay) teuer

death [dɛθ] n Tod m; (of project, hopes) Ende nt; (in accident etc) Todesfall m, Todesopfer nt; **death certificate** n Totenschein m;

death penalty n Todesstrafe f;
death toll n Zahl f der
Todesopfer; **death trap** n
Todesfalle f
debatable [dɪ'beɪtəbl] adj
fraglich; (question) strittig; **debate**
[dɪ'beɪt] n Debatte f ▷ vt
debattieren
debauched [dɪ'bɔːtʃt] adj
ausschweifend
debit ['debɪt] n Soll nt ▷ vt
(account) belasten; **debit card** n
Geldkarte f
debris ['debriː] n Trümmer pl
debt [det] n Schuld f; **to be in
~** verschuldet sein
decade ['dekeɪd] n Jahrzehnt nt
decadent ['dekədənt] adj
dekadent
decaff ['diːkæf] n (fam)
koffeinfreier Kaffee;
decaffeinated [diː'kæfɪneɪtɪd]
adj koffeinfrei
decanter [dɪ'kæntə*] n Dekanter
m, Karaffe f
decay [dɪ'keɪ] n Verfall m;
(rotting) Verwesung f; (of tooth)
Karies f ▷ vi verfallen; (rot)
verwesen; (wood) vermodern;
(teeth) faulen; (leaves) verrotten
deceased [dɪ'siːst] n: **the ~**
der/die Verstorbene
deceit [dɪ'siːt] n Betrug m;
deceive [dɪ'siːv] vt täuschen
December [dɪ'sembə*] n
Dezember m; see also **September**
decent ['diːsənt] adj anständig
deception [dɪ'sepʃən] n Betrug
m; **deceptive** [dɪ'septɪv] adj
täuschend, irreführend
decide [dɪ'saɪd] vt (question)
entscheiden; (body of people)
beschließen; **I can't ~ what to do**
ich kann mich nicht entscheiden,
was ich tun soll ▷ vi sich
entscheiden; **to ~ on sth** (in favour
of sth) sich für etw entscheiden,

sich zu etw entschließen; **decided**
adj entschieden; (clear) deutlich;
decidedly adv entschieden
decimal ['desɪməl] adj Dezimal-;
decimal system n
Dezimalsystem nt
decipher [dɪ'saɪfə*] vt entziffern
decision [dɪ'sɪʒən] n Entscheidung f (on über +akk); (of committee,
jury etc) Beschluss m; **to make a
~** eine Entscheidung treffen;
decisive [dɪ'saɪsɪv] adj entscheidend; (person)
entscheidungsfreudig
deck [dek] n (Naut) Deck nt; (of
cards) Blatt nt; **deckchair** n
Liegestuhl m
declaration [deklə'reɪʃən] n
Erklärung f; **declare** [dɪ'klɛə*] vt
erklären; (state) behaupten (that
dass); (at customs) **have you
anything to ~?** haben Sie etwas
zu verzollen?
decline [dɪ'klaɪn] n Rückgang m
▷ vt (invitation, offer) ablehnen ▷ vi
(become less) sinken, abnehmen;
(health) sich verschlechtern
decode [diː'kəʊd] vt
entschlüsseln
decompose [diːkəm'pəʊz] vi sich
zersetzen
decontaminate
[diːkən'tæmɪneɪt] vt entgiften;
(from radioactivity) entseuchen
decorate ['dekəreɪt] vt
(aus)schmücken; (wallpaper)
tapezieren; (paint) anstreichen;
decoration [dekə'reɪʃən] n
Schmuck m; (process) Schmücken
nt; (wallpapering) Tapezieren nt;
(painting) Anstreichen nt;
Christmas ~s Weihnachts-
schmuck m; **decorator** n
Maler(in) m(f)
decrease ['diːkriːs] n Abnahme f
▷ [diː'kriːs] vi abnehmen
dedicate ['dedɪkeɪt] vt widmen

(to sb jdm); **dedicated** *adj (person)*
engagiert; **dedication**
[dedɪ'keɪʃən] *n* Widmung *f*;
(commitment) Hingabe *f*,
Engagement *nt*
deduce [dɪ'djuːs] *vt* folgern,
schließen *(from* aus, *that* dass)
deduct [dɪ'dʌkt] *vt* abziehen
(from von); **deduction** [dɪ'dʌkʃən]
n (of money) Abzug *m; (conclusion)*
(Schluss)folgerung *f*
deed [diːd] *n* Tat *f*
deep [diːp] *adj* tief; **deepen** *vt*
vertiefen; **deep-freeze** *n*
Tiefkühltruhe *f; (upright)*
Gefrierschrank *m*; **deep-fry** *vt*
frittieren
deer [dɪə*] *n* Reh *nt; (with stag)*
Hirsch *m*
defeat [dɪ'fiːt] *n* Niederlage *f*; **to
admit ~** sich geschlagen geben
▷ *vt* besiegen
defect [*'*diːfekt] *n* Defekt *m*,
Fehler *m*; **defective** [dɪ'fektɪv]
adj fehlerhaft
defence [dɪ'fens] *n* Verteidigung
f; **defend** [dɪ'fend] *vt*
verteidigen; **defendant**
[dɪ'fendənt] *n (Jur)* Angeklagte(r)
mf; **defender** *n (Sport)*
Verteidiger(in) *m(f)*; **defensive**
[dɪ'fensɪv] *adj* defensiv
deficiency [dɪ'fɪʃənsɪ] *n* Mangel
m; **deficient** *adj* mangelhaft;
deficit [*'*defɪsɪt] *n* Defizit *nt*
define [dɪ'faɪn] *vt (word)*
definieren; *(duties, powers)*
bestimmen; **definite** [*'*defɪnɪt]
adj (clear) klar, eindeutig; *(certain)*
sicher; **it's ~** es steht fest;
definitely *adv* bestimmt;
definition [defɪ'nɪʃən] *n* Definition *f; (Foto)* Schärfe *f*
defrost [diː'frɒst] *vt (fridge)*
abtauen; *(food)* auftauen
degrading [dɪ'greɪdɪŋ] *adj*
erniedrigend

degree [dɪ'griː] *n* Grad *m; (at
university)* akademischer Grad; **a
certain/high ~ of** ein
gewisses/hohes Maß an +*dat*; **to a
certain ~** einigermaßen; **I have a
~ in chemistry** ≈ ich habe einen
Abschluss in Chemie
dehydrated [diːhaɪ'dreɪtɪd] *adj
(food)* getrocknet, Trocken-;
(person) ausgetrocknet
de-ice [diː'aɪs] *vt* enteisen
delay [dɪ'leɪ] *vt (postpone)*
verschieben, aufschieben; **to be
~ed** *(event)* sich verzögern; **the
train/flight was ~ed** der Zug/die
Maschine hatte Verspätung ▷ *vi*
warten; *(hesitate)* zögern ▷ *n*
Verzögerung *f; (of train etc)*
Verspätung *f*; **without ~**
unverzüglich; **delayed** *adj (train
etc)* verspätet
delegate *n* [*'*delɪgət] Dele-
gierte(r) *mf* ▷ [*'*delɪgeɪt] *vt*
delegieren; **delegation**
[delɪ'geɪʃən] *n* Abordnung *f*;
(foreign) Delegation *f*
delete [dɪ'liːt] *vt (aus)*streichen;
(Inform) löschen; **deletion** *n*
Streichung *f; (Inform)* Löschung *f*
deli [*'*delɪ] *n (fam)*
Feinkostgeschäft *nt*
deliberate [dɪ'lɪbərət] *adj
(intentional)* absichtlich;
deliberately *adv* mit Absicht,
extra
delicate [*'*delɪkɪt] *adj (fine)* fein;
(fragile) zart; *(a. Med)* empfindlich;
(situation) heikel
delicatessen [delɪkə'tesn] *nsing*
Feinkostgeschäft *nt*
delicious [dɪ'lɪʃəs] *adj* köstlich,
lecker
delight [dɪ'laɪt] *n* Freude *f* ▷ *vt*
entzücken; **delighted** *adj* sehr
erfreut *(with* über +*akk)*; **delightful**
adj entzückend; *(weather, meal etc)*
herrlich

deliver [dɪ'lɪvə*] vt (goods) liefern
(to sb jdm); (letter, parcel) zustellen;
(speech) halten; (baby) entbinden;
delivery n Lieferung f; (of letter,
parcel) Zustellung f; (of baby)
Entbindung f; **delivery van** n
Lieferwagen m

delude [dɪ'luːd] vt täuschen;
don't ~ yourself mach dir nichts
vor; **delusion** n Irrglaube m

de luxe [dɪ'lʌks] adj Luxus-

demand [dɪ'mɑːnd] vt verlangen
(from von); (time, patience etc)
erfordern ▷ n (request) Forderung
f, Verlangen nt (for nach); (Comm:
for goods) Nachfrage f; **on ~** auf
Wunsch; **very much in ~** sehr
gefragt; **demanding** adj
anspruchsvoll

demented [dɪ'mentɪd] adj
wahnsinnig

demerara [demə'rɛərə] n:
~ (sugar) brauner Zucker

demister n Defroster m

demo ['deməʊ] (pl **-s**) n (fam)
Demo f

democracy [dɪ'mɒkrəsɪ] n
Demokratie f; **democrat,
Democrat** (US Pol) ['deməkræt]
Demokrat(in) m(f); **democratic**
adj demokratisch; **the
Democratic Party** (US Pol) die
Demokratische Partei

demolish [dɪ'mɒlɪʃ] vt abreißen;
(fig) zerstören; **demolition**
[demə'lɪʃən] n Abbruch m

demonstrate ['demənstreɪt] vt,
vi demonstrieren, beweisen;
demonstration n Demonstration f

demoralize [dɪ'mɒrəlaɪz] vt
demoralisieren

denial [dɪ'naɪəl] n Leugnung f;
(official ~) Dementi nt

denim ['denɪm] n Jeansstoff m;
denim jacket n Jeansjacke f;
denims npl Bluejeans pl

Denmark ['denmɑːk] n Dänemark nt

denomination [dɪnɒmɪ'neɪʃən]
n (Rel) Konfession f; (Comm)
Nennwert m

dense [dens] adj dicht; (fam:
stupid) schwer von Begriff; **density**
['densɪtɪ] n Dichte f

dent [dent] n Beule f, Delle f ▷ vt
einbeulen

dental ['dentl] adj Zahn-; **~ care**
Zahnpflege f; **~ floss** Zahnseide f;
dentist ['dentɪst] n Zahnarzt m,
Zahnärztin; **dentures** ['dentʃəz]
npl Zahnprothese f; (full) Gebiss nt

deny [dɪ'naɪ] vt leugnen,
bestreiten; (refuse) ablehnen

deodorant [diː'əʊdərənt] n
Deo(dorant) nt

depart [dɪ'pɑːt] vi abreisen; (bus,
train) abfahren (for nach, from von);
(plane) abfliegen (for nach, from
von)

department [dɪ'pɑːtmənt] n
Abteilung f; (at university) Institut
nt; (Pol: ministry) Ministerium nt;
department store n Kaufhaus nt

departure [dɪ'pɑːtʃə*] n (of
person) Weggang m; (on journey)
Abreise f (for nach); (of train etc)
Abfahrt f (for nach); (of plane)
Abflug m (for nach); **departure
lounge** n (Aviat) Abflughalle f;
departure time n Abfahrtzeit f;
(Aviat) Abflugzeit f

depend [dɪ'pend] vi: **it ~s** es
kommt darauf an (whether, if ob);
depend on vt (thing) abhängen
von; (person: rely on) sich verlassen
auf +akk; (person, area etc)
angewiesen sein auf +akk; **it ~s on
the weather** es kommt auf das
Wetter an; **dependable** adj
zuverlässig; **dependence** n
Abhängigkeit f (on von);
dependent adj abhängig (on von)

deport [dɪ'pɔːt] vt ausweisen,

abschieben; **deportation** [diːpɔː'teɪʃən] n Abschiebung f

deposit [dɪ'pɒzɪt] n (down payment) Anzahlung f; (security) Kaution f; (for bottle) Pfand nt; (to bank account) Einzahlung f; (in river etc) Ablagerung f ▷ vt (put down) abstellen, absetzen; (to bank account) einzahlen; (sth valuable) deponieren; **deposit account** n Sparkonto nt

depot ['depəʊ] n Depot nt

depreciate [dɪ'priːʃieɪt] vi an Wert verlieren

depress [dɪ'pres] vt (in mood) deprimieren; **depressed** adj (person) niedergeschlagen, deprimiert; **~ area** Notstandsgebiet nt; **depressing** adj deprimierend; **depression** [dɪ'preʃən] n (mood) Depression f; (Meteo) Tief nt

deprive [dɪ'praɪv] vt: **to ~ sb of sth** jdn einer Sache berauben; **deprived** adj (child) (sozial) benachteiligt

dept abbr = **department** Abt.

depth [depθ] n Tiefe f

deputy ['depjʊti] adj stell-vertretend, Vize- ▷ n Stellvertreter(in) m(f); (US Pol) Abgeordnete(r) mf

derail [dɪ'reɪl] vt entgleisen lassen; **to be ~ed** entgleisen

deranged [dɪ'reɪndʒd] adj geistesgestört

derivation [derɪ'veɪʃən] n Ableitung f; **derive** [dɪ'raɪv] vt ableiten (from von) ▷ abstammen (from von)

dermatitis [dɜːmə'taɪtɪs] n Hautentzündung f

derogatory [dɪ'rɒgətərɪ] adj abfällig

descend [dɪ'send] vt, vi hinabsteigen, hinuntergehen; (person) **to ~ o** be **~ed from**

abstammen von; **descendant** n Nachkomme m; **descent** [dɪ'sent] n (coming down) Abstieg m; (origin) Abstammung f

describe [dɪs'kraɪb] vt be-schreiben; **description** [dɪ'skrɪpʃən] n Beschreibung f

desert ['dezət] n Wüste f ▷ [dɪ'zɜːt] vt verlassen; (abandon) im Stich lassen; **deserted** adj verlassen; (empty) menschenleer

deserve [dɪ'zɜːv] vt verdienen

design [dɪ'zaɪn] n (plan) Entwurf m; (of vehicle, machine) Konstruktion f; (of object) Design nt; (planning) Gestaltung f ▷ vt entwerfen; (machine etc) konstruieren; **~ed for sb/sth** (intended) für jdn/etw konzipiert

designate ['dezɪgneɪt] vt bestimmen

designer [dɪ'zaɪnə*] n Designer(in) m(f); (Tech) Konstrukteur(in) m(f); **designer drug** n Designerdroge f

desirable [dɪ'zaɪərəbl] n wünschenswert; (person) begehrenswert; **desire** [dɪ'zaɪə*] n Wunsch m (for nach); (esp sexual) Begierde f (for nach) ▷ vt wünschen; (ask for) verlangen; **if ~d** auf Wunsch

desk [desk] n Schreibtisch m; (reception ~) Empfang m; (at airport etc) Schalter m; **desktop publishing** n Desktoppublishing nt

desolate ['desəlɪt] adj trostlos

despair [dɪs'peə*] n Verzweif-lung f (at über +akk) ▷ vi verzweifeln (of an +dat)

despatch [dɪ'spætʃ] see **dispatch**

desperate ['despərɪt] adj verzweifelt; (situation) hoffnungslos; **to be ~ for sth** etw dringend brauchen, unbedingt wollen; **desperation**

[despə'reɪʃən] n Verzweiflung f

despicable [dɪ'spɪkəbl] adj verachtenswert; **despise** [dɪ'spaɪz] vt verachten

despite [dɪ'spaɪt] prep trotz +gen

dessert [dɪ'zɜːt] n Nachtisch m; **dessert spoon** n Dessertlöffel m

destination [destɪ'neɪʃən] n (of person) (Reise)ziel nt; (of goods) Bestimmungsort m

destiny ['destɪnɪ] n Schicksal nt

destroy [dɪ'strɔɪ] vt zerstören; (completely) vernichten; **destruction** [dɪ'strʌkʃən] n Zerstörung f; (complete) Vernichtung f; **destructive** [dɪ'strʌktɪv] adj zerstörerisch; (esp fig) destruktiv

detach [dɪ'tætʃ] vt abnehmen; (from form etc) abtrennen; (free) lösen (from von); **detachable** adj abnehmbar; (from form etc) abtrennbar; **detached** adj (attitude) distanziert, objektiv; **~ house** Einzelhaus nt

detail ['diːteɪl, (US) dɪ'teɪl] n Einzelheit f, Detail nt; (further) **~s from ...** Näheres erfahren Sie bei ...; **to go into ~** ins Detail gehen; **in ~** ausführlich; **detailed** adj detailliert, ausführlich

detain [dɪ'teɪn] vt aufhalten; (police) in Haft nehmen

detect [dɪ'tekt] vt entdecken; (notice) wahrnehmen; **detective** [dɪ'tektɪv] n Detektiv(in) m(f); **detective story** n Krimi m

detention [dɪ'tenʃən] n Haft f; (Sch) Nachsitzen nt

deter [dɪ'tɜː] vt abschrecken (from von)

detergent [dɪ'tɜːdʒənt] n Reinigungsmittel nt; (soap powder) Waschmittel nt

deteriorate [dɪ'tɪərɪəreɪt] vi sich verschlechtern

determination [dɪtɜːmɪ'neɪʃən] n Entschlossenheit f; **determine** [dɪ'tɜːmɪn] vt bestimmen; **determined** adj (fest) entschlossen

deterrent [dɪ'terənt] n Abschreckungsmittel nt

detest [dɪ'test] vt verabscheuen; **detestable** adj abscheulich

detour ['diːtʊə*] n Umweg m; (of traffic) Umleitung f

deuce [djuːs] n (Tennis) Einstand m

devalue [diː'væljuː] vt abwerten

devastate ['devəsteɪt] vt verwüsten; **devastating** ['devəsteɪtɪŋ] adj verheerend

develop [dɪ'veləp] vt entwickeln; (illness) bekommen ▷ vi sich entwickeln; **developing country** n Entwicklungsland nt; **development** n Entwicklung f; (of land) Erschließung f

device [dɪ'vaɪs] n Vorrichtung f, Gerät nt

devil ['devl] n Teufel m; **devilish** adj teuflisch

devote [dɪ'vəʊt] vt widmen (to dat); **devoted** adj liebend; (servant etc) treu ergeben; **devotion** n Hingabe f

devour [dɪ'vaʊə*] vt verschlingen

dew [djuː] n Tau m

diabetes [daɪə'biːtiːz] n Diabetes m, Zuckerkrankheit f; **diabetic** [daɪə'betɪk] adj zuckerkrank, für Diabetiker ▷ n Diabetiker(in) m(f)

diagnosis (diagnoses) [daɪəg'nəʊsɪs] (pl **diagnoses**) n Diagnose f

diagonal [daɪ'ægənl] adj diagonal

diagram ['daɪəgræm] n Diagramm nt

dial ['daɪəl] n Skala f; (of clock)

Zifferblatt nt ▷ vt (Tel) wählen;
dial code n (US) Vorwahl f
dialect ['daɪəlekt] n Dialekt m
dialling code n (Brit) Vorwahl f;
dialling tone n (Brit) Amtszeichen nt
dialogue, dialog (US) ['daɪəlɒg]
n Dialog m
dial tone n (US) Amtszeichen nt
dialysis [daɪˈælərsɪs] n (Med)
Dialyse f
diameter [daɪˈæmɪtə*] n
Durchmesser m
diamond ['daɪəmənd] n Diamant m; (Cards) Karo nt
diaper ['daɪpə*] n (US) Windel f
diarrhoea [daɪəˈriːə] n Durchfall
m
diary ['daɪərɪ] n (Taschen)kalender m; (account) Tagebuch nt
dice [daɪs] npl Würfel pl; **diced**
adj in Würfel geschnitten
dictate [dɪkˈteɪt] vt diktieren;
dictation [dɪkˈteɪʃən] n Diktat nt
dictator [dɪkˈteɪtə*] n Diktator(in) m(f); **dictatorship**
[dɪkˈteɪtəʃɪp] n Diktatur f
dictionary ['dɪkʃənrɪ] n
Wörterbuch nt
did [dɪd] pt of **do**
didn't ['dɪdnt] contr of **did not**
die [daɪ] vi sterben (of an +dat);
(plant, animal) eingehen; (engine)
absterben; **to be dying to do sth**
darauf brennen, etw zu tun; **I'm
dying for a drink** ich brauche
unbedingt was zu trinken; **die
away** vi schwächer werden;
(wind) sich legen; **die down** vi
nachlassen; **die out** vi aussterben
diesel ['diːzəl] n (fuel, car) Diesel
m; **~ engine** Dieselmotor m
diet ['daɪət] n Kost f; (special food)
Diät f ▷ vi eine Diät machen
differ ['dɪfə*] vi (be different) sich
unterscheiden; (disagree) anderer
Meinung sein; **difference**

['dɪfrəns] n Unterschied m; **it
makes no ~ (to me)** es ist (mir)
egal; **it makes a big ~** es macht
viel aus; **different** adj andere(r, s);
(with pl) verschieden; **to be quite
~** ganz anders sein (from als); (two
people, things) völlig verschieden
sein; **a ~ person** ein anderer
Mensch; **differentiate**
[dɪfəˈrenʃɪeɪt] vt, vi
unterscheiden; **differently**
['dɪfrəntlɪ] adv anders (from als);
(from one another) unterschiedlich
difficult ['dɪfɪkəlt] adj schwierig; **I find it ~** es fällt mir schwer;
difficulty n Schwierigkeit f; **with
~** nur schwer; **to have ~ in doing
sth** etw nur mit Mühe machen
können
dig [dɪg] (dug, dug) vt, vi (hole)
graben; **dig in** vi (fam: to food)
reinhauen; **~!** greif(t) zu!; **dig up** vt
ausgraben
digest [daɪˈdʒest] vt (a. fig)
verdauen; **digestible** [dɪˈdʒestəbl]
adj verdaulich; **digestion**
[dɪˈdʒestʃən] n Verdauung f;
digestive [dɪˈdʒestɪv] adj: **~ biscuit** (Brit) Vollkornkeks m
digit ['dɪdʒɪt] n Ziffer f; **digital**
['dɪdʒɪtəl] adj digital; **~ computer**
Digitalrechner m; **~ watch/clock**
Digitaluhr f; **digital camera** n
Digitalkamera f; **digital
television, digital TV** n
Digitalfernsehen nt
dignified ['dɪgnɪfaɪd] adj
würdevoll; **dignity** ['dɪgnɪtɪ] n
Würde f
dilapidated [dɪˈlæpɪdeɪtɪd] adj
baufällig
dilemma [daɪˈlemə] n Dilemma
nt
dill [dɪl] n Dill m
dilute [daɪˈluːt] vt verdünnen
dim [dɪm] adj (light) schwach;
(outline) undeutlich; (stupid)

schwer von Begriff ▷ vt
verdunkeln; (US Auto) abblenden;
~med headlights (US)
Abblendlicht nt
dime [daɪm] n (US)
Zehncentstück nt
dimension [daɪˈmenʃən] n
Dimension f; **~s** pl Maße pl
diminish [dɪˈmɪnɪʃ] vt
verringern ▷ vi sich verringern
dimple [ˈdɪmpl] n Grübchen nt
dine [daɪn] vi speisen; **dine out**
vi außer Haus essen; **diner** n Gast
m; (Rail) Speisewagen m; (US)
Speiselokal nt
dinghy [ˈdɪŋɪ] n Ding(h)i nt;
(inflatable) Schlauchboot nt
dingy [ˈdɪndʒɪ] adj düster; (dirty)
schmuddelig
dining car [ˈdaɪnɪŋkɑː] n
Speisewagen m; **dining room** n
Esszimmer nt; (in hotel)
Speiseraum m; **dining table** n
Esstisch m
dinner [ˈdɪnə] n Abendessen nt;
(lunch) Mittagessen nt; (public)
Diner nt; **to be at ~** beim Essen
sein; **to have ~** zu Abend/Mittag
essen; **dinner jacket** n Smoking
m; **dinner party** n
Abendgesellschaft f (mit Essen);
dinnertime n Essenszeit f
dinosaur [ˈdaɪnəsɔː] n Dinosaurier m
dip [dɪp] vt tauchen (in in +akk);
to ~ (one's headlights) (Brit Auto)
abblenden; **~ped headlights**
Abblendlicht nt ▷ n (in ground)
Bodensenke f; (sauce) Dip m
diploma [dɪˈpləʊmə] n Diplom
nt
diplomat [ˈdɪpləmæt] n Diplo-
mat(in) m(f); **diplomatic**
[dɪpləˈmætɪk] adj diplomatisch
dipstick [ˈdɪpstɪk] n Ölmessstab
m
direct [daɪˈrekt] adj direkt;

(cause, consequence) unmittelbar;
~ debit (mandate)
Einzugsermächtigung f;
(transaction) Abbuchung f im
Lastschriftverfahren; **~ train**
durchgehender Zug ▷ vt (aim,
send) richten (at, to an +akk); (film)
die Regie führen bei; (traffic)
regeln; **direct current** n (Elec)
Gleichstrom m
direction [dɪˈrekʃən] n (course)
Richtung f; (Cine) Regie f; **in
the ~ of ...** in Richtung ...; **~s**
pl (to a place) Wegbeschreibung f
directly [dɪˈrektlɪ] adv direkt; (at
once) sofort
director [dɪˈrektə] n Direk-
tor(in) m(f), Leiter(in) m(f); (of film)
Regisseur(in) m(f)
directory [dɪˈrektərɪ] n Adressbuch nt; (Tel) Telefonbuch nt;
~ enquiries o (US) **assistance** (Tel)
Auskunft f
dirt [dɜːt] n Schmutz m, Dreck m;
dirt cheap adj spottbillig; **dirt
road** n unbefestigte Straße; **dirty**
adj schmutzig
disability [dɪsəˈbɪlɪtɪ] n
Behinderung f; **disabled**
[dɪsˈeɪbld] adj behindert,
Behinderten- ▷ npl: **the ~** die
Behinderten
disadvantage [dɪsədˈvɑːntɪdʒ]
n Nachteil m; **at a ~** benachteiligt;
disadvantageous [dɪsædvɑːn-
ˈteɪdʒəs] adj unvorteilhaft,
ungünstig
disagree [dɪsəˈɡriː] vi anderer
Meinung sein; (two people) sich
nicht einig sein; (two reports etc)
nicht übereinstimmen; **to ~ with
sb** mit jdm nicht übereinstimmen;
(food) jdm nicht bekommen;
disagreeable adj unangenehm;
(person) unsympathisch;
disagreement n Meinungsverschiedenheit f

disappear [dɪsə'pɪə*] vi verschwinden; **disappearance** n Verschwinden nt

disappoint [dɪsə'pɔɪnt] vt enttäuschen; **disappointing** adj enttäuschend; **disappointment** n Enttäuschung f

disapproval [dɪsə'pru:vl] n Missbilligung f; **disapprove** [dɪsə'pru:v] vi missbilligen (of akk)

disarm [dɪs'ɑ:m] vt entwaffnen ▷ vi (Pol) abrüsten; **disarmament** n Abrüstung f; **disarming** adj (smile, look) gewinnend

disaster [dɪ'zɑ:stə*] n Katastrophe f; **disastrous** [dɪ'zɑ:strəs] adj katastrophal

disbelief [dɪsbə'li:f] n Ungläubigkeit f

disc [dɪsk] n Scheibe f, CD f; see also **disk**; (Anat) Bandscheibe f; **disc brake** n Scheibenbremse f

discharge ['dɪstʃɑ:dʒ] n (Med) Ausfluss m ▷ [dɪs'tʃɑ:dʒ] vt (person) entlassen; (emit) ausstoßen; (Med) ausscheiden

discipline ['dɪsɪplɪn] n Disziplin f

disc jockey ['dɪskdʒɒkɪ] n Diskjockey m

disclose [dɪs'kləʊz] vt bekannt geben; (secret) enthüllen

disco ['dɪskəʊ] (pl -s) n Disko f, Diskomusik f

discomfort [dɪs'kʌmfət] n (slight pain) leichte Schmerzen pl; (unease) Unbehagen nt

disconnect [dɪskə'nekt] vt (electricity, gas, phone) abstellen; (unplug) **to ~ the TV (from the mains)** den Stecker des Fernsehers herausziehen; (Tel) **I've been ~ed** das Gespräch ist unterbrochen worden

discontent [dɪskən'tent] n Unzufriedenheit f; **discontented** adj unzufrieden

discontinue [dɪskən'tɪnju:] vt einstellen; (product) auslaufen lassen

discount ['dɪskaʊnt] n Rabatt m

discover [dɪs'kʌvə*] vt entdecken; **discovery** n Entdeckung f

discredit [dɪs'kredɪt] vt in Verruf bringen ▷ n Misskredit m

discreet [dɪs'kri:t] adj diskret

discrepancy [dɪs'krepənsɪ] n Unstimmigkeit f, Diskrepanz f

discriminate [dɪs'krɪmɪneɪt] vi unterscheiden; **to ~ against sb** jdn diskriminieren; **discrimination** [dɪskrɪmɪ'neɪʃən] n (different treatment) Diskriminierung f

discus ['dɪskəs] n Diskus m

discuss [dɪs'kʌs] vt diskutieren, besprechen; **discussion** [dɪs'kʌʃən] n Diskussion f

disease [dɪ'zi:z] n Krankheit f

disembark [dɪsɪm'bɑ:k] vi von Bord gehen

disentangle [dɪsɪn'tæŋgl] vt entwirren

disgrace [dɪs'greɪs] n Schande f ▷ vt Schande machen +dat; (family etc) Schande bringen über +akk; (less strong) blamieren; **disgraceful** adj skandalös

disguise [dɪs'gaɪz] vt verkleiden; (voice) verstellen ▷ n Verkleidung f; **in ~** verkleidet

disgust [dɪs'gʌst] n Abscheu m; (physical) Ekel m ▷ vt anekeln, anwidern; **disgusting** adj widerlich; (physically) ekelhaft

dish [dɪʃ] n Schüssel f; (food) Gericht nt; **~es** pl (crockery) Geschirr nt; **to do/wash the ~es** abwaschen; **dishcloth** n (for washing) Spültuch nt; (for drying) Geschirrtuch nt

dishearten [dɪs'hɑːtən] *vt*
entmutigen; **don't be ~ed** lass den
Kopf nicht hängen!
dishonest [dɪs'ɒnɪst] *adj*
unehrlich
dishonour [dɪs'ɒnə°] *n* Schande
f
dish towel *n* (*US*) Geschirrtuch
nt; **dish washer** *n*
Geschirrspülmaschine *f*
dishy ['dɪʃɪ] *adj* (*Brit fam*) gut
aussehend
disillusioned [dɪsɪ'luːʒənd] *adj*
desillusioniert
disinfect [dɪsɪn'fekt] *vt* desinfizieren; **disinfectant** *n*
Desinfektionsmittel *nt*
disintegrate [dɪs'ɪntɪgreɪt]
vi zerfallen; (*group*) sich
auflösen
disjointed [dɪs'dʒɔɪntɪd] *adj*
unzusammenhängend
disk [dɪsk] *n* (*Inform: floppy*)
Diskette *f*; **disk drive** *n*
Diskettenlaufwerk *nt*; **diskette**
[dɪ'sket] *n* Diskette *f*
dislike [dɪs'laɪk] *n* Abneigung *f*
▷ *vt* nicht mögen; **to ~ doing sth**
etw ungern tun
dislocate ['dɪsləʊkeɪt] *vt* (*Med*)
verrenken, ausrenken
dismal ['dɪzməl] *adj* trostlos
dismantle [dɪs'mæntl] *vt*
auseinandernehmen; (*machine*)
demontieren
dismay [dɪs'meɪ] *n* Bestürzung *f*;
dismayed *adj* bestürzt
dismiss [dɪs'mɪs] *vt* (*employee*)
entlassen; **dismissal** *n*
Entlassung *f*
disobedience [dɪsə'biːdɪəns] *n*
Ungehorsam *m*; **disobedient** *adj*
ungehorsam; **disobey** [dɪsə'beɪ]
vt nicht gehorchen +*dat*
disorder [dɪs'ɔːdə°] *n* (*mess*)
Unordnung *f*; (*riot*) Aufruhr *m*;
(*Med*) Störung *f*, Leiden *nt*

disorganized [dɪs'ɔːgənaɪzd] *adj*
chaotisch
disparaging *adj* geringschätzig
dispatch [dɪ'spætʃ] *vt* abschicken, abfertigen
dispensable [dɪ'spensəbl] *adj*
entbehrlich; **dispense** *vt*
verteilen; **dispense with** *vt*
verzichten auf +*akk*; **dispenser** *n*
Automat *m*
disperse [dɪ'spɜːs] *vi* sich
zerstreuen
display [dɪ'spleɪ] *n* (*exhibition*)
Ausstellung *f*, Show *f*; (*of goods*)
Auslage *f*; (*Tech*) Anzeige *f*, Display
nt ▷ *vt* zeigen; (*goods*) ausstellen
disposable [dɪ'spəʊzəbl] *adj*
(*container, razor etc*) Wegwerf-;
~ nappy Wegwerfwindel *f*;
disposal [dɪ'spəʊzəl] *n* Loswerden *nt*; (*of waste*) Beseitigung *f*; **to
be at sb's ~** jdm zur Verfügung
stehen; **to have at one's
~** verfügen über; **dispose of** *vt*
loswerden; (*waste etc*) beseitigen
dispute [dɪ'spjuːt] *n* Streit *m*;
(*industrial*) Auseinandersetzung *f*
▷ *vt* bestreiten
disqualification
[dɪskwɒlɪfɪ'keɪʃən] *n* Disquali-
fikation *f*; **disqualify**
[dɪs'kwɒlɪfaɪ] *vt* disqualifizieren
disregard [dɪsrɪ'gɑːd] *vt* nicht
beachten
disreputable [dɪs'repjʊtəbl] *adj*
verrufen
disrespect [dɪsrɪ'spekt] *n*
Respektlosigkeit *f*
disrupt [dɪs'rʌpt] *vt* stören;
(*interrupt*) unterbrechen;
disruption [dɪs'rʌpʃən] *n*
Störung *f*; (*interruption*)
Unterbrechung *f*
dissatisfied [dɪs'sætɪsfaɪd] *adj*
unzufrieden
dissent [dɪ'sent] *n* Widerspruch
m

dissolve [dɪ'zɒlv] vt auflösen
▷ vi sich auflösen

dissuade [dɪ'sweɪd] vt (davon abbringen) **to ~ sb from doing sth** jdn davon abbringen, etw zu tun

distance ['dɪstəns] n Entfernung f; **in the/from a ~** in/aus der Ferne; **distant** adj (a. in time) fern; (relative etc) entfernt; (person) distanziert

distaste [dɪs'teɪst] n Abneigung f (for gegen)

distil [dɪ'stɪl] vt destillieren; **distillery** n Brennerei f

distinct [dɪ'stɪŋkt] adj verschieden; (clear) klar, deutlich; **distinction** [dɪ'stɪŋkʃən] n (difference) Unterschied m; (in exam etc) Auszeichnung f; **distinctive** adj unverkennbar; **distinctly** adv deutlich

distinguish [dɪ'stɪŋgwɪʃ] vt unterscheiden (sth from sth etw von etw)

distort [dɪ'stɔːt] vt verzerren; (truth) verdrehen

distract [dɪ'strækt] vt ablenken; **distraction** [dɪ'strækʃən] n Ablenkung f; (diversion) Zerstreuung f

distress [dɪ'stres] n (need, danger) Not f; (suffering) Leiden nt; (mental) Qual f; (worry) Kummer m ▷ vt mitnehmen, erschüttern; **distressed area** n Notstandsgebiet nt; **distress signal** n Notsignal nt

distribute [dɪ'strɪbjuːt] vt verteilen; (Comm: goods) vertreiben; **distribution** [dɪstrɪ'bjuːʃən] n Verteilung f; (Comm: of goods) Vertrieb m; **distributor** [dɪ'strɪbjʊtə°] n (Auto) Verteiler m; (Comm) Händler(in) m(f)

district ['dɪstrɪkt] n Gegend f; (administrative) Bezirk m; **district attorney** n (US) Staatsanwalt m, Staatsanwältin f

distrust [dɪs'trʌst] vt misstrauen +dat ▷ n Misstrauen nt

disturb [dɪ'stɜːb] vt stören; (worry) beunruhigen; **disturbance** n Störung f; **disturbing** adj beunruhigend

ditch [dɪtʃ] n Graben m ▷ vt (fam: person) den Laufpass geben +dat; (plan etc) verwerfen

ditto ['dɪtəʊ] n dito, ebenfalls

dive [daɪv] n (into water) Kopfsprung m; (Aviat) Sturzflug m; (fam) zwielichtiges Lokal ▷ vi (under water) tauchen; **diver** n Taucher(in) m(f)

diverse [daɪ'vɜːs] adj verschieden; **diversion** [daɪ'vɜːʃən] n (of traffic) Umleitung f; (distraction) Ablenkung f; **divert** [daɪ'vɜːt] vt ablenken; (traffic) umleiten

divide [dɪ'vaɪd] vt teilen; (in several parts, between people) aufteilen ▷ vi sich teilen; **dividend** ['dɪvɪdend] n Dividende f

divine [dɪ'vaɪn] adj göttlich

diving ['daɪvɪŋ] n (Sport)-tauchen nt; (jumping in) Springen nt; (Sport: from board) Kunstspringen nt; **diving board** n Sprungbrett nt; **diving goggles** npl Taucherbrille f; **diving mask** n Tauchmaske f

division [dɪ'vɪʒən] n Teilung f; (Math) Division f; (department) Abteilung f; (Sport) Liga f

divorce [dɪ'vɔːs] n Scheidung f ▷ vt sich scheiden lassen von; **divorced** adj geschieden; **to get ~** sich scheiden lassen; **divorcee** [dɪvɔː'siː] n Geschiedene(r) mf

DIY [diːaɪ'waɪ] abbr =

do-it-yourself; **DIY centre** n
Baumarkt m
dizzy ['dɪzɪ] adj schwindlig
DJ [diː'dʒeɪ] abbr = **dinner jacket**
Smoking m ▷ abbr = **disc jockey**
Diskjockey m, DJ m
DNA abbr = **desoxyribonucleic
acid** DNS f

⭕ **KEYWORD**

do [duː] (pt **did**, pp **done**) n (inf)
(party etc) Fete f
▷ vb aux **1** (in negative constructions
and questions) **I don't understand**
ich verstehe nicht; **didn't you
know?** wusstest du das nicht?;
what do you think? was meinen
Sie?
2 (for emphasis, in polite phrases) **she
does seem rather tired** sie
scheint wirklich sehr müde zu
sein; **do sit down/help yourself**
setzen Sie sich doch hin/greifen
Sie doch zu
3 (used to avoid repeating vb) **she
swims better than I do** sie
schwimmt besser als ich; **she
lives in Glasgow — so do I** sie
wohnt in Glasgow — ich auch
4 (in tag questions) **you like him,
don't you?** du magst/Sie mögen
ihn doch, oder?
▷ vt **1** (carry out, perform etc) tun,
machen; **what are you doing
tonight?** was machst du/machen
Sie heute Abend?; **I've got
nothing to do** ich habe nichts zu
tun; **to do one's hair/nails** sich
die Haare/Nägel machen
2 (car etc) fahren
▷ vi **1** (act, behave) **do as I do** mach
es wie ich
2 (get on, fare) **he's doing
well/badly at school** er ist
gut/schlecht in der Schule; **how
do you do?** guten Tag

3 (be suitable) gehen; (be sufficient)
reichen; **to make do (with)**
auskommen mit
do away with vt (kill)
umbringen; (abolish: law etc)
abschaffen
do up vt (laces, dress, buttons)
zumachen; (renovate: room, house)
renovieren
do with vt (need) brauchen; (be
connected) zu tun haben mit
do without vt, vi auskommen
ohne
do up vt (fasten) zumachen;
(parcel) verschnüren; (renovate)
wiederherrichten
do with vt (need) brauchen; **I
could ~ a drink** ich könnte einen
Drink gebrauchen
do without vt auskommen
ohne; **I can ~ your comments**
auf deine Kommentare kann ich
verzichten

dock [dɒk] n Dock nt; (Jur)
Anklagebank f; **docker** n
Hafenarbeiter m; **dockyard** n
Werft f
doctor ['dɒktə°] n Arzt m, Ärztin;
(in title, also academic) Doktor m
document ['dɒkjʊmənt] n
Dokument nt; **documentary**
[dɒkjʊ'mentərɪ] n Dokumentarfilm m; **documentation**
[dɒkjʊmen'teɪʃən] n Dokumen-
tation f
docusoap ['dɒkjʊsəʊp] n
Reality-Serie f, Dokusoap f
doddery ['dɒdərɪ] adj tatterig
dodgem ['dɒdʒəm] n Auto-
skooter m
dodgy [dɒdʒɪ] adj nicht ganz in
Ordnung; (dishonest, unreliable)
zwielichtig; **he has a ~ stomach**
er hat sich den Magen verdorben
dog [dɒg] n Hund m; **dog food** n
Hundefutter nt; **doggie bag**

['dɒgɪ'bæg] n Tüte oder Box, in der
Essensreste aus dem Restaurant
mit nach Hause genommen werden
können

do-it-yourself [ˈduːɪtjəˈself] n
Heimwerken nt, Do-it-yourself nt
▷ adj Heimwerker-;
do-it-yourselfer n Bastler(in)
m(f), Heimwerker(in) m(f)

doll [dɒl] n Puppe f

dollar [ˈdɒləʳ] n Dollar m

dolphin [ˈdɒlfɪn] n Delphin m

domain n Domäne f; (Inform)
Domain f

dome [dəʊm] n Kuppel f

domestic [dəˈmestɪk] adj häuslich; (within country) Innen-,
Binnen-; **domestic animal** n
Haustier nt; **domesticated**
[dəˈmestɪkeɪtɪd] adj (person)
häuslich; (animal) zahm; **domestic
flight** n Inlandsflug m

domicile [ˈdɒmɪsaɪl] n (ständi-
ger) Wohnsitz

dominant [ˈdɒmɪnənt] adj
dominierend, vorherrschend;
dominate [ˈdɒmɪneɪt] vt
beherrschen

dominoes [ˈdɒmɪnəʊz] npl
Domino(spiel) nt

donate [dəʊˈneɪt] vt spenden;
donation n Spende f

done [dʌn] pp of **do** ▷ adj (cooked)
gar; **well ~** durchgebraten

döner (kebab) [ˈdɒnəkəˈbæb] n
Döner (Kebab) m

donkey [ˈdɒŋkɪ] n Esel m

donor [ˈdəʊnə] n Spender(in)
m(f)

don't [dəʊnt] contr of **do not**

doom [duːm] n Schicksal nt;
(downfall) Verderben nt

door [dɔːʳ] n Tür f; **doorbell** n
Türklingel f; **door handle** n
Türklinke f; **doorknob** n Türknauf
m; **doormat** n Fußabtreter m;
doorstep n Türstufe f; **right**

on our ~ direkt vor unserer
Haustür

dope [dəʊp] (Sport) n (for athlete)
Aufputschmittel nt ▷ vt dopen

dormitory [ˈdɔːmɪtrɪ] n Schlafsaal m; (US) Studentenwohnheim
nt

dosage [ˈdəʊsɪdʒ] n Dosierung f;
dose [dəʊs] n Dosis f ▷ vt
dosieren

dot [dɒt] n Punkt m; **on the ~** auf
die Minute genau, pünktlich

dotcom [ˈdɒtkɒm] n: **~ (company)** Internetfirma f,
Dotcom-Unternehmen nt

dote on [dəʊt ɒn] vt abgöttisch
lieben

dotted line n punktierte Linie

double [ˈdʌbl] adj, adv doppelt;
~ the quantity die zweifache
Menge, doppelt so viel ▷ vt
verdoppeln ▷ n (person)
Doppelgänger(in) m(f); (Cine)
Double nt; **double bass** n
Kontrabass m; **double bed** n
Doppelbett nt; **double-click** vt
(Inform) doppelklicken; **double
cream** n Sahne mit hohem
Fettgehalt; **doubledecker** n
Doppeldecker m; **double glazing**
n Doppelverglasung f;
double-park vi in zweiter Reihe
parken; **double room** n
Doppelzimmer nt; **doubles** npl
(Sport: also match) Doppel nt

doubt [daʊt] n Zweifel m; **no
~** ohne Zweifel, zweifellos,
wahrscheinlich; **to have one's ~s**
Bedenken haben ▷ vt bezweifeln;
(statement, word) anzweifeln; **I ~ it**
das bezweifle ich; **doubtful** adj
zweifelhaft, zweifelnd; **it is
~ whether ...** es ist fraglich, ob ...;
doubtless adv ohne Zweifel,
sicherlich

dough [dəʊ] n Teig m; **doughnut**
n Donut m (rundes Hefegebäck)

dove [dʌv] n Taube f

down [daʊn] n Daunen pl; (fluff) Flaum m ▷ adv unten; (motion) nach unten; (towards speaker) herunter; (away from speaker) hinunter; **~ here/there** hier/dort unten; (downstairs) **they came ~ for breakfast** sie kamen zum Frühstück herunter; (southwards) **he came ~ from Scotland** er kam von Schottland herunter ▷ prep (towards speaker) herunter; (away from speaker) hinunter; **to drive ~ the hill/road** den Berg/die Straße hinunter fahren; (along) **to walk ~ the street** die Straße entlang gehen; **he's ~ the pub** (fam) er ist in der Kneipe ▷ vt (fam: drink) runterkippen ▷ adj niedergeschlagen, deprimiert

down-and-out adj heruntergekommen ▷ n Obdachlose(r) mf, Penner(in) m(f); **downcast** adj niedergeschlagen; **downfall** n Sturz m; **down-hearted** adj entmutigt; **downhill** adv bergab; **he's going ~** (fig) mit ihm geht es bergab

- **DOWNING STREET**
-
- **Downing Street** ist die Straße
- in London, die von Whitehall
- zum St James's Park führt, und
- in der sich der offizielle
- Wohnsitz des Premierministers
- (Nr. 10) und des Finanzministers
- (Nr. 11) befindet. Im weiteren
- Sinne bezieht sich der Begriff
- „Downing Street" auf die
- britische Regierung.

download [ˈdaʊnləʊd] vt downloaden, herunterladen; **downmarket** adj für den Massenmarkt; **down payment** n Anzahlung f; **downpour** n Platzregen m; **downs** npl Hügelland nt; **downsize** vt (business) verkleinern ▷ vi sich verkleinern

Down's syndrome [ˈdaʊnzˈsɪndrəʊm] n (Med) Downsyndrom nt

downstairs [daʊnˈstɛəz] adv unten; (motion) nach unten; **downstream** adv flussabwärts; **downtime** n Ausfallzeit f; **downtown** adv (be, work etc) in der Innenstadt; (go) in die Innenstadt ▷ adj (US) in der Innenstadt; **~ Chicago** die Innenstadt von Chicago; **down under** adv (fam: in/to Australia) in/nach Australien; (in/to New Zealand) in/nach Neuseeland; **downwards** adv, adj nach unten; (movement, trend) Abwärts-

doze [dəʊz] vi dösen ▷ n Nickerchen nt

dozen [ˈdʌzn] n Dutzend nt; **two ~ eggs** zwei Dutzend Eier; **~s of times** x-mal

DP abbr = **data processing** DV f

drab [dræb] adj trist; (colour) düster

draft [drɑːft] n (outline) Entwurf m; (US Mil) Einberufung f

drag [dræg] vt schleppen ▷ n (fam) **to be a ~** (boring) stinklangweilig sein; (laborious) ein ziemlicher Schlauch sein; **drag on** vi sich in die Länge ziehen

dragon [ˈdrægən] n Drache m; **dragonfly** n Libelle f

drain [dreɪn] n Abfluss m ▷ vt (water, oil) ablassen; (vegetables etc) abgießen; (land) entwässern, trockenlegen ▷ vi (of water) abfließen; **drainpipe** n Abflussrohr nt

drama [ˈdrɑːmə] n (a. fig) Drama nt; **dramatic** [drəˈmætɪk] adj dramatisch

drank [dræŋk] *pt of* **drink**
drapes [dreɪps] *npl* (*US*)
Vorhänge *pl*
drastic ['dræstɪk] *adj* drastisch
draught [drɑːft] *n* (Luft)zug *m*;
there's a ~ es zieht; **on ~** (*beer*)
vom Fass; **draughts** *nsing*
Damespiel *nt*; **draughty** *adj*
zugig
draw [drɔː] (**drew, drawn**) *vt*
(*pull*) ziehen; (*crowd*) anlocken,
anziehen; (*picture*) zeichnen ▷ *vi*
(*Sport*) unentschieden spielen ▷ *n*
(*Sport*) Unentschieden *nt*;
(*attraction*) Attraktion *f*; (*for lottery*)
Ziehung *f*; **draw out** *vt*
herausziehen; (*money*) abheben;
draw up *vt* (*formulate*) entwerfen;
(*list*) erstellen ▷ *vi* (*car*) anhalten;
drawback *n* Nachteil *m*;
drawbridge *n* Zugbrücke *f*
drawer ['drɔː°] *n* Schublade *f*
drawing ['drɔːɪŋ] *n* Zeichnung *f*;
drawing pin *n* Reißzwecke *f*
drawn [drɔːn] *pp of* **draw**
dread [dred] *n* Furcht *f* (*of* vor
+*dat*) ▷ *vt* sich fürchten vor +*dat*;
dreadful *adj* furchtbar;
dreadlocks *npl* Rastalocken *pl*
dream [driːm] *n* (**dreamed** *o*
dreamt, dreamed *o* **dreamt**) *vt, vi*
träumen (*about* von) ▷ *n* Traum *m*;
dreamt [dremt] *pt, pp of* **dream**
dreary ['drɪərɪ] *adj* (*weather,
place*) trostlos; (*book etc*) langweilig
drench [drentʃ] *vt* durchnässen
dress [dres] *n* Kleidung *f*;
(*garment*) Kleid *nt* ▷ *vt* anziehen;
(*Med: wound*) verbinden; **to get
~ed** sich anziehen; **dress up** *vi*
sich fein machen; (*in costume*) sich
verkleiden (*as* als); **dress circle** *n*
(*Theat*) erster Rang; **dresser** *n*
Anrichte *f*; (*US: dressing table*)
(Frisier)kommode *f*; **dressing** *n*
(*Gastr*) Dressing *nt*, Soße *f*; (*Med*)
Verband *m*; **dressing gown** *n*

Bademantel *m*; **dressing room** *n*
(*Theat*) Künstlergarderobe *f*;
dressing table *n*
Frisierkommode *f*; **dress
rehearsal** *n* (*Theat*) Generalprobe
f
drew [druː] *pt of* **draw**
dried [draɪd] *adj* getrocknet;
(*milk, flowers*) Trocken-; **~ fruit**
Dörrobst *nt*; **drier** ['draɪə°] *n see*
dryer
drift [drɪft] *vi* treiben ▷ *n* (*of
snow*) Verwehung *f*; (*fig*) Tendenz *f*;
if you get my ~ wenn du mich
richtig verstehst/wenn Sie mich
richtig verstehen
drill [drɪl] *n* Bohrer *m* ▷ *vt, vi*
bohren
drink [drɪŋk] (**drank, drunk**) *vt,
vi* trinken ▷ *n* Getränk *nt*;
(*alcoholic*) Drink *m*; **drink-driving**
n (*Brit*) Trunkenheit *f* am Steuer;
drinking water *n* Trinkwasser
nt
drip [drɪp] *n* Tropfen *m* ▷ *vi*
tropfen; **drip-dry** *adj* bügelfrei;
dripping *n* Bratenfett *nt* ▷ *adj*:
~ (wet) tropfnass
drive [draɪv] (**drove, driven**) *vt*
(*car, person in car*) fahren; (*force:
person, animal*) treiben; (*Tech*)
antreiben; **to ~ sb mad** jdn
verrückt machen ▷ *vi* fahren ▷ *n*
Fahrt *f*; (*entrance*) Einfahrt *f*,
Auffahrt *f*; (*Inform*) Laufwerk *nt*; **to
go for a ~** spazieren fahren; **drive
away, drive off** *vi* wegfahren
▷ *vt* vertreiben
drive-in *adj* Drive-in-; **~ cinema**
(*US*) Autokino *nt*
driven ['drɪvn] *pp of* **drive**
driver ['draɪvə°] *n* Fahrer(in)
m(f); (*Inform*) Treiber *m*; **~'s license**
(*US*) Führerschein *m*; **~'s seat**
Fahrersitz *m*; **driving** ['draɪvɪŋ]
n (*Auto*)fahren *nt*; **he likes ~** er
fährt gern Auto; **driving lesson** *n*

Fahrstunde f; **driving licence** n (Brit) Führerschein m; **driving school** n Fahrschule f; **driving seat** n (Brit) Fahrersitz m; **to be in the ~** alles im Griff haben; **driving test** n Fahrprüfung f

drizzle ['drɪzl] n Nieselregen m ▷ vi nieseln

drop [drɒp] n (of liquid) Tropfen m; (fall in price etc) Rückgang m ▷ vt (a. fig: give up) fallen lassen ▷ vi (fall) herunterfallen; (figures, temperature) sinken, zurückgehen; **drop by, drop in** vi vorbeikommen; **drop off** vi (to sleep) einnicken; **drop out** vi (withdraw) aussteigen; (university) das Studium abbrechen; **dropout** n Aussteiger(in) m(f)

drought [draʊt] n Dürre f

drove [drəʊv] pt of **drive**

drown [draʊn] vi ertrinken ▷ vt ertränken

drowsy ['draʊzɪ] adj schläfrig

drug [drʌg] n (Med) Medikament nt, Arznei f; (addictive) Droge f; (narcotic) Rauschgift nt; **to be on ~s** drogensüchtig sein ▷ vt (mit Medikamenten) betäuben; **drug addict** n Rauschgiftsüchtige(r) mf; **drug dealer** n Drogenhändler(in) m(f); **druggist** n (US) Drogist(in) m(f); **drugstore** n (US) Drogerie f

drum [drʌm] n Trommel f; **~s** pl Schlagzeug nt; **drummer** n Schlagzeuger(in) m(f)

drunk [drʌŋk] pp of **drink** ▷ adj betrunken; **to get ~** sich betrinken ▷ n Betrunkene(r) mf; (alcoholic) Trinker(in) m(f); **drunk-driving** n (US) Trunkenheit f am Steuer; **drunken** adj betrunken, besoffen

dry [draɪ] adj trocken ▷ vt trocknen; (dishes, oneself, one's hands etc) abtrocknen ▷ vi trocknen, trocken werden; **dry out**

vi trocknen; **dry up** vi austrocknen; **dry-clean** vt chemisch reinigen; **dry-cleaning** n chemische Reinigung; **dryer** n Trockner m; (for hair) Föhn m; (over head) Trockenhaube f

DTP abbr = **desktop publishing** DTP nt

dual ['djʊəl] adj doppelt; **~ carriageway** (Brit) zweispurige Schnellstraße f; **~ nationality** doppelte Staatsangehörigkeit

dubbed [dʌbd] adj (film) synchronisiert

dubious ['dju:bɪəs] adj zweifelhaft

duchess ['dʌtʃəs] n Herzogin f

duck [dʌk] n Ente f

dude [du:d] n (US fam) Typ m; **a cool ~** ein cooler Typ

due [dju:] adj (time) fällig; (fitting) angemessen; **in ~ course** zu gegebener Zeit; **~ to** infolge +gen, wegen +gen ▷ adv: **~ south/north** etc direkt nach Norden/Süden etc

dug [dʌg] pt, pp of **dig**

duke [dju:k] n Herzog m

dull [dʌl] adj (colour, light, weather) trübe; (boring) langweilig

duly ['dju:lɪ] adv ordnungs- gemäß; (as expected) wie erwartet

dumb [dʌm] adj stumm; (fam: stupid) doof, blöde

dumb-bell ['dʌmbel] n Hantel f

dummy ['dʌmɪ] n (sham) Attrappe f; (in shop) Schaufensterpuppe f; (Brit: teat) Schnuller m; (fam: person) Dummkopf m ▷ adj unecht, Schein-; **~ run** Testlauf m

dump [dʌmp] n Abfallhaufen m; (fam: place) Kaff nt ▷ vt (lit, fig) abladen; (fam) **he ~ed her** er hat mir ihr Schluss gemacht

dumpling ['dʌmplɪŋ] n Kloß m, Knödel m

dune [dju:n] n Düne f

dung [dʌŋ] n (*manure*) Mist m
dungarees [dʌŋgəˈriːz] npl
Latzhose f
dungeon [ˈdʌndʒən] n Kerker m
duplex [ˈdjuːpleks] n
zweistöckige Wohnung; (*US*)
Doppelhaushälfte f
duplicate [ˈdjuːplɪkɪt] n Dup-
likat nt ▷ [ˈdjuːplɪkeɪt] vt (*make
copies of*) kopieren; (*repeat*)
wiederholen
durable [ˈdjʊərəbl] adj haltbar;
duration [djʊəˈreɪʃən] n Dauer f
during [ˈdjʊərɪŋ] prep (*time*)
während +gen
dusk [dʌsk] n Abenddämmerung f
dust [dʌst] n Staub m ▷ vt
abstauben; **dustbin** n (*Brit*)
Mülleimer m; **dustcart** n (*Brit*)
Müllwagen m; **duster** n
Staubtuch nt; **dust jacket** n
Schutzumschlag m; **dustman** n
(*Brit*) Müllmann m; **dustpan** n
Kehrschaufel f; **dusty** adj staubig
Dutch [dʌtʃ] adj holländisch ▷ n
(*language*) Holländisch nt; **to
speak/talk double ~** (*fam*)
Quatsch reden; **the ~** pl die
Holländer; **Dutchman** (pl **-men**)
n Holländer m; **Dutchwoman** (pl
-women) n Holländerin f
duty [ˈdjuːtɪ] n Pflicht f; (*task*)
Aufgabe f; (*tax*) Zoll m; **on/off ~** im
Dienst/nicht im Dienst; **to be on
~** Dienst haben; **duty-free** adj
zollfrei; **~ shop** Dutyfreeshop m
duvet [ˈduːveɪ] n Federbett nt
DVD n abbr = **digital versatile
disk** DVD f; **DVD player** n
DVD-Player m; **DVD recorder** n
DVD-Rekorder m
dwelling [ˈdwelɪŋ] n Wohnung f
dwindle [ˈdwɪndl] vi schwinden
dye [daɪ] n Farbstoff m ▷ vt
färben
dynamic [daɪˈnæmɪk] adj
dynamisch

dynamo [ˈdaɪnəməʊ] n Dynamo m
dyslexia [dɪsˈleksɪə] n Legasthenie
f; **dyslexic** adj legasthenisch; **to
be ~** Legastheniker(in) sein

e

E [i:] *abbr* = **east** (*geo*) O; *abbr* = **ecstasy** (*drug*) Ecstasy *nt*

E111 form *n* ≈ Auslandskrankenschein *m*

each [i:tʃ] *adj* jeder/jede/jedes ▷ *pron* jeder/jede/jedes; **I'll have one of ~** ich nehme von jedem eins; **they ~ have a car** jeder von ihnen hat ein Auto; **~ other** einander, sich; **for/against ~ other** füreinander/gegeneinander ▷ *adv* je; **they cost 10 euros ~** sie kosten je 10 Euro, sie kosten 10 Euro das Stück

eager ['i:gə°] *adj* eifrig; **to be ~ to do sth** darauf brennen, etw zu tun

eagle ['i:gl] *n* Adler *m*

ear [ɪə°] *n* Ohr *nt*; **earache** *n* Ohrenschmerzen *pl*; **eardrum** *n* Trommelfell *nt*

earl [ɜ:l] *n* Graf *m*

early ['ɜ:lɪ] *adj, adv* früh; **to be 10 minutes ~** 10 Minuten zu früh kommen; **at the earliest** frühestens; **in ~ June/2008** Anfang Juni/2008; **~ retirement** vorzeitiger Ruhestand; **~ warning system** Frühwarnsystem *nt*

earn [ɜ:n] *vt* verdienen

earnest ['ɜ:nɪst] *adj* ernst; **in ~** im Ernst

earnings ['ɜ:nɪŋz] *npl* Verdienst *m*, Einkommen *nt*

earplug *n* Ohrenstöpsel *m*, Ohropax® *nt*; **earring** *n* Ohrring *m*

earth [ɜ:θ] *n* Erde *f*; **what on ~ ...?** was in aller Welt ...? ▷ *vt* erden; **earthenware** *n* Tonwaren *pl*; **earthquake** *n* Erdbeben *nt*

earwig ['ɪəwɪg] *n* Ohrwurm *m*

ease [i:z] *vt* (*pain*) lindern; (*burden*) erleichtern ▷ *n* (*easiness*) Leichtigkeit *f*; **to feel at ~** sich wohlfühlen; **to feel ill at ~** sich nicht wohlfühlen; **easily** ['i:zɪlɪ] *adv* leicht; **he is ~ the best** er ist mit Abstand der Beste

east [i:st] *n* Osten *m*; **to the ~ of** östlich von ▷ *adv* (*go, face*) nach Osten ▷ *adj* Ost-; **~ wind** Ostwind *m*; **eastbound** *adj* (in) Richtung Osten

Easter ['i:stə°] *n* Ostern *nt*; **at ~** zu Ostern; **Easter egg** *n* Osterei *nt*; **Easter Sunday** *n* Ostersonntag *m*

eastern ['i:stən] *adj* Ost-, östlich; **Eastern Europe** Osteuropa *nt*; **East Germany** *n* Ostdeutschland *nt*; **former ~** die ehemalige DDR, die neuen Bundesländer; **eastwards** ['i:stwədz] *adv* nach Osten

easy ['i:zɪ] *adj* leicht; (*task, solution*) einfach; (*life*) bequem; (*manner*) ungezwungen; **easy-going** *adj* gelassen

eat [i:t] (**ate, eaten**) *vt* essen; (*animal*) fressen; **eat out** *vi* zum

Essen ausgehen; **eat up** *vt* aufessen; (*animal*) auffressen

eaten ['i:tn] *pp of* **eat**

eavesdrop ['i:vzdrɒp] *vi* (heimlich) lauschen; **to ~ on sb** jdn belauschen

eccentric [ɪk'sentrɪk] *adj* exzentrisch

echo ['ekəʊ] (*pl* **-es**) *n* Echo *nt* ▷ *vi* widerhallen

ecological [i:kə'lɒdʒɪkl] *adj* ökologisch; **~ disaster** Umweltkatastrophe *f*; **ecology** [ɪ'kɒlədʒɪ] *n* Ökologie *f*

economic [i:kə'nɒmɪk] *adj* wirtschaftlich, Wirtschafts-; **~ aid** Wirtschaftshilfe *f*; **economical** *adj* wirtschaftlich; (*person*) sparsam; **economics** *nsing o pl* Wirtschaftswissenschaft *f*; **economist** [ɪ'kɒnəmɪst] *n* Wirtschaftswissenschaftler(in) *m(f)*; **economize** [ɪ'kɒnəmaɪz] *vi* sparen (*on* an +*dat*); **economy** [ɪ'kɒnəmɪ] *n* (*of state*) Wirtschaft *f*; (*thrift*) Sparsamkeit *f*; **economy class** *n* (*Aviat*) Economyclass *f*

ecstasy ['ekstəsɪ] *n* Ekstase *f*; (*drug*) Ecstasy *f*

eczema ['eksɪmə] *n* Ekzem *nt*

edge [edʒ] *n* Rand *m*; (*of knife*) Schneide *f*; **on ~** nervös; **edgy** ['edʒɪ] *adj* nervös

edible ['edɪbl] *adj* essbar

Edinburgh ['edɪnbərə] *n* Edinburg *nt*

edit ['edɪt] *vt* (*series, newspaper etc*) herausgeben; (*text*) redigieren; (*film*) schneiden; (*Inform*) editieren; **edition** [ɪ'dɪʃən] *n* Ausgabe *f*; **editor** *n* Redakteur(in) *m(f)*; (*of series etc*) Herausgeber(in) *m(f)*; **editorial** [edɪ'tɔ:rɪəl] *adj* Redaktions- ▷ *n* Leitartikel *m*

educate ['edjʊkeɪt] *vt* (*child*) erziehen; (*at school, university*) ausbilden; (*public*) aufklären;

educated *adj* gebildet; **education** [edjʊ'keɪʃən] *n* Erziehung *f*; (*studies, training*) Ausbildung *f*; (*subject of study*) Pädagogik *f*; (*system*) Schulwesen *nt*; (*knowledge*) Bildung *f*; **educational** *adj* pädagogisch; (*instructive*) lehrreich; **~ television** Schulfernsehen *nt*

eel [i:l] *n* Aal *m*

eerie ['ɪərɪ] *adj* unheimlich

effect [ɪ'fekt] *n* Wirkung *f* (*on* auf +*akk*); **to come into ~** in Kraft treten; **effective** *adj* wirksam, effektiv

effeminate [ɪ'femɪnət] *adj* (*of man*) tuntig

efficiency [ɪ'fɪʃənsɪ] *n* Leistungsfähigkeit *f*; (*of method*) Wirksamkeit *f*; **efficient** *adj* (*Tech*) leistungsfähig; (*method*) wirksam, effizient

effort ['efət] *n* Anstrengung *f*; (*attempt*) Versuch *m*; **to make an ~** sich anstrengen; **effortless** *adj* mühelos

e.g. *abbr* = **exempli gratia (for example)** z. B.

egg [eg] *n* Ei *nt*; **eggcup** *n* Eierbecher *m*; **eggplant** *n* (*US*) Aubergine *f*; **eggshell** *n* Eierschale *f*

ego ['i:gəʊ] (*pl* **-s**) *n* Ich *nt*; (*self-esteem*) Selbstbewusstsein *nt*; **ego(t)ist** ['egəʊ(t)ɪst] *n* Egozentriker(in) *m(f)*

Egypt ['i:dʒɪpt] *n* Ägypten *nt*; **Egyptian** [ɪ'dʒɪpʃən] *adj* ägyptisch ▷ *n* Ägypter(in) *m(f)*

eiderdown ['aɪdədaʊn] *n* Daunendecke *f*

eight [eɪt] *num* acht; **at the age of ~** im Alter von acht Jahren; **it's ~ (o'clock)** es ist acht Uhr ▷ *n* (*a. bus etc*) Acht *f*; (*boat*) Achter *m*; **eighteen** [eɪ'ti:n] *num* achtzehn ▷ *n* Achtzehn *f*; *see also* **eight**;

eighteenth adj achtzehnte(r, s); see also **eighth**; **eighth** [eɪtθ] adj achte(r, s); **the ~ of June** der achte Juni ▷ n (fraction) Achtel nt; **an ~ of a litre** ein Achtelliter; **eightieth** ['eɪtɪəθ] adj achtzigste(r, s); see also **eighth**; **eighty** ['eɪtɪ] num achtzig ▷ n Achtzig f; see also **eight**

Eire ['eərə] n die Republik Irland

either ['aɪðə*] conj: **~ ... or** entweder ... oder ▷ pron: **~ of the two** eine(r, s) von beiden ▷ adj: **on ~ side** auf beiden Seiten ▷ adv: **I won't go ~** ich gehe auch nicht

eject [ɪ'dʒekt] vt ausstoßen; (person) vertreiben

elaborate [ɪ'læbərət] adj (complex) kompliziert; (plan) ausgeklügelt; (decoration) kunstvoll ▷ vi [ɪ'læbəreɪt] **could you ~ on that?** könntest du/könnten Sie mehr darüber sagen?

elastic [ɪ'læstɪk] adj elastisch; **~ band** Gummiband nt

elbow ['elbəʊ] n Ellbogen m; **to give sb the ~** (fam) jdm den Laufpass geben

elder ['eldə*] adj (of two) älter ▷ n Ältere(r) mf; (Bot) Holunder m; **elderly** adj ältere(r, s) ▷ n: **the ~** die älteren Leute; **eldest** ['eldɪst] adj älteste(r, s)

elect [ɪ'lekt] vt wählen; **he was ~ed chairman** er wurde zum Vorsitzenden gewählt; **election** [ɪ'lekʃən] n Wahl f; **election campaign** n Wahlkampf m; **electioneering** [ɪlekʃə'nɪərɪŋ] n Wahlpropaganda f; **electorate** [ɪ'lektərɪt] n Wähler pl

electric [ɪ'lektrɪk] adj elektrisch; (car, motor, razor etc) Elektro-; **~ blanket** Heizdecke f; **~ cooker** Elektroherd m; **~ current** elektrischer Strom; **~ shock** Stromschlag m; **electrical** adj elektrisch; **~ goods/appliances** Elektrogeräte; **electrician** [ɪlek'trɪʃən] n Elektriker(in) m(f); **electricity** [ɪlek'trɪsɪtɪ] n Elektrizität f; **electrocute** [ɪ'lektrəʊkjuːt] vt durch einen Stromschlag töten; **electronic** [ɪlek'trɒnɪk] adj elektronisch

elegance ['elɪɡəns] n Eleganz f; **elegant** adj elegant

element ['elɪmənt] n Element nt; **an ~ of truth** ein Körnchen Wahrheit; **elementary** [elɪ'mentərɪ] adj einfach; (basic) grundlegend; **~ stage** Anfangsstadium nt; **~ school** (US) Grundschule f; **~ maths/French** Grundkenntnisse in Mathematik/Französisch

elephant ['elɪfənt] n Elefant m

elevator ['elɪveɪtə*] n (US) Fahrstuhl m

eleven [ɪ'levn] num elf ▷ n (team, bus etc) Elf f see **eight**; **eleventh** [ɪ'levnθ] adj elfte(r, s) ▷ n (fraction) Elftel nt see **eighth**

eligible ['elɪdʒəbl] adj infrage kommend; (for grant etc) berechtigt; **~ for a pension/competition** pensions-/teilnahmeberechtigt; **~ bachelor** begehrter Junggeselle

eliminate [ɪ'lɪmɪneɪt] vt ausschließen; (from aus), ausschalten; (problem etc) beseitigen; **elimination** n Ausschluss m (from aus); (of problem etc) Beseitigung f

elm [elm] n Ulme f

elope [ɪ'ləʊp] vi durchbrennen (with sb mit jdm)

eloquent ['eləkwənt] adj redegewandt

else [els] adv: **anybody/anything ~** (in addition) sonst (noch) jemand/etwas; (other) ein anderer/etwas anderes; **somebody ~** jemand anders; **everyone ~** alle anderen; **or ~** sonst; **elsewhere** adv anderswo, woanders; (direction) woandershin

ELT abbr = **English Language Teaching**

e-mail, **E-mail** ['i:meɪl] vi, vt mailen (sth to sb jdm etw) ▷ n E-Mail f; **e-mail address** n E-Mail-Adresse f

emancipated [ɪ'mænsɪpeɪtɪd] adj emanzipiert

embankment [ɪm'bæŋkmənt] n Böschung f; (for railway) Bahndamm m

embargo [ɪm'bɑːɡəʊ] (pl **-es**) n Embargo nt

embark [ɪm'bɑːk] vi an Bord gehen

embarrass [ɪm'bærəs] vt in Verlegenheit bringen; **embarrassed** adj verlegen; **embarrassing** adj peinlich

embassy ['embəsɪ] n Botschaft f

embrace [ɪm'breɪs] vt umarmen ▷ n Umarmung f

embroider [ɪm'brɔɪdə*] vt besticken; **embroidery** n Stickerei f

embryo ['embrɪəʊ] (pl **-s**) n Embryo m

emerald ['emərəld] n Smaragd m

emerge [ɪ'mɜːdʒ] vi auftauchen; **it ~d that ...** es stellte sich heraus, dass ...

emergency [ɪ'mɜːdʒənsɪ] n Notfall m ▷ adj Not-; **~ exit** Notausgang m; **~ landing** Notlandung f; **~ room** (US) Unfallstation f; **~ service** Notdienst m; **~ stop** Vollbremsung f

emigrate ['emɪɡreɪt] vi auswandern

emit [ɪ'mɪt] vt ausstoßen; (heat) abgeben

emotion [ɪ'məʊʃən] n Emotion f, Gefühl nt; **emotional** adj (person) emotional; (experience, moment, scene) ergreifend

emperor ['empərə*] n Kaiser m

emphasis ['emfəsɪs] n Betonung f; **emphasize** ['emfəsaɪz] vt betonen; **emphatic**, **emphatically** [ɪm'fætɪk, -lɪ] adj, adv nachdrücklich

empire ['empaɪə*] n Reich nt

employ [ɪm'plɔɪ] vt beschäftigen; (hire) anstellen; (use) anwenden; **employee** [emplɔɪ'iː] n Angestellte(r) mf; **employer** n Arbeitgeber(in) m(f); **employment** n Beschäftigung f; (position) Stellung f; **employment agency** n Stellenvermittlung f

empress ['emprɪs] n Kaiserin f

empty ['emptɪ] adj leer ▷ vt (contents) leeren; (container) ausleeren

enable [ɪ'neɪbl] vt: **to ~ sb to do sth** es jdm ermöglichen, etw zu tun

enamel [ɪ'næməl] n Email nt; (of teeth) Zahnschmelz m

enchanting [ɪn'tʃɑːntɪŋ] adj bezaubernd

enclose [ɪn'kləʊz] vt einschließen; (in letter) beilegen (in, with dat); **enclosure** [ɪn'kləʊʒə*] n (for animals) Gehege nt; (in letter) Anlage f

encore ['ɒŋkɔː*] n Zugabe f

encounter [ɪn'kaʊntə*] n Begegnung f ▷ vt (person) begegnen +dat; (difficulties) stoßen auf +akk

encourage [ɪn'kʌrɪdʒ] vt ermutigen; **encouragement** n Ermutigung f

encyclopaedia
[ensaɪkləʊ'piːdɪə] n Lexikon nt, Enzyklopädie f

end [end] n Ende nt; (of film, play etc) Schluss m; (purpose) Zweck m; **at the ~ of May** Ende Mai; **in the ~** schließlich; **to come to an ~** zu Ende gehen ▷ vt beenden ▷ vi enden; **end up** vi enden

endanger [ɪn'deɪndʒə°] vt gefährden; **~ed species** vom Aussterben bedrohte Art

endeavour [ɪn'devə°] n Bemühung f ▷ vi sich bemühen (to do sth etw zu tun)

ending ['endɪŋ] n (of book) Ausgang m; (last part) Schluss m; (of word) Endung f; **endless** ['endlɪs] adj endlos; (possibilities) unendlich

endurance [ɪn'djʊərəns] n Ausdauer f; **endure** [ɪn'djʊə°] vt ertragen

enemy ['enɪmɪ] n Feind(in) m(f) ▷ adj feindlich

energetic [enə'dʒetɪk] adj energiegeladen; (active) aktiv; **energy** ['enədʒɪ] n Energie f

enforce [ɪn'fɔːs] vt durchsetzen; (obedience) erzwingen

engage [ɪn'geɪdʒ] vt (employ) einstellen; (singer, performer) engagieren; **engaged** adj verlobt; (toilet, telephone line) besetzt; **to get ~** sich verloben (to mit); **engaged tone** n (Brit Tel) Belegtzeichen nt; **engagement** n (to marry) Verlobung f; **~ ring** Verlobungsring m; **engaging** adj gewinnend

engine ['endʒɪn] n (Auto) Motor m; (Rail) Lokomotive f; **~ failure** (Auto) Motorschaden m; **~ trouble** (Auto) Defekt m am Motor; **engineer** [endʒɪ'nɪə°] n Ingenieur(in) m(f); (US Rail) Lokomotivführer(in) m(f);

engineering [endʒɪ'nɪərɪŋ] n Technik f; (mechanical ~) Maschinenbau m; (subject) Ingenieurwesen nt; **engine immobilizer** n (Auto) Wegfahrsperre f

England ['ɪŋglənd] n England nt; **English** adj englisch; **he's ~** er ist Engländer; **the ~ Channel** der Ärmelkanal ▷ n (language) Englisch nt; **in ~** auf Englisch; **to translate into ~** ins Englische übersetzen; (people) **the ~** pl die Engländer; **Englishman** (pl **-men**) n Engländer m; **Englishwoman** (pl **-women**) n Engländerin f

engrave [ɪn'greɪv] vt eingravieren; **engraving** n Stich m

engrossed [ɪn'grəʊst] adj vertieft (in sth in etw akk)

enigma [ɪ'nɪgmə] n Rätsel nt

enjoy [ɪn'dʒɔɪ] vt genießen; **I ~ reading** ich lese gern; **he ~s teasing her** es macht ihm Spaß, sie aufzuziehen; **did you ~ the film?** hat dir der Film gefallen?; **enjoyable** adj angenehm; (entertaining) unterhaltsam; **enjoyment** n Vergnügen nt; (stronger) Freude f (of an +dat)

enlarge [ɪn'lɑːdʒ] vt vergrößern; (expand) erweitern; **enlargement** n Vergrößerung f

enormous, enormously [ɪ'nɔːməs, -lɪ] adj, adv riesig, ungeheuer

enough [ɪ'nʌf] adj genug; **that's ~** das reicht!; (stop it) Schluss damit!; **I've had ~** das hat mir gereicht; (to eat) ich bin satt ▷ adv genug, genügend

enquire [ɪn'kwaɪə°] vi sich erkundigen (about nach); **enquiry** [ɪn'kwaɪərɪ] n (question) Anfrage f; (for information) Erkundigung f (about über +akk); (investigation)

Untersuchung f; **"Enquiries"**
„Auskunft"

enrol [ɪnˈrəʊl] vi sich
einschreiben; (for course, school)
sich anmelden; **enrolment** n
Einschreibung f, Anmeldung f

en suite [ɒnˈswiːt] adj, n: **room
with ~** (**bathroom**) Zimmer nt mit
eigenem Bad

ensure [ɪnˈʃʊə*] vt sicherstellen

enter [ˈentə*] vt eintreten in
+akk, betreten; (drive into)
einfahren in +akk; (country)
einreisen in +akk; (in list)
eintragen; (Inform) eingeben; (race,
contest) teilnehmen an +dat ▷ vi
(towards speaker) hereinkommen;
(away from speaker) hineingehen

enterprise [ˈentəpraɪz] n
(Comm) Unternehmen nt

entertain [entəˈteɪn] vt (guest)
bewirten; (amuse) unterhalten;
entertaining adj unterhaltsam;
entertainment n (amusement)
Unterhaltung f

enthusiasm [ɪnˈθjuːzɪæzəm] n
Begeisterung f; **enthusiastic**
[ɪnθjuːzɪˈæstɪk] adj begeistert
(about von)

entice [ɪnˈtaɪs] vt locken; (lead
astray) verleiten

entire, **entirely** [ɪnˈtaɪə*, -lɪ] adj,
adv ganz

entitle [ɪnˈtaɪtl] vt (qualify)
berechtigen (to zu); (name)
betiteln

entrance [ˈentrəns] n Eingang
m; (for vehicles) Einfahrt f; (entering)
Eintritt m; (Theat) Auftritt m;
entrance exam n
Aufnahmeprüfung f; **entrance fee**
n Eintrittsgeld nt

entrust [ɪnˈtrʌst] vt: **to ~ sb
with sth** jdm etw anvertrauen

entry [ˈentrɪ] n (way in) Eingang
m; (entering) Eintritt m; (in vehicle)
Einfahrt f; (into country) Einreise f;
(admission) Zutritt m; (in diary,
accounts) Eintrag m; **"no ~"**
„Eintritt verboten"; (for vehicles)
„Einfahrt verboten"; **entry phone**
n Türsprechanlage f

E-number n (food additive)
E-Nummer f

envelope [ˈenvələʊp] n
(Brief)umschlag m

enviable [ˈenvɪəbl] adj benei-
denswert; **envious** [ˈenvɪəs] adj
neidisch

environment [ɪnˈvaɪərənmənt]
n Umgebung f; (ecology) Umwelt f;
environmental [ɪnvaɪərənˈmen-
təl] adj Umwelt-; **~ pollution**
Umweltverschmutzung f;
environmentalist n Umwelt-
schützer(in) m(f)

envy [ˈenvɪ] n Neid m (of auf
+akk) ▷ vt beneiden (sb sth jdn um
etw)

epic [ˈepɪk] n Epos nt; (film)
Monumentalfilm m

epidemic [epɪˈdemɪk] n Epidemie f

epilepsy [ˈepɪlepsɪ] n Epilepsie f;
epileptic [epɪˈleptɪk] adj
epileptisch

episode [ˈepɪsəʊd] n Episode f;
(TV) Folge f

epoch [ˈiːpɒk] n Zeitalter nt,
Epoche f

equal [ˈiːkwl] adj gleich (to +dat)
▷ n Gleichgestellte(r) mf ▷ vt
gleichen; (match) gleichkommen
+dat; **two times two ~s four** zwei
mal zwei ist gleich vier; **equality**
[ɪˈkwɒlɪtɪ] n Gleichheit f; (equal
rights) Gleichberechtigung f;
equalize vi (Sport) ausgleichen;
equalizer n (Sport)
Ausgleichstreffer m; **equally** adv
gleich; (on the other hand)
andererseits; **equation**
[ɪˈkweɪʒən] n (Math) Gleichung f

equator [ɪˈkweɪtə*] n Äquator m

equilibrium [iːkwɪˈlɪbrɪəm] n
Gleichgewicht nt
equip [ɪˈkwɪp] vt ausrüsten;
(kitchen) ausstatten; **equipment** n
Ausrüstung f; (for kitchen)
Ausstattung f; **electrical**
~ Elektrogeräte pl
equivalent [ɪˈkwɪvələnt] adj
gleichwertig (to dat);
(corresponding) entsprechend (to
dat) ▷ n Äquivalent nt; (amount)
gleiche Menge; (in money)
Gegenwert m
era [ˈɪərə] n Ära f, Zeitalter nt
erase [ɪˈreɪz] vt ausradieren;
(tape, disk) löschen; **eraser** n
Radiergummi m
erect [ɪˈrekt] adj aufrecht ▷ vt
(building, monument) errichten;
(tent) aufstellen; **erection** n
Errichtung f; (Anat) Erektion f
erode [ɪˈrəʊd] vt zerfressen;
(land) auswaschen; (rights, power)
aushöhlen; **erosion** [ɪˈrəʊʒən] n
Erosion f
erotic [ɪˈrɒtɪk] adj erotisch
err [ɜː°] vi sich irren
errand [ˈerənd] n Besorgung f
erratic [ɪˈrætɪk] adj (behaviour)
unberechenbar; (bus link etc)
unregelmäßig; (performance)
unbeständig
error [ˈerə°] n Fehler m; **in**
~ irrtümlicherweise; **error
message** n (Inform)
Fehlermeldung f
erupt [ɪˈrʌpt] vi ausbrechen
escalator [ˈeskəleɪtə°] n Rolltreppe f
escalope [ˈeskələp] n Schnitzel
nt
escape [ɪˈskeɪp] n Flucht f; (from
prison etc) Ausbruch m; **to have a
narrow** ~ gerade noch
davonkommen; **there's no** ~ (fig)
es gibt keinen Ausweg ▷ vt
(pursuers) entkommen +dat;

(punishment etc) entgehen +dat ▷ vi
(from pursuers) entkommen (from
dat); (from prison etc) ausbrechen
(from dat); (leak: gas) ausströmen;
(water) auslaufen
escort [ˈeskɔːt] n (companion)
Begleiter(in) m(f); (guard) Eskorte f
▷ vt [ɪˈskɔːt] (lady) begleiten
especially [ɪˈspeʃəlɪ] adv
besonders
espionage [ˈespɪənɑːʒ] n Spio-
nage f
Esquire [ɪˈskwaɪə°] n (Brit: in
address): **J. Brown, Esq** Herrn J.
Brown
essay [ˈeseɪ] n Aufsatz m;
(literary) Essay m
essential [ɪˈsenʃəl] adj (necessary) unentbehrlich,
unverzichtbar; (basic) wesentlich
▷ n **the ~s** pl das Wesentliche;
essentially adv im Wesentlichen
establish [ɪˈstæblɪʃ] vt (set up)
gründen; (introduce) einführen;
(relations) aufnehmen; (prove)
nachweisen; **to ~ that ...**
feststellen, dass ...;
establishment n Institution f;
(business) Unternehmen nt
estate [ɪˈsteɪt] n Gut nt; (of
deceased) Nachlass m; (housing ~)
Siedlung f; (country house) Landsitz
m; **estate agent** n (Brit)
Grundstücksmakler(in) m(f),
Immobilienmakler(in) m(f); **estate
car** n (Brit) Kombiwagen m
estimate [ˈestɪmət] n Schätzung
f; (Comm: of price)
Kostenvoranschlag m ▷ [ˈestɪmeɪt]
vt schätzen
Estonia [eˈstəʊnɪə] n Estland nt;
Estonian [eˈstəʊnɪən] ▷ adj
estnisch; ▷ n (person) Este m;
Estin f; (language) Estnisch nt
estuary [ˈestjʊərɪ] n Mündung f
etching [ˈetʃɪŋ] n Radierung f
eternal, eternally [ɪˈtɜːnl, -nəlɪ]

adj, adv ewig; **eternity** *n* Ewigkeit *f*

ethical ['eθɪkəl] *adj* ethisch; **ethics** ['eθɪks] *npl* Ethik *f*

Ethiopia [i:θɪ'əʊpɪə] *n* Äthiopien *nt*

ethnic ['eθnɪk] *adj* ethnisch; (*clothes etc*) landesüblich; **~ minority** ethnische Minderheit

EU *abbr* = **European Union** EU *f*

euphemism ['ju:fɪmɪzəm] *n* Euphemismus *m*

euro ['jʊərəʊ] (*pl* **-s**) *n* (*Fin*) Euro *m*; **~ symbol** Eurozeichen *nt*; **Eurocheque** ['jʊərəʊtʃek] *n* Euroscheck *m*; **Europe** ['jʊərəp] *n* Europa *nt*; **European** [jʊərə'pi:ən] *adj* europäisch; **~ Parliament** Europäisches Parlament; **~ Union** Europäische Union ▷ *n* Europäer(in) *m(f)*; **Eurosceptic** ['jʊərəʊskeptɪk] *n* Euroskeptiker(in) *m(f)*; **Eurotunnel** *n* Eurotunnel *m*

evacuate [ɪ'vækjʊeɪt] *vt* (*place*) räumen; (*people*) evakuieren

evade [ɪ'veɪd] *vt* ausweichen +*dat*; (*pursuers*) sich entziehen +*dat*

evaluate [ɪ'væljʊeɪt] *vt* auswerten

evaporate [ɪ'væpəreɪt] *vi* verdampfen; (*fig*) verschwinden; **~d milk** Kondensmilch *f*

even ['i:vən] *adj* (*flat*) eben; (*regular*) gleichmäßig; (*equal*) gleich; (*number*) gerade; **the score is ~** es steht unentschieden ▷ *adv* sogar; **~ you** selbst (*o* sogar) du/Sie; **~ if** selbst wenn, wenn auch; **~ though** obwohl; **not ~** nicht einmal; **~ better** noch besser; **even out** *vi* (*prices*) sich einpendeln

evening ['i:vnɪŋ] *n* Abend *m*; **in the ~** abends, am Abend; **this ~** heute Abend; **evening class** *n* Abendkurs *m*; **evening dress** *n* (*generally*) Abendkleidung *f*; (*woman's*) Abendkleid *nt*

evenly ['i:vənlɪ] *adv* gleichmäßig

event [ɪ'vent] *n* Ereignis *nt*; (*organized*) Veranstaltung *f*; (*Sport: discipline*) Disziplin *f*; **in the ~ of** im Falle +*gen*; **eventful** *adj* ereignisreich

eventual [ɪ'ventʃʊəl] *adj* (*final*) letztendlich; **eventually** [ɪ'ventʃʊəlɪ] *adv* (*at last*) am Ende; (*given time*) schließlich

ever ['evə°] *adv* (*at any time*) je(mals); **don't ~ do that again** tu das ja nie wieder; **he's the best ~** er ist der Beste, den es je gegeben hat; **have you ~ been to the States?** bist du schon einmal in den Staaten gewesen?; **for ~** (für) immer; **for ~ and ~** auf immer und ewig; **~ so ...** (*fam*) äußerst ...; **~ so drunk** ganz schön betrunken

every ['evrɪ] *adj* jeder/jede/jedes; **~ day** jeden Tag; **~ other day** jeden zweiten Tag; **~ five days** alle fünf Tage; **I have ~ reason to believe that ...** ich habe allen Grund anzunehmen, dass ...; **everybody** *pron* jeder, alle *pl*; **everyday** *adj* (*commonplace*) alltäglich; (*clothes, language etc*) Alltags-; **everyone** *pron* jeder, alle *pl*; **everything** *pron* alles; **everywhere** *adv* überall; (*with direction*) überallhin

evidence ['evɪdəns] *n* Beweise *pl*; (*single piece*) Beweis *m*; (*testimony*) Aussage *f*; (*signs*) Spuren *pl*; **evident, evidently** *adj, adv* offensichtlich

evil ['i:vl] *adj* böse ▷ *n* Böse(s) *nt*; **an ~** ein Übel

evolution [i:və'lu:ʃən] *n* Entwicklung *f*; (*of life*) Evolution *f*; **evolve** [ɪ'vɒlv] *vi* sich entwickeln

ex- [eks] *pref* Ex-, ehemalig;

~boyfriend Exfreund m; **~wife** frühere Frau, Exfrau f; **ex** n (fam) Verflossene(r) mf, Ex mf

exact [ɪgˈzækt] adj genau; **exactly** adv genau; **not ~ fast** nicht gerade schnell

exaggerate [ɪgˈzædʒəreɪt] vt, vi übertreiben; **exaggerated** adj übertrieben; **exaggeration** n Übertreibung f

exam [ɪgˈzæm] n Prüfung f; **examination** [ɪgzæmɪˈneɪʃən] n (Med etc) Untersuchung f, Prüfung f; (at university) Examen nt; (at customs etc) Kontrolle f; **examine** [ɪgˈzæmɪn] vt untersuchen (for auf +akk); (check) kontrollieren, prüfen; **examiner** n Prüfer(in) m(f)

example [ɪgˈzɑːmpl] n Beispiel nt (of für +akk); **for ~** zum Beispiel

excavation [ekskəˈveɪʃən] n Ausgrabung f

exceed [ɪkˈsiːd] vt überschreiten, übertreffen; **exceedingly** adv äußerst

excel [ɪkˈsel] vt übertreffen; **he ~led himself** er hat sich selbst übertroffen ▷ vi sich auszeichnen (in in +dat, at bei); **excellent, excellently** [ˈeksələnt, -lɪ] adj, adv ausgezeichnet

except [ɪkˈsept] prep: **~** außer +dat; **~ for** abgesehen von ▷ vt ausnehmen; **exception** [ɪkˈsepʃən] n Ausnahme f; **exceptional, exceptionally** [ɪkˈsepʃənl, -nəlɪ] adj, adv außergewöhnlich

excess [ekˈses] n Übermaß nt (of an +dat); **excess baggage** n Übergepäck nt; **excesses** npl Exzesse pl; (drink, sex) Ausschweifungen pl; **excessive, excessively** adj, adv übermäßig; **excess weight** n Übergewicht nt

exchange [ɪksˈtʃeɪndʒ] n Austausch m (for gegen); (of bought items) Umtausch m (for gegen); (Fin) Wechsel m; (Tel) Vermittlung f, Zentrale f ▷ vt austauschen; (goods) tauschen; (bought items) umtauschen (for gegen); (money, blows) wechseln; **exchange rate** n Wechselkurs m

excite [ɪkˈsaɪt] vt erregen; **excited** adj aufgeregt; **to get ~** sich aufregen; **exciting** adj aufregend; (book, film) spannend

exclamation [ekskləˈmeɪʃən] n Ausruf m; **exclamation mark**, **exclamation point** (US) n Ausrufezeichen nt

exclude [ɪksˈkluːd] vt ausschließen; **exclusion** [ɪksˈkluːʒən] n Ausschluss m; **exclusive** [ɪksˈkluːsɪv] adj (select) exklusiv; (sole) ausschließlich; **exclusively** adv ausschließlich

excrement [ˈekskrɪmənt] n Kot m, Exkremente pl

excruciating [ɪksˈkruːʃieɪtɪŋ] adj fürchterlich, entsetzlich

excursion [ɪksˈkɜːʃən] n Ausflug m

excusable [ɪksˈkjuːzəbl] adj entschuldbar; **excuse** [ɪksˈkjuːz] vt entschuldigen; **~ me** Entschuldigung!; **to ~ sb for sth** jdm etw verzeihen; **to ~ sb from sth** jdn von etw befreien ▷ [ɪksˈkjuːs] n Entschuldigung f, Ausrede f

ex-directory [eksdaɪˈrektərɪ] adj: **to be ~** (Brit Tel) nicht im Telefonbuch stehen

execute [ˈeksɪkjuːt] vt (carry out) ausführen; (kill) hinrichten; **execution** n (killing) Hinrichtung f; (carrying out) Ausführung f; **executive** [ɪgˈzekjutɪv] n (Comm) leitender Angestellter, leitende Angestellte

exemplary [ɪg'zemplərɪ] adj beispielhaft

exempt [ɪg'zempt] adj befreit (from von) ▷ vt befreien

exercise ['eksəsaɪz] n (in school, sports) Übung f; (movement) Bewegung f; **to get more ~** mehr Sport treiben; **exercise bike** n Heimtrainer m; **exercise book** n Heft nt

exert [ɪg'zɜːt] vt (influence) ausüben

exhaust [ɪg'zɔːst] n (fumes) Abgase pl; (Auto) **~ (pipe)** Auspuff m; **exhausted** adj erschöpft; **exhausting** adj anstrengend

exhibit [ɪg'zɪbɪt] n (in exhibition) Ausstellungsstück nt; **exhibition** [eksɪ'bɪʃən] n Ausstellung f; **exhibitionist** [eksɪ'bɪʃənɪst] n Selbstdarsteller(in) m(f); **exhibitor** n Aussteller(in) m(f)

exhilarating [ɪg'zɪləreɪtɪŋ] adj belebend, erregend

exile ['eksaɪl] n Exil nt; (person) Verbannte(r) mf ▷ vt verbannen

exist [ɪg'zɪst] vi existieren; (live) leben (on von); **existence** n Existenz f; **to come into ~** entstehen; **existing** adj bestehend

exit ['eksɪt] n Ausgang m; (for vehicles) Ausfahrt f; **exit poll** n Umfrage direkt nach dem Wahlgang

exorbitant [ɪg'zɔːbɪtənt] adj astronomisch

exotic [ɪg'zɒtɪk] adj exotisch

expand [ɪks'pænd] vt ausdehnen, erweitern ▷ vi sich ausdehnen; **expansion** [ɪks'pænʃən] n Expansion f, Erweiterung f

expect [ɪk'spekt] vt erwarten; (suppose) annehmen; **he ~s me to do it** er erwartet, dass ich es mache; **I ~ it'll rain** es wird wohl regnen; **I ~ so** ich denke schon ▷ vi: **she's ~ing** sie bekommt ein Kind

expedition [ekspɪ'dɪʃən] n Expedition f

expenditure [ɪk'spendɪtʃə*] n Ausgaben pl

expense [ɪk'spens] n Kosten pl; (single cost) Ausgabe f; (business) **~s** pl Spesen pl; **at sb's ~** auf jds Kosten; **expensive** [ɪk'spensɪv] adj teuer

experience [ɪk'spɪərɪəns] n Erfahrung f; (particular incident) Erlebnis nt; **by/from ~** aus Erfahrung ▷ vt erfahren, erleben; (hardship) durchmachen; **experienced** adj erfahren

experiment [ɪk'sperɪmənt] n Versuch m, Experiment nt ▷ vi experimentieren

expert ['ekspɜːt] n Experte m, Expertin f; (professional) Fachmann m, Fachfrau f; (Jur) Sachverständige(r) mf ▷ adj fachmännisch, Fach-; **expertise** [ekspə'tiːz] n Sachkenntnis f

expire [ɪk'spaɪə*] vi (end) ablaufen; **expiry date** [ɪk'spaɪərɪdeɪt] n Verfallsdatum nt

explain [ɪk'spleɪn] vt erklären (sth to sb jdm etw); **explanation** [eksplə'neɪʃən] n Erklärung f

explicit [ɪk'splɪsɪt] adj ausdrücklich, eindeutig

explode [ɪk'spləʊd] vi explodieren

exploit [ɪk'splɔɪt] vt ausbeuten

explore [ɪk'splɔː*] vt erforschen

explosion [ɪk'spləʊʒən] n Explosion f; **explosive** [ɪk'spləʊsɪv] adj explosiv ▷ n Sprengstoff m

export [ek'spɔːt] vt, vi exportieren ▷ ['ekspɔːt] n Export m ▷ adj (trade) Export-

expose [ɪk'spəʊz] vt (to danger

etc) aussetzen (*to dat*); (*uncover*) freilegen; (*imposter*) entlarven; **exposed** *adj* (*position*) ungeschützt; **exposure** [ɪkˈspəʊʒə*] *n* (*Med*) Unterkühlung *f*; (*Foto: time*) Belichtung(szeit) *f*; **24 ~s** 24 Aufnahmen

express [ɪkˈspres] *adj* (*speedy*) Express-, Schnell-; **~ delivery** Eilzustellung *f* ▷ *n* (*Rail*) Schnellzug *m* ▷ *vt* ausdrücken ▷ *vr*: **to ~ oneself** sich ausdrücken; **expression** [ɪkˈspreʃən] *n* (*phrase*) Ausdruck *m*; (*look*) Gesichtsausdruck *m*; **expressive** *adj* ausdrucksvoll; **expressway** *n* (*US*) Schnellstraße *f*

extend [ɪkˈstend] *vt* (*arms*) ausstrecken; (*lengthen*) verlängern; (*building*) vergrößern, ausbauen; (*business, limits*) erweitern; **extension** [ɪkˈstenʃən] *n* (*lengthening*) Verlängerung *f*; (*of building*) Anbau *m*; (*Tel*) Anschluss *m*; (*of business, limits*) Erweiterung *f*; **extensive** [ɪkˈstensɪv] *adj* (*knowledge*) umfangreich; (*use*) häufig; **extent** [ɪkˈstent] *n* (*length*) Länge *f*; (*size*) Ausdehnung *f*; (*scope*) Umfang *m*, Ausmaß *nt*; **to a certain/large ~** in gewissem/hohem Maße

exterior [ekˈstɪərɪə*] *n* Äußere(s) *nt*

external [ekˈstɜːnl] *adj* äußere(r, s), Außen-; **externally** *adv* äußerlich

extinct [ɪkˈstɪŋkt] *adj* (*species*) ausgestorben

extinguish [ɪkˈstɪŋgwɪʃ] *vt* löschen; **extinguisher** *n* Löschgerät *nt*

extra [ˈekstrə] *adj* zusätzlich; **~ charge** Zuschlag *m*; **~ time** (*Sport*) Verlängerung *f* ▷ *adv*

besonders; **~ large** (*clothing*) übergroß ▷ *npl*: **~s** zusätzliche Kosten *pl*; (*food*) Beilagen *pl*; (*accessories*) Zubehör *nt*; (*for car etc*) Extras *pl*

extract [ɪkˈstrækt] *vt* herausziehen (*from* aus); (*tooth*) ziehen ▷ [ˈekstrækt] *n* (*from book etc*) Auszug *m*

extraordinary [ɪkˈstrɔːdnɪrɪ] *adj* außerordentlich; (*unusual*) ungewöhnlich; (*amazing*) erstaunlich

extreme [ɪkˈstriːm] *adj* äußerste(r, s); (*drastic*) extrem ▷ *n* Extrem *nt*; **extremely** *adv* äußerst, höchst; **extreme sports** *npl* Extremsportarten *pl*; **extremist** [ɪkˈstriːmɪst] *adj* extremistisch ▷ *n* Extremist *m*

extricate [ˈekstrɪkeɪt] *vt* befreien (*from* aus)

extrovert [ˈekstrəʊvɜːt] *adj* extrovertiert

exuberance [ɪgˈzuːbərəns] *n* Überschwang *m*; **exuberant** *adj* überschwänglich

exultation [egzʌlˈteɪʃən] *n* Jubel *m*

eye [aɪ] *n* Auge *nt*; **to keep an ~ on sb/sth** auf jdn/etw aufpassen ▷ *vt* mustern; **eyebrow** *n* Augenbraue *f*; **eyelash** *n* Wimper *f*; **eyelid** *n* Augenlid *nt*; **eyeliner** *n* Eyeliner *m*; **eyeopener** *n*: **that was an ~** das hat mir die Augen geöffnet; **eyeshadow** *n* Lidschatten *m*; **eyesight** *n* Sehkraft *f*; **eyesore** *n* Schandfleck *m*; **eye witness** *n* Augenzeuge *m*, Augenzeugin *f*

f

fabric ['fæbrɪk] *n* Stoff *m*
fabulous ['fæbjʊləs] *adj* sagenhaft
façade [fə'sɑːd] *n* (*a. fig*) Fassade *f*
face [feɪs] *n* Gesicht *nt*; (*of clock*) Zifferblatt *nt*; (*of mountain*) Wand *f*; **in the ~ of** trotz +*gen*; **to be ~ to ~** (*people*) einander gegenüberstehen ▷ *vt, vi* (*person*) gegenüberstehen +*dat*; (*at table*) gegenübersitzen +*dat*; **to ~ north** (*room*) nach Norden gehen; **to ~ (up to) the facts** den Tatsachen ins Auge sehen; **to be ~d with sth** mit etw konfrontiert sein; **face lift** *n* Gesichtsstraffung *f*; (*fig*) Verschönerung *f*; **face powder** *n* Gesichtspuder *m*
facet ['fæsɪt] *n* (*fig*) Aspekt *m*
face value *n* Nennwert *m*
facial ['feɪʃəl] *adj* Gesichts- ▷ *n* (*fam*) (kosmetische) Gesichtsbehandlung

facilitate [fə'sɪlɪteɪt] *vt* erleichtern
facility [fə'sɪlɪtɪ] *n* (*building etc to be used*) Einrichtung *f*, Möglichkeit *f*; (*installation*) Anlage *f*; (*skill*) Gewandtheit *f*
fact [fækt] *n* Tatsache *f*; **as a matter of ~, in ~** eigentlich, tatsächlich
factor ['fæktə°] *n* Faktor *m*
factory ['fæktərɪ] *n* Fabrik *f*; **factory outlet** *n* Fabrikverkauf *m*
factual ['fæktjʊəl] *adj* sachlich
faculty ['fækəltɪ] *n* Fähigkeit *f*; (*at university*) Fakultät *f*; (*US: teaching staff*) Lehrkörper *m*
fade [feɪd] *vi* (*a. fig*) verblassen; **faded** *adj* verblasst, verblichen
faff about ['fæfəbaʊt] *vi* (*Brit fam*) herumwursteln
fag [fæg] *n* (*Brit fam: cigarette*) Kippe *f*; (*US fam pej*) Schwule(r) *m*
Fahrenheit ['færənhaɪt] *n* Fahrenheit
fail [feɪl] *vt* (*exam*) nicht bestehen ▷ *vi* versagen; (*plan, marriage*) scheitern; (*student*) durchfallen; (*eyesight*) nachlassen; **words ~ me** ich bin sprachlos; **failing** *n* Schwäche *f*; **failure** ['feɪljə°] *n* (*person*) Versager(in) *m(f)*; (*act, a. Tech*) Versagen *nt*; (*of engine etc*) Ausfall *m*; (*of plan, marriage*) Scheitern *nt*
faint [feɪnt] *adj* schwach; (*sound*) leise; (*fam*) **I haven't the ~est** (**idea**) ich habe keinen blassen Schimmer ▷ *vi* ohnmächtig werden (**with** vor +*dat*); **faintness** *n* (*Med*) Schwächegefühl *nt*
fair [fɛə°] *adj* (*hair*) (dunkel)blond; (*skin*) hell; (*just*) gerecht, fair; (*reasonable*) ganz ordentlich; (*in school*) befriedigend; (*weather*) schön; (*wind*) günstig; **a ~ number/amount of** ziemlich viele/viel ▷ *adv*: **to play ~** fair

spielen; (*fig*) fair sein; **~ enough** in Ordnung! ▷ *n* (*fun~*) Jahrmarkt *m*; (*Comm*) Messe *f*; **fair-haired** *adj* (dunkel)blond; **fairly** *adv* (*honestly*) fair; (*rather*) ziemlich

fairy ['fɛərɪ] *n* Fee *f*; **fairy tale** *n* Märchen *nt*

faith [feɪθ] *n* (*trust*) Vertrauen *nt* (*in sb* zu jdm); (*Rel*) Glaube *m*; **faithful, faithfully** *adj*, *adv* treu; **Yours ~ly** Hochachtungsvoll

fake [feɪk] *n* (*thing*) Fälschung *f* ▷ *adj* vorgetäuscht ▷ *vt* fälschen

falcon ['fɔːlkən] *n* Falke *m*

fall [fɔːl] *vi* (**fell, fallen**) *vi* fallen; (*from a height, badly*) stürzen; **to ~ ill** krank werden; **to ~ asleep** einschlafen; **to ~ in love** sich verlieben ▷ *n* Fall *m*; (*accident, fig: of regime*) Sturz *m*; (*decrease*) Sinken *nt* (*in* +*gen*); (*US: autumn*) Herbst *m*; **fall apart** *vi* auseinanderfallen; **fall behind** *vi* zurückbleiben; (*with work, rent*) in Rückstand geraten; **fall down** *vi* (*person*) hinfallen; **fall off** *vi* herunterfallen; (*decrease*) zurückgehen; **fall out** *vi* herausfallen; (*quarrel*) sich streiten; **fall over** *vi* hinfallen; **fall through** *vi* (*plan etc*) ins Wasser fallen

fallen ['fɔːlən] *pp of* **fall**

fallout ['fɔːlaʊt] *n* radioaktiver Niederschlag, Fall-out *m*

false [fɔːls] *adj* falsch; (*artificial*) künstlich; **false alarm** *n* blinder Alarm; **false start** *n* (*Sport*) Fehlstart *m*; **false teeth** *npl* (künstliches) Gebiss

fame [feɪm] *n* Ruhm *m*

familiar [fə'mɪlɪə*] *adj* vertraut, bekannt; **to be ~ with** vertraut sein mit, gut kennen; **familiarity** [fəmɪlɪ'ærɪtɪ] *n* Vertrautheit *f*

family ['fæmɪlɪ] *n* Familie *f*; (*including relations*) Verwandtschaft

f; **family man** *n* Familienvater *m*; **family name** *n* Familienname *m*, Nachname *m*; **family practitioner** *n* (*US*) Allgemeinarzt *m*, Allgemeinärztin *f*

famine ['fæmɪn] *n* Hungersnot *f*; **famished** ['fæmɪʃt] *adj* ausgehungert

famous ['feɪməs] *adj* berühmt

fan [fæn] *n* (*hand-held*) Fächer *m*; (*Elec*) Ventilator *m*; (*admirer*) Fan *m*

fanatic [fə'nætɪk] *n* Fanatiker(in) *m(f)*

fancy ['fænsɪ] *adj* (*elaborate*) kunstvoll; (*unusual*) ausgefallen ▷ *vt* (*like*) gernhaben; **he fancies her** er steht auf sie; **~ that!** stell dir vor!, so was!; **fancy dress** *n* Kostüm *nt*

fan heater ['fænhiːtə*] *n* Heizlüfter *m*; **fanlight** *n* Oberlicht *nt*

fan mail *n* Fanpost *f*

fantasise ['fæntəsaɪz] *vi* träumen (*about* von); **fantastic** [fæn'tæstɪk] *adj* (*a. fam*) fantastisch; **that's ~** (*fam*) das ist ja toll!; **fantasy** ['fæntəzɪ] *n* Fantasie *f*

far [fɑː*] (**further** *o* **farther, furthest** *o* **farthest**) *adj* weit; **the ~ end of the room** das andere Ende des Zimmers; **the Far East** der Ferne Osten ▷ *adv* weit; **~ better** viel besser; **by ~ the best** bei weitem der/die/das Beste; **as ~ as ...** bis zum *o* zur ...; (*with place name*) bis nach ...; **as ~ as I'm concerned** was mich betrifft, von mir aus; **so ~** soweit, bisher; **faraway** *adj* weit entfernt; (*look*) verträumt

fare [fɛə*] *n* Fahrpreis *m*; (*money*) Fahrgeld *nt*

farm [fɑːm] *n* Bauernhof *m*, Farm *f*; **farmer** *n* Bauer *m*, Bäuerin *f*, Landwirt(in) *m(f)*; **farmhouse** *n*

Bauernhaus nt; **farming** n Landwirtschaft f; **farmland** n Ackerland nt; **farmyard** n Hof m

far-reaching ['fɑːriːtʃɪŋ] adj weit reichend; **far-sighted** adj weitsichtig; (fig) weitblickend

fart [fɑːt] n (fam) Furz m; **old ~** (fam: person) alter Sack ▷ vi (fam) furzen

farther ['fɑːðə*] adj, adv comparative of **far**; see **further**

farthest ['fɑːðɪst] adj, adv superlative of **far**; see **furthest**

fascinating ['fæsɪneɪtɪŋ] adj faszinierend; **fascination** n Faszination f

fascism ['fæʃɪzəm] n Faschismus m; **fascist** ['fæʃɪst] adj faschistisch ▷ Faschist(in) m(f)

fashion ['fæʃən] n (clothes) Mode f; (manner) Art (und Weise) f; **to be in ~** (in) Mode sein; **out of ~** unmodisch; **fashionable, fashionably** adj, adv (clothes, person) modisch; (author, pub etc) in Mode

fast [fɑːst] adj schnell; **to be ~** (clock) vorgehen ▷ adv schnell; (firmly) fest; **to be ~ asleep** fest schlafen ▷ n Fasten nt ▷ vi fasten; **fastback** n (Auto) Fließheck nt

fasten ['fɑːsn] vt (attach) befestigen (to an +dat); (do up) zumachen; **~ your seatbelts** bitte anschnallen; **fastener, fastening** n Verschluss m

fast food n Fast Food nt; **fast forward** n (for tape) Schnellvorlauf m; **fast lane** n Überholspur f

fat [fæt] adj dick; (meat) fett ▷ n Fett nt

fatal ['feɪtl] adj tödlich

fate [feɪt] n Schicksal nt

fat-free adj (food) fettfrei

father ['fɑːðə*] n Vater m; (priest)

Pfarrer m ▷ vt (child) zeugen; **Father Christmas** n der Weihnachtsmann; **father-in-law** (pl **fathers-in-law**) n Schwiegervater m

fatigue [fə'tiːg] n Ermüdung f

fattening ['fætnɪŋ] adj: **to be ~** dick machen; **fatty** ['fætɪ] adj (food) fettig

faucet ['fɔːsɪt] n (US) Wasserhahn m

fault [fɔːlt] n Fehler m; (Tech) Defekt m; (Elec) Störung f; (blame) Schuld f; **it's your ~** du bist daran schuld; **faulty** adj fehlerhaft; (Tech) defekt

favor (US), **favour** ['feɪvə*] n (approval) Gunst f; (kindness) Gefallen m; **in ~ of** für; **I'm in ~ (of going)** ich bin dafür(, dass wir gehen); **to do sb a ~** jdm einen Gefallen tun ▷ vt (prefer) vorziehen; **favourable** adj günstig (to, for für); **favourite** ['feɪvərɪt] n Liebling m, Favorit(in) m(f) ▷ adj Lieblings-

fax [fæks] vt faxen ▷ n Fax nt; **fax number** n Faxnummer f

faze [feɪz] vt (fam) aus der Fassung bringen

FBI abbr = **Federal Bureau of Investigation** FBI nt

fear [fɪə*] n Angst f (of vor +dat) ▷ vt befürchten; **fearful** adj (timid) ängstlich, furchtsam; (terrible) fürchterlich; **fearless** adj furchtlos

feasible ['fiːzəbl] adj machbar

feast [fiːst] n Festessen nt

feather ['feðə*] n Feder f

feature ['fiːtʃə*] n (facial) (Gesichts)zug m; (characteristic) Merkmal nt; (of car etc) Ausstattungsmerkmal nt; (in the press) (Cine) Feature nt ▷ vt bringen, (als Besonderheit) zeigen; **feature film** n Spielfilm m

February ['februərı] n Februar m; see also **September**

fed [fed] pt, pp of **feed**

federal ['fedərəl] adj Bundes-; **the Federal Republic of Germany** die Bundesrepublik Deutschland

fed-up [fed'ʌp] adj: **to be ~ with sth** etw satthaben; **I'm ~** ich habe die Nase voll

fee [fiː] n Gebühr f; (of doctor, lawyer) Honorar nt

feeble ['fiːbl] adj schwach

feed [fiːd] (**fed, fed**) vt (baby, animal) füttern; (support) ernähren ▷ n (for baby) Mahlzeit f; (for animals) Futter nt; (Inform: paper ~) Zufuhr f; **feed in** vt (information) eingeben; **feedback** n (information) Feed-back nt

feel [fiːl] (**felt, felt**) vt (sense) fühlen; (pain) empfinden; (touch) anfassen; (think) meinen ▷ vi (person) sich fühlen; **I ~ cold** mir ist kalt; **do you ~ like a walk?** hast du Lust, spazieren zu gehen?; **feeling** n Gefühl nt

feet [fiːt] pl of **foot**

fell [fel] pt of **fall** ▷ vt (tree) fällen

fellow ['feləʊ] n Kerl m, Typ m; **~ citizen** Mitbürger(in) m(f); **~ countryman** Landsmann m; **~ worker** Mitarbeiter(in) m(f)

felt [felt] pt, pp of **feel** ▷ n Filz m; **felt tip, felt-tip pen** n Filzstift m

female ['fiːmeɪl] n (of animals) Weibchen nt ▷ adj weiblich; **~ doctor** Ärztin f; **feminine** ['feminin] adj weiblich; **feminist** ['feminist] n Feminist(in) m(f) ▷ adj feministisch

fence [fens] n Zaun m

fencing n (Sport) Fechten nt

fender ['fendə*] n (US Auto) Kotflügel m

fennel ['fenl] n Fenchel m

fern [fɜːn] n Farn m

ferocious [fə'rəʊʃəs] adj wild

ferry ['ferı] n Fähre f ▷ vt übersetzen

fertile ['fɜːtaɪl] adj fruchtbar; **fertility** [fə'tɪlɪtɪ] n Fruchtbarkeit f; **fertilize** ['fɜːtɪlaɪz] vt (Bio) befruchten; (Agr: land) düngen; **fertilizer** n Dünger m

festival ['festɪvəl] n (Rel) Fest nt; (Art, Mus) Festspiele pl; (pop music) Festival nt; **festive** ['festɪv] adj festlich; **festivities** [fe'stɪvɪtɪz] n Feierlichkeiten pl

fetch [fetʃ] vt holen; (collect) abholen; (in sale, money) einbringen; **fetching** adj reizend

fetish ['fetɪʃ] n Fetisch m

fetus ['fiːtəs] n (US) Fötus m

fever ['fiːvə*] n Fieber nt; **feverish** adj (Med) fiebrig; (fig) fieberhaft

few [fjuː] adj, pron pl wenige pl; **a ~ pl** ein paar; **fewer** adj weniger; **fewest** adj wenigste(r, s)

fiancé [fɪ'ɒnseɪ] n Verlobte(r) m; **fiancée** n Verlobte f

fiasco [fɪ'æskəʊ] (pl **-s** o US **-es**) n Fiasko nt

fiber (US), **fibre** ['faɪbə*] n Faser f; (material) Faserstoff m

fickle ['fɪkl] adj unbeständig

fiction ['fɪkʃən] n (novels) Prosaliteratur f; **fictional**, **fictitious** [fɪk'tɪʃəs] adj erfunden

fiddle ['fɪdl] n Geige f; (trick) Betrug m ▷ vt (accounts, results) frisieren; **fiddle with** vt herumfummeln an +dat; **fiddly** adj knifflig

fidelity [fɪ'delɪtɪ] n Treue f

fidget ['fɪdʒɪt] vi zappeln; **fidgety** adj zappelig

field [fiːld] n Feld nt; (grass-covered) Wiese f; (fig: of work) (Arbeits)gebiet nt

fierce [fɪəs] *adj* heftig; (*animal, appearance*) wild; (*criticism, competition*) scharf

fifteen [fɪf'tiːn] *num* fünfzehn ▷ *n* Fünfzehn *f; see also* **eight**; **fifteenth** *adj* fünfzehnte(r, s); *see also* **eighth**; **fifth** [fɪfθ] *adj* fünfte(r, s) ▷ *n* (*fraction*) Fünftel *nt; see also* **eighth**; **fifty** ['fɪftɪ] *num* fünfzig ▷ *n* Fünfzig *f; see also* **eight**; **fiftieth** *adj* fünfzigste(r, s); *see also* **eighth**

fig [fɪg] *n* Feige *f*

fight [faɪt] (**fought, fought**) *vi* kämpfen (*with, against* gegen, *for, over* um) ▷ *vt* (*person*) kämpfen mit; (*fig: disease, fire etc*) bekämpfen ▷ *n* Kampf *m*; (*brawl*) Schlägerei *f*; (*argument*) Streit *m*; **fight back** *vi* zurückschlagen; **fight off** *vt* abwehren; **fighter** *n* Kämpfer(in) *m(f)*

figurative ['fɪgərətɪv] *adj* übertragen

figure ['fɪgə*] *n* (*person*) Gestalt *f*; (*of person*) Figur *f*; (*number*) Zahl *f*, Ziffer *f*; (*amount*) Betrag *m*; **a four-figure sum** eine vierstellige Summe ▷ *vt* (*US: think*) glauben ▷ *vi* (*appear*) erscheinen; **figure out** *vt* (*work out*) herausbekommen; **I can't figure him out** ich werde aus ihm nicht schlau; **figure skating** *n* Eiskunstlauf *m*

file [faɪl] *n* (*tool*) Feile *f*; (*dossier*) Akte *f*; (*Inform*) Datei *f*; (*folder*) Aktenordner *m*; **on ~** in den Akten ▷ *vt* (*metal, nails*) feilen; (*papers*) ablegen (*under* unter) ▷ *vi*: **to ~ in/out** hintereinander hereinkommen/hinausgehen; **filing cabinet** *n* Aktenschrank *m*

fill [fɪl] *vt* füllen; (*tooth*) plombieren; (*post*) besetzen; **fill in** *vt* (*hole*) auffüllen; (*form*) ausfüllen; (*tell*) informieren (*on* über); **fill out** *vt* (*form*) ausfüllen; **fill up** *vi* (*Auto*) volltanken

fillet ['fɪlɪt] *n* Filet *nt*

filling ['fɪlɪŋ] *n* (*Gastr*) Füllung *f*; (*for tooth*) Plombe *f*; **filling station** *n* Tankstelle *f*

film [fɪlm] *n* Film *m* ▷ *vt* (*scene*) filmen; **film star** *n* Filmstar *m*; **film studio** *n* Filmstudio *nt*

filter ['fɪltə*] *n* Filter *m*; (*traffic lane*) Abbiegespur *f* ▷ *vt* filtern

filth [fɪlθ] *n* Dreck *m*; **filthy** *adj* dreckig

fin [fɪn] *n* Flosse *f*

final ['faɪnl] *adj* letzte(r, s); (*stage, round*) End-; (*decision, version*) endgültig; **~ score** Schlussstand *m* ▷ *n* (*Sport*) Endspiel *nt*; (*competition*) Finale *nt*; **~s** *pl* Abschlussexamen *nt*; **finalize** *vt* die endgültige Form geben +*dat*; **finally** *adv* (*lastly*) zuletzt; (*eventually*) schließlich, endlich

finance [faɪ'næns] *n* Finanzwesen *nt*; **~s** *pl* Finanzen *pl* ▷ *vt* finanzieren; **financial** [faɪ'nænʃəl] *adj* finanziell; (*adviser, crisis, policy etc*) Finanz-

find [faɪnd] (**found, found**) *vt* finden; **he was found dead** er wurde tot aufgefunden; **I ~ myself in difficulties** ich befinde mich in Schwierigkeiten; **she ~s it difficult/easy** es fällt ihr schwer/leicht; **find out** *vt* herausfinden; **findings** *npl* (*Jur*) Ermittlungsergebnis *nt*; (*of report, Med*) Befund *m*

fine [faɪn] *adj* (*thin*) dünn, fein; (*good*) gut; (*splendid*) herrlich; (*clothes*) elegant; (*weather*) schön; **I'm ~** es geht mir gut; **that's ~** das ist OK ▷ *adv* (*well*) gut ▷ *n* (*Jur*) Geldstrafe *f* ▷ *vt* (*Jur*) mit einer Geldstrafe belegen; **fine arts** *npl*: **the ~** die schönen Künste *pl*;

finely adv (cut) dünn; (ground) fein

finger ['fɪŋgə*] n Finger m ▷ vt herumfingern an +dat; **fingernail** n Fingernagel m; **fingerprint** n Fingerabdruck m; **fingertip** n Fingerspitze f

finicky ['fɪnɪkɪ] adj (person) pingelig; (work) knifflig

finish ['fɪnɪʃ] n Ende nt; (Sport) Finish nt; (line) Ziel nt; (of product) Verarbeitung f ▷ vt beenden; (book etc) zu Ende lesen; (food) aufessen; (drink) austrinken ▷ vi zu Ende gehen; (song, story) enden; (person) fertig sein; (stop) aufhören; **have you ~ed?** bist du fertig?; **to ~ first/second** (Sport) als erster/zweiter durchs Ziel gehen; **finishing line** n Ziellinie f

Finland ['fɪnlənd] n Finnland nt; **Finn** n Finne m, Finnin f; **Finnish** adj finnisch ▷ n (language) Finnisch nt

fir [fɜ:*] n Tanne f

fire [faɪə*] n Feuer nt; (house etc) Brand m; **to set ~ to sth** etw in Brand stecken; **to be on ~** brennen ▷ vt (bullets, rockets) abfeuern; (fam: dismiss) feuern ▷ vi (Auto: engine) zünden; **~ at sb** auf jdn schießen; **fire alarm** n Feuermelder m; **fire brigade** n Feuerwehr f; **fire engine** n Feuerwehrauto nt; **fire escape** n Feuerleiter f; **fire extinguisher** n Feuerlöscher m; **firefighter** n Feuerwehrmann m, Feuerwehrfrau f; **fireman** n Feuerwehrmann m; **fireplace** n (offener) Kamin; **fireproof** adj feuerfest; **fire station** n Feuerwache f; **firewood** n Brennholz nt; **fireworks** npl Feuerwerk nt

firm [fɜ:m] adj fest; (person) **to be ~** entschlossen auftreten ▷ n Firma f

first [fɜ:st] adj erste(r, s) ▷ adv (at first) zuerst; (firstly) erstens; (arrive, finish) als erste(r); (happen) zum ersten Mal; **~ of all** zuallererst ▷ n (person) Erste(r) mf; (Auto: gear) erster Gang; **at ~** zuerst, anfangs; **first aid** n erste Hilfe; **first-class** adj erstklassig; (compartment, ticket) erster Klasse; **~ mail** (Brit) bevorzugt beförderte Post ▷ adv (travel) erster Klasse; **first floor** n (Brit) erster Stock; (US) Erdgeschoss nt; **first lady** n (US) Frau f des Präsidenten; **firstly** adv erstens; **first name** n Vorname m; **first night** n (Theat) Premiere f; **first-rate** adj erstklassig

fir tree n Tannenbaum m

fish [fɪʃ] n Fisch m; **~ and chips** (Brit) frittierter Fisch mit Pommes frites ▷ vi fischen; (with rod) angeln; **to go ~ing** fischen/angeln gehen; **fishbone** n Gräte f; **fishcake** n Fischfrikadelle f; **fish farm** n Fischzucht f; **fish finger** n (Brit) Fischstäbchen nt; **fishing** ['fɪʃɪŋ] n Fischen nt; (with rod) Angeln nt; (as industry) Fischerei f; **fishing boat** n Fischerboot nt; **fishing line** n Angelschnur f; **fishing rod** n Angelrute f; **fishing village** n Fischerdorf nt; **fishmonger** ['fɪʃmʌŋgə*] n Fischhändler(in) m(f); **fish stick** n (US) Fischstäbchen nt; **fish tank** n Aquarium nt

fishy ['fɪʃɪ] adj (fam: suspicious) faul

fist [fɪst] n Faust f

fit [fɪt] adj (Med) gesund; (Sport) in Form, fit; (suitable) geeignet; **to keep ~** sich in Form halten ▷ vt passen +dat; (attach) anbringen (to an +dat); (install) einbauen (in in +akk) ▷ vi passen; (in space, gap) hineinpassen ▷ n (of clothes) Sitz m; (Med) Anfall m; **it's a good ~** es passt gut; **fit in** vt (accommodate) unterbringen; (find time for) einschieben ▷ vi (in space) hineinpassen; (plans, ideas) passen; **he doesn't ~ (here)** er passt nicht hierher; **to ~ with sb's plans** sich mit jds Plänen vereinbaren lassen; **fitness** n (Med) Gesundheit f; (Sport) Fitness f; **fitness trainer** n (Sport) Fitnesstrainer(in) m(f); **fitted carpet** n Teppichboden m; **fitted kitchen** n Einbauküche f; **fitting** adj passend ▷ n (of dress) Anprobe f; **~s** pl Ausstattung f

five [faɪv] num fünf ▷ n Fünf f; see also **eight**; **fiver** n (Brit fam) Fünfpfundschein m

fix [fɪks] vt befestigen (to an +dat); (settle) festsetzen; (place, time) ausmachen; (repair) reparieren; **fixer** n (drug addict) Fixer(in) m(f); **fixture** ['fɪkstʃə°] n (Sport) Veranstaltung f; (match) Spiel nt; (in building) Installationsteil nt; **~s (and fittings)** pl Ausstattung f

fizzy ['fɪzɪ] adj sprudelnd; **~ drink** Limo f

flabbergasted ['flæbəgɑːstɪd] adj (fam) platt

flabby ['flæbɪ] adj (fat) wabbelig

flag [flæg] n Fahne f; **flagstone** n Steinplatte f

flake [fleɪk] n Flocke f ▷ vi: **to ~ (off)** abblättern

flamboyant [flæm'bɔɪənt] adj extravagant

flame [fleɪm] n Flamme f; (person) **an old ~** eine alte Liebe

flan [flæn] n (fruit ~) Obstkuchen m

flannel ['flænl] n Flanell m; (Brit: face ~) Waschlappen m; (fam: waffle) Geschwafel nt ▷ vi herumlabern

flap [flæp] n Klappe f; (fam) **to be in a ~** rotieren ▷ vt (wings) schlagen mit ▷ vi flattern

flared [fleəd] adj (trousers) mit Schlag; **flares** npl Schlaghose f

flash [flæʃ] n Blitz m; (news ~) Kurzmeldung f; (Foto) Blitzlicht nt; **in a ~** im Nu ▷ vt: **to ~ one's (head)lights** die Lichthupe betätigen ▷ vi aufblinken; (brightly) aufblitzen; **flashback** n Rückblende f, Flashback m; **flashlight** ['flæʃlaɪt] n (Photo) Blitzlicht nt; (US: torch) Taschenlampe f; **flashy** adj grell, schrill; (pej) protzig

flat [flæt] adj flach; (surface) eben; (drink) abgestanden; (tyre) platt; (battery) leer; (refusal) glatt ▷ n (Brit: rooms) Wohnung f; (Auto) Reifenpanne f; **flat screen** n (Inform) Flachbildschirm m; **flatten** vt platt machen, einebnen

flatter ['flætə°] vt schmeicheln +dat; **flattering** adj schmeichelhaft

flatware ['flætweə] n (US) Besteck nt

flavor (US), **flavour** ['fleɪvə°] n Geschmack m ▷ vt Geschmack geben +dat; (with spices) würzen; **flavouring** n Aroma nt

flaw [flɔː] n Fehler m; **flawless** adj fehlerlos; (complexion) makellos

flea [fliː] n Floh m

fled [fled] pt, pp of **flee**

flee [fliː] (**fled, fled**) vi fliehen

fleece [fliːs] n (of sheep) Vlies nt; (soft material) Fleece m; (jacket) Fleecejacke f

fleet [fliːt] n Flotte f

Flemish ['flemɪʃ] adj flämisch ▷ n (language) Flämisch nt

flesh [fleʃ] n Fleisch nt

flew [fluː] pt of **fly**

flex [fleks] n (Brit Elec) Schnur f

flexibility [fleksɪ'bɪlɪtɪ] n Biegsamkeit f; (fig) Flexibilität f; **flexible** ['fleksɪbl] adj biegsam;

(*plans, person*) flexibel; **flexitime** n
gleitende Arbeitszeit, Gleitzeit f
flicker ['flɪkə*] vi flackern; (*TV*)
flimmern
flies [flaɪz] pl of **fly** ▷ n
flight [flaɪt] n Flug m; (*escape*)
Flucht f; **~ of stairs** Treppe f; **flight
attendant** n Flugbegleiter(in)
m(f); **flight recorder** n
Flugschreiber m
flimsy ['flɪmzɪ] adj leicht gebaut,
nicht stabil; (*thin*) hauchdünn;
(*excuse*) fadenscheinig
fling [flɪŋ] (**flung, flung**) vt
schleudern ▷ n: **to have a ~** eine
(kurze) Affäre haben
flip [flɪp] vt schnippen; **to ~ a
coin** eine Münze werfen; **flip
through** vt (*book*) durchblättern;
flipchart n Flipchart nt
flipper ['flɪpə*] n Flosse f
flirt [flɜːt] vi flirten
float [fləʊt] n (*for fishing*)
Schwimmer m; (*in procession*)
Festwagen m; (*money*)
Wechselgeld nt ▷ vi schwimmen;
(*in air*) schweben
flock [flɒk] n (*of sheep*) (*Rel*) Herde
f; (*of birds*) Schwarm m; (*of people*)
Schar f
flog [flɒg] vt auspeitschen; (*Brit
fam*) verscheuern
flood [flʌd] n Hochwasser nt,
Überschwemmung f; (*fig*) Flut f
▷ vt überschwemmen; **floodlight**
n Flutlicht nt; **floodlit** adj
(*building*) angestrahlt
floor [flɔː*] n Fußboden m;
(*storey*) Stock m; **ground ~** (*Brit*),
first ~ (*US*) Erdgeschoss nt; **first
~** (*Brit*), **second ~** (*US*) erster Stock;
floorboard n Diele f
flop [flɒp] n (*fam: failure*) Reinfall
m, Flop m ▷ vi misslingen, floppen
floppy disk ['flɒpɪ'dɪsk] n
Diskette f
Florence ['flɒrəns] n Florenz nt

florist ['flɒrɪst] n Blumenhänd-
ler(in) m(f); **florist's (shop)**
['flɒrɪsts] n Blumengeschäft
m(f)
flounder ['flaʊndə*] n (*fish*)
Flunder f
flour ['flaʊə*] n Mehl nt
flourish ['flʌrɪʃ] vi gedeihen;
(*business*) gut laufen; (*boom*)
florieren ▷ vt (*wave about*)
schwenken; **flourishing** adj
blühend
flow [fləʊ] n Fluss m; **to go with
the ~** mit dem Strom schwimmen
▷ vi fließen
flower ['flaʊə*] n Blume f ▷ vi
blühen; **flower bed** n Blumenbeet
nt; **flowerpot** n Blumentopf
m
flown [fləʊn] pp of **fly**
flu [fluː] n (*fam*) Grippe f
fluent adj (*Italian etc*) fließend; **to
be ~ in German** fließend Deutsch
sprechen
fluid ['fluːɪd] n Flüssigkeit f ▷ adj
flüssig
flung [flʌŋ] pt, pp of **fling**
fluorescent [flʊə'resnt] adj fluo-
reszierend, Leucht-
flush [flʌʃ] n (*lavatory*)
Wasserspülung f; (*blush*) Röte f
▷ vi (*lavatory*) spülen
flute [fluːt] n Flöte f
fly [flaɪ] (**flew, flown**) vt, vi
fliegen; **how time flies** wie die Zeit
vergeht! ▷ n (*insect*) Fliege f;
~/flies (pl) (*on trousers*)
Hosenschlitz m; **fly-drive** n
Urlaub m mit Flug und
Mietwagen; **flyover** n (*Brit*)
Straßenüberführung f,
Eisenbahnüberführung f; **flysheet**
n Überzelt nt
FM abbr = **frequency modulation**
≈ UKW
FO abbr = **Foreign Office** ≈ AA nt
foal [fəʊl] n Fohlen nt

foam [fəʊm] n Schaum m ▷ vi schäumen
fob off [fɒb ɒf] vt: **to fob sb off with sth** jdm etw andrehen
focus ['fəʊkəs] n Brennpunkt m; **in/out of ~** (photo) scharf/unscharf; (camera) scharf/unscharf eingestellt ▷ vt (camera) scharf stellen ▷ vi sich konzentrieren (on auf +akk)
foetus ['fiːtəs] n Fötus m
fog [fɒg] n Nebel m; **foggy** adj neblig; **fog light** n (Auto: at rear) Nebelschlussleuchte f
foil [fɔɪl] vt vereiteln ▷ n Folie f
fold [fəʊld] vt falten ▷ vi (fam: business) eingehen ▷ n Falte f; **fold up** vt (map etc) zusammenfalten; (chair etc) zusammenklappen ▷ vi (fam: business) eingehen; **folder** n (portfolio) Aktenmappe f; (pamphlet) Broschüre f; (Inform) Ordner m; **folding** adj zusammenklappbar; (bicycle, chair) Klapp-
folk [fəʊk] n Leute pl; (Mus) Folk m; **my ~s** pl (fam) meine Leute ▷ adj Volks-
follow ['fɒləʊ] vt folgen +dat; (pursue) verfolgen; (understand) folgen können +dat; (career, news etc) verfolgen; **as ~s** wie folgt ▷ vi folgen; (result) sich ergeben (from aus); **follow up** vt (request, rumour) nachgehen +dat, weiter verfolgen; **follower** n Anhänger(in) m(f); **following** adj folgend; **the ~ day** am (darauf)folgenden Tag ▷ prep nach; **follow up** n (event, book etc) Fortsetzung f
fond [fɒnd] adj: **to be ~ of** gernhaben; **fondly** adv (with love) liebevoll; **fondness** n Vorliebe f; (for people) Zuneigung f
fondue ['fɒnduː] n Fondue nt

font [fɒnt] n Taufbecken nt; (Typo) Schriftart f
food [fuːd] n Essen nt, Lebensmittel pl; (for animals) Futter nt; (groceries) Lebensmittel pl; **food poisoning** n Lebensmittelvergiftung f; **food processor** n Küchenmaschine f; **foodstuff** n Lebensmittel nt
fool [fuːl] n Idiot m, Narr m; **to make a ~ of oneself** sich blamieren ▷ vt (deceive) hereinlegen ▷ vi: **to ~ around** herumalbern; (waste time) herumtrödeln; **foolish** adj dumm; **foolproof** adj idiotensicher
foot [fʊt] (pl **feet** [fiːt]) n Fuß m; (measure) Fuß m (30,48 cm); **on ~** zu Fuß ▷ vt (bill) bezahlen; **foot-and-mouth disease** n Maul- und Klauenseuche f; **football** n Fußball m; (US: American ~) Football m; **footballer** n Fußballspieler(in) m(f); **footbridge** n Fußgängerbrücke f; **footing** n (hold) Halt m; **footlights** npl Rampenlicht nt; **footnote** n Fußnote f; **footpath** n Fußweg m; **footprint** n Fußabdruck m; **footwear** n Schuhwerk nt

---

⊙ **KEYWORD**

for [fɔː*] prep **1** für; **is this for me?** ist das für mich?; **the train for London** der Zug nach London; **he went for the paper** er ging die Zeitung holen; **give it to me — what for?** gib es mir — warum? **2** (because of) wegen; **for this reason** aus diesem Grunde **3** (referring to distance) **there are roadworks for 5 km** die Baustelle ist 5 km lang; **we walked for miles** wir sind meilenweit gegangen

4 (referring to time) seit; (with future sense) für; **he was away for 2 years** er war zwei Jahre lang weg **5** (+infin clauses) **it is not for me to decide** das kann ich nicht entscheiden; **for this to be possible ...** damit dies möglich wird/wurde ... **6** (in spite of) trotz +gen o (inf) dat; **for all his complaints** obwohl er sich ständig beschwert ▷ conj denn

forbade [fəˈbæd] pt of **forbid**

forbid [fəˈbɪd] (**forbade, forbidden**) vt verbieten

force [fɔːs] n Kraft f; (compulsion) Zwang m, Gewalt; **to come into ~** in Kraft treten; **the Forces** pl die Streitkräfte ▷ vt zwingen; **forced** adj (smile) gezwungen; **~ landing** Notlandung f; **forceful** adj kraftvoll

forceps [ˈfɔːseps] npl Zange f

forearm [ˈfɔːrɑːm] n Unterarm m

forecast [ˈfɔːkɑːst] vt voraussagen; (weather) vorhersagen ▷ n Vorhersage f

forefinger [ˈfɔːfɪŋɡəʳ] n Zeigefinger m

foreground [ˈfɔːɡraʊnd] n Vordergrund m

forehand [ˈfɔːhænd] n (Sport) Vorhand f

forehead [ˈfɔːhed, ˈfɒrɪd] n Stirn f

foreign [ˈfɒrən] adj ausländisch; **foreigner** n Ausländer(in) m(f); **foreign exchange** n Devisen pl; **foreign language** n Fremdsprache f; **foreign minister** n Außenminister(in) m(f); **Foreign Office** n (Brit) Außenministerium nt; **Foreign Secretary** n (Brit) Außenminister(in) m(f); **foreign policy** n Außenpolitik f

foremost [ˈfɔːməʊst] adj erste(r, s); (leading) führend

forerunner [ˈfɔːrʌnəʳ] n Vorläufer(in) m(f)

foresee [fɔːˈsiː] irr vt vorhersehen; **foreseeable** adj absehbar

forest [ˈfɒrɪst] n Wald m; **forestry** [ˈfɒrɪstrɪ] n Forstwirtschaft f

forever [fəˈrevəʳ] adv für immer

forgave [fəˈɡeɪv] pt of **forgive**

forge [fɔːdʒ] n Schmiede f ▷ vt schmieden; (fake) fälschen; **forger** n Fälscher(in) m(f); **forgery** n Fälschung f

forget [fəˈɡet] (**forgot, forgotten**) vt, vi vergessen; **to ~ about sth** etw vergessen; **forgetful** adj vergesslich; **forgetfulness** n Vergesslichkeit f; **forget-me-not** n Vergissmeinnicht nt

forgive [fəˈɡɪv] (**forgave, forgiven**) irr vt verzeihen; **to ~ sb for sth** jdm etw verzeihen

forgot [fəˈɡɒt] pt of **forget**

forgotten [fəˈɡɒtn] pp of **forget**

fork [fɔːk] n Gabel f; (in road) Gabelung f ▷ vi (road) sich gabeln

form [fɔːm] n (shape) Form f, Klasse f; (document) Formular nt; (person) **to be in (good) ~** in Form sein ▷ vt bilden

formal [ˈfɔːməl] adj förmlich, formell; **formality** [fɔːˈmælɪtɪ] n Formalität f

format [ˈfɔːmæt] n Format nt ▷ vt (Inform) formatieren

former [ˈfɔːməʳ] adj frühere(r, s); (opposite of latter) erstere(r, s); **formerly** adv früher

formidable [ˈfɔːmɪdəbl] adj gewaltig; (opponent) stark

formula [ˈfɔːmjʊlə] n Formel f

formulate [ˈfɔːmjʊleɪt] vt formulieren

forth [fɔːθ] *adv*: **and so ~** und so
weiter; **forthcoming**
[fɔːθ'kʌmɪŋ] *adj* kommend,
bevorstehend

fortify ['fɔːtɪfaɪ] *vt* verstärken;
(for protection) befestigen

fortieth ['fɔːtɪəθ] *adj* vierzigs-
te(r, s); *see also* **eighth**

fortnight ['fɔːtnaɪt] *n* vierzehn
Tage *pl*

fortress ['fɔːtrɪs] *n* Festung *f*

fortunate ['fɔːtʃənɪt] *adj* glücklich; **I was ~** ich hatte Glück;
fortunately *adv* zum Glück;
fortune ['fɔːtʃən] *n (money)*
Vermögen *nt*; **good ~** Glück *nt*;
fortune-teller *n* Wahrsager(in)
m(f)

forty ['fɔːtɪ] *num* vierzig ▷ *n*
Vierzig *f*; *see also* **eight**

forward ['fɔːwəd] *adv* vorwärts
▷ *n (Sport)* Stürmer(in) *m(f)* ▷ *vt*
(send on) nachsenden; *(Inform)*
weiterleiten; **forwards** *adv*
vorwärts

foster child ['fɒstətʃaɪld] *n*
Pflegekind *nt*; **foster parents** *npl*
Pflegeeltern *pl*

fought [fɔːt] *pt, pp of* **fight**

foul [faʊl] *adj (weather)* schlecht;
(smell) übel ▷ *n (Sport)* Foul *nt*

found [faʊnd] *pt, pp of* **find** ▷ *vt*
(establish) gründen; **foundations**
[faʊn'deɪʃənz] *npl* Fundament *nt*

fountain ['faʊntɪn] *n* Springbrunnen *m*; **fountain pen** *n* Füller
m

four [fɔː*] *num* vier ▷ *n* Vier *f*; *see
also* **eight**; **fourteen** ['fɔːtiːn]
num vierzehn ▷ *n* Vierzehn *f*; *see
also* **eight**; **fourteenth** *adj*
vierzehnte(r, s); *see also* **eighth**;
fourth [fɔːθ] *adj* vierte(r, s); *see
also* **eighth**

four-wheel drive *n*
Allradantrieb *m*; *(car)*
Geländewagen *m*

fowl [faʊl] *n* Geflügel *nt*

fox [fɒks] *n (a. fig)* Fuchs *m*

fraction ['frækʃən] *n (Math)*
Bruch *m*; *(part)* Bruchteil *m*;
fracture ['fræktʃə*] *n (Med)*
Bruch *m* ▷ *vt* brechen

fragile ['frædʒaɪl] *adj*
zerbrechlich

fragment ['frægmənt] *n* Bruch-
stück *nt*

fragrance ['freɪgrəns] *n* Duft *m*;
fragrant *adj* duftend

frail [freɪl] *adj* gebrechlich

frame [freɪm] *n* Rahmen *m*; *(of
spectacles)* Gestell *nt*; **~ of mind**
Verfassung *f* ▷ *vt* einrahmen; **to
~ sb** *(fam: incriminate)* jdm etwas
anhängen; **framework** *n*
Rahmen *m*, Struktur *f*

France [frɑːns] *n* Frankreich *nt*

frank [fræŋk] *adj* offen

frankfurter ['fræŋkfɜːtə*] *n*
(Frankfurter) Würstchen *nt*

frankly ['fræŋklɪ] *adv* offen
gesagt; **quite ~** ganz ehrlich;
frankness *n* Offenheit *f*

frantic ['fræntɪk] *adj (activity)*
hektisch; *(effort)* verzweifelt;
~ with worry außer sich vor Sorge

fraud [frɔːd] *n (trickery)* Betrug *m*;
(person) Schwindler(in) *m(f)*

freak [friːk] *n* Anomalie *f*;
(animal, person) Missgeburt *f*; *(fam:
fan)* Fan *m*, Freak *m* ▷ *adj*
(conditions) außergewöhnlich,
seltsam; **freak out** *vi (fam)*
ausflippen

freckle ['frekl] *n* Sommersprosse
f

free [friː] *adj, adv* frei; *(without
payment)* gratis, kostenlos; **for
~** umsonst ▷ *vt* befreien; **freebie**
['friːbɪ] *n (fam)* Werbegeschenk
nt; **it was a ~** es war gratis;
freedom ['friːdəm] *n* Freiheit *f*;
freefone ['friːfəʊn] *adj*: **a
~ number** eine gebührenfreie

Nummer; **free kick** n (Sport) Freistoß m

freelance ['fri:lɑ:ns] adj freiberuflich tätig; (artist) freischaffend ▷ n Freiberufler(in) m(f)

free-range ['fri:reɪndʒ] adj (hen) frei laufend; **~ eggs** pl Freilandeier pl

freeway ['fri:weɪ] n (US) (gebührenfreie) Autobahn

freeze [fri:z] (froze, frozen) vi (feel cold) frieren; (of lake etc) zufrieren; (water etc) gefrieren ▷ vt einfrieren; **freezer** n Tiefkühltruhe f; (in fridge) Gefrierfach nt; **freezing** adj eiskalt; **I'm ~** mir ist eiskalt; **freezing point** n Gefrierpunkt m

freight [freɪt] n (goods) Fracht f; (money charged) Frachtgebühr f; **freight car** n (US) Güterwagen m; **freight train** n (US) Güterzug m

French [frentʃ] adj französisch ▷ n (language) Französisch nt; **the ~** pl die Franzosen; **French bean** n grüne Bohne; **French bread** n Baguette f; **French dressing** n Vinaigrette f; **French fries** (US) npl Pommes frites pl; **French kiss** n Zungenkuss m; **Frenchman** (pl **-men**) n Franzose m; **French toast** n (US) in Ei und Milch getunktes gebratenes Brot; **French window(s)** n(pl) Balkontür f, Terrassentür f; **Frenchwoman** (pl **-women**) n Französin f

frequency ['fri:kwənsɪ] n Häufigkeit f; (Phys) Frequenz f; **frequent** ['fri:kwənt] adj häufig; **frequently** adv häufig

fresco ['freskəʊ] (pl **-es**) n Fresko nt

fresh [freʃ] adj frisch; (new) neu; **freshen** vi: **to ~ (up)** (person) sich frisch machen; **fresher, freshman** (pl **-men**) n Erstsemester nt;

freshwater fish n Süßwasserfisch m

Fri abbr = **Friday** Fr

friction ['frɪkʃən] n (a. fig) Reibung f

Friday ['fraɪdeɪ] n Freitag m; see also **Tuesday**

fridge [frɪdʒ] n Kühlschrank m

fried [fraɪd] adj gebraten; **~ potatoes** Bratkartoffeln pl; **~ egg** Spiegelei nt; **~ rice** gebratener Reis

friend [frend] n Freund(in) m(f); (less close) Bekannte(r) mf; **to make ~s with sb** sich mit jdm anfreunden; **we're good ~s** wir sind gut befreundet; **friendly** adj freundlich; **to be ~ with sb** mit jdm befreundet sein ▷ n (Sport) Freundschaftsspiel nt; **friendship** ['frendʃɪp] n Freundschaft f

fright [fraɪt] n Schrecken m; **frighten** vt erschrecken; **to be ~ed** Angst haben; **frightening** adj beängstigend

frill [frɪl] n Rüsche f; **~s** (fam) Schnickschnack

fringe [frɪndʒ] n (edge) Rand m; (on shawl etc) Fransen pl; (hair) Pony m

frivolous ['frɪvələs] adj leichtsinnig; (remark) frivol

frizzy ['frɪzɪ] adj kraus

frog [frɒg] n Frosch m

O KEYWORD

from [frɒm] prep **1** (indicating starting place) von; (indicating origin etc) aus +dat; **a letter/telephone call from my sister** ein Brief/Anruf von meiner Schwester; **where do you come from?** woher kommen Sie?; **to drink from the bottle** aus der Flasche trinken

2 (indicating time) von ... an; (past) seit; **from one o'clock to** 0 **until** 0 **till two** von ein Uhr bis zwei; **from January (on)** ab Januar
3 (indicating distance) von ... (entfernt)
4 (indicating price, number etc) ab +dat; **from £10** ab £10; **there were from 20 to 30 people there** es waren zwischen 20 und 30 Leute da
5 (indicating difference) **he can't tell red from green** er kann nicht zwischen Rot und Grün unterscheiden; **to be different from sb/sth** anders sein als jd/etw
6 (because of, based on) **from what he says** aus dem, was er sagt; **weak from hunger** schwach vor Hunger

front [frʌnt] n Vorderseite f; (of house) Fassade f; (in war, of weather) Front f; (at seaside) Promenade f; **in ~, at the ~** vorne; **in ~ of** vor; **up ~** (in advance) vorher, im Voraus ▷ adj vordere(r, s), Vorder-; (first) vorderste(r, s); **~ door** Haustür f; **~ page** Titelseite f; **~ seat** Vordersitz m; **~ wheel** Vorderrad nt
frontier ['frʌntɪə*] n Grenze f
front-wheel drive n (Auto) Frontantrieb m
frost [frɒst] n Frost m; (white ~) Reif m; **frosting** n (US) Zuckerguss m; **frosty** adj frostig
froth [frɒθ] n Schaum m; **frothy** adj schaumig
frown [fraʊn] vi die Stirn runzeln
froze [frəʊz] pt of **freeze**
frozen [frəʊzn] pp of **freeze** ▷ adj (food) tiefgekühlt, Tiefkühl-
fruit [fruːt] n (as collective, a. type) Obst nt; (single ~, a. fig) Frucht f;

fruit machine n Spielautomat m; **fruit salad** n Obstsalat m
frustrated [frʌˈstreɪtɪd] adj frustriert; **frustratration** n Frustration f, Frust m
fry [fraɪ] vt braten; **frying pan** n Bratpfanne f
fuchsia ['fjuːʃə] n Fuchsie f
fuck [fʌk] vt (vulg) ficken; **~ off** verpiss dich!; **fucking** adj (vulg) Scheiß-
fudge [fʌdʒ] n weiche Karamellsüßigkeit
fuel [fjʊəl] n Kraftstoff m; (for heating) Brennstoff m; **fuel consumption** n Kraftstoffverbrauch m; **fuel gauge** n Benzinuhr f; **fuel oil** n Gasöl nt; **fuel rod** n Brennstab m; **fuel tank** n Tank m; (for oil) Öltank m
fugitive ['fjuːdʒɪtɪv] n Flüchtling m
fulfil [fʊlˈfɪl] vt erfüllen
full [fʊl] adj voll; (person: satisfied) satt; (member, employment) Voll(zeit)-; (complete) vollständig; **~ of ...** voller ... gen; **full beam** n (Auto) Fernlicht nt; **full moon** n Vollmond m; **full stop** n Punkt m; **full-time** adj: **~ job** Ganztagsarbeit f; **fully** adv völlig; (recover) voll und ganz; (discuss) ausführlich
fumble ['fʌmbl] vi herumfummeln (with, at an +dat)
fumes [fjuːmz] npl Dämpfe pl; (of car) Abgase pl
fun [fʌn] n Spaß m; **for ~** zum Spaß; **it's ~** es macht Spaß; **to make ~ of** sich lustig machen über +akk
function ['fʌŋkʃən] n Funktion f; (event) Feier f; (reception) Empfang m ▷ vi funktionieren; **function key** n (Inform) Funktionstaste f
fund [fʌnd] n Fonds m; **~s** pl Geldmittel pl

fundamental [fʌndə'mentl] *adj* grundlegend; **fundamentally** *adv* im Grunde

funding ['fʌndɪŋ] *n* finanzielle Unterstützung

funeral ['fju:nərəl] *n* Beerdigung *f*

funfair ['fʌnfɛə*] *n* Jahrmarkt *m*

fungus ['fʌŋgəs] (*pl* **fungi** *o* **funguses**) *n* Pilz *m*

funicular [fju:'nɪkjʊlə*] *n* Seilbahn *f*

funnel ['fʌnl] *n* Trichter *m*; (*of steamer*) Schornstein *m*

funny ['fʌnɪ] *adj* (*amusing*) komisch, lustig; (*strange*) seltsam

fur [fɜ:*] *n* Pelz *m*; (*of animal*) Fell *nt*

furious ['fjʊərɪəs] *adj* wütend (*with sb* auf jdn)

furnished ['fɜ:nɪʃd] *adj* möbliert; **furniture** ['fɜ:nɪtʃə*] *n* Möbel *pl*; **piece of ~** Möbelstück *nt*

further ['fɜ:ðə*] *comparative of* **far**
▷ *adj* weitere(r, s); **~ education** Weiterbildung *f*; **until ~ notice** bis auf weiteres ▷ *adv* weiter; **furthest** ['fɜ:ðɪst] *superlative of* **far** ▷ *adj* am weitesten entfernt ▷ *adv* am weitesten

fury ['fjʊərɪ] *n* Wut *f*

fuse [fju:z] *n* (*Elec*) Sicherung *f* ▷ *vi* (*Elec*) durchbrennen; **fuse box** *n* Sicherungskasten *m*

fuss [fʌs] *n* Theater *nt*; **to make a ~** (ein) Theater machen; **fussy** *adj* (*difficult*) schwierig, kompliziert; (*attentive to detail*) pingelig

future ['fju:tʃə*] *adj* künftig ▷ *n* Zukunft *f*

fuze (*US*) *see* **fuse**

fuzzy ['fʌzɪ] *adj* (*indistinct*) verschwommen; (*hair*) kraus

g

gable ['geɪbl] *n* Giebel *m*

gadget ['gædʒɪt] *n* Vorrichtung *f*, Gerät *nt*

Gaelic ['geɪlɪk] *adj* gälisch ▷ *n* (*language*) Gälisch *nt*

gain [geɪn] *vt* (*obtain, win*) gewinnen; (*advantage, respect*) sich verschaffen; (*wealth*) erwerben; (*weight*) zunehmen ▷ *vi* (*improve*) gewinnen (*in an* +*dat*); (*clock*) vorgehen ▷ *n* Gewinn *m* (*in an* +*dat*)

gale [geɪl] *n* Sturm *m*

gall bladder ['gɔ:lblædə*] *n* Gallenblase *f*

gallery ['gælərɪ] *n* Galerie *f*, Museum *nt*

gallon ['gælən] *n* Gallone *f*; ((*Brit*) 4,546 l, (*US*) 3,79 l)

gallop ['gæləp] *n* Galopp *m* ▷ *vi* galoppieren

gallstone ['gɔ:lstəʊn] *n* Gallenstein *m*

Gambia ['gæmbɪə] n Gambia nt

gamble ['gæmbl] vi um Geld spielen, wetten ▷ n: **it's a ~** es ist riskant; **gambling** n Glücksspiel nt

game [geɪm] n Spiel nt; (animals) Wild nt; **a ~ of chess** eine Partie Schach; **~s** (in school) Sport m; **game show** n (TV) Gameshow f

gammon ['gæmən] n geräucherter Schinken

gang [gæŋ] n (of criminals, youths) Bande f, Gang f, Clique f ▷ vt: **to ~ up on** sich verschwören gegen

gangster ['gæŋstə*] n Gangster m

gangway ['gæŋweɪ] n (for ship) Gangway f; (Brit: aisle) Gang m, Gangway f

gap [gæp] n (hole) Lücke f; (in time) Pause f; (in age) Unterschied m

gape [geɪp] vi (mit offenem Mund) starren

gap year n Jahr zwischen Schulabschluss und Studium, das oft zu Auslandsaufenthalten genutzt wird

garage ['gærɑːʒ] n Garage f; (for repair) (Auto)werkstatt f; (for fuel) Tankstelle f

garbage ['gɑːbɪdʒ] n (US) Müll m; (fam: nonsense) Quatsch m; **garbage can** n (US) Mülleimer m; (outside) Mülltonne f; **garbage truck** n (US) Müllwagen m

garden ['gɑːdn] n Garten m; **(public) ~s** Park m; **garden centre** n Gartencenter nt; **gardener** n Gärtner(in) m(f); **gardening** n Gartenarbeit f

gargle ['gɑːgl] vi gurgeln

gargoyle ['gɑːgɔɪl] n Wasserspeier m

garlic ['gɑːlɪk] n Knoblauch m; **garlic bread** n Knoblauchbrot nt; **garlic butter** n Knoblauchbutter f

gas [gæs] n Gas nt; (US: petrol)

Benzin nt; **to step on the ~** Gas geben; **gas cooker** n Gasherd m; **gas cylinder** n Gasflasche f; **gas fire** n Gasofen m

gasket ['gæskɪt] n Dichtung f

gas lighter n (for cigarettes) Gasfeuerzeug nt; **gas mask** n Gasmaske f; **gas meter** n Gaszähler m

gasoline ['gæsəliːn] n (US) Benzin nt

gasp [gɑːsp] vi keuchen; (in surprise) nach Luft schnappen

gas pedal n (US) Gaspedal nt; **gas pump** n (US) Zapfsäule f; **gas station** n (US) Tankstelle f; **gas tank** n (US) Benzintank m

gastric ['gæstrɪk] adj Magen-; **~ flu** Magen-Darm-Grippe f; **~ ulcer** Magengeschwür nt

gasworks ['gæswɜːks] n Gaswerk nt

gate [geɪt] n Tor nt; (barrier) Schranke f; (Aviat) Gate nt, Flugsteig m

gateau ['gætəʊ] (pl **gateaux**) n Torte f

gateway n Tor nt

gather ['gæðə*] vt (collect) sammeln; **to ~ speed** beschleunigen ▷ vi (assemble) sich versammeln; (understand) schließen (from aus); **gathering** n Versammlung f

gauge [geɪdʒ] n Meßgerät nt

gauze [gɔːz] n Gaze f; (for bandages) Mull m

gave [geɪv] pt of **give**

gay [geɪ] adj (homosexual) schwul; **~ marriage** (fam) Homoehe f

gaze [geɪz] n Blick m ▷ vi starren

GCSE abbr = **general certificate of secondary education** (school) Abschlussprüfung f der Sekundarstufe, ≈ mittlere Reife

gear [gɪə*] n (Auto) Gang m; (equipment) Ausrüstung f; (clothes)

Klamotten pl; **to change ~** schalten; **gearbox** n Getriebe nt; **gear change**, **gear shift** (US) n Gangschaltung f; **gear lever**, **gear stick** (US) n Schalthebel m

geese [giːs] pl of **goose**

gel [dʒel] n Gel nt ▷ vi gelieren; **they really ~led** sie verstanden sich auf Anhieb

gem [dʒem] n Edelstein m; (fig) Juwel nt

Gemini ['dʒemɪniː] nsing (Astr) Zwillinge pl

gender ['dʒendə*] n Geschlecht nt

gene [dʒiːn] n Gen nt

general ['dʒenərəl] adj allgemein; **~ knowledge** Allgemeinbildung f; **~ election** Parlamentswahlen pl; **generalize** ['dʒenərəlaɪz] vi verallgemeinern; **generally** ['dʒenərəlɪ] adv im Allgemeinen

generation [dʒenə'reɪʃən] n Generation f; **generation gap** n Generationsunterschied m

generator ['dʒenəreɪtə*] n Generator m

generosity [dʒenə'rɒsɪtɪ] n Großzügigkeit f; **generous** ['dʒenərəs] adj großzügig; (portion) reichlich

genetic [dʒɪ'netɪk] adj genetisch; **~ research** Genforschung f; **~ technology** Gentechnik f; **genetically modified** adj gentechnisch verändert, genmanipuliert; see also **GM**

Geneva [dʒɪ'niːvə] n Genf nt; **Lake ~** der Genfer See

genitals ['dʒenɪtlz] npl Geschlechtsteile pl

genitive ['dʒenɪtɪv] n Genitiv m

genius ['dʒiːnɪəs] n Genie nt

gentle ['dʒentl] adj sanft; (touch) zart; **gentleman** (pl **-men**) n

Herr m; (polite man) Gentleman m

gents [dʒents] n: **"~"** (lavatory) „Herren"; **the ~** pl die Herrentoilette

genuine ['dʒenjʊɪn] adj echt

geographical [dʒɪə'græfɪkəl] adj geografisch; **geography** [dʒɪ'ɒɡrəfɪ] n Geografie f; (at school) Erdkunde f

geological [dʒɪəʊ'lɒdʒɪkəl] adj geologisch; **geology** [dʒɪ'ɒlədʒɪ] n Geologie f

geometry [dʒɪ'ɒmɪtrɪ] n Geometrie f

geranium [dʒɪ'reɪnɪəm] n Geranie f

gerbil ['dʒɜːbəl] n (Zool) Wüstenrennmaus f

germ [dʒɜːm] n Keim m; (Med) Bazillus m

German ['dʒɜːmən] adj deutsch; **she's ~** sie ist Deutsche; **~ shepherd** Deutscher Schäferhund ▷ n (person) Deutsche(r) mf; (language) Deutsch nt; **in ~** auf Deutsch; **German measles** n sing Röteln pl; **Germany** ['dʒɜːmənɪ] n Deutschland nt

gesture ['dʒestʃə*] n Geste f

KEYWORD

get [get] (pt, pp **got**, pp **gotten** (US)) vi 1 (become, be) werden; **to get old/tired** alt/müde werden; **to get married** heiraten 2 (go) (an)kommen, gehen 3 (begin) **to get to know sb** jdn kennenlernen; **let's get going** o **started!** fangen wir an! 4 (modal vb aux) **you've got to do it** du musst/Sie müssen es tun ▷ vt 1 **to get sth done** (do) etw machen; (have done) etw machen lassen; **to get sth going** o **to go** etw in Gang bringen;

to get sb to do sth jdn dazu bringen, etw zu tun
2 (*obtain: money, permission, results*) erhalten; (*find: job, flat*) finden; (*fetch: person, object*) holen; **to get sth for sb** jdm etw besorgen; **get me Mr Jones, please** (*Tel*) verbinde/verbinden Sie mich bitte mit Mr Jones; **get a life!** (*annoyed*) mach dich mal locker!, reg dich bloß ab!
3 (*receive: present, letter*) bekommen, kriegen; (*acquire: reputation etc*) erwerben
4 (*catch*) bekommen, kriegen; (*hit*) (*target etc*) treffen, erwischen; **get him!** (*to dog*) fass!
5 (*take, move*) bringen; **to get sth to sb** jdm etw bringen
6 (*understand*) verstehen; (*hear*) mitbekommen; **I've got it!** ich hab's!
7 (*have, possess*) **to have got sth** etw haben
get about vi herumkommen, (*news*) sich verbreiten
get across vi: **to sth** über etw akk kommen; vt: **to get sth across** (*communicate*) etw klarmachen
get along vi (*people*) (*gut*) zurecht-/auskommen (*with*) mit; (*depart*) sich akk auf den Weg machen
get at vt (*reach*) herankommen an +akk; (*facts*) herausbekommen; **what are you getting at?** worauf wollen Sie hinaus?, was meinst du damit?; **to get at sb** (*nag*) an jdm herumnörgeln
get away vi (*leave*) sich akk davonmachen, wegkommen (*escape*); **to get away from sth** von etw dat entkommen; **to get away with sth** mit etw davonkommen
get back vi (*return*) zurückkommen; (*Tel*) **to get back**

to s.o. jdn zurückrufen
▷ vt zurückbekommen
get by vi (*pass*) vorbeikommen; (*manage*) zurecht-/auskommen (*on*) mit
get down vi (*her*)untergehen; **to get down to** in Angriff nehmen, (*find time to do*) kommen zu;
▷ vt (*depress*) fertigmachen; **it gets me down** (*fam*) es macht mich fertig; **to get sth down** (*write*) etw aufschreiben
get in vi (*train*) ankommen; (*arrive home*) heimkommen
get into vt (*enter*) hinein-/ hereinkommen in +akk; (*car, train etc*) einsteigen in +akk; (*clothes*) anziehen; (*rage, panic etc*) geraten in +akk; **to get into trouble** in Schwierigkeiten kommen
get off vi (*from train etc*) aussteigen; (*from horse etc*) absteigen; (*fam: be enthusiastic*) **to get off on sth** auf etw abfahren;
▷ vt (*nail, sticker*) los-/abbekommen; (*clothes*) ausziehen
get on vi (*progress*) vorankommen; (*be friends*) auskommen; (*age*) alt werden; (*onto train etc*) einsteigen; (*onto horse etc*) aufsteigen
▷ vt etw +akk vorantreiben, mit etw akk loslegen
get out vi (*of house*) herauskommen; (*of vehicle*) aussteigen; **get out!** raus!
▷ vt (*take out*) herausholen; (*stain, nail*) herausbekommen
get out of vi (*duty etc*) herumkommen um
get over vi (*illness*) sich akk erholen von; (*surprise*) verkraften; (*news*) fassen; (*loss*) sich abfinden mit
get round vi herumkommen um; vt (*fig*) (*person*) herumkriegen

get through vi (Tel) durchkommen (to) zu
get together vi zusammenkommen
get up vi aufstehen ▷ vt hinaufbringen; (go up) hinaufgehen; (organize) auf die Beine stellen
get up to vi (reach) erreichen; (prank etc) anstellen

getaway n Flucht f;
get-together n Treffen nt
Ghana ['gɑːnə] n Ghana nt
gherkin ['gɜːkɪn] n Gewürzgurke f
ghetto ['getəʊ] (pl **-es**) n Ghetto nt
ghost [gəʊst] n Gespenst nt; (of sb) Geist m
giant ['dʒaɪənt] n Riese m ▷ adj riesig
giblets ['dʒɪblɪts] npl Geflügelinnereien pl
Gibraltar [dʒɪ'brɔːltə*] n Gibraltar nt
giddy ['gɪdɪ] adj schwindlig
gift [gɪft] n Geschenk nt; (talent) Begabung f; **gifted** adj begabt; **giftwrap** vt als Geschenk verpacken
gigantic [dʒaɪ'gæntɪk] adj riesig
giggle ['gɪgl] vi kichern ▷ n Gekicher nt
gill [gɪl] n (of fish) Kieme f
gimmick ['gɪmɪk] n (for sales, publicity) Gag m
gin [dʒɪn] n Gin m
ginger ['dʒɪndʒə*] n Ingwer m ▷ adj (colour) kupferrot; (cat) rötlichgelb; **ginger ale** n Gingerale nt; **ginger beer** n Ingwerlimonade f; **gingerbread** n Lebkuchen m (mit Ingwergeschmack); **ginger(-haired)** adj rotblond; **gingerly** adv (move) vorsichtig

gipsy ['dʒɪpsɪ] n Zigeuner(in) m(f)
giraffe [dʒɪ'rɑːf] n Giraffe f
girl [gɜːl] n Mädchen nt; **girlfriend** n (feste) Freundin f; **girl guide** n (Brit), **girl scout** (US) Pfadfinderin f
gist [dʒɪst] n: **to get the ~ (of it)** das Wesentliche verstehen
give [gɪv] (**gave, given**) vt geben; (as present) schenken (to sb jdm); (state: name etc) angeben; (speech) halten; (blood) spenden; **to ~ sb sth** jdm etw geben/schenken ▷ vi (yield) nachgeben; **give away** vt (give free) verschenken; (secret) verraten; **give back** vt zurückgeben; **give in** vi aufgeben; **give up** vt, vi aufgeben; **give way** vi (collapse, yield) nachgeben; (traffic) die Vorfahrt beachten
given ['gɪvn] pp of **give** ▷ adj (fixed) festgesetzt; (certain) bestimmt; **~ name** (US) Vorname m ▷ conj: **~ that ...** angesichts der Tatsache, dass ...
glacier ['glæsɪə*] n Gletscher m
glad [glæd] adj froh (about über); **I was ~ (to hear) that ...** es hat mich gefreut, dass ...; **gladly** ['glædlɪ] adv gerne
glance [glɑːns] n Blick m ▷ vi einen Blick werfen (at auf +akk)
gland [glænd] n Drüse f; **glandular fever** n Drüsenfieber nt
glare [gleə*] n grelles Licht; (stare) stechender Blick ▷ vi (angrily) **to ~ at sb** jdn böse anstarren; **glaring** adj (mistake) krass
glass [glɑːs] n Glas nt; **~es** pl Brille f
glen [glen] n (Scot) (enges) Bergtal nt

glide [glaɪd] vi gleiten; (hover) schweben; **glider** n Segelflugzeug nt; **gliding** n Segelfliegen nt

glimmer ['glɪmə*] n (of hope) Schimmer m

glimpse [glɪmps] n flüchtiger Blick

glitter ['glɪtə*] vi glitzern; (eyes) funkeln

glitzy [glɪtsɪ] adj (fam) glanzvoll, Schickimicki-

global ['gləʊbəl] adj global, Welt-; **~ warming** die Erwärmung der Erdatmosphäre; **globe** [gləʊb] sp2; n (sphere) Kugel f; (world) Erdball m; (map) Globus m

gloomily ['gluːmɪlɪ] , **gloomy** adv, adj düster

glorious ['glɔːrɪəs] adj (victory, past) ruhmreich; (weather, day) herrlich; **glory** ['glɔːrɪ] n Herrlichkeit f

gloss [glɒs] n (shine) Glanz m

glossary ['glɒsərɪ] n Glossar nt

glossy ['glɒsɪ] adj (surface) glänzend ▷ n (magazine) Hochglanzmagazin nt

glove [glʌv] n Handschuh m; **glove compartment** n Handschuhfach nt

glow [gləʊ] vi glühen

glucose ['gluːkəʊs] n Traubenzucker m

glue [gluː] n Klebstoff m ▷ vt kleben

glutton ['glʌtn] n Vielfraß m; **a ~ for punishment** (fam) Masochist m

GM abbr = **genetically modified** Gen-; **~ foods** gentechnisch veränderte Lebensmittel

GMT abbr = **Greenwich Mean Time** WEZ f

go [gəʊ] (**went, gone**) vi gehen; (in vehicle, travel) fahren; (plane) fliegen; (road) führen (to nach); (depart: train, bus) (ab)fahren;

(person) (fort)gehen; (disappear) verschwinden; (time) vergehen; (function) gehen, funktionieren; (machine, engine) laufen; (fit, suit) passen (with zu); (fail) nachlassen; **I have to ~ to the doctor/to London** ich muss zum Arzt/nach London; **to ~ shopping** einkaufen gehen; **to ~ for a walk/swim** spazieren/schwimmen gehen; **has he gone yet?** ist er schon weg?; **the wine ~es in the cupboard** der Wein kommt in den Schrank; **to get sth ~ing** etw in Gang setzen; **to keep ~ing** weitermachen; (machine etc) weiterlaufen; **how's the job ~ing?** was macht der Job?; **his memory/eyesight is going** sein Gedächtnis lässt nach/seine Augen werden schwach; **to ~ deaf/mad/grey** taub/verrückt/grau werden ▷ vb aux: **to be ~ing to do sth** etw tun werden; **I was ~ing to do it** ich wollte es tun ▷ n (pl **-es**) (attempt) Versuch m; **can I have another ~?** darf ich noch mal (probieren)?; **it's my ~** ich bin dran; **in one ~** auf einen Schlag; (drink) in einem Zug; **go after** vt nachlaufen +dat; (in vehicle) nachfahren +dat; **go ahead** vi (in front) vorausgehen; (start) anfangen; **go away** vi weggehen; (on holiday, business) verreisen; **go back** vi (return) zurückgehen; **we ~ a long way** (fam) wir kennen uns schon ewig; **go by** vi vorbeigehen; (vehicle) vorbeifahren; (years, time) vergehen ▷ vt (judge by) gehen nach; **go down** vi (sun, ship) untergehen; (flood, temperature) zurückgehen; (price) sinken; **to ~ well/badly** gut/schlecht ankommen; **go in** vi hineingehen; **go into** vt (enter) hineingehen in +akk; (crash) fahren gegen, hineinfahren in +akk; **to ~ teaching/politics/the army** Lehrer werden/in die Politik gehen/zum Militär gehen; **go off** vi (depart) weggehen; (in vehicle) wegfahren; (lights) ausgehen; (milk etc) sauer werden; (gun, bomb, alarm) losgehen ▷ vt (dislike) nicht mehr mögen; **go on** vi (continue) weitergehen; (lights) angehen; **to ~ with** o **doing sth** etw weitermachen; **go out** vi (leave house) hinausgehen; (fire, light, person socially) ausgehen; **to ~ for a meal** essen gehen; **go up** vi (temperature, price) steigen; (lift) hochfahren; **go without** vt verzichten auf +akk; (food, sleep) auskommen ohne

go-ahead ['gəʊəhed] adj (progressive) fortschrittlich ▷ n grünes Licht

goal [gəʊl] n (aim) Ziel nt; (Sport) Tor nt; **goalie, goalkeeper** n Torwart m, Torfrau f; **goalpost** n Torpfosten m

goat [gəʊt] n Ziege f

gob [gɒb] n (Brit fam) Maul nt; **shut your ~** halt's Maul! ▷ vi spucken; **gobsmacked** (fam: surprised) platt

god [gɒd] n Gott m; **thank God** Gott sei Dank; **godchild** (pl **-children**) n Patenkind nt; **goddaughter** n Patentochter f; **goddess** ['gɒdes] n Göttin f; **godfather** n Pate m; **godmother** n Patin f; **godson** n Patensohn m

goggles npl Schutzbrille f; (for skiing) Skibrille f; (for diving) Taucherbrille f

going ['gəʊɪŋ] adj (rate) üblich; **goings-on** npl Vorgänge pl

go-kart ['gəʊkɑːt] n Gokart m

gold [gəʊld] n Gold nt; **golden** adj golden; **goldfish** n Goldfisch m; **gold-plated** adj vergoldet

golf [gɒlf] n Golf nt; **golf ball** n Golfball m; **golf club** n Golfschläger m; (association) Golfklub m; **golf course** n Golfplatz m; **golfer** n Golfspieler(in) m(f)

gone [gɒn] pp of **go**; **he's ~** er ist weg ▷ prep: **just ~ three** kurz nach drei

good [gʊd] n (benefit) Wohl nt; (morally good things) Gute(s) nt; **for the ~ of** zum Wohle +gen; **it's for your own ~** es ist zu deinem/Ihrem Besten o Vorteil; **it's no ~** (doing sth) es hat keinen Sinn o Zweck; (thing) es taugt nichts; **for ~** für immer ▷ adj (better, best) gut; (suitable) passend; (thorough) gründlich; (well-behaved) brav; (kind) nett, lieb; **to be ~ at sport/maths** gut in Sport/Mathe sein; **to be no ~ at sport/maths** schlecht in Sport/Mathe sein; **it's ~ for you** tut dir gut; **this is ~ for colds** das ist gut gegen Erkältungen; **too ~ to be true** zu schön, um wahr zu sein; **this is just not ~ enough** so geht das nicht; **a ~ three hours** gute drei Stunden; **~ morning/evening** guten Morgen/Abend; **~ night** gute Nacht; **to have a ~ time** sich gut amüsieren

goodbye [gʊd'baɪ] interj auf Wiedersehen

Good Friday n Karfreitag m

good-looking adj gut aussehend

goods [gʊdz] npl Waren pl, Güter pl; **goods train** n (Brit) Güterzug m

goodwill [gʊd'wɪl] n Wohlwollen nt

goose [guːs] (pl **geese**) n Gans f

▷ vt (fam) **to ~ s.o.** jdn in den Arsch kneifen; **gooseberry** ['gʊzbərɪ] n Stachelbeere f; **goose bumps** n, **goose pimples** npl Gänsehaut f

gorge [gɔːdʒ] n Schlucht f

gorgeous ['gɔːdʒəs] adj wunderschön; **he's ~** er sieht toll aus

gorilla [gəˈrɪlə] n Gorilla m

gossip ['gɒsɪp] n (talk) Klatsch m; (person) Klatschtante f ▷ vi klatschen, tratschen

got [gɒt] pt, pp of **get**

gotten ['gɒtn] (US) pp of **get**

govern ['gʌvən] vt regieren; (province etc) verwalten; **government** n Regierung f; **governor** n Gouverneur(in) m(f); **govt** abbr = **government** Regierung f

gown [gaʊn] n Abendkleid nt; (academic) Robe f

GP abbr = **General Practitioner** Allgemeinarzt, Allgemeinärztin

GPS n abbr = **global positioning system** GPS nt

grab [græb] vt packen; (person) schnappen

grace [greɪs] n Anmut f; (prayer) Tischgebet nt; **5 days' ~** 5 Tage Aufschub; **graceful** adj anmutig

grade [greɪd] n Niveau nt; (of goods) Güteklasse f; (mark) Note f; (US: year) Klasse f; **to make the ~** es schaffen; **grade crossing** n (US) Bahnübergang m; **grade school** n (US) Grundschule f

gradient ['greɪdɪənt] n (upward) Steigung f; (downward) Gefälle nt

gradual, **gradually** ['grædjʊəl, -lɪ] adj, adv allmählich

graduate ['grædjʊɪt] n Uniabsolvent(in) m(f), Hochschulabsolvent(in) m(f) ▷ ['grædjʊeɪt] vi einen akademischen Grad erwerben

grain [greɪn] n (cereals) Getreide nt; (of corn, sand) Korn nt; (in wood) Maserung f

gram [græm] n Gramm nt

grammar ['græmə*] n Grammatik f; **grammar school** n (Brit) ≈ Gymnasium nt

gran [græn] n (fam) Oma f

grand [grænd] adj (pej) hochnäsig; (posh) vornehm ▷ n (fam) 1000 Pfund bzw. 1000 Dollar

grand(d)ad n (fam) Opa m; **granddaughter** n Enkelin f; **grandfather** n Großvater m; **grandma** n (fam) Oma f; **grandmother** n Großmutter f; **grandpa** n (fam) Opa m; **grandparents** npl Großeltern pl; **grandson** n Enkel m

grandstand n (Sport) Tribüne f

granny ['grænɪ] n (fam) Oma f

grant [grɑːnt] vt gewähren (sb sth jdm etw); **to take sb/sth for ~ed** jdn/etw als selbstverständlich hinnehmen ▷ n Subvention f, finanzielle Unterstützung f; (for university) Stipendium nt

grape [greɪp] n Weintraube f; **grapefruit** n Grapefruit f; **grape juice** n Traubensaft m

graph [grɑːf] n Diagramm nt; **graphic** ['græfɪk] adj grafisch; (description) anschaulich

grasp [grɑːsp] vt ergreifen; (understand) begreifen

grass [grɑːs] n Gras nt; (lawn) Rasen m; **grasshopper** n Heuschrecke f

grate [greɪt] n Feuerrost m ▷ vi kratzen ▷ vt (cheese) reiben

grateful, **gratefully** ['greɪtfʊl, -fəlɪ] adj, adv dankbar

grater ['greɪtə*] n Reibe f

gratifying ['grætɪfaɪɪŋ] adj erfreulich

gratitude ['grætɪtjuːd] n Dankbarkeit f

grave [greɪv] n Grab nt ▷ adj
ernst; (mistake) schwer
gravel ['grævəl] n Kies m
graveyard ['greɪvjɑːd] n Friedhof m
gravity ['grævɪtɪ] n Schwerkraft
f; (seriousness) Ernst m
gravy ['greɪvɪ] n Bratensoße
f
gray [greɪ] adj (US) grau
graze [greɪz] vi (of animals)
grasen ▷ vt (touch) streifen; (Med)
abschürfen ▷ n (Med)
Abschürfung f
grease [griːs] n (fat) Fett nt;
(lubricant) Schmiere f ▷ vt
einfetten; (Tech) schmieren;
greasy ['griːsɪ] adj fettig; (hands,
tools) schmierig; (fam: person)
schleimig
great [greɪt] adj groß; (fam: good)
großartig, super; **a ~ deal of** viel;
Great Britain ['greɪt'brɪtn] n
Großbritannien nt;
great-grandfather n Urgroß-
vater m; **great-grandmother** n
Urgroßmutter f; **greatly** adv sehr;
~ disappointed zutiefst
enttäuscht
Greece [griːs] n Griechenland nt
greed [griːd] n Gier f (for nach);
(for food) Gefräßigkeit f; **greedy**
adj gierig; (for food) gefräßig
Greek [griːk] adj griechisch ▷ n
(person) Grieche m, Griechin f;
(language) Griechisch nt; **it's all
~ to me** ich verstehe nur
Bahnhof
green [griːn] adj grün; **~ with
envy** grün/gelb vor Neid ▷ n
(colour; for golf) Grün nt; (village ~)
Dorfwiese f; **~s** (vegetables) grünes
Gemüse; **the Greens, the Green
Party** (Pol) die Grünen; **green card**
n (US: work permit)
Arbeitserlaubnis f; (Brit: for car)
grüne Versicherungskarte;

greengage n Reneklode f;
greengrocer n Obst- und
Gemüsehändler(in) m(f);
greenhouse n Gewächshaus nt;
~ effect Treibhauseffekt m;
Greenland n Grönland nt; **green
pepper** n grüner Paprika; **green
salad** n grüner Salat
Greenwich Mean Time
['grenɪdʒ'miːntaɪm] n west-
europäische Zeit
greet [griːt] vt grüßen; **greeting**
n Gruß m
grew [gruː] pt of **grow**
grey [greɪ] adj grau; **grey-haired**
adj grauhaarig; **greyhound** n
Windhund m
grid [grɪd] n Gitter nt; **gridlock** n
Verkehrsinfarkt m; **gridlocked** adj
(roads) völlig verstopft; (talks)
festgefahren
grief [griːf] n Kummer m; (over
loss) Trauer f
grievance ['griːvəns] n
Beschwerde f
grieve [griːv] vi trauern (for um)
grill [grɪl] n (on cooker) Grill m ▷ vt
grillen
grim [grɪm] adj (face, humour)
grimmig; (situation, prospects)
trostlos
grin [grɪn] n Grinsen nt ▷ vi
grinsen
grind [graɪnd] (**ground, ground**)
vt mahlen; (sharpen) schleifen; (US:
meat) durchdrehen, hacken
grip [grɪp] n Griff m; **get a
~** nimm dich zusammen!; **to get
to ~s with sth** etw in den Griff
bekommen ▷ vt packen; **gripping**
adj (exciting) spannend
groan [grəʊn] vi stöhnen (with
vor +dat)
grocer ['grəʊsə*] n Lebensmit-
telhändler(in) m(f); **groceries** npl
Lebensmittel pl
groin [grɔɪn] n (Anat) Leiste f;

groin strain n (Med) Leistenbruch m
groom [gru:m] n Bräutigam m
▷ vt: **well ~ed** gepflegt
grope [grəʊp] vi tasten ▷ vt
(sexually harrass) befummeln
gross [grəʊs] adj (coarse) derb;
(extreme: negligence, error) grob;
(disgusting) ekelhaft; (Comm)
brutto; **~ national product**
Bruttosozialprodukt nt; **~ salary**
Bruttogehalt nt
grotty ['grɒtɪ] adj (fam) mies,
vergammelt
ground [graʊnd] pt, pp of **grind**
▷ n Boden m, Erde f; (Sport) Platz
m; **~s** pl (around house)
(Garten)anlagen pl; (reasons)
Gründe pl; (of coffee) Satz m; **on
(the) ~s of** aufgrund von; **ground
floor** n (Brit) Erdgeschoss nt;
ground meat n (US) Hackfleisch
nt
group [gru:p] n Gruppe f ▷ vt
gruppieren
grouse [graʊs] (pl -) n (bird)
Schottisches Moorhuhn;
(complaint) Nörgelei f
grow [grəʊ] (**grew, grown**) vi
wachsen; (increase) zunehmen (in
an); (become) werden; **to ~ old** alt
werden; **to ~ into ...** sich
entwickeln zu ... ▷ vt (crop, plant)
ziehen; (commercially) anbauen;
I'm ~ing a beard ich lasse mir
einen Bart wachsen; **grow up** vi
aufwachsen; (mature) erwachsen
werden; **growing** adj wachsend;
a ~ number of people immer
mehr Leute
growl [graʊl] vi knurren
grown [grəʊn] pp of **grow**
grown-up [grəʊn'ʌp] adj
erwachsen ▷ n Erwachsene(r) mf;
growth [grəʊθ] n Wachstum nt;
(increase) Zunahme f; (Med)
Wucherung f

grubby ['grʌbɪ] adj schmuddelig
grudge [grʌdʒ] n Abneigung f
(against gegen); **to ~ sb sth**
jdm etw nicht gönnen
gruelling ['grʊəlɪŋ] adj
aufreibend; (pace) mörderisch
gruesome ['gru:səm] adj
grausig
grumble ['grʌmbl] vi murren
(about über +akk)
grumpy ['grʌmpɪ] adj (fam)
mürrisch, grantig
grunt [grʌnt] vi grunzen
G-string ['dʒiːstrɪŋ] n String m,
Stringtanga m
guarantee [gærən'tiː] n Garantie f (of für); **it's still under ~** es ist
noch Garantie darauf ▷ vt
garantieren
guard [gɑːd] n (sentry) Wache f;
(in prison) Wärter(in) m(f); (Brit
Rail) Schaffner(in) m(f) ▷ vt
bewachen; **a closely ~ed
secret** ein streng gehütetes
Geheimnis
guardian ['gɑːdɪən] n Vormund
m; **~ angel** Schutzengel m
guess [ges] n Vermutung f;
(estimate) Schätzung f; **have a
~ rate mal!** ▷ vt, vi raten;
(estimate) schätzen; **I ~ you're
right** du hast wohl recht; **I ~ so** ich
glaube schon
guest [gest] n Gast m; **be my
~** nur zu!; **guest-house** n Pension
f; **guest room** n Gästezimmer
nt
guidance ['gaɪdəns] n (direction)
Leitung f; (advice) Rat m;
(counselling) Beratung f; **for your
~** zu Ihrer Orientierung; **guide**
[gaɪd] n (person) Führer(in) m(f);
(tour) Reiseleiter(in) m(f); (book)
Führer m; (girl ~) Pfadfinderin f
▷ vt führen; **guidebook** n
Reiseführer m; **guide dog** n
Blindenhund m; **guided tour** n

Führung f (of durch); **guidelines**
npl Richtlinien pl
guilt [gɪlt] n Schuld f; **guilty** adj
schuldig (of gen); (look)
schuldbewusst; **to have a
~ conscience** ein schlechtes
Gewissen haben
guinea pig ['gɪnɪ pɪg] n
Meerschweinchen nt; (person)
Versuchskaninchen nt
guitar [gɪ'tɑ:ʳ] n Gitarre f
gulf [gʌlf] n Golf m; (gap) Kluft f;
Gulf States npl Golfstaaten pl
gull [gʌl] n Möwe f
gullible ['gʌlɪbl] adj
leichtgläubig
gulp [gʌlp] n (kräftiger) Schluck
▷ vi schlucken
gum [gʌm] n (around teeth, usu pl)
Zahnfleisch nt; (chewing ~)
Kaugummi m
gun [gʌn] n Schusswaffe f; (rifle)
Gewehr nt; (pistol) Pistole f;
gunfire n Schüsse pl,
Geschützfeuer nt; **gunpowder** n
Schießpulver nt; **gunshot** n
Schuss m
gush [gʌʃ] vi (heraus)strömen
(from aus)
gut [gʌt] n Darm m; **~s** pl
(intestines) Eingeweide; (courage)
Mumm m
gutter ['gʌtəʳ] n (for roof)
Dachrinne f; (in street) Rinnstein m,
Gosse f; **gutter press** n
Skandalpresse f
guy [gaɪ] n (man) Typ m, Kerl m; **~s**
pl (US) Leute pl
gym [dʒɪm] n Turnhalle f; (for
working out) Fitnesscenter nt;
gymnasium [dʒɪm'neɪzɪəm] n
Turnhalle f; **gymnastics**
[dʒɪm'næstɪks] nsing Turnen nt;
gym-toned adj durchtrainiert
gynaecologist [gaɪnɪ'kɒlədʒɪst]
n Frauenarzt m, Frauenärztin f,
Gynäkologe m, Gynäkologin f;

gynaecology n Gynäkologie f,
Frauenheilkunde f
gypsy ['dʒɪpsɪ] n Zigeuner(in)
m(f)

h

habit ['hæbɪt] n Gewohnheit f; **habitual** [hə'bɪtjʊəl] adj gewohnt; (drinker, liar) gewohnheitsmäßig

hack [hæk] vt hacken; **hacker** n (Inform) Hacker(in) m(f)

had [hæd] pt, pp of **have**

haddock ['hædək] n Schellfisch m

hadn't ['hædnt] contr of **had not**

haemophiliac, **hemophiliac** (US) [hiːməʊ'fɪliæk] n Bluter(in) m(f); **haemorrhage**, **hemorrhage** (US) ['hemərɪdʒ] n Blutung f ▷ vi bluten; **haemorrhoids**, **hemorrhoids** (US) ['heməroɪdz] npl Hämorrhoiden pl

haggis ['hægɪs] n (Scot) mit gehackten Schafsinnereien und Haferschrot gefüllter Schafsmagen

Hague [heɪg] n: **the ~** Den Haag

hail [heɪl] n Hagel m ▷ vi hageln ▷ vt: **to ~ sb as sth** jdn als etw feiern; **hailstone** n Hagelkorn nt; **hailstorm** n Hagelschauer m

hair [hɛə*] n Haar nt, Haare pl; **to do one's ~** sich frisieren; **to get one's ~ cut** sich dat die Haare schneiden lassen; **hairbrush** n Haarbürste f; **hair conditioner** n Haarspülung f; **haircut** n Haarschnitt m; **to have a ~** sich dat die Haare schneiden lassen; **hairdo** (pl **-s**) n Frisur f; **hairdresser** n Friseur m, Friseuse f; **hairdryer** n Haartrockner m; (hand-held) Fön® m; (over head) Trockenhaube f; **hair gel** n Haargel nt; **hairpin** n Haarnadel f; **hair remover** n Enthaarungsmittel nt; **hair spray** n Haarspray nt; **hair style** n Frisur f; **hairy** adj haarig, behaart; (fam: dangerous) brenzlig

hake [heɪk] n Seehecht m

half [hɑːf] (pl **halves**) n Hälfte f; (Sport: of game) Halbzeit f; **to cut in ~** halbieren ▷ adj halb; **three and a ~ pounds** dreieinhalb Pfund; **~ an hour, a ~ hour** eine halbe Stunde; **one and a ~** eineinhalb, anderthalb ▷ adv halb, zur Hälfte; **~ past three, ~ three** halb vier; **at ~ past** um halb; **~ asleep** fast eingeschlafen; **she's ~ German** sie ist zur Hälfte Deutsche; **~ as big (as)** halb so groß (wie); **half board** n Halbpension f; **half fare** n halber Fahrpreis; **half-hearted** adj halbherzig; **half-hour** n halbe Stunde; **half moon** n Halbmond m; **half pint** n ≈ Viertelliter m o nt; **half price** n: (**at**) **~** zum halben Preis; **half-term** n (at school) Ferien pl in der Mitte des Trimesters; **half-time** n Halbzeit f; **halfway** adv auf halbem Wege; **halfwit** n (fam) Trottel m

halibut ['hælɪbət] n Heilbutt m

hall [hɔːl] n (building) Halle f; (for

audience) Saal *m*; *(entrance ~)* Flur *m*; *(large)* Diele *f*; **~ of residence** *(Brit)* Studentenwohnheim *nt*
hallmark ['hɔːlmɑːk] *n* Stempel *m*; *(fig)* Kennzeichen *nt*
hallo [hʌ'ləʊ] *interj* hallo
Hallowe'en [hæləʊ'iːn] *n* Halloween *nt* *(Tag vor Allerheiligen, an dem sich Kinder verkleiden und von Tür zu Tür gehen)*

- **HALLOWE'EN**
-
- **Hallowe'en** ist der 31. Oktober,
- der Vorabend von Allerheiligen,
- und nach altem Glauben der
- Abend, an dem man Geister und
- Hexen sehen kann. In
- Großbritannien und vor allem in
- den USA feiern die Kinder
- Hallowe'en, indem sie sich
- verkleiden und mit selbst
- gemachten Laternen aus
- Kürbissen von Tür zu Tür
- ziehen.

halo ['heɪləʊ] *(pl* **-es**) *n (of saint)* Heiligenschein *m*
halt [hɔːlt] *n* Pause *f*, Halt *m*; **to come to a ~** zum Stillstand kommen ▷ *vt, vi* anhalten
halve [hɑːv] *vt* halbieren
ham [hæm] *n* Schinken *m*; **~ and eggs** Schinken mit Spiegelei
hamburger ['hæmbɜːɡə*] *n (Gastr)* Hamburger *m*
hammer ['hæmə*] *n* Hammer *m* ▷ *vt, vi* hämmern
hammock ['hæmək] *n* Hängematte *f*
hamper ['hæmpə*] *vt* behindern ▷ *n (as gift)* Geschenkkorb *m*; *(for picnic)* Picknickkorb *m*
hamster ['hæmstə*] *n* Hamster *m*
hand [hænd] *n* Hand *f*; *(of clock, instrument)* Zeiger *m*; *(in card game)* Blatt *nt*; **to be made by**

~ Handarbeit sein; **~s up!** Hände hoch!; *(at school)* meldet euch!; **~s off!** Finger weg!; **on the one ~ ..., on the other ~...** einerseits ..., andererseits ...; **to give sb a ~** jdm helfen *(with* bei*)*; **it's in his ~s** er hat es in der Hand; **to be in good ~s** gut aufgehoben sein; **to get out of ~** außer Kontrolle geraten ▷ *vt (pass)* reichen *(to sb* jdm*)*; **hand down** *vt (tradition)* überliefern; *(heirloom)* vererben; **hand in** *vt* einreichen; *(at school, university etc)* abgeben; **hand out** *vt* verteilen; **hand over** *vt* übergeben
handbag *n* Handtasche *f*; **handbook** *n* Handbuch *nt*; **handbrake** *n (Brit)* Handbremse *f*; **handcuffs** *npl* Handschellen *pl*; **handful** *n* Handvoll *f*; **handheld PC** *n* Handheld *m*
handicap ['hændɪkæp] *n* Behinderung *f*, Handikap *nt* ▷ *vt* benachteiligen; **handicapped** *adj* behindert; **the ~** die Behinderten
handicraft ['hændɪkrɑːft] *n* Kunsthandwerk *nt*
handkerchief ['hæŋkətʃɪf] *n* Taschentuch *nt*
handle ['hændl] *n* Griff *m*; *(of door)* Klinke *f*; *(of cup etc)* Henkel *m*; *(for winding)* Kurbel *f* ▷ *vt (touch)* anfassen; *(deal with: matter)* sich befassen mit; *(people, machine etc)* umgehen mit; *(situation, problem)* fertig werden mit; **handlebars** *npl* Lenkstange *f*
hand luggage ['hændlʌɡɪdʒ] *n* Handgepäck *nt*; **handmade** *adj* handgefertigt; **to be ~** Handarbeit sein; **handout** *n (sheet)* Handout *nt*, Thesenpapier *nt*; **handset** *n* Hörer *m*; **please replace the ~** bitte legen Sie auf; **hands-free phone** *n* Freisprechanlage *f*; **handshake** *n* Händedruck *m*

handsome ['hænsəm] adj (man) gut aussehend

hands-on [hændz'ɒn] adj praxisorientiert; **~ experience** praktische Erfahrung

handwriting ['hændraɪtɪŋ] n Handschrift f

handy ['hændɪ] adj (useful) praktisch

hang [hæŋ] (**hung, hung**) vt (auf)hängen; (execute: hanged, hanged) hängen; **to ~ sth on sth** etw an etw akk hängen ▷ vi hängen ▷ n: **he's got the ~ of it** er hat den Dreh raus; **hang about** vi sich herumtreiben, rumhängen; **hang on** vi sich festhalten (to an +dat); (fam: wait) warten; **to ~ to sth** etw behalten; **hang up** vi (Tel) auflegen ▷ vt aufhängen

hangar ['hæŋə*] n Flugzeughalle f

hanger ['hæŋə*] n Kleiderbügel m

hang glider ['hæŋglaɪdə*] n (Flug)drachen m; (person) Drachenflieger(in) m(f); **hang-gliding** n Drachenfliegen nt

hangover ['hæŋəʊvə*] n (bad head) Kater m; (relic) Überbleibsel nt

hankie ['hæŋkɪ] n (fam) Taschentuch nt

happen ['hæpən] vi geschehen; (sth strange, unpleasant) passieren; **if anything should ~ to me** wenn mir etwas passieren sollte; **it won't ~ again** es wird nicht wieder vorkommen; **I ~ed to be passing** ich kam zufällig vorbei; **happening** n Ereignis nt, Happening nt

happily ['hæpɪlɪ] adv fröhlich, glücklich; (luckily) glücklicherweise; **happiness** ['hæpɪnəs] n Glück nt; **happy** ['hæpɪ] adj glücklich; (satisfied)

~ with sth mit etw zufrieden; (willing) **to be ~ to do sth** etw gerne tun; **Happy Christmas** fröhliche Weihnachten!; **Happy New Year** ein glückliches Neues Jahr!; **Happy Birthday** herzlichen Glückwunsch zum Geburtstag!; **happy hour** n Happy Hour f (Zeit, in der man in Bars Getränke zu günstigeren Preisen bekommt)

harass ['hærəs] vt (ständig) belästigen; **harassment** n Belästigung f; (at work) Mobbing nt; **sexual ~** sexuelle Belästigung

harbor (US), **harbour** ['hɑːbə*] n Hafen m

hard [hɑːd] adj hart; (difficult) schwer, schwierig; (harsh) hart(herzig); **don't be ~ on him** sei nicht zu streng zu ihm; **it's ~ to believe** es ist kaum zu glauben ▷ adv (work) schwer; (run) schnell; (rain, snow) stark; **to try ~/~er** sich dat große/mehr Mühe geben; **hardback** n gebundene Ausgabe; **hard-boiled** adj (egg) hart gekocht; **hard copy** n (Inform) Ausdruck m; **hard disk** n (Inform) Festplatte f; **harden** vt härten ▷ vi hart werden; **hardened** adj (person) abgehärtet (to gegen); **hard-hearted** adj hartherzig; **hardliner** n Hardliner(in) m(f); **hardly** ['hɑːdlɪ] adv kaum; **~ ever** fast nie; **hardship** ['hɑːdʃɪp] n Not f; **hard shoulder** n (Brit) Standspur f; **hardware** n (Inform) Hardware f, Haushalts- und Eisenwaren pl; **hard-working** adj fleißig, tüchtig

hare [heə*] n Hase m

harm [hɑːm] n Schaden m; (bodily) Verletzung f; **it wouldn't do any ~** es würde nicht schaden ▷ vt schaden +dat; (person) verletzen; **harmful** adj schädlich; **harmless** adj harmlos

harp [hɑːp] *n* Harfe *f*
harsh [hɑːʃ] *adj* (*climate, voice*) rau; (*light, sound*) grell; (*severe*) hart, streng
harvest ['hɑːvɪst] *n* Ernte *f*; (*time*) Erntezeit *f* ▷ *vt* ernten
has [hæz] *pres of* **have**
hash [hæʃ] *n* (*Gastr*) Haschee *nt*; (*fam: hashish*) Haschisch *nt*; **to make a ~ of sth** etw vermasseln; **hash browns** *npl* (*US*) ≈ Kartoffelpuffer/Rösti mit Zwiebeln *pl*
hassle ['hæsl] *n* Ärger *m*; (*fuss*) Theater *nt*; **no ~** kein Problem ▷ *vt* bedrängen
hasn't ['hæznt] *contr of* **has not**
haste [heɪst] *n* Eile *f*; **hastily**, **hasty** *adv, adj* hastig; (*rash*) vorschnell
hat [hæt] *n* Hut *m*
hatch [hætʃ] *n* (*Naut*) Luke *f*; (*in house*) Durchreiche *f*; **hatchback** ['hætʃbæk] *n* (*car*) Wagen *m* mit Hecktür
hate [heɪt] *vt* hassen; **I ~ doing this** ich mache das sehr ungern ▷ *n* Hass *m* (*of auf +akk*)
haul [hɔːl] *vt* ziehen, schleppen ▷ *n* (*booty*) Beute *f*; **haulage** ['hɔːlɪdʒ] *n* Transport *m*; (*trade*) Spedition *f*; **haunted** *adj*: **a ~ house** ein Haus, in dem es spukt

O **KEYWORD**

have [hæv] (*pt, pp* **had**) *vb aux* **1** haben; (*esp with vbs of motion*) sein; **to have arrived/slept** angekommen sein/geschlafen haben; **to have been** gewesen sein; **having eaten** *o* **when he had eaten, he left** nachdem er gegessen hatte, ging er
2 (*in tag questions*) **you've done it, haven't you?** du hast/Sie haben es doch gemacht, oder nicht?

3 (*in short answers and questions*) **you've made a mistake — so I have/no I haven't** du hast/Sie haben einen Fehler gemacht — ja, stimmt/nein; **we haven't paid — yes we have!** wir haben nicht bezahlt — doch!; **I've been there before, have you?** ich war schon einmal da, du/Sie auch?
▷ *modal vb aux* (*be obliged*): **to have (got) to do sth** etw tun müssen; **you haven't to tell her** du darfst es ihr nicht erzählen
▷ *vt* **1** (*possess*) haben; **he has (got) blue eyes** er hat blaue Augen; **I have (got) an idea** ich habe eine Idee
2 (*referring to meals etc*) **to have breakfast/a cigarette** frühstücken/eine Zigarette rauchen
3 (*receive, obtain etc*) haben; **may I have your address?** kann ich deine/Ihre Adresse haben?; **to have a baby** ein Kind bekommen
4 (*maintain, allow*) **he will have it that he is right** er besteht darauf, dass er recht hat; **I won't have it** das lasse ich mir nicht bieten
5 to have sth done etw machen lassen; **to have sb do sth** jdn etw machen lassen; **he soon had them all laughing** er brachte sie alle zum Lachen
6 (*experience, suffer*) **she had her bag stolen** man hat ihr die Tasche gestohlen; **he had his arm broken** er hat sich den Arm gebrochen
7 (*+noun: take, hold etc*) **to have a walk/rest** spazieren gehen/sich ausruhen; **to have a meeting/party** eine Besprechung/Party haben; **have on** *vt* (*be wearing*) anhaben; (*have arranged*) vorhaben; (*Brit*) **you're having me on** du verarschst mich doch;

have out vt: **to have it out with sb** (settle problem) etw mit jdm bereden

Hawaii [həˈwaɪiː] n Hawaii nt

hawk [hɔːk] n Habicht m

hay [heɪ] n Heu nt; **hay fever** n Heuschnupfen m

hazard [ˈhæzəd] n Gefahr f; (risk) Risiko nt; **hazardous** adj gefährlich; **~ waste** Sondermüll m; **hazard warning lights** npl Warnblinkanlage f

haze [heɪz] n Dunst m

hazelnut [ˈheɪzlnʌt] n Haselnuss f

hazy [ˈheɪzɪ] adj (misty) dunstig; (vague) verschwommen

he [hiː] pron er

head [hed] n Kopf m; (leader) Leiter(in) m(f); (at school) Schulleiter(in) m(f); **~ of state** Staatsoberhaupt nt; **at the ~ of** an der Spitze von; (tossing coin) **~s or tails?** Kopf oder Zahl? ▷ adj (leading) Ober-; **~ boy** Schulsprecher m; **~ girl** Schulsprecherin f ▷ vt anführen; (organization) leiten; **head for** vt zusteuern auf +akk; **he's heading for trouble** er wird Ärger bekommen

headache [ˈhedeɪk] n Kopfschmerzen pl, Kopfweh nt; **header** n (football) Kopfball m; (dive) Kopfsprung m; **headfirst** adj kopfüber; **headhunt** vt (Comm) abwerben; **heading** n Überschrift f; **headlamp, headlight** n Scheinwerfer m; **headline** n Schlagzeile f; **headmaster** n Schulleiter m; **headmistress** n Schulleiterin f; **head-on collision** adj Frontalzusammenstoß m; **headphones** npl Kopfhörer m; **headquarters** npl (of firm) Zentrale f; **headrest, head**restraint n Kopfstütze f; **headscarf** (pl **-scarves**) n Kopftuch nt; **head teacher** n Schulleiter(in) m(f)

heal [hiːl] vt, vi heilen

health [helθ] n Gesundheit f; **good/bad for one's ~** gesund/ungesund; **your ~!** zum Wohl!; **~ and beauty** Wellness; **health centre** n Ärztezentrum nt; **health club** n Fitnesscenter nt; **health food** n Reformkost f; **~ shop, ~ store** Bioladen m; **health insurance** n Krankenversicherung f; **health service** n Gesundheitswesen nt; **healthy** adj gesund

heap [hiːp] n Haufen m; **~s of** (fam) jede Menge ▷ vt, vi häufen

hear [hɪə*] n (**heard, heard**) vt, vi hören; **to ~ about sth** von etw erfahren; **I've ~d of it/him** ich habe schon davon/von ihm gehört; **hearing** n Gehör nt; (Jur) Verhandlung f; **hearing aid** n Hörgerät nt; **hearsay** n: **from ~** vom Hörensagen

heart [hɑːt] n Herz nt; **to lose/take ~** den Mut verlieren/Mut fassen; **to learn by ~** auswendig lernen; (cards) **~s** Herz nt; **queen of ~s** Herzdame f; **heart attack** n Herzanfall m; **heartbeat** n Herzschlag m; **heartbreaking** adj herzzerreißend; **heartbroken** adj todunglücklich, untröstlich; **heartburn** n Sodbrennen nt; **heart failure** n Herzversagen nt; **heartfelt** adj tief empfunden; **heartless** adj herzlos; **heart-throb** n (fam) Schwarm m; **heart-to-heart** n offene Aussprache; **hearty** [hɑːtɪ] adj (meal, appetite) herzhaft; (welcome) herzlich

heat [hiːt] n Hitze f; (pleasant) Wärme f; (temperature) Temperatur f; (Sport) Vorlauf m ▷ vt (house, room) heizen; **heat up** vi warm werden ▷ vt aufwärmen; **heated** adj beheizt; (fig) hitzig; **heater** n Heizofen m; (Auto) Heizung f

heath [hi:θ] n (Brit) Heide f; **heather** ['heðə*] n Heidekraut nt

heating ['hi:tɪŋ] n Heizung f; **heat resistant** adj hitzebeständig; **heatwave** n Hitzewelle f

heaven ['hevn] n Himmel m; **heavenly** adj himmlisch

heavily ['hevɪlɪ] adv (rain, drink etc) stark; **heavy** ['hevɪ] adj schwer; (rain, traffic, smoker etc) stark; **heavy goods vehicle** n Lastkraftwagen m

Hebrew ['hi:bru:] adj hebräisch ▷ n (language) Hebräisch nt

hectic ['hektɪk] adj hektisch

he'd [hi:d] contr of **he had**; **he would**

hedge [hedʒ] n Hecke f

hedgehog ['hedʒhɒg] n Igel m

heel [hi:l] n (Anat) Ferse f; (of shoe) Absatz m

hefty ['heftɪ] adj schwer; (person) stämmig; (fine, amount) saftig

height [haɪt] n Höhe f; (of person) Größe f

heir [ɛə*] n Erbe m; **heiress** ['ɛərɪs] n Erbin f

held [held] pt, pp of **hold**

helicopter ['helɪkɒptə*] n Hubschrauber m; **heliport** ['helɪpɔ:t] n Hubschrauber-landeplatz m

hell [hel] n Hölle f; **go to ~** scher dich zum Teufel ▷ interj verdammt; **that's a ~ of a lot of money** das ist verdammt viel Geld

he'll [hi:l] contr of **he will**; **he shall**

hello [hʌ'ləʊ] interj hallo

helmet ['helmɪt] n Helm m

help [help] n Hilfe f ▷ vt, vi helfen +dat (with bei); **to ~ sb (to) do sth** jdm helfen, etw zu tun; **can I ~?** kann ich (Ihnen) behilflich sein?; **I couldn't ~ laughing** ich musste einfach lachen; **I can't ~ it** ich kann nichts dafür; **~ yourself** bedienen Sie sich; **helpful** adj (person) hilfsbereit; (useful) nützlich; **helping** n Portion f; **helpless** adj hilflos

hem [hem] n Saum m

hemophiliac [hi:məʊ'fɪlɪæk] n (US) Bluter m; **hemorrhage** ['hemərɪdʒ] n (US) Blutung f; **hemorrhoids** ['hemərɔɪdz] npl (US) Hämorrhoiden pl

hen [hen] n Henne f

hen night n (Brit) Junggesellinnenabschied m

hence [hens] adv (reason) daher

henpecked ['henpekt] adj: **to be ~** unter dem Pantoffel stehen

hepatitis [hepə'taɪtɪs] n Hepatitis f

her [hɜ:*] adj ihr; **she's hurt ~ leg** sie hat sich dat das Bein verletzt ▷ pron (direct object) sie; (indirect object) ihr; **do you know ~?** kennst du sie?; **can you help ~?** kannst du ihr helfen?; **it's ~** sie ist's

herb [hɜ:b] n Kraut nt

herbal medicine ['hɜ:bəl-] n Pflanzenheilkunde f; **herbal tea** n Kräutertee m

herd [hɜ:d] n Herde f; **herd instinct** n Herdentrieb m

here [hɪə*] adv hier; (to this place) hierher; **come ~** komm her; **I won't be ~ for lunch** ich bin zum Mittagessen nicht da; **~ and there** hier und da, da und dort

hereditary [hɪ'redɪtərɪ] adj erblich; **hereditary disease** n Erbkrankheit f; **heritage** ['herɪtɪdʒ] n Erbe nt

hernia ['hɜːnɪə] n Leistenbruch m, Eingeweidebruch m

hero ['hɪərəʊ] (pl **-es**) n Held m

heroin ['herəʊɪn] n Heroin nt

heroine ['herəʊɪn] n Heldin f; **heroism** ['herəʊɪzəm] n Heldentum nt

herring ['herɪŋ] n Hering m

hers [hɜːz] pron ihre(r, s); **this is ~** das gehört ihr; **a friend of ~** ein Freund von ihr

herself [hɜː'self] pron (reflexive) sich; **she's bought ~ a flat** sie hat sich eine Wohnung gekauft; **she needs it for ~** sie braucht es für sich (selbst); (emphatic) **she did it ~** sie hat es selbst gemacht; (**all**) **by ~** allein

he's [hiːz] contr of **he is**; **he has**

hesitant ['hezɪtənt] adj zögernd; **hesitate** ['hezɪteɪt] vi zögern; **don't ~ to ask** fragen Sie ruhig; **hesitation** n Zögern nt; **without ~** ohne zu zögern

heterosexual [hetərəʊ'sekʃʊəl] adj heterosexuell ▷ n Heterosexuelle(r) mf

HGV abbr = **heavy goods vehicle** LKW m

hi [haɪ] interj hi, hallo

hiccup ['hɪkʌp] n Schluckauf m; (minor problem) Problemchen nt; **to have (the) ~s** Schluckauf haben

hid [hɪd] pt of **hide**

hidden ['hɪdn] pp of **hide**

hide [haɪd] (**hid, hidden**) vt verstecken (from vor +dat); (feelings, truth) verbergen; (cover) verdecken ▷ vi sich verstecken (from vor +dat)

hideous ['hɪdɪəs] adj scheußlich

hiding ['haɪdɪŋ] n (beating) Tracht f Prügel; (concealment) **to be in ~** versteckt halten; **hiding place** n Versteck nt

hi-fi ['haɪfaɪ] n Hi-Fi nt; (system) Hi-Fi-Anlage f

high [haɪ] adj hoch; (wind) stark; (living) im großen Stil; (on drugs) high ▷ adv hoch ▷ n (Meteo) Hoch nt; **highchair** n Hochstuhl m; **higher** adj höher; **higher education** n Hochschulbildung f; **high flier** n Hochbegabte(r) (m)f; **high heels** npl Stöckelschuhe pl; **high jump** n Hochsprung m; **Highlands** npl (schottisches) Hochland nt; **highlight** n (in hair) Strähnchen nt; (fig) Höhepunkt m ▷ vt (with pen) hervorheben; **highlighter** n Textmarker m; **highly** adj hoch, sehr; **~ paid** hoch bezahlt; **I think ~ of him** ich habe eine hohe Meinung von ihm; **high-performance** adj Hochleistungs-; **high school** n (US) Highschool f, ≈ Gymnasium nt; **high-speed** adj Schnell-; **~ train** Hochgeschwindigkeitszug m; **high street** n Hauptstraße f; **high tech** adj Hightech- ▷ n Hightech nt; **high tide** n Flut f; **highway** n (US) ≈ Autobahn f; (Brit) Landstraße f

hijack ['haɪdʒæk] vt entführen, hijacken; **hijacker** n Entführer(in) m(f), Hijacker m

hike [haɪk] vi wandern ▷ n Wanderung f; **hiker** n Wanderer m, Wanderin f; **hiking** n Wandern nt

hilarious [hɪ'leərɪəs] adj zum Schreien komisch

hill [hɪl] n Hügel m; (higher) Berg m; **hilly** adj hügelig

him [hɪm] pron (direct object) ihn; (indirect object) ihm; **do you know ~?** kennst du ihn?; **can you help ~?** kannst du ihm helfen?; **it's ~** er ist's; **~ too** er auch

himself [hɪm'self] pron (reflexive) sich; **he's bought ~ a flat** er hat sich eine Wohnung gekauft; **he needs it for ~** er braucht es für sich (selbst); (emphatic) **he did it**

~ er hat es selbst gemacht; (**all**) **by** ~ allein

hinder ['hɪndə*] vt behindern; **hindrance** ['hɪndrəns] n Behinderung f

Hindu ['hɪnduː] adj hinduistisch ▷ n Hindu m; **Hinduism** ['hɪnduːɪzəm] n Hinduismus m

hinge [hɪndʒ] n Scharnier nt; (on door) Angel f

hint [hɪnt] n Wink m, Andeutung f; (trace) Spur f ▷ vi andeuten (at akk)

hip [hɪp] n Hüfte f

hippopotamus [hɪpə'pɒtəməs] n Nilpferd nt

hire ['haɪə*] vt (worker) anstellen; (car, bike etc) mieten ▷ n Miete f; **for** ~ (taxi) frei; **hire car** n Mietwagen m; **hire charge** n Benutzungsgebühr f; **hire purchase** n Ratenkauf m

his [hɪz] adj sein; **he's hurt ~ leg** er hat sich dat das Bein verletzt ▷ pron seine(r, s); **it's** ~ es gehört ihm; **a friend of** ~ ein Freund von ihm

historic [hɪ'stɒrɪk] adj (significant) historisch; **historical** adj (monument etc) historisch; (studies etc) geschichtlich; **history** ['hɪstərɪ] n Geschichte f

hit [hɪt] n (blow) Schlag m; (on target) Treffer m; (successful film, CD etc) Hit m ▷ vt (**hit, hit**) schlagen; (bullet, stone etc) treffen; **the car ~ the tree** das Auto fuhr gegen einen Baum; **to ~ one's head on sth** sich dat den Kopf an etw dat stoßen; **hit (up)on** vt stoßen auf +akk; **hit-and-run** adj: ~ **accident** Unfall m mit Fahrerflucht

hitch [hɪtʃ] vt (pull up) hochziehen ▷ n Schwierigkeit f; **without a** ~ reibungslos

hitch-hike ['hɪtʃhaɪk] vi trampen; **hitch-hiker** n Tramper(in)

m(f); **hitchhiking** n Trampen nt

HIV abbr = **human immunodeficiency virus** HIV nt; ~ **positive/negative** HIV-positiv/negativ

hive [haɪv] n Bienenstock m

HM abbr = **His/Her Majesty**

HMS abbr = **His/Her Majesty's Ship**

hoarse [hɔːs] adj heiser

hoax [həʊks] n Streich m, Jux m; (false alarm) blinder Alarm

hob [hɒb] n (of cooker) Kochfeld nt

hobble ['hɒbl] vi humpeln

hobby ['hɒbɪ] n Hobby nt

hobo ['həʊbəʊ] (pl **-es**) n (US) Penner(in) m(f)

hockey ['hɒkɪ] n Hockey nt

hold [həʊld] (**held, held**) vt halten; (contain) enthalten; (be able to contain) fassen; (post, office) innehaben; (value) behalten; (meeting) abhalten; (person as prisoner) gefangen halten; **to ~ one's breath** den Atem anhalten; **to ~ hands** Händchen halten; ~ **the line** (Tel) bleiben Sie am Apparat ▷ vi halten; (weather) sich halten ▷ n (grasp) Halt m; (of ship, aircraft) Laderaum m; **hold back** vt zurückhalten; (keep secret) verheimlichen; **hold on** vi sich festhalten; (wait) warten; (Tel) dranbleiben; **to ~ to sth** etw festhalten; **hold out** vt ausstrecken; (offer) hinhalten; (offer) bieten ▷ vi durchhalten; **hold up** vt hochhalten; (support) stützen; (delay) aufhalten; **holdall** n Reisetasche f; **holder** n Inhaber(in) m(f); **holdup** n (in traffic) Stau m; (robbery) Überfall m

hole [həʊl] n Loch nt; (of fox, rabbit) Bau m; ~ **in the wall** (cash dispenser) Geldautomat m

holiday ['hɒlɪdər] n (day off)
freier Tag; (public ~) Feiertag m;
(vacation) Urlaub m; (at school)
Ferien pl; **on ~** im Urlaub; **to go on
~** Urlaub machen; **holiday camp**
n Ferienlager nt; **holiday home** n
Ferienhaus nt; (flat)
Ferienwohnung f; **holidaymaker**
n Urlauber(in) m(f); **holiday
resort** n Ferienort m
Holland ['hɒlənd] n Holland nt
hollow ['hɒləʊ] adj hohl; (words)
leer ▷ n Vertiefung f
holly ['hɒlɪ] n Stechpalme f
holy ['həʊlɪ] adj heilig; **Holy
Week** n Karwoche f
home [həʊm] n Zuhause nt;
(area, country) Heimat f; (institution)
Heim nt; **at ~** zu Hause; **to make
oneself at ~** es sich dat bequem
machen; **away from ~** verreist
▷ adv: **to go ~** nach Hause
gehen/fahren; **home address** n
Heimatadresse f; **home country**
n Heimatland nt; **home game** n
(Sport) Heimspiel nt; **homeless** adj
obdachlos; **homely** adj häuslich;
(US: ugly) unscheinbar;
home-made adj selbst gemacht;
home movie n Amateurfilm m;
Home Office n (Brit)
Innenministerium nt
homeopathic adj (US) see
homoeopathic
home page ['həʊmpeɪdʒ] n
(Inform) Homepage f; **Home
Secretary** n (Brit)
Innenminister(in) m(f); **homesick**
adj: **to be ~** Heimweh haben;
home town n Heimatstadt f;
homework n Hausaufgaben pl
homicide ['hɒmɪsaɪd] n (US)
Totschlag m
homoeopathic
[həʊmɪəʊ'pæθɪk] adj
homöopathisch
homosexual [hɒməʊ'sekʃʊəl]

adj homosexuell ▷ n Homosex-
uelle(r) mf
Honduras [hɒn'djʊərəs] n
Honduras nt
honest ['ɒnɪst] adj ehrlich;
honesty n Ehrlichkeit f
honey ['hʌnɪ] n Honig m;
honeycomb n Honigwabe f;
honeydew melon n
Honigmelone f; **honeymoon** n
Flitterwochen pl
Hong Kong [hɒŋ 'kɒŋ] n
Hongkong nt
honor (US) see **honour**; **honorary**
['ɒnərərɪ] adj (member, title etc)
Ehren-, ehrenamtlich; **honour**
['ɒnə°] vt ehren; (cheque) einlösen;
(contract) einhalten ▷ n Ehre f; **in
~ of** zu Ehren von; **honourable** adj
ehrenhaft; **honours degree** n
akademischer Grad mit Prüfung im
Spezialfach
hood [hʊd] n Kapuze f; (Auto)
Verdeck nt; (US Auto) Kühlerhaube
f
hoof [hu:f] (pl **hooves**) n Huf
m
hook [hʊk] n Haken m; **hooked**
adj (keen) besessen (on von);
(drugs) abhängig sein (on von)
hooligan ['hu:lɪgən] n Hooligan
m
hoot [hu:t] vi (Auto) hupen
Hoover® ['hu:və] n Staubsauger
m; **hoover** vi, vt staubsaugen
hop [hɒp] vi hüpfen ▷ n (Bot)
Hopfen m
hope [həʊp] vi, vt hoffen (for auf
+akk); **I ~ so/~ not**
hoffentlich/hoffentlich nicht; **I
~ (that) we'll meet** ich hoffe, dass
wir uns sehen werden ▷ n
Hoffnung f; **there's no ~** es ist
aussichtslos; **hopeful** adj
hoffnungsvoll; **hopefully** adv (full
of hope) hoffnungsvoll; (I hope so)
hoffentlich; **hopeless** adj

hoffnungslos; (*incompetent*) miserabel

horizon [hə'raızn] *n* Horizont *m*; **horizontal** [hɒrı'zɒntl] *adj* horizontal

hormone ['hɔ:məʊn] *n* Hormon *nt*

horn [hɔ:n] *n* Horn *nt*; (*Auto*) Hupe *f*

hornet ['hɔ:nıt] *n* Hornisse *f*

horny ['hɔ:nı] *adj* (*fam*) geil

horoscope ['hɒrəskəʊp] *n* Horoskop *nt*

horrible, horribly ['hɒrıbl, -blı] *adj, adv* schrecklich; **horrid, horridly** ['hɒrıd, -lı] *adj, adv* abscheulich; **horrify** ['hɒrıfaı] *vt* entsetzen; **horror** ['hɒrə*] *n* Entsetzen *nt*; **~s** (*things*) Schrecken *pl*

hors d'oeuvre [ɔː'dɜːvr] *n* Vorspeise *f*

horse [hɔːs] *n* Pferd *nt*; **horse chestnut** *n* Rosskastanie *f*; **horsepower** *n* Pferdestärke *f*, PS *nt*; **horse racing** *n* Pferderennen *nt*; **horseradish** *n* Meerrettich *m*; **horse riding** *n* Reiten *nt*; **horseshoe** *n* Hufeisen *nt*

horticulture ['hɔːtıkʌltʃə*] *n* Gartenbau *m*

hose, hosepipe [həʊz, 'həʊzpaıp] *n* Schlauch *m*

hospitable [hɒ'spıtəbl] *adj* gastfreundlich

hospital ['hɒspıtl] *n* Krankenhaus *nt*

hospitality [hɒspı'tælıtı] *n* Gastfreundschaft *f*

host [həʊst] *n* Gastgeber *m*; (*TV: of show*) Moderator(in) *m(f)*, Talkmaster(in) *m(f)* ▷ *vt* (*party*) geben; (*TV: TV show*) moderieren

hostage ['hɒstıdʒ] *n* Geisel *f*

hostel ['hɒstəl] *n* Wohnheim *nt*; (*youth ~*) Jugendherberge *f*

hostess ['həʊstıs] *n* (*of a party*) Gastgeberin *f*

hostile ['hɒstaıl] *adj* feindlich; **hostility** [hɒs'tılıtı] *n* Feindseligkeit *f*

hot [hɒt] *adj* heiß; (*drink, food, water*) warm; (*spiced*) scharf; **I'm (feeling) ~** mir ist heiß; **hot cross bun** *n* Rosinenbrötchen mit einem Kreuz darauf, hauptsächlich zu Ostern gegessen; **hot dog** *n* Hotdog *m*

hotel [həʊ'tel] *n* Hotel *nt*; **hotel room** *n* Hotelzimmer *nt*

hothouse *n* Treibhaus *nt*; **hotline** *n* Hotline *f*; **hotplate** *n* Kochplatte *f*; **hotpot** *n* Fleischeintopf mit Kartoffeleinlage; **hot-water bottle** *n* Wärmflasche *f*

hour ['aʊə*] *n* Stunde *f*; **to wait for ~s** stundenlang warten; **~s** *pl* (*of shops etc*) Geschäftszeiten *pl*; **hourly** *adj* stündlich

house [haʊs] (*pl* **houses**) *n* Haus *nt*; **at my ~** bei mir (zu Hause); **to my ~** zu mir (nach Hause); **on the ~** auf Kosten des Hauses; **the House of Commons/Lords** das britische Unterhaus/Oberhaus; **the Houses of Parliament** das britische Parlamentsgebäude ▷ [haʊz] *vt* unterbringen; **houseboat** *n* Hausboot *nt*; **household** *n* Haushalt *m*; **~ appliance** Haushaltsgerät *nt*; **house-husband** *n* Hausmann *m*; **housekeeping** *n* Haushaltung *f*; (*money*) Haushaltsgeld *nt*; **house-trained** *adj* stubenrein; **house-warming (party)** *n* Einzugsparty *f*; **housewife** (*pl* **-wives**) *n* Hausfrau *f*; **house wine** *n* Hauswein *m*; **housework** *n* Hausarbeit *f*

housing ['haʊzıŋ] *n* (*houses*) Wohnungen *pl*; (*house building*) Wohnungsbau *m*; **housing**

benefit n Wohngeld nt; **housing development, housing estate** (Brit) n Wohnsiedlung f
hover ['hɒvə*] vi schweben; **hovercraft** n Luftkissenboot nt
how [haʊ] adv wie; **~ many** wie viele; **~ much** wie viel; **~ are you?** wie geht es Ihnen?; **~ are things?** wie geht's?; **~'s work?** was macht die Arbeit?; **~ about ...?** wie wäre es mit ...?; **however** [haʊ'evə*] conj (but) jedoch, aber ▷ adv (no matter how) wie ... auch; **~ much it costs** wie viel es auch kostet; **~ you do it** wie man es auch macht
howl [haʊl] vi heulen; **howler** ['haʊlə*] n (fam) grober Schnitzer
HP, hp (Brit) abbr = **hire purchase** Ratenkauf m ▷ abbr = **horsepower** PS
HQ abbr = **headquarters**
hubcap ['hʌbkæp] n Radkappe f
hug [hʌg] vt umarmen ▷ n Umarmung f
huge [hju:dʒ] adj riesig
hum [hʌm] vi, vt summen
human ['hju:mən] adj menschlich; **~ rights** Menschenrechte pl ▷ n: **~ (being)** Mensch m; **humanitarian** [hju:mænɪ'tɛərɪən] adj humanitär; **humanity** [hju:'mænɪtɪ] n Menschheit f; (kindliness) Menschlichkeit f; **humanities** Geisteswissenschaften pl
humble ['hʌmbl] adj demütig; (modest) bescheiden
humid ['hju:mɪd] adj feucht; **humidity** [hju:'mɪdɪtɪ] n (Luft)feuchtigkeit f
humiliate [hju:'mɪlɪeɪt] vt demütigen; **humiliation** [hju:mɪlɪ'eɪʃn] n Erniedrigung f, Demütigung f
humor (US) see **humour**;

humorous ['hju:mərəs] adj humorvoll; (story) lustig, witzig;
humour ['hju:mə*] n Humor m; **sense of ~** Sinn m für Humor
hump [hʌmp] n Buckel m
hunch [hʌntʃ] n Gefühl nt, Ahnung f ▷ vt (back) krümmen; **hunchback** n Bucklige(r) mf
hundred ['hʌndrəd] num: **one ~, a ~** (ein)hundert; **a ~ and one** hundert(und)eins; **two ~** zweihundert; **hundredth** adj hundertste(r, s) ▷ n (fraction) Hundertstel nt; **hundredweight** n Zentner m (50,8 kg)
hung [hʌŋ] pt, pp of **hang**
Hungarian [hʌŋ'gɛərɪən] adj ungarisch ▷ n (person) Ungar(in) m(f); (language) Ungarisch nt; **Hungary** ['hʌŋgərɪ] n Ungarn nt
hunger ['hʌŋgə*] n Hunger m; **hungry** ['hʌŋgrɪ] adj hungrig; **to be ~** Hunger haben
hunk [hʌŋk] n (fam) gut gebauter Mann; **hunky** ['hʌŋkɪ] adj (fam) gut gebaut
hunt [hʌnt] n Jagd f; (search) Suche f (for nach) ▷ vt, vi jagen; (search) suchen (for nach); **hunting** n Jagen nt, Jagd f
hurdle ['hɜ:dl] n (a. fig) Hürde f; **the 400m ~s** der 400m-Hürdenlauf
hurl [hɜ:l] vt schleudern
hurricane ['hʌrɪkən] n Orkan m
hurried ['hʌrɪd] adj eilig; **hurry** ['hʌrɪ] n Eile f; **to be in a ~** es eilig haben; **there's no ~** es eilt nicht ▷ vi sich beeilen; **~ (up)** mach schnell! ▷ vt antreiben
hurt [hɜ:t] (hurt, hurt) vt wehtun +dat; (wound: person, feelings) verletzen; **I've ~ my arm** ich habe mir am Arm wehgetan ▷ vi wehtun; **my arm ~s** mir tut der Arm weh

husband ['hʌzbənd] *n* Ehemann *m*

husky ['hʌskɪ] *adj* rau ▷ *n* Schlittenhund *m*

hut [hʌt] *n* Hütte *f*

hyacinth ['haɪəsɪnθ] *n* Hyazinthe *f*

hybrid ['haɪbrɪd] *n* Kreuzung *f*

hydroelectric ['haɪdrəʊɪ'lektrɪk] *adj*: **~ power station** Wasserkraftwerk *nt*

hydrofoil ['haɪdrəʊfɔɪl] *n* Tragflächenboot *nt*

hydrogen ['haɪdrədʒən] *n* Wasserstoff *m*

hygiene ['haɪdʒiːn] *n* Hygiene *f*; **hygienic** [haɪ'dʒiːnɪk] *adj* hygienisch

hymn [hɪm] *n* Kirchenlied *nt*

hypermarket ['haɪpəmɑːkɪt] *n* Großmarkt *m*; **hypersensitive** *adj* überempfindlich

hyphen ['haɪfən] *n* Bindestrich *m*

hypnosis [hɪp'nəʊsɪs] *n* Hypnose *f*; **hypnotize** ['hɪpnətaɪz] *vt* hypnotisieren

hypochondriac [haɪpəʊ'kɒndriæk] *n* eingebildete(r) Kranke(r), eingebildete Kranke

hypocrisy ['hɪ'pəkrəsɪ] *n* Heuchelei *f*; **hypocrite** ['hɪpəkrɪt] *n* Heuchler(in) *m(f)*

hypodermic [haɪpə'dɜːmɪk] *adj*, *n*: **~ (needle)** Spritze *f*

hypothetical [haɪpəʊ'θetɪkəl] *adj* hypothetisch

hysteria [hɪ'stɪərɪə] *n* Hysterie *f*; **hysterical** [hɪ'sterɪkəl] *adj* hysterisch; *(amusing)* zum Totlachen

I [aɪ] *pron* ich

ice [aɪs] *n* Eis *nt* ▷ *vt (cake)* glasieren; **iceberg** *n* Eisberg *m*; **iceberg lettuce** *n* Eisbergsalat *m*; **icebox** *n (US)* Kühlschrank *m*; **icecold** *adj* eiskalt; **ice cream** *n* Eis *nt*; **ice cube** *n* Eiswürfel *m*; **iced** *adj* eisgekühlt; *(coffee, tea)* Eis-; *(cake)* glasiert; **ice hockey** *n* Eishockey *nt*

Iceland ['aɪslənd] *n* Island *nt*; **Icelander** *n* Isländer(in) *m(f)*; **Icelandic** [aɪs'lændɪk] *adj* isländisch ▷ *n (language)* Isländisch

ice lolly ['aɪslɒlɪ] *n (Brit)* Eis *nt* am Stiel; **ice rink** *n* Kunsteisbahn *f*; **ice skating** *n* Schlittschuhlaufen *nt*

icing ['aɪsɪŋ] *n (on cake)* Zuckerguss *m*

icon ['aɪkɒn] *n* Ikone *f*; *(Inform)* Icon *nt*, Programmsymbol *nt*

icy [ˈaɪsɪ] *adj* (*slippery*) vereist; (*cold*) eisig

I'd [aɪd] *contr of* **I would; I had**

ID *abbr* = **identification** Ausweis *m*

idea [aɪˈdɪə] *n* Idee *f*; (**I've**) **no** ~ (ich habe) keine Ahnung; **that's my ~ of ...** so stelle ich mir ... vor

ideal [aɪˈdɪəl] *n* Ideal *nt* ▷ *adj* ideal; **ideally** *adv* ideal; (*before statement*) idealerweise

identical [aɪˈdentɪkəl] *adj* identisch; ~ **twins** eineiige Zwillinge

identify [aɪˈdentɪfaɪ] *vt* identifizieren; **identity** [aɪˈdentɪtɪ] *n* Identität *f*; **identity card** *n* Personalausweis *m*

idiom [ˈɪdɪəm] *n* Redewendung *f*; **idiomatic** *adj* idiomatisch

idiot [ˈɪdɪət] *n* Idiot(in) *m(f)*

idle [ˈaɪdl] *adj* (*doing nothing*) untätig; (*worker*) unbeschäftigt; (*machines*) außer Betrieb; (*lazy*) faul; (*promise, threat*) leer

idol [ˈaɪdl] *n* Idol *nt*; **idolize** [ˈaɪdəlaɪz] *vt* vergöttern

idyllic [ɪˈdɪlɪk] *adj* idyllisch

i.e. *abbr* = **id est** d.h.

○ **KEYWORD**

if [ɪf] *conj* **1** wenn; (*in case also*) falls; **if I were you** wenn ich Sie wäre

2 (*although*) (**even**) **if** (selbst *o* auch) wenn

3 (*whether*) ob

4 if so/not wenn ja/nicht; **if only ...** wenn ... doch nur ...; **if only I could** wenn ich doch nur könnte; *see also* **as**

ignition [ɪgˈnɪʃən] *n* Zündung *f*; **ignition key** *n* (*Auto*) Zündschlüssel *m*

ignorance [ˈɪgnərəns] *n* Unwissenheit *f*; **ignorant** *adj* unwissend; **ignore** [ɪgˈnɔː*] *vt* ignorieren, nicht beachten

I'll [aɪl] *contr of* **I will; I shall**

ill [ɪl] *adj* krank; ~ **at ease** unbehaglich

illegal [ɪˈliːgəl] *adj* illegal

illegitimate [ɪlɪˈdʒɪtɪmət] *adj* unzulässig; (*child*) unehelich

illiterate [ɪˈlɪtərət] *adj*: **to be** ~ Analphabet(in) sein

illness [ˈɪlnəs] *n* Krankheit *f*

illuminate [ɪˈluːmɪneɪt] *vt* beleuchten; **illuminating** *adj* (*remark*) aufschlussreich

illusion [ɪˈluːʒən] *n* Illusion *f*; **to be under the ~ that ...** sich einbilden, dass ...

illustrate [ˈɪləstreɪt] *vt* illustrieren; **illustration** *n* Abbildung *f*, Bild *nt*

I'm [aɪm] *contr of* **I am**

image [ˈɪmɪdʒ] *n* Bild *nt*; (*public ~*) Image *nt*; **imaginable** [ɪˈmædʒɪnəbl] *adj* denkbar; **imaginary** [ɪˈmædʒɪnərɪ] *adj* eingebildet; ~ **world** Fantasiewelt *f*; **imagination** [ɪmædʒɪˈneɪʃən] *n* Fantasie *f*; (*mistaken*) Einbildung *f*; **imaginative** [ɪˈmædʒɪnətɪv] *adj* fantasievoll; **imagine** [ɪˈmædʒɪn] *vt* sich vorstellen; (*wrongly*) sich einbilden; ~! stell dir vor!

imbecile [ˈɪmbəsiːl] *n* Trottel *m*

imitate [ˈɪmɪteɪt] *vt* nachahmen, nachmachen; **imitation** *n* Nachahmung *f* ▷ *adj* imitiert, Kunst-

immaculate [ɪˈmækjʊlɪt] *adj* tadellos; (*spotless*) makellos

immature [ɪməˈtjʊə*] *adj* unreif

immediate [ɪˈmiːdɪət] *adj* unmittelbar; (*instant*) sofortig; (*reply*) umgehend; **immediately** *adv* sofort

immense, immensely [ɪˈmens, -lɪ] *adj, adv* riesig, enorm

immersion heater [ɪ'mɜːʃn
hiːtə] n Boiler m
immigrant ['ɪmɪgrənt] n Ein-
wanderer m, Einwanderin f;
immigration [ɪmɪ'greɪʃən] n
Einwanderung f; (facility)
Einwanderungskontrolle f
immobilize [ɪ'məʊbɪlaɪz] vt
lähmen; **immobilizer** n (Auto)
Wegfahrsperre f
immoral [ɪ'mɒrəl] adj
unmoralisch
immortal [ɪ'mɔːtl] adj
unsterblich
immune [ɪ'mjuːn] adj (Med)
immun (from, to gegen); **immune
system** n Immunsystem nt
impact ['ɪmpækt] n Aufprall m;
(effect) Auswirkung f (on auf +akk)
impatience [ɪm'peɪʃəns] n
Ungeduld f; **impatient,
impatiently** adj, adv ungeduldig
impeccable [ɪm'pekəbl] adj
tadellos
impede [ɪm'piːd] vt behindern
imperative [ɪm'perətɪv] adj
unbedingt erforderlich ▷ n (Ling)
Imperativ m
imperfect [ɪm'pɜːfɪkt] adj
unvollkommen; (goods) fehlerhaft
▷ n (Ling) Imperfekt nt;
imperfection [ɪmpə'fekʃən] n
Unvollkommenheit f; (fault) Fehler
m
imperial [ɪm'pɪərɪəl] adj kaiser-
lich, Reichs-; **imperialism** n
Imperialismus m
impertinence [ɪm'pɜːtɪnəns] n
Unverschämtheit f, Zumutung f;
impertinent adj unverschämt
implant ['ɪmplaːnt] n (Med)
Implantat nt
implausible [ɪm'plɔːzəbl] adj
unglaubwürdig
implement ['ɪmplɪmənt] n
Werkzeug nt, Gerät nt
▷ [ɪmplɪ'ment] vt durchführen

implication [ɪmplɪ'keɪʃən] n
Folge f, Auswirkung f; (logical)
Schlussfolgerung f; **implicit**
[ɪm'plɪsɪt] adj implizit,
unausgesprochen; **imply**
[ɪm'plaɪ] vt (indicate) andeuten;
(mean) bedeuten; **are you ~ing
that ...** wollen Sie damit sagen,
dass ...
impolite [ɪmpə'laɪt] adj
unhöflich
import [ɪm'pɔːt] vt einführen,
importieren ▷ n ['ɪmpɔːt] Einfuhr f, Import m
importance [ɪm'pɔːtəns] n
Bedeutung f; **of no ~** unwichtig;
important adj wichtig (to sb für
jdn); (significant) bedeutend;
(influential) einflussreich
import duty ['ɪmpɔːt djuːtɪ] n
Einfuhrzoll m; **import licence** n
Einfuhrgenehmigung f
impose [ɪm'pəʊz] vt (conditions)
auferlegen (on dat); (penalty,
sanctions) verhängen (on gegen);
imposing [ɪm'pəʊzɪŋ] adj eindrucksvoll, imposant
impossible [ɪm'pɒsəbl] adj
unmöglich
impotence ['ɪmpətəns] n
Machtlosigkeit f; (sexual)
Impotenz f; **impotent** adj
machtlos; (sexually) impotent
impractical [ɪm'præktɪkəl] adj
unpraktisch; (plan)
undurchführbar
impress [ɪm'pres] vt beeindrucken; **impression** [ɪm'preʃən]
n Eindruck m; **impressive** adj
eindrucksvoll
imprison [ɪm'prɪzn] vt inhaf-
tieren; **imprisonment** n
Inhaftierung f
improbability [ɪmprɒbə'bɪlɪtɪ]
n Unwahrscheinlichkeit f;
improbable [ɪm'prɒbəbl] adj
unwahrscheinlich

improper [ɪmˈprɒpə*] *adj*
(*indecent*) unanständig; (*use*)
unsachgemäß
improve [ɪmˈpruːv] *vt*
verbessern ▷ *vi* sich verbessern,
besser werden; (*patient*)
Fortschritte machen;
improvement *n* Verbesserung *f*
(*in* +gen; *on* gegenüber); (*in
appearance*) Verschönerung *f*
improvise [ˈɪmprəvaɪz] *vt, vi*
improvisieren
impulse [ˈɪmpʌls] *n* Impuls *m*;
impulsive [ɪmˈpʌlsɪv] *adj*
impulsiv

O **KEYWORD**

in [ɪn] *prep* **1** (*indicating place,
position*) in +dat; (*with motion*) in
+akk; **in here/there** hier/dort; **in
London** in London; **in the United
States** in den Vereinigten Staaten
2 (*indicating time: during*) in +dat; **in
summer** im Sommer; **in 1988** (im
Jahre) 1988; **in the afternoon**
nachmittags, am Nachmittag
3 (*indicating time: in the space of*)
innerhalb von; **I'll see you in 2
weeks** *o* **in 2 weeks' time** ich sehe
dich/Sie in zwei Wochen
4 (*indicating manner, circumstances,
state etc*) in +dat; **in the sun/rain**
in der Sonne/im Regen; **in
English/French** auf
Englisch/Französisch; **in a
loud/soft voice** mit lauter/leiser
Stimme
5 (*with ratios, numbers*) **1 in 10** jeder
Zehnte; **20 pence in the pound** 20
Pence pro Pfund; **they lined up in
twos** sie stellten sich in
Zweierreihe auf
6 (*referring to people, works*) **the
disease is common in children**
die Krankheit ist bei Kindern
häufig; **in Dickens** bei Dickens;

we have a loyal friend in him er
ist uns ein treuer Freund
7 (*indicating profession etc*) **to be in
teaching/the army** Lehrer,
Lehrerin/beim Militär sein; **to be
in publishing** im Verlagswesen
arbeiten
8 (*with present participle*) **in saying
this, I ...** wenn ich das sage, ... ich;
in accepting this view, he ... weil
er diese Meinung akzeptierte, ...
er
▷ *adv*: **to be in** (*person: at home,
work*) da sein; (*train, ship, plane*)
angekommen sein; (*in fashion*) in
sein; **to ask sb in** jdn hereinbitten;
to run/limp etc in
hereingerannt/gehumpelt *etc*
kommen
▷ *n*: **the ins and outs** (*of proposal,
situation etc*) die Feinheiten

inability [ɪnəˈbɪlɪtɪ] *n* Unfähig-
keit *f*
inaccessible [ɪnækˈsesəbl] *adj*
(*a. fig*) unzugänglich
inaccurate [ɪnˈækjʊrɪt] *adj*
ungenau
inadequate [ɪnˈædɪkwət] *adj*
unzulänglich
inapplicable [ɪnəˈplɪkəbl] *adj*
unzutreffend
inappropriate [ɪnəˈprəʊprɪət]
adj unpassend; (*clothing*)
ungeeignet; (*remark*)
unangebracht
inborn [ˈɪnˈbɔːn] *adj* angeboren
incapable [ɪnˈkeɪpəbl] *adj*
unfähig (*of* zu); **to be ~ of doing
sth** nicht imstande sein, etw zu
tun
incense [ˈɪnsens] *n* Weihrauch
m
incentive [ɪnˈsentɪv] *n* Anreiz *m*
incessant, incessantly [ɪnˈsesnt,
-lɪ] *adj, adv* unaufhörlich
incest [ˈɪnsest] *n* Inzest *m*

inch [ɪntʃ] n Zoll m (2,54 cm)
incident ['ɪnsɪdənt] n Vorfall m;
(disturbance) Zwischenfall m;
incidentally [ɪnsɪ'dentlɪ]
adv nebenbei bemerkt,
übrigens
inclination [ɪnklɪ'neɪʃən] n
Neigung f; **inclined** ['ɪnklaɪnd]
adj: **to be ~ to do sth** dazu neigen,
etw zu tun
include [ɪn'klu:d] vt einschließen; (on list, in group)
aufnehmen; **including** prep
einschließlich (+gen); **not
~ service** Bedienung nicht
inbegriffen; **inclusive** [ɪn'klu:sɪv]
adj einschließlich (of +gen); (price)
Pauschal-
incoherent [ɪnkəʊ'hɪərənt] adj
zusammenhanglos
income ['ɪnkʌm] n Einkommen
nt; (from business) Einkünfte pl;
income tax n Einkommensteuer
f; (on wages, salary) Lohnsteuer f;
incoming ['ɪnkʌmɪŋ] adj an-
kommend; (mail) eingehend
incompatible [ɪnkəm'pætəbl]
adj unvereinbar; (people)
unverträglich; (Inform) nicht
kompatibel
incompetent [ɪn'kɒmpɪtənt]
adj unfähig
incomplete [ɪnkəm'pli:t] adj
unvollständig
incomprehensible
[ɪnkɒmprɪ'hensəbl] adj
unverständlich
inconceivable [ɪnkən'si:vəbl]
adj unvorstellbar
inconsiderate [ɪnkən'sɪdərət]
adj rücksichtslos
inconsistency [ɪnkən'sɪstənsɪ]
n Inkonsequenz f; (contradictory)
Widersprüchlichkeit f;
inconsistent adj inkonsequent;
(contradictory) widersprüchlich;
(work) unbeständig

inconvenience [ɪnkən'vi:nɪəns]
n Unannehmlichkeit f; (trouble)
Umstände pl; **inconvenient** adj
ungünstig, unbequem; (time) **it's
~ for me** es kommt mir
ungelegen; **if it's not too ~ for
you** wenn es dir/Ihnen passt
incorporate [ɪn'kɔ:pəreɪt] vt
aufnehmen (into in +akk); (include)
enthalten
incorrect ['ɪnkərekt] adj falsch;
(improper) inkorrekt
increase ['ɪnkri:s] n Zunahme f
(in an +dat); (in amount, speed)
Erhöhung f (in +gen) ▷ [ɪn'kri:s] vt
(price, taxes, salary, speed etc)
erhöhen; (wealth) vermehren;
(number) vergrößern; (business)
erweitern ▷ vi zunehmen (in an
+dat); (prices) steigen; (in size)
größer werden; (in number) sich
vermehren; **increasingly**
[ɪn'kri:sɪŋlɪ] adv zunehmend
incredible, **incredibly**
[ɪn'kredəbl, -blɪ] adj, adv
unglaublich; (very good)
fantastisch
incredulous [ɪn'kredjʊləs] adj
ungläubig, skeptisch
incriminate [ɪn'krɪmɪneɪt] vt
belasten
incubator ['ɪnkjʊbeɪtə*] n
Brutkasten m
incurable [ɪn'kjʊərəbl] adj
unheilbar
indecent [ɪn'di:snt] adj
unanständig
indecisive [ɪndɪ'saɪsɪv] adj
(person) unentschlossen; (result)
nicht entscheidend
indeed [ɪn'di:d] adv tatsächlich;
(as answer) allerdings; **very hot
~** wirklich sehr heiß
indefinite [ɪn'defɪnɪt] adj
unbestimmt; **indefinitely** adv
endlos; (postpone) auf
unbestimmte Zeit

independence [ɪndɪ'pendəns]
n Unabhängigkeit *f*

independent [ɪndɪ'pendənt]
adj unabhängig (*of* von); (*person*)
selbstständig
indescribable [ɪndɪ'skraɪbəbl]
adj unbeschreiblich
index ['ɪndeks] *n* Index *m*,
Verzeichnis *nt*; **index finger** *n*
Zeigefinger *m*
India ['ɪndɪə] *n* Indien *nt*; **Indian**
['ɪndɪən] *adj* indisch; (*Native
American*) indianisch ▷ *n* Inder(in)
m(f); (*Native American*) Indianer(in)
m(f); **Indian Ocean** *n* Indischer
Ozean; **Indian summer** *n* Spät-
sommer *m*, Altweibersommer *m*
indicate ['ɪndɪkeɪt] *vt* (*show*)
zeigen; (*instrument*) anzeigen;
(*suggest*) hinweisen auf +*akk* ▷ *vi*
(*Auto*) blinken; **indication**
[ɪndɪ'keɪʃn] *n* (*sign*) Anzeichen *nt*
(*of* für); **indicator** ['ɪndɪkeɪtə*] *n*
(*Auto*) Blinker *m*
indifferent [ɪn'dɪfrənt] *adj* (*not
caring*) gleichgültig (*to, towards*
gegenüber); (*mediocre*)
mittelmäßig
indigestible [ɪndɪ'dʒestəbl] *adj*
unverdaulich; **indigestion**
[ɪndɪ'dʒestʃən] *n* Verdau-
ungsstörung *f*
indignity [ɪn'dɪgnɪtɪ] *n* Demütigung *f*

indirect, indirectly [ɪndɪ'rekt, -lɪ]
adj, adv indirekt
indiscreet [ɪndɪ'skriːt] *adj*
indiskret
indispensable [ɪndɪ'spensəbl]
adj unentbehrlich
indisposed [ɪndɪ'spəuzd] *adj*
unwohl
indisputable [ɪndɪ'spjuːtəbl]
adj unbestreitbar; (*evidence*)
unanfechtbar
individual [ɪndɪ'vɪdjuəl] *n*
Einzelne(r) *mf* ▷ *adj* einzeln;
(*distinctive*) eigen, individuell;
~ case Einzelfall *m*; **individually**
adv (*separately*) einzeln
Indonesia [ɪndəʊ'niːzjə] *n*
Indonesien *nt*
indoor ['ɪndɔː*] *adj* (*shoes*)
Haus-; (*plant, games*) Zimmer-;
(*Sport: football, championship, record
etc*) Hallen-; **indoors** *adv* drinnen,
im Haus
indulge [ɪn'dʌldʒ] *vi*: **to ~ in sth**
sich *dat* etw gönnen; **indulgence**
n Nachsicht *f*; (*enjoyment*)
(übermäßiger) Genuss; (*luxury*)
Luxus *m*; **indulgent** *adj*
nachsichtig (*with* gegenüber)
industrial [ɪn'dʌstrɪəl] *adj*
Industrie-, industriell; **~ estate**
Industriegebiet *nt*; **industry**
['ɪndəstrɪ] *n* Industrie *f*
inedible [ɪn'edɪbl] *adj* nicht
essbar, ungenießbar
ineffective [ɪnɪ'fektɪv] *adj*
unwirksam, wirkungslos;
inefficient *adj* unwirksam; (*use,
machine*) unwirtschaftlich; (*method
etc*) unrationell
ineligible [ɪn'elɪdʒəbl] *adj* nicht
berechtigt (*for* zu)
inequality [ɪnɪ'kwɒlɪtɪ] *n*
Ungleichheit *f*
inevitable [ɪn'evɪtəbl] *adj*
unvermeidlich; **inevitably** *adv*
zwangsläufig

inexcusable [ɪnɪks'kjuːzəbl]
adj unverzeihlich; **that's ~** das
kann man nicht verzeihen
inexpensive [ɪnɪks'pensɪv] adj
preisgünstig
inexperience [ɪnɪks'pɪərɪəns]
n Unerfahrenheit f;
inexperienced adj unerfahren
inexplicable [ɪnɪks'plɪkəbl] adj
unerklärlich
infallible [ɪn'fæləbl] adj
unfehlbar
infamous ['ɪnfəməs] adj (person)
berüchtigt (for wegen); (deed)
niederträchtig
infancy ['ɪnfənsɪ] n frühe
Kindheit; **infant** ['ɪnfənt] n
Säugling m; (small child)
Kleinkind nt; **infant school** n
Vorschule f
infatuated [ɪn'fætjʊeɪtɪd] adj
vernarrt (with in +akk), verknallt
(with in +akk)
infect [ɪn'fekt] vt (person)
anstecken; (wound) infizieren;
infection [ɪn'fekʃən] n Infektion
f; **infectious** [ɪn'fekʃəs] adj
ansteckend
inferior [ɪn'fɪərɪə*] adj (in quality)
minderwertig; (in rank)
untergeordnet; **inferiority**
[ɪnfɪərɪ'ɒrɪtɪ] n Minderwertigkeit
f; **~ complex** Minderwertigkeitskomplex m
infertile [ɪn'fɜːtaɪl] adj
unfruchtbar
infidelity [ɪnfɪ'delɪtɪ] n Untreue
f
infinite ['ɪnfɪnɪt] adj unendlich
infinitive [ɪn'fɪnɪtɪv] n (Ling)
Infinitiv m
infinity [ɪn'fɪnɪtɪ] n Unend-
lichkeit f
infirmary [ɪn'fɜːmərɪ] n
Krankenhaus nt
inflame [ɪn'fleɪm] vt (Med)
entzünden; **inflammation**

[ɪnflə'meɪʃən] n (Med)
Entzündung f
inflatable [ɪn'fleɪtəbl] adj auf-
blasbar; **~ dinghy** Schlauchboot
nt; **inflate** [ɪn'fleɪt] vt
aufpumpen; (by blowing)
aufblasen; (prices) hochtreiben
inflation [ɪn'fleɪʃən] n Inflation
f
inflexible [ɪn'fleksɪbl] adj
unflexibel
inflict [ɪn'flɪkt] vt: **to ~ sth on sb**
jdm etw zufügen; (punishment)
jdm etw auferlegen; (wound) jdm
etw beibringen
in-flight [ɪn'flaɪt] adj (catering,
magazine) Bord-; **~ entertainment**
Bordprogramm nt
influence ['ɪnflʊəns] n Einfluss
m (on auf +akk) ▷ vt beeinflussen;
influential [ɪnflʊ'enʃəl] adj
einflussreich
influenza [ɪnflʊ'enzə] n Grippe
f
inform [ɪn'fɔːm] vt informieren
(of, about über +akk); **to keep sb**
~ed jdn auf dem Laufenden halten
informal [ɪn'fɔːməl] adj zwanglos, ungezwungen
information [ɪnfə'meɪʃən] n
Auskunft f, Informationen pl; **for**
your ~ zu deiner/Ihrer
Information; **further ~** weitere
Informationen, Weiteres;
information desk n
Auskunftsschalter m; **information**
technology n Informations-
technik f; **informative**
[ɪn'fɔːmətɪv] adj aufschlussreich
infra-red ['ɪnfrə'red] adj infrarot
infrastructure n Infrastruktur
f
infuriate [ɪn'fjʊərɪeɪt] vt wütend
machen; **infuriating** adj äußerst
ärgerlich
infusion [ɪn'fjuːʒən] n (herbal
tea) Aufguss m; (Med) Infusion f

ingenious [ɪn'dʒiːnɪəs] *adj* (*person*) erfinderisch; (*device*) raffiniert; (*idea*) genial
ingredient [ɪn'griːdɪənt] *n* (*Gastr*) Zutat *f*
inhabit [ɪn'hæbɪt] *vt* bewohnen; **inhabitant** *n* Einwohner(in) *m(f)*
inhale [ɪn'heɪl] *vt* einatmen; (*cigarettes, Med*) inhalieren; **inhaler** *n* Inhalationsgerät *nt*
inherit [ɪn'herɪt] *vt* erben; **inheritance** *n* Erbe *nt*
inhibited [ɪn'hɪbɪtɪd] *adj* gehemmt; **inhibition** [ɪnhɪ'bɪʃən] *n* Hemmung *f*
in-house ['ɪnhaʊs] *adj* intern
inhuman [ɪn'hjuːmən] *adj* unmenschlich
initial [ɪ'nɪʃəl] *adj* anfänglich; ~ **stage** Anfangsstadium *nt* ▷ *vt* mit Initialen unterschreiben; **initially** *adv* anfangs; **initials** *npl* Initialen *pl*
initiative [ɪ'nɪʃətɪv] *n* Initiative *f*
inject [ɪn'dʒekt] *vt* (*drug etc*) einspritzen; **to ~ sb with sth** jdm etw (ein)spritzen; **injection** *n* Spritze *f*, Injektion *f*
in-joke ['ɪndʒəʊk] *n* Insiderwitz *m*
injure ['ɪndʒə*] *vt* verletzen; **to ~ one's leg** sich *dat* das Bein verletzen; **injury** ['ɪndʒərɪ] *n* Verletzung *f*
injustice [ɪn'dʒʌstɪs] *n* Ungerechtigkeit *f*
ink [ɪŋk] *n* Tinte *f*; **ink-jet printer** *n* Tintenstrahldrucker *m*
inland ['ɪnlənd] *adj* Binnen- ▷ *adv* landeinwärts; **inland revenue** *n* (*Brit*) Finanzamt *nt*
in-laws ['ɪnlɔːz] *npl* (*fam*) Schwiegereltern *pl*
inline skates ['ɪnlaɪnskeɪts] *npl* Inlineskates *pl*, Inliner *pl*
inmate ['ɪnmeɪt] *n* Insasse *m*
inn [ɪn] *n* Gasthaus *nt*

innate [ɪ'neɪt] *adj* angeboren
inner ['ɪnə*] *adj* innere(r, s); ~ **city** Innenstadt *f*
innocence ['ɪnəsns] *n* Unschuld *f*; **innocent** *adj* unschuldig
innovation [ɪnəʊ'veɪʃən] *n* Neuerung *f*
innumerable [ɪ'njuːmərəbl] *adj* unzählig
inoculate [ɪ'nɒkjʊleɪt] *vt* impfen (*against* gegen); **inoculation** [ɪnɒkjʊ'leɪʃən] *n* Impfung *f*
in-patient ['ɪnpeɪʃənt] *n* stationärer Patient, stationäre Patientin
input ['ɪnpʊt] *n* (*contribution*) Beitrag *m*; (*Inform*) Eingabe *f*
inquest ['ɪnkwest] *n* gerichtliche Untersuchung (einer Todesursache)
inquire [ɪn'kwaɪə*] *see* **enquire**; **inquiry** [ɪn'kwaɪərɪ] *see* **enquiry**
insane [ɪn'seɪn] *adj* wahnsinnig; (*Med*) geisteskrank; **insanity** [ɪn'sænɪtɪ] *n* Wahnsinn *m*
insatiable [ɪn'seɪʃəbl] *adj* unersättlich
inscription [ɪn'skrɪpʃən] *n* (*on stone etc*) Inschrift *f*
insect ['ɪnsekt] *n* Insekt *nt*; **insecticide** [ɪn'sektɪsaɪd] *n* Insektenbekämpfungsmittel *nt*; **insect repellent** *n* Insektenschutzmittel *nt*
insecure [ɪnsɪ'kjʊə*] *adj* (*person*) unsicher; (*shelves*) instabil
insensitive [ɪn'sensɪtɪv] *adj* unempfindlich (*to* gegen); (*unfeeling*) gefühllos; **insensitivity** [ɪnsensɪ'tɪvɪtɪ] *n* Unempfindlichkeit *f* (*to* gegen); (*unfeeling nature*) Gefühllosigkeit *f*
inseparable [ɪn'sepərəbl] *adj* unzertrennlich
insert [ɪn'sɜːt] *vt* einfügen; (*coin*) einwerfen; (*key etc*) hineinstecken

▷ *n* (*in magazine*) Beilage *f*;
insertion *n* (*in text*) Einfügen *nt*
inside ['ɪn'saɪd] *n*: **the ~** das
Innere; (*surface*) die Innenseite;
from the ~ von innen ▷ *adj*
innere(r, s), Innen-; **~ lane** (*Auto*)
Innenspur *f*; (*Sport*) Innenbahn *f*
▷ *adv* (*place*) innen; (*direction*)
hinein; **to go ~** hineingehen
▷ *prep* (*place*) in +*dat*; (*into*) in +*akk*
... hinein; (*time, within*) innerhalb
+*gen*; **inside out** *adv* verkehrt
herum; (*know*) in- und auswendig;
insider *n* Eingeweihte(r) *mf*,
Insider(in) *m(f)*
insight ['ɪnsaɪt] *n* Einblick *m*
(*into* in +*akk*)
insignificant [ɪnsɪg'nɪfɪkənt]
adj unbedeutend
insincere [ɪnsɪn'sɪə*] *adj* un-
aufrichtig, falsch
insinuate [ɪn'sɪnjʊeɪt] *vt*
andeuten; **insinuation**
[ɪnsɪnjʊ'eɪʃən] *n* Andeutung *f*
insist [ɪn'sɪst] *vi* darauf bestehen;
to ~ on sth auf etw *dat* bestehen;
insistent *adj* hartnäckig
insoluble [ɪn'sɒljʊbl] *adj*
unlösbar
insomnia [ɪn'sɒmnɪə] *n* Schlaflosigkeit *f*
inspect [ɪn'spekt] *vt* prüfen,
kontrollieren; **inspection** *n*
Prüfung *f*; (*check*) Kontrolle *f*;
inspector *n* (*police ~*)
Inspektor(in) *m(f)*; (*senior*)
Kommissar(in) *m(f)*; (*on bus etc*)
Kontrolleur(in) *m(f)*
inspiration [ɪnspɪ'reɪʃən] *n*
Inspiration *f*; **inspire** [ɪn'spaɪə*]
vt (*respect*) einflößen (*in dat*);
(*person*) inspirieren
install [ɪn'stɔːl] *vt* (*software*)
installieren; (*furnishings*) einbauen
installment, instalment
[ɪn'stɔːlmənt] *n* Rate *f*; (*of story*)
Folge *f*; **to pay in ~s** auf Raten

zahlen; **installment plan** *n* (*US*)
Ratenkauf *m*
instance ['ɪnstəns] *n* (*of
discrimination*) Fall *m*; (*example*)
Beispiel *nt* (*of* für +*akk*); **for ~** zum
Beispiel
instant ['ɪnstənt] *n* Augenblick
m ▷ *adj* sofortig; **instant coffee**
n löslicher Kaffee *m*; **instantly** *adv*
sofort
instead [ɪn'sted] *adv* stattdes-
sen; **instead of** *prep* (an)statt
+*gen*; **~ of me** an meiner Stelle;
~ of going (an)statt zu gehen
instinct ['ɪnstɪŋkt] *n* Instinkt *m*;
instinctive, instinctively
[ɪn'stɪŋktɪv, -lɪ] *adj, adv*
instinktiv
institute ['ɪnstɪtjuːt] *n* Institut
nt; **institution** [ɪnstɪ'tjuːʃən] *n*
(*organisation*) Institution *f*,
Einrichtung *f*; (*home*) Anstalt *f*
instruct [ɪn'strʌkt] *vt* anweisen;
instruction [ɪn'strʌkʃən] *n*
(*teaching*) Unterricht *m*; (*command*)
Anweisung *f*; **~s for use**
Gebrauchsanweisung *f*;
instructor *n* Lehrer(in) *m(f)*; (*US*)
Dozent(in) *m(f)*
instrument ['ɪnstrʊmənt] *n*
Instrument *nt*; **instrument panel**
n Armaturenbrett *nt*
insufficient [ɪnsə'fɪʃənt] *adj*
ungenügend
insulate ['ɪnsjʊleɪt] *vt* (*Elec*)
isolieren; **insulating tape** *n*
Isolierband *nt*; **insulation**
[ɪnsjʊ'leɪʃən] *n* Isolierung *f*
insulin ['ɪnsjʊlɪn] *n* Insulin *nt*
insult ['ɪnsʌlt] *n* Beleidigung *f*
▷ [ɪn'sʌlt] *vt* beleidigen;
insulting [ɪn'sʌltɪŋ] *adj*
beleidigend
insurance [ɪn'ʃʊərəns] *n* Versicherung *f*; **~ company**
Versicherungsgesellschaft *f*;
~ policy Versicherungspolice *f*;

insure [ɪnˈʃʊəʳ] vt versichern (against gegen)

intact [ɪnˈtækt] adj intakt

intake [ˈɪnteɪk] n Aufnahme f

integrate [ˈɪntɪˈgreɪt] vt integrieren (into in +akk); **integration** n Integration f

integrity [ɪnˈtegrɪtɪ] n Integrität f, Ehrlichkeit f

intellect [ˈɪntɪlekt] n Intellekt m; **intellectual** [ɪntɪˈlektjʊəl] adj intellektuell; (interests etc) geistig

intelligence [ɪnˈtelɪdʒəns] n (understanding) Intelligenz f; **intelligent** adj intelligent

intend [ɪnˈtend] vt beabsichtigen; **to ~ to do sth** vorhaben, etw zu tun

intense [ɪnˈtens] adj intensiv; (pressure) enorm; (competition) heftig; **intensity** n Intensität f; **intensive** adj intensiv; **intensive care unit** n Intensivstation f; **intensive course** n Intensivkurs m

intent [ɪnˈtent] adj: **to be ~ on doing sth** fest entschlossen sein, etw zu tun; **intention** [ɪnˈtenʃən] n Absicht f; **intentional**, **intentionally** adj, adv absichtlich

interact [ɪntərˈækt] vi aufeinander einwirken; **interaction** n Interaktion f, Wechselwirkung f; **interactive** adj interaktiv

interchange [ˈɪntətʃeɪndʒ] n (of motorways) Autobahnkreuz nt; **interchangeable** [ɪntəˈtʃeɪndʒəbl] adj austauschbar

intercity [ɪntəˈsɪtɪ] n Intercityzug m, IC m

intercom [ˈɪntəkɒm] n (Gegen)sprechanlage f

intercourse [ˈɪntəkɔːs] n (sexual) Geschlechtsverkehr m

interest [ˈɪntrest] n Interesse nt;

(Fin: on money) Zinsen pl; (Comm: share) Anteil m; **to be of ~** von Interesse sein (to für) ▷ vt interessieren; **interested** adj interessiert (in an +dat); **to be ~ed in** sich interessieren für; **are you ~ in coming?** hast du Lust, mitzukommen?; **interest-free** adj zinsfrei; **interesting** adj interessant; **interest rate** n Zinssatz m

interface [ˈɪntəfeɪs] n (Inform) Schnittstelle f

interfere [ɪntəˈfɪəʳ] vi (meddle) sich einmischen (with, in in +akk); **interference** n Einmischung f; (TV, Radio) Störung f

interior [ɪnˈtɪərɪəʳ] adj Innen- ▷ n Innere(s) nt; (of car) Innenraum m; (of house) Innenausstattung f

intermediate [ɪntəˈmiːdɪət] adj Zwischen-; **~ stage** Zwischenstadium nt

intermission [ɪntəˈmɪʃən] n Pause f

intern [ɪnˈtɜːn] n Assistent(in) m(f)

internal [ɪnˈtɜːnl] adj innere(r, s); (flight) Inlands-; **~ revenue** (US) Finanzamt nt; **internally** adv innen; (in body) innerlich

international [ɪntəˈnæʃnəl] adj international; **~ match** Länderspiel nt; **~ flight** Auslandsflug m ▷ n (Sport: player) Nationalspieler(in) m(f)

Internet [ˈɪntənet] n (Inform) Internet nt; **Internet access** n Internetzugang m; **Internet auction** n Internetauktion f; **Internet banking** n Onlinebanking nt; **Internet café** n Internetcafé nt; **Internet connection** n Internetanschluss m; **Internet provider** n Internetprovider m

interpret [ɪnˈtɜːprɪt] vi, vt

(*translate*) dolmetschen; (*explain*) interpretieren; **interpretation** [ɪntɜːprɪˈteɪʃən] n Interpretation f; **interpreter** [ɪnˈtɜːprɪtə*] n Dolmetscher(in) m(f)

interrogate [ɪnˈterəgeɪt] vt verhören; **interrogation** n Verhör nt

interrupt [ɪntəˈrʌpt] vt unterbrechen; **interruption** [ɪntəˈrʌpʃən] n Unterbrechung f

intersection [ɪntəˈsekʃən] n (*of roads*) Kreuzung f

interstate [ɪntəˈsteɪt] n (US) zwischenstaatlich; **~ highway** ≈ Bundesautobahn f

interval [ˈɪntəvəl] n (*space, time*) Abstand m; (*theatre etc*) Pause f

intervene [ɪntəˈviːn] vi eingreifen (*in* in); **intervention** [ɪntəˈvenʃən] n Eingreifen nt; (*Pol*) Intervention f

interview [ˈɪntəvjuː] n Interview nt; (*for job*) Vorstellungsgespräch nt ▷ vt interviewen; (*job applicant*) ein Vorstellungsgespräch führen mit; **interviewer** n Interviewer(in) m(f)

intestine [ɪnˈtestɪn] n Darm m; **~s** pl Eingeweide pl

intimate [ˈɪntɪmət] adj (*friends*) vertraut, eng; (*atmosphere*) gemütlich; (*sexually*) intim

intimidate [ɪnˈtɪmɪdeɪt] vt einschüchtern; **intimidation** n Einschüchterung f

into [ˈɪntʊ] prep in +akk; (*crash*) gegen; **to change ~ sth** (*turn ~*) zu etw werden; (*put on*) sich dat etw anziehen; **to translate ~ French** ins Französische übersetzen; **to be ~ sth** (*fam*) auf etw akk stehen

intolerable [ɪnˈtɒlərəbl] adj unerträglich

intolerant [ɪnˈtɒlərənt] adj intolerant

intoxicated [ɪnˈtɒksɪkeɪtɪd] adj betrunken; (*fig*) berauscht

intricate [ˈɪntrɪkət] adj kompliziert

intrigue [ɪnˈtriːg] vt faszinieren; **intriguing** adj faszinierend, fesselnd

introduce [ɪntrəˈdjuːs] vt (*person*) vorstellen (*to sb* jdm); (*sth new*) einführen (*to* in +akk); **introduction** [ɪntrəˈdʌkʃən] n Einführung f (*to* in +akk); (*to book*) Einleitung f (*to* zu); (*to person*) Vorstellung f

introvert [ˈɪntrəʊvɜːt] n Introvertierte(r) mf

intuition [ɪntjuːˈɪʃn] n Intuition f

invade [ɪnˈveɪd] vt einfallen in +akk

invalid [ˈɪnvəlɪd] n Kranke(r) mf; (*disabled*) Invalide m ▷ adj [ɪnˈvælɪd] (*not valid*) ungültig

invaluable [ɪnˈvæljʊəbl] adj äußerst wertvoll, unschätzbar

invariably [ɪnˈveərɪəblɪ] adv ständig; (*every time*) jedes Mal, ohne Ausnahme

invasion [ɪnˈveɪʒən] n Invasion f (*of* in +akk), Einfall m (*of* in +akk)

invent [ɪnˈvent] vt erfinden; **invention** [ɪnˈvenʃən] n Erfindung f; **inventor** n Erfinder(in) m(f)

inverted commas [ɪnˈvɜːtɪd ˈkɒməz] npl Anführungszeichen pl

invest [ɪnˈvest] vt, vi investieren (*in* in +akk)

investigate [ɪnˈvestɪgeɪt] vt untersuchen; **investigation** [ɪnvestɪˈgeɪʃən] n Untersuchung f (*into* +gen)

investment [ɪnˈvestmənt] n Investition f; **it's a good ~** es ist eine gute Anlage; (*it'll be useful*) es macht sich bezahlt

invigorating [ɪn'vɪgəreɪtɪŋ] *adj*
erfrischend, belebend; (*tonic*)
stärkend

invisible [ɪn'vɪzəbl] *adj*
unsichtbar

invitation [ɪnvɪ'teɪʃən] *n* Ein-
ladung *f*; **invite** [ɪn'vaɪt] *vt*
einladen

invoice ['ɪnvɔɪs] *n* (*bill*)
Rechnung *f*

involuntary [ɪn'vɒləntərɪ] *adj*
unbeabsichtigt

involve [ɪn'vɒlv] *vt* verwickeln
(*in sth* in etw *akk*); (*entail*) zur Folge
haben; **to be ~d in sth** (*participate
in*) an etw *dat* beteiligt sein; **I'm
not ~d** (*affected*) ich bin nicht
betroffen

inward ['ɪnwəd] *adj* innere(r, s);
inwardly *adv* innerlich; **inwards**
adv nach innen

iodine ['aɪədi:n] *n* Jod *nt*

IOU [aɪəʊ'ju:] *abbr* = **I owe you**
Schuldschein *m*

IQ *abbr* = **intelligence quotient** IQ
m

Iran [ɪ'rɑ:n] *n* der Iran

Iraq [ɪ'rɑ:k] *n* der Irak

Ireland ['aɪələnd] *n* Irland *nt*

iris ['aɪrɪs] *n* (*flower*) Schwertlilie
f; (*of eye*) Iris *f*

Irish ['aɪrɪʃ] *adj* irisch; **~ coffee**
Irish Coffee *m*; **~ Sea** die Irische
See ▷ *n* (*language*) Irisch *nt*; **the
~** *pl* die Iren *pl*; **Irishman** (*pl* **-men**)
n Ire *m*; **Irishwoman** (*pl* **-women**)
n Irin *f*

iron ['aɪən] *n* Eisen *nt*; (*for ironing*)
Bügeleisen *nt* ▷ *adj* eisern ▷ *vt*
bügeln

ironic(al) [aɪ'rɒnɪk(əl)] *adj*
ironisch

ironing board *n* Bügelbrett
nt

irony ['aɪrənɪ] *n* Ironie *f*

irrational [ɪ'ræʃənl] *adj*
irrational

irregular [ɪ'regjələ*] *adj*
unregelmäßig; (*shape*)
ungleichmäßig

irrelevant [ɪ'reləvənt] *adj*
belanglos, irrelevant

irreplaceable [ɪrɪ'pleɪsəbl] *adj*
unersetzlich

irresistible [ɪrɪ'zɪstəbl] *adj*
unwiderstehlich

irrespective of [ɪrɪ'spektɪv ɒv]
prep ungeachtet +*gen*

irresponsible [ɪrɪ'spɒnsəbl] *adj*
verantwortungslos

irretrievable [ɪrɪ'tri:vəbl] *adv*
unwiederbringlich; (*loss*)
unersetzlich

irritable ['ɪrɪtəbl] *adj* reizbar;
irritate ['ɪrɪteɪt] *vt* (*annoy*)
ärgern; (*deliberately*) reizen;
irritation [ɪrɪ'teɪʃən] *n* (*anger*)
Ärger *m*; (*Med*) Reizung *f*

IRS *abbr* = **Internal Revenue
Service** (*US*) Finanzamt *nt*

is [ɪz] *present of* **be** ist

Islam ['ɪzlɑ:m] *n* Islam *m*; **Islamic**
[ɪz'læmɪk] *adj* islamisch

island ['aɪlənd] *n* Insel *f*; **Isle**
[aɪl] *n* (*in names*) **the ~ of Man** die
Insel Man; **the ~ of Wight** die Insel
Wight; **the British ~s** die
Britischen Inseln

isn't ['ɪznt] *contr of* **is not**

isolate ['aɪsəleɪt] *vt* isolieren;
isolated *adj* (*remote*) abgelegen;
(*cut off*) abgeschnitten (*from von*);
an ~ case ein Einzelfall; **isolation**
[aɪsə'leɪʃən] *n* Isolierung *f*

Israel ['ɪzreɪl] *n* Israel *nt*; **Israeli**
[ɪz'reɪlɪ] *adj* israelisch ▷ *n* Israeli
m o f

issue ['ɪʃu:] *n* (*matter*) Frage *f*;
(*problem*) Problem *nt*; (*subject*)
Thema *nt*; (*of newspaper etc*)
Ausgabe *f*; **that's not the ~** darum
geht es nicht ▷ *vt* ausgeben;
(*document*) ausstellen; (*orders*)
erteilen; (*book*) herausgeben

it [ɪt] *pron* **1** (*specific: subject*)
er/sie/es; (*direct object*) ihn/sie/es;
(*indirect object*) ihm/ihr/ihm;
about/from/in/of it
darüber/davon/darin/davon
2 (*impers*) es; **it's raining** es regnet;
it's Friday tomorrow morgen ist
Freitag; **who is it? — it's me** wer ist
da? — ich (bin's)

IT *abbr* = **information technology**
IT *f*

Italian [ɪ'tæljən] *adj* italienisch
▷ *n* Italiener(in) *m(f)*; (*language*)
Italienisch *nt*

italic [ɪ'tælɪk] *adj* kursiv ▷ *npl*: **in
~s** kursiv

Italy ['ɪtəlɪ] *n* Italien *nt*

itch [ɪtʃ] *n* Juckreiz *m*; **I have an
~** mich juckt es ▷ *vi* jucken; **he is
~ing to ...** es juckt ihn, zu ...; **itchy**
adj juckend

it'd ['ɪtd] *contr of* **it would; it had**

item ['aɪtəm] *n* (*article*)
Gegenstand *m*; (*in catalogue*)
Artikel *m*; (*on list, in accounts*)
Posten *m*; (*on agenda*) Punkt *m*; (*in
show programme*) Nummer *f*; (*in
news*) Bericht *m*; (*TV, radio*)
Meldung *f*

itinerary [aɪ'tɪnərərɪ] *n* Reiseroute *f*

it'll ['ɪtl] *contr of* **it will; it shall**

its [ɪts] *pron* sein; (*feminine form*)
ihr

it's [ɪts] *contr of* **it is; it has**

itself [ɪt'self] *pron* (*reflexive*) sich;
(*emphatic*) **the house ~** das Haus
selbst *o* an sich; **by ~** allein; **the
door closes (by) ~** die Tür schließt
sich von selbst

I've [aɪv] *contr of* **I have**

ivory ['aɪvərɪ] *n* Elfenbein *nt*

ivy ['aɪvɪ] *n* Efeu *m*

J

jab [dʒæb] *vt* (*needle, knife*)
stechen (*into* in +*akk*) ▷ *n* (*fam*)
Spritze *f*

jack [dʒæk] *n* (*Auto*) Wagenheber
m; (*Cards*) Bube *m*; **jack in** *vt* (*fam*)
aufgeben, hinschmeißen; **jack up**
vt (*car etc*) aufbocken

jacket ['dʒækɪt] *n* Jacke *f*; (*of
man's suit*) Jackett *nt*; (*of book*)
Schutzumschlag *m*; **jacket potato**
(*pl* **-es**) *n* (in der Schale)
gebackene Kartoffel

jack-knife ['dʒæknaɪf] (*pl
jack-knives*) *n* Klappmesser *nt*
▷ *vi* (*truck*) sich quer stellen

jackpot ['dʒækpɒt] *n* Jackpot *m*

jacuzzi® [dʒə'kuːzɪ] *n* (*bath*)
Whirlpool® *m*

jail [dʒeɪl] *n* Gefängnis *nt* ▷ *vt*
einsperren

jam [dʒæm] *n* Konfitüre *f*,
Marmelade *f*; (*traffic ~*) Stau *m* ▷ *vt*
(*street*) verstopfen; (*machine*)

blockieren; **to be ~med** (*stuck*) klemmen; **to ~ on the brakes** eine Vollbremsung machen

Jamaica [dʒə'meɪkə] *n* Jamaika *nt*

jam-packed *adj* proppenvoll

janitor ['dʒænɪtə*'] *n* (*US*) Hausmeister(in) *m(f)*

Jan *abbr* = **January** Jan

January ['dʒænjʊərɪ] *n* Januar *m*

Japan [dʒə'pæn] *n* Japan *nt*; **Japanese** [dʒæpə'niːz] *adj* japanisch ▷ *n* (*person*) Japaner(in) *m(f)*; (*language*) Japanisch *nt*

jar [dʒɑː*'] *n* Glas *nt*

jaundice ['dʒɔːndɪs] *n* Gelbsucht *f*

javelin ['dʒævlɪn] *n* Speer *m*; (*Sport*) Speerwerfen *nt*

jaw [dʒɔː] *n* Kiefer *m*

jazz [dʒæz] *n* Jazz *m*

jealous ['dʒeləs] *adj* eifersüchtig (*of* auf +*akk*); **don't make me ~** mach mich nicht neidisch; **jealousy** *n* Eifersucht *f*

jeans [dʒiːnz] *npl* Jeans *pl*

jeep® [dʒiːp] *n* Jeep® *m*

jelly ['dʒelɪ] *n* Gelee *nt*; (*on meat*) Gallert *f*; (*dessert*) Götterspeise *f*; (*US: jam*) Marmelade *f*; **jelly baby** *n* (*sweet*) Gummibärchen *nt*; **jellyfish** *n* Qualle *f*

jeopardize ['dʒepədaɪz] *vt* gefährden

jerk [dʒɜːk] *n* Ruck *m*; (*fam: idiot*) Trottel *m* ▷ *vt* ruckartig bewegen ▷ *vi* (*rope*) rucken; (*muscles*) zucken

Jerusalem [dʒə'ruːsələm] *n* Jerusalem *nt*

jet [dʒet] *n* (*of water etc*) Strahl *m*; (*nozzle*) Düse *f*; (*aircraft*) Düsenflugzeug *nt*; **jet foil** *n* Tragflächenboot *nt*; **jetlag** *n* Jetlag *m* (*Müdigkeit nach langem Flug*)

Jew [dʒuː] *n* Jude *m*, Jüdin *f*

jewel ['dʒuːəl] *n* Edelstein *m*; (*esp fig*) Juwel *nt*; **jeweller**, **jeweler** (*US*) *n* Juwelier(in) *m(f)*; **jewellery**, **jewelry** (*US*) *n* Schmuck *m*

Jewish ['dʒuːɪʃ] *adj* jüdisch; **she's ~** sie ist Jüdin

jigsaw (puzzle) ['dʒɪgsɔː(pʌzl)] *n* Puzzle *nt*

jilt [dʒɪlt] *vt* den Laufpass geben +*dat*

jingle ['dʒɪŋgl] *n* (*advert*) Jingle *m*; (*verse*) Reim *m*

jitters ['dʒɪtərz] *npl* (*fam*) **to have the ~** Bammel haben; **jittery** *adj* (*fam*) ganz nervös

job [dʒɒb] *n* (*piece of work*) Arbeit *f*; (*task*) Aufgabe *f*; (*occupation*) Stellung *f*, Job *m*; **what's your ~?** was machen Sie beruflich?; **it's a good ~ you did that** gut, dass du das gemacht hast; **jobcentre** *n* Arbeitsvermittlungsstelle *f*, Arbeitsamt *nt*; **job-hunting** *n*: **to go ~** auf Arbeitssuche gehen; **jobless** *adj* arbeitslos; **job seeker** *n* Arbeitssuchende(r) *mf*; **jobseeker's allowance** *n* Arbeitslosengeld *nt*; **job-sharing** *n* Arbeitsplatzteilung *f*

jockey ['dʒɒkɪ] *n* Jockey *m*

jog [dʒɒg] *vt* (*person*) anstoßen ▷ *vi* (*run*) joggen; **jogging** *n* Jogging *nt*; **to go ~** joggen gehen

john [dʒɒn] *n* (*US fam*) Klo *nt*

join [dʒɔɪn] *vt* (*put together*) verbinden (*to* mit); (*club etc*) beitreten +*dat*; (*sit with*) sich jdm anschließen; (*sit with*) sich zu jdm setzen ▷ *vi* (*unite*) sich vereinigen; (*rivers*) zusammenfließen ▷ *n* Verbindungsstelle *f*; (*seam*) Naht *f*; **join in** *vi*, *vt* mitmachen (*sth* bei etw)

joint [dʒɔɪnt] *n* (*of bones*) Gelenk *nt*; (*in pipe etc*) Verbindungsstelle *f*; (*of meat*) Braten *m*; (*of marijuana*)

Joint m ▷ adj gemeinsam; **joint account** n Gemeinschaftskonto nt; **jointly** adv gemeinsam

joke [dʒəʊk] n Witz m; (prank) Streich m; **for a ~** zum Spaß; **it's no ~** das ist nicht zum Lachen ▷ vi Witze machen; **you must be joking** das ist ja wohl nicht dein Ernst!

jolly ['dʒɒlɪ] adj lustig, vergnügt

Jordan ['dʒɔːdən] n (country) Jordanien nt; (river) Jordan m

jot down [dʒɒt daʊn] vt sich notieren; **jotter** n Notizbuch nt

journal ['dʒɜːnl] n (diary) Tagebuch nt; (magazine) Zeitschrift f; **journalism** n Journalismus m; **journalist** n Journalist(in) m(f)

journey ['dʒɜːnɪ] n Reise f; (esp on stage, by car, train) Fahrt f

joy [dʒɔɪ] n Freude f (at über +akk); **joystick** n (Inform) Joystick m; (Aviat) Steuerknüppel m

judge [dʒʌdʒ] n Richter(in) m(f); (Sport) Punktrichter(in) m(f) ▷ vt beurteilen (by nach); **as far as I can ~** meinem Urteil nach ▷ vi urteilen (by nach); **judg(e)ment** n (Jur) Urteil nt; (opinion) Ansicht f; **an error of ~** Fehleinschätzung f

judo ['dʒuːdəʊ] n Judo nt

jug [dʒʌg] n Krug m

juggle ['dʒʌgl] vi (lit, fig) jonglieren (with mit)

juice [dʒuːs] n Saft m; **juicy** adj saftig; (story, scandal) pikant

July [dʒuːˈlaɪ] n Juli m; see also **September**

jumble ['dʒʌmbl] n Durch-einander nt ▷ vt: **to ~ (up)** durcheinanderwerfen; (facts) durcheinanderbringen; **jumble sale** n (for charity) Flohmarkt m; Wohltätigkeitsbasar m

jumbo ['dʒʌmbəʊ] adj (sausage etc) Riesen-; **jumbo jet** n Jumbojet m

jump [dʒʌmp] vi springen; (nervously) zusammenzucken; **to ~ to conclusions** voreilige Schlüsse ziehen; **to ~ from one thing to another** dauernd das Thema wechseln ▷ vt (a. fig: omit) überspringen; **to ~ the lights** bei Rot über die Kreuzung fahren; **to ~ the queue** sich vordrängen ▷ n Sprung m; (for horses) Hindernis nt; **jumper** n Pullover m; (US: dress) Trägerkleid nt; (person, horse) Springer(in) m(f); **jumper cable** n (US), **jump lead** n (Brit Auto) Starthilfekabel nt

junction ['dʒʌŋkʃən] n (of roads) Kreuzung f; (Rail) Knotenpunkt m

June [dʒuːn] n Juni m; see also **September**

jungle ['dʒʌŋgl] n Dschungel m

junior ['dʒuːnɪə°] adj (younger) jünger; (lower position) untergeordnet (to sb jdm) ▷ n: **she's two years my ~** sie ist zwei Jahre jünger als ich; **junior high (school)** n (US) ≈ Mittelschule f; **junior school** n (Brit) Grundschule f

junk [dʒʌŋk] n (trash) Plunder m; **junk food** n Nahrungsmittel pl mit geringem Nährwert, Junkfood nt; **junkie** n (fam) Junkie m, Fixer(in) m(f); (fig: fan) Freak m; **junk mail** n Reklame f; (Inform) Junkmail f; **junk shop** n Trödelladen m

jury ['dʒʊərɪ] n Geschworene pl; (in competition) Jury f

just [dʒʌst] adj gerecht ▷ adv (recently) gerade; (exactly) genau; **~ as expected** genau wie erwartet; **~ as nice** genauso nett; (barely) **~ in time** gerade noch rechtzeitig; (immediately) **~ before/after ...** gleich vor/nach ...; (small distance) **~ round the corner** gleich um die Ecke; (a little)

~ over an hour etwas mehr als eine Stunde; (*only*) **~ the two of us** nur wir beide; **~ a moment** Moment mal; (*absolutely, simply*) **it was ~ fantastic** es war einfach klasse; **~ about** so etwa; (*more or less*) mehr oder weniger; **~ about ready** fast fertig

justice ['dʒʌstɪs] *n* Gerechtigkeit *f*; **justifiable** [dʒʌstɪ'faɪəbl] *adj* berechtigt; **justifiably** *adv* zu Recht; **justify** ['dʒʌstɪfaɪ] *vt* rechtfertigen

jut [dʒʌt] *vi:* **to ~ (out)** herausragen

juvenile ['dʒuːvənaɪl] *n adj* Jugend-, jugendlich ▷ *n* . Jugendliche(r) *mf*

k *abbr* = **thousand**; **15k** 15 000

K *abbr* = **kilobyte** KB

kangaroo [kæŋgə'ruː] *n* Känguru *nt*

karaoke [kærɪ'əʊkɪ] *n* Karaoke *nt*

karate [kə'rɑːtɪ] *n* Karate *nt*

kart [kɑːt] *n* Gokart *m*

kayak ['kaɪæk] *n* Kajak *m* o *nt*; **kayaking** ['kaɪækɪŋ] *n* Kajakfahren *nt*

Kazakhstan [kæzæk'stɑːn] *n* Kasachstan *nt*

kebab [kə'bæb] *n* (*shish ~*) Schaschlik *nt* o *m*; (*doner ~*) Kebab *m*

keel [kiːl] *n* (*Naut*) Kiel *m*; **keel over** *vi* (*boat*) kentern; (*person*) umkippen

keen [kiːn] *adj* begeistert (*on* von); (*hardworking*) eifrig; (*mind, wind*) scharf; (*interest, feeling*) stark; **to be ~ on sb** von jdm angetan sein; **she's ~ on riding** sie reitet gern; **to be ~ to do sth** darauf erpicht sein, etw zu tun

keep [kiːp] **(kept, kept)** *vt* (*retain*) behalten; (*secret*) für sich behalten; (*observe*) einhalten; (*promise*) halten; (*run: shop, diary, accounts*) führen; (*animals*) halten; (*support, family etc*) unterhalten, versorgen; (*store*) aufbewahren; **to ~ sb waiting** jdn warten lassen; **to ~ sb from doing sth** jdn davon abhalten, etw zu tun; **to ~ sth clean/secret** etw sauber/geheim halten; **"~ clear"** „(bitte) frei halten"; **~ this to yourself** behalten Sie das für sich ▷ *vi* (*food*) sich halten; (*remain, with adj*) bleiben; **~ quiet** sei ruhig!; **~ left** links fahren; **to ~ doing sth** (*repeatedly*) etw immer wieder tun; **~ at it** mach weiter so!; **it ~s happening** es passiert immer wieder ▷ *n* (*livelihood*) Unterhalt *m*; **keep back** *vi* zurückbleiben ▷ *vt* zurückhalten; (*information*) verschweigen (*from sb* jdm); **keep off** *vt* (*person, animal*) fernhalten; **"~ off the grass"** „Betreten des Rasens verboten"; **keep on** *vi* weitermachen; (*walking*) weitergehen; (*in car*) weiterfahren; **to ~ doing sth** (*persistently*) etw immer wieder tun ▷ *vt* (*coat etc*) anbehalten; **keep out** *vt* nicht hereinlassen ▷ *vi* draußen bleiben; **~** (*on sign*) Eintritt verboten; **keep to** *vt* (*road, path*) bleiben auf +*dat*; (*plan etc*) sich halten an +*akk*; **to ~ the point** bei der Sache bleiben; **keep up** *vi* Schritt halten (*with* mit) ▷ *vt* (*maintain*) aufrechterhalten; (*speed*) halten; **to ~ appearances** den Schein wahren; **keep it up!** (*fam*) weiter so!

keeper *n* (*museum etc*) Aufseher(in) *m(f)*; (*goal~*) Torwart *m*; (*zoo ~*) Tierpfleger(in) *m(f)*; **keep-fit** *n* Fitnesstraining *nt*; **~ exercises** Gymnastik *f*

kennel ['kenl] *n* Hundehütte *f*; **kennels** *n* Hundepension *f*

Kenya ['kenjə] *n* Kenia *nt*

kept [kept] *pt, pp of* **keep**

kerb ['kɜːb] *n* Randstein *m*

kerosene ['kerəsiːn] *n* (*US*) Petroleum *nt*

ketchup ['ketʃʌp] *n* Ketchup *nt o m*

kettle ['ketl] *n* Kessel *m*

key [kiː] *n* Schlüssel *m*; (*of piano, computer*) Taste *f*; (*Mus*) Tonart *f*; (*for map etc*) Zeichenerklärung *f* ▷ *vt*: **to ~ (in)** (*Inform*) eingeben ▷ *adj* entscheidend; **keyboard** *n* (*piano, computer*) Tastatur *f*; **keyhole** *n* Schlüsselloch *nt*; **keypad** *n* (*Inform*) Nummernblock *m*; **keyring** *n* Schlüsselring *m*

kick [kɪk] *n* Tritt *m*; (*Sport*) Stoß *m*; **I get a ~ out of it** (*fam*) es turnt mich an ▷ *vt, vi* treten; **kick out** *vt* (*fam*) rausschmeißen (*of* aus); **kick-off** *n* (*Sport*) Anstoß *m*

kid [kɪd] *n* (*child*) Kind *nt* ▷ *vt* (*tease*) auf den Arm nehmen ▷ *vi* Witze machen; **you're ~ding** das ist doch nicht dein Ernst!; **no ~ding** aber echt!

kidnap ['kɪdnæp] *vt* entführen; **kidnapper** *n* Entführer(in) *m(f)*; **kidnapping** *n* Entführung *f*

kidney ['kɪdnɪ] *n* Niere *f*; **kidney machine** *n* künstliche Niere

kill [kɪl] *vt* töten; (*esp intentionally*) umbringen; (*weeds*) vernichten; **killer** *n* Mörder(in) *m(f)*

kilo ['kiːləʊ] (*pl* **-s**) *n* Kilo *nt*; **kilobyte** *n* Kilobyte *nt*; **kilogramme** *n* Kilogramm *nt*; **kilometer** (*US*), **kilometre** *n* Kilometer *m*; **~s per hour**

Stundenkilometer *pl*; **kilowatt** *n* Kilowatt *nt*

kilt [kɪlt] *n* Schottenrock *m*

kind [kaɪnd] *adj* nett, freundlich (*to* zu) ▷ *n* Art *f*; (*of coffee, cheese etc*) Sorte *f*; **what ~ of ...?** was für ein(e) ...?; **this ~ of ...** so ein(e) ...; **~ of** (+ *adj*) irgendwie

kindergarten ['kɪndəgɑːtn] *n* Kindergarten *m*

kindly ['kaɪndlɪ] *adj* nett, freundlich ▷ *adv* liebenswürdigerweise; **kindness** ['kaɪndnəs] *n* Freundlichkeit *f*

king [kɪŋ] *n* König *m*; **kingdom** *n* Königreich *nt*; **kingfisher** *n* Eisvogel *m*; **king-size** *adj* im Großformat; (*bed*) extra groß

kipper ['kɪpə*] *n* Räucherhering *m*

kiss [kɪs] *n* Kuss *m*; **~ of life** Mund-zu-Mund-Beatmung *f* ▷ *vt* küssen

kit [kɪt] *n* (*equipment*) Ausrüstung *f*; (*fam*) Sachen *pl*; (*sports ~*) Sportsachen *pl*; (*belongings, clothes*) Sachen *pl*; (*for building sth*) Bausatz *m*

kitchen ['kɪtʃɪn] *n* Küche *f*; **kitchen foil** *n* Alufolie *f*; **kitchen scales** *n* Küchenwaage *f*; **kitchen unit** *n* Küchenschrank *m*; **kitchenware** *n* Küchengeschirr *nt*

kite [kaɪt] *n* Drachen *m*

kitten ['kɪtn] *n* Kätzchen *nt*

kiwi ['kiːwiː] *n* (*fruit*) Kiwi *f*

km *abbr* = **kilometres** km

knack [næk] *n* Dreh *m*, Trick *m*; **to get/have got the ~** den Dreh herauskriegen/heraushaben; **knackered** ['nækəd] *adj* (*Brit fam*) fix und fertig, kaputt

knee [niː] *n* Knie *nt*; **kneecap** *n* Kniescheibe *f*; **knee-jerk** *adj* (*reaction*) reflexartig; **kneel** [niːl] (**knelt** *o* **kneeled, knelt** *o* **kneeled**)

vi knien; (*action, ~ down*) sich hinknien

knelt [nelt] *pt, pp of* **kneel**

knew [njuː] *pt of* **know**

knickers ['nɪkəz] *npl* (*Brit fam*) Schlüpfer *m*

knife [naɪf] *n* (*pl* **knives**) *n* Messer *nt*

knight [naɪt] *n* Ritter *m*; (*in chess*) Pferd *nt*, Springer *m*

knit [nɪt] *vt, vi* stricken; **knitting** *n* (*piece of work*) Strickarbeit *f*; (*activity*) Stricken *nt*; **knitting needle** *n* Stricknadel *f*; **knitwear** *n* Strickwaren *pl*

knob [nɒb] *n* (*on door*) Knauf *m*; (*on radio etc*) Knopf *m*

knock [nɒk] *vt* (*with hammer etc*) schlagen; (*accidentally*) stoßen; **to ~ one's head** sich *dat* den Kopf anschlagen ▷ *vi* klopfen (*on, at* an +*akk*) ▷ *n* (*blow*) Schlag *m*; (*on door*) Klopfen *nt*; **there was a ~ (at the door)** es hat geklopft; **knock down** *vt* (*object*) umstoßen; (*person*) niederschlagen; (*with car*) anfahren; (*building*) abreißen; **knock out** *vt* (*stun*) bewusstlos schlagen; (*boxer*) k.o. schlagen; **knock over** *vt* umstoßen; (*with car*) anfahren; **knocker** *n* Türklopfer *m*; **knockout** *n* Knockout *m*, K.o. *m*

knot [nɒt] *n* Knoten *m*

know [nəʊ] (**knew, known**) *vt, vi* wissen; (*be acquainted with: people, places*) kennen; (*recognize*) erkennen; (*language*) können; **I'll let you ~** ich sage dir Bescheid; **I ~ some French** ich kann etwas Französisch; **to get to ~ sb** jdn kennenlernen; **to be ~n as** bekannt sein als; **know about** *vt* Bescheid wissen über +*akk*; (*subject*) sich auskennen in +*dat*; (*cars, horses etc*) sich auskennen mit; **know of** *vt* kennen; **not that**

I ~ nicht dass ich wüsste;
know-all n (fam) Klugscheißer m;
know-how n Kenntnis f,
Know-how nt; **knowing** adj
wissend; (look, smile) vielsagend;
knowledge ['nɒlɪdʒ] n Wissen
nt; (of a subject) Kenntnisse pl; **to
(the best of) my ~** meines
Wissens
known [nəʊn] pp of **know**
knuckle ['nʌkl] n (Finger)knöchel m; (Gastr) Hachse f;
knuckle down vi sich an die
Arbeit machen
Koran [kɒˈrɑːn] n Koran m
Korea [kəˈrɪə] n Korea nt
Kosovo ['kɒsɒvəʊ] n der Kosovo
kph abbr = **kilometres per hour**
km/h
Kremlin ['kremlɪn] n: **the ~** der
Kreml
Kurd [kɜːd] n Kurde m, Kurdin f;
Kurdish adj kurdisch
Kuwait [kʊˈweɪt] n Kuwait nt

L abbr (Brit Auto) = **learner**
LA abbr = **Los Angeles**
lab [læb] n (fam) Labor nt
label ['leɪbl] n Etikett nt; (tied)
Anhänger m; (adhesive) Aufkleber
m; (record ~) Label nt ▷ vt
etikettieren; (pej) abstempeln
laboratory [ləˈbɒrətərɪ] n Labor
nt

● **LABOR DAY**
●
● Der **Labor Day** ist in den USA
● und Kanada der Name für den
● Tag der Arbeit. Er wird dort als
● gesetzlicher Feiertag am ersten
● Montag im September
● begangen.

laborious [ləˈbɔːrɪəs] adj
mühsam; **labor** (US), **labour**
['leɪbə*] n Arbeit f; (Med) Wehen
pl; **to be in ~** Wehen haben ▷ adj

(*Pol*) Labour-; **~ Party** Labour Party
f; **labor union** n (*US*)
Gewerkschaft f; **labourer** n
Arbeiter(in) m(f)
lace [leɪs] n (*fabric*) Spitze f; (*of
shoe*) Schnürsenkel m ▷ vt: **to
~ (up)** zuschnüren; **lace-up** n
Schnürschuh m
lack [læk] vt, vi: **to be ~ing** fehlen;
sb ~s o **is ~ing in sth** es fehlt jdm
an etw dat; **we ~ the time** uns
fehlt die Zeit ▷ n Mangel m (*of* an
+dat)
lacquer [ˈlækə*] n Lack m; (*Brit:
hair ~*) Haarspray nt
lad [læd] n Junge m
ladder [ˈlædə*] n Leiter f; (*in tight*)
Laufmasche f
laddish [ˈlædɪʃ] adj (*Brit*)
machohaft
laden [ˈleɪdn] adj beladen (*with*
mit)
ladies [ˈleɪdɪz], **ladies' room** n
Damentoilette f
lad mag n Männerzeitschrift f
lady [ˈleɪdɪ] n Dame f; (*as title*)
Lady f; **ladybird, ladybug** (*US*) n
Marienkäfer m; **Ladyshave®** n
Epiliergerät nt
lag [læg] vi: **to ~ (behind)**
zurückliegen ▷ vt (*pipes*) isolieren
lager [ˈlɑːgə*] n helles Bier;
~ lout betrunkener Rowdy
lagging [ˈlægɪŋ] n Isolierung f
laid [leɪd] pt, pp of **lay**; **laid-back**
adj (*fam*) cool, gelassen
lain [leɪn] pp of **lie**
lake [leɪk] n See m; **the Lake
District** Seengebiet im Nordwesten
Englands
lamb [læm] n Lamm nt; (*meat*)
Lammfleisch nt; **lamb chop** n
Lammkotelett nt
lame [leɪm] adj lahm; (*excuse*)
faul; (*argument*) schwach
lament [ləˈment] n Klage f ▷ vt
beklagen

laminated [ˈlæmɪneɪtɪd] adj
beschichtet
lamp [læmp] n Lampe f; (*in street*)
Laterne f; (*in car*) Licht nt,
Scheinwerfer m; **lamppost** n
Laternenpfahl m; **lampshade** n
Lampenschirm m
land [lænd] n Land nt ▷ vi (*from
ship*) an Land gehen; (*Aviat*) landen
▷ vt (*passengers*) absetzen; (*goods*)
abladen; (*plane*) landen; **landing** n
Landung f; (*on stairs*)
Treppenabsatz m; **landing stage**
n Landesteg m; **landing strip** n
Landebahn f
landlady n Hauswirtin f,
Vermieterin f; **landlord** n (*of
house*) Hauswirt m, Vermieter m;
(*of pub*) Gastwirt m; **landmark** n
Wahrzeichen nt; (*event*)
Meilenstein m; **landowner** n
Grundbesitzer(in) m(f); **landscape**
n Landschaft f; (*format*)
Querformat nt; **landslide** n (*Geo*)
Erdrutsch m
lane [leɪn] n (*in country*) enge
Landstraße, Weg m; (*in town*) Gasse
f; (*of motorway*) Spur f; (*Sport*) Bahn
f; **to get in ~** (*in car*) sich einordnen
language [ˈlæŋgwɪdʒ] n Sprache
f; (*style*) Ausdrucksweise f
lantern [ˈlæntən] n Laterne f
lap [læp] n Schoß m; (*in race*)
Runde f ▷ vt (*in race*) überholen
lapse [læps] n (*mistake*) Irrtum m;
(*moral*) Fehltritt m ▷ vi ablaufen
laptop [ˈlæptɒp] n Laptop m
large [lɑːdʒ] adj groß; **by and
~** im Großen und Ganzen; **largely**
adv zum größten Teil; **large-scale**
adj groß angelegt, Groß-
lark [lɑːk] n (*bird*) Lerche f
laryngitis [lærɪnˈdʒaɪtɪs] n Kehl-
kopfentzündung f; **larynx**
[ˈlærɪŋks] n Kehlkopf m
laser [ˈleɪzə*] n Laser m; **laser
printer** n Laserdrucker m

lash [læʃ] vt peitschen; **lash out** vi (with fists) um sich schlagen; (spend money) sich in Unkosten stürzen (on mit)

lass [læs] n Mädchen nt

last [lɑːst] adj letzte(r, s); **the ~ but one** der/die/das vorletzte; **~ night** gestern Abend; **~ but not least** nicht zuletzt ▷ adv zuletzt; (last time) das letzte Mal; **at ~** endlich ▷ n (person) Letzte(r) mf; (thing) Letzte(s) nt; **he was the ~ to leave** er ging als Letzter ▷ vi (continue) dauern; (remain in good condition) durchhalten; (remain good) sich halten; (money) ausreichen; **lasting** adj dauerhaft; (impression) nachhaltig; **lastly** adv schließlich; **last-minute** adj in letzter Minute; **last name** n Nachname m

late [leɪt] adj spät; (after proper time) zu spät; (train etc) verspätet; (dead) verstorben; **to be ~** zu spät kommen; (train etc) Verspätung haben ▷ adv spät; (after proper time) zu spät; **late availibility flight** n Last-Minute-Flug m; **lately** adv in letzter Zeit; **late opening** n verlängerte Öffnungszeiten pl; **later** ['leɪtə°] adj, adv später; **see you ~** bis später; **latest** ['leɪtɪst] adj späteste(r, s); (most recent) neueste(r, s) ▷ n: **the ~** (news) das Neueste; **at the ~** spätestens

Latin ['lætɪn] n Latein nt ▷ adj lateinisch; **Latin America** n Lateinamerika nt; **Latin-American** adj lateinamerikanisch ▷ n Latein-amerikaner(in) m(f)

latter ['lætə°] adj (second of two) letztere(r, s); (last: part, years) letzte(r, s), später

Latvia ['lætvɪə] n Lettland nt;

Latvian ['lætvɪən] ▷ adj lettisch; ▷ n (person) Lette m; Lettin f; (language) Lettisch nt

laugh [lɑːf] n Lachen nt; **for a ~** aus Spaß ▷ vi lachen (at, about über +akk); **to ~ at sb** sich über jdn lustig machen; **it's no ~ing matter** es ist nicht zum Lachen; **laughter** ['lɑːftə°] n Gelächter nt

launch [lɔːntʃ] n (launching, of ship) Stapellauf m; (of rocket) Abschuss m; (of product) Markteinführung f; (with hype) Lancierung f; (event) Eröffnungsfeier f ▷ vt (ship) vom Stapel lassen; (rocket) abschießen; (product) einführen; (with hype) lancieren; (project) in Gang setzen

launder ['lɔːndə°] vt waschen und bügeln; (fig: money) waschen; **laundrette** [lɔːn'dret] n (Brit), **laundromat** ['lɔːndrəmæt] n (US) Waschsalon m; **laundry** ['lɔːndrɪ] n (place) Wäscherei f; (clothes) Wäsche f

lavatory ['lævətrɪ] n Toilette f

lavender ['lævɪndə°] n Lavendel m

lavish ['lævɪʃ] adj verschwende-risch; (furnishings etc) üppig; (gift) großzügig

law [lɔː] n Gesetz nt; (system) Recht nt; (for study) Jura; (of sport) Regel f; **against the ~** gesetzwidrig; **law-abiding** adj gesetzestreu; **law court** n Gerichtshof m; **lawful** adj rechtmäßig

lawn [lɔːn] n Rasen m; **lawnmower** n Rasenmäher m

lawsuit ['lɔːsuːt] n Prozess m; **lawyer** ['lɔːjə°] n Rechtsanwalt m, Rechtsanwältin f

laxative ['læksətɪv] n Abführ-mittel nt

lay [leɪ] pt of **lie** ▷ vt (**laid**, **laid**) legen; (table) decken; (vulg) poppen, bumsen; (egg) legen ▷ adj Laien-; **lay down** vt hinlegen; **lay off** vt (workers) (vorübergehend) entlassen; (stop attacking) in Ruhe lassen; **lay on** vt (provide) anbieten; (organize) veranstalten, bereitstellen; **layabout** n Faulenzer(in) m(f); **lay-by** n Parkbucht f; (bigger) Parkplatz m

layer ['leɪə°] n Schicht f

layman ['leɪmən] n Laie m

layout ['leɪaʊt] n Gestaltung f; (of book etc) Lay-out nt

laze [leɪz] vi faulenzen; **laziness** ['leɪzɪnɪs] n Faulheit f; **lazy** ['leɪzɪ] adj faul; (day, time) gemütlich

lb abbr = **pound** Pfd.

lead [led] n Blei nt ▷ vt, vi [liːd] (**led, led**) führen; (group etc) leiten; **to ~ the way** vorangehen; **this is ~ing us nowhere** das bringt uns nicht weiter ▷ [liːd] n (race) Führung f; (distance, time ahead) Vorsprung m (over vor +dat); (of police) Spur f; (Theat) Hauptrolle f; (dog's) Leine f; (Elec: flex) Leitung f; **lead astray** vt irreführen; **lead away** vt wegführen; **lead back** vi zurückführen; **lead on** vt anführen; **lead to** vt (street) hinführen nach; (result in) führen zu; **lead up to** vt (drive) führen zu

leaded ['ledɪd] adj (petrol) verbleit

leader ['liːdə°] n Führer(in) m(f); (of party) Vorsitzende(r) mf; (of project, expedition) Leiter(in) m(f); (Sport: in race) der/die Erste; (in league) Tabellenführer m; **leadership** ['liːdəʃɪp] n Führung f

lead-free ['led'friː] adj (petrol) bleifrei

leading ['liːdɪŋ] adj führend, wichtig

leaf [liːf] (pl **leaves**) n Blatt nt;

leaflet ['liːflɪt] n Prospekt m; (pamphlet) Flugblatt nt; (with instructions) Merkblatt nt

league [liːg] n Bund m; (Sport) Liga f

leak [liːk] n (gap) undichte Stelle; (escape) Leck nt; **to take a ~** (fam) pinkeln gehen ▷ vi (pipe etc) undicht sein; (liquid etc) auslaufen; **leaky** adj undicht

lean [liːn] adj (meat) mager; (face) schmal; (person) drahtig ▷ vi (**leant** o **leaned, leant** o **leaned**) (not vertical) sich neigen; (rest) **to ~ against sth** sich an etw akk lehnen; (support oneself) **to ~ on sth** sich auf etw akk stützen ▷ vt lehnen (on, against an +akk); **lean back** vi sich zurücklehnen; **lean forward** vi sich vorbeugen; **lean over** vi sich hinüberbeugen; **lean towards** vt tendieren zu

leant [lent] pt, pp of **lean**

leap [liːp] n Sprung m ▷ vi (**leapt** o **leaped, leapt** o **leaped**) springen; **leapt** [lept] pt, pp of **leap; leap year** n Schaltjahr nt

learn [lɜːn] (**learnt** o **learned, learnt** o **learned**) vt, vi lernen; (find out) erfahren; **to ~ (how) to swim** schwimmen lernen; **learned** ['lɜːnɪd] adj gelehrt; **learner** n Anfänger(in) m(f); (Brit: driver) Fahrschüler(in) m(f)

learnt [lɜːnt] pt, pp of **learn**

lease [liːs] n (of land, premises etc) Pacht f; (contract) Pachtvertrag m; (of house, car etc) Miete f; (contract) Mietvertrag m ▷ vt pachten; (house, car etc) mieten; **lease out** vt vermieten; **leasing** ['liːsɪŋ] n Leasing nt

least [liːst] adj wenigste(r, s); (slightest) geringste(r, s) ▷ adv am wenigsten; **~ expensive** billigste(r, s) ▷ n: **the ~** das Mindeste; **not in the ~** nicht im geringsten; **at ~** wenigstens; (*with number*) mindestens

leather ['leðə*] *n* Leder *nt* ▷ *adj* ledern, Leder-

leave [li:v] *n* (*time off*) Urlaub *m*; **on ~** auf Urlaub; **to take one's ~** Abschied nehmen (*of* von) ▷ *vt* (**left, left**) (*place, person*) verlassen; (*not remove, not change*) lassen; (*~ behind: message, scar etc*) hinterlassen; (*forget*) hinter sich lassen; (*after death*) hinterlassen (*to sb* jdm); (*entrust*) überlassen (*to sb* jdm); **to be left** (*remain*) übrig bleiben; **~ me alone** lass mich in Ruhe!; **don't ~ it to the last minute** warte nicht bis zur letzten Minute ▷ *vi* (*weg*)gehen, (*weg*)fahren; (*on journey*) abreisen; (*bus, train*) abfahren (*for* nach); **leave behind** *vt* zurücklassen; (*scar etc*) hinterlassen; (*forget*) hinter sich lassen; **leave out** *vt* auslassen; (*person*) ausschließen (*of* von)

leaves [li:vz] *pl of* **leaf**

leaving do [li:vɪŋ du:] *n* Abschiedsfeier *f*

Lebanon ['lebənən] *n*: **the ~** der Libanon

lecture ['lektʃə*] *n* Vortrag *m*; (*at university*) Vorlesung *f*; **to give a ~** einen Vortrag/eine Vorlesung halten; **lecturer** *n* Dozent(in) *m(f)*; **lecture theatre** *n* Hörsaal *m*

led [led] *pt, pp of* **lead**

LED *abbr* = **light-emitting diode** Leuchtdiode *f*

ledge [ledʒ] *n* Leiste *f*; (*window ~*) Sims *m* o *nt*

leek [li:k] *n* Lauch *m*

left [left] *pt, pp of* **leave** ▷ *adj* linke(r, s) ▷ *adv* (*position*) links; (*movement*) nach links ▷ *n* (*side*) linke Seite; **the Left** (*Pol*) die Linke; **on/to the ~** links (*of* von); **move/fall to the ~** nach links

rücken/fallen; **left-hand** *adj* linke(r, s); **~ bend** Linkskurve *f*; **~ drive** Linkssteuerung *f*; **left-handed** *adj* linkshändig; **left-hand side** *n* linke Seite

left-luggage locker *n* Gepäckschließfach *nt*; **left-luggage office** *n* Gepäckaufbewahrung *f*

leftovers *npl* Reste *pl*

left wing *n* linker Flügel; **left-wing** *adj* (*Pol*) linksgerichtet

leg [leg] *n* Bein *nt*; (*of meat*) Keule *f*

legacy ['legəsɪ] *n* Erbe *nt*, Erbschaft *f*

legal ['li:gəl] *adj* Rechts-, rechtlich; (*allowed*) legal; (*limit, age*) gesetzlich; **~ aid** Rechtshilfe *f*; **legalize** *vt* legalisieren; **legally** *adv* legal

legend ['ledʒənd] *n* Legende *f*

legible, legibly ['ledʒəbl, -blɪ] *adj, adv* leserlich

legislation [ledʒɪs'leɪʃn] *n* Gesetze *pl*

legitimate [lɪ'dʒɪtɪmət] *adj* rechtmäßig, legitim

legroom ['legrʊm] *n* Beinfreiheit *f*

leisure ['leʒə*] *n* (*time*) Freizeit *f* ▷ *adj* Freizeit-; **~ centre** Freizeitzentrum *nt*; **leisurely** ['leʒəlɪ] *adj* gemächlich

lemon ['lemən] *n* Zitrone *f*; **lemonade** [lemə'neɪd] *n* Limonade *f*; **lemon curd** *n* Brotaufstrich aus Zitronen, Butter, Eiern und Zucker; **lemon juice** *n* Zitronensaft *m*; **lemon sole** *n* Seezunge *f*

lend [lend] (**lent, lent**) *vt* leihen; **to ~ sb sth** jdm etw leihen; **to (sb) ~ a hand** (jdm) behilflich sein; **lending library** *n* Leihbücherei *f*

length [leŋθ] *n* Länge *f*; **4 metres ~** 4 Meter lang; **what**

~ is it? wie lange ist es?; **for any ~ of time** für längere Zeit; **at ~** (*lengthily*) ausführlich; **lengthen** ['leŋθən] *vt* verlängern; **lengthy** *adj* sehr lange; (*dragging*) langwierig

lenient ['liːnɪənt] *adj* nachsichtig

lens [lenz] *n* Linse *f*; (*Foto*) Objektiv *nt*

lent [lent] *pt, pp of* **lend**

Lent [lent] *n* Fastenzeit *f*

lentil ['lentl] *n* (*Bot*) Linse *f*

Leo ['liːəʊ] (*pl* **-s**) *n* (*Astr*) Löwe *m*

leopard ['lepəd] *n* Leopard *m*

lesbian ['lezbɪən] *adj* lesbisch ▷ *n* Lesbe *f*

less [les] *adj, adv, n* weniger; **~ and ~** immer weniger; (*~ often*) immer seltener; **lessen** ['lesn] *vi* abnehmen, nachlassen ▷ *vt* verringern; (*pain*) lindern; **lesser** ['lesə*] *adj* geringer; (*amount*) kleiner

lesson ['lesn] *n* (*at school*) Stunde *f*; (*unit of study*) Lektion *f*; (*fig*) Lehre *f*; (*Rel*) Lesung *f*; **~s start at 9** der Unterricht beginnt um 9

let [let] (**let, let**) *vt* lassen; (*lease*) vermieten; **to ~ sb have sth** jdm etw geben; **~'s go** gehen wir; **to ~ go (of sth)** (etw) loslassen; **let down** *vt* herunterlassen; (*fail to help*) im Stich lassen; (*disappoint*) enttäuschen; **let in** *vt* hereinlassen; **let off** *vt* (*bomb*) hochgehen lassen; (*person*) laufen lassen; **let out** *vt* hinauslassen; (*secret*) verraten; (*scream etc*) ausstoßen; **let up** *vi* nachlassen; (*stop*) aufhören

lethal ['liːθəl] *adj* tödlich

let's *contr* = **let us**

letter ['letə*] *n* (*of alphabet*) Buchstabe *m*; (*message*) Brief *m*; (*official ~*) Schreiben *nt*; **letter**

bomb *n* Briefbombe *f*; **letterbox** *n* Briefkasten *m*

lettuce ['letɪs] *n* Kopfsalat *m*

leukaemia, leukemia (US) [luːˈkiːmɪə] *n* Leukämie *f*

level ['levl] *adj* (*horizontal*) waagerecht; (*ground*) eben; (*two things, two runners*) auf selber Höhe; **to be ~ with sb/sth** mit jdm/etw auf gleicher Höhe sein; **~ on points** punktgleich ▷ *adv* (*run etc*) auf gleicher Höhe, gleich auf; **to draw ~** (*in race*) gleichziehen (*with* mit); (*in game*) ausgleichen ▷ *n* (*altitude*) Höhe *f*; (*standard*) Niveau *nt*; (*amount, degree*) Grad *m*; **to be on a ~ with** auf gleicher Höhe sein mit ▷ *vt* (*ground*) einebnen; **level crossing** *n* (*Brit*) (schienengleicher) Bahnübergang *m*; **level-headed** *adj* vernünftig

lever ['liːvə*, (US) 'levə*] *n* Hebel *m*; (*fig*) Druckmittel *nt*; **lever up** *vt* hochstemmen

liability [laɪəˈbɪlɪtɪ] *n* Haftung *f*; (*burden*) Belastung *f*; (*obligation*) Verpflichtung *f*; **liable** ['laɪəbl] *adj*: **to be ~ for sth** (*responsible*) für etw haften; **~ for tax** steuerpflichtig

liar ['laɪə*] *n* Lügner(in) *m(f)*

Lib Dem [lɪbˈdem] *abbr* = **Liberal Democrat**

liberal ['lɪbərəl] *adj* (*generous*) großzügig; (*broad-minded*) liberal; **Liberal Democrat** *n* (*Brit Pol*) Liberaldemokrat(in) *m(f)* ▷ *adj* liberaldemokratisch

liberate ['lɪbəreɪt] *vt* befreien; **liberation** [lɪbəˈreɪʃn] *n* Befreiung *f*

Liberia [laɪˈbɪərɪə] *n* Liberia *nt*

liberty ['lɪbətɪ] *n* Freiheit *f*

Libra ['liːbrə] *n* (*Astr*) Waage *f*

library ['laɪbrərɪ] *n* Bibliothek *f*; (*lending ~*) Bücherei *f*

Libya ['lɪbɪə] n Libyen nt
lice [laɪs] pl of **louse**
licence ['laɪsəns] n (permit) Genehmigung f; (Comm) Lizenz f; (driving ~) Führerschein m; **license** ['laɪsəns] n (US) see **licence** ▷ vt genehmigen; **licensed** adj (restaurant etc) mit Schankerlaubnis; **license plate** n (US Auto) Nummernschild nt; **licensing hours** npl Ausschankzeiten pl
lick [lɪk] vt lecken ▷ n Lecken nt
licorice ['lɪkərɪs] n Lakritze f
lid [lɪd] n Deckel m; (eye~) Lid nt
lie [laɪ] n Lüge f; **~ detector** Lügendetektor m ▷ vi lügen; **to ~ to sb** jdn belügen ▷ vi (lay, lain) (rest, be situated) liegen; (~ down) sich legen; (snow) liegen bleiben; **to be lying third** an dritter Stelle liegen; **lie about** vi herumliegen; **lie down** vi sich hinlegen
Liechtenstein ['lɪktənstaɪn] n Liechtenstein nt
lie in [laɪ'ɪn] n: **to have a ~** ausschlafen
life [laɪf] (pl **lives**) n Leben nt; **to get ~** lebenslänglich bekommen; **there isn't much ~ here** hier ist nicht viel los; **how many lives were lost?** wie viele sind ums Leben gekommen?; **life assurance** n Lebensversicherung f; **lifebelt** n Rettungsring m; **lifeboat** n Rettungsboot nt; **lifeguard** n Bademeister(in) m(f), Rettungsschwimmer(in) m(f); **life insurance** n Lebensversicherung f; **life jacket** n Schwimmweste f; **lifeless** adj (dead) leblos; **lifelong** adj lebenslang; **life preserver** n (US) Rettungsring m; **life-saving** adj lebensrettend; **life-size(d)** adj in Lebensgröße; **life span** n Lebensspanne f; **life style** n

Lebensstil m; **lifetime** n Lebenszeit f
lift [lɪft] vt (hoch)heben; (ban) aufheben ▷ n (Brit: elevator) Aufzug m, Lift m; **to give sb a ~** jdn im Auto mitnehmen; **lift up** vt hochheben; **lift-off** n Start m
ligament ['lɪgəmənt] n Band nt
light [laɪt] (lit o **lighted, lit** o **lighted**) vt beleuchten; (fire, cigarette) anzünden ▷ n Licht nt; (lamp) Lampe f; **~s** pl (Auto) Beleuchtung f; (traffic ~s) Ampel f; **in the ~ of** angesichts +gen ▷ adj (bright) hell; (not heavy, easy) leicht; (punishment) milde; (taxes) niedrig; **~ blue/green** hellblau/hellgrün; **light up** vt (illuminate) beleuchten ▷ vi (a. eyes) aufleuchten
light bulb n Glühbirne f
lighten ['laɪtn] vi hell werden ▷ vt (give light to) erhellen; (make less heavy) leichter machen; (fig) erleichtern
lighter ['laɪtə°] n (cigarette ~) Feuerzeug nt
light-hearted adj unbeschwert; **lighthouse** n Leuchtturm m; **lighting** n Beleuchtung f; **lightly** adv leicht; **light meter** n (Foto) Belichtungsmesser m
lightning ['laɪtnɪŋ] n Blitz m
lightweight adj leicht
like [laɪk] vt mögen, gernhaben; **he ~s swimming** er schwimmt gern; **would you ~ ...?** hättest du/hätten Sie gern ...?; **I'd ~ to go home** ich möchte nach Hause (gehen); **I don't ~ the film** der Film gefällt mir nicht ▷ prep wie; **what's it/he ~?** wie ist es/er?; **he looks ~ you** er sieht dir/Ihnen ähnlich; **~ that/this** so; **likeable** ['laɪkəbl] adj sympathisch
likelihood ['laɪklɪhʊd] n Wahrscheinlichkeit f; **likely** ['laɪklɪ] adj wahrscheinlich; **the bus is**

~ to be late der Bus wird wahrscheinlich Verspätung haben; **he's not (at all) ~ to come** (höchst)wahrscheinlich kommt er nicht

like-minded [laɪkˈmaɪndɪd] *adj* gleich gesinnt

likewise [ˈlaɪkwaɪz] *adv* ebenfalls; **to do ~** das Gleiche tun

liking [ˈlaɪkɪŋ] *n* (*for person*) Zuneigung *f*; (*for type, things*) Vorliebe *f* (*for* für)

lilac [ˈlaɪlək] *n* Flieder *m* ⊳ *adj* fliederfarben

lily [ˈlɪlɪ] *n* Lilie *f*; **~ of the valley** Maiglöckchen *nt*

limb [lɪm] *n* Glied *nt*

limbo [ˈlɪmbəʊ] *n*: **in ~** (*plans*) auf Eis gelegt

lime [laɪm] *n* (*tree*) Linde *f*; (*fruit*) Limone *f*; (*substance*) Kalk *m*; **lime juice** *n* Limonensaft *m*; **limelight** *n* (*fig*) Rampenlicht *nt*

limerick [ˈlɪmərɪk] *n* Limerick *m* (*fünfzeiliges komisches Gedicht*)

limestone [ˈlaɪmstəʊn] *n* Kalkstein *m*

limit [ˈlɪmɪt] *n* Grenze *f*; (*for pollution etc*) Grenzwert *m*; **there's a ~ to that** dem sind Grenzen gesetzt; **to be over the ~** (*speed*) das Tempolimit überschreiten; (*alcohol consumption*) fahruntüchtig sein; **that's the ~** jetzt reicht's!, das ist die Höhe! ⊳ *vt* beschränken (*to* auf +*akk*); (*freedom, spending*) einschränken; **limitation** [lɪmɪˈteɪʃən] *n* Beschränkung *f*; (*of freedom, spending*) Einschränkung *f*; **limited** *adj* begrenzt; **~ liability company** Gesellschaft *f* mit beschränkter Haftung, GmbH *f*; **public ~ company** Aktiengesellschaft *f*

limousine [ˈlɪməziːn] *n* Limousine *f*

limp [lɪmp] *vi* hinken ⊳ *adj* schlaff

line [laɪn] *n* Linie *f*; (*written*) Zeile *f*; (*rope*) Leine *f*; (*on face*) Falte *f*; (*row*) Reihe *f*; (*US: queue*) Schlange *f*; (*Rail*) Bahnlinie *f*; (*between A and B*) Strecke *f*; (*Tel*) Leitung *f*; (*range of items*) Kollektion *f*; **hold the ~** bleiben Sie am Apparat; **to stand in ~** Schlange stehen; **in ~ with** in Übereinstimmung mit; **something along those ~s** etwas in dieser Art; **drop me a ~** schreib mir ein paar Zeilen; **~s** (*Theat*) Text *m* ⊳ *vt* (*clothes*) füttern; (*streets*) säumen; **lined** *adj* (*paper*) liniert; (*face*) faltig; **line up** *vi* sich aufstellen; (*US: form queue*) sich anstellen

linen [ˈlɪnɪn] *n* Leinen *nt*; (*sheets etc*) Wäsche *f*

liner [ˈlaɪnə*] *n* Überseedampfer *m*, Passagierschiff *nt*

linger [ˈlɪŋgə*] *vi* verweilen; (*smell*) nicht weggehen

lingerie [ˈlænʒəriː] *n* Damenunterwäsche *f*

lining [ˈlaɪnɪŋ] *n* (*of clothes*) Futter *nt*; (*brake ~*) Bremsbelag *m*

link [lɪŋk] *n* (*connection*) Verbindung *f*; (*of chain*) Glied *nt*; (*relationship*) Beziehung *f* (*with* zu); (*between events*) Zusammenhang *m*; (*Internet*) Link *m* ⊳ *vt* verbinden

lion [ˈlaɪən] *n* Löwe *m*; **lioness** *n* Löwin *f*

lip [lɪp] *n* Lippe *f*; **lipstick** *n* Lippenstift *m*

liqueur [lɪˈkjʊə*] *n* Likör *m*

liquid [ˈlɪkwɪd] *n* Flüssigkeit *f* ⊳ *adj* flüssig

liquidate [ˈlɪkwɪdeɪt] *vt* liquidieren

liquidizer [ˈlɪkwɪdaɪzə*] *n* Mixer *m*

liquor [ˈlɪkə*] *n* Spirituosen *pl*

liquorice ['lɪkərɪs] n Lakritze f
Lisbon ['lɪzbən] n Lissabon nt
lisp [lɪsp] vt, vi lispeln
list [lɪst] n Liste f ▷ vi (ship)
Schlagseite haben ▷ vt auflisten,
aufzählen; **~ed building** unter
Denkmalschutz stehendes
Gebäude
listen ['lɪsn] vi zuhören, horchen
(for sth auf etw akk); **listen to** vt
(person) zuhören +dat; (radio)
hören; (advice) hören auf; **listener**
n Zuhörer(in) m(f); (to radio)
Hörer(in) m(f)
lit [lɪt] pt, pp of **light**
liter ['liːtə*] n (US) Liter m
literacy ['lɪtərəsɪ] n Fähigkeit f
zu lesen und zu schreiben; **literal**
['lɪtərəl] adj (translation, meaning)
wörtlich; (actual) buchstäblich;
literally adv (translate, take sth)
wörtlich; (really) buchstäblich,
wirklich; **literary** ['lɪtərərɪ] adj
literarisch; (critic, journal etc)
Literatur-; (language) gehoben;
literature ['lɪtrətʃə*] n Literatur
f; (brochures etc)
Informationsmaterial nt
Lithuania [lɪθjuːˈeɪnjə] n Litauen
nt; **Lithuanian** [lɪθjuːˈeɪnjən]
▷ adj litauisch; ▷ n (person)
Litauer(in) m(f); (language)
Litauisch nt
litre ['liːtə*] n Liter m
litter ['lɪtə*] n Abfälle pl; (of
animals) Wurf m ▷ vt: **to be ~ed
with** übersät sein mit; **litter bin** n
Abfalleimer m
little ['lɪtl] adj (**smaller,
smallest**) klein; (in quantity)
wenig; **a ~ while ago** vor kurzer
Zeit ▷ adv, n (**fewer, fewest**)
wenig; **a ~** ein bisschen, ein
wenig; **as ~ as possible** so wenig
wie möglich; **for as ~ as £5** ab nur
5 Pfund; **I see very ~ of them** ich
sehe sie sehr selten; **~ by ~** nach

und nach; **little finger** n kleiner
Finger
live [laɪv] adj lebendig; (Elec)
geladen, unter Strom; (TV, Radio:
event) live; **~ broadcast**
Direktübertragung f ▷ [lɪv] vi
leben; (not die) überleben; (dwell)
wohnen; **you ~ and learn** man
lernt nie aus ▷ vt (life) führen; **to
~ a life of luxury** im Luxus leben;
live on vi weiterleben ▷ vt: **to
~ sth** von etw leben; (feed) sich von
etw ernähren; **to earn enough to
~** genug verdienen, um davon zu
leben; **live together** vi
zusammenleben; **live up to** vt
(reputation) gerecht werden +dat;
(expectations) entsprechen +dat;
live with vt (parents etc) wohnen
bei; (partner) zusammenleben mit;
(difficulty) **you'll just have to ~ it**
du musst dich/Sie müssen sich
eben damit abfinden
liveliness ['laɪvlɪnɪs] n Lebhaf-
tigkeit f; **lively** ['laɪvlɪ] adj
lebhaft
liver ['lɪvə*] n Leber f
lives [laɪvz] pl of **life**
livestock ['laɪvstɒk] n Vieh nt
living ['lɪvɪŋ] n Lebensunterhalt
m; **what do you do for a ~?** was
machen Sie beruflich? ▷ adj
lebend; **living room** n
Wohnzimmer nt
lizard ['lɪzəd] n Eidechse f
llama ['lɑːmə] n (Zool) Lama nt
load [ləʊd] n Last f; (cargo)
Ladung f; (Tech, Elec) Belastung f; **~s
of** (fam) massenhaft; **it was a ~ of
rubbish** (fam) es war
grottenschlecht ▷ vt (vehicle)
beladen; (Inform) laden; (film)
einlegen
loaf [ləʊf] (pl **loaves**) n: **a ~ of
bread** ein (Laib) Brot (m)nt
loan [ləʊn] n (item leant)
Leihgabe f; (Fin) Darlehen nt; **on**

~ geliehen ▷ vt leihen (to sb
jdm)
loathe [ləʊð] vt verabscheuen
loaves [ləʊvz] pl of **loaf**
lobby ['lɒbɪ] n Vorhalle f; (Pol)
Lobby f
lobster ['lɒbstə*] n Hummer m
local ['ləʊkəl] adj (traffic, time etc)
Orts-; (radio, news, paper) Lokal-;
(government, authority) Kommunal-;
(anaesthetic) örtlich; **~ call** (Tel)
Ortsgespräch nt; **~ elections**
Kommunalwahlen pl; **~ time**
Ortszeit f; **~ train** Nahverkehrszug
m; **the ~ shops** die Geschäfte am
Ort ▷ n (pub) Stammlokal nt; **the
~s** pl die Ortsansässigen pl; **locally**
adv örtlich, am Ort
locate [ləʊ'keɪt] vt (find)
ausfindig machen; (position)
legen; (establish) errichten; **to be
~d** sich befinden (in, at in +dat);
location [ləʊ'keɪʃən] n (position)
Lage f; (Cine) Drehort m
loch [lɒx] n (Scot) See m
lock [lɒk] n Schloss nt; (Naut)
Schleuse f; (of hair) Locke f ▷ vt
(door etc) abschließen ▷ vi (door
etc) sich abschließen lassen;
(wheels) blockieren; **lock in** vt
einschließen, einsperren; **lock out**
vt aussperren; **lock up** vt (house)
abschließen; (person) einsperren
locker ['lɒkə*] n Schließfach nt;
locker room n (US)
Umkleideraum m
locksmith ['lɒksmɪθ] n Schlos-
ser(in) m(f)
locust ['ləʊkəst] n Heuschrecke f
lodge [lɒdʒ] n (small house)
Pförtnerhaus nt; (porter's ~)
Pförtnerloge f ▷ vi in Untermiete
wohnen (with bei); (get stuck)
stecken bleiben; **lodger** n
Untermieter(in) m(f); **lodging** n
Unterkunft f
loft [lɒft] n Dachboden m

log [lɒg] n Klotz m; (Naut) Log nt;
to keep a ~ of sth über etw Buch
führen; **log in** vi (Inform) sich
einloggen; **log off** vi (Inform) sich
ausloggen; **log on** vi (Inform) sich
einloggen; **log out** vi (Inform) sich
ausloggen
logic ['lɒdʒɪk] n Logik f; **logical**
adj logisch
logo ['ləʊgəʊ] (pl **-s**) n Logo nt
loin [lɔɪn] n Lende f
loiter ['lɔɪtə*] vi sich herumtreiben
lollipop ['lɒlɪpɒp] n Lutscher m;
~ man/lady (Brit) Schülerlotse m,
Schülerlotsin f
lolly ['lɒlɪ] n Lutscher m
London ['lʌndən] n London nt;
Londoner n Londoner(in) m(f)
loneliness ['ləʊnlɪnɪs] n Einsamkeit f; **lonely** ['ləʊnlɪ], (esp
US) **lonesome** ['ləʊnsəm] adj
einsam
long [lɒŋ] adj lang; (distance)
weit; **it's a ~ way** es ist weit (to
nach); **for a ~ time** lange; **how ~ is
the film?** wie lange dauert der
Film? ▷ adv lange; **not for ~** nicht lange;
~ ago vor langer Zeit; **before
~** bald; **all day ~** den ganzen Tag;
no ~er nicht mehr; **as ~ as** solange
▷ vi sich sehnen (for nach); (be
waiting) sehnsüchtig warten (for
auf); **long-distance call** n
Ferngespräch nt; **long drink** n
Longdrink m; **long-haul flight** n
Langstreckenflug m; **longing** n
Sehnsucht f (for nach); **longingly**
adv sehnsüchtig; **longitude**
['lɒŋgɪtjuːd] n Länge f; **long jump**
n Weitsprung m; **long-life milk** n
H-Milch f; **long-range** adj
Langstrecken-, Fern-; **~ missile**
Langstreckenrakete f;
long-sighted adj weitsichtig;
long-standing adj alt,
langjährig; **long-term** adj

langfristig; (car park, effect etc) Langzeit-; **~ unemployment** Langzeitarbeitslosigkeit f; **long wave** n Langwelle f
loo [luː] n (Brit fam) Klo nt
look [lʊk] n Blick m; (appearance) **~(s)** pl Aussehen nt; **I'll have a ~** ich schau mal nach; **to have a ~ at sth** sich dat etw ansehen; **can I have a ~?** darf ich mal sehen? ▷ vi schauen, gucken; (with prep) sehen; (search) nachsehen; (appear) aussehen; (**I'm**) **just ~ing** ich schaue nur; **it ~s like rain** es sieht nach Regen aus ▷ vt: **~ what you've done** sieh dir mal an, was du da angestellt hast; (appear) **he ~s his age** man sieht ihm sein Alter an; **to ~ one's best** sehr vorteilhaft aussehen; **look after** vt (care for) sorgen für; (keep an eye on) aufpassen auf +akk; **look at** vt ansehen, anschauen; **look back** vi sich umsehen; (fig) zurückblicken; **look down on** vt (fig) herabsehen auf +akk; **look for** vt suchen; **look forward to** vt sich freuen auf +akk; **look into** vt (investigate) untersuchen; **look out** vi hinaussehen (of the window zum Fenster); (watch out) Ausschau halten (for nach); (be careful) aufpassen, Acht geben (for auf +akk); **~!** Vorsicht!; **look up** vi aufsehen ▷ vt (word etc) nachschlagen; **look up to** vt aufsehen zu
loony ['luːnɪ] adj (fam) bekloppt
loop [luːp] n Schleife f
loose [luːs] adj locker; (knot, button) lose; **loosen** vt lockern; (knot) lösen
loot [luːt] n Beute f
lop-sided ['lɒp'saɪdɪd] adj schief
lord [lɔːd] n (ruler) Herr m; (Brit: title) Lord m; **the Lord** (God) Gott der Herr; **the (House of) Lords** (Brit) das Oberhaus

lorry ['lɒrɪ] n (Brit) Lastwagen m
lose [luːz] (**lost, lost**) vt verlieren; (chance) verpassen; **to ~ weight** abnehmen; **to ~ one's life** umkommen ▷ vi verlieren; (clock, watch) nachgehen; **loser** n Verlierer(in) m(f); **loss** [lɒs] n Verlust m; **lost** [lɒst] pt, pp of **lose**; **we're ~** wir haben uns verlaufen ▷ adj verloren; **lost-and-found** (US), **lost property (office)** n Fundbüro nt
lot [lɒt] n (fam: batch) Menge f, Haufen m, Stoß m; **this is the first ~** das ist die erste Ladung; **a ~ viel(e)**; **a ~ of money** viel Geld; **~s of people** viele Leute; **the (whole) ~** alles; (people) alle
lotion ['ləʊʃən] n Lotion f
lottery ['lɒtərɪ] n Lotterie f
loud [laʊd] adj laut; (colour) schreiend; **loudspeaker** n Lautsprecher m; (of stereo) Box f
lounge [laʊndʒ] n Wohnzimmer nt; (in hotel) Aufenthaltsraum m; (at airport) Warteraum m ▷ vi sich herumlümmeln
louse [laʊs] (pl lice) n Laus f; **lousy** ['laʊzɪ] adj (fam) lausig
lout [laʊt] n Rüpel m
lovable ['lʌvəbl] adj liebenswert
love [lʌv] n Liebe f (of zu); (person, address) Liebling m, Schatz m; (Sport) null; **to be in ~** verliebt sein (with sb in jdn); **to fall in ~** sich verlieben (with sb in jdn); **to make ~** (sexually) sich lieben; **to make ~ to** (o with) **sb** mit jdm schlafen; (in letter) **he sends his ~** er lässt grüßen; **give her my ~** grüße sie von mir; **~, Tom** liebe Grüße, Tom ▷ vt (person) lieben; (activity) sehr gerne mögen; **to ~ to do sth** etw für sein Leben gerne tun; **I'd ~ a cup of tea** ich hätte liebend gern eine Tasse Tee; **love affair** n (Liebes)verhältnis nt; **love letter** n

Liebesbrief m; **love life** n Liebesleben nt; **lovely** ['lʌvlɪ] adj schön, wunderschön; (charming) reizend; **we had a ~ time** es war sehr schön; **lover** ['lʌvə] n Liebhaber(in) m(f); **loving** adj liebevoll

low [ləʊ] adj niedrig; (rank) niedere(r, s); (level, note, neckline) tief; (intelligence, density) gering; (quality, standard) schlecht; (not loud) leise; (depressed) niedergeschlagen; **we're ~ on petrol** wir haben kaum noch Benzin ▷ n (Meteo) Tief nt; **low-calorie** adj kalorienarm; **lowcut** adj (dress) tief ausgeschnitten; **low-emission** adj schadstoffarm; **lower** ['ləʊə°] adj niedriger; (storey, class etc) untere(r, s) ▷ vt herunterlassen; (eyes, price) senken; (pressure) verringern; **low-fat** adj fettarm; **low tide** [ləʊ'taɪd] n Ebbe f

loyal ['lɔɪəl] adj treu; **loyalty** n Treue f

lozenge ['lɒzɪndʒ] n Pastille f

Als **L-Plates** werden in Großbritannien die weißen Schilder mit einem roten „L" bezeichnet, die vorn und hinten an jedem von einem Fahrschüler gesteuerten Fahrzeug befestigt werden müssen. Fahrschüler müssen einen vorläufigen Führerschein beantragen und dürfen damit unter der Aufsicht eines erfahrenen Autofahrers auf allen Straßen außer Autobahnen fahren.

Ltd abbr = **limited** ≈ GmBH f

lubricant ['lu:brɪkənt] n Schmiermittel nt, Gleitmittel nt

luck [lʌk] n Glück nt; **bad ~** Pech

nt; **luckily** adv glücklicherweise, zum Glück; **lucky** adj (number, day etc) Glücks-; **to be ~** Glück haben

ludicrous ['lu:dɪkrəs] adj grotesk

luggage ['lʌgɪdʒ] n Gepäck nt; **luggage compartment** n Gepäckraum m; **luggage rack** n Gepäcknetz nt

lukewarm ['lu:kwɔ:m] adj lauwarm

lullaby ['lʌləbaɪ] n Schlaflied nt

lumbago [lʌm'beɪgəʊ] n Hexenschuss m

luminous ['lu:mɪnəs] adj leuchtend

lump [lʌmp] n Klumpen m; (Med) Schwellung f; (in breast) Knoten m; (of sugar) Stück nt; **lump sum** n Pauschalsumme f; **lumpy** adj klumpig

lunacy ['lu:nəsɪ] n Wahnsinn m; **lunatic** ['lu:nətɪk] adj wahnsinnig ▷ n Wahnsinnige(r) mf

lunch, luncheon [lʌntʃ, -ən] n Mittagessen nt; **to have ~** zu Mittag essen; **lunch break, lunch hour** n Mittagspause f; **lunchtime** n Mittagszeit f

lung [lʌŋ] n Lunge f

lurch [lɜːtʃ] n: **to leave sb in the ~** jdn im Stich lassen

lurid ['ljʊərɪd] adj (colour) grell; (details) widerlich

lurk [lɜːk] vi lauern

lust [lʌst] n (sinnliche) Begierde (for nach)

Luxembourg ['lʌksəmbɜːg] n Luxemburg nt; **Luxembourger** [lʌksəm'bɜːgə°] n Luxemburger(in) m(f)

luxurious [lʌg'ʒʊərɪəs] adj luxuriös, Luxus-; **luxury** ['lʌkʃərɪ] n (a. luxuries pl) Luxus m; **~ goods** Luxusgüter pl

lynx [lɪŋks] n Luchs m

lyrics ['lɪrɪks] npl Liedtext m

m

m *abbr* = **metre** m

M *abbr* (*street*) = **Motorway** A; (*size*) = **medium** M

MA *abbr* = **Master of Arts** Magister Artium *m*

ma [ma:] *n* (*fam*) Mutti *f*

mac [mæk] *n* (*Brit fam*) Regenmantel *m*

macaroon [mækə'ru:n] *n* Makrone *f*

Macedonia [masɪdəʊnɪə] *n* Mazedonien *nt*

machine [mə'ʃi:n] *n* Maschine *f*; **machine gun** *n* Maschinengewehr *nt*; **machinery** [mə'ʃi:nərɪ] *n* Maschinen *pl*; (*fig*) Apparat *m*; **machine washable** *adj* waschmaschinenfest

mackerel ['mækrəl] *n* Makrele *f*

macro ['mækrəʊ] (*pl* **-s**) *n* (*Inform*) Makro *nt*

mad [mæd] *adj* wahnsinnig, verrückt; (*dog*) tollwütig; (*angry*)

wütend, sauer (*at* auf +*akk*); (*fam*) **~ about** (*fond of*) verrückt nach; **to work like ~** wie verrückt arbeiten; **are you ~?** spinnst du/spinnen Sie?

madam ['mædəm] *n* gnädige Frau

mad cow disease [mæd'kaʊdɪ'zi:z] *n* Rinderwahnsinn *m*; **maddening** *adj* zum Verrücktwerden

made [meɪd] *pt, pp of* **make**

made-to-measure ['meɪdtə'meʒə*] *adj* nach Maß; **~ suit** Maßanzug *m*

madly ['mædlɪ] *adv* wie verrückt; (*with adj*) wahnsinnig; **madman** ['mædmən] (*pl* **-men**) *n* Verrückte(r) *m*; **madwoman** ['mædwʊmən] (*pl* **-women**) *n* Verrückte *f*; **madness** ['mædnɪs] *n* Wahnsinn *m*

magazine ['mægəzi:n] *n* Zeitschrift *f*

maggot ['mægət] *n* Made *f*

magic ['mædʒɪk] *n* Magie *f*; (*activity*) Zauberei *f*; (*fig: effect*) Zauber *m*; **as if by ~** wie durch Zauberei ▷ *adj* Zauber-; (*powers*) magisch; **magician** [mə'dʒɪʃən] *n* Zauberer *m*, Zaub(r)erin *f*

magnet ['mægnɪt] *n* Magnet *m*; **magnetic** [mæg'netɪk] *adj* magnetisch; **magnetism** ['mægnɪtɪzəm] *n* (*fig*) Anziehungskraft *f*

magnificent, magnificently [mæg'nɪfɪsənt, -lɪ] *adj, adv* herrlich, großartig

magnify ['mægnɪfaɪ] *vt* vergrößern; **magnifying glass** *n* Vergrößerungsglas *nt*, Lupe *f*

magpie ['mægpaɪ] *n* Elster *f*

maid [meɪd] *n* Dienstmädchen *nt*; **maiden name** *n* Mädchenname *m*; **maiden voyage** *n* Jungfernfahrt *f*

mail [meɪl] n Post f; (e-mail) Mail f ▷ vt (post) aufgeben; (send) mit der Post schicken (to an +akk); **mailbox** n (US) Briefkasten m; (Inform) Mailbox f; **mailing list** n Adressenliste f; **mailman** n (pl **-men**) (US) Briefträger m; **mail order** n Bestellung f per Post; **mail order firm** n Versandhaus nt; **mailshot** n Mailing nt

main [meɪn] adj Haupt-; **~ course** Hauptgericht nt; **the ~ thing** die Hauptsache ▷ n (pipe) Hauptleitung f; **mainframe** n Großrechner m; **mainland** n Festland nt; **mainly** adv hauptsächlich; **main road** n Hauptverkehrsstraße f; **main street** n (US) Hauptstraße f

maintain [meɪnˈteɪn] vt (keep up) aufrechterhalten; (machine, roads) instand halten; (service) warten; (claim) behaupten; **maintenance** [ˈmeɪntənəns] n Instandhaltung f; (Tech) Wartung f

maize [meɪz] n Mais m

majestic [məˈdʒestɪk] adj majestätisch; **majesty** [ˈmædʒɪstɪ] n Majestät f; **Your/His/Her Majesty** Eure/Seine/Ihre Majestät

major [ˈmeɪdʒə°] adj (bigger) größer; (important) bedeutend; **~ part** Großteil m; (role) wichtige Rolle; **~ road** Hauptverkehrsstraße f; (Mus) **A ~** A-Dur nt ▷ vi (US) **to ~ in sth** etw als Hauptfach studieren

Majorca [məˈjɔːkə] n Mallorca nt

majority [məˈdʒɒrɪtɪ] n Mehrheit f; **to be in the ~** in der Mehrzahl sein

make [meɪk] n Marke f ▷ vt (made, made) machen; (manufacture) herstellen; (clothes) anfertigen; (dress) nähen; (soup) zubereiten; (bread, cake) backen; (tea, coffee) kochen; (speech) halten; (earn) verdienen; (decision) treffen; **it's made of gold** es ist aus Gold; **to ~ sb do sth** jdn dazu bringen, etw zu tun; (force) jdn zwingen, etw zu tun; **she made us wait** sie ließ uns warten; **what ~s you think that?** wie kommen Sie darauf?; **it ~s the room look smaller** es lässt den Raum kleiner wirken; **to ~ (it to) the airport** (reach) den Flughafen erreichen; (in time) es zum Flughafen schaffen; **he never really made it** er hat es nie zu etwas gebracht; **she didn't ~ it through the night** sie hat die Nacht nicht überlebt; (calculate) **I ~ it £5/a quarter to six** nach meiner Rechnung kommt es auf 5 Pfund/nach meiner Uhr ist es dreiviertel sechs; **he's just made for this job** er ist für diese Arbeit wie geschaffen; **make for** vt zusteuern auf +akk; **make of** vt (think of) halten von; **I couldn't ~ anything of it** ich wurde daraus nicht schlau; **make off** vi sich davonmachen (with mit); **make out** vi zurechtkommen ▷ vt (cheque) ausstellen; (list) aufstellen; (understand) verstehen; (discern) ausmachen; **to ~ (that) ...** es so hinstellen, als ob ...; **make up** vt (team etc) bilden; (face) schminken; (invent: story etc) erfinden; **to ~ one's mind** sich entscheiden; **to ~ (it) up with sb** sich mit jdm aussöhnen ▷ vi sich versöhnen; **make up for** vt ausgleichen; (time) aufholen

make-believe adj Fantasie-; **makeover** n gründliche Veränderung, Verschönerung f; **maker** n (Comm) Hersteller(in) m(f); **makeshift** adj behelfsmäßig; **make-up** n

Make-up nt, Schminke f; **making**
['meɪkɪŋ] n Herstellung f
maladjusted [mælə'dʒʌstɪd] adj
verhaltensgestört
malaria [mə'leərɪə] n Malaria f
Malaysia [mə'leɪʒɪə] n Malaysia
nt
male [meɪl] n Mann m; (animal)
Männchen nt ▷ adj männlich;
~ chauvinist Chauvi m, Macho m;
~ nurse Krankenpfleger m
malfunction [mæl'fʌŋkʃən] vi
nicht richtig funktionieren ▷ n
Defekt m
malice ['mælɪs] n Bosheit f;
malicious [mə'lɪʃəs] adj boshaft;
(behaviour, action) böswillig;
(damage) mutwillig
malignant [mə'lɪgnənt] adj
bösartig
mall [mɔːl] n (US)
Einkaufszentrum nt
malnutrition [mælnjʊ'trɪʃən] n
Unterernährung f
malt [mɔːlt] n Malz nt
Malta ['mɔːltə] n Malta nt;
Maltese [mɔːl'tiːz] adj
maltesisch ▷ n (person)
Malteser(in) m(f); (language)
Maltesisch nt
maltreat [mæl'triːt] vt schlecht
behandeln; (violently) misshandeln
mammal ['mæməl] n Säugetier
nt
mammoth ['mæməθ] adj
Mammut-, Riesen-
man [mæn] (pl **men**) n (male)
Mann m; (human race) der Mensch,
die Menschen pl; (in chess) Figur f
▷ vt besetzen
manage ['mænɪdʒ] vi zurechtkommen; **can you ~?** schaffst du
es?; **to ~ without sth** ohne etw
auskommen, auf etw verzichten
können ▷ vt (control) leiten;
(musician, sportsman) managen;
(cope with) fertig werden mit; (task,

portion, climb etc) schaffen; **to ~ to
do sth** es schaffen, etw zu tun;
manageable adj (object)
handlich; (task) zu bewältigen;
management n Leitung f;
(directors) Direktion f; (subject)
Management nt,
Betriebswirtschaft f;
management consultant n
Unternehmensberater(in) m(f);
manager n Geschäftsführer(in)
m(f); (departmental ~)
Abteilungsleiter(in) m(f); (of
branch, bank) Filialleiter(in) m(f); (of
musician, sportsman) Manager(in)
m(f); **managing director** n
Geschäftsführer(in) m(f)
mane [meɪn] n Mähne f
maneuver (US) see **manoeuvre**
mango ['mæŋgəʊ] (pl **-es**) n
Mango f
man-hour n Arbeitsstunde f
manhunt n Fahndung f
mania ['meɪnɪə] n Manie f;
maniac ['meɪnɪæk] n Wahnsin-
nige(r) mf; (fan) Fanatiker(in)
m(f)
manicure ['mænɪkjʊə*] n
Maniküre f
manipulate [mə'nɪpjʊleɪt] vt
manipulieren
mankind [mæn'kaɪnd] n
Menschheit f
manly ['mænlɪ] adj männlich
man-made ['mænmeɪd] adj
(product) künstlich
manner ['mænə*] n Art f; **in this
~** auf diese Art und Weise; **~s** pl
Manieren pl
manoeuvre [mə'nuːvə*] n
Manöver nt ▷ vt, vi manövrieren
manor ['mænə*] n: **~ (house)**
Herrenhaus nt
manpower ['mænpaʊə*] n
Arbeitskräfte pl
mansion ['mænʃən] n Villa f; (of
old family) Herrenhaus nt

manslaughter ['mænslɔːtə*] n
Totschlag m

mantelpiece ['mæntlpiːs] n
Kaminsims m

manual ['mænjʊəl] adj manuell,
Hand- ▷ n Handbuch nt

manufacture [mænjʊ'fæktʃə*]
vt herstellen ▷ n Herstellung f;
manufacturer n Hersteller m

manure [mə'njʊə*] n Dung m;
(esp artificial) Dünger m

many ['menɪ] (**more, most**) adj,
pron viele; **~ times** oft; **not
~ people** nicht viele Leute; **too
~ problems** zu viele Probleme

map [mæp] n Landkarte f; (of
town) Stadtplan m

maple ['meɪpl] n Ahorn m

marathon ['mærəθən] n Marathon m

marble ['mɑːbl] n Marmor m; (for
playing) Murmel f

march [mɑːtʃ] vi marschieren
▷ n Marsch m; (protest)
Demonstration f

March [mɑːtʃ] n März m; see also
September

mare [meə] n Stute f

margarine [mɑːdʒə'riːn] n
Margarine f

margin ['mɑːdʒɪn] n Rand m;
(extra amount) Spielraum m;
(Comm) Gewinnspanne f;
marginal adj (difference etc)
geringfügig

marijuana [mærjʊ'ɑːnə] n
Marihuana nt

marine [mə'riːn] adj Meeres-

marital ['mærɪtl] adj ehelich;
~ status Familienstand m

maritime ['mærɪtaɪm] adj See-

marjoram ['mɑːdʒərəm] n
Majoran m

mark [mɑːk] n (spot) Fleck m; (at
school) Note f; (sign) Zeichen nt
▷ vt (make ~) Flecken machen auf
+akk; (indicate) markieren;

(schoolwork) benoten, korrigieren,
Flecken machen auf +akk;
markedly ['mɑːkɪdlɪ] adv merk-
lich; (with comp adj) wesentlich;
marker n (in book) Lesezeichen nt;
(pen) Marker m

market ['mɑːkɪt] n Markt m;
(stock ~) Börse f ▷ vt (Comm: new
product) auf den Markt bringen;
(goods) vertreiben; **marketing** n
Marketing nt; **market leader** n
Marktführer m; **market place** n
Marktplatz m; **market research** n
Marktforschung f

marmalade ['mɑːməleɪd] n
Orangenmarmelade f

maroon [mə'ruːn] adj rötlich
braun

marquee [mɑː'kiː] n großes Zelt

marriage ['mærɪdʒ] n Ehe f;
(wedding) Heirat f (to mit);
married ['mærɪd] adj (person)
verheiratet

marrow ['mærəʊ] n (bone ~)
Knochenmark nt; (vegetable) Kürbis
m

marry ['mærɪ] vt heiraten; (join)
trauen; (take as husband, wife)
heiraten ▷ vi: **to ~ / to get
married** heiraten

marsh [mɑːʃ] n Marsch f, Sumpf m

marshal ['mɑːʃəl] n (at rally etc)
Ordner m; (US: police)
Bezirkspolizeichef m

martial arts ['mɑːʃəl'ɑːts] npl
Kampfsportarten pl

martyr ['mɑːtə*] n Märtyrer(in)
m(f)

marvel ['mɑːvəl] n Wunder nt
▷ vi staunen (at über +akk);
marvellous, marvelous (US) adj
wunderbar

marzipan [mɑːzɪ'pæn] n Marzipan nt o m

mascara [mæ'skɑːrə] n Wimperntusche f

mascot ['mæskɒt] n Maskott-chen nt

masculine ['mæskjʊlɪn] adj männlich

mashed [mæʃt] adj ~ **potatoes** pl Kartoffelbrei m, Kartoffelpüree nt

mask [mɑːsk] n (a. Inform) Maske f ▷ vt (feelings) verbergen

masochist ['mæsəʊkɪst] n Masochist(in) m(f)

mason ['meɪsn] n (stone~) Steinmetz(in) m(f); **masonry** n Mauerwerk nt

mass [mæs] n Masse f; (of people) Menge f; (Rel) Messe f; **~es of** massenhaft

massacre ['mæsəkə*] n Blutbad nt

massage ['mæsɑːʒ] n Massage f ▷ vt massieren

massive ['mæsɪv] adj (powerful) gewaltig; (very large) riesig

mass media ['mæs'miːdɪə] npl Massenmedien pl; **mass-produce** vt in Massenproduktion herstellen; **mass production** n Massenproduktion f

master ['mɑːstə*] n Herr m; (of dog) Besitzer m, Herrchen nt; (teacher) Lehrer m; (artist) Meister m ▷ vt meistern; (language etc) beherrschen; **masterly** adj meisterhaft; **masterpiece** n Meisterwerk nt

masturbate ['mæstəbeɪt] vi masturbieren

mat [mæt] n Matte f; (for table) Untersetzer m

match [mætʃ] n Streichholz nt; (Sport) Wettkampf m; (ball games) Spiel nt; (tennis) Match nt ▷ vt (be like, suit) passen zu; (equal) gleichkommen +dat ▷ vi zusammenpassen; **matchbox** n Streichholzschachtel f; **matching** adj (one item)

passend; (two items) zusammenpassend

mate [meɪt] n (companion) Kumpel m; (of animal) Weibchen nt/Männchen nt ▷ vi sich paaren

material [mə'tɪərɪəl] n Material nt; (for book etc, cloth) Stoff m; **materialistic** [mətɪərɪə'lɪstɪk] adj materialistisch; **materialize** [mə'tɪərɪəlaɪz] vi zustande kommen; (hope) wahr werden

maternal [mə'tɜːnl] adj mütterlich; **maternity** [mə'tɜːnɪtɪ] adj: ~ **dress** Umstandskleid nt; ~ **leave** Elternzeit f (der Mutter); ~ **ward** Entbindungsstation f

math [mæθ] n (US fam) Mathe f; **mathematical** [mæθə'mætɪkəl] adj mathematisch; **mathematics** [mæθə'mætɪks] nsing Mathematik f; **maths** [mæθs] nsing (Brit fam) Mathe f

matinée ['mætɪneɪ] n Nachmit-tagsvorstellung f

matter ['mætə*] n (substance) Materie f; (affair) Sache f; **a personal ~** eine persönliche Angelegenheit; **a ~ of taste** eine Frage des Geschmacks; **no ~ how/what** egal wie/was; **what's the ~?** was ist los?; **as a ~ of fact** eigentlich; **a ~ of time** eine Frage der Zeit ▷ vi darauf ankommen, wichtig sein; **it doesn't ~** es macht nichts; **matter-of-fact** adj sachlich, nüchtern

mattress ['mætrəs] n Matratze f

mature [mə'tjʊə*] adj reif ▷ vi reif werden; **maturity** [mə'tjʊərɪtɪ] n Reife f

maximum ['mæksɪməm] adj Höchst-, höchste(r, s); ~ **speed** Höchstgeschwindigkeit f ▷ n Maximum nt

may [meɪ] (**might**) vb aux (be

possible) können; (*have permission*) dürfen; **it ~ rain** es könnte regnen; **~ I smoke?** darf ich rauchen?; **it ~ not happen** es passiert vielleicht gar nicht; **we ~ as well go** wir können ruhig gehen

May [meɪ] *n* Mai *m; see also* **September**

maybe ['meɪbiː] *adv* vielleicht

May Day ['meɪdeɪ] *n* der erste Mai

mayo ['meɪəʊ] (*US fam*), **mayonnaise** [meɪə'neɪz] *n* Mayo *f*, Mayonnaise *f*, Majonäse *f*

mayor [mɛə*] *n* Bürgermeister *m*

maze [meɪz] *n* Irrgarten *m*; (*fig*) Wirrwarr *nt*

MB *abbr* = **megabyte** MB *nt*

○ **KEYWORD**

me [miː] *pron* **1** (*direct*) mich; **it's me** ich bin's

2 (*indirect*) mir; **give them to me** gib sie mir

3 (*after prep*) (*+akk*) mich; (*+dat*) mir; **with/without me** mit mir/ohne mich

meadow ['medəʊ] *n* Wiese *f*

meal [miːl] *n* Essen *nt*, Mahlzeit *f*; **to go out for a ~** essen gehen; **meal pack** *n* (*US*) tiefgekühltes Fertiggericht; **meal time** *n* Essenszeit *f*

mean [miːn] *vt* (*signify*) bedeuten; (*have in mind*) meinen; (*intend*) vorhaben; **I ~ it** ich meine das ernst; **what do you ~ (by that)?** was willst du damit sagen?; **to ~ to do sth** etw tun wollen; **it was ~t for you** es war für dich bestimmt (*o* gedacht); **it was ~t to be a joke** es sollte ein Witz sein ▷ *vi*: **he ~s well** er

meint es gut ▷ *adj* (*stingy*) geizig; (*spiteful*) gemein (*to* zu); **meaning** ['miːnɪŋ] *n* Bedeutung *f*; (*of life, poem*) Sinn *m*; **meaningful** *adj* sinnvoll; **meaningless** *adj* (*text*) ohne Sinn

means [miːnz] (*pl* **means**) *n* Mittel *nt*; (*pl: funds*) Mittel *pl*; **by ~ of** durch, mittels; **by all ~** selbstverständlich; **by no ~** keineswegs; **~ of transport** Beförderungsmittel

meant [ment] *pt, pp of* **mean**

meantime [miːn'taɪm] *adv*: **in the ~** inzwischen; **meanwhile** [miːn'waɪl] *adv* inzwischen

measles ['miːzlz] *nsing* Masern *pl*; **German ~** Röteln *pl*

measure ['meʒə*] *vt, vi* messen ▷ *n* (*unit, device for measuring*) Maß *nt*; (*step*) Maßnahme *f*; **to take ~s** Maßnahmen ergreifen; **measurement** *n* (*amount measured*) Maß *nt*

meat [miːt] *n* Fleisch *nt*; **meatball** *n* Fleischbällchen *nt*

mechanic [mɪ'kænɪk] *n* Mechaniker(in) *m(f)*; **mechanical** *adj* mechanisch; **mechanics** *nsing* Mechanik *f*; **mechanism** ['mekənɪzəm] *n* Mechanismus *m*

medal ['medl] *n* Medaille *f*; (*decoration*) Orden *m*; **medalist** (*US*), **medallist** ['medəlɪst] *n* Medaillengewinner(in) *m(f)*

media ['miːdɪə] *npl* Medien *pl*

median strip ['miːdɪən strɪp] *n* (*US*) Mittelstreifen *m*

mediate ['miːdɪeɪt] *vi* vermitteln

medical ['medɪkəl] *adj* medizinisch; (*treatment etc*) ärztlich; **~ student** Medizinstudent(in) *m(f)* ▷ *n* Untersuchung *f*; **Medicare** ['medɪkeə*] *n* (*US*) Krankenkasse *f* für ältere Leute; **medication**

[medɪ'keɪʃən] n Medikamente pl;
to be on ~ Medikamente nehmen;
medicinal [me'dɪsɪnl] adj Heil-;
~ herbs Heilkräuter pl; **medicine**
['medsɪn] n Arznei f; (science)
Medizin f

medieval [medɪ'iːvəl] adj
mittelalterlich

mediocre [miːdɪ'əʊkə°] adj
mittelmäßig

meditate ['medɪteɪt] vi meditieren; (fig) nachdenken (on über
+akk)

Mediterranean
[medɪtə'reɪnɪən] n (sea)
Mittelmeer nt; (region)
Mittelmeerraum m

medium ['miːdɪəm] adj (quality,
size) mittlere(r, s); (steak)
halbdurch; **~ (dry)** (wine)
halbtrocken; **~ sized** mittelgroß;
~ wave Mittelwelle f ▷ n (pl
media) Medium nt; (means) Mittel
nt

meet [miːt] (**met, met**) vt
treffen; (by arrangement) sich
treffen mit; (difficulties) stoßen auf
+akk; (get to know) kennenlernen;
(requirement, demand) gerecht
werden +dat; (deadline) einhalten;
pleased to ~ you sehr angenehm!;
to ~ sb at the station jdn vom
Bahnhof abholen ▷ vi sich
treffen; (become acquainted) sich
kennenlernen; **we've met**
(**before**) wir kennen uns schon;
meet up vt sich treffen (with
mit); **meet with** vt (group)
zusammenkommen mit;
(difficulties, resistance etc) stoßen
auf +akk; **meeting** n Treffen nt;
(business ~) Besprechung f; (of
committee) Sitzung f; (assembly)
Versammlung f; **meeting place**,
meeting point n Treffpunkt m

megabyte ['megəbaɪt] n
Megabyte nt

melody ['melədɪ] n Melodie f

melon ['melən] n Melone f

melt [melt] vt, vi schmelzen

member ['membə°] n Mitglied
nt; (of tribe, species) Angehörige(r)
mf; **Member of Parliament**
Parlamentsabgeordnete(r) mf;
membership n Mitgliedschaft f;
membership card n
Mitgliedskarte f

memento [mə'mentəʊ] (pl **-es**)
n Andenken nt (of an +akk)

memo ['meməʊ] (pl **-s**) n
Mitteilung f, Memo nt; **memo pad**
n Notizblock m

memorable ['memərəbl] adj
unvergesslich; **memorial**
[mɪ'mɔːrɪəl] n Denkmal nt (to
für); **memorize** ['meməraɪz] vt
sich einprägen, auswendig lernen;
memory ['memərɪ] n Gedächtnis nt; (Inform: of computer)
Speicher m; (sth recalled)
Erinnerung f; **in ~ of** zur
Erinnerung an +akk

men [men] pl of **man**

menace ['menɪs] n Bedrohung f;
(danger) Gefahr f

mend [mend] vt reparieren;
(clothes) flicken ▷ n: **to be on the
~** auf dem Wege der Besserung
sein

meningitis [menɪn'dʒaɪtɪs] n
Hirnhautentzündung f

menopause ['menəʊpɔːz] n
Wechseljahre pl

mental ['mentl] adj geistig;
mentality [men'tælɪtɪ] n Mentalität f; **mentally** ['mentəlɪ] adv
geistig; **~ handicapped** geistig
behindert; **~ ill** geisteskrank

mention ['menʃən] n Erwäh-
nung f ▷ vt erwähnen (to sb jdm
gegenüber); **don't ~ it** bitte sehr,
gern geschehen

menu ['menjuː] n Speisekarte f;
(Inform) Menü nt

merchandise ['mɜːtʃəndaɪz] *n*
Handelsware *f*; **merchant**
['mɜːtʃənt] *adj* Handels-
merciful ['mɜːsɪfʊl] *adj* gnädig;
mercifully *adv* glücklicherweise
mercury ['mɜːkjʊrɪ] *n* Queck-
silber *nt*
mercy ['mɜːsɪ] *n* Gnade *f*
mere [mɪə*] *adj* bloß; **merely**
['mɪəlɪ] *adv* bloß, lediglich
merge [mɜːdʒ] *vi* verschmelzen;
(*Auto*) sich einfädeln; (*Comm*)
fusionieren; **merger** *n* (*Comm*)
Fusion *f*
meringue [məˈræŋ] *n* Baiser *nt*
merit ['merɪt] *n* Verdienst *nt*;
(*advantage*) Vorzug *m*
merry ['merɪ] *adj* fröhlich; (*fam*:
tipsy) angeheitert; **Merry**
Christmas Fröhliche
Weihnachten!; **merry-go-round** *n*
Karussell *nt*
mess [mes] *n* Unordnung *f*;
(*muddle*) Durcheinander *nt*; (*dirty*)
Schweinerei *f*; (*trouble*)
Schwierigkeiten *pl*; **in a**
~ (*muddled*) durcheinander; (*untidy*)
unordentlich; (*fig*: *person*) in der
Klemme; **to make a ~ of sth** etw
verpfuschen; **to look a**
~ unmöglich aussehen; **mess**
about *vi* (*tinker with*)
herummurksen (*with an* +*dat*);
(*play the fool*) herumalbern; (*do*
nothing in particular)
herumgammeln; **mess up** *vt*
verpfuschen; (*make untidy*) in
Unordnung bringen; (*dirty*)
schmutzig machen
message ['mesɪdʒ] *n* Mitteilung
f, Nachricht *f*; (*meaning*) Botschaft
f; **can I give him a ~?** kann ich
ihm etwas ausrichten?; **please**
leave a ~ (*on answerphones*)
bitte hinterlassen Sie eine
Nachricht; **I get the ~** ich hab's
verstanden

messenger ['mesɪndʒə*] *n* Bote
m
messy ['mesɪ] *adj* (*untidy*)
unordentlich; (*situation etc*)
verfahren
met [met] *pt*, *pp of* **meet**
metal ['metl] *n* Metall *nt*;
metallic [mɪˈtælɪk] *adj*
metallisch
meteorology [miːtɪəˈrɒlədʒɪ] *n*
Meteorologie *f*
meter ['miːtə*] *n* Zähler *m*;
(*parking meter*) Parkuhr *f*; (*US*) *see*
metre
method ['meθəd] *n* Methode *f*;
methodical [mɪˈθɒdɪkəl] *adj*
methodisch
meticulous [mɪˈtɪkjʊləs] *adj*
(*peinlich*) genau
metre ['miːtə*] *n* Meter *m* o *nt*;
metric ['metrɪk] *adj* metrisch;
~ system Dezimalsystem *nt*
Mexico ['meksɪkəʊ] *n* Mexiko *nt*
mice [maɪs] *pl of* **mouse**
mickey ['mɪkɪ] *n*: **to take the**
~ (**out of sb**) (*fam*) (jdn) auf den
Arm nehmen
microchip ['maɪkrəʊtʃɪp] *n*
(*Inform*) Mikrochip *m*; **microphone**
n Mikrofon *nt*; **microscope** *n*
Mikroskop *nt*; **microwave** (**oven**)
n Mikrowelle(nherd) *f*(*m*)
mid [mɪd] *adj*: **in ~ January**
Mitte Januar; **he's in his ~ forties**
er ist Mitte vierzig
midday ['mɪddeɪ] *n* Mittag *m*;
at ~ mittags
middle ['mɪdl] *n* Mitte *f*; (*waist*)
Taille *f*; **in the ~ of** mitten in +*dat*;
to be in the ~ of doing sth gerade
dabei sein, etw zu tun ▷ *adj*
mittlere(r, s), Mittel-; **the ~ one**
der/die/das Mittlere;
middle-aged *adj* mittleren
Alters; **Middle Ages** *npl*: **the**
~ das Mittelalter; **middle-class**
adj mittelständisch; (*bourgeois*)

bürgerlich; **middle classes** npl: **the ~** der Mittelstand; **Middle East** n: **the ~** der Nahe Osten; **middle name** n zweiter Vorname

Midlands ['mɪdləndz] npl: **the ~** Mittelengland nt

midnight ['mɪdnaɪt] n Mitternacht f

midst [mɪdst] n: **in the ~ of** mitten in +dat

midsummer ['mɪdsʌmə*] n Hochsommer m; **Midsummer's Day** Sommersonnenwende f

midway [mɪd'weɪ] adv auf halbem Wege; **~ through the film** nach der Hälfte des Films; **midweek** [mɪd'wiːk] adj, adv in der Mitte der Woche

midwife ['mɪdwaɪf] (pl **-wives**) n Hebamme f

midwinter [mɪd'wɪntə*] n tiefster Winter

might [maɪt] pt of **may**; (possibility) könnte; (permission) dürfte; (would) würde; **they ~ still come** sie könnten noch kommen; **he ~ have let me know** er hätte mir doch Bescheid sagen können; **I thought she ~ change her mind** ich dachte schon, sie würde sich anders entscheiden ▷ n Macht f, Kraft f

mighty ['maɪtɪ] adj gewaltig; (powerful) mächtig

migraine ['miːgreɪn] n Migräne f

migrant ['maɪgrənt] n (bird) Zugvogel m; **~ worker** Gastarbeiter(in) m(f); Migrant(in) m(f); **migrate** [maɪ'greɪt] vi abwandern; (birds) nach Süden ziehen

mike [maɪk] n (fam) Mikro nt

Milan [mɪ'læn] n Mailand nt

mild [maɪld] adj mild; (person) sanft; **mildly** adv: **to put it**

~ gelinde gesagt; **mildness** n Milde f

mile [maɪl] n Meile f (= 1,609 km); **for ~s (and ~s)** ≈ kilometerweit; **~s per hour** Meilen pro Stunde; **~s better than** hundertmal besser als; **mileage** n Meilen pl, Meilenzahl f; **mileometer** [maɪ'lɒmɪtə*] n ≈ Kilometerzähler m; **milestone** n (a. fig) Meilenstein m

militant ['mɪlɪtənt] adj militant; **military** ['mɪlɪtərɪ] adj Militär-, militärisch

milk [mɪlk] n Milch f ▷ vt melken; **milk chocolate** n Vollmilchschokolade f; **milkman** (pl **-men**) n Milchmann m; **milk shake** n Milchshake m, Milchmixgetränk nt

mill [mɪl] n Mühle f; (factory) Fabrik f

millennium [mɪ'lenɪəm] n Jahrtausend nt

milligramme ['mɪlɪgræm] n Milligramm nt; **milliliter** (US), **millilitre** n Milliliter m; **millimeter** (US), **millimetre** n Millimeter m

million ['mɪljən] n Million f; **five ~** fünf Millionen; **~s of people** Millionen von Menschen; **millionaire** [mɪljə'nɛə*] n Millionär(in) m(f)

mime [maɪm] n Pantomime f ▷ vt, vi mimen; **mimic** ['mɪmɪk] n Imitator(in) m(f) ▷ vt, vi nachahmen; **mimicry** ['mɪmɪkrɪ] n Nachahmung f

mince [mɪns] vt (zer)hacken ▷ n (meat) Hackfleisch nt; **mincemeat** n süße Gebäckfüllung aus Rosinen, Äpfeln, Zucker, Gewürzen und Talg; **mince pie** n mit 'mincemeat' gefülltes süßes Weihnachtsgebäck

mind [maɪnd] n (intellect)

Verstand m; (also person) Geist m; **out of sight, out of ~** aus den Augen, aus dem Sinn; **he is out of his ~** er ist nicht bei Verstand; **to keep sth in ~** etw im Auge behalten; **do you have sth in ~?** denken Sie an etwas Besonderes?; **I've a lot on my ~** mich beschäftigt so vieles im Moment; **to change one's ~** es sich dat anders überlegen ▷ vt (look after) aufpassen auf +akk; (object to) etwas haben gegen; **~ you, ...** allerdings ...; **I wouldn't ~ ...** ich hätte nichts gegen ...; **"~ the step"** „Vorsicht Stufe!" ▷ vi etwas dagegen haben; **do you ~ if I ...** macht es Ihnen etwas aus, wenn ich ...; **I don't ~** es ist mir egal, meinetwegen; **never ~** macht nichts

mine [maɪn] pron meine(r, s); **this is ~** das gehört mir; **a friend of ~** ein Freund von mir ▷ n (coalmine) Bergwerk nt; (Mil) Mine f; **miner** n Bergarbeiter(in) m(f)

mineral ['mɪnərəl] n Mineral nt; **mineral water** n Mineralwasser nt

mingle ['mɪŋgl] vi sich mischen (with unter +akk)

miniature ['mɪnɪtʃə°] adj Miniatur-

minibar ['mɪnɪbɑ:] n Minibar f; **minibus** n Kleinbus m; **minicab** n Kleintaxi nt

minimal ['mɪnɪml] adj minimal; **minimize** ['mɪnɪmaɪz] vt auf ein Minimum reduzieren; **minimum** ['mɪnɪməm] n Minimum nt ▷ adj Mindest-

mining ['maɪnɪŋ] n Bergbau m

miniskirt n Minirock m

minister ['mɪnɪstə°] n (Pol) Minister(in) m(f); (Rel) Pastor(in) m(f), Pfarrer(in) m(f); **ministry** ['mɪnɪstri] n (Pol) Ministerium nt

minor ['maɪnə°] adj kleiner; (insignificant) unbedeutend; (operation, offence) harmlos; **~ road** Nebenstraße f; (Mus) **A ~** a-Moll nt ▷ n (Brit: under 18) Minderjährige(r) mf; **minority** [maɪ'nɒrɪti] n Minderheit f

mint [mɪnt] n Minze f; (sweet) Pfefferminz(bonbon) nt; **mint sauce** n Minzsoße f

minus ['maɪnəs] prep minus; (without) ohne

minute [maɪ'nju:t] adj winzig; **in ~ detail** genauestens ▷ ['mɪnɪt] n Minute f; **just a ~** Moment mal!; **any ~** jeden Augenblick; **~s** pl (of meeting) Protokoll nt

miracle ['mɪrəkl] n Wunder nt; **miraculous** [mɪ'rækjʊləs] adj unglaublich

mirage ['mɪrɑ:ʒ] n Fata Morgana f, Luftspiegelung f

mirror ['mɪrə°] n Spiegel m

misbehave [mɪsbɪ'heɪv] vi sich schlecht benehmen

miscalculation ['mɪskælkjʊ'leɪʃən] n Fehlkalkulation f; (misjudgement) Fehleinschätzung f

miscarriage [mɪs'kærɪdʒ] n (Med) Fehlgeburt f

miscellaneous [mɪsɪ'leɪnɪəs] adj verschieden

mischief ['mɪstʃɪf] n Unfug m; **mischievous** ['mɪstʃɪvəs] adj (person) durchtrieben; (glance) verschmitzt

misconception [mɪskən'sepʃən] n falsche Vorstellung

misconduct [mɪs'kɒndʌkt] n Vergehen nt

miser ['maɪzə°] n Geizhals m

miserable ['mɪzərəbl] adj (person) todunglücklich; (conditions, life) elend; (pay, weather) miserabel

miserly ['maɪzəli] adj geizig

misery ['mɪzərɪ] n Elend nt;
(suffering) Qualen pl
misfit ['mɪsfɪt] n Außensei-
ter(in) m(f)
misfortune [mɪs'fɔːtʃən] n Pech
nt
misguided [mɪs'gaɪdɪd] adj irrig;
(optimism) unangebracht
misinform [mɪsɪn'fɔːm] vt falsch
informieren
misinterpret [mɪsɪn'tɜːprɪt] vt
falsch auslegen
misjudge [mɪs'dʒʌdʒ] vt falsch
beurteilen
mislay [mɪs'leɪ] irr vt verlegen
mislead [mɪs'liːd] irr vt
irreführen; **misleading** adj
irreführend
misprint ['mɪsprɪnt] n Druck-
fehler m
mispronounce [mɪsprə'naʊns]-
vt falsch aussprechen
miss [mɪs] vt (fail to hit, catch)
verfehlen; (not notice, hear) nicht
mitbekommen; (be too late for)
verpassen; (chance) versäumen;
(regret the absence of) vermissen; **I
~ you** du fehlst mir ▷ vi nicht
treffen; (shooting) daneben-
schießen; (ball, shot etc) daneben-
gehen; **miss out** vt auslassen
▷ vi: **to ~ on sth** etw verpassen
Miss [mɪs] n (unmarried woman)
Fräulein nt
missile ['mɪsaɪl] n Geschoss nt;
(rocket) Rakete f
missing ['mɪsɪŋ] adj (person)
vermisst; (thing) fehlend; **to be/go
~** vermisst werden, fehlen
mission ['mɪʃən] n (Pol, Mil, Rel)
Auftrag m, Mission f; **missionary**
['mɪʃənrɪ] n Missionar(in) m(f)
mist [mɪst] n (feiner) Nebel m;
(haze) Dunst m; **mist over**, **mist up**
vi sich beschlagen
mistake [mɪ'steɪk] n Fehler m;
by ~ aus Versehen ▷ irr vt

(**mistook, mistaken**)
(misunderstand) falsch verstehen;
(mix up) verwechseln (for mit);
there's no mistaking ... ... ist
unverkennbar; (meaning) ...
ist unmissverständlich;
mistaken adj (idea, identity)
falsch; **to be ~** sich irren,
falschliegen
mistletoe ['mɪsltəʊ] n Mistel f
mistreat [mɪs'triːt] vt schlecht
behandeln
mistress ['mɪstrɪs] n (lover)
Geliebte f
mistrust [mɪs'trʌst] n Misstrauen nt (of gegen) ▷ vt
misstrauen +dat
misty ['mɪstɪ] adj neblig; (hazy)
dunstig
misunderstand
[mɪsʌndə'stænd] irr vt, vi falsch
verstehen; **misunderstanding** n
Missverständnis nt; (disagreement)
Differenz f
mitten ['mɪtn] n Fausthandschuh m
mix [mɪks] n (mixture) Mischung f
▷ vt mischen; (blend) vermischen
(with mit); (drinks, music) mixen; **to
~ business with pleasure** das
Angenehme mit dem Nützlichen
verbinden ▷ vi (liquids) sich
vermischen lassen; **mix up** vt
(mix) zusammenmischen; (confuse)
verwechseln (with mit); **mixed** adj
gemischt; **a ~ bunch** eine bunt
gemischte Truppe; **~ grill** Mixed
Grill m; **~ vegetables**
Mischgemüse nt; **mixer** n (for
food) Mixer m; **mixture** ['mɪkstʃə*]
n Mischung f; (Med) Saft m;
mix-up n Durcheinander nt,
Missverständnis nt
ml abbr = **millilitre** ml
mm abbr = **millimetre** mm
moan [məʊn] n Stöhnen nt;
(complaint) Gejammer nt ▷ vi

stöhnen; (*complain*) jammern, meckern (*about* über +*akk*)
mobile ['məʊbaɪl] *adj* beweglich; (*on wheels*) fahrbar ▷ *n* (*phone*) Handy *nt*; **mobile phone** *n* Mobiltelefon *nt*, Handy *nt*
mobility [məʊ'bɪlɪtɪ] *n* Beweglichkeit *f*
mock [mɒk] *vt* verspotten ▷ *adj* Schein-; **mockery** *n* Spott *m*
mod cons ['mɒd'kɒnz] *abbr* = **modern conveniences** (moderner) Komfort
mode [məʊd] *n* Art *f*; (*Inform*) Modus *m*
model ['mɒdl] *n* Modell *nt*; (*example*) Vorbild *nt*; (*fashion ~*) Model *nt* ▷ *adj* (*miniature*) Modell-; (*perfect*) Muster- ▷ *vt* (*make*) formen ▷ *vi*: **she ~s for Versace** sie arbeitet als Model bei Versace
modem ['məʊdem] *n* Modem *nt*
moderate ['mɒdərət] *adj* mäßig; (*views, politics*) gemäßigt; (*income, success*) mittelmäßig ▷ *n* (*Pol*) Gemäßigte(r) *mf* ▷ ['mɒdəreɪt] *vt* mäßigen; **moderation** [mɒdə'reɪʃən] *n* Mäßigung *f*; **in ~** mit Maßen
modern ['mɒdən] *adj* modern; **~ history** neuere Geschichte; **~ Greek** Neugriechisch *nt*; **modernize** ['mɒdənaɪz] *vt* modernisieren
modest ['mɒdɪst] *adj* bescheiden; **modesty** *n* Bescheidenheit *f*
modification [mɒdɪfɪ'keɪʃən] *n* Abänderung *f*; **modify** ['mɒdɪfaɪ] *vt* abändern
moist [mɔɪst] *adj* feucht; **moisten** ['mɔɪsn] *vt* befeuchten; **moisture** ['mɔɪstʃə*] *n* Feuchtigkeit *f*; **moisturizer** *n* Feuchtigkeitscreme *f*
molar ['məʊlə*] *n* Backenzahn *m*
mold (*US*) *see* **mould**

mole [məʊl] *n* (*spot*) Leberfleck *m*; (*animal*) Maulwurf *m*
molecule ['mɒlɪkjuːl] *n* Molekül *nt*
molest [məʊ'lest] *vt* belästigen
molt (*US*) *see* **moult**
molten ['məʊltən] *adj* geschmolzen
mom [mɒm] *n* (*US*) Mutti *f*
moment ['məʊmənt] *n* Moment *m*, Augenblick *m*; **just a ~** Moment mal!; **at** (*o* **for**) **the ~** im Augenblick; **in a ~** gleich
momentous [məʊ'mentəs] *adj* bedeutsam
Monaco ['mɒnəkəʊ] *n* Monaco *nt*
monarchy ['mɒnəkɪ] *n* Monarchie *f*
monastery ['mɒnəstrɪ] *n* (*for monks*) Kloster *nt*
Monday ['mʌndeɪ] *n* Montag *m*; *see also* **Tuesday**
monetary ['mʌnɪtərɪ] *adj* (*reform, policy, union*) Währungs-; **~ unit** Geldeinheit *f*
money ['mʌnɪ] *n* Geld *nt*; **to get one's ~'s worth** auf seine Kosten kommen; **money order** *n* Postanweisung *f*
mongrel ['mʌŋgrəl] *n* Promenadenmischung *f*
monitor ['mɒnɪtə*] *n* (*screen*) Monitor *m* ▷ *vt* (*progress etc*) überwachen; (*broadcasts*) abhören
monk [mʌŋk] *n* Mönch *m*
monkey ['mʌŋkɪ] *n* Affe *m*; **~ business** Unfug *m*
monopolize [mə'nɒpəlaɪz] *vt* monopolisieren; (*fig: person, thing*) in Beschlag nehmen; **monopoly** [mə'nɒpəlɪ] *n* Monopol *nt*
monotonous [mə'nɒtənəs] *adj* eintönig, monoton
monsoon [mɒn'suːn] *n* Monsun *m*
monster ['mɒnstə*] *n* (*animal,*

thing) Monstrum *nt* ▷ *adj* Riesen-;
monstrosity [mɒnˈstrɒsɪtɪ] *n*
Monstrosität *f*; *(thing)* Ungetüm
nt

Montenegro [mɒntɪˈniːgrəʊ] *n*
Montenegro *nt*

month [mʌnθ] *n* Monat *m*;
monthly *adj* monatlich; *(ticket, salary)* Monats- ▷ *adv* monatlich
▷ *n* *(magazine)* Monatsschrift *f*

monty [ˈmɒntɪ] *n*: **to go the full**
~ *(fam: strip)* alle Hüllen fallen
lassen; *(go the whole hog)* aufs
Ganze gehen

monument [ˈmɒnjʊmənt] *n*
Denkmal *nt* *(to* für); **monumental**
[mɒnjʊˈmentl] *adj* *(huge)*
gewaltig

mood [muːd] *n* *(of person)*
Laune *f*; *(a. general)* Stimmung *f*;
to be in a good/bad
~ gute/schlechte Laune haben;
to be in the ~ for sth zu etw
aufgelegt sein; **I'm not in the**
~ ich fühle mich nicht danach;
moody *adj* launisch

moon [muːn] *n* Mond *m*; **to be**
over the ~ *(fam)* überglücklich
sein; **moonlight** *n* Mondlicht *nt*
▷ *vi* schwarzarbeiten; **moonlit**
adj *(night, landscape)* mondhell

moor [mɔː*] *n* Moor *nt* ▷ *vt, vi*
festmachen; **moorings** *npl*
Liegeplatz *m*; **moorland** *n*
Moorland *nt*, Heideland *nt*

moose [muːs] *(pl* -) *n* Elch *m*

mop [mɒp] *n* Mopp *m*; **mop up**
vt aufwischen

mope [məʊp] *vi* Trübsal blasen

moped [ˈməʊped] *n* *(Brit)* Moped
nt

moral [ˈmɒrəl] *adj* moralisch;
(values) sittlich ▷ *n* Moral *f*; **~s** *pl*
Moral *f*; **morale** [mɒˈrɑːl] *n*
Stimmung *f*, Moral *f*; **morality**
[məˈrælɪtɪ] *n* Moral *f*, Ethik *f*

morbid [ˈmɔːbɪd] *adj* krankhaft

◯ **KEYWORD**

more [mɔː*] *adj* *(greater in number*
etc) mehr; *(additional)* noch mehr;
do you want (some) more tea?
möchtest du/möchten Sie noch
etwas Tee?; **I have no** *o* **I don't**
have any more money ich habe
kein Geld mehr
▷ *pron* *(greater amount)* mehr;
(further o additional amount) noch
mehr; **is there any more?** gibt es
noch mehr?; *(left over)* ist noch
etwas da?; **there's no more** es ist
nichts mehr da
▷ *adv* mehr; **more**
dangerous/easily *etc* **(than)**
gefährlicher/einfacher *etc* (als);
more and more immer mehr;
more and more excited immer
aufgeregter; **more or less** mehr
oder weniger; **more than ever**
mehr denn je; **more beautiful**
than ever schöner denn je

moreish *adj* *(food)* **these**
crisps are really ~ ich kann mit
diesen Chips einfach nicht
aufhören; **moreover** *adv*
außerdem

morgue [mɔːg] *n* Leichen-
schauhaus *nt*

morning [ˈmɔːnɪŋ] *n* Morgen *m*;
in the ~ am Morgen, morgens;
(tomorrow) morgen früh; **this**
~ heute morgen ▷ *adj* Morgen-;
(early) Früh-; *(walk etc)*
morgendlich; **morning after pill**
n die Pille danach; **morning**
sickness *n* Schwangerschafts-
übelkeit *f*

Morocco [məˈrɒkəʊ] *n* Marokko
nt

moron [ˈmɔːrɒn] *n* Idiot(in) *m(f)*

morphine [ˈmɔːfiːn] *n* Morphium *nt*

morsel ['mɔːsl] *n* Bissen *m*

mortal ['mɔːtl] *adj* sterblich; (*wound*) tödlich ▷ *n* Sterbliche(r) *mf*; **mortality** [mɔː'tælɪtɪ] *n* (*death rate*) Sterblichkeitsziffer *f*; **mortally** *adv* tödlich

mortgage ['mɔːɡɪdʒ] *n* Hypothek *f* ▷ *vt* mit einer Hypothek belasten

mortified ['mɔːtɪfaɪd] *adj*: **I was ~** es war mir schrecklich peinlich

mortuary ['mɔːtjʊərɪ] *n* Leichenhalle *f*

mosaic [məʊ'zeɪɪk] *n* Mosaik *nt*

Moscow ['mɒskəʊ] *n* Moskau *nt*

Moslem ['mɒzləm] *adj*, *n see* **Muslim**

mosque [mɒsk] *n* Moschee *f*

mosquito [mɒ'skiːtəʊ] (*pl* **-es**) *n* (Stech)mücke *f*; (*tropical*) Moskito *m*; **~ net** Moskitonetz *nt*

moss [mɒs] *n* Moos *nt*

most [məʊst] *adj* meiste *pl*, die meisten; **in ~ cases** in den meisten Fällen ▷ *adv* (*with verbs*) am meisten; (*with adj*) ...ste; (*with adv*) am ...sten; (*very*) äußerst, höchst; **he ate (the) ~** er hat am meisten gegessen; **the ~ beautiful/interesting** der/die/das schönste/interessanteste; **~ interesting** hochinteressant! ▷ *n* das meiste, der größte Teil; (*people*) die meisten; **~ of the money/players** das meiste Geld/die meisten Spieler; **for the ~ part** zum größten Teil; **five at the ~** höchstens fünf; **to make the ~ of sth** etw voll ausnützen; **mostly** *adv* (*most of the time*) meistens; (*mainly*) hauptsächlich; (*for the most part*) größtenteils

MOT *abbr* = **Ministry of Transport; ~ (test)** ≈ TÜV *m*

motel [məʊ'tel] *n* Motel *nt*

moth [mɒθ] *n* Nachtfalter *m*; (*wool-eating*) Motte *f*; **mothball** *n* Mottenkugel *f*

mother ['mʌðə*] *n* Mutter *f* ▷ *vt* bemuttern; **mother-in-law** (*pl* **mothers-in-law**) *n* Schwiegermutter *f*; **mother-to-be** (*pl* **mothers-to-be**) *n* werdende Mutter

motif [məʊ'tiːf] *n* Motiv *nt*

motion ['məʊʃən] *n* Bewegung *f*; (*in meeting*) Antrag *m*; **motionless** *adj* bewegungslos

motivate ['məʊtɪveɪt] *vt* motivieren; **motive** ['məʊtɪv] *n* Motiv *nt*

motor ['məʊtə*] *n* Motor *m*; (*fam: car*) Auto *nt* ▷ *adj* Motor-; **Motorail train®** *n* (*Brit*) Autoreisezug *m*; **motorbike** *n* Motorrad *nt*; **motorboat** *n* Motorboot *nt*; **motorcycle** *n* Motorrad *nt*; **motor industry** *n* Automobilindustrie *f*; **motoring** ['məʊtərɪŋ] *n* Autofahren *nt*; **~ organization** Automobilklub *m*; **motorist** ['məʊtərɪst] *n* Autofahrer(in) *m(f)*; **motor oil** *n* Motorenöl *nt*; **motor racing** *n* Autorennsport *m*; **motor scooter** *n* Motorroller *m*; **motor show** *n* Automobilausstellung *f*; **motor vehicle** *n* Kraftfahrzeug *nt*; **motorway** *n* (*Brit*) Autobahn *f*

motto ['mɒtəʊ] (*pl* **-es**) *n* Motto *nt*

mould [məʊld] *n* Form *f*; (*mildew*) Schimmel *m* ▷ *vt* (*a. fig*) formen; **mouldy** ['məʊldɪ] *adj* schimmelig

moult [məʊlt] *vi* sich mausern, haaren

mount [maʊnt] *vt* (*horse*) steigen auf *+akk*; (*exhibition etc*) organisieren; (*painting*) mit einem Passepartout versehen ▷ *vi*: **to ~ (up)** (an)steigen ▷ *n* Passepartout *nt*

mountain ['maʊntɪn] n Berg m;
mountain bike n Mountainbike
nt; **mountaineer** [maʊntɪ'nɪə*]
n Bergsteiger(in) m(f);
mountaineering [maʊntɪ'nɪərɪŋ]
n Bergsteigen nt; **mountainous**
adj bergig; **mountainside** n
Berghang m

mourn [mɔːn] vt betrauern ▷ vi
trauern (for um); **mourner** n
Trauernde(r) mf; **mournful** adj
trauervoll; **mourning** n Trauer f;
to be in ~ trauern (for um)

mouse [maʊs] (pl **mice**) n (a.
Inform) Maus f; **mouse mat**,
mouse pad (US) n Mauspad nt;
mouse trap n Mausefalle f

mousse [muːs] n (Gastr) Creme f;
(styling ~) Schaumfestiger m

moustache [mə'stæʃ] n
Schnurrbart m

mouth [maʊθ] n Mund m; (of
animal) Maul nt; (of cave) Eingang
m; (of bottle etc) Öffnung f; (of river)
Mündung f; **to keep one's ~ shut**
(fam) den Mund halten; **mouthful**
n (of drink) Schluck m; (of food)
Bissen m; **mouth organ** n
Mundharmonika f; **mouthwash** n
Mundwasser nt; **mouthwatering**
adj appetitlich, lecker

move [muːv] n (movement)
Bewegung f; (in game) Zug m; (step)
Schritt m; (moving house) Umzug m;
to make a ~ (in game) ziehen;
(leave) sich auf den Weg machen;
to get a ~ on (with sth) sich (mit
etw) beeilen ▷ vt bewegen;
(object) rücken; (car) wegfahren;
(transport: goods) befördern;
(people) transportieren; (in job)
versetzen; (emotionally) bewegen,
rühren; **I can't ~ it** (stuck, too heavy)
ich bringe es nicht von der Stelle;
to ~ (house) umziehen ▷ vi sich
bewegen; (change place) gehen;
(vehicle, ship) fahren; (move house,

town etc) umziehen; (in game)
ziehen; **move about** vi sich
bewegen; (travel) unterwegs sein;
move away vi weggehen; (move
town) wegziehen; **move in** vi (to
house) einziehen; **move off** vi
losfahren; **move on** vi
weitergehen; (vehicle)
weiterfahren; **move out** vi
ausziehen; **move up** vi (in queue
etc) aufrücken; **movement** n
Bewegung f

movie ['muːvɪ] n Film m; **the ~s**
(the cinema) das Kino; **movie
theatre** n (US) Kino nt

moving ['muːvɪŋ] adj (emotionally) ergreifend, berührend

mow [məʊ] (**mowed, mown** o
mowed) vt mähen; **mower** n
(lawn~) Rasenmäher m

mown [məʊn] pp of **mow**

Mozambique [məʊzæm'biːk] n
Mosambik m

MP abbr = **Member of Parliament**
Parlamentsabgeordnete(r) mf

mph abbr = **miles per hour** Meilen
pro Stunde

MPV abbr = **multi-purpose
vehicle** Mehrzweckfahrzeug nt

MP3 player [empiː'θriː 'pleɪə*]
n MP3-Player m

Mr [mɪstə*] n (written form of
address) Herr

Mrs ['mɪsɪz] n (written form of
address) Frau

Ms [məz] n (written form of address
for any woman, married or unmarried)
Frau

MS n abbr = **multiple sclerosis** MS
f

Mt abbr = **Mount** Berg m

much [mʌtʃ] adj (**more, most**) adj
viel; **we haven't got ~ time** wir
haben nicht viel Zeit; **how
~ money?** wie viel Geld? ▷ adv
viel; (with verb) sehr; **~ better** viel
besser; **I like it very ~** es gefällt

mir sehr gut; **I don't like it ~** ich mag es nicht besonders; **thank you very ~** danke sehr; **I thought as ~** das habe ich mir gedacht; **~ as I like him** so sehr ich ihn mag; **we don't see them ~** wir sehen sie nicht sehr oft; **~ the same** fast gleich ▷ *n* viel; **as ~ as you want** so viel du willst; **he's not ~ of a cook** er ist kein großer Koch

muck [mʌk] *n* (*fam*) Dreck *m*; **muck about** *vi* (*fam*) herumalbern; **muck up** *vt* (*fam*) dreckig machen; (*spoil*) vermasseln; **mucky** *adj* dreckig

mucus ['mjuːkəs] *n* Schleim *m*

mud [mʌd] *n* Schlamm *m*

muddle ['mʌdl] *n* Durcheinander *nt*; **to be in a ~** ganz durcheinander sein ▷ *vt*: **to ~ (up)** durcheinanderbringen; **muddled** *adj* konfus

muddy ['mʌdɪ] *adj* schlammig; (*shoes*) schmutzig; **mudguard** ['mʌdgɑːd] *n* Schutzblech *nt*

muesli ['muːzlɪ] *n* Müsli *nt*

muffin ['mʌfɪn] *n* Muffin *m*; (*Brit*) *weiches, flaches Milchbrötchen aus Hefeteig, das meist getoastet und mit Butter gegessen wird*

muffle ['mʌfl] *vt* (*sound*) dämpfen; **muffler** *n* (*US*) Schalldämpfer *m*

mug [mʌg] *n* (*cup*) Becher *m*; (*fam: fool*) Trottel *m* ▷ *vt* (*attack and rob*) überfallen; **mugging** *n* Raubüberfall *m*

muggy ['mʌgɪ] *adj* (*weather*) schwül

mule [mjuːl] *n* Maulesel *m*

mull over [mʌl 'əʊvə*] *vt* nachdenken über +*akk*

mulled [mʌld] *adj*: **~ wine** Glühwein *m*

multicolored (*US*), **multicoloured** ['mʌltɪ'kʌləd] *adj* bunt; **multicultural** *adj*

multikulturell; **multi-grade** *adj*: **~ oil** Mehrbereichsöl *nt*; **multilingual** *adj* mehrsprachig; **multinational** *n* (*company*) Multi *m*

multiple ['mʌltɪpl] *n* Vielfache(s) *nt* ▷ *adj* mehrfach; (*several*) mehrere; **multiple-choice (method)** *n* Multiple-Choice-Verfahren *nt*; **multiple sclerosis** ['mʌltɪplskle'rəʊsɪs] *n* Multiple Sklerose *f*

multiplex ['mʌltɪpleks] *adj, n*: **~ (cinema)** Multiplexkino *nt*

multiplication [mʌltɪplɪ'keɪʃən] *n* Multiplikation *f*; **multiply** ['mʌltɪplaɪ] *vt* multiplizieren (*by* mit) ▷ *vi* sich vermehren

multi-purpose ['mʌltɪ'pɜːpəs]-*adj* Mehrzweck-; **multistorey (car park)** *n* Parkhaus *nt*; **multitasking** *n* (*Inform*) Multitasking *nt*

mum [mʌm] *n* (*fam: mother*) Mutti *f*, Mami *f*

mumble ['mʌmbl] *vt, vi* murmeln

mummy ['mʌmɪ] *n* (*dead body*) Mumie *f*; (*fam: mother*) Mutti *f*, Mami *f*

mumps [mʌmps] *nsing* Mumps *m*

munch [mʌntʃ] *vt, vi* mampfen

Munich ['mjuːnɪk] *n* München *nt*

municipal [mjuː'nɪsɪpəl] *adj* städtisch

mural ['mjʊərəl] *n* Wandgemälde *nt*

murder ['mɜːdə*] *n* Mord *m*; **the traffic was ~** der Verkehr war die Hölle ▷ *vt* ermorden; **murderer** *n* Mörder(in) *m(f)*

murky ['mɜːkɪ] *adj* düster; (*water*) trüb

murmur ['mɜːmə*] *vt, vi* murmeln

muscle ['mʌsl] n Muskel m;
muscular ['mʌskjʊlə°] adj (strong)
muskulös; (cramp, pain etc) Muskel-
museum [mjuː'zɪəm] n Museum
nt
mushroom ['mʌʃruːm] n (ess-
barer) Pilz; (button ~) Champignon
m ▷ vi (fig) emporschießen
mushy ['mʌʃi] adj breiig; **~ peas**
Erbsenmus nt
music ['mjuːzɪk] n Musik f;
(printed) Noten pl; **musical** adj
(sound) melodisch; (person)
musikalisch; **~ instrument**
Musikinstrument nt ▷ n (show)
Musical nt; **musically** adv
musikalisch; **musician**
[mjuː'zɪʃən] n Musiker(in) m(f)
Muslim ['mʊzlɪm] adj
moslemisch ▷ n Moslem m,
Muslime f
mussel ['mʌsl] n Miesmuschel f
must [mʌst] (**had to, had to**) vb
aux (need to) müssen; (in negation)
dürfen; **I ~n't forget that** ich darf
das nicht vergessen; (certainty) **he
~ be there by now** er ist
inzwischen bestimmt schon da;
(assumption) **I ~ have lost it** ich
habe es wohl verloren; **~ you?**
muss das sein? ▷ n Muss nt
mustache ['mʌstæʃ] n (US)
Schnurrbart m
mustard ['mʌstəd] n Senf m; **to
cut the ~** es bringen
mustn't ['mʌsnt] contr of **must
not**
mute [mjuːt] adj stumm
mutter ['mʌtə°] vt, vi murmeln
mutton ['mʌtn] n Ham-
melfleisch nt
mutual ['mjuːtjʊəl] adj gegenseitig; **by ~ consent** in
gegenseitigem Einvernehmen
my [maɪ] adj mein; **I've hurt
~ leg** ich habe mir das Bein
verletzt

Myanmar ['maɪænmaː] n
Myanmar nt
myself [maɪ'self] pron (reflexive)
mich akk, mir dat; **I've hurt ~** ich
habe mich verletzt; **I've bought
~ a flat** ich habe mir eine
Wohnung gekauft; **I need it for
~** ich brauche es für mich (selbst);
(emphatic) **I did it ~** ich habe es
selbst gemacht; (**all**) **by ~** allein
mysterious [mɪ'stɪərɪəs] adj
geheimnisvoll, mysteriös;
(inexplicable) rätselhaft; **mystery**
['mɪstəri] n Geheimnis nt; (puzzle)
Rätsel nt; **it's a ~ to me** es ist mir
schleierhaft; **mystify** ['mɪstɪfaɪ]
vt verblüffen
myth [mɪθ] n Mythos m; (fig:
untrue story) Märchen nt; **mythical**
adj mythisch; (fig: untrue)
erfunden; **mythology**
[mɪ'θɒlədʒi] n Mythologie f

n

N *abbr* = **north** N

nag [næg] *vt, vi* herumnörgeln (*sb* an jdm); **nagging** *n* Nörgelei *f*

nail [neɪl] *n* Nagel *m* ▷ *vt* nageln (*to* an); **nail down** *vt* festnageln; **nailbrush** *n* Nagelbürste *f*; **nail clippers** *npl* Nagelknipser *m*; **nailfile** *n* Nagelfeile *f*; **nail polish** *n* Nagellack *m*; **nail polish remover** *n* Nagellackentferner *m*; **nail scissors** *npl* Nagelschere *f*; **nail varnish** *n* Nagellack *m*

naive [naɪˈiːv] *adj* naiv

naked [ˈneɪkɪd] *adj* nackt

name [neɪm] *n* Name *m*; **his ~ is ...** er heißt ...; **what's your ~?** wie heißen Sie?; (*reputation*) **to have a good/bad ~** einen guten/schlechten Ruf haben ▷ *vt* nennen (*after* nach); (*sth new*) benennen; (*nominate*) ernennen (*as* als/zu); **a boy ~d ...** ein Junge

namens ...; **namely** *adv* nämlich; **name plate** *n* Namensschild *nt*

nan bread [ˈnɑːnˈbred] *n (warm serviertes) indisches Fladenbrot*

nanny [ˈnænɪ] *n* Kindermädchen *nt*

nap [næp] *n*: **to have/take a ~** ein Nickerchen machen

napkin [ˈnæpkɪn] *n* (*at table*) Serviette *f*

Naples [ˈneɪplz] *n* Neapel *nt*

nappy [ˈnæpɪ] *n* (*Brit*) Windel *f*

narcotic [nɑːˈkɒtɪk] *n* Rauschgift *nt*

narrate [nəˈreɪt] *vt* erzählen; **narration** [nəˈreɪʃən], **narrative** [ˈnærətɪv] *n* Erzählung *f*; **narrator** [nəˈreɪtə*] *n* Erzähler(in) *m(f)*

narrow [ˈnærəʊ] *adj* eng, schmal; (*victory, majority*) knapp; **to have a ~ escape** mit knapper Not davonkommen ▷ *vi* sich verengen; **narrow down** *vt* einschränken (*to sth* auf etw *akk*); **narrow-minded** *adj* engstirnig

nasty [ˈnɑːstɪ] *adj* ekelhaft; (*person*) fies; (*remark*) gehässig; (*accident, wound etc*) schlimm

nation [ˈneɪʃən] *n* Nation *f*; **national** [ˈnæʃənl] *adj* national; **~ anthem** Nationalhymne *f*; **National Health Service** (*Brit*) staatlicher Gesundheitsdienst; **~ insurance** (*Brit*) Sozialversicherung *f*; **~ park** Nationalpark *m*; **~ service** Wehrdienst *m*; **~ socialism** (*Hist*) Nationalsozialismus *m* ▷ *n* Staatsbürger(in) *m(f)*

○ **NATIONAL TRUST**
○
○ Der **National Trust** ist ein 1895
○ gegründeter Natur- und
○ Denkmalschutzverband in
○ Großbritannien, der Gebäude
○ und Gelände von besonderem

- historischen oder ästhetischen
- Interesse erhält und der
- Öffentlichkeit zugänglich
- macht.

nationality [næʃˈnælɪtɪ] n Staatsangehörigkeit f, Nationalität f; **nationalize** [ˈnæʃnəlaɪz] vt verstaatlichen; **nationwide** adj, adv landesweit

native [ˈneɪtɪv] adj einheimisch; (inborn) angeboren, natürlich; **Native American** Indianer(in) m(f); **~ country** Heimatland nt; **a ~ German** ein gebürtiger Deutscher, eine gebürtige Deutsche; **~ language** Muttersprache f; **~ speaker** Muttersprachler(in) m(f) ▷ n Einheimische(r) mf; (in colonial context) Eingeborene(r) mf

nativity play [nəˈtɪvətɪpleɪ] n Krippenspiel nt

NATO [ˈneɪtəʊ] acr = **North Atlantic Treaty Organization** Nato f

natural [ˈnætʃrəl] adj natürlich; (law, science, forces etc) Natur-; (inborn) angeboren; **~ gas** Erdgas nt; **~ resources** Bodenschätze pl; **naturally** adv natürlich; (by nature) von Natur aus; **it comes ~ to her** es fällt ihr leicht

nature [ˈneɪtʃə*] n Natur f; (type) Art f; **it is not in my ~** es entspricht nicht meiner Art; **by ~** von Natur aus; **nature reserve** n Naturschutzgebiet nt

naughty [ˈnɔːtɪ] adj (child) ungezogen; (cheeky) frech

nausea [ˈnɔːsɪə] n Übelkeit f

nautical [ˈnɔːtɪkəl] adj nautisch; **~ mile** Seemeile f

nave [neɪv] n Hauptschiff nt

navel [ˈneɪvəl] n Nabel m

navigate [ˈnævɪgeɪt] vi navigieren; (in car) lotsen, dirigieren;

navigation [nævɪˈgeɪʃən] n Navigation f; (in car) Lotsen nt

navy [ˈneɪvɪ] n Marine f; **~ blue** Marineblau nt

Nazi [ˈnɑːtsɪ] n Nazi m

NB abbr = **nota bene** NB

NE abbr = **northeast** NO

near [nɪə*] adj nahe; **in the ~ future** in nächster Zukunft; **that was a ~ miss** (o thing) das war knapp; (with price) **... or ~est offer** Verhandlungsbasis ... ▷ adv in der Nähe; **so ~** so nahe; **come ~er** näher kommen; (event) näher rücken ▷ prep: ~ (**to**) (space) nahe an +dat; (vicinity) in der Nähe +gen; **~ the sea** nahe am Meer; **~ the station** in der Nähe des Bahnhofs, in Bahnhofsnähe; **nearby** adj nahe gelegen ▷ adv in der Nähe; **nearly** adv fast; **nearside** n (Auto) Beifahrerseite f; **near-sighted** adj kurzsichtig

neat [niːt] adj ordentlich; (work, writing) sauber; (undiluted) pur

necessarily [nesəˈserəlɪ] adv notwendigerweise; **not ~** nicht unbedingt; **necessary** [ˈnesəsərɪ] adj notwendig, nötig; **it's ~ to ...** man muss ...; **it's not ~ for him to come** er braucht nicht mitzukommen; **necessity** [nɪˈsesɪtɪ] n Notwendigkeit f; **the bare necessities** das absolut Notwendigste; **there is no ~ to ...** man braucht nicht (zu) ..., man muss nicht ...

neck [nek] n Hals m; (size) Halsweite f; **back of the ~** Nacken m; **necklace** [ˈneklɪs] n Halskette f; **necktie** n (US) Krawatte f

nectarine [ˈnektərɪn] n Nektarine f

née [neɪ] adj geborene

need [niːd] n (requirement) Bedürfnis nt (for für); (necessity)

431 | **New England**

Notwendigkeit f; (*poverty*) Not f; **to be in ~ of sth** etw brauchen; **if ~(s) be** wenn nötig; **there is no ~ to ...** man braucht nicht (zu) ..., man muss nicht ... ▷ *vt* brauchen; **I ~ to speak to you** ich muss mit dir reden; **you ~n't go** du brauchst nicht (zu) gehen, du musst nicht gehen

needle ['niːdl] n Nadel f

needless, needlessly ['niːdlɪs, -lɪ] *adj, adv* unnötig; **~ to say** selbstverständlich

needy ['niːdɪ] *adj* bedürftig

negative ['negətɪv] n (*Ling*) Verneinung f; (*Foto*) Negativ nt ▷ *adj* negativ; (*answer*) verneinend

neglect [nɪ'glekt] n Vernachlässigung f ▷ *vt* vernachlässigen; **to ~ to do sth** es versäumen, etw zu tun; **negligence** ['neglɪdʒəns] n Nachlässigkeit f; **negligent** *adj* nachlässig

negligible ['neglɪdʒəbl] *adj* unbedeutend; (*amount*) geringfügig

negotiate [nɪ'gəʊʃɪeɪt] vi verhandeln; **negotiation** [nɪgəʊʃɪ'eɪʃən] n Verhandlung f

neigh [neɪ] vi (*horse*) wiehern

neighbor (US), **neighbour** ['neɪbə*] n Nachbar(in) m(f); **neighbo(u)rhood** n Nachbarschaft f; **neighbo(u)ring** *adj* benachbart

neither ['naɪðə*] *adj, pron* keine(r, s) von beiden; **~ of you/us** keiner von euch/uns beiden ▷ *adv*: **~ ... nor ...** weder ... noch ... ▷ *conj*: **I'm not going - ~ am I** ich gehe nicht - ich auch nicht

neon ['niːɒn] n Neon nt; **~ sign** (*advertisement*) Leuchtreklame f

nephew ['nefjuː] n Neffe m

nerd [nɜːv] n (*fam*) Schwachkopf m; **he's a real computer ~** er ist ein totaler Computerfreak

nerve [nɜːv] n Nerv m; **he gets on my ~s** er geht mir auf die Nerven; (*courage*) **to keep/lose one's ~** die Nerven behalten/verlieren; (*cheek*) **to have the ~ to do sth** die Frechheit besitzen, etw zu tun; **nerve-racking** *adj* nervenaufreibend; **nervous** ['nɜːvəs] *adj* (*apprehensive*) ängstlich; (*on edge*) nervös; **nervous breakdown** n Nervenzusammenbruch m

nest [nest] n Nest nt ▷ vi nisten

net [net] n Netz nt; **the Net** (*Internet*) das Internet; **on the ~** im Netz ▷ *adj* (*price, weight*) Netto-; **~ profit** Reingewinn m; **netball** n Netzball m

Netherlands ['neðələndz] npl: **the ~** die Niederlande pl

nettle ['netl] n Nessel f

network ['netwɜːk] n Netz nt; (*TV, Radio*) Sendenetz nt; (*Inform*) Netzwerk nt; **networking** n Networking n (*das Knüpfen und Pflegen von Kontakten, die dem beruflichen Fortkommen dienen*)

neurosis [njʊə'rəʊsɪs] n Neurose f; **neurotic** [njʊə'rɒtɪk] *adj* neurotisch

neuter ['njuːtə*] *adj* (*Bio*) geschlechtslos; (*Ling*) sächlich

neutral ['njuːtrəl] *adj* neutral ▷ n (*gear in car*) Leerlauf m

never ['nevə*] *adv* nie(mals); **~ before** noch nie; **~ mind** macht nichts!; **never-ending** *adj* endlos; **nevertheless** [nevəðə'les] *adv* trotzdem

new [njuː] *adj* neu; **this is all ~ to me** das ist für mich noch ungewohnt; **newcomer** n Neuankömmling m; (*in job, subject*) Neuling m

New England [njuː'ɪŋglənd] n Neuengland nt

Newfoundland ['nju:fəndlənd] *n* Neufundland *nt*
newly ['nju:lɪ] *adv* neu; **~ made** (*cake*) frisch gebacken; **newly-weds** *npl* Frischvermählte *pl*; **new moon** *n* Neumond *m*
news [nju:z] *nsing* (*item of ~*) Nachricht *f*; (*Radio, TV*) Nachrichten *pl*; **good ~** ein erfreuliche Nachricht; **what's the ~?** was gibt's Neues?; **have you heard the ~?** hast du das Neueste gehört?; **that's ~ to me** das ist mir neu; **newsagent**, **news dealer** (*US*) *n* Zeitungshändler(in) *m(f)*; **news bulletin** *n* Nachrichtensendung *f*; **news flash** *n* Kurzmeldung *f*; **newsgroup** *n* (*Inform*) Diskussionsforum *nt*, Newsgroup *f*; **newsletter** *n* Mitteilungsblatt *nt*; **newspaper** ['nju:speɪpə*] *n* Zeitung *f*
New Year ['nju:'jɪə*] *n* das neue Jahr; **Happy ~** (ein) frohes Neues Jahr!; (*toast*) Prosit Neujahr!; **~'s Day** Neujahr *nt*, Neujahrstag *m*; **~'s Eve** Silvesterabend *m*; **~'s resolution** guter Vorsatz fürs neue Jahr
New York [nju:'jɔ:k] *n* New York *nt*
New Zealand [nju:'zi:lənd] *n* Neuseeland *nt* ▷ *adj* neuseeländisch; **New Zealander** *n* Neuseeländer(in) *m(f)*
next [nekst] *adj* nächste(r, s); **the week after ~** übernächste Woche; **~ time I see him** wenn ich ihn das nächste Mal sehe; **you're ~** du bist jetzt dran ▷ *adv* als Nächstes; (*then*) dann, darauf; **~ to** neben +*dat*; **~ to last** vorletzte(r, s); **~ to impossible** nahezu unmöglich; **the ~ best thing** das Nächstbeste; **~ door** nebenan
NHS *abbr* = **National Health Service**

Niagara Falls [naɪ'ægrə'fɔ:lz] *npl* Niagarafälle *pl*
nibble ['nɪbl] *vt* knabbern an +*dat*; **nibbles** *npl* Knabberzeug *nt*
Nicaragua [nɪkə'rægjʊə] *n* Nicaragua *nt*
nice [naɪs] *adj* nett, sympathisch; (*taste, food, drink*) gut; (*weather*) schön; **~ and ...** schön ...; **be ~ to him** sei nett zu ihm; **have a ~ day** (*US*) schönen Tag noch!; **nicely** *adv* nett; (*well*) gut; **that'll do ~** das genügt vollauf
nick [nɪk] *vt* (*fam: steal*) klauen; (*capture*) schnappen
nickel ['nɪkl] *n* (*Chem*) Nickel *nt*; (*US: coin*) Nickel *m*
nickname ['nɪkneɪm] *n* Spitzname *m*
nicotine ['nɪkəti:n] *n* Nikotin *nt*; **nicotine patch** *n* Nikotinpflaster *nt*
niece [ni:s] *n* Nichte *f*
Nigeria [naɪ'dʒɪərɪə] *n* Nigeria *nt*
night [naɪt] *n* Nacht *f*; (*before bed*) Abend *m*; **good ~** gute Nacht!; **at** (*o by*) **~** nachts; **to have an early ~** früh schlafen gehen; **nightcap** *n* Schlummertrunk *m*; **nightclub** *n* Nachtklub *m*; **nightdress** *n* Nachthemd *nt*; **nightie** ['naɪtɪ] *n* (*fam*) Nachthemd *nt*
nightingale ['naɪtɪŋgeɪl] *n* Nachtigall *f*
night life ['naɪtlaɪf] *n* Nachtleben *nt*; **nightly** *adv* (*every evening*) jeden Abend; (*every night*) jede Nacht; **nightmare** ['naɪtmeə*] *n* Albtraum *m*; **nighttime** *n* Nacht *f*; **at ~** nachts
nil [nɪl] *n* (*Sport*) null
Nile [naɪl] *n* Nil *m*
nine [naɪn] *num* neun; **~ times out of ten** so gut wie immer ▷ *n* (*a. bus etc*) Neun *f*; *see also* **eight**; **nineteen** [naɪn'ti:n] *num*

neunzehn ▷ n (a. bus etc)
Neunzehn f; see also **eight**;
nineteenth adj neunzehnte(r, s);
see also **eighth**; **ninetieth**
['naɪntɪəθ] adj neunzigste(r, s);
see also **eighth**; **ninety** ['naɪntɪ]
num neunzig ▷ n Neunzig f; see
also **eight**; **ninth** [naɪnθ] adj
neunte(r, s) ▷ n (fraction) Neuntel
nt; see also **eighth**

nipple ['nɪpl] n Brustwarze f

nitrogen ['naɪtrədʒən] n Stick-
stoff m

KEYWORD

no [nəʊ] (pl **noes**) adv (opposite of
yes) nein; **to answer no** (to
question) mit Nein antworten; (to
request) Nein o nein sagen; **no
thank you** nein, danke
▷ adj (not any) kein(e); **I have no
money/time** ich habe kein
Geld/keine Zeit; **"no smoking"**
„Rauchen verboten"
▷ n Nein nt; (no vote) Neinstimme f

nobility [nəʊ'bɪlɪtɪ] n Adel m;
noble ['nəʊbl] adj (rank) adlig;
(quality) edel ▷ n Adlige(r)
mf

nobody ['nəʊbədɪ] pron niemand; (emphatic) keiner; **~ knows**
keiner weiß es; **~ else** sonst
niemand, kein anderer ▷ n
Niemand m

no-claims bonus
[nəʊ'kleɪmzbəʊnəs] n Schadenfreiheitsrabatt m

nod [nɒd] vi, vt nicken; **nod off** vi
einnicken

noise [nɔɪz] n (loud) Lärm m;
(sound) Geräusch nt; **noisy** adj
laut; (crowd) lärmend

nominate ['nɒmɪneɪt] vt (in
election) aufstellen; (appoint)
ernennen

nominative ['nɒmɪnətɪv] n
(Ling) Nominativ m

nominee [nɒmɪ'ni:] n Kandi-
dat(in) m(f)

non- [nɒn] pref Nicht-; (with adj)
nicht-, un-; **non-alcoholic** adj
alkoholfrei

none [nʌn] pron keine(r, s); **~ of
them** keiner von ihnen; **~ of it is
any use** nichts davon ist
brauchbar; **there are ~ left** es sind
keine mehr da; (with comparative)
to be ~ the wiser auch nicht
schlauer sein; **I was ~ the worse
for it** es hat mir nichts geschadet

nonentity [nɒ'nentɪtɪ] n Null
f

nonetheless [nʌnðə'les] adv
nichtsdestoweniger, dennoch

non-event n Reinfall m;
non-existent adj nicht
vorhanden; **non-fiction** n
Sachbücher pl; **non-iron** adj
bügelfrei; **non-polluting** adj
schadstofffrei; **non-resident** n:
"open to ~s" „auch für
Nichthotelgäste"; **non-returnable**
adj: **~ bottle** Einwegflasche f

nonsense ['nɒnsəns] n Unsinn
m; **don't talk ~** red keinen Unsinn

non-smoker [nɒn'sməʊkə*] n
Nichtraucher(in) m(f);
non-smoking adj Nichtraucher-;
~ area Nichtraucherbereich m;
nonstop adj (train) durchgehend;
(flight) Nonstop- ▷ adv (talk)
ununterbrochen; (travel) ohne
Unterbrechung; (fly) ohne
Zwischenlandung; **non-violent**
adj gewaltfrei

noodles ['nu:dlz] npl Nudeln pl

noon [nu:n] n Mittag m; **at ~** um
12 Uhr mittags

no one ['nəʊwʌn] pron
niemand; (emphatic) keiner; **~ else**
sonst niemand, kein anderer

nor [nɔ:] conj: **neither ... ~ ...**

weder ... noch ...; **I don't smoke, ~ does he** ich rauche nicht, er auch nicht

norm [nɔːm] *n* Norm *f*

normal ['nɔːməl] *adj* normal; **to get back to ~** sich wieder normalisieren; **normally** *adv* (*usually*) normalerweise

north [nɔːθ] *n* Norden *m*; **to the ~ of** nördlich von ▷ *adv* (*go, face*) nach Norden ▷ *adj* Nord-; **~ wind** Nordwind *m*; **North America** *n* Nordamerika *nt*; **northbound** *adj* (in) Richtung Norden; **northeast** *n* Nordosten *m*; **to the ~ of** nordöstlich von ▷ *adv* (*go, face*) nach Nordosten ▷ *adj* Nordost-; **northern** ['nɔːðən] *adj* nördlich; **~ France** Nordfrankreich *nt*; **Northern Ireland** *n* Nordirland *nt*; **North Pole** *n* Nordpol *m*; **North Sea** *n* Nordsee *f*; **northwards** *adv* nach Norden; **northwest** *n* Nordwesten *m*; **to the ~ of** nordwestlich von ▷ *adv* (*go, face*) nach Nordwesten ▷ *adj* Nordwest-

Norway ['nɔːweɪ] *n* Norwegen *nt*; **Norwegian** [nɔːˈwiːdʒən] *adj* norwegisch ▷ *n* (*person*) Norweger(in) *m(f)*; (*language*) Norwegisch *nt*

nos. *abbr* = **numbers** Nr.

nose [nəʊz] *n* Nase *f*; **nose around** *vi* herumschnüffeln; **nosebleed** *n* Nasenbluten *nt*; **nose-dive** *n* Sturzflug *m*; **to take a ~** abstürzen

nosey ['nəʊzɪ] *see* **nosy**

nostalgia [nɒˈstældʒɪə] *n* Nostalgie *f* (*for* nach); **nostalgic** *adj* nostalgisch

nostril ['nɒstrɪl] *n* Nasenloch *nt*

nosy ['nəʊzɪ] *adj* neugierig

not [nɒt] *adv* nicht; **~ a** kein; **~ one of them** kein einziger von ihnen; **he is ~ an expert** er ist kein

Experte; **I told him ~ to** (**do it**) ich sagte ihm, er solle es nicht tun; **~ at all** überhaupt nicht, keineswegs; (*don't mention it*) gern geschehen; **~ yet** noch nicht

notable ['nəʊtəbl] *adj* bemerkenswert; **note** [nəʊt] *n* (*written*) Notiz *f*; (*short letter*) paar Zeilen *pl*; (*on scrap of paper*) Zettel *m*; (*comment in book etc*) Anmerkung *f*; (*bank~*) Schein *m*; (*Mus: sign*) Note *f*; (*sound*) Ton *m*; **to make a ~ of sth** sich *dat* etw notieren; **~s** (*of lecture etc*) Aufzeichnungen *pl*; **to take ~s** sich *dat* Notizen machen (*of* über +*akk*) ▷ *vt* (*notice*) bemerken (*that* dass); (*write down*) notieren; **notebook** *n* Notizbuch *nt*; (*Inform*) Notebook *nt*; **notepad** *n* Notizblock *m*; **notepaper** *n* Briefpapier *nt*

nothing ['nʌθɪŋ] *n* nichts; **~ but ...** lauter ...; **for ~** umsonst; **he thinks ~ of it** er macht sich nichts daraus

notice ['nəʊtɪs] *n* (*announcement*) Bekanntmachung *f*; (*on ~ board*) Anschlag *m*; (*attention*) Beachtung *f*; (*advance warning*) Ankündigung *f*; (*to leave job, flat etc*) Kündigung *f*; **at short ~** kurzfristig; **until further ~** bis auf weiteres; **to give sb ~** jdm kündigen; **to hand in one's ~** kündigen; **to take (no) ~ of** (**sth**) etw (nicht) beachten; **take no ~** kümmere dich nicht darum! ▷ *vt* bemerken; **noticeable** *adj* erkennbar; (*visible*) sichtbar; **to be ~** auffallen; **notice board** *n* Anschlagtafel *f*

notification [nəʊtɪfɪˈkeɪʃən] *n* Benachrichtigung *f* (*of* von); **notify** ['nəʊtɪfaɪ] *vt* benachrichtigen (*of* von)

notion ['nəʊʃən] *n* Idee *f*

notorious [nəʊˈtɔːrɪəs] *adj* berüchtigt

nought [nɔːt] n Null f
noun [naʊn] n Substantiv nt
nourish ['nʌrɪʃ] vt nähren;
  nourishing adj nahrhaft;
  nourishment n Nahrung f
novel ['nɒvəl] n Roman m ▷ adj
  neuartig; **novelist** n
  Schriftsteller(in) m(f); **novelty** n
  Neuheit f
November [nəʊ'vembə°] n
  November m; see also **September**
novice ['nɒvɪs] n Neuling m
now [naʊ] adv (at the moment)
  jetzt; (introductory phrase) also;
  right ~ jetzt gleich; **just ~** gerade;
  by ~ inzwischen; **from ~ on** ab
  jetzt; **~ and again** (o then) ab und
  zu; **nowadays** adv heutzutage
nowhere ['nəʊwɛə°] adv nirgends; **we're getting ~** wir
  kommen nicht weiter; **~ near**
  noch lange nicht
nozzle ['nɒzl] n Düse f
nuclear ['njuːklɪə°] adj (energy
  etc) Kern-; **~ power station**
  Kernkraftwerk nt; **nuclear waste**
  n Atommüll m
nude [njuːd] adj nackt ▷ n (person) Nackte(r) mf; (painting etc) Akt
  m
nudge [nʌdʒ] vt stupsen; **nudist**
  ['njuːdɪst] n Nudist(in) m(f),
  FKK-Anhänger(in) m(f); **nudist
  beach** n FKK-Strand m
nuisance ['njuːsns] n Ärgernis
  nt; (person) Plage f; **what a ~** wie
  ärgerlich!
nuke [njuːk] (US fam) n (bomb)
  Atombombe f ▷ vt eine
  Atombombe werfen auf +akk
numb [nʌm] adj taub, gefühllos
  ▷ vt betäuben
number ['nʌmbə°] n Nummer f;
  (Math) Zahl f; (quantity) (An)zahl f;
  in small/large ~s in
  kleinen/großen Mengen; **a ~ of
  times** mehrmals ▷ vt (give a

number to) nummerieren; (count)
  zählen (among zu); **his days are
  ~ed** seine Tage sind gezählt;
  number plate n (Brit Auto)
  Nummernschild nt
numeral ['njuːmərəl] n Ziffer f;
  numerical [njuː'merɪkəl] adj
  numerisch; (superiority)
  zahlenmäßig; **numerous**
  ['njuːmərəs] adj zahlreich
nun [nʌn] n Nonne f
Nuremberg ['njʊərəmbɜːg] n
  Nürnberg nt
nurse [nɜːs] n Krankenschwester
  f; (male ~) Krankenpfleger m ▷ vt
  (patient) pflegen; (baby) stillen;
  nursery n Kinderzimmer nt; (for
  plants) Gärtnerei f; (tree)
  Baumschule f; **nursery rhyme** n
  Kinderreim m; **nursery school** n
  Kindergarten m; **~ teacher**
  Kindergärtner(in) m(f),
  Erzieher(in) m(f); **nursing** n
  (profession) Krankenpflege f;
  ~ home Privatklinik f
nut [nʌt] n Nuss f; (Tech: for bolt)
  Mutter f; **nutcase** n (fam)
  Spinner(in) m(f); **nutcracker** n,
  nutcrackers npl Nussknacker m
nutmeg ['nʌtmeg] n Muskat m,
  Muskatnuss f
nutrient ['njuːtrɪənt] n Nährstoff
  m
nutrition [njuː'trɪʃən] n Ernährung f; **nutritious** [njuː'trɪʃəs]
  adj nahrhaft
nuts [nʌts] (fam) adj verrückt; **to
  be ~ about sth** nach etw verrückt
  sein ▷ npl (testicles) Eier pl
nutshell ['nʌtʃel] n Nussschale f;
  in a ~ kurz gesagt
nutter ['nʌtə°] n (fam)
  Spinner(in) m(f); **nutty** ['nʌtɪ]
  adj (fam) verrückt
NW abbr = **northwest** NW
nylon® ['naɪlɒn] n Nylon® nt
  ▷ adj Nylon-

O

O [əʊ] *n* (*Tel*) Null *f*

oak [əʊk] *n* Eiche *f* ▷ *adj* Eichen-

OAP *abbr* = **old-age pensioner** Rentner(in) *m(f)*

oar [ɔː°] *n* Ruder *nt*

oasis [əʊˈeɪsɪs] (*pl* **oases**) *n* Oase *f*

oatcake [ˈəʊtkeɪk] *n* Haferkeks *m*

oath [əʊθ] *n* (*statement*) Eid *m*

oats [əʊts] *npl* Hafer *m*; (*Gastr*) Haferflocken *pl*

obedience [əˈbiːdɪəns] *n* Gehorsam *m*; **obedient** *adj* gehorsam; **obey** [əˈbeɪ] *vt, vi* gehorchen +*dat*

object [ˈɒbdʒekt] *n* Gegenstand *m*; (*abstract*) Objekt *nt*; (*purpose*) Ziel *nt* ▷ [əbˈdʒekt] *vi* dagegen sein; (*raise objection*) Einwände erheben (*to* gegen); (*morally*) Anstoß nehmen (*to* an +*dat*); **do you ~ to my smoking?** haben Sie etwas dagegen, wenn ich rauche?; **objection** [əbˈdʒekʃən] *n* Einwand *m*

objective [əbˈdʒektɪv] *n* Ziel *nt* ▷ *adj* objektiv; **objectivity** [ɒbdʒekˈtɪvɪtɪ] *n* Objektivität *f*

obligation [ɒblɪˈɡeɪʃən] *n* (*duty*) Pflicht *f*; (*commitment*) Verpflichtung *f*; **no ~** unverbindlich; **obligatory** [əˈblɪɡətərɪ] *adj* obligatorisch; **oblige** [əˈblaɪdʒ] *vt*: **to ~ sb to do sth** jdn (dazu) zwingen, etw zu tun; **he felt ~d to accept the offer** er fühlte sich verpflichtet, das Angebot anzunehmen

oblique [əˈbliːk] *adj* schräg; (*angle*) schief

oboe [ˈəʊbəʊ] *n* Oboe *f*

obscene [əbˈsiːn] *adj* obszön

obscure [əbˈskjʊə°] *adj* unklar; (*unknown*) unbekannt

observant [əbˈzɜːvənt] *adj* aufmerksam; **observation** [ɒbzəˈveɪʃən] *n* (*watching*) Beobachtung *f*; (*remark*) Bemerkung *f*; **observe** [əbˈzɜːv] *vt* (*notice*) bemerken; (*watch*) beobachten; (*customs*) einhalten

obsessed [əbˈsest] *adj* besessen (*with an idea etc* von einem Gedanken etc); **obsession** [əbˈseʃən] *n* Manie *f*

obsolete [ˈɒbsəliːt] *adj* veraltet

obstacle [ˈɒbstəkl] *n* Hindernis *nt* (*to* für); **to be an ~ to sth** einer Sache im Weg stehen

obstinate [ˈɒbstɪnət] *adj* hartnäckig

obstruct [əbˈstrʌkt] *vt* versperren; (*pipe*) verstopfen; (*hinder*) behindern, aufhalten; **obstruction** [əbˈstrʌkʃən] *n* Blockierung *f*; (*of pipe*) Verstopfung *f*; (*obstacle*) Hindernis *nt*

obtain [əbˈteɪn] *vt* erhalten; **obtainable** *adj* erhältlich

obvious ['ɒbvɪəs] *adj*
offensichtlich; **it was ~ to me
that ...** es war mir klar, dass ...;
obviously *adj* offensichtlich

occasion [ə'keɪʒən] *n* Gelegenheit *f*; (*special event*) (großes)
Ereignis; **on the ~ of** anlässlich
+*gen*; **special ~** besonderer Anlass;
occasional, **occasionally** *adj*, *adv*
gelegentlich

occupant ['ɒkjʊpənt] *n* (*of
house*) Bewohner(in) *m(f)*; (*of
vehicle*) Insasse *m*, Insassin *f*;
occupation [ɒkjʊ'peɪʃən] *n*
Beruf *m*; (*pastime*) Beschäftigung *f*;
(*of country etc*) Besetzung *f*;
occupied *adj* (*country, seat, toilet*)
besetzt; (*person*) beschäftigt; **to
keep sb/oneself ~** jdn/sich
beschäftigen; **occupy** ['ɒkjʊpaɪ]
vt (*country*) besetzen; (*time*)
beanspruchen; (*mind, person*)
beschäftigen

occur [ə'kɜː*] *vi* vorkommen;
~ to sb jdm einfallen; **occurrence**
[ə'kʌrəns] *n* (*event*) Ereignis *nt*;
(*presence*) Vorkommen *nt*

ocean ['əʊʃən] *n* Ozean *m*; (*US:
sea*) das Meer *nt*

o'clock [ə'klɒk] *adv*: **5 ~** 5 Uhr; **at
10 ~** um 10 Uhr

octagon ['ɒktəgən] *n* Achteck
nt

October [ɒk'təʊbə*] *n* Oktober
m; *see also* **September**

octopus ['ɒktəpəs] *n* Tintenfisch *m*

odd [ɒd] *adj* (*strange*) sonderbar;
(*not even*) ungerade; (*one missing*)
einzeln; **to be the ~ one out** nicht
dazugehören; **~ jobs**
Gelegenheitsarbeiten *pl*; **odds** *npl*
Chancen *pl*; **against all
~** entgegen allen Erwartungen;
~ and ends (*fam*) Kleinkram *pl*

odometer [əʊ'dɒmətə*] *n* (*US
Auto*) Meilenzähler *m*

odor (*US*), **odour** ['əʊdə*] *n*
Geruch *m*

O **KEYWORD**

of [ɒv, əv] *prep* **1** von +*dat* ≈ use of
gen; **the history of Germany** die
Geschichte Deutschlands; **a friend
of ours** ein Freund von uns; **a boy
of 10** ein 10-jähriger Junge;
that was kind of you das war
sehr freundlich von Ihnen
2 (*expressing quantity, amount,
dates etc*) **a kilo of flour** ein Kilo
Mehl; **how much of this do you
need?** wie viel brauchen Sie
(davon)?; **there were 3 of them**
(*people*) sie waren zu dritt; (*objects*)
es gab 3 (davon); **a cup of
tea/vase of flowers** eine
Tasse Tee/Vase mit Blumen;
the 5th of July der 5. Juli
3 (*from, out of*) aus; **a bridge made
of wood** eine Holzbrücke, eine
Brücke aus Holz

off [ɒf] *adv* (*away*) weg, fort; (*free*)
frei; (*switch*) ausgeschaltet; (*milk*)
sauer; **a mile ~** eine Meile
entfernt; **I'll be ~ now** ich gehe
jetzt; **to have the day/Monday
~** heute/Montag freihaben; **the
lights are ~** die Lichter sind aus;
the concert is ~ das Konzert fällt
aus; **I got 10 % ~** ich habe 10 %
Nachlass bekommen ▷ *prep* (*away
from*) von; **to jump/fall ~ the roof**
vom Dach springen/fallen; **to get
~ the bus** aus dem Bus
aussteigen; **he's ~ work/school** er
hat frei/schulfrei; **to take £20
~ the price** den Preis um 20 Pfund
herabsetzen

offence [ə'fens] *n* (*crime*)
Straftat *f*; (*minor*) Vergehen *nt*; (*to
feelings*) Kränkung *f*; **to
cause/take ~** Anstoß

erregen/nehmen; **offend** [ə'fend]
vt kränken; (eye, ear) beleidigen;
offender n Straffällige(r) mf;
offense (US) see **offence**;
offensive [ə'fensɪv] adj anstößig;
(insulting) beleidigend; (smell) übel,
abstoßend ▷ n (Mil) Offensive f
offer ['ɒfə°] n Angebot nt; **on
~** (Comm) im Angebot ▷ vt
anbieten (to sb jdm); (money, a
chance etc) bieten
offhand [ɒf'hænd] adj lässig
▷ adv (say) auf Anhieb
office ['ɒfɪs] n Büro nt; (position)
Amt nt; **doctor's ~** (US) Arztpraxis
f; **office block** n Bürogebäude nt;
office hours npl Dienstzeit f;
(notice) Geschäftszeiten pl; **officer**
['ɒfɪsə°] n (Mil) Offizier(in) m(f);
(official) Polizeibeamte(r) m,
Polizeibeamtin f; **office worker**
['ɒfɪswɜːkə°] n Büroangestellte(r)
mf; **official** [ə'fɪʃəl] adj offiziell;
(report etc) amtlich; **~ language**
Amtssprache f ▷ n Beamte(r) m,
Beamtin f, Repräsentant(in)
m(f)
off-licence ['ɒflaɪsəns] n (Brit)
Wein- und Spirituosenhandlung f;
off-line adj (Inform) offline;
off-peak adj außerhalb der
Stoßzeiten; (rate, ticket) verbilligt;
off-putting adj abstoßend,
entmutigend, irritierend;
off-season adj außerhalb der
Saison
offshore ['ɒfʃɔː°] adj küstennah,
Küsten-; (oil rig) im Meer; **offside**
['ɒfsaɪd] n (Auto) Fahrerseite f;
(Sport) Abseits nt
often ['ɒfən] adv oft; **every so
~** von Zeit zu Zeit
oil [ɔɪl] n Öl nt ▷ vt ölen; **oil level**
n Ölstand m; **oil painting** n
Ölgemälde nt; **oil-rig** n
(Öl)bohrinsel f; **oil slick** n
Ölteppich m; **oil tanker** n

Öltanker m; (truck) Tankwagen m;
oily adj ölig; (skin, hair) fettig
ointment ['ɔɪntmənt] n Salbe f
OK, okay [əʊ'keɪ] adj (fam) okay,
in Ordnung; **that's ~ by** (o **with**)
me das ist mir recht
old [əʊld] adj alt; **old age** n Alter
nt; **~ pension** Rente f; **~ pensioner**
Rentner(in) m(f); **old-fashioned**
adj altmodisch; **old people's
home** n Altersheim nt
olive ['ɒlɪv] n Olive f; **olive oil** n
Olivenöl nt
Olympic [əʊ'lɪmpɪk] adj olympisch; **the ~ Games, the ~s** pl die
Olympischen Spiele pl, die
Olympiade
omelette ['ɒmlət] n Omelett nt
omission [əʊ'mɪʃən] n Auslas-
sung f; **omit** [əʊ'mɪt] vt
auslassen

O   **KEYWORD**

on [ɒn] prep **1** (indicating position)
auf +dat; (with vb of motion) auf
+akk; (on vertical surface, part of
body) an +dat/akk; **it's on the table**
es ist auf dem Tisch; **she put the
book on the table** sie legte das
Buch auf den Tisch; **on the left**
links
2 (indicating means, method,
condition etc) **on foot** (go, be) zu
Fuß; **on the train/plane** (go) mit
dem Zug/Flugzeug; (be) im
Zug/Flugzeug; **on the
telephone/television** am
Telefon/im Fernsehen; **to be on
drugs** Drogen nehmen; **to be on
holiday/business** im Urlaub/auf
Geschäftsreise sein
3 (referring to time) **on Friday** (am)
Freitag; **on Fridays** freitags; **on
June 20th** am 20. Juni; **a week on
Friday** Freitag in einer Woche; **on
arrival he ...** als er ankam, ... er ...

4 (*about, concerning*) über +*akk*
▷ *adv* **1** (*referring to dress*) an; **she put her boots/hat on** sie zog ihre Stiefel an/setzte ihren Hut auf
2 (*further, continuously*) weiter; **to walk on** weitergehen
▷ *adj* **1** (*functioning, in operation: machine, TV, light*) an; (*tap*) aufgedreht; (*brakes*) angezogen; **is the meeting still on?** findet die Versammlung noch statt?; **there's a good film on** es läuft ein guter Film
2 that's not on! (*inf*) (*of behaviour*) das ist nicht drin!

once [wʌns] *adv* (*one time, in the past*) einmal; **at ~** sofort; (*at the same time*) gleichzeitig; **~ more** noch einmal; **for ~** ausnahmsweise (einmal); **~ in a while** ab und zu mal ▷ *conj* wenn ... einmal; **~ you've got used to it** sobald Sie sich daran gewöhnt haben
oncoming [ˈɒnkʌmɪŋ] *adj* entgegenkommend; **~ traffic** Gegenverkehr *m*

⊙ **KEYWORD**

one [wʌn] *num* eins; (*with noun, referring back to noun*) ein/eine/ein; **it is one (o'clock)** es ist eins, es ist ein Uhr; **one hundred and fifty** einhundertfünfzig
▷ *adj* **1** (*sole*) einzige(r, s); **the one book which** das einzige Buch, welches
2 (*same*) derselbe/dieselbe/dasselbe; **they came in the one car** sie kamen alle in dem einen Auto
3 (*indef*) **one day I discovered ...** eines Tages bemerkte ich ...
▷ *pron* **1** eine(r, s); **do you have a red one?** haben Sie einen

roten/eine rote/ein rotes?; **this one** diese(r, s); **that one** der/die/das; **which one?** welche(r, s)?; **one by one** einzeln
2 one another einander; **do you two ever see one another?** seht ihr beide euch manchmal?
3 (*impers*) man; **one never knows** man kann nie wissen; **to cut one's finger** sich in den Finger schneiden

one-off *adj* einmalig ▷ *n*: **a ~** etwas Einmaliges; **one-parent family** *n* Einelternfamilie *f*; **one-piece** *adj* einteilig; **oneself** *pron* (*reflexive*) sich; **one-way** *adj*: **~ street** Einbahnstraße *f*; **~ ticket** (*US*) einfache Fahrkarte
onion [ˈʌnjən] *n* Zwiebel *f*
on-line [ˈɒnlaɪn] *adj* (*Inform*) online; **~ banking** Homebanking *nt*
only [ˈəʊnlɪ] *adv* nur; (*with time*) erst; **~ yesterday** erst gestern; **he's ~ four** er ist erst vier; **~ just arrived** gerade erst angekommen
▷ *adj* einzige(r, s); **~ child** Einzelkind *nt*
o.n.o. *abbr* = **or nearest offer** VB
onside [ɒnˈsaɪd] *adv* (*Sport*) nicht im Abseits
onto [ˈɒntʊ] *prep* auf +*akk*; (*vertical surface*) an +*akk*; **to be ~ sb** jdm auf die Schliche gekommen sein
onwards [ˈɒnwədz] *adv* voran, vorwärts; **from today ~** von heute an, ab heute
open [ˈəʊpən] *adj* offen; **in the ~ air** im Freien; **~ to the public** für die Öffentlichkeit zugänglich; **the shop is ~ all day** das Geschäft hat den ganzen Tag offen ▷ *vt* öffnen, aufmachen; (*meeting, account, new building*)

eröffnen; (*road*) dem Verkehr übergeben ▷ vi (*door, window etc*) aufgehen, sich öffnen; (*shop, bank*) öffnen, aufmachen; (*begin*) anfangen (*with* mit); **open-air** adj Freiluft-; **open day** n Tag m der offenen Tür; **opening** n Öffnung f; (*beginning*) Anfang m; (*official, of exhibition etc*) Eröffnung f; (*opportunity*) Möglichkeit f; **~ hours** (o **times**) Öffnungszeiten pl; **openly** adv offen; **open-minded** adj aufgeschlossen; **open-plan** adj: **~ office** Großraumbüro nt

opera ['ɒpərə] n Oper f; **opera glasses** npl Opernglas nt; **opera house** n Oper f, Opernhaus nt; **opera singer** n Opernsänger(in) m(f)

operate ['ɒpəreɪt] vt (*machine*) bedienen; (*brakes, lights*) betätigen ▷ vi (*machine*) laufen; (*bus etc*) verkehren (*between* zwischen); **to ~ (on sb)** (*Med*) (jdn) operieren; **operating theatre** n Operationssaal m; **operation** [ɒpəˈreɪʃən] n (*of machine*) Bedienung f; (*functioning*) Funktionieren nt; (*Med*) Operation f (*on* an +dat); (*undertaking*) Unternehmen nt; **in ~** (*machine*) in Betrieb; **to have an ~** operiert werden (*for* wegen); **operator** ['ɒpəreɪtə*] n: **to phone the ~** die Vermittlung anrufen

opinion [əˈpɪnjən] n Meinung f (*on* zu); **in my ~** meiner Meinung nach

opponent [əˈpəʊnənt] n Gegner(in) m(f)

opportunity [ɒpəˈtjuːnɪtɪ] n Gelegenheit f

oppose [əˈpəʊz] vt sich widersetzen +dat; (*idea*) ablehnen; **opposed** adj: **to be ~ to sth** gegen etw sein; **as ~ to** im

Gegensatz zu; **opposing** adj (*team*) gegnerisch; (*points of view*) entgegengesetzt

opposite ['ɒpəzɪt] adj (*house*) gegenüberliegend; (*direction*) entgegengesetzt; **the ~ sex** das andere Geschlecht ▷ adv gegenüber ▷ prep gegenüber +dat; **~ me** mir gegenüber ▷ n Gegenteil nt

opposition [ɒpəˈzɪʃən] n Widerstand m (*to* gegen); (*Pol*) Opposition f

oppress [əˈpres] vt unterdrücken; **oppressive** adj (*heat*) drückend

opt [ɒpt] vi: **to ~ for sth** sich für etw entscheiden; **to ~ to do sth** sich entscheiden, etw zu tun

optician [ɒpˈtɪʃən] n Optiker(in) m(f)

optimist ['ɒptɪmɪst] n Optimist(in) m(f); **optimistic** [ɒptɪˈmɪstɪk] adj optimistisch

option ['ɒpʃən] n Möglichkeit f; (*Comm*) Option f; **to have no ~** keine Wahl haben; **optional** adj freiwillig; **~ extras** (*Auto*) Extras pl

or [ɔː*] conj oder; (*otherwise*) sonst; (*after neg*) noch; **hurry up, ~ (else) we'll be late** beeil dich, sonst kommen wir zu spät

oral ['ɔːrəl] adj mündlich; **~ sex** Oralverkehr m ▷ n (*exam*) Mündliche(s) nt; **oral surgeon** n Kieferchirurg(in) m(f)

orange ['ɒrɪndʒ] n Orange f ▷ adj orangefarben; **orange juice** n Orangensaft m

orbit ['ɔːbɪt] n Umlaufbahn f; **to be out of ~** (*fam*) nicht zu erreichen sein ▷ vt umkreisen

orchard ['ɔːtʃəd] n Obstgarten m

orchestra ['ɔːkɪstrə] n Orchester nt; (*US Theat*) Parkett nt

orchid ['ɔːkɪd] n Orchidee f

ordeal [ɔːˈdiːl] n Tortur f;
(emotional) Qual f
order [ˈɔːdə°] n (sequence)
Reihenfolge f; (good arrangement)
Ordnung f; (command) Befehl m;
(Jur) Anordnung f; (condition)
Zustand m; (Comm), Bestellung f;
out of ~ (not functioning) außer
Betrieb; (unsuitable) nicht
angebracht; **in ~** (items) richtig
geordnet; (all right) in Ordnung; **in
~ to do sth** um etw zu tun ▷ vt
(arrange) ordnen; (command)
befehlen; **to ~ sb to do sth** jdm
befehlen, etw zu tun; (food,
product) bestellen; **order form** n
Bestellschein m
ordinary [ˈɔːdnrɪ] adj gewöhnlich, normal; (average)
durchschnittlich
ore [ɔː°] n Erz nt
organ [ˈɔːgən] n (Mus) Orgel f;
(Anat) Organ nt
organic [ɔːˈgænɪk] adj organisch;
(farming, vegetables) Bio-, Öko-;
~ farmer Biobauer m, Biobäuerin
f; **~ food** Biokost f
organization [ɔːgənaɪˈzeɪʃən] n
Organisation f; (arrangement)
Ordnung f; **organize** [ˈɔːgənaɪz]
vt organisieren; **organizer** n
(elektronisches) Notizbuch
orgasm [ˈɔːgæzəm] n Orgasmus
m
orgy [ˈɔːdʒɪ] n Orgie f
oriental [ɔːrɪˈentəl] adj
orientalisch
orientation [ˈɔːrɪenteɪʃən] n
Orientierung f
origin [ˈɒrɪdʒɪn] n Ursprung
m; (of person) Herkunft f;
original [əˈrɪdʒɪnl] adj (first)
ursprünglich; (painting) original;
(idea) originell ▷ n Original nt;
originality [ərɪdʒɪˈnælɪtɪ] n
Originalität f; **originally** adv
ursprünglich

Orkneys [ˈɔːknɪz] npl, **Orkney
Islands** npl Orkneyinseln pl
ornament [ˈɔːnəmənt] n
Schmuckgegenstand m;
ornamental [ɔːnəˈmentl] adj
dekorativ
orphan [ˈɔːfən] n Waise f,
Waisenkind nt; **orphanage**
[ˈɔːfənɪdʒ] n Waisenhaus nt
orthodox [ˈɔːθədɒks] adj
orthodox
orthopaedic, **orthopedic** (US)
[ɔːθəʊˈpiːdɪk] adj orthopädisch
ostentatious [ɒstenˈteɪʃəs] adj
protzig
ostrich [ˈɒstrɪtʃ] n (Zool) Strauß
m
other [ˈʌðə°] adj, pron andere(r,
s); **any ~ questions?** sonst noch
Fragen?; **the ~ day** neulich; **every
~ day** jeden zweiten Tag; **any
person ~ than him** alle außer ihm;
**someone/something or
~** irgendjemand/irgendetwas;
otherwise adv sonst; (differently)
anders
OTT adj abbr = **over the top**
übertrieben
otter [ˈɒtə°] n Otter m
ought [ɔːt] vb aux (obligation)
sollte; (probability) dürfte; (stronger)
müsste; **you ~ to do that** du
solltest/Sie sollten das tun; **he
~ to win** er müsste gewinnen;
that ~ to do das müsste reichen
ounce [aʊns] n Unze f (28,35 g)
our [aʊə°] adj unser; **ours** pron
unsere(r, s); **this is ~** das gehört
uns; **a friend of ~** ein Freund von
uns; **ourselves** pron (reflexive)
uns; **we enjoyed ~** wir haben uns
amüsiert; **we've got the house
to ~** wir haben das Haus für uns;
(emphatic) **we did it ~** wir haben
es selbst gemacht; (**all**) **by
~** allein
out [aʊt] adv hinaus/heraus; (not

indoors) draußen; (*not at home*) nicht zu Hause; (*not alight*) aus; (*unconscious*) bewusstlos; (*published*) herausgekommen; (*results*) bekannt gegeben; **have you been ~ yet?** warst du/waren Sie schon draußen?; **I was ~ when they called** ich war nicht da, als sie vorbeikamen; **to be ~ and about** unterwegs sein; **the sun is ~** die Sonne scheint; **the fire is ~** das Feuer ist ausgegangen; (*wrong*) **the calculation is (way) ~** die Kalkulation stimmt (ganz und gar) nicht; **they're ~ to get him** sie sind hinter ihm her ▷ *vt* (*fam*) outen

outback ['aʊtbæk] *n* (*in Australia*) **the ~** das Hinterland

outboard ['aʊtbɔːd] *adj*: **~ motor** Außenbordmotor *m*

outbreak ['aʊtbreɪk] *n* Ausbruch *m*

outburst ['aʊtbɜːst] *n* Ausbruch *m*

outcome ['aʊtkʌm] *n* Ergebnis *nt*

outcry ['aʊtkraɪ] *n* (*public protest*) Protestwelle *f* (*against* gegen)

outdo [aʊt'duː] *irr vt* übertreffen

outdoor ['aʊtdɔː*] *adj* Außen-; (*Sport*) im Freien; **~ swimming pool** Freibad *nt*; **outdoors** [aʊt'dɔːz] *adv* draußen, im Freien

outer ['aʊtə*] *adj* äußere(r, s); **outer space** Weltraum *m*

outfit ['aʊtfɪt] *n* Ausrüstung *f*; (*clothes*) Kleidung *f*

outgoing ['aʊtgəʊɪŋ] *adj* kontaktfreudig

outgrow [aʊt'grəʊ] *irr vt* (*clothes*) herauswachsen aus

outing ['aʊtɪŋ] *n* Ausflug *m*

outlet ['aʊtlet] *n* Auslass *m*, Abfluss *m*; (*US*) Steckdose *f*; (*shop*) Verkaufsstelle *f*

outline ['aʊtlaɪn] *n* Umriss *m*; (*summary*) Abriss *m*

outlive [aʊt'lɪv] *vt* überleben

outlook ['aʊtlʊk] *n* Aussicht(en) *f(pl)*; (*prospects*) Aussichten *pl*; (*attitude*) Einstellung *f* (*on* zu)

outnumber [aʊt'nʌmbə*] *vt* zahlenmäßig überlegen sein +*dat*; **~ed** zahlenmäßig unterlegen

out of ['aʊtɒv] *prep* (*motion, motive, origin*) aus; (*position, away from*) außerhalb +*gen*; **~ danger/sight/breath** außer Gefahr/Sicht/Atem; **made ~ wood** aus Holz gemacht; **we are ~ bread** wir haben kein Brot mehr; **out-of-date** *adj* veraltet; **out-of-the-way** *adj* abgelegen

outpatient ['aʊtpeɪʃənt] *n* ambulanter Patient, ambulante Patientin

output ['aʊtpʊt] *n* Produktion *f*; (*of engine*) Leistung *f*; (*Inform*) Ausgabe *f*

outrage ['aʊtreɪdʒ] *n* (*great anger*) Empörung *f* (*at* über); (*wicked deed*) Schandtat *f*; (*crime*) Verbrechen *nt*; (*indecency*) Skandal *m*; **outrageous** [aʊt'reɪdʒəs] *adj* unerhört; (*clothes, behaviour etc*) unmöglich, schrill

outright ['aʊtraɪt] *adv* (*killed*) sofort ▷ *adj* total; (*denial*) völlig; (*winner*) unbestritten

outside [aʊt'saɪd] *n* Außenseite *f*; **on the ~** außen ▷ *adj* äußere(r, s), Außen-; (*chance*) sehr gering ▷ *adv* außen; **to go ~** nach draußen gehen ▷ *prep* außerhalb +*gen*; **outsider** *n* Außenseiter(in) *m(f)*

outskirts ['aʊtskɜːts] *npl* (*of town*) Stadtrand *m*

outstanding [aʊt'stændɪŋ] *adj* hervorragend; (*debts etc*) ausstehend

outward ['aʊtwəd] *adj* äußere(r, s); **~ journey** Hinfahrt *f*;

outwardly adv nach außen hin;
outwards adv nach außen

oval ['əʊvəl] adj oval

ovary ['əʊvərɪ] n Eierstock m

ovation [əʊ'veɪʃən] n Ovation f,
Applaus m

oven ['ʌvn] n Backofen m; **oven
glove** n Topfhandschuh m;
ovenproof adj feuerfest;
oven-ready adj bratfertig

over ['əʊvə*] prep (position) über
+dat; (motion) über +akk; **they
spent a long time ~ it** sie haben
lange dazu gebraucht; **from all
~ England** aus ganz England;
~ £20 mehr als 20 Pfund; **~ the
phone/radio** am Telefon/im
Radio; **to talk ~ a glass of wine**
sich bei einem Glas Wein
unterhalten; **~ and above this**
darüber hinaus; **~ the summer**
während des Sommers ▷ adv
(across) hinüber/herüber; (finished)
vorbei; (match, play etc) zu Ende;
(left) übrig; (more) mehr;
~ there/in America da
drüben/drüben in Amerika; **~ to
you** du bist/Sie sind dran; **it's (all)
~ between us** es ist aus zwischen
uns; **~ and ~ again** immer wieder;
to start (all) ~ again noch einmal
von vorn anfangen; **children of 8
and ~** Kinder ab 8 Jahren

over- ['əʊvə*] pref über-

overall ['əʊvərɔːl] n (Brit) Kittel
m ▷ adj (situation) allgemein;
(length) Gesamt-; **~ majority**
absolute Mehrheit ▷ adv
insgesamt; **overalls** npl Overall
m

overboard ['əʊvəbɔːd] adv über
Bord

overbooked [əʊvə'bʊkt] adj
überbucht; **overbooking** n
Überbuchung f

overcharge [əʊvə'tʃɑːdʒ] vt zu
viel verlangen von

overcoat ['əʊvəkəʊt] n Wintermantel m

overcome [əʊvə'kʌm] irr vt
überwinden; **~ by sleep/emotion**
von Schlaf/Rührung übermannt;
we shall ~ wir werden siegen

overcooked [əʊvə'kʊkt] adj
verkocht; (meat) zu lange gebraten

overcrowded [əʊvə'kraʊdɪd]
adj überfüllt

overdo [əʊvə'duː] irr vt übertreiben; **overdone** adj
übertrieben; (food) zu lange
gekocht; (meat) zu lange gebraten

overdose ['əʊvədəʊs] n Über-
dosis f

overdraft ['əʊvədrɑːft] n Kon-
toüberziehung f; **overdrawn**
[əʊvə'drɔːn] adj überzogen

overdue [əʊvə'djuː] adj
überfällig

overestimate [əʊvər'estɪmeɪt]
vt überschätzen

overexpose [əʊvərɪks'pəʊz] vt (Foto)
überbelichten

overflow [əʊvə'fləʊ] vi
überlaufen

overhead ['əʊvəhed] adj (Aviat)
~ locker Gepäckfach nt;
~ projector Overheadprojektor m;
~ railway Hochbahn f
▷ [əʊvə'hed] adv oben;
overhead, (Brit) **overheads** n
(Comm) allgemeine
Geschäftskosten pl

overhear [əʊvə'hɪə*] irr vt zufällig
mit anhören

overheat [əʊvə'hiːt] vi (engine)
heiß laufen

overjoyed [əʊvə'dʒɔɪd] adj
überglücklich (at über)

overland ['əʊvəlænd] adj Über-
land- ▷ [əʊvə'lænd] adv (travel)
über Land

overlap [əʊvə'læp] vi (dates etc)
sich überschneiden; (objects) sich
teilweise decken

overload [əʊvə'ləʊd] vt
überladen

overlook [əʊvə'lʊk] vt (view from
above) überblicken; (not notice)
übersehen; (pardon) hinwegsehen
über +akk

overnight [əʊvə'naɪt] adj (jour-
ney, train) Nacht-; **~ bag**
Reisetasche f; **~ stay**
Übernachtung f ▷ adv über Nacht

overpass ['əʊvəpɑːs] n
Überführung f

overpay [əʊvə'peɪ] vt
überbezahlen

overrule [əʊvə'ruːl] vt verwerfen; (decision) aufheben

overseas [əʊvə'siːz] adj Über-
see-; ausländisch; (fam) Auslands-
▷ adv (go) nach Übersee; (live,
work) in Übersee

oversee [əʊvə'siː] irr vt
beaufsichtigen

overshadow [əʊvə'ʃædəʊ] vt
überschatten

overshoot [əʊvə'ʃuːt] irr vt
(runway) hinausschießen über
+akk; (turning) vorbeifahren
+dat

oversight ['əʊvəsaɪt] n Versehen nt

oversimplify [əʊvə'sɪmplɪfaɪ]
vt zu sehr vereinfachen

oversleep [əʊvə'sliːp] irr vi
verschlafen

overtake [əʊvə'teɪk] irr vt, vi
überholen

overtime ['əʊvətaɪm] n Überstunden pl

overturn [əʊvə't3ːn] vt, vi
umkippen

overweight [əʊvə'weɪt] adj: **to
be ~** Übergewicht haben

overwhelm [əʊvə'welm] vt
überwältigen; **overwhelming** adj
überwältigend

overwork [əʊvə'w3ːk] n
Überarbeitung f ▷ vi sich

überarbeiten; **overworked** adj
überarbeitet

owe [əʊ] vt schulden; **to ~ sth to
sb** (money) jdm etw schulden;
(favour etc) jdm etw verdanken;
how much do I ~ you? was bin ich
dir/Ihnen schuldig?; **owing to**
prep wegen +gen

owl [aʊl] n Eule f

own [əʊn] vt besitzen ▷ adj eigen;
on one's ~ allein; **he has a flat of
his ~** er hat eine eigene Wohung;
own up vi: **to ~ to sth** etw
zugeben; **owner** n Besitzer(in)
m(f); (of business) Inhaber(in) m(f);
ownership n Besitz m; **under
new ~** unter neuer Leitung

ox [ɒks] (pl **oxen**) n Ochse m;
oxtail ['ɒksteɪl] n Ochsen-
schwanz m; **~ soup**
Ochsenschwanzsuppe f; **oxygen**
['ɒksɪdʒən] n Sauerstoff m

oyster ['ɔɪstə*] n Auster f

oz abbr = **ounces** Unzen pl

Oz ['ɒz] n (fam) Australien nt

ozone ['əʊzəʊn] n Ozon nt;
~ layer Ozonschicht f

p

p abbr = **page** S.; abbr = **penny, pence**

p.a. abbr = **per annum**

pace [peɪs] n (speed) Tempo nt; (step) Schritt m; **pacemaker** n (Med) Schrittmacher m

Pacific [pə'sɪfɪk] n: **the ~ (Ocean)** der Pazifik; **Pacific Standard Time** n pazifische Zeit

pacifier ['pæsɪfaɪə] n (US: for baby) Schnuller m

pack [pæk] n (of cards) Spiel nt; (esp US: of cigarettes) Schachtel f; (gang) Bande f; (US: backpack) Rucksack m ▷ vt (case) packen; (clothes) einpacken ▷ vi (for holiday) packen; **pack in** vt (Brit fam: job) hinschmeißen; **package** ['pækɪdʒ] n (a. Inform, fig) Paket nt; **package deal** n Pauschalangebot nt; **package holiday**, **package tour** n Pauschalreise f; **packaging** n (material) Verpackung f; **packed lunch** n (Brit) Lunchpaket nt; **packet** n Päckchen nt; (of cigarettes) Schachtel f

pad [pæd] n (of paper) Schreibblock m; (padding) Polster nt; **padded envelope** n wattierter Umschlag; **padding** n (material) Polsterung f

paddle ['pædl] n (for boat) Paddel nt ▷ vi (in boat) paddeln; **paddling pool** n (Brit) Planschbecken nt

padlock ['pædlɒk] n Vorhängeschloss nt

page [peɪdʒ] n (of book etc) Seite f

pager ['peɪdʒə*] n Piepser m

paid [peɪd] pt, pp of **pay** ▷ adj bezahlt

pain [peɪn] n Schmerz m; **to be in ~** Schmerzen haben; **she's a (real) ~** sie nervt; **painful** adj (physically) schmerzhaft; (embarrassing) peinlich; **painkiller** n schmerzstillendes Mittel

painstaking adj sorgfältig

paint [peɪnt] n Farbe f ▷ vt anstreichen; (picture) malen; **paintbrush** n Pinsel m; **painter** n Maler(in) m(f); **painting** n (picture) Bild nt, Gemälde nt

pair [pɛə*] n Paar nt; **a ~ of shoes** ein Paar Schuhe; **a ~ of scissors** eine Schere; **a ~ of trousers** eine Hose

pajamas [pə'dʒɑːməz] npl (US) Schlafanzug m

Pakistan [pɑːkɪ'stɑːn] n Pakistan nt

pal [pæl] n (fam) Kumpel m

palace ['pæləs] n Palast m

pale [peɪl] adj (face) blass, bleich; (colour) hell

palm [pɑːm] n (of hand) Handfläche f; **~ (tree)** Palme f; **palmtop (computer)** n Palmtop(computer) m

pamper ['pæmpə*] vt
verhätscheln

pan [pæn] n (saucepan) Topf m;
(frying pan) Pfanne f; **pancake**
['pænkeɪk] n Pfannkuchen m;
Pancake Day n (Brit)
Fastnachtsdienstag m

pandemic [pæn'demɪk] n Pandemie f

panel ['pænl] n (of wood) Tafel f;
(in discussion) Diskussionsteil-
nehmer pl; (in jury) Jurymitglieder
pl

panic ['pænɪk] n Panik f ▷ vi in
Panik geraten; **panicky** ['pænɪkɪ]
adj panisch

pansy ['pænzɪ] n (flower)
Stiefmütterchen nt

panties ['pæntɪz] npl (Damen)-
slip m

pantomime ['pæntəmaɪm] n
(Brit) um die Weihnachtszeit
aufgeführte Märchenkomödie

pants [pænts] npl Unterhose f;
(esp US: trousers) Hose f

pantyhose ['pæntɪhəʊz] npl
(US) Strumpfhose f; **panty-liner** n
Slipeinlage f

paper ['peɪpə*] n Papier nt;
(newspaper) Zeitung f; (exam)
Klausur f; (for reading at conference)
Referat nt; **~s** pl (identity papers)
Papiere pl; **~ bag** Papiertüte f;
~ cup Pappbecher m ▷ vt (wall)
tapezieren; **paperback** n
Taschenbuch nt; **paper clip** n
Büroklammer f; **paper feed** n (of
printer) Papiereinzug m; **paper
round** n: **to do a ~** Zeitungen
austragen; **paperwork** n
Schreibarbeit f

parachute ['pærəʃuːt] n Fallschirm m ▷ vi abspringen

paracetamol [pærə'siːtəmɒl] n
(tablet) Paracetamoltablette
f

parade [pə'reɪd] n (procession)

Umzug m; (Mil) Parade f ▷ vi
vorbeimarschieren

paradise ['pærədaɪs] n Paradies
nt

paragliding ['pærəglaɪdɪŋ] n
Gleitschirmfliegen nt

paragraph ['pærəgrɑːf] n Absatz
m

parallel ['pærəlel] adj parallel
▷ n (Math, fig) Parallele f

paralyze ['pærəlaɪz] vt lähmen;
(fig) lahmlegen

paranoid ['pærənɔɪd] adj
paranoid

paraphrase ['pærəfreɪz] vt
umschreiben; (sth spoken) anders
ausdrücken

parasailing ['pærəseɪlɪŋ] n
Parasailing nt

parasol ['pærəsɒl] n Sonnenschirm m

parcel ['pɑːsl] n Paket nt

pardon ['pɑːdn] n (Jur)
Begnadigung f; **~ me/I beg your
~** verzeih/verzeihen Sie bitte;
(objection) aber ich bitte dich/Sie; **I
beg your ~?/~ me?** wie bitte?

parent ['peərənt] n Elternteil m;
~s pl Eltern pl; **~s-in-law** pl
Schwiegereltern pl; **parental**
[pə'rentl] adj elterlich, Eltern-

parish ['pærɪʃ] n Gemeinde f

park [pɑːk] n Park m ▷ vt, vi
parken; **parking** n Parken nt; **"no
~"** „Parken verboten"; **parking
brake** n (US) Handbremse f;
parking disc n Parkscheibe f;
parking fine n Geldbuße f für
falsches Parken; **parking lights**
npl (US) Standlicht nt; **parking lot**
n (US) Parkplatz m; **parking meter**
n Parkuhr f; **parking place**,
parking space n Parkplatz m;
parking ticket n Strafzettel m

parliament ['pɑːləmənt] n Parlament nt

parrot ['pærət] n Papagei m

parsley ['pɑːslɪ] n Petersilie f

parsnip ['pɑːsnɪp] n Pastinake f (längliches, weißes Wurzelgemüse)

part [pɑːt] n Teil m; (of machine) Teil nt; (Theat) Rolle f; (US: in hair) Scheitel m; **to take ~** teilnehmen (in an +dat); **for the most ~** zum größten Teil ▷ adj Teil- ▷ vt (separate) trennen; (hair) scheiteln ▷ vi (people) sich trennen

partial ['pɑːʃəl] adj (incomplete) teilweise, Teil-

participant [pɑːˈtɪsɪpənt] n Teilnehmer(in) m(f); **participate** [pɑːˈtɪsɪpeɪt] vi teilnehmen (in an +dat)

particular [pəˈtɪkjʊlə*] adj (specific) bestimmt; (exact) genau; (fussy) eigen; **in ~** insbesondere ▷ n **~s** pl (details) Einzelheiten pl; (about person) Personalien pl; **particularly** adv besonders

parting ['pɑːtɪŋ] n (farewell) Abschied m; (Brit: in hair) Scheitel m

partly ['pɑːtlɪ] adv teilweise

partner ['pɑːtnə*] n Partner(in) m(f); **partnership** n Partnerschaft f

partridge ['pɑːtrɪdʒ] n Rebhuhn nt

part-time ['pɑːtˈtaɪm] adj Teilzeit- ▷ adv: **to work ~** Teilzeit arbeiten

party ['pɑːtɪ] n (celebration) Party f; (Pol, Jur) Partei f; (group) Gruppe f ▷ vi feiern

pass [pɑːs] vt (on foot) vorbeigehen an +dat; (in car etc) vorbeifahren an +dat; (time) verbringen; (exam) bestehen; (law) verabschieden; **to ~ sth to sb, to ~ sb sth** jdm etw reichen; **to ~ the ball to sb** jdm den Ball zuspielen ▷ vi (on foot) vorbeigehen; (in car etc) vorbeifahren; (years) vergehen; (in exam) bestehen ▷ n (document) Ausweis m; (Sport) Pass m; **pass**

away vi (die) verscheiden; **pass by** vi (on foot) vorbeigehen; (in car etc) vorbeifahren ▷ vt (on foot) vorbeigehen an +dat; (in car etc) vorbeifahren an +dat; **pass on** vt weitergeben (to auf +akk); (disease) übertragen (to auf +akk); **pass out** vi (faint) ohnmächtig werden; **pass round** vt herumreichen

passage ['pæsɪdʒ] n (corridor) Gang m; (in book, music) Passage f; **passageway** n Durchgang m

passenger ['pæsɪndʒə*] n Passagier(in) m(f); (on bus) Fahrgast m; (on train) Reisende(r) mf; (in car) Mitfahrer(in) m(f)

passer-by ['pɑːsəˈbaɪ] (pl **passers-by**) n Passant(in) m(f)

passion ['pæʃən] n Leidenschaft f; **passionate** ['pæʃənɪt] adj leidenschaftlich; **passion fruit** n Passionsfrucht

passive ['pæsɪv] adj passiv; **~ smoking** Passivrauchen nt ▷ n: **~ (voice)** (Ling) Passiv nt

passport ['pɑːspɔːt] n (Reise)-pass m; **passport control** n Passkontrolle f

password ['pɑːswɜːd] n (Inform) Passwort nt

past [pɑːst] n Vergangenheit f ▷ adv (by) vorbei; **it's five ~** es ist fünf nach ▷ adj (years) vergangen; (president etc) ehemalig; **in the ~ two months** in den letzten zwei Monaten ▷ prep (telling time) nach; **half ~ 10** halb 11; **to go ~ sth** an etw dat vorbei-/-fahren

pasta ['pæstə] n Nudeln pl

paste [peɪst] vt (stick) kleben; (Inform) einfügen ▷ n (glue) Kleister m

pastime ['pɑːstaɪm] n Zeitvertreib m

pastry ['peɪstrɪ] n Teig m; (cake) Stückchen

pasty ['pæstɪ] n (Brit) Pastete f

patch [pætʃ] n (area) Fleck m; (for mending) Flicken ▷ vt flicken; **patchy** adj (uneven) ungleichmäßig

pâté ['pæteɪ] n Pastete f

paternal [pə'tɜ:nl] adj väterlich; **~ grandmother** Großmutter f väterlicherseits; **paternity leave** [pə'tɜ:nɪtɪli:v] n Elternzeit f (des Vaters)

path [pɑ:θ] n (a. Inform) Pfad m; (a. fig) Weg m

pathetic [pə'θetɪk] adj (bad) kläglich, erbärmlich; **it's ~** es ist zum Heulen

patience ['peɪʃəns] n Geduld f; (Brit Cards) Patience f; **patient** adj geduldig ▷ n Patient(in) m(f)

patio ['pætɪəʊ] n Terrasse f

patriotic [pætrɪ'ɒtɪk] adj patriotisch

patrol car [pə'trəʊlkɑ:*] n Streifenwagen m; **patrolman** (pl **-men**) n (US) Streifenpolizist m

patron ['peɪtrən] n (sponsor) Förderer m, Förderin f; (in shop) Kunde m, Kundin f

patronize ['pætrənaɪz] vt (treat condescendingly) von oben herab behandeln; **patronizing** adj (attitude) herablassend

pattern ['pætən] n Muster nt

pause [pɔ:z] n Pause f ▷ vi (speaker) innehalten

pavement n (Brit) Bürgersteig m; (US) Pflaster nt

pay [peɪ] (**paid, paid**) vt bezahlen; **he paid (me) £20 for it** er hat (mir) 20 Pfund dafür gezahlt; **to ~ attention** Acht geben (to auf +akk); **to ~ sb a visit** jdn besuchen ▷ vi zahlen; (be profitable) sich bezahlt machen; **to ~ for sth** etw bezahlen ▷ n Bezahlung f, Lohn m; **pay back** vt (money) zurückzahlen; **pay in** vt (into account) einzahlen; **payable** adj zahlbar; (due) fällig; **payday** n Zahltag m; **payee** [peɪ'i:] n Zahlungsempfänger(in) m(f); **payment** n Bezahlung f; (money) Zahlung f; **pay-per-view** adj Pay-per-View-; **pay phone** n Münzfernsprecher m; **pay TV** n Pay-TV nt

PC abbr = **personal computer** PC m; abbr = **politically correct** politisch korrekt

PDA abbr = **personal digital assistant** PDA m

PE abbr = **physical education** (school) Sport m

pea [pi:] n Erbse f

peace [pi:s] n Frieden m; **peaceful** adj friedlich

peach [pi:tʃ] n Pfirsich m

peacock ['pi:kɒk] n Pfau m

peak [pi:k] n (of mountain) Gipfel m; (fig) Höhepunkt m; **peak period** n Stoßzeit f; (season) Hochsaison

peanut ['pi:nʌt] n Erdnuss f; **peanut butter** n Erdnussbutter f

pear [peə*] n Birne f

pearl [pɜ:l] n Perle f

pebble ['pebl] n Kiesel m

pecan [pɪ'kæn] n Pekannuss f

peck [pek] vt, vi picken; **peckish** adj (Brit fam) ein bisschen hungrig

peculiar [pɪ'kju:lɪə*] adj (odd) seltsam; **~ to** charakteristisch für; **peculiarity** [pɪkjʊlɪ'ærɪtɪ] n (singular quality) Besonderheit f; (strangeness) Eigenartigkeit f

pedal ['pedl] n Pedal nt

pedestrian [pɪ'destrɪən] n Fußgänger(in) m(f); **pedestrian crossing** n Fußgängerüberweg m

pee [pi:] vi (fam) pinkeln

peel [pi:l] n Schale f ▷ vt schälen ▷ vi (paint etc) abblättern; (skin etc) sich schälen

peer [pɪə*] n Gleichaltrige(r) mf ▷ vi starren

peg [peg] n (for coat etc) Haken m; (for tent) Hering m; (**clothes**) ~ (Wäsche)klammer f

pelvis ['pelvɪs] n Becken nt

pen [pen] n (ball-point) Kuli m, Kugelschreiber; (fountain ~) Füller m

penalize ['pi:nəlaɪz] vt (punish) bestrafen; **penalty** ['penltɪ] n (punishment) Strafe f; (in football) Elfmeter m

pence [pens] pl of **penny**

pencil ['pensl] n Bleistift m; **pencil sharpener** n (Bleistift)spitzer m

penetrate ['penɪtreɪt] vt durchdringen; (enter into) eindringen in +akk

penfriend ['penfrend] n Brieffreund(in) m(f)

penguin ['peŋgwɪn] n Pinguin m

penicillin [penɪ'sɪlɪn] n Penizillin nt

peninsula [pɪ'nɪnsjʊlə] n Halbinsel f

penis ['pi:nɪs] n Penis m

penknife ['pennaɪf] (pl **penknives**) n Taschenmesser nt

penny ['penɪ] n (pl **pence** o **pennies**) (Brit) Penny m; (US) Centstück nt

pension ['penʃən] n Rente f; (for civil servants, executives etc) Pension f; **pensioner** n Rentner(in) m(f); **pension plan**, **pension scheme** n Rentenversicherung f

penultimate [pɪ'nʌltɪmət] adj vorletzte(r, s)

people ['pi:pl] npl (persons) Leute pl; (von Staat) Volk nt; (inhabitants) Bevölkerung f; **people carrier** n Minivan m

pepper ['pepə*] n Pfeffer m; (vegetable) Paprika m; **peppermint** n (sweet) Pfefferminz nt

per [pɜ:*] prep pro; ~ **annum** pro Jahr; ~ **cent** Prozent nt

percentage [pə'sentɪdʒ] n Prozentsatz m

perceptible [pə'septəbl] adj wahrnehmbar

percolator ['pɜ:kəleɪtə*] n Kaffeemaschine f

percussion [pɜ:'kʌʃən] n (Mus) Schlagzeug nt

perfect ['pɜ:fɪkt] adj perfekt; (utter) völlig ▷ [pə'fekt] vt vervollkommnen; **perfectly** adv perfekt; (utterly) völlig

perform [pə'fɔ:m] vt (task) ausführen; (play) aufführen; (Med: operation) durchführen ▷ vi (Theat) auftreten; **performance** n (show) Vorstellung f; (efficiency) Leistung f

perfume ['pɜ:fju:m] n Duft m; (substance) Parfüm nt

perhaps [pə'hæps] adv vielleicht

period ['pɪərɪəd] n (length of time) Zeit f; (in history) Zeitalter nt; (school) Stunde f; (Med) Periode f; (US: full stop) Punkt m; **for a ~ of three years** für einen Zeitraum von drei Jahren; **periodical** [pɪərɪ'ɒdɪkəl] n Zeitschrift f

peripheral [pə'rɪfərəl] n (Inform) Peripheriegerät nt

perjury ['pɜ:dʒərɪ] n Meineid m

perm [pɜ:m] n Dauerwelle f

permanent, **permanently** ['pɜ:mənənt, -lɪ] adj, adv ständig

permission [pə'mɪʃən] n Erlaubnis f; **permit** ['pɜ:mɪt] n Genehmigung f ▷ [pə'mɪt] vt erlauben, zulassen; **to ~ sb to do sth** jdm erlauben, etw zu tun

persecute ['pɜ:sɪkju:t] vt verfolgen

perseverance [pɜ:sɪ'vɪərəns] n Ausdauer f

persist [pə'sɪst] vi (in belief etc) bleiben (in bei); (rain, smell) andauern; **persistent** adj beharrlich

person ['pɜːsn] n Mensch m; (in
official context) Person f; **in ~**
persönlich; **personal** adj
persönlich; (private) privat;
personality [pɜːsə'nælətɪ] n
Persönlichkeit f; **personal
organizer** n Organizer m;
personal stereo (pl **-s**) n
Walkman® m; **personnel**
[pɜːsə'nel] n Personal nt
perspective [pə'spektɪv] n
Perspektive f
persuade [pə'sweɪd] vt überreden; (convince) überzeugen;
persuasive [pə'sweɪsɪv] adj
überzeugend
perverse [pə'vɜːs] adj
eigensinnig; abwegig; **pervert**
['pɜːvɜːt] n Perverse(r) mf
▷ [pə'vɜːt] vt (morally) verderben;
perverted [pə'vɜːtɪd] adj pervers
pessimist ['pesɪmɪst] n Pes-
simist(in) m(f); **pessimistic**
[pesɪ'mɪstɪk] adj pessimistisch
pest [pest] n (insect) Schädling m;
(fig: person) Nervensäge f; (thing)
Plage f; **pester** ['pestə°] vt
plagen; **pesticide** ['pestɪsaɪd] n
Schädlingsbekämpfungsmittel nt
pet [pet] n (animal) Haustier nt;
(person) Liebling m
petal ['petl] n Blütenblatt nt
petition [pə'tɪʃən] n Petition f
petrol ['petrəl] n (Brit) Benzin nt;
petrol pump n (at garage)
Zapfsäule f; **petrol station** n
Tankstelle f; **petrol tank** n
Benzintank m
pharmacy ['fɑːməsɪ] n (shop)
Apotheke f; (science) Pharmazie f
phase [feɪz] n Phase f
PhD abbr = **Doctor of Philosophy**
Dr. phil; (dissertation) Doktorarbeit
f; **to do one's ~** promovieren
pheasant ['feznt] n Fasan m
phenomenon [fɪ'nɒmɪnən] (pl
phenomena) n Phänomen nt

Philippines ['fɪlɪpiːnz] npl
Philippinen pl
philosophical [fɪlə'sɒfɪkəl] adj
philosophisch; (fig) gelassen;
philosophy [fɪ'lɒsəfɪ] n Philosophie f
phone [fəʊn] n Telefon nt ▷ vt, vi
anrufen; **phone book** n
Telefonbuch nt; **phone bill** n
Telefonrechnung f; **phone booth**,
phone box (Brit) n Telefonzelle f;
phonecall n Telefonanruf m;
phonecard n Telefonkarte f;
phone-in n Rundfunkprogramm, bei
dem Hörer anrufen können; **phone
number** n Telefonnummer f
photo ['fəʊtəʊ] (pl **-s**) n Foto nt;
photo booth n Fotoautomat m;
photocopier ['fəʊtəʊˈkɒpɪə°] n
Kopiergerät nt; **photocopy**
['fəʊtəʊkɒpɪ] n Fotokopie f ▷ vt
fotokopieren; **photograph**
['fəʊtəgrɑːf] n Fotografie f,
Aufnahme f ▷ vt fotografieren;
photographer [fə'tɒgrəfə°] n
Fotograf(in) m(f); **photography**
[fə'tɒgrəfɪ] n Fotografie f
phrase [freɪz] n (expression)
Redewendung f, Ausdruck m;
phrase book n Sprachführer m
physical ['fɪzɪkəl] adj (bodily)
körperlich, physisch ▷ n ärztliche
Untersuchung; **physically** adv
(bodily) körperlich, physisch;
~ handicapped körperbehindert
physics ['fɪzɪks] nsing Physik f
physiotherapy [fɪzɪə'θerəpɪ] n
Physiotherapie f
physique [fɪ'ziːk] n Körperbau m
piano ['pjɑːnəʊ] (pl **-s**) n Klavier
nt
pick [pɪk] vt (flowers, fruit)
pflücken; (choose) auswählen;
(team) aufstellen; **pick out** vt
auswählen; **pick up** vt (lift up)
aufheben; (collect) abholen; (learn)
lernen

pickle ['pɪkl] n (food) (Mixed) Pickles pl ▷ vt einlegen

pickpocket ['pɪkpɒkɪt] n Taschendieb(in) m(f)

picnic ['pɪknɪk] n Picknick nt

picture ['pɪktʃə°] n Bild nt; **to go to the ~s** (Brit) ins Kino gehen ▷ vt (visualize) sich vorstellen; **picture book** n Bilderbuch nt; **picturesque** [pɪktʃə'resk] adj malerisch

pie [paɪ] n (meat) Pastete f; (fruit) Kuchen m

piece [piːs] n Stück nt; (part) Teil nt; (in chess) Figur f; (in draughts) Stein m; **a ~ of cake** ein Stück Kuchen; **to fall to ~s** auseinanderfallen

pier [pɪə°] n Pier m

pierce [pɪəs] vt durchstechen, durchbohren; (cold, sound) durchdringen; **pierced** adj (part of body) gepierct; **piercing** adj durchdringend

pig [pɪg] n Schwein nt

pigeon ['pɪdʒən] n Taube f; **pigeonhole** n (compartment) Ablegefach nt

piggy ['pɪgɪ] adj (fam) verfressen; **pigheaded** ['pɪg'hedɪd] adj dickköpfig; **piglet** ['pɪglət] n Ferkel nt; **pigsty** ['pɪgstaɪ] n Schweinestall m; **pigtail** ['pɪgteɪl] n Zopf m

pile [paɪl] n (heap) Haufen m; (one on top of another) Stapel m; **pile up** vi (accumulate) sich anhäufen

piles [paɪlz] npl Hämorr(ho)iden pl

pile-up ['paɪlʌp] n (Auto) Massenkarambolage f

pilgrim ['pɪlgrɪm] n Pilger(in) m(f)

pill [pɪl] n Tablette f; **the ~** die (Antibaby)pille; **to be on the ~** die Pille nehmen

pillar ['pɪlə°] n Pfeiler m

pillow ['pɪləʊ] n (Kopf)kissen nt; **pillowcase** n (Kopf)kissenbezug m

pilot ['paɪlət] n (Aviat) Pilot(in) m(f)

pimple ['pɪmpl] n Pickel m

pin [pɪn] n (for fixing) Nadel f; (in sewing) Stecknadel f; (Tech) Stift m; **I've got ~s and needles in my leg** mein Bein ist mir eingeschlafen ▷ vt (fix with ~) heften (to an +akk)

PIN [pɪn] acr = **personal identification number ~ (number)** PIN f, Geheimzahl f

pinch [pɪntʃ] n (of salt) Prise f ▷ vt zwicken; (fam: steal) klauen ▷ vi (shoe) drücken

pine [paɪn] n Kiefer f

pineapple ['paɪnæpl] n Ananas f

pink [pɪŋk] adj rosa

pinstripe(d) ['pɪnstraɪp(t)] adj Nadelstreifen-

pint [paɪnt] n Pint nt (Brit: 0,57 l, US: 0,473l); (Brit: glass of beer) Bier nt

pious ['paɪəs] adj fromm

pip [pɪp] n (of fruit) Kern m

pipe [paɪp] n (for smoking) Pfeife f; (for water, gas) Rohrleitung f

pirate ['paɪərɪt] n Pirat(in) m(f); **pirated copy** n Raubkopie f

Pisces ['paɪsiːz] nsing (Astr) Fische pl; **she's a ~** sie ist Fisch

piss [pɪs] vi (vulg) pissen ▷ n (vulg) Pisse f; **to take the ~ out of sb** jdn verarschen; **piss off** vi (vulg) sich verpissen; **~!** verpiss dich!; **pissed** adj (Brit fam: drunk) sturzbesoffen; (US fam: annoyed) stocksauer

pistachio [pɪ'staːʃɪəʊ] (pl -s) n Pistazie f

piste [piːst] n (Ski) Piste f

pistol ['pɪstl] n Pistole f

pit [pɪt] n (hole) Grube f; (coalmine) Zeche f; **the ~s** (motor racing) die Box; **to be the ~s** (fam) grottenschlecht sein

pitch [pɪtʃ] n (Sport) Spielfeld nt; (Mus: of instrument) Tonlage f; (of voice) Stimmlage f ▷ vt (tent)

aufschlagen; (*throw*) werfen;
pitch-black *adj* pechschwarz
pitcher ['pɪtʃə*] *n* (*US: jug*) Krug *m*
pitiful ['pɪtɪfʊl] *adj* (*contemptible*)
jämmerlich
pitta bread ['pɪtə] *n* Pittabrot *nt*
pity ['pɪtɪ] *n* Mitleid *nt*; **what a
~** wie schade; **it's a ~** es ist schade
▷ *vt* Mitleid haben mit
pizza ['piːtsə] *n* Pizza *f*
place [pleɪs] *n* (*spot, in text*)
Stelle *f*; (*town etc*) Ort; (*house*) Haus
nt; (*position, seat, on course*) Platz *m*;
~ of birth Geburtsort *m*; **at my
~** bei mir; **in third ~** auf dem dritten
Platz; **to three decimal ~s** bis auf
drei Stellen nach dem Komma; **out
of ~** nicht an der richtigen Stelle;
(*fig: remark*) unangebracht; **in ~ of**
anstelle von; **in the first ~** (*firstly*)
erstens; (*immediately*) gleich; (*in any
case*) überhaupt ▷ *vt* (*put*) stellen,
setzen; (*lay flat*) legen; (*advertisement*) setzen (*in* in +*akk*); (*Comm:
order*) aufgeben; **place mat** *n* Set *nt*
plague [pleɪg] *n* Pest *f*
plaice [pleɪs] *n* Scholle *f*
plain [pleɪn] *adj* (*clear*) klar,
deutlich; (*simple*) einfach; (*not
beautiful*) unattraktiv; (*yoghurt*)
Natur-; (*Brit: chocolate*)
(Zart)bitter- ▷ *n* Ebene *f*; **plainly**
adv (*frankly*) offen; (*simply*) einfach;
(*obviously*) eindeutig
plait [plæt] *n* Zopf *m* ▷ *vt*
flechten
plan [plæn] *n* Plan *m*; (*for essay
etc*) Konzept *nt* ▷ *vt* planen; **to
~ to do sth, to ~ on doing sth**
vorhaben, etw zu tun ▷ *vi* planen
plane [pleɪn] *n* (*aircraft*)
Flugzeug *nt*; (*tool*) Hobel *m*
planet ['plænɪt] *n* Planet *m*
plank [plæŋk] *n* Brett *nt*
plant [plɑːnt] *n* Pflanze *f*;
(*equipment*) Maschinen *pl*; (*factory*)
Werk *nt* ▷ *vt* (*tree etc*) pflanzen;

plantation [plæn'teɪʃən] *n* Plan-
tage *f*
plaque [plæk] *n* Gedenktafel *f*;
(*on teeth*) Zahnbelag *m*
plaster ['plɑːstə*] *n* (*Brit Med:
sticking ~*) Pflaster *nt*; (*on wall*)
Verputz *m*; **to have one's arm in
~** den Arm in Gips haben
plastered ['plɑːstəd] *adj* (*fam*)
besoffen; **to get (absolutely)
~** sich besaufen
plastic ['plæstɪk] *n* Kunststoff *m*;
to pay with ~ mit Kreditkarte
bezahlen ▷ *adj* Plastik-; **plastic
bag** *n* Plastiktüte *f*; **plastic
surgery** *n* plastische Chirurgie *f*
plate [pleɪt] *n* (*for food*) Teller *m*;
(*flat sheet*) Platte *f*; (*plaque*) Schild
nt
platform ['plætfɔːm] *n* (*Rail*)
Bahnsteig *m*; (*at meeting*) Podium
nt
platinum ['plætɪnəm] *n* Platin *nt*
play [pleɪ] *n* Spiel *nt*; (*Theat*)
(Theater)stück *nt* ▷ *vt* spielen;
(*another player or team*) spielen
gegen; **to ~ the piano** Klavier
spielen; **to ~ a part in** (*fig*) eine
Rolle spielen bei ▷ *vi* spielen;
play at: *vt*: **what are you ~ing at?**
was soll das?; **play back** *vt*
abspielen; **play down** *vt*
herunterspielen
playacting *n* Schauspielerei *f*;
playback *n* Wiedergabe *f*; **player**
n Spieler(in) *m(f)*; **playful** *adj*
(*person*) verspielt; (*remark*)
scherzhaft; **playground** *n*
Spielplatz *m*; (*in school*) Schulhof *m*;
playgroup *n* Spielgruppe *f*;
playing card *n* Spielkarte *f*;
playing field *n* Sportplatz *m*;
playmate *n* Spielkamerad(in)
m(f); **playwright** *n*
Dramatiker(in) *m(f)*
plc *abbr* = **public limited company**
AG *f*

plea [pli:] n Bitte f (for um)

plead [pli:d] vi dringend bitten (with sb jdn); (Jur) **to ~ guilty** sich schuldig bekennen

pleasant, pleasantly ['pleznt, -lı] adj, adv angenehm

please [pli:z] adv bitte; **more tea? - yes, ~** noch Tee? - ja, bitte ▷ vt (be agreeable to) gefallen +dat; **~ yourself** wie du willst/Sie wollen; **pleased** adj zufrieden; (glad) erfreut; **~ to meet you** freut mich, angenehm; **pleasing** adj erfreulich; **pleasure** ['pleʒə*] n Vergnügen nt, Freude f; **it's a ~** gern geschehen

pledge [pledʒ] n (promise) Versprechen nt ▷ vt (promise) versprechen

plenty ['plentı] n: **~ of** eine Menge, viel(e); **to be ~** genug sein, reichen; **I've got ~** ich habe mehr als genug ▷ adv (US fam) ganz schön

pliable ['plaıəbl] adj biegsam

pliers ['plaıəz] npl (Kombi)zange f

plimsoll ['plımsəl] n (Brit) Turnschuh m

plonk [plɒŋk] n (Brit fam: wine) billiger Wein ▷ vt: **to ~ sth (down)** etw hinknallen

plot [plɒt] n (of story) Handlung f; (conspiracy) Komplott nt; (of land) Stück nt Land, Grundstück nt ▷ vi ein Komplott schmieden

plough, plow (US) [plaʊ] n Pflug m ▷ vt, vi (Agr) pflügen; **ploughman's lunch** n (Brit) in einer Kneipe serviertes Gericht aus Käse, Brot, Mixed Pickles etc

pluck [plʌk] vt (eyebrows, guitar) zupfen; (chicken) rupfen; **pluck up** vt: **to ~ (one's) courage** Mut aufbringen

plug [plʌg] n (for sink, bath) Stöpsel m; (Elec) Stecker m; (Auto) (Zünd)kerze f; (fam: publicity) Schleichwerbung f ▷ vt (fam: advertise) Reklame machen für; **plug in** vt anschließen

plum [plʌm] n Pflaume f ▷ adj (fam: job etc) Super-

plumber ['plʌmə*] n Klempner(in) m(f); **plumbing** ['plʌmıŋ] n (fittings) Leitungen pl; (craft) Installieren nt

plump [plʌmp] adj rundlich

plunge [plʌndʒ] vt (knife) stoßen; (into water) tauchen ▷ vi stürzen; (into water) tauchen

plural ['plʊərəl] n Plural m

plus [plʌs] prep plus; (as well as) und ▷ adj Plus-; **20 ~** mehr als 20 ▷ n (fig) Plus nt

plywood ['plaıwʊd] n Sperrholz nt

pm abbr = **post meridiem; at 3 ~** um 3 Uhr nachmittags; **at 8 ~** um 8 Uhr abends

pneumonia [njuːˈməʊnıə] n Lungenentzündung f

poached [pəʊtʃt] adj (egg) pochiert, verloren

PO Box abbr = **post office box** Postfach nt

pocket ['pɒkıt] n Tasche f ▷ vt (put in ~) einstecken; **pocketbook** n (US: wallet) Brieftasche f; **pocket calculator** n Taschenrechner m; **pocket money** n Taschengeld nt

poem ['pəʊəm] n Gedicht nt; **poet** ['pəʊıt] n Dichter(in) m(f); **poetic** [pəʊˈetık] adj poetisch; **poetry** ['pəʊıtrı] f (art) Dichtung f; (poems) Gedichte pl

point [pɔınt] n Punkt m; (spot) Stelle f; (sharp tip) Spitze f; (moment) Zeitpunkt m; (purpose) Zweck m; (idea) Argument nt; (decimal) Dezimalstelle f; **~s** pl (Rail) Weiche f; **~ of view** Standpunkt m; **three ~ two** drei Komma zwei; **at some ~** irgendwann (mal); **to get**

to the ~ zur Sache kommen; **there's no ~** es hat keinen Sinn; **I was on the ~ of leaving** ich wollte gerade gehen ▷ vt (gun etc) richten (at auf +akk); **to ~ one's finger at** mit dem Finger zeigen auf +akk ▷ vi (with finger etc) zeigen (at, to auf +akk); **point out** vt (indicate) aufzeigen; (mention) hinweisen auf +akk; **pointed** adj spitz; (question) gezielt; **pointer** n (on dial) Zeiger m; (tip) Hinweis m; **pointless** adj sinnlos

poison ['pɔɪzn] n Gift nt ▷ vt vergiften; **poisonous** adj giftig

poke [pəʊk] vt (with stick, finger) stoßen, stupsen; (put) stecken

Poland ['pəʊlənd] n Polen nt

polar ['pəʊlə*] adj Polar-, polar; **~ bear** Eisbär m

pole [pəʊl] n Stange f; (Geo, Elec) Pol m

Pole [pəʊl] n Pole m, Polin f

pole vault n Stabhochsprung m

police [pə'li:s] n Polizei f; **police car** n Polizeiwagen m; **policeman** (pl **-men**) n Polizist m; **police station** n (Polizei)wache f; **policewoman** (pl **-women**) n Polizistin f

policy ['pɒlɪsɪ] n (plan) Politik f; (principle) Grundsatz m; (insurance ~) (Versicherungs)police f

polio ['pəʊlɪəʊ] n Kinderlähmung f

polish ['pɒlɪʃ] n (for furniture) Politur f; (for floor) Wachs nt; (for shoes) Creme f; (shine) Glanz m; (fig) Schliff m ▷ vt polieren; (shoes) putzen; (fig) den letzten Schliff geben +dat

Polish ['pəʊlɪʃ] adj polnisch ▷ n Polnisch nt

polite [pə'laɪt] adj höflich; **politeness** n Höflichkeit f

political, politically [pə'lɪtɪkəl, -ɪ] adj, adv politisch; **~ly correct** politisch korrekt; **politician**

[pɒlɪ'tɪʃən] n Politiker(in) m(f);
politics ['pɒlɪtɪks] nsing o pl Politik f

poll [pəʊl] n (election) Wahl f; (opinion ~) Umfrage f

pollen ['pɒlən] n Pollen m, Blütenstaub m; **pollen count** n Pollenflug m

polling station ['pəʊlɪŋsteɪʃən] n Wahllokal nt

pollute [pə'lu:t] vt verschmutzen; **pollution** [pə'lu:ʃən] n Verschmutzung f

pompous ['pɒmpəs] adj aufgeblasen; (language) geschwollen

pond [pɒnd] n Teich m

pony ['pəʊnɪ] n Pony nt; **ponytail** n Pferdeschwanz m

poodle ['pu:dl] n Pudel m

pool [pu:l] n (swimming ~) Schwimmbad nt; (private) Schwimmpool m; (of spilt liquid, blood) Lache f; (game) Poolbillard nt ▷ vt (money etc) zusammenlegen

poor [pɔ:*] adj arm; (not good) schlecht ▷ npl: **the ~** die Armen pl; **poorly** adv (badly) schlecht ▷ adj (Brit) krank

pop [pɒp] n (music) Pop m; (noise) Knall m ▷ vt (put) stecken; (balloon) platzen lassen ▷ vi (balloon) platzen; (cork) knallen; **to ~ in** (person) vorbeischauen; **pop concert** n Popkonzert nt; **popcorn** n Popcorn nt

Pope [pəʊp] n Papst m

pop group ['pɒpgru:p] n Popgruppe f; **pop music** n Popmusik f

poppy ['pɒpɪ] n Mohn m

Popsicle® ['pɒpsɪkl] n (US) Eis nt am Stiel

pop star ['pɒpstɑ:*] n Popstar m

popular ['pɒpjʊlə*] adj (well-liked) beliebt (with bei); (widespread) weit verbreitet

population [pɒpjʊ'leɪʃən] *n*
Bevölkerung *f*; (*of town*) Einwohner
pl

porcelain ['pɔːslɪn] *n* Porzellan
nt

porch [pɔːtʃ] *n* Vorbau *m*; (*US: verandah*) Veranda *f*

porcupine ['pɔːkjʊpaɪn] *n*
Stachelschwein *nt*

pork [pɔːk] *n* Schweinefleisch *nt*;
pork chop *n* Schweinekotelett;
pork pie *n* Schweinefleischpastete
f

porn [pɔːn] *n* Porno *m*;
pornographic [pɔːnə'græfɪk] *adj*
pornografisch; **pornography**
[pɔː'nɒgrəfɪ] *n* Pornografie *f*

porridge ['pɒrɪdʒ] *n* Haferbrei *m*

port [pɔːt] *n* (*harbour*) Hafen *m*;
(*town*) Hafenstadt *f*; (*Naut: left side*)
Backbord *nt*; (*wine*) Portwein *m*;
(*Inform*) Anschluss *m*

portable ['pɔːtəbl] *adj* tragbar;
(*radio*) Koffer-

portal ['pɔːtl] *n* (*Inform*) Portal *nt*

porter ['pɔːtə°] *n* Pförtner(in)
m(f); (*for luggage*) Gepäckträger *m*

porthole ['pɔːthəʊl] *n* Bullauge
nt

portion ['pɔːʃən] *n* Teil *m*; (*of food*) Portion *f*

portrait ['pɔːtrɪt] *n* Porträt *nt*

portray [pɔː'treɪ] *vt* darstellen

Portugal ['pɔːtʃʊgl] *n* Portugal
nt; **Portuguese** [pɔːtʃʊ'giːz] *adj*
portugiesisch ▷ *n* Portugiese *m*,
Portugiesin *f*; (*language*)
Portugiesisch *nt*

pose [pəʊz] *n* Haltung *f* ▷ *vi*
posieren ▷ *vt* (*threat, problem*)
darstellen

posh [pɒʃ] *adj* (*fam*) piekfein

position [pə'zɪʃən] *n* Stellung *f*;
(*place*) Position *f*, Lage *f*; (*job*) Stelle
f; (*opinion*) Standpunkt *m*; **to be in
a ~ to do sth** in der Lage sein, etw
zu tun; **in third ~** auf dem dritten

Platz ▷ *vt* aufstellen; (*Inform: cursor*) positionieren

positive ['pɒzɪtɪv] *adj* positiv;
(*convinced*) sicher

possess [pə'zes] *vt* besitzen;
possession [pə'zeʃən] *n* **~(s** *pl*)
Besitz *m*; **possessive** *adj* (*person*)
besitzergreifend

possibility [pɒsə'bɪlɪtɪ] *n*
Möglichkeit *f*; **possible** ['pɒsəbl]
adj möglich; **if ~** wenn möglich; **as
big/soon as ~** so groß/bald wie
möglich; **possibly** *adv* (*perhaps*)
vielleicht; **I've done all I ~ can** ich
habe mein Möglichstes getan

post [pəʊst] *n* (*mail*) Post *f*; (*pole*)
Pfosten *m*; (*job*) Stelle *f* ▷ *vt*
(*letters*) aufgeben; **to keep sb ~ed**
jdn auf dem Laufenden halten;
postage ['pəʊstɪdʒ] *n* Porto *nt*;
~ and packing Porto und
Verpackung; **postal** *adj* Post-;
(*Brit*) **~ order** Postanweisung *f*;
postbox *n* Briefkasten *m*;
postcard *n* Postkarte *f*; **postcode**
n (*Brit*) Postleitzahl *f*

poster ['pəʊstə°] *n* Plakat *nt*,
Poster *nt*

postgraduate [pəʊst'grædjuɪt]
*n jmd, der seine Studien nach dem
ersten akademischen Grad weiterführt*

postman ['pəʊstmən] (*pl* **-men**)
n Briefträger *m*; **postmark** *n*
Poststempel *m*

postmortem [pəʊst'mɔːtəm] *n*
Autopsie *f*

post office ['pəʊstɒfɪs] *n* Post® *f*

postpone [pə'spəʊn] *vt* verschieben (*till auf +akk*)

posture ['pɒstʃə°] *n* Haltung *f*

pot [pɒt] *n* Topf *m*; (*tea~, coffee ~*)
Kanne *f*; (*fam: marijuana*) Pot *nt*
▷ *vt* (*plant*) eintopfen

potato [pə'teɪtəʊ] (*pl* **-es**) *n*
Kartoffel *f*; **potato chips** (*US*) *npl*
Kartoffelchips *pl*; **potato peeler** *n*
Kartoffelschäler *m*

potent ['pəʊtənt] *adj* stark
potential [pəʊ'tenʃəl] *adj* potenziell ▷ *n* Potenzial *nt*; **potentially** *adv* potenziell
pothole ['pɒthəʊl] *n* Höhle *f*; *(in road)* Schlagloch *nt*
potter about ['pɒtərəbaʊt] *vi* herumhantieren
pottery ['pɒtərɪ] *n (objects)* Töpferwaren *pl*
potty ['pɒtɪ] *adj (Brit fam)* verrückt ▷ *n* Töpfchen *nt*
poultry ['pəʊltrɪ] *n* Geflügel *nt*
pounce [paʊns] *vi:* **to ~ on** sich stürzen auf +*akk*
pound [paʊnd] *n (money)* Pfund *nt*; *(weight)* Pfund *nt (0,454 kg)*; **a ~ of cherries** ein Pfund Kirschen; **ten-~ note** Zehnpfundschein *m*
pour [pɔː*] *vt (liquid)* gießen; *(rice, sugar etc)* schütten; **to ~ sb sth** *(drink)* jdm etw eingießen; **pouring** *adj (rain)* strömend
poverty ['pɒvətɪ] *n* Armut *f*
powder ['paʊdə*] *n* Pulver *nt*; *(cosmetic)* Puder *m*; **powdered milk** *n* Milchpulver *nt*; **powder room** *n* Damentoilette *f*
power ['paʊə*] *n* Macht *f*; *(ability)* Fähigkeit *f*; *(strength)* Stärke *f*; *(Elec)* Strom *m*; **to be in ~** an der Macht sein ▷ *vt* betreiben, antreiben; **power-assisted steering** *n* Servolenkung *f*; **power cut** *n* Stromausfall *m*; **powerful** *adj (politician etc)* mächtig; *(engine, government)* stark; *(argument)* durchschlagend; **powerless** *adj* machtlos; **power station** *n* Kraftwerk *nt*
p&p *abbr* = **postage and packing**
PR *abbr* = **public relations** ▷ *abbr* = **proportional representation**
practical, practically ['præktɪkəl,

-ɪ] *adj, adv* praktisch; **practice** ['præktɪs] *n (training)* Übung *f*; *(custom)* Gewohnheit *f*; *(doctor's, lawyer's)* Praxis *f*; **in ~** *(in reality)* in der Praxis; **out of ~** außer Übung; **to put sth into ~** etw in die Praxis umsetzen ▷ *vt, vi (US) see*
practise; practise ['præktɪs] *vt (instrument, movement)* üben; *(profession)* ausüben ▷ *vi* üben; *(doctor, lawyer)* praktizieren
Prague [prɑːg] *n* Prag *nt*
praise [preɪz] *n* Lob *nt* ▷ *vt* loben
pram [præm] *n (Brit)* Kinderwagen *m*
prawn [prɔːn] *n* Garnele *f*, Krabbe *f*; **prawn crackers** *npl* Krabbenchips *pl*
pray [preɪ] *vi* beten; **to ~ for sth** *(fig)* stark auf etw *akk* hoffen; **prayer** ['preə*] *n* Gebet *nt*
pre- [priː] *pref* vor-, prä-
preach [priːtʃ] *vi* predigen
prearrange [priːə'reɪndʒ] *vt* im Voraus vereinbaren
precaution [prɪ'kɔːʃən] *n* Vorsichtsmaßnahme *f*
precede [prɪ'siːd] *vt* vorausgehen +*dat*; **preceding** *adj* vorhergehend
precinct ['priːsɪŋkt] *n (Brit: pedestrian ~)* Fußgängerzone *f*; *(Brit: shopping ~)* Einkaufsviertel *nt*; *(US: district)* Bezirk *m*
precious ['preʃəs] *adj* kostbar; **~ stone** Edelstein *m*
précis ['preɪsiː] *n* Zusammenfassung *f*
precise, precisely [prɪ'saɪs, -lɪ] *adj, adv* genau
precondition [priːkən'dɪʃən] *n* Vorbedingung *f*
predecessor ['priːdɪsesə*] *n* Vorgänger(in) *m(f)*
predicament [prɪ'dɪkəmənt] *n* missliche Lage

predict [prɪ'dɪkt] vt voraussage-n; **predictable** adj vorhersehbar; (person) berechenbar

predominant [prɪ'dɒmɪnənt] adj vorherrschend; **predominantly** adv überwiegend

preface ['prefɪs] n Vorwort nt

prefer [prɪ'fɜ:*] vt vorziehen (to dat), lieber mögen (to als); **to ~ to do sth** etw lieber tun; **preferably** ['prefrəblɪ] adv vorzugsweise, am liebsten; **preference** ['prefərəns] n (liking) Vorliebe f; **preferential** [prefə'renʃəl] adj: **to get ~ treatment** bevorzugt behandelt werden

prefix ['pri:fɪks] n (US Tel) Vorwahl f

pregnancy ['pregnənsɪ] n Schwangerschaft f; **pregnant** ['pregnənt] adj schwanger; **two months ~** im zweiten Monat schwanger

prejudice ['predʒʊdɪs] n Vor-urteil nt; **prejudiced** adj (person) voreingenommen

preliminary [prɪ'lɪmɪnərɪ] adj (measures) vorbereitend; (results) vorläufig; (remarks) einleitend

premature ['premətʃʊə*] adj vorzeitig; (hasty) voreilig

premiere ['premɪɛə*] n Premiere f

premises ['premɪsɪz] npl (offices) Räumlichkeiten pl; (of factory, school) Gelände nt

premium-rate ['pri:mɪəmreɪt] adj (Tel) zum Höchsttarif

preoccupied [pri:'ɒkjʊpaɪd] adj: **to be ~ with sth** mit etw sehr beschäftigt sein

prepaid [pri:'peɪd] adj voraus-bezahlt; (envelope) frankiert

preparation [prepə'reɪʃən] n Vorbereitung f; **prepare** [prɪ'pɛə*] vt vorbereiten (for auf +akk); (food)

zubereiten; **to be ~d to do sth** bereit sein, etw zu tun ▷ vi sich vorbereiten (for auf +akk)

prerequisite [pri:'rekwɪzɪt] n Voraussetzung f

prescribe [prɪ'skraɪb] vt vor-schreiben; (Med) verschreiben; **prescription** [prɪ'skrɪpʃən] n Rezept nt

presence ['prezns] n Gegenwart f; **present** ['preznt] adj (in attendance) anwesend (at bei); (current) gegenwärtig; **~ tense** Gegenwart f, Präsens nt ▷ n Gegenwart f; (gift) Geschenk nt; **at ~** zurzeit ▷ [prɪ'zent] vt (TV, Radio) präsentieren; (problem) darstellen; (report etc) vorlegen; **to ~ sb with sth** jdm etw überreichen; **present-day** adj heutig; **presently** adv bald; (at present) zurzeit

preservative [prɪ'zɜ:vətɪv] n Konservierungsmittel nt; **preserve** [prɪ'zɜ:v] vt erhalten; (food) einmachen, konservieren

president ['prezɪdənt] n Präsi-dent(in) m(f); **presidential** [prezɪ'denʃəl] adj Präsidenten-; (election) Präsidentschafts-

press [pres] n (newspapers, machine) Presse f ▷ vt (push) drücken; **to ~ a button** auf einen Knopf drücken ▷ vi (push) drücken; **pressing** adj dringend; **press-stud** n Druckknopf m; **press-up** n (Brit) Liegestütz m; **pressure** ['preʃə*] n Druck m; **to be under ~** unter Druck stehen; **to put ~ on sb** jdn unter Druck setzen; **pressure cooker** n Schnellkochtopf m; **pressurize** ['preʃəraɪz] vt (person) unter Druck setzen

presumably [prɪ'zju:məblɪ] adv vermutlich; **presume** [prɪ'zju:m] vt, vi annehmen

presumptuous [prɪˈzʌmptʃʊəs] adj anmaßend

presuppose [priːsəˈpəʊz] vt voraussetzen

pretend [prɪˈtend] vt: **to ~ that** so tun als ob; **to ~ to do sth** vorgeben, etw zu tun ▷ vi: **she's ~ing** sie tut nur so

pretentious [prɪˈtenʃəs] adj anmaßend; (person) wichtigtuerisch

pretty [ˈprɪtɪ] adj hübsch ▷ adv ziemlich

prevent [prɪˈvent] vt verhindern; **to ~ sb from doing sth** jdn daran hindern, etw zu tun

preview [ˈpriːvjuː] n (Cine) Voraufführung f; (trailer) Vorschau f

previous, previously [ˈpriːvɪəs, -lɪ] adj, adv früher

prey [preɪ] n Beute f

price [praɪs] n Preis m ▷ vt: **it's ~d at £10** es ist mit 10 Pfund ausgezeichnet; **priceless** adj unbezahlbar; **price list** n Preisliste f; **price tag** n Preisschild nt

prick [prɪk] n Stich m; (vulg: penis) Schwanz m; (vulg: person) Arsch m ▷ vt stechen in +akk; **to ~ one's finger** sich dat in den Finger stechen; **prickly** [ˈprɪklɪ] adj stachelig

pride [praɪd] n Stolz m; (arrogance) Hochmut m ▷ vt: **to ~ oneself on sth** auf etw akk stolz sein

priest [priːst] n Priester m

primarily [ˈpraɪmərɪlɪ] adv vorwiegend; **primary** [ˈpraɪmərɪ] adj Haupt-; **~ education** Grundschulausbildung f; **~ school** Grundschule f

prime [praɪm] adj Haupt-; (excellent) erstklassig ▷ n: **in one's ~** in den besten Jahren; **prime minister** n Premierminister(in) m(f); **prime time** n (TV) Hauptsendezeit f

primitive [ˈprɪmɪtɪv] adj primitiv

primrose [ˈprɪmrəʊz] n Schlüsselblume f

prince [prɪns] n Prinz m; (ruler) Fürst m; **princess** [prɪnˈses] n Prinzessin f; Fürstin f

principal [ˈprɪnsɪpəl] adj Haupt-, wichtigste(r, s) ▷ n (school) Rektor(in) m(f)

principle [ˈprɪnsəpl] n Prinzip nt; **in ~** im Prinzip; **on ~** aus Prinzip

print [prɪnt] n (picture) Druck m; (Foto) Abzug m; (made by feet, fingers) Abdruck m; **out of ~** vergriffen ▷ vt drucken; (photo) abziehen; (write in block letters) in Druckschrift schreiben; **print out** vt (Inform) ausdrucken; **printed matter** n Drucksache f; **printer** n Drucker m; **printout** n (Inform) Ausdruck m

prior [ˈpraɪə⁎] adj früher; **a ~ engagement** eine vorher getroffene Verabredung; **~ to sth** vor etw dat; **~ to going abroad, she had ...** bevor sie ins Ausland ging, hatte sie ...

priority [praɪˈɒrɪtɪ] n (thing having precedence) Priorität f

prison [ˈprɪzn] n Gefängnis nt; **prisoner** n Gefangene(r) mf; **~ of war** Kriegsgefangene(r) mf

privacy [ˈprɪvəsɪ] n Privatleben nt; **private** [ˈpraɪvɪt] adj privat; (confidential) vertraulich ▷ n einfacher Soldat; **in ~** privat; **privately** adv privat; (confidentially) vertraulich; **privatize** [ˈpraɪvətaɪz] vt privatisieren

privilege [ˈprɪvɪlɪdʒ] n Privileg nt; **privileged** adj privilegiert

prize [praɪz] n Preis m; **prize money** n Preisgeld nt; **prizewinner** n Gewinner(in) m(f); **prizewinning** adj preisgekrönt

pro [prəʊ] (*pl* **-s**) *n* (*professional*) Profi *m*; **the ~s and cons** *pl* das Für und Wider

pro- [prəʊ] *pref* pro-

probability [prɒbə'bɪlətɪ] *n* Wahrscheinlichkeit *f*; **probable**, **probably** ['prɒbəbl, -blɪ] *adj*, *adv* wahrscheinlich

probation [prə'beɪʃən] *n* Probezeit *f*; (*Jur*) Bewährung *f*

probe [prəʊb] *n* (*investigation*) Untersuchung *f* ▷ *vt* untersuchen

problem ['prɒbləm] *n* Problem *nt*; **no ~** kein Problem!

procedure [prə'siːdʒə*] *n* Verfahren *nt*

proceed [prə'siːd] *vi* (*continue*) fortfahren; (*set about sth*) vorgehen ▷ *vt*: **to ~ to do sth** anfangen, etw zu tun; **proceedings** *npl* (*Jur*) Verfahren *nt*; **proceeds** ['prəʊsiːdz] *npl* Erlös *m*

process ['prəʊses] *n* Prozess *m*, Vorgang *m*; (*method*) Verfahren *nt* ▷ *vt* (*application etc*) bearbeiten; (*food, data*) verarbeiten; (*film*) entwickeln

procession [prə'seʃən] *n* Umzug *m*

processor ['prəʊsesə*] *n* (*Inform*) Prozessor *m*; (*Gastr*) Küchenmaschine *f*

produce ['prɒdjuːs] *n* (*Agr*) Produkte *pl*, Erzeugnisse *pl* ▷ [prə'djuːs] *vt* (*manufacture*) herstellen, produzieren; (*on farm*) erzeugen; (*film, play, record*) produzieren; (*cause*) hervorrufen; (*evidence, results*) liefern; **producer** *n* (*manufacturer*) Hersteller(in) *m(f)*; (*of film, play, record*) Produzent(in) *m(f)*; **product** ['prɒdʌkt] *n* Produkt *nt*, Erzeugnis *nt*; **production** [prə'dʌkʃən] *n* Produktion *f*; (*Theat*) Inszenierung *f*; **productive** [prə'dʌktɪv] *adj* produktiv; (*land*) ertragreich

prof [prɒf] *n* (*fam*) Prof *m*

profession [prə'feʃən] *n* Beruf *m*; **professional** [prə'feʃənl] *n* Profi *m* ▷ *adj* beruflich; (*expert*) fachlich; (*sportsman, actor etc*) Berufs-

professor [prə'fesə*] *n* Professor(in) *m(f)*; (*US: lecturer*) Dozent(in) *m(f)*

proficient [prə'fɪʃənt] *adj* kompetent (*in* in +*dat*)

profile ['prəʊfaɪl] *n* Profil *nt*; **to keep a low ~** sich rarmachen

profit ['prɒfɪt] *n* Gewinn *m* ▷ *vi* profitieren (*by, from* von); **profitable** *adj* rentabel

profound [prə'faʊnd] *adj* tief; (*idea, thinker*) tiefgründig; (*knowledge*) profund

program ['prəʊgræm] *n* (*Inform*) Programm *nt*; (*US*) *see* **programme** ▷ *vt* (*Inform*) programmieren; (*US*) *see* **programme**

programme ['prəʊgræm] *n* Programm *nt*; (*TV, Radio*) Sendung *f* ▷ *vt* programmieren; **programmer** *n* Programmierer(in) *m(f)*; **programming** *n* (*Inform*) Programmieren *nt*; **~ language** Programmiersprache *f*

progress ['prəʊgres] *n* Fortschritt *m*; **to make ~** Fortschritte machen ▷ [prə'gres] *vi* (*work, illness etc*) fortschreiten; (*improve*) Fortschritte machen; **progressive** [prə'gresɪv] *adj* (*person, policy*) fortschrittlich; **progressively** [prə'gresɪvlɪ] *adv* zunehmend

prohibit [prə'hɪbɪt] *vt* verbieten

project ['prɒdʒekt] *n* Projekt *nt*

projector [prə'dʒektə*] *n* Projektor *m*

prolong [prə'lɒŋ] *vt* verlängern

prom [prɒm] *n* (*at seaside*) Promenade *f*; (*Brit: concert*) Konzert *nt* (*bei dem ein Großteil des Publikums im Parkett Stehplätze hat*); (*US:*

*dance) Ball für die Schüler und
Studenten von Highschools oder
Colleges*

prominent ['prɒmɪnənt] *adj*
(politician, actor etc) prominent;
(easily seen) auffallend

promiscuous [prə'mɪskjʊəs]
adj promisk

promise ['prɒmɪs] *n* Versprechen *nt* ▷ *vt* versprechen; **to
~ sb sth** jdm etw versprechen; **to
~ to do sth** versprechen, etw zu
tun ▷ *vi* versprechen; **promising**
adj vielversprechend

promote [prə'məʊt] *vt (in rank)*
befördern; *(help on)* fördern;
(Comm) werben für; **promotion**
[prə'məʊʃən] *n (in rank)*
Beförderung *f; (Comm)* Werbung *f*
(of für)

prompt [prɒmpt] *adj* prompt;
(punctual) pünktlich ▷ *adv:* **at two
o'clock ~** Punkt zwei Uhr ▷ *vt*
(Theat: actor) soufflieren +*dat*

prone [prəʊn] *adj:* **to be ~ to sth**
zu etw neigen

pronounce [prə'naʊns] *vt*
(word) aussprechen; **pronounced**
adj ausgeprägt; **pronunciation**
[prənʌnsɪ'eɪʃən] *n* Aussprache *f*

proof [pru:f] *n* Beweis *m; (of
alcohol)* Alkoholgehalt *m*

prop [prɒp] *n* Stütze *f; (Theat)*
Requisit *nt* ▷ *vt:* **to ~ sth
against sth** etw gegen etw
lehnen; **prop up** *vt* stützen; *(fig)*
unterstützen

proper ['prɒpə*] *adj* richtig;
(morally correct) anständig

property ['prɒpətɪ] *n (possession)*
Eigentum *nt; (house)* Haus *nt; (land)*
Grundbesitz *m; (characteristic)*
Eigenschaft *f*

proportion [prə'pɔ:ʃən] *n*
Verhältnis *nt; (share)* Teil *m;* **~s** *pl*
(size) Proportionen *pl;* **in ~ to** im
Verhältnis zu; **proportional** *adj*

proportional; **~ representation**
Verhältniswahlrecht *nt*

proposal [prə'pəʊzl] *n* Vorschlag
m; **~ (of marriage)** (Heirats)antrag
m; **propose** [prə'pəʊz] *vt*
vorschlagen ▷ *vi (offer marriage)*
einen Heiratsantrag machen *(to sb*
jdm)

proprietor [prə'praɪətə*] *n*
Besitzer(in) *m(f); (of pub, hotel)*
Inhaber(in) *m(f)*

prose [prəʊz] *n* Prosa *f*

prosecute ['prɒsɪkju:t] *vt* verfolgen *(for* wegen)

prospect ['prɒspekt] *n* Aussicht
f

prosperity [prɒ'sperɪtɪ] *n*
Wohlstand *m;* **prosperous** *adj*
wohlhabend; *(business)* gut
gehend

prostitute ['prɒstɪtju:t] *n* Pros-
tituierte(r) *mf*

protect [prə'tekt] *vt* schützen
(from, against vor +*dat,* gegen);
protection [prə'tekʃən] *n* Schutz
m (from, against vor +*dat,* gegen);
protective *adj* beschützend;
(clothing etc) Schutz-

protein ['prəʊti:n] *n* Protein *nt*

protest ['prəʊtest] *n* Protest *m;*
(demonstration)
Protestkundgebung *f* ▷ [prə'test]
vi protestieren *(against* gegen);
(demonstrate) demonstrieren

Protestant ['prɒtəstənt] *adj*
protestantisch ▷ *n* Protestant(in)
m(f)

proud, **proudly** [praʊd, -lɪ] *adj*,
adv stolz *(of* auf +*akk)*

prove [pru:v] *vt* beweisen; *(turn
out to be)* sich erweisen als

proverb ['prɒvɜ:b] *n* Sprichwort
nt

provide [prə'vaɪd] *vt* zur
Verfügung stellen; *(drinks, music
etc)* sorgen für; *(person)* versorgen
(with mit); **provide for** *vt (family*

etc) sorgen für; **provided** *conj*:
~ (**that**) vorausgesetzt, dass;
provider *n* (*Inform*) Provider *m*
provision [prə'vɪʒən] *n* (*condition*) Bestimmung *f*; **~s** *pl* (*food*)
Proviant *m*
provisional, provisionally
[prə'vɪʒənl, -l] *adj, adv*
provisorisch
provoke [prə'vəʊk] *vt*
provozieren; (*cause*) hervorrufen
proximity [prɒk'sɪmɪtɪ] *n* Nähe *f*
prudent ['pruːdənt] *adj* klug;
(*person*) umsichtig
prudish ['pruːdɪʃ] *adj* prüde
prune [pruːn] *n* Backpflaume *f*
▷ *vt* (*tree etc*) zurechtstutzen
PS *abbr* = **postscript** PS *nt*
psalm [sɑːm] *n* Psalm *m*
pseudo ['sjuːdəʊ] *adj* pseudo-,
Pseudo-; **pseudonym** ['sjuːdə-
nɪm] *n* Pseudonym *nt*
PST *abbr* = **Pacific Standard Time**
psychiatric [saɪkɪ'ætrɪk] *adj*
psychiatrisch; (*illness*) psychisch;
psychiatrist [saɪ'kaɪətrɪst] *n*
Psychiater(in) *m(f)*; **psychiatry**
[saɪ'kaɪətrɪ] *n* Psychiatrie *f*;
psychic ['saɪkɪk] *adj* über-
sinnlich; **I'm not ~** ich kann keine
Gedanken lesen; **psychoanalysis**
[saɪkəʊə'næləsɪs] *n* Psychoanalyse *f*; **psychoanalyst**
[saɪkəʊ'ænəlɪst] *n* Psychoanaly-
tiker(in) *m(f)*; **psychological** [saɪ-
kə'lɒdʒɪkəl] *adj* psychologisch;
psychology [saɪ'kɒlədʒɪ] *n* Psychologie *f*; **psychopath** ['saɪkəʊ-
pæθ] *n* Psychopath(in) *m(f)*
pt *abbr* = **pint**
pto *abbr* = **please turn over** b.w.
pub [pʌb] *n* (*Brit*) Kneipe *f*

  ● **PUB**
  ●
  ● Ein **pub** ist ein Gasthaus mit
  ● einer Lizenz zum Ausschank von

  ● alkoholischen Getränken. Ein
  ● „Pub" besteht meist aus
  ● verschiedenen gemütlichen
  ● (**lounge, snug**) oder
  ● einfacheren (**public bar**)
  ● Räumen, in denen oft auch
  ● Spiele wie Darts, Domino und
  ● Poolbillard zur Verfügung
  ● stehen. In „Pubs" werden vor
  ● allem mittags zum Mahlzeiten
  ● angeboten (**pub lunch**). Die
  ● Sperrstunde wurde 2005
  ● aufgehoben. Dennoch sind
  ● „Pubs" oft nur von 11 bis 23 Uhr
  ● geöffnet. Nachmittags bleiben
  ● sie häufig geschlossen.

puberty ['pjuːbətɪ] *n* Pubertät
f
public ['pʌblɪk] *n*: **the** (**general**)
~ die (breite) Öffentlichkeit; **in**
~ in der Öffentlichkeit ▷ *adj*
öffentlich; (*relating to the State*)
Staats-; **~ convenience** (*Brit*)
öffentliche Toilette; **~ holiday**
gesetzlicher Feiertag; **~ opinion**
die öffentliche Meinung;
~ relations *pl*
Öffentlichkeitsarbeit *f*, Public
Relations *pl*; **~ school** (*Brit*)
Privatschule *f*; **publication**
[pʌblɪ'keɪʃən] *n* Veröffentlichung
f; **publicity** [pʌb'lɪsɪtɪ] *n*
Publicity *f*; (*advertisements*)
Werbung *f*; **publish** ['pʌblɪʃ] *vt*
veröffentlichen; **publisher** *n*
Verleger(in) *m(f)*; (*company*) Verlag
m; **publishing** *n* Verlagswesen *nt*
pub lunch ['pʌb'lʌntʃ] *n* (*oft
einfacheres*) Mittagessen in einer
Kneipe
pudding ['pʊdɪŋ] *n* (*course*)
Nachtisch *m*
puddle ['pʌdl] *n* Pfütze *f*
puff [pʌf] *vi* (*pant*) schnaufen
puffin ['pʌfɪn] *n* Papageien-
taucher *m*

puff paste (US), **puff pastry** ['pʌf'peɪstrɪ] n Blätterteig m
pull [pʊl] n Ziehen nt; **to give sth a ~** an etw dat ziehen ▷ vt (cart, tooth) ziehen; (rope, handle) ziehen an +dat; (fam: date) abschleppen; **to ~ a muscle** sich dat einen Muskel zerren; **to ~ sb's leg** jdn auf den Arm nehmen ▷ vi ziehen; **pull apart** vt (separate) auseinanderziehen; **pull down** vt (blind) herunterziehen; (house) abreißen; **pull in** vi hineinfahren; (stop) anhalten; **pull off** vt (deal etc) zuwege bringen; (clothes) ausziehen; **pull on** vt (clothes) anziehen; **pull out** vi (car from lane) ausscheren; (train) abfahren; (withdraw) aussteigen (of aus) ▷ vt herausziehen; (tooth) ziehen; (troops) abziehen; **pull round, pull through** vi durchkommen; **pull up** vt (raise) hochziehen; (chair) heranziehen ▷ vi anhalten
pullover ['pʊləʊvə*] n Pullover m
pulp [pʌlp] n Brei m; (of fruit) Fruchtfleisch nt
pulpit ['pʊlpɪt] n Kanzel f
pulse [pʌls] n Puls m
pump [pʌmp] n Pumpe f; (in petrol station) Zapfsäule f; **pump up** vt (tyre etc) aufpumpen
pumpkin ['pʌmpkɪn] n Kürbis m
pun [pʌn] n Wortspiel nt
punch [pʌntʃ] n (blow) (Faust)schlag m; (tool) Locher m; (hot drink) Punsch m; (cold drink) Bowle f ▷ vt (strike) schlagen; (ticket, paper) lochen
punctual, punctually ['pʌŋktjʊəl, -ɪ] adj, adv pünktlich
punctuation [pʌŋktjʊ'eɪʃən] n Interpunktion f; **punctuation mark** n Satzzeichen nt
puncture ['pʌŋktʃə*] n (flat tyre) Reifenpanne f

punish ['pʌnɪʃ] vt bestrafen; **punishment** n Strafe f; (action) Bestrafung f
pupil ['pju:pl] n (school) Schüler(in) m(f)
puppet ['pʌpɪt] n Marionette f
puppy ['pʌpɪ] n junger Hund
purchase ['pɜːtʃɪs] n Kauf m ▷ vt kaufen
pure [pjʊə*] adj rein; (clean) sauber; (utter) pur; **purely** ['pjʊəlɪ] adv rein; **purify** ['pjʊərɪfaɪ] vt reinigen; **purity** ['pjʊərɪtɪ] n Reinheit f
purple ['pɜːpl] adj violett
purpose ['pɜːpəs] n Zweck m; (of person) Absicht f; **on ~** absichtlich
purr [pɜː*] vi (cat) schnurren
purse [pɜːs] n Geldbeutel m; (US: handbag) Handtasche f
pursue [pə'sjuː] vt (person, car) verfolgen; (hobby, studies) nachgehen +dat; **pursuit** [pə'sjuːt] n (chase) Verfolgung f; (occupation) Beschäftigung f; (hobby) Hobby nt
pus [pʌs] n Eiter m
push [pʊʃ] n Stoß m ▷ vt (person) stoßen; (car, chair etc) schieben; (button) drücken; (drugs) dealen ▷ vi (in crowd) drängeln; **push in** vi (in queue) sich vordrängeln; **push off** vi (fam: leave) abhauen; **push on** vi (with job) weitermachen; **push up** vt (prices) hochtreiben; **pushchair** n (Brit) Sport(kinder)wagen m; **pusher** n (of drugs) Dealer(in) m(f); **push-up** n (US) Liegestütz m; **pushy** adj (fam) aufdringlich, penetrant
put [pʊt] (**put, put**) vt tun; (upright) stellen; (flat) legen; (express) ausdrücken; (write) schreiben; **he ~ his hand in his pocket** er steckte die Hand in die Tasche; **he ~ his hand on her shoulder** er legte ihr die Hand auf

die Schulter; **to ~ money into one's account** Geld auf sein Konto einzahlen; **put aside** vt (money) zurücklegen; **put away** vt (tidy away) wegräumen; **put back** vt zurücklegen; (clock) zurückstellen; **put down** vt (in writing) aufschreiben; (Brit: animal) einschläfern; (rebellion) niederschlagen; **to put the phone down** (den Hörer) auflegen; **to put one's name down for sth** sich für etw eintragen; **put forward** vt (idea) vorbringen; (name) vorschlagen; (clock) vorstellen; **put in** vt (install) einbauen; (submit) einreichen; **put off** vt (switch off) ausschalten; (postpone) verschieben; **to put sb off doing sth** jdn davon abbringen, etw zu tun; **put on** vt (switch on) anmachen; (clothes) anziehen; (hat, glasses) aufsetzen; (make-up, CD) auflegen; (play) aufführen; **to put the kettle on** Wasser aufsetzen; **to put weight on** zunehmen; **put out** vt (hand, foot) ausstrecken; (light, cigarette) ausmachen; **put up** vt (hand) hochheben; (picture) aufhängen; (tent) aufstellen; (building) errichten; (price) erhöhen; (person) unterbringen; **to ~ with** sich abfinden mit; **I won't ~ with it** das lasse ich mir nicht gefallen

putt [pʌt] vt, vi (Sport) putten
puzzle ['pʌzl] n Rätsel nt; (toy) Geduldsspiel nt; (jigsaw) **~** Puzzle nt ▷ vt vor ein Rätsel stellen; **it ~s me** es ist mir ein Rätsel; **puzzling** adj rätselhaft
pyjamas [pɪ'dʒɑːməz] npl Schlafanzug m
pylon ['paɪlən] n Mast m
pyramid ['pɪrəmɪd] n Pyramide f

q

quack [kwæk] vi quaken
quaint [kweɪnt] adj (idea, tradition) kurios; (picturesque) malerisch
qualification [kwɒlɪfɪ'keɪʃən] n (for job) Qualifikation f; (from school, university) Abschluss m; **qualified** ['kwɒlɪfaɪd] adj (for job) qualifiziert; **qualify** vt (limit) einschränken; **to be qualified to do sth** berechtigt sein, etw zu tun ▷ vi (finish training) seine Ausbildung abschließen; (contest etc) sich qualifizieren
quality ['kwɒlɪtɪ] n Qualität f; (characteristic) Eigenschaft f
quantity ['kwɒntɪtɪ] n Menge f, Quantität f
quarantine ['kwɒrəntiːn] n Quarantäne f
quarrel ['kwɒrəl] n Streit m ▷ vi sich streiten
quarter ['kwɔːtə*] n Viertel nt;

(*of year*) Vierteljahr *nt*; (*US: coin*) Vierteldollar *m*; **a ~ of an hour** eine Viertelstunde; **~ to/past** (*Brit*) (*o ~ of/after* (*US*)) **three** Viertel vor/nach drei ▷ *vt* vierteln; **quarter final** *n* Viertelfinale *nt*; **quarters** *npl* (*Mil*) Quartier *nt*

quartet [kwɔːˈtet] *n* Quartett *nt*

quay [kiː] *n* Kai *m*

queasy [ˈkwiːzɪ] *adj*: **I feel ~** mir ist übel

queen [kwiːn] *n* Königin *f*; (*in cards, chess*) Dame *f*

queer [kwɪəʳ] *adj* (*strange*) seltsam, sonderbar; (*pej: homosexual*) schwul ▷ *n* (*pej*) Schwule(r) *m*

quench [kwentʃ] *vt* (*thirst*) löschen

query [ˈkwɪərɪ] *n* Frage *f* ▷ *vt* infrage stellen; (*bill*) reklamieren

question [ˈkwestʃən] *n* Frage *f*; **that's out of the ~** das kommt nicht infrage ▷ *vt* (*person*) befragen; (*suspect*) verhören; (*express doubt about*) bezweifeln; **questionable** *adj* zweifelhaft; (*improper*) fragwürdig; **question mark** *n* Fragezeichen *nt*; **questionnaire** [kwestʃəˈnɛəʳ] *n* Fragebogen *m*

queue [kjuː] *n* (*Brit*) Schlange *f*; **to jump the ~** sich vordrängeln ▷ *vi*: **to ~ (up)** Schlange stehen

quibble [ˈkwɪbl] *vi* kleinlich sein; (*argue*) streiten

quiche [kiːʃ] *n* Quiche

quick [kwɪk] *adj* schnell; (*short*) kurz; **be ~** mach schnell!; **quickly** *adv* schnell

quid [kwɪd] (*pl* **quid**) *n* (*Brit fam*) Pfund *nt*; **20 ~** 20 Pfund

quiet [ˈkwaɪət] *adj* (*not noisy*) leise; (*peaceful, calm*) still, ruhig; **be ~** sei still!; **to keep ~ about sth** über etw *akk* nichts sagen ▷ *n*

Stille *f*, Ruhe *f*; **quiet down** (*US*), **quieten down** [ˈkwaɪətənˈdaʊn] *vi* sich beruhigen ▷ *vt* beruhigen; **quietly** *adv* leise; (*calmly*) ruhig

quilt [kwɪlt] *n* (Stepp)decke *f*

quit [kwɪt] (**quit** *o* **quitted, quit** *o* **quitted**) *vt* (*leave*) verlassen; (*job*) aufgeben; **to ~ doing sth** aufhören, etw zu tun ▷ *vi* aufhören; (*resign*) kündigen

quite [kwaɪt] *adv* (*fairly*) ziemlich; (*completely*) ganz, völlig; **I don't ~ understand** ich verstehe das nicht ganz; **~ a few** ziemlich viele; **~ so** richtig!

quits [kwɪts] *adj*: **to be ~ with sb** mit jdm quitt sein

quiver [ˈkwɪvəʳ] *vi* zittern

quiz [kwɪz] *n* (*competition*) Quiz *nt*

quota [ˈkwəʊtə] *n* Anteil *m*; (*Comm, Pol*) Quote *f*

quotation [kwəʊˈteɪʃən] *n* Zitat *nt*; (*price*) Kostenvoranschlag *m*; **quotation marks** *npl* Anführungszeichen *pl*; **quote** [kwəʊt] *vt* (*text, author*) zitieren; (*price*) nennen ▷ *n* Zitat *nt*; (*price*) Kostenvoranschlag *m*; **in ~s** in Anführungszeichen

r

rabbi ['ræbaɪ] n Rabbiner m
rabbit ['ræbɪt] n Kaninchen nt
rabies ['reɪbiːz] nsing Tollwut f
raccoon [rə'kuːn] n Waschbär m
race [reɪs] n (competition) Rennen
nt; (people) Rasse f ⊳ vt um die
Wette laufen/fahren ⊳ vi (rush)
rennen; **racecourse** n Rennbahn
f; **racehorse** n Rennpferd nt;
racetrack n Rennbahn f
racial ['reɪʃəl] adj Rassen-;
~ discrimination
Rassendiskriminierung f
racing ['reɪsɪŋ] n: (**horse**)
~ Pferderennen nt; (**motor**)
~ Autorennen nt; **racing car** n
Rennwagen m
racism ['reɪsɪzəm] n Rassismus
m; **racist** n Rassist(in) m(f) ⊳ adj
rassistisch
rack [ræk] n Ständer m, Gestell nt
⊳ vt: **to ~ one's brains** sich dat
den Kopf zerbrechen

racket ['rækɪt] n (Sport) Schläger
m; (noise) Krach m
radar ['reɪdɑː*] n Radar nt o m;
radar trap n Radarfalle f
radiation [reɪdɪ'eɪʃən] n (radio-
active) Strahlung f
radiator ['reɪdɪeɪtə*] n Heizkörper m; (Auto) Kühler m
radical ['rædɪkəl] adj radikal
radio ['reɪdɪəʊ] (pl **-s**) n
Rundfunk m, Radio nt
radioactivity [reɪdɪəʊæk'tɪvɪtɪ]
n Radioaktivität f
radio alarm ['reɪdɪəʊə'lɑːm] n
Radiowecker m; **radio station** n
Rundfunkstation f
radiotherapy [reɪdɪəʊ'θerəpɪ]
n Strahlenbehandlung f
radish ['rædɪʃ] n Radieschen nt
radius ['reɪdɪəs] n Radius m;
within a five-mile ~ im Umkreis
von fünf Meilen (of um)
raffle ['ræfl] n Tombola f; **raffle**
ticket n Los nt
raft [rɑːft] n Floß nt
rag [ræg] n Lumpen m; (for
cleaning) Lappen m
rage [reɪdʒ] n Wut f; **to be all the**
~ der letzte Schrei sein ⊳ vi toben;
(disease) wüten
raid [reɪd] n Überfall m (on auf
+akk); (by police) Razzia f (on gegen)
⊳ vt (bank etc) überfallen; (by
police) eine Razzia machen in +dat
rail [reɪl] n (on stairs, balcony etc)
Geländer nt; (of ship) Reling f; (Rail)
Schiene f; **railcard** n (Brit) ≈
Bahncard® f; **railing** n Geländer
nt; **~s** pl (fence) Zaun m; **railroad** n
(US) Eisenbahn f; **railroad station**
n (US) Bahnhof m; **railway** n (Brit)
Eisenbahn f; **railway line** n
Bahnlinie f; (track) Gleis m; **railway**
station n Bahnhof m
rain [reɪn] n Regen m ⊳ vi
regnen; **it's ~ing** es regnet;
rainbow n Regenbogen m;

raincoat n Regenmantel m;
rainfall n Niederschlag m;
rainforest n Regenwald m; **rainy**
adj regnerisch
raise [reiz] n (US: of wages/salary)
Gehalts-/Lohnerhöhung f ▷ vt
(lift) hochheben; (increase)
erhöhen; (family) großziehen;
(livestock) züchten; (money)
aufbringen; (objection) erheben; **to
~ one's voice** laut werden
raisin ['reizən] n Rosine f
rally ['ræli] n (Pol) Kundgebung f;
(Auto) Rallye f; (Tennis) Ballwechsel
m
RAM [ræm] acr = **random access
memory** RAM m
ramble ['ræmbl] n Wanderung f
▷ vi (walk) wandern; (talk)
schwafeln
ramp [ræmp] n Rampe f
ran [ræn] pt of **run**
ranch [rɑːntʃ] n Ranch f
rancid ['rænsɪd] adj ranzig
random ['rændəm] adj
willkürlich ▷ n: **at ~** (choose)
willkürlich; (fire) zieilos
rang [ræŋ] pt of **ring**
range [reɪndʒ] n (selection)
Auswahl f (of an +dat); (Comm)
Sortiment nt (of an +dat); (of
missile, telescope) Reichweite f; (of
mountains) Kette f; **in this price
~** in dieser Preisklasse ▷ vi: **to
~ from ... to ...** gehen von ... bis ...;
(temperature, sizes, prices) liegen
zwischen ... und ...
rank [ræŋk] n (Mil) Rang m; (social
position) Stand m ▷ vt einstufen
ransom ['rænsəm] n Lösegeld nt
rap [ræp] n (Mus) Rap m
rape [reɪp] n Vergewaltigung f
▷ vt vergewaltigen
rapid, rapidly ['ræpɪd, -lɪ] adj, adv
schnell
rapist ['reɪpɪst] n Vergewaltiger
m

rare [rɛə°] adj selten, rar;
(especially good) vortrefflich; (steak)
blutig; **rarely** adv selten; **rarity**
['rɛərɪtɪ] n Seltenheit f
rash [ræʃ] adj unbesonnen ▷ n
(Med) (Haut)ausschlag m
rasher ['ræʃə°] n: **~ (of bacon)**
(Speck)scheibe f
raspberry ['rɑːzbərɪ] n Himbeere f
rat [ræt] n Ratte f; (pej: person)
Schwein nt
rate [reɪt] n (proportion, frequency)
Rate f; (speed) Tempo nt; **~ (of
exchange)** (Wechsel)kurs m; **~ of
inflation** Inflationsrate f; **~ of
interest** Zinssatz m; **at any ~** auf
jeden Fall ▷ vt (evaluate)
einschätzen (as als)
rather ['rɑːðə°] adv (in preference)
lieber; (fairly) ziemlich; **I'd ~ stay
here** ich würde lieber hierbleiben;
I'd ~ not lieber nicht; **or ~** (more
accurately) vielmehr
ratio ['reɪʃɪəʊ] (pl -s) n Verhältnis
nt
rational ['ræʃənl] adj rational;
rationalize ['ræʃnəlaɪz] vt
rationalisieren
rattle ['rætl] n (toy) Rassel f ▷ vt
(keys, coins) klimpern mit; (person)
durcheinanderbringen ▷ vi (window) klappern; (bottles) klirren;
rattle off vt herunterrasseln;
rattlesnake n Klapperschlange
f
rave [reɪv] vi (talk wildly)
fantasieren; (rage) toben; (enthuse)
schwärmen (about von) ▷ n (Brit:
event) Raveparty f
raven ['reɪvn] n Rabe m
raving ['reɪvɪŋ] adv: **~ mad** total
verrückt
ravishing ['rævɪʃɪŋ] adj
hinreißend
raw [rɔː] adj (food) roh; (skin)
wund; (climate) rau

ray [reɪ] n (of light) Strahl m; **~ of hope** Hoffnungsschimmer m

razor ['reɪzə*] n Rasierapparat m; **razor blade** n Rasierklinge f

Rd n abbr = **road** Str.

re [ri:] prep (Comm) betreffs +gen

RE abbr = **religious education**

reach [ri:tʃ] n: **within/out of (sb's) ~** in/außer (jds) Reichweite; **within easy ~ of the shops** nicht weit von den Geschäften ▷ vt (arrive at, contact) erreichen; (come down/up as far as) reichen bis zu; (contact) **can you ~ it?** kommst du/kommen Sie dran?; **reach for** vt greifen nach; **reach out** vi die Hand ausstrecken; **to ~ for** greifen nach

react [ri:'ækt] vi reagieren (to auf +akk); **reaction** [ri:'ækʃən] n Reaktion f (to auf +akk); **reactor** [rɪ'æktə*] n Reaktor m

read [ri:d] (**read, read**) vt lesen; (meter) ablesen; **to ~ sth to sb** jdm etw vorlesen ▷ vi lesen; **to ~ to sb** jdm vorlesen; **it ~s well** es liest sich gut; **it ~s as follows** es lautet folgendermaßen; **read out** vt vorlesen; **read through** vt durchlesen; **read up on** vt nachlesen über +akk; **readable** adj (book) lesenswert; (handwriting) lesbar; **reader** n Leser(in) m(f); **readership** n Leserschaft f

readily ['redɪlɪ] adv (willingly) bereitwillig; **~ available** leicht erhältlich

reading ['ri:dɪŋ] n (action) Lesen nt; (from meter) Zählerstand m; **reading glasses** npl Lesebrille f; **reading lamp** n Leselampe f; **reading list** n Leseliste f; **reading matter** n Lektüre f

readjust [ri:ə'dʒʌst] vt (mechanism etc) neu einstellen ▷ vi sich wieder anpassen (to an +akk)

ready ['redɪ] adj fertig, bereit; **to be ~ to do sth** (willing) bereit sein, etw zu tun; **are you ~ to go?** bist du so weit?; **to get sth ~** etw fertig machen; **to get (oneself) ~** sich fertig machen; **ready cash** n Bargeld nt; **ready-made** adj (product) Fertig-; (clothes) Konfektions-; **~ meal** Fertiggericht nt

real [rɪəl] adj wirklich; (actual) eigentlich; (genuine) echt; (idiot etc) richtig ▷ adv (fam, esp US) echt; **for ~** echt; **this time it's for ~** diesmal ist es ernst; **get ~** sei realistisch!; **real ale** n Ale nt; **real estate** n Immobilien pl

realistic, realistically [rɪə'lɪstɪk, -əlɪ] adj, adv realistisch; **reality** [rɪ'ælɪtɪ] n Wirklichkeit f; **in ~** in Wirklichkeit; **reality TV** n Reality-TV nt; **realization** [rɪəlaɪ'zeɪʃən] n (awareness) Erkenntnis f; **realize** ['rɪəlaɪz] vt (understand) begreifen; (plan, idea) realisieren; **I ~d (that)** ... mir wurde klar, dass ...

really ['rɪəlɪ] adv wirklich

real time [rɪəl'taɪm] n (Inform) **in ~** in Echtzeit

realtor ['rɪəltə*] n (US) Grundstücksmakler(in) m(f)

reappear [ri:ə'pɪə*] vi wieder erscheinen

rear [rɪə*] adj hintere(r, s), Hinter- ▷ n (of building, vehicle) hinterer Teil; **at the ~ of** hinter +dat; (inside) hinten in +dat; **rear light** n (Auto) Rücklicht nt

rearm [ri:'ɑ:m] vi wieder aufrüsten

rearrange [ri:ə'reɪndʒ] vt (furniture, system) umstellen; (meeting) verlegen (for auf +akk)

rear-view mirror ['rɪəvju:'mɪrə*] n Rückspiegel m; **rear window** n (Auto) Heckscheibe f

reason ['riːzn] n (cause) Grund m (for für); (ability to think) Verstand m; (common sense) Vernunft f; **for some ~** aus irgendeinem Grund ▷ vi: **to ~ with sb** mit jdm vernünftig reden; **reasonable** adj (person, price) vernünftig; (offer) akzeptabel; (chance) reell; (food, weather) ganz gut; **reasonably** adv vernünftig; (fairly) ziemlich

reassure [riːəˈʃʊəʳ] vt beruhigen; **she ~d me that ...** sie versicherte mir, dass ...

rebel ['rebl] n Rebell(in) m(f) ▷ [rɪˈbel] vi rebellieren; **rebellion** [rɪˈbelɪən] n Aufstand m

reboot [riːˈbuːt] vt, vi (Inform) rebooten

rebound [rɪˈbaʊnd] vi (ball etc) zurückprallen

rebuild [riːˈbɪld] irr vt wieder aufbauen

recall [rɪˈkɔːl] vt (remember) sich erinnern an +akk; (call back) zurückrufen

recap ['riːkæp] vt, vi rekapitulieren

receipt [rɪˈsiːt] n (document) Quittung f; (receiving) Empfang m; **~s** pl (money) Einnahmen pl

receive [rɪˈsiːv] vt (news etc) erhalten, bekommen; (visitor) empfangen; **receiver** n (Tel) Hörer m; (Radio) Empfänger m

recent ['riːsnt] adj (event) vor Kurzem stattgefunden; (photo) neueste(r,s); (invention) neu; **in ~ years** in den letzten Jahren; **recently** adv vor Kurzem; (in the last few days or weeks) in letzter Zeit

reception [rɪˈsepʃən] n Empfang m; **receptionist** n (in hotel) Empfangschef m, Empfangsdame f; (woman in firm) Empfangsdame f; (Med) Sprechstundenhilfe f

recess [rɪˈses] n (in wall) Nische f; (US: in school) Pause f

recession [rɪˈseʃən] n Rezession f

recharge [riːˈtʃɑːdʒ] vt (battery) aufladen; **rechargeable** [riːˈtʃɑːdʒəbl] adj wiederaufladbar

recipe ['resɪpɪ] n Rezept nt (for für)

recipient [rɪˈsɪpɪənt] n Empfänger(in) m(f)

reciprocal [rɪˈsɪprəkəl] adj gegenseitig

recite [rɪˈsaɪt] vt vortragen; (details) aufzählen

reckless ['rekləs] adj leichtsinnig; (driving) gefährlich

reckon ['rekən] vt (calculate) schätzen; (think) glauben ▷ vi: **to ~ with/on** rechnen mit

reclaim [rɪˈkleɪm] vt (baggage) abholen; (expenses, tax) zurückverlangen

recline [rɪˈklaɪn] vi (person) sich zurücklehnen; **reclining seat** n Liegesitz m

recognition [rekəgˈnɪʃən] n (acknowledgement) Anerkennung f; **in ~ of** in Anerkennung +gen; **recognize** ['rekəgnaɪz] vt erkennen; (approve officially) anerkennen

recommend [rekəˈmend] vt empfehlen; **recommendation** [rekəmenˈdeɪʃən] n Empfehlung f

reconfirm [riːkənˈfɜːm] vt (flight etc) rückbestätigen

reconsider [riːkənˈsɪdəʳ] vt noch einmal überdenken ▷ vi es sich dat noch einmal überlegen

reconstruct [riːkənˈstrʌkt] vt wieder aufbauen; (crime) rekonstruieren

record ['rekɔːd] n (Mus) (Schall)platte f; (best performance) Rekord m; **~s** pl (files) Akten pl; **to keep a ~ of** Buch führen über +akk ▷ adj (time etc) Rekord- ▷ [rɪˈkɔːd] vt (write down) aufzeichnen; (on *tape etc)* aufnehmen; **~ed message** Ansage *f;* **recorded delivery** *n* (Brit) **by ~** per Einschreiben

recorder [rɪˈkɔːdə*] *n* (Mus) Blockflöte *f;* (**cassette**) ~ (Kassetten)rekorder *m;*

recording [rɪˈkɔːdɪŋ] *n* (on tape *etc)* Aufnahme *f;* **record player** [ˈrekɔːdpleɪə*] *n* Plattenspieler *m*

recover [rɪˈkʌvə*] *vt* (money, item) zurückbekommen; (appetite, strength) wiedergewinnen ▷ *vi* sich erholen

recreation [rekrɪˈeɪʃən] *n* Erholung *f;* **recreational** *adj* Freizeit-; **~ vehicle** (US) Wohnmobil *nt*

recruit [rɪˈkruːt] *n* (Mil) Rekrut(in) *m(f);* (in firm, organization) neues Mitglied ▷ *vt* (Mil) rekrutieren; (members) anwerben; (staff) einstellen; **recruitment agency** *n* Personalagentur *f*

rectangle [ˈrektæŋgl] *n* Rechteck *nt;* **rectangular** [rekˈtæŋgʊlə*] *adj* rechteckig

rectify [ˈrektɪfaɪ] *vt* berichtigen

recuperate [rɪˈkuːpəreɪt] *vi* sich erholen

recyclable [riːˈsaɪkləbl] *adj* recycelbar, wiederverwertbar; **recycle** [riːˈsaɪkl] *vt* recyceln, wiederverwerten; **~d paper** Recyclingpapier *nt;* **recycling** *n* Recycling *nt,* Wiederverwertung *f*

red [red] *adj* rot ▷ *n:* **in the ~** in den roten Zahlen; **Red Cross** *n* Rotes Kreuz; **red cabbage** *n* Rotkohl *m;* **redcurrant** *n* (rote) Johannisbeere

redeem [rɪˈdiːm] *vt* (Comm) einlösen

red-handed [redˈhændɪd] *adj:* **to catch sb ~** jdn auf frischer Tat ertappen; **redhead** *n* Rothaarige(r) *mf*

redial [riːˈdaɪəl] *vt, vi* nochmals wählen

redirect [riːdaɪˈrekt] *vt* (traffic) umleiten; (forward) nachsenden

red light [redˈlaɪt] *n* (traffic signal) rotes Licht; **to go through the ~** bei Rot über die Ampel fahren; **red meat** *n* Rind-, Lamm-, Rehfleisch

redo [riːˈduː] *irr vt* nochmals machen

reduce [rɪˈdjuːs] *vt* reduzieren (to auf +akk, by um); **reduction** [rɪˈdʌkʃən] *n* Reduzierung *f;* (in price) Ermäßigung *f*

redundant [rɪˈdʌndənt] *adj* überflüssig; **to be made ~** entlassen werden

red wine [redˈwaɪn] *n* Rotwein *m*

reef [riːf] *n* Riff *nt*

reel [riːl] *n* Spule *f;* (on fishing rod) Rolle *f;* **reel off** *vt* herunterrasseln *f*

ref [ref] *n* (fam: referee) Schiri *m*

refectory [rɪˈfektərɪ] *n* (at college) Mensa *f*

refer [rɪˈfɜː*] *vt:* **to ~ sb to sb/sth** jdn an jdn/etw verweisen; **to ~ sth to sb** (query, problem) etw an jdn weiterleiten ▷ *vi:* **to ~ to** (mention, allude to) sich beziehen auf +akk; (book) nachschlagen in +dat

referee [refəˈriː] *n* Schiedsrichter(in) *m(f);* (in boxing) Ringrichter *m;* (Brit: for job) Referenz *f*

reference [ˈrefrəns] *n* (allusion) Anspielung *f* (to auf +akk); (for job) Referenz *f;* (in book) Verweis *m;* **~ (number)** (in document) Aktenzeichen *nt;* **with ~ to** mit Bezug auf +akk; **reference book** *n* Nachschlagewerk *nt*

referendum [refəˈrendəm] *(pl* **referenda**) *n* Referendum *nt*

refill [ˈriːfɪl] *vt* [riːˈfɪl] nachfüllen ▷ *n* (for ballpoint pen) Ersatzmine *f*

refine [rɪ'faɪn] vt (purify) raffinieren; (improve) verfeinern; **refined** adj (genteel) fein

reflect [rɪ'flekt] vt reflektieren; (fig) widerspiegeln ▷ vi nachdenken (on über +akk); **reflection** [rɪ'flekʃən] n (image) Spiegelbild nt; (thought) Überlegung f; **on ~** nach reiflicher Überlegung

reflex ['riːfleks] n Reflex m

reform [rɪ'fɔːm] n Reform f ▷ vt reformieren; (person) bessern

refrain [rɪ'freɪn] vi: **to ~ from doing sth** es unterlassen, etw zu tun

refresh [rɪ'freʃ] vt erfrischen; **refresher course** n Auffrischungskurs m; **refreshing** adj erfrischend; **refreshments** npl Erfrischungen pl

refrigerator [rɪ'frɪdʒəreɪtə*] n Kühlschrank m

refuel [riː'fjʊəl] vt, vi auftanken

refugee [refjʊ'dʒiː] n Flüchtling m

refund ['riːfʌnd] n (of money) Rückerstattung f; **to get a ~ (on sth)** sein Geld (für etw) zurückbekommen ▷ [rɪ'fʌnd] vt zurückerstatten

refusal [rɪ'fjuːzəl] n (to do sth) Weigerung f; **refuse** ['refjuːs] n Müll m, Abfall m ▷ [rɪ'fjuːz] vt ablehnen; **to ~ sb sth** jdm etw verweigern; **to ~ to do sth** sich weigern, etw zu tun ▷ vi sich weigern

regain [rɪ'geɪn] vt wiedergewinnen, wiedererlangen; **to ~ consciousness** wieder zu Bewusstsein kommen

regard [rɪ'gɑːd] n: **with ~ to** in Bezug auf +akk; **in this ~** in dieser Hinsicht; **~s** (at end of letter) mit freundlichen Grüßen; **give my ~s to ...** viele Grüße an ... +akk ▷ vt:

to ~ sb/sth as sth jdn/etw als etw betrachten; **as ~s ...** was ... betrifft; **regarding** prep bezüglich +gen; **regardless** adj: **~ of** ohne Rücksicht auf +akk ▷ adv trotzdem; **to carry on ~** einfach weitermachen

regime [reɪ'ʒiːm] n (Pol) Regime nt

region ['riːdʒən] n (of country) Region f, Gebiet nt; **in the ~ of** (about) ungefähr; **regional** adj regional

register ['redʒɪstə*] n Register nt; (school) Namensliste f ▷ vt (with an authority) registrieren lassen; (birth, death, vehicle) anmelden ▷ vi (at hotel, for course) sich anmelden; (at university) sich einschreiben; **registered** adj eingetragen; (letter) eingeschrieben; **by ~ post** per Einschreiben; **registration** [redʒɪ'streɪʃən] n (for course) Anmeldung f; (at university) Einschreibung f; (Auto: number) (polizeiliches) Kennzeichen; **registration form** n Anmeldeformular nt; **registration number** n (Auto) (polizeiliches) Kennzeichen; **registry office** ['redʒɪstrɪɒfɪs] n Standesamt nt

regret [rɪ'gret] n Bedauern nt ▷ vt bedauern; **regrettable** adj bedauerlich

regular ['regjʊlə*] adj regelmäßig; (size) normal ▷ n (client) Stammkunde m, Stammkundin f; (in bar) Stammgast m; (petrol) Normalbenzin nt; **regularly** adv regelmäßig

regulate ['regjʊleɪt] vt regulieren; (using rules) regeln; **regulation** [regjʊ'leɪʃən] n (rule) Vorschrift f

rehabilitation [riːəbɪlɪ'teɪʃən] n Rehabilitation f

rehearsal [rɪ'hɜːsəl] *n* Probe *f*; **rehearse** *vt, vi* proben

reign [reɪn] *n* Herrschaft *f* ▷ *vi* herrschen (*over* über +*akk*)

reimburse [riːɪm'bɜːs] *vt* (*person*) entschädigen; (*expenses*) zurückerstatten

reindeer ['reɪndɪə*] *n* Rentier *nt*

reinforce [riːɪn'fɔːs] *vt* verstärken

reinstate [riːɪn'steɪt] *vt* (*employee*) wieder einstellen; (*passage in text*) wieder aufnehmen

reject ['riːdʒekt] *n* (*Comm*) Ausschussartikel *m* ▷ [rɪ'dʒekt] *vt* ablehnen; **rejection** [rɪ'dʒekʃən] *n* Ablehnung *f*

relapse [rɪ'læps] *n* Rückfall *m*

relate [rɪ'leɪt] *vt* (*story*) erzählen; (*connect*) in Verbindung bringen (*to* mit) ▷ *vi*: **to ~ to** (*refer*) sich beziehen auf +*akk*; **related** *adj* verwandt (*to* mit); **relation** [rɪ'leɪʃən] *n* (*relative*) Verwandte(r) *mf*; (*connection*) Beziehung *f*; **~s** *pl* (*dealings*) Beziehungen *pl*; **relationship** *n* (*connection*) Beziehung *f*; (*between people*) Verhältnis *nt*

relative ['relətɪv] *n* Verwandte(r) *mf* ▷ *adj* relativ; **relatively** *adv* relativ, verhältnismäßig

relax [rɪ'læks] *vi* sich entspannen; **~!** reg dich nicht auf! ▷ *vt* (*grip, conditions*) lockern; **relaxation** [riːlæk'seɪʃən] *n* (*rest*) Entspannung *f*; **relaxed** *adj* entspannt; **relaxing** *adj* entspannend

release [rɪ'liːs] *n* (*from prison*) Entlassung *f*; **new/recent ~** (*film, CD*) Neuerscheinung *f* ▷ *vt* (*animal, hostage*) freilassen; (*prisoner*) entlassen; (*handbrake*) lösen; (*news*) veröffentlichen; (*film, CD*) herausbringen

relent [rɪ'lent] *vi* nachgeben;

relentless, relentlessly *adj, adv* (*merciless*) erbarmungslos; (*neverending*) unaufhörlich

relevance ['reləvəns] *n* Relevanz *f* (*to* für); **relevant** *adj* relevant (*to* für)

reliable, reliably [rɪ'laɪəbl, -blɪ] *adj, adv* zuverlässig; **reliant** [rɪ'laɪənt] *adj*: **~ on** abhängig von

relic ['relɪk] *n* (*from past*) Relikt *nt*

relief [rɪ'liːf] *n* (*from anxiety, pain*) Erleichterung *f*; (*assistance*) Hilfe *f*; **relieve** [rɪ'liːv] *vt* (*pain*) lindern; (*boredom*) überwinden; (*take over from*) ablösen; **I'm ~d** ich bin erleichtert

religion [rɪ'lɪdʒən] *n* Religion *f*; **religious** [rɪ'lɪdʒəs] *adj* religiös

relish ['relɪʃ] *n* (*for food*) würzige Soße ▷ *vt* (*enjoy*) genießen; **I don't ~ the thought of it** der Gedanke behagt mir gar nicht

reluctant [rɪ'lʌktənt] *adj* widerwillig; **to be ~ to do sth** etw nur ungern tun; **reluctantly** *adv* widerwillig

rely on [rɪ'laɪ ɒn] *vt* sich verlassen auf +*akk*; (*depend on*) abhängig sein von

remain [rɪ'meɪn] *vi* bleiben; (*be left over*) übrig bleiben; **remainder** *n* (*a. Math*) Rest *m*; **remaining** *adj* übrig; **remains** *npl* Überreste *pl*

remark [rɪ'mɑːk] *n* Bemerkung *f* ▷ *vt*: **to ~ that** bemerken, dass ▷ *vi*: **to ~ on sth** über etw *akk* eine Bemerkung machen; **remarkable, remarkably** *adj, adv* bemerkenswert

remarry [riː'mærɪ] *vi* wieder heiraten

remedy ['remədɪ] *n* Mittel *nt* (*for* gegen) ▷ *vt* abhelfen +*dat*

remember [rɪ'membə*] *vt* sich erinnern an +*akk*; **to ~ to do sth** daran denken, etw zu tun; **I ~ seeing her** ich erinnere mich daran, sie gesehen zu haben; **I must ~ that** das muss ich mir merken ▷ *vi* sich erinnern

Remembrance Day [rɪ'membrəns'deɪ] *n* (*Brit*) ≈ Volkstrauertag *m*

● REMEMBRANCE DAY
●
● **Remembrance Sunday/Day** ist
● der britische Gedenktag für die
● Gefallenen der beiden
● Weltkriege und anderer Kriege.
● Er fällt auf einen Sonntag vor
● oder nach dem 11. November
● (am 11.11.1918 endete der Erste
● Weltkrieg) und wird mit einer
● Schweigeminute,
● Kranzniederlegungen an
● Kriegerdenkmälern und dem
● Tragen von Anstecknadeln in
● Form einer Mohnblume
● begangen.

remind [rɪ'maɪnd] *vt*: **to ~ sb of/about sth/sth** jdn an jdn/etw erinnern; **to ~ sb to do sth** jdn daran erinnern, etw zu tun; **that ~s me** dabei fällt mir ein ...; **reminder** *n* (*to pay*) Mahnung *f*

reminisce [remɪ'nɪs] *vi* in Erinnerungen schwelgen (*about* an +*akk*); **reminiscent** [remɪ'nɪsənt] *adj*: **to be ~ of** erinnern an +*akk*

remittance *n* Überweisung *f* (*to* an +*akk*)

remnant ['remnənt] *n* Rest *m*

remote [rɪ'məʊt] *adj* (*place*) abgelegen; (*slight*) gering ▷ *n* (*TV*) Fernbedienung *f*; **remote control** *n* Fernsteuerung *f*; (*device*) Fernbedienung *f*

removal [rɪ'muːvəl] *n* Entfernung *f*; (*Brit*: *move from house*) Umzug *m*; **removal firm** *n* (*Brit*) Spedition *f*; **remove** [rɪ'muːv] *vt* entfernen; (*lid*) abnehmen; (*clothes*) ausziehen; (*doubt, suspicion*) zerstreuen

rename [riː'neɪm] *vt* umbenennen

renew [rɪ'njuː] *vt* erneuern; (*licence, passport, library book*) verlängern lassen

renounce [rɪ'naʊns] *vt* verzichten auf +*akk*; (*faith, opinion*) abschwören +*dat*

renovate ['renəveɪt] *vt* renovieren

renowned [rɪ'naʊnd] *adj* berühmt (*for* für)

rent [rent] *n* Miete *f*; **for ~** (*US*) zu vermieten ▷ *vt* (*as hirer, tenant*) mieten; (*as owner*) vermieten; **~ed car** Mietwagen *m*; **rent out** *vt* vermieten; **rental** *n* Miete *f*; (*for car, TV etc*) Leihgebühr *f* ▷ *adj* Miet-

reorganize [riː'ɔːgənaɪz] *vt* umorganisieren

rep [rep] *n* (*Comm*) Vertreter(in) *m(f)*

repair [rɪ'peə*] *n* Reparatur *f* ▷ *vt* reparieren; (*damage*) wiedergutmachen; **repair kit** *n* Flickzeug *nt*

repay [riː'peɪ] *irr vt* (*money*) zurückzahlen; **to ~ sb for sth** (*fig*) sich bei jdm für etw revanchieren

repeat [rɪ'piːt] *n* (*Radio, TV*) Wiederholung *f* ▷ *vt* wiederholen; **repetition** [repə'tɪʃən] *n* Wiederholung *f*; **repetitive** [rɪ'petɪtɪv] *adj* sich wiederholend

rephrase [riː'freɪz] *vt* anders formulieren

replace [rɪ'pleɪs] *vt* ersetzen (*with* durch); (*put back*) zurückstellen; **replacement** *n* (*thing, person*) Ersatz *m*; (*temporarily in job*) Vertretung *f*; **replacement part** *n* Ersatzteil *nt*

replay ['riːpleɪ] *n*: (*action*)

~ Wiederholung f ▷ [riːˈpleɪ] vt (game) wiederholen

replica [ˈreplɪkə] n Kopie f

reply [rɪˈplaɪ] n Antwort f ▷ vi antworten; **to ~ to sb/sth** jdm/auf etw akk antworten ▷ vt: **to ~ that** antworten, dass

report [rɪˈpɔːt] n Bericht m; (school) Zeugnis nt ▷ vt (tell) berichten; (give information against) melden; (to police) anzeigen ▷ vi (present oneself) sich melden; **to ~ sick** sich krankmelden; **report card** n (US: school) Zeugnis nt; **reporter** n Reporter(in) m(f)

represent [reprɪˈzent] vt darstellen; (speak for) vertreten; **representation** [reprɪzenˈteɪʃən] n (picture etc) Darstellung f; **representative** [reprɪˈzentətɪv] n Vertreter(in) m(f); (US Pol) Abgeordnete(r) mf ▷ adj repräsentativ (of für)

reprimand [ˈreprɪmɑːnd] n Tadel m ▷ vt tadeln

reprint [ˈriːprɪnt] n Nachdruck m

reproduce [riːprəˈdjuːs] vt (copy) reproduzieren ▷ vi (Bio) sich fortpflanzen; **reproduction** [riːprəˈdʌkʃən] n (copy) Reproduktion f; (Bio) Fortpflanzung f

reptile [ˈreptaɪl] n Reptil nt

republic [rɪˈpʌblɪk] n Republik f; **republican** adj republikanisch ▷ n Republikaner(in) m(f)

repulsive [rɪˈpʌlsɪv] adj abstoßend

reputable [ˈrepjʊtəbl] adj seriös

reputation [repjʊˈteɪʃən] n Ruf m; **he has a ~ for being difficult** er hat den Ruf, schwierig zu sein

request [rɪˈkwest] n Bitte f (for um); **on ~** auf Wunsch ▷ vt bitten um; **to ~ sb to do sth** jdn bitten, etw zu tun

require [rɪˈkwaɪə*] vt (need)

brauchen; (desire) verlangen; **what qualifications are ~d?** welche Qualifikationen sind erforderlich?; **required** adj erforderlich; **requirement** n (condition) Anforderung f; (need) Bedingung f

rerun [ˈriːrʌn] n Wiederholung f

rescue [ˈreskjuː] n Rettung f; **to come to sb's ~** jdm zu Hilfe kommen ▷ vt retten; **rescue party** n Rettungsmannschaft f

research [rɪˈsɜːtʃ] n Forschung f ▷ vi forschen (into über +akk) ▷ vt erforschen; **researcher** n Forscher(in) m(f)

resemblance [rɪˈzembləns] n Ähnlichkeit f (to mit); **resemble** [rɪˈzembl] vt ähneln +dat

resent [rɪˈzent] vt übel nehmen

reservation [rezəˈveɪʃən] n (booking) Reservierung f; (doubt) Vorbehalt m; **I have a ~** (in hotel, restaurant) ich habe reserviert; **reserve** [rɪˈzɜːv] n (store) Vorrat m (of an +dat); (manner) Zurückhaltung f; (Sport) Reservespieler(in) m(f); (game ~) Naturschutzgebiet nt ▷ vt (book in advance) reservieren; **reserved** adj reserviert

reservoir [ˈrezəvwɑː*] n (for water) Reservoir nt

reside [rɪˈzaɪd] vi wohnen; **residence** [ˈrezɪdəns] n Wohnsitz m; (living) Aufenthalt m; **~ permit** Aufenthaltsgenehmigung f; **~ hall** Studentenwohnheim nt; **resident** [ˈrezɪdənt] n (in house) Bewohner(in) m(f); (in town, area) Einwohner(in) m(f)

resign [rɪˈzaɪn] vt (post) zurücktreten von; (job) kündigen ▷ vi (from post) zurücktreten; (from job) kündigen; **resignation** [rezɪgˈneɪʃən] n (from post)

Rücktritt m; (from job) Kündigung f; **resigned** adj resigniert; **he is ~ to it** er hat sich damit abgefunden

resist [rɪ'zɪst] vt widerstehen +dat; **resistance** n Widerstand m (to gegen)

resit [riː'sɪt] (Brit) irr vt wiederholen ▷ ['riːsɪt] n Wiederholungsprüfung f

resolution [rezə'luːʃən] n (intention) Vorsatz m; (decision) Beschluss m

resolve [rɪ'zɒlv] vt (problem) lösen

resort [rɪ'zɔːt] n (holiday ~) Urlaubsort m; (health ~) Kurort m; **as a last ~** als letzter Ausweg ▷ vi: **to ~ to** greifen zu; (violence) anwenden

resources [rɪ'sɔːsɪz] npl (money) (Geld)mittel pl; (mineral ~) Bodenschätze pl

respect [rɪ'spekt] n Respekt m (for vor +dat); (consideration) Rücksicht f (for auf +akk); **with ~ to** in Bezug auf +akk; **in this ~** in dieser Hinsicht; **with all due ~** bei allem Respekt ▷ vt respektieren; **respectable** [rɪ'spektəbl] adj (person, family) angesehen; (district) anständig; (achievement, result) beachtlich; **respected** [rɪ'spektɪd] adj angesehen

respective [rɪ'spektɪv] adj jeweilig; **respectively** adv: **5 % and 10 % ~** 5 % beziehungsweise 10 %

respiratory [rɪ'spɪrətərɪ] adj: **~ problems** (o **trouble**) Atembeschwerden pl

respond [rɪ'spɒnd] vi antworten (to auf +akk); (react) reagieren (to auf +akk); (to treatment) ansprechen (to auf +akk); **response** [rɪ'spɒns] n Antwort f; (reaction) Reaktion f; **in ~ to** als Antwort auf +akk

responsibility [rɪspɒnsə'bɪlɪtɪ] n Verantwortung f; **that's her ~** dafür ist sie verantwortlich; **responsible** [rɪ'spɒnsəbl] adj verantwortlich (for für); (trustworthy) verantwortungsbewusst; (job) verantwortungsvoll

rest [rest] n (relaxation) Ruhe f; (break) Pause f; (remainder) Rest m; **to have** (o **take**) **a ~** sich ausruhen; (break) Pause machen; **the ~ of the wine/the people** der Rest des Weins/der Leute ▷ vi (relax) sich ausruhen; (lean) lehnen (on, against an +dat, gegen)

restaurant ['restərɒnt] n Restaurant nt; **restaurant car** n (Brit) Speisewagen m

restful ['restfʊl] adj (holiday etc) erholsam, ruhig; **restless** ['restləs] adj unruhig

restore [rɪ'stɔː*] vt (painting, building) restaurieren; (order) wiederherstellen; (give back) zurückgeben

restrain [rɪ'streɪn] vt (person, feelings) zurückhalten; **to ~ oneself** sich beherrschen

restrict [rɪ'strɪkt] vt beschränken (to auf +akk); **restricted** adj beschränkt; **restriction** [rɪ'strɪkʃən] n Einschränkung f (on +gen)

rest room ['restruːm] n (US) Toilette f

result [rɪ'zʌlt] n Ergebnis nt; (consequence) Folge f; **as a ~ of** infolge +gen ▷ vi: **to ~ in** führen zu; **to ~ from** sich ergeben aus

resume [rɪ'zjuːm] vt (work, negotiations) wieder aufnehmen; (journey) fortsetzen

résumé ['rezjʊmeɪ] n Zusammenfassung f; (US: curriculum vitae) Lebenslauf m

resuscitate [rɪˈsʌsɪteɪt] vt
wiederbeleben
retail [ˈriːteɪl] adv im
Einzelhandel; **retailer** n
Einzelhändler(in) m(f)
retain [rɪˈteɪn] vt behalten; (heat)
halten
rethink [riːˈθɪŋk] irr vt noch
einmal überdenken
retire [rɪˈtaɪə*] vi (from work) in
den Ruhestand treten; (withdraw)
sich zurückziehen; **retired** adj
(person) pensioniert; **retirement** n
(time of life) Ruhestand m;
retirement age n Rentenalter nt
retrace [rɪˈtreɪs] vt
zurückverfolgen
retrain [riːˈtreɪn] vi sich
umschulen lassen
retreat [rɪˈtriːt] n (Mil) Rückzug
m (from aus); (refuge) Zufluchtsort
m ▷ vi (Mil) sich zurückziehen;
(step back) zurückweichen
retrieve [rɪˈtriːv] vt (recover)
wiederbekommen; (rescue) retten;
(data) abrufen
retrospect [ˈretrəʊspekt] n: **in
~** rückblickend; **retrospective**
[retrəʊˈspektɪv] adj rückblickend;
(pay rise) rückwirkend
return [rɪˈtɜːn] n (going back)
Rückkehr f; (giving back)
Rückgabe f; (profit) Gewinn m;
(Brit: ~ ticket) Rückfahrkarte f;
(plane ticket) Rückflugticket nt;
(Tennis), Return m; **in ~** als
Gegenleistung (for für); **many
happy ~s (of the day)** herzlichen
Glückwunsch zum Geburtstag!
▷ vi (person) zurückkehren;
(doubts, symptoms) wieder
auftreten; **to ~ to school/work**
wieder in die Schule/die Arbeit
gehen ▷ vt (give back)
zurückgeben; **I ~ed his call** ich
habe ihn zurückgerufen;
returnable adj (bottle) Pfand-;

return flight n (Brit) Rückflug m;
(both ways) Hin- und Rückflug m;
return key n (Inform)
Eingabetaste f; **return ticket** n
(Brit) Rückfahrkarte f; (for plane)
Rückflugticket nt
reunification [riːjuːnɪfɪˈkeɪʃən]
n Wiedervereinigung f
reunion [riːˈjuːnjən] n (party)
Treffen nt; **reunite** [riːjuːˈnaɪt] vt
wieder vereinigen
reusable [riːˈjuːzəbl] adj
wiederverwendbar
reveal [rɪˈviːl] vt (make known)
enthüllen; (secret) verraten; (show)
zeigen; **revealing** adj
aufschlussreich; (dress) freizügig
revenge [rɪˈvendʒ] n Rache f; (in
game) Revanche f; **to take ~ on sb
(for sth)** sich an jdm (für etw)
rächen
revenue [ˈrevənjuː] n Einnahmen pl
reverse [rɪˈvɜːs] n (back)
Rückseite f; (opposite) Gegenteil nt;
(Auto) **~ (gear)** Rückwärtsgang m
▷ adj: **in ~ order** in umgekehrter
Reihenfolge ▷ vt (order)
umkehren; (decision) umstoßen;
(car) zurücksetzen; **to ~ the
charges** (Brit) ein R-Gespräch
führen ▷ vi (Auto)
rückwärtsfahren
review [rɪˈvjuː] n (of book, film
etc) Rezension f; Kritik f; **to be
under ~** überprüft werden ▷ vt
(book, film etc) rezensieren;
(re-examine) überprüfen
revise [rɪˈvaɪz] vt revidieren;
(text) überarbeiten; (Brit: in school)
wiederholen ▷ vi (Brit, in school)
(für eine Prüfung) lernen; **revision**
[rɪˈvɪʒən] n (of text)
Überarbeitung f; (Brit, in school)
Wiederholung f
revitalize [riːˈvaɪtəlaɪz] vt neu
beleben

revive [rɪ'vaɪv] vt (person) wiederbeleben; (tradition, interest) wieder aufleben lassen ▷ vi (regain consciousness) wieder zu sich kommen

revolt [rɪ'vəʊlt] n Aufstand m; **revolting** adj widerlich

revolution [revə'luːʃən] n (Pol, fig) Revolution f; (turn) Umdrehung f; **revolutionary** adj revolutionär ▷ n Revolutionär(in) m(f)

revolve [rɪ'vɒlv] vi sich drehen (around um); **revolver** n Revolver m; **revolving door** n Drehtür f

reward [rɪ'wɔːd] n Belohnung f ▷ vt belohnen; **rewarding** adj lohnend

rewind [riː'waɪnd] irr vt (tape) zurückspulen

rewrite [riː'raɪt] irr vt (write again; recast) umschreiben

rheumatism ['ruːmətɪzəm] n Rheuma nt

Rhine [raɪn] n Rhein m

rhinoceros [raɪ'nɒsərəs] n Nashorn nt

Rhodes [rəʊdz] n Rhodos nt

rhubarb ['ruːbɑːb] n Rhabarber m

rhyme [raɪm] n Reim m ▷ vi sich reimen (with auf +akk)

rhythm ['rɪðəm] n Rhythmus m

rib [rɪb] n Rippe f

ribbon ['rɪbən] n Band nt

rice [raɪs] n Reis m; **rice pudding** n Milchreis m

rich [rɪtʃ] adj reich; (food) schwer ▷ npl: **the ~** die Reichen pl

rickety ['rɪkɪtɪ] adj wackelig

rid [rɪd] (**rid, rid**) vt: **to get ~ of sb/sth** jdn/etw loswerden

ridden ['rɪdn] pp of **ride**

riddle ['rɪdl] n Rätsel nt

ride [raɪd] (**rode, ridden**) vt (horse) reiten; (bicycle) fahren ▷ vi (on horse) reiten; (on bike) fahren ▷ n (in vehicle, on bike) Fahrt f; (on horse) (Aus)ritt m; **to go for a ~** (in car, on bike) spazieren fahren; (on horse) reiten gehen; **to take sb for a ~** (fam) jdn verarschen; **rider** n (on horse) Reiter(in) m(f); (on bike) Fahrer(in) m(f)

ridiculous [rɪ'dɪkjʊləs] adj lächerlich; **don't be ~** red keinen Unsinn!

riding ['raɪdɪŋ] n Reiten nt; **to go ~** reiten gehen ▷ adj Reit-

rifle ['raɪfl] n Gewehr nt

rig [rɪg] n: **oil ~** Bohrinsel f ▷ vt (election etc) manipulieren

right [raɪt] adj (correct, just) richtig; (opposite of left) rechte(r, s); (clothes, job etc) passend; **to be ~** (person) recht haben; (clock) richtig gehen; **that's ~** das stimmt! ▷ n Recht nt (to auf +akk); (side) rechte Seite; **the Right** (Pol) die Rechte; **to take a ~** (Auto) rechts abbiegen; **on the ~** rechts (of von); **to the ~** nach rechts; (on the ~) rechts (of von) ▷ adv (towards the ~) nach rechts; (directly) direkt; (exactly) genau; **to turn ~** (Auto) rechts abbiegen; **~ away** sofort; **~ now** im Moment; (immediately) sofort; **right angle** n rechter Winkel; **right-hand drive** n Rechtssteuerung f ▷ adj rechtsgesteuert; **right-handed** adj: **he is ~** er ist Rechtshänder; **right-hand side** n rechte Seite; **on the ~** auf der rechten Seite; **rightly** adv zu Recht; **right of way** n: **to have ~** (Auto) Vorfahrt haben; **right wing** n (Pol, Sport) rechter Flügel; **right-wing** adj Rechts-; **~ extremist** Rechtsradikale(r) mf

rigid ['rɪdʒɪd] adj (stiff) starr; (strict) streng

rigorous, **rigorously** ['rɪgərəs, -lɪ] *adj, adv* streng

rim [rɪm] *n* (*of cup etc*) Rand *m*; (*of wheel*) Felge *f*

rind [raɪnd] *n* (*of cheese*) Rinde *f*; (*of bacon*) Schwarte *f*; (*of fruit*) Schale *f*

ring [rɪŋ] (**rang, rung**) *vt, vi* (*bell*) läuten; (*Tel*) anrufen ▷ *n* (*on finger, in boxing*) Ring *m*; (*circle*) Kreis *m*; (*at circus*) Manege *f*; **to give sb a ~** (*Tel*) jdn anrufen; **ring back** *vt, vi* zurückrufen; **ring up** *vt, vi* anrufen

ring binder *n* Ringbuch *nt*

ringleader *n* Anführer(in) *m(f)*

ring road *n* (*Brit*) Umgehungsstraße *f*

ringtone *n* Klingelton *m*

rink [rɪŋk] *n* (*ice ~*) Eisbahn *f*; (*for roller-skating*) Rollschuhbahn *f*

rinse [rɪns] *vt* spülen

riot ['raɪət] *n* Aufruhr *m*

rip [rɪp] *n* Riss *m* ▷ *vt* zerreißen; **to ~ sth open** etw aufreißen ▷ *vi* reißen; **rip off** *vt* (*fam: person*) übers Ohr hauen; **rip up** *vt* zerreißen

ripe [raɪp] *adj* (*fruit*) reif; **ripen** *vi* reifen

rip-off ['rɪpɔf] *n*: **that's a ~** (*fam: too expensive*) das ist Wucher

rise [raɪz] (**rose, risen**) *vi* (*from sitting, lying*) aufstehen; (*sun*) aufgehen; (*prices, temperature*) steigen; (*ground*) ansteigen; (*in revolt*) sich erheben ▷ *n* (*increase*) Anstieg *m* (*in +gen*); (*pay ~*) Gehaltserhöhung *f*; (*to power, fame*) Aufstieg *m* (*to zu*); (*slope*) Steigung *f*; **risen** ['rɪzn] *pp of* **rise**

risk [rɪsk] *n* Risiko *nt* ▷ *vt* riskieren; **to ~ doing sth** es riskieren, etw zu tun; **risky** *adj* riskant

risotto [rɪ'zɒtəʊ] (*pl* **-s**) *n* Risotto *nt*

ritual ['rɪtjʊəl] *n* Ritual *nt* ▷ *adj* rituell

rival ['raɪvəl] *n* Rivale *m*, Rivalin *f* (*for um*); (*Comm*) Konkurrent(in) *m(f)*; **rivalry** *n* Rivalität *f*; (*Comm, Sport*) Konkurrenz *f*

river ['rɪvə*] *n* Fluss *m*; **the River Thames** (*Brit*), **the Thames River** (*US*) die Themse; **riverside** *n* Flussufer *nt* ▷ *adj* am Flussufer

road [rəʊd] *n* Straße *f*; (*fig*) Weg *m*; **on the ~** (*travelling*) unterwegs, mit dem Auto/Bus *etc* fahren; **roadblock** *n* Straßensperre *f*; **roadmap** *n* Straßenkarte *f*; **road rage** *n* *aggressives Verhalten im Straßenverkehr*; **roadside** *n*: **at** (*o* **by**) **the ~** am Straßenrand; **roadsign** *n* Verkehrsschild *nt*; **road tax** *n* Kraftfahrzeugsteuer *f*; **roadworks** *npl* Bauarbeiten *pl*; **roadworthy** *adj* fahrtüchtig

roar [rɔː*] *n* (*of person, lion*) Brüllen *nt*; (*von Verkehr*) Donnern *nt* ▷ *vi* (*person, lion*) brüllen (*with vor* +*dat*)

roast [rəʊst] *n* Braten *m* ▷ *adj*: **~ beef** Rinderbraten *m*; **~ chicken** Brathähnchen *nt*; **~ pork** Schweinebraten *m*; **~ potatoes** *pl im Backofen gebratene Kartoffeln* ▷ *vt* (*meat*) braten

rob [rɒb] *vt* bestehlen; (*bank, shop*) ausrauben; **robber** *n* Räuber(in) *m(f)*; **robbery** *n* Raub *m*

robe [rəʊb] *n* (*US: dressing gown*) Morgenrock *m*; (*of judge, priest etc*) Robe *f*, Talar *m*

robin ['rɒbɪn] *n* Rotkehlchen *nt*

robot ['rəʊbɒt] *n* Roboter *m*

robust [rəʊ'bʌst] *adj* robust; (*defence*) stark

rock [rɒk] *n* (*substance*) Stein *m*; (*boulder*) Felsbrocken *m*; (*Mus*) Rock *m*; **stick of ~** (*Brit*) Zuckerstange *f*; **on the ~s** (*drink*)

mit Eis; (*marriage*) gescheitert
▷ *vt, vi* (*swing*) schaukeln; (*dance*)
rocken; **rock climbing** *n* Klettern
nt; **to go ~** klettern gehen
rocket ['rɒkɪt] *n* Rakete *f*; (*in salad*) Rucola *m*
rocking chair ['rɒkɪntʃeə*] *n*
Schaukelstuhl *m*
rocky ['rɒkɪ] *adj* (*landscape*) felsig;
(*path*) steinig
rod [rɒd] *n* (*bar*) Stange *f*; (*fishing ~*) Rute *f*
rode [rəʊd] *pt of* **ride**
rogue [rəʊg] *n* Schurke *m*,
Gauner *m*
role [rəʊl] *n* Rolle *f*; **role model** *n*
Vorbild *nt*
roll [rəʊl] *n* (*of film, paper etc*)
Rolle *f*; (*bread ~*) Brötchen *nt* ▷ *vt*
(*move by ~ing*) rollen; (*cigarette*)
drehen ▷ *vi* (*move by ~ing*) rollen;
(*ship*) schlingern; (*camera*) laufen;
roll out *vt* (*pastry*) ausrollen; **roll over** *vi* (*person*) sich umdrehen;
roll up *vi* (*fam: arrive*) antanzen
▷ *vt* (*carpet*) aufrollen; **to roll one's sleeves up** die Ärmel
hochkrempeln
roller *n* (*hair ~*) (Locken)wickler *m*;
Rollerblades® *npl* Inlineskates
pl; **rollerblading** *n* Inlineskaten
nt; **roller coaster** *n* Achterbahn *f*;
roller skates *npl* Rollschuhe *pl*;
roller-skating *n* Rollschuhlaufen
nt; **rolling pin** *n* Nudelholz *nt*;
roll-on (deodorant) *n* Deoroller
m
ROM [rɒm] *acr* = **read only memory** ROM *m*
Roman ['rəʊmən] *adj* römisch
▷ *n* Römer(in) *m(f)*; **Roman Catholic** *adj* römisch-katholisch
▷ *n* Katholik(in) *m(f)*
romance [rəʊ'mæns] *n* Romantik *f*; (*love affair*) Romanze *f*
Romania [rəʊ'meɪnɪə] *n*
Rumänien *nt*; **Romanian** *adj*

rumänisch ▷ *n* Rumäne *m*,
Rumänin *f*; (*language*) Rumänisch
nt
romantic [rəʊ'mæntɪk] *adj*
romantisch
roof [ruːf] *n* Dach *nt*; **roof rack** *n*
Dachgepäckträger *m*
rook [rʊk] *n* (*in chess*) Turm *m*
room [ruːm] *n* Zimmer *nt*, Raum
m; (*large, for gatherings etc*) Saal *m*;
(*space*) Platz *m*; (*fig*) Spielraum *m*;
to make ~ for Platz machen für;
roommate *n* Zimmergenosse *m*,
Zimmergenossin *f*;
Mitbewohner(in) *m(f)*; **room service** *n* Zimmerservice *m*;
roomy *adj* geräumig; (*garment*)
weit
root [ruːt] *n* Wurzel *f*; **root out** *vt*
(*eradicate*) ausrotten; **root vegetable** *n* Wurzelgemüse *nt*
rope [rəʊp] *n* Seil *nt*; **to know the ~s** (*fam*) sich auskennen
rose [rəʊz] *pt of* **rise** ▷ *n* Rose *f*
rosé ['rəʊzeɪ] *n* Rosé(wein) *m*
rot [rɒt] *vi* verfaulen
rota ['rəʊtə] *n* (*Brit*) Dienstplan *m*
rotate [rəʊ'teɪt] *vt* (*turn*) rotieren
lassen ▷ *vi* rotieren; **rotation**
[rəʊ'teɪʃən] *n* (*turning*) Rotation *f*;
in ~ abwechselnd
rotten ['rɒtn] *adj* (*decayed*) faul;
(*mean*) gemein; (*unpleasant*)
scheußlich; (*ill*) elend
rough [rʌf] *adj* (*not smooth*) rau;
(*path*) uneben; (*coarse, violent*)
grob; (*crossing*) stürmisch; (*without comforts*) hart; (*unfinished, makeshift*) grob; (*approximate*)
ungefähr; **~ draft** Rohentwurf *m*; **I have a ~ idea** ich habe eine
ungefähre Vorstellung ▷ *adv*: **to sleep ~** im Freien schlafen ▷ *vt*:
to ~ it primitiv leben ▷ *n*: **to write sth in ~** etw ins Unreine
schreiben; **roughly** *adv* grob;
(*approximately*) ungefähr

round [raʊnd] *adj* rund ▷ *adv*: **all ~** (*on all sides*) rundherum; **the long way ~** der längere Weg; **I'll be ~ at 8** ich werde um acht Uhr da sein; **the other way ~** umgekehrt ▷ *prep* (*surrounding*) um (... herum); **~ (about)** (*approximately*) ungefähr; **~ the corner** um die Ecke; **to go ~ the world** um die Welt reisen; **she lives ~ here** sie wohnt hier in der Gegend ▷ *n* Runde *f*; (*of bread, toast*) Scheibe *f*; **it's my ~** (*of drinks*) die Runde geht auf mich ▷ *vt* (*corner*) biegen um; **round off** *vt* abrunden; **round up** *vt* (*number, price*) aufrunden

roundabout *n* (*Brit Auto*) Kreisverkehr *m*; (*Brit: merry-go-round*) Karussell *nt* ▷ *adj* umständlich; **round-the-clock** *adj* rund um die Uhr; **round trip** *n* Rundreise *f*; **round-trip ticket** *n* (*US*) Rückfahrkarte *f*; (*for plane*) Rückflugticket *nt*

rouse [raʊz] *vt* (*from sleep*) wecken

route [ruːt] *n* Route *f*; (*bus, plane etc service*) Linie *f*; (*fig*) Weg *m*

routine [ruːˈtiːn] *n* Routine *f* ▷ *adj* Routine-

row [rəʊ] *n* (*line*) Reihe *f*; **three times in a ~** dreimal hintereinander ▷ *vt, vi* (*boat*) rudern ▷ [raʊ] *n* (*noise*) Krach *m*; (*dispute*) Streit *m*

rowboat ['rəʊbəʊt] *n* (*US*) Ruderboot *nt*

row house ['rəʊhaʊs] *n* (*US*) Reihenhaus *nt*

rowing ['rəʊɪŋ] *n* Rudern *nt*; **rowing boat** *n* (*Brit*) Ruderboot *nt*; **rowing machine** *n* Rudergerät *nt*

royal ['rɔɪəl] *adj* königlich; **royalty** *n* (*family*) Mitglieder *pl* der königlichen Familie; **royalties** *pl* (*from book, music*) Tantiemen *pl*

RSPCA *abbr* = **Royal Society for the Prevention of Cruelty to Animals** britischer Tierschutzverein

RSPCC *abbr* = **Royal Society for the Prevention of Cruelty to Children** britischer Kinderschutzverein

RSVP *abbr* = **répondez s'il vous plaît** u. A. w. g.

rub [rʌb] *vt* reiben; **rub in** *vt* einmassieren; **rub out** *vt* (*with eraser*) ausradieren

rubber ['rʌbə*] *n* Gummi *m*; (*Brit: eraser*) Radiergummi *m*; (*US fam: contraceptive*) Gummi *m*; **rubber band** *n* Gummiband *nt*; **rubber stamp** *n* Stempel *m*

rubbish ['rʌbɪʃ] *n* Abfall *m*; (*nonsense*) Quatsch *m*; (*poor-quality thing*) Mist *m*; **don't talk ~** red keinen Unsinn!; **rubbish bin** *n* Mülleimer *m*; **rubbish dump** *n* Müllablageplatz *m*

rubble ['rʌbl] *n* Schutt *m*

ruby ['ruːbɪ] *n* (*stone*) Rubin *m*

rucksack ['rʌksæk] *n* Rucksack *m*

rude [ruːd] *adj* (*impolite*) unhöflich; (*indecent*) unanständig

rug [rʌg] *n* Teppich *m*; (*next to bed*) Bettvorleger *m*; (*for knees*) Wolldecke *f*

rugby ['rʌgbɪ] *n* Rugby *nt*

rugged ['rʌgɪd] *adj* (*coastline*) zerklüftet; (*features*) markant

ruin ['ruːɪn] *n* Ruine *f*; (*financial, social*) Ruin *m* ▷ *vt* ruinieren

rule [ruːl] *n* Regel *f*; (*governing*) Herrschaft *f*; **as a ~** in der Regel ▷ *vt, vi* (*govern*) regieren; (*decide*) entscheiden; **ruler** *n* Lineal *nt*; (*person*) Herrscher(in) *m(f)*

rum [rʌm] *n* Rum *m*

rumble ['rʌmbl] *vi* (*stomach*) knurren; (*train, truck*) rumpeln

rummage ['rʌmɪdʒ] *vi*: **~ (around)** herumstöbern

rumor (US), **rumour** ['ruːmə°] n Gerücht nt

run [rʌn] (**ran**, **run**) vt (race, distance) laufen; (machine, engine, computer program, water) laufen lassen; (manage) leiten, führen; (car) unterhalten; **I ran her home** ich habe sie nach Hause gefahren ▷ vi laufen; (move quickly) rennen; (bus, train) fahren; (path etc) verlaufen; (machine, engine, computer program) laufen; (flow) fließen; (colours, make-up) verlaufen; **to ~ for President** für die Präsidentschaft kandidieren; **to be ~ning low** knapp werden; **my nose is ~ning** mir läuft die Nase; **it ~s in the family** es liegt in der Familie ▷ n (on foot) Lauf m; (in car) Spazierfahrt f; (series) Reihe f; (sudden demand) Ansturm m (on auf +akk); (in tights) Laufmasche f; (in cricket, baseball) Lauf m; **to go for a ~** laufen gehen; (in car) eine Spazierfahrt machen; **in the long ~** auf die Dauer; **on the ~** auf der Flucht (from vor +dat); **run about** vi herumlaufen; **run away** vi weglaufen; **run down** vt (with car) umfahren; (criticize) heruntermachen; **to be ~** (tired) abgespannt sein; **run into** vt (meet) zufällig treffen; (problem) stoßen auf +akk; **run off** vi weglaufen; **run out** vi (person) hinausrennen; (liquid) auslaufen; (lease, time) ablaufen; (money, supplies) ausgehen; **he ran ~ of money** ihm ging das Geld aus; **run over** vt (with car) überfahren; **run up** vt (debt, bill) machen

rung [rʌŋ] pp of **ring**

runner ['rʌnə°] n (athlete) Läufer(in) m(f); **to do a ~** (fam) wegrennen; **runner bean** n (Brit) Stangenbohne f

running ['rʌnɪŋ] n (Sport) Laufen nt; (management) Leitung f, Führung f ▷ adj (water) fließend; **~ costs** Betriebskosten pl; (for car) Unterhaltskosten pl; **3 days ~** 3 Tage hintereinander

runny ['rʌnɪ] adj (food) flüssig; (nose) laufend

runway ['rʌnweɪ] n Start- und Landebahn f

rural ['rʊərəl] adj ländlich

rush [rʌʃ] n Eile f; (for tickets etc) Ansturm m (for auf +akk); **to be in a ~** es eilig haben; **there's no ~** es eilt nicht ▷ vt (do too quickly) hastig machen; (meal) hastig essen; **to ~ sb to hospital** jdn auf dem schnellsten Weg ins Krankenhaus bringen; **don't ~ me** dräng mich nicht ▷ vi (hurry) eilen; **don't ~** lass dir Zeit; **rush hour** n Hauptverkehrszeit f

rusk [rʌsk] n Zwieback m

Russia ['rʌʃə] n Russland nt; **Russian** adj russisch ▷ n Russe m, Russin f; (language) Russisch nt

rust [rʌst] n Rost m ▷ vi rosten; **rustproof** ['rʌstpruːf] adj rostfrei; **rusty** ['rʌstɪ] adj rostig

ruthless ['ruːθləs] adj rücksichtslos; (treatment, criticism) schonungslos

rye [raɪ] n Roggen m; **rye bread** n Roggenbrot nt

S

S *abbr* = **south** S

sabotage ['sæbətɑːʒ] *vt* sabotieren

sachet ['sæʃeɪ] *n* Päckchen *nt*

sack [sæk] *n* (*bag*) Sack *m*; **to get the ~** (*fam*) rausgeschmissen werden ▷ *vt* (*fam*) rausschmeißen

sacred ['seɪkrɪd] *adj* heilig

sacrifice ['sækrɪfaɪs] *n* Opfer *nt* ▷ *vt* opfern

sad [sæd] *adj* traurig

saddle ['sædl] *n* Sattel *m*

sadistic [sə'dɪstɪk] *adj* sadistisch

sadly ['sædlɪ] *adv* (*unfortunately*) leider

safari [sə'fɑːrɪ] *n* Safari

safe [seɪf] *adj* (*free from danger*) sicher; (*out of danger*) in Sicherheit; (*careful*) vorsichtig; **have a ~ journey** gute Fahrt! ▷ *n* Safe *m*; **safeguard** *n* Schutz *m* ▷ *vt* schützen (*against* vor +*dat*); **safely** *adv* sicher; (*arrive*) wohlbehalten;

(*drive*) vorsichtig; **safety** *n* Sicherheit *f*; **safety belt** *n* Sicherheitsgurt *m*; **safety pin** *n* Sicherheitsnadel *f*

Sagittarius [sædʒɪ'tɛərɪəs] *n* (*Astr*) Schütze *m*

Sahara [sə'hɑːrə] *n*: **the ~** (**Desert**) die (Wüste) Sahara

said [sed] *pt, pp of* **say**

sail [seɪl] *n* Segel *nt*; **to set ~** losfahren (*for* nach) ▷ *vi* (*in yacht*) segeln; (*on ship*) mit dem Schiff fahren; (*ship*) auslaufen (*for* nach) ▷ *vt* (*yacht*) segeln mit; (*ship*) steuern; **sailboat** *n* (*US*) Segelboot *nt*; **sailing** *n*: **to go ~** segeln gehen; **sailing boat** *n* (*Brit*) Segelboot *nt*; **sailor** *n* Seemann *m*; (*in navy*) Matrose *m*

saint [seɪnt] *n* Heilige(r) *mf*

sake [seɪk] *n*: **for the ~ of** um +*gen* ... willen; **for your ~** deinetwegen, dir zuliebe

salad ['sæləd] *n* Salat *m*; **salad cream** *n* (*Brit*) majonäseartige Salatsoße; **salad dressing** *n* Salatsoße *f*

salary ['sælərɪ] *n* Gehalt *nt*

sale [seɪl] *n* Verkauf *m*; (*at reduced prices*) Ausverkauf *m*; **the ~s** *pl* (*in summer, winter*) der Schlussverkauf; **for ~** zu verkaufen; **sales clerk** *n* (*US*) Verkäufer(in) *m(f)*; **salesman** (*pl* **-men**) *n* Verkäufer *m*; (*rep*) Vertreter *m*; **sales rep** *n* Vertreter(in) *m(f)*; **sales tax** *n* (*US*) Verkaufssteuer *f*; **saleswoman** (*pl* **-women**) *n* Verkäuferin *f*; (*rep*) Vertreterin *f*

salmon ['sæmən] *n* Lachs *m*

saloon [sə'luːn] *n* (*ship's lounge*) Salon *m*; (*US: bar*) Kneipe *f*

salt [sɔːlt] *n* Salz *nt* ▷ *vt* (*flavour*) salzen; (*roads*) mit Salz streuen; **salt cellar**, **salt shaker** (*US*) *n* Salzstreuer *m*; **salty** *adj* salzig

salvage ['sælvɪdʒ] vt bergen (*from* aus); (*fig*) retten
same [seɪm] adj: **the ~** (*similar*) der/die/das gleiche, die gleichen pl; (*identical*) der-/die-/dasselbe, dieselben pl; **they live in the ~ house** sie wohnen im selben Haus ▷ pron: **the ~** (*similar*) der/die/das Gleiche, die Gleichen pl; (*identical*) der-/die-/dasselbe, dieselben pl; **all the ~** trotzdem; **the ~ to you** gleichfalls; **it's all the ~ to me** es ist mir egal ▷ adv: **the ~** gleich; **they look the ~** sie sehen gleich aus
sample ['sɑːmpl] n Probe f; (*of fabric*) Muster nt ▷ vt probieren
sanctions ['sæŋkʃənz] npl (*Pol*) Sanktionen pl
sanctuary ['sæŋktjʊərɪ] n (*refuge*) Zuflucht f; (*for animals*) Schutzgebiet nt
sand [sænd] n Sand m
sandal ['sændl] n Sandale f
sandpaper n Sandpapier nt ▷ vt schmirgeln
sandwich ['sænwɪdʒ] n Sandwich nt
sandy ['sændɪ] adj (*full of sand*) sandig; **~ beach** Sandstrand m
sane [seɪn] adj geistig gesund, normal; (*sensible*) vernünftig
sang [sæŋ] pt of **sing**
sanitary ['sænɪtərɪ] adj hygienisch; **sanitary napkin** (US), **sanitary towel** n Damenbinde f
sank [sæŋk] pt of **sink**
Santa (Claus) ['sæntə('klɔːz)] n der Weihnachtsmann
sarcastic [sɑːˈkæstɪk] adj sarkastisch
sardine [sɑːˈdiːn] n Sardine f
Sardinia [sɑːˈdɪnɪə] n Sardinien nt
sari [sɑːrɪ] n Sari m (*von indischen Frauen getragenes Gewand*)
sat [sæt] pt, pp of **sit**

Sat abbr = **Saturday** Sa.
satellite ['sætəlaɪt] n Satellit m; **satellite dish** n Satellitenschüssel f; **satellite TV** n Satellitenfernsehen nt
satin ['sætɪn] n Satin m
satisfaction [sætɪsˈfækʃən] n (*contentment*) Zufriedenheit f; **is that to your ~?** bist du/sind Sie damit zufrieden?; **satisfactory** [sætɪsˈfæktərɪ] adj zufriedenstellend; **satisfied** ['sætɪsfaɪd] adj zufrieden (*with* mit); **satisfy** ['sætɪsfaɪ] vt zufriedenstellen; (*convince*) überzeugen; (*conditions*) erfüllen; (*need, demand*) befriedigen; **satisfying** adj befriedigend
Saturday ['sætədeɪ] n Samstag m, Sonnabend m; *see also* **Tuesday**
sauce [sɔːs] n Soße f; **saucepan** n Kochtopf m; **saucer** n Untertasse f
saucy ['sɔːsɪ] adj frech
Saudi Arabia ['saudɪəˈreɪbɪə] n Saudi-Arabien nt
sauna ['sɔːnə] n Sauna f
sausage ['sɒsɪdʒ] n Wurst f; **sausage roll** n mit Wurst gefülltes Blätterteigröllchen
savage ['sævɪdʒ] adj (*person, attack*) brutal; (*animal*) wild
save [seɪv] vt (*rescue*) retten (*from* vor +dat); (*money, time, electricity etc*) sparen; (*strength*) schonen; (*Inform*) speichern; **to ~ sb's life** jdm das Leben retten ▷ vi sparen ▷ n (*in football*) Parade f; **save up** vi sparen (*for* auf +akk); **saving** n (*of money*) Sparen nt; **~s** pl Ersparnisse pl; **~s account** Sparkonto nt
savory (US), **savoury** ['seɪvərɪ] adj (*not sweet*) pikant
saw [sɔː] (**sawed, sawn**) vt, vi sägen ▷ n (*tool*) Säge f ▷ pt of **see**; **sawdust** n Sägemehl nt

saxophone ['sæksəfəʊn] n
Saxophon nt

say [seɪ] (**said, said**) vt sagen (to
sb jdm); (prayer) sprechen; **what
does the letter ~?** was steht im
Brief?; **the rules ~ that ...** in den
Regeln heißt es, dass ...; **he's said
to be rich** er soll reich sein ▷ n: **to
have a ~ in sth** bei etw ein
Mitspracherecht haben ▷ adv
zum Beispiel; **saying** n
Sprichwort nt

scab [skæb] n (on cut) Schorf m

scaffolding ['skæfəʊldɪŋ] n
(Bau)gerüst nt

scale [skeɪl] n (of map etc)
Maßstab m; (on thermometer etc)
Skala f; (of pay) Tarifsystem nt;
(Mus) Tonleiter f; (of fish, snake)
Schuppe f; **to ~** maßstabsgerecht;
on a large/small ~ in
großem/kleinem Umfang; **scales**
npl (for weighing) Waage f

scalp [skælp] n Kopfhaut f

scan [skæn] vt (examine) genau
prüfen; (read quickly) überfliegen;
(Inform) scannen ▷ n (Med)
Ultraschall m; **scan in** vt (Inform)
einscannen

scandal ['skændl] n Skandal m;
scandalous adj skandalös

Scandinavia [skændɪ'neɪvɪə] n
Skandinavien nt; **Scandinavian**
adj skandinavisch ▷ n Skandi-
navier(in) m(f)

scanner ['skænə*] n Scanner m

scapegoat ['skeɪpgəʊt] n
Sündenbock m

scar [skɑ:*] n Narbe f

scarce ['skeəs] adj selten; (in
short supply) knapp; **scarcely** adv
kaum

scare ['skeə*] n (general alarm)
Panik f ▷ vt erschrecken; **to be ~d**
Angst haben (of vor +dat)

scarf [skɑ:f] (pl **-scarves**) n Schal
m; (on head) Kopftuch nt

scarlet ['skɑ:lət] adj schar-
lachrot; **scarlet fever** n Scharlach
m

scary ['skɛərɪ] adj (film, story)
gruselig

scatter ['skætə*] vt verstreuen;
(seed, gravel) streuen; (disperse)
auseinandertreiben

scene [si:n] n (location) Ort m;
(division of play) (Theat) Szene f;
(view) Anblick m; **to make a ~** eine
Szene machen; **scenery** ['si:nərɪ]
n (landscape) Landschaft f; (Theat)
Kulissen pl; **scenic** ['si:nɪk] adj
(landscape) malerisch; **~ route**
landschaftlich schöne Strecke

scent [sent] n (perfume) Parfüm
nt; (smell) Duft m

sceptical ['skeptɪkəl] adj (Brit)
skeptisch

schedule ['ʃedju:l, 'skedʒʊəl] n
(plan) Programm nt; (of work)
Zeitplan m; (list) Liste f; (US: of
trains, buses, air traffic)
Fahr-, Flugplan m; **on
~** planmäßig; **to be behind ~ with
sth** etw in Verzug sein ▷ vt:
**the meeting is ~d for next
Monday** die Besprechung ist für
nächsten Montag angesetzt;
scheduled adj (departure, arrival)
planmäßig; **~ flight** Linienflug m

scheme [ski:m] n (plan) Plan m;
(project) Projekt nt; (dishonest)
Intrige f ▷ vi intrigieren

schizophrenic [skɪtsə'frenɪk]
adj schizophren

scholar ['skɒlə*] n Gelehrte(r)
mf; **scholarship** n (grant)
Stipendium nt

school [sku:l] n Schule f;
(university department) Fachbereich
m; (US: university) Universität f;
school bag n Schultasche f;
schoolbook n Schulbuch nt;
schoolboy n Schüler m; **school
bus** n Schulbus m; **schoolgirl** n

Schülerin f; **schoolteacher** n Lehrer(in) m(f); **schoolwork** n Schularbeiten pl

sciatica [saɪˈætɪkə] n Ischias m

science [ˈsaɪəns] n Wissenschaft f; (natural ~) Naturwissenschaft f; **science fiction** n Sciencefiction f; **scientific** [saɪənˈtɪfɪk] adj wissenschaftlich; **scientist** [ˈsaɪəntɪst] n Wissenschaftler(in) m(f); (in natural sciences) Naturwissenschaftler(in) m(f)

scissors [ˈsɪzəz] npl Schere f

scone [skɒn] n kleines süßes Hefebrötchen mit oder ohne Rosinen, das mit Butter oder Dickrahm und Marmelade gegessen wird

scoop [skuːp] n (exclusive story) Exklusivbericht m; **a ~ of ice-cream** eine Kugel Eis ▷ vt: **to ~ (up)** schaufeln

scooter [ˈskuːtə*] n (Motor)-roller m; (toy) (Tret)roller m

scope [skəʊp] n Umfang m; (opportunity) Möglichkeit f

score [skɔː*] n (Sport) Spielstand m; (final result) Spielergebnis nt; (in quiz etc) Punktestand m; (Mus) Partitur f; **to keep (the) ~** mitzählen ▷ vt (goal) schießen; (points) punkten ▷ vi (keep ~) mitzählen; **scoreboard** n Anzeigetafel f

scorn [skɔːn] n Verachtung f; **scornful** adj verächtlich

Scorpio [ˈskɔːpɪəʊ] (pl -s) n (Astr) Skorpion m

scorpion [ˈskɔːpɪən] n Skorpion m

Scot [skɒt] n Schotte m, Schottin f; **Scotch** [skɒtʃ] n (whisky) schottischer Whisky, Scotch m

Scotch tape® n (US) Tesafilm® m

Scotland [ˈskɒtlənd] n Schottland nt; **Scotsman** (pl -men) n Schotte m; **Scotswoman** (pl -women) n Schottin f; **Scottish** adj schottisch

scout [skaʊt] n (boy ~) Pfadfinder m

scowl [skaʊl] vi finster blicken

scrambled eggs npl Rührei nt

scrap [skræp] n (bit) Stückchen nt, Fetzen m; (metal) Schrott m ▷ vt (car) verschrotten; (plan) verwerfen; **scrapbook** n Sammelalbum nt

scrape [skreɪp] n (scratch) Kratzer m ▷ vt (car) schrammen; (wall) streifen; **to ~ one's knee** sich das Knie schürfen; **scrape through** vi (exam) mit knapper Not bestehen

scrap heap [ˈskræphiːp] n Schrotthaufen m; **scrap metal** n Schrott m; **scrap paper** n Schmierpapier nt

scratch [skrætʃ] n (mark) Kratzer m; **to start from ~** von vorne anfangen ▷ vt kratzen; (car) zerkratzen; **to ~ one's arm** sich am Arm kratzen ▷ vi kratzen; (~ oneself) sich kratzen

scream [skriːm] n Schrei m ▷ vi schreien (with vor +dat); **to ~ at sb** jdn anschreien

screen [skriːn] n (TV, Inform) Bildschirm m; (Cine) Leinwand f ▷ vt (protect) abschirmen; (hide) verdecken; (film) zeigen; (applicants, luggage) überprüfen; **screenplay** n Drehbuch nt; **screensaver** n (Inform) Bildschirmschoner m

screw [skruː] n Schraube f ▷ vt (vulg: have sex with) ficken; **to ~ sth to sth** etw an etw akk schrauben; **to ~ off/on** (lid) ab-/aufschrauben; **screw up** vt (paper) zusammenknüllen; (make a mess of) vermasseln; **screwdriver** n Schraubenzieher m; **screw top** n Schraubverschluss m

scribble ['skrɪbl] vt, vi kritzeln

script [skrɪpt] n (of play) Text m; (of film) Drehbuch nt; (style of writing) Schrift f

scroll down ['skrəʊl'daʊn] vi (Inform) runterscrollen; **scroll up** vi (Inform) raufscrollen; **scroll bar** n (Inform) Scrollbar f

scrub [skrʌb] vt schrubben; **scrubbing brush**, **scrub brush** (US) n Scheuerbürste f

scruffy ['skrʌfɪ] adj vergammelt

scrupulous, scrupulously ['skruːpjʊləs, -lɪ] adj, adv gewissenhaft; (painstaking) peinlich genau

scuba-diving ['skuːbədaɪvɪŋ] n Sporttauchen nt

sculptor ['skʌlptə*] n Bildhauer(in) m(f); **sculpture** ['skʌlptʃə*] n (Art) Bildhauerei f; (statue) Skulptur f

sea [siː] n Meer nt, See f; **seafood** n Meeresfrüchte pl; **sea front** n Strandpromenade f; **seagull** n Möwe f

seal [siːl] n (animal) Robbe f; (stamp, impression) Siegel nt; (Tech) Verschluss m; (ring etc) Dichtung f ▷ vt versiegeln; (envelope) zukleben

seam [siːm] n Naht f

search [sɜːtʃ] n Suche f (for nach); **to do a ~ for** (Inform) suchen nach; **in ~ of** auf der Suche nach ▷ vi suchen (for nach) ▷ vt durchsuchen; **search engine** n (Inform) Suchmaschine f

seashell ['siːʃel] n Muschel f; **seashore** n Strand m; **seasick** adj seekrank; **seaside** n: **at the ~** am Meer; **to go to the ~** ans Meer fahren; **seaside resort** n Seebad nt

season ['siːzn] n Jahreszeit f; (Comm) Saison f; **high/low**

~ Hoch-/Nebensaison f ▷ vt (flavour) würzen

seasoning n Gewürz nt

season ticket n (Rail) Zeitkarte f; (Theat) Abonnement nt; (Sport) Dauerkarte f

seat [siːt] n (place) Platz m; (chair) Sitz m; **take a ~** setzen Sie sich ▷ vt: **the hall ~s 300** der Saal hat 300 Sitzplätze; **please be ~ed** bitte setzen Sie sich; **to remain ~ed** sitzen bleiben; **seat belt** n Sicherheitsgurt m

sea view ['siːvjuː] n Seeblick m; **seaweed** n Seetang m

secluded [sɪ'kluːdɪd] adj abgelegen

second ['sekənd] adj zweite(r, s); **the ~ of June** der zweite Juni ▷ adv (in ~ position) an zweiter Stelle; (secondly) zweitens; **he came ~** er ist Zweiter geworden ▷ n (of time) Sekunde f; (moment) Augenblick m; **~ (gear)** der zweite Gang; (~ helping) zweite Portion; **just a ~** (einen) Augenblick!; **secondary** adj (less important) zweitrangig; **~ education** höhere Schulbildung f; **~ school** weiterführende Schule; **second-class** adj (ticket) zweiter Klasse; **~ stamp** Briefmarke für nicht bevorzugt beförderte Sendungen ▷ adv (travel) zweiter Klasse; **second-hand** adj, adv gebraucht; (information) aus zweiter Hand; **secondly** adv zweitens; **second-rate** adj (pej) zweitklassig

secret ['siːkrət] n Geheimnis nt ▷ adj geheim; (admirer) heimlich

secretary ['sekrətrɪ] n Sekretär(in) m(f); (minister) Minister(in) m(f); **Secretary of State** n (US) Außenminister(in) m(f); **secretary's office** n Sekretariat nt

secretive ['si:krətɪv] *adj* (*person*) geheimnistuerisch; **secretly** ['si:krətlɪ] *adv* heimlich
sect [sekt] *n* Sekte *f*
section ['sekʃən] *n* (*part*) Teil *m*; (*of document*) Abschnitt *m*; (*department*) Abteilung *f*
secure [sɪ'kjʊə*] *adj* (*safe*) sicher (*from* vor +*dat*); (*firmly fixed*) fest ▷ *vt* (*make firm*) befestigen; (*window, door*) fest verschließen; **securely** *adv* fest; (*safely*) sicher; **security** [sɪ'kjʊərɪtɪ] *n* Sicherheit *f*
sedative ['sedətɪv] *n* Beruhigungsmittel *nt*
seduce [sɪ'dju:s] *vt* verführen; **seductive** [sɪ'dʌktɪv] *adj* verführerisch; (*offer*) verlockend
see [si:] (**saw, seen**) *vt* sehen; (*understand*) verstehen; (*check*) nachsehen; (*accompany*) bringen; (*visit*) besuchen; (*talk to*) sprechen; **to ~ the doctor** zum Arzt gehen; **to ~ sb home** jdn nach Hause begleiten; **I saw him swimming** ich habe ihn schwimmen sehen; **~ you** tschüs!; **~ you on Friday** bis Freitag! ▷ *vi* sehen; (*understand*) verstehen; (*check*) nachsehen; (**you**) **~** siehst du!; **we'll ~** mal sehen; **see about** *vt* (*attend to*) sich kümmern um; **see off** *vt* (*say goodbye to*) verabschieden; **see out** *vt* (*show out*) zur Tür bringen; **see through** *vt*: **to see sth through** etw zu Ende bringen; **to ~ sb/sth** jdn/etw durchschauen; **see to** *vt* sich kümmern um; **~ it that ...** sieh zu, dass ...
seed [si:d] *n* (*of plant*) Samen *m*; (*in fruit*) Kern *m*; **seedless** *adj* kernlos
seedy ['si:dɪ] *adj* zwielichtig
seek [si:k] (**sought, sought**) *vt* suchen; (*fame*) streben nach; **to ~ sb's advice** jdn um Rat fragen

seem [si:m] *vi* scheinen; **he ~s (to be) honest** er scheint ehrlich zu sein; **it ~s to me that ...** es scheint mir, dass ...
seen [si:n] *pp of* **see**
seesaw ['si:sɔ:] *n* Wippe *f*
see-through *adj* durchsichtig
segment ['segmənt] *n* Teil *m*
seize [si:z] *vt* packen; (*confiscate*) beschlagnahmen; (*opportunity, power*) ergreifen
seldom ['seldəm] *adv* selten
select [sɪ'lekt] *adj* (*exclusive*) exklusiv ▷ *vt* auswählen; **selection** [sɪ'lekʃən] *n* Auswahl *f* (*of* an +*dat*); **selective** *adj* (*choosy*) wählerisch
self [self] (*pl* **selves**) *n* Selbst *nt*, Ich *nt*; **he's his old ~ again** er ist wieder ganz der Alte; **self-adhesive** *adj* selbstklebend; **self-assured** *n* selbstsicher; **self-catering** *adj* für Selbstversorger; **self-centred** *adj* egozentrisch; **self-confidence** *n* Selbstbewusstsein *nt*; **self-confident** *adj* selbstbewusst; **self-conscious** *adj* befangen, verklemmt; **self-contained** *adj* (*flat*) separat; **self-control** *n* Selbstbeherrschung *f*; **self-defence** *n* Selbstverteidigung *f*; **self-employed** *adj* selbstständig; **self-evident** *adj* offensichtlich
selfish, selfishly ['selfɪʃ, -lɪ] *adj, adv* egoistisch, selbstsüchtig; **selfless, selflessly** *adj, adv* selbstlos
self-pity [self'pɪtɪ] *n* Selbstmitleid *nt*; **self-portrait** *n* Selbstporträt *nt*; **self-respect** *n* Selbstachtung *f*; **self-service** *n* Selbstbedienung *f* ▷ *adj* Selbstbedienungs-
sell [sel] (**sold, sold**) *vt* verkaufen; **to ~ sb sth, to ~ sth to**

sb jdm etw verkaufen; **do you ~ postcards?** haben Sie Postkarten? ▷ vi (product) sich verkaufen; **sell out** vt: **to be sold ~** ausverkauft sein; **sell-by date** n Haltbarkeitsdatum nt

Sellotape® ['seləteɪp] n (Brit) Tesafilm® m

semester [sɪ'mestə*] n Semester nt

semi ['semɪ] n (Brit: house) Doppelhaushälfte f; **semicircle** n Halbkreis m; **semicolon** n Semikolon nt; **semidetached (house)** (Brit) Doppelhaushälfte f; **semifinal** n Halbfinale nt

seminar ['semɪnɑː*] n Seminar nt

semiskimmed milk ['semɪskɪmd'mɪlk] n Halbfettmilch f

senate ['senət] n Senat m; **senator** n Senator(in) m(f)

send [send] (**sent, sent**) vt schicken; **to ~ sb sth, to ~ sth to sb** jdm etw schicken; **~ her my best wishes** grüße sie von mir; **send away** vt wegschicken ▷ vi: **to ~ for** anfordern; **send back** vt zurückschicken; **send for** vt (person) holen lassen; (by post) anfordern; **send off** vt (by post) abschicken; **send out** vt (invitations etc) verschicken ▷ vi: **to ~ for sth** etw holen lassen

sender ['sendə*] n Absender(in) m(f)

senior ['siːnɪə*] adj (older) älter; (high-ranking) höher; (pupils) älter; **he is ~ to me** er ist mir übergeordnet ▷ n: **he's eight years my ~** er ist acht Jahre älter als ich; **senior citizen** n Senior(in) m(f)

sensation [sen'seɪʃən] n Gefühl nt; (excitement, person, thing)

Sensation f; **sensational** adj sensationell

sense [sens] n (faculty, meaning) Sinn m; (feeling) Gefühl nt; (understanding) Verstand m; **~ of smell/taste** Geruchs-/Geschmackssinn m; **to have a ~ of humour** Humor haben; **to make ~** (sentence etc) einen Sinn ergeben; (be sensible) Sinn machen; **in a ~** gewissermaßen ▷ vt spüren; **senseless** adj (stupid) sinnlos

sensible, sensibly ['sensəbl, -blɪ] adj, adv vernünftig

sensitive ['sensɪtɪv] adj empfindlich (to gegen); (easily hurt) sensibel; (subject) heikel

sensual ['sensjʊəl] adj sinnlich

sensuous ['sensjʊəs] adj sinnlich

sent [sent] pt, pp of **send**

sentence ['sentəns] n (Ling) Satz m; (Jur) Strafe f ▷ vt verurteilen (to zu)

sentiment ['sentɪmənt] n (sentimentality) Sentimentalität f; (opinion) Ansicht f; **sentimental** [sentɪ'mentl] adj sentimental

separate ['seprət] adj getrennt, separat; (individual) einzeln ▷ ['sepəreɪt] vt trennen (from von); **they are ~d** (couple) sie leben getrennt ▷ vi sich trennen; **separately** adv getrennt; (singly) einzeln

September [sep'tembə*] n September m; **in ~** im September; **on the 2nd of ~** am 2. September; **at the beginning/in the middle/at the end of ~** Anfang/Mitte/Ende September; **last/next ~** letzten/nächsten September

septic ['septɪk] adj vereitert

sequel ['siːkwəl] n (to film, book) Fortsetzung f (to von)

sequence ['siːkwəns] n (order)
Reihenfolge f
Serbia ['sɜːbjə] n Serbien nt
sergeant ['sɑːdʒənt] n Polizei-
meister(in) m(f); (Mil)
Feldwebel(in) m(f)
serial ['sɪərɪəl] n (TV) Serie f; (in
newspaper etc) Fortsetzungsroman
m ▷ adj (Inform) seriell; **~ number**
Seriennummer f
series ['sɪərɪz] nsing Reihe f; (TV,
Radio) Serie f
serious ['sɪərɪəs] adj ernst;
(injury, illness, mistake) schwer;
(discussion) ernsthaft; **are you ~?**
ist das dein Ernst?; **seriously** adv
ernsthaft; (hurt) schwer; **~?** im
Ernst?; **to take sb ~** jdn ernst
nehmen
sermon ['sɜːmən] n (Rel) Predigt f
servant ['sɜːvənt] n Diener(in)
m(f); **serve** [sɜːv] vt (customer)
bedienen; (food) servieren; (one's
country etc) dienen +dat; (sentence)
verbüßen; **I'm being ~d** ich werde
schon bedient; **it ~s him right** es
geschieht ihm recht ▷ vi dienen
(as als), aufschlagen ▷ n
Aufschlag m
server n (Inform) Server m
service ['sɜːvɪs] n (in shop, hotel)
Bedienung f; (activity, amenity)
Dienstleistung f; (set of dishes)
Service nt; (Auto) Inspektion f;
(Tech) Wartung f; (Rel)
Gottesdienst m, Aufschlag m;
train/bus ~ Zug-/Busverbindung
f; **"~ not included"** „Bedienung
nicht inbegriffen" ▷ vt (Auto, Tech)
warten; **service area** n (on
motorway) Raststätte f (mit
Tankstelle); **service charge** n
Bedienung f; **service provider** n
(Inform) Provider m; **service
station** n Tankstelle f
session ['seʃən] n (of court,
assembly) Sitzung f

set [set] (**set, set**) vt (place)
stellen; (lay flat) legen; (arrange)
anordnen; (table) decken; (trap,
record) aufstellen; (time, price)
festsetzen; (watch, alarm) stellen
(for auf +akk); **to ~ sb a task** jdm
eine Aufgabe stellen; **to ~ free**
freilassen; **to ~ a good example**
ein gutes Beispiel geben; **the
novel is ~ in London** der Roman
spielt in London ▷ vi (sun)
untergehen; (become hard) fest
werden; (bone)
zusammenwachsen ▷ n (collection
of things) Satz m; (of cutlery,
furniture) Garnitur f; (group of
people) Kreis m; (Radio, TV) Apparat
m, Satz m; (Theat) Bühnenbild nt;
(Cine) (Film)kulisse f ▷ adj (agreed,
prescribed) festgelegt; (ready)
bereit; **~ meal** Menü nt; **set aside**
vt (money) beiseitelegen; (time)
einplanen; **set off** vi aufbrechen
(for nach) ▷ vt (alarm) auslösen;
(enhance) hervorheben; **set out** vi
aufbrechen (for nach) ▷ vt (chairs,
chesspieces etc) aufstellen; (state)
darlegen; **to ~ to do sth** (intend)
beabsichtigen, etw zu tun; **set up**
vt (firm, organization) gründen;
(stall, tent, camera) aufbauen;
(meeting) vereinbaren ▷ vi: **to ~ as
a doctor** sich als Arzt niederlassen
setback n Rückschlag m
settee [se'tiː] n Sofa nt, Couch f
setting ['setɪŋ] n (of novel, film)
Schauplatz m; (surroundings)
Umgebung f
settle ['setl] vt (bill, debt)
begleichen; (dispute) beilegen;
(question) klären; (stomach)
beruhigen ▷ vi: **to ~ (down)** (feel
at home) sich einleben; (calm down)
sich beruhigen; **settle in** vi (in
place) sich einleben; (in job) sich
eingewöhnen; **settle up** vi
(be)zahlen; **to ~ with sb** mit jdm

abrechnen; **settlement** n (of bill, debt) Begleichung f; (colony) Siedlung f; **to reach a ~** sich einigen

setup ['setʌp] n (organization) Organisation f; (situation) Situation f

seven ['sevn] num sieben ▷ n Sieben f; see also **eight**; **seventeen** ['sevn'ti:n] num siebzehn ▷ n Siebzehn f; see also **eight**; **seventeenth** adj siebzehnte(r, s); see also **eighth**; **seventh** ['sevnθ] adj siebte(r, s) ▷ n (fraction) Siebtel nt; see also **eighth**; **seventieth** ['sevntɪɪθ] adj siebzigste(r, s); see also **eighth**; **seventy** ['sevntɪ] num siebzig; **~-one** einundsiebzig ▷ n Siebzig f; **to be in one's seventies** in den Siebzigern sein; see also **eight**

several ['sevrəl] adj, pron mehrere

severe [sɪ'vɪə*] adj (strict) streng; (serious) schwer; (pain) stark; (winter) hart; **severely** adv (harshly) hart; (seriously) schwer

sew [səʊ] (**sewed, sewn**) vt, vi nähen

sewage ['su:ɪdʒ] n Abwasser nt; **sewer** ['sʊə*] n Abwasserkanal m

sewing ['səʊɪŋ] n Nähen nt; **sewing machine** n Nähmaschine f

sewn [səʊn] pp of **sew**

sex [seks] n Sex m; (gender) Geschlecht nt; **to have ~** Sex haben (with mit); **sexism** ['seksɪzəm] n Sexismus m; **sexist** ['seksɪst] adj sexistisch ▷ n Sexist(in) m(f); **sex life** n Sex(ual)leben nt

sexual ['seksjʊəl] adj sexuell; **~ discrimination/harassment** sexuelle Diskriminierung/Belästigung; **~ intercourse** Geschlechtsverkehr m; **sexuality**

[seksjʊ'ælɪtɪ] n Sexualität f; **sexually** adv sexuell

sexy ['seksɪ] adj sexy, geil

Seychelles ['seɪʃelz] npl Seychellen pl

shabby ['ʃæbɪ] adj schäbig

shack [ʃæk] n Hütte f

shade [ʃeɪd] n (shadow) Schatten m; (for lamp) (Lampen)schirm m; (colour) Farbton m; **~s** (US: sunglasses) Sonnenbrille f ▷ vt (from sun) abschirmen; (in drawing) schattieren

shadow ['ʃædəʊ] n Schatten m

shady ['ʃeɪdɪ] adj schattig; (fig) zwielichtig

shake [ʃeɪk] (**shook, shaken**) vt schütteln; (shock) erschüttern; **to ~ hands with sb** jdm die Hand geben; **to ~ one's head** den Kopf schütteln ▷ vi (tremble) zittern; (building, ground) schwanken; **shake off** vt abschütteln; **shaken** ['ʃeɪkn] pp of **shake**; **shaky** ['ʃeɪkɪ] adj (trembling) zittrig; (table, chair, position) wackelig; (weak) unsicher

shall [ʃæl] (**should**) vb aux werden; (in questions) sollen; **I ~ do my best** ich werde mein Bestes tun; **~ I come too?** soll ich mitkommen?; **where ~ we go?** wo gehen wir hin?

shallow ['ʃæləʊ] adj (a. fig) seicht; (person) oberflächlich

shame [ʃeɪm] n (feeling of ~) Scham f; (disgrace) Schande f; **what a ~!** wie schade!; **~ on you!** schäm dich/schämen Sie sich!; **it's a ~ that ...** schade, dass ...

shampoo [ʃæm'pu:] n Shampoo nt; **to have a ~ and set** sich die Haare waschen und legen lassen ▷ vt (hair) waschen; (carpet) schamponieren

shandy ['ʃændɪ] n Radler m, Alsterwasser nt

shan't [ʃɑ:nt] contr of **shall not**

shape [ʃeɪp] n Form f;
(unidentified figure) Gestalt f; **in
the ~ of** in Form +gen; **to be in
good ~** (healthwise) in guter
Verfassung sein; **to take ~** (plan,
idea) Gestalt annehmen ▷ vt (clay,
person) formen; **-shaped** [ʃeɪpt]
suf -förmig; **shapeless** adj
formlos

share [ʃeə*] n Anteil +dat (in, of an
m); (Fin) Aktie f ▷ vt, vi teilen;
shareholder n Aktionär(in) m(f)

shark [ʃɑːk] n (Zool) Haifisch m

sharp [ʃɑːp] adj scharf; (pin) spitz;
(person) scharfsinnig; (pain) heftig;
(increase, fall) abrupt; **C/F ~** (Mus)
Cis/Dis nt ▷ adv: **at 2 o'clock
~** Punkt 2 Uhr; **sharpen** vt (knife)
schärfen; (pencil) spitzen;
sharpener n (pencil ~) Spitzer m

shatter [ʃætə*] vt zerschmet-
tern; (fig) zerstören ▷ vi
zerspringen; **shattered** adj
(exhausted) kaputt

shave [ʃeɪv] (**shaved, shaved** o
shaven) vt rasieren ▷ vi sich
rasieren ▷ n Rasur f; **that was a
close ~** (fig) das war knapp; **shave
off** vt: **to shave one's beard off**
sich den Bart abrasieren; **shaven**
[ʃeɪvn] pp of **shave** ▷ adj (head)
kahl geschoren; **shaver** n (Elec)
Rasierapparat m; **shaving brush**
n Rasierpinsel m; **shaving foam** n
Rasierschaum m; **shaving tackle**
n Rasierzeug nt

shawl [ʃɔːl] n Tuch nt

she [ʃiː] pron sie

shed [ʃed] (**shed, shed**) n
Schuppen m ▷ vt (tears, blood)
vergießen; (hair, leaves) verlieren

she'd [ʃiːd] contr of **she had; she
would**

sheep [ʃiːp] (pl -) n Schaf nt;
sheepdog n Schäferhund m;
sheepskin n Schaffell nt

sheer [ʃɪə*] adj (madness) rein;
(steep) steil; **by ~ chance** rein
zufällig

sheet [ʃiːt] n (on bed) Betttuch nt;
(of paper) Blatt nt; (of metal) Platte f;
(of glass) Scheibe f; **a ~ of paper**
ein Blatt Papier

shelf [ʃelf] (pl **shelves**) n
Bücherbord nt, Regal nt; **shelves** pl
(item of furniture) Regal nt

she'll [ʃiːl] contr of **she will; she
shall**

shell [ʃel] n (of egg, nut) Schale f;
(sea~) Muschel f ▷ vt (peas, nuts)
schälen; **shellfish** n (as food)
Meeresfrüchte pl

shelter [ʃeltə*] n (protection)
Schutz m; (accommodation)
Unterkunft f; (bus ~)
Wartehäuschen nt ▷ vt schützen
(from vor +dat) ▷ vi sich
unterstellen; **sheltered** adj (spot)
geschützt; (life) behütet

shelve [ʃelv] vt (fig) aufschieben;
shelves pl of **shelf**

shepherd [ʃepəd] n Schäfer m;
shepherd's pie n
Hackfleischauflauf mit Decke aus
Kartoffelpüree

sherry [ʃerɪ] n Sherry m

she's [ʃiːz] contr of **she is; she has**

shield [ʃiːld] n Schild m; (fig)
Schutz m ▷ vt schützen (from vor
+dat)

shift [ʃɪft] n (change)
Veränderung f; (period at work,
workers) Schicht f; (on keyboard)
Umschalttaste f ▷ vt (furniture etc)
verrücken; (stain) entfernen; **to
~ gear(s)** (US Auto) schalten ▷ vi
(move) sich bewegen; (move up)
rutschen; **shift key** n
Umschalttaste f

shin [ʃɪn] n Schienbein nt

shine [ʃaɪn] (**shone, shone**) vi
(be shiny) glänzen; (sun) scheinen;
(lamp) leuchten ▷ vt (polish)
polieren ▷ n Glanz m

shingles ['ʃɪŋglz] *nsing* (*Med*)
Gürtelrose *f*
shiny ['ʃaɪnɪ] *adj* glänzend
ship [ʃɪp] *n* Schiff *nt* ▷ *vt* (*send*)
versenden; (*by ship*) verschiffen;
shipment *n* (*goods*) Sendung *f*;
(*sent by ship*) Ladung *f*; **shipwreck**
n Schiffbruch *m*; **shipyard** *n*
Werft *f*
shirt [ʃɜːt] *n* Hemd *nt*
shit [ʃɪt] *n* (*vulg*) Scheiße *f*;
(*person*) Arschloch *nt*; **~!** Scheiße!;
shitty ['ʃɪtɪ] *adj* (*fam*) beschissen
shiver ['ʃɪvə°] *vi* zittern (*with* vor
+*dat*)
shock [ʃɒk] *n* (*mental, emotional*)
Schock *m*; **to be in ~** unter Schock
stehen; **to get a ~** (*Elec*) einen
Schlag bekommen ▷ *vt*
schockieren; **shock absorber** *n*
Stoßdämpfer *m*; **shocked** *adj*
schockiert (*by* über +*akk*);
shocking *adj* schockierend;
(*awful*) furchtbar
shoe [ʃuː] *n* Schuh *m*; **shoehorn**
n Schuhlöffel *m*; **shoelace** *n*
Schnürsenkel *m*; **shoe polish** *n*
Schuhcreme *f*
shone [ʃɒn] *pt, pp of* **shine**
shook [ʃʊk] *pt of* **shake**
shoot [ʃuːt] (**shot, shot**) *vt*
(*wound*) anschießen; (*kill*)
erschießen; (*Cine*) drehen; (*fam:*
heroin) drücken ▷ *vi* (*with gun,*
move quickly) schießen; **to ~ at sb**
auf jdn schießen ▷ *n* (*of plant*)
Trieb *m*; **shooting** *n* (*exchange of*
gunfire) Schießerei *f*; (*killing*)
Erschießung *f*
shop [ʃɒp] *n* Geschäft *nt*, Laden *m*
▷ *vi* einkaufen; **shop assistant** *n*
Verkäufer(in) *m(f)*; **shopkeeper** *n*
Geschäftsinhaber(in) *m(f)*;
shoplifting *n* Ladendiebstahl *m*;
shopper *n* Käufer(in) *m(f)*;
shopping *n* (*activity*) Einkaufen
nt; (*goods*) Einkäufe *pl*; **to do the**

~ einkaufen; **to go ~** einkaufen
gehen; **shopping bag** *n*
Einkaufstasche *f*; **shopping cart** *n*
(*US*) Einkaufswagen *m*; **shopping
center** (*US*), **shopping centre** *n*
Einkaufszentrum *nt*; **shopping list**
n Einkaufszettel *m*; **shopping
trolley** *n* (*Brit*) Einkaufswagen *m*;
shop window *n* Schaufenster *nt*
shore [ʃɔː°] *n* Ufer *nt*; **on ~** an
Land
short [ʃɔːt] *adj* kurz; (*person*)
klein; **to be ~ of money** knapp bei
Kasse sein; **to be ~ of time** wenig
Zeit haben; **~ of breath**
kurzatmig; **to cut ~** (*holiday*)
abbrechen; **we are two ~** wir
haben zwei zu wenig; **it's ~ for ...**
das ist die Kurzform von ... ▷ *n*
(*drink, Elec*) Kurze(r) *m*; **shortage** *n*
Knappheit *f* (*of* an +*dat*);
shortbread *n* Buttergebäck *nt*;
short circuit *n* Kurzschluss *m*;
shortcoming *n* Unzulänglichkeit
f; (*of person*) Fehler *m*; **shortcut** *n*
(*quicker route*) Abkürzung *f*; (*Inform*)
Shortcut *m*; **shorten** *vt* kürzen;
(*in time*) verkürzen; **shorthand** *n*
Stenografie *f*; **shortlist** *n*: **to be
on the ~** in der engeren Wahl sein;
shortly *adv* bald; **shorts** *npl*
Shorts *pl*; **short-sighted** *adj* (*a.*
fig) kurzsichtig; **short-sleeved**
adj kurzärmelig; **short-stay car
park** *n* Kurzzeitparkplatz *m*;
short story *n* Kurzgeschichte *f*;
short-term *adj* kurzfristig; **short
wave** *n* Kurzwelle *f*
shot [ʃɒt] *pt, pp of* **shoot** ▷ *n*
(*from gun, in football*) Schuss *m*;
(*Foto, Cine*) Aufnahme *f*; (*injection*)
Spritze *f*; (*of alcohol*) Schuss *m*
should [ʃʊd] *pt of* **shall** ▷ *vb aux*:
I ~ go now ich sollte jetzt gehen;
what ~ I do? was soll ich tun?; **you
~n't have said that** das hättest

du/hätten Sie nicht sagen sollen; **that ~ be enough** das müsste reichen

shoulder [ˈʃəʊldə*] n Schulter f

shouldn't [ˈʃʊdnt] contr of **should not**

should've [ˈʃʊdəv] contr of **should have**

shout [ʃaʊt] n Schrei m; (call) Ruf m ▷ vt rufen; (order) brüllen ▷ vi schreien; **to ~ at** anschreien; **to ~ for help** um Hilfe rufen

shove [ʃʌv] vt (person) schubsen; (car, table etc) schieben ▷ vi (in crowd) drängeln

shovel [ˈʃʌvl] n Schaufel f ▷ vt schaufeln

show [ʃəʊ] (showed, shown) vt zeigen; **to ~ sb sth, to ~ sth to sb** jdm etw zeigen; **to ~ sb in** jdn hereinführen; **to ~ sb out** jdn zur Tür bringen ▷ n (Cine, Theat) Vorstellung f; (TV) Show f; (exhibition) Ausstellung f; **show off** vi (pej) angeben; **show round** vt herumführen; **to show sb round the house/the town** jdm das Haus/die Stadt zeigen; **show up** vi (arrive) auftauchen

shower [ˈʃaʊə*] n Dusche f; (rain) Schauer m; **to have** (o **take**) **a ~** duschen ▷ vi (wash) duschen

showing [ˈʃəʊɪŋ] n (Cine) Vorstellung f

shown [ʃəʊn] pp of **show**

showroom [ˈʃəʊruːm] n Ausstellungsraum m

shrank [ʃræŋk] pt of **shrink**

shred [ʃred] n (of paper, fabric) Fetzen m ▷ vt (in shredder) (im Reißwolf) zerkleinern; **shredder** n (for paper) Reißwolf m

shrimp [ʃrɪmp] n Garnele f

shrink [ʃrɪŋk] (shrank, shrunk) vi schrumpfen; (clothes) eingehen

shrivel [ˈʃrɪvl] vi: **to ~ (up)**

schrumpfen; (skin) runzlig werden; (plant) welken

Shrove Tuesday [ˈʃrəʊvˈtjuːzdeɪ] n Fastnachtsdienstag m

shrub [ʃrʌb] n Busch m, Strauch m

shrug [ʃrʌg] vt, vi: **to ~ (one's shoulders)** die Achseln zucken

shrunk [ʃrʌŋk] pp of **shrink**

shudder [ˈʃʌdə*] vi schaudern; (ground, building) beben

shuffle [ˈʃʌfl] vt, vi mischen

shut [ʃʌt] (shut, shut) vt zumachen, schließen; **~ your face!** (fam) halt den Mund! ▷ vi schließen ▷ adj geschlossen; **we're ~** wir haben geschlossen; **shut down** vt schließen; (computer) ausschalten ▷ vi schließen; (computer) sich ausschalten; **shut in** vt einschließen; **shut out** vt (lock out) aussperren; **to shut oneself out** sich aussperren; **shut up** vt (lock up) abschließen; (silence) zum Schweigen bringen ▷ vi (keep quiet) den Mund halten; **~!** halt den Mund!; **shutter** n (on window) (Fenster)laden m; **shutter release** n Auslöser m; **shutter speed** n Belichtungszeit f

shuttle bus [ˈʃʌtlbʌs] n Shuttlebus m

shuttlecock [ˈʃʌtlkɒk] n Federball m

shuttle service [ˈʃʌtlsɜːvɪs] n Pendelverkehr m

shy [ʃaɪ] adj schüchtern; (animal) scheu

Siberia [saɪˈbɪərɪə] n Sibirien nt

Sicily [ˈsɪsɪlɪ] n Sizilien nt

sick [sɪk] adj krank; (joke) makaber; **to be ~** (Brit: vomit) sich übergeben; **to be off ~** wegen Krankheit fehlen; **I feel ~** mir ist schlecht; **to be ~ of sb/sth** jdn/etw satthaben; **it makes me**

~ (fig) es ekelt mich an; **sickbag** n Spucktüte f; **sick leave** n: **to be on ~** krankgeschrieben sein; **sickness** n Krankheit f; (Brit: nausea) Übelkeit f; **sickness benefit** n (Brit) Krankengeld nt

side [saɪd] n Seite f; (of road) Rand m; (of mountain) Hang m; (Sport) Mannschaft f; **by my ~** neben mir; **~ by ~** nebeneinander ▷ adj (door, entrance) Seiten-; **sideboard** n Anrichte f; **sideburns** npl Koteletten pl; **side dish** n Beilage f; **side effect** n Nebenwirkung f; **sidelight** n (Brit Auto) Parklicht nt; **side order** n Beilage f; **side road** n Nebenstraße f; **side street** n Seitenstraße f; **sidewalk** n (US) Bürgersteig m; **sideways** adv seitwärts

sieve [sɪv] n Sieb nt

sift [sɪft] vt (flour etc) sieben

sigh [saɪ] vi seufzen

sight [saɪt] n (power of seeing) Sehvermögen nt; (view, thing seen) Anblick m; **~s** pl (of city etc) Sehenswürdigkeiten pl; **to have bad ~** schlecht sehen; **to lose ~ of** aus den Augen verlieren; **out of ~** außer Sicht; **sightseeing** n: **to go ~** Sehenswürdigkeiten besichtigen; **~ tour** Rundfahrt f

sign [saɪn] n Zeichen nt; (notice, road ~) Schild nt ▷ vt unterschreiben ▷ vi unterschreiben; **to ~ for sth** den Empfang einer Sache gen bestätigen; **to ~ in/out** sich ein-/austragen; **sign on** vi (Brit: register as unemployed) sich arbeitslos melden; **sign up** vi (for course) sich einschreiben; (Mil) sich verpflichten

signal ['sɪgnl] n Signal nt ▷ vi (car driver) blinken

signature ['sɪgnətʃə*] n Unterschrift f

significant [sɪg'nɪfɪkənt] adj (important) bedeutend, wichtig; (meaning sth) bedeutsam; **significantly** adv (considerably) bedeutend

sign language ['saɪnlæŋgwidʒ] n Zeichensprache f; **signpost** n Wegweiser m

silence ['saɪləns] n Stille f; (of person) Schweigen nt; **~!** Ruhe! ▷ vt zum Schweigen bringen; **silent** adj still; (taciturn) schweigsam; **she remained ~** sie schwieg

silk [sɪlk] n Seide f ▷ adj Seiden-

silly ['sɪlɪ] adj dumm, albern; **don't do anything ~** mach keine Dummheiten; **the ~ season** das Sommerloch

silver ['sɪlvə*] n Silber nt; (coins) Silbermünzen pl ▷ adj Silber-, silbern; **silver-plated** adj versilbert; **silver wedding** n silberne Hochzeit

similar ['sɪmɪlə*] adj ähnlich (to dat); **similarity** [sɪmɪ'lærɪtɪ] n Ähnlichkeit f (to mit); **similarly** adv (equally) ebenso

simple ['sɪmpl] adj einfach; (unsophisticated) schlicht; **simplify** ['sɪmplɪfaɪ] vt vereinfachen; **simply** adv einfach; (merely) bloß; (dress) schlicht

simulate ['sɪmjʊleɪt] vt simulieren

simultaneous, simultaneously [sɪməl'teɪnɪəs, -lɪ] adj, adv gleichzeitig

sin [sɪn] n Sünde f ▷ vi sündigen

since [sɪns] adv seitdem; (in the meantime) inzwischen ▷ prep seit +dat; **ever ~ 1995** schon seit 1995 ▷ conj (time) seit, seitdem; (because) da, weil; **ever ~ I've known her** seit ich sie kenne; **it's ages ~ I've seen him** ich habe ihn seit Langem nicht mehr gesehen

sincere [sɪn'sɪə°] adj aufrichtig;
sincerely adv aufrichtig;
Yours ~ mit freundlichen
Grüßen
sing [sɪŋ] (**sang, sung**) vt, vi
singen
Singapore [sɪŋgə'pɔː°] n Singapur nt
singer ['sɪŋə°] n Sänger(in) m(f)
single ['sɪŋgl] adj (one only)
einzig; (not double) einfach; (bed,
room) Einzel-; (unmarried) ledig;
(Brit: ticket) einfach ⊳ n (Brit:
ticket) einfache Fahrkarte; (Mus)
Single f; **a ~ to London, please**
(Brit Rail) einfach nach London,
bitte; **single out** vt (choose)
auswählen; **single-handed,
single-handedly** adv im
Alleingang; **single parent** n
Alleinerziehende(r) mf; **single
supplement** n (for hotel room)
Einzelzimmerzuschlag m
singular ['sɪŋgjʊlə°] n Singular
m
sinister ['sɪnɪstə°] adj
unheimlich
sink [sɪŋk] (**sank, sunk**) vt (ship)
versenken ⊳ vi sinken ⊳ n
Spülbecken nt; (in bathroom)
Waschbecken nt
sip [sɪp] vt nippen an +dat
sir [sɜː°] n: **yes, ~** ja(, mein Herr);
can I help you, ~? kann ich Ihnen
helfen?; **Sir James** (title) Sir James
sister ['sɪstə°] n Schwester f;
(Brit: nurse) Oberschwester f;
sister-in-law (pl **sisters-in-law**) n
Schwägerin f
sit [sɪt] (**sat, sat**) vi (be sitting)
sitzen; (~ down) sich setzen;
(committee, court) tagen ⊳ vt (Brit:
exam) machen; **sit down** vi sich
hinsetzen; **sit up** vi (from lying
position) sich aufsetzen
sitcom ['sɪtkɒm] n Situ-
ationskomödie f

site [saɪt] n Platz m; (building ~)
Baustelle f; (web~) Site f
sitting ['sɪtɪŋ] n (meeting, for
portrait) Sitzung f; **sitting room** n
Wohnzimmer nt
situated ['sɪtjʊeɪtɪd] adj: **to be
~** liegen
situation [sɪtjʊ'eɪʃən] n (circumstances) Situation f, Lage f; (job)
Stelle f; **"~s vacant/wanted"** (Brit)
„Stellenangebote/Stellengesuche"
six [sɪks] num sechs ⊳ n Sechs f;
see also **eight**; **sixpack** n (of beer
etc) Sechserpack nt; **sixteen**
['sɪks'tiːn] num sechzehn ⊳ n
Sechzehn f; see also **eight**;
sixteenth adj sechzehnte(r, s); see
also **eighth**; **sixth** [sɪksθ] adj
sechste(r, s); **~ form** ≈
Oberstufe f ⊳ n (fraction) Sechstel
nt; see also **eighth**; **sixtieth**
['sɪkstɪθ] adj sechzigste(r, s); see
also **eighth**; **sixty** ['sɪkstɪ] num
sechzig; **~-one** einundsechzig ⊳ n
Sechzig f; **to be in one's sixties** in
den Sechzigern sein; see also **eight**
size [saɪz] n Größe f; **what ~ are
you?** welche Größe hast du/haben
Sie?; **a ~ too big** eine Nummer zu
groß
sizzle ['sɪzl] vi (Gastr) brutzeln
skate [skeɪt] n Schlittschuh m;
(roller ~) Rollschuh m ⊳ vi
Schlittschuh laufen; (roller-~)
Rollschuh laufen; **skateboard** n
Skateboard nt; **skating** n Eislauf
m; (roller-~) Rollschuhlauf m;
skating rink n Eisbahn f; (for
roller-skating) Rollschuhbahn f
skeleton ['skelɪtn] n (a. fig)
Skelett nt
skeptical n (US) see **sceptical**
sketch [sketʃ] n Skizze f; (Theat)
Sketch m ⊳ vt skizzieren;
sketchbook n Skizzenbuch nt
ski [skiː] n Ski m ⊳ vi Ski laufen;
ski boot n Skistiefel m

skid [skɪd] vi (Auto) schleudern
skier ['skiːəʳ] n Skiläufer(in) m(f); **skiing** n Skilaufen nt; **to go ~** Ski laufen gehen; **~ holiday** Skiurlaub m; **skiing instructor** n Skilehrer(in) m(f)
skilful, skilfully ['skɪlfʊl, -fəlɪ] adj, adv geschickt
ski-lift ['skiːlɪft] n Skilift m
skill [skɪl] n Geschick nt; (acquired technique) Fertigkeit f; **skilled** adj geschickt (at, in in +dat); (worker) Fach-; (work) fachmännisch
skim [skɪm] vt: **to ~ (off)** (fat etc) abschöpfen; **to ~ (through)** (read) überfliegen; **skimmed milk** n Magermilch f
skin [skɪn] n Haut f; (fur) Fell nt; (peel) Schale f; **skin diving** n Sporttauchen nt; **skinny** adj dünn
skip [skɪp] vi hüpfen; (with rope) seilspringen ▷ vt (miss out) überspringen; (meal) ausfallen lassen; (school, lesson) schwänzen
ski pants ['skiːpænts] npl Skihose f; **ski pass** n Skipass m; **ski pole** n Skistock m; **ski resort** n Skiort m
skirt [skɜːt] n Rock m
ski run ['skiːrʌn] n (Ski)abfahrt f; **ski stick** n Skistock m; **ski tow** n Schlepplift m
skittle ['skɪtl] n Kegel m; **~s** (game) Kegeln nt
skive [skaɪv] vi: **to ~ (off)** (Brit) (from school) schwänzen; (from work) blaumachen
skull [skʌl] n Schädel m
sky [skaɪ] n Himmel m; **skydiving** n Fallschirmspringen nt; **skylight** n Dachfenster nt; **skyscraper** n Wolkenkratzer m
slam [slæm] vt (door) zuschlagen; **slam on** vt: **to slam the brakes on** voll auf die Bremse treten
slander ['slɑːndəʳ] n Verleumdung f ▷ vt verleumden

slang [slæŋ] n Slang m
slap [slæp] n Klaps m; (across face) Ohrfeige f ▷ vt schlagen; **to ~ sb's face** jdn ohrfeigen
slash [slæʃ] n (punctuation mark) Schrägstrich m ▷ vt (face, tyre) aufschlitzen; (prices) stark herabsetzen
slate [sleɪt] n (rock) Schiefer m; (roof ~) Schieferplatte f
slaughter ['slɔːtəʳ] vt (animals) schlachten; (people) abschlachten
Slav [slɑːv] adj slawisch ▷ n Slawe m, Slawin f
slave [sleɪv] n Sklave m, Sklavin f; **slave away** vi schuften; **slave-driver** n (fam) Sklaventreiber(in) m(f); **slavery** ['sleɪvərɪ] n Sklaverei f
sleaze [sliːz] n (corruption) Korruption f; **sleazy** adj (bar, district) zwielichtig
sledge ['sledʒ] n Schlitten m
sleep [sliːp] (**slept, slept**) vi schlafen; **to ~ with sb** mit jdm schlafen ▷ n Schlaf m; **to put to ~** (animal) einschläfern; **sleep in** vi (lie in) ausschlafen; **sleeper** n (Rail: train) Schlafwagenzug m; (carriage) Schlafwagen m; **sleeping bag** n Schlafsack m; **sleeping car** n Schlafwagen m; **sleeping pill** n Schlaftablette f; **sleepless** adj schlaflos; **sleepy** adj schläfrig; (place) verschlafen
sleet [sliːt] n Schneeregen m
sleeve [sliːv] n Ärmel m; **sleeveless** adj ärmellos
sleigh [sleɪ] n (Pferde)schlitten m
slender ['slendəʳ] adj schlank; (fig) gering
slept [slept] pt, pp of **sleep**
slice [slaɪs] n Scheibe f; (of cake, tart, pizza) Stück nt ▷ vt: **to ~ (up)** in Scheiben schneiden; **sliced bread** n geschnittenes Brot

slid [slɪd] *pt, pp of* **slide**

slide [slaɪd] (**slid, slid**) *vt* gleiten lassen; (*push*) schieben ▷ *vi* gleiten; (*slip*) rutschen ▷ *n* (*Foto*) Dia *nt*; (*in playground*) Rutschbahn *f*; (*Brit: for hair*) Spange *f*

slight [slaɪt] *adj* leicht; (*problem, difference*) klein; **not in the ~est** nicht im Geringsten; **slightly** *adv* etwas; (*injured*) leicht

slim [slɪm] *adj* (*person*) schlank; (*book*) dünn; (*chance, hope*) gering ▷ *vi* abnehmen

slime [slaɪm] *n* Schleim *m*; **slimy** *adj* schleimig

sling [slɪŋ] (**slung, slung**) *vt* werfen ▷ *n* (*for arm*) Schlinge *f*

slip [slɪp] *n* (*mistake*) Flüchtigkeitsfehler *m*; **~ of paper** Zettel *m* ▷ *vt* (*put*) stecken; **to ~ on/off** (*garment*) an-/ausziehen; **it ~ped my mind** ich habe es vergessen ▷ *vi* (*lose balance*) (aus)rutschen; **slip away** *vi* (*leave*) sich wegstehlen; **slipper** *n* Hausschuh *m*; **slippery** *adj* (*path, road*) glatt; (*soap, fish*) glitschig; **slip-road** *n* (*Brit: onto motorway*) Auffahrt *f*; (*off motorway*) Ausfahrt *f*

slit [slɪt] (**slit, slit**) *vt* aufschlitzen ▷ *n* Schlitz *m*

slope [sləʊp] *n* Neigung *f*; (*side of hill*) Hang *m* ▷ *vi* (*be sloping*) schräg sein; **sloping** *adj* (*floor, roof*) schräg

sloppy ['slɒpɪ] *adj* (*careless*) schlampig; (*sentimental*) rührselig

slot [slɒt] *n* (*opening*) Schlitz *m*; (*Inform*) Steckplatz *m*; **we have a ~ free at 2** (*free time*) um 2 ist noch ein Termin frei; **slot machine** *n* Automat *m*; (*for gambling*) Spielautomat *m*

Slovak ['sləʊvæk] *adj* slowakisch ▷ *n* (*person*) Slowake *m*, Slowakin *f*; (*language*) Slowakisch *nt*; **Slovakia** [sləʊ'vækɪə] *n* Slowakei *f*

Slovene ['sləʊviːn], **Slovenian** [sləʊ'viːnɪən] *adj* slowenisch ▷ *n* (*person*) Slowene *m*, Slowenin *f*; (*language*) Slowenisch *nt*; **Slovenia** [sləʊ'viːnɪə] *n* Slowenien *nt*

slow [sləʊ] *adj* langsam; (*business*) flau; **to be ~** (*clock*) nachgehen; (*stupid*) begriffsstutzig sein; **slow down** *vi* langsamer werden; (*when driving/walking*) langsamer fahren/gehen; **slowly** *adv* langsam; **slow motion** *n*: **in ~** in Zeitlupe

slug [slʌg] *n* (*Zool*) Nacktschnecke *f*

slum [slʌm] *n* Slum *m*

slump [slʌmp] *n* Rückgang *m* (*in an +dat*) ▷ *vi* (*onto chair etc*) sich fallen lassen; (*prices*) stürzen

slung [slʌŋ] *pt, pp of* **sling**

slur [slɜː°] *n* (*insult*) Verleumdung *f*; **slurred** [slɜːd] *adj* undeutlich

slush [slʌʃ] *n* (*snow*) Schneematsch *m*; **slushy** *adj* matschig; (*fig*) schmalzig

slut [slʌt] *n* (*pej*) Schlampe *f*

smack [smæk] *n* Klaps *m* ▷ *vt*: **to ~ sb** jdm einen Klaps geben ▷ *vi*: **to ~ of** riechen nach

small [smɔːl] *adj* klein; **small ads** *npl* (*Brit*) Kleinanzeigen *pl*; **small change** *n* Kleingeld *nt*; **small letters** *npl*: **in ~** in Kleinbuchstaben; **smallpox** *n* Pocken *pl*; **small print** *n*: **the ~** das Kleingedruckte; **small-scale** *adj* (*map*) in kleinem Maßstab; **small talk** *n* Konversation *f*, Smalltalk *m*

smart [smɑːt] *adj* (*elegant*) schick; (*clever*) clever; **smartarse**, **smartass** (*US*) *n* (*fam*) Klugscheißer (in) *m(f)*; **smart card** *n* Chipkarte *f*; **smartly** *adv* (*dressed*) schick

smash [smæʃ] *n* (*car crash*) Zusammenstoß *m*, Schmetterball *m* ▷ *vt* (*break*) zerschlagen; (*fig: record*) brechen, deutlich übertreffen ▷ *vi* (*break*) zerbrechen; **to ~ into** (*car*) krachen gegen

smear [smɪə*] *n* (*mark*) Fleck *m*; (*Med*) Abstrich *m*; (*fig*) Verleumdung *f* ▷ *vt* (*spread*) schmieren; (*make dirty*) beschmieren; (*fig*) verleumden

smell [smel] (**smelt** *o* **smelled, smelt** *o* **smelled**) *vt* riechen ▷ *vi* riechen (*of* nach); (*unpleasantly*) stinken ▷ *n* Geruch *m*; (*unpleasant*) Gestank *m*; **smelly** *adj* übel riechend; **smelt** [smelt] *pt, pp of* **smell**

smile [smaɪl] *n* Lächeln *nt* ▷ *vi* lächeln; **to ~ at sb** jdn anlächeln

smock [smɒk] *n* Kittel *m*

smog [smɒg] *n* Smog *m*

smoke [sməʊk] *n* Rauch *m* ▷ *vt* rauchen; (*food*) räuchern ▷ *vi* rauchen; **smoke alarm** *n* Rauchmelder *m*; **smoked** *adj* (*food*) geräuchert; **smoke-free** *adj* (*zone, building*) rauchfrei; **smoker** *n* Raucher(in) *m(f)*; **smoking** *n* Rauchen *nt*; **"no ~"** „Rauchen verboten"

smooth [smuːð] *adj* glatt; (*flight, crossing*) ruhig; (*movement*) geschmeidig; (*without problems*) reibungslos; (*pej: person*) aalglatt ▷ *vt* (*hair, dress*) glatt streichen; (*surface*) glätten; **smoothly** *adv* reibungslos; **to run ~** (*engine*) ruhig laufen

smudge [smʌdʒ] *vt* (*writing, lipstick*) verschmieren

smug [smʌg] *adj* selbstgefällig

smuggle ['smʌgl] *vt* schmuggeln; **to ~ in/out** herein-/herausschmuggeln

smutty ['smʌtɪ] *adj* (*obscene*) schmutzig

snack [snæk] *n* Imbiss *m*; **to have**
a ~ eine Kleinigkeit essen; **snack bar** *n* Imbissstube *f*

snail [sneɪl] *n* Schnecke *f*; **snail mail** *n* (*fam*) Schneckenpost *f*

snake [sneɪk] *n* Schlange *f*

snap [snæp] *n* (*photo*) Schnappschuss *m* ▷ *adj* (*decision*) spontan ▷ *vt* (*break*) zerbrechen; (*rope*) zerreißen ▷ *vi* (*break*) brechen; (*rope*) reißen; (*bite*) schnappen (*at* nach); **snap off** *vt* (*break*) abbrechen; **snap fastener** *n* (*US*) Druckknopf *m*; **snapshot** *n* Schnappschuss *m*

snatch [snætʃ] *vt* (*grab*) schnappen

sneak [sniːk] *vi* (*move*) schleichen; **sneakers** *npl* (*US*) Turnschuhe *pl*

sneeze [sniːz] *vi* niesen

sniff [snɪf] *vi* schniefen; (*smell*) schnüffeln (*at* an +*dat*) ▷ *vt* schnuppern an +*dat*; (*glue*) schnüffeln

snob [snɒb] *n* Snob *m*; **snobbish** *adj* versnobt

snog [snɒg] *vi, vt* knutschen

snooker ['snuːkə*] *n* Snooker *nt*

snoop [snuːp] *vi*: **to ~ (around)** (herum)schnüffeln

snooze [snuːz] *n, vi*: **to (have a) ~** ein Nickerchen machen

snore [snɔː*] *vi* schnarchen

snorkel ['snɔːkl] *n* Schnorchel *m*; **snorkelling** *n* Schnorcheln *nt*; **to go ~** schnorcheln gehen

snout [snaʊt] *n* Schnauze *f*

snow [snəʊ] *n* Schnee *m* ▷ *vi* schneien; **snowball** *n* Schneeball *m*; **snowboard** *n* Snowboard *nt*; **snowboarding** *n* Snowboarding *nt*; **snowdrift** *n* Schneewehe *f*; **snowdrop** *n* Schneeglöckchen *nt*; **snowflake** *n* Schneeflocke *f*; **snowman** (*pl* **-men**) *n* Schneemann *m*; **snowplough**,

snowplow (US) n Schneepflug m;
snowstorm n Schneesturm m;
snowy adj (region) schneereich;
(landscape) verschneit
snug [snʌg] adj (person, place)
gemütlich
snuggle up ['snʌgl'ʌp] vi: **to
~ to sb** sich an jdn ankuscheln

O **KEYWORD**

so [səʊ] adv 1 (thus) so; (likewise)
auch; **so saying he walked away**
indem er das sagte, ging er; **if so**
wenn ja; **I didn't do it — you did
so!** ich hab das nicht gemacht —
hast du wohl!; **so do I, so am I** etc
ich auch; **so it is!** tatsächlich!; **I
hope/think so** hoffentlich/ich
glaube schon; **so far** bis jetzt
2 (in comparisons etc: to such a
degree): **so quickly/big (that)**
so schnell/groß, dass; **I'm so glad
to see you** ich freue mich so,
dich/Sie zu sehen
3 **so many** so viele; **so much work**
so viel Arbeit; **I love you so much**
ich liebe dich so sehr
4 (phrases) **10 or so** etwa 10; **so
long!** (inf) (goodbye) tschüss!
▷ conj 1 (expressing purpose) **so as to**
um ... zu; **so (that)** damit
2 (expressing result) also; **so I was
right after all** ich hatte also doch
recht; **so you see ...** wie du
siehst/Sie sehen ...

soak [səʊk] vt durchnässen;
(leave in liquid) einweichen; **I'm ~ed**
ich bin klatschnass; **soaking** adj:
~ (wet) klatschnass
soap [səʊp] n Seife f; **soap
(opera)** n Seifenoper f; **soap
powder** n Waschpulver nt
sob [sɒb] vi schluchzen
sober ['səʊbə*] adj nüchtern;
sober up vi nüchtern werden

so-called ['səʊ'kɔːld] adj
sogenannt
soccer ['sɒkə*] n Fußball m
sociable ['səʊʃəbl] adj gesellig
social ['səʊʃəl] adj sozial;
(sociable) gesellig; **socialist** adj
sozialistisch ▷ n Sozialist(in)
m(f); **socialize** vi unter die Leute
gehen; **social security** n (Brit)
Sozialhilfe f; (US)
Sozialversicherung f
society [sə'saɪətɪ] n Gesellschaft
f; (club) Verein m
sock [sɒk] n Socke f
socket ['sɒkɪt] n (Elec) Steckdose
f
soda ['səʊdə] n (~ water) Soda f;
(US: pop) Limo f; **soda water** n
Sodawasser nt
sofa ['səʊfə] n Sofa nt; **sofa bed**
n Schlafcouch f
soft [sɒft] adj weich; (quiet) leise;
(lighting) gedämpft; (kind)
gutmütig; (weak) nachgiebig;
~ drink alkoholfreies Getränk;
softly adv sanft; (quietly) leise;
software n (Inform) Software f
soil [sɔɪl] n Erde f; (ground) Boden
m
solar ['səʊlə*] adj Sonnen-, Solar-
solarium [sə'lɛərɪəm] n
Solarium nt
sold [səʊld] pt, pp of **sell**
soldier ['səʊldʒə*] n Soldat(in)
m(f)
sole [səʊl] n Sohle f; (fish)
Seezunge f ▷ vt besohlen ▷ adj
einzig; (owner, responsibility)
alleinig; **solely** adv nur
solemn ['sɒləm] adj feierlich;
(person) ernst
solicitor [sə'lɪsɪtə*] n (Brit)
Rechtsanwalt m, Rechtsanwältin f
solid ['sɒlɪd] adj (hard) fest; (gold,
oak etc) massiv; (~ly built) solide;
(meal) kräftig; **three hours ~** drei
volle Stunden

solitary ['sɒlɪtərɪ] *adj* einsam; (*single*) einzeln; **solitude** ['sɒlɪtjuːd] *n* Einsamkeit *f*

solo ['səʊləʊ] *n* (*Mus*) Solo *nt*

soluble ['sɒljʊbl] *adj* löslich; **solution** [sə'luːʃən] *n* Lösung *f* (*to +gen*); **solve** [sɒlv] *vt* lösen

somber (*US*), **sombre** ['sɒmbə*] *adj* düster

O **KEYWORD**

some [sʌm] *adj* **1** (*a certain amount o number of*) einige; (*a few*) ein paar; (*with singular nouns*) etwas; **some tea/biscuits** etwas Tee/ein paar Kekse; **I've got some money, but not much** ich habe ein bisschen Geld, aber nicht viel
2 (*certain: in contrasts*) manche(r, s); **some people say that ...** manche Leute sagen, dass ...
3 (*unspecified*) irgendein(e); **some woman was asking for you** da hat eine Frau nach dir/Ihnen gefragt; **some day** eines Tages; **some day next week** irgendwann nächste Woche
▷ *pron* **1** (*a certain number*) einige; **have you got some?** hast du/haben Sie welche?
2 (*a certain amount*) etwas; **I've read some of the book** ich habe das Buch teilweise gelesen
▷ *adv*: **some 10 people** etwa 10 Leute

somebody *pron* jemand; **~ (or other)** irgendjemand; **~ else** jemand anders; **someday** *adv* irgendwann; **somehow** *adv* irgendwie; **someone** *pron see* **somebody**; **someplace** *adv* (*US*) *see* **somewhere**; **something** ['sʌmθɪŋ] *pron* etwas; **~ (or other)** irgendetwas; **~ else** etwas anderes; **~ nice** etwas Nettes;

would you like ~ to drink? möchtest du/möchten Sie etwas trinken? ▷ *adv*: **~ like 20** ungefähr 20; **sometime** *adv* irgendwann; **sometimes** *adv* manchmal; **somewhat** *adv* ein wenig; **somewhere** *adv* irgendwo; (*to a place*) irgendwohin; **~ else** irgendwo anders; (*to another place*) irgendwo anders hin

son [sʌn] *n* Sohn *m*

song [sɒŋ] *n* Lied *nt*; Song *m*

son-in-law ['sʌnɪnlɔː] (*pl* **sons-in-law**) *n* Schwiegersohn *m*

soon [suːn] *adv* bald; (*early*) früh; **too ~** zu früh; **as ~ as I ...** sobald ich ...; **as ~ as possible** so bald wie möglich; **sooner** *adv* (*time*) früher; (*for preference*) lieber

soot [sʊt] *n* Ruß *m*

soothe [suːð] *vt* beruhigen; (*pain*) lindern

sophisticated [sə'fɪstɪkeɪtɪd] *adj* (*person*) kultiviert; (*machine*) hoch entwickelt; (*plan*) ausgeklügelt

sophomore ['sɒfəmɔː*] *n* (*US*) College-Student(in) *m(f)* im zweiten Jahr

soppy ['sɒpɪ] *adj* (*fam*) rührselig

soprano [sə'prɑːnəʊ] *n* Sopran *m*

sore [sɔː*] *adj*: **to be ~** wehtun; **to have a ~ throat** Halsschmerzen haben ▷ *n* wunde Stelle

sorrow ['sɒrəʊ] *n* Kummer *m*

sorry ['sɒrɪ] *adj* (*sight, figure*) traurig; (**I'm**) **~** (*excusing*) Entschuldigung!; **I'm ~** (*regretful*) es tut mir leid; **~?** wie bitte?; **I feel ~ for him** er tut mir leid

sort [sɔːt] *n* Art *f*; **what ~ of film is it?** was für ein Film ist das?; **a ~ of** eine Art *+gen*; **all ~s of things** alles Mögliche ▷ *adv*: **~ of** (*fam*) irgendwie ▷ *vt* sortieren; **everything's ~ed** (*dealt with*) alles

ist geregelt; **sort out** vt (classify etc) sortieren; (problems) lösen
sought [sɔːt] pt, pp of **seek**
soul [səʊl] n Seele f; (music) Soul m
sound [saʊnd] adj (healthy) gesund; (safe) sicher; (sensible) vernünftig; (theory) stichhaltig; (thrashing) tüchtig ▷ n (noise) Geräusch nt; (Mus) Klang m; (TV) Ton m ▷ vt: **to ~ the alarm** Alarm schlagen; **to ~ one's horn** hupen ▷ vi (seem) klingen (like wie); **soundcard** n (Inform) Soundkarte f; **sound effects** npl Klangeffekte pl; **soundproof** adj schalldicht; **soundtrack** n (of film) Filmmusik f, Soundtrack m
soup [suːp] n Suppe f
sour ['saʊəʳ] adj sauer; (fig) mürrisch
source [sɔːs] n Quelle f; (fig) Ursprung m
sour cream [saʊəˈkriːm] n saure Sahne
south [saʊθ] n Süden m; **to the ~ of** südlich von ▷ adv (go, face) nach Süden ▷ adj Süd-; **South Africa** n Südafrika nt; **South African** adj südafrikanisch ▷ n Südafrikaner(in) m(f); **South America** n Südamerika nt; **South American** adj südamerikanisch ▷ n Südamerikaner(in) m(f); **southbound** adj (in) Richtung Süden; **southern** ['sʌðən] adj Süd-, südlich; **~ Europe** Südeuropa nt; **southwards** ['saʊθwədz] adv nach Süden
souvenir [suːvəˈnɪəʳ] n Andenken nt (of an +akk)
sow [saʊ] (**sowed, sown** o **sowed**) vt (a. fig) säen; (field) besäen ▷ [saʊ] n (pig) Sau f
soya bean ['sɔɪəˈbiːn] n Sojabohne f
soy sauce ['sɔɪˈsɔːs] n Sojasoße f

spa [spɑː] n (place) Kurort m
space [speɪs] n (room) Platz m, Raum m; (outer ~) Weltraum m; (gap) Zwischenraum m; (for parking) Lücke f; **space bar** n Leertaste f; **spacecraft** (pl -) n Raumschiff nt; **space ship** n Raumschiff nt; **space shuttle** n Raumfähre f
spacing ['speɪsɪŋ] n (in text) Zeilenabstand m; **double ~** zweizeiliger Abstand
spacious ['speɪʃəs] adj geräumig
spade [speɪd] n Spaten m; **~s** Pik nt
spaghetti [spəˈgetɪ] nsing Spaghetti pl
Spain [speɪn] n Spanien nt
spam [spæm] n (Inform) Spam m
Spaniard ['spænɪəd] n Spanier(in) m(f); **Spanish** ['spænɪʃ] adj spanisch ▷ n (language) Spanisch nt
spanner ['spænəʳ] n (Brit) Schraubenschlüssel m
spare [speəʳ] adj (as replacement) Ersatz-; **~ part** Ersatzteil nt; **~ room** Gästezimmer nt; **~ time** Freizeit f; **~ tyre** Ersatzreifen m ▷ n (~ part) Ersatzteil nt ▷ vt (lives, feelings) verschonen; **can you ~ (me) a moment?** hättest du/hätten Sie einen Moment Zeit?
spark [spɑːk] n Funke m; **sparkle** ['spɑːkl] vi funkeln; **sparkling wine** n Schaumwein m, Sekt m; **spark plug** ['spɑːkplʌg] n Zündkerze f
sparrow ['spærəʊ] n Spatz m
sparse [spɑːs] adj spärlich; **sparsely** adv: **~ populated** dünn besiedelt
spasm ['spæzəm] n Krampf m
spat [spæt] pt, pp of **spit**
speak [spiːk] (**spoke, spoken**) vt sprechen; **can you ~ French?** sprechen Sie Französisch?; **to**

~ **one's mind** seine Meinung sagen ▷ vi sprechen (to mit, zu); (make speech) reden; ~**ing** (Tel) am Apparat; **so to** ~ sozusagen; ~ **for yourself** das meinst auch nur du!; **speak up** vi (louder) lauter sprechen; **speaker** n Sprecher(in) m(f); (public ~) Redner(in) m(f); (loud~) Lautsprecher m, Box f

special ['speʃəl] adj besonde-re(r, s), speziell ▷ n (on menu) Tagesgericht nt; (TV, Radio) Sondersendung f; **special delivery** n Eilzustellung f; **special effects** npl Spezialeffekte pl; **specialist** n Spezialist(in) m(f); (Tech) Fachmann m, Fachfrau f; (Med) Facharzt m, Fachärztin f; **speciality** [speʃɪ'ælɪtɪ] n Spezi-alität f; **specialize** vi sich spezialisieren (in auf +akk); **specially** adv besonders; (specifically) extra; **special offer** n Sonderangebot nt; **specialty** n (US) see **speciality**

species ['spiːʃiːz] nsing Art f

specific [spə'sɪfɪk] adj spezi-fisch; (precise) genau; **specify** ['spesɪfaɪ] vt genau angeben

specimen ['spesɪmən] n (sample) Probe f; (example) Exemplar nt

specs [speks] npl (fam) Brille f

spectacle ['spektəkl] n Schauspiel nt

spectacles npl Brille f

spectacular [spek'tækjʊlə°] adj spektakulär

spectator [spek'teɪtə°] n Zuschauer(in) m(f)

sped [sped] pt, pp of **speed**

speech [spiːtʃ] n (address) Rede f; (faculty) Sprache f; **to make a** ~ eine Rede halten; **speechless** adj sprachlos (with vor +dat)

speed [spiːd] n (**sped** o **speeded**, **sped** o **speeded**) vi rasen; (exceed ~ limit) zu schnell fahren ▷ n Geschwindigkeit f; (of film) Lichtempfindlichkeit f; **speed up** vt beschleunigen ▷ vi schneller werden/fahren; (drive faster) schneller fahren; **speedboat** n Rennboot nt; **speed bump** n Bodenschwelle f; **speed camera** n Blitzgerät nt; **speed limit** n Geschwindigkeitsbegrenzung f; **speedometer** [spɪ'dɒmɪtə°] n Tachometer m; **speed trap** n Radarfalle f; **speedy** adj schnell

spell [spel] (**spelt** o **spelled**, **spelt** o **spelled**) vt buchstabieren; **how do you** ~ **...?** wie schreibt man ...? ▷ n (period) Weile f; (enchantment) Zauber m; **a cold/hot** ~ (weather) ein Kälteeinbruch/eine Hitzewelle; **spellchecker** n (Inform) Rechtschreibprüfung f; **spelling** n Rechtschreibung f; (of a word) Schreibweise f; ~ **mistake** Schreibfehler m

spelt [spelt] pt, pp of **spell**

spend [spend] (**spent, spent**) vt (money) ausgeben (on für); (time) verbringen; **spending money** n Taschengeld nt

spent [spent] pt, pp of **spend**

sperm [spɜːm] n Sperma nt

sphere [sfɪə°] n (globe) Kugel f; (fig) Sphäre f

spice [spaɪs] n Gewürz nt; (fig) Würze f ▷ vt würzen; **spicy** ['spaɪsɪ] adj würzig; (fig) pikant

spider ['spaɪdə°] n Spinne f

spike [spaɪk] n (on railing etc) Spitze f; (on shoe, tyre) Spike m

spill [spɪl] (**spilt** o **spilled**, **spilt** o **spilled**) vt verschütten

spin [spɪn] (**spun, spun**) vi (turn) sich drehen; (washing) schleudern; **my head is** ~**ning** mir dreht sich alles ▷ vt (turn) drehen; (coin) hochwerfen ▷ n (turn) Drehung f

spinach ['spɪnɪtʃ] n Spinat m

spin doctor n Spindoktor m (*Verantwortlicher für die schönrednerische Öffentlichkeitsarbeit besonders von Politikern*)

spin-drier ['spɪndraɪə*] n Wäscheschleuder f; **spin-dry** vt schleudern

spine [spaɪn] n Rückgrat nt; (*of animal, plant*) Stachel m; (*of book*) Rücken m

spiral ['spaɪrəl] n Spirale f ▷ adj spiralförmig; **spiral staircase** n Wendeltreppe f

spire ['spaɪə*] n Turmspitze f

spirit ['spɪrɪt] n (*essence, soul*) Geist m; (*humour, mood*) Stimmung f; (*courage*) Mut m; (*verve*) Elan m; **~s** pl (*drinks*) Spirituosen pl

spiritual ['spɪrɪtjʊəl] adj geistig; (*Rel*) geistlich

spit [spɪt] (**spat, spat**) vi spucken ▷ n (*for roasting*) (Brat)spieß m; (*saliva*) Spucke f; **spit out** vt ausspucken

spite [spaɪt] n Boshaftigkeit f; **in ~ of** trotz +gen; **spiteful** adj boshaft

spitting image ['spɪtɪŋ'ɪmɪdʒ] n: **he's the ~ of you** er ist dir/Ihnen wie aus dem Gesicht geschnitten

splash [splæʃ] vt (*person, object*) bespritzen ▷ vi (*liquid*) spritzen; (*play in water*) planschen

splendid ['splendɪd] adj herrlich

splinter ['splɪntə*] n Splitter m

split [splɪt] (**split, split**) vt (*stone, wood*) spalten; (*share*) teilen ▷ vi (*stone, wood*) sich spalten; (*seam*) platzen ▷ n (*in stone, wood*) Spalt m; (*in clothing*) Riss m; (*fig*) Spaltung f; **split up** vi (*couple*) sich trennen ▷ vt (*divide up*) aufteilen; **split ends** npl (Haar)spliss m; **splitting** adj (*headache*) rasend

spoil [spɔɪl] (**spoiled** o **spoilt,**

spoiled o **spoilt**) vt verderben; (*child*) verwöhnen ▷ vi (*food*) verderben

spoilt [spɔɪlt] pt, pp of **spoil**

spoke [spəʊk] pt of **speak** ▷ n Speiche f

spoken ['spəʊkən] pp of **speak**

spokesperson ['spəʊkspɜ:sən] (pl **-people**) n Sprecher(in) m(f)

sponge [spʌndʒ] n (*for washing*) Schwamm m; **sponge bag** n Kulturbeutel m; **sponge cake** n Biskuitkuchen m

sponsor ['spɒnsə*] n (*of event, programme*) Sponsor(in) m(f) ▷ vt unterstützen; (*event, programme*) sponsern

spontaneous, spontaneously [spɒn'teɪnɪəs, -lɪ] adj, adv spontan

spool [spu:l] n Spule f

spoon [spu:n] n Löffel m

sport [spɔ:t] n Sport m; **sports car** n Sportwagen m; **sports centre** n Sportzentrum nt; **sports club** n Sportverein m; **sportsman** (pl **-men**) n Sportler m; **sportswear** n Sportkleidung f; **sportswoman** (pl **-women**) n Sportlerin f; **sporty** adj sportlich

spot [spɒt] n (*dot*) Punkt m; (*of paint, blood etc*) Fleck m; (*place*) Stelle f; (*pimple*) Pickel m; **on the ~** vor Ort; (*at once*) auf der Stelle ▷ vt (*notice*) entdecken; (*difference*) erkennen; **spotless** adj (*clean*) blitzsauber; **spotlight** n (*lamp*) Scheinwerfer m; **spotty** adj (*pimply*) pickelig

spouse [spaʊs] n Gatte m, Gattin f

spout [spaʊt] n Schnabel m

sprain [spreɪn] n Verstauchung f ▷ vt: **to ~ one's ankle** sich den Knöchel verstauchen

sprang [spræŋ] pt of **spring**

spray [spreɪ] n (*liquid in can*)

Spray nt o m; (~ (can)) Spraydose f
▷ vt (plant, insects) besprühen;
(car) spritzen
spread [spred] (**spread, spread**)
vt (open out) ausbreiten; (news,
disease) verbreiten; (butter, jam)
streichen; (bread, surface)
bestreichen ▷ vi (news, disease,
fire) sich verbreiten ▷ n (of disease,
religion etc) Verbreitung f; (for bread)
Aufstrich m; **spreadsheet** n
(Inform) Tabellenkalkulation f
spring [sprɪŋ] (**sprang, sprung**)
vi (leap) springen ▷ n (season)
Frühling m; (coil) Feder f; (water)
Quelle f; **springboard** n
Sprungbrett nt; **spring onion** n
(Brit) Frühlingszwiebel f; **spring
roll** n (Brit) Frühlingsrolle f;
springy adj (mattress) federnd
sprinkle ['sprɪŋkl] vt streuen;
(liquid) (be)träufeln; **to ~ sth with
sth** etw mit etw bestreuen; (with
liquid) etw mit etw besprengen;
sprinkler n (for lawn)
Rasensprenger m; (for fire)
Sprinkler m
sprint [sprɪnt] vi rennen; (Sport)
sprinten
sprout [spraʊt] n (of plant) Trieb
m; (from seed) Keim m; (**Brussels**)
~s pl Rosenkohl m ▷ vi sprießen
sprung [sprʌŋ] pp of **spring**
spun [spʌn] pt, pp of **spin**
spy [spaɪ] n Spion(in) m(f) ▷ vi
spionieren; **to ~ on sb** jdm
nachspionieren ▷ vt erspähen
squad [skwɒd] n (Sport) Kader m;
(police ~) Kommando nt
square [skwɛəʳ] n (shape)
Quadrat nt; (open space) Platz m;
(on chessboard etc) Feld nt ▷ adj (in
shape) quadratisch; **2 ~ metres** 2
Quadratmeter; **2 metres ~** 2 Meter
im Quadrat ▷ vt: **3 ~d** 3 hoch 2;
square root n Quadratwurzel f
squash [skwɒʃ] n (drink)

Fruchtsaftgetränk nt; (Sport)
Squash nt; (US: vegetable) Kürbis m
▷ vt zerquetschen
squat [skwɒt] vi (be crouching)
hocken; **to ~ (down)** sich
(hin)hocken
squeak [skwiːk] vi (door, shoes
etc) quietschen; (animal) quieken
squeal [skwiːl] vi (person)
kreischen (with vor +dat)
squeeze [skwiːz] vt drücken;
(orange) auspressen ▷ vi: **to ~ into
the car** sich in den Wagen
hineinzwängen; **squeeze up** vi
(on bench etc) zusammenrücken
squid [skwɪd] n Tintenfisch m
squint [skwɪnt] vi schielen; (in
bright light) blinzeln
squirrel ['skwɪrəl] n Eichhörnchen nt
squirt [skwɜːt] vt, vi (liquid)
spritzen
Sri Lanka [sriː'læŋkə] n Sri
Lanka nt
st abbr = **stone** Gewichtseinheit (6,35
kg)
St abbr = **saint** St.; abbr = **street** Str.
stab [stæb] vt (person) einstechen
auf +akk; (to death) erstechen;
stabbing adj (pain) stechend
stabilize ['steɪbəlaɪz] vt
stabilisieren ▷ vi sich
stabilisieren
stable ['steɪbl] n Stall m ▷ adj
stabil
stack [stæk] n (pile) Stapel m
▷ vt: **to ~ (up)** (auf)stapeln
stadium ['steɪdɪəm] n Stadion
nt
staff [stɑːf] n (personnel) Personal
nt, Lehrkräfte pl
stag [stæg] n Hirsch m
stag night n (Brit)
Junggesellenabschied m
stage [steɪdʒ] n (Theat) Bühne f;
(of project, life etc) Stadium nt; (of
journey) Etappe f; **at this ~** zu

diesem Zeitpunkt ▷ vt (Theat) aufführen, inszenieren; (demonstration) veranstalten

stagger ['stægə*] vi wanken ▷ vt (amaze) verblüffen; **staggering** adj (amazing) umwerfend; (amount, price) schwindelerregend

stagnate [stæg'neɪt] vi (fig) stagnieren

stain [steɪn] n Fleck m; **stained-glass window** n Buntglasfenster nt; **stainless steel** n rostfreier Stahl; **stain remover** n Fleck(en)entferner m

stair [steə*] n (Treppen)stufe f; **~s** pl Treppe f; **staircase** n Treppe f

stake [steɪk] n (post) Pfahl m; (in betting) Einsatz m; (Fin) Anteil m (in an +dat); **to be at ~** auf dem Spiel stehen

stale [steɪl] adj (bread) alt; (beer) schal

stalk [stɔːk] n Stiel m ▷ vt (wild animal) sich anpirschen an +akk; (person) nachstellen +dat

stall [stɔːl] n (in market) (Verkaufs)stand m; (in stable) Box f; **~s** pl (Theat) Parkett nt ▷ vt (engine) abwürgen ▷ vi (driver) den Motor abwürgen; (car) stehen bleiben; (delay) Zeit schinden

stamina ['stæmɪnə] n Durchhaltevermögen nt

stammer ['stæmə*] vi, vt stottern

stamp [stæmp] n (postage ~) Briefmarke f; (for document) Stempel m ▷ vt (passport etc) stempeln; (mail) frankieren; **stamped addressed envelope** n frankierter Rückumschlag

stand [stænd] (**stood, stood**) vi stehen; (as candidate) kandidieren ▷ vt (place) stellen; (endure) aushalten; **I can't ~ her** ich kann sie nicht ausstehen ▷ n (stall)

Stand m; (seats in stadium) Tribüne f; (for coats, bicycles) Ständer m; (for small objects) Gestell nt; **stand around** vi herumstehen; **stand by** vi (be ready) sich bereithalten; (be inactive) danebenstehen ▷ vt (fig: person) halten zu; (decision, promise) stehen zu; **stand for** vt (represent) stehen für; (tolerate) hinnehmen; **stand in for** vt einspringen für; **stand out** vi (be noticeable) auffallen; **stand up** vi (get up) aufstehen ▷ vt (girlfriend, boyfriend) versetzen; **stand up for** vt sich einsetzen für; **stand up to** vt: **to ~ sb** jdm die Stirn bieten

standard ['stændəd] n (norm) Norm f; **~ of living** Lebensstandard m ▷ adj Standard-

standardize ['stændədaɪz] vt vereinheitlichen

stand-by ['stændbaɪ] n (thing in reserve) Reserve f; **on ~** in Bereitschaft ▷ adj (flight, ticket) Stand-by-; **standing order** n (at bank) Dauerauftrag m; **standpoint** ['stændpɔɪnt] n Standpunkt m; **standstill** ['stændstɪl] n Stillstand m; **to come to a ~** stehen bleiben; (fig) zum Erliegen kommen

stank [stæŋk] pt of **stink**

staple ['steɪpl] n (for paper) Heftklammer f ▷ vt heften (to an +akk); **stapler** n Hefter m

star [stɑː*] n Stern m; (person) Star m ▷ vt: **the film ~s Hugh Grant** der Film zeigt Hugh Grant in der Hauptrolle ▷ vi die Hauptrolle spielen

starch [stɑːtʃ] n Stärke f

stare [steə*] vi starren; **to ~ at** anstarren

starfish ['stɑːfɪʃ] n Seestern m

star sign ['stɑːsaɪn] n Sternzeichen nt

start [stɑːt] n (beginning) Anfang m, Beginn m; (Sport) Start m; (lead) Vorsprung m; **from the ~** von Anfang an ⊳ vt (car, engine) starten; (business, family) gründen; **to ~ to do sth, to ~ doing sth** anfangen, etw zu tun ⊳ vi (begin) anfangen; (car) anspringen; (on journey) aufbrechen; (Sport) starten; (jump) zusammenfahren; **~ing from Monday** ab Montag; **start off** vt (discussion, process etc) anfangen, beginnen ⊳ vi (begin) anfangen, beginnen; (on journey) aufbrechen; **start over** vi (US) wieder anfangen; **start up** vi (in business) anfangen ⊳ vt (car, engine) starten; (business) gründen; **starter** n (Brit: first course) Vorspeise f; (Auto) Anlasser m; **starting point** n (a. fig) Ausgangspunkt m

startle ['stɑːtl] vt erschrecken; **startling** adj überraschend

starve [stɑːv] vi hungern; (to death) verhungern; **I'm starving** ich habe einen Riesenhunger

state [steɪt] n (condition) Zustand m; (Pol) Staat m; **the (United) States** die (Vereinigten) Staaten ⊳ adj Staats-; (control, education) staatlich ⊳ vt erklären; (facts, name etc) angeben; **stated** adj (fixed) festgesetzt

statement ['steɪtmənt] n (official declaration) Erklärung f; (to police) Aussage f; (from bank) Kontoauszug m

state-of-the-art [steɪtəvðiːˈɑːt] adj hochmodern, auf dem neuesten Stand der Technik

static ['stætɪk] adj (unchanging) konstant

station ['steɪʃən] n (for trains, buses) Bahnhof m; (underground ~) Station f; (police ~, fire ~) Wache f;

(TV, Radio) Sender m ⊳ vt (Mil) stationieren

stationer's ['steɪʃənəz] n: **~ (shop)** Schreibwarengeschäft nt; **stationery** n Schreibwaren pl

station wagon ['steɪʃənwægən] n (US) Kombiwagen m

statistics [stəˈtɪstɪks] nsing (science) Statistik f; (figures) Statistiken pl

statue ['stætjuː] n Statue f

status ['steɪtəs] n Status m; (prestige) Ansehen nt; **status bar** n (Inform) Statuszeile f

stay [steɪ] n Aufenthalt m ⊳ vi bleiben; (with friends, in hotel) wohnen (with bei); **to ~ the night** übernachten; **stay away** vi wegbleiben; **to ~ from sb** sich von jdm fernhalten; **stay behind** vi zurückbleiben; (at work) länger bleiben; **stay in** vi (at home) zu Hause bleiben; **stay out** vi (not come home) wegbleiben; **stay up** vi (at night) aufbleiben

steady ['stedɪ] adj (speed) gleichmäßig; (progress, increase) stetig; (job, income, girlfriend) fest; (worker) zuverlässig; (hand) ruhig; **they've been going ~ for two years** sie sind seit zwei Jahren fest zusammen ⊳ vt (nerves) beruhigen; **to ~ oneself** Halt finden

steak [steɪk] n Steak nt; (of fish) Filet nt

steal [stiːl] **(stole, stolen)** vt stehlen; **to ~ sth from sb** jdm etw stehlen

steam [stiːm] n Dampf m ⊳ vt (Gastr) dämpfen; **steam up** vi (window) beschlagen; **steamer** n (Gastr) Dampfkochtopf m; (ship) Dampfer m; **steam iron** n Dampfbügeleisen nt

steel [stiːl] n Stahl m ⊳ adj Stahl-

steep [sti:p] *adj* steil
steeple ['sti:pl] *n* Kirchturm *m*
steer [stɪə*] *vt, vi* steuern; (*car, bike etc*) lenken; **steering** *n* (*Auto*) Lenkung *f*; **steering wheel** *n* Steuer *nt*, Lenkrad *nt*
stem [stem] *n* (*of plant, glass*) Stiel *m*
step [step] *n* Schritt *m*; (*stair*) Stufe *f*; (*measure*) Maßnahme *f*; ~ **by** ~ Schritt für Schritt ▷ *vi* treten; ~ **this way, please** hier entlang, bitte; **step down** *vi* (*resign*) zurücktreten
stepbrother *n* Stiefbruder *m*; **stepchild** (*pl* **-children**) *n* Stiefkind *nt*; **stepfather** *n* Stiefvater *m*
stepladder *n* Trittleiter *f*
stepmother *n* Stiefmutter *f*; **stepsister** *n* Stiefschwester *f*
stereo ['sterɪəʊ] (*pl* **-s**) *n*: ~ (**system**) Stereoanlage *f*
sterile ['sterail] *adj* steril; **sterilize** ['sterɪlaɪz] *vt* sterilisieren
sterling ['stɜ:lɪŋ] *n* (*Fin*) das Pfund Sterling
stew [stju:] *n* Eintopf *m*
steward ['stju:əd] *n* (*on plane, ship*) Steward *m*; **stewardess** *n* Stewardess *f*
stick [stɪk] (**stuck, stuck**) *vt* (*with glue etc*) kleben; (*pin etc*) stecken; (*fam: put*) tun ▷ *vi* (*get jammed*) klemmen; (*hold fast*) haften ▷ *n* Stock *m*; (*hockey ~*) Schläger *m*; (*of chalk*) Stück *nt*; (*of celery, rhubarb*) Stange *f*; **stick out** *vt*: **to stick one's tongue out** (**at sb**) (jdm) die Zunge herausstrecken ▷ *vi* (*protrude*) vorstehen; (*ears*) abstehen; (*be noticeable*) auffallen; **stick to** *vt* (*rules, plan etc*) sich halten an +*akk*; **sticker** ['stɪkə*] *n* Aufkleber *m*; **sticky** ['stɪkɪ] *adj* klebrig;

(*weather*) schwül; ~ **label** Aufkleber *m*; ~ **tape** Klebeband *nt*
stiff [stɪf] *adj* steif
stifle ['staɪfl] *vt* (*yawn etc, opposition*) unterdrücken; **stifling** *adj* drückend
still [stɪl] *adj* still; (*drink*) ohne Kohlensäure ▷ *adv* (*yet, even now*) (immer) noch; (*all the same*) immerhin; (*sit, stand*) still; **he ~ doesn't believe me** er glaubt mir immer noch nicht; **keep ~** halt still!; **bigger/better ~** noch größer/besser
still life (*pl* **still lives**) *n* Stillleben *nt*
stimulate ['stɪmjʊleɪt] *vt* anregen, stimulieren; **stimulating** *adj* anregend
sting [stɪŋ] (**stung, stung**) *vt* (*wound with ~*) stechen ▷ *vi* (*eyes, ointment etc*) brennen ▷ *n* (*insect wound*) Stich *m*
stingy ['stɪndʒɪ] *adj* (*fam*) geizig
stink [stɪŋk] (**stank, stunk**) *vi* stinken (*of* nach) ▷ *n* Gestank *m*
stir [stɜ:*] *vt* (*mix*) (um)rühren; **stir up** *vt* (*mob*) aufhetzen; (*memories*) wachrufen; **to ~ trouble** Unruhe stiften; **stir-fry** *vt* (unter Rühren) kurz anbraten
stitch [stɪtʃ] *n* (*in sewing*) Stich *m*; (*in knitting*) Masche *f*; **to have a ~** (*pain*) Seitenstechen haben; **he had to have ~es** er musste genäht werden; **she had her ~es out** ihr wurden die Fäden gezogen; **to be in ~es** (*fam*) sich kaputtlachen ▷ *vt* nähen; **stitch up** *vt* (*hole, wound*) nähen
stock [stɒk] *n* (*supply*) Vorrat *m* (*of* an +*dat*); (*of shop*) Bestand *m*; (*for soup etc*) Brühe *f*; ~**s and shares** *pl* Aktien und Wertpapiere *pl*; **to be in/out of** ~ vorrätig/nicht vorrätig sein; **to**

take ~ Inventur machen; (*fig*)
Bilanz ziehen ▷ *vt* (*keep in shop*)
führen; **stock up** *vi* sich
eindecken (*on,* with mit)
stockbroker *n* Börsenmakler(in)
m(f)
stock cube *n* Brühwürfel *m*
stock exchange *n* Börse *f*
stocking ['stɒkɪŋ] *n* Strumpf *m*
stock market ['stɒkmɑːkɪt] *n*
Börse *f*
stole [stəʊl] *pt of* **steal; stolen**
['stəʊlən] *pp of* **steal**
stomach ['stʌmək] *n* Magen *m;*
(*belly*) Bauch *m;* **on an empty ~** auf
leeren Magen; **stomach-ache** *n*
Magenschmerzen *pl;* **stomach
upset** *n* Magenverstimmung *f*
stone [stəʊn] *n* Stein *m;* (*seed*)
Kern *m,* Stein *m;* (*weight*) britische
Gewichtseinheit (6,35 kg) ▷ *adj*
Stein-, aus Stein; **stony** *adj*
(*ground*) steinig
stood [stʊd] *pt, pp of* **stand**
stool [stuːl] *n* Hocker *m*
stop [stɒp] *n* Halt *m;* (*for bus,
tram, train*) Haltestelle *f;* **to come
to a ~** anhalten ▷ *vt* (*vehicle,
passer-by*) anhalten; (*put an end to*)
ein Ende machen +dat; (*cease*)
aufhören mit; (*prevent from
happening*) verhindern; (*bleeding*)
stillen; (*engine, machine*) abstellen;
(*payments*) einstellen; (*cheque*)
sperren; **to ~ doing sth** aufhören,
etw zu tun; **to ~ sb (from) doing
sth** jdn daran hindern, etw zu tun;
~ it hör auf (damit)! ▷ *vi* (*vehicle*)
anhalten; (*during journey*) Halt
machen; (*pedestrian, clock, heart*)
stehen bleiben; (*rain, noise*)
aufhören; (*stay*) bleiben; **stop by**
vi vorbeischauen; **stop over** *vi*
Halt machen; (*overnight*)
übernachten; **stopgap** *n*
Provisorium *nt,* Zwischenlösung *f;*
stopover *n* (*on journey*)

Zwischenstation *f;* **stopper** *n*
Stöpsel *m;* **stop sign** *n*
Stoppschild *nt;* **stopwatch** *n*
Stoppuhr *f*
storage ['stɔːrɪdʒ] *n* Lagerung *f;*
store [stɔː*] *n* (*supply*) Vorrat *m*
(*of an* +dat); (*place for storage*) Lager
nt; (*large shop*) Kaufhaus *nt;* (*US:
shop*) Geschäft *nt* ▷ *vt* lagern;
(*Inform*) speichern; **storecard** *n*
Kundenkreditkarte *f;* **storeroom**
n Lagerraum *m*
storey ['stɔːrɪ] *n* (*Brit*) Stock *m,*
Stockwerk *nt*
storm [stɔːm] *n* Sturm *m;*
(*thunder~*) Gewitter *nt* ▷ *vt, vi*
(*with movement*) stürmen; **stormy**
adj stürmisch
story ['stɔːrɪ] *n* Geschichte *f;*
(*plot*) Handlung *f;* (*US: of building*)
Stock *m,* Stockwerk *nt*
stout [staʊt] *adj* (*fat*) korpulent
stove [stəʊv] *n* Herd *m;* (*for
heating*) Ofen *m*
stow [stəʊ] *vt* verstauen;
stowaway *n* blinder Passagier
straight [streɪt] *adj* (*not curved*)
gerade; (*hair*) glatt; (*honest*) ehrlich
(*with zu*); (*fam: heterosexual*) hetero
▷ *adv* (*directly*) direkt; (*immediately*)
sofort; (*drink*) pur; (*think*) klar;
~ ahead geradeaus; **to go ~ on**
geradeaus weitergehen/
weiterfahren; **straightaway** *adv*
sofort; **straightforward** *adj*
einfach; (*person*) aufrichtig,
unkompliziert
strain [streɪn] *n* Belastung *f* ▷ *vt*
(*eyes*) überanstrengen; (*rope,
relationship*) belasten; (*vegetables*)
abgießen; **to ~ a muscle** sich
einen Muskel zerren; **strained** *adj*
(*laugh, smile*) gezwungen;
(*relations*) gespannt; **~ muscle**
Muskelzerrung *f;* **strainer** *n* Sieb
nt
strand [strænd] *n* (*of wool*) Faden

m; (of hair) Strähne f ▷ vt: **to be (left) ~ed** (person) festsitzen

strange [streɪndʒ] adj seltsam; (unfamiliar) fremd; **strangely** adv seltsam; **~ enough** seltsamerweise; **stranger** n Fremde(r) mf; **I'm a ~ here** ich bin hier fremd

strangle ['stræŋgl] vt (kill) erdrosseln

strap [stræp] n Riemen m; (on dress etc) Träger m; (on watch) Band nt ▷ vt (fasten) festschnallen (to an +dat); **strapless** adj trägerlos

strategy ['strætɪdʒɪ] n Strategie f

straw [strɔ:] n Stroh nt; (drinking ~) Strohhalm m

strawberry n Erdbeere f

stray [streɪ] n streunendes Tier ▷ adj (cat, dog) streunend ▷ vi streunen

streak ['stri:k] n (of colour, dirt) Streifen m; (in hair) Strähne f; (in character) Zug m

stream [stri:m] n (flow of liquid) Strom m; (brook) Bach m ▷ vi strömen; **streamer** n (of paper) Luftschlange f

street [stri:t] n Straße f; **streetcar** n (US) Straßenbahn f; **street lamp**, **street light** n Straßenlaterne f; **street map** n Stadtplan m

strength [streŋθ] n Kraft f, Stärke f; **strengthen** vt verstärken; (fig) stärken

strenuous ['strenjʊəs] adj anstrengend

stress [stres] n Stress m; (on word) Betonung f; **to be under ~** im Stress sein ▷ vt betonen; (put under ~) stressen; **stressed** adj: **~ (out)** gestresst

stretch [stretʃ] n (of land) Stück nt; (of road) Strecke f ▷ vt (material, shoes) dehnen; (rope, canvas)

spannen; (person in job etc) fordern; **to ~ one's legs** (walk) sich die Beine vertreten ▷ vi (person) sich strecken; (area) sich erstrecken (to bis zu); **stretch out** vt: **to stretch one's hand/legs out** die Hand/die Beine ausstrecken, ausstrecken ▷ vi (reach) sich strecken; (lie down) sich ausstrecken; **stretcher** n Tragbahre f

strict, **strictly** [strɪkt, -lɪ] adj, adv (severe(ly)) streng; (exact(ly)) genau; **~ speaking** genauer gesagt

strike [straɪk] (**struck**, **struck**) vt (match) anzünden; (hit) schlagen; (find) finden; **it struck me as strange** es kam mir seltsam vor ▷ vi (stop work) streiken; (attack) zuschlagen; (clock) schlagen ▷ n (by workers) Streik m; **to be on ~** streiken; **strike up** vt (conversation) anfangen; (friendship) schließen; **striking** adj auffallend

string [strɪŋ] n (for tying) Schnur f; (Mus, Tennis) Saite f; **the ~s** pl (section of orchestra) die Streicher pl

strip [strɪp] n Streifen m; (Brit: of footballer etc) Trikot nt ▷ vi (undress) sich ausziehen, strippen

stripe [straɪp] n Streifen m; **striped** adj gestreift

stripper ['strɪpə*] n Stripper(in) m(f); (paint ~) Farbentferner m

strip-search ['strɪpsɜ:tʃ] n Leibesvisitation f (bei der man sich ausziehen muss)

striptease ['strɪpti:z] n Striptease m

stroke [strəʊk] n (Med, Tennis etc) Schlag m; (of pen, brush) Strich m ▷ vt streicheln

stroll [strəʊl] n Spaziergang m ▷ vi spazieren; **stroller** n (US: for baby) Buggy m

strong [strɒŋ] adj stark; (healthy)

robust; (*wall, table*) stabil; (*shoes*) fest; (*influence, chance*) groß; **strongly** *adv* stark; (*believe*) fest; (*constructed*) stabil

struck [strʌk] *pt, pp of* **strike**

structural ['strʌktʃərəl, -lɪ] *adj* strukturell; **structure** ['strʌktʃə*] *n* Struktur *f*; (*building, bridge*) Konstruktion *f*, Bau *m*

struggle ['strʌgl] *n* Kampf *m* (*for* um) ▷ *vi* (*fight*) kämpfen (*for* um); (*do sth with difficulty*) sich abmühen; **to ~ to do sth** sich abmühen, etw zu tun

stub [stʌb] *n* (*of cigarette*) Kippe *f*; (*of ticket, cheque*) Abschnitt *m* ▷ *vt*: **to ~ one's toe** sich *dat* den Zeh stoßen (*on an* +*dat*)

stubble ['stʌbl] *n* Stoppelbart *m*; (*field*) Stoppeln *pl*

stubborn ['stʌbən] *adj* (*person*) stur

stuck [stʌk] *pt, pp of* **stick** ▷ *adj*: **to be ~** (*jammed*) klemmen; (*at a loss*) nicht mehr weiterwissen; **to get ~** (*car in snow etc*) stecken bleiben

student ['stjuːdənt] *n* Student(in) *m(f)*, Schüler(in) *m(f)*

studio ['stjuːdɪəʊ] (*pl* **-s**) *n* Studio *nt*

studious ['stjuːdɪəs] *adj* fleißig

study ['stʌdɪ] *n* (*investigation*) Untersuchung *f*; (*room*) Arbeitszimmer *nt* ▷ *vt, vi* studieren

stuff [stʌf] *n* Zeug *nt*, Sachen *pl* ▷ *vt* (*push*) stopfen; (*Gastr*) füllen; **to ~ oneself** (*fam*) sich vollstopfen; **stuffing** *n* (*Gastr*) Füllung *f*

stuffy ['stʌfɪ] *adj* (*room*) stickig; (*person*) spießig

stumble ['stʌmbl] *vi* stolpern; (*when speaking*) stocken

stun [stʌn] *vt* (*shock*) fassungslos

machen; **I was ~ned** ich war fassungslos (*o* völlig überrascht)

stung [stʌŋ] *pt, pp of* **sting**

stunk [stʌŋk] *pp of* **stink**

stunning ['stʌnɪŋ] *adj* (*marvellous*) fantastisch; (*beautiful*) atemberaubend; (*very surprising, shocking*) überwältigend; unfassbar

stunt [stʌnt] *n* (*Cine*) Stunt *m*

stupid ['stjuːpɪd] *adj* dumm; **stupidity** [stjuː'pɪdɪtɪ] *n* Dummheit *f*

sturdy ['stɜːdɪ] *adj* robust; (*building, car*) stabil

stutter ['stʌtə*] *vi, vt* stottern

stye [staɪ] *n* (*Med*) Gerstenkorn *nt*

style [staɪl] *n* Stil *m* ▷ *vt* (*hair*) stylen; **styling mousse** *n* Schaumfestiger *m*; **stylish** ['staɪlɪʃ] *adj* elegant, schick

subconscious [sʌb'kɒnʃəs] *adj* unterbewusst ▷ *n*: **the ~** das Unterbewusstsein

subdivide [sʌbdɪ'vaɪd] *vt* unterteilen

subject ['sʌbdʒɪkt] *n* (*topic*) Thema *nt*; (*in school*) Fach *nt*; (*citizen*) Staatsangehörige(r) *mf*; (*of kingdom*) Untertan(in) *m(f)*; (*Ling*) Subjekt *nt*; **to change the ~** das Thema wechseln ▷ *adj* [səb'dʒekt] **to be ~ to** (*dependent on*) abhängen von; (*under control of*) unterworfen sein +*dat*

subjective [səb'dʒektɪv] *adj* subjektiv

sublet [sʌb'let] *irr vt* untervermieten (*to an* +*akk*)

submarine [sʌbmə'riːn] *n* U-Boot *nt*

submerge [səb'mɜːdʒ] *vt* (*put in water*) eintauchen ▷ *vi* tauchen

submit [səb'mɪt] *vt* (*application, claim*) einreichen ▷ *vi* (*surrender*) sich ergeben

subordinate [sə'bɔːdɪnət] *adj*

untergeordnet (to +dat) ▷ n Untergebene(r) mf

subscribe [səb'skraɪb] vi: **to ~ to** (magazine etc) abonnieren; **subscription** [səb'skrɪpʃən] n (to magazine etc) Abonnement nt; (to club etc) (Mitglieds)beitrag m

subsequent ['sʌbsɪkwənt] adj nach(folgend); **subsequently** adv später, anschließend

subside [səb'saɪd] vi (floods) zurückgehen; (storm) sich legen; (building) sich senken

substance ['sʌbstəns] n Substanz f

substantial [səb'stænʃəl] adj beträchtlich; (improvement) wesentlich; (meal) reichhaltig; (furniture) solide

substitute ['sʌbstɪtjuːt] n Ersatz m; (Sport) Ersatzspieler(in) m(f) ▷ vt: **to ~ A for B** B durch A ersetzen

subtitle ['sʌbtaɪtl] n Untertitel m

subtle ['sʌtl] adj (difference, taste) fein; (plan) raffiniert

subtotal ['sʌbtəʊtl] n Zwischensumme f

subtract [səb'trækt] vt abziehen (from von)

suburb ['sʌbɜːb] n Vorort m; **in the ~s** am Stadtrand; **suburban** [sə'bɜːbən] adj vorstädtisch, Vorstadt-

subway ['sʌbweɪ] n (Brit) Unterführung f; (US Rail) U-Bahn f

succeed [sək'siːd] vi erfolgreich sein; **he ~ed (in doing it)** es gelang ihm(, es zu tun) ▷ vt nachfolgen +dat; **succeeding** adj nachfolgend; **success** [sək'ses] n Erfolg m; **successful, successfully** adj, adv erfolgreich

successive [sək'sesɪv] adj aufeinanderfolgend; **successor** n Nachfolger(in) m(f)

succulent ['sʌkjʊlənt] adj saftig

succumb [sə'kʌm] vi erliegen (to +dat)

such [sʌtʃ] adj solche(r, s); **~ a book** so ein Buch, ein solches Buch; **it was ~ a success that ...** es war solch ein Erfolg, dass ...; **~ as** wie ▷ adv so; **~ a hot day** so ein heißer Tag ▷ pron: **as ~** als solche(r, s)

suck [sʌk] vt (toffee etc) lutschen; (liquid) saugen; **it ~s** (fam) das ist beschissen

Sudan [sʊ'dɑːn] n: **(the) ~** der Sudan

sudden ['sʌdn] adj plötzlich; **all of a ~** ganz plötzlich; **suddenly** adv plötzlich

sue [suː] vt verklagen

suede [sweɪd] n Wildleder nt

suffer ['sʌfə*] vt erleiden ▷ vi leiden; **to ~ from** (Med) leiden an +dat

sufficient, sufficiently [sə'fɪʃənt, -lɪ] adj, adv ausreichend

suffocate ['sʌfəkeɪt] vt, vi ersticken

sugar ['ʃʊgə*] n Zucker m ▷ vt zuckern; **sugar bowl** n Zuckerdose f; **sugary** adj (sweet) süß

suggest [sə'dʒest] vt vorschlagen; (imply) andeuten; **I ~ saying nothing** ich schlage vor, nichts zu sagen; **suggestion** [sə'dʒestʃən] n (proposal) Vorschlag m; **suggestive** adj vielsagend; (sexually) anzüglich

suicide ['sʊɪsaɪd] n (act) Selbstmord m; **suicide bomber** n Selbstmordattentäter(in) m(f); **suicide bombing** n Selbstmordattentat nt

suit [suːt] n (man's clothes) Anzug m; (lady's clothes) Kostüm nt; (Cards) Farbe f ▷ vt (be convenient for) passen +dat; (clothes, colour) stehen +dat; (climate, food) bekommen +dat; **suitable** adj geeignet (for für); **suitcase** n Koffer m

suite [swi:t] n (of rooms) Suite f; (sofa and chairs) Sitzgarnitur f

sulk [sʌlk] vi schmollen; **sulky** adj eingeschnappt

sultana [sʌl'tɑ:nə] n (raisin) Sultanine f

sum [sʌm] n Summe f; (money a.) Betrag m; (calculation) Rechenaufgabe f; **sum up** vt, vi (summarize) zusammenfassen

summarize ['sʌməraiz] vt, vi zusammenfassen; **summary** n Zusammenfassung f

summer ['sʌmə*] n Sommer m; **summer camp** n (US) Ferienlager nt; **summer holidays** n Sommerferien pl; **summertime** n: **in (the)** ~ im Sommer

summit ['sʌmɪt] n (a. Pol) Gipfel m

summon ['sʌmən] vt (doctor, fire brigade etc) rufen; (to one's office) zitieren; **summon up** vt (courage, strength) zusammennehmen

summons ['sʌmənz] nsing (Jur) Vorladung f

sumptuous ['sʌmptjʊəs] adj luxuriös; (meal) üppig

sun [sʌn] n Sonne f ▷ vt: **to** ~ **oneself** sich sonnen

Sun abbr = **Sunday** So.

sunbathe vi sich sonnen; **sunbathing** n Sonnenbaden nt; **sunbed** n Sonnenbank f; **sunblock** n Sunblocker m; **sunburn** n Sonnenbrand m; **sunburnt** adj: **to be/get** ~ einen Sonnenbrand haben/bekommen

sundae ['sʌndeɪ] n Eisbecher m

Sunday ['sʌndɪ] n Sonntag m; see also **Tuesday**

sung [sʌŋ] pp of **sing**

sunglasses ['sʌnglɑ:sɪz] npl

Sonnenbrille f; **sunhat** n Sonnenhut m

sunk [sʌŋk] pp of **sink**

sunlamp ['sʌnlæmp] n Höhensonne f; **sunlight** n Sonnenlicht nt; **sunny** ['sʌnɪ] adj sonnig; **sun protection factor** n Lichtschutzfaktor m; **sunrise** n Sonnenaufgang m; **sunroof** n (Auto) Schiebedach nt; **sunscreen** n Sonnenschutzmittel nt; **sunset** n Sonnenuntergang m; **sunshade** n Sonnenschirm m; **sunshine** n Sonnenschein m; **sunstroke** n Sonnenstich m; **suntan** n (Sonnen)bräune f; **to get/have a** ~ braun werden/sein; ~ **lotion** (o **oil**) Sonnenöl nt

super ['su:pə*] adj (fam) toll

superb, superbly [su'pɜ:b, -lɪ] adj, adv ausgezeichnet

superficial, superficially [su:pə'fɪʃəl, -ɪ] adj, adv oberflächlich

superfluous [sʊ'pɜ:flʊəs] adj überflüssig

superglue ['su:pəglu:] n Sekundenkleber m

superior [sʊ'pɪərɪə*] adj (better) besser (to als); (higher in rank) höhergestellt (to als), höher ▷ n (in rank) Vorgesetzte(r) mf

supermarket ['su:pəmɑ:kɪt] n Supermarkt m

supersede [su:pə'si:d] vt ablösen

supersonic [su:pə'sɒnɪk] adj Überschall-

superstition [su:pə'stɪʃən] n Aberglaube m; **superstitious** [su:pə'stɪʃəs] adj abergläubisch

superstore ['su:pəstɔ:*] n Verbrauchermarkt m

supervise ['su:pəvaɪz] vt beaufsichtigen; **supervisor** ['su:pəvaɪzə] n Aufsicht f; (at university) Doktorvater m

supper ['sʌpə*] n Abendessen nt; (late-night snack) Imbiss

supplement ['sʌplɪmənt] n (extra payment) Zuschlag m; (of newspaper) Beilage f ▷ vt ergänzen; **supplementary** [sʌplɪ'mentərɪ] adj zusätzlich

supplier [sə'plaɪə*] n Lieferant(in) m(f); **supply** [sə'plaɪ] vt (deliver) liefern; (drinks, music etc) sorgen für; **to ~ sb with sth** (provide) jdn mit etw versorgen ▷ n (stock) Vorrat m (of an +dat)

support [sə'pɔ:t] n Unterstützung f; (Tech) Stütze f ▷ vt (hold up) tragen, stützen; (provide for) ernähren, unterhalten; (speak in favour of) unterstützen; **he ~s Manchester United** er ist Manchester-United-Fan

suppose [sə'pəʊz] vt (assume) annehmen; **I ~ so** ich denke schon; **I ~ not** wahrscheinlich nicht; **you're not ~d to smoke here** du darfst/Sie dürfen hier nicht rauchen; **supposedly** [sə'pəʊzɪdlɪ] adv angeblich; **supposing** conj angenommen

suppress [sə'pres] vt unterdrücken

surcharge ['sɜ:tʃɑ:dʒ] n Zuschlag m

sure [ʃʊə*] adj sicher; **I'm (not) ~** ich bin mir (nicht) sicher; **make ~ you lock up** vergiss/vergessen Sie nicht abzuschließen ▷ adv: **~!** klar!; **~ enough** tatsächlich; **surely** adv: **~ you don't mean it?** das ist nicht dein/Ihr Ernst, oder?

surf [sɜ:f] n Brandung f ▷ vi (Sport) surfen ▷ vt: **to ~ the net** im Internet surfen

surface ['sɜ:fɪs] n Oberfläche f ▷ vi auftauchen; **surface mail** n: **by ~** auf dem Land-/Seeweg

surfboard ['sɜ:fbɔ:d] n Surfbrett nt; **surfer** n Surfer(in) m(f);

surfing n Surfen nt; **to go ~** surfen gehen

surgeon ['sɜ:dʒən] n Chirurg(in) m(f); **surgery** ['sɜ:dʒərɪ] n (operation) Operation f; (room) Praxis f, Sprechzimmer nt; (consulting time) Sprechstunde f; **to have ~** operiert werden

surname ['sɜ:neɪm] n Nachname m

surpass [sɜ:'pɑ:s] vt übertreffen

surplus ['sɜ:pləs] n Überschuss m (of an +dat)

surprise [sə'praɪz] n Überraschung f ▷ vt überraschen; **surprising** adj überraschend; **surprisingly** adv überraschenderweise, erstaunlicherweise

surrender [sə'rendə*] vi sich ergeben (to +dat) ▷ vt (weapon, passport) abgeben

surround [sə'raʊnd] vt umgeben; (stand all round) umringen; **surrounding** adj (countryside) umliegend ▷ n ~s pl Umgebung f

survey ['sɜ:veɪ] n (opinion poll) Umfrage f; (of literature etc) Überblick m (of über +akk); (of land) Vermessung f ▷ [sɜ:'veɪ] vt (look out over) überblicken; (land) vermessen

survive [sə'vaɪv] vt, vi überleben

susceptible [sə'septəbl] adj empfänglich (to für); (Med) anfällig (to für)

sushi ['su:ʃɪ] n Sushi nt

suspect ['sʌspekt] n Verdächtige(r) mf ▷ adj verdächtig ▷ [sə'spekt] vt verdächtigen (of +gen); (think likely) vermuten

suspend [sə'spend] vt (from work) suspendieren; (payment) vorübergehend einstellen; (player) sperren; (hang up) aufhängen; **suspender** n (Brit) Strumpfhalter

m; **~s** pl (US: for trousers)
Hosenträger pl

suspense [sə'spens] n Spannung f

suspicious [sə'spɪʃəs] adj misstrauisch (of sb/sth jdm/etw gegenüber); (causing suspicion) verdächtig

swallow ['swɒləʊ] n (bird) Schwalbe f ▷ vt, vi schlucken

swam [swæm] pt of **swim**

swamp [swɒmp] n Sumpf m

swan [swɒn] n Schwan m

swap [swɒp] vt, vi tauschen; **to ~ sth for sth** etw gegen etw eintauschen

sway [sweɪ] vi schwanken

swear [sweə*] (**swore, sworn**) vi (promise) schwören; (curse) fluchen; **to ~ at sb** jdn beschimpfen; **swear by** vt (have faith in) schwören auf +akk; **swearword** n Fluch m

sweat [swet] n Schweiß m ▷ vi schwitzen; **sweatband** n Schweißband nt; **sweater** n Pullover m; **sweatshirt** n Sweatshirt nt; **sweaty** adj verschwitzt

swede [swiːd] n Steckrübe f

Swede [swiːd] n Schwede m, Schwedin f; **Sweden** n Schweden nt; **Swedish** adj schwedisch ▷ n (language) Schwedisch nt

sweep [swiːp] (**swept, swept**) vt, vi (with brush) kehren, fegen; **sweep up** vt (dirt etc) zusammenkehren, zusammenfegen

sweet [swiːt] n (Brit: candy) Bonbon nt; (dessert) Nachtisch m ▷ adj süß; (kind) lieb; **sweet-and-sour** adj süßsauer; **sweetcorn** n Mais m; **sweeten** vt (tea etc) süßen; **sweetener** n (substance) Süßstoff m; **sweet potato** n Süßkartoffel f

swell [swel] (**swelled, swollen** o **swelled**) vi: **to ~ (up)** (an)schwellen ▷ adj (US fam) toll; **swelling** n (Med) Schwellung f

sweltering ['sweltərɪŋ] adj (heat) drückend

swept [swept] pt, pp of **sweep**

swift, **swiftly** [swɪft] adj, adv schnell

swig [swɪg] n (fam) Schluck m

swim [swɪm] (**swam, swum**) vi schwimmen ▷ n: **to go for a ~** schwimmen gehen; **swimmer** n Schwimmer(in) m(f); **swimming** n Schwimmen nt; **to go ~** schwimmen gehen; **swimming cap** n (Brit) Badekappe f; **swimming costume** n (Brit) Badeanzug m; **swimming pool** n Schwimmbad nt; (private, in hotel) Swimmingpool m; **swimming trunks** npl (Brit) Badehose f; **swimsuit** n Badeanzug m

swindle ['swɪndl] vt betrügen (out of um)

swine [swaɪn] n (person) Schwein nt

swing [swɪŋ] (**swung, swung**) vt, vi (object) schwingen ▷ n (for child) Schaukel f

swipe [swaɪp] vt (credit card etc) durchziehen; (fam: steal) klauen; **swipe card** n Magnetkarte f

Swiss [swɪs] adj schweizerisch ▷ n Schweizer(in) m(f)

switch [swɪtʃ] n (Elec) Schalter m ▷ vi (change) wechseln (to zu); **switch off** vt abschalten, ausschalten; **switch on** vt anschalten, einschalten; **switchboard** n (Tel) Vermittlung f

Switzerland ['swɪtsələnd] n die Schweiz

swivel ['swɪvl] vi sich drehen ▷ vt drehen; **swivel chair** n Drehstuhl m

swollen ['swəʊlən] pp of **swell**

▷ adj (Med) geschwollen; (stomach) aufgebläht

swop [swɒp] see **swap**

sword [sɔːd] n Schwert nt

swore [swɔː*] pt of **swear**

sworn [swɔːn] pp of **swear**

swot [swɒt] vi (Brit fam) büffeln (for für)

swum [swʌm] pp of **swim**

swung [swʌŋ] pt, pp of **swing**

syllable ['sɪləbl] n Silbe f

syllabus ['sɪləbəs] n Lehrplan m

symbol ['sɪmbəl] n Symbol nt; **symbolic** [sɪm'bɒlɪk] adj symbolisch; **symbolize** vt symbolisieren

symmetrical [sɪ'metrɪkəl] adj symmetrisch

sympathetic [sɪmpə'θetɪk] adj mitfühlend; (understanding) verständnisvoll; **sympathize** ['sɪmpəθaɪz] vi mitfühlen (with sb mit jdm); **sympathy** ['sɪmpəθɪ] n Mitleid nt; (after death) Beileid nt; (understanding) Verständnis nt

symphony ['sɪmfənɪ] n Sinfonie f

symptom ['sɪmptəm] n (a. fig) Symptom nt

synagogue ['sɪnəgɒg] n Synagoge f

synonym ['sɪnənɪm] n Synonym nt; **synonymous** [sɪ'nɒnɪməs] adj synonym (with mit)

synthetic [sɪn'θetɪk] adj (material) synthetisch

syphilis ['sɪfɪlɪs] n Syphilis f

Syria ['sɪrɪə] n Syrien nt

syringe [sɪ'rɪndʒ] n Spritze f

system ['sɪstəm] n System nt; **systematic** [sɪstə'mætɪk] adj systematisch; **system disk** n (Inform) Systemdiskette f; **system(s) software** n (Inform) Systemsoftware f

t

tab [tæb] n (for hanging up coat etc) Aufhänger m; (Inform) Tabulator m; **to pick up the ~** (fam) die Rechnung übernehmen

table ['teɪbl] n Tisch m; (list) Tabelle f; **~ of contents** Inhaltsverzeichnis nt; **tablecloth** n Tischdecke f; **tablelamp** n Tischlampe f; **tablemat** n Set nt; **tablespoon** n Servierlöffel m; (in recipes) Esslöffel m

tablet ['tæblət] n (Med) Tablette f

table tennis ['teɪbltenɪs] n Tischtennis nt; **table wine** n Tafelwein m

tabloid ['tæblɔɪd] n Boulevardzeitung f

taboo [tə'buː] n Tabu nt ▷ adj tabu

tacit, tacitly ['tæsɪt, -lɪ] adj, adv stillschweigend

tack [tæk] n (small nail) Stift m; (US: thumb~) Reißzwecke f

tackle ['tækl] n (Sport) Angriff m; (equipment) Ausrüstung f ▷ vt (deal with) in Angriff nehmen; (Sport) angreifen; (verbally) zur Rede stellen (about wegen)

tacky ['tækɪ] adj trashig, heruntergekommen

tact [tækt] n Takt m; **tactful**, **tactfully** adj, adv taktvoll; **tactic(s)** ['tæktɪk(s)] n(pl) Taktik f; **tactless**, **tactlessly** ['tæktləs, -lɪ] adj, adv taktlos

tag [tæg] n (label) Schild nt; (with maker's name) Etikett nt

Tahiti [tɑː'hiːtɪ] n Tahiti nt

tail [teɪl] n Schwanz m; **heads or ~s?** Kopf oder Zahl?; **tailback** n (Brit) Rückstau m; **taillight** n (Auto) Rücklicht nt

tailor ['teɪlə*] n Schneider(in) m(f)

tailpipe ['teɪlpaɪp] n (US Auto) Auspuffrohr nt

tainted ['teɪntɪd] adj (US: food) verdorben

Taiwan [taɪ'wæn] n Taiwan nt

take [teɪk] (**took, taken**) vt nehmen; (~ along with one) mitnehmen; (~ to a place) bringen; (subtract) abziehen (from von); (capture: person) fassen; (gain, obtain) bekommen; (Fin, Comm) einnehmen; (train, taxi) nehmen, fahren mit; (trip, walk, holiday, exam, course, photo) machen; (bath) nehmen; (phone call) entgegennehmen; (decision, precautions) treffen; (risk) eingehen; (advice, job) annehmen; (consume) zu sich nehmen; (tablets) nehmen; (heat, pain) ertragen; (react to) aufnehmen; (have room for) Platz haben für; **I'll ~ it** (item in shop) ich nehme es; **how long does it ~?** wie lange dauert es?; **it ~s 4 hours** man braucht 4 Stunden; **do you ~ sugar?** nimmst

du/nehmen Sie Zucker?; **I ~ it that ...** ich nehme an, dass ...; **to ~ part in** teilnehmen an; **to ~ place** stattfinden; **take after** vt nachschlagen +dat; **take along** vt mitnehmen; **take apart** vt auseinandernehmen; **take away** vt (remove) wegnehmen (from sb jdm); (subtract) abziehen (from von); **take back** vt (return) zurückbringen; (retract) zurücknehmen; (remind) zurückversetzen (to in +akk); **take down** vt (picture, curtains) abnehmen; (write down) aufschreiben; **take in** vt (understand) begreifen; (give accommodation to) aufnehmen; (deceive) hereinlegen; (include) einschließen; (show, film etc) mitnehmen; **take off** vi (plane) starten ▷ vt (clothing) ausziehen; (hat, lid) abnehmen; (deduct) abziehen; (Brit: imitate) nachmachen; **to take a day off** sich einen Tag freinehmen; **take on** vt (undertake) übernehmen; (employ) einstellen; (Sport) antreten gegen; **take out** vt (wallet etc) herausnehmen; (person, dog) ausführen; (insurance) abschließen; (money from bank) abheben; (book from library) ausleihen; **take over** vt übernehmen ▷ vi: **he took over (from me)** er hat mich abgelöst; **take to** vt: **I've taken to her/it** ich mag sie/es; **to ~ doing sth** (begin) anfangen, etw zu tun; **take up** vt (carpet) hochnehmen; (space) einnehmen; (time) in Anspruch nehmen; (hobby) anfangen mit; (new job) antreten; (offer) annehmen

takeaway n (Brit: meal) Essen nt zum Mitnehmen

taken ['teɪkn] pp of **take** ▷ adj

(*seat*) besetzt; **to be ~ with** angetan sein von

takeoff ['teɪkɒf] n (*Aviat*) Start m; (*imitation*) Nachahmung f; **takeout** (*US*) see **takeaway**; **takeover** n (*Comm*) Übernahme f

takings ['teɪkɪŋz] npl Einnahmen pl

tale [teɪl] n Geschichte f

talent ['tælənt] n Talent nt; **talented** adj begabt

talk [tɔːk] n (*conversation*) Gespräch nt; (*rumour*) Gerede nt; (*to audience*) Vortrag m ▷ vi sprechen, reden; (*have conversation*) sich unterhalten; **to ~ to** (*o with*) **sb** (**about sth**) mit jdm (über etw akk) sprechen ▷ vt (*language*) sprechen; (*nonsense*) reden; (*politics, business*) reden über +akk; **to ~ sb into doing/out of doing sth** jdn überreden/jdm ausreden, etw zu tun; **talk over** vt besprechen

talkative adj gesprächig; **talk show** n Talkshow f

tall [tɔːl] adj groß; (*building, tree*) hoch; **he is 6ft ~** er ist 1,80m groß

tame [teɪm] adj zahm; (*joke, story*) fade ▷ vt (*animal*) zähmen

tampon ['tæmpɒn] n Tampon m

tan [tæn] n (*on skin*) (Sonnen)bräune f; **to get/have a ~** braun werden/sein ▷ vi braun werden

tangerine [tændʒə'riːn] n Mandarine f

tango ['tæŋgəʊ] n Tango m

tank [tæŋk] n Tank m; (*for fish*) Aquarium nt; (*Mil*) Panzer m

tanker ['tæŋkə*] n (*ship*) Tanker m; (*vehicle*) Tankwagen m

tanned [tænd] adj (*by sun*) braun

tantalizing ['tæntəlaɪzɪŋ] adj verlockend

Tanzania [tænzə'nɪə] n Tansania nt

tap [tæp] n (*for water*) Hahn m ▷ vt, vi (*strike*) klopfen; **to ~ sb on the shoulder** jdm auf die Schulter klopfen; **tap-dance** vi steppen

tape [teɪp] n (*adhesive ~*) Klebeband nt; (*for tape recorder*) Tonband nt; (*cassette*) Kassette f; (*video*) Video nt ▷ vt (*record*) aufnehmen; **tape up** vt (*parcel*) zukleben; **tape measure** n Maßband nt; **tape recorder** n Tonbandgerät nt

tapestry ['tæpɪstrɪ] n Wandteppich m

tap water ['tæpwɔːtə*] n Leitungswasser nt

target ['tɑːgɪt] n Ziel nt; (*board*) Zielscheibe f; **target group** n Zielgruppe f

tariff ['tærɪf] n (*price list*) Preisliste f; (*tax*) Zoll m

tarmac ['tɑːmæk] n (*Aviat*) Rollfeld nt

tart [tɑːt] n (*fruit ~*) (Obst)kuchen m; (*small*) (Obst)törtchen nt; (*fam, pej: prostitute*) Nutte f; (*fam: promiscuous person*) Schlampe f

tartan ['tɑːtən] n Schottenkaro nt; (*material*) Schottenstoff m

tartar(e) sauce ['tɑːtə'sɔːs] n Remouladensoße f

task [tɑːsk] n Aufgabe f; (*duty*) Pflicht f; **taskbar** n (*Inform*) Taskbar f

Tasmania [tæz'meɪnɪə] n Tasmanien nt

taste [teɪst] n Geschmack m; (*sense of ~*) Geschmackssinn m; (*small quantity*) Kostprobe f; **it has a strange ~** es schmeckt komisch ▷ vt schmecken; (*try*) probieren ▷ vi (*food*) schmecken (*of* nach); **to ~ good/strange** gut/komisch schmecken; **tasteful, tastefully** adj, adv geschmackvoll; **tasteless**, **tastelessly** adj, adv geschmacklos; **tasty** adj lecker

tattered ['tætəd] adj (clothes) zerlumpt; (fam: person) angespannt; **I'm absolutely ~** ich bin mit den Nerven am Ende

tattoo [tə'tu:] n (on skin) Tätowierung f

taught [tɔ:t] pt, pp of **teach**

Taurus ['tɔ:rəs] n (Astr) Stier m

tax [tæks] n Steuer f (on auf +akk) ▷ vt besteuern; **taxable** adj steuerpflichtig; **taxation** [tæk'seɪʃən] n Besteuerung f; **tax bracket** n Steuerklasse f; **tax disc** n (Brit Auto) Steuermarke f; **tax-free** adj steuerfrei

taxi ['tæksɪ] n Taxi nt ▷ vi (plane) rollen; **taxi driver** n Taxifahrer(in) m(f); **taxi rank** (Brit), **taxi stand** n Taxistand m

tax return ['tæksrɪ'tɜ:n] n Steuererklärung f

tea [ti:] n Tee m; (afternoon ~) ≈ Kaffee und Kuchen; (meal) frühes Abendessen; **teabag** n Teebeutel m; **tea break** n (Tee)pause f

teach [ti:tʃ] (**taught, taught**) vt (person, subject) unterrichten; **to ~ sb** (**how**) **to dance** jdm das Tanzen beibringen ▷ vi unterrichten; **teacher** n Lehrer(in) m(f); **teaching** n (activity) Unterrichten nt; (profession) Lehrberuf m

teacup ['ti:kʌp] n Teetasse f

team [ti:m] n (Sport) Mannschaft f, Team nt; **teamwork** n Teamarbeit f

teapot ['ti:pɒt] n Teekanne f

tear [tɪə*] n (in eye) Träne f

tear [tɛə*] (**tore, torn**) vt zerreißen; **to ~ a muscle** sich einen Muskel zerren ▷ n (in material etc) Riss m; **tear down** vt (building) abreißen; **tear up** vt (paper) zerreißen

tearoom ['ti:rʊm] n Teestube f,

Café, in dem in erster Linie Tee serviert wird

tease [ti:z] vt (person) necken (about wegen)

tea set ['ti:set] n Teeservice nt; **teashop** n Teestube f; **teaspoon** n Teelöffel m; **tea towel** n Geschirrtuch nt

technical ['teknɪkəl] adj technisch; (knowledge, term, dictionary) Fach-; **technically** adv technisch; **technique** [tek'ni:k] n Technik f

techno ['teknəʊ] n Techno f

technological [teknə'lɒdʒɪkəl] adj technologisch; **technology** [tek'nɒlədʒɪ] n Technologie f, Technik f

tedious ['ti:dɪəs] adj langweilig

teen(age) ['ti:n(eɪdʒ)] adj (fashions etc) Teenager-; **teenager** n Teenager m; **teens** [ti:nz] npl: **in one's ~** im Teenageralter

teeth [ti:θ] pl of **tooth**

teetotal ['ti:'təʊtl] adj abstinent

telegraph pole ['telɪgrɑ:fpəʊl] n (Brit) Telegrafenmast m

telephone ['telɪfəʊn] n Telefon nt ▷ vi telefonieren ▷ vt anrufen; **telephone banking** n Telefonbanking nt; **telephone book** n Telefonbuch nt; **telephone booth, telephone box** (Brit) n Telefonzelle f; **telephone call** n Telefonanruf m; **telephone directory** n Telefonbuch nt; **telephone number** n Telefonnummer f

telephoto lens ['telɪfəʊtəʊ'lenz] n Teleobjektiv nt

telescope ['telɪskəʊp] n Teleskop nt

televise ['telɪvaɪz] vt im Fernsehen übertragen; **television** ['telɪvɪʒən] n Fernsehen nt; **television programme** n Fernsehsendung f; **television (set)** n Fernseher m

teleworking ['telɪwɜːkɪŋ] n
Telearbeit f

tell [tel] vt (told, told) vt (say,
inform) sagen (sb sth jdm etw);
(story) erzählen; (truth) sagen;
(difference) erkennen; (reveal secret)
verraten; **to ~ sb about sth** jdm
von etw erzählen; **to ~ sth from
sth** etw von etw unterscheiden
▷ vi (be sure) wissen; **tell apart** vt
unterscheiden; **tell off** vt
schimpfen

telling adj aufschlussreich

telly ['telɪ] n (Brit fam) Glotze f; **on
(the) ~** in der Glotze

temp [temp] n Aushilfskraft f
▷ vi als Aushilfskraft arbeiten

temper ['tempə°] n (anger) Wut f;
(mood) Laune f; **to lose one's ~** die
Beherrschung verlieren; **to have a
bad ~** jähzornig sein;
temperamental
[tempərə'mentl] adj (moody)
launisch

temperature ['temprɪtʃə°] n
Temperatur f; (Med: high ~) Fieber
nt; **to have a ~** Fieber haben

temple ['templ] n Tempel m;
(Anat) Schläfe f

temporarily ['tempərərɪlɪ] adv
vorübergehend; **temporary**
['tempərərɪ] adj vorübergehend;
(road, building) provisorisch

tempt [tempt] vt in Versuchung
führen; **I'm ~ed to accept** ich bin
versucht anzunehmen;
temptation [temp'teɪʃən] n
Versuchung f; **tempting** adj
verlockend

ten [ten] num zehn ▷ n Zehn f;
see also **eight**

tenant ['tenənt] n Mieter(in)
m(f); (of land) Pächter(in) m(f)

tend [tend] vi: **to ~ to do sth**
(person) dazu neigen, etw zu tun;
to ~ towards neigen zu;
tendency ['tendənsɪ] n Tendenz

f; **to have a ~ to do sth** (person)
dazu neigen, etw zu tun

tender ['tendə°] adj (loving)
zärtlich; (sore) empfindlich; (meat)
zart

tendon ['tendən] n Sehne f

Tenerife [tenə'riːf] n Teneriffa nt

tenner ['tenə°] n (Brit fam: note)
Zehnpfundschein m; (amount) zehn
Pfund

tennis ['tenɪs] n Tennis nt;
tennis ball n Tennisball m; **tennis
court** n Tennisplatz m; **tennis
racket** n Tennisschläger m

tenor ['tenə°] n Tenor m

tenpin bowling, tenpins (US)
['tenpɪn'bəʊlɪŋ, 'tenpɪnz] n
Bowling nt

tense [tens] adj angespannt;
(stretched tight) gespannt; **tension**
['tenʃən] n Spannung f; (strain)
Anspannung f

tent [tent] n Zelt nt

tenth [tenθ] adj zehnte(r, s) ▷ n
(fraction) Zehntel nt; see also **eighth**

tent peg ['tentpeg] n Hering m;
tent pole n Zeltstange f

term [tɜːm] n (in school, at
university) Trimester nt; (expression)
Ausdruck m; (conditions)
Bedingungen pl; **to be on good ~s
with sb** mit jdm gut auskommen;
to come to ~s with sth sich mit
etw abfinden; **in the long/short
~** langfristig/kurzfristig; **in ~s
of ...** was ... betrifft

terminal ['tɜːmɪnl] n (bus ~ etc)
Endstation f; (Aviat) Terminal m;
(Inform) Terminal nt; (Elec) Pol m
▷ adj (Med) unheilbar; **terminally**
adv (ill) unheilbar

terminate ['tɜːmɪneɪt] vt (contract) lösen; (pregnancy) abbrechen
▷ vi (train, bus) enden

terminology [tɜːmɪ'nɒlədʒɪ] n
Terminologie f

terrace ['terəs] n (of houses)

Häuserreihe f; (in garden etc)
Terrasse f; **terraced** adj (garden)
terrassenförmig angelegt;
terraced house n (Brit)
Reihenhaus nt

terrible ['tɛrəbl] adj schrecklich

terrific [tə'rɪfɪk] adj (very good)
fantastisch

terrify ['tɛrɪfaɪ] vt erschrecken;
to be terrified schreckliche Angst
haben (of vor +dat)

territory ['tɛrɪtərɪ] n Gebiet nt

terror ['tɛrə*] n Schrecken m;
(Pol) Terror m; **terrorism** n
Terrorismus m; **terrorist** n
Terrorist(in) m(f)

test [tɛst] n Test m, Klassenarbeit
f; (driving ~) Prüfung f; **to put to
the ~** auf die Probe stellen ▷ vt
testen, prüfen; (patience, courage
etc) auf die Probe stellen

Testament ['tɛstəmənt] n: **the
Old/New ~** das Alte/Neue
Testament

test-drive ['tɛstdraɪv] vt Probe
fahren

testicle ['tɛstɪkl] n Hoden m

testify ['tɛstɪfaɪ] vi (Jur)
aussagen

test tube ['tɛsttjuːb] n
Reagenzglas nt

tetanus ['tɛtənəs] n Tetanus m

text [tɛkst] n Text m; (of
document) Wortlaut m; (sent by
mobile phone) SMS f ▷ vt (message)
simsen, SMSen; **to ~ sb** jdm
simsen, jdm eine SMS schicken;
I'll ~ it to you ich schicke es dir per
SMS

textbook n Lehrbuch nt

texting ['tɛkstɪŋ] n SMS-
Messaging nt; **text message** n
SMS f; **text messaging** n
SMS-Messaging nt

texture ['tɛkstʃə*] n
Beschaffenheit f

Thailand ['taɪlænd] n Thailand nt

Thames [tɛmz] n Themse f

than [ðæn] prep, conj als;
bigger/faster ~ me
größer/schneller als ich; **I'd rather
walk ~ drive** ich gehe lieber zu
Fuß als mit dem Auto

thank [θæŋk] vt danken +dat;
~ you danke; **~ you very much**
vielen Dank; **thankful** adj
dankbar; **thankfully** adv (luckily)
zum Glück; **thankless** adj
undankbar; **thanks** npl Dank m;
~ danke!; ~ to dank +gen

● **THANKSGIVING DAY**
●
●
● **Thanksgiving (Day)** ist ein
● Feiertag in den USA, der auf den
● vierten Donnerstag im
● November fällt. Er soll daran
● erinnern, wie die Pilgerväter die
● gute Ernte im Jahre 1621
● feierten. In Kanada gibt es einen
● ähnlichen Erntedanktag (der
● aber nichts mit den Pilgervätern
● zu tun hat) am zweiten Montag
● im Oktober.

O KEYWORD

that [ðæt, ðət] adj (demonstrative)
(pl those) der/die/das, jene(r, s);
that one das da
▷ pron 1 (demonstrative) (pl those)
das; **who's/what's that?** wer ist
da/was ist das?; **is that you?** bist
du/sind Sie das?; **that's what he
said** genau das hat er gesagt;
what happened after that? was
passierte danach?; **that is** das
heißt
2 (relative) (subj) der/die/das, die;
(direct obj) den/die/das, die;
(indirect obj) dem/der/dem, denen;
all (that) I have alles, was ich
habe
3 (relative) (of time); **the day (that)**

an dem Tag, als; **the winter (that) he came** in dem Winter, in dem er kam
▷ *conj* dass; **he thought that I was ill** er dachte, dass ich krank sei, er dachte, ich sei krank
▷ *adv* (*demonstrative*) so; **I can't work that much** ich kann nicht so viel arbeiten

that's [ðæts] *contr of* **that is; that has**

thaw [θɔː] *vi* tauen; (*frozen food*) auftauen ▷ *vt* auftauen lassen

O **KEYWORD**

the [ðə, ðiː] *def art* **1** der/die/das; **to play the piano/violin** Klavier/Geige spielen; **I'm going to the butcher's/the cinema** ich gehe zum Fleischer/ins Kino; **Elizabeth the First** Elisabeth die Erste
2 (+*adj to form noun*) das, die; **the rich and the poor** die Reichen und die Armen
3 (*in comparisons*) **the more he works the more he earns** je mehr er arbeitet, desto mehr verdient er

theater (*US*), **theatre** [ˈθɪətə*] *n* Theater *nt*; (*for lectures etc*) Saal *m*
theft [θeft] *n* Diebstahl *m*
their [ðɛə*] *adj* ihr; (*unidentified person*) sein; **they cleaned ~ teeth** sie putzten sich die Zähne; **someone has left ~ umbrella here** jemand hat seinen Schirm hier vergessen; **theirs** *pron* ihre(r, s); (*unidentified person*) seine(r, s); **it's ~** es gehört ihnen; **a friend of ~** ein Freund von ihnen; **someone has left ~ here** jemand hat seins hier liegen lassen
them [ðem, ðəm] *pron* (*direct object*) sie; (*indirect object*) ihnen;

(*unidentified person*) ihn/ihm, sie/ihr; **do you know ~?** kennst du/kennen Sie sie?; **can you help ~?** kannst du/können Sie ihnen helfen?; **it's ~** sie sind's; **if anyone has a problem you should help ~** wenn jemand ein Problem hat, solltest du/sollten Sie ihm helfen
theme [θiːm] *n* Thema *nt*; (*Mus*) Motiv *nt*; **~ park** Themenpark *m*; **~ song** Titelmusik *f*
themselves [ðəm'selvz] *pron* sich; **they hurt ~** sie haben sich verletzt; **they ~ were not there** sie selbst waren nicht da; **they did it ~** sie haben es selbst gemacht; **they are not dangerous in ~** an sich sind sie nicht gefährlich; (**all**) **by ~** allein
then [ðen] *adv* (*at that time*) damals; (*next*) dann; (*therefore*) also; (*furthermore*) ferner; **from ~ on** von da an; **by ~** bis dahin
▷ *adj* damalig
theoretical, **theoretically** [θɪə'retɪkəl, -ɪ] *adj*, *adv* theoretisch
theory [ˈθɪərɪ] *n* Theorie *f*; **in ~** theoretisch
therapy [ˈθerəpɪ] *n* Therapie *f*

O **KEYWORD**

there [ðɛə*] *adv* **1** **there is/there are** es *o* da ist/sind; (*there exists/exist also*) es gibt; **there are 3 of them** (*people, things*) es gibt 3 davon; **there has been an accident** da war ein Unfall
2 (*place*) da, dort; (*direction*) dahin, dorthin; **put it in/on there** leg es dahinein/dorthinauf
3 **there, there** (*esp to child*) na, na

thereabouts *adv* (*approximately*) so ungefähr; **therefore** *adv* daher, deshalb

thermometer [θə'mɒmɪtə*] *n*
Thermometer *nt*

Thermos® ['θɜːməs] *n*: **~ (flask)**
Thermosflasche® *f*

these [ðiːz] *pron, adj* diese; **I
don't like ~ apples** ich mag diese
Äpfel nicht; **~ are not my books**
das sind nicht meine Bücher

thesis ['θiːsɪs] (*pl* **theses**) *n* (*for
PhD*) Doktorarbeit *f*

they [ðeɪ] *pron pl* sie; (*people in
general*) man; (*unidentified person*)
er/sie; **~ are rich** sie sind reich;
~ say that ... man sagt, dass ...; **if
anyone looks at this, ~ will see
that ...** wenn sich jemand dies
ansieht, wird er erkennen, dass ...

they'd [ðeɪd] *contr of* **they had;
they would**

they'll [ðeɪl] *contr of* **they will;
they shall**

they've [ðeɪv] *contr of* **they have**

thick [θɪk] *adj* dick; (*fog*) dicht;
(*liquid*) dickflüssig; (*fam: stupid*)
dumm; **thicken** *vi* (*fog*) dichter
werden; (*sauce*) dick werden ▷ *vt*
(*sauce*) eindicken

thief [θiːf] (*pl* **thieves**) *n*
Dieb(in) *m(f)*

thigh [θaɪ] *n* Oberschenkel *m*

thimble ['θɪmbl] *n* Fingerhut *m*

thin [θɪn] *adj* dünn

thing [θɪŋ] *n* Ding *nt*; (*affair*)
Sache *f*; **my ~s** *pl* meine Sachen *pl*;
how are ~s? wie geht's?; **I can't
see a ~** ich kann nichts sehen; **he
knows a ~ or two about cars** er
kennt sich mit Autos aus

think [θɪŋk] (**thought, thought**)
vt, vi denken; (*believe*) meinen; **I
~ so** ich denke schon; **I don't ~ so**
ich glaube nicht; **think about** *vt*
denken an +*akk*; (*reflect on*)
nachdenken über +*akk*; (*have
opinion of*) halten von; **think of** *vt*
denken an +*akk*; (*devise*) sich
ausdenken; (*have opinion of*) halten

von; (*remember*) sich erinnern an
+*akk*; **think over** *vt* überdenken;
think up *vt* sich ausdenken

third [θɜːd] *adj* dritte(r, s); **the
Third World** die Dritte Welt ▷ *n*
(*fraction*) Drittel *nt*; **in ~ (gear)** im
dritten Gang; *see also* **eighth**;
thirdly *adv* drittens; **third-party
insurance** *n* Haftpflichtver-
sicherung *f*

thirst [θɜːst] *n* Durst *m* (*for* nach);
thirsty *adj*: **to be ~** Durst haben

thirteen ['θɜː'tiːn] *num* dreizehn
▷ *n* Dreizehn *f*; *see also* **eight**;
thirteenth *adj* dreizehnte(r, s);
see also **eighth**; **thirtieth** ['θɜːtɪɪθ]
adj dreißigste(r, s); *see also* **eighth**;
thirty ['θɜːtɪ] *num* dreißig;
~-one einunddreißig ▷ *n* Dreißig
f; **to be in one's thirties** in den
Dreißigern sein; *see also* **eight**

KEYWORD

this [ðɪs] *adj* (*demonstrative*) (*pl*
these) diese(r, s); **this evening**
heute Abend; **this one** diese(r, s)
(da)
▷ *pron* (*demonstrative*) (*pl these*)
dies, das; **who/what is this?**
wer/was ist das?; **this is where I
live** hier wohne ich; **this is what
he said** das hat er gesagt; **this is
Mr Brown** dies ist Mr Brown; (*on
telephone*) hier ist Mr Brown
▷ *adv* (*demonstrative*) **this
high/long** *etc* so groß/lang *etc*

thistle [θɪsl] *n* Distel *f*

thong [θɒŋ] *n* String *m*

thorn [θɔːn] *n* Dorn *m*, Stachel *m*

thorough ['θʌrə] *adj* gründlich;
thoroughly *adv* gründlich; (*agree
etc*) völlig

those [ðəʊz] *pron* die da, jene;
~ who diejenigen, die ▷ *adj* die,
jene

though [ðəʊ] *conj* obwohl; **as ~** als ob ▷ *adv* aber

thought [θɔːt] *pt, pp of* **think** ▷ *n* Gedanke *m*; (*thinking*) Überlegung *f*; **thoughtful** *adj* (*kind*) rücksichtsvoll; (*attentive*) aufmerksam; (*in Gedanken versunken*) nachdenklich; **thoughtless** *adj* (*unkind*) rücksichtslos, gedankenlos

thousand ['θaʊzənd] *num*: (**one**) **~, a ~** tausend; **five ~** fünftausend; **~s of** Tausende von

thrash [θræʃ] *vt* (*hit*) verprügeln; (*defeat*) vernichtend schlagen

thread [θred] *n* Faden *m* ▷ *vt* (*needle*) einfädeln; (*beads*) auffädeln

threat [θret] *n* Drohung *f*; (*danger*) Bedrohung *f* (*to* für); **threaten** *vt* bedrohen; **threatening** *adj* bedrohlich

three [θriː] *num* drei ▷ *n* Drei *f*; *see also* **eight**; **three-dimensional** *adj* dreidimensional; **three-piece suit** *n* Anzug *m* mit Weste; **three-quarters** *npl* drei Viertel *pl*

threshold ['θreʃhəʊld] *n* Schwelle *f*

threw [θruː] *pt of* **throw**

thrifty ['θrɪftɪ] *adj* sparsam

thrilled [θrɪld] *adj*: **to be ~ (with sth)** sich (über etw *akk*) riesig freuen; **thriller** *n* Thriller *m*; **thrilling** *adj* aufregend

thrive [θraɪv] *vi* gedeihen (*on* bei); (*fig, business*) florieren

throat [θrəʊt] *n* Hals *m*, Kehle *f*

throbbing ['θrɒbɪŋ] *adj* (*pain, headache*) pochend

thrombosis [θrɒm'bəʊsɪs] *n* Thrombose *f*; **deep vein ~** tiefe Venenthrombose *f*

throne [θrəʊn] *n* Thron *m*

through [θruː] *prep* durch; (*time*) während +*gen*; (*because of*) aus, durch; (*US: up to and including*) bis;

arranged **~ him** durch ihn arrangiert ▷ *adv* durch; **to put sb ~** (*Tel*) jdn verbinden (*to* mit) ▷ *adj* (*ticket, train*) durchgehend; **~ flight** Direktflug *m*; **to be ~ with sb/sth** mit jdm/etw fertig sein;

throughout [θruː'aʊt] *prep* (*place*) überall in +*dat*; (*time*) während +*gen*; **~ the night** die ganze Nacht hindurch ▷ *adv* überall; (*time*) die ganze Zeit

throw [θrəʊ] (**threw, thrown**) *vt* werfen; (*rider*) abwerfen; (*party*) geben; **to ~ sth to sb, to ~ sb sth** jdm etw zuwerfen; **I was ~n by his question** seine Frage hat mich aus dem Konzept gebracht ▷ *n* Wurf *m*; **throw away** *vt* wegwerfen; **throw in** *vt* (*include*) dazugeben; **throw out** *vt* (*unwanted object*) wegwerfen; (*person*) hinauswerfen (*of* aus); **throw up** *vt, vi* (*fam: vomit*) sich übergeben; **throw-in** *n* Einwurf *m*

thrown [θrəʊn] *pp of* **throw**

thru (*US*) *see* **through**

thrush [θrʌʃ] *n* Drossel *f*

thrust [θrʌst] (**thrust, thrust**) *vt, vi* (*push*) stoßen

thruway ['θruːweɪ] *n* (*US*) Schnellstraße *f*

thumb [θʌm] *n* Daumen *m* ▷ *vt*: **to ~ a lift** per Anhalter fahren; **thumbtack** *n* (*US*) Reißzwecke *f*

thunder ['θʌndə*] *n* Donner *m* ▷ *vi* donnern; **thunderstorm** *n* Gewitter *nt*

Thur(s) *abbr* = **Thursday** Do.

Thursday ['θɜːzdɪ] *n* Donnerstag *m*; *see also* **Tuesday**

thus [ðʌs] *adv* (*in this way*) so; (*therefore*) somit, also

thyme [taɪm] *n* Thymian *m*

Tibet [tɪ'bet] *n* Tibet *nt*

tick [tɪk] *n* (*Brit: mark*) Häkchen *nt* ▷ *vt* (*name*) abhaken; (*box, answer*) ankreuzen ▷ *vi* (*clock*) ticken

ticket ['tɪkɪt] n (for train, bus) (Fahr)karte f; (plane ~) Flugschein m, Ticket nt; (for theatre, match, museum etc) (Eintritts)karte f; (price ~) (Preis)schild nt; (raffle ~) Los nt; (for car park) Parkschein m; (for traffic offence) Strafzettel m; **ticket collector, ticket inspector** (Brit) n Fahrkartenkontrolleur(in) m(f); **ticket machine** n (for public transport) Fahrscheinautomat m; (in car park) Parkscheinautomat m; **ticket office** n (Rail) Fahrkartenschalter m; (Theat) Kasse f

tickle ['tɪkl] vt kitzeln; **ticklish** ['tɪklɪʃ] adj kitzlig

tide [taɪd] n Gezeiten pl; **the ~ is in/out** es ist Flut/Ebbe

tidy ['taɪdɪ] adj ordentlich ▷ vt aufräumen; **tidy up** vt, vi aufräumen

tie [taɪ] n (neck~) Krawatte f; (Sport) Unentschieden nt; (bond) Bindung f ▷ vt (attach, do up) binden (to an +akk); (~ together) zusammenbinden; (knot) machen ▷ vi (Sport) unentschieden spielen; **tie down** vt festbinden (to an +dat); (fig) binden; **tie up** vt (dog) anbinden; (parcel) verschnüren; (shoelace) binden; (boat) festmachen; **I'm tied up** (fig) ich bin beschäftigt

tiger ['taɪgə*] n Tiger m

tight [taɪt] adj (clothes) eng; (knot) fest; (screw, lid) fest sitzend; (control, security measures) streng; (timewise) knapp; (schedule) eng ▷ adv (shut) fest; (pull) stramm; **hold ~** festhalten!; **sleep ~** schlaf gut!; **tighten** vt (knot, rope, screw) anziehen; (belt) enger machen; (restrictions, control) verschärfen; **tights** npl (Brit) Strumpfhose f

tile [taɪl] n (on roof) Dachziegel m;

(on wall, floor) Fliese f; **tiled** adj (roof) Ziegel-; (floor, wall) gefliest

till [tɪl] n Kasse f ▷ prep, conj see **until**

tilt [tɪlt] vt kippen; (head) neigen ▷ vi sich neigen

time [taɪm] n Zeit f; (occasion) Mal nt; (Mus) Takt m; **local ~** Ortszeit; **what ~ is it?, what's the ~?** wie spät ist es?, wie viel Uhr ist es?; **to take one's ~** (over sth) sich (bei etw) Zeit lassen; **to have a good ~** Spaß haben; **in two weeks' ~** in zwei Wochen; **at ~s** manchmal; **at the same ~** gleichzeitig; **all the ~** die ganze Zeit; **by the ~ he ...** bis er ...; (in past) als er ...; **for the ~ being** vorläufig; **in ~** (not late) rechtzeitig; **on ~** pünktlich; **the first ~** das erste Mal; **this ~** diesmal; **five ~s** fünfmal; **five ~s six** fünf mal sechs; **four ~s a year** viermal im Jahr; **three at a ~** drei auf einmal ▷ vt (with stopwatch) stoppen; **you ~d that well** das hast du/haben Sie gut getimt; **time difference** n Zeitunterschied m; **time limit** n Frist f; **timer** n Timer m; (switch) Schaltuhr f; **time-saving** adj zeitsparend; **time switch** n Schaltuhr f; **timetable** n (for public transport) Fahrplan m; (school) Stundenplan m; **time zone** n Zeitzone f

timid ['tɪmɪd] adj ängstlich

timing ['taɪmɪŋ] n (coordination) Timing nt, zeitliche Abstimmung

tin [tɪn] n (metal) Blech nt; (Brit: can) Dose f; **tinfoil** n Alufolie f; **tinned** [tɪnd] adj (Brit) aus der Dose; **tin opener** n (Brit) Dosenöffner m

tinsel ['tɪnsəl] n ≈ Lametta nt

tint [tɪnt] n (Farb)ton m; (in hair) Tönung f; **tinted** adj getönt

tiny ['taɪnɪ] *adj* winzig

tip [tɪp] *n* (*money*) Trinkgeld *nt*; (*hint*) Tipp *m*; (*end*) Spitze *f*; (*of cigarette*) Filter *m*; (*Brit: rubbish ~*) Müllkippe *f* ▷ *vt* (*waiter*) Trinkgeld geben +*dat*; **tip over** *vt, vi* (*overturn*) umkippen

tipsy ['tɪpsɪ] *adj* beschwipst

tiptoe ['tɪptəʊ] *n*: **on ~** auf Zehenspitzen

tire ['taɪə*] *n* (*US*) *see* **tyre** ▷ *vt* müde machen ▷ *vi* müde werden; **tired** *adj* müde; **to be ~ of sb/sth** jdn/etw satthaben; **to be ~ of doing sth** es satthaben, etw zu tun; **tireless, tirelessly** *adv* unermüdlich; **tiresome** *adj* lästig; **tiring** *adj* ermüdend

Tirol [tɪ'rəʊl] *see* **Tyrol**

tissue ['tɪʃuː] *n* (*Anat*) Gewebe *nt*; (*paper handkerchief*) Tempotaschentuch® *nt*, Papier(taschen)tuch *nt*; **tissue paper** *n* Seidenpapier *nt*

tit [tɪt] *n* (*bird*) Meise *f*; (*fam: breast*) Titte *f*

title ['taɪtl] *n* Titel *m*

titter ['tɪtə] *vi* kichern

○ **KEYWORD**

to [tuː, tə] *prep* **1** (*direction*) zu, nach; **I go to France/school** ich gehe nach Frankreich/zur Schule; **to the left** nach links
2 (*as far as*) bis
3 (*with expressions of time*) vor; **a quarter to 5** Viertel vor 5
4 (*for, of*) für; **secretary to the director** Sekretärin des Direktors
5 (*expressing indirect object*) **to give sth to sb** jdm etw geben; **to talk to sb** mit jdm sprechen; **I sold it to a friend** ich habe es einem Freund verkauft
6 (*in relation to*) zu; **30 miles to the gallon** 30 Meilen pro Gallone

7 (*purpose, result*) zu; **to my surprise** zu meiner Überraschung ▷ *with vb* **1** (*infin*) zu; **to go/eat** gehen/essen; **to want to do sth** etw tun wollen; **to try/start to do sth** versuchen/anfangen, etw zu tun; **he has a lot to lose** er hat viel zu verlieren
2 (*with vb omitted*) **I don't want to** ich will (es) nicht
3 (*purpose, result*) um; **I did it to help you** ich tat es, um dir/Ihnen zu helfen
4 (*after adj etc*) **ready to use** gebrauchsfertig; **too old/young to ...** zu alt/jung, um ... zu ...
▷ *adv*: **push/pull the door to** die Tür zuschieben/zuziehen

toad [təʊd] *n* Kröte *f*; **toadstool** *n* Giftpilz *m*

toast [təʊst] *n* (*bread, drink*) Toast *m*; **a piece** (o **slice**) **of ~** eine Scheibe Toast; **to propose a ~ to sb** einen Toast auf jdn ausbringen ▷ *vt* (*bread*) toasten; (*person*) trinken auf +*akk*; **toaster** *n* Toaster *m*

tobacco [tə'bækəʊ] (*pl* **-es**) *n* Tabak *m*; **tobacconist's** [tə'bækənɪsts] *n*: **~ (shop)** Tabakladen *m*

toboggan [tə'bɒgən] *n* Schlitten *m*

today [tə'deɪ] *adv* heute; **a week ~** heute in einer Woche; **~'s newspaper** die Zeitung von heute

toddler ['tɒdlə*] *n* Kleinkind *nt*

toe [təʊ] *n* Zehe *f*, Zeh *m*; **toenail** *n* Zehennagel *m*

toffee ['tɒfɪ] *n* (*sweet*) Karamellbonbon *nt*; **toffee apple** *n* kandierter Apfel; **toffee-nosed** *adj* hochnäsig

tofu ['təʊfuː] *n* Tofu *m*

together [tə'geðə*] *adv*

zusammen; **I tied them ~** ich habe sie zusammengebunden

toilet ['tɔɪlət] *n* Toilette *f*; **to go to the ~** auf die Toilette gehen; **toilet bag** *n* Kulturbeutel *m*; **toilet paper** *n* Toilettenpapier *nt*; **toiletries** ['tɔɪlətrɪz] *npl* Toilettenartikel *pl*; **toilet roll** *n* Rolle *f* Toilettenpapier

token ['təʊkən] *n* Marke *f*; (*in casino*) Spielmarke *f*; (*voucher, gift ~*) Gutschein *m*; (*sign*) Zeichen *nt*

Tokyo ['təʊkɪəʊ] *n* Tokio *nt*

told [təʊld] *pt, pp of* **tell**

tolerant ['tɒlərənt] *adj* tolerant (*of* gegenüber); **tolerate** ['tɒləreɪt] *vt* tolerieren; (*noise, pain, heat*) ertragen

toll [təʊl] *n* (*charge*) Gebühr *f*; **the death ~** die Zahl der Toten; **toll-free** *adj, adv* (*US Tel*) gebührenfrei; **toll road** *n* gebührenpflichtige Straße

tomato [tə'mɑːtəʊ] (*pl* **-es**) *n* Tomate *f*; **tomato juice** *n* Tomatensaft *m*; **tomato ketchup** *n* Tomatenketchup *m o nt*; **tomato sauce** *n* Tomatensoße *f*; (*Brit: ketchup*) Tomatenketchup *m o nt*

tomb [tuːm] *n* Grabmal *nt*; **tombstone** *n* Grabstein *m*

tomorrow [tə'mɒrəʊ] *adv* morgen; **~ morning** morgen früh; **~ evening** morgen Abend; **the day after ~** übermorgen; **a week (from) ~/~ week** morgen in einer Woche

ton [tʌn] *n* (*Brit*) Tonne *f* (1016 kg); (*US*) Tonne *f* (907 kg); **~s of books** (*fam*) eine Menge Bücher

tone [təʊn] *n* Ton *m*; **tone down** *vt* mäßigen; **toner** ['təʊnə*] *n* (*for printer*) Toner *m*; **toner cartridge** *n* Tonerpatrone *f*

tongs [tɒŋz] *npl* Zange *f*; (*curling ~*) Lockenstab *m*

tongue [tʌŋ] *n* Zunge *f*

tonic ['tɒnɪk] *n* (*Med*) Stärkungsmittel *nt*; **~ (water)** Tonic *nt*; **gin and ~** Gin *m* Tonic

tonight [tə'naɪt] *adv* heute Abend; (*during night*) heute Nacht

tonsils ['tɒnslz] *n* Mandeln *pl*; **tonsillitis** [tɒnsɪ'laɪtɪs] *n* Mandelentzündung *f*

too [tuː] *adv* zu; (*also*) auch; **~ fast** zu schnell; **~ much/many** zu viel/viele; **me ~** ich auch; **she liked it ~** ihr gefiel es auch

took [tʊk] *pt of* **take**

tool [tuːl] *n* Werkzeug *nt*; **toolbar** *n* (*Inform*) Symbolleiste *f*; **toolbox** *n* Werkzeugkasten *m*

tooth [tuːθ] (*pl* **teeth**) *n* Zahn *m*; **toothache** *n* Zahnschmerzen *pl*; **toothbrush** *n* Zahnbürste *f*; **toothpaste** *n* Zahnpasta *f*; **toothpick** *n* Zahnstocher *m*

top [tɒp] *n* (*of tower, class, company etc*) Spitze *f*; (*of mountain*) Gipfel *m*; (*of tree*) Krone *f*; (*of street*) oberes Ende; (*of tube, pen*) Kappe *f*; (*of box*) Deckel *m*; (*of bikini*) Oberteil *nt*; (*sleeveless*) Top *nt*; **at the ~ of the page** oben auf der Seite; **at the ~ of the league** an der Spitze der Liga; **on ~** oben; **on ~ of** auf +*dat*; (*in addition to*) zusätzlich zu; **in ~ (gear)** im höchsten Gang; **over the ~** übertrieben ▷ *adj* (*floor, shelf*) oberste(r, s); (*price, note*) höchste(r, s); (*best*) Spitzen-; (*pupil, school*) beste(r, s) ▷ *vt* (*exceed*) übersteigen; (*be better than*) übertreffen; (*league*) an erster Stelle liegen in +*dat*; **~ped with cream** mit Sahne obendrauf; **top up** *vt* auffüllen; **can I top you up?** darf ich dir nachschenken?

topic ['tɒpɪk] *n* Thema *nt*; **topical** *adj* aktuell

topless ['tɒpləs] adj, adv oben ohne

topping ['tɒpɪŋ] n (on top of pizza, ice-cream etc) Belag m, Garnierung f

top-secret ['tɒp'si:krət] adj streng geheim

torch [tɔːtʃ] n (Brit) Taschenlampe f

tore [tɔː*] pt of **tear**

torment ['tɔːment] vt quälen

torn [tɔːn] pp of **tear**

tornado [tɔː'neɪdəʊ] n (pl **-es**) n Tornado m

torrential [tə'renʃəl] adj (rain) sintflutartig

tortoise ['tɔːtəs] n Schildkröte f

torture ['tɔːtʃə*] n Folter f; (fig) Qual f ▷ vt foltern

Tory ['tɔːrɪ] (Brit) n Tory m, Konservative(r) mf ▷ adj Tory-

toss [tɒs] vt (throw) werfen; (salad) anmachen; **to ~ a coin** eine Münze werfen ▷ n: **I don't give a ~** (fam) es ist mir scheißegal

total ['təʊtl] n (of figures, money) Gesamtsumme f; **a ~ of 30** insgesamt 30; **in ~** insgesamt ▷ adj total; (sum etc) Gesamt- ▷ vt (amount to) sich belaufen auf +akk; **totally** adv total

touch [tʌtʃ] n (act of ~ing) Berührung f; (sense of ~) Tastsinn m; (trace) Spur f; **to be/keep in ~ with sb** mit jdm in Verbindung stehen/bleiben; **to get in ~ with sb** sich mit jdm in Verbindung setzen; **to lose ~ with sb** den Kontakt zu jdm verlieren ▷ vt (feel) berühren; (emotionally) bewegen; **touch on** vt (topic) berühren; **touchdown** n (Aviat) Landung f; (Sport) Touchdown m; **touching** adj (moving) rührend; **touch screen** n Touchscreen m, Berührungsbildschirm m; **touchy** adj empfindlich, zickig

tough [tʌf] adj hart; (meat) zäh; (material) robust; (meat) zäh

tour ['tʊə*] n Tour f (of durch); (of town, building) Rundgang m (of durch); (of pop group etc) Tournee f ▷ vt eine Tour/einen Rundgang/eine Tournee machen durch ▷ vi (on holiday) umherreisen; **tour guide** n Reiseleiter(in) m(f)

tourism ['tʊərɪzəm] n Tourismus m, Fremdenverkehr m; **tourist** n Tourist(in) m(f); **tourist class** n Touristenklasse f; **tourist guide** n (book) Reiseführer m; (person) Fremdenführer(in) m(f); **tourist office** n Fremdenverkehrsamt nt

tournament ['tʊənəmənt] n Tournier nt

tour operator ['tʊərɒpəreɪtə*] n Reiseveranstalter m

tow [təʊ] vt abschleppen; (caravan, trailer) ziehen; **tow away** vt abschleppen

towards [tə'wɔːdz] prep: **~ me** mir entgegen, auf mich zu; **we walked ~ the station** wir gingen in Richtung Bahnhof; **my feelings ~ him** meine Gefühle ihm gegenüber; **she was kind ~ me** sie war nett zu mir

towel ['taʊəl] n Handtuch nt

tower ['taʊə*] n Turm m; **tower block** n (Brit) Hochhaus nt

town [taʊn] n Stadt f; **town center** (US), **town centre** n Stadtmitte f, Stadtzentrum nt; **town hall** n Rathaus nt

towrope ['təʊrəʊp] n Abschleppseil nt; **tow truck** n (US) Abschleppwagen m

toxic ['tɒksɪk] adj giftig, Gift-

toy [tɔɪ] n Spielzeug nt; **toy with** vt spielen mit; **toyshop** n Spielwarengeschäft nt

trace [treɪs] n Spur f; **without**

~ spurlos ▷ *vt* (*find*) ausfindig machen; **tracing paper** *n* Pauspapier *nt*

track [træk] *n* (*mark*) Spur *f*; (*path*) Weg *m*; (*Rail*) Gleis *nt*; (*on CD, record*) Stück *nt*; **to keep/lose ~ of sb/sth** jdn/etw im Auge behalten/aus den Augen verlieren; **track down** *vt* ausfindig machen; **trackball** *n* (*Inform*) Trackball *m*; **tracksuit** *n* Trainingsanzug *m*

tractor ['træktə*] *n* Traktor *m*

trade [treɪd] *n* (*commerce*) Handel *m*; (*business*) Geschäft *nt*; (*skilled job*) Handwerk *nt* ▷ *vi* handeln (*in* mit) ▷ *vt* (*exchange*) tauschen (*for* gegen); **trademark** *n* Warenzeichen *nt*; **tradesman** (*pl* **-men**) *n* (*shopkeeper*) Geschäftsmann *m*; (*workman*) Handwerker *m*; **trade(s) union** *n* (*Brit*) Gewerkschaft *f*

tradition [trə'dɪʃən] *n* Tradition *f*; **traditional, traditionally** *adj, adv* traditionell

traffic ['træfɪk] *n* Verkehr *m*; (*pej: trading*) Handel *m* (*in* mit); **traffic circle** *n* (*US*) Kreisverkehr *m*; **traffic island** *n* Verkehrsinsel *f*; **traffic jam** *n* Stau *m*; **traffic lights** *npl* Verkehrsampel *f*; **traffic warden** *n* (*Brit*) ≈ Politesse *f*

tragedy ['trædʒədɪ] *n* Tragödie *f*; **tragic** ['trædʒɪk] *adj* tragisch

trail [treɪl] *n* Spur *f*; (*path*) Weg *m* ▷ *vt* (*follow*) verfolgen; (*drag*) schleppen; (*drag behind*) hinter sich herziehen; (*Sport*) zurückliegen hinter +*dat* ▷ *vi* (*hang loosely*) schleifen; (*Sport*) weit zurückliegen; **trailer** *n* Anhänger *m*; (*US: caravan*) Wohnwagen *m*; (*Cine*) Trailer *m*

train [treɪn] *n* (*Rail*) Zug *m* ▷ *vt* (*teach*) ausbilden; (*Sport*) trainieren ▷ *vi* (*Sport*) trainieren; **to ~ as** (*o to be*) **a teacher** eine Ausbildung als Lehrer machen; **trained** *adj* (*person, voice*) ausgebildet; **trainee** *n* Auszubildende(r) *mf*; (*academic, practical*) Praktikant(in) *m(f)*; **traineeship** *n* Praktikum *nt*; **trainer** *n* (*Sport*) Trainer(in) *m(f)*; **~s** (*Brit: shoes*) Turnschuhe *pl*; **training** *n* Ausbildung *f*; (*Sport*) Training *nt*; **train station** *n* Bahnhof *m*

tram ['træm] *n* (*Brit*) Straßenbahn *f*

tramp [træmp] *n* Land-streicher(in) *m(f)* ▷ *vi* trotten

tranquillizer ['træŋkwɪlaɪzə*] *n* Beruhigungsmittel *nt*

transaction *n* (*piece of business*) Geschäft *nt*

transatlantic ['trænzət'læntɪk] *adj* transatlantisch; **~ flight** Transatlantikflug *m*

transfer ['trænsfə*] *n* (*of money*) Überweisung *f*; (*US: ticket*) Umsteigekarte *f* ▷ [træns'fɜː*] *vt* (*money*) überweisen (*to sb* an jdn); (*patient*) verlegen; (*employee*) versetzen; (*Sport*) transferieren ▷ *vi* (*on journey*) umsteigen; **transferable** [træns'fɜːrəbl] *adj* übertragbar

transform [træns'fɔːm] *vt* umwandeln; **transformation** [trænsfə'meɪʃən] *n* Umwandlung *f*

transfusion [træns'fjuːʒən] *n* Transfusion *f*

transistor [træn'zɪstə*] *n* Transistor *m*; **~ (radio)** Transistorradio *nt*

transition [træn'zɪʃən] *n* Übergang *m* (*from ... to* von ... zu)

transit lounge ['trænzɪtlaʊndʒ] *n* Transitraum *m*; **transit passenger** *n* Transitreisende(r) *mf*

translate [trænz'leɪt] vt, vi
übersetzen; **translation**
[trænz'leɪʃən] n Übersetzung f;
translator [trænz'leɪtə*] n
Übersetzer(in) m(f)
transmission [trænz'mɪʃən] n
(Auto) Getriebe nt
transparent [træns'pærənt] adj
durchsichtig; (fig) offenkundig
transplant [træns'plɑːnt] (Med)
vt transplantieren ▷ ['trænsplɑːnt]
n (operation) Transplantation f
transport ['trænspɔːt] n (of
goods, people) Beförderung f; **public
~** öffentliche Verkehrsmittel pl
▷ [træns'pɔːt] vt befördern,
transportieren; **transportation**
[trænspɔː'teɪʃən] n see **transport**
trap [træp] n Falle f ▷ vt: **to be
~ped** (in snow, job etc) festsitzen
trash [træʃ] n (book, film etc)
Schund m; (US: refuse) Abfall m;
trash can n (US) Abfalleimer m;
trashy adj niveaulos; (novel)
Schund-
traumatic [trɔː'mætɪk] adj
traumatisch
travel ['trævl] n Reisen nt ▷ vi
(journey) reisen ▷ vt (distance)
zurücklegen; (country) bereisen;
travel agency, travel agent n
(company) Reisebüro nt; **traveler**
(US) see **traveller**; **traveler's
check** (US) see **traveller's cheque**;
travel insurance n
Reiseversicherung f; **traveller** n
Reisende(r) mf; **traveller's cheque**
n (Brit) Reisescheck m; **travelsick**
n reisekrank
tray [treɪ] n Tablett nt; (for mail
etc) Ablage f; (of printer, photocopier)
Fach nt
tread [tred] n (on tyre) Profil nt;
tread on [tred] (**trod, trodden**)
vt treten auf +akk
treasure ['treʒə*] n Schatz m
▷ vt schätzen

treat [triːt] n besondere Freude;
it's my ~ das geht auf meine
Kosten ▷ vt behandeln; **to ~ sb
(to sth)** jdn (zu etw) einladen; **to
~ oneself to sth** sich etw leisten;
treatment ['triːtmənt] n
Behandlung f
treaty ['triːtɪ] n Vertrag m
tree [triː] n Baum m
tremble ['trembl] vi zittern
tremendous [trə'mendəs] adj
gewaltig; (fam: very good) toll
trench [trentʃ] n Graben m
trend [trend] n Tendenz f;
(fashion) Mode f, Trend m; **trendy**
adj trendy
trespass ['trespəs] vi: **"no ~ing"**
„Betreten verboten"
trial ['traɪəl] n (Jur) Prozess m;
(test) Versuch m; **by ~ and error**
durch Ausprobieren; **trial period**
n (for employee) Probezeit f
triangle ['traɪæŋgl] n Dreieck nt;
(Mus) Triangel m; **triangular**
[traɪ'æŋgjʊlə*] adj dreieckig
tribe [traɪb] n Stamm m
trick [trɪk] n Trick m; (mischief)
Streich m ▷ vt hereinlegen
tricky ['trɪkɪ] adj (difficult)
schwierig, heikel; (situation)
verzwickt
trifle ['traɪfl] n Kleinigkeit f; (Brit
Gastr) Trifle nt (Nachspeise aus
Biskuit, Wackelpudding, Obst,
Vanillesoße und Sahne)
trigger ['trɪgə*] n (of gun) Abzug
m ▷ vt: **to ~ (off)** auslösen
trim [trɪm] vt (hair, beard)
nachschneiden; (nails) schneiden;
(hedge) stutzen ▷ n: **just a ~,
please** nur etwas nachschneiden,
bitte; **trimmings** npl (decorations)
Verzierungen pl; (extras) Zubehör
nt; (Gastr) Beilagen pl
trip [trɪp] n Reise f; (outing)
Ausflug m ▷ vi stolpern (over über
+akk)

triple ['trɪpl] adj dreifach ▷ adv:
~ **the price** dreimal so teuer ▷ vi
sich verdreifachen; **triplet**
['trɪplɪt] n Drilling m
tripod ['traɪpɒd] n (Foto) Stativ
nt
trite [traɪt] adj banal
triumph ['traɪʌmf] n Triumph m
trivial ['trɪvɪəl] adj trivial
trod [trɒd] pt of **tread**
trodden pp of **tread**
trolley ['trɒlɪ] n (Brit: in shop)
Einkaufswagen m; (for luggage)
Kofferkuli m; (serving ~) Teewagen
m
trombone [trɒm'bəʊn] n
Posaune f
troops [tru:ps] npl (Mil) Truppen
pl
trophy ['trəʊfɪ] n Trophäe f
tropical ['trɒpɪkl] adj tropisch
trouble ['trʌbl] n (problems)
Schwierigkeiten pl; (worry) Sorgen
pl; (effort) Mühe f; (unrest) Unruhen
pl; (Med) Beschwerden pl; **to be in**
~ in Schwierigkeiten sein; **to get**
into ~ (with authority) Ärger
bekommen; **to make**
~ Schwierigkeiten machen ▷ vt
(worry) beunruhigen; (disturb)
stören; **my back's troubling me**
mein Rücken macht mir zu
schaffen; **sorry to ~ you** ich muss
dich/Sie leider kurz stören;
troubled adj (worried)
beunruhigt; **trouble-free** adj
problemlos; **troublemaker** n
Unruhestifter(in) m(f);
troublesome adj lästig
trousers ['traʊzəz] npl Hose f;
trouser suit n (Brit) Hosenanzug
m
trout [traʊt] n Forelle f
truck [trʌk] n Lastwagen m; (Brit
Rail) Güterwagen m; **trucker** n
(US: driver) Lastwagenfahrer(in)
m(f)

true [tru:] adj (factually correct)
wahr; (genuine) echt; **to come**
~ wahr werden
truly ['tru:lɪ] adv wirklich; **Yours**
~ (in letter) mit freundlichen
Grüßen
trumpet ['trʌmpɪt] n Trompete
f
trunk [trʌŋk] n (of tree) Stamm
m; (Anat) Rumpf m; (of elephant)
Rüssel m; (piece of luggage)
Überseekoffer m; (US Auto)
Kofferraum m; **trunks** npl:
(**swimming**) ~ Badehose f
trust [trʌst] n (confidence)
Vertrauen nt (in zu) ▷ vt vertrauen
+dat; **trusting** adj vertrauensvoll;
trustworthy adj
vertrauenswürdig
truth [tru:θ] n Wahrheit f;
truthful adj ehrlich; (statement)
wahrheitsgemäß
try [traɪ] n Versuch m ▷ vt
(attempt) versuchen; (~ out)
ausprobieren; (sample) probieren;
(Jur: person) vor Gericht stellen;
(courage, patience) auf die Probe
stellen ▷ vi versuchen; (make
effort) sich bemühen; **~ and come**
versuch zu kommen; **try on** vt
(clothes) anprobieren; **try out** vt
ausprobieren
T-shirt ['ti:ʃɜ:t] n T-Shirt nt
tub [tʌb] n (for ice-cream,
margarine) Becher m
tube [tju:b] n (pipe) Rohr nt; (of
rubber, plastic) Schlauch m; (for
toothpaste, glue etc) Tube f; **the**
Tube (in London) die U-Bahn
tube station ['tju:bsteɪʃən] n
U-Bahn-Station f
tuck [tʌk] vt (put) stecken; **tuck**
in vt (shirt) in die Hose stecken;
(blanket) feststecken; (person)
zudecken ▷ vi (eat) zulangen
Tue(s) abbr = **Tuesday** Di.
Tuesday ['tju:zdɪ] n Dienstag m;

on ~ (am) Dienstag; **on ~s** dienstags; **this/last/next ~** diesen/letzten/nächsten Dienstag; (**on**) **~ morning/ afternoon/evening** (am) Dienstagmorgen/-nachmittag/ -abend; **every ~** jeden Dienstag; **a week on ~/~ week** Dienstag in einer Woche

tug [tʌg] *vt* ziehen; **she ~ged his sleeve** sie zog an seinem Ärmel ▷ *vi* ziehen (*at* an +*dat*)

tuition [tjuˈɪʃən] *n* Unterricht *m*; (*US: fees*) Studiengebühren *pl*; **~ fees** *pl* Studiengebühren *pl*

tulip [ˈtjuːlɪp] *n* Tulpe *f*

tumble [ˈtʌmbl] *vi* (*person, prices*) fallen; **tumble dryer** *n* Wäschetrockner *m*; **tumbler** *n* (*glass*) (Becher)glas *nt*

tummy [ˈtʌmɪ] *n* (*fam*) Bauch *m*; **tummyache** *n* (*fam*) Bauchweh *nt*

tumor (*US*), **tumour** [ˈtjuːmə*] *n* Tumor *m*

tuna [ˈtjuːnə] *n* Thunfisch *m*

tune [tjuːn] *n* Melodie *f*; **to be in/out of ~** (*instrument*) gestimmt/verstimmt sein; (*singer*) richtig/falsch singen ▷ *vt* (*instrument*) stimmen; (*radio*) einstellen (*to* auf +*akk*); **tuner** *n* (*in stereo system*) Tuner *m*

Tunisia [tjuˈnɪzɪə] *n* Tunesien *nt*

tunnel [ˈtʌnl] *n* Tunnel *m*; (*under road, railway*) Unterführung *f*

turban [ˈtɜːbən] *n* Turban *m*

turbulence [ˈtɜːbjʊləns] *n* (*Aviat*) Turbulenzen *pl*; **turbulent** *adj* stürmisch

Turk [tɜːk] *n* Türke *m*, Türkin *f*

turkey [ˈtɜːkɪ] *n* Truthahn *m*

Turkey [ˈtɜːkɪ] *n* die Türkei; **Turkish** *adj* türkisch ▷ *n* (*language*) Türkisch *nt*

turmoil [ˈtɜːmɔɪl] *n* Aufruhr *m*

turn [tɜːn] *n* (*rotation*) Drehung *f*; (*performance*) Nummer *f*; **to make a left ~** nach links abbiegen; **at the ~ of the century** um die Jahrhundertwende; **it's your ~** du bist/Sie sind dran; **in ~, by ~s** abwechselnd; **to take ~s** sich abwechseln ▷ *vt* (*wheel, key, screw*) drehen; (*to face other way*) umdrehen; (*corner*) biegen um; (*page*) umblättern; (*transform*) verwandeln (*into* in +*akk*) ▷ *vi* (*rotate*) sich drehen; (*to face other way*) sich umdrehen; (*change direction: driver, car*) abbiegen; (*become*) werden; (*weather*) umschlagen; **to ~ into sth** (*become*) sich in etw *akk* verwandeln; **to ~ cold/green** kalt/grün werden; **to ~ left/right** links/rechts abbiegen; **turn away** *vt* (*person*) abweisen; **turn back** *vt* (*person*) zurückweisen ▷ *vi* (*go back*) umkehren; **turn down** *vt* (*refuse*) ablehnen; (*radio, TV*) leiser stellen; (*heating*) kleiner stellen; **turn off** *vi* abbiegen ▷ *vt* (*switch off*) ausschalten; (*tap*) zudrehen; (*engine, electricity*) abstellen; **turn on** *vt* (*switch on*) einschalten; (*tap*) aufdrehen; (*engine, electricity*) anstellen; (*fam: person*) anmachen, antörnen; **turn out** *vt* (*light*) ausmachen; (*pockets*) leeren ▷ *vi* (*develop*) sich entwickeln; **as it turned out** wie sich herausstellte; **turn over** *vt* umdrehen; (*page*) umblättern ▷ *vi* (*person*) sich umdrehen; (*car*) sich überschlagen; (*TV*) umschalten (*to* auf +*akk*); **turn round** *vt* umdrehen ▷ *vi* (*to face other way*) sich umdrehen; (*go back*) umkehren; **turn to** *vt* sich zuwenden +*dat*; **turn up** *vi* (*person, lost object*) auftauchen ▷ *vt* (*radio, TV*) lauter stellen; (*heating*) höher stellen; **turning** n (in road) Abzweigung f; **turning point** n Wendepunkt m

turnip ['tɜːnɪp] n Rübe f

turnover ['tɜːnəʊvə*] n (Fin) Umsatz m

turnpike ['tɜːnpaɪk] n (US) gebührenpflichtige Autobahn

turntable ['tɜːnteɪbl] n (on record player) Plattenteller m

turn-up ['tɜːnʌp] n (Brit: on trousers) Aufschlag m

turquoise ['tɜːkwɔɪz] adj türkis

turtle ['tɜːtl] n (Brit) Wasserschildkröte f; (US) Schildkröte f

tutor ['tjuːtə*] n (private) Privatlehrer(in) m(f); (Brit: at university) Tutor(in) m(f)

tux [tʌks] , **tuxedo** [tʌk'siːdəʊ] (pl **-s**) n (US) Smoking m

TV ['tiːviː] n Fernsehen nt; (~ set) Fernseher m; **to watch ~** fernsehen; **on ~** im Fernsehen ⊳ adj Fernseh-; **~ programme** Fernsehsendung f

tweed [twiːd] n Tweed m

tweezers ['twiːzəz] npl Pinzette f

twelfth [twelfθ] adj zwölfte(r, s); see also **eighth**; **twelve** [twelv] num zwölf ⊳ n Zwölf f; see also **eight**

twentieth ['twentɪɪθ] adj zwanzigste(r, s); see also **eighth**; **twenty** ['twentɪ] num zwanzig; **~-one** einundzwanzig ⊳ n Zwanzig f; **to be in one's twenties** in den Zwanzigern sein; see also **eight**

twice [twaɪs] adv zweimal; **~ as much/many** doppelt so viel/viele

twig [twɪg] n Zweig m

twilight ['twaɪlaɪt] n (in evening) Dämmerung f

twin [twɪn] n Zwilling m ⊳ adj (brother etc) Zwillings-; **~ beds** zwei Einzelbetten ⊳ vt: **York is ~ned with Münster** York ist eine Partnerstadt von Münster

twinge [twɪndʒ] n (pain) stechender Schmerz

twinkle ['twɪŋkl] vi funkeln

twin room ['twɪn'ruːm] n Zweibettzimmer nt; **twin town** n Partnerstadt f

twist [twɪst] vt (turn) drehen, winden; (distort) verdrehen; **I've ~ed my ankle** ich bin mit dem Fuß umgeknickt

two [tuː] num zwei; **to break sth in ~** etw in zwei Teile brechen ⊳ n Zwei f; **the ~ of them** die beiden; see also **eight**; **two-dimensional** adj zweidimensional; (fig) oberflächlich; **two-faced** adj falsch, heuchlerisch; **two-piece** adj zweiteilig; **two-way** adj: **~ traffic** Gegenverkehr

type [taɪp] n (sort) Art f; (typeface) Schrift(art) f; **what ~ of car is it?** was für ein Auto ist das?; **he's not my ~** er ist nicht mein Typ; **typeface** n Schrift(art) f; **typewriter** n Schreibmaschine f

typhoid ['taɪfɔɪd] n Typhus m

typhoon [taɪ'fuːn] n Taifun m

typical ['tɪpɪkəl] adj typisch (of für)

typing error ['taɪpɪŋerə*] n Tippfehler m

tyre [taɪə*] n (Brit) Reifen m; **tyre pressure** n Reifendruck m

Tyrol [tɪ'rəʊl] n: **the ~** Tirol nt

u

UFO ['juːfəʊ] *acr* = **unidentified flying object**

Uganda [juːˈgændə] *n* Uganda *nt*

ugly ['ʌglɪ] *adj* hässlich

UHT *adj abbr* = **ultra-heat treated** ~ **milk** H-Milch *f*

UK *abbr* = **United Kingdom**

Ukraine [juːˈkreɪn] *n*: **the** ~ die Ukraine

ulcer ['ʌlsə*] *n* Geschwür *nt*

ulterior [ʌlˈtɪərɪə*] *adj*: ~ **motive** Hintergedanke *m*

ultimate ['ʌltɪmət] *adj (final)* letzte(r, s); *(authority)* höchste(r, s); **ultimately** *adv* letzten Endes; *(eventually)* schließlich; **ultimatum** [ʌltɪˈmeɪtəm] *n* Ultimatum *nt*

ultra- ['ʌltrə] *pref* ultra-

ultrasound ['ʌltrəsaʊnd] *n (Med)* Ultraschall *m*

umbrella [ʌmˈbrelə] *n* Schirm *m*

umpire ['ʌmpaɪə*] *n* Schieds-richter(in) *m(f)*

umpteen ['ʌmptiːn] *num (fam)* zig; ~ **times** zigmal

un- [ʌn] *pref* un-

UN *nsing abbr* = **United Nations** VN, Vereinte Nationen *pl*

unable [ʌnˈeɪbl] *adj*: **to be** ~ **to do sth** etw nicht tun können

unacceptable [ʌnəˈkseptəbl] *adj* unannehmbar

unaccountably [ʌnəˈkaʊntəblɪ] *adv* unerklärlicherweise

unaccustomed [ʌnəˈkʌstəmd] *adj*: **to be** ~ **to sth** etw nicht gewohnt sein

unanimous, unanimously [juːˈnænɪməs, -lɪ] *adj, adv* einmütig

unattached [ʌnəˈtætʃt] *adj (without partner)* ungebunden

unattended [ʌnəˈtendɪd] *adj (luggage, car)* unbeaufsichtigt

unauthorized [ʌnˈɔːθəraɪzd] *adj* unbefugt

unavailable [ʌnəˈveɪləbl] *adj* nicht erhältlich; *(person)* nicht erreichbar

unavoidable [ʌnəˈvɔɪdəbl] *adj* unvermeidlich

unaware [ʌnəˈweə*] *adj*: **to be** ~ **of sth** sich einer Sache *dat* nicht bewusst sein; **I was** ~ **that ...** ich wusste nicht, dass ...

unbalanced [ʌnˈbælənst] *adj* unausgewogen; *(mentally)* gestört

unbearable [ʌnˈbɛərəbl] *adj* unerträglich

unbeatable [ʌnˈbiːtəbl] *adj* unschlagbar

unbelievable [ʌnbɪˈliːvəbl] *adj* unglaublich

unblock [ʌnˈblɒk] *vt (pipe)* frei machen

unbutton [ʌnˈbʌtn] *vt* aufknöpfen

uncertain [ʌnˈsɜːtən] *adj*
unsicher

uncle [ˈʌŋkl] *n* Onkel *m*

uncomfortable [ʌnˈkʌmfətəbl]
adj unbequem

unconditional [ʌnkənˈdɪʃənl]
adj bedingungslos

unconscious [ʌnˈkɒnʃəs] *adj*
(*Med*) bewusstlos; **to be ~ of sth**
sich einer Sache *dat* nicht bewusst
sein; **unconsciously** *adv*
unbewusst

uncork [ʌnˈkɔːk] *vt* entkorken

uncover [ʌnˈkʌvə*] *vt*
aufdecken

undecided [ʌndɪˈsaɪdɪd] *adj*
unschlüssig

undeniable [ʌndɪˈnaɪəbl] *adj*
unbestreitbar

under [ˈʌndə*] *prep* (*beneath*)
unter +*dat*; (*with motion*) unter
+*akk*; **children ~ eight** Kinder
unter acht; **~ an hour** weniger als
eine Stunde ▷ *adv* (*beneath*)
unten; (*with motion*) darunter;
children aged eight and ~ Kinder
bis zu acht Jahren; **under-age** *adj*
minderjährig

undercarriage [ˈʌndəkærɪdʒ] *n*
Fahrgestell *nt*

underdog [ˈʌndədɒg] *n* (*outsider*)
Außenseiter(in) *m(f)*

underdone [ʌndəˈdʌn] *adj*
(*Gastr*) nicht gar, durch;
(*deliberately*) nicht durchgebraten

underestimate [ʌndər-
ˈestɪmeɪt] *vt* unterschätzen

underexposed [ʌndərɪksˈpəʊzd]
adj (*Foto*) unterbelichtet

undergo [ʌndəˈgəʊ] *irr vt*
(*experience*) durchmachen;
(*operation, test*) sich unterziehen
+*dat*

undergraduate [ʌndəˈgrædjʊət]
n Student(in) *m(f)*

underground [ˈʌndəgraʊnd] *adj*
unterirdisch ▷ *n* (*Brit Rail*) U-Bahn

f; **underground station** *n*
U-Bahn-Station *f*

underlie [ʌndəˈlaɪ] *irr vt*
zugrunde liegen +*dat*

underline [ʌndəˈlaɪn] *vt*
unterstreichen

underlying [ʌndəˈlaɪɪŋ] *adj*
zugrunde liegend

underneath [ʌndəˈniːθ] *prep*
unter; (*with motion*) unter +*akk*
▷ *adv* darunter

underpants [ˈʌndəpænts] *npl*
Unterhose *f*; **undershirt**
[ˈʌndəʃɜːt] *n* (*US*) Unterhemd *nt*;
undershorts [ˈʌndəʃɔːts] *npl* (*US*)
Unterhose *f*

understand [ʌndəˈstænd] *irr vt,
vi* verstehen; **I ~ that …** (*been told*)
ich habe gehört, dass …;
(*sympathize*) ich habe Verständnis
dafür, dass …; **to make oneself
understood** sich verständlich
machen; **understandable** *adj*
verständlich; **understanding** *adj*
verständnisvoll

undertake [ʌndəˈteɪk] *irr vt*
(*task*) übernehmen; **to ~ to do sth**
sich verpflichten, etw zu tun;
undertaker *n* Leichenbestat-
ter(in) *m(f)*; **~'s** (*firm*)
Bestattungsinstitut *nt*

underwater [ʌndəˈwɔːtə*] *adv*
unter Wasser ▷ *adj* Unterwasser-

underwear [ˈʌndəwɛə*] *n*
Unterwäsche *f*

undesirable [ʌndɪˈzaɪərəbl] *adj*
unerwünscht

undo [ʌnˈduː] *irr vt* (*unfasten*)
aufmachen; (*work*)
zunichtemachen; (*Inform*)
rückgängig machen

undoubtedly [ʌnˈdaʊtɪdlɪ] *adv*
zweifellos

undress [ʌnˈdres] *vt* ausziehen;
to get ~ed sich ausziehen ▷ *vi*
sich ausziehen

undue [ʌnˈdjuː] *adj* übermäßig

unduly [ʌn'djuːlɪ] *adv*
übermäßig

unearth [ʌn'ɜːθ] *vt* (*dig up*)
ausgraben; (*find*) aufstöbern

unease [ʌn'iːz] *n* Unbehagen *nt*;
uneasy *adj* (*person*) unbehaglich;
I'm ~ about it mir ist nicht wohl
dabei

unemployed [ʌnɪm'plɔɪd] *adj*
arbeitslos ▷ ▷ *npl*: **the ~** die
Arbeitslosen *pl*; **unemployment**
[ʌnɪm'plɔɪmənt] *n* Arbeitslosigkeit *f*; **unemployment**
benefit *n* Arbeitslosengeld *nt*

unequal [ʌn'iːkwəl] *adj*
ungleich

uneven [ʌn'iːvən] *adj* (*surface,*
road) uneben; (*contest*) ungleich

unexpected [ʌnɪk'spektɪd] *adj*
unerwartet

unfair [ʌn'feə*] *adj* unfair

unfamiliar [ʌnfə'mɪljə*] *adj*: **to**
be ~ with sb/sth jdn/etw nicht
kennen

unfasten [ʌn'fɑːsn] *vt*
aufmachen

unfit [ʌn'fɪt] *adj* ungeeignet (*for*
für); (*in bad health*) nicht fit

unforeseen [ʌnfɔː'siːn] *adj*
unvorhergesehen

unforgettable [ʌnfə'getəbl] *adj*
unvergesslich

unforgivable [ʌnfə'gɪvəbl] *adj*
unverzeihlich

unfortunate [ʌn'fɔːtʃnət] *adj*
(*unlucky*) unglücklich; **it is ~**
that ... es ist bedauerlich, dass ...;
unfortunately *adv* leider

unfounded [ʌn'faʊndɪd] *adj*
unbegründet

unhappy [ʌn'hæpɪ] *adj* (*sad*)
unglücklich, unzufrieden; **to be**
~ with sth mit etw unzufrieden
sein

unhealthy [ʌn'helθɪ] *adj*
ungesund

unheard-of [ʌn'hɜːdɒv] *adj*

(*unknown*) gänzlich unbekannt;
(*outrageous*) unerhört

unhelpful [ʌn'helpfʊl] *adj* nicht
hilfreich

unhitch [ʌn'hɪtʃ] *vt* (*caravan,*
trailer) abkoppeln

unhurt [ʌn'hɜːt] *adj* unverletzt

uniform ['juːnɪfɔːm] *n* Uniform
f ▷ *adj* einheitlich

unify ['juːnɪfaɪ] *vt* vereinigen

unimportant [ʌnɪm'pɔːtənt]-
adj unwichtig

uninhabited [ʌnɪn'hæbɪtɪd] *adj*
unbewohnt

uninstall [ʌnɪn'stɔːl] *vt* (*Inform*)
deinstallieren

unintentional [ʌnɪn'tenʃənl]
adj unabsichtlich

union ['juːnjən] *n* (*uniting*)
Vereinigung *f*; (*alliance*) Union *f*;
Union Jack *n* Union Jack *m*
(*britische Nationalflagge*)

unique [juː'niːk] *adj* einzigartig

unit ['juːnɪt] *n* Einheit *f*; (*of*
system, machine) Teil *nt*; (*in school*)
Lektion *f*

unite [juː'naɪt] *vt* vereinigen;
the United Kingdom das
Vereinigte Königreich; **the United**
Nations *pl* die Vereinten Nationen
pl; **the United States (of**
America) *pl* die Vereinigten
Staaten (von Amerika) *pl* ▷ *vi* sich
vereinigen

universe ['juːnɪvɜːs] *n* Univer-
sum *nt*

university [juːnɪ'vɜːsɪtɪ] *n*
Universität *f*

unkind [ʌn'kaɪnd] *adj* unfreundlich (*to* zu)

unknown [ʌn'nəʊn] *adj*
unbekannt (*to* +dat)

unleaded [ʌn'ledɪd] *adj* bleifrei

unless [ən'les] *conj* es sei denn,
wenn ... nicht; **don't do it ~ I tell**
you to mach das nicht, es sei
denn, ich sage es dir; **~ I'm**

mistaken ... wenn ich mich nicht irre ...

unlicensed [ʌn'laɪsənst] adj (to sell alcohol) ohne Lizenz

unlike [ʌn'laɪk] prep (in contrast to) im Gegensatz zu; **it's ~ her to be late** es sieht ihr gar nicht ähnlich, zu spät zu kommen; **unlikely** [ʌn'laɪklɪ] adj unwahrscheinlich

unload [ʌn'ləʊd] vt ausladen

unlock [ʌn'lɒk] vt aufschließen

unlucky [ʌn'lʌkɪ] adj unglücklich; **to be ~** Pech haben

unmistakable [ʌnmɪ'steɪkəbl] adj unverkennbar

unnecessary [ʌn'nesəsərɪ] adj unnötig

unobtainable [ʌnəb'teɪnəbl] adj nicht erhältlich

unoccupied [ʌn'ɒkjʊpaɪd] adj (seat) frei; (building, room) leer stehend

unpack [ʌn'pæk] vt, vi auspacken

unpleasant [ʌn'pleznt] adj unangenehm

unplug [ʌn'plʌg] vt: **to ~ sth** den Stecker von etw herausziehen

unprecedented [ʌn'presɪdəntɪd] adj beispiellos

unpredictable [ʌnprɪ'dɪktəbl] adj (person, weather) unberechenbar

unreasonable [ʌn'riːznbl] adj unvernünftig; (demand) übertrieben

unreliable [ʌnrɪ'laɪəbl] adj unzuverlässig

unsafe [ʌn'seɪf] adj nicht sicher; (dangerous) gefährlich

unscrew [ʌn'skruː] vt abschrauben

unsightly [ʌn'saɪtlɪ] adj unansehnlich

unskilled [ʌn'skɪld] adj (worker) ungelernt

unsuccessful [ʌnsək'sesfʊl] adj erfolglos

unsuitable [ʌn'suːtəbl] adj ungeeignet (for für)

until [ən'tɪl] prep bis; **not ~** erst; **from Monday ~ Friday** von Montag bis Freitag; **he didn't come home ~ midnight** er kam erst um Mitternacht nach Hause; **~ then** bis dahin ▷ conj bis; **she won't come ~ you invite her** sie kommt erst, wenn du sie einlädst/wenn Sie sie einladen

unusual, unusually [ʌn'juːʒʊəl, -ɪ] adj, adv ungewöhnlich

unwanted [ʌn'wɒntɪd] adj unerwünscht, ungewollt

unwell [ʌn'wel] adj krank; **to feel ~** sich nicht wohlfühlen

unwilling [ʌn'wɪlɪŋ] adj: **to be ~ to do sth** nicht bereit sein, etw zu tun

unwind [ʌn'waɪnd] irr vt abwickeln ▷ vi (relax) sich entspannen

unwrap [ʌn'ræp] vt auspacken

unzip [ʌn'zɪp] vt den Reißverschluss aufmachen an +dat; (Inform) entzippen

● **KEYWORD**

up [ʌp] prep: **to be up sth** oben auf etw dat sein; **to go up sth** (auf) etw akk hinaufgehen; **go up that road** gehen Sie die Straße hinauf

▷ adv **1** (upwards, higher) oben; **put it up a bit higher** stell es etwas weiter nach oben; **up there** da oben, dort oben; **up above** hoch oben

2 to be up (out of bed) auf sein; (prices, level) gestiegen sein; (building, tent) stehen

3 up to (as far as) bis; **up to now** bis jetzt

4 to be up to (*depending on*): **it's up to you** das hängt von dir ab; (*equal to*): **he's not up to it** (*job, task etc*) er ist dem nicht gewachsen; (*inf: be doing*) (*showing disapproval, suspicion*) **what is he up to?** was führt er im Schilde?; **it's not up to me to decide** die Entscheidung liegt nicht bei mir; **his work is not up to the required standard** seine Arbeit entspricht nicht dem geforderten Niveau
▷ *n*: **ups and downs** (*in life, career*) Höhen und Tiefen *pl*

upbringing [ˈʌpbrɪŋɪŋ] *n* Erziehung *f*

update [ʌpˈdeɪt] *n* (*list etc*) Aktualisierung *f*; (*software*) Update *nt* ▷ *vt* (*list etc, person*) auf den neuesten Stand bringen, aktualisieren

upgrade [ʌpˈgreɪd] *vt* (*computer*) aufrüsten; **we were ~d** das Hotel hat uns ein besseres Zimmer gegeben

upheaval [ʌpˈhiːvəl] *n* Aufruhr *m*; (*Pol*) Umbruch *m*

uphill [ʌpˈhɪl] *adv* bergauf

upon [əˈpɒn] *prep see* **on**

upper [ˈʌpəʳ] *adj* obere(r, s); (*arm, deck*) Ober-

upright [ˈʌpraɪt] *adj, adv* aufrecht

uprising [ˈʌpraɪzɪŋ] *n* Aufstand *m*

uproar [ˈʌprɔːʳ] *n* Aufruhr *m*

upset [ʌpˈset] *irr vt* (*overturn*) umkippen; (*disturb*) aufregen; (*sadden*) bestürzen; (*offend*) kränken; (*plans*) durcheinanderbringen ▷ *adj* (*disturbed*) aufgeregt; (*sad*) bestürzt; (*offended*) gekränkt; **~ stomach** [ˈʌpset] Magenverstimmung *f*

upside down [ʌpsaɪdˈdaʊn]

adv verkehrt herum; (*fig*) drunter und drüber; **to turn sth ~** (*box etc*) etw umdrehen/durchwühlen

upstairs [ʌpˈstɛəz] *adv* oben; (*go, take*) nach oben

up-to-date [ˈʌptəˈdeɪt] *adj* modern; (*fashion, information*) aktuell; **to keep sb ~** jdn auf dem Laufenden halten

upwards [ˈʌpwədz] *adv* nach oben

urban [ˈɜːbən] *adj* städtisch, Stadt-

urge [ɜːdʒ] *n* Drang *m* ▷ *vt*: **to ~ sb to do sth** jdn drängen, etw zu tun; **urgent, urgently** [ˈɜːdʒənt, -lɪ] *adj, adv* dringend

urine [ˈjʊərɪn] *n* Urin *m*

us [ʌs] *pron* uns; **do they know ~?** kennen sie uns?; **can he help ~?** kann er uns helfen?; **it's ~** wir sind's; **both of ~** wir beide

US, USA *nsing abbr* = **United States (of America)** USA *pl*

use [juːs] *n* (*using*) Gebrauch *m*; (*for specific purpose*) Benutzung *f*; **to make ~ of** Gebrauch machen von; **in/out of ~** in/außer Gebrauch; **it's no ~ (doing that)** es hat keinen Zweck(, das zu tun); **it's (of) no ~ to me** das kann ich nicht brauchen ▷ [juːz] *vt* benutzen, gebrauchen; (*for specific purpose*) verwenden; (*method*) anwenden; **use up** *vt* aufbrauchen

used [juːzd] *adj* (*secondhand*) gebraucht ▷ *vb aux*: **to be ~d to sb/sth** an jdn/etw gewöhnt sein; **to get ~d to sb/sth** sich an jdn/etw gewöhnen; **she ~d to live here** sie hat früher mal hier gewohnt; **useful** *adj* nützlich; **useless** *adj* nutzlos; (*unusable*) unbrauchbar; (*pointless*) zwecklos; **user** [ˈjuːzəʳ] *n* Benutzer(in) *m(f)*;

user-friendly *adj*
benutzerfreundlich
usual [ˈjuːʒʊəl] *adj* üblich,
gewöhnlich; **as ~** wie üblich;
usually *adv* normalerweise
utensil [juːˈtensl] *n* Gerät *nt*
uterus [ˈjuːtərəs] *n* Gebärmutter
f
utilize [ˈjuːtɪlaɪz] *vt* verwenden
utmost [ˈʌtməʊst] *adj* äußerst;
to do one's ~ sein Möglichstes
tun
utter [ˈʌtəʳ] *adj* völlig ▷ *vt* von
sich geben; **utterly** *adv* völlig
U-turn [ˈjuːtɜːn] *n* (*Auto*) Wende
f; **to do a ~** wenden; (*fig*) eine
Kehrtwendung machen

vacancy [ˈveɪkənsɪ] *n* (*job*)
offene Stelle; (*room*) freies Zimmer;
vacant [ˈveɪkənt] *adj* (*room,
toilet*) frei; (*post*) offen; (*building*)
leer stehend; **vacate** [vəˈkeɪt] *vt*
(*room, building*) räumen; (*seat*) frei
machen
vacation [vəˈkeɪʃən] *n* (*US*)
Ferien *pl*, Urlaub *m*; (*at university*)
(Semester)ferien *pl*; **to go on ~** in
Urlaub fahren; **~ course**
Ferienkurs *m*
vaccinate [ˈvæksɪneɪt] *vt*
impfen; **vaccination**
[væksɪˈneɪʃən] *n* Impfung *f*; **~ card**
Impfpass *m*
vacuum [ˈvækjʊm] *n* Vakuum *nt*
▷ *vt, vi* (staub)saugen; **vacuum
(cleaner)** *n* Staubsauger *m*
vagina [vəˈdʒaɪnə] *n* Scheide *f*
vague [veɪg] *adj* (*imprecise*) vage;
(*resemblance*) entfernt; **vaguely**
adv in etwa, irgendwie

vain [veɪn] *adj* (*attempt*)
vergeblich; (*conceited*) eitel; **in
~** vergeblich, umsonst; **vainly** *adv*
(*in vain*) vergeblich
valentine (card)
['væləntaɪn(kɑːd)] *n* Valentins-
karte *f*; **Valentine's Day** *n*
Valentinstag *m*
valid ['vælɪd] *adj* (*ticket, passport
etc*) gültig; (*argument*) stichhaltig;
(*claim*) berechtigt
valley ['vælɪ] *n* Tal *nt*
valuable ['væljʊəbl] *adj* wertvoll;
(*time*) kostbar; **valuables** *npl*
Wertsachen *pl*
value ['væljuː] *n* Wert *m* ▷ *vt*
(*appreciate*) schätzen; **value added
tax** *n* Mehrwertsteuer *f*
valve [vælv] *n* Ventil *nt*
van [væn] *n* (*Auto*) Lieferwagen *m*
vanilla [vəˈnɪlə] *n* Vanille *f*
vanish ['vænɪʃ] *vi* verschwinden
vanity ['vænɪtɪ] *n* Eitelkeit *f*;
vanity case *n* Schminkkoffer *m*
vapor (*US*), **vapour** ['veɪpə*] *n*
(*mist*) Dunst *m*; (*steam*) Dampf
m
variable ['vɛərɪəbl] *adj* (*weather,
mood*) unbeständig; (*quality*)
unterschiedlich; (*speed, height*)
regulierbar; **varied** ['vɛərɪd] *adj*
(*interests, selection*) vielseitig;
(*career*) bewegt; (*work, diet*)
abwechslungsreich; **variety**
[vəˈraɪətɪ] *n* (*diversity*)
Abwechslung *f*; (*assortment*)
Vielfalt *f* (*of* an +*dat*); (*type*) Art *f*;
various ['vɛərɪəs] *adj*
verschieden
varnish ['vɑːnɪʃ] *n* Lack *m* ▷ *vt*
lackieren
vary ['vɛərɪ] *vt* (*alter*) verändern
▷ *vi* (*be different*) unterschiedlich
sein; (*fluctuate*) sich verändern;
(*prices*) schwanken
vase [vɑːz, ?? veɪz] (*US*) *n* Vase *f*
vast [vɑːst] *adj* riesig; (*area*) weit

VAT [væt] *abbr* = **value added tax**
Mehrwertsteuer *f*, MwSt.
Vatican ['vætɪkən] *n*: **the ~** der
Vatikan
VCR [viːsiːˈɑː*] *abbr* = **video
cassette recorder** Videorekorder
m
VD [viːˈdiː] *abbr* = **venereal
disease** Geschlechtskrankheit *f*
VDU [viːdiːˈjuː] *abbr* = **visual
display unit**
veal [viːl] *n* Kalbfleisch *nt*
vegan ['viːgən] *n* Veganer(in)
m(f)
vegetable ['vedʒtəbl] *n* Gemüse
nt
vegetarian [vedʒɪˈtɛərɪən] *n*
Vegetarier(in) *m(f)* ▷ *adj*
vegetarisch
veggie ['vedʒɪ] *n* (*fam*)
Vegetarier(in) *m(f)*; Gemüse *nt*
▷ *adj* vegetarisch; **veggieburger**
n Veggieburger *m*, Gemüseburger
m
vehicle ['viːɪkl] *n* Fahrzeug *nt*
veil [veɪl] *n* Schleier *m*
vein [veɪn] *n* Ader *f*
Velcro® ['velkrəʊ] *n* Klettband
nt
velvet ['velvɪt] *n* Samt *m*
vending machine
['vendɪŋməʃiːn] *n* Automat *m*
venetian blind [vɪˈniːʃənˈblaɪnd]
n Jalousie *f*
Venezuela [veneˈzweɪlə] *n*
Venezuela *nt*
Venice ['venɪs] *n* Venedig *nt*
venison ['venɪsn] *n* Rehfleisch
nt
vent [vent] *n* Öffnung *f*
ventilate ['ventɪleɪt] *vt* lüften;
ventilation [ventɪˈleɪʃən] *n*
Belüftung *f*; **ventilator**
['ventɪleɪtə*] *n* (*in room*)
Ventilator *m*; **to be on a ~** (*Med*)
künstlich beatmet werden
venture ['ventʃə*] *n* (*project*)

Unternehmung f; (Comm)
Unternehmen nt ▷ vi (go) (sich)
wagen
venue ['venjuː] n (for concert etc)
Veranstaltungsort m; (Sport)
Austragungsort m
verb [vɜːb] n Verb nt; **verbal** adj
(agreement) mündlich; (skills)
sprachlich; **verbally** adv
mündlich
verdict ['vɜːdɪkt] n Urteil nt
verge [vɜːdʒ] n (of road)
(Straßen)rand m; **to be on the ~ of
doing sth** im Begriff sein, etw zu
tun ▷ vi: **to ~ on** grenzen an +akk
verification [verɪfɪ'keɪʃən] n
(confirmation) Bestätigung f;
(check) Überprüfung f; **verify**
['verɪfaɪ] vt (confirm) bestätigen;
(check) überprüfen
vermin ['vɜːmɪn] npl Schädlinge
pl; (insects) Ungeziefer nt
verruca [ve'ruːkə] n Warze f
versatile ['vɜːsətaɪl] adj
vielseitig
verse [vɜːs] n (poetry) Poesie f;
(stanza) Strophe f
version ['vɜːʃən] n Version f
versus ['vɜːsəs] prep gegen
vertical ['vɜːtɪkəl] adj senkrecht,
vertikal
very ['verɪ] adv sehr; **~ much** sehr
▷ adj: **the ~ book I need** genau
das Buch, das ich brauche; **at that
~ moment** gerade in dem
Augenblick; **at the ~ top** ganz
oben; **the ~ best** der/die/das
Allerbeste
vest [vest] n (Brit) Unterhemd nt;
(US: waistcoat) Weste f
vet [vet] n Tierarzt m, Tierärztin f
veto ['viːtəʊ] (pl **-es**) n Veto nt
▷ vt sein Veto einlegen gegen
VHF abbr = **very high frequency**
UKW
via ['vaɪə] prep über +akk
viable ['vaɪəbl] adj (plan)

realisierbar; (company) rentabel
vibrate [vaɪ'breɪt] vi vibrieren;
vibration [vaɪ'breɪʃən] n Vibration f
vicar ['vɪkə*] n Pfarrer(in) m(f)
vice [vaɪs] n (evil) Laster nt; (Tech)
Schraubstock m ▷ pref Vize-;
~~chairman stellvertretender
Vorsitzender; **~~president**
Vizepräsident(in) m(f)
vice versa ['vaɪs'vɜːsə] adv
umgekehrt
vicinity [vɪ'sɪnɪtɪ] n: **in the ~** in
der Nähe (of +gen)
vicious ['vɪʃəs] adj (violent)
brutal; (malicious) gemein; **vicious
circle** n Teufelskreis m
victim ['vɪktɪm] n Opfer nt
Victorian [vɪk'tɔːrɪən] adj
viktorianisch
victory ['vɪktərɪ] n Sieg m
video ['vɪdɪəʊ] (pl **-s**) adj Video-
▷ n Video nt; (recorder)
Videorekorder m ▷ vt (auf Video)
aufnehmen; **video camera** n
Videokamera f; **video cassette** n
Videokassette f; **video clip** n
Videoclip m; **video game** n
Videospiel nt; **video recorder** n
Videorekorder m; **video shop** n
Videothek f; **videotape** n
Videoband nt ▷ vt (auf Video)
aufnehmen
Vienna [vɪ'enə] n Wien nt
Vietnam [vjet'næm] n Vietnam
nt
view [vjuː] n (sight) Blick m (of auf
+akk); (vista) Aussicht f; (opinion)
Ansicht f, Meinung f; **in ~ of**
angesichts +gen ▷ vt (situation,
event) betrachten; (house)
besichtigen; **viewer** n (for slides)
Diabetrachter m; (TV)
Zuschauer(in) m(f); **viewpoint** n
(fig) Standpunkt m
vigilant ['vɪdʒɪlənt] adj
wachsam

vile [vaɪl] *adj* abscheulich; (*weather, food*) scheußlich

village ['vɪlɪdʒ] *n* Dorf *nt*; **villager** *n* Dorfbewohner(in) *m(f)*

villain ['vɪlən] *n* Schurke *m*; (*in film, story*) Bösewicht *m*

vine [vaɪn] *n* (Wein)rebe *f*

vinegar ['vɪnɪgəʳ] *n* Essig *m*

vineyard ['vɪnjəd] *n* Weinberg *m*

vintage ['vɪntɪdʒ] *n* (*of wine*) Jahrgang *m*; **vintage wine** *n* edler Wein

vinyl ['vaɪnɪl] *n* Vinyl *nt*

viola [vɪ'əʊlə] *n* Bratsche *f*

violate ['vaɪəleɪt] *vt* (*treaty*) brechen; (*rights, rule*) verletzen

violence ['vaɪələns] *n* (*brutality*) Gewalt *f*; (*of person*) Gewalttätigkeit *f*; **violent** *adj* (*brutal*) brutal; (*death*) gewaltsam

violet ['vaɪələt] *n* Veilchen *nt*

violin [vaɪə'lɪn] *n* Geige *f*, Violine *f*

VIP *abbr* = **very important person** VIP *mf*

virgin ['vɜːdʒɪn] *n* Jungfrau *f*

Virgo ['vɜːgəʊ] *n* (*Astr*) Jungfrau *f*

virile ['vɪraɪl] *adj* (*man*) männlich

virtual ['vɜːtjʊəl] *adj* (*Inform*) virtuell; **virtually** *adv* praktisch; **virtual reality** *n* virtuelle Realität

virtue ['vɜːtjuː] *n* Tugend *f*; **by ~ of** aufgrund +*gen*; **virtuous** ['vɜːtjʊəs] *adj* tugendhaft

virus ['vaɪrəs] *n* (*Med, Inform*) Virus *nt*

visa ['viːzə] *n* Visum *nt*

visibility [vɪzɪ'bɪlɪtɪ] *n* (*Meteo*) Sichtweite *f*; **good/poor ~** gute/schlechte Sicht; **visible** ['vɪzəbl] *adj* sichtbar; (*evident*) sichtlich; **visibly** *adv* sichtlich

vision ['vɪʒən] *n* (*power of sight*) Sehvermögen *nt*; (*foresight*) Weitblick *m*; (*dream, image*) Vision *f*

visit ['vɪzɪt] *n* Besuch *m*; (*stay*) Aufenthalt *m* ▷ *vt* besuchen; **visiting hours** *npl* Besuchszeiten *pl*; **visitor** *n* Besucher(in) *m(f)*; **~s' book** Gästebuch *nt*; **visitor centre** *n* Informationszentrum *nt*

visor ['vaɪzəʳ] *n* (*on helmet*) Visier *nt*; (*Auto*) Blende *f*

visual ['vɪzjʊəl] *adj* Seh-; (*image, joke*) visuell; **~ aid** Anschauungsmaterial *nt*; **~ display unit** Monitor *m*; **visualize** *vt* sich vorstelle; **visually** *adv* visuell; **~ impaired** sehbehindert

vital ['vaɪtl] *adj* (*essential*) unerlässlich, wesentlich; (*argument, moment*) entscheidend; **vitality** [vaɪ'tælɪtɪ] *n* Vitalität *f*; **vitally** *adv* äußerst

vitamin ['vɪtəmɪn] *n* Vitamin *nt*

vivacious [vɪ'veɪʃəs] *adj* lebhaft

vivid ['vɪvɪd] *adj* (*description*) anschaulich; (*memory*) lebhaft; (*colour*) leuchtend

V-neck ['viːnek] *n* V-Ausschnitt *m*

vocabulary [vəʊ'kæbjʊlərɪ] *n* Wortschatz *m*, Vokabular *nt*

vocal ['vəʊkəl] *adj* (*of the voice*) Stimm-; (*group*) Gesangs-; (*protest, person*) lautstark

vocation [vəʊ'keɪʃən] *n* Berufung *f*; **vocational** *adj* Berufs-

vodka ['vɒdkə] *n* Wodka *m*

voice [vɔɪs] *n* Stimme *f* ▷ *vt* äußern; **voice mail** *n* Voicemail *f*

void [vɔɪd] *n* Leere *f* ▷ *adj* (*Jur*) ungültig; **~ of** (ganz) ohne

volcano [vɒl'keɪnəʊ] *n* (*pl* **-es**) *n* Vulkan *m*

volley ['vɒlɪ] *n* (*Tennis*) Volley *m*; **volleyball** *n* Volleyball *m*

volt [vəʊlt] *n* Volt *nt*; **voltage** *n* Spannung *f*

volume ['vɒljuːm] *n* (*of sound*) Lautstärke *f*; (*space occupied by sth*)

Volumen nt; (size, amount) Umfang m; (book) Band m; **volume control** n Lautstärkeregler m

voluntary, **voluntarily** ['vɒləntərı, -lı] adj, adv freiwillig; (unpaid) ehrenamtlich; **volunteer** [vɒlən'tıə*] n Freiwillige(r) mf ▷ vi sich freiwillig melden ▷ vt: **to ~ to do sth** sich anbieten, etw zu tun

voluptuous [və'lʌptjʊəs] adj sinnlich

vomit ['vɒmıt] vi sich übergeben

vote [vəʊt] n Stimme f; (ballot) Wahl f; (result) Abstimmungsergebnis nt; (right to vote) Wahlrecht nt ▷ vt (elect) wählen; **they ~d him chairman** sie wählten ihn zum Vorsitzenden ▷ vi wählen; **to ~ for/against sth** für/gegen etw stimmen; **voter** n Wähler(in) m(f)

voucher ['vaʊtʃə*] n Gutschein m

vow [vaʊ] n Gelöbnis nt ▷ vt: **to ~ to do sth** geloben, etw zu tun

vowel ['vaʊəl] n Vokal m

voyage ['vɔııdʒ] n Reise f

vulgar ['vʌlgə*] adj vulgär, ordinär

vulnerable ['vʌlnərəbl] adj verwundbar; (sensitive) verletzlich

vulture ['vʌltʃə*] n Geier m

W abbr = **west** W

wade [weıd] vi (in water) waten

wafer ['weıfə*] n Waffel f; (Rel) Hostie f; **wafer-thin** adj hauchdünn

waffle ['wɒfl] n Waffel f; (Brit fam: empty talk) Geschwafel nt ▷ vi (Brit fam) schwafeln

wag [wæg] vt (tail) wedeln mit

wage [weıdʒ] n Lohn m

waggon (Brit), **wagon** ['wægən] n (horse-drawn) Fuhrwerk nt; (Brit Rail) Waggon m; (US Auto) Wagen m

waist [weıst] n Taille f; **waistcoat** n (Brit) Weste f; **waistline** n Taille f

wait [weıt] n Wartezeit f ▷ vi warten (for auf +akk); **to ~ and see** abwarten; **~ a minute** Moment mal!; **wait up** vi aufbleiben

waiter n Kellner m; **~!** Herr Ober!

waiting n. **"no ~"** „Halteverbot";

waiting list n Warteliste f;
waiting room n (Med)
Wartezimmer nt; (Rail) Wartesaal
m
waitress n Kellnerin f
wake [weɪk] (**woke** o **waked**,
woken o **waked**) vt wecken ▷ vi
aufwachen; **wake up** vt
aufwecken ▷ vi aufwachen;
wake-up call n (Tel) Weckruf m
Wales [weɪlz] n Wales nt
walk [wɔːk] n Spaziergang m;
(ramble) Wanderung f; (route) Weg
m; **to go for a ~** spazieren gehen;
it's only a five-minute ~ es sind
nur fünf Minuten zu Fuß ▷ vi
gehen; (stroll) spazieren gehen;
(ramble) wandern ▷ vt (dog)
ausführen; **walking** n: **to go
~** wandern; **walking shoes** npl
Wanderschuhe pl; **walking stick** n
Spazierstock m
Walkman® (pl **-s**) n Walkman®
m
wall [wɔːl] n (inside) Wand f;
(outside) Mauer f
wallet ['wɒlɪt] n Brieftasche
f
wallpaper ['wɔːlpeɪpə⁰] n
Tapete f; (Inform)
Bildschirmhintergrund m ▷ vt
tapezieren
walnut ['wɔːlnʌt] n (nut)
Walnuss f
waltz [wɔːlts] n Walzer m
wander ['wɒndə⁰] vi (person)
herumwandern
want [wɒnt] n (lack) Mangel m
(of an +dat); (need) Bedürfnis nt;
for ~ of aus Mangel an +dat ▷ vt
(desire) wollen; (need) brauchen; **I
~ to stay here** ich will hier
bleiben; **he doesn't ~ to** er will
nicht
WAP phone ['wæpfəʊn] n
WAP-Handy nt
war [wɔː⁰] n Krieg m

ward [wɔːd] n (in hospital)
Station f; (child) Mündel nt
warden ['wɔːdən] n Aufseher(in)
m(f); (in youth hostel) Herbergsvater
m, Herbergsmutter f
wardrobe ['wɔːdrəʊb] n
Kleiderschrank m
warehouse ['wɛəhaʊs] n
Lagerhaus nt
warfare ['wɔːfɛə⁰] n Krieg m;
(techniques) Kriegsführung f
warm [wɔːm] adj warm;
(welcome) herzlich; **I'm ~** mir ist
warm ▷ vt wärmen; (food)
aufwärmen; **warm over** vt (US:
food) aufwärmen; **warm up** vt
(food) aufwärmen; (room)
erwärmen ▷ vi (food, room) warm
werden; (Sport) sich aufwärmen;
warmly adv warm; (welcome)
herzlich; **warmth** n Wärme f; (of
welcome) Herzlichkeit f
warn [wɔːn] vt warnen (of,
against vor +dat); **to ~ sb not to do
sth** jdn davor warnen, etw zu tun;
warning n Warnung f; **warning
light** n Warnlicht nt; **warning
triangle** n (Auto) Warndreieck nt
warranty ['wɒrəntɪ] n Garantie
f
wart [wɔːt] n Warze f
wary ['wɛərɪ] adj vorsichtig;
(suspicious) misstrauisch
was [wɒz, wəz] pt of **be**
wash [wɒʃ] n: **to have a ~** sich
waschen; **it's in the ~** es ist in der
Wäsche ▷ vt waschen; (plates,
glasses etc) abwaschen; **to ~ one's
hands** sich dat die Hände
waschen; **to ~ the dishes** (das
Geschirr) abwaschen ▷ vi (clean
oneself) sich waschen; **wash off** vt
abwaschen; **wash up** vi (Brit:
wash dishes) abwaschen; (US: clean
oneself) sich waschen; **washable**
adj waschbar; **washbag** n (US)
Kulturbeutel m; **washbasin** n

Waschbecken nt; **washcloth** n (US) Waschlappen m; **washer** n (Tech) Dichtungsring m; (washing machine) Waschmaschine f; **washing** n (laundry) Wäsche f; **washing machine** n Waschmaschine f; **washing powder** n Waschpulver nt; **washing-up** n (Brit) Abwasch m; **to do the ~** abwaschen; **washing-up liquid** n (Brit) Spülmittel nt; **washroom** n (US) Toilette f

wasn't ['wɒznt] contr of **was not**

wasp [wɒsp] n Wespe f

waste [weɪst] n (materials) Abfall m; (wasting) Verschwendung f; **it's a ~ of time** das ist Zeitverschwendung ▷ adj (superfluous) überschüssig ▷ vt verschwenden (on an +akk); (opportunity) vertun; **waste bin** n Abfalleimer m; **wastepaper basket** n Papierkorb m

watch [wɒtʃ] n (timepiece) (Armband)uhr f ▷ vt (observe) beobachten; (guard) aufpassen auf +akk; (film, play, programme) sich dat ansehen; **to ~ TV** fernsehen ▷ vi zusehen; (guard) Wache halten; **to ~ for sb/sth** nach jdm/etw Ausschau halten; **~ out** pass auf!; **watchdog** n Wachhund m; (fig) Aufsichtsbehörde f; **watchful** adj wachsam

water ['wɔːtə*] n Wasser nt ▷ vt (plant) gießen ▷ vi (eye) tränen; **my mouth is ~ing** mir läuft das Wasser im Mund zusammen; **water down** vt verdünnen; **watercolor** (US), **watercolour** n (painting) Aquarell nt; (paint) Wasserfarbe f; **watercress** n (Brunnen)kresse f; **waterfall** n Wasserfall m; **watering can** n Gießkanne f; **water level** n

Wasserstand m; **watermelon** n Wassermelone f; **waterproof** adj wasserdicht; **water-skiing** n Wasserskilaufen nt; **water sports** npl Wassersport m; **watertight** adj wasserdicht; **water wings** npl Schwimmflügel pl; **watery** adj wässerig

wave [weɪv] n Welle f ▷ vt (move to and fro) schwenken; (hand, flag) winken mit ▷ vi (person) winken; (flag) wehen; **wavelength** n Wellenlänge f; **to be on the same ~** (fig) die gleiche Wellenlänge haben; **wavy** ['weɪvɪ] adj wellig

wax [wæks] n Wachs nt; (in ear) Ohrenschmalz nt

way [weɪ] n Weg m; (direction) Richtung f; (manner) Art f; **can you tell me the ~ to … ?** wie komme ich (am besten) zu … ?; **we went the wrong ~** wir sind in die falsche Richtung gefahren/gegangen; **to lose one's ~** sich verirren; **to make ~ for sb/sth** jdm/etw Platz machen; **to get one's own ~** seinen Willen durchsetzen; **"give ~"** (Auto) „Vorfahrt achten"; **the other ~ round** andersherum; **one ~ or another** irgendwie; **in a ~** in gewisser Weise; **in the ~** im Weg; **by the ~** übrigens; **"~ in"** „Eingang"; **"~ out"** „Ausgang"; **no ~** (fam) kommt nicht infrage!

we [wiː] pron wir

weak [wiːk] adj schwach; **weaken** vt schwächen ▷ vi schwächer werden

wealth [welθ] n Reichtum m; **wealthy** adj reich

weapon ['wepən] n Waffe f

wear [weə*] (wore, worn) vt (have on) tragen; **what shall I ~?** was soll ich anziehen? ▷ vi (become worn) sich abnutzen ▷ n: **~ (and tear)** Abnutzung f; **wear**

off vi (diminish) nachlassen; **wear out** vt abnutzen; (person) erschöpfen ▷ vi sich abnutzen

weather ['weðə*] n Wetter nt; **I'm feeling under the ~** ich fühle mich nicht ganz wohl; **weather forecast** n Wettervorhersage f

weave [wi:v] (**wove** o **weaved, woven** o **weaved**) vt (cloth) weben; (basket etc) flechten

web [web] n (a. fig) Netz nt; **the Web** das Web, das Internet; **webcam** ['webkæm] n Webcam f; **web page** n Webseite f; **website** n Website f

we'd [wi:d] contr of **we had; we would**

Wed abbr = **Wednesday** Mi.

wedding ['wedɪŋ] n Hochzeit f; **wedding anniversary** n Hochzeitstag m; **wedding dress** n Hochzeitskleid nt; **wedding ring** n Ehering m

wedding shower n (US) Party für die zukünftige Braut

wedge [wedʒ] n (under door etc) Keil m; (of cheese etc) Stück nt, Ecke f

Wednesday ['wenzdeɪ] n Mittwoch m; see also **Tuesday**

wee [wi:] adj klein ▷ vi (fam) Pipi machen

weed [wi:d] n Unkraut nt ▷ vt jäten

week [wi:k] n Woche f; **twice a ~** zweimal in der Woche; **a ~ on Friday/Friday ~** Freitag in einer Woche; **a ~ last Friday** letzten Freitag vor einer Woche; **in two ~s' time, in two ~s** in zwei Wochen; **for ~s** wochenlang; **weekday** n Wochentag m; **weekend** n Wochenende nt; **weekend break** n Wochenendurlaub m; **weekly** adj,

adv wöchentlich; (magazine) Wochen-

weep [wi:p] (**wept, wept**) vi weinen

weigh [weɪ] vt, vi wiegen; **it ~s 20 kilos** es wiegt 20 Kilo; **weigh up** vt abwägen; (person) einschätzen; **weight** [weɪt] n Gewicht nt; **to lose/put on ~** abnehmen/zunehmen; **weightlifting** n Gewichtheben nt; **weight training** n Krafttraining nt; **weighty** adj (important) schwerwiegend

weird [wɪəd] adj seltsam; **weirdo** ['wɪədəʊ] n Spinner(in) m(f)

welcome ['welkəm] n Empfang m ▷ adj willkommen; (news) angenehm; **~ to London** willkommen in London! ▷ vt begrüßen; **welcoming** adj freundlich

welfare ['welfɛə*] n Wohl nt; (US: social security) Sozialhilfe f; **welfare state** n Wohlfahrtsstaat m

well [wel] n Brunnen m ▷ adj (in good health) gesund; **are you ~?** geht es dir/Ihnen gut?; **to feel ~** sich wohlfühlen; **get ~ soon** gute Besserung! ▷ interj nun; **~, I don't know** nun, ich weiß nicht ▷ adv gut; **~ done!** gut gemacht!; **it may ~ be** das kann wohl sein; **as ~ (in addition)** auch; **~ over 60** weit über 60

we'll [wi:l] contr of **we will; we shall**

well-behaved [welbɪ'heɪvd] adj brav; **well-being** n Wohl nt; **well-built** adj (person) gut gebaut; **well-done** adj (steak) durchgebraten; **well-earned** adj wohlverdient

wellingtons ['welɪŋtənz] npl Gummistiefel pl

well-known [wel'nəʊn] adj bekannt; **well-off** adj (wealthy)

wohlhabend; **well-paid** adj gut
bezahlt

Welsh [welʃ] adj walisisch ▷ n
(language) Walisisch nt; **the ~** pl die
Waliser pl; **Welshman** (pl **-men**) n
Waliser m; **Welshwoman** (pl
-women) n Waliserin f

went [went] pt of **go**

wept [wept] pt, pp of **weep**

were [wɜ:] pt of **be**

we're [wɪəʳ] contr of **we are**

weren't [wɜ:nt] contr of **were not**

west [west] n Westen m; **the
West** (Pol) der Westen ▷ adv (go,
face) nach Westen ▷ adj West-;
westbound adj (in) Richtung
Westen; **western** adj
West-, westlich; **Western Europe**
Westeuropa nt ▷ n (Cine) Western
m; **West Germany** n: (**the
former**) **~** (das ehemalige)
Westdeutschland,
Westdeutschland n; **westwards**
['westwədz] adv nach Westen

wet [wet] (**wet, wet**) vt: **to
~ oneself** in die Hose machen
▷ adj nass, feucht; **"~ paint"**
„frisch gestrichen"; **wet suit** n
Taucheranzug m

we've [wi:v] contr of **we have**

whale [weɪl] n Wal m

wharf [wɔ:f] (pl **-s** o **wharves**) n
Kai m

KEYWORD

what [wɒt] adj **1** (in questions)
welche(r, s) was für ein(e);
what size is it? welche Größe ist
das?
2 (in exclamations) was für ein(e);
what a mess! was für ein
Durcheinander!
▷ pron (interrogative/relative) was;
what are you doing? was machst
du/machen Sie gerade?; **what are
you talking about?** wovon redest

du/reden Sie?; **what's your
name?** wie heißt du/heißen Sie?;
what is it called? wie heißt das?;
what about ...? wie wär's mit ...?;
I saw what you did ich habe
gesehen, was du gemacht
hast/Sie gemacht haben
▷ excl (disbelieving) wie, was;
what, no coffee! wie, kein
Kaffee?; **I've crashed the car —
what!** ich hatte einen
Autounfall — was!

whatever pron: **I'll do ~ you
want** ich tue alles, was du
willst/Sie wollen; **~ he says** egal,
was er sagt

what's [wɒts] contr of **what is;
what has**

wheat [wi:t] n Weizen m

wheel [wi:l] n Rad nt; (steering
wheel) Lenkrad nt ▷ vt (bicycle,
trolley) schieben; **wheelbarrow** n
Schubkarren m; **wheelchair** n
Rollstuhl m; **wheel clamp** n
Parkkralle f

KEYWORD

when [wen] adv wann
▷ conj **1** (at, during, after the time
that) wenn; (in past) als; **she was
reading when I came in** sie las,
als ich hereinkam; **be careful
when you cross the road** sei
vorsichtig, wenn du über die
Straße gehst/seien Sie vorsichtig,
wenn Sie über die Straße gehen
2 (on, at which) als; **on the day
when I met him** an dem Tag, an
dem ich ihn traf
3 (whereas) wo ... doch

whenever adv (every time) immer
wenn; **come ~ you like** komm,
wann immer du willst/kommen
Sie, wann immer sie wollen

where [wεə°] *adv* wo; **~ are you going?** wohin gehst du/gehen Sie?; **~ are you from?** woher kommst du/kommen Sie? ▷ *conj* wo; **that's ~ I used to live** da habe ich früher gewohnt; **whereabouts** [wεərə'bauts] *adv* wo ▷ *n* ['wεərəbauts] Aufenthaltsort *m*; **whereas** [wεər'æz] *conj* während, wohingegen; **whereby** *adv* wodurch; **wherever** [wεər'evə°] *conj* wo immer; **~ that may be** wo immer das sein mag; **~ I go** überall, wohin ich gehe

whether ['wεðə°] *conj* ob

○ **KEYWORD**

which [wɪtʃ] *adj* **1** (*interrogative*) (*direct, indirect*) welche(r, s); **which one?** welche(r, s)?
2 in which case in diesem Fall; **by which time** zu dieser Zeit
▷ *pron* **1** (*interrogative*) welche(r, s); (*of people also*) wer
2 (*relative*) der/die/das; (*referring to people*) was; **the apple which you ate/which is on the table** der Apfel, den du gegessen hast/der auf dem Tisch liegt; **he said he saw her, which is true** er sagte, er habe sie gesehen, was auch stimmt

whichever *adj, pron* welche(r, s) auch immer
while [waɪl] *n*: **a ~** eine Weile; **for a ~** eine Zeit lang; **a short ~ ago** vor Kurzem ▷ *conj* während; (*although*) obwohl
whine [waɪn] *vi* (*person*) jammern
whip [wɪp] *n* Peitsche *f* ▷ *vt* (*beat*) peitschen; **~ped cream** Schlagsahne *f*
whirl [wɜːl] *vt, vi* herumwirbeln;

whirlpool *n* (*in river, sea*) Strudel *m*; (*pool*) Whirlpool *m*
whisk [wɪsk] *n* Schneebesen *m* ▷ *vt* (*cream etc*) schlagen
whisker ['wɪskə°] *n* (*of animal*) Schnurrhaar *nt*; **~s** *pl* (*of man*) Backenbart *m*
whisk(e)y ['wɪskɪ] *n* Whisky *m*
whisper ['wɪspə°] *vi, vt* flüstern; **to ~ sth to sb** jdm etw zuflüstern
whistle ['wɪsl] *n* Pfiff *m*; (*instrument*) Pfeife *f* ▷ *vt, vi* pfeifen
white [waɪt] *n* (*of egg*) Eiweiß *nt*; (*of eye*) Weiße *nt* ▷ *adj* weiß; (*with fear*) blass; (*coffee*) mit Milch/Sahne; **White House** *n*: **the ~** das Weiße Haus; **white lie** *n* Notlüge *f*; **white meat** *n* helles Fleisch; **white sauce** *n* weiße Soße; **white water rafting** *n* Rafting *nt*; **white wine** *n* Weißwein *m*
Whitsun ['wɪtsn] *n* Pfingsten *nt*

○ **KEYWORD**

who [huː] *pron* **1** (*interrogative*) wer; (*akk*) wen; (*dat*) wem; **who is it?, who's there?** wer ist da?
2 (*relative*) der/die/das; **the woman/man who spoke to me** die Frau/der Mann, die/der mit mir sprach

whoever [huː'evə°] *pron* wer auch immer; **~ you choose** wen auch immer du wählst/Sie wählen
whole [həul] *adj* ganz ▷ *n* Ganze(s) *nt*; **the ~ of my family** meine ganze Familie; **on the ~** im Großen und Ganzen; **wholefood** *n* (*Brit*) Vollwertkost *f*; **~ store** Bioladen *m*; **wholeheartedly** *adv* voll und ganz; **wholemeal** *adj* (*Brit*) Vollkorn-; **wholesale** *adv* (*buy, sell*) im Großhandel; **wholesome**

adj gesund; **whole wheat** *adj* Vollkorn-; **wholly** ['həʊlɪ] *adv* völlig

 KEYWORD

whom [huːm] *pron* **1**
(*interrogative*) (*akk*) wen; (*dat*) wem; **whom did you see?** wen hast du/haben Sie gesehen?; **to whom did you give it?** wem hast du/haben Sie es gegeben?
2 (*relative*) (*akk*) den/die/das; (*dat*) dem/der/dem; **the man whom I saw/to whom I spoke** der Mann, den ich sah/mit dem ich sprach

whooping cough ['huːpɪŋkɒf] *n* Keuchhusten *m*
whose [huːz] *adj* (*in questions*) wessen; (*in relative clauses*) dessen/deren/dessen, deren *pl*; **~ bike is that?** wessen Fahrrad ist das? ▷ *pron* (*in questions*) wessen; **~ is this?** wem gehört das?

 KEYWORD

why [waɪ] *adv* warum, weshalb ▷ *conj* warum, weshalb; **that's not why I'm here** ich bin nicht deswegen hier; **that's the reason why** deshalb ▷ *excl* (*expressing surprise, shock*) na so was; (*explaining*) also dann; **why, it's you!** na so was, du bist/Sie sind es!

wicked ['wɪkɪd] *adj* böse; (*fam: great*) geil
wide [waɪd] *adj* breit; (*skirt, trousers*) weit; (*selection*) groß ▷ *adv* weit; **wide-angle lens** *n* Weitwinkelobjektiv *nt*; **wide-awake** *adj* hellwach; **widely** *adv* weit; **~ known**

allgemein bekannt; **widen** *vt* verbreitern; (*fig*) erweitern; **wide-open** *adj* weit offen; **widescreen TV** *n* Breitbildfernseher *m*; **widespread** *adj* weit verbreitet
widow ['wɪdəʊ] *n* Witwe *f*; **widowed** *adj* verwitwet; **widower** *n* Witwer *m*
width [wɪdθ] *n* Breite *f*
wife [waɪf] (*pl* **wives**) *n* (Ehe)frau *f*
wig [wɪg] *n* Perücke *f*
wiggle ['wɪgl] *vt* wackeln mit
wild [waɪld] *adj* wild; (*violent*) heftig; (*plan, idea*) verrückt ▷ *n*: **in the ~** in freier Wildbahn; **wildlife** *n* Tier- und Pflanzenwelt *f*; **wildly** *adv* wild; (*exaggerated*) maßlos

 KEYWORD

will [wɪl] *vb aux* **1** (*forms future tense*) werden; **I will finish it tomorrow** ich mache es morgen zu Ende
2 (*in conjectures, predictions*) **he will** *o* **he'll be there by now** er dürfte jetzt da sein; **that will be the postman** das wird der Postbote sein
3 (*in commands, requests, offers*) **will you be quiet!** sei/seien Sie endlich still!; **will you help me?** hilfst du/helfen Sie mir?; **will you have a cup of tea?** trinkst du/trinken Sie eine Tasse Tee?; **I won't put up with it!** das lasse ich mir nicht gefallen!
▷ *vt* wollen
▷ *n* Wille *m*; (*jur*) Testament *nt*

willing *adj* bereitwillig; **to be ~ to do sth** bereit sein, etw zu tun; **willingly** *adv* gern(e)
willow ['wɪləʊ] *n* Weide *f*

willpower ['wɪlpaʊə*] n Willenskraft f

wimp [wɪmp] n Weichei nt

win [wɪn] (**won, won**) vt, vi gewinnen ▷ n Sieg m; **win over**, **win round** vt für sich gewinnen

wind [waɪnd] (**wound, wound**) vt (rope, bandage) wickeln; **wind down** vt (car window) herunterkurbeln; **wind up** vt (clock) aufziehen; (car window) hochkurbeln; (meeting, speech) abschließen; (person) aufziehen, ärgern

wind [wɪnd] n Wind m; (Med) Blähungen pl

wind instrument ['wɪndɪnstrʊmənt] n Blasinstrument nt; **windmill** n Windmühle f

window ['wɪndəʊ] n Fenster nt; (counter) Schalter m; **~ of opportunity** Chance f, Gelegenheit f; **window box** n Blumenkasten m; **windowpane** n Fensterscheibe f; **window-shopping** n: **to go ~** einen Schaufensterbummel machen; **windowsill** n Fensterbrett nt

windpipe ['wɪndpaɪp] n Luftröhre f; **windscreen** n (Brit) Windschutzscheibe f; **windscreen wiper** n (Brit) Scheibenwischer m; **windshield** n (US) Windschutzscheibe f; **windshield wiper** n (US) Scheibenwischer m; **windsurfer** n Windsurfer(in) m(f); (board) Surfbrett nt; **windsurfing** n Windsurfen nt

windy ['wɪndɪ] adj windig

wine [waɪn] n Wein m; **wine bar** n Weinlokal nt; **wineglass** n Weinglas nt; **wine list** n Weinkarte f; **wine tasting** n (event) Weinprobe f

wing [wɪŋ] n Flügel m; (Brit Auto) Kotflügel m; **~s** pl (Theat) Kulissen pl

wink [wɪŋk] vi zwinkern; **to ~ at sb** jdm zuzwinkern

winner ['wɪnə*] n Gewinner(in) m(f); (Sport) Sieger(in) m(f); **winning** adj (team, horse etc) siegreich; **~ number** Gewinnzahl f ▷ n **~s** pl Gewinn m

winter ['wɪntə*] n Winter m; **winter sports** npl Wintersport m; **wint(e)ry** ['wɪntrɪ] adj winterlich

wipe [waɪp] vt abwischen; **to ~ one's nose** sich dat die Nase putzen; **to ~ one's feet** (on mat) sich dat die Schuhe abtreten; **wipe off** vt abwischen; **wipe out** vt (destroy) vernichten; (data, debt) löschen; (epidemic etc) ausrotten

wire ['waɪə*] n Draht m; (Elec) Leitung f; (US: telegram) Telegramm nt ▷ vt (plug in) anschließen; (US Tel) telegrafieren (sb sth jdm etw); **wireless** ['waɪələs] adj drahtlos

wisdom ['wɪzdəm] n Weisheit f; **wisdom tooth** n Weisheitszahn m

wise, wisely [waɪz, -lɪ] adj, adv weise

wish [wɪʃ] n Wunsch m (for nach); **with best ~es** (in letter) herzliche Grüße ▷ vt wünschen, wollen; **to ~ sb good luck/Merry Christmas** jdm viel Glück/frohe Weihnachten wünschen; **I ~ I'd never seen him** ich wünschte, ich hätte ihn nie gesehen

witch [wɪtʃ] n Hexe f

◯ **KEYWORD**

with [wɪð] prep **1** (accompanying, in the company of) mit; **we stayed with friends** wir übernachteten

bei Freunden; **I'll be with you in a minute** einen Augenblick, ich bin sofort da; **I'm not with you** (*I don't understand*) das verstehe ich nicht; **to be with it** (*inf*) (*up-to-date*) auf dem Laufenden sein; (*alert*) (voll) da sein *inf*
2 (*descriptive, indicating manner etc*) mit; **the man with the grey hat** der Mann mit dem grauen Hut; **red with anger** rot vor Wut

withdraw [wɪð'drɔː] *irr vt* zurückziehen; (*money*) abheben; (*comment*) zurücknehmen ▷ *vi* sich zurückziehen

wither ['wɪðə°] *vi* (*plant*) verwelken

withhold [wɪð'həʊld] *irr vt* vorenthalten (*from sb* jdm)

within [wɪð'ɪn] *prep* innerhalb +*gen*; **~ walking distance** zu Fuß erreichbar

without [wɪð'aʊt] *prep* ohne; **~ asking** ohne zu fragen

withstand [wɪð'stænd] *irr vt* standhalten +*dat*

witness ['wɪtnəs] *n* Zeuge *m*, Zeugin *f* ▷ *vt* Zeuge sein; **witness box, witness stand** (*US*) *n* Zeugenstand *m*

witty ['wɪtɪ] *adj* geistreich

wives [waɪvz] *pl of* **wife**

WMD *abbr* = **weapon of mass destruction** Massenvernichtungswaffe

wobble ['wɒbl] *vi* wackeln; **wobbly** *adj* wackelig

wok [wɒk] *n* Wok *m*

woke [wəʊk] *pt of* **wake**

woken ['wəʊkn] *pp of* **wake**

wolf [wʊlf] (*pl* **wolves**) *n* Wolf *m*

woman ['wʊmən] (*pl* **women**) *n* Frau *f*

womb [wuːm] *n* Gebärmutter *f*

women ['wɪmɪn] *pl of* **woman**

won [wʌn] *pt, pp of* **win**

wonder ['wʌndə°] *n* (*marvel*) Wunder *nt*; (*surprise*) Staunen *nt* ▷ *vt, vi* (*speculate*) sich fragen; **I ~ what/if ...** ich frage mich, was/ob ...; **wonderful, wonderfully** *adj, adv* wunderbar

won't [wəʊnt] *contr of* **will not**

wood [wʊd] *n* Holz *nt*; **~s** Wald *m*; **wooden** *adj* Holz-; (*fig*) hölzern; **woodpecker** *n* Specht *m*; **woodwork** *n* (*wooden parts*) Holzteile *pl*; (*in school*) Werken *nt*

wool [wʊl] *n* Wolle *f*; **woollen, woolen** (*US*) *adj* Woll-

word [wɜːd] *n* Wort *nt*; (*promise*) Ehrenwort *nt*; **~s** *pl* (*of song*) Text *m*; **to have a ~ with sb** mit jdm sprechen; **in other ~s** mit anderen Worten ▷ *vt* formulieren; **wording** *n* Wortlaut *m*, Formulierung *f*; **word processing** *n* Textverarbeitung *f*; **word processor** *n* (*program*) Textverarbeitungsprogramm *nt*

wore [wɔː°] *pt of* **wear**

work [wɜːk] *n* Arbeit *f*; (*of art, literature*) Werk *nt*; **~ of art** Kunstwerk *nt*; **he's at ~** er ist in/auf der Arbeit; **out of ~** arbeitslos ▷ *vi* arbeiten (*at, on* an +*dat*); (*machine, plan*) funktionieren; (*medicine*) wirken; (*succeed*) klappen ▷ *vt* (*machine*) bedienen; **work out** *vi* (*plan*) klappen; (*sum*) aufgehen; (*person*) trainieren ▷ *vt* (*price, speed etc*) ausrechnen; (*plan*) ausarbeiten; **work up** *vt*: **to get worked up** sich aufregen; **workaholic** [wɜːkə'hɒlɪk] *n* Arbeitstier *nt*; **worker** *n* Arbeiter(in) *m(f)*; **working class** *n* Arbeiterklasse *f*; **workman** (*pl* **-men**) *n* Handwerker *m*; **workout** *n* (*Sport*) Fitnesstraining *nt*, Konditionstraining *nt*; **work permit** *n* Arbeitserlaubnis *f*;

workplace n Arbeitsplatz m;
workshop n Werkstatt f;
(meeting) Workshop m; **work
station** n (Inform) Workstation
f

world [wɜ:ld] n Welt f; **world
championship** n Weltmeisterschaft f; **World War** n: ~ **I/II, the
First/Second ~** der Erste/Zweite
Weltkrieg; **world-wide** adj, adv
weltweit; **World Wide Web** n
World Wide Web nt

worm [wɜ:m] n Wurm m

worn [wɔ:n] pp of **wear** ▷ adj
(clothes) abgetragen; (tyre)
abgefahren; **worn-out** adj
abgenutzt; (person) erschöpft

worried ['wʌrɪd] adj besorgt; **be
~ about** sich dat Sorgen machen
um; **worry** ['wʌrɪ] n Sorge f ▷ vt
Sorgen machen +dat ▷ vi sich
Sorgen machen (about um); **don't
~!** keine Sorge!; **worrying** adj
beunruhigend

worse [wɜ:s] adj comparative of
bad; schlechter; (pain, mistake etc)
schlimmer ▷ adv comparative of
badly; schlechter; **worsen** vt
verschlechtern ▷ vi sich
verschlechtern

worship ['wɜ:ʃɪp] vt anbeten,
anhimmeln

worst [wɜ:st] adj superlative of
bad; schlechteste(r, s); (pain,
mistake etc) schlimmste(r, s) ▷ adv
superlative of **badly**; am
schlechtesten ▷ n: **the ~ is over**
das Schlimmste ist vorbei; **at (the)
~** schlimmstenfalls

worth [wɜ:θ] n Wert m; **£10 ~ of
food** Essen für 10 Pfund ▷ adj: **it is
~ £50** es ist 50 Pfund wert;
~ seeing sehenswert; **it's ~ it**
(rewarding) es lohnt sich;
worthless adj wertlos;
worthwhile adj lohnend,
lohnenswert; **worthy** ['wɜ:ði]

adj (deserving respect) würdig; **to
be ~ of sth** etw verdienen

KEYWORD

would [wʊd] vb aux **1** (conditional
tense) **if you asked him he would
do it** wenn du ihn fragtest/Sie ihn
fragten, würde er es tun; **if you
had asked him he would have
done it** wenn du ihn gefragt
hättest/Sie ihn gefragt hätten,
hätte er es getan
2 (in offers, invitations, requests)
would you like a biscuit?
möchtest du/möchten Sie einen
Keks?; **would you ask him to
come in?** würdest du/würden Sie
ihn bitte hereinbitten?
3 (in indirect speech) **I said I would
do it** ich sagte, ich würde es tun
4 (emphatic) **it WOULD have to
snow today!** es musste ja
ausgerechnet heute schneien!
5 (insistence) **she wouldn't behave**
sie wollte sich partout nicht
anständig benehmen
6 (conjecture) **it would have been
midnight** es mag ungefähr
Mitternacht gewesen sein; **it
would seem so** es sieht wohl so
aus
7 (indicating habit) **he would go
there on Mondays** er ging jeden
Montag dorthin

wouldn't ['wʊdnt] contr of
would not
would've ['wʊdəv] contr of
would have
wound [wu:nd] n Wunde f ▷ vt
verwunden; (fig) verletzen
▷ [waʊnd] pt, pp of **wind**
wove [wəʊv] pt of **weave**
woven ['wəʊvn] pp of **weave**
wrap [ræp] vt (parcel, present)
einwickeln; **to ~ sth round sth**

etw um etw wickeln; **wrap up** *vt* (*parcel, present*) einwickeln ▷ *vi* (*dress warmly*) sich warm anziehen; **wrapper** *n* (*of sweet*) Papier *nt*; **wrapping paper** *n* Packpapier *nt*; (*giftwrap*) Geschenkpapier *nt*

wreath [riːθ] *n* Kranz *m*

wreck [rek] *n* (*ship, plane, car*) Wrack *nt*; **a nervous ~** ein Nervenbündel *m* ▷ *vt* (*car*) zu Schrott fahren; (*fig*) zerstören; **wreckage** ['rekɪdʒ] *n* Trümmer *pl*

wrench [rentʃ] *n* (*tool*) Schraubenschlüssel *m*

wrestling ['reslɪŋ] *n* Ringen *nt*

wring out ['rɪŋ'aʊt] (**wrung, wrung**) *vt* auswringen

wrinkle ['rɪŋkl] *n* Falte *f*

wrist [rɪst] *n* Handgelenk *nt*; **wristwatch** *n* Armbanduhr *f*

write [raɪt] (**wrote, written**) *vt* schreiben; (*cheque*) ausstellen ▷ *vi* schreiben; **to ~ to sb** jdm schreiben; **write down** *vt* aufschreiben; **write off** *vt* (*debt, person*) abschreiben; (*car*) zu Schrott fahren ▷ *vi*: **to ~ off for sth** etw anfordern; **write out** *vt* (*name etc*) ausschreiben; (*cheque*) ausstellen; **write-protected** *adj* (*Inform*) schreibgeschützt; **writer** *n* Verfasser(in) *m(f)*; (*author*) Schriftsteller(in) *m(f)*; **writing** *n* Schrift *f*; (*profession*) Schreiben *nt*; **in ~** schriftlich; **writing paper** *n* Schreibpapier *nt*

written ['rɪtən] *pp of* **write**

wrong [rɒŋ] *adj* (*incorrect*) falsch; (*morally*) unrecht; **you're ~** du hast/Sie haben unrecht; **what's ~ with your leg?** was ist mit deinem/Ihrem Bein los?; **you've got the ~ number** du bist/Sie sind falsch verbunden; **I dialled the ~ number** ich habe mich verwählt; **don't get me ~** versteh/verstehen Sie mich

nicht falsch; **to go ~** (*plan*) schiefgehen; **wrongly** *adv* falsch; (*unjustly*) zu Unrecht

wrote [rəʊt] *pt of* **write**

WWW *abbr* = **World Wide Web** WWW

xenophobia [zenə'fəʊbɪə] *n*
Ausländerfeindlichkeit *f*
XL *abbr* = **extra large** XL, übergroß
Xmas ['krɪsməs] *n* Weihnachten
nt
X-ray ['eksreɪ] *n* (*picture*)
Röntgenaufnahme *f* ▷ *vt* röntgen
xylophone ['zaɪləfəʊn] *n* Xylo

yacht [jɒt] *n* Jacht *f*; **yachting** *n*
Segeln *nt*; **to go ~** segeln gehen
yam [jæm] *n* (*US*) Süßkartoffel
f
yard [jɑːd] *n* Hof *m*; (*US: garden*)
Garten *m*; (*measure*) Yard *nt* (0,91 m)
yawn [jɔːn] *vi* gähnen
yd *abbr* = **yard(s)**
year ['jɪə*] *n* Jahr *nt*; **this/last/
next ~** dieses/letztes/nächstes
Jahr; **he is 28 ~s old** er ist 28 Jahre
alt; **~s ago** vor Jahren; **a
five-year-old** ein(e)
Fünfjährige(r); **yearly** *adj, adv*
jährlich
yearn [jɜːn] *vi* sich sehnen (*for*
nach +*dat*); **to ~ to do sth** sich
danach sehnen, etw zu tun
yeast [jiːst] *n* Hefe *f*
yell [jel] *vi, vt* schreien; **to ~ at sb**
jdn anschreien
yellow ['jeləʊ] *adj* gelb; **~ card**

(*Sport*) gelbe Karte; **~ fever** Gelbfieber *nt*; **~ line** (*Brit*) ≈ Halteverbot *nt*; **double ~ line** (*Brit*) ≈ absolutes Halteverbot; **the Yellow Pages®** *pl* die Gelben Seiten *pl*

yes [jes] *adv* ja; (*answering negative question*) doch; **to say ~ to sth** ja zu etw sagen ⊳ *n* Ja *nt*

yesterday ['jestədeɪ] *adv* gestern; **~ morning/evening** gestern Morgen/Abend; **the day before ~** vorgestern; **~'s newspaper** die Zeitung von gestern

yet [jet] *adv* (*still*) noch; (*up to now*) bis jetzt; (*in a question: already*) schon; **he hasn't arrived ~** er ist noch nicht gekommen; **have you finished ~?** bist du/sind Sie schon fertig?; **~ again** schon wieder; **as ~** bis jetzt ⊳ *conj* doch

yield [jiːld] *n* Ertrag *m* ⊳ *vt* (*result, crop*) hervorbringen; (*profit, interest*) bringen ⊳ *vi* nachgeben (*to +dat*); (*Mil*) sich ergeben (*to +dat*); **"~"** (*US Auto*) „Vorfahrt beachten"

yoga ['jəʊgə] *n* Yoga *nt*

yog(h)urt [jɒgət] *n* Jog(h)urt *m*

yolk [jəʊk] *n* Eigelb *nt*

Yorkshire pudding ['jɔːkʃə'pʊdɪŋ] *n* gebackener Eierteig, der meist zum Roastbeef gegessen wird

 KEYWORD

you [juː] *pron* **1** (*subj, in comparisons*) (*familiar form*) (*sg*) du; (*pl*) ihr; (*in letters*) Du, Ihr; (*polite form*) Sie; **you Germans** ihr Deutschen; **she's younger than you** sie ist jünger als du/ihr/Sie

2 (*direct object, after prep +akk*) (*familiar form*) (*sg*) dich; (*pl*) euch; (*in letters*) Dich, Euch; (*polite form*)

Sie; **I know you** ich kenne dich/euch/Sie

3 (*indirect object, after prep +dat*) (*familiar form*) (*sg*) dir; (*pl*) euch; (*in letters*) Dir, Euch; (*polite form*) Ihnen; **I gave it to you** ich gab es dir/euch/Ihnen

4 (*impers*) (*one*) (*subj*) man; (*direct object*) einen; (*indirect object*) einem; **fresh air does you good** frische Luft tut (einem) gut

you'd [juːd] *contr of* **you had; you would**; **~ better leave** du solltest/Sie sollten gehen

you'll [juːl] *contr of* **you will; you shall**

young [jʌŋ] *adj* jung ⊳ *n* **the ~** *pl* (*~ people*) die jungen Leute *pl*; (*animals*) die Jungen *pl*; **youngster** ['jʌŋstə*] *n* Jugendliche(r) *mf*

your ['jɔː*] *adj sing* dein; *polite form* Ihr; *pl* euer; *polite form* Ihr; **have you hurt ~ leg?** hast du dir/haben Sie sich das Bein verletzt?

you're ['jʊə*] *contr of* **you are**

yours ['jɔːz] *pron sing* deine(r, s); *polite form* Ihre(r, s); *pl* eure(r, s); *polite form* Ihre(r, s); **is this ~?** gehört das dir/Ihnen?; **a friend of ~** ein Freund von dir/Ihnen

yourself [jɔː'self] *pron sing* dich; *polite form* sich; **have you hurt ~?** hast du dich/haben Sie sich verletzt?; **did you do it ~?** hast du/haben Sie es selbst gemacht?; **(all) by ~** allein; **yourselves** *pron pl* euch; *polite form* sich; **have you hurt ~?** habt ihr euch/haben Sie sich verletzt?; **did you do it ~?** habt ihr/haben Sie es selbst gemacht?; **(all) by ~** allein

youth [juːθ] *n* (*period*) Jugend *f*; (*young man*) junger Mann; (*young people*) Jugend *f*; **youth group** *n*

Jugendgruppe f; **youth hostel** n
Jugendherberge f
you've [juːv] contr of **you have**
yucky ['jʌkɪ] adj (fam) eklig
yummy ['jʌmɪ] adj (fam) lecker
yuppie, **yuppy** ['jʌpɪ] n Yuppie
m

Z

zap [zæp] vt (Inform) löschen; (in
computer game) abknallen ▷ vi (TV)
zappen; **zapper** n (TV)
Fernbedienung f; **zapping** n (TV)
ständiges Umschalten, Zapping nt
zebra ['zebrə, ?? 'ziːbrə] (US) n
Zebra nt; **zebra crossing** n (Brit)
Zebrastreifen m
zero [zɪərəʊ] (pl -es) n Null f; **10
degrees below ~** 10 Grad unter
null
zest [zest] n (enthusiasm)
Begeisterung f
zigzag ['zɪgzæg] n Zickzack m
▷ vi (person, vehicle) im Zickzack
gehen/fahren; (path) im Zickzack
verlaufen
zinc [zɪŋk] n Zink nt
zip [zɪp] n (Brit) Reißverschluss m
▷ vt: **to ~ (up)** den Reißverschluss
zumachen; (Inform) zippen; **zip
code** n (US) Postleitzahl f; **Zip
disk®** n (Inform) ZIP-Diskette® f;

Zip drive® n (Inform)
ZIP-Laufwerk® nt; **Zip file®** n
(Inform) ZIP-Datei® f; **zipper** n
(US) Reißverschluss m

zit [zɪt] n (fam) Pickel m

zodiac ['zəʊdɪæk] n Tierkreis m;
sign of the ~ Tierkreiszeichen
nt

zone [zəʊn] n Zone f; (area)
Gebiet nt; (in town) Bezirk m

zoo [zuː] n Zoo m

zoom [zuːm] vi (move fast)
brausen, sausen ▷ n: ~ (**lens**)
Zoomobjektiv nt; **zoom in** vi
(Foto) heranzoomen (on an +akk)

zucchini [zuːˈkiːnɪ] (pl -(**s**)) n
(US) Zucchini f

VERB TABLES

Introduction

The **Verb Tables** in the following section contain 31 tables of German verbs in alphabetical order. Each table shows you the following forms: **Present**, **Perfect**, **Future**, **Subjunctive**, **Imperfect**, **Conditional**, **Imperative** and the **Present** and **Past Participles**.

In order to help you use the verbs shown in the Verb Tables correctly, there are also a number of example phrases at the bottom of each page to show the verb as it is used in context.

In German there are **regular** verbs or **weak** verbs (their forms follow the normal rules) and **irregular** or **strong** verbs (their forms do not follow the normal rules) and **mixed** verbs (their forms have features of both **weak** and **strong** verbs).

The **Verb Tables** given show one **weak** verb – machen, Verb Table 19 and three **mixed** verbs – bringen, Verb Table 2; denken, Verb Table 3 and kennen Verb Table 13. The rest of the verbs shown are **strong** verbs.

▶ **bleiben** (to remain)

PRESENT

ich	bleibe
du	bleibst
er	bleibt
wir	bleiben
ihr	bleibt
sie	bleiben

PRESENT SUBJUNCTIVE

ich	bleibe
du	bleibest
er	bleibe
wir	bleiben
ihr	bleibet
sie	bleiben

PERFECT

ich	bin geblieben
du	bist geblieben
er	ist geblieben
wir	sind geblieben
ihr	seid geblieben
sie	sind geblieben

IMPERFECT

ich	blieb
du	bliebst
er	blieb
wir	blieben
ihr	bliebt
sie	blieben

FUTURE

ich	werde bleiben
du	wirst bleiben
er	wird bleiben
wir	werden bleiben
ihr	werdet bleiben
sie	werden bleiben

CONDITIONAL

ich	würde bleiben
du	würdest bleiben
er	würde bleiben
wir	würden bleiben
ihr	würdet bleiben
sie	würden bleiben

IMPERATIVE

bleib(e)!/bleiben wir!/bleibt!
bleiben Sie!

PAST PARTICIPLE

geblieben

PRESENT PARTICIPLE

bleibend

EXAMPLE PHRASES

*Hoffentlich **bleibt** das Wetter schön.* I hope the weather will stay fine.
*Vom Kuchen **ist** nur noch ein Stück **geblieben**.* There's only one piece of cake left.
*Dieses Erlebnis **blieb** in meiner Erinnerung.* This experience stayed with me.

---

ich = I **du** = you **er** = he **wir** = we/one **ihr** = you **sie** = they

▶ bringen (to bring)

PRESENT

ich	bringe
du	bringst
er	bringt
wir	bringen
ihr	bringt
sie	bringen

PRESENT SUBJUNCTIVE

ich	bringe
du	bringest
er	bringe
wir	bringen
ihr	bringet
sie	bringen

PERFECT

ich	habe gebracht
du	hast gebracht
er	hat gebracht
wir	haben gebracht
ihr	habt gebracht
sie	haben gebracht

IMPERFECT

ich	brachte
du	brachtest
er	brachte
wir	brachten
ihr	brachtet
sie	brachten

FUTURE

ich	werde bringen
du	wirst bringen
er	wird bringen
wir	werden bringen
ihr	werdet bringen
sie	werden bringen

CONDITIONAL

ich	würde bringen
du	würdest bringen
er	würde bringen
wir	würden bringen
ihr	würdet bringen
sie	würden bringen

IMPERATIVE

bring(e)!/bringen wir!/bringt!
bringen Sie!

PAST PARTICIPLE

gebracht

PRESENT PARTICIPLE

bringend

EXAMPLE PHRASES

*Kannst du mich zum Flughafen **bringen**?* Can you take me to the airport?
*Max **hat** mir Blumen **gebracht**.* Max brought me flowers.
*Das **brachte** mich auf eine Idee.* It gave me an idea.

ich = I **du** = you **er** = he **wir** = we/one **ihr** = you **sie** = they

▶ denken (to think)

PRESENT

ich	denke
du	denkst
er	denkt
wir	denken
ihr	denkt
sie	denken

PRESENT SUBJUNCTIVE

ich	denke
du	denkest
er	denke
wir	denken
ihr	denket
sie	denken

PERFECT

ich	habe gedacht
du	hast gedacht
er	hat gedacht
wir	haben gedacht
ihr	habt gedacht
sie	haben gedacht

IMPERFECT

ich	dachte
du	dachtest
er	dachte
wir	dachten
ihr	dachtet
sie	dachten

FUTURE

ich	werde denken
du	wirst denken
er	wird denken
wir	werden denken
ihr	werdet denken
sie	werden denken

CONDITIONAL

ich	würde denken
du	würdest denken
er	würde denken
wir	würden denken
ihr	würdet denken
sie	würden denken

IMPERATIVE

denk(e)!/denken wir!/denkt!
denken Sie!

PAST PARTICIPLE

gedacht

PRESENT PARTICIPLE

denkend

EXAMPLE PHRASES

*Wie **denken** Sie darüber?* What do you think about it?
*Das war für ihn **gedacht**.* It was meant for him.
*Es war das Erste, woran ich **dachte**.* It was the first thing I thought of.

ich = I **du** = you **er** = he **wir** = we/one **ihr** = you **sie** = they

▶ dürfen (to be allowed to)

PRESENT		PRESENT SUBJUNCTIVE	
ich	darf	ich	dürfe
du	darfst	du	dürfest
er	darf	er	dürfe
wir	dürfen	wir	dürfen
ihr	dürft	ihr	dürfet
sie	dürfen	sie	dürfen

PERFECT		IMPERFECT	
ich	habe gedurft/dürfen	ich	durfte
du	hast gedurft/dürfen	du	durftest
er	hat gedurft/dürfen	er	durfte
wir	haben gedurft/dürfen	wir	durften
ihr	habt gedurft/dürfen	ihr	durftet
sie	haben gedurft/dürfen	sie	durften

FUTURE		CONDITIONAL	
ich	werde dürfen	ich	würde dürfen
du	wirst dürfen	du	würdest dürfen
er	wird dürfen	er	würde dürfen
wir	werden dürfen	wir	würden dürfen
ihr	werdet dürfen	ihr	würdet dürfen
sie	werden dürfen	sie	würden dürfen

IMPERATIVE

PAST PARTICIPLE

gedurft/dürfen*

PRESENT PARTICIPLE

dürfend

The second form is used when combined with an infinitive construction.

EXAMPLE PHRASES

Darf ich ins Kino? Can I go to the cinema?
Das *würde* ich zu Hause nicht dürfen. I wouldn't be allowed to do that at home.
Das *dürfen* Sie mir glauben. You can take my word for it.

ich = I **du** = you **er** = he **wir** = we/one **ihr** = you **sie** = they

▶ **fahren** (to drive/to go)

PRESENT

ich	fahre
du	fährst
er	fährt
wir	fahren
ihr	fahrt
sie	fahren

PRESENT SUBJUNCTIVE

ich	fahre
du	fahrest
er	fahre
wir	fahren
ihr	fahret
sie	fahren

PERFECT

ich	bin gefahren*
du	bist gefahren
er	ist gefahren
wir	sind gefahren
ihr	seid gefahren
sie	sind gefahren

IMPERFECT

ich	fuhr
du	fuhrst
er	fuhr
wir	fuhren
ihr	fuhrt
sie	fuhren

FUTURE

ich	werde fahren
du	wirst fahren
er	wird fahren
wir	werden fahren
ihr	werdet fahren
sie	werden fahren

CONDITIONAL

ich	würde fahren
du	würdest fahren
er	würde fahren
wir	würden fahren
ihr	würdet fahren
sie	würden fahren

IIMPERATIVE

fahr(e)!/fahren wir!/fahrt!
fahren Sie!
OR: ich habe/hätte gefahren
etc (*when transitive*).

PAST PARTICIPLE

gefahren

PRESENT PARTICIPLE

fahrend

EXAMPLE PHRASES

*Sie **fahren** mit dem Bus in die Schule.* They go to school by bus.
*Rechts **fahren**!* Drive on the right!
*Ich **bin** mit der Familie nach Spanien **gefahren**.* I went to Spain with my family.

---

ich = I   **du** = you   **er** = he   **wir** = we/one   **ihr** = you   **sie** = they

▶ fallen (to fall)

PRESENT

ich	falle
du	fällst
er	fällt
wir	fallen
ihr	fallt
sie	fallen

PRESENT SUBJUNCTIVE

ich	falle
du	fallest
er	falle
wir	fallen
ihr	fallet
sie	fallen

PERFECT

ich	bin gefallen
du	bist gefallen
er	ist gefallen
wir	sind gefallen
ihr	seid gefallen
sie	sind gefallen

IMPERFECT

ich	fiel
du	fielst
er	fiel
wir	fielen
ihr	fielt
sie	fielen

FUTURE

ich	werde fallen
du	wirst fallen
er	wird fallen
wir	werden fallen
ihr	werdet fallen
sie	werden fallen

CONDITIONAL

ich	würde fallen
du	würdest fallen
er	würde fallen
wir	würden fallen
ihr	würdet fallen
sie	würden fallen

IMPERATIVE

fall(e)!/fallen wir!/fallt!
fallen Sie!

PAST PARTICIPLE

gefallen

PRESENT PARTICIPLE

fallend

EXAMPLE PHRASES

*Er **fiel** vom Fahrrad.* He fell off his bike.
*Ich **bin** durch die Prüfung **gefallen**.* I failed my exam.
*Die Aktien **fielen** im Kurs.* Share prices went down.

---

ich = I **du** = you **er** = he **wir** = we/one **ihr** = you **sie** = they

▶ finden (to find)

PRESENT

ich	finde
du	findest
er	findet
wir	finden
ihr	findet
sie	finden

PRESENT SUBJUNCTIVE

ich	finde
du	findest
er	finde
wir	finden
ihr	findet
sie	finden

PERFECT

ich	habe gefunden
du	hast gefunden
er	hat gefunden
wir	haben gefunden
ihr	habt gefunden
sie	haben gefunden

IMPERFECT

ich	fand
du	fand(e)st
er	fand
wir	fanden
ihr	fandet
sie	fanden

FUTURE

ich	werde finden
du	wirst finden
er	wird finden
wir	werden finden
ihr	werdet finden
sie	werden finden

CONDITIONAL

ich	würde finden
du	würdest finden
er	würde finden
wir	würden finden
ihr	würdet finden
sie	würden finden

IMPERATIVE

find(e)!/finden wir!/findet!
finden Sie!

PAST PARTICIPLE

gefunden

PRESENT PARTICIPLE

findend

EXAMPLE PHRASES

Hast du deine Brieftasche **gefunden?** Have you found your wallet?
Er **fand** den Mut, sie zu fragen. He found the courage to ask her.
Ich **finde**, sie ist eine gute Lehrerin. I think she's a good teacher.

---

ich = I **du** = you **er** = he **wir** = we/one **ihr** = you **sie** = they

▶ geben (to give)

PRESENT

ich	gebe
du	gibst
er	gibt
wir	geben
ihr	gebt
sie	geben

PRESENT SUBJUNCTIVE

ich	gebe
du	gebest
er	gebe
wir	geben
ihr	gebet
sie	geben

PERFECT

ich	habe gegeben
du	hast gegeben
er	hat gegeben
wir	haben gegeben
ihr	habt gegeben
sie	haben gegeben

IMPERFECT

ich	gab
du	gabst
er	gab
wir	gaben
ihr	gabt
sie	gaben

FUTURE

ich	werde geben
du	wirst geben
er	wird geben
wir	werden geben
ihr	werdet geben
sie	werden geben

CONDITIONAL

ich	würde geben
du	würdest geben
er	würde geben
wir	würden geben
ihr	würdet geben
sie	würden geben

IMPERATIVE

gib!/geben wir!/gebt!
geben Sie!

PAST PARTICIPLE

gegeben

PRESENT PARTICIPLE

gebend

EXAMPLE PHRASES

*Er **gab** mir das Geld für die Bücher.* He gave me the money for the books.
*Was **gibt** es im Kino?* What's on at the cinema?
*Wir **würden** alles darum **geben**, ins Finale zu kommen.* We would give anything
  to reach the finals.

ich = I **du** = you **er** = he **wir** = we/one **ihr** = you **sie** = they

▶ gehen (to go)

PRESENT

ich	gehe
du	gehst
er	geht
wir	gehen
ihr	geht
sie	gehen

PRESENT SUBJUNCTIVE

ich	gehe
du	gehest
er	gehe
wir	gehen
ihr	gehet
sie	gehen

PERFECT

ich	bin gegangen
du	bist gegangen
er	ist gegangen
wir	sind gegangen
ihr	seid gegangen
sie	sind gegangen

IMPERFECT

ich	ging
du	gingst
er	ging
wir	gingen
ihr	gingt
sie	gingen

FUTURE

ich	werde gehen
du	wirst gehen
er	wird gehen
wir	werden gehen
ihr	werdet gehen
sie	werden gehen

CONDITIONAL

ich	würde gehen
du	würdest gehen
er	würde gehen
wir	würden gehen
ihr	würdet gehen
sie	würden gehen

IMPERATIVE

geh(e)!/gehen wir!/geht!
gehen Sie!

PAST PARTICIPLE

gegangen

PRESENT PARTICIPLE

gehend

EXAMPLE PHRASES

*Die Kinder **gingen** ins Haus.* The children went into the house.
*Wie **geht** es dir?* How are you?
*Wir **sind** gestern schwimmen **gegangen**.* We went swimming yesterday.

---

ich = I **du** = you **er** = he **wir** = we/one **ihr** = you **sie** = they

▶ **haben** (to have)

PRESENT

ich	habe
du	hast
er	hat
wir	haben
ihr	habt
sie	haben

PRESENT SUBJUNCTIVE

ich	habe
du	habest
er	habe
wir	haben
ihr	habet
sie	haben

PERFECT

ich	habe gehabt
du	hast gehabt
er	hat gehabt
wir	haben gehabt
ihr	habt gehabt
sie	haben gehabt

IMPERFECT

ich	hatte
du	hattest
er	hatte
wir	hatten
ihr	hattet
sie	hatten

FUTURE

ich	werde haben
du	wirst haben
er	wird haben
wir	werden haben
ihr	werdet haben
sie	werden haben

CONDITIONAL

ich	würde haben
du	würdest haben
er	würde haben
wir	würden haben
ihr	würdet haben
sie	würden haben

IMPERATIVE

hab(e)!/haben wir!/habt!
haben Sie!

PAST PARTICIPLE

gehabt

PRESENT PARTICIPLE

habend

EXAMPLE PHRASES

Hast du eine Schwester? Have you got a sister?
Er hatte Hunger. He was hungry.
Ich hätte gern ein Eis. I'd like an ice cream.
Sie hat heute Geburtstag. It's her birthday today.

ich = I **du** = you **er** = he **wir** = we/one **ihr** = you **sie** = they

▶ halten (to hold)

PRESENT		PRESENT SUBJUNCTIVE	
ich	halte	ich	halte
du	hältst	du	haltest
er	hält	er	halte
wir	halten	wir	halten
ihr	haltet	ihr	haltet
sie	halten	sie	halten

PERFECT		IMPERFECT	
ich	habe gehalten	ich	hielt
du	hast gehalten	du	hielt(e)st
er	hat gehalten	er	hielt
wir	haben gehalten	wir	hielten
ihr	habt gehalten	ihr	hieltet
sie	haben gehalten	sie	hielten

FUTURE		CONDITIONAL	
ich	werde halten	ich	würde halten
du	wirst halten	du	würdest halten
er	wird halten	er	würde halten
wir	werden halten	wir	würden halten
ihr	werdet halten	ihr	würdet halten
sie	werden halten	sie	würden halten

IMPERATIVE

halt(e)!/halten wir!/haltet!
halten Sie!

PAST PARTICIPLE

gehalten

PRESENT PARTICIPLE

haltend

EXAMPLE PHRASES

*Kannst du das mal **halten**?* Can you hold that for a moment?
*Der Bus **hielt** vor dem Rathaus.* The bus stopped in front of the town hall.
*Ich **habe** sie für deine Mutter **gehalten**.* I took her for your mother.

---

ich = I   **du** = you   **er** = he   **wir** = we/one   **ihr** = you   **sie** = they

▶ **helfen** (to help)

PRESENT

ich	helfe
du	hilfst
er	hilft
wir	helfen
ihr	helft
sie	helfen

PRESENT SUBJUNCTIVE

ich	helfe
du	helfest
er	helfe
wir	helfen
ihr	helfet
sie	helfen

PERFECT

ich	habe geholfen
du	hast geholfen
er	hat geholfen
wir	haben geholfen
ihr	habt geholfen
sie	haben geholfen

IMPERFECT

ich	half
du	halfst
er	half
wir	halfen
ihr	halft
sie	halfen

FUTURE

ich	werde helfen
du	wirst helfen
er	wird helfen
wir	werden helfen
ihr	werdet helfen
sie	werden helfen

CONDITIONAL

ich	würde helfen
du	würdest helfen
er	würde helfen
wir	würden helfen
ihr	würdet helfen
sie	würden helfen

IMPERATIVE

hilf!/helfen wir!/helft!
helfen Sie!

PAST PARTICIPLE

geholfen

PRESENT PARTICIPLE

helfend

EXAMPLE PHRASES

*Er **hat** mir dabei **geholfen**.* He helped me with it.
*Diese Arznei **hilft** gegen Kopfschmerzen.* This medicine is good for headaches.
*Sein Vorschlag **half** mir wenig.* His suggestion was not much help to me.

ich = I **du** = you **er** = he **wir** = we/one **ihr** = you **sie** = they

▶ **kennen** (to know) *(be acquainted with)*

PRESENT

ich	kenne
du	kennst
er	kennt
wir	kennen
ihr	kennt
sie	kennen

PRESENT SUBJUNCTIVE

ich	kenne
du	kennest
er	kenne
wir	kennen
ihr	kennet
sie	kennen

PERFECT

ich	habe gekannt
du	hast gekannt
er	hat gekannt
wir	haben gekannt
ihr	habt gekannt
sie	haben gekannt

IMPERFECT

ich	kannte
du	kanntest
er	kannte
wir	kannten
ihr	kanntet
sie	kannten

FUTURE

ich	werde kennen
du	wirst kennen
er	wird kennen
wir	werden kennen
ihr	werdet kennen
sie	werden kennen

CONDITIONAL

ich	würde kennen
du	würdest kennen
er	würde kennen
wir	würden kennen
ihr	würdet kennen
sie	würden kennen

IMPERATIVE

kenn(e)!/kennen wir!/kennt!
kennen Sie!

PAST PARTICIPLE

gekannt

PRESENT PARTICIPLE

kennend

EXAMPLE PHRASES

*Ich **kenne** ihn nicht.* I don't know him.
*Er **kannte** kein Erbarmen.* He knew no mercy.
***Kennst** du mich noch?* Do you remember me?

---

ich = I **du** = you **er** = he **wir** = we/one **ihr** = you **sie** = they

▶ **kommen** (to come)

PRESENT

ich	komme
du	kommst
er	kommt
wir	kommen
ihr	kommt
sie	kommen

PRESENT SUBJUNCTIVE

ich	komme
du	kommest
er	komme
wir	kommen
ihr	kommet
sie	kommen

PERFECT

ich	bin gekommen
du	bist gekommen
er	ist gekommen
wir	sind gekommen
ihr	seid gekommen
sie	sind gekommen

IMPERFECT

ich	kam
du	kamst
er	kam
wir	kamen
ihr	kamt
sie	kamen

FUTURE

ich	werde kommen
du	wirst kommen
er	wird kommen
wir	werden kommen
ihr	werdet kommen
sie	werden kommen

CONDITIONAL

ich	würde kommen
du	würdest kommen
er	würde kommen
wir	würden kommen
ihr	würdet kommen
sie	würden kommen

IMPERATIVE

komm(e)!/kommen wir!
kommt!/kommen Sie!

PAST PARTICIPLE

gekommen

PRESENT PARTICIPLE

kommend

EXAMPLE PHRASES

*Er **kam** die Straße entlang.* He was coming along the street.
*Ich **komme** zu deiner Party.* I'm coming to your party.
*Woher **kommst** du?* Where do you come from?

ich = I **du** = you **er** = he **wir** = we/one **ihr** = you **sie** = they

▶ **können** (to be able to)

PRESENT

ich	kann
du	kannst
er	kann
wir	können
ihr	könnt
sie	können

PRESENT SUBJUNCTIVE

ich	könne
du	könnest
er	könne
wir	können
ihr	könnet
sie	können

PERFECT

ich	habe gekonnt/können
du	hast gekonnt/können
er	hat gekonnt/können
wir	haben gekonnt/können
ihr	habt gekonnt/können
sie	haben gekonnt/können

IMPERFECT

ich	konnte
du	konntest
er	konnte
wir	konnten
ihr	konntet
sie	konnten

FUTURE

ich	werde können
du	wirst können
er	wird können
wir	werden können
ihr	werdet können
sie	werden können

CONDITIONAL

ich	würde können
du	würdest können
er	würde können
wir	würden können
ihr	würdet können
sie	würden können

IMPERATIVE

PAST PARTICIPLE

gekonnt/können*

PRESENT PARTICIPLE

könnend

The second form is used when combined with an infinitive construction.

EXAMPLE PHRASES

*Er **kann** gut schwimmen.* He can swim well.
*Sie **konnte** kein Wort Deutsch.* She couldn't speak a word of German.
***Kann** ich gehen?* Can I go?

---

ich = I **du** = you **er** = he **wir** = we/one **ihr** = you **sie** = they

▶ **lassen** (to leave; to allow)

PRESENT

ich	lasse
du	lässt
er	lässt
wir	lassen
ihr	lasst
sie	lassen

PRESENT SUBJUNCTIVE

ich	lasse
du	lassest
er	lasse
wir	lassen
ihr	lasset
sie	lassen

PERFECT

ich	habe gelassen
du	hast gelassen
er	hat gelassen
wir	haben gelassen
ihr	habt gelassen
sie	haben gelassen

IMPERFECT

ich	ließ
du	ließest
er	ließ
wir	ließen
ihr	ließt
sie	ließen

FUTURE

ich	werde lassen
du	wirst lassen
er	wird lassen
wir	werden lassen
ihr	werdet lassen
sie	werden lassen

CONDITIONAL

ich	würde lassen
du	würdest lassen
er	würde lassen
wir	würden lassen
ihr	würdet lassen
sie	würden lassen

IMPERATIVE

lass!/lassen wir!/lasst!
lassen Sie!

PAST PARTICIPLE

gelassen/lassen*

PRESENT PARTICIPLE

lassend

The second form is used when combined with an infinitive construction.

EXAMPLE PHRASES

*Sie **ließ** uns warten.* She kept us waiting.
*Ich **lasse** den Hund nicht auf das Sofa.* I won't let the dog get up on the sofa.
*Sie **haben** ihn allein im Auto **gelassen**.* They left him alone in the car.

ich = I **du** = you **er** = he **wir** = we/one **ihr** = you **sie** = they

▶ laufen (to run)

PRESENT

ich	laufe
du	läufst
er	läuft
wir	laufen
ihr	lauft
sie	laufen

PRESENT SUBJUNCTIVE

ich	laufe
du	laufest
er	laufe
wir	laufen
ihr	laufet
sie	laufen

PERFECT

ich	bin gelaufen
du	bist gelaufen
er	ist gelaufen
wir	sind gelaufen
ihr	seid gelaufen
sie	sind gelaufen

IMPERFECT

ich	lief
du	liefst
er	lief
wir	liefen
ihr	lieft
sie	liefen

FUTURE

ich	werde laufen
du	wirst laufen
er	wird laufen
wir	werden laufen
ihr	werdet laufen
sie	werden laufen

CONDITIONAL

ich	würde laufen
du	würdest laufen
er	würde laufen
wir	würden laufen
ihr	würdet laufen
sie	würden laufen

IIMPERATIVE

lauf(e)!/laufen wir!/lauft!
laufen Sie!

PAST PARTICIPLE

gelaufen

PRESENT PARTICIPLE

laufend

EXAMPLE PHRASES

*Er **lief** so schnell er konnte.* He ran as fast as he could.
*Sie **läuft** ständig zur Polizei.* She's always going to the police.
*Das Schiff **ist** auf Grund **gelaufen**.* The ship ran aground.

---

ich = I **du** = you **er** = he **wir** = we/one **ihr** = you **sie** = they

▶ liegen (to lie)

PRESENT

ich	liege
du	liegst
er	liegt
wir	liegen
ihr	liegt
sie	liegen

PRESENT SUBJUNCTIVE

ich	liege
du	liegest
er	liege
wir	liegen
ihr	lieget
sie	liegen

PERFECT

ich	habe gelegen
du	hast gelegen
er	hat gelegen
wir	haben gelegen
ihr	habt gelegen
sie	haben gelegen

IMPERFECT

ich	lag
du	lagst
er	lag
wir	lagen
ihr	lagt
sie	lagen

FUTURE

ich	werde liegen
du	wirst liegen
er	wird liegen
wir	werden liegen
ihr	werdet liegen
sie	werden liegen

CONDITIONAL

ich	würde liegen
du	würdest liegen
er	würde liegen
wir	würden liegen
ihr	würdet liegen
sie	würden liegen

IMPERATIVE

lieg(e)!/liegen wir!/liegt!
liegen Sie!

PAST PARTICIPLE

gelegen

PRESENT PARTICIPLE

liegend

EXAMPLE PHRASES

Wir lagen den ganzen Tag am Strand. We lay on the beach all day.
Köln liegt am Rhein. Cologne is on the Rhine.
Es hat daran gelegen, dass ich krank war. It was because I was ill.

ich = I **du** = you **er** = he **wir** = we/one **ihr** = you **sie** = they

▶ **machen** (to do *or* to make)

PRESENT

ich	mache
du	machst
er	macht
wir	machen
ihr	macht
sie	machen

PRESENT SUBJUNCTIVE

ich	mache
du	machest
er	mache
wir	machen
ihr	machet
sie	machen

PERFECT

ich	habe gemacht
du	hast gemacht
er	hat gemacht
wir	haben gemacht
ihr	habt gemacht
sie	haben gemacht

IMPERFECT

ich	machte
du	machtest
er	machte
wir	machten
ihr	machtet
sie	machten

FUTURE

ich	werde machen
du	wirst machen
er	wird machen
wir	werden machen
ihr	werdet machen
sie	werden machen

CONDITIONAL

ich	würde machen
du	würdest machen
er	würde machen
wir	würden machen
ihr	würdet machen
sie	würden machen

IMPERATIVE

mach!/macht!/machen Sie!

PAST PARTICIPLE

gemacht

PRESENT PARTICIPLE

machend

EXAMPLE PHRASES

*Was **machst** du?* What are you doing?
*Ich **habe** die Betten **gemacht**.* I made the beds.
*Ich **werde** es morgen **machen**.* I'll do it tomorrow.

---

ich = I **du** = you **er** = he **wir** = we/one **ihr** = you **sie** = they

▶ mögen (to like)

PRESENT

ich	mag
du	magst
er	mag
wir	mögen
ihr	mögt
sie	mögen

PRESENT SUBJUNCTIVE

ich	möge
du	mögest
er	möge
wir	mögen
ihr	möget
sie	mögen

PERFECT

ich	habe gemocht/mögen
du	hast gemocht/mögen
er	hat gemocht/mögen
wir	haben gemocht/mögen
ihr	habt gemocht/mögen
sie	haben gemocht/mögen

IMPERFECT

ich	mochte
du	mochtest
er	mochte
wir	mochten
ihr	mochtet
sie	mochten

FUTURE

ich	werde mögen
du	wirst mögen
er	wird mögen
wir	werden mögen
ihr	werdet mögen
sie	werden mögen

CONDITIONAL

ich	würde mögen
du	würdest mögen
er	würde mögen
wir	würden mögen
ihr	würdet mögen
sie	würden mögen

IMPERATIVE

PAST PARTICIPLE

gemocht/mögen*

PRESENT PARTICIPLE

mögend

The second form is used when combined with an infinitive construction.

EXAMPLE PHRASES

*Ich **mag** gern Vanilleeis.* I like vanilla ice cream.
*Er **mochte** sie nicht danach fragen.* He didn't want to ask her about it.
*Ich **habe** ihn noch nie **gemocht**.* I never liked him.

ich = I **du** = you **er** = he **wir** = we/one **ihr** = you **sie** = they

▶ **müssen** (to have to)

PRESENT

ich	muss
du	musst
er	muss
wir	müssen
ihr	müsst
sie	müssen

PRESENT SUBJUNCTIVE

ich	müsse
du	müssest
er	müsse
wir	müssen
ihr	müsset
sie	müssen

PERFECT

ich	habe gemusst/müssen
du	hast gemusst/müssen
er	hat gemusst/müssen
wir	haben gemusst/müssen
ihr	habt gemusst/müssen
sie	haben gemusst/müssen

IMPERFECT

ich	musste
du	musstest
er	musste
wir	mussten
ihr	musstet
sie	mussten

FUTURE

ich	werde müssen
du	wirst müssen
er	wird müssen
wir	werden müssen
ihr	werdet müssen
sie	werden müssen

CONDITIONAL

ich	würde müssen
du	würdest müssen
er	würde müssen
wir	würden müssen
ihr	würdet müssen
sie	würden müssen

IMPERATIVE

PAST PARTICIPLE

gemusst/müssen*

PRESENT PARTICIPLE

müssend

The second form is used when combined with an infinitive construction.

EXAMPLE PHRASES

*Ich **muss** aufs Klo.* I must go to the loo.
*Wir **müssen** jeden Abend unsere Hausaufgaben machen.* We have to do our homework every night.
*Sie **hat** abwaschen **müssen**.* She had to wash up.

ich = I **du** = you **er** = he **wir** = we/one **ihr** = you **sie** = they

▶ **nehmen** (to take)

PRESENT

ich	nehme
du	nimmst
er	nimmt
wir	nehmen
ihr	nehmt
sie	nehmen

PRESENT SUBJUNCTIVE

ich	nehme
du	nehmest
er	nehme
wir	nehmen
ihr	nehmet
sie	nehmen

PERFECT

ich	habe genommen
du	hast genommen
er	hat genommen
wir	haben genommen
ihr	habt genommen
sie	haben genommen

IMPERFECT

ich	nahm
du	nahmst
er	nahm
wir	nahmen
ihr	nahmt
sie	nahmen

FUTURE

ich	werde nehmen
du	wirst nehmen
er	wird nehmen
wir	werden nehmen
ihr	werdet nehmen
sie	werden nehmen

CONDITIONAL

ich	würde nehmen
du	würdest nehmen
er	würde nehmen
wir	würden nehmen
ihr	würdet nehmen
sie	würden nehmen

IMPERATIVE

nimm!/nehmen wir!/nehmt!
nehmen Sie!

PAST PARTICIPLE

genommen

PRESENT PARTICIPLE

nehmend

EXAMPLE PHRASES

Hast du den Bus in die Stadt **genommen?** Did you take the bus into town?
*Wie viel **nimmst** du dafür?* How much will you take for it?
*Er **nahm** sich vom Brot.* He helped himself to bread.

---

ich = I **du** = you **er** = he **wir** = we/one **ihr** = you **sie** = they

▶ **sein** (to be)

PRESENT

ich	bin
du	bist
er	ist
wir	sind
ihr	seid
sie	sind

PRESENT SUBJUNCTIVE

ich	sei
du	sei(e)st
er	sei
wir	seien
ihr	seiet
sie	seien

PERFECT

ich	bin gewesen
du	bist gewesen
er	ist gewesen
wir	sind gewesen
ihr	seid gewesen
sie	sind gewesen

IMPERFECT

ich	war
du	warst
er	war
wir	waren
ihr	wart
sie	waren

FUTURE

ich	werde sein
du	wirst sein
er	wird sein
wir	werden sein
ihr	werdet sein
sie	werden sein

CONDITIONAL

ich	würde sein
du	würdest sein
er	würde sein
wir	würden sein
ihr	würdet sein
sie	würden sein

IMPERATIVE

sei!/seien wir!/seid!/seien Sie!

PAST PARTICIPLE

gewesen

PRESENT PARTICIPLE

seiend

EXAMPLE PHRASES

*Er **ist** zehn Jahre alt.* He is ten years old.
*Mir **ist** kalt.* I'm cold.
*Wir **waren** gestern im Theater.* We were at the theatre yesterday.
***Seid** ruhig!* Be quiet!

ich = I   **du** = you   **er** = he   **wir** = we/one   **ihr** = you   **sie** = they

▶ **sitzen** (to sit)

PRESENT

ich	sitze
du	sitzt
er	sitzt
wir	sitzen
ihr	sitzt
sie	sitzen

PRESENT SUBJUNCTIVE

ich	sitze
du	sitzest
er	sitze
wir	sitzen
ihr	sitzet
sie	sitzen

PERFECT

ich	habe gesessen
du	hast gesessen
er	hat gesessen
wir	haben gesessen
ihr	habt gesessen
sie	haben gesessen

IMPERFECT

ich	saß
du	saßest
er	saß
wir	saßen
ihr	saßt
sie	saßen

FUTURE

ich	werde sitzen
du	wirst sitzen
er	wird sitzen
wir	werden sitzen
ihr	werdet sitzen
sie	werden sitzen

CONDITIONAL

ich	würde sitzen
du	würdest sitzen
er	würde sitzen
wir	würden sitzen
ihr	würdet sitzen
sie	würden sitzen

IMPERATIVE

sitz(e)!/sitzen wir!/sitzt!
sitzen Sie!

PAST PARTICIPLE

gesessen

PRESENT PARTICIPLE

sitzend

EXAMPLE PHRASES

Er saß auf meinem Stuhl. He was sitting on my chair.
Deine Krawatte sitzt nicht richtig. Your tie isn't straight.
Ich habe zwei Jahre über dieser Arbeit gesessen. I've spent two years on this piece
of work.

---

ich = I **du** = you **er** = he **wir** = we/one **ihr** = you **sie** = they

▶ **sprechen** (to speak)

PRESENT

ich	spreche
du	sprichst
er	spricht
wir	sprechen
ihr	sprecht
sie	sprechen

PRESENT SUBJUNCTIVE

ich	spreche
du	sprechest
er	spreche
wir	sprechen
ihr	sprechet
sie	sprechen

PERFECT

ich	habe gesprochen
du	hast gesprochen
er	hat gesprochen
wir	haben gesprochen
ihr	habt gesprochen
sie	haben gesprochen

IMPERFECT

ich	sprach
du	sprachst
er	sprach
wir	sprachen
ihr	spracht
sie	sprachen

FUTURE

ich	werde sprechen
du	wirst sprechen
er	wird sprechen
wir	werden sprechen
ihr	werdet sprechen
sie	werden sprechen

CONDITIONAL

ich	würde sprechen
du	würdest sprechen
er	würde sprechen
wir	würden sprechen
ihr	würdet sprechen
sie	würden sprechen

IMPERATIVE

sprich!/sprechen wir!/sprecht!
sprechen Sie!

PAST PARTICIPLE

gesprochen

PRESENT PARTICIPLE

sprechend

EXAMPLE PHRASES

*Er **spricht** kein Italienisch.* He doesn't speak Italian.
*Ich **würde** dich gern privat **sprechen**.* I would like to speak to you privately.
***Hast** du mit ihr **gesprochen**?* Have you spoken to her?

ich = I **du** = you **er** = he **wir** = we/one **ihr** = you **sie** = they

▶ **stehen** (to stand)

PRESENT

ich	stehe
du	stehst
er	steht
wir	stehen
ihr	steht
sie	stehen

PRESENT SUBJUNCTIVE

ich	stehe
du	stehest
er	stehe
wir	stehen
ihr	stehet
sie	stehen

PERFECT

ich	habe gestanden
du	hast gestanden
er	hat gestanden
wir	haben gestanden
ihr	habt gestanden
sie	haben gestanden

IMPERFECT

ich	stand
du	stand(e)st
er	stand
wir	standen
ihr	standet
sie	standen

FUTURE

ich	werde stehen
du	wirst stehen
er	wird stehen
wir	werden stehen
ihr	werdet stehen
sie	werden stehen

CONDITIONAL

ich	würde stehen
du	würdest stehen
er	würde stehen
wir	würden stehen
ihr	würdet stehen
sie	würden stehen

IMPERATIVE

steh(e)!/stehen wir!/steht!
stehen Sie!

PAST PARTICIPLE

gestanden

PRESENT PARTICIPLE

stehend

EXAMPLE PHRASES

*Wir **standen** an der Bushaltestelle.* We stood at the bus stop.
*Es **hat** in der Zeitung **gestanden**.* It was in the newspaper.
*Dieses Kleid **würde** dir gut **stehen**.* This dress would suit you.

ich = I **du** = you **er** = he **wir** = we/one **ihr** = you **sie** = they

▶ **tragen** (to wear, to carry)

PRESENT

ich	trage
du	trägst
er	trägt
wir	tragen
ihr	tragt
sie	tragen

PRESENT SUBJUNCTIVE

ich	trage
du	tragest
er	trage
wir	tragen
ihr	traget
sie	tragen

PERFECT

ich	habe getragen
du	hast getragen
er	hat getragen
wir	haben getragen
ihr	habt getragen
sie	haben getragen

IMPERFECT

ich	trug
du	trugst
er	trug
wir	trugen
ihr	trugt
sie	trugen

FUTURE

ich	werde tragen
du	wirst tragen
er	wird tragen
wir	werden tragen
ihr	werdet tragen
sie	werden tragen

CONDITIONAL

ich	würde tragen
du	würdest tragen
er	würde tragen
wir	würden tragen
ihr	würdet tragen
sie	würden tragen

IMPERATIVE

trag(e)!/tragen wir!/tragt!
tragen Sie!

PAST PARTICIPLE

getragen

PRESENT PARTICIPLE

tragend

EXAMPLE PHRASES

*Ich **trug** ihren Koffer zum Bahnhof.* I carried her case to the station.
*Du **trägst** die ganze Verantwortung dafür.* You bear the full responsibility for it.
*Ich **würde** meine Haare gern länger **tragen**.* I'd like to wear my hair longer.

---

ich = I **du** = you **er** = he **wir** = we/one **ihr** = you **sie** = they

▶ **tun** (to do)

PRESENT

ich	tue
du	tust
er	tut
wir	tun
ihr	tut
sie	tun

PRESENT SUBJUNCTIVE

ich	tue
du	tuest
er	tue
wir	tuen
ihr	tuet
sie	tuen

PERFECT

ich	habe getan
du	hast getan
er	hat getan
wir	haben getan
ihr	habt getan
sie	haben getan

IMPERFECT

ich	tat
du	tat(e)st
er	tat
wir	taten
ihr	tatet
sie	taten

FUTURE

ich	werde tun
du	wirst tun
er	wird tun
wir	werden tun
ihr	werdet tun
sie	werden tun

CONDITIONAL

ich	würde tun
du	würdest tun
er	würde tun
wir	würden tun
ihr	würdet tun
sie	würden tun

IMPERATIVE

tu(e)!/tun wir!/tut!/tun Sie!

PAST PARTICIPLE

getan

PRESENT PARTICIPLE

tuend

EXAMPLE PHRASES

Ich **werde** das auf keinen Fall **tun**. There is no way I'll do that.
So etwas **tut** man nicht! That is just not done!
Sie **tat**, als ob sie schliefe. She pretended to be sleeping.

ich = I **du** = you **er** = he **wir** = we/one **ihr** = you **sie** = they

▶ **werden** (to become)

PRESENT

    ich werde
    du wirst
    er wird
    wir werden
    ihr werdet
    sie werden

PRESENT SUBJUNCTIVE

    ich werde
    du werdest
    er werde
    wir werden
    ihr werdet
    sie werden

PERFECT

    ich bin geworden/worden
    du bist geworden/worden
    er ist geworden/worden
    wir sind geworden/worden
    ihr seid geworden/worden
    sie sind geworden/worden

IMPERFECT

    ich wurde
    du wurdest
    er wurde
    wir wurden
    ihr wurdet
    sie wurden

FUTURE

    ich werde werden
    du wirst werden
    er wird werden
    wir werden werden
    ihr werdet werden
    sie werden werden

CONDITIONAL

    ich würde werden
    du würdest werden
    er würde werden
    wir würden werden
    ihr würdet werden
    sie würden werden

IMPERATIVE

werde!/werden wir!/werdet!
werden Sie!

PAST PARTICIPLE

geworden/worden*

PRESENT PARTICIPLE

werdend

The second form is used when combined with an infinitive construction.

EXAMPLE PHRASES

*Mir **wird** schlecht.* I feel ill.
*Ich will Lehrerin **werden**.* I want to be a teacher.
*Der Kuchen **ist** gut **geworden**.* The cake turned out well.

---

ich = I **du** = you **er** = he **wir** = we/one **ihr** = you **sie** = they

▶ **wissen** (to know)

PRESENT

ich	weiß
du	weißt
er	weiß
wir	wissen
ihr	wisst
sie	wissen

PRESENT SUBJUNCTIVE

ich	wisse
du	wissest
er	wisse
wir	wissen
ihr	wisset
sie	wissen

PERFECT

ich	habe gewusst
du	hast gewusst
er	hat gewusst
wir	haben gewusst
ihr	habt gewusst
sie	haben gewusst

IMPERFECT

ich	wusste
du	wusstest
er	wusste
wir	wussten
ihr	wusstet
sie	wussten

FUTURE

ich	werde wissen
du	wirst wissen
er	wird wissen
wir	werden wissen
ihr	werdet wissen
sie	werden wissen

CONDITIONAL

ich	würde wissen
du	würdest wissen
er	würde wissen
wir	würden wissen
ihr	würdet wissen
sie	würden wissen

IMPERATIVE

wisse!/wissen wir!/wisset!
wissen Sie!

PAST PARTICIPLE

gewusst

PRESENT PARTICIPLE

wissend

EXAMPLE PHRASES

*Ich **weiß** nicht.* I don't know.
*Er **hat** nichts davon **gewusst**.* He didn't know anything about it.
*Sie **wussten**, wo das Kino war.* They knew where the cinema was.

ich = I **du** = you **er** = he **wir** = we/one **ihr** = you **sie** = they

▶ **wollen** (to want)

PRESENT

ich	will
du	willst
er	will
wir	wollen
ihr	wollt
sie	wollen

PRESENT SUBJUNCTIVE

ich	wolle
du	wollest
er	wolle
wir	wollen
ihr	wollet
sie	wollen

PERFECT

ich	habe gewollt/wollen
du	hast gewollt/wollen
er	hat gewollt/wollen
wir	haben gewollt/wollen
ihr	habt gewollt/wollen
sie	haben gewollt/wollen

IMPERFECT

ich	wollte
du	wolltest
er	wollte
wir	wollten
ihr	wolltet
sie	wollten

FUTURE

ich	werde wollen
du	wirst wollen
er	wird wollen
wir	werden wollen
ihr	werdet wollen
sie	werden wollen

CONDITIONAL

ich	würde wollen
du	würdest wollen
er	würde wollen
wir	würden wollen
ihr	würdet wollen
sie	würden wollen

IMPERATIVE

wolle!/wollen wir!/wollt!
wollen Sie!

PAST PARTICIPLE

gewollt/wollen*

PRESENT PARTICIPLE

wollend

The second form is used when combined with an infinitive construction.

EXAMPLE PHRASES

*Er **will** nach London gehen.* He wants to go to London.
*Das **habe** ich nicht **gewollt**.* I didn't want this to happen.
*Sie **wollten** nur mehr Geld.* All they wanted was more money.

ich = I   **du** = you   **er** = he   **wir** = we/one   **ihr** = you   **sie** = they